PEOPLE IN WORLD HISTORY

PEOPLE IN WORLD HISTORY

An Index to Biographies in History Journals and Dissertations Covering All Countries of the World Except Canada and the U.S.

Volume 1: A-M

1989 Edition

Susan K. Kinnell
Editor

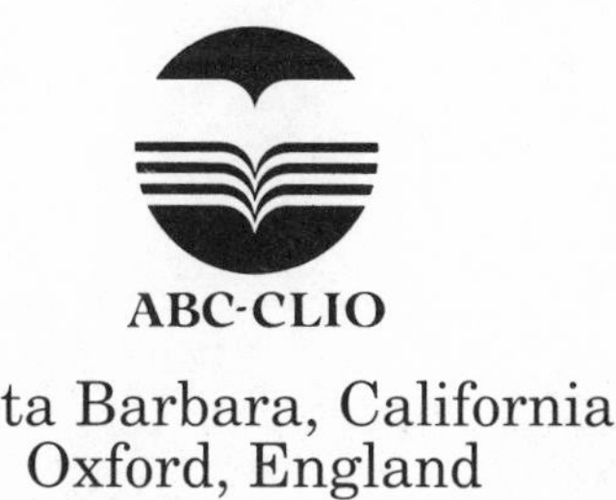

Santa Barbara, California
Oxford, England

ISBN 0-87436-551-1 (v. 1)
ISBN 0-87436-550-3 (set)
ISSN 1041-066X

10 9 8 7 6 5 4 3 2 1

ABC-CLIO, Inc.
130 Cremona Drive, Box 1911
Santa Barbara, California 93116

Clio Press Ltd.
55 St. Thomas' Street
Oxford, OX1 1JG, England

This book is printed on acid free paper ♾.
Manufactured in the United States of America.

CONTENTS

Volume 1

Introduction vii
Sample Entries ix
List of Abbreviations x
Entries, A-M 1

Volume 2

Sample Entries vii
List of Abbreviations viii
Entries, N-Z 1
Subject Index 263
Author Index 469
List of Periodicals 489

INTRODUCTION

Biographical information in history journals and dissertations has long been underutilized by social historians, genealogists, and students. Usually difficult to access because biographical material is scattered throughout many issues of these journals, the articles in these periodicals nevertheless contain a wealth of information about the lives of famous, relatively obscure, and almost unknown people. Extracts from letters, diaries, and family journals, detailed analyses of little-known incidents from the lives of more famous people, and summaries of the contributions of politicians, historians, and others through tributes and obituaries provide material about the lives of many people in many walks of life. The purpose of this publication is to make this wealth of material available to the student or researcher, not only by name of the individual, but also by field of work, ethnic group, region, or contribution. In addition, the abstracts included for each article entry will give readers considerable biographical information without consulting the original articles.

Scope

For this compilation the editors consulted ABC-CLIO's *Historical Abstracts* database, scanning all of the entries from 1983 to 1988 to find dissertation citations and article abstracts in which the focus was primarily biographical. Of these, they chose only those entries that covered a significant portion of the person's life—usually at least four years unless a shorter period of time represented a period of great interest or importance. In the end, material was selected from over 1200 periodicals, resulting in 7713 entries on over 6000 men and women in world history.

The subjects of these entries range from the very prominent to the obscure and relatively unknown—from Andres Bello and Clara Zetkin to Laurence Binyon and Otakar Zich. The historical time frame covered by these entries is from 1450 to the present.

People from the United States and Canada have not been included in these volumes unless they have contributed significantly to the history or culture of other countries. (For more information of the lives of U.S. and Canadian people, see *People in History: An Index to U.S. and Canadian Biographies in History Journals and Dissertations*, ABC-CLIO, 1988.) The dissertation citations are among those previously selected from *Dissertation Abstracts International* by the editors of *Historical Abstracts*. A list of the over 1200 periodicals from which the article entries were selected is included at the end of the second volume.

Arrangement

All people discussed are listed alphabetically by name, with *See* references from all variant names such as pseudonyms or nicknames. Multiple entries for each name are listed alphabetically by author following the biographical name.

For works that treat the lives of two or more persons, a complete citation appears under each name; however, the abstract of the article is given only under the name of the primary subject with a *See* reference from all other names. If all persons receive equal treatment in the article, the abstract is found with the citation for the person whose name is first alphabetically.

The dates following the text of the abstract identify the time period covered in the article or dissertation, and do not necessarily reflect the dates of the subject's life.

Indexes

At the end of Volume 2, there is a multi-level subject index that provides additional access to all of the people in these two volumes by occupation, ethnic group, religion, interests, national origin, source of materials, etc. Within this index, there are *See* and *See also* references to help locate all relevant material. For more information on the subject index, see the note at the beginning of the index.

An index to all authors of the article entries and dissertations follows the subject index.

Future Plans

These two volumes are intended as companion volumes to the earlier two-volume set: *People in History: An Index to U.S. and Canadian Biographies in History Journals and Dissertations*. Future plans include regular supplements to both titles to maintain currency.

SAMPLE ENTRIES

ACCESS BY ENTRY:

Colville, Olivia ← Primary Biographical Subject

1455. Baker, Colin. NYASALAND 1905-1909: THE JOURNEYS OF MARY HALL, OLIVIA COLVILLE AND CHARLOTTE MANSFIELD. *Soc. of Malawi J. [Malawi] 1982 35(1): 11-29.* Compares the travel accounts of three English women in Nyasaland, 1905-09, then a British protectorate. The women traveled a common route between Chinde on the coast and Liwonde on the Shire; the writings reflect their distinct personalities and the differing health and transportation conditions encountered during this four-year period. 62 notes. 1905-09

Entry Number
Article Author
Article Citation
Article Abstract
Dates Covered by Article

Hall, Mary ← Secondary Biographical Subject

2819. Baker, Colin. NYASALAND 1905-1909: THE JOURNEYS OF MARY HALL, OLIVIA COLVILLE AND CHARLOTTE MANSFIELD. *Soc. of Malawi J. [Malawi] 1982 35(1): 11-29.* 1905-09
For abstract see ***Colville, Olivia***

Entry Number
Article Author
Article Citation
Dates Covered by Article
Cross Reference to Primary Biographical Subject

Nakajima Atsushi ← Primary Biographical Subject

4868. Ochner, Nobuko Miyama. "Nakajima Atsushi: His Life and Work." University of Hawaii 1984. 681 pp. *DAI 1984 45(6): 1757-A.* DA8421226 1930's-42

Entry Number
Dissertation Author
Dissertation Citation
Dates Covered by Dissertation
DAI Order Number

Nemrych, Iurii ← Variant Name of Primary Biographical Subject
See Niemirycz, Jerzy ← Cross Reference to Primary Biographical Subject

ACCESS THROUGH SUBJECT AND AUTHOR INDEXES:

Women. *See also* Feminism.
—. Absolutism. France. Historians. 17c. 1902-80. *4060*
—. British. Nyasaland. Travel accounts. 1905-09. *1455*

Entry Number
Subject, under "Women"

Nyasaland. British. Travel accounts. Women. 1905-09. *1455*
—. Colonialism. Personal narratives. 1925-39. *2017*

Entry Number
Geographical Subject, under "Nyasaland"

Bajtschinski, Kostadin 1773
Bak, Joan L. 7123
Baker, Colin 1455
Baker, Donald C. 719
Baker, Frank 7401 7402

Entry Number
Article Author

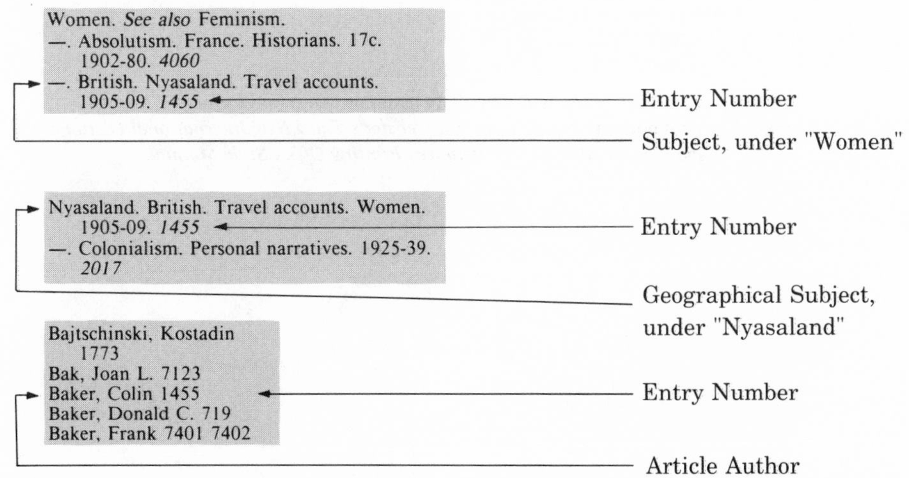

LIST OF ABBREVIATIONS

A. .... Author-prepared Abstract
Acad. .... Academy, Académie, Academia
Agric. .... Agriculture, Agricultural
AIA .... Abstracts in Anthropology
Akad. .... Akademie
Am. .... America, American
Ann. .... Annals, Annales, Annual, Annali
Anthrop. .... Anthropology, Anthropological
Arch. .... Archives
Archaeol. .... Archaeology, Archaeological
Art. .... Article
Assoc. .... Association, Associate
Biblio. .... Bibliography, Bibliographical
Biog. .... Biography, Biographical
Bol. .... Boletim, Boletín
Bull. .... Bulletin
c. .... century (in index)
ca. .... circa
Can. .... Canada, Canadian, Canadien
Cent. .... Century
Coll. .... College
Com. .... Committee
Comm. .... Commission
Comp. .... Compiler
DAI .... Dissertation Abstracts International
Dept. .... Department
Dir. .... Director, Direktor
Econ. .... Economy, Econom-.
Ed. .... Editor, Edition
Educ. .... Education, Educational
Geneal. .... Genealogy, Genealogical, Généalogique
Grad. .... Graduate
Hist. .... History, Hist-.
IHE .... Indice Histórico Español
Illus. .... Illustrated, Illustration
Inst. .... Institute, Institut-.
Int. .... International, Internacional, Internationaal, Internationaux, Internazionale
J. .... Journal, Journal-prepared Abstract
Lib. .... Library, Libraries
Mag. .... Magazine
Mus. .... Museum, Musée, Museo
Nac. .... Nacional
Natl. .... National, Nationale
Naz. .... Nazionale
Phil. .... Philosophy, Philosophical
Photo. .... Photograph
Pol. .... Politics, Political, Politique, Politico
Pr. .... Press
Pres. .... President
Pro. .... Proceedings
Publ. .... Publishing, Publication
Q. .... Quarterly
Rev. .... Review, Revue, Revista, Revised
Riv. .... Rivista
Res. .... Research
RSA .... Romanian Scientific Abstracts
S. .... Staff-prepared Abstract
Sci. .... Science, Scientific
Secy. .... Secretary
Soc. .... Society, Société, Sociedad, Societá
Sociol. .... Sociology, Sociological
Tr. .... Transactions
Transl. .... Translator, Translation
U. .... University, Universi-.
US .... United States
Vol. .... Volume
Y. .... Yearbook

Abbreviations also apply to feminine and plural forms.
Abbreviations not noted above are based on *Webster's Third New International Dictionary* and the *United States Government Printing Office Style Manual.*

PEOPLE IN WORLD HISTORY

Aaland, Jacob

1. Djupedal, Reidar. JACOB AALAND [Jacob Aaland]. *Heimen [Norway] 1983 20(1): 15-19.* A summary of the life and work of Jacob Aaland (1865-1950), whose pioneering research into the community traditions of Nordfjord founded a new school of local history. Based on a speech delivered 10 July 1977. 19c-20c

Abarca de Bolea, Pedro Pablo

See Aranda, Conde de

Abbas I

2. Savory, R. M. "VERY DULL AND ARDUOUS READING": A REAPPRAISAL OF *THE HISTORY OF SHĀH 'ABBĀS THE GREAT* BY ISKANDAR BEG MUNSHĪ. *Hamdard Islamicus [Pakistan] 1980 3(1): 19-37.* Reappraises Munshī's detailed historical account of the reign of Abbas I the Great, 1588-1629, who was of the Safavid dynasty, which came to power in 1501 and ruled Persia until 1736. Praises Iskandar Beg Munshī as a historiographer and master of dramatic narrative while criticizing Iranian scholars and Western orientalists who have ignored the rich historiography of this book as well as of this dynasty. 16c-18c

'Abd al-'Alī Bahr Al-'Ulūm

3. Ansārī, Muhammad Iqbāl. MULLĀ 'ABD AL-'ALĪ BAHR AL-'ULŪM *Hamdard Islamicus [Pakistan] 1983 6(2): 69-96.* A short biography and list of the major works of Indian Islamic teacher 'Abd al-'Alī Bahr al-'Ulūm (1729-1812), including a list of his more important pupils. 1729-1810

'Abd al-'Azīz al-Dihlawī, Shāh

4. Mushir-ul-Haq. SHĀH 'ABD AL-'AZĪZ AL-DIHLAWĪ AND HIS TIMES. *Hamdard Islamicus [Pakistan] 1984 7(1): 51-96, (2): 77-103.* Prints a biography of Shāh 'Abd al-'Azīz al-Dihlawī (1746-1824), focusing on his perceptions of the relationship between Indian Muslims and other religious communities during a period of increasing colonialism by Christians from the British Empire. Based on letters and other primary sources; 206 notes. 1762-1824

'Abd Allāh Al-Sunnī, Muḥammad

5. Jibrān, Muḥammad Mas'ūd. AL-SHAYKH MUḤAMMAD 'ABD ALLĀH AL-SUNNĪ, MUJĀHIDAN BI-'L-SAYF WA-'L-ḤARF 1851-1932 M [Shaykh Muhammad 'Abd Allāh al-Sunnī (1851-1932), fighter with sword and pen]. *Majallat al-Buhūth al-Tārīkhīya [Libya] 1984 6(1): 71-101.* Shaykh 'Abd Allāh al-Sunnī came to Libya from Sennar, Sudan to work with al-Sanūsī. His son Muḥammad 'Abd Allāh al-Sunnī was born in 1851 in Mazda, educated in his father's *zawiya* (Islamic missionary center), and then studied abroad, returning to take up his father's missionary and educational work. In 1895, he moved to French West Africa, where he led resistance against the French for six years, returning to support Libyan resistance against the Italians in 1913. He died on 13 December 1932. He left behind some classical poetry, and traces of his political and religious preaching can be found in some letters of the period. 97 notes. 1851-1932

'Abd al-Rāziq, 'Alī

6. Binder, Leonard. 'ALĪ 'ABD AL-RĀZIQ AND ISLAMIC LIBERALISM. *Asian and African Studies [Israel] 1982 16(1): 31-57.* 'Alī 'Abd al-Rāziq was a leading Egyptian intellectual whose liberal analysis of the history of the Caliphate concluded with a call for the separation of church and state. His arguments spurred on the Islamic fundamentalists to greater endeavors. 42 notes. 1925

Abdel Kader

7. Khmeleva, N. G. ABD AL'-KADIR—NATSIONAL'NYI GEROI ALZHIRA [Abdel Kader—national hero of Algeria]. *Narody Azii i Afriki [USSR] 1983 (5): 100-106.* Describes the Algerian resistance to French occupation in the 1830's and 1840's led by Abdel Kader (1808-83). After a university education in Tunisia, Egypt, Iraq and Syria, Abdel Kader was elected to lead the tribes in Oran against the French. He was successful until 1844, when he was forced to flee to Morocco. He tried to establish a regular army, and introduced economic and political reforms that strengthened his country. The resistance movement took on an Islamic character, although Abdel Kader tried to establish a balance between reason and faith. Secondary sources; 19 notes. 1830's-83

8. Michelbach, Pierre. ABD EL-KADER, GUERRIER ET MYSTIQUE [Abdel Kader, warrior and mystic]. *Histoire [France] 1982 (43): 93-95.* Reviews Michel Chodkiewicz's *Emir Abd el-kader: Ecrits Spirituels Présentés et Traduits de l'Arabe* (1982); the writings of the famous Algerian warrior and leader, Abdel Kader (1807?-83), reveal his deep mysticism. 1832-83

9. Nagy, László J. ABD EL KADER (1807?-1883) [Abdel Kader (1807?-83)]. *Világtörténet [Hungary] 1984 (2): 102-116.* Relates the most important periods in the life of Abdel Kader ('Abd al-Qādir) Algeria's most popular national hero, and includes an article on his relationship with the Porte and Great Britain and a letter written by him to the British prime minister dated 10 December 1841. On 22 November 1832 Abdel Kader was elected commander by 10,000 soldiers representing 32 tribes in their stand against France, and three days later he took Mascara. The 1837 Treaty of Tafna, signed by General Bugeaud of France, gave Abdel Kader, all of Algeria except a few cities. By 1841 he had completed the administrative structure of his empire. In 1839 war broke out again, and in 1843 Abdel Kader was captured. He was placed under house arrest in Pau and later in Amboise. Napoleon III released him in 1852 with a pension. He died 24 May 1883 in Damascus. His twofold goal was to rid the country of the French and to esbablish an Arab-Islamic state. Biblio. 1832-83

Abdul Latif

10. Justyński, Janusz. NARÓD I PAŃSTWO W DOKTRYNIE INDYJSKICH REPREZENTANTÓW ODRODZENIA MUZUŁMAŃSKIEGO [The nation and the state in the doctrine of Indian representatives of the Muslim revival]. *Czasopismo Prawno-Historyczne [Poland] 1983 35(1): 119-134.* Examines the roles of four prominent Muslims of India—Sayyid Ahmad Khan, Abdul Latif, Muhammad Iqbal, and Muhammad Ali Jinnah—in the Islamic revival and their importance in the politics of the subcontinent during the period of colonialism, including the emergence of Pakistan as a sovereign Muslim state. 1833-1940's

Abdülgani Seni

11. Kreiser, Klaus. ABDULGANI SENI (1871-1951) COMME OBSERVATEUR DE L'ADMINISTRATION OTTOMANE AU YEMEN [Abdülgani Seni (1871-1951) as an observer of Ottoman administration in Yemen]. *Revue d'Histoire Maghrebine [Tunisia] 1983 10(31-32): 315-319.* Abdülgani Seni (1871-1951) was sent to Yemen by the Turkish interior minister in 1909 to fulfill the duties of *vilâyet mektubcusu* (an administrative post). This region had been conquered by the Turks in 1869, but resistance still continued. Discusses Abdülgani's early life and career, his preparations for his journey to Yemen, his administrative duties, his writings on Yemen, and his political ideas. Provides a list of the books and articles written by Abdülgani Seni. 1871-1910's

Abel, Charles W.

12. Wetherell, David. THE FORTUNES OF CHARLES W. ABEL OF KWATO 1891-1930. *J. of Pacific Hist. [Australia] 1982 17(4): 195-217.* Abel was one of the earliest English residents in the China Strait at the eastern tip of New Guinea, arriving in 1891. As an agent of the London Missionary Society (LMS), he was an exemplar of the pioneering Nonconformist. Initially engaging in missionary activity, Abel quickly acquired an intense concern for the Papuan people and the danger of their decline and final extinction in the face of European culture. He was both the seer of their future salvation and a prophetic architect along the path to "inevitable" progress. This obsession led to his involvement in commerce, land deals, and the founding of the Kwato Extension Association, independent of the LMS, and eventual recruitment of wealthy backers among American evangelicals in the 1920's. His career's marriage of social conscience and a desire for personal success were unique, with Abel's self-interest and his mission becoming identical. 117 notes. 1891-1930

Abel, Wilhelm

13. —. NEKROLOG: WILHELM ABEL (25. 8. 1904-27. 4. 1985) [Obituary: Wilhelm Abel (25 August 1904-27 April 1985)]. *Historische Zeitschrift [West Germany] 1985 241(3): 758-763.* Summarizes the career of an important German economic and social historian. At Göttingen, Abel developed methodology and wrote significant works on agricultural history, handicrafts, poverty, and hunger in medieval and modern times. 1930's-85

Abendroth, Wolfgang

14. Bock, Hans Manfred. WOLFGANG ABENDROTH (1906-1985)—NACHRUF UND BIBLIOGRAPHISCHER ÜBERBLICK [Wolfgang Abendroth (1906-85): memorial and bibliographical overview]. *Internationale Wissenschaftliche Korrespondenz zur Geschichte der Deutschen Arbeiterbewegung [West Germany] 1985 21(4): 482-500.* Discusses the life of the German socialist political scientist Wolfgang Abendroth and prints a bibliography of 325 of his publications. 1920-85

Abisoghomian, Hovhannēs

15. Hakobjanian, H. A. ONNIK CHIFTĒ-SARAFI GĔRAKAN-KĔNNADATAKAN ZHARANGUTYUNĔ [The legacy of literary criticism of Onnik Chiftē-Saraf]. *Patma-Banasirakan Handes. Istoriko-Filologicheskii Zhurnal [USSR] 1981 (4): 167-181.* Chiftē-Saraf (pseud. for Hovhannēs Abisoghomian, b. 1874 in Constantinople, d. 1932 in Switzerland), Armenian writer and literary critic, believed that literature should be close to the people so as to ennoble them and raise their standards. As a writer he portrayed characters of humble background, true love, harmonious family life, and moral principles. Apart from his chief novel, *Miamiti mĕ Arkadznērĕ,* his contributions to Armenian periodicals, and translations from French classical literature, he wrote literary criticism applauding realism and sincerity in contemporary Armenian writers. After 1918 his pen-name was Hovhannēs Aspēt. Primary sources; 29 notes. Russian summary. 1900-32

Abrate, Mario

16. —. NOS AMIS DISPARUS: MARIO ABRATE [Mario Abrate, deceased]. *Revue Internationale d'Histoire de la Banque [Switzerland] 1982 (24-25): 329-331.* Born in Carmagnola (Torino) in 1927, Mario Abrate, Professor of Economic History at the University of Turin, passed away 7 June 1983. Focusing on the history of banking, metallurgical industries, and agriculture, his works covered the 16th to the 20th century. Biblio. 1550-1980

Acciaiuoli, Donato

17. Ganz, Margery A. DONATO ACCIAIUOLI AND THE MEDICI: A STRATEGY FOR SURVIVAL IN '400 FLORENCE. *Rinascimento [Italy] 1982 22: 33-73.* An examination of the political career, intellectual interests, and relationships with the Medici family of Donato Acciaiuoli (1428-78) reveals how he and others of the Florentine elite supported the Medici regime while at the same time maximizing family honor and power. Acciaiuoli participated in the political affairs of the Medici government, but he and others of the elite were excluded from decisionmaking. Devoted to early 15th-century civic humanism, Acciaiuoli maintained a precarious balance between loyalty to these essentially republican ideals and to the Medici. Primary documents in the state archive, Florence; 109 notes. 1400-78

Achilli, Giacinto

18. Paz, D. G. APOSTATE PRIESTS AND VICTORIAN RELIGIOUS TURMOIL: GAVAZZI, ACHILLI, CONNELLY. *Proceedings of the South Carolina Historical Association 1985: 57-69.* Discusses three prominent Roman Catholic priests—Alessandro Gavazzi (1809-89), Giacinto Achilli (1803-60?), and Pierce Connelly (1804-83)—who left the Church during the mid-19th century. The Bolognese Gavazzi was exiled to the United States for his part in the nationalist revolution in Italy in 1848. Achilli, a Dominican from Viterbo, Italy, was also accused of participation in Risorgimento politics, among other things, and he left for England after a brief imprisonment. Connelly was an Episcopal priest from Mississippi who converted to Catholicism, but eventually became dissatisfied with his role in the Catholic Church. All three were used by anti-Catholic societies, who sponsored them for lecture tours and lionized them. Secondary sources; 61 notes. 1840's-60's

Acosta, Cecilio

19. Beltrán Guerrero, Luis. EN EL CENTENARIO DE LA MUERTE DE CECILIO ACOSTA: HUMANIDAD Y HUMANISMO, FACETAS DE CECILIO ACOSTA [On the centenary of the death of Cecilio Acosta: humanity and humanism, facets of Cecilio Acosta]. *Bol. de la Acad. Nac. de la Hist. [Venezuela] 1981 64(255): 521-540.* Venezuelan Cecilio Acosta (1818-81) was a priest, agronomist, professor of law and philosophy, jurist, journalist, historian, and orator. He was deeply human and well loved. This tribute attempts to illustrate his human facets with examples of his attitudes toward women, food, hunting, friendship, truth, democracy, violence, and other matters. 1840's-81

20. Castellanos, Rafael Ramón. CECILIO ACOSTA EN LA INTIMIDAD [The private life of Cecilio Acosta]. *Bol. de la Acad. Nac. de la Hist. [Venezuela] 1981 64(256): 915-925.* Although the private papers of the priest, philospher, historian, and jurist Acosta have not survived, it is possible to reconstruct his private history and the influences which helped shape his personality. Beside his widowed mother and his tutor, the strongest influences were his deep Christian faith and his seminary formation. He was a retiring, emotionally unstable, and dependent character but he was able to keep his private feelings out of his intense and fruitful career as a thinker, teacher, and publicist. 33 notes. 1818-81

Adam, Gregorio

21. Manzo Núñez, Torcuato. VIDA UTIL Y OBRA GRANDE [A useful life and a great work]. *Bol. de la Acad. Nac. de la Hist. [Venezuela] 1981 64(256): 869-875.* This is a eulogy of Gregorio Adam, bishop of Valencia and former member of the Venezuelan Language Academy. Adam was also a historian and his writings on ecclesiastical subjects are imbued with a deep religious emotion which at times clouded his judgment. He founded many institutions of higher education. 1893-1961

Adami, Edward Fenech

22. Hatherley, John. MALTA: THE OPPOSITION STANDPOINT. *Contemporary Rev. [Great Britain] 1984 244(1420): 231-233.* Examines the political aims and discusses the political and academic career of Dr. Edward Fenech Adami, leader of the Nationalist Party, 1977-83, in Malta. 1977-83

Adams, Herbert Baxter

23. Cunningham, Raymond J. THE GERMAN HISTORICAL WORLD OF HERBERT BAXTER ADAMS: 1874-1876. *J. of Am. Hist. 1981 68(2): 261-275.* Traces the postgraduate career of Herbert Baxter Adams as he pursued his doctorate at Heidelberg and Berlin Universities. Adams's training in German historical scholarship determined the direction and content of his professional approach in training historians at Johns Hopkins. In Germany Adams acquired a lifelong enthusiasm for *Kulturgeschichte.* 54 notes. 1874-76

Adams, John

24. Tyson, Blake. JOHN ADAMS'S CARTOGRAPHIC CORRESPONDENCE TO SIR DANIEL FLEMING OF RYDAL HALL, CUMBRIA, 1676-1687. *Geographical Journal [Great Britain] 1985 151(1): 21-39.* Previously the cartographic career of John Adams has been studied largely from his *Index Villaris* (1680), scarce maps, and scattered secondary sources, so that considerable gaps existed in our understanding of his work. The discovery of a collection of original letters and supporting material in Cumbria allows a much closer study of his working methods, problems, and personality. Details of his preparation of publications, his relationships with contemporaries, and his remarkable triangulation survey of England and Wales become much clearer. In addition there are exciting clues which suggest that he appreciated several concepts, now an accepted part of modern studies in locational theory. Although this deserves closer examination, the present article accumulates and discusses a mass of evidence from which future studies might spring and which is necessary to our better appreciation of John Adams's contribution to seventeenth century geography. 1676-87

Addenbrooke, John

25. Rook, Arthur and Martin, Laurence. JOHN ADDENBROOKE M.D. (1680-1719). *Medical History [Great Britain] 1982 26(2): 169-178.* Provides a biographical sketch of a little-known public benefactor, John Addenbrooke (1680-1719), founder of the hospital which bears his name, including his medical education at Cambridge where he was successively scholar, fellow and bursar of Catharine Hall (later St. Catharine's College), an account of the available teaching in Cambridge, Addenbrooke's contemporary students and his teachers, marriage, medical practice in London, premature retirement through ill-health, and the provision in his will for the establishment of one of the first voluntary general hospitals. Based on J. Venn and J. A. Venn's *Alumni Cantabrigiensis* (1924) and other sources; 3 illus., 47 notes. 1680-1766

Adenauer, Konrad

26. Merkl, Peter H. THE LEGITIMIZING ROLE OF THE LEADER: KONRAD ADENAUER, 1949-1976. *Hist. Social Res. [West Germany] 1982 (21): 12-26.* *See preceding entry.* 1949-76

27. Merkl, Peter H. LA FUNCION LEGITIMADORA DEL LIDER (KONRAD ADENAUER, 1949-1976) [The legitimizing function of the leader: Konrad Adenauer, 1949-76]. *Rev. de Estudios Pol. [Spain] 1981 (21): 7-25.* Using recent academic theories on the nature and function of leadership, examines the role of Konrad Adenauer during West Germany's first 14 years. Adenauer managed to remain in power long enough to leave his mark on the system. He faced and resolved important problems, such as external security, prosperity, and international respect for his country, and thus helped create a functioning system as legitimate as any other. Based in part on Institut für Demoskopie public opinion polls, 1949-76; 35 notes. 1949-76

Ader, Clement

28. Christienne, Charles. DEUX PENSEURS AERONAUTIQUES: ADER ET MITCHELL [Two aviation theorists: Ader and Mitchell]. *Rev. Hist. des Armées [France] 1982 (1): 24-41.* While Clement Ader (1841-1925), French engineer and inventor, and General William E. Mitchell (1879-1936) differed in many significant ways, such as their careers and personalities, they shared an absolute faith in the primacy of air power in the conduct of war. In his prophetic work, *L'Aviation Militaire,* Ader described the future employment of military aircraft, the construction of airfields, the design and operation of aircraft carriers, and the organization of the air force as a separate and independent arm. Before his death, Ader was acclaimed the "father of French aviation." Mitchell, on the other hand, whose views revolved around the concepts of grand strategy, the employment of aircraft in war and the reorganization of the defense system—views which were eventually vindicated by subsequent developments—was convicted by a court martial because he had accused army and navy leaders of gross incompetence. Illus., 12 photos, biblio. 1896-1926

Adıvar, Halide Edip

29. Tatarlı, İbrahim. LES GRANDES ETAPES DANS L'EVOLUTION CREATIVE DE HALİDE EDİP ADIVAR [Main stages in the creative evolution of Halide Edip Adıvar]. *Etudes Balkaniques [Bulgaria] 1984 20(2): 15-40.* Traces the literary biography of Turkish author Halide Edip Adıvar (1884-1964). During her formative years, 1896-1908, she was influenced by romanticism, especially that of Byron and Shelley. She was interested in the Turkish romantic authors Şeyh

Galip and Abdülhak Hamit Tarhan, and she was permanently affected by Shakespeare and the Christian Gospels. Her enthusiasm for the revolutionary movements of 1908 led to 10 years of advocacy of reform and social change. After World War I, she advanced Turkish nationalism. She opposed Atatürk, and from 1924 until his death lived in exile in France, England, the United States, and India. She returned to Turkey in 1939 and contributed to the literature, education, and politics of the country. 39 notes. 1896-1963

Adornes, Anselm

30. Macquarrie, Alan. ANSELM ADORNES OF BRUGES: TRAVELLER IN THE EAST AND FRIEND OF JAMES III. *Innes Rev. [Great Britain] 1982 33: 15-22.* Presents the facts of the Bruges merchant Anselm Adornes's activities in Scotland between 1468 and 1483, including some new evidence, with differences of emphasis from previous accounts of his career. 1468-83

Ady, Endre

31. Kiss, Endre. VON DER "SCHAFFENDEN ZERSTÖRUNG" BIS ZUR METHODE DES "ZARATHUSTRA" (FRIEDRICH NIETZSCHES WIRKUNG AUF DEN JUNGEN ENDRE ADY) [From "creative destruction" to the methods of *Zarathustra:* Friedrich Nietzsche's influence on young Endre Ady]. *Ann. U. Sci. Budapestinensis de Rolando Eötvös Nominatae: Sectio Phil. et Sociol. [Hungary] 1981 15: 121-135.* Nietzsche's influence on the poet Endre Ady from 1899 on can be clearly demonstrated. In Nagyvárad, Ady heard a great deal about Nietzsche and by 1903 came to admire him greatly. Traces of *Zarathustra* in his style are documented. Primary sources. 1896-1908

Aehrenthal, Alois Lexa von

32. Wank, Solomon. A CASE OF ARISTOCRATIC ANTISEMITISM IN AUSTRIA: COUNT AEHRENTHAL AND THE JEWS, 1878-1907. *Leo Baeck Institute. Year Book [Great Britain] 1985 30: 435-456.* Count Alois Lexa von Aehrenthal (1854-1912) was an Austrian career diplomat who served in several high-level posts. When this Austrian aristocrat entered the diplomatic service in 1877, his attitude toward Jews was mildly negative, but it was typical of his conservative class. As revealed in his letters, this vague anti-Semitism changed radically by the end of the century. By then, Aehrenthal was finding it convenient to blame "International Jewry" for much of the political turmoil that was agitating European society. Based on published and unpublished writings of Count Aehrenthal in several European archives and secondary sources; 135 notes. 1878-1907

Aemilius, George

33. Holzberg, Niklas. EIN VERGESSENER SCHÜLER PHILIPP MELANCHTHONS: GEORG AEMILIUS (1517-1569) [A forgotten student of Philipp Melanchthon: George Aemilius (1517-69)]. *Arch. für Reformationsgeschichte [West Germany] 1982 73: 94-122.* Surveys the life and works of one of Melanchthon's lesser known pupils, George Aemilius (1517-69). Born in Mansfeld and distantly related to Luther, Aemilius studied from 1532 until 1540 in Wittenberg, where, along with Johannes Stigel, Simon Lemnius, Melchior Acontius, and others, he belonged to a circle of Neo-Latin poets and published numerous verses. While rector of the Siegen grammar school, 1540-53, he composed epigrams for the Latin edition of Hans Holbein the Younger's *Dance of Death* and many books for use in the school, including the gospels and epistles of the church year in Latin hexameters. As the first superintendent in the county of Stolberg, 1553-69, he wrote hymns in German, translated Luther's chorales into Latin, and took a deep interest in botany. His work is essentially Lutheran, but also betrays humanist tendencies. 1517-69

Afanas'ev, Fedor A.

34. Zhuravlev, V. V. ON NE MYSLIL SEBIA VNE REVOLIUTSII [He could not imagine himself outside the revolution]. *Voprosy Istorii KPSS [USSR] 1984 (2): 121-124.* Provides a brief political biography of Fedor Afanas'evich Afanas'ev (1859-1905). Contrary to Western claims the Bolshevik Party contained dedicated proletarian revolutionaries, one of whose best examples was Fedor A. Afanas'ev. He worked in poor conditions in factories in different areas of Russia. One of Russia's first Marxists, he spent time in jail, in exile, and in illegal underground party activities. During a demonstration in Ivanovo Voznesensk in 1905, he was killed by the Black Hundreds. Based on memoirs and secondary sources in Russian and English; 25 notes. 1859-1905

Agca, Mehmet Ali

35. Henze, Paul. QUEST FOR AN ASSASSIN: REPORT FROM MALATYA: MEHMET ALI AGCA. *Encounter [Great Britain] 1983 60(5): 9-18.* Presents impressions of a trip to Malatya, Turkey, home of Mehmet Ali Agca, would-be assassin of Pope John Paul II. Discusses interviews regarding Mehmet Ali Agca with his relatives, friends, and officials. 1982

36. Kudriavtsev, V. N. "DELO ANTONOVA": PRAVOSUDIE ILI POLITICHESKAIA AKTSIIA? [The Antonov case: justice or political action?]. *Sovetskoe Gosudarstvo i Pravo [USSR] 1985 (9): 88-93.* 1985
For abstract see ***Antonov, Sergei***

37. Ledeen, Michael. THE BULGARIAN CONNECTION AND THE MEDIA. *Commentary 1983 75(6): 45-50.* Uses the assassination attempt on Pope John Paul II to explore the media reaction and quick acceptance of the story offered by Mehmet Ali Agca, the would-be assassin. Agca's Bulgarian connection to the Kremlin and conspiracy was discovered by an American journalist, Claire Sterling. 1981-83

Aghayan, Tsatour

38. Tavakalian, N. A. TS. P. AGHAYAN (TSĔNĔNDYAN 70-AMYAKI ARTIV) [Tsatour Pavēli Aghayan: on the 70th anniversary of his birth]. *Patma-Banasirakan Handes. Istoriko-Filologicheskii Zhurnal [USSR] 1981 (4): 289-292.* Tribute to the historian Tsatour Aghayan on his 70th birthday. Educated in Moscow and Erevan, Aghayan specialized in Soviet history, particularly of the Caucasian peoples, who are the subject of some of his works. During the past 40 years he has held responsible posts in the cultural departments of the Communist Party in Armenia and has been a prolific writer on the October Revolution, Lenin's Armenian allies, the struggles of Caucasian peoples to establish Soviet rule, their mutual friendship, and other aspects of Soviet history. For his services Aghayan has been awarded several state honors. Primary sources. 1931-81

Aghayian, Edward B.

39. Abrahamian, S. G. E. B. AGHAYIAN (DZĔNĔNDYAN 70-AMYAKI ARTIV) [E. B. Aghayian (his 70th birthday)]. *Patma-Banasirakan Handes. Istoriko-Filologicheskii Zhurnal [USSR] 1983 (2-3): 229-301.* Tribute to Edward Bagradi Aghayian, scholar, member of the Arme-

nian Academy of Sciences, and professor of linguistics at Erevan University and Institute of Languages. During the past 50 years his works on Armenian and comparative linguistics have earned him state honors. He has been an innovator in the methodology of his research into the history of ancient and modern Armenian linguistics. Notable among his works is *Explanatory Dictionary of Modern Armenian.* Primary sources; photo. 1933-83

Agricola, Michael

40. Gallén, Jarl. BRYTNINGSTIDENS MÄN: MARTIN SKYTTE OCH MIKAEL AGRICOLA: FESTTAL VID AGRICOLA-DAGARNA 7.-8.4.1984 (BANDUPPTAGNING) [A time of upheaval indeed: Martin Skytte and Michael Agricola: keynote speech of the Agricola Days, 7-8 April 1984 (introduction)]. *Opusculum [Finland] 1984 4(3-4): 99-105.* In April 1984 a special celebration was held in Pernå to commemorate Michael Agricola. The author considers Agricola's life, paying particular attention to his role as secretary to Bishop Martin Skytte in Åbo. Skytte influenced Agricola's views on European culture and theology. Agricola's greatest contribution was in creating literary Finnish and in laying the foundation of Finland's modern culture during the Reformation. 1509-57

41. Knuutila, Jyrki. MIKAEL AGRICOLAA KÄSITTELEVÄT TIETEELLISET TUTKIMUKSET VUOSILTA 1961-1984 [Research on Michael Agricola, 1961-84]. *Opusculum [Finland] 1984 4(3-4): 130-140.* 1509-57

42. Pirinen, Kauko. MIKAEL AGRICOLA USKONPUHDISTAJANA [Michael Agricola as a reformer]. *Opusculum [Finland] 1984 4(3-4): 89-98.* Describes the life and works of Michael Agricola (1509-57), Finnish author and theologian, emphasizing his translations of liturgical texts into Finnish and noting his religious reforms. Agricola created the basis of literary Finnish with his publications, and his translations made the scriptures accessible to the Finns. Agricola supported the Lutheran Reformation, but tried to avoid all the great disputes. In 1554-57, a period of warfare throughout the region, he was bishop of Turku. He died in 1557, after attending peace negotiations in Russia. 1528-57

43. Pirinen, Kauko. MIKAEL AGRICOLA, PERNAJAN POIKA [Michael Agricola, the boy from Pernaja]. *Opusculum [Finland] 1984 4(3-4): 83-88.* The Reformation in Finland and Michael Agricola's life work are closely connected with Sweden. Finland was part of Sweden and all changes in Swedish society also applied to Finland. The author describes Agricola's early life, noting the importance of Swedish influences on this important Finnish prelate, theologian, and writer. 1509-57

Aguilera Malta, Demetrio

44. Flores Jaramillo, Renán. DEMETRIO AGUILERA MALTA [Demetrio Aguilera Malta]. *Cuadernos Hispanoamericanos [Spain] 1979 116(348): 623-638.* Provides biographical information on the Ecuadoran writer Demetrio Aguilera Malta (b. 1909), including his education, newspaper work in Panama, studies in Spain, journalistic activities in Mexico, contributions to international reviews and periodicals, cultural and teaching missions in various countries, and authorship of poetry, short stories, novels, essays, and literary criticism. Discusses his historical novels and other works, with particular reference to *Un Nuevo Mar para el Rey, La Caballeresa del Sol, Don Goyo, Infierno Negro, Jaguar,* and *Siete Lunas y Siete Serpientes.* Based mainly on the works of Demetrio Aguilera Malta. 1930's-79

Agursky, Mikhail

45. Agursky, Mikhail. "GOD" IS DEAD! *Midstream 1985 31(1): 38-41.* The author details his life as a Jew in the Soviet Union. 1919-53

Agustič, Imre

46. Barbarič, Štefan. SLOVENSKOMADŽARSKI PUBLICIST IMRE AGUSTIČ [Slovene-Hungarian publicist Imre Agustič]. *Časopis za Zgodovino in Narodopisje [Yugoslavia] 1985 21(2): 212-221.* Imre Agustič (1837-79) earned fame among both Hungarians and Slovenes. Describes his journalism and his liberal thought and the resonance of his journal *Prijatel* in Slovenia. 1860's-79

Ahmad Rasim

47. Martin, B. G. AHMAD RASIM PASHA AND THE SUPPRESSION OF THE FAZZAN SLAVE TRADE, 1881-1896. *Africa [Italy] 1983 38(4): 545-579.* After a long career in the Ottoman administration Ahmad Rasim Pasha became governor of Tripolitania in 1881 and held the office until 1896. His most serious problem was the traffic in African slaves across the Fezzan to North Africa, which had existed since antiquity. Despite all the vested interests involved, Ahmad Rasim did not hesitate in attacking the slave trade, which declined in a decisive fashion during his administration. He broke up the trade wherever he could and forcibly freed slaves from their owners' control. The combination of his energy and long period in office made his measures effective. Based on published primary sources and secondary works; 100 notes. 1881-96

Ahmet Cezzar Paşa

48. Bakr, 'Abd al-Wahhāb. AḤMAD BĀSHĀ AL-JAZZĀR WA-MIṢR: RU'YAH JADĪDAH [Ahmet Cezzar Paşa and Egypt: a new view]. *Revue d'Histoire Maghrebine [Tunisia] 1983 10(29-30): 61-70.* Ahmet Paşa was not actually more bloody than others, and had to flee from Egypt because of his loyalty to his chief. In Syria, he loyally served Ottoman interests against local lords, rising high in the Ottoman administration. But his fixed ambition was to return to Egypt, and when he was not given command of the Ottoman expeditions there in 1786 and 1799, he rebelled. However, the sultan later "forgave" him and appointed him to a post in Syria. Based on French archives and Ottoman documents; 11 notes. 1755-1804

Åhrén, Uno

49. Tudberg, E. "Uno Åhrén, en Föregåangsman inom 1900-Talets Arkitektur och Samhällsplanering" [Uno Åhrén, a pioneer of architecture and planning in Sweden during the 20th century]. Royal Inst. of Tech. [Sweden] 1981. 291 pp. *DAI-C 1982 43(4): 671; 7/4208c.* 20c

Aiken, Frank

50. Raymond, Raymond James. DAVID GRAY, THE AIKEN MISSION, AND IRISH NEUTRALITY, 1940-41. *Diplomatic History 1985 9(1): 55-71.* Discusses the circumstances surrounding Irish emissary Frank Aiken's mission to the United States during the early stages of World War II. The United States was heavily involved in supporting the British war effort but Ireland was following neutralist policies that hindered the British. The mission was arranged by the

newly appointed US minister to Ireland, David Gray, who had suggested it as a means to obtain needed ships and supplies from the United States. When Aiken transformed his mission into a propaganda junket to undermine US policies, he was rebuffed. Irish leaders blamed Gray for the failure, and Irish-American relations deteriorated. Based on documents in the Franklin D. Roosevelt Library, the Harry S Truman Library, the University of Wyoming Library, Washington National Records Center, and Ireland's State Paper Office. 1940-41

51. Rosenberg, Joseph L. THE 1941 MISSION OF FRANK AIKEN TO THE UNITED STATES: AN AMERICAN PERSPECTIVE. *Irish Hist. Studies [Ireland] 1980 22(86): 162-177.* Frank Aiken, the Irish Minister for Coordination of Defensive Measures, was sent by Eamon de Valera to purchase American food and weapons. As he was distinctly anti-British, Franklin D. Roosevelt received him coolly. His visit became a propaganda tour for American neutrality. Although Aiken was warmly received by Irish-American societies and by American politicians of Irish descent, his mission really widened the gap between the United States and Ireland. Based on manuscripts in the F. D. Roosevelt Library, National Archives, and numerous other collections; 125 notes. 1941

Ainsworth, Henry

52. Moody, Michael E. "A MAN OF A THOUSAND": THE REPUTATION AND CHARACTER OF HENRY AINSWORTH, 1569/70-1622. *Huntington Lib. Q. 1982 45(3): 200-214.* Henry Ainsworth (1569-1622), a minister in the English Separatist Church in Amsterdam, was involved in frequent controversies with other ministers and with church members. In 1610, he and others seceded and formed another congregation, but controversies continued. Examination of his career shows that Ainsworth sought moderation and compromise, which led to charges of weakness and apostasy. Perhaps his chief character trait was diffidence. 61 notes. 1597-1622

Aitken, Maxwell

See Beaverbrook, 1st Baron

Ajassa, Kitoye

53. Okonkwor, R. Chude. SIR KITOYE AJASSA AND THE PIONEER: A REASSESSMENT. *Nigeria Mag. [Nigeria] 1982 (140): 44-53.* Established in 1914, Sir Kitoye Ajassa's *Nigerian Pioneer* became unpopular more for its conservatism and a certain lack of realism than for the toadyism of which he and it were accused. 1914-36

Akamatsu Katsumaro

54. Large, Stephen S. BUDDHISM AND POLITICAL RENOVATION IN PREWAR JAPAN: THE CASE OF AKAMATSU KATSUMARO. *J. of Japanese Studies 1983 9(1): 33-66.* Akamatsu Katsumaro (1894-1955) was one of the political activists who advocated *kakushin* or "renovation," meaning defiant opposition to standpat bureaucracy, reorganization of state power to build a nation based on social and political justice, and mobilization of the masses. Akamatsu consistently interpreted *kakushin* in the light of his True Pure Land Buddhist faith, but his political approach went from socialism to national socialism and then to his "scientific Japanism." He believed that the spiritually awakened "creativity of the people" would help attain social egolessness. Elected to the Diet, he helped form the Japan Renovation Party. Defeated for re-election in 1942, he retired from active political life. 122 notes. 1920-55

Akbar

55. Jaffrey, Madhur. THE EMPEROR AKBAR. *Art & Antiques 1985 (Dec): 60-65.* India experienced a cultural renaissance under the reign of Muslim Mogul Emperor Jalal-ud-Din Akbar, who encouraged diverse forms of literature, religion, music, architecture, and painting. Scenes of Akbar's cultural activities are reflected in miniature paintings the ruler commissioned that combine Persian format with Akbar's desire for naturalism and drama. 1556-1605

Åkerhielm, Samuel, Jr.

56. Åkerhielm, Samuel; Cavallie, James, ed. ETT MEMOARFRAGMENT AV SAMUEL ÅKERHIELM D.Y. [The fragmentary memoirs of Samuel Åkerhielm Jr.]. *Karolinska Förbundets Årsbok [Sweden] 1979-80: 142-167.* An introduction to 18th-century Swedish politician Samuel Åkerhielm Jr., followed by publication of the entire manuscript of his fragmentary memoirs. Intrigues caused Åkerhielm's dismissal from politics in 1747 and he began his memoirs the ensuing year. The memoirs contain some historically valuable statements and information, in particular descriptions of Åkerhielm's duties in the chancellery and the functioning of the same in Sweden and abroad during the military campaigns of Charles XII. Included in these observations is an account of the drafting of the new plans for the chancellery, ratified in 1713. 1685-1765

Åkerman, Joachim

57. Wallberg, Evabritta. JOACHIM ÅKERMANS ARKIV [Joachim Åkerman's archive]. *RA-nytt [Sweden] 1986 (1): 56-59.* Describes the papers of Gustaf Richard Joachim Åkerman (1868-1958), a Swedish army general who also held civilian appointments, whose archive is now deposited in the Swedish National Military Archives in Stockholm. 1905-58

Akiko, Yosano

58. Larson, Phyllis Hyland. "Yosano Akiko: The Early Years." U. of Minnesota 1985. 180 pp. *DAI 1986 46(7): 1944-A.* DA8519283 1900-12

Alameda y Brea, Cirilo

59. Pobladura, Melchor de. APUNTES Y DOCUMENTOS PARA LA BIOGRAFIA DEL CARDENAL FRANCISCANO ALAMEDA Y BREA (1781-1872) [Notes and documents for the biography of the Franciscan cardinal Alameda y Brea, 1781-1872]. *Arch. Ibero-Americano [Spain] 1981 41(163-164): 279-319.* Friar Cirilo Alameda y Brea, the son of affluent farmers, was among other things political adviser to the governor of La Plata, go-between in the marriages of two Bourbon princes with two Braganza princesses, member of the Supreme Council of the Inquisition, superior general of the Franciscan order, grandee of Spain, archbishop of Santiago de Cuba, member of the Council of State, archbishop of Burgos, archbishop of Toledo, and cardinal. Partly based on primary material in the Vatican Secret Archive; documentary appendix, 64 notes. 1800-72

Alas, Leopoldo

60. Bouzo, Carlos. NOTAS SOBRE LA ENFERMEDAD DE CLARIN Y ALGUNOS REFRANES MEDICOS [Notes on the sickness of Clarín and some medical proverbs]. *Estudios [Spain] 1985 41(148): 177-184.* Leopoldo Alas y Ureña (pseudonym, Clarín), a Spanish 19th-century author, was naturally left-handed but forced to write with his right hand, an effort for which he paid with headaches, digestive disorders, and sexual peculiarities. 19c

Alavedra, Joseph Pablo María

61. Perazzo, Nicolás. CRONICA DE SAN FELIPE: EL PADRE JOSEPH PABLO MARIA ALAVEDRA [Chronicle of San Felipe: Father Joseph Pablo María Alavedra]. *Bol. de la Acad. Nac. de la Hist. [Venezuela] 1981 64(256): 845-848.* Alavedra belonged to one of the leading families of San Felipe; he distinguished himself in the service of the Catholic Church and in his educational career. Based on documents in the archives of the Central University of Venezuela. 1780's-90's

Albada, Aggaeus van

62. Bergsma, W. AGGAEUS VAN ALBADA (CIRCA 1525-1587) [Aggaeus van Albada (ca. 1525-87)]. *Spiegel Historiael [Netherlands] 1985 20(1): 21-27.* Discusses Aggaeus (Agge) van Albada, a brilliant statesman from Friesland, States General delegate to the Keulen peace congress, 1579, and editor of its documents, advocate of religious tolerance, and follower of the German spiritualist Caspar von Schenckfeld (1489-1561), a fact which ended his political career. ca 1525-87

Albert, Prince Consort

63. Grigg, John. BENEVOLENT FOREIGNER. ON PRINCE ALBERT. *Encounter [Great Britain] 1984 63(1): 64-69.* Reviews Hermione Hobhouse's *Prince Albert: His Life and Work* (1984) and Robert Rhodes James's *Albert, Prince Consort* (1984), two new studies throwing light on different aspects of Prince Albert, especially as politician and patron of the arts. 1819-61

Albert-Birot, Pierre

64. Eichhorn, Linda. THE VOICE OF A NEW AGE: PIERRE ALBERT-BIROT AND "SIC." *Library Chronicle of the University of Texas at Austin 1986 (35): 44-59.* Pierre Albert-Birot—poet, painter, sculptor, editor, publisher, printer, and founder of the avant-garde review *SIC* (Sounds, Ideas and Colors)—did much to usher in the modern era of literature, art, music, and theater by creating one of the primary publication outlets for most of the leading French writers of the period—Guillaume Apollinaire, Louis Aragon, Tristan Tzara, Pierre Reverdy, and a host of others. 1916-19

Alberti, Giovanni

65. Witcombe, Christopher Lewis Charles Ewart. "Giovanni and Cherubino Alberti." Bryn Mawr Coll. 1981. 651 pp. *DAI 1982 43(6): 1731-A.* DA8220697 1589-1601

Alberti, Joan

66. Sandt, H. van de. "Joan Alberti, een Nederlandse Theoloog en Classicus in de Achttiende Eeuw" [Joan Alberti, a Dutch theologian and classicist in the 18th century]. State U. of Utrecht [Netherlands] 1984. 405 pp. *DAI-C 1986 47(1): 25; 47/117c.* 18c

Albertini, Georges

67. Assouline, Pierre. GEORGES ALBERTINI, L'EMINENCE GRISE DE L'ANTICOMMUNISME [Georges Albertini, the *eminence grise* of anticommunism]. *Histoire [France] 1986 (90): 14-28.* A polemicist and personal friend of French banker Hippolyte Worms, whom he met in prison in 1946, Georges Albertini (1911-83) was particularly influential in French politics, 1948-58, as private consultant to Fourth Republic left-of-center, centrist, and Gaullist political figures Guy Mollet, Georges Bidault, and Robert Lacoste, persuading them to fight communism at all costs; however, because of his collaborationist past in the Pétain government, he did not run for public office, and his personal papers were said to have been burned on his death. 1931-74

Albrecht, Heinrich Christoph

68. Koch, Walter. HEINRICH CHRISTOPH ALBRECHT UND CHRISTINE WESTPHALEN: EINE NEUENTDECKTE QUELLE ÜBER DEN NORDDEUTSCHEN JAKOBINER [Heinrich Christoph Albrecht and Christine Westphalen: a newly discovered source on North German Jacobins]. *Jahrbuch des Inst. für Deutsche Gesch. [Israel] 1982 11: 381-385.* The Hamburg democratic publicist Heinrich Christoph Albrecht (1763-1800) is already known from some of his publications, but an unpublished book of poetry from the period 1785-1801 by Engel Christine von Axen (1758-1840), who married the merchant Johann Westphalen, expands our knowledge of Albrecht considerably. The poems show that Albrecht was married to Christine's sister Margarete von Axen in 1794. Christine herself wrote poetry in a highly emotional style, but she soon turned against the Jacobins. In 1804 she published a play on Charlotte Corday anonymously. Manuscript of poems by Engel Christine Westphalen and Heinrich Christoph Albrecht and archival and printed primary materials; 17 notes. 1785-1801

Albret, Jeanne d'

69. Castelot, André. JEANNE D'ALBRET, "LA BREBIS ACCOUCHE D'UN LION" [Jeanne d'Albret: "the sheep gives birth to a lion"]. *Historama [France] 1984 (9): 74-78.* Narrates events connected with the marriage of Jeanne d'Albret, whose family ruled the Kingdom of Navarre, with Antoine de Bourbon, and tells how her giving birth to a male child who later became France's Henry IV resulted in Spain's giving up its claim to the possession of the lower part of the small Kingdom of Navarre. 1548-1610

Albuquerque, Pedro Autran da Matta

70. Winz, Antônio Pimentel. CONSELHEIRO DR. PEDRO AUTRAN DA MATTA ALBUQUERQUE [Councillor Dr. Pedro Autran da Matta Albuquerque]. *Rev. do Inst. Hist. e Geog. Brasileiro [Brazil] 1982 (334): 177-182.* Notes the centenary of the death of Councillor Albuquerque and gives a brief chronology of his life, including his most important post as director of the Faculty of Law at Recife. The author includes a bibliography of this law professor's works. Secondary sources; 2 plates, biblio. 1805-81

Alcón, Andrés

71. Puerto Sarmiento, F. Javier. ANDRES ALCON (1782-1850), FARMACEUTICO, POLITICO Y PROFESOR DE QUIMICA [Andrés Alcón (1782-1850), pharmacist, politician, and professor of chemistry]. *Boletín de la Sociedad Española de Historia de la Farmacia [Spain] 1984 35(139): 143-164.* A chronology of the scientific training and teaching career of Andrés Alcón (1782-1850), including his work at the

Spanish Royal Pharmacy, provides evidence of the harmful effect of political upheaval on medical research in 19th-century Spain. 1800-50

Aldama Pruaño, Antonio María de

72. Ruiz Jurado, Manuel. ANTONIO MARIA DE ALDAMA PRUAÑO S.I. [Antonio María de Aldama Pruaño S.J.]. *Arch. Hist. Societatis Iesu [Italy] 1983 52(104): 447-450.* Presents a brief biography of Aldama Pruaño and bibliography of his works. 1908-82

Alegría, Claribel

73. Arenal, Electa. TWO POETS OF THE SANDINISTA STRUGGLE. *Feminist Studies 1981 7(1): 19-27.* Poetic volumes *Sobrevivo* [I Survive] by Claribel Alegría and *Linea de fuego* [Firing Line] by Gioconda Belli, which recaptured elements of the people's war against Somozas' dictatorship, received the 1978 poetry prize of the prestigious Casa de las Americas in Havana. Alegría and Belli filled the role of "spokespoet" for a period of revolution and reconstruction, a role few women poets have fulfilled. Alegría's volume is characterized by a distilled and abstracted simplicity which interweaves complex historical and personal themes. Belli's volume expresses the fragility and fleetingness of life, woman's erotic sensuality amidst strife, and the ongoing resistance of a united people. 7 notes. 1926-78

Aleijadinho

74. Hogan, James E. THE CONTEMPORARIES OF ANTÔNIO FRANCISCO LISBOA: AN ANNOTATED BIBLIOGRAPHY. *Latin Am. Res. Rev. 1981 16(3): 138-145.* The study of Antônio Francisco Lisbôa (Aleijadinho) should be placed in the context of the general cultural environment of 18th-century Minas Gerais. The article provides an extensive bibliographic base to broaden this study. 2 notes, biblio. ca 1690-1830

Alekseev, Mikhail Pavlovich

75. Boss, Valentin. ALEKSEEV AND ANGLO-RUSSIAN STUDIES. *Russian Review 1984 43(4): 393-404.* Reviews two works by M. P. Alekseev: *Russko-Angliiskie Literaturnye Sviazi (XVIII vek-pervaia Polovina XIX veka)* (1982) and *Sravnitel'noe Literaturovedenie* (1983). Briefly recounts Alekseev's career and his leading role in the study of comparative literature in Russia. The disparate views held by the Russians and the English about one another's culture and country for the past 500 years are compared in light of Alekseev's work. 18 notes. 15c-20c

76. Cross, A. G. ACADEMICIAN M. P. ALEKSEEV (1896-1981): A TRIBUTE. *Oxford Slavonic Papers [Great Britain] 1983 16: 1-9.* A tribute to the late Mikhail Pavlovich Alekseev, noted as an expert in English literature and the doyen of researchers into Anglo-Russian literary and cultural relations. Based on the publications of Alekseev; 17 notes. 15c-20c

Alekseev, Nikolai N.

77. Shabanov, V. MARSHAL VOISK SVIAZI N. N. ALEKSEEV (K 70-LETIIU SO DNIA ROZHDENIIA) [Marshal of Communications N. N. Alekseev on his 70th birthday]. *Voenno-Istoricheskii Zhurnal [USSR] 1984 (6): 88-90.* Sketches the military career of Marshal Nikolai N. Alekseev. A graduate from the Leningrad Military School, he became by 1942 an expert in radiolocation. After World War II he took part in establishing artillery surveillance posts and headed the Main Artillery Directorate. Photo. 1914-84

Alençon, Duc d'

78. Holt, Mack Parker. "A Prince of the Blood in the French Wars of Religion: François de Valois, Duke of Alençon and Anjou, 1555-1584." Emory U. 1981. 528 pp. *DAI 1983 43(7): 2422-A.* DA8221526 1555-84

Aleramo, Sibilla

79. Melandri, Lea. LA SPUDORATEZZA: VITA E OPERE DI SIBILLA ALERAMO [Shamelessness: life and works of Sibilla Aleramo]. *Memoria: Riv. di Storia delle Donne [Italy] 1983 (8): 5-23.* Through autobiographical and other narratives by Sibilla Aleramo, 20th-century Italian feminist writer, the author traces the struggles of Aleramo and of women in general to break through the restrictions within which they have been confined. Aleramo paid particular attention in her works to the role of shame, modesty, and other such feelings inculcated by society to keep women in their place. Biblio. 20c

Alesius, Alexander

80. Wiedermann, Gotthelf. ALEXANDER ALESIUS' LECTURES ON THE PSALMS AT CAMBRIDGE, 1536. *Journal of Ecclesiastical History [Great Britain] 1986 37(1): 15-41.* Alesius (1500-65), a Scottish reformer, spent three years at Wittenberg, where he was in direct contact with Luther and Melanchthon. Melanchthon sent him to England in 1535, where he was warmly received by Henry VIII, Cromwell, and Cranmer. He was appointed lecturer on the scriptures at Cambridge, and represented an important link between Reformation England and Germany. His theological views, and his indebtedness to Luther, are here traced on the basis of his Cambridge commentary on the first 25 psalms. Based on a manuscript in the Salisbury collection at Hatfield House, Hertfordshire; 192 notes. 1532-36

Alessandri, Arturo

81. Ciria, Alberto. THE INDIVIDUAL IN HISTORY: FIVE LATIN AMERICAN BIOGRAPHIES. *Latin American Research Review 1985 20(3): 247-267.* ca 1920-70
For abstract see ***Sandino, Augusto César***

Alexander, Daniel William

82. Newman, Richard. ARCHBISHOP DANIEL WILLIAM ALEXANDER AND THE AFRICAN ORTHODOX CHURCH. *Int. J. of African Hist. Studies 1983 16(4): 615-630.* The African Orthodox Church, which originated in the United States, became a link between Garveyite separatism and African nationalism. Daniel William Alexander, long active in South African nationalist organizations, including independent black church movements, became a bishop in the African Orthodox Church in 1927, a position which he held until his death in 1970. Based on Alexander's papers and the records of the church; 66 notes. 1927-70

Alexander, Gertrud

83. Alexander, Gertrud. AN DER KULTURFRONT [On the cultural front]. *Beiträge zur Gesch. der Arbeiterbewegung [East Germany] 1981 23(5): 714-721.* An excerpt from the memoirs of Gertrud Alexander in which she explains the reasons for her selection as editor of *Rote Fahne* [Red banner], 1919-23, and describes her job as art critic for the journal and her task in putting forward the Marxist viewpoint

on culture, literature, and art. Based on the memoirs of Gertrud Alexander in the Institute for Marxism-Leninism, Berlin and secondary sources; 5 notes. 1919-23

84. Endler, Brunhild. "ICH STEHE IM POLITISCHEN TAGESKAMPF": GERTRUD ALEXANDER ["I am in the daily political struggle": Gertrud Alexander]. *Beiträge zur Gesch. der Arbeiterbewegung [East Germany] 1982 24(4): 588-594.* Traces the life, career, and political activities of German Communist and writer Gertrud Alexander (1882-1967). Traces the development of Alexander's political ideas during her studies at Jena University, through the influence of her father-in-law, and in her friendship with leading German Communists such as Karl Kautsky, Rosa Luxemburg, and Franz Mehring. Assesses the impact of her meeting with Clara Zetkin and her joining the Communist Party in 1918. Discusses her work as editor of the Communist newspaper *Die Rote Fahne,* 1920-25. In 1925 she traveled to Moscow and became involved in the international women's movement. Despite some serious illness she continued to work in Moscow and retired in 1949. Based on documents in Susanne Alexander's possession in Moscow and secondary sources; 21 notes. 1882-1967

Alexander I (1777-1825)

85. Dragunov, G. P. PEREPISKA LAGARPA S ALEKSANDROM I [Correspondence between de la Harpe and Alexander I]. *Istoriia SSSR [USSR] 1983 (4): 184-187.* Traces the development of the correspondence between the Russian Tsar Alexander I and the distinguished Swiss politician and philosopher Frédéric César de la Harpe (1754-1838). De la Harpe was brought to Leningrad by Alexander's mother, Catherine II, in 1783 as a French language tutor. He stayed for 11 years and exerted a strong influence on his charge. A lively correspondence was maintained until 1824, when de la Harpe wrote to Alexander that he was disappointed in him, since he had given up the values so painstakingly instilled in him. There was no reply. Based on documents from the Library of Lausanne University; 17 notes. 1783-1824

86. Nichols, Irby C., Jr. TSAR ALEXANDER I: PACIFIST, AGGRESSOR, OR VACILLATOR. *East European Q. 1982 16(1): 33-44.* Reviews the debate on whether or not Alexander I planned an attack on Turkey at the time of his death in 1825. Systematically disproves arguments that Alexander had decided for war and concludes that no evidence exists to show that Alexander's pacifist position toward Turkey in 1821-22 had changed. Based largely on published material; 38 notes. 1820-25

Alexander I (1888-1934)

87. Biber, Dušan. SIR NEVILE HENDERSON O POLITIKI KRALJA ALEKSANDRA DO NACISTIČNE NEMČIJE [Sir Nevile Henderson on the policy of King Alexander I toward Nazi Germany]. *Prispevki za Zgodovino Delavskega Gibanja [Yugoslavia] 1980 20(1-2): 23-29.* 1932-34

*For abstract see **Henderson, Nevile***

Alexandridis, Dimitrios

88. Tabaki, Anna. UN ASPECT DES LUMIERES NEOHELLENIQUES: L'APPROCHE SCIENTIFIQUE DE L'ORIENT. LE CAS DE DIMITRIOS ALEXANDRIDIS [An aspect of the Neo-Hellenic Enlightenment: the scientific study Orient: the case of Dimitrios Alexandridis]. *Ellēnika [Greece] 1984 35(2): 316-337.* It is widely accepted that the Greek Enlightenment of the 18th and 19th centuries began with the study of the culture of Western Europe. In reality, educated Greeks of this period, like the phanariotes, were influenced greatly by Turkish, Persian, and Arabic culture. The influence of Near Eastern culture on the Greek Enlightenment has not been fully appreciated. Dimitrios Alexandridis, who flourished in the first quarter of the 19th century, was one of the leading Greek figures in this movement. Alexandridis was born in Thessaly and studied philology and medicine in Germany. While practicing medicine, he published (from Vienna) the *Greek Telegraph* (1818) and the *Philological Telegraph* (1821) in which he wrote about cultural developments in the Turkish, Persian and Arabic world. In 1802 he translated an Arabic work, *The Geography of Abu al-Fida,* into modern Greek and in 1812 published a Greek-Turkish grammar. 18c-19c

Alföldi, Andreas

89. Alföldi, Maria-R. NEKROLOG: ANDREAS ALFÖLDI (1895-1981) [Obituary: Andreas Alföldi (1895-1981)]. *Hist. Zeits. [West Germany] 1981 233(3): 781-786.* Reviews the career of Hungarian historian, Alföldi who, despite worldwide recognition, was unable to remain in Hungary after 1947. 1895-1981

Alfonso V

90. Ashtor, E. ALFONSO IL MAGNANIMO E I MAMLUCCHI [Alfonso the Magnanimous and the Mamelukes]. *Archivio Storico Italiano [Italy] 1984 142(1): 3-29.* Traces the foreign policy of Alfonso V, the Magnanimous (1396-1458), king of Aragon and Sicily (1416-58), and of Naples (1442-58), toward the Mamelukes, particularly in the Levant. He dreamed of restoring the Eastern Roman Empire and of establishing a new Latin kingdom in Palestine (following a successful crusade). He wished to evict the Turks from the Balkans. Nevertheless, he also engaged in diplomacy and established treaties with the Sultan of Cairo protecting trade between Egypt and Catalonia. 87 notes. 1420-53

Alfonso XIII

91. Gamboa Sánchez-Barcáiztegui, Marcial. MIS RECUERDOS DE DON ALFONSO XIII EN RELACION CON LA ARMADA [My memories of Don Alfonso XIII with respect to the navy]. *Revista General de Marina [Spain] 1986 210(Apr): 493-508.* Recollects anecdotes demonstrating the interest of Spanish King Alfonso XIII in his navy, 1902-31, and his continued interest even while in exile. Includes a final interview with the author in 1939. 1902-30's

92. Marías, Julián. LA ATENCION AL MAR EN EL REINADO DE ALFONSO XIII [Attention to the sea in the reign of Alfonso XIII]. *Revista General de Marina [Spain] 1986 210(Apr): 509-515.* Spanish King Alfonso XIII, who reigned from 1902 to 1931, loved the sea and supported the rebuilding of Spanish naval power after the disastrous Spanish-American War of 1898. 1902-31

'Ali ben Ibrahim

93. LaRue, G. Michael. KHABIR 'ALI AT HOME IN KUBAYH: THE BRIEF BIOGRAPHY OF A DAR FUR CARAVAN LEADER. *African Economic History 1984 13: 56-83.* The life of 'Ali ben Ibrahim, the foremost caravan leader *(khabir)* of mid-19th century Dār Fūr, and an important *hakura* landowner and slaveholder in the Kubayh region, illuminates the nexus between long-distance trade and changes in the control over land and social stratification. As the Dār Fūr sultans moved into nearby al-Fashir, communal landholding gave way to *hakura,* or sultanic land grants.

Khabir 'Ali made the most of the situation by using his commercial success and marriage connections to gain sultanic favor and thereby control the best land around Kubayh. Based on field interviews in 1979-80; 134 notes. 1820-1910

Ali Pasha of Janina

94. Naçi, S. N. RRETH BURIMEVE TË HISTORIOGRAFISË MBI PERJARDHJEN E ALI PASHË TEPELENËS DHE FILLIMET E VEPRIMTARISË SË TIJ [The beginning of the activities of Ali Pasha of Tepelenë]. *Studime Hist. [Albania] 1981 35(2): 219-237.* Contrary to oral tradition and some early biographies, documents prove that Ali Pasha of Janinina was not a descendant of an Anatolian bandit but was the scion of a powerful Albanian family from Tepelenë. His successes and offices were achieved not through crime and banditry, but by legitimate means in a career open to a member of a great family. The biographies by de Pouqueville—*Histoire de Regénération de la Grece* (1925)—and Ahmet Myfit—*Tepedelenli Ali Paşa* (1908)—are inspired by anti-Albanian attitudes and personal ambitions and contribute to the embellishment and perpetuation of inaccurate oral traditions. Secondary sources and official documents; 52 notes. 18c-19c

Alikhanov, Abram I.

95. Frenkel', V. Ia. and Gasparian, B. G. AKADEMIK A. I. ALIKHANOV (MATERIALY K NAUCHNOI BIOGRAFII) [Materials for a scientific biography of Academician A. I. Alikhanov]. *Voprosy Istorii Estestvoznaniia i Tekhniki [USSR] 1984 (2): 75-84.* Between 1927 and 1943 Abram Isaakovich Alikhanov (1904-70) worked at the Leningrad Physico-Technical Institute, and from 1932 concentrated on nuclear physics. He helped develop such fields as proton acceleration and heavy water reactors. His character and achievements are evaluated on the basis of contemporary archival material. Archival materials and secondary literature. 1927-70

Alimjan, Hamid

96. Montgomery, David C. ONCE AGAIN IN TASHKENT. *Asian Affairs [Great Britain] 1983 14(2): 132-147.* Presents an account of the political, professional, and personal problems of an American scholar undertaking biographical research on the Uzbek poet Hamid Alimjan (1909-44). Despite earlier sojourns in Tashkent in 1969 and 1977-78, in 1982 access to archives, securing documents, interviews, and even simple transportation proved to be difficult. The author also comments on religion, the Soviet military, and the Uzbek culture. Based on personal travel and experience; 4 notes. 1909-82

Alkalai, Judah ben Solomon Hai

97. Loker, Zvi. LE RABBIN JUDA BEN SOLOMON HAY ALCALAY ET L'ALLIANCE ISRAELITE UNIVERSELLE A PROPOS DE SES LETTRES INEDITES [Unpublished letters of Rabbi Judah ben Solomon Hay Alcalay and the Universal Jewish Alliance]. *Revue des Etudes Juives [France] 1985 144(1-3): 127-144.* Prints four letters in Hebrew, written between 1868 and 1872, by Judah Hai Alkalai, illustrating his position as a precursor of Zionism. 1868-72

Allāh, Thanā

98. Ali, Yusuf Talal. THE LIFE AND WORKS OF QĀDĪ THANĀ' ALLĀH OF PANIPAT. *Hamdard Islamicus [Pakistan] 1980 3(3): 45-59.* Lists the works of Qādī Thanā Allāh (1731-1810) and describes his diverse and unflagging efforts for the advancement of Islam in his native Panipat. He was a teacher, a spiritual leader, an author, and, for a time, a soldier in the holy war to rid northern India of the Maratha invaders. 1731-1810

Allan, Thomas

99. Hempton, David N. THOMAS ALLAN AND METHODIST POLITICS, 1800-1840. *History [Great Britain] 1982 67(219): 13-31.* Appointed a general solicitor for Methodism in England in 1803, Thomas Allan served as his denomination's foremost lay spokesman in national debates on religious toleration. He organized opposition among dissenting Protestants to bills in Parliament in 1811-12 to restrict the licensing of non-Anglican ministers. In contrast to the English popular radicals, Allan and the Methodists based their claims to liberty not on natural rights but in the constitutional liberty guaranteed by law. Allan tempered the traditional Methodist stance against Catholic rights in the 1820's and ultimately lost influence to a more professional, institutionalized Methodist ministry. Based on Allan's extensive private correspondence; 80 notes. 1803-30's

Allatios, Leon

100. Frazee, Charles. LEON ALLATIOS, A GREEK SCHOLAR OF THE SEVENTEENTH CENTURY. *Modern Greek Studies Yearbook 1985 1: 63-78.* A short life history of Leon Allatios (1587-1669), an important but unknown Catholic Greek scholar who emigrated to Italy in the 17th century and who attempted to unite the Eastern and Western churches. 1600's-69

Almansa, Bernardino de

101. Briceño Jáuregui, Manuel. DON BERNARDINO DE ALMANSA, PERSONALIDAD DISCUTIDA [Don Bernardino de Almansa, a controversial personality]. *Boletín de Historia y Antigüedades [Colombia] 1985 72(748): 9-37.* Bernardino de Almansa, Peruvian-born cleric who served as Archbishop of Santa Fe in 1631-33, has been praised by some for his rectitude and condemned by others for tactless self-will. During his brief tenure as archbishop he engaged in frequent controversies with civil authorities over protocol and jurisdiction. In one of these controversies the Jesuits became involved, in opposition to him. Based on documents in Archivo de Indias, Archivo Nacional de Colombia, and Jesuit archives; 105 notes. 1631-33

Almeida, Cândido Mendes de

102. Lacombe, Americo Jacobina. CANDIDO MENDES DE ALMEIDA [Cândido Mendes de Almeida]. *Rev. do Inst. Hist. e Geog. Brasileiro [Brazil] 1981 (332): 193-203.* Reviews the career and contributions of Cândido Mendes de Almeida, a noted Brazilian senator and jurist of the mid-19th century. He is especially remembered for his work in Brazilian civil law legislation, and in the organization of the Brazilian judiciary. His importance to contemporary Brazil is emphasized. 19c

Almeida, Renato

103. Mariz, Vasco. RENATO ALMEIDA [Renato Almeida]. *Revista do Instituto Histórico e Geográfico Brasileiro [Brazil] 1983 (340): 111-122.* Renato Almeida (1895-1981) was a historian of Brazilian music and folklore. He was the author of a monumental *History of Brazilian Music* and organizer of a campaign in defense of his country's folklore which led to the establishment of the National Folklore Institute. This is a description of his career. 1895-1981

Almirall, Juan

104. Moreno Martin, Armando. VENTURAS Y DESVENTURAS DE FRAY ALMIRALL [Adventures and mishaps of Brother Almirall]. *Rev. Chilena de Hist. y Geog. [Chile] 1980 (148): 137-154.* Brother Juan Almirall was a Franciscan who served as secretary to two Spanish officers leading an expedition to reconquer a rebellious Chile. Almirall actually favored the cause of independence, working with Carrera and O'Higgins. Because of his support for the Chileans, the Spanish authorities confined him to a convent. He would subsequently die, apparently while on a trip, although the date and circumstances remain unknown. 1812-29

Almon, John

105. Rogers, Deborah Dee. "John Almon: A Study of the Literary Career of an Eighteenth-Century Political Bookseller." Columbia U. 1983 186 pp. *DAI 1984 44(8): 2478-A.* DA8327284 1763-84

Alós family

106. Pérez Samper, Maria Angeles. LA FAMILIA ALOS, UNA DINASTIA CATALANA AL SERVICIO DEL ESTADO (SIGLO XVIII) [The Alós family, a Catalan dynasty in the service of the state in the 18th century]. *Cuadernos de Investigación Hist. [Spain] 1982 6: 195-239.* Studies the Alós family, 1617-1844, numerous members of which distinguished themselves in regional and local administration, the Church, the military, and university and cultural life. Provides short biographies of family members, particularly Juan de Alós y Serradora (1617-95), Antonio de Alós y Ríus (1693-1780), and José María de Alós y de Mora (1765-1844). Although the prominence of the family owed a good deal to mutual support, the success of its members was primarily due to the good service they rendered the state. Communication to the Colloquium on the Upper Administration of Spain in the 18th Century, Madrid, 1980. Based on material in the Archivo Histórico Nacional, Archivo Histórico de Protocolos de Barcelona, Archivo de la Historia de la Ciudad (Barcelona), Archivo de la Corona de Aragón; 170 notes. 1617-1844

Alpári, Gyula

107. Varga, Lajos. ALPÁRI GYULA SZÜLETÉSÉNEK CENTENÁRIUMÁRA [For the centennial of the birth of Gyula Alpári]. *Társadalmi Szemle [Hungary] 1982 37(1): 83-87.* Born in 1882, Alpári was a journalist and international organizer and propagandist of socialism. He joined the Hungarian Social Democratic Party in 1901 and published reports on the situation in the army in its organ *Népszava.* Expelled from the party in 1911, he led an opposition group that was the forerunner of the Hungarian Communist Party. In the Hungarian Soviet Republic he headed the press bureau. After the fall of the Soviet republic, he fled, eventually becoming head of the Comintern's *Internationale Presse Korrespondenz* (Inprekorr, Berlin), but he maintained his contact with the Hungarian Party. He was arrested by the Gestapo in Paris in 1940 and executed in 1944. 1901-44

Alpatov, Mikhail A.

108. Vandalkovskaia, M. G. and Kireeva, R. A. TVORCHESKII PUT' MIKHAILA ANTONOVICHA ALPATOVA [The scholarly career of Mikhail Antonovich Alpatov]. *Istoriia SSSR [USSR] 1982 (2): 86-94.* Surveys the life and scholarship of the Soviet historian Mikhail A. Alpatov (1903-80). Born in Rostov-na-Donu, Alpatov joined the Communist Party in 1930, participated in the campaign for the collectivization of agriculture, and conducted political agitation as a Party propagandist. Although most of his scholarly work was devoted to Russian and Western historiography, Alpatov also studied the Cossacks and the Civil War. In addition, Alpatov wrote journalism and film criticism and published at least one successful historical novel. 16 notes. 1903-80

109. —. MIKHAIL ANTONOVICH ALPATOV [Mikhail Antonovich Alpatov]. *Voprosy Istorii [USSR] 1981 (6): 189.* Obituary notice of the Soviet historian Mikhail Antonovich Alpatov (1903-80). He combined his historical work with teaching and a number of editorial and administrative appointments. His main research concern was the history of historical science, in particular the work of 19th-century French Medievalists such as Fustel de Coulanges. He also enjoyed success as a writer of popular fiction with two novels to his credit. 1920's-80

Alquézar, Francisco de

110. Herrera García, Antonio. LA RIQUEZA DE ALGUNOS DESCENDIENTES DE CONVERSOS: LOS MAYORAZGOS FUNDADOS POR EL SEVILLANO FRANCISCO DE ALCAZAR (SIGLO XVI) [The wealth of some descendants of converted Jews: the entailed estates established by Francisco de Alquézar of Seville, 16th century]. *Sefarad [Spain] 1981 41(1): 95-110.* Francisco de Alquézar was the descendant of a family of converted Jews of the city of Seville who enjoyed the patronage and protection of the Guzmans, hereditary dukes of Medina Sidonia. He held high official positions (mayor of the city, overseer of municipal lands, and treasurer of the mint) and was active in trade with the New World. The extent of his wealth is illustrated by the entailed estates he established, 1528-37, for each of his four sons. The author summarizes the lands, houses, rents and encumbrances of these four estates—La Palma, Gelo, Collera, and Puñana—located in and around Seville, and cites some of the documents related to later litigation over their descent. Utilizes material from the Archivo Histórico Nacional; 32 notes. 1528-37

Alt, Franz

111. Schuppanz. "Franz Alt (1821-1914)" [Franz Alt (1821-1914)]. U. of Vienna [Austria] 1980. 310 pp. *DAI-C 1984 45(3): 580; 9/2346c.* 19c

Althusser, Louis

112. Mari, Giovanni. LOUIS ALTHUSSER [Louis Althusser]. *Belfagor [Italy] 1980 35(4): 407-442.* Discusses the main themes in the theoretical work of the French Marxist philosopher Louis Althusser in the context of discussions within the French Communist Party during the past 20 years. 1953-79

Altmann, Adolf

113. Altmann, Alexander. ADOLF ALTMANN (1879-1944): A FILIAL MEMOIR. *Leo Baeck Inst. Year Book [Great Britain] 1981 26: 145-167.* Adolf (Abraham) Altmann, the scion of a Hassidic family, combined traditional piety with the best of Western culture. After study in Pressburg and Vienna, he earned his doctorate with a dissertation on the history of Jewish Salzburg, where he served as rabbi. Eventually he assumed the post of *Oberrabbiner* of Trier, Germany, in which position he remained until his emigration to Holland in 1938. He died at Auschwitz. 2 photos, 76 notes. 1890's-1944

Altunian, Genrikh

114. Geiber, Isak. HENRIKH ALTUNIAN: V ZHYTTI, V SUDI I V SERTSI [The life, trial, and heart of Genrikh Altunian]. *Sučasnist [West Germany] 1982 (1-2): 178-187.* Half-Armenian and half-German, a major in the Soviet army and lecturer in a military academy, Altunian regarded the Soviet system as good but in need of some improvements. His help to those persecuted by the authorities led to his imprisonment. 1967-80

Alured, Lucy

115. Burdon, Pauline. THE SECOND MRS. MARVELL. *Notes and Queries [Great Britain] 1982 29(1): 33-44.* Describes the lineage and relations of Lucy Alured, who married the elder Marvell in 1638, and shows what place the Alureds had in the life of the poet Andrew Marvell (1621-78). 1538-1647

Alvarado, Beatriz de

116. Montezuma Hurtado, Alberto. LA SIN VENTURA DOÑA BEATRIZ [The unfortunate Doña Beatriz]. *Bol. Cultural y Biblio. [Colombia] 1982 19(4): 93-99.* Doña Beatriz, wife of Pedro de Alvarado, suffered when her husband died and shortly thereafter died herself following a volcanic eruption in Guatemala. 1540-41

Alvarado, Lisandro

117. Felice Cardot, Carlos. LISANDRO ALVARADO EN BARQUISIMETO [Lisandro Alvarado in Barquisimeto]. *Bol. de la Acad. Nac. de la Hist. [Venezuela] 1982 65(260): 863-877.* Lisandro Alvarado (1856-1929) was a physician, agronomist, historian, linguist, and anthropologist, for whom a high school and then the University of Barquisimeto were named. Article recalls his connections with the life and people of the city. 22 notes. 1856-1929

118. Octavio, Octavia. ALGUNOS MOMENTOS FAMILIARES DE DON LISANDRO ALVARADO [Some family moments of Don Lisandro Alvarado]. *Bol. de la Acad. Nac. de la Hist. [Venezuela] 1981 64(254): 419-423.* The author, who, as a little girl, knew the noted historian and physician Lisandro Alvarado, remembers the great man, who was a friend of her family, and publishes a letter he wrote to her father and one to herself. 2 unpublished letters, 1 in facsimile. 1920's

Alvarado, Salvador

119. Chacon, Ramon D. SALVADOR ALVARADO AND THE ROMAN CATHOLIC CHURCH: CHURCH-STATE RELATIONS IN REVOLUTIONARY YUCATAN, 1914-1918. *Journal of Church and State 1985 27(2): 245-266.* The role of the Roman Catholic Church in Mexico during the 19th century was one of the issues that led to conflict between the liberals and conservatives. In the revolution of 1910, the Church was again the target of the liberals. Conditions in Yucatan before Salvador Alvarado became governor in 1915 are described. Yucatan had escaped the progressive changes experienced in other areas, and Alvarado saw as his task bringing about these changes, including curbing the Church as a necessary task to succeed in bringing about change. He weakened the Church's political power, associated the Church with the "old order," and eliminated the Church's control over education. Based on government documents and other material; 76 notes. 1857-1922

120. Richmond, Douglas W. SALVADOR ALVARADO AND THE YUCATAN DURING THE MEXICAN REVOLUTION, 1914-1920. *Maryland Historian 1984 15(2): 1-10.* Summarizes the brief career of Salvador Alvarado as governor of Yucatán for Venustiano Carranza. Alvarado mobilized peasants and proletariat by instituting reforms that broke the oligarchy. Based on the Alvarado-Carranza correspondence and secondary sources; 41 notes. 1914-20

Alvarez Bravo, Manuel

121. Masuoka, Susan N. MEXICO'S MASTER IMAGE-MAKER. *Américas (Organization of American States) 1984 36(4): 9-13.* Reviews the career and art of Manuel Alvarez Bravo, Mexico's most famous creative photographer. 1920's-84

Alves de Lima e Silva, Luis

122. Calmon, Pedro. IMAGEM E GLORIA DO DUQUE DE CAXIAS [Portrait and glory of the Duke of Caxias]. *Rev. do Inst. Hist. e Geog. Brasileiro [Brazil] 1980 (327): 227-234.* Luis Alves de Lima e Silva, Duke of Caxias (1803-80), father of the Brazilian army, fought in the early wars for the unification of the country against fissiparous tendencies and in the war against Paraguay. 1820's-80

123. Moreira Bento, Cláudio. FONTES DA CULTURA EM ARTE DA GUERRA DO DUQUE DE CAXIAS [Sources of the Duque de Caxias's culture in the art of war]. *Rev. do Inst. Hist. e Geog. Brasileiro [Brazil] 1980 (328): 121-130.* Luis Alves de Lima e Silva, Duque de Caxias, was one of Brazil's greatest statesmen and military men. He is the patron of the Brazilian army and is considered by some as the founder of its nationality. On the centenary of his death, describes his military culture and the way in which he acquired it. 9 notes. 1803-80

124. —. [The Duke of Caxias]. *Revista do Instituto Histórico e Geográfico Brasileiro [Brazil] 1983 (338): 175-196.*

Pondé, Francisco de Paula e Azevedo. O DUQUE DE CAXIAS [The Duke of Caxias], *pp. 175-184.* On the occasion of the Brazilian army's yearly commemoration of its patron's birthday, recalls the life and career of the great leader (1803-80). 10 notes.

Moreira Bento, Cláudio. CENTENARIO DA MORTE DO DUQUE DE CAXIAS [Centenary of the death of the Duke of Caxias], *pp. 185-196.* Recalls the last days, death, and funeral of the 19th-century national leader and gives a list of objects belonging to the Duke that are preserved in various national museums. 1803-80

Alvinczi, Péter

125. Kocsis, Attila. "AZ IGAZNAK EMLÉKEZETE ÁLDOTT!" ["Blessed is the memory of the just!"]. *Theologiai Szemle [Hungary] 1985 28(3): 165-169.* Péter Alvinczi (1570-1634), initiator of the Protestant union, refused to accept the existence of separate denominations within the Protestant Church. His attempt to reconcile the Calvinists with the Lutherans across the country was unsuccessful. He refused all political assignments, but as chaplain in the court of István Bocskai, prince of Transylvania, 1605-06, and later in that of his successor, Gábor Bethlen, 1613-29, he was taken into the confidence of both rulers and had far-reaching political influence. Biblio. 1600-34

Amado, Jorge

126. Ortiz, Griselda. JORGE AMADO: CINCUENTA AÑOS DE NOVELAR [Jorge Amado: fifty years as a novelist]. *U. de La Habana [Cuba] 1981 (215): 78-98.* Reviews the novels of Jorge Amado and discusses the various stages of his career as a writer in Brazil. 1912-79

Ambedkar, Bhimrao Ramji

127. Kuber, W. N. DR. AMBEDKAR COLLECTION IN BOMBAY UNIVERSITY. *Indian Arch. [India] 1980 29(1): 38-40.* Lists the contents of a collection consisting of books, leaflets, periodicals, newspapers, and press clippings donated by Bhimrao Ramji Ambedkar's biographer, C. B. Khairmoday, to the Bombay University library. These materials throw light on some aspects of political and educational work as well as on the Hindu reaction to his decision regarding the mass conversion of Untouchables to Buddhism. Ref. 1924-59

Amel'ko, Nikolai N.

128. Kasatonov, V. ADMIRAL N. N. AMEL'KO (K 70-LETIIU SO DNIA ROZHDENIIA) [Admiral N. N. Amel'ko: on his 70th birthday]. *Voenno-Istoricheskii Zhurnal [USSR] 1984 (11): 89-92.* Outlines the career of Soviet admiral Nikolai N. Amel'ko (b. 1914), who took part in the defense of Tallin in 1941 and the evacuation of the Tallin troops to Kronstadt. Secondary sources; 2 photos, 7 notes. 1930's-84

Amend, Edward John

129. Amend, Edward John. ESCAPE FROM STARVING RUSSIA. *J. of the Am. Hist. Soc. of Germans from Russia 1981 4(3): 17-24; 1982 5(1): 17-20, (3): 49-54.* Part 1. Edward John Amend, a German Russian living in Walter, which was located on the Volga Bergseite, provides an account of his plans for escaping to Austria in 1921. Part 2. Posing as an Austrian prisoner of war and accompanied by two Hungarian prisoners of war, German settler Edward John Amend began his escape from Russia. Part 3. On the beginning leg of his escape, Amend was first impressed by Moscow, but then became disillusioned with Communism during the 1921 May-Day fete. 1921

Amendola, Giovanni

130. D'Auria, Elio. FILOSOFIA, POLITICA E TRADIZIONE NAZIONALE IN GIOVANNI AMENDOLA [Philosophy, politics, and national tradition in Giovanni Amendola]. *Veltro [Italy] 1982 26(3-4): 179-193.* Examines the life of the Italian scholar and politician Giovanni Amendola (1882-1926), who at the beginning of the 20th century fought for liberty and democracy. 1904-25

131. Quagliariello, Ernesto. LA TESTIMONIANZA DI GIOVANNI AMENDOLA [The witness of Giovanni Amendola]. *Studium [Italy] 1982 78(5): 545-554.* Recalls the memory of a politician who during the critical period of the decline of the liberal state and the rise of Fascism was conspicuous by his high moral standards and sense of public responsibility and was assassinated by a Fascist squad in 1925. 1920-25

Amiel, Henri-Frédéric

132. Ferenczi, László. AMIEL ÉS A MAGYAROK [Amiel and the Hungarians]. *Helikon Világirodalmi Figyelő [Hungary] 1984 30(2-4): 298-302.* Genevan Henri-Frédéric Amiel's (1821-81) diary was one of the outstanding products of classical literature in the French language. Amiel was very interested in political and literary developments in Hungary. In his diary in 1857 he mentioned the famous Hungarian poet Sándor Petőfi, and on 12 May 1860 he wrote at great length about Petőfi, whom he considered a genius and whose work he read in the German translation by Kertbeny. 19c

133. Monnier, Philippe M. ENFANT SOUS LA RESTAURATION: LES PREMIERS ÉCRITS DE HENRI-FRÉDÉRIC AMIEL [Child of the Restoration: the first writings of Henri-Frédéric Amiel]. *Mus. de Genève [Switzerland] 1981 (215): 2-8.* Commemorates the 100th anniversary of the death of Genevan moralist and poet Henri-Frédéric Amiel (d. 1881), providing a brief history, texts, and facsimiles of his early writings from age 7 to 17. 1821-38

Amīn ud-Dawlah, Mīrza Alī Khān

134. Farmayan, Hafez. PORTRAIT OF A NINETEENTH-CENTURY IRANIAN STATESMAN: THE LIFE AND TIMES OF GRAND VIZIER AMĪN UD-DAWLAH, 1844-1904. *Int. J. of Middle East Studies [Great Britain] 1983 15(3): 337-351.* Examines the life and times of Mīrza Alī Khān Amīn ud-Dawlah, and the working of late 19th century Iranian power politics. Amīn ud-Dawlah's policies exacerbated the two basic factors that underlined the decline of modern Iran: Russo-British rivalry and in-fighting among Iranian political figures at the Shah's court in Tehran. Based on Amīn ud-Dawlah's *Memoirs* and other primary sources; 46 notes. 1844-1904

Amīr 'Ali, Sayyid

135. Ahsan, Abdullah. A LATE NINETEENTH CENTURY MUSLIM RESPONSE TO THE WESTERN CRITICISM OF ISLAM—AN ANALYSIS OF AMĪR 'ALI'S LIFE AND WORKS. *American Journal of Islamic Social Sciences 1985 2(2): 179-206.* In the 19th century, in response to Sir William Muir's European biases against Islam as expressed in his *Life of Mahomet,* Sayyid Amīr 'Ali wrote about Islam in India in Western terms, partially to present the Muslim case to the British authorities; his writings inspired hero worship of himself and a new self-confidence among Indian Muslims. 1870's-90's

Amiras, Alexander

136. Karathanassis, Athanassios E. L'EXEMPLE D'UN ERUDIT GREC EN MOLDOVALACHIE: ALEXANDRE AMIRAS (1679-1740) [The example of a Greek scholar established in Moldo-Wallachia: Alexander Amiras, 1679-1740]. *Balkan Studies [Greece] 1982 23(2): 321-340.* Alexander Amiras, a distinguished scholar of the Phanariote period, is well known for the important role he played in the political and cultural affairs of the Romanian principalities. After an initial period of studies in Rome and Constan-

tinople, he worked as a Counsellor to Charles XII, king of Sweden, at his court at Bendari, and later, to Prince Gr. Grikas at his court at Iaşi, in Moldavia. During this period Amiras translated from Moldavian to Modern Greek the chronicle of Miron and Nicolas Costin on the history of Moldavia (1729), wrote the history of the life of Charles XII during his exile at Bendari, and compiled a small treatise about the names of the Turkish Sultans. 1679-1740

Amorim, Enrique

137. Rojas, Santiago. ENRIQUE AMORIM Y EL GRUPO DE BOEDO [Enrique Amorim and the Boedo group]. *Inter-American Rev. of Biblio. 1981 31(3): 378-384.* The literary Generation of 1922 in Buenos Aires was composed of two groups, named for the streets of Florida and Boedo. Those of Florida, rich and aristocratic, were interested in aesthetics and were in the literary vanguard. Those of Boedo, humble and proletarian, wanted to change the world—some called them anarchists and communists. Enrique Amorim (1900-60) came to Buenos Aires from Uruguay and published his first work there in 1920. Although from a rich family, his works showed a sympathy with the poor, and he was first aligned with the Boedo group. His writings on the poor of the rural areas deromanticized them. Many of Amorim's later works were about city dwellers and written in the Florida style. Amorim represents a synthesis for the two groups of the Generation of 22. Based on a study of Amorim's works; 24 notes. 1922-28

Amort, Čestmir

138. *Slovanský Přehled* editors. ŠEDESÁTINY ČESTMÍRA AMORTA [Čestmír Amort's 60th birthday]. *Slovanský Přehled [Czechoslovakia] 1982 68(2): 165-168.* A member of the Communist Party since 1943 and involved in the antifascist struggles of the time, after the war Amort devoted himself to the studies of other socialist countries, especially Czechoslovak-Bulgarian relations. His latest book is *Georgi Dimitrov a Československý Lid* [Georgi Dimitrov and the Czechoslovakian people]. He has also been a prolific producer of history textbooks and the recipient of many Czech and Bulgarian academic prizes. 1943-82

139. Vasiliev, Vasil A. PROFESOR CHESTMIR AMORT NA 60 GODINI [Professor Čestmir Amort's 60th birthday]. *Istoricheski Pregled [Bulgaria] 1982 38(5): 178-181.* Čestmir Amort, the Czech historian of Bulgaria, celebrated his 60th birthday on 21 March 1982. He joined the Communist Party of Czechoslovakia in 1943, visited Bulgaria for the first time in 1946, and from 1960 devoted himself to Bulgarian affairs. He published a biography of Georgi Dimitrov in 1960, *Bulgarian People in the Struggle against Fascism from 1923* in 1973, and *On the Freedom of the Bulgarian People* in 1978. He also wrote a 765 page *History of Bulgaria.* He was awarded the order of Cyril and Methodius on the 90th anniversary of Georgi Dimitrov's death. Based on biographical sources and the works of Chestmir Amort. 1943-82

Amrein, Josef Georg

140. Suter, Heinrich. EIN ORDENSGRÜNDER UND PIONIER DER ENTWICKLUNGSHILFE [Founder of an order and pioneer in developmental aid]. *Civitas [Switzerland] 1984 39(4): 128-132.* A biography of Josef Georg Amrein (1844-1927) who, as Andreas Amrhein, joined the Benedictine Order in Beuron, Germany in 1870 and in 1884 founded the Benedictine Congregation for Foreign Missions, which from small beginnings has grown into a vast missionary operation of developmental aid all over the world. 1844-1927

Anand, Mulk Raj

141. Kalinnikova, E. INDIISKII DANKO [The Indian Danko]. *Aziia i Afrika Segodnia [USSR] 1985 (12): 52-54.* Discusses the life and works of Indian author and International Peace Prize winner Mulk Raj Anand (born 1905). Introduction to translations of two Anand stories, "The Dreamer" and "The Witch," in the same issue (pp. 54-56). English summary. 1935-85

Anastasia

142. Duhamel, Catherine. JE L'AFFIRME: MME ANDERSON ETAIT ANASTASIA [I affirm it: Mme. Anderson was Anastasia]. *Historama [France] 1985 (14): 52-58.* Examines the possibility of Anna Anderson being Anastasia Romanovna, the missing grand duchess of Russia, and discusses the search for the escaped Anastasia by the Bolsheviks in 1918, the imperial Russian family's refusal to recognize Anderson (alias Mme. Chaikovskaia) as the true Anastasia, the psychological state of Anderson, the belief that she may have actually been a missing Polish worker, Franziska Schanzkowska, and the hostility of the Romanovs on the subject of Anastasia. 1918-84

Anchieta, José de

143. Rumeu de Armas, Antonio. UNA CARTA INEDITA DEL APOSTOL DEL BRASIL, BEATO JOSE DE ANCHIETA AL REY FELIPE II: LA EXPEDICION DE DIEGO FLORES DE VALDES AL MAGALLANES [An unpublished letter of José de Anchieta, apostle to Brazil, to King Philip II: the expedition of Diego Flores de Valdés to the Straits of Magellan]. *Hispania [Spain] 1985 45(159): 5-32.* Publishes facsimile and transcription of an unpublished letter dated 7 August 1583 from St. José de Anchieta (1534-1597), prolific author, Jesuit Provincial, and missionary to Brazil, to Philip II of Spain. Sets the historical background for the letter, particularly early settlement and missionary activity in Brazil, and the Spanish expedition led by Diego Flores de Valdés and Pedro Sarmiento de Gamboa to establish forts and settlements in the Straits of Magellan. Their fleet laid over at Rio de Janeiro March-November 1582, and Anchieta provided them assistance. The author provides information on the Spanish response to French and English pirates in the region as well as Anchieta's views on the progress of conversion in Brazil. Based on a MS in the Archivo General de Simancas, Guerra Antigua section; 46 notes. 1582-83

144. Viotti, Hélio Abranches. A VIDA DO PADRE ANCHIETA [The life of Father Anchieta]. *Revista do Instituto Histórico e Geográfico Brasileiro [Brazil] 1983 (339): 91-103.* José de Anchieta (1534-97) was among the first Jesuits sent to Brazil. He played a pioneering role in its colonization and conversion. He learned and codified the main local language and wrote on the art of preaching and catechizing as well as on native customs. 6 notes. 1534-97

Ancízar, Manuel

145. Perazzo, Nicolás. MANUEL ANCIZAR: COLOMBIANO ILUSTRE, AMIGO DE VENEZUELA [Manuel Ancízar: illustrious Colombian, friend of Venezuela]. *Bol. de la Acad. Nac. de la Hist. [Venezuela] 1982 65(259): 615-617.* Manuel Ancízar (1812-82) taught philosophy and political

economy in Caracas and Valencia. His political ideas made it difficult for him to reside permanently in Venezuela. 1812-82

Andersen, Hans Christian

146. Jansen, Steen. H. C. ANDERSEN: NOTE SULLE AUTOBIOGRAFIE [Hans Christian Andersen: notes on autobiographies]. *Veltro [Italy] 1981 25(1-3): 169-180.* Analyzes Hans Christian Andersen's *Ricordi,* which remained unpublished in his own lifetime, and compares it with his official portraits of himself published in 1847 and 1855, all of which carry a common conviction that superior gifts, given the help of Providence, can carry an individual in society. 1832-55

Anderson, Anna

147. Duhamel, Catherine. JE L'AFFIRME: MME ANDERSON ETAIT ANASTASIA [I affirm it: Mme. Anderson was Anastasia]. *Historama [France] 1985 (14): 52-58.* 1918-84
For abstract see ***Anastasia***

Anderson, Vernon

148. Sanders, James. THE VERNON ANDERSON PAPERS. *Hist. in Africa 1981 8: 361-364.* Vernon Anderson was a Presbyterian missionary in the Congo from 1921 until 1946. A collection of his letters, notebooks, and other materials is inventoried here. Primary source; note. 1921-46

Andersson, Otto

149. Rosas, John. OTTO ANDERSSONS VÄG FRÅN VÅRDÖ TILL ÅBO AKADEMI [Otto Andersson's path from Vårdö to Åbo Akademy]. *Hist. och Litteraturhistoriska Studier [Finland] 1983 58: 99-136.* Traces the academic career of the Finnish music scholar Otto Andersson (1879-1969) from his birth as a farmer's son in the Åland Islands, through music studies in Turku and Helsinki, to his appointment in 1926 as professor of music and folk poetry at Åbo Academy in Turku, Finland. Based on private papers in various Finnish archives; 3 illus., 83 notes. 1879-1926

Andics, Erzsébet

150. Gergely, András. ZUM 80. GEBURTSTAG VON ERZSÉBET ANDICS [Erzsébet Andic's 80th birthday]. *Ann. U. Sci. Budapestinensis de Rolando Eötvös Nominatae: Sectio Hist. [Hungary] 1982 22: 267-276.* A tribute to Erzsébet Andics (b. 1902), including a biography of her professional career. She is one of the historians specializing in revolutionary movements of 1848-49 and 1918-19 in Hungary. 11 notes. 1848-49

Andrade, Olegario

151. Castagnino, Raúl A. OLEGARIO V. ANDRADE: OLVIDO Y RESCATE DE UNA LIRA [Olegario V. Andrade: recovering his poetry from oblivion]. *Bol. de la Acad. Argentina de Letras [Argentina] 1982 47(185-186): 235-248.* The memory of Olegario Andrade (d. 1882) has fallen into unmerited oblivion, and not even his biographical data have been carefully researched. Assembles what is known of his early years, his career as a journalist, and the sources of his inspiration and pleads for a better study of his poetry. 1840's-82

152. Marcos, Juan Manuel. RELECTURA DE OLEGARIO VICTOR ANDRADE [A reevaluation of Olegario Victor Andrade]. *Cuadernos Hispanoamericanos [Spain] 1986 (427): 139-145.* Olegario Victor Andrade (1839-82) is known in the literary history of Argentina as the singer of the nation's glories through his allegorical poems, since that was the role the Buenos Aires oligarchy entrusted to him in his mature years; in contrast, it was in his juvenile Entre Ríos sojourn, when he adhered to revolutionary federalism, that he reached his highest literary quality, both in poetry and journalism. 19c

Andranik, General

153. Nersissian, M.; Harutyunian, A.; and Mouradian, D. MATERIALY O GENERALE ANDRANIKE [Documents on General Andranik]. *Patma-Banasirakan Handes. Istoriko-Filologicheskii Zhurnal [USSR] 1981 (4): 242-248.* Three documents on General Andranik (1865-1927). 1) Torgom Gevorgian's memoirs state that, upon witnessing the famine and misery in Daralagiaz (April 1919), Andranik publicly expressed his anger to Major Gibbon for Britain's failure to keep its promises of help. 2) A letter dated 12 July 1918 by two Russian officers, Bort and Kolmakovi, stresses that Andranik took measures to prevent racial conflicts, contrary to Turkish rumors that he organized Moslem massacres in Nakhichevan and Zangezur. 3) Andranik's letter (1926, from Fresno) to representatives of the Committee of Assistance to Armenia, who were in New York to raise money. Andranik welcomes their initiative and reveals his decision to present his sword to the Erevan History Museum. Primary sources; 10 notes. Armenian summary. 1918-26

Andreas, Cardinal

154. Maier, Konstantin. RESIDENZ, KOADJUTORIE ODER RESIGNATION: DER KAMPF ERZHERZOG FERDINANDS VON ÖSTERREICH UM DAS BISTUM KONSTANZ [Residence, coadjustorship, or resignation: Archduke Ferdinand of Austria's campaign for the bishopric of Constance]. *Zeitschrift für Kirchengeschichte [West Germany] 1985 96(3): 344-376.* ca 1525-85
For abstract see ***Ferdinand II***

Andreas-Salomé, Lou

155. Jimeno Valdés, Agustín. LA MUJER ANTE EL CAMBIO SOCIO-CULTURAL Y LOU ANDREAS SALOME [Woman before sociocultural change and Lou Andreas-Salomé]. *Folia Humanistica [Spain] 1982 20(231): 241-259.* Discusses the changing status of women, and the life of Lou Andreas-Salomé, mistress of Rainer Maria Rilke. 19c-20c

Andrei, Petre

156. Eşanu, L. PETRE ANDREI, ESQUISSE DE PORTRAIT COMMÉMORATIF [Petre Andrei, a commemorative portrait]. *Rev. Roumaine d'Hist. [Romania] 1981 20(2): 329-338.* Reviews the life and political career of the remarkable Petre Andrei (1891-1940) whose work *Sociologie Générale* in 1936 was considered a cultural event of inestimable value for Romanian philosophical literature. After studies in Iaşi under Dimitrie Gusti and research in Leipzig and Berlin, Andrei enjoyed a brilliant teaching career at the University of Iaşi while participating in antifascist movements such as the National Committee for Peace and serving the National Peasant Party in various elective capacities. He became Minister of Education in the Miron Cristea government, but intense opposition from the Legionary regime led to his suicide. Based on state archives in Iaşi and Bucharest and secondary works; 36 notes. 1891-1940

Andrén, Georg

157. Hessler, Carl Arvid. ATT LÄRA KÄNNA SAMHÄLLET [Learning to know society]. *Statsvetenskaplig Tidskrift [Sweden] 1982 85(3): 149-153.* Describes teaching and scholarship of three Swedish professors at the University of Göteborg around 1925-35: the sociologist Gustaf Steffen (1864-1929), the historian Curt Weibull (b. 1886), and the political scientist Georg Andrén (1890-1969). 1925-35

Andreu, Pierre

158. Hoffman, Robert L.; Rice-Maximin, Edward (commentary). WILD SWINGS, AND OTHER ODDITIES OF POLITICAL COMMITMENT. *Proceedings of the Annual Meeting of the Western Society for French History 1983 11: 361-369.* Briefly examines the political careers and writings of several Frenchmen of the first half of the 20th century. These include Georges Valois (1878-1945), Edouard Berth (1875-1939), Georges Soulès (b. 1907), and Pierre Andreu (b. 1909), among others. These individuals were similar in that at various times in their careers they made abrupt shifts in their political beliefs. The groups that they belonged to, at different times, included conservatives, fascists, communists, anarchists, and liberals. A person's family and educational background could have a complex influence on radical shifts in political allegiance. Comments, pp. 370-371. Based on printed primary sources and secondary works; 14 notes. 1900-40

Andrew, Charles Kenneth Croft

159. Ashcroft, M. Y. CHARLES KENNETH CROFT ANDREW 1899-1981. *J. of the Soc. of Arch. [Great Britain] 1982 7(1): 66-68.* An obituary of Charles Kenneth Croft Andrew, outlining his early career, his antiquarian studies, and particularly his achievements in organizing and improving the accommodation of the archives of North Riding, Yorkshire, as county archivist, 1949-65. 1899-1981

Andrewes, Thomas (Governor)

160. Elliot, David C. SOME SLIGHT CONFUSION: A NOTE ON THOMAS ANDREWES AND THOMAS ANDREWES. *Huntington Library Quarterly 1984 47(2): 129-132.* 1640-64

*For abstract see **Andrewes, Thomas (Lord Mayor of London)***

Andrewes, Thomas (Lord Mayor)

161. Elliot, David C. SOME SLIGHT CONFUSION: A NOTE ON THOMAS ANDREWES AND THOMAS ANDREWES. *Huntington Library Quarterly 1984 47(2): 129-132.* Thomas Andrewes (d. 1659), Lord Mayor of London under the Commonwealth, was not the same Thomas Andrewes who served as Governor of the East India Company in 1659. Based on primary sources; 14 notes. 1640-64

Andrić, Ivo

162. Butler, Thomas. BETWEEN EAST AND WEST: THREE BOSNIAN WRITER-REBELS. *Cross Currents 1984 3: 339-357.* Compares the lives and literature of three Bosnian authors who advanced independence movements against the Habsburg Empire and/or the Nazi military occupation: Serbian Orthodox Peter Kočić (1877-1916), Croatian Catholic Ivo Andrić (1892-1975), and Muslim Communist Meša Selimović (1910-82). All three transformed the oral tradition to promote Bosnian nationalism. 1878-82

163. Dimić, Milan V. IVO ANDRIĆ AND WORLD LITERATURE. *Canadian Slavonic Papers [Canada] 1985 27(3): 269-283.* Ivo Andrić (1892-1975) was born in Bosnia under Austrian rule, wrote in the "ijekavian" form of Serbo-Croatian, and became one of the star authors of the Yugoslav socialist regime, winning the Nobel prize for literature in 1961. Andrić belongs to world literature, both in the Goethean sense of *Weltliteratur*, at home in the international literary tradition, and in T. S. Eliot's typology as one of those adding something unique to the open-ended, permanently evolving system of letters constituting a universal heritage. In his narrative fiction Andrić combined traditional mimetic concerns with a distinctively modernist stance and form. His Bosnian landscapes were archetypes, metaphors, or at least similes for man's existential predicament. Based on analysis of Andrić's own theoretical essays, his unpublished papers, secondary studies; 39 notes. 1913-75

164. Mihailovich, Vasa D. THE RECEPTION OF THE WORKS OF IVO ANDRIĆ IN THE ENGLISH-SPEAKING WORLD. *Southeastern Europe 1982 9(1-2): 41-52.* The interest in the writing of Yugoslav author Ivo Andrić in the English-speaking world expanded only in the late 1950's, reaching a peak immediately after his receipt of the Nobel Prize in 1961. 72 notes. 1960-79

Androić, Mirko

165. Rastić, Marijan. MIRKO ANDROIĆ [Mirko Androić]. *Arhivski Vjesnik [Yugoslavia] 1982 25: 117-118.* Mirko Androić was born on 8 July 1922 in Varaždin, Yugoslavia and died on 7 June 1982. He studied history at the Philosophy Faculty in Zagreb, and became an archivist in the Varaždin History Archive. His principal interest was the history, industrial development, and workers' movement of Varaždin and Northwest Croatia. 1952-82

Andropov, Yuri

166. Glazov, Yuri. YURI ANDROPOV: A NEW LEADER OF RUSSIA. *Studies in Soviet Thought [Netherlands] 1983 26(3): 173-215.* Traces the life and career of Yuri Andropov, examining his diplomatic achievements, his rise in the state security apparatus to chief of the KGB in 1967, and, finally, his emergence in 1982 as head of the Politburo, de facto ruler of the USSR. Based on memoirs and press sources; 18 notes. 1914-83

167. Schneider, Eberhard. JURIJ WLADIMIROWITSCH ANDROPOW [Yuri Vladimirovich Andropov]. *Osteuropa [West Germany] 1983 33(3-4): 194-200.* Describes Yuri Andropov's life and the phases of his activity in the Communist Party. 1914-82

Ange, Brother

168. Hanna, Blake T. LA FRERE ANGE, CARME DECHAUSSE, ET DENIS DIDEROT [Brother Ange, a Discalced Carmelite, and Denis Diderot]. *Revue d'Histoire Littéraire de la France [France] 1984 84(3): 373-389.* A biographical study of Brother Ange, centering on this Discalced Carmelite's relations with French philosopher Denis Diderot (1713-84). 18c

Angeles, Carlos Antonio de los

169. Brunet, José. MERCEDARIOS EN EL EJERCICIO DE LA MEDICINA EN EL SIGLO XVIII [Mercedarians in the practice of medicine in the 18th century]. *Estudios [Spain] 1985 41(148): 101-106.* Traces the lives of two Mercedarian priests active in South American missions from

which the Jesuits had been expelled who practiced medicine and pharmacy for the benefit of both Indians and Spaniards: Carlos Antonio de los Angeles and José Felipe Sánchez del Castillo. 1730's-90's

Angell, Norman

170. Biocca, Dario. IL NUOVO PACIFISMO E IL DIBATTITO SULLE CONSEQUENZE ECONOMICHE DELL' IMPERIALISMO E DELLA GUERRA: 1913-1915 [The new pacifism and the debate on the economic consequences of imperialism and war: 1913-15]. *Nuova Riv. Storica [Italy] 1982 66(5-6): 547-563.* Focuses on Norman Angell's career in order to rebut A. J. P. Taylor's description of the new pacifists as "trouble makers." His economic analysis, drawn largely from J. H. Hobson, was not only largely accurate, but very popular. He differed from Hobson only in calling war stupidity, not the product of conspiracy. It could be averted only by explaining its impact to the powerful. He thus distanced himself from traditional pacifism; his largest backers were the Carnegie Foundation and the Rowntree Trust. The high point of his movement came at the La Toquet conference in 1913. An attempt to issue a strong statement for neutrality before the outbreak of war was abortive. 26 notes. 1913-15

Angoulême, Marguerite d'

171. Vose, Heather M. MARGUERITE OF NAVARRE: THAT "RIGHTE ENGLISH WOMAN." *Sixteenth Century Journal 1985 16(3): 315-333.* Marguerite d' Angoulême, sister to Francis I and daughter of Louise of Savoy, "enhanced" rather than dominated the court, which meant that she was more flexible and charming than her domineering mother and was a more effective promoter of the king's interests. In dealing with the court of Henry VIII, she emerges as an incorruptible diplomat whose own individualized approach to spiritual matters made her sympathize with the religious difficulties of Henry VIII and Anne Boleyn. She preferred compromise and negotiation to fanaticism and war, and therefore she looks especially attractive to us. Based on state papers from the reign of Henry VIII and secondary sources; 106 notes. 1520-40's

Angulo, Gonzalo de

172. —. [THE LABOR OF BISHOP GONZALO DE ANGULO]. *Boletin de la Academia Nacional de la Historia [Venezuela] 1984 67(267): 457-473.*

Quintero, José Humberto. LA LABOR DEL OBISPO GONZALO DE ANGULO [The labor of Bishop Gonzalo de Angulo], *pp. 457-469.* Describes the efforts of Bishop Angulo of Caracas in defense of the rights of Indians in Venezuela, in discharge of an order from the king.

Mendoza, Cristobal L. CONTESTACION [Reply], *pp. 469-473.* Responds to the preceding presentation by Cardinal Quintero on the occasion of the latter's reception as a member of the Academia Nacional de la Historia. Based on material in the Caracas archdiocesan archive. 1619-33

Anikulapo-Kuti, Fela

173. Labijoh, Justin. FELA ANIKULAPO-KUTI: PROTEST MUSIC AND SOCIAL PROCESSES IN NIGERIA. *J. of Black Studies 1982 13(1): 119-135.* Applies the life history methodology of J. Dollard on the life of Fela Anikulapo-Kuti to critique the culture of modern Nigeria. After studying music in England, Fela worked for the Nigerian Broadcasting Corporation, 1963-68. He then led a band, playing first highlife, then jazz, soul, and finally Afrobeat music, which was experimental in style and increasingly protest in content. Lower-class youths adopted Fela as a symbol of their protest against the Nigerian establishment and flocked to his commune, the Kalukuta Republic, until the military burned it in 1977. Based on interviews; 2 notes, biblio. 1963-77

Anna of Saxony

174. Ridder-Symoens, Hilde de. VROUWEN ROND WILLEM VAN ORANJE [Women around William of Orange]. *Spiegel Historiael [Netherlands] 1984 19(4): 181-186.* 1533-84

*For abstract see **William the Silent***

Anne of Austria

175. Pasteur, Claude. LES MEDECINS ET LE SEIN D'ANNE D'AUTRICHE [The physicians and Anne of Austria's breast]. *Historama [France] 1984 (6): 40-45.* Traces the evolution of the disease of the French queen (1601-66), who died of breast cancer. 1664-66

Anne of France

176. Decaux, Alain. ANNE DE BEAUJEU, "LA MOINS FOLLE FEMME DE FRANCE" [Anne of Beaujeu, "the least deluded woman of France"]. *Historama [France] 1985 (13): 36-42.* Anne of Beaujeu (1461-1522) effectively ruled France for eight years following the death of her father, King Louis XI, in 1483. Charles VIII was of age to rule, but had been left uneducated; Anne tutored him skillfully and wisely, but Charles eventually shook off her influence, drove her from court, and went his own ineffective way. 1483-91

Annesley, Samuel

177. Newton, John A. SAMUEL ANNESLEY (1620-1696) (THE WESLEY HISTORICAL SOCIETY LECTURE, 1985). *Proceedings of the Wesley Historical Society [Great Britain] 1985 45(2): 29-45.* Gives a history of the life and ministry of the 17th-century Nonconformist Samuel Annesley (1620-96), John Wesley's maternal grandfather. Explores the relationship between Annesley and his favorite daughter Susanna and examines Annesley's impact on Wesley as a Puritan divine. 1620-96

Annesley family

178. Young, Betty I. SOURCES FOR THE ANNESLEY FAMILY. *Proceedings of the Wesley Historical Society [Great Britain] 1985 45(2): 46-57.* Provides information about the Annesley family in 17th-century England, Susanna Annesley being John Wesley's mother. 17c

Antheil, George

179. Whitesitt, Linda. "The Life and Music of George Antheil (1900-1959). (Vol. 1 & 2) U. of Maryland 1981. 767 pp. *DAI 1982 43(6): 1743-A.* DA8214492 1920's-59

Anthemos VI

180. Charamanta, Geōrgiou Dr. ANTHEMOS Z' [Anthemos VI]. *Ēpeirōtikē Estia [Greece] 1985 85(397-399): 177-191.* Anthemos VI (1828-1913), Ecumenical Patriarch from 1885 to 1897, studied at the Zosimias school in Ioannina. He received his theological training at the theological school of Halkidikē, and was then appointed professor at the Zosimias school. He served as metropolitan of Leros and Kalymnos before becoming patriarch. As patriarch he raised funds for a new wing of his theological school. In 1897, due to ecclesiastical politics, he was forced to resign. Primary sources; 32 notes. 1828-1913

Antoir, Joseph

181. Gasparri, Aulo. IL DIARIO DI UN PROFUGO DELLA RIVOLUZIONE FRANCESE [The diary of a fugitive from the French Revolution]. *Riv. Italiana di Studi Napoleonici [Italy] 1980 17(2): 103-108.* The author of the diary was Joseph Antoir, born in Toulon in 1781. Antoir describes himself as "an unpretentious man who wishes no more than to record his memories." The French Revolution forced his family to leave their home in 1803. They found shelter on a British warship and went to Portoferraio, on the island of Elba, then to Corsica, then to Florence. In Florence Antoir met the poet Alphonse Lamartine and other French literary figures. His diary ends in 1836. Based on a manuscript preserved in the Foresiana of Portoferraio, 11 notes. 1824-36

Antonescu, Ion

182. Ionescu, Mihail E. APOGEUL CRIZEI POLITICO-MILITARE A REGIMULUI ANTONESCIAN ÎN PREAJMA DECLANŞĂRII INSURECŢIEI DIN AUGUST 1944 [The apogee of the political and military crisis of the Antonescu regime on the eve of the outbreak of the August 1944 uprising]. *Rev. de Istorie [Romania] 1980 33(9): 1651-1667.* Details the activities and plans of Ion Antonescu during his final days as fascist dictator of Romania, 20-23 August 1944, just before the antifascist uprising. It appears that Antonescu intended to maintain power by establishing an armistice with the Soviet Union after stabilizing the East Carpathian-Danube Delta military front, either with German consent or by initiating hostilities against the Germans, but his plans were foiled by the uprising. Based on archival documents and published primary and secondary sources; 64 notes. French summary. 1944

Antonio

183. Orgel, Irene. THE TWENTY-FIRST KING OF PORTUGAL. *Midstream 1985 31(3): 33-36.* Long misrepresented as an illegitimate pretender, Portugal's King Antonio (1531-95), who ruled in 1580 before the Spanish annexation of Portugal, was the legitimate offspring of a secret marriage between Don Luis, second son of King Manoel of Portugal, and one Violante Gomez, the daughter of Christianized Spanish Jews. Antonio may have provided English playwright William Shakespeare (1564-1616) with inspiration for several less anti-Semitic plays as well as *The Merchant of Venice* (1598), which like Christopher Marlowe's *The Jew of Malta* appeared during a 1590's wave of anti-Semitism in Britain following the failure of a 1589 English attempt to reinstate Antonio as king of Portugal. 1492-1589

Antonov, Sergei

184. Kudriavtsev, V. N. "DELO ANTONOVA": PRAVOSUDIE ILI POLITICHESKAIA AKTSIIA? [The Antonov case: justice or political action?]. *Sovetskoe Gosudarstvo i Pravo [USSR] 1985 (9): 88-93.* Since the 1985 trial of the would-be assassin of Pope John Paul II, a legal case has been mounted against Bulgarian citizen Sergei Antonov as Mehmet Ali Agca's accomplice, despite evidence of the latter's insanity, for clearly political reasons. 1985

Antonov-Ovseenko, Vladimir A.

185. Hoshuliak, I. L. DO 100-RICHCHIA Z DNIA NARODZHENNIA V. O. ANTONOVA-OVSIIENKA [On the 100th birthday anniversary of Vladimir A. Antonov-Ovseenko]. *Ukrains'kyi Istorychnyi Zhurnal [USSR] 1983 (3): 116-122.* V. A. Ovseenko, also well known under his underground name of Antonov, joined the Social Democratic Workers' Party in 1903 after having graduated from the Petersburg officers' school and for a long time supported the Party's Menshevik wing. He actively participated in the 1905 revolution, inciting sailors against the tsarist regime. In 1907 he realized the correctness of the Lenin line and became a Bolshevik. During the civil war he distinguished himself as commander of various Bolshevik forces. In 1921 he was appointed head of the Red Army's political directorate but sided with the Trotskyite opposition and was dismissed in 1929. From 1934 to 1937 he served abroad as a diplomat. Secondary sources; 23 notes. 1903-37 -Ovseenko

186. Polikarpov, V. V. A. ANTONOV-OVSEENKO (K 100-LETIIU SO DNIA ROZHDENIIA) [V. A. Antonov-Ovseenko: on the 100th anniversary of his birth]. *Voenno-Istoricheskii Zhurnal [USSR] 1983 (3): 94-96.* Many victories of the Red Army during the Civil War are connected with the name of Vladimir A. Antonov-Ovseenko (1883-1938). He was directly responsible for the defeat of the counterrevolution in the South in 1918 and in 1919 took part in the crushing of the uprising in Tambov. After the Civil War he held a number of responsible government posts. Though he was associated with the Trotskyists, 1923-27, he did not take part in factional activities and eventually broke with them. 11 notes. 1917-27

Antonovych, Volodymyr

187. Hrushevsky, Mikhail S. VOLODYMYR ANTONOVYCH, OSNOVNI IDEI IOHO TVORCHOSTY I DIIAL'NOSTY [Volodymyr Antonovych: basic ideas of his creativity and activity]. *Ukrains'kyi Istoryk 1984 21(1-4): 193-199.* Outlines the many accomplishments of Ukrainian historian Volodymyr Antonovych (1834-1908), one of the most outstanding Ukrainian figures in the second half of the 19th century, and discusses certain ideas and interests such as love of scholarship and political, social, and national concerns, which contributed to his great creativity and multifaceted activity. Proposes that Antonovych's memory be honored with the publication of a major monograph. Reprinted from *Zapysky Ukrains'koho Naukovoho Tovarystva* 1909 3: 5-14. 1850's-1908

188. Hrushevsky, Mikhail S. Z SOTSIIAL'NO-NATSIONAL'NYKH KONTSEPTSII ANTONOVYCHA [On the socionational concepts of Antonovych]. *Ukrains'kyi Istoryk 1984 21(1-4): 200-218.* As a scholar and a civic and political leader, Ukrainian historian Volodymyr Antonovych (1834-1908) played an active role in Ukrainian life for over 50 years. Antonovych's populist and nationalist ideals were revealed in his autobiography *Confession* (1862) and in many other publications. 11 notes. Reprinted from *Ukraina* 1928 5: 3-16. 1850's-1908

189. Hrushevsky, Mikhail S. PAM'IATY VOLODYMYRA ANTONOVYCHA [In memory of Volodymyr Antonovych]. *Ukrains'kyi Istoryk 1984 21(1-4): 191-192.* A eulogy delivered on 24 March 1908 at the funeral of Ukrainian historian Volodymyr Antonovych (1834-1908). Reprinted from *Literaturno-Naukovyi Vistnyk* 1908 42: 20-21. 1834-1908

Antschel, Paul

See Celan, Paul

Anyi, Wang

190. Yang, Gladys. RESEARCH NOTE: WOMEN WRITERS. *China Quarterly [Great Britain] 1985 (103): 510-517.* Briefly comments on seven contemporary Chinese women writers; Zong Pu, Shen Rong, Dai Houying, Yu Luojin, Zhang Jie, Zhang Xinxin, and Wang Anyi. All seem to base their fiction on events they have witnessed or experienced. Based on a paper presented at the University of Leeds in November 1983; 14 notes. 1957-83

Aparisi y Guijarro, Antonio

191. Ferrer Garcia, Francisco Blas. APARISI Y GUIJARRO (1815-1872): NOTAS SOBRE EL QUEHACER DE UN PUBLICISTA DEL SIGLO XIX [Aparisi y Guijarro (1815-72): notes on the activity of a 19th-century publicist]. *Anuario de Historia Contemporánea [Spain] 1982 9: 121-144.* Antonio Aparisi y Guijarro, poet, orator, and publicist, was an important political figure in the period of Spain's transition from the old regime in the mid-19th century. ca 1840-72

Apfaltrern family

192. Demšar, Viktorijan. GRAJSKO ŽIVLJENJE APFALTRERNOV NA KRIŽU V 19. STOLETJU [The castle life of the Apfaltrern family in Križ in the 19th century]. *Kronika [Yugoslavia] 1980 28(3): 191-194.* The Schreibkalender, or castle diary, of the Apfaltrern family provides the basis for this account of the daily life and social intercourse of a baronial family in the 19th century. 19c

Apollinaire, Guillaume

193. Décaudin, Michel. APOLLINAIRE ET PICASSO [Apollinaire and Picasso]. *Esprit [France] 1982 (1): 80-84.* Analyzes the deep mutual admiration, professional relationship, and affinities that united French poet and art critic, Guillaume Apollinaire (1880-1918), and Spanish painter and sculptor, Pablo Picasso (1881-1973). ca 1905-20

194. Pallister, Janis L. APOLLINAIRE AND MAYAKOVSKY: SOME PARALLELS. *East European Quarterly 1985 19(1): 95-103.* Discusses similarities in the lives and poetry of Vladimir Mayakovski (1893-1930) and Guillaume Apollinaire (1880-1918). Both were contemptuous of bourgeois values and believed in the future of man. In several cases their poems are very similar. Based on a comparison of the published works in French of Mayakovski and Apollinaire; 22 notes. ca 1900-30

Aponte, Carlos

195. —. DOCUMENTO DE AUGUSTO CESAR SANDINO SOBRE CARLOS APONTE [A document of Augusto César Sandino on Carlos Aponte]. *Casa de las Américas [Cuba] 1982 22(130): 132-133.* The Venezuelan Carlos Aponte fought with Sandino in his guerrilla army in Nicaragua during the 1920's. He was executed in Cuba in 1935 during the Batista dictatorship with the leader of the revolutionary organization *Joven Cuba.* A letter of Sandino commending Aponte is reproduced here. 1929

Apostolov, Aleksandar

196. Velkov, Dragan. SHEESET GODINI OD ZHIVOTOT I DEJNOSTA NA PROFESOROT D-R ALEKSANDAR APOSTOLOV [On Professor Aleksandar Apostolov's 60th birthday]. *Istorija [Yugoslavia] 1980 16(2): 7-11.* Tribute to Aleksandar Apostolov (b. 1920), professor of history at the University of Skopje, on his 60th birthday. Apostolov is celebrated for his research into Macedonian history, especially his study of archival material in France and Belgium. A former partisan, he is a leading party activist in the university's philosophy department. 1920-80

Appar, Petr Andreevich

197. —. GEROI GRAZHDANSKOI VOINY [Heroes of the Civil War]. *Voenno-Istoricheskii Zhurnal [USSR] 1982 (8): 57-60.* In connection with the USSR's 60th anniversary records the military and civilian services to the USSR of Akim Kononovich Korol' (1896-1969), Petr Andreevich Appar (1889-1956), Iosif Ivanovich Popov (1896-1962), Khasan Mukhamedzhanovich Mukhamedzhanov (1889-1963), Olim Pochoev (1904-57), Nikifor Petrovich Romashkin (1897-1942), Vasili Ambrosievich Strepko (1900-58), and Semën Adamovich Khmaladze (1885-1938). The eight men represent eight nationalities. Based on Soviet military and biographical sources; 8 notes. 1917-69

Aquarone, Alberto

198. DeFelice, Renzo. LA SCOMPARSA DI UN AMICO: ALBERTO AQUARONE [The disappearance of a friend: Alberto Aquarone]. *Storia Contemporanea [Italy] 1985 16(3): 653-654.* Provides a tribute to the late Italian historian, Alberto Aquarone. Although his contributions included several subjects, Aquarone is best known for his work on contemporary Italian and European history. 19c-20c

Aquino, Francisco Radler de

199. Oliveira, Antônio Camillo de. CENTENÁRIO DO COMANDANTE FRANCISCO RADLER DE AQUINO [Centenary of Commander Francisco Radler de Aquino]. *Rev. do Inst. Hist. e Geog. Brasileiro [Brazil] 1979 (322): 257-267.* Admiral Francisco Radler de Aquino, born in New York of an American mother and Brazilian father, was a seaman with a reputation as a brilliant technician. He was the author of many original technical works on navigation and a member of the Institute of History and Geography. 1894-1935

Aragon, Alonso de

200. Navarro Latorre, José. DON ALONSO DE ARAGON, LA "ESPADA" O "LANZA" DE JUAN II. ESQUEMA BIOGRÁFICA DE UNO DE LOS MEJORES GUERREROS ESPAÑOLES DEL SIGLO XV [Don Alonso de Aragon, the "sword" or "lance" of John II: biographical sketch of one of the best Spanish warriors of the 15th century]. *Jerónimo Zurita. Cuadernos de Historia [Spain] 1982 (41-42): 159-204.* Provides a biographical sketch of Don Alonso de Aragon (1415-85), illegitimate son of John II, king of Aragon, 1458-79. Alonso developed into one of the best warriors of his time and was of invaluable assistance to his father and later to his half-brother Ferdinand of Aragon (1452-1516) in the numerous wars of the period. He became Master of the Order of Calatrava, (1443-55), Count of Ribagorza, and 1st Duke of Villahermosa. Based on a manuscript biography of the Real Biblioteca de la Academia de Historia of Madrid; illus., 32 notes, biblio. 1415-85

Aragon, Louis

201. Boisdeffre, Pierre de. ARAGON [Aragon]. *Rev. des Deux Mondes [France] 1983 (4): 100-112.* A literary biographical comment on Louis Aragon (1897-1983), which stresses the dichotomous character of his personality and multifaceted style—a talented "bourgeois" and militant Communist. 1897-1983

Aranda, Conde de

202. Varela Marcos, Jesús. ARANDA Y SU SUEÑO DE LA INDEPENDENCIA SURAMERICANA [Aranda and his dream of South American independence]. *Anuario de Estudios Americanos [Spain] 1980 37: 351-368.* Pedro Pablo Abarca de Bolea, the count of Aranda, served as Spanish ambassador to France during the American Revolution. In 1780 he concluded that Spain could not maintain its possessions in South America and suggested liberating Peru and establishing an independent nation in Buenos Aires. 26 notes, appendix. 1770-90

Aranha, Bento

203. Reis, Arthur Cézar Ferreira. PARA A BIOGRAFIA DE BENTO ARANHA [For the biography of Bento Aranha]. *Rev. do Inst. Hist. e Geog. Brasileiro [Brazil] 1980 (329): 5-9.* Bento Aranha (1769-1811), member of a well-known family and a noted government servant in Amazonia, was also a poet and playwright of merit. Reproduced here are a few documents pertaining to his career as a civil servant. They throw light on his character and illustrate the opinion his superiors had of him. 3 documents. 1804

Aranha, Francisco

204. Velinkar, J. FRANCISCO ARANHA, BUILDER OF SALSETE CHURCHES. *Indica [India] 1980 17(2): 139-145.* Discusses the life of Jesuit priest Francisco Aranha in Goa India. Leaving his native Portugal in 1568, he arrived in Goa and entered the Jesuit seminary. By 1583 he had built churches at many sites in Goa. Many of the Hindu inhabitants resisted the Christianization of their culture, and in 1583 Aranha was killed by an angry mob of Hindus. Primary sources; 4 fig., 35 notes. 1568-83

Arany, János

205. Keresztury, Dezső. JÁNOS ARANY AND ENGLISH LITERATURE. *New Hungarian Quarterly [Hungary] 1985 26(100): 67-77.* János Arany (1817-82), the great poet and man of letters of Hungary, was strongly influenced by English literature. William Shakespeare exercised the greatest effect on his literary production, which culminated in his direction of the complete Hungarian edition of the works of Shakespeare. 1840's-82

Arató, Endre

206. Diószegi, István. ENDRE ARATÓ (1921-1977) [Endre Arató (1921-77)]. *Ann. U. Sci. Budapestinensis de Rolando Eötvös Nominatae. Sectio Hist. [Hungary] 1981 21: 5-11.* A tribute to the Hungarian historian Endre Arató (1921-77). The author considers his childhood and early life, his university studies in Budapest, his membership of the Communist Party, and his academic career, and pays particular attention to his studies on nationalism. 1921-77

207. Diószegi, István. ARATÓ ENDRE EMLÉKEZETE (1921-1977) [Remembrance of Endre Arató, 1921-77]. *Századok [Hungary] 1981 115(4): 820-825.* Tribute to Endre Arató, Czechoslovakian historian. 1945-77

Araújo, José Tomás Nabuco de

208. Rodrigues, José Honório. CENTENÁRIO DA MORTE DE JOSÉ TOMÁS NABUCO DE ARAÚJO [The centenary of the death of José Tomás Nabuco de Araújo]. *Rev. do Inst. Hist. e Geog. Brasileiro [Brazil] 1979 (323): 142-159.* Nabuco de Araujo (1813-78) was a jurist and statesman of note. He was senator, councilor of state, and government minister. He was a great liberal who fought for the representative system of government, for constitutional guarantees, against the monopoly of power and oligarchies of all types. He was a patriot, a humanitarian, and an advocate of social justice. Biblio. of his writings; 25 notes. 1813-78

Araújo Porto-Alegre, Manuel de

209. Barata, Mário. ALGUNS ASPECTOS DA VIDA DE MANUEL DE ARAUJO PORTO ALEGRE [Some aspects of the life of Manuel de Araújo Porto-Alegre]. *Rev. do Inst. Hist. e Geog. Brazileiro [Brazil] 1980 (327): 215-225.* Remarks on the friendship of Araújo Porto-Alegre with Claudio Luis da Costa, author of a manual of anatomy for the use of painters, and with Almeida Garrett, noted Portuguese writer and poet. Also describes Araújo's feeling for nature, as seen in some of his landscapes and sketches for the stage, and his contribution to a national feeling in the arts. 7 notes. 1820's-79

Arbeláez, Vicente

210. Tisnés J., Roberto. EL ARZOBISPO MONSEÑOR VICENTE ARBELAEZ (1822-1884) [Archbishop Vicente Arbeláez (1822-84)]. *Boletín de Historia y Antigüedades [Colombia] 1984 71(747): 901-905.* Vicente Arbeláez, after an active ecclesiastical career and two instances of political exile, became archbishop of Bogotá in 1868 and served until his death in a period of difficult church-state relations. 1840's-84

Arboleda Pombo, Julio

211. Hernández de Alba, Guillermo. LAS POSTRIMERIAS DE JULIO ARBOLEDA [The last years of Julio Arboleda]. *Bol. Cultural y Biblio. [Colombia] 1982 19(4): 62-69.* The last years of the life of General Julio Arboleda Pombo and the circumstances of his death were described in a 1914 account written by his cousin. 1861-62

Arbuthnot, Malcolm

212. Parsons, Melinda Boyd. "Malcolm Arbuthnot (1877-1967) British Post-Impressionist." University of Delaware 1984. 492 pp. *DAI 1984 45(6): 1560-A.* DA8420973 1890's-1967

Arce, Agustín

213. Barcena, Emilio. P. AGUSTIN ARCE (1884-1984) [Father Agustín Arce, 1884-1984]. *Archivo Ibero-Americano [Spain] 1984 44(175): 378-381.* An obituary of the Spanish cleric Agustín Arce (1884-1984). Born in Rioseras, Burgos, Arce served in Peru, Italy, and Spain during the early years of his career. Moving to Jerusalem in 1922, he made significant contributions to historical research and publication concerning Spanish and Franciscan relations with the Holy Lands. 1884-1984

Arciniegas, Germán

214. Belaúnde Moreyra, Antonio. GERMAN ARCINIEGAS—GRAN AMERICANISTA [Germán Arciniegas—great Americanist]. *Bol. de Hist. y Antigüedades [Colombia] 1981 68(733): 519-527.* Tribute to the Colombian historian Germán Arciniegas by the Peruvian ambassador to Colombia emphasizing his contributions to general American history. 20c

215. —. EN LOS OCHENTA AÑOS DE DON GERMAN ARCINIEGAS [On the 80th birthday of Germán Arciniegas]. *Bol. de Hist. y Antigüedades [Colombia] 1980 67(731): 673-690.* Biobibliographical note on the Colombian historian, journalist, and literary figure Germán Arciniegas, followed by addresses of tribute from Eduardo Guzmán Esponda, president of the Academia Colombiana de la Lengua, and from former president Carlos Lleras Restrepo. 1920's-80

Arellano family

216. Arellano, Jorge Eduardo. LOS ARELLANO DE GRANADA (MEMORIAL DE LOS ANTEPASADOS) [The Arellanos of Granada (memorial to some ancestors)]. *Revista del Pensamiento Centroamericano [Nicaragua] 1984 39(185): 59-81.* Recalls five members of the Arellano family of Granada, Nicaragua, and the 19th-century society in which they lived. Besides being a family portrait, the article is a celebration of people who lived a full life on the land. 2 portraits, 3 facsimile documents, note on sources. 19c

Aretino, Pietro

217. Palladino, Lora Anne. "Pietro Aretino: Orator and Art Theorist." Yale U. 1981. 461 pp. *DAI 1983 43(7): 2140-A.* DA8210748 1530's-56

Arguedas, José María

218. Irish, J. A. George. J. M. ARGUEDAS AND PERUVIAN NEO-INDIGENISMO. *Revista/Review Interamericana [Puerto Rico] 1980 10(2): 173-187.* José María Arguedas has brought to Peruvian letters a new kind of indigenismo that transcends local and regional considerations. He attempts to make the Peruvian Indian a universal man with all the problems that face men elsewhere on the globe. 43 notes. 1900-80

Arias, Desiderio

219. González, María F. DESIDERIO ARIAS Y EL CAUDILLISMO [Desiderio Arias and caudillismo]. *Estudios Sociales [Dominican Republic] 1985 18(61): 29-50.* Describes the principal characteristics of Desiderio Arias's political leadership—his code of honor and nationalist sentiments—and compares him with other leaders of the Dominican Republic. 1902-31

Ariès, Philippe

220. Chaunu, Pierre. SUR LE CHEMIN DE PHILIPPE ARIES, HISTORIEN DE LA MORT [On the path of Philippe Ariès, historian of death]. *Histoire, Economie et Société [France] 1984 3(4): 651-664.* An obituary for Philippe Ariès, whose historical contributions include approximately 40 articles and a dozen books in the period 1945-84, relating to the historical interpretation of death. Discusses the influence of Ariès's studies of death and dying and the contemporary critical response to his ideas. Illus., 43 notes. 20c

221. Chaunu, Pierre. LE PARCOURS SOLITAIRE: IN PIAM MEMORIAM [The solitary path: in piam memoriam]. *Histoire, Économie et Société [France] 1984 3(1): 3-5.* Obituary of Philippe Ariès (1914-84), pioneer historian of the family, and author of studies of French social attitudes and of death and dying. 1930's-84

222. Poussou, J.-P. IN MEMORIAM: PHILIPPE ARIES (1914-1984) [In memoriam: Philippe Ariès]. *Annales de Démographie Historique [France] 1984: 5-6.* Philippe Ariès (1914-84) was one of the founders of historical demography. He was first of all a historian of the evolution of French society between the 17th and the 19th centuries. The child, the family, death were at the heart of his concerns. Beyond quantitative history, Ariès meditated on the meaning societies gave to life and death. His work, though in part to be revised, remains fundamental. 1914-84

223. —. IN MEMORIAM [In memoriam]. *Bulletin d'Information de la Société de Démographie Historique [France] 1984 (40): 3.* Obituary of Philippe Ariès, one of the founders of historical demography and a cultural anthropologist who emphasized that society was not immobile, that behaviors perpetually modified themselves, and that the civilization of moral values was flexible. 20c

Arismendi, Rodney

224. Kozlov, Iu. K. BOEVOI RUKOVODITEL' URUGVAISKIKH KOMMUNISTOV (K 70-LETIIU SO DNIA ROZHDENIIA PERVOGO SEKRETARIA TSK KOMPARTII URUGVAIA RODNEIA ARISMENDI) [Militant leader of the Uruguayan Communists: on the 70th birthday of Rodney Arismendi, First Secretary of the Central Committee of the Communist Party of Uruguay]. *Voprosy Istorii KPSS [USSR] 1983 (3): 118-121.* Charts the political career of Rodney Arismendi, particularly his participation in the Communist youth movement and his parliamentary work. Examines his writings on various aspects of the struggle for socialism. Note. 1913-83

Arista, Mariano

225. Sanchez, Joseph P. GENERAL MARIANO ARISTA AT THE BATTLE OF PALO ALTO, TEXAS, 1846: MILITARY REALIST OR FAILURE? *Journal of the West 1985 24(2): 8-21.* Summarizes the battle of Palo Alto, Texas, in 1846, the first major battle of the Mexican War, and evaluates the military strategy of Mexican General Mariano Arista. A Mexican board of inquiry heard charges leveled by Arista's subordinates that Arista's mismanagement of his troops led to Mexico's defeat at the hands of the smaller US army, led by General Zachary Taylor. Arista defended himself, arguing that his troop alignment and deployment followed a sound battle plan and that his retreat caused the US army to lose their advantage. Finally, in 1848, the Supreme Tribunal of War granted Arista vindication from all charges. Based on archival sources in the Biblioteca Nacional de Mexico and at Yale University as well as secondary sources; 3 maps, 2 illus., 126 notes. 1845-48

Aristotle

226. Muccillo, Maria. LA VITA E LE OPERE DI ARISTOTELE NELLA "DISCUSSIONES PERIPATETICAE" DI FRANCESCO PATRIZI DA CHERSO [The life and works of Aristotle in the *Discussiones Peripateticae* by Francesco Patrizi da Cherso]. *Rinascimento [Italy] 1981 21: 53-119.* Francesco Patrizi (1529-97), in his 1571 work, utilized the critical historical tools of Renaissance philology to demystify Aristotle in an attempt to destroy his moral and intellectual authority. Patrizi denied to Aristotle a place in the honorable tradition of pious and occult philosophy that culminates in Christ. Rather, he reduced the Greek writer to a student of physics. Patrizi examined the Aristotelian school from its beginnings to his own day, asserting that the Aristotelians, excepting the immediate heirs, misunderstood or misrepresented their master due to their slavish imitation of

him. Patrizi attacked Aristotle and his school in order to affirm the freedom of inquiry from any authority. Based on the printed text of *Discussiones* and other primary sources; 157 notes. 1571-81

Aristov, Fedor F.

227. Aristova, T. F. FEDOR FEDOROVICH ARISTOV [Fedor Fedorovich Aristov]. *Narody Azii i Afriki [USSR] 1985 (1): 79-80.* Biography of F. F. Aristov (1888-1932), orientalist and professor at Moscow State University whose pedagogic career, begun in 1907, continued unabated in the Soviet era. Paper shortage in 1921 prevented the publication in book form of his studies of the Far East, published later only as essays. Most of his papers perished during World War II, yet even the few that survived in state archives are a valuable contribution to the study of East Asia and the Soviet Far East. 5 notes. 1907-32

Arkhipenko, Aleksandr

228. Kapitaykin, Eduard. OLEKSANDER ARKHYPENKO V TEL-AVIVI [Aleksandr Arkhipenko in Tel Aviv]. *Sučasnist [West Germany] 1981 (10): 45-53.* Describes Arkhipenko's early involvement with sculptural cubism and the background of a display of nearly 50 of his works at the Tel Aviv Museum in 1976, which became such a success that the management decided to run it as a permanent exhibition. 5 photos. 1910-23

Arlosoroff, Chaim

229. Avineri, Shlomo. THE SOCIALIST ZIONISM OF CHAIM ARLOSOROFF. *Jerusalem Quarterly [Israel] 1985 (34): 68-87.* Explores the life and work of Zionist socialist Chaim Arlosoroff. 1920's-33

230. Black, Edwin. THE STRANGE CASE OF CHAIM ARLOSOROFF. *Present Tense 1984 12(1): 30-36.* Details the life and work of Chaim Arlosoroff, who had supported a binational state of Jews and Arabs in Palestine. 1899-1933

Armero y Fernández de Peñaranda, Francisco

231. Gómez Flores, Alfonso. EL PRIMER MARQUES DEL NERVION [The 1st Marquess del Nervión]. *Rev. General de Marina [Spain] 1983 204[i.e., 205](Aug-Sept): 379-381.* Biographical note on Francisco Armero y Fernández de Peñaranda, 1st Marquess del Nervión, 19th-century Spanish naval officer, who served as Captain General of the Fleet, Captain General of Madrid, Captain General of Andalucía, Navy Minister, Minister of Commerce and Overseas, President of the Council of Ministers, Senator, and Vice President of the Senate. 19c

Armstrong, John

232. Langham-Carter, R. R. THE ARMSTRONG CHAPEL: A LIFE OF UPS AND DOWNS. *Africana Notes and News [South Africa] 1981 24(7): 234-238.* John Armstrong, the first Anglican bishop of Grahamstown, South Africa died 16 May 1856. He was buried near his daughter, and a collection was taken up to build a memorial chapel over their graves. The chapel was built but suffered from vandalism and was eventually destroyed in 1950. The graves were moved to another location. Primary sources. 19c-20c

Arnesen, Baard

233. Fossberg, Jorunn. BAARD: GULLSMED I FREDERIKSTAD [Baard: goldsmith in Frederikstad]. *By og Bygd [Norway] 1983-84 30: 99-103.* Baard Arnesen practiced his trade of goldsmith in the Norwegian city of Frederikstad in the years 1661-83, producing ecclesiastical chalices, Baroque tankards, spoons, and other objects of gold and silver in the typical Danish-Norwegian style of his day. Based on artifacts and secondary sources; 4 photos, 8 notes, appendix, biblio. English summary. 1635-1700

Arnold, Ethel M.

234. Wachter, Phyllis E. "Surname Arnold; Occupation: Spinster; Avocation: New Victorian Woman." Temple University 1984. 192 pp. *DAI 1984 45(6): 1763-A.* DA8419791 1880's-1930

Arnold, Matthew

235. Honan, Park. THE YOUNG MATTHEW ARNOLD. *Contemporary Review [Great Britain] 1984 245(1425): 191-198.* Discusses the early years of the English poet and critic Matthew Arnold (1822-88), referring to his family life and education. 1830's-40's

236. Letwin, Shirley Robin. MATTHEW ARNOLD: ENEMY OF TRADITION. *Pol. Theory 1982 10(3): 333-351.* Discusses the philosophies of Matthew Arnold, his contributions to Western culture and thought, and resistance to certain of his ideas. 1822-88

Arnold, Thomas, Jr.

237. Macpherson, Carmel R. THOMAS ARNOLD THE YOUNGER: SOME COMMON MISCONCEPTIONS REDRESSED. *Hist. of Educ. Rev. [Australia] 1983 12(1): 29-41.* As the son of Rugby's famed headmaster, Thomas Arnold the younger faced great expectations which did not materialize in teaching convicts' children in Australia. 1849-56

Arnott, Neil

238. Bayliss, Robert A. and Ellis, C. William. NEIL ARNOTT, F.R.S., REFORMER, INNOVATOR AND POPULARIZER OF SCIENCE, 1788-1874. *Notes and Records of the Royal Soc. of London [Great Britain] 1981 36(1): 103-124.* Neil Arnott, physician to the French and Spanish embassies in England from 1816 until his death, developed an early zeal for scientific education, publishing a popular *Elements of Physics* in 1827. Active in arousing public awareness about heating and ventilation problems, he was also concerned with public education and was a noted philanthropist. Perhaps because he held to public office, the long and significant career of Dr. Arnott has been overlooked by historians. 87 notes. 1816-74

Aron, Raymond

239. Boisdeffre, Pierre de. VIE ET MORT DE RAYMOND ARON (1905-1983) [The life and death of Raymond Aron (1905-83)]. *Rev. des Deux Mondes [France] 1983 (12): 570-583.* Describes the career of this noted French philosopher, his place in French intellectual life of the 20th century, and his thoughts on this century's political events. 1930's-83

240. Fourastie, Jean. RAYMOND ARON ET SES "MEMOIRES" [Raymond Aron and his *Memoirs]. Rev. des Deux Mondes [France] 1983 (11): 271-278.* Describes the career of Raymond Aron as journalist, economist, sociologist, and philosopher and his thoughts on French and European economics and intellectual life in the 20th century. 20c

241. Hassner, Pierre. RAYMOND ARON AND THE HISTORY OF THE TWENTIETH CENTURY. *International Studies Quarterly [Great Britain] 1985 29(1): 29-37.* As both a philosopher of historical understanding and an interpreter of contemporary history, Raymond Aron was able to identify better than any of his contemporaries the fundamental features of the 20th century, to put them into perspective and to inquire about their ultimate significance. Perhaps his central perception, which grew out of his experience with war and totalitarianism, was the ambivalence of progress. Aron suggested that the advance of science and of the Enlightenment itself had produced its own negation: a need for order and community and, accordingly, the suppression of liberty and equality. 8 notes. 1933-76

242. Hoffmann, Stanley. RAYMOND ARON AND THE THEORY OF INTERNATIONAL RELATIONS. *International Studies Quarterly [Great Britain] 1985 29(1): 13-27.* Raymond Aron's main contribution to our understanding of the new era of nuclear weapons consists of a series of analyses dealing with deterrence, the need for strategic calculations, and the necessity of the Cold War. Nobody has more persistently tried to understand and to measure the extent to which the invention of these weapons has revolutionized world politics. Aron was convinced that a pacified world was impossible, but that nuclear war was unlikely. 13 notes. 1945-76

243. Kolodziej, Edward A. RAYMOND ARON: A CRITICAL RETROSPECTIVE AND PROSPECTIVE. *International Studies Quarterly [Great Britain] 1985 29(1): 5-11.* Raymond Aron almost singlehandedly created the field of international relations in postwar France and defined both its scope and the appropriate methods and concepts for analysis. A symposium, to which this is the introduction, aims at a critical evaluation rather than a eulogy and is intended to identify the principal elements in Aron's work that merit attention and preservation. 5 notes. 1945-76

244. Luterbacher, Urs. THE FRUSTRATED COMMENTATOR: AN EVALUATION OF THE WORK OF RAYMOND ARON. *International Studies Quarterly [Great Britain] 1985 29(1): 39-49.* Like many French intellectuals of his generation, Raymond Aron was first and foremost an accomplished essayist and commentator—a frustrated commentator never completely satisfied with the writings he was reviewing nor his own. He represents a whole generation of scholars who came to adopt German historicism, a mode of thinking that postulates that social and political events are understandable only within their own particular context. Aron's eclecticism and skepticism prevented him from initiating a new French scientific approach to the study of social behavior in general and to international politics in particular. 19 notes. 1933-76

245. McConnell, Scott. HOMAGE TO RAYMOND ARON. *Commentary 1984 77(5): 39-46.* Reviews the life and contributions of Raymond Aron, French philosopher, historian, and sociologist. 1930's-80's

246. Schieder, Theodor. NEKROLOG: RAYMOND ARON 14.3.1905-17.10.1983 [Obituary: Raymond Aron (14 March 1905-17 October 1983)]. *Historische Zeitschrift [West Germany] 1984 239(2): 491-496.* Evaluates the historical contributions of Raymond Aron, the French sociologist-publicist who ranks as an analyst with Montesquieu, Tocqueville, and Weber. His works on peace and war and on Carl von Clausewitz are especially significant for contemplation of the current world situation, historical context, and implications for the future. 1905-83

247. Shils, Edward. RAYMOND ARON. *American Scholar 1985 54(2): 161-178.* Raymond Aron is unique among contemporary intellectuals, but not just for his scholarship and analysis. This is true specifically because of Aron's *Verantwortungsethik,* or ethics of conscience. Aron's most salient quality was his indominability. Personal misfortunes, public obloquy, and social chaos did not extinguish his Enlightenment view of human reason. 1930's-83

Arouet, François-Marie

See Voltaire

Arquien, Marie d'

248. Ribardière, Diane. PENDANT 50 ANS, DEUX FRANÇAISES REINES DE POLOGNE [For 50 years, two French queens of Poland]. *Historama [France] 1985 (16): 48-54, (17): 62-68.* Part 1. MARIE DE GONZAGUE LA VOLONTAIRE [Marie de Gonzague the volunteer]. Part 2. MARIE D'ARQUIEN: MEDIOCRE MAS...[Marie d'Arquien, mediocre but...]. Retraces the lives of two French women, Marie de Gonzague and Marie Casimir de La Grange d'Arquien, who became queens of Poland in the 17th century. The author pays particular attention to their political influences. 1640's-83

Artel, Jean

249. Mattéi, Xavier. EVOCATIONS [Recalls]. *Revue Historique des Armées [France] 1985 (2): 54-57.* A former "enfant de troupe" (child educated in a French military school) and vice-president of the Enfants de Troupe Association highlights in biographical accounts the patriotic and heroic behavior of Roger Barbé (1920-41) and Jean Artel (1927-44) during World War II. Also quotes *in extenso* the farewell message written by Henri Martrice (1924-44) to his parents shortly before being shot by the Germans. 2 photos. 1940-44

Artëm

250. Ovsii, I. O. DO 100-RICHCHIA Z DNIA NAROD-ZHENNIA F. A. SERHEIEVA (ARTEMA) [On the 100th birthday anniversary of F. A. Sergeev (Artëm)]. *Ukrains'kyi Istorychnyi Zhurnal [USSR] 1983 (3): 110-116.* Fedor A. Sergeev joined the Bolsheviks in 1902 while still at the Moscow technical college, from which he was eventually expelled for his revolutionary fervor. He became an organizer of clandestine revolutionary groups in the south of the Ukraine. In the thick of the 1905 revolution he showed himself a leader and became widely known under the party name of Artëm. During the civil war he commanded Bolshevik units in battles with forces of the Ukrainian Central Rada. When the Ukrainian SSR was proclaimed in Kharkov in December 1917, he became People's Commissar for Industry. He died in an aviation accident in 1921. Based on the Party Archives of the Party History Institute attached to the Ukrainian CP Central Committee and secondary sources; 12 notes. 1902-21

251. Poole, Tom R. and Fried, Eric. ARTEM: A BOLSHEVIK IN BRISBANE. *Australian Journal of Politics and History [Australia] 1985 31(2): 243-254.* A brief biography of Fedor Andreevich Sergeyev (1883-1921), or "Artem," who directed Bolshevik forces in the Ukraine in 1905 and again in 1917. After imprisonment he escaped to China and later Australia, where he lived in Brisbane from 1911 to 1917. There he sought to raise the class consciousness of workers and worked for the Russian emigre community. After the tsar's overthrow in 1917 he returned to Russia and was a loyal supporter of Lenin, who valued him for his dependability and "decorative value as a proletarian." Concludes with an annotated translation of a seven-page sketch about Australia, "A Lucky Country," written in Brisbane and published in St. Petersburg in 1913-14. Based on Queensland archives, newspapers, and monographs; 43 notes. ca 1900-21

Artigas, José

252. Abdala, Miguel H. JOSE ARTIGAS, REVOLUCIONARIO LATINOAMERICANO [José Artigas, Latin American revolutionary]. *Investigación Econ. [Mexico] 1982 41(162): 197-218.* José Artigas (1764-1850) must be seen as a national revolutionary in Uruguay and a Latin American in tune with the difficult demands of the continental popular revolution which had matured by 1810. Attempts to demystify ruling class efforts to create a national history by distorting the true continental significance of events and their actors. 26 notes. 1810-20

Artukovic, Andrija

253. —. PER NON DIMENTICARE. UN CRIMINALE DI GUERRA USTASCIA [May we never forget. A Ustaši war criminal]. *Balcanica [Italy] 1984 3(2): 104-122.* Reprints the text of a suit filed in California by a group of former Yugoslav citizens against the unlawful presence in the United States of war criminal Andrija Artukovic, former interior minister in the Nazi-controlled Ustaši government of Ante Pavelic in Croatia during World War II. 1941-45

Arvelo, Carlos

254. Vargas, Francisco Alejandro. CIRUJANO MAYOR Y COMANDANTE CARLOS ARVELO [Chief surgeon and commander Carlos Arvelo]. *Boletin de la Academia Nacional de la Historia [Venezuela] 1984 67(266): 303-315.* Carlos Arvelo (1784-1862) played an important role in establishing health services. During the war of independence he was surgeon-major of the Liberator's armies, director of the military hospital, and founder of the Faculty of Medicine of Caracas. He was also elected to the legislative assembly. 4 notes. ca 1800-62

Asachi, Gheorghe

255. Cernatoni, Alexandru. GH. ASACHI—UN "DESCĂLECĂTOR" AL CULTURII NAȚIONALE [Gh. Asachi: founder of national culture]. *Magazin Istoric [Romania] 1980 14(12): 23-27.* Gheorghe Asachi (1788-1871), diplomat, author, editor, and educator, played a major role in building cultural life in Moldavia, especially by encouraging the study of foreign languages. 2 illus. 1800-70

Ashley, Lord

256. Mandler, Peter. CAIN AND ABEL: TWO ARISTOCRATS AND THE EARLY VICTORIAN FACTORY ACTS. *Historical Journal [Great Britain] 1984 27(1): 83-109.* 1820's-50's

*For abstract see **Howard, George (Viscount Morpeth)***

Askenazy, Szymon

257. Guterman, Aleksander. SZCZEGÓŁ W BIOGRAFII PROFESORA SZYMONA ASKENAZEGO [A detail from the biography of Professor Szymon Askenazy]. *Biuletyn Żydowskiego Instytutu Hist. w Polsce [Poland] 1981 (4): 57-59.* Relates details of the early childhood of Askenazy, his confirmation, and connections with Jewry, from which he later departed considerably, although never renouncing the faith of his fathers and not concealing his descent. Information about Askenazy's bar mitzvah was first published in *Izraelita* [Poland] 1878/79 (1): 5. 1865-79

Åsling, Nils G.

258. Åsling, Nils G. NÅGRA ERFARENHETER AV REGERINGSPOLITIK [Some experiences in the work of the government]. *Statsvetenskaplig Tidskrift [Sweden] 1985 88(2): 147-149.* Discusses the author's experience as minister of industry in Swedish cabinets from 1979 to 1981. 1979-81

Asproni, Giorgio

259. Corona, Maria Corrias. CATTANEO E ASPRONI: L'INCONTRO DI DUE DEMOCRATICI [Cattaneo and Asproni: the meeting of two democrats]. *Politico [Italy] 1982 47(2): 387-402.* On the basis of Giorgio Asproni's *Political Diary,* on Carlo Cattaneo's *Letters* and on some unpublished letters of theirs, reconstructs the beginning and the consolidation of a deep friendship between the two exponents of the democracy in the Italian Risorgimento. Underlines the influence that this friendship had on Cattaneo's behavior and on Asproni's political ideas. 1860-67

Asquith, Herbert Henry

260. Adams, R. J. Q. ASQUITH'S CHOICE: THE MAY COALITION AND THE COMING OF CONSCRIPTION, 1915-1916. *Journal of British Studies 1986 25(3): 243-263.* Although the passage of the first Military Service Act in 1916 has usually been portrayed as either a measure forced on the weakening British Liberal prime minister, Herbert Henry Asquith, or as the result of his typical procrastination, it was, in fact, legislation for which Asquith had carefully and deliberately prepared the way. Asquith acted out of expediency—if conscription were rejected, the same would happen to his leadership. He stacked the committee to investigate manpower with supporters of conscription, and when its report increased pressure for a draft, he stalled allowing the Derby Scheme to finally discredit voluntarism. He used the time won to fashion a compromise satisfactory to himself. Based on cabinet papers at the Public Record Office, London; 65 notes. 1915-16

261. Ball, Stuart R. ASQUITH'S DECLINE AND THE GENERAL ELECTION OF 1918. *Scottish Hist. Rev. [Great Britain] 1982 61(1): 44-61.* In the period following his resignation in December 1916 until the election of 1918, Herbert Henry Asquith had become overly cautious, arrogant about his own indispensability, and insulated from the political realities of the Reform Act of 1918. His personal defeat in 1918 was the result of a broadened franchise, an increasing disenchantment with political organization, a failure to address local issues, and an uninspiring and cautious response to his opposition. Asquith's defeat had a debilitating effect on the Liberal Party, for despite his absence from the Commons, he refused to give up his role as leader. Disintegration of the party ensued, which he himself blamed on the Coupon Election of 1918. 38 notes. 1916-18

Assad, Hafiz al-

262. Olson, Robert W. SYRIA: THE CONSOLIDATION OF THE ASAD REGIME, 1970-75. *Indiana Social Studies Q. 1982 35(2): 52-64.* Hafiz al-Assad uses a private army of his own Alawi tribesmen, judicious high level appointments to members of other groups, and skillful diplomacy to maintain his minority regime in Syria. 1970-75

Assad Khan

263. Velinkar, J. ASSAD KHAN IN PORTUGUESE SOURCES. *Indian Arch. [India] 1981 30(2): 79-88.* Describes the military career of Assad Khan, 16th-century general of the Adil Shahi army at Belgaum, the entrance from the southern coastal region to Adil Shah's kingdom in India. Assad Khan fought several battles resisting the Portuguese at Goa. He died of fever at the age of 90 in 1544. Based on primary Portuguese sources; 36 notes. 1516-44

Astell, Mary

264. Perry, Ruth. MARY ASTELL'S RESPONSE TO THE ENLIGHTENMENT. *Women & History 1984 (9): 13-40.* A conservative Tory and devout defender of the Church of England, Mary Astell disputed Locke, Shaftesbury, and others, insisting on women's intellectual equality and advocating education for all women. She argued against artificial, feminine qualities of vanity, pettiness, and greed, and instead stressed feminine emancipation through intellectual development in a near celibate state. Astell's success as an intellectual writer was helped by the growing emphasis on intellectual activity in early 18th-century London, but as a woman, she lived the intellectual life in personal solitude. 38 notes. 1666-1731

265. Perry, Ruth. TWO FORGOTTEN WITS. *Antioch Rev. 1981 39(4): 431-438.* Reviews the lives and novels of English feminists Mary Astell (1668-1731) and Lady Mary Wortley Montague (1689-1762). ca 1690-1762

Aston, Trevor H.

266. Hilton, R. H.; Philpin, C. H. E.; and Vaisey, M. A. T. H. ASTON. *Past & Present [Great Britain] 1986 (110): 3-5. Past & Present* records the loss of its editor Trevor Aston, who served since 1963. He not only fitted in with but vigorously developed the particular editorial style of the journal. His creative drive and the breadth of his historical interests and imagination sustained *Past & Present* for almost a generation. 1963-86

Astrid

267. Huas, Jeanine. IL Y A 50 ANS, LE MONDE ENTIER PLEURAIT LA REINE ASTRID [Fifty years ago, the entire world mourned for Queen Astrid]. *Historama [France] 1985 (18): 80-84.* Princess Astrid of Sweden (1905-35) became queen of Belgium by her marriage to the Duke of Brabant in 1926 and died in an automobile accident. 1905-35

Aström, Sven-Erik

268. Schybergson, Per. FORSKAREN SVEN-ERIK ÅSTRÖM [The scholar Sven-Erik Åström]. *Hist. Arkisto [Finland] 1981 (76): 19-36.* Surveys research by the Finnish historian, Sven-Erik Åström, professor of social and economic history in the faculty of political science at the University of Helsinki from 1960 to 1981. Åström has written on the social, urban, commercial, and ecological history of northern Europe from the 17th to 19th centuries. Based on Åström's published writings. English translation. 17c-19c

Astuti, Guido

269. Pauli, Lesław. GUIDO ASTUTI 1910-1980 [Guido Astuti (1910-80)]. *Czasopismo Prawno-Historyczne [Poland] 1982 34(1): 201-202.* An obituary of Guido Astuti, 1910-80, a distinguished Italian historian of law and jurist. 1910-80

Atatürk, Kemal

270. Arar, Ismail. LA PLACE D'ATATÜRK DANS LES GRANDS COURANTS DE L'HISTOIRE [Atatürk's place in the great currents of history]. *Rev. des Études Sud-Est Européennes [Romania] 1982 20(1): 43-49.* Shows how Kemal Atatürk (1881-1938) changed his country's and the world's destinies. He honored science and attached great importance to historical research and conceived the role of history and of life as aiming toward the existence, happiness, and glory of future generations. From May 1981 speech to the International Law and International Relations Association. 1914-38

271. Băluță-Kiss, Lucreția. LE CENTENAIRE DE LA NAISSANCE DE MUSTAPHA KEMAL ATATÜRK, LE FONDATEUR DE LA TURQUIE MODERNE [The centenary of Mustafa Kemal Atatürk's birth, founder of modern Turkey]. *Rev. Roumaine d'Etudes Int. [Romania] 1981 15(6): 619-623.* Reports on a symposium held at the Romanian Association for International Law and International Relations on 19 June 1981. Papers read included: "The Place of Atatürk in the Great Currents of History;" "Atatürk, the Great Reformer of Modern Turkey;" "Atatürk and Historical Research;" "Mustafa Kemal Atatürk, Humanistic Thinker"; and "Major Consonances in Romanian-Turkish Relations between the Two Wars." 1906-38

272. Blanco Villalta, J. G. ATATÜRK N'APPARTIENT PAS SEULEMENT A LA TURQUIE MAIS A L'HUMANITE [Atatürk belongs not only to Turkey, but to all humanity]. *Rev. Int. d'Hist. Militaire [France] 1981 (50): 101-106.* Recalls impressions of Kemal Atatürk's personality, relates anecdotes, and quotes his remarks that give evidence not only of great patriotism, but above all, exemplary humanism. 1921-38

273. Chernikov, I. F. MUSTAFA KEMAL ATATURK I RADIANSKO-TURETSKE SPIVROBITNYTSTVO U HALUZI KULTURY I NAUKY [Mustafa Kemal Atatürk and Soviet-Turkish cooperation in the field of culture and science]. *Ukrains'kyi Istorychnyi Zhurnal [USSR] 1982 (4): 112-118.* While retaining the privileges of the ruling classes, Kemal Atatürk at the same time enacted many innovations and reforms of progressive character, such as abolishing the sultanate and declaring Turkey a republic, separating church from state, and introducing the Latin alphabet. But his recognition of Soviet Russia as a friend and his steering of Turkey toward closer relations with the northern neighbor, especially in the field of culture and science was probably his greatest achievement—many examples of cooperation and mutual exchange are cited. 1920-30

274. Ekrem, Mehmet Ali. CONSIDERATIONS SUR LES REFORMES INTERIEURES ET SUR LA POLITIQUE ETRANGERE DE KEMAL ATATÜRK [The internal reforms and foreign policy of Kemal Atatürk]. *Rev. Roumaine*

d'Hist. [Romania] 1981 20(3): 435-454. Commemorating the centenary of Mustafa Kemal Atatürk, founder of modern Turkey, reviews the many fundamental reforms that brought the country, within the span of two decades, from a medieval Ottoman state to a modern nation. With the economic modernization outlines at the Izmir Congress of 1923, the laicization of the juridical and educational system, the creation of a new civil code in 1926, the political and social equality granted to women, and the all-important adoption of the Latin alphabet, Atatürk brought his people into the 20th century. His foreign policy rested on the key elements of eliminating the capitulations system and abandoning the pan-Islamic and pan-Turkic ideologies while working for Balkan peace and unity. Based on Turkish and Romanian secondary materials; 60 notes. 1914-34

275. Enginsoy, Cemal; Uysal, Ahmet E., transl. ATATÜRK AS A SOLDIER AND STATESMAN. *Rev. Int. d'Hist. Militaire [France] 1981 (50): 11-40.* Praises the greatness of Mustafa Kemal Atatürk (1881-1938), analyzes his political concepts, and relates the salient actions in which the liberator of his country and the creator of modern Turkey applied his qualities of military genius and superior statesmanship. In the Turkish War of Independence (1919-23) he formulated both military and psychological strategies for success in warfare and applied the principles of maneuver and surprise. As a statesman, beginning in 1923, he adopted an economic policy upholding private enterprise and introduced various reforms in keeping with western standards. Translated from Turkish; 81 notes. 1919-23

276. Enginsoy, Cemal. ASKER VE DEVLET ADAMI ATATÜRK (1881-1938) [Atatürk, soldier and statesman (1881-1938)]. *Belleten [Turkey] 1982 46(181): 133-143.* An appreciation of the life of Mustafa Kemal Atatürk, with first-hand anecdotes. Identifies his military qualities as personal bravery, capacity to discern the actions of others, patience and timing, bluff and feint, and realism toward the enemy and sees his political genius in a combination of idealism and realism. 1910-38

277. Erikan, Celal. ATATÜRK ET LA GUERRE TOTALE [Atatürk and total warfare]. *Rev. Int. d'Hist. Militaire [France] 1981 (50): 145-165.* Studies the Turkish War of Independence, 1919-22, focusing on the strategy of its leader, Mustafa Kemal Atatürk (1881-1938), who was the first general to apply the notion of total warfare. It included the people's participation, careful selection of objectives, a combination of offensive and defensive maneuvers, surprise tactics, careful preparation, and propaganda. The battle of Afyonkarahisar, Turkey's last military operation against the Greeks, is examined as an example of Atatürk's military strategy. Based on Atatürk's speeches; map, 46 notes. 1919-22

278. Hazai, György. MUSZTAFA KEMÁL ATATÜRK [Mustafa Kemal Atatürk]. *Világtörténet [Hungary] 1983 (2): 67-74.* Gives a brief biography and lists the accomplishments as prime minister of Turkey of Mustapha Kemal Atatürk (1881-1938). At the time of his birth, Turkey was referred to as the "sick man of Europe" due to its social, economic and political difficulties. In 1923, when he became prime minister, Atatürk instituted massive reforms that brought Turkey into the 20th century. Based on a paper presented at the Magyar Tudományos Akadémia conference on the 100th anniversary of Atatürk's birth, 28 October 1981. 1923-38

279. İğdemir, Uluğ. ATATÜRK: A GREAT MAN AND A THINKER. *Rev. Int. d'Hist. Militaire [France] 1981 (50): 97-100.* Mustafa Kemal Atatürk, during his career as a military man and a statesman, demonstrated great leadership and a reformer's love of freedom, independence, humanity, and peace. Based on Atatürk's speeches and writings. 1922-38

280. İnan, M. Rauf, Uysal, Ahmet E., transl. ATATÜRK AS A TEACHER AND LEADER. *Rev. Int. d'Hist. Militaire [France] 1981 (50): 207-224.* Analyzes the character and leadership of Kemal Atatürk. The hero of Turkish independence showed his talent as an educator early in his military career and later on a national and international level. His original qualities resided in a modest birth, accomplishment of victories with limited material means, a good psychological knowledge of the Turkish people, unusual foresight, and great strategic expertise. Article translated from Turkish; 29 notes. 1920-38

281. Jäschke, Gotthard. MUSTAFA KEMAL, EIN GEBORENER SOLDAT [Mustafa Kemal, a born soldier]. *Rev. Int. d'Hist. Militaire [France] 1981 (50): 107-111.* Sketches the military career of Mustafa Kemal Atatürk, using quotations from his speeches and from persons who knew him to show how he inspired his soldiers and to testify to his strategic cunning and skillful leadership. 1914-35

282. Karal, Enver Ziya; Uysal, Ahmet E., transl. ATATÜRK AS A SOLDIER. *Rev. Int. d'Hist. Militaire [France] 1981 (50): 113-132.* After a review of the military background of Mustafa Kemal Atatürk (1881-1938), analyzes his outstanding military qualities and quotes from the speeches in which the hero of Turkish independence expressed his views on military science and the art of war. His main concept was that war is justified only when waged for the defense of the country and the right of the nation. His great achievements and victories were due to his respect for ideas, love of his country, and confidence in the Turkish nation and the Turkish army. 1905-38

283. Karpat, Kemal H. THE PERSONALITY OF ATATÜRK. *American Historical Review 1985 90(4): 893-899.* Reviews Vamik D. Volkan and Norman Itzkowitz, *The Immortal Atatürk—a Psychobiography,* which attempts to analyze Atatürk's life and public career from a Freudian perspective. This is one of the most important sources in English on modern Turkish history and on Atatürk, as well as the first to apply psychological analysis to Turkish history. 6 notes. 1880's-1938

284. Koşay, Hâmit Z. PRESENTATION TO ATATÜRK. *Rev. des Études Sud-Est Européennes [Romania] 1982 20(1): 85-91.* Tribute to Kemal Atatürk (1881-1938) on the 100th anniversary of his birth. Centers on his interest in the preservation of archaeological treasures, Turkey's origins, its language as a source of history, the question of the Turkish homeland, Turkish civilization, and the relation between the Turkish and Basque languages. Cites Atatürk's action to promote historical investigations about Turkey. Photo. 1920's-30's

285. Maxim, Mihai. ATATÜRK SI MAREA LUI DRAGOSTE—ISTORIA [Atatürk and his great love, history]. *Magazin Istoric [Romania] 1981 15(11): 21-23.* Throughout his life, Kemal Atatürk (1881-1938) showed his

interest in the history of Turkey by the encouragement he gave to universities, museums, and societies devoted to the study of history. Illus. 1900-38

286. Ozankaya, Özer. ATATÜRK: THE ARCHITECT OF TURKISH RENAISSANCE. *Rev. Int. d'Hist. Militaire [France] 1981 (50): 225-232.* On the occasion of the 100th anniversary of the birth of Kemal Atatürk (1881-1938), expresses recognition for his contribution to human culture and to the development of democratic societies. 1923-38

287. Shpuza, Gazmend. ATATURC ET LES RELATIONS ALBANO-TURQUES [Atatürk and Albanian-Turkish relations]. *Studia Albanica [Albania] 1981 18(2): 127-138.* Discusses the relationship between Albania and Turkey, 1924-45, and examines specifically the active involvement of the Turkish statesman Kemal Atatürk (1881-1938) during the period of Albania's independence. The author also examines Atatürk's attitude to the Zog monarchy in Albania after 1928, and the reaction of the Albanian press to Atatürk's political and social reforms in Turkey. Secondary sources and newspaper reports; 71 notes. 1924-45

288. Şimşir, Bilâl N. MUSTAFA KEMAL ATATÜRK, HOMME DE GUERRE—HOMME DE PAIX (SEPTEMBER 1922) [Mustafa Kemal Atatürk—man of war, man of peace: September 1922]. *Rev. Int. d'Hist. Militaire [France] 1981 (50): 41-95.* Relates the memorable military and diplomatic events of September 1922 connected with the actions of Kemal Atatürk (1881-1938), victor over the Greeks who were occupying his country, and leader in time of peace. Centers on his great military skill in opening the way to Turkey's liberation and his brilliant political realism in isolating Great Britain and its bellicose policies from its European allies. The hero of Turkish independence prevented more bloodshed and gained the admiration of leaders of the Western and Eastern worlds. Based on Turkish Foreign Ministry archives and other official documents; 135 notes. 1922

289. Sūrī, Salāh al-Dīn Hasan al-. AL-TAHDĪTH 'INDA MUSTAFĀ KAMĀL ATĀTŪRK: DIRĀSAH TAHLĪLĪYAH [Mustafa Kemal Atatürk's modernization: an analysis]. *Majallat al-Buhūth al-Tārīkhīya [Libya] 1982 4(2): 277-292.* Kemal Atatürk's reforms from 1922 to 1934 were intended to make Turkey into a modern state on a par with Europe. He adopted European patterns, not only in the separation of religion and state, but also in all administrative institutions, economic structure, and cultural, social and psychological aspects. The abolition of the Caliphate, the liberation of women, and the romanization of the alphabet were meant to cut the link with the Ottoman past and change people's whole way of life and thought. 23 notes. 1922-34

290. Velikov, Stefan. MUSTAFA KEMAL ATATURK (CENTENARY OF HIS BIRTH). *Études Balkaniques [Bulgaria] 1981 17(1): 22-33.* Describes the life and career of Mustafa Kemal Atatürk (1881-1938), his part in the establishment of the Turkish Republic, and his domestic and foreign policies as its first president, with particular reference to the Balkans and Bulgaria. Ataturk had been a military attache in Sofia between 1913 and 1915 and advocated cooperation and friendship between the Bulgarian and Turkish peoples. Bulgaria supported the cause of the Turkish people in Anatolia and Thrace, Bulgarian builders helped in the transformation of Ankara into a modern city, and a series of treaties from 1925 onward confirmed a sincere and lasting friendship. Secondary sources. 1913-38

Athanasios I

291. Papadopoulos, Stephanos. LES DEMARCHES DE L'ARCHEVEQUE ATHANASE D'OCHRID POUR LA LIBERATION DES PEUPLES BALKANIQUES (FIN XVI[e]-DEBUT XVII[e] SIECLE) [The contribution of Archbishop Athanasios of Ohrid to the liberation of the Balkan people]. *Balkan Studies [Greece] 1983 24(2): 559-564.* The contribution of the Orthodox Eastern Church to the enslaved Balkan peoples during the Turkish occupation was important in the preservation and cultivation of national consciousness, education, and fighting morale. The Archbishop of Ohrid, Athanasios I, was for 20 years, 1595-1615, active in many revolutionary spheres. In order to ensure the support of the European sovereigns for the realization of his plans, Athanasios came into contact with the Venetians, the Spaniards, the Catholic Church, the Emperor of Austria, and others. For the same reason, he travelled abroad for many years and visited Rome, Naples, Milan, Prague, Moscow, and other cities. His activities continued up to 1615, at which point all trace of him is lost. Biblio. English summary, p. 689. 1595-1615

Atkinson, Theophilus and Henrietta

292. Wolpowitz, Lily. A MISSIONARY FAMILY: THE ATKINSONS OF PACALTSDORP AND THEIR ALBUMS. *Quarterly Bulletin of the South African Library [South Africa] 1985 39(4): 133-142.* Sketches the lives and work of the Reverend Theophilus Atkinson and his wife Henrietta, missionaries who settled in South Africa in the early 19th century, and examines excerpts from a music album, photo albums, and two autograph books of poetry belonging to Mrs. Atkinson and her daughter Elizabeth which are in the collection of the South African Library. 1795-1890

Atl, Dr.

293. Cherney, Lawrence and Bennett, Manuel. DR. ATL: FATHER OF MEXICAN MURALISM. *Américas (Organization of Am. States) 1981 33(2): 26-33.* Discusses the artistic career of Dr. Atl (Gerardo Murillo), born in 1875 in Guadalajara, Mexico, especially his studies in Europe, his teaching activities, and the murals he painted of Mexican landscapes. 1900-80

Attlee, Clement

294. Golant, William. MR. ATTLEE. *Hist. Today [Great Britain] 1983 33(Aug): 12-17.* Both the personality and ideology of Clement Attlee, Britain's first socialist prime minister, fit the needs of the British electorate in 1945. 1945-55

Aubigné, Agrippa d'

295. Schrenk, Gilbert. ASPECTS DE L'ECRITURE AUTOBIOGRAPHIQUE AU XVIe SIECLE: AGRIPPA D'AUBIGNE ET *SA VIE A SES ENFANTS* [Aspects of 16th-century autobiography: Agrippa d'Aubigné and *Sa Vie à Ses Enfants*]. *Nouvelle Revue du Seizième Siècle [France] 1985 3: 33-51.* Autobiography in the 16th century was a heterogeneous activity, involving several genres. The two fundamental concepts of autobiographical creation were the desire for narrative exactitude and for unity and structure within the text. In his *Sa Vie à Ses Enfants,* Agrippa d'Aubigné (1552-1630), by the use of satire, omissions, shifted chronology, and the retelling of incidents narrated earlier elsewhere, created a portrait that differs in several respects from historical fact. 90 notes. 1570's-1630

Aubigné, Francoişe de

See Maintenon, Marquise de

Auclert, Hubertine

296. Hause, Steven C.; McBride, Theresa (commentary). CITIZENESS OF THE REPUBLIC: CLASS AND SEX IDENTITY IN THE FEMINIST CAREER OF HUBERTINE AUCLERT, 1848-1914. *Proceedings of the Annual Meeting of the Western Society for French History 1984 12: 235-242.* Hubertine Auclert (1848-1914) was the founder of the women's suffrage movement in France. She worked indefatigably for that cause beginning in the 1870's; she wrote, organized demonstrations, and gave speeches. Her career demonstrates that she combined an interest in women's rights with a concern for the rights of the working class. Although at different times she worked with various republican or socialist groups, she never felt comfortable with any of them. She remained fiercely independent. Nevertheless, she did help to demonstrate the connection between gender interests and class interests. Comments, pp. 257-259. Based on documents in the departmental archives of the Allier and in the Parisian Prefecture of Police; 21 notes. 1870's-1914

Auden, W. H.

297. Warren, Austin. THE POETRY OF AUDEN. *Southern Rev. 1981 17(3): 461-478.* Discusses the growth and development of W. H. Auden's poetry, his career in England and America, and his place in 20th-century letters. 1927-73

Audibert, Paul

298. Rollandi, Maria Stella. IL SISTEMA BEDAUX NELLE MINIERE SARDE DELLA "PERTUSOLA" (1927-1935) [The Bedaux system and the Sardinian miners of "Pertusola," 1927-35]. *Studi Storici [Italy] 1985 26(1): 69-106.* Discusses the role of the engineer Paul Audibert in introducing the Bedaux system into Sardinian mining communities where Communist and Socialist loyalties were traditionally strong. Charles Bedaux, a French-born naturalized American, developed Frederick Taylor's economic theories into a system that included time compensation and productivity incentives. Audibert also attempted to control the leisure activities of his workers and to keep tensions at a minimum by introducing his own newspaper. His management techniques were endorsed by the new-age Fascist syndicate, Pertusola. Based on archives of the industrial associations, Sardinian mining associations, and the Geology Office; 4 tables, 104 notes. 1927-35

Auer, Anna Margaretha

See Pickelmann, John and Anna

Aurangzeb

299. Husain, S. M. Azizuddin. *KALIMAT-I-TAIYIBAT:* A SOURCE OF AURANGZEB'S REIGN. *Indian Arch. [India] 1980 29(1): 41-43.* The *Kalimat-i-Taiyibat* is a collection of royal orders or a precis of points, including scraps of verses and Arabic texts, dictated by Emperor Aurangzeb to his *munshi* (secretary) for inclusion in formal letters (compiled after Aurangzeb's death) to persons whose names are not always given. The style of these notes throws light on the emperor's manner, which was not always direct but made its point by quoting the Koran, the four caliphs, or other classics. 10 notes. ca 1708-19

Aurelian, Petre S.

300. Vlad, Radu-Dan. L'INDUSTRIALISATION DE LA ROUMANIE DANS LA VISION DE PETRE S. AURELIAN [The industrialization of Romania in the vision of Petre S. Aurelian]. *Revue Roumaine d'Histoire [Romania] 1984 23(3): 257-273.* Reviews the career of Petre S. Aurelian (1833-1909), one of the most notable economists of 19th-century Romania. An honors student, he studied political theory and political economy in France, 1856-60. Familiar with economic theory protecting the interests of industrialized countries at the expense of developing nations, such as Romania, he advocated industrialization as a means of promoting national unity. He became a driving force for the modernization of his country. 75 notes. 1850's-1909

Ausländer, Rose

301. Lermen, Birgit. "AUSGEGRABENE WURZELN": DIE LYRIKERIN ROSE AUSLÄNDER ["Dug up roots": the lyric poet Rose Ausländer]. *Stimmen der Zeit [West Germany] 1985 203(9): 632-638.* Discusses the life and prints poems of the German Jewish poet Rose Ausländer (born Rosalie Scherzer in 1901), who lived in Czernowitz, Romania during World War II. Having survived the Holocaust, her poems dealt with the themes of lost homeland, loneliness, and persecution, as well as hope. 1920's-85

Austen, Jane

302. Halperin, John. UNENGAGED LAUGHTER: JANE AUSTEN'S JUVENILIA. *South Atlantic Q. 1982 81(3): 286-299.* The juvenilia of Jane Austen (1775-1817), of which about 90,000 words still survive, were written in three slim quarto notebooks between 1787 and 1793. They are mostly farcical and satirical in nature, short stories, sketches, fictional letters, scraps of epistolary novels, bits of plays, and other materials. They show that as a girl Jane Austen was well read, and that by the time she was in her teens her literary taste was already set. The juvenilia are the surest guide to the things she thought about and interested herself in during her adolescence. The earlier pieces are largely literary satire, the later ones largely social comedy. Based on literary studies of Jane Austen; 24 notes. 1787-93

303. Honan, Park. JANE AUSTEN AND MARRIAGE. *Contemporary Review [Great Britain] 1984 245(1426): 253-259.* Describes the marriage proposal made by Harris Biggs-Wither to the English writer Jane Austen in December 1802. Also considers Jane Austen's acceptance and speedy rejection of the proposal with regard to the customs and attitudes of the contemporary society in which she lived. 1802

304. Kaplan, Deborah. THE DISAPPEARANCE OF THE WOMAN WRITER: JANE AUSTEN AND HER BIOGRAPHERS. *Prose Studies [Great Britain] 1984 7(2): 129-147.* Considers the disservice done to Jane Austen by biographers who have treated her life as uneventful. The author suggests that Austen's domestic experiences and social values must be incorporated into any study of her life as a woman novelist. 1775-1817

305. LeFaye, Deirdre. THREE AUSTEN FAMILY LETTERS. *Notes and Queries [Great Britain] 1985 32(3): 329-335.* Contains three previously unpublished letters written by and to members of Jane Austen's family circle, containing fresh information on the life of the Austens during the 1770's and 1780's. 1771-86

Avanesov

306. Gharibjanian, G. B. V. I. LENINI HAY ZINAKITS-NĒRN U ASHAKĒRTNĒRĒ [V. I. Lenin's Armenian comrades-in-arms and disciples]. *Patma-Banasirakan Handes. Istoriko-Filologicheskii Zhurnal [USSR] 1980 (1): 13-20.* Describes briefly the careers of Isahak Lalayants, Knunyants, Shahumian, Suren Spandarian, Kamo, Alexander Bekzadian, Kasparyants, Miasnikian, S. Ter-Gabrielian, Kasian, Avanesov, Baghdatian and Vahan Terian, who, convinced that the interests of the Armenian working people were linked to the interests of the working masses in Russia, were among Lenin's most loyal comrades-in-arms and disciples. Lenin personally appreciated their work; he described Lalayants as a dedicated revolutionary, sent a wreath to Kamo's tomb in Tiflis, and appointed Shahumian as Extraordinary Commissar for the Caucasus. Secondary sources; 18 notes.
ca 1890-1917

Avdalbēgyan, T'adevos

307. Darbinyan, H. D. T'ADEVOS AVDALBĒGYAN (TSNNDYAN 100-AMYAKI AṚT'IV) [T'adevos Avdalbēgyan: on the centenary of his birth]. *Patma-Banasirakan Handes. Istoriko-Filologicheskii Zhurnal [USSR] 1985 (4): 85-93.* T'adevos Avdalbēgyan (1885-1937) was trained as an economist but had wide-ranging interests. He selected problems for study that were apparently intractable, such as the determination of the income of Armenian and European peasants in the 5th century. His publications include translations, perceptive literary studies such as *The Armenian Village in Hovhannēs T'umanyan's Works* (1925), and historical investigations. Based on the author's writings; photo, 5 notes. Russian summary. 1907-37

Aveline, Claude

308. Jacobs, Gabriel. CLAUDE AVELINE: A PUBLISHER OF FINE EDITIONS IN THE PARIS OF THE 1920S. *Publishing Hist. [Great Britain] 1982 (12): 5-15.* Reviews the Paris publishing career of Claude Aveline, who, after 1930, became better known as a writer. His specialty was limited editions of high quality, personally selected and produced. He prospered due to the 1920's vogue of collecting such publications but had turned to writing by 1930. Biblio. 1920's

Avendaño, Diego de

309. Losada, Angel. "DIEGO DE AVENDAÑO S.I. MORALISTA Y JURISTA, DEFENSOR DE LA DIGNIDAD HUMANA DE INDIOS Y NEGROS EN AMERICA" (SEGOVIA 27 O 29.IX.1594-LIMA 30.VIII.1688) ["Diego de Avendaño S.J. moralist and jurist, defender of the human dignity of Indians, and blacks in America" (Segovia 27 or 29.IX.1594-Lima 30.VIII.1688)]. *Missionalia Hispanica [Spain] 1982 39(115): 1-18.* Fr. Diego de Avendaño, the Spanish-born Jesuit, has been almost forgotten, yet his work in Peru is memorable, if only for his defense of the human rights of slaves, especially in his *Thesaurus Indicus* (1668-86). In addition, he held high offices in his order, and published other books. Biblio. 1594-1688

Avezzana, Giuseppe

310. Pontecorvo, A. PER IL CENTENARIO DELLA MORTE DEL GEN. GIUSEPPE AVEZZANA [For the centenary of the death of General Giuseppe Avezzana]. *Rassegna Storica del Risorgimento [Italy] 1979 66(4): 411-414.* Reproduces an account written by General Giuseppe Avezzana (1797-1879), a noted fighter for liberty, which recounts his activities with Napoleon's army, the Piedmontese army, and the liberal circle at Genoa, and travel to Spain, the United States, and Mexico where he again fought. He returned to Italy twice to fight for freedom, in 1848, and in 1860 to join Garibaldi's campaign. He was a member of the Italian parliament from 1861 to 1879. 11 notes. 1822-79

Avila Camacho, Manuel

311. Carrillo Flores, Antonio. SEMBLANZA DEL PRESIDENTE AVILA CAMACHO [Profile of President Manuel Avila Camacho]. *Memoria del Colegio Nacional [Mexico] 1983 10(2): 121-128.* An overview of Manuel Avila Camacho's presidency. Text of speech delivered in Mexico City, 13 October 1983. 1940-55

Avis, Johan George

312. Buijtenen, M. P. van. IN MEMORIAM JOHAN GEORGE AVIS [In memoriam: Johan George Avis]. *Nederlands Archievenblad [Netherlands] 1982 86(1): 18-22.* An appreciation of the character and work of Johan George Avis (1893-1981), a Mennonite and since 1930 inventory archivist at various Dutch national archives, who in 1947 became provincial archives inspector in Overijssel. 1893-1981

Ayalon-Eizland, Yeḥezqel

313. Ayalon-Eizland, Yeḥezqel. ŠNATAYIM BE-MAḤANEH-HA-KFIYAH MIYELEṢ: PIRQEY YOMAN [Two years in the Mielec work camp: excerpts from a diary]. *Yalkut Moreshet Periodical [Israel] 1985 (39): 91-108.* The author describes his experiences in the Mielec work camp, where he was imprisoned from July 1942 to January 1944, discussing other prisoners and the conduct of the Germans and Poles in charge of the camp. 1942-44

Aydemır, Şevket Süreyya

314. MacLeod, William Allister. "Şevket Süreyya Aydemır, Modern Turkish Biographer." University of Michigan 1984. 175 pp. *DAI 1985 45(7): 2123-A.* DA8422282
1959-76

Ayscue, George

315. LeFevre, Peter. SIR GEORGE AYSCUE, COMMONWEALTH AND RESTORATION ADMIRAL. *Mariner's Mirror [Great Britain] 1982 68(2): 189-202.* Notes there is not a complete biography of Admiral Ayscue and briefly sketches his career. His exact date of birth is unknown, as is the date of his marriage. He was knighted for unknown reasons in 1641 and joined the parliamentary side during the Civil War, going to sea for the first time in 1646 as commander of a major vessel. He was promoted to admiral in 1649, served in various expeditions, then with distinction during the first Dutch war of the mid-1650's. He was pensioned in the late 1650's and politics may have been involved since his reputation as a seaman was high. He lived quietly until the second Dutch war of the 1660's, when he again served and was taken prisoner in 1666. He was ransomed in 1667 and returned to England where he died in 1672. Based mainly on HMC and CSP calendars and secondary sources; 21 biblio. notes. 1615-72

Azaña, Manuel

316. Suero Roca, María Teresa. AZAÑA Y LOS GENERALES [Azaña and the generals]. *Historia y Vida [Spain] 1984 17(195): 92-105.* Based on Manuel Azaña's diaries, analyzes the opinions and the relationship of the Spanish Republican prime minister and minister of war with

Generals José Sanjurjo, Goded, Gonzalo Queipo de Llano, and Francisco Franco during the early years of the Second Republic. 1931-36

Azorín

317. Ouimette, Victor. FROM DICTATORSHIP TO REPUBLIC: AZORIN AND THE FORCE OF THE INTELLECT. *Hispanic Review 1986 54(1): 1-25.* In 1929, 26 young writers appealed for leadership in the effort to rescue Spain from its political malaise, and the prominent author and critic Azorín was interested in the enthusiasm for political action among young intellectuals. Incorrectly perceived as a conservative because of his emphasis on historical tradition, Azorín was actually an orthodox liberal individualist opposed to the collectivist ideologies popular with contemporaries. He resisted the notion that action and thought were antithetical, but warned that political involvement could disrupt the tranquility in which creativity thrived. By 1936 he had personally experienced such results. Based on newspapers, periodicals, and other contemporary published works; 68 notes. 1907-36

Azoury, Negib

318. Kramer, Martin. AZOURY: A FURTHER EPISODE. *Middle Eastern Studies [Great Britain] 1982 18(4): 351-358.* Discusses the political activities of Negib Azoury, who attempted to draw Europe into financial and logistical support for an Arab uprising against the Ottoman Empire. These activities were directed at the French government from 1907 to 1910. France also found him a useful source of data about British policies, though there was some doubt as to where Azoury's allegiances lay. Based on French diplomatic papers and secondary sources; 32 notes. 1906-10

Azuela, Mariano

319. Mejia, G. "The Novels of Mariano Azuela: A Process against a Revolution." U. of Essex [England] 1984. *DAI-C 1985 46(4): 861; 46/4143c.* 1910's-52

B

Ba Jin

320. Zhelokhovtsev, A. BA JIN: WRITER AND PATRIOT. *Far Eastern Affairs [USSR] 1984 (1): 120-131.* Prints a biography of China's long-suffering novelist and translator, Ba Jin (b. 1904), who took his pseudonym from the first and last syllables respectively of the family names of the anarchists Bakunin and Kropotkin, whom he admired. Focuses on his suffering under political repression by the Nationalists, military occupation and deportation by Japan, and the Cultural Revolution. 1928-82

Babel, Isaac

321. Lvov, Arkady. BABEL THE JEW. *Commentary 1983 75(3): 40-49.* Profiles the life of Jewish writer Isaac Babel, and his search for identity. Focuses on political influences on Babel's literature. 1916-39

322. Sicher, Efraim. THE JEW ON HORSEBACK: ON THE QUESTION OF ISAAK BABEL'S PLACE IN SOVIET JEWISH LITERATURE. *Soviet Jewish Affairs [Great Britain] 1983 13(1): 37-50.* Describes Isaac Babel's (1894-1941) writings and Zionism in the early USSR, as well as the effect on the writing and distribution of Jewish literature under the new régime. 1918-39

323. Sicher, Efraim. MAUPASSANT EN RUSSIE: UN EXEMPLE D'INFLUENCE LITTERAIRE CHEZ ISAAK BABEL' [Maupassant in Russia: an example of one of Isaac Babel's literary influences]. *Revue des Etudes Slaves [France] 1985 57(3): 385-395.* Discusses the influence of 19th-century French novelist and short-story writer Guy de Maupassant on Russian writer Isaac Babel, born in Odessa in 1894. Babel probably first read de Maupassant in the Russian edition that included an introduction by Leo Tolstoy; he has often been called the Russian de Maupassant. 30 notes. 19c-20c

324. Souvarine, Boris. LAST CONVERSATIONS WITH ISAAC BABEL. *Dissent 1981 28(3): 319-330.* Notes on three conversations in 1932 with Soviet writer Isaac Babel (1894-1941) covering the Communist Party and politics in the USSR. 1932

Babeuf, Gracchus

325. Tønnesson, Kåre. KOMMUNISMENS RØTTER: TO BØKER OM BABEUF [Communism's roots: two books on Babeuf]. *Hist. Tidsskrift [Norway] 1982 61(2): 162-167.* Reviews two recent books on Gracchus Babeuf: V. Dalin's *Grakkh Babeuf: Nakanune i vo vremai Velikoi Frantsuzskoi Revoliutsii, 1789-1794* [1963] [French translation: *Gracchus Babeuf à la Veille et Pendant la Grande Révolution Française 1785-1794* (1976)] and R. B. Rose's *Gracchus Babeuf: The First Revolutionary Communist* (1978). These books differ, among other things, on the time when Babeuf's ideas can clearly be regarded as a truly communist program and the length of the temporary dictatorship Babeuf came to propose before the masses ruled. Dalin's book provides the most thorough presentation of Babeuf's thought based on his writings while Rose's work presents a more comprehensive picture of his life, thought, and career. 1790-96

Babics, András

326. Mérey, Klára T. BABICS ANDRÁS (1906-1984) [András Babics (1906-84)]. *Történelmi Szemle [Hungary] 1985 28(3): 553-554.* This obituary commemorates the life and career of András Babics (1906-84), Hungarian historian and founder of the Trans-Danubia Institute of the Hungarian Academy of Sciences. 1906-84

Babini, José

327. Ortiz, Eduardo L. and Pyenson, Lewis. ELOGE: JOSÉ BABINI, 11 MAY 1897-18 MAY 1984. *Isis 1985 76(284): 567-569.* Babini was an influential Argentine educator, mathematician, and historian of science and a prolific writer in the latter field. 1930's-84

Babushkin, I. V.

328. Varhatiuk, P. L. I. V. BABUSHKIN U KATERYNOSLAVI—DO 110-RICHCHIA Z DNIA NARODZHENNIA [I. V. Babushkin in Ekaterinoslav—his 110th birthday anniversary]. *Ukrains'kyi Istorychnyi Zhurnal [USSR] 1983 (1): 133-136.* Without such people as I. V. Babushkin, V. I. Lenin stated once, the Russian people would remain forever a nation of slaves. As one of the founders of the Bolshevik Party he actively participated in its clandestine work, including publishing and illegal transportation of weapons. He was executed without trial in Chita in 1906. Describes his activities in the Ukraine, particularly in Ekaterinoslav. Secondary sources; 15 notes. 1890-1906

Bacchini, B.

329. Casari, Umberto. NOTE SUL BACCHINI GIORNALISTA [Notes on the journalist Bacchini]. *Studi Secenteschi [Italy] 1979 20: 99-120.* Reflects on the life and work of Italian literary journalist B. Bacchini. 47 notes. 17c-18c

Bacchini, Benedetto

330. Sacchelli, Abramo. BENEDETTO BACCHINI (1651-1721) VOCE NUOVA E IMPORTANTE NEL SEICENTO [Benedetto Bacchini (1651-1721), a new and important voice in the 17th century]. *Arch. Storico per le Province Parmensi [Italy] 1980 32: 165-177.* The Benedictine monk Bacchini was a humanist and the teacher of the great scholar Lodovico Muratori, whom he discovered and initiated in the art of paleography; he was one of the early representatives of the Enlightenment. 1680-1721

Bach, Johann Sebastian

331. Jarlert, Anders. JOHANN SEBASTIAN BACH I KYRKOHISTORISKT PERSPEKTIV: ETT BIDRAG TILL 300-ÅRSJUBILEETS BACHBILD [Johann Sebastian Bach from the standpoint of church history: a contribution to the 300-Year Jubilee view of Bach]. *Kyrkohistorisk Årsskrift [Sweden] 1985: 11-28.* Swedish Archbishop Nathan Söderblom, usually credited with (and criticized for) first calling Johann Sebastian Bach (1685-1750) "the fifth evangelist" in the 1920's, actually said that Bach's passions sound like a fifth gospel, and perhaps over-emphasized the importance of music as opposed to text. Older church historians assumed that Bach was a pietist, but every age has taken its own view (our own secular and post-Romantic one being influenced by Söderblom and Albert Schweitzer), and therefore no definitive picture can ever be achieved. Secondary sources; 103 notes. German summary. 1700's-50

332. Máté, János. JOHANN SEBASTIAN BACH SZÜLETÉSÉNEK 300. ÉVFORDULÓJÁRA [Johann Sebastian Bach: 300th anniversary of his birth]. *Theologiai Szemle [Hungary] 1985 28(3): 171-172.* Discusses Bach's desire to fulfill his everyday obligation to his religion through music and the importance of theological comprehension to the proper understanding of his music. 1700-50

333. Mila, Massimo. LA VECCHIAIA DI BACH [Bach's old age]. *Belfagor [Italy] 1983 38(3): 253-264.* Describes the reasons which moved Johann Sebastian Bach to retire to Leipzig at the age of 38 and his gradual disenchantment with the meanness of the surrounding life and the influence it had on his music. 1723-50

334. Sorozábal Serrano, Pablo. JUAN SEBASTIAN BACH O EL ARTE COMO OFICIO [Johann Sebastian Bach or art as craft]. *Cuadernos Hispanoamericanos [Spain] 1985 (426): 6-19.* Johann Sebastian Bach's (1685-1750) music has been valued by the 20th-century bourgeois avant garde as an elitist, dehumanized, scientific study of sounds; the wide acceptance of Bach since the 1960's bears witness to the radical worldliness of his compositions, even the religious ones. He experienced the transition from the hegemony of the feudal aristocracy to the beginnings of the bourgeois revolution which was a time when artists were still skilled craftsmen in the service of church and civil authorities, with a functional, utilitarian concept of art. From this dialectic arose that blend of reason and passion that was characteristic of Bach's music. ca 1700-50

335. Wolff, Christoph. PROBLEMS AND NEW PERSPECTIVES OF BACH BIOGRAPHY. *Proteus 1985 2(1): 1-7.* Discusses the structure and techniques of 19th-century German music scholar Philipp Spitta's definitive 2-volume biography *Johann Sebastian Bach* (1873, 1880) and research in the 1980's that challenged some of Spitta's assumptions. Spitta's five-part periodization of Bach's life oversimplified or ignored certain crucial turning points in the composer's life and his analysis of musical influences on Bach's development was incomplete. 1707-40's

336. —. BACH AS SEEN BY HIS CONTEMPORARIES. *Proteus 1985 2(1): 14-18.* Selections from *The Bach Reader* (1966), edited by Hans T. David and Arthur Mendel, ranging from a poem of 1731 to a reminiscence by the last of Bach's pupils, Johann Christian Kittel, in 1808. 1731-1808

Bachmann family

337. Bachmann-Dick, Fritz. THE RELATIONSHIP BETWEEN THE FAMILY OF JOHANN JAKOB KAPPELER AND THE BACHMANN FAMILIES AT THUNDORF AND STETTFURT. *Swiss American Historical Society Newsletter 1984 20(2): 21-47.* History and genealogy of the Kappeler and Bachmann families of Canton Thurgau, Switzerland, from the 14th century to the 19th. Appends several documents on the history of the Bachman family in the United States, 1852-1971. 14c-19c

Badet, Arnaud de

338. Montagnes, Bernard. UN INQUISITEUR DE TOULOUSE ACCUSE D'HERESIE EN 1534: LE DOMINICAIN ARNAUD DE BADET [An inquisitor of Toulouse accused of heresy in 1534: the Dominican Arnaud de Badet]. *Revue d'Histoire de l'Eglise de France [France] 1985 71(187): 233-251.* Dominicans in southwestern France in the 1530's, although fighting the common enemy of Lutheran heresy, were divided between reformed and traditional monasteries, the former constituting the Congregation of France, the latter remaining under the jurisdiction of the Province of Toulouse. This division led to Badet's brief rise to the office of inquisitor, but also to a charge of heresy against him in 1534. Surely no Lutheran, he was nevertheless a scholar open to secular culture, and not immune to German ideas. Although acquitted, his career as inquisitor fell victim to the sectarianism of his age. Based on documents in departmental archives and archives of religious orders; 68 notes, biblio. 1530-39

Baeck, Leo

339. Altmann, Alexander. LEO BAECK AND THE JEWISH MYSTICAL TRADITION. *Essays in Jewish Intellectual History* (Hanover, N.H.: Published for Brandeis U. Pr. by U. Pr. of New England, 1981): 293-311. Discusses the role of liberal Jewish scholar and rabbi Leo Baeck in the resurrection of the mystical cabalistic and Hasidic teachings of Judaism in the 20th century. 1895-1927

Baer, Gabriel

340. Gilbar, Gad G. NOTES AND COMMUNICATIONS. *Int. J. of Middle East Studies [Great Britain] 1983 15(1): 129-130.* An obituary of Gabriel Baer (1919-82), who possessed an extraordinary knowledge of Islamic history and civilization as well as mastery of the Arabic and Turkish languages. His publications have become cornerstones in the study of the social history of the modern Middle East. Moreover his contributions have been recognized by many honors and he inspired many young scholars in the Middle East as well as in the West. 1919-82

341. Warburg, Gabriel R. IN MEMORIAM GABRIEL BAER, 1919-1982. *Asian and African Studies [Israel] 1981 15(2): 161-163.* Obituary of Gabriel Baer, the editor of *Asian and African Studies.* 1940's-82

Baerdes, Willem Dirkszoon

342. Tracy, James D. HABSBURG GRAIN POLICY AND AMSTERDAM POLITICS: THE CAREER OF SHERIFF WILLEM DIRKSZOON BAERDES, 1542-1606. *Sixteenth Cent. J. 1983 14(3): 293-319.* Willem Dirkszoon Baerdes was the nucleus around whom a party formed that would eventually gain control and guide Amsterdam to greatness as a Calvinist republic. Baerdes' appointment as *schout* (sheriff) surprised the older generation and some modern scholars because Baerdes had been associated with the ousted sheriff, but this appointment was a compromise between factions of the burgher elite, who closed ranks in the face of violence from riots and external forces. As sheriff, Baerdes gained the confidence of both the central government and the merchant elite, which was unusual at that time. Amsterdam archives and secondary sources; 139 notes. 1520's-1606

Bagalei, Dimitri Ivanovich

See Bahalii, Dmytro Ivanovych

Bagdash, Khalid

343. Vavilov, A. I. VERNYI SYN BORIUSHCHEGOSIA NARODA (K 70-LETIIU KH. BAGDASHA) [A true son of a fighting people: the 70th birthday of Kh. Bagdash]. *Voprosy Istorii KPSS [USSR] 1982 (11): 129-132.* Briefly records the life and exploits of Khalid Bagdash (b. 1912), the general secretary of the Syrian Communist Party. He was first elected to the post in 1937. From time to time the Party became illegal, but by 1977 Bagdash was able to serve openly as a member of the Syrian parliament. The Syrian Communist Party closely supported Leonid Brezhnev's initiatives toward peace in the Middle East. Bagdash was granted the Order of the October Revolution in 1972. Several references to the press in Russian and Arabic; 4 notes. 1930's-82

Bagdonas, Juozas

344. —. JUOZAS BAGDONAS—PROFILE OF AN ARTIST. *Lituanus 1983 29(4): 50-62.* Lithuanian-born artist Juozas Bagdonas studied both in his homeland and in the major art capitals of Europe prior to the second world war. During this period his style was realistic-impressionistic. His subjects included nature, peasant life, and fishermen at work. Toward the end of the war Bagdonas became a refugee, moving to Vienna, then Germany, Colombia and, in 1958, the United States, where he has lived in Washington, D.C. and New York City. By 1960 his style had become completely abstract. More recent works are often characterized by the use of large canvases (conveying a sense of immensity), a variety of textures, and the mixture of paints with other materials. 10 plates. 1930's-70's

Bagford, John

345. Gatch, Milton McC. JOHN BAGFORD AS A COLLECTOR AND DISSEMINATOR OF MANUSCRIPT FRAGMENTS. *Library [Great Britain] 1985 7(2): 95-114.* John Bagford (d.1716) was a London bookseller who has mistakenly been identified as a mutilator of printed books in order to collect a large number of manuscript fragments. The examination of two Bagford fragment collections, one housed at the University of Missouri and the other in the University Library, Cambridge, fails to convict him convincingly of such destruction. Bagford gathered the fragments for a planned history of printing and the printed book. 60 notes. 1699-1716

Baghdatian

346. Gharibjanian, G. B. V. I. LENINI HAY ZINAKITSNĒRN U ASHAKĒRTNĒRĒ [V. I. Lenin's Armenian comrades-in-arms and disciples]. *Patma-Banasirakan Handes. Istoriko-Filologicheskii Zhurnal [USSR] 1980 (1): 13-20.* ca 1890-1917

For abstract see ***Avanesov***

Bahalii, Dmytro Ivanovych

347. Sarbei, V. H. and Kravchenko, V. V. AKADEMIK AN URSR D. I. BAHALII [Dmytro I. Bahalii, academician of the Ukrainian Academy of Sciences]. *Ukrains'kyi Istorychnyi Zhurnal [USSR] 1982 (11): 154-158.* Dmytro Ivanovych Bahalii (known also by the Russian variant of his name, Dmitri Ivanovich Bagalei) was hailed as an outstanding Soviet Ukrainian historian as far back as 1927, when the Ukraine named a research establishment after him in Kharkov. By his own admission, he started his vocation as a bourgeois Ukrainophile and later went over to the proletarian revolution. Unlike Hrushevskyi, Bahalii adhered to the concept that the Russian and Ukrainian peoples originated from the same Kiev roots. Although he failed in his attempt to produce a history of the Ukraine on the basis of Marxist-Leninist methodology, his striving to master the basics of the scientific materialistic perception of history was sincere. 1919-32

Bahr, Hermann

348. Daviau, Donald G. HERMANN BAHR AND THE RADICAL POLITICS OF AUSTRIA IN THE 1880'S. *German Studies Rev. 1982 5(2): 163-185.* In his university years at Vienna and Berlin, Hermann Bahr (d. 1918) was passionately involved in political radicalism, first as an adherent of Georg von Schönerer's Pan-German movement and later as a follower of the Marxist Socialist Viktor Adler. After Bismarck rejected Austrian Pan-Germanism, Bahr became an Austrian patriot. He later became disillusioned with socialism as he concluded that it was unlikely that a "new man" would be created, since people were firmly rooted in the past. 63 notes. 1881-88

Bahrdt, Karl Friedrich

349. Mühlpfordt, Günter. BAHRDTS WEG ZUM REVOLUTIONÄREN DEMOKRATISMUS: DAS WERDEN SEINER LEHRE VON STAAT DES VOLKSWOHLS [Bahrdt's way to revolutionary democratism: the development of his theory of the welfare state]. *Zeits. für Geschichtswissenschaft [East Germany] 1981 29(11): 996-1017.* Karl Friedrich Bahrdt (1741-92) was a product of the mid-German Enlightenment of Leipzig, Halle, and Erfurt. He was a theologian, a classical philologist, a philosopher, and a writer. His books were banned in 1779. He was inspired by the French Revolution. In 1791, he published in Riga his *System of a Moral Religion, Part 3,* in which his views on the welfare state are expounded. 98 notes. 1770-92

Bai Rubing

350. —. PAI JU-PING—FIRST SECRETARY OF THE CCP SHANTUNG PROVINCIAL COMMITTEE. *Issues & Studies [Taiwan] 1982 18(10): 93-98.* Bai Rubing (Pai Juping, 1916-) is one of the two provincial secretaries retaining their posts after the fall of the Gang of Four. Bai, who has had important assignments since 1949, specializes in finance.

In 1977 he was elected a member of the 11th CCP Central Committee and deputy for Shandong to the 5th National People's Congress. Based on Mainland media reports; 9 notes. 1949-82

Baidukov, G. F.

351. Beliakov, A. CHEREZ SEVERNYI POLIUS AMERIKU [Across the North Pole to America]. *Voenno-Istoricheskii Zhurnal [USSR] 1981 23(5): 38-43.* Informal account of the flight in June 1937 of V. P. Chkalov, G. F. Baidukov, and A. Beliakov across the North Pole to the United States. Beginning with brief details of previous endurance flights in the North, describes the origin of the idea for the flight to America, Stalin's interest in the plan, and concentrates in detail on the actual flight, recording the precise time of particular events, personal feelings at given moments, and a description of the arrival and reception in the United States. Considers the importance of the flight not only for the history of aviation but for the development of Soviet-American relations and thus to the promotion of peace between East and West. Based on personal experience; 2 notes. 1937

Bailey, Benjamin

352. Ryan, Robert M. THE FALL OF ONE OF THE NOBLEST MEN ALIVE: BENJAMIN BAILEY. ARCHDEACON OF COLOMBO. *Bull. of Res. in the Humanities 1982 85(1): 9-26.* Although in his youth a churchman of great promise and moral tutor of English poet John Keats, Benjamin Bailey's later career in Ceylon was one of insubordination, ambition, greed, and spite. 1817-48

Bailey, David C.

353. Beezley, William H. DAVID C. BAILEY (1930-82). *Hispanic Am. Hist. Rev. 1983 63(3): 591-592.* David C. Bailey, Professor of Latin American history at Michigan State University, was a specialist in the history of Mexico. 1930-82

Bailey, Jackson

354. Shimomura, Mitsuko. TANOHATA VILLAGE: SCHOOL OF INTERNATIONAL LIVING. *Japan Q. [Japan] 1983 30(2): 140-144.* Tanohata, a village of 5,000 in northeastern Japan, has been the home of Mr. and Mrs. Jackson Bailey, who initiated there a student exchange with Earlham College and began a program in cross-cultural education. Generations of students have engaged in manual labor, taught English, and learned Japanese. The program has contributed uniquely to international understanding. 1960's-83

Baillet, Thibault

355. Yver, Jean. LE PRESIDENT THIBAULT BAILLET ET LA REDACTION DES COUTUMES (1496-1514) [President Thibault Baillet and the drawing up of legal customs, 1496-1514]. *Revue Historique de Droit Français et Etranger [France] 1986 64(1): 19-42.* Analyzes the work of Thibault Baillet from 1496 to 1514. Baillet was president of the Parlement of Paris. Following the orders of kings Charles VIII and Louis XII, he led commissions that reformed and put into writing 15 of the most important regional legal customs that were under the jurisdiction of his Parlement. The aim was to bring greater uniformity and efficiency and to make clear exactly what the customs were. Baillet was a conscientious jurist, and he accomplished much that was beneficial. Based on printed primary sources; 81 notes. 1496-1514

Baillie, Joanna

356. Noble, Aloma E. "Joanna Baillie as a Dramatic Artist." U. of Iowa 1983. 226 pp. *DAI 1984 44(7): 1974-A.* DA8325170 1790's-1851

Bairaktares, Ioannes

357. Mitakē, Dionysē. IŌANNĒS BAIRAKTARĒS [Ioannes Bairaktares]. *Ēpeirōtikē Hestia [Greece] 1982 31[i.e., 32](160-161): 166-170.* There has been no study made of Ioannes Bairaktares, (1798-1853). He was an Albanian Christian born in the mountain fortress of Souli. When Ali Pasha, the tyrant of Epirus, forced the Souliotes out of his realm, Bairaktares joined the Greek army to fight in the war of independence. In 1826 he distinguished himself at the siege of Messolonghi both as a soldier and translator. When the city fell he escaped to the forces of D. Ypsilanti in Eastern Greece. He eventually attained the office of general, and was noted for his patriotic zeal. 19 notes. 1798-1853

Baker, Samuel

358. Casada, Jim. SAMUEL BAKER: VICTORIAN ADVENTURER. *Sporting Classics 1985 3(6): 16-17, 75-82.* The adventurous life of sporting writer, African explorer, and imperial administrator, Samuel Baker, made him one of Victorian England's most popular and controversial figures. 1821-93

Baker, Thomas

359. Korsten, Frans. THOMAS BAKER AND HIS BOOKS. *Transactions of the Cambridge Bibliographical Society [Great Britain] 1985 8(5): 491-513.* The correspondence of the scholar and antiquary Thomas Baker (1656-1740) is almost entirely concerned with books, and from it Baker emerges as occupying a unique position in the scholarly world in the early 18th century by virtue of his friendly relations with both Whig and Tory scholars. His own collection, partly donated at his death to St. John's College, Cambridge, reflected his interest in the history of Cambridge University, incanabula, religion, and English history and politics. He also had a great interest and expertise in bibliography. Based on corresondence in the British Library and Bodleian Library and books in St. John's College, Cambridge; 109 notes. 1680's-1740

Baker, William

360. LeSueur, Thomas D. A. WILLIAM BAKER, SHOPKEEPER. *Journal of the Royal Australian Historical Society [Australia] 1984 70(2): 112-123.* Distinguishes between the careers of William Baker, storekeeper, and William Baker, settler, who were both contemporary Hawkesbury, New South Wales residents ca. 1810. The storekeeper, a First Fleet marine's sergeant turned farmer and government storekeeper at Hawkesbury until dismissed by Lachlan Macquarie (1810) for associating with the Rum Rebels, migrated to Hobart and died in 1836. The settler, a Second Fleet convict, became a publican and died a respected citizen of Windsor in 1829. Based on New South Wales Colonial Secretary papers, *Sydney Gazette,* and other primary sources; 74 notes. 1788-1836

Bakhuizen, Ludolf

361. Vorstman, R. M. LUDOLF BAKHUIZEN. *Mariner's Mirror [Great Britain] 1985 71(4): 474-477.* Describes an exhibition of the marine painter Ludolf Bakhuizen (1630-1708) held in the Netherlands' Maritime Museum in Amsterdam in 1985. Born in Germany, Bakhuizen went to Am-

sterdam in 1650 and became well-known for his paintings of ships and sea battles. He was also commissioned to do portraits of Amsterdam's elite during his long and successful career. 2 illus. 1650-1708

Bakri Sapalō, Shaykh

362. Hayward, R. J. and Hassan, Mohammed. THE OROMO ORTHOGRAPHY OF SHAYKH BAKRI SAPALŌ *Bull. of the School of Oriental and African Studies [Great Britain] 1981 44(3): 550-566.* Discusses the indigenous alphabet devised in about 1956 by Shaykh Bakri Sapalō for writing the hitherto exclusively oral language of his native Oromo districts of the Hagar region of Ethiopia. Bakri (1895-1980), a prolific writer in Arabic, poet, teacher, theologian, and historian, was for more than 50 years a leading intellectual and political figure in Oromo society, an ardent nationalist and fierce critic of Ethiopian rule in the Hagar. His Oromo alphabet was intended to stimulate the growth of a sense of separate ethnic identity among the Oromo, and to bring their plight to world attention. Consequently, its diffusion was strenuously opposed by the Aramaic-speaking officials of successive imperial and military-Marxist Ethiopian regimes determined to stamp out separatist movements in the region. Based on Shaykh Bakri's letters and political tracts in Oromo, oral information, and secondary sources; plate, 5 fig., 27 notes, ref., appendix. 1875-1980

Bakšev, Petur Bogdan

363. Dimitrov, Božidar. PETUR BOGDAN BAKŠEV—ACTIVITE POLITIQUE [Petur Bogdan Bakšev's political activity]. *Etudes Balkaniques [Bulgaria] 1984 20(2): 41-66.* Relates the politics of the Bulgarian translator of literature and archbishop of the Catholic Church Petur Bogdan Bakšev (d. 1674) to trends in 17th-century Europe. He lived part of his life in Venetian territories in Italy and the Balkans and tried to enlist the help of the Habsburg Empire and Poland in Bulgaria's independence movements against the Ottoman Empire. He also sought to strengthen the position of the Catholic minority groups in Bulgaria by encouraging conversions from the Orthodox Eastern Church. 111 notes. 1630-73

Bakunin, Mikhail

364. Furlani, Silvio. ANCORA UN PO' DI LUCE SU BAKUNIN E LA SUA ASSOCIAZIONE SEGRETA SCANDINAVA: CHI ERA MARKUS? [Again a little light on Bakunin and his Scandinavian secret association: who was Markus?]. *Riv. Storica Italiana [Italy] 1981 93(3): 795-808.* Criticizes the traditional view that Markus, the only one of three Swedish members of Mikhail Bakunin's association to send him reports after his 1863 visit to Sweden, was the prominent Liberal and literary figure August Blanche (1811-68). A list of code names in Bakunin's hand reveals that his Swedish correspondent was Carl Rudolf Löwstädt (b. 1820), a follower of Etienne Cabet (1788-1856) and probably translator of the Communist Manifesto. Based on documents in the Kungliga Bibliotek, Stockholm; 62 notes. 1844-70

365. Mervaud, Michel. LETTRES DE BAKUNIN A ADOLF REICHEL ET A ADOLF VOGT [Letters of Bakunin to Adolf Reichel and Adolf Vogt]. *Revue des Etudes Slaves [France] 1984 56(4): 495-571.* Edits, annotates, and translates into French 21 letters of Mikhail Bakunin. Twelve have never been before published in full, and for nine others more accurate readings are offered. Adolf Reichel (1816-96), a composer and musician of West Prussia, was politically conservative but kept up a friendship with Bakunin. Adolf Vogt (1823-1907), a doctor and brother of the famous naturalist Carl Vogt, brought Bakunin to the clinic in Berne where he died in 1876. Based on Bakunin's letters in the National Library of Paris; the Bakunin Archives; secondary sources; 186 notes. 1840's-76

Balaban, Meyer

366. Horn, Maurycy. MEYER BAŁABAN—SHEFER FUN GESHIKHTE-SHUL VEGN YIDN IN POYLN [Meyer Balaban—head of the historical school of Polish Jewry]. *Bleter far Geszichte [Poland] 1983 21: 7-55.* Meyer Balaban (1877-1942) was the preeminent historian of Polish Jewry. In a career that spanned four decades, Balaban published 20 books, over 100 articles in learned journals, and another 100 in popular magazines. Balaban was a follower of Simon Dubnow, who stands in apposition to Heinrich Gratz, the first comprehensive Jewish historian. Balaban specialized in local Jewish histories, Hasidism in Poland, Polish-Jewish history as reflected in legal documents, Jewish sectarians, and the bibliography of Polish Jewish history, particularly in primary source materials. English and Polish summaries. ca 13c-20c

367. Horn, Maurycy. MAJER BAŁABAN—WYBITNY HISTORYK ŻYDÓW POLSKICH I PEDAGOG 1877-1942 (W CZTERDZIESTOLECIE ŚMIERCI) [Majer Bałaban (1877-1942) on the 40th anniversary of his death: outstanding historian of the Jews of Poland and pedagog]. *Biuletyn Żydowskiego Instytutu Hist. w Polsce [Poland] 1982 (3-4): 3-15.* Meyer Balaban was the founder of the Warsaw school of Jewish history in Poland. Balaban's pedagogical activity and his tremendous role as an organizer of Jewish scholarly life in the interwar period, his creative participation in Polish international scholarly conferences and meetings, his editing of scholarly periodicals, as well as services rendered in publishing and popularizing work are recounted. The last years of life and work of the scholar in Warsaw during the Nazi occupation are described. 1877-1942

Balabanoff, Angelica

368. Mullaney, Marie Marmo. GENDER AND THE SOCIALIST REVOLUTIONARY ROLE, 1871-1921: A GENERAL THEORY OF THE FEMALE REVOLUTIONARY PERSONALITY. *Historical Reflections [Canada] 1984 11(2): 99-151.* Examines five female revolutionaries—Louise Michel (1830-1905), Eleanor Marx (1855-98), Alexandra Kollontai (1872-1952), Rosa Luxemburg (1860-1919), and Angelica Balabanoff (1878-1965)—in the light of four elements of standard revolutionary behavior theory: the socialization, motivation, "Machiavellianism," and asceticism of revolutionaries. Traditional, male-based theory does not apply to these women. Their patterns of revolutionary involvement, their resistance to personal power, and their pursuit of a richer life beyond socialist activity force reconsideration of the older model. The question of revolution and feminism is also discussed. 189 notes. 1871-1921

Balassa, Bálint

369. Némethy, Sándor. A DELEGATUM JUDICIUM EXTRAORDINARIUM POSONIENSE ANNO 1674. TÖRTÉNETE ES JOGÁSZI KRITIKÁJA (10) [The history and juristic critique of the Delegatum Judicium Extraordinarium Posoniense, 1674: part 10]. *Theológiai Szemle [Hungary] 1984 27(2): 97-102.* Continued from previous articles. Describes the life of the eccentric Hungarian aristocrat Count Bálint Balassa who—despite his Lutheran roots—in 1672 became one of the judges in the anti-Protestant trials of the Delegatum Judicium Extraordinarium. In his private life he demonstrated a remarkable tolerance to all religions, yet as a

judge he sealed the fates of thousands of Protestants. Based on documents in the Hungarian National Archives; biblio. 1626-84

Balassa, Franz

370. Kállay, István. EIN GEHEIMBERICHT ÜBER DEN TOD MARIA THERESIAS [A confidential report concerning the death of Empress Maria Theresa]. *Mitteilungen des Österreichischen Staatsarchivs [Austria] 1981 34: 342-344.* Traces the life and career of Hungarian Count Franz Balassa (1736-1807), royal commissioner in Fiume in the 1780's, noting also his work in Croatia and his reports on the royal family and life at court in Vienna, which he gleaned from numerous sources. The author examines and reproduces a letter Balassa received from one of his sources concerning the death of the Empress Maria Theresa in 1780. Based on a document in the Hungarian State Archives in Budapest; 5 notes. 1760's-1807

Balbo, Italo

371. Michaelis, Meir. IL MARESCIALLO DELL'ARIA ITALO BALBO E LA POLITICA MUSSOLINIANA. IL FRONDISMO DI BALBO ALLA LUCE DI ALCUNE DOCUMENTI E TESTIMONIANZE INEDITI [Air Marshall Italo Balbo and the politics of Mussolini: the opposition of Balbo in the light of unpublished documents]. *Storia Contemporanea [Italy] 1983 14(2): 333-357.* Italo Balbo emerged as an opponent of Benito Mussolini, who sent him to govern Libya. Suspicious and critical of poor organization, Balbo criticized the African venture in 1935-36. Later he had to protest his loyalty to Mussolini (who had already tested this by forcing him to become a Freemason in 1924). Balbo, who had a reputation for friendship with Jews, had reservations about the Rome-Berlin axis and Nazism. When he visited Germany in 1938 he was celebrated as a famous aviator who had assisted the German air force. Primary sources; 60 notes. 1930's

Bălcescu, Nicolae

372. Vătămanu, Nicolae. PE URMELE LUI BĂLCESCU IN FRANŢA [On the tracks of Bălcescu in France]. *Magazin Istoric [Romania] 1982 16(11): 5-11.* An account of the last days in France of Nicolae Bălcescu, historian, patriot, and Romanian revolutionary. 1830-52

Balčikonis, Juozas

373. Schmalstieg, William R. A NOTE ON JUOZAS BALČIKONIS' CONTRIBUTION TO THE STANDARDIZATION OF LITHUANIAN. *Lituanus 1981 27(4): 35-43.* Reviews the life and work of Juozas Balčikonis (1885-1969), linguist, translator, and teacher of Lithuanian. Balcikonis was a prime mover in beginning the *Academic Dictionary of Lithuanian* and succeeded Kazimieras Būga as editor, a position Balčikonis held from 1930 to 1952. 20c

Baldwin, William

374. Gresham, Stephen. WILLIAM BALDWIN, LITERARY VOICE OF THE REIGN OF EDWARD VI. *Huntington Lib. Q. 1981 44(2): 101-116.* William Baldwin (fl. 1537-53), perhaps the most representative religious and moral writer of his era, coupled moral teaching with a concern for literary form. Works discussed include: *A Treatise of Morall Philosophie* (1548), a collection of biographical sketches of great philosophers; *The Canticles or Balades of Salomon* (1549), a metrical paraphrase of the Song of Solomon; *Wonderfull Newes of the Death of Paule the III* (ca. 1552), a translation of an attack on the pope; *Beware the Cat* (ca. 1553), an anti-Roman Catholic satire; and *The Funeralles of King Edward the Sixt* (1553), a comment on social and political ills. 39 notes. 1547-53

Ball, Hannah

375. Boulton, David J. WOMEN AND EARLY METHODISM. *Pro. of the Wesley Hist. Soc. [Great Britain] 1981 43(2): 13-17.* 18c
*For abstract see **Bolton, Nancy***

Ball, Robert Stawell

376. Davies, Gordon L. Herries. SIR ROBERT STAWELL BALL, 1840-1913. *Hermathena [Ireland] 1985 (138): 41-56.* Outlines the life of Robert Stawell Ball, Irish astronomer and mathematician, particularly noted for his *Treatise on the Theory of Screws* (1900), which explained the movement of rigid bodies around fixed points. 1860's-1913

Ballin, Albert

377. Neveux, Jean Baptiste. SUR LES ROUTES OCEANES—BALLIN ET L'IMPÉRIALISME MARITIME DE L'EMPIRE ALLEMAND [On the sea routes: Ballin and the growing naval power of the German empire]. *Rev. d'Allemagne [France] 1981 13(3): 512-526.* Albert Ballin (1857-1918), an ocean shipping lines entrepreneur, helped to transform Hamburg into a center of world commerce. He expanded the passenger service agency that his father, Samuel Joel Ballin (1804-74), had founded for immigrants from Germany to the United States. He became the sole owner of the firm of Morris and Company. After an association with the firm of Carr and Sloman, he became a director of the Hamburg-American Line Company. Because he was a frequent guest of William II (1859-1951), he was known in some circles as a *Kaiserjude.* 45 notes. 1871-1918

Ballinger, Margaret

378. Scher, D. M. TEACHING AND MAKING HISTORY: THE REMARKABLE CAREER OF MARGARET BALLINGER. *Kleio [South Africa] 1981 13(1-2): 32-40.* Margaret Ballinger was born Margaret Violet Livingstone Hodgson in 1894. She came to South Africa at the age of 10 and there engaged in a brilliant academic career, becoming head of the department of history at Rhodes College, and later moving on to the University of Witwatersrand. She received the support of the African National Congress for election by the Cape division in 1936. During her 23 years as a representative to parliament she impressed whites and blacks with her honesty and skillful support of racial equality. She died in 1980. Primary sources; 23 notes. 1919-80

Ballios, Stavros

379. Mōralidēs, Giannēs G. O MAKEDONOMAHOS-ODĒGOS STAVROS BALLIOS KAI O EPISKOPOS KITROUS THEOKLĒTOS B' [A soldier and military scout in the Macedonian struggle, Stavros Ballios, and Bishop Theoklētos II of Kitros]. *Makedonika [Greece] 1984 24: 209-216.* Stavros Ballios (1872-1908) was a soldier and reconnaissance officer for the Greeks during the Macedonian War (1903-08). Ballios, whose name was originally Stefou, came from a prominent Macedonian family. His uncle was Bishop of Kitros. The Turks arrested Ballios and imprisoned him in Veroia. Maltreated during detention, his health was broken, and he died at the age of 36. 29 notes. 1890's-1908

Balogh, József

380. Boldizsár, Iván. THE FRENCH COLONEL: ONE OF THE BITTER-SWEET STORIES. *New Hungarian Quarterly [Hungary] 1985 26(97): 89-93.* Reminisces about experiences in the Hungarian underground in 1944 and his acquaintance with the Jewish man of letters and French colonel, József Balogh, the editor of the *Nouvelle Revue de Hongrie* and the *Hungarian Quarterly.* Many people risked their lives to hide him from the Germans, but his own desire to continue working and his inability to remain in inactivity and seclusion led to his arrest in 1944. 1944

Balogh, Thomas

381. Csikós-Nagy, Béla. THOMAS BALOGH: AN OBITUARY. *New Hungarian Quarterly [Hungary] 1985 26(98): 145-147.* Obituary of Hungarian-born British economist, ennobled in 1968, Thomas Balogh (1905-85). He studied in Budapest, Berlin, and Harvard University. His first book, *A Német Pénzromlás Oknyomozó Története* [An investigative history of the deterioration of money in Germany] (1928) was published immediately after his study in Berlin. After a term in Geneva with the financial commission of the League of Nations, he moved to Great Britain, where he was a confidant of Keynes. He became internationally respected for his humanistic and historical approach to economics and for his special interest in the problems of the developing nations. Despite frequent returns to Hungary after World War II, he remained in Great Britain. He advocated mixed economies for both capitalist and Communist countries. 1927-85

Baltrušaitis, Jurgis, Sr.

382. Baltrušaitis, Jurgis, Sr.; Vitas, Robert A. et al., transl. THE POLISH ULTIMATUM TO LITHUANIA—THE DESPATCH OF LITHUANIAN MINISTER J. BALTRUŠAITIS IN MOSCOW. *Lituanus 1985 31(4): 23-46.* Jurgis Baltrušaitis, Sr. (1873-1944) was the minister of Lithuania to the Soviet Union from 1920 until 1939. On 12 May 1938, he wrote a lengthy dispatch about the ultimatum of Poland to Lithuania demanding the restoration of diplomatic relations between the two countries in March 1938. The dispatch described the unfolding of the crisis and analyzed the reactions of Britain, France, and the USSR. Baltrušaitis urged that the Lithuanian government seek help from the Soviet Union, which he regarded as the best potential guarantor of Lithuanian independence. However, the Lithuanian government rejected his advice in favor of a policy of neutrality. 54 notes. 1938

Bambridge, William

383. Etherington, Ruth. WILLIAM BAMBRIDGE (1819-1879): SCHOOLMASTER—MISSIONARY—ROYAL PHOTOGRAPHER—ARTIST. *Hist. J. [New Zealand] 1982 (41): 5-9.* Biography of William Bambridge (1819-79), who was Bishop of New Zealand for five years and appointed Royal Photographer by Queen Victoria in 1846. 1840-79

Bán, Antal

384. Strassenreiter, Erzsébet. BÁN ANTAL [Antal Bán]. *Társadalmi Szemle [Hungary] 1983 38(3): 88-98.* As a prominent member of the Social Democratic Party, Antal Bán, unlike other Party members, felt that cooperation with the Communist Party was of utmost importance. As postwar minister of industrial development he was instrumental in nationalizing private industry. In 1948, when the Socialists joined the Communist Party, it was decided that his orientation was misaligned and he was forced to leave the country. In Switzerland, and later in England, he established the first foreign representation of the Hungarian Social Democratic Party. By the time he was elected a member of COMISCO, his attitude had changed completely, and he was very outspoken in his criticism of Communism. Bán died in 1945 in Zurich. 1903-45

Banerjea, Surendranath

385. Flora, Giuseppe. SURENDRA NATH BANERJEA E MAZZINI [Surendranath Banerjea and Mazzini]. *Rassegna Storica del Risorgimento [Italy] 1982 69(3): 297-323.* Moderate liberal Indian leader Surendranath Banerjea (1848-1925) admitted to being deeply influenced by Italian statesman Giuseppe Mazzini. This influence led Banerjea to work for the unification of India. He points out in his autobiography, *A Nation in the Making* (1925), how profoundly he was influenced by the writings of Mazzini. Primary sources; 44 notes, appendix. 1860-1925

Bánki, Donát

386. Varga, József. BÁNKI DONÁT SZÜLETÉSÉNEK 125. ÉVFORDULÓJA [The 125th anniversary of Donát Bánki's birth]. *Magyar Tudomány [Hungary] 1984 29(7-8): 634-636.* Donát Bánki, the internationally renowned inventor and teacher at the Budapesti Műegyetem, was born on 6 June 1859 in Bakonybánk. He was chief engineer at the Ganz manufacturing company and with János Csonka invented the carburetor. The Bánki turbine, his invention, is manufactured to this day. His principles in the fields of hydraulic motors, steam turbines, and aviation are universally accepted. He was also an excellent teacher who published hundreds of books and articles in his field. Bánki died in 1922. Photo. 1859-1922

Banks, Joseph

387. Marshall, John Braybrooke. DANIEL CARL SOLANDER, FRIEND, LIBRARIAN AND ASSISTANT TO SIR JOSEPH BANKS. *Archives of Natural History [Great Britain] 1984 11(3): 451-456.* 1760-82
For abstract see ***Solander, Daniel***

Bar, François Nicolas de

388. Choné, Paulette. FRANÇOIS NICOLAS DE BAR, "NICOLO LORENESE" (1632-1695) [François Nicolas de Bar, "Nicolo Lorenese" (1632-95)]. *Mélanges de l'Ecole Française de Rome. Moyen Age-Temps Modernes [Italy] 1982 94(2): 995-1017.* Recounts the career and apprenticeship and describes the works of this noted French painter in Rome, where several expatriate artists gathered during the 17th century. 17c

Barabasz, Feliks

389. Tryniszewski, Eugeniusz. FELIKS BARABASZ: 1919-1982 [Feliks Barabasz (1919-82)]. *Komunikaty Mazursko-Warmińskie [Poland] 1983 (1): 190-193.* An obituary of Feliks Barabasz, who belonged to a patriotic Polish family living in East Prussia. He was a member of parliament, a member of the city and county councils in Olsztyn, the director of the Olsztyn branch of the Polish Bank, and an activist in local Olsztyn organizations. In 1940 he was drafted into the German army and then sent to a labor camp near Olsztyn. After the war he worked in banking until his retirement. Throughout this period he actively participated in the social, cultural, and economic development of the Olsztyn region. Based on unpublished manuscripts and documents held by F. Barabasz's family and friends; 15 notes. 1940-82

Baratz, Barbara

390. Baratz, Barbara. HATZALA BE'UKRAINA HA'MIZRAHIT [Rescue in eastern Ukraine]. *Yalkut Moreshet Periodical [Israel] 1982 (34): 63-84.* The author's memoirs cover the period from the Nazi invasion into Russia until the liberation of eastern Ukraine and her return to her husband and son. The writer and her daughter Mira were saved from the Nazis by a Ukrainian named Suchenko, who gave them his name and helped them find a new hiding place whenever necessary. Barbara Baratz and her daughter were the only ones saved, though many other Jews were aided by Suchenko. English summary. 1941-44

Barba-Jacob, Porfirio

391. Santa, Eduardo. BARBA-JACOB, POETA EXISTENCIAL [Barba-Jacob, existential poet]. *Bol. de Hist. y Antigüedades [Colombia] 1983 70(742): 765-786.* The Colombian poet Porfirio Barba-Jacob (1883-1942), in a life of wandering and bohemianism, left only a small corpus of published poems. Nevertheless, these poems are a supreme expression of both existential philosophy and Spanish lyricism. 43 notes. 1883-1942

Barbé, Roger

392. Mattéi, Xavier. EVOCATIONS [Recalls]. *Revue Historique des Armées [France] 1985 (2): 54-57.* 1940-44

For abstract see ***Artel, Jean***

Barber, Henry

393. Schuhmacher, W. Wilfried. MERCHANT CAPTAIN OF THE PACIFIC. *Am. Neptune 1981 41(3): 224-230.* Reports the scattered evidence of Captain Henry Barber's trading activities in Hawaii, Alaska, British Columbia, and China. Little is known about Barber except that he traded in the Pacific area for a decade. 13 notes. 1794-1807

Barbèra, Gaspero and Pietro

394. DiLoreto d'Alfonso, Rosaria. LE CARTE BARBERA DELLA BIBLIOTECA NAZIONALE DI FIRENZE [The Barbèra papers in the Biblioteca Nazionale Centrale in Florence]. *Rassegna Storica Toscana [Italy] 1982 28(1): 39-114.* The papers consist of 300 letters addressed to the publisher Gaspero Barbèra and his son Pietro Barbèra from 1851 to 1881, of which 123 are here reproduced. Many of these highlight the human qualities as well as the professional talents of the publisher. Most often the subject of these letters is the publication of works of fiction. 7 notes. Article to be continued. 1851-81

Barbie, Klaus

395. Delarue, Jacques. UN SS NOMME BARBIE [An SS named Barbie]. *Histoire [France] 1985 (82): 52-65.* A comprehensive account of the career of Klaus Barbie (b. 1913), including the complicities and protections from which the former SS officer has benefited; now imprisoned in Lyons, Barbie awaits trial for war crimes committed in occupied France, 1940-44. 1940-44

396. Ruzié, David. THE KLAUS BARBIE CASE: WAR CRIMES VERSUS CRIMES AGAINST HUMANITY. *Patterns of Prejudice [Great Britain] 1986 20(3): 27-33.* Discusses the case of Klaus Barbie (b. 1913), the "Butcher of Lyon," who could not be prosecuted for his war crimes because the French could not extradite him from Bolivia until 1983, by which time the statute of limitations had expired. The prosecutor thus charged Barbie with crimes against humanity—a charge that has been successfully challenged in the Court of Cassation (supreme court of appeal). 1930's-86

Barbosa, Ruy

397. Macedo, Roberto. DOIS AMIGOS: RUI E FLORIANO [Two friends: Ruy and Floriano]. *Rev. do Inst. Hist. e Geog. Brasileiro [Brazil] 1979 (322): 185-211.* The jurist and statesman Ruy Barbosa and Marshal Floriano Vieira Peixoto were good friends despite differences in temperament and training. Recalls their attitudes and activities during the events leading to the proclamation of the republic in 1889, in which both played a prominent part. Many quotations in the text. 1870-89

398. Moraes Filho, Evaristo de. RUI BARBOSA E A FILOSOFIA EXISTENCIA CRISTÃ [Ruy Barbosa and Christian existential philosophy]. *Revista do Instituto Histórico e Geográfico Brazileiro [Brazil] 1983 (338): 137-172.* Ruy Barbosa, politician, statesman, and publicist of the first Brazilian republic (1889-1930), who fought for the separation of church and state, was a profoundly religious man, in the line of the Christian existentialist philosophers. He was a follower of Döllinger and the Old Catholics, who opposed the dogma of papal infallibility, but not an atheist, as he is sometimes portrayed. 67 notes. 1880's-1923

Barclay de Tolly, Mikhail

399. Thun-Hohenstein, Romedio. DIE ROLLE DES LIVLÄNDERS FELDMARSCHALL FÜRST MICHAEL ANDREAS BARCLAY DE TOLLY IM RUSSISCH-FRANZÖSISCHEN KRIEG VON 1812: ZUR FRAGE EINER NATIONALRUSSISCHEN LEGENDE [The part of the Livonian Field Marshal Prince Mikhail Barclay de Tolly in the Russian-French War of 1812: a Russian national legend]. *Zeits. für Ostforschung [West Germany] 1982 31(4): 517-529.* In the first quarter of the 19th century, Field-Marshal Prince Michael Barclay de Tolly (1761-1818) held an exceptional position among the Russian generals. Without doubt he can be called the architect of the victory over Napoleon. However, in his own country Barclay de Tolly was shown enmity, and consequently he was always thrust into the background by Kutusov. Barclay's strategy of orderly retreat led to animosities and intrigues against him, but after Kutusov's death in 1813 the tsar conferred upon him the command of the Russian troops in the campaign from Leipzig to France. The French admired his leadership, and the British military strategist Lidell Hart called it an example of successful indirect approach. Contrary to this, Clausewitz gave an unfavorable description of Barclay, and Tolstoy presented a caricature of Barclay in *War and Peace.* 1807-15

Barcroft, Joseph

400. Irzhak, Lev Isaakovich. SVIAZI DZHOZEFA BARKROFTA S SOVETSKOI FIZIOLOGIEI [Joseph Barcroft's ties with Soviet physiology]. *Voprosy Istorii Estestvoznaniia i Tekhniki [USSR] 1983 (1): 139-146.* In 1910, Leon A. Orbeli (1882-1952) met in Cambridge with Joseph Barcroft (1872-1947) where they collaborated in laboratory tests on blood oxygenation. Collaboration, interrupted by World War I, resumed in the 1920's. Barcroft's influence on Soviet physiological research grew in the 1930's through repeated contacts with Soviet scholars, and was further enhanced by Barcroft's attendance of the 15th International Physiological Congress, held in Leningrad in 1935. Note, biblio. 1910-1930's

Barczewski, Walenty

401. Ogrodziński, Władysław. MIEJSCE WALENTEGO BARCZEWSKIEGO W KULTURZE POLSKIEJ [The place of Walenty Barczewski in Polish culture]. *Komunikaty Mazursko-Warmińskie [Poland] 1981 (2-4): 423-427.* Walenty Barczewski (1856-1928) was a priest, a student of the folk culture of Ermland, an educator, and a discreet champion of the Polish cause in the officially hostile environment of East Prussia. The record concerning him is very incomplete, and while it is questionable whether that can be rectified, an attempt should be made. Based on a lecture given at a conference entitled Interrelations of Ermland and Masuria with Polish Lands in Olsztyn on 28 October 1980 and secondary sources; 10 notes. German summary. 1910's-20's

Bardin, Ivan P.

402. Krivonosov, Iu. I. IVAN PAVLOVICH BARDIN (1883-1960) [Ivan Pavlovich Bardin (1883-1960)]. *Voprosy Istorii Estestvoznaniia i Tekhniki [USSR] 1984 (1): 92-97.* A biographical sketch of the Soviet engineer prominent in the field of metallurgy, Ivan P. Bardin (1883-1960). In 1944 he founded the Central Institute for Metallurgic Research in Moscow and became a member of the Soviet Academy of Sciences, combining active research with writing on the history of science. 2 photos; 4 notes. 1910's-60

Baring, Maurice

403. Heussler, Robert. MAURICE BARING AND THE PASSING OF THE VICTORIAN AGE. *Biography 1984 7(2): 134-157.* An overview of Maurice Baring's values is set in the context of a life experience that extended from the last years of the Victorian era to the 1940's. Baring was an original and at the same time a representative of England's literary and ruling classes at the height of their influence. 1890's-1940's

Barishanski, Rabbi

404. Altshuler, Mordechai. THE RABBI OF HOMEL'S TRIAL IN 1922. *Michael: On the Hist. of the Jews in the Diaspora [Israel] 1980 6: 9-61.* Examines and reproduces three documents relating to the trial of Rabbi Barishanski of Homel in the USSR in 1922. Homel, situated on a tributary of the Dnieper, had one of the oldest Jewish communities in Polesye. After 1919, a branch of the Party Jewish section *(Yevsektsiia)* was established in Homel. This was a group of mainly atheistic Jews, previously members of Jewish socialist parties, who intensified their campaign against the Jewish religion to prove their loyalty to the Communist Party. The author examines the antireligious propaganda and anti-Jewish activities of this group, 1919-22, which culminated in the arrest and trial of the Rabbi and 10 others accused of "preparing organized resistance to the Soviet regime and conducting anti-Soviet propaganda." The accused were all found guilty of the charges, but the sentences were less than the maximum prescribed by law in order to avoid antagonism and to prevent harsh protest from abroad. After a number of appeals the Rabbi was pardoned and in 1923 went to live in the United States. Based on trial documents held in the Central Archives for the History of the Jewish People, Jerusalem; 29 notes. 1919-23

Barkan, Ömer Lûtfi

405. Mélikoff, Irène. IN MEMORIAM ÖMER LÛTFI BARKAN [In memory of Ömer Lûtfi Barkan]. *Turcica [France] 1981 13: 7-9.* Commemorates Ömer Lûtfi Barkan (1903-79), founder and head of the Institute of the Economic History of Turkey at the University of Istanbul. He is most noted for his archival research on the economic and social history of the Ottoman Empire. Photo. 1903-79

Barker, Thomas

406. Waites, Bryan. THOMAS BARKER OF LYNDON: EIGHTEENTH-CENTURY WEATHERMAN. *Local Hist. [Great Britain] 1982 15(2): 70-72.* Biography of British meteorologist Thomas Barker (d. 1809), who kept careful records on temperature, barometric pressure, rainfall, and wind, from March 1748 to August 1763, and wrote *An Account of the Discoveries Concerning Comets, with the Way to Find Their Orbits* (1757). 18c

Barlach, Ernst

407. Carls, Carl Dietrich. "ENTARTETE KUNST": ZUM BEISPIEL: ERNST BARLACH ["Degenerate Art": for example Ernst Barlach]. *Frankfurter Hefte [West Germany] 1983 38(4): 51-58.* Describes Barlach's work and life, his philosophy of life, reaction to Nazism, and his death in 1938. 1906-38

Barlicki, Norbert

408. Tomicki, Jan. NORBERT BARLICKI (1880-1941) W STULECIE URODZIN [Norbert Barlicki (1880-1941): on the centenary of his birth] *Nowe Drogi [Poland] 1980 (6): 83-94.* Analyzes the life and work of Norbert Barlicki (1880-1914), a leading member of the Polish Socialist Party, and his contribution to the establishment of socialism in Poland. 3 notes. 1900's-41

Barnard, Anne

409. Robinson, A. M. L. LADY ANNE BARNARD'S MORGANATIC MARRIAGE. *Quarterly Bulletin of the South African Library [South Africa] 1984 38(3): 131-133.* There is a belief that Lady Anne Lindsay (afterwards Barnard), the eldest child of the 5th Earl of Balcarres, contracted a morganatic marriage with the future King George IV of England and had two sons by him. In such a marriage, while the children are recognized as being legitimate, neither they nor their mother would have claim to the father's superior rank or property. It is unlikely that this was the case, as Lady Anne married the impecunious Andrew Barnard and sailed for Cape Town with him in 1797, two years after the prince married Princess Caroline of Brunswick. Based on secondary sources. 1750-1807

Barnes, Albert C.

410. Helbling, Mark. AFRICAN ART: ALBERT C. BARNES AND ALAIN LOCKE. *Phylon 1982 43(1): 57-67.* Albert C. Barnes and Alain Locke met in Paris, France, in December 1923. From that friendship evolved a complex relationship that resulted in the promotion of African art. Barnes, a rich collector, responded to the ideas of John Locke and Charles S. Johnson. African art was understood not as artifact, but as the historical expression of the Afro-American artistic mind. 1920's

Barneveld, Willem van

411. Snelders, H. A. M. THE AMSTERDAM PHARMACIST WILLEM VAN BARNEVELD (1747-1826) AND THE DISCOVERY OF PHOTOSYNTHESIS (1778). *Janus [Netherlands] 1981 68(1-3): 1-14.* Willem van Barneveld, pharmacist in Amsterdam, 1770-1819, and burgher of Hatten, 1819-26, was a diligent student of the experimental natural sciences. He repeated in 1778 Priestley's experiment showing

that plants can restore putrid air, but as Barneveld recorded in his *Proeve van Onderzoek* (1781), only in the presence of sunlight. This was a year earlier than Jan Ingen-Housz (1730-99), who is generally credited with the discovery of photosynthesis, performed his experiments leading to a similar discovery. The later controversy concerning priority is further documented. Based on publications and archives of the Provinciaal Utregtsch Genootschap van Kunsten en Wetenschappen and other published works; 53 notes.
1770's-80's

Baroja, Pío

412. Golson, Emily Becker. "Pío Baroja and John Dos Passos: The Evolution of Two Political Novelists." Brandeis U. 1982. 316 pp. *DAI 1982 43(4): 1138-A.* DA8220103
1900-56

413. Golson, Emily Becker. "Pío Baroja and John Dos Passos: The Evolution of Two Political Novelists." Brandeis U. 1982. 316 pp. *DAI 1982 43(4): 1138-A.* DA8220103
1900-56

Barons, Krišjānis

414. Greble, V. VĒRTĪGS SASNIEGUMS KRIŠJĀŅA BARONA DARBĪBAS IZPĒTĒ [Valuable achievement in the study of Krišjānis Barons's activity]. *Latvijas PSR Zinātņu Akadēmijas Vēstis [USSR] 1985 (10): 138-140.* Reviews Kārlis Arājs's *Krišjānis Barons* (2d ed., 1985) and *Krišjānis Barons un "Latvju Dainas"* (1985), in which a detailed biography of the collector of Latvian folk songs Krišjānis Barons (1835-1923) and his methods of systematization of Latvian folklore are analyzed. 19c-20c

Barozzi, Pietro

415. Gasparini, Giuseppina de Sandre. UNO STUDIO SULL'EPISCOPATO PADOVANO DI PIETRO BAROZZI (1487-1507) E ALTRI CONTRIBUTI SUI VESCOVI VENETI NEL QUATTROCENTO: PROBLEMI E LINEE DI RICERCA [A study of the Paduan bishopric of Pietro Barozzi (1487-1507) and other contributions to the Venetian diocese in the 15th century: problems and guides to research]. *Riv. di Storia della Chiesa in Italia [Italy] 1980 34(1): 81-122.* Discussion of Denys Hay's *The Church in Italy in the 15th Century* (1977), with analysis of the diocese of the humanist and Paduan bishop Pietro Barozzi (1487-1507). Considers the institutional, social, cultural, and religious problems of the age and indicates lines of further research by means of comparison with other 15th-century Venetian bishops. Based on state and episcopal archives; 197 notes. 1487-1507

Barres, Maurice

416. Sirinelli, Jean-Francois. LITTERATURE ET POLITIQUE: LE CAS BURDEAU-BOUTEILLER [Literature and politics: the case of Burdeau-Bouteiller]. *Revue Historique [France] 1984 272(1): 91-111.* 1851-1920's
For abstract see ***Burdeau, Auguste***

Barrett, Rafael

417. Herken Krauer, Juan Carlos. DIPLOMACIA BRITANICA EN EL RIO DE LA PLATA: EL "CASO RAFAEL BARRET" (1908-1910) [British diplomacy in the Río de la Plata: Rafael Barrett, 1908-10]. *Cahiers du Monde Hispanique et Luso-Brésilien [France] 1983 (41): 39-62.* Rafael Barrett entered Paraguay to educate and organize workers. He was arrested and deported in the course of a coup which resulted in rioting. British efforts to support Barrett were unavailing and were not particularly vigorous because they were interested in preserving their presence in the Río de la Plata. Based on Rafael Barrett's writing, diplomatic documents, press reports, and secondary sources; 105 notes. 1904-10

Barrios, Gerardo

418. Kuhn, Gary G. EL POSITIVISMO DE GERARDO BARRIOS [The positivism of Gerardo Barrios]. *Rev. del Pensamiento Centroamericano [Costa Rica] 1981 36(172-173): 87-88.* Notes elements of positivism in the policies of Gerardo Barrios, president of El Salvador, 1858-63. 15 notes.
1858-63

Barros, Luisa Margarida Portugal de

419. Matos Pedreira Cerqueira, Paulo de. D. PEDRO II E A CONDESSA DE BARRAL [King Pedro II and the countess of Barral]. *Rev. do Inst. Hist. e Geog. Brasileiro [Brazil] 1980 (326): 377-394.* The relations between the Emperor Pedro II and Luisa Margarida Portugal de Barros, daughter of the viscount of Pedra Branca and later countess of Barral, who for eight years was in charge of the education of the imperial princesses, went beyond simple friendship or platonic love, as a study of the emperor's correspondence reveals. Based on the royal correspondence published by the National Archive, 1977. 1856-64

Barrucand, Victor

420. Drouot, Christine and Vergniot, Olivier. VICTOR BARRUCAND, UN INDESIRABLE A ALGER [Victor Barrucand, an undesirable in Algiers]. *Revue de l'Occident Musulman et de la Méditerranée [France] 1984 (37): 31-36.* Victor Barrucand (1868-1934) was sent to Algeria by the League of the Rights of Man in 1900 to combat the anti-Semitic movement in the colony. Settling permanently, he ran the review *Akhbar* between 1902 and 1934, seeking to reconcile French and Arab and attempting to fight racism. His literary activity was as controversial as his journalism, especially his editing of the works of Isabelle Eberhardt after her death in 1904. Biblio., 25 notes. 1900-34

Barry, Maltman

421. Martinez, Paul. THE "PEOPLE'S CHARTER" AND THE ENIGMATIC MR. MALTMAN BARRY. *Bull. of the Soc. for the Study of Labour Hist. [Great Britain] 1980 (41): 34-45.* Discusses the career and beliefs of the British socialist Maltman Barry with particular reference to his journalism, his relations with Marx and Engels, and "The People's Charter," in which he set out a distinctly "modern," if not Marxist, socialist program. Reproduces the text of the charter, which was published in 1876 in Barry's *The People's Advocate.* 1871-92

Bart, Jean

422. Villiers, Patrick. LES CORSAIRES ET LA GUERRE DE COURSE [Corsairs and their war on commerce]. *Histoire [France] 1981 (36): 26-34.* Relates the achievements of Sir Francis Drake (1545-96), Jean Bart (1650-1702), René Duguay-Trouin (1673-1736), and Robert Surcouf (1673-1736). 16c-19c

Barteau, Louis

423. Malafeev, K. A. STRANITSY ZHIZNI I DEIATEL'NOSTI LUI BARTU [Pages from the life and political activity of Louis Barteau]. *Novaia i Noveishaia Istoriia [USSR] 1982 (4): 118-136.* Louis Barteau (1862-

1934) belonged to a group of French bourgeois politicians who, in the period after World War I, considered alliance with the USSR as the main guarantee of French security against the German threat. Barteau saw French-Soviet friendship as part of a larger plan, as a means to strengthen France's position in Europe and establish more firmly the territorial and political status quo embodied in the Treaty of Versailles. As Minister of Foreign Affairs he sought a European treaty of collective security, but was murdered by Fascist terrorists, 9 October 1934, before he could achieve his aim. Secondary sources; 107 notes. 1917-34

Bartel, Horst

424. G. S. and H. K. HORST BARTEL ZUM GEDENKEN [To the memory of Horst Bartel]. *Zeitschrift für Geschichtswissenschaft [East Germany] 1984 32(10): 900-901.* Born in 1928, Horst Bartel became a teacher in 1946, and in 1956 he wrote a thesis at the Institut für Gesellschaftswissenschaft on the influence of Marx and Engels in the German worker movement during the Sozialistengesetz. He eventually was appointed to the Chair of the History of the Labor Movement. He gathered material about August Bebel and the German labor movement and researched Marxism, opportunism, and 19th-century history. He was a member of the German Academy and a corresponding member of the Soviet Academy. 1940's-80's

Barth, Karl

425. Wall, Donald D. KARL BARTH AND NATIONAL SOCIALISM, 1921-1946. *Fides et Hist. 1983 15(2): 80-95.* While Karl Barth voiced opposition to national socialism as early as 1931, and counseled the German Evangelical Church to avoid its link with natural theology in 1933, he did not equate Nazism with injustice until 1939. His essay, *The Church and the State* (1938) argued that the purpose of the state was to assure church freedom. Disgusted with their lack of response to Crystal Night, Barth broke relations with the Confessing Church and began to denounce Nazism publicly. An essay entitled *The Church and the Political Problem of Our Day.* (1939) counseled church members that they were under no obligation to obey Hitler. Through the war period, Barth's attacks on Nazism and antisemitism were unmitigated, however, his theological thrust gave German Christians no concrete direction on how to thwart totalitarianism. 59 notes. 1921-46

Barthes, Roland

426. Kennedy, J. Gerald. ROLAND BARTHES, AUTOBIOGRAPHY, AND THE END OF WRITING. *Georgia Rev. 1981 35(2): 381-398.* The mask of erudition and implacable theory worn by Roland Barthes (d. 1980) gave way to an expression of his elemental anxieties and irreducible essence in his final works. Barthes, appointed to the Collége de France Chair of Semiology in 1977, had evolved a complex theory of writing as a species of imposture, discourse as artificiality, and the writer as a poseur. Works from 1971-77 *(Sade Fournier Loyola, The Pleasure of the Text,* and *Roland Barthes)* included fragments of self-disclosure. *La Chambre Claire* (1980) revealed that grief over his mother's death in 1977 radically changed his view of the nature and purpose of writing. 20 notes. 1970's

427. Rybalka, Michel. BARTHES AND SARTRE. *Contemporary French Civilization 1986 10(1): 50-63.* Discusses the influence on French intellectual life of philosopher and writer Jean Paul Sartre (1905-80) and literary critic Roland Barthes (1915-80). 20c

Bartók, Béla

428. Bartók, Béla, Jr. BARTÓK AND THE VISUAL ARTS. *New Hungarian Q. [Hungary] 1981 22(81): 44-49.* Hungarian composer Béla Bartók (1881-1945) took an interest in all branches of art, visiting museums wherever his concert tours took him. He himself also interested visual artists, both for the inspiration of his music and the intensity of his countenance as a subject. A drawing was done by Cézár Kunwald, a statue by Ervin Voit, and another statue by Géza Csorba. Vedrődy-Vogyerázky painted Bartók in Vienna in 1905. Many attempted to paint, sculpt, or draw Bartók after his death. 1900-45

429. Fontrodona, Linus. BÉLA BARTÓK [Béla Bartók]. *Historia y Vida [Spain] 1984 17(195): 83-88.* A life of Hungarian composer Béla Bartók (1881-1945). 1900-45

430. Király, István. TÉNYEK ÉS DOKUMENTUMOK A MAGYAR AGRÁROKTATÁS MULTJÁBOL. BARTÓK BÉLA CSALÁDJA ÉS A PARASZTSÁG [Facts and documents from the history of Hungarian agricultural education: the family of Béla Bartók and the peasantry]. *Agrártörténeti Szemle [Hungary] 1981 23(3-4): 532-541.* The father of the composer Béla Bartók was the principal of an agricultural school in Torontál County, Hungary, in the 1880's. His concern for the peasantry left a deep impression on his son. Based on the Baranya County Archives and secondary sources; 17 notes, document. English summary. 1880's

431. Lipman, Samuel. BARTÓK AT THE PIANO. *Commentary 1984 77(5): 54-58.* Discusses the contributions of Béla Bartók, both as a composer and performer in Hungary and the United States. 1900's-45

432. Staud, Géza. BARTÓK AND THE STAGE. *New Hungarian Q. [Hungary] 1981 22(84): 93-102.* In 1911 Béla Bartók wrote his first work for the stage, the opera *Blue Beard,* but it was not performed until 1918, the year after the opening performance in Budapest of his ballet, *The Wooden Prince.* These works could not be performed under the Horthy regime, and his next work, a dance pantomime entitled *The Miraculous Mandarin,* premiered in Germany, where its alleged immorality aroused controversy. Based partly on Bartók's writings; 9 pictures of stage sets and costume designs, 23 notes. 1911-30's

433. Ujfalussy, József. BARTÓK BÉLA SZÁZADIK SZÜLETÉSNAPJÁN [On Béla Bartók's 100th birthday]. *Magyar Tudomány [Hungary] 1981 26(6): 440-443.* Béla Bartók (1881-1945) felt a great affinity to folk songs and the peasant life-style. He feared that with increasing urbanization authentic folk music would die out. In stressing the beauty of folk music he did not deny the value of composed music. He wrote in 1931 that folk music has artistic merit only when a superior musical talent can permeate composed music with it and thereby affect the composed music. Béla Bartók was that superior musical talent. Based on a lecture at the Hungarian Music Academy, Budapest; 25 March 1981. 1921-45

434. Vargyas, Lajos. BARTÓK AND FOLK MUSIC RESEARCH. *New Hungarian Q. [Hungary] 1981 22(83): 58-70.* Folk songs were an important influence on Béla Bartók's (1881-1945) musical thinking. Folk song research brought contact with the people, and this interest resulted in the collection, notation, arrangement, and comparison of East European folk songs. His work led to a new discipline, comparative ethnomusicology, while also explaining the role of

folk music in Hungarian musical art. Based on Hungarian sources, and especially on Bartók's collected writings; 23 notes. 1900-40

435. Zoltai, Dénes. BARTÓK BÉLA. EGY OSZTHATATLAN ÉETMŰ [Béla Bartók: an indivisible oeuvre]. *Társadalmi Szemle [Hungary] 1981 36(2): 47-57.* Discarding such middle-class illusions as the romantic approach of German composers and the dictatorial system of minor and major chords, Bartók managed to find the "newest" in the most ancient form of music in Hungary, among the poor and downtrodden peasantry. The new 7/8 measure, the formation of new sounds in the concert hall, and many other new musical concepts helped Bartók to create music that placed him in a leading position in the cultural life of the country. 1881-1945

Barton, John

436. Greenwald, Michael Lester. "The Scholar's Eye: John Barton of the Royal Shakespeare Company." U. of California, Santa Barbara 1981. 651 pp. *DAI 1982 43(1): 18-A.* DA8209766 1960's-80

Barton, John (economist)

437. Sturges, R. P. THE CAREER OF JOHN BARTON, ECONOMIST AND STATISTICIAN. *Hist. of Pol. Econ. 1982 14(3): 366-384.* Most commentators recognized the high quality of much of Barton's early work. He stressed the priority of moral and humane imperatives over purely economic ones. He did not care for commerce and manufacturing and had a great dislike for cities. His concerns, directed to the poor, developed into a nostalgia for an idealized pastoral society. Table, 57 notes. 1814-50

Barvins'kyi, Oleksander

438. Hrushevsky, Mikhail S. IAK MENE SPROVADZHENO DO L'VOVA [How I came to Lvov]. *Ukrains'kyi Istoryk 1984 21(1-4): 230-235.* 1891-98
*For abstract see **Hrushevsky, Mikhail S.***

Basadre Grohmann, Jorge

439. Buse de la Guerre, Hermann. HA FALLECIDO ILUSTRE HISTORIADOR PERUANO: EL DOCTOR JORGE BASADRE GROHMANN [The illustrious Peruvian historian, Doctor Jorge Basadre Grohmann, has died]. *Jahrbuch für Gesch. von Staat, Wirtschaft und Gesellschaft Lateinamerikas [West Germany] 1982 19: 439-443.* Doctor Jorge Basadre Grohmann was a professor and historian; his best known work is the monumental 16-volume *Historia de la Republica del Perú,* recently appearing in the 7th edition. Besides writing and teaching at the Universidad Mayor de San Marcos, Basadre became director of the Biblioteca Central de la Universidad de San Marcos and, following the earthquake and fire that destroyed the Biblioteca Nacional in 1943, he directed the rebuilding of this library. Later he served as minister of education, and just before his death, he planned to visit Germany. 1903-80

440. Llosa, Jorge Guillermo. JORGE BASADRE, HISTORIADOR DE LA REPÚBLICA DEL PERÚ [Jorge Basadre, historian of the republic of Peru]. *Bol. de la Acad. Nac. de la Hist. [Venezuela] 1981 64(253): 111-112.* Jorge Basadre (1903-80) was called "the historian of the republic." He was a professor at the University of San Marcos, director of the National Library, minister of education, and member of the UNESCO commission charged with writing the History of Mankind. His *History of the Republic of Peru,* originally a one-volume edition, covered 16 volumes in the sixth edition (1968). He was also the author of several volumes on themes connected with history. 1903-80

Basak, Radhagovinda

441. Dasgupta, Kalyan Kumar. RADHAGOVINDA BASAK (1885-1982). *Journal of Indian History [India] 1982 60: 265-275.* Summarizes the life and work of Radhagovinda Basak, noteworthy Sanskritist, epigraphist, and historian. Educated at Dhākā College and Calcutta University, he broke new ground in the 1920's with his interpretations of ancient inscriptions as found on such antiquities as a series of copper plates of the Gupta Period bearing land sale records. In 1934, he completed his *History of North-Eastern India,* the first in-depth study of this area in ancient times. In the years which followed, he authored in English and Bengali numerous books and articles of Sanskrit language and literature, translations of ancient works, and historical works. 21 notes. 1885-1982

Basarab, Matei

442. Gheorghe, Constantin. MATEI BASARAB: AN EPOCH, A RULER (1632-1654). *Romania [Romania] 1982 7(4): 105-111.* Although a soldier by inclination, Matei Basarab respected scholarship and religion and was a compassionate ruler who was able to unite the Romanian countries of Transylvania, Wallachia, and Moldavia. 1632-54

443. Giurescu, Dinu C. MATEI BASARAB—DIPLOMAT [Matei Basarab, the diplomat]. *Magazin Istoric [Romania] 1983 17(10): 8-11.* The reign of Matei Basarab, voivode of Wallachia 1632-54, was comparatively peaceful, due to the diplomatic ability with which he held his Turkish overlords at bay and fended off other threats to his rule. 1632-54

444. Stoicescu, Nicolae. LUPTA LUI MATEI DIN BRÎNCOVENI PENTRU OCUPAREA TRONULUI ȚĂRII ROMÂNEȘTI [The struggle of Matei from Brîncoveni for the conquest of Wallachia's throne]. *Revista de Istorie [Romania] 1982 35(9): 985-1002.* The author examines the circumstances which led Matei Basarab from Brîncoveni to Wallachia's throne on 20 September 1632. Matei's first failed attempt at conquering the throne in August 1631, was followed by his escape to Transylvania. He returned to Wallachia in August 1632, supported also by Banat's population and occupied the throne without fighting. In October 1632, he defeated the army which supported Radu Iliaș, the new prince appointed by the sultan. In February 1633, Matei Basarab's rule was recognized by the Ottoman Empire as well. Secondary sources; 82 notes. French summary. 1630-33

Basarab Brâncoveanu family

445. Nastovici, A. FONDUL FAMILIAL "BASARAB BRÂNCOVEANU" [The archives of the Basarab Brâncoveanu family]. *Revista Arhivelor [Romania] 1985 47(1): 60-62.* Discusses the Basarab Brâncoveanu family archives, found in the archives of the city of Bucharest, which include documents pertaining to the Basarab dynasty (which ruled Wallachia intermittently after the 13th century) during the period of 1864-1964. 1864-1964

Bashkirov, Viacheslav Filippovich

446. —. GEROI STALINGRADSKOI BITVY [Heroes of the battle of Stalingrad]. *Voenno-Istoricheskii Zhurnal [USSR] 1982 (9): 42-45.* Assesses the efforts of six of the 112 Soviet soldiers awarded the title Hero of the Soviet Union

after the battle of Stalingrad (1942-43). Viacheslav Filippovich Bashkirov, a political commissar and pilot, a Russian, shot down six enemy aircraft single-handed. Chichiko Kaisarovich Bendeliani, pilot, a Georgian, introduced new methods of navigation and successfully led squadrons into battle. Ivan Prokop'evich Malozemov, Guards lieutenant and tank commander, a Russian, achieved a massive tally of enemy victims on the streets of Stalingrad. Khanpasha Nuradilovich Nuradilov, cavalry sergeant, a Tatar, despite serious wounds led an artillery attack on enemy positions. Vasilii Nikolaevich Prokatov, rifleman sergeant, a Russian, was killed in a grenade attack on a hopelessly stronger enemy position. Georgii Andreevich Khachin, artillery warrant officer, a Russian, despite his wounds, destroyed enemy tanks in a grenade attack. Documents from Central Archives of the Soviet Defense Ministry; 7 notes; 3 photos. 1942-43

Bataillon, Marcel

447. Braudel, Fernand. LA VIDA EJEMPLAR DE MARCEL BATAILLON [The exemplary life of Marcel Bataillon]. *Cuadernos de Investigación Hist. [Spain] 1981 5: 8-13.* A brief sketch, with personal reminisences, of the scholarly life of Marcel Bataillon (1895-1980), prominent French historian of Spain. 1920-75

448. Nerva, Marquis de. HOMENAJE POSTUMO A MARCEL BATAILLON [A posthumous homage to Marcel Bataillon]. *Cuadernos de Investigación Hist. [Spain] 1981 5: 5-7.* Address in memory of Marcel Bataillon (1895-1980), eminent French historian of Spain, who specialized in the influence of Erasmus in Spain, Bartolomé de las Casas, and the spiritual growth of the 16th century. 1925-70

Bateson, Gregory

449. Pogliano, Claudio. GREGORY BATESON [Gregory Bateson]. *Belfagor [Italy] 1984 39(5): 545-564.* Traces Gregory Bateson's education, intellectual influences, work in New Guinea and Bali, as well as his academic experience, as an introduction to his innovative ethnographies. 1904-80

Bathori, Jane

450. Cueno-Laurent, Linda. "The Performer as Catalyst: The Role of the Singer Jane Bathori (1877-1970) in the Careers of Debussy, Ravel, *Les Six,* and Their Contemporaries in Paris, 1904-1926." New York U. 1982. 274 pp. *DAI 1983 43(7): 2149-A.* DA8226746 1904-26

Batlle y Ordóñez, José

451. Claps, Manuel A. and Lamas, Mario Daniel. ALGUNOS ASPECTOS DE LA ESTRUCTURA IDEOLOGICA DEL BATLLISMO [Some aspects of the ideological structure of Batllismo]. *Investigación Econ. [Mexico] 1982 41(162): 219-266.* Batllismo, from the name of its founder José Batlle y Ordóñez (1856-1929) was a political movement of the early 20th century in Uruguay Beginning in 1903 Batlle stabilized the country by instituting bourgeois democratic reforms and by strengthening the state. He also promulgated an advanced social legislation that substantially improved workers' living conditions. He used state power to arbitrate class conflicts in an effort to achieve social harmony. His ideology affected every aspect of Uruguayan society. 110 notes. 1903-29

Batthyány, Josef

452. Sill, Ferenc. JOSEF BATTHYÁNY—PROPST VON EISENBURG [Josef Batthyány, provost of Eisenburg]. *Burgenländische Heimatblätter [Austria] 1983 45(1): 9-18.* Traces the life and career of the Hungarian Cardinal Josef Batthyány (1727-99). Batthyány worked in the Eisenburg diocese, 1753-58, as provost and regularly inspected the churches in the area. 1753-58

Batthyány, Lajos

453. Ács, Tibor. BATTHYÁNY LAJOS KATONAI SZOLGÁLATÁNAK TÖRTÉNETE 1826. AUGUSZTUS 5-1831. ÁPRILIS 30. [The military service of Lajos Batthyány: 5 August 1826 to 30 April 1831]. *Hadtörténelmi Közlemények [Hungary] 1984 31(4): 716-752.* Hungary's first prime minister, Lajos Batthyány, spent five years in the service of the Habsburg army before taking over the management of the family estate bequeathed to him by his father. His career in the army is chronicled in this paper, with details of the circumstances in which he joined and copies of reports by higher officers dealing with his performance. Based on military documents kept at the Kriegsarchiv, Vienna, contemporary correspondence, and other sources; 5 plates, 110 notes. 1826-31

454. Urbán, Aladár. BATTHYÁNY LAJOSNÉ VISSZAEMLÉKEZÉSEI FÉRJE FOGSÁGÁRA ÉS HALÁLÁRA [The memoirs of the wife of Lajos Batthyány on the imprisonment and death of her husband]. *Századok [Hungary] 1981 115(3): 587-620.* Publishes two letters: one written by the widow of Lajos Batthyány and the second by Count János Zichy. The widow's letter addressed to her children tells of the difficult days between the time her husband was arrested and his execution. Her small dagger which she left with him was used by Batthyány to take his own life and thus avoid the shame of being hanged in public. Due to the small size of the dagger he was only able to sever his arteries at three different places. The wounds were sufficient to prevent his death on the gallows and he was subsequently executed by a firing squad. Baron Zichy's note confirmed the happening as described by Batthyány's widow. 18 notes. 1849-82

Batthyány I, Ádam

455. Koppány, Tibor. BATTHYÁNY I. ÁDÁM ÉPITKEZÉSEI (1629-1659) [The buildings of Ádám Batthyány I, 1629-59]. *Történelmi Szemle [Hungary] 1984 27(4): 539-555.* Ádam Batthyány I (1609-59) was one of the great Hungarian patrons of the arts of the late Renaissance and early Baroque. He invited Italian and German artists and artisans to Hungary, including the architect Filiberto Lucchese. The most notable structures resulting from his patronage were located in Németújvár, Rohonc, and Szalonak. Based primarily on the Batthyány Family archives and secondary sources; 6 illus., 49 notes. 1629-59

Batz, Charles de

456. Bordes, Maurice. D'ARTAGNAN ET LES D'ARTAGNAN DANS L'HISTOIRE ET LE ROMAN [D'Artagnan and the "D'Artagnans" in history and novel]. *Information Historique [France] 1984 46(3): 105-112.* A biographical essay on Gascon soldier Charles de Batz, Comte d'Artagnan (1611?-73), and his cousin, Pierre de Montesquieu, Comte d'Artagnan, Marshal of France (1645-1725) and a comment on the various novels, such as Alexandre Dumas's *The Three Musketeers,* which have romanticized and made famous these noble gentlemen. 1611-1725

Baudin, Nicolas Thomas

457. Ly-Tio-Fane, Madeleine. CONTACTS BETWEEN SCHÖNBRUNN AND THE JARDIN DU ROI AT ISLE DE FRANCE (MAURITIUS) IN THE 18TH CENTURY. AN EPISODE IN THE CAREER OF NICOLAS THOMAS BAUDIN. *Mitteilungen des Österreichischen Staatsarchivs [Austria] 1982 35: 85-109.* Nicolas Thomas Baudin (b. 1754) performed military service in India and the Caribbean. Both military expeditions were failures, but while in the Caribbean Baudin obtained the captaincy of *La Pepita,* a merchant vessel. In 1785 Joseph II sent his chief gardener, Franz Boos, to Africa to gather exotic plants for his gardens at Schönbrunn. Since Baudin was willing to carry plants, in 1787 he took the commission to transport the plants from Mauritius to Trieste. The journey was a catastrophe: Boos's assistant, Georg Scholl was abandoned at the Cape and the ship sandbanked. Ironically, Baudin's career prospered after this failure. He became commander-in-chief of two vessels on a voyage of discovery to the "Terrae Australes." Primary sources; 72 notes. 1780's-1800

Baudouin de Courtenay, Jan

458. Ondrášková, Karla. K VÝROČÍ JAZÝKOVĚDCE JANA BAUDOINA DE COURTENAY [On the anniversary of Polish linguist Jan Baudouin de Courtenay]. *Slovanský Přehled [Czechoslovakia] 1985 71(6): 526-528.* 1985 was the 140th anniversary of the birth of the great Polish linguist Jan Baudouin de Courtenay (1845-1929). One of the first great Slavists, he was also a great historian, patriot, and critic of jingoist nationalism. Baudouin de Courtenay had many personal friends among Czech scholars, such as Adolf Černý. Of 19th-century Czech leaders, he had the greatest interest in the work of Karel Havlíček, especially his anticlerical writing, such as *Ěpistoly Kutnohorské.* Baudouin de Courtenay shared with Havlíček a conviction that one must fight for one's rights and principles. 16 notes. 1870's-1929

Bauer, Bruno

459. Pepperle, Heinz. BRUNO BAUER AN DER BERLINER UNIVERSITÄT (1828-1839) [Bruno Bauer at the University of Berlin, 1828-39]. *Wissenschaftliche Zeitschrift der Humboldt-Universität zu Berlin. Gesellschaftswissenschaftliche Reihe [East Germany] 1984 33(1): 19-23.* Discusses Bruno Bauer's early development during his years at the University of Berlin up until his move to Bonn, with particular focus on his position in regard to the opposed factions within the faculty at Berlin. 1828-39

Bauer, Francis

460. Meynell, Guy. FRANCIS BAUER, JOSEPH BANKS, EVERARD HOME AND OTHERS. *Archives of Natural History [Great Britain] 1983 11(2): 209-221.* Austrian-born botanical artist Francis Bauer (1758-1840) spent the latter part of his life as draftsman at Kew Gardens on the invitation of his patron and friend, Joseph Banks, custodian of the gardens. Many of his drawings, celebrated for their accuracy, found their way to the British Museum through Banks's, and later Bauer's, bequests, although some are now at the Göttingen University Library. Based on collections of the British Museum and the Göttingen University Library; 44 notes, biblio. 1758-1840

Bauer, Otto

461. Lauridsen, John T. OTTO BAUER-SYMPOSIUM I 100-ÅRET FOR HANS FØDSEL [Otto Bauer: symposium on the centenary of his birth]. *Arbejder Hist. [Denmark] 1982 19: 13-19.* Tributes to Austrian socialist leader Otto Bauer (1881-1938) by the members of a symposium held at the Karl Renner Institute, Vienna, 20-22 October 1981. Newspaper articles, unpublished material, secondary sources; 18 notes. 1881-1938

Baumont, Maurice

462. Batowski, Henryk. MAURICE BAUMONT (28 II 1892-12 VI 1981) [Maurice Baumont: 28 February 1892-12 June 1981]. *Kwartalnik Historyczny [Poland] 1983 90(3): 699-700.* An obituary of a French historian, Maurice Baumont (1892-1981), a specialist in international and German issues, and a credit to French scholarship. 1892-1981

Bautier, Robert Henri

463. Hurmuzache, S., ed. CONVORBIRE CU R. H. BAUTIER [Conversation with R. H. Bautier]. *Rev. Arhivelor [Romania] 1980 42(3-4): 398-405.* The French historian and archivist Robert Henri Bautier looks back over his career, describes his activity in international historical organizations, and gives his opinions on the training of specialists in the auxiliary historical sciences. 1950-80

Bavaev, Tadzhiali

464. —. GEROI BITVY ZA BERLIN [Heroes of the battle for Berlin]. *Voenno-Istoricheskii Zhurnal [USSR] 1981 23(5): 33-37.* Stressing the importance of the heroic action of Soviet forces in the battle against fascism, dwells briefly on the lives and contribution to the Soviet victory in the battle for Berlin of six individuals subsequently named Heroes of the Soviet Union: Sergeant Tadzhiali Bavaev, 2d Lieutenant Konstantin Grigorevich Gromov, Lieutenant Colonel Nikolai Nikolaevich Radaev, Lieutenant Valentin Ivanovich Shaburov, Captain Grigori Ivanovich Shevchenko, and Master Sergeant Makar Ivanovich Shkuro. Provides basic biographical details of each man, outlines their military positions at the time, and their heroic action during the battle for Berlin. Based on Soviet military archival material; 7 notes. 1945

Baxter, Richard

465. Keeble, N. H. RICHARD BAXTER'S PREACHING MINISTRY: ITS HISTORY AND TEXTS. *Journal of Ecclesiastical History [Great Britain] 1984 35(4): 539-559.* Traces the history of the preaching ministry of Richard Baxter (1615-91), English Puritan clergyman. The author describes the structure and quality of his sermons, and appends an annotated checklist of 34 published sermons. Based on Baxter's published works; 72 notes. 1640-82

Bayer, Gottlieb Siegfried

466. Dubowoj, Sina M. GOTTLIEB SIEGFRIED BAYER (1694-1738): FROM KÖNIGSBERG TO THE IMPERIAL ACADEMY OF SCIENCES IN ST. PETERSBURG. *Canadian Slavonic Papers [Canada] 1985 27(2): 123-139.* Gottlieb Siegfried Bayer (1694-1738) was professor of Oriental languages and antiquity at the Imperial Academy of Sciences in St. Petersburg from February 1726 until his death. His many works ranged from Greek, Roman, Biblical, Oriental, and Russian history to biographies of eminent Prussians, descriptions of ancient artifacts, and a Chinese lexicon. His name became linked primarily to the Varangian or Normanist theory of Russian history, which, however misjudged, helped lay the foundations of a systematic study of Russian history from its origins to the time of Peter. His influence on his friend and pupil Gerhard Friedrich Müller (1705-83) helped produce one of Russia's greatest historians, and Bay-

er's role in the fledgling Academy of Sciences was instrumental in helping it to survive. Based on the author's unpublished MA thesis and secondary works; 59 notes. 1720's-38

Bayerová, Anna

467. Nečas, Ctibor. PRVNÍ ÚŘEDNÍ LÉKAŘKA V BOSNĚ [The first official woman doctor in Bosnia]. *Časopis Matice Moravské [Czechoslovakia] 1983 102(3-4): 245-257.* Under the Turks there had been little medical care in Bosnia and Herzegovina; there was only one hospital and four doctors when the territory passed under Austrian control. By 1892 there were 29 doctors. In 1891 the idea of "official women doctors" was instituted to cater to the health of Muslim women and children. The first appointee, in January 1892, was Anna Bayerová (1853-1924), a Czech trained and practicing in Switzerland. Her pay, accommodation, status, and conditions of work were highly unsatisfactory, and she had to cope with ill-health and bureaucratic obstruction, helped only by the minister of finance Kállay. Soon after her probationary year was over she returned to Bohemia. A product of her stay was an important collection of handcrafts. Based on contemporary press reports, official documents, and Anna Bayerova's correspondence; 38 notes. 1891-93

Bayo, Ciro

468. Redondo Goicoechea, Alicia. VIDA Y OBRA DE CIRO BAYO: COSTUMBRISMO O NOVELA [Life and works of Ciro Bayo: genre writing or novel]. *Bol. de la Biblioteca de Menéndez Pelayo [Spain] 1981 57: 253-294.* Analyzes the life and works of Ciro Bayo (1859?-1939), a minor Spanish author. Addresses whether Ciro was a novelist or a describer of customs by examining his most important works. He was a traditionalist, with little creativity, whose efforts in literature were more directed at presenting descriptions and customs than developing works based on character and plot. He did help continue a genre of which Camilo José Cela is the modern representative. 119 notes. 1910-35

Bays, Anthoni

469. Křížová, Květa. ANTHONI BAYS UND DIE BILDERGALERIE DER HOHENEMSER [Anthoni Bays and the Hohenems picture gallery]. *Montfort [Austria] 1981 33(2): 134-144.* Between 1574 and 1578 the Flemish painter Anthoni Bays (1550?-?1600) was employed by Jakob Hannibal I von Hohenems (1530-87) to paint portraits of members of the Hohenems family and later became the court painter of Archduke Ferdinand von Tyrol (1529-95) at Innsbruck. 1574-80's

Bazhanov, Boris

470. Urban, George R. and Bazhanov, Boris. STALIN CLOSELY OBSERVED. *Survey [Great Britain] 1980 25(3): 86-109.* Interview with Boris Bazhanov, who was Joseph Stalin's secretary between 1923 and 1926 and the author of *Stalin, der rote Diktator* (1930). His observations and comments cover the period of his secretaryship, and among the main topics are the triumvirate of Stalin, Zinoviev, and Kamenev, Stalin and his path to power, Lenin's "testament," and Stalinism. 1923-26

Bazhno, Mikola

471. Koszeliweć, Iwan. TRAGEDIA MYKOLY BAŻNA [The tragedy of Mikola Bazhno]. *Kultura [France] 1984 (7-8): 136-142.* The public attack by the Ukrainian poet Mikola Bazhno (1904-83) on his best friend Iurii Ianowski in the 1940's to please Stalinist authorities caused him lifelong guilt. 1940's-83

Bazin, André

472. Mesnil, Michel. ANDRE BAZIN OU LE DROIT DE QUESTION [André Bazin, or the right to question]. *Esprit [France] 1983 (1): 37-45.* Recounts the career of French film critic André Bazin from 1951-58 and his discerning appreciation of modern film as a legitimate art form. 1951-58

Bazin, Guillaume Erasme

473. Clémens, Jacques. DOSSIER D'UN ETUDIANT ORIGINAIRE DE MARMANDE A L'UNIVERSITE DE PAU (FIN XVIIIe SIECLE) [The record of a student, a native of Marmande, at the University of Pau in the late 18th century]. *Rev. de Pau et du Béarn [France] 1981 (9): 77-79.* Gives the texts of letters of recommendation which illuminate the career, 1762-84, of Guillaume Erasme Bazin, a lawyer. 1762-84

Bazylow, Ludwik

474. Serczyk, Władysław A. LUDWIK BAZYLOW: 14 IV 1915-17 I 1985. [Ludwik Bazylow, 14 April 1915-17 January 1985]. *Studia Historyczne [Poland] 1985 28(3): 502-505.* Obituary of an outstanding Polish historian, Ludwik Bazylow. Bazylow spent most of his active life of scholarship at Warsaw University, where he was dean of the history faculty and vice-rector. His main subject was the history of Russia, 1801-1917. 1801-1917

475. Sobczak, Jan. PROFESOR LUDWIK BAZYLOW (1915-1985) [Professor Ludwik Bazylow (1915-85)]. *Z Pola Walki [Poland] 1985 29[i.e., 28](1): 197-203.* An obituary of Polish historian Bazylow, whose 300 publications include an outstanding history of 19th-century Russia, as well as works on cooperation between Polish and Russian revolutionaries, 1900-07 and on aspects of Polish history since the 15th century. 15c-20c

Bea, Augustin

476. Köhler, Oskar. "EXPLOSION" IM LEBEN AUGUSTIN BEAS. ZUR 100. WIEDERKEHR SEINES GEBURTSTAGS EINE ERINNERUNG AN DIE ÖKUMENISCHE HOFFNUNG [Explosion in Augustin Bea's life: on his 100th anniversary, a memoir on ecumenical hope]. *Stimmen der Zeit [West Germany] 1981 199(5): 301-313.* Describes Bea's relationship to Pope John XXIII, who made him cardinal in 1959. Explores Bea's work for the Jesuits, Vatican Council II, and his prior life and education. 1881-1968

Beale, John

477. Stubbs, Mayling. JOHN BEALE, PHILOSOPHICAL GARDENER OF HEREFORDSHIRE: PART 1: PRELUDE TO THE ROYAL SOCIETY (1608-1663). *Ann. of Sci. [Great Britain] 1982 39(5): 463-489.* Outlines the pre-1663 biography and intellectual development of the Herefordshire minister and horticulturalist who played an active role in the Hartlib Circle in the late 1650's. Central to Beale's enduring Baconianism, and possibly to his mechanical and hermetic

philosophy, was his close association at Eton with Sir Henry Wotton. He became a major contributor to Hartlib's compilation of Baconian histories through his treatises on horticulture, natural history, astronomy, optics, mechanics, prophecy, and mnemonics. A pragmatic visionary, Beale's kinship with the Hartlib Circle—both in scientific and in religious matters—stemmed from a blend of idealism and utilitarianism. 1608-63

Beals, Carleton

478. Britton, John. CARLETON BEALS AND CENTRAL AMERICA AFTER SANDINO: STRUGGLE TO PUBLISH. *Journalism Q. 1983 60(2): 240-245, 310.* Traces the career of leftist US journalist Carleton Beals (1893-1979), who vigorously opposed US intervention in Nicaragua in 1928. He was an outspoken supporter of Augusto César Sandino's guerrilla revolutionary movements. He also opposed US-backed regimes throughout Central America and faced subsequent difficulty in getting his reports published between World War II and the era of the Vietnam War. 27 notes. 1928-70's

Beamish, Henry Hamilton

479. Lebzelter, Gisela C. HENRY HAMILTON BEAMISH AND THE BRITONS: CHAMPIONS OF ANTI-SEMITISM. Lunn, Kenneth and Thurlow, Richard C., ed. *British Fascism: Essays on the Radical Right in Inter-War Britain* (New York: St. Martin's Pr., 1980): 41-56. Examines the career and ideas of Henry Hamilton Beamish, founder of the Britons, an anti-Semitic, proto-fascist organization most active during the 1920's. 1919-36

Beatty, Hugh

480. Trench, C. E. F. HUGH BEATTY, AN IRISH SOLDIER IN PORTUGAL. *Irish Sword [Ireland] 1981 14(56): 216-220.* Hugh Beatty (1742-89), a native of Dublin, served as an officer in regiments of the Portuguese army from 1762 to 1789. Information on his activities in Portugal is included. List of sources; 2 illustrations. 1762-89

Beauchamp family

481. McGoldrick, L. "The Literary Manuscripts and Literary Patronage of the Beauchamp and Neville Families in the Late Middle Ages." Newcastle upon Tyne Polytechnic [England] 1985. 310 pp. *DAI-C 1986 47(2): 283; 47/1369c.* ca 1390-1500

Beauduin, Lambert

482. Haquin, André. L'EXIL DE DOM LAMBERT BEAUDUIN AU MONASTERE D'EN-CALCAT (1932-1934) [The exile of Dom Lambert Beauduin to the Monastery of En-Calcat, 1932-34]. *Revue d'Histoire Ecclésiastique [Belgium] 1985 80(1): 51-99, (2): 415-440.* Part 1. Beauduin (1873-1960), a central figure of the Liturgical Revival and early ecumenism, was a diocesan priest and activist (from 1899), Benedictine monk at Mont-César (from 1906), theology professor at Rome (from 1914), founder of the ecumenist monastery of Amay-sur-Meuse near Liège (1925), and founder of the Byzantino-Slav section of the Bibliothèque Royale at Brussels (1931). The scope and manner of his monastery's ecumenism roused violent controversy on theological, financial, canonical, and personal levels, causing the Roman authorities to exile him to En-Calcat monastery near Dourgne in southeastern France. Part 2. Concentrates on the brief years of exile. Describes the physical rigors and psychological costs and Beaudin's projects, writing, correspondence, and pastoral activity, as well as schemes by friends to reverse the injustice and to secure a post for Beaudin in Paris or Beirut. Based on materials in archives in Rome, Belgium, and France. 1925-34

Beaufort, Henry

483. Hicks, M. A. EDWARD IV, THE DUKE OF SOMERSET AND LANCASTRIAN LOYALISM IN THE NORTH. *Northern History [Great Britain] 1984 20: 23-37.* Analyzes motives behind the 1463 desertion to the Lancastrian forces of alleged Yorkist Henry Beaufort, third Duke of Somerset (1436-64), from a Lancastrian perspective. As a supporter of the Lancastrian King Henry VI (1421-71), Somerset was attainted after the former's 1461 Towton defeat by Edward IV. Having become close friends with King Edward IV (1461-83) and participated in an anti-Lancastrian siege, Somerset was pardoned in 1463 and offered money and favors by the Yorkist monarch, but nonetheless rejoined the Lancastrians in December 1463. He was captured and executed. Somerset's "betrayal" of Edward IV was motivated by dynastic loyalty, not the self-interest that 20th-century historians have tended to attribute to him. 40 notes, appendix. 1461-71

Beaufort, Margaret

484. Jones, Michael and Underwood, Malcolm. LADY MARGARET BEAUFORT, 1443-1509. *History Today [Great Britain] 1985 35(Aug): 23-30.* Lady Margaret Beaufort, mother of Henry VII, was a master of political intrigue in 15th-century England. Her interest in public policy and her position as great landowner aided her son and provided patronage to many worthy causes and educational institutions. 1457-1509

485. Underwood, Malcolm G. THE LADY MARGARET AND HER CAMBRIDGE CONNECTIONS. *Sixteenth Cent. J. 1982 13(1): 67-81.* Lady Margaret Beaufort, Countess of Richmond and Derby, was the principal benefactor of Cambridge University. The controversy from 1501 to 1503 over the wounding of a prominent fishmonger named Hugh Rankyn, a former town treasurer, resulted in litigation between the town and the university. Lady Margaret was involved in the matter during the last years of her life, and her enduring concern is demonstrated. Based on Cambridge University and Cambridge town records, the *University Grace Book,* the *Annals of Cambridge,* and secondary sources; 73 notes. 1490-1509

Beaujeu, Anne de

486. Hilgar, Marie-France. ANNE DE BEAUJEU, UNOFFICIAL REGENT, 1483-1492 (ABSTRACT). *Proceedings of the Annual Meeting of the Western Society for French History 1984 11: 53.* Were it not for the salic law, Anne de Beaujeu would be as famous today as Elizabeth of England and Catherine of Russia. Before his death, Louis XI had entrusted to his oldest daughter Anne, and to her husband, the entire charge of his son, Charles VIII. From 1483 to 1492, Anne exercised the regency unofficially. Energetic, obstinate, and intelligent, Anne succeeded in triumphing over feudal intrigues, coalitions, and plots against her and the king. The fact that her adversaries repeatedly asked for her removal shows that they were well aware Anne was the moving force and the brains of the family and of the government of France. Abstract only. 1483-92

Beaumarchais, Pierre Caron de

487. Farley, M. Foster. BEAUMARCHAIS AND THE AMERICAN REVOLUTION. *Daughters of the Am. Revolution Mag. 1983 117(3): 236-241.* Under the name Roderique Hortaliz and Company, Pierre-Augustin Caron de Beaumarchais (1732-99), confidential French agent of Louis XVI, channeled gunpowder and other military goods to the colonies during the early days of the American Revolution.
1757-99

Beaupréau, Marquis de

488. Béchu, Philippe. NOBLESSE D'EPEE ET TRADITION MILITAIRE AU XVIIIeme SIECLE [The *noblesse d'épée* and military tradition in the 18th century]. *Histoire, Economie et Société [France] 1983 2(4): 507-548.* The family of Jacques-Bertrand de Scépeaux, Marquis de Beaupréau, were landholders in Anjou and had been ennobled in the Middle Ages. The 18th-century Beaupréau increased his fortunes through marriage, had a military career, and was appointed lieutenant-general of Anjou. He retained his provincial estates but lived in Paris and maintained a large household (with resulting indebtedness). His career shows the overlapping nature of the *noblesse d'épée* with the worlds of the military and bureaucracy in the old regime. Based on family records and other sources in the Archives Nationales, Paris; 153 notes. 1704-78

Beauvoir, Simone de

489. McCall, Dorothy Kaufman. SIMONE DE BEAUVOIR, IL FEMMINISMO E SARTRE [Simone de Beauvoir, feminism, and Sartre]. *Comunità [Italy] 1980 34(182): 226-243.* Discusses the earlier phase of de Beauvoir's feminism, that of *The Second Sex,* and Jean Paul Sartre's position on the women's liberation movement.
1949-70

Beaverbrook, 1st Baron

490. McEwen, J. M. LLOYD GEORGE'S ACQUISITION OF THE *DAILY CHRONICLE* IN 1918. *J. of British Studies 1983 22(1): 127-144.* 1918
For abstract see ***Donald, Robert***

491. Stubbs, John O. BEAVERBROOK AS HISTORIAN: *POLITICIANS AND THE WAR, 1914-1916* RECONSIDERED. *Albion 1982 14(3-4): 235-253.* Although Lord Beaverbrook's history is now considered essential reading, it was met with criticism when published, especially for its favorable treatment of Andrew Bonar Law. Its chief weakness as history is its exclusive concentration of the political elites and their crises. Although Beaverbrook was much more than the "chronicler" he styled himself in the difficult field of contemporary history, there are real problems of interpretation and emphasis. He is on firmer ground when discussing the world of senior politicians. In sum, the book is neither an accurate record nor detached scholarship, but required reading nonetheless. Based in part on the Beaverbrook MSS; 53 notes. 1910-72

Bebel, August

492. Borodin, E. I. NOVYI FAKT BIOGRAFII V. I. LENINA [New detail for the biography of V. I. Lenin]. *Voprosy Istorii KPSS [USSR] 1984 (11): 120-124.* 1910
For abstract see ***Lenin, V. I.***

493. Nishikawa, Masao. FUJIN-RON TO AUGUSUTO BĒBERU: HAKKAN (1879) HYAKUSHŪNEN NI YOSETE [*Women and Socialism* and August Bebel: at the 100th anniversary of its publication]. *Rekishi Hyōron [Japan] 1980 (359): 3-18.* A survey of the life of August Bebel and the follow-up observation of revisions of his major work, *Women and Socialism.* Discusses the positions of the German Social Democratic Party (SDP) and Bebel on women's liberation. The frequent revision of *Women and Socialism* precisely shows the process of accepting Marxism in the SDP. Detailed introduction of references touches upon the introduction of Bebel and his work in Japan; 38 notes.
1860's-1913

Beccaria, Cesare

494. Hotta, Seizō. BEKKARIA NI OKERU "HIHANTEKI KEIZAIGAKU" NO KEISEI: KENEI KARA HYUMU [Formation of Beccaria's *Elements of Public Economy:* from Quesnay to Hume]. *Shisō [Japan] 1984 (722): 127-144.* Cesare Beccaria's *Essays on Crimes and Punishments* (1764) was not only a study of criminal laws but also a book about broader social phenomena. It demanded completion of law as a precondition of modern society but did not offer a theory of the structure of modern society. His *Elements of Public Economy* (1804) was intended to solve this problem. The manuscript of *Elements of Public Economy* reveals that David Hume, rather than François Quesnay, as is generally believed, had the greater influence on Beccaria's economic theory. Beccaria transformed Hume's introductory study of the formation of modern society as learning for the establishment into a critical study of the established order based on the feudal land system. Primary sources; 79 notes.
1750's-1804

Becher, Ulrich

495. Zeller, Nancy Anne McClure. "Ulrich Becher: A Computer-Assisted Case Study of the Reception of an Exile." U. of Texas, Austin 1981. 423 pp. *DAI 1982 42(7): 3173-A.* 8128718 1930's-60's

Beck, Joseph

496. Gromada, Thaddeus V. JOSEPH BECK IN THE LIGHT OF RECENT POLISH HISTORIOGRAPHY. *Polish Rev. 1981 26(3): 65-73.* A review and analysis of interpretations post-1956 Polish historians have given to Joseph Beck (1894-1944), Poland's foreign minister 1932-39, and his "third Europe" project. This was an attempt to achieve security, independent of Germany and the Soviet Union, through a political association among Poland, Hungary, Romania, Yugoslavia, and Italy. As part of this project, Beck sought the creation of a common Polish-Hungarian border at the expense of Czechoslovakia. Because of Poland's relative weakness, modern Polish historians tend to view this policy as unrealistic, suggesting the preferability of an alternative policy in cooperation with the USSR. Western scholars, however, believe that Beck had no feasible alternative if Poland was to remain independent of the two powers. Beck followed a policy of "every country for itself" based on the diplomacy of absolute state sovereignty. Secondary sources; 39 notes.
1932-39

Bečka, Jiří

497. Křikavová, Adéla. JIŘÍ BEČKA TURNS SEVENTY. *Archív Orientální [Czechoslovakia] 1986 54(1): 77-88.* Jiří Bečka (born 1915 in Prague) graduated from the Law Faculty of Charles University in 1945, after which he pursued an interest in oriental studies. He completed his thesis on *Margi Sudkhūr* [The death of the usurer] by Sadriddīn Aynī

in 1954 at the Faculty of Arts of the Czechoslovak Academy of Sciences. He specialized in Iranian studies, particularly the history of Tadzhik literature, and coauthored and edited the *Dictionary of Oriental Literatures* published in 1974. Bečka was a skilled linguist and produced translations of Eastern Iranian literary and oral folk works and wrote reviews of Czechoslovakian books on the literature of the Near East. Bibliography. 1945-85

Becker, Carl

498. McNeill, William H. CARL BECKER, HISTORIAN. *History Teacher 1985 19(1): 89-100.* Presents a brief biographical sketch of Carl Becker's life and intellectual interests. A persistent global viewpoint and concern for the future of liberal democracy and American society and government were Becker's dominant preoccupations. Becker's greatest influence may lie in his textbook, *Modern History* (1931), which emphasizes the influence of France over England and presents a strong secular perspective. Based on published sources and personal experience. 1900's-45

Becker, Jack Ellerton

499. Rogers, W. P. JACK ELLERTON BECKER 1904-1979. *Hist. Records of Australian Sci. [Australia] 1982 5(3): 92-107.* A biography of Jack Ellerton Becker, an Australian entrepreneur who was knighted in recognition of his support for the Australian Academy of Science. A person of humble background, his early career involved making musical instruments, organizing musical events, and establishing a music school. His first riches were achieved through agriculture, on land that was worthless until the soil was supplemented with trace elements. Further prosperity accrued from other agricultural and real estate pursuits. 1925-79

Beckford, Slim

500. Taylor, Godfrey. A PRELIMINARY LOOK AT SLIM AND SAM: JAMAICAN STREET SINGERS. *Jamaica J. [Jamaica] 1983 16(3): 39-45.* Describes the lives and art of two of Jamaica's great folk singers and composers, popularly known as Slim and Sam (Slim Beckford and Sam Blackwood), who made their living selling their song sheets for a penny each at their street performances during the 1930's and early 1940's. 1930's-40's

Beddoes, Thomas

501. Levere, Trevor H. THOMAS BEDDOES AT OXFORD: RADICAL POLITICS AND THE REGIUS CHAIR IN CHEMISTRY. *Ambix [Great Britain] 1981 28(2): 61-69.* Thomas Beddoes had attended the University of Edinburgh before arriving at Oxford University. In 1787 he held the post of Reader in Chemistry, seemingly satisfactorily. In the 1790's his attitudes toward the French Revolution made him politically suspect and therefore undesirable. Attendance at his classes dwindled. These factors cost him a Regius professorship when it was proposed to establish one in 1792, and he resigned the following year. During this period he was on the secret government list of Disaffected and Seditious Persons. Extracts from some of his writings are given. Mainly primary sources from letter collections; 54 notes. 1790-95

502. Levere, Trevor H. DR. THOMAS BEDDOES (1750-1808): SCIENCE AND MEDICINE IN POLITICS AND SOCIETY. *British Journal for the History of Science [Great Britain] 1984 17(2): 187-204.* Reviews the political and professional activities of British physician and chemist Thomas Beddoes during the years following the French Revolution. Beddoes was a liberal and a reformer who sympathized with the spirit of the French Revolution although he deplored the mob violence that accompanied it. His persuasions placed him at odds with British authorities and, when they cost him his Oxford chair, he opened a clinic in Bristol with the help of other well-known republican sympathizers. The clinic was founded in the mistaken belief that some of the gasses then being discovered by Joseph Priestly would prove to be curative. Later, he addressed the political and physical aspects of proper nutrition and public health and, throughout, continued to be a prominent agitator for humanitarian causes. Based on papers in the Cornwall Record Office, Bristol Record Office, Public Record Office, and secondary sources. 1792-1808

Beerbohm, Max

503. Danson, Lawrence. MAX BEERBOHM AND *THE MIRROR OF THE PAST. Princeton U. Lib. Chronicle 1982 43(2): 77-153.* Discusses the life and work of Max Beerbohm, British writer, drama critic for the *Saturday Review* for 12 years, and BBC broadcaster in the 1950's. Focuses on his unfinished manuscript, *The Mirror of the Past* (1913-16) in the Princeton University Library's Robert H. Taylor Collection. It is a "fascinating hodgepodge" of verbal sketches and elaborations of the sketches. 1890's-1956

Beethoven, Ludwig van

504. Brauneis, Walther. DAS PASQUALATIHAUS AUF DER MÖLKERBASTEI: EINE BAUGESCHICHTLICHE STUDIE [The Pasqualati house in the Mölkerbastei: a historical architectural study]. *Wiener Geschichtsblätter [Austria] 1982 37(2): 97-104.* Describes one of Ludwig van Beethoven's residences in Vienna, its owner, the Pasqualati family, and Beethoven's life and work during his residence there. 18c-19c

505. Horward, Donald D. NAPOLEON AND BEETHOVEN. *Consortium on Revolutionary Europe 1750-1850: Pro. 1980 2: 3-13.* Napoleon and Beethoven never met, and it is probable that the former never became aware of the music of the latter. But Napoleon's career had a significant impact on Beethoven's life and music. Up to 1804, Beethoven greatly admired the Frenchman, seeing in him the epitome of rationalism and the ideals of the French Revolution. But Napoleon's acquisition of the title of emperor and his numerous victories over Austrian troops led Beethoven to oppose him. Between 1804 and 1814, Beethoven composed numerous nationalistic works that contained direct or indirect attacks against Napoleon. Once the Frenchman was defeated, however, Beethoven gradually reversed his opinions once again, and saw Napoleon as a champion of reason and artistic freedom. Based on printed primary sources; 33 notes. 1796-1827

Bega, Cornelis

506. Scott, Mary Ann. "Cornelis Bega (1631/32-1664) as Painter and Draughtsman." U. of Maryland 1984. 628 pp. *DAI 1985 46(4): 823-A.* DA8510280 1650-64

Beguin, Albert

507. Cosgrove, Brian. THE CRITICISM OF ALBERT BEGUIN AND THE POETRY OF WILLIAM WORDSWORTH. *Studies [Ireland] 1983 72(286): 170-184.* Albert Beguin, (d. 1957) was a major critic of romanticism of the kind seen in Wordsworthian Nature and Imagination. The author traces Beguin's development as a gifted and stimulating critic and his quest for spiritual reality. 65 notes. 19c-20c

Beil'shtein, Fedor

508. Kochetova, E. K. and Potapov, V. M. O BEIL'SHTEINE I "BEIL'SHTEINE" [On Beil'shtein and "the Beil'shtein"]. *Voprosy Istorii Estestvoznaniia i Tekhniki [USSR] 1984 (2): 62-67.* Fedor Beil'shtein (1838-1906) gave his name to his lifework, a reference book on organic chemistry which has expanded from his initial 2,000 pages covering all the then known organic compounds, published in 1881-1883, to the present 250 volumes. Aspects of Beil'shtein's life and the genesis of the work in competition with German scientist E. Erlenmeier are described. Based on documents in the USSR Academy of Science's archive and secondary sources. 1860's-1906

Beimler, Hans

509. Haferkorn, Katja. BIOGRAPHISCHE SKIZZEN. "WIR HABEN DAS RECHT, STOLZ ZU SEIN AUF EINEN SOLCHEN KÄMPFER...": HANS BEIMLER [Biographical sketches. "We have the right to be proud of such a fighter...": Hans Beimler]. *Beiträge zur Gesch. der Arbeiterbewegung [East Germany] 1981 23(1): 84-93.* Hans Beimler (1895-1936), a Bavarian mechanic, joined the Spartacists in 1918, participated in the navy uprising, became a member of the Bavarian Soviet Republic, a union activist, city councilman at Augsburg, and representative in the Bavarian state parliament. In April 1933, he was arrested and held at Dachau. He escaped to the Soviet Union and from there went to Prague, Zurich, and Paris to support German exiles and strengthen the anti-fascist forces. He was killed during the Spanish Civil War. Based on party archives and published sources; 43 notes. 1918-36

Bek-Nazarov, Amo

510. Birkos, Alexander S. ROMANCE, REFORM AND REVOLUTION: THE EARLY ARMENIAN CINEMA OF AMO BEK-NAZAROV. *Armenian Rev. 1982 35(3): 276-283.* Born Ambartsum Bek-Nazarian, Amo Bek-Nazarov is recalled as the father of the first generation of Armenian film actors and producer-director of films with Armenian relevance. 1915-35

Bekzadian, Alexander

511. Gharibjanian, G. B. V. I. LENINI HAY ZINAKITSNĔRN U ASHAKĔRTNĔRĔ [V. I. Lenin's Armenian comrades-in-arms and disciples]. *Patma-Banasirakan Handes. Istoriko-Filologicheskii Zhurnal [USSR] 1980 (1): 13-20.* ca 1890-1917

For abstract see ***Avanesov***

Bél, Mátyás

512. Čapková, Dagmar. VÝROČÍ VÝZNAMNÉHO POLYHISTORA [Anniversary of an important polyhistor]. *Studia Comeniana et Historica [Czechoslovakia] 1985 15(30): 129-132.* Matej Bel (1684-1749), a representative of the early Enlightenment, was a Slovak Protestant, alumnus of the Halle Pietists, impressive spokesman for education and toleration, and author of *Notitia Hungariae Novae Historico-Geographica* (1735-42). A patriot of old Hungary, but mindful of his Slavic roots, he contributed to the revival of Czech and Slovak culture. 1710's-49

513. Wellmann, Imre. MÁTYÁS BÉL, A POLYGRAPH IN HUNGARY IN THE 18TH CENTURY. *Hungarian Studies [Hungary] 1985 1(2): 191-204.* Examines the life and writings of Mátyás Bél (1684-1749), Hungarian educator, historian, and geographer, whose most famous work was the extensive *Notitia Hungariae novae historico geographica* (1735-42). 1700's-49

Belalcázar, Sebastián de

514. Paz Otero, Gerardo. EL CARISMA DE LOS CONQUISTADORES [The conquerors' charisma]. *Bol. de la Acad. Nac. de la Hist. [Venezuela] 1980 63(249): 151-158.* Reviews a number of references on the personality of Sebastián de Belalcázar, founder of Quito, Popayán, and Cali. 11 notes. 1471-1551

Beliakov, A.

515. Beliakov, A. CHEREZ SEVERNYI POLIUS AMERIKU [Across the North Pole to America]. *Voenno-Istoricheskii Zhurnal [USSR] 1981 23(5): 38-43.* 1937

For abstract see ***Baidukov, G. F.***

Belinski, Vissarion

516. Dunn, Patrick P.; Schoenwald, Richard L. (commentary). BELINSKII, BAKUNIN, AND THE QUEST FOR REVOLUTIONARY IMMORTALITY. *Consortium on Revolutionary Europe 1750-1850: Proceedings 1983: 464-476.* Presents a psychohistorical analysis of the career of 19th-century Russian writer Vissarion Belinsky. He was stunned by the premature deaths of his friends Liubov' Bakunina and Nikolai Stankevich in 1838 and 1840. In the anxiety caused by these two deaths, Belinsky finally rejected the Hegelianism that he had formerly espoused. Eventually he came to advocate revolution. Comments, pp. 495-508. Based on printed primary sources; 38 notes. 1830's-40's

Bell, Charles Davidson

517. Warner, Brian. LITHOGRAPHS BY CHARLES DAVIDSON BELL. *Africana Notes and News [South Africa] 1981 24(6): 195-199.* A brief history of South African lithographer Charles Davidson Bell and a listing of his lithographs, the latter task not definitively possible prior to a recent discovery of a major collection of his works. Bell was an artist for an African exploring expedition, 1834-36. Here he made contact with Charles Smyth, who soon returned to Scotland where he became interested in lithography. Bell later visited Smyth and became taken with the art as well. Most of his lithographs were done in Scotland; his production fell sharply after his return to South Africa. The listing of his works contains 29 lithographs. 2 photos, 10 notes. ca 1834-39

Bell, George

518. Best, Geoffrey. THE BISHOP AND THE BOMBER. *Hist. Today [Great Britain] 1983 33(Sept): 28-32.* Anglican Bishop George Bell became an unpopular figure in World War II Great Britain for his opposition to the saturation bombing of German cities by the Royal Air Force. 1939-45

Bell, Vanessa

519. Gillespie, Diane Filby, interviewer. VANESSA BELL, VIRGINIA WOOLF, AND DUNCAN GRANT: CONVERSATION WITH ANGELICA GARNETT. *Modernist Studies [Canada] 1979 3(1-3): 151-158.* Although Vanessa Bell is generally remembered for her relationship with other people, including her father Sir Leslie Stephen, her sister Virginia Woolf, her husband Clive Bell, and her lover Roger Fry, she was a formidable painter and personality in her own

right; her life provides insight into the group of artists known as the Bloomsbury Group. In this interview, Angelica Garnett discusses her biography of Vanessa Bell. 1879-1930's

Bella, Stefano della

520. Romani, Luigi. STEFANO DELLA BELLA, INCISORE FIORENTINO DEL XVII SECOLO AMANTE DEL MARE [Stefano della Bella, 17th-century Florentine engraver and lover of the sea]. *Rivista Marittima [Italy] 1985 118(11): 61-72.* A biography of early 17th-century Florentine engraver Stefano della Bella (1610-64) attempts to establish the itinerary that led him to illustrate scenes of harbor life in Livorno, Amsterdam, Piombino, Saint-Omer, and La Rochelle; his work has been catalogued in part by Alexandre de Vesme (Collectors' Editions, New York, 1971). 1639-50

Bellarmine, Robert

521. Galeota, Gustavo. ROBERTO BELLARMINO, ABBATE COMMENDATARIO DI PROCIDA [Robert Bellarmine, usufructuary abbot of Procida]. *Arch. Hist. Societatis Iesu [Italy] 1982 51(102): 209-246.* Bellarmine was made a cardinal in 1599 and being poor by religious profession was given the benefice of the abbey of the island of Procida in the bay of Naples; he sold the benefice five years later because it involved too many economic problems. 1600-06

Bellegarde, Louis-Dantès

522. Bellegarde-Smith, Patrick D. DANTES BELLEGARDE AND PAN-AFRICANISM. *Phylon 1981 42(3): 233-244.* Louis-Dantés Bellegarde (1877-1966) led the struggle for the political liberation of Haiti and made a significant contribution to worldwide black awareness. At various times he was a presidential adviser, cabinet member, diplomat, and public speaker. He worked against United States occupation of Haiti and for black consciousness. 1877-1966

523. Bellegarde-Smith, Patrick. INTERNATIONAL RELATIONS/SOCIAL THEORY IN A SMALL STATE: AN ANALYSIS OF THE THOUGHT OF DANTÈS BELLEGARDE. *Americas (Acad. of Am. Franciscan Hist.) 1982 39(2): 167-184.* The Haitian intellectual and diplomat Louis-Dantès Bellegarde (1877-1966) both in his official service and in his writing promoted international cooperation and cultural westernization. The first of these, on a basis of strict adherence to international law, he saw as particularly essential to the survival of small states. His devotion to French and Catholic culture reflected in part his elite status, but he was a Haitian nationalist in his own fashion. 82 notes. ca 1920-60

Belli, Gioconda

524. Arenal, Electa. TWO POETS OF THE SANDINISTA STRUGGLE. *Feminist Studies 1981 7(1): 19-27.* 1926-78

*For abstract see **Alegría, Claribel***

Bellido, María Luisa

525. López Pérez, Manuel. MARÍA LUISA BELLIDO, LA HEROÍNA DE BAILÉN (2A PARTE) [María Luisa Bellido, the heroine of Bailén, Part 2]. *Rev. de Hist. Militar [Spain] 1981 25(50): 51-67.* Continued from a previous article. Discusses the revival of the legend of María Bellido, her place in the city traditions, and the historical arguments for and against her authenticity. The evidence favors the historicity of Bellido. Primary sources; 3 plates, 22 notes, biblio. 1808

Bello, Andrés

526. Bortone Goitía, Alfonso. ANDRES BELLO: UNA GRAN FIGURA AMERICANA [Andrés Bello: a great American figure]. *Rev. de la Soc. Bolivariana de Venezuela [Venezuela] 1981 38(132): 108-111.* Reviews the life and work of Bello, a Venezuelan writer and humanist who once taught Bolívar. 1781-1829

527. Cacua Prada, Antonio. DON ANDRES BELLO, PERIODISTA [Andrés Bello, journalist]. *Bol. de Hist. y Antigüedades [Colombia] 1981 68(734): 763-771.* Venezuelan-born Andrés Bello had a distinguished career as a journalist, beginning in Caracas, continuing through a period of collaboration in Spanish-language periodicals published in London, and culminating in Chile, where he finally made his home. Biblio. 1810-65

528. Caldera, Rafael. EL SENADOR DON ANDRÉS BELLO [Senator Andrés Bello]. *Rev. Nac. de Cultura [Venezuela] 1982 43(249): 31-48.* Andrés Bello was not only a man of letters but also a great legislator, organizer, and executive. In 1832, Chile granted him honorary citizenship. A member of the Chilean Senate for more than 20 years, Bello worked to shape the legislation of the American states and dedicated himself to international relations, education, and the abolition of the slave trade. 1830's-40's

529. Carilla, Emilio. BELLO Y EL RÍO DE LA PLATA [Bello and the Río de la Plata]. *Inter-American Rev. of Biblio. 1982 32(2): 168-178.* Examines Andrés Bello's (1781-1865) works for Argentine themes and discusses Argentine opinions of Bello's writings, although there is no evidence that Bello ever went to Argentina. Born in Venezuela, Bello lived in England from 1811 to 1829. In 1815 he considered moving to Argentina, but, perhaps because of his English wife, Mary Anne Boyland, did not do so. In a letter to the Mexican friar Servando Teresa de Mier in 1821 he was very critical of the intellectual climate of Buenos Aires. In 1829 Bello moved to Chile, where he became famous as a poet, educator, jurist, and orthographer. Based on Bello's works and contemporary publications; 31 notes. 1811-65

530. Galich López, Luis Fernando. D. ANDRES BELLO Y LOPEZ [Don Andrés Bello y Lopez]. *Anales de la Acad. de Geog. e Hist. de Guatemala [Guatemala] 1981 55: 183-194.* It has been said that if Bolívar was the political emancipator of Spanish America, Andrés Bello (1781-1865) was its literary and cultural emancipator. He was a poet, grammarian, cosmographer, jurist, writer, and diplomat. Like Bolívar, he was born in Caracas; he accepted a government post in Chile in 1829. Presented to the Chamber of Commerce of Guatemala 13 March 1981. Biblio. 1781-1865

531. Grases, Pedro. BELLO, HUMANISTA Y UNIVERSITARIO [Bello: humanist and university professor]. *Rev. Nac. de Cultura [Venezuela] 1982 43(249): 68-80.* Implicit in the liberal humanism of Andrés Bello was a new view of people as individuals and participants in the new American societies. On his return to Chile from London, Bello concentrated on education to create a society based on liberty and new styles of government. 19c

532. Herrera Campíns, Luis. AQUI Y AFUERA SEGUIREMOS VENERANDO A BELLO [Here and abroad we shall continue to venerate Bello]. *Bol. de la Acad. Nac. de la Hist. [Venezuela] 1981 64(256): 801-809.* Andrés Bello (1781-1865), scholar, humanist, poet, philosopher, university professor and rector, senator, jurist, and critic is one of the fathers of Latin American independence. This speech by the Venezuelan president was delivered on the occasion of the inauguration of a monument in his honor celebrating the bicentennial of his birth. 1781-1865

533. Herrera Campíns, Luis. BICENTENARIO DEL NACIMIENTO DE ANDRES BELLO [The bicentennial of the birth of Andrés Bello]. *Rev. Nac. de Cultura [Venezuela] 1982 43(249): 15-29.* Bello prepared for his life of intellectual activity in Caracas. In London, where he lived for several years, he established contact with classical and romantic European culture. It was from London that he began the revolutionary work of transforming the language of the new American nations. The statue unveiled by Venezuelan President Luis Herrera Campíns in Caracas honors Bello as an educator. 1781-1865

534. Lezcano, Julio. ANDRES BELLO, UN AMERICANO UNIVERSAL [Andrés Bello, a universal American]. *Estudios Paraguayos [Paraguay] 1983 11(2): 45-168.* This biographical study of one of the most important Latin American figures of the independence era focuses on his multifaceted intellectual activities. Andrés Bello (1781-1865), born in Caracas, was a poet, educator, jurist, and diplomat. He wrote on grammar, education, literature, philosophy, and Roman, civil, and international law. He was also the author of the Chilean Civil Code. 353 notes, biblio. 1804-65

535. Lovera De-Sola, R. J. BELLO EN CARACAS [Bello in Caracas]. *Bol. de la Acad. Nac. de la Hist. [Venezuela] 1983 66(261): 195-212.* Andrés Bello was born in Caracas and lived there till the age of 28. In 1810 he was appointed secretary to Bolívar's mission in London, where he stayed until 1829. In that year, pressed by economic problems, he accepted a post in Chile, where he was to play an important role as a jurist, professor of law, and framer of the constitution. To the end of his life, however, he remained attached to his native country, considering himself an exile among "foreigners" who thought of him as a fellow "citizen." 73 notes. ca 1810-65

536. Murillo Rubiera, Fernando. ANDRES BELLO EN INGLATERRA [Andrés Bello in England]. *Cuadernos Hispanoamericanos [Spain] 1982 (388): 5-44.* Andrés Bello's stay in London from 1810 to 1829 is a major event in his biography, for although he knew periods of extreme difficulty due to political insecurity in the South American Spanish colonies, he also found in London the friendship of Spanish exiles and representatives of the newly independent South American republics. These relationships and the London environment provided the intellectual and cultural background needed to develop his interests in philology and the diplomatic experiences that made him an expert in international relations. 50 notes. 1810-29

537. Temeltas de Calcaño, Josefina. ANDRÉS BELLO Y EL PODER JUDICIAL [Andrés Bello and the judicial power]. *Rev. Nac. de Cultura [Venezuela] 1982 43(249): 241-254.* Between 1832 and 1865, Andrés Bello was widely known on the American continent for his contribution to the formulation of international law. He was distinguished also for his work in the codification and renewal of civil law and for the teaching of law in Latin America. 5 notes. 1832-65

538. Tenreiro, Salvador. EPISTOLARIO DE BELLO EN CHILE. [Bello's letters in Chile]. *Rev. Nac. de Cultura [Venezuela] 1982 43(248): 88-103.* The 605 extant letters of Andrés Bello (1781-1865) have been classified into five categories: letters to his friends with autobiographical, literary, and political themes; letters to his family from London, Chile, and Spain; official activities and educational themes; his activities as a journalist; and his relationship with the Royal Spanish Academy, of which he was made an honorary member in 1851. Primary sources; 23 notes. 1829-65

539. Uslar Pietri, Arturo. BELLO EL VENEZOLANO [Bello the Venezuelan]. *Rev. Nac. de Cultura [Venezuela] 1982 43(249): 51-66.* In 1802, Andrés Bello received recognition of his intellectual ability in his appointment as a colonial official of the region. That position brought Bello into contact with events throughout Venezuela and Europe. In 1810, with Simón Bolívar and Luis Méndez, he left for England to seek support for independence. Bello interpreted his mission as that of serving the American continent by bringing to it liberty and modern civilization. 1802-10

540. Uslar Pietri, Arturo. BELLO, EL VENEZOLANO [Bello the Venezuelan]. *Bol. de la Acad. Nac. de la Hist. [Venezuela] 1981 64(256): 811-819.* On the occasion of the bicentennial of the birth of Andrés Bello, recounts the career of the great academic, historian, and publicist from his birth to his departure to Europe, to his life in Chile. Describes his family background, education, his meeting with Alexander von Humboldt, employment in the Capitania General, his editorship of the first Caracas newspaper, and finally his appointment at the age of 28 as secretary to the mission sent to England to canvass support for the revolutionaries of 1810. 1781-1810

541. Zea, Leopoldo. EL AMERICANISMO DE BELLO [Bello's Americanism]. *Rev. Nac. de Cultura [Venezuela] 1982 43(248): 24-40.* Although during his years in London, Andrés Bello assimilated the culture of Europe, he did not impose that culture on the new American reality. He considered that neither Europe nor the United States could resolve the unique problems of South America. Bello repudiated Spanish colonial dominion. However, he did not reject the heritage of Iberian vigor and values which he believed to have supplied the impetus and spirit of the struggle for liberation. Primary sources; 7 notes. 19c

542. —. BICENTENARIO DEL NACIMIENTO DE DON ANDRES BELLO [Bicentennial of the birth of Andrés Bello]. *Bol. de la Acad. Argentina de Letras [Argentina] 1981 46(179-182): 179-209.*

Canal Feijóo, Bernardo. PALABRAS DE APERTURA [Opening words], *pp. 179-182.* The president of the academy opens a special session to honor the memory of Andres Bello, an eminent figure in the history of Latin American culture.

Risolía, Marco Aurelio. ANDRES BELLO JURISTA: SU GRAVITACION EN NUESTRA LEGISLACION CIVIL [Andrés Bello, jurist: his influence on our civil legislation], *pp. 183-193.* Describes Bello's role in compiling the Argentine civil code as well as the Chilean.

Barba, Enrique M. ANDRES BELLO HISTORIADOR [Andrés Bello, historian], *pp. 195-204.* Though born in

Spain, Bello was the creator of the Chilean historical school.

Ghiano, Juan Carlos. VIGENCIA DE ANDRES BELLO [Permanence of Andrés Bello], *pp. 205-209.* This jurist and historian, example of a modern humanist, continues to teach his truths and his scientific methods through the transparency of his didactic prose and the poems of his maturity. 1781-1865

543. —. BICENTENARIO DEL NACIMIENTO DE DON ANDRES BELLO [Bicentennial of the birth of Don Andrés Bello]. *Bol. de Hist. y Antigüedades [Colombia] 1981 68(735): 977-1028.*

Mier, José M. de. DISERTACION SOBRE ANDRES BELLO [Dissertation on Andrés Bello], *pp. 978-985.* Biographical note with special emphasis on Bello's influence in Colombia.

Balmes Arteaga, Enrique. EL CODIGO DE BELLO EN COLOMBIA [Bello's law code in Colombia], *pp. 1001-1028.* After independence Colombia continued observing Spanish legislation save where expressly superseded or incompatible with republican principles. Early codification projects had no practical effect. New republican legislation continually added to the existing body of law, but private law underwent few changes. Starting with Santander in 1858, one state after another adopted modified versions of the Chilean code drafted by Andrés Bello (1781-1865). The federal government in 1873 issued its own version for territories under national jurisdiction, which in turn was extended to the entire nation in 1887. Additional changes in civil law since then have preserved the original code's defense of property rights and the family, but with modernization of details. Includes also various tributes to the Venezuelan-born publicist, diplomat, and scholar, who eventually settled in Chile. Biblio. 19c

Belloc, Hilaire

544. McCarthy, John P. THE HISTORICAL VISION OF CHESTERBELLOC. *Modern Age 1982 26(2): 175-182.* G. K. Chesterton and Hilaire Belloc came of age in a world torn between the realpolitik of authoritarian regimes and revolutionary skepticism. Chesterton was a radical liberal democrat whose democratic radicalism emerged as conservatism in his pleas to return to roots or first principles. His philosophical and psychological perspective was transformed into a complete historical vision by contact with Belloc. The most celebrated statement of Belloc's historical vision is his *Europe and the Faith,* in which he argues that Catholicism engendered certain values in the people of Europe from which their civilization developed. To the degree that Europe becomes less Christian, the less it remains a distinct civilization. The Chesterbelloc view of history interprets past and future by reference to ideological and cultural challenges to the Church. Based on the writings of Chesterton and Belloc; 25 notes. 1900-40

Beloborodov, Atanasi P.

545. Rudenko, S. GENERAL ARMII A. P. BELOBORODOV (K 80-LETIIU SO DNIA ROZHDENIIA) [Army General A. P. Beloborodov: on the 80th anniversary of his birth]. *Voenno-Istoricheskii Zhurnal [USSR] 1983 (1): 93-96.* Atanasi P. Beloborodov joined the Red Army when he was 16 years old and fought in the Civil War. After graduation from the Frunze military academy in 1936 he served in the Far East. His military talent flowered during the 1941-45 war when he commanded first a division, then a corps, and finally a number of armies. In the postwar period he held a number of responsible posts, including that of head of the Main Personnel Administration of the USSR Defense Ministry. Since 1968 he has been adviser to the ministry. Based on secondary sources; 2 notes, 2 photos. 1918-82

Belov, Avraham

546. Belov, Avraham. MISHPAT EICHMANN B-MOSKVA (SKIRA TIODIT-EPISTOLARIT) [The Eichman trial in Moscow (a documentary-epistolary survey)]. *Shvut [Israel] 1981 8: 99-107.* In 1962 the Soviet government contracted with the author to produce a book for the legal publishing house Gosiurizdat on the trial of Adolf Eichmann in Jerusalem. A publishing schedule was set and 60,000 copies were to have been printed. Just before the book went to press, the Communist leadership suppressed publication on the grounds that publication would be harmful to the state. Belov was not paid the full fee. He took the payment issue through the Soviet judicial system and finally prevailed at his third appearance before the RSFSR Supreme Court. The book has not yet been published. Based on the author's correspondence with various agencies of the Soviet government; 5 notes. 1962-66

Belov, Ivan

547. —. KOMANDARM 1 RANGA I. P. BELOV [Commander of the army of the first rank I. P. Belov]. *Voenno-Istoricheskii Zhurnal [USSR] 1983 (6): 94-96.* Reviews the career of Ivan Belov (1893-1938) on the 90th anniversary of his birth. Rising from birth in a poor peasant family, Belov served in the tsarist army and then distinguished himself in the revolutionary year of 1917 and during the Civil War. Thereafter he made substantial contributions to the strengthening of the defensive capacities of the USSR. Based on Soviet secondary and archival sources; photo, 6 notes. 1916-38

Belov, Mikhail I.

548. —. MIKHAIL IVANOVICH BELOV [Mikhail Ivanovich Belov]. *Voprosy Istorii [USSR] 1982 (1): 189.* Obituary of Professor Mikhail I. Belov (1916-81), a leading historian of early Russian study and settlement of Siberia, the Russian north, and the Far East. 1916-81

Beluche, Renato

549. Vargas, Francisco Alejandro. HOMENAJE AL CONTRALMIRANTE RENATO BELUCHE [Tribute to Rear Admiral Renato Beluche]. *Bol. de la Acad. Nac. de la Hist. [Venezuela] 1981 64(254): 335-343.* Renato Beluche (1780-1860) was born in New Orleans of French and Italian ancestry. He fought in the French revolutionary wars and was awarded the Legion of Honor in 1802. Returning to North America, he was captain of a ship that sailed in the service of Napoleon. In 1814 he was among the 3,283 defenders of New Orleans against a besieging army of 15,000 British soldiers. He then sailed to the Caribbean and joined the forces of Simón Bolívar in the war of independence of the Spanish colonies. Plate of the Beluche family coat of arms. 1780-1860

Bely, Andrei

550. Malmstad, John E. BELYI: A CENTENARY UNOBSERVED. *Slavic Rev. 1983 42(2): 266-271.* Presents an overview of Andrei Bely's (1880-1934) career and accomplishments within the perspective of Russian symbolism. 1904-81

Ben-Chorin, Shalom

551. Barkenings, Hans-Joachim. LEONHARD RAGAZ UND SCHALOM BEN-CHORIN: ZUR FRÜHGESCHICHTE DES CHRISTLICH-JÜDISCHEN DIALOGS [Leonhard Ragaz and Shalom Ben-Chorin: the early history of the Christian-Jewish dialogue]. *Zeits. für Religions- und Geistesgeschichte [West Germany] 1982 34(1): 46-70.* Noteworthy among the earlier Christian-Jewish dialogues is the one carried out from 1930 to 1945 between the Swiss religious socialist Leonhard Ragaz and Shalom Ben-Chorin. The latter, an author and poet, was born Fritz Rosenthal in Germany and took the Jewish name after he moved to Palestine in 1935. On the spiritual plane, Martin Buber was the person with whom Ragaz exchanged ideas, while Ben-Chorin represented a multifarious, more personal contact. Their exchange of letters, introduced in chronological order and with comments, widened Ragaz's perspectives and gave him new insights with which to further and develop the Christian-Jewish dialogue and relationship. 1930-45

Bendeliani, Chichiko Kaisarovich

552. —. GEROI STALINGRADSKOI BITVY [Heroes of the battle of Stalingrad]. *Voenno-Istoricheskii Zhurnal [USSR] 1982 (9): 42-45.* 1942-43
*For abstract see **Bashkirov, Viacheslav Filippovich***

Benderev, Anastas

553. Shalaverova, Mariia and Vulkov, Georgi. ANASTAS BENDEREV KATO VOENEN ISTORIK [Anastas Benderev as military historian]. *Istoricheski Pregled [Bulgaria] 1981 37(1): 73-81.* Examines the career of Anastas Benderev (1859-1946). Benderev was born in Gorna Oriakhovitsa in central Bulgaria and lived through the period of liberation, development of capitalism, and the beginning of socialism. A career officer, he served in both the Bulgarian and Russian armies. His historical works deal with the Bulgarian war of liberation (1877-78), the Serbo-Bulgarian War, and the Macedonian revolutionary movement. Based on the works of Benderev, some archival material, and secondary works. 1877-1946

Bendigo

See Thompson, William

Benditer, Janeta

554. Saizu, I. JANETA BENDITER [Janeta Benditer]. *Anuarul Institutului de Istorie şi Arheologie "A. D. Xenopol" [Romania] 1981 18: 863.* Janeta Benditer (1917-80) studied at Iaşi and in Moscow. She was in turn lecturer and professor of history at Iaşi, 1952-75. At the A. D. Xenopol Institute she was responsible for contemporary history. Her published work covered Xenopol himself and the institute named after him, but mainly German, English, and Italian politics as they affected Romania from the 1920's to 1947. 1920's-80

Benedictsson, Victoria

555. Moberg, Verne. "The Truth and Work of Victoria Benedictsson: Levels of Reality in Her Writing Life." U. of Wisconsin, Madison 1984. 305 pp. *DAI 1985 45(10): 3139-A.* DA8417968 1870's-88

Benedikt, Heinrich

556. Stourzh, Gerald. HEINRICH BENEDIKT (1886-1981). *Austrian Hist. Y. 1981-82 17-18: 579-580.* Born in Vienna in 1886, Heinrich Benedikt became a lawyer and businessman with an interest in history, writing several works in the 1920's. He did not begin his academic career until 1947 at the age of 61. Among his published works are *Die Friedensaktion der Meinl-Gruppe 1917/18* (1962), *Als Belgien Österreichish War* (1965) and *Die Monarchie des Hauses Österreich* (1968). Note. 1920's-81

Beneš, Eduard

557. Bruegel, J. W. DR. BENEŠ ON HIS POSITION AFTER FEBRUARY, 1948. *East Central Europe 1981 8(1-2): 103-105.* Conversations between Eduard Beneš of Czechoslovakia and British diplomats reveal that in 1948 before the Communist coup President Beneš was optimistic about the possibility of preserving a democratic state; after the coup he blamed himself and his ministers for not comprehending the extent of the Communist plot. Based mostly on communications from British Ambassador Dixon to Foreign Minister Bevin in the Public Record Office, London; 5 notes. 1948

558. Hochman, Jiří; Anderle, Josef (commentary). PRESIDENT EDUARD BENEŠ AND THE SOVIET ALLIANCE. *Kosmas 1986 5(1): 15-23.* Though President Eduard Beneš perceived the failure of the Czechoslovak-Soviet defensive pact of 1935 to save Czechoslovakia in 1938, he resorted to another alliance with the USSR in 1943, in hopes of restoring a Czechoslovak nation-state after World War II. Comments, pp. 35-53. 1934-43

Ben-Gurion, David

559. Ben-Aharon, Yizhak. REMEMBERING BEN-GURION. *Jerusalem Q. [Israel] 1980 (16): 40-53.* Israeli political leader Yizhak Ben-Aharon gives his personal recollections of David Ben-Gurion from their initial meeting in 1924 to Ben-Gurion's death in 1973. 1924-73 -Gurion

560. Tzahor, Zeev. DAVID BEN-GURION: FROM SOCIALISM TO STATEHOOD. *Midstream 1986 32(1): 36-38.* Profiles David Ben-Gurion (1886-1973) throughout his political life. 1900-63

Beni, Paolo

561. Diffley, Paul B. A NOTE ON PAOLO BENI'S BIRTHPLACE. *Studi Secenteschi [Italy] 1983 24: 51-56.* Disproves the notion that poet Paolo Beni (d. 1625) was born in Greece; he was a native of Italy. 16 notes. Italian summary. 16c-17c

Benjamin, Walter

562. Bewell, Alan J. PORTRAITS AT GREYFRIARS: PHOTOGRAPHY, HISTORY, AND MEMORY IN WALTER BENJAMIN. *Clio 1982 12(1): 17-29.* For Walter Benjamin (1892-1940) photography, historical reflection, and memory shared the same "image-space" provided by 19th-century cities like Paris, London, and Berlin. In *A Short History of Photography* (1931), Benjamin argued that these cities provided images that allowed the historian to reconstruct the past. 31 notes. 19c

563. Mandalari, Maria Teresa. WALTER BENJAMIN: L'AMICIZIA CON GERSHOM SCHOLEM E L'ANGELO DI KLEE [Walter Benjamin: his friendship with Gershom Scholem and Klee's angel]. *Belfagor [Italy] 1982 37(1): 55-73.* Scholem's friendship for Benjamin was deep but not always very insightful, and there were serious ideological differences between them; Klee's watercolor of the *Angelus Novus* accompanied Benjamin for most of his life and was the subject of some of his profound meditations.
1920's-30's

564. Scholem, Gershom. AHNEN UND VERWANDTE WALTER BENJAMINS [Ancestors and relatives of Walter Benjamin]. *Bull. des Leo Baeck Inst. [Israel] 1982 (61): 29-55.* Adds to previous studies of the ancestors and relatives of Walter Benjamin using new source material. He has divided his study into three parts: the father's ancestors; the mother's ancestors; and other relatives. German Jewish family and daily life are a continuing part of this investigation.
18c-1940

565. Scholem, Gershom. MY FRIEND WALTER BENJAMIN. *Commentary 1981 72(6): 58-69.* A memoir of literary critic Walter Benjamin (1892-1940). 1916-40

Benjedid, Chadli

566. Mortimer, Robert A. THE POLITICS OF REASSURANCE IN ALGERIA. *Current History 1985 84(502): 201-204, 228-229.* Algeria's President Chadli Benjedid, in contrast to his radical and aggressive predecessor Houari Boumedienne, practiced a policy of moderate reform at home while seeking to reassure and conciliate Algeria's neighbors.
1982-84

Benkovski, Georgi

567. Spasov, Liudmil. GEORGI BENKOVSKI I UZSTANOVLIAVANETO NA BULGARSKATA DURZHAVNOST [Georgi Benkovski and the rise of the Bulgarian state]. *Istoricheski Pregled [Bulgaria] 1982 38(1): 21-29.* Discusses Georgi Benkovski who has been regarded as a dictator, adventurer, firebrand, and revolutionary democrat. His Romanian travels, education, and discussions on German social democracy and the Paris Commune show that he had a coherent revolutionary ideology. He understood that Bulgaria had to be liberated from Turkish oppression, probably with Russian help. Benkovski sought a republic based on communal principles, national equality, and religious freedom. His ideas emphasized egalitarian socialism and complemented his basic democratic revolutionary aims. 57 notes.
1870-76

Bennett, Arnold

568. Zarzana, James A. "Arnold Bennett Reconsidered: His Literary Theories and Fiction." U. of Notre Dame 1985. 199 pp. *DAI 1985 46(4): 991-A.* DA8513503
1890's-1931

Benoist-Méchin, Jacques

569. Florenne, Yves. OMBRES POUR UN PORTRAIT [Background for a portrait]. *Rev. des Deux Mondes [France] 1983 (7): 102-104.* Recounts the role of Jacques Benoist-Méchin as a minister of the Vichy regime and attaché to the Nazis during the German occupation. 1940's

Benso, Camillo

See Cauour, Conte di

Benson, Bobby

570. Omibiyi-Obidike, M. A. BOBBY BENSON: THE ENTERTAINER-MUSICIAN. *Nigeria Magazine [Nigeria] 1983 (147): 18-27.* Bernard Olabanji Shobowale Benson (1921-83), Nigerian musician, performer, and teacher, introduced new forms of Western-style popular entertainment into Nigeria beginning in the 1940's. He remained a leading cultural figure in his country until his tragic death.
1940's-83

Bentham, Jeremy

571. Crimmins, James E. BENTHAM ON RELIGION: ATHEISM AND THE SECULAR SOCIETY. *Journal of the History of Ideas 1986 47(1): 95-111.* Between 1809 and 1823, Jeremy Bentham undertook an extensive examination and critique of the development and nature of religion. Basically, he wished to extirpate it from the civilization of the future, a future that would be influenced by the stridently secular social science of his Utilitarian followers. In his lifelong hostility toward religion, his views were shaped by reading the French philosophes, especially Helvetius and Holbach. 51 notes. 1770's-1820's

572. Rosen, Frederick. JEREMY BENTHAM: RECENT INTERPRETATIONS. *Pol. Studies [Great Britain] 1982 30(4): 575-581.* Reviews recent works that provide new insights into the life and thought of the English philosopher, jurist, political theorist, and founder of utilitarianism, Jeremy Bentham (1748-1832). Much of this work has been indebted in one way or another to the Bentham Project associated with University College, London. The reviewer concentrates on publications connected with Bentham's concept of liberty, his theory of constitutional democracy, his radicalism and liberalism, his jurisprudence, and the influence of H. L. A. Hart on the revival of interest in Bentham's philosophy of law. Among the works referred to are three volumes of Bentham's *Collected Works* edited by J. Burns and H. L. A. Hart (1970-77), Douglas Long's *Bentham and Liberty* (1977), L. J. Hume's *Bentham and Bureaucracy* (1981), and David Lyons's *In the Interest of the Governed, A Study in Bentham's Philosophy of Utility and Law* (1973). Secondary sources; 32 notes. 1768-1832

573. Taylor, Brian W. THE HERMIT OF QUEEN'S SQUARE PLACE? *Vitae Scholasticae 1984 4[i.e., 3](2): 461-475.* Jeremy Bentham referred to himself as the "Hermit of Queen's Square Place," and this became a popularly held image in the works of John Bowring, a Bentham biographer. The hermit image is refuted through the use of the diaries and manuscript autobiography of George Bentham, Jeremy's nephew and close collaborator in his writings. Bowring does not mention George Bentham in any of his works. George Bentham was suspicious of Bowring's influence over Jeremy Bentham, and both were hostile toward each other. Lengthy litigation developed. Concludes that there is insufficient evidence to say that Jeremy Bentham was a hermit. 54 notes.
1826-42

Bentham, Samuel

574. Morriss, R. A. SAMUEL BENTHAM AND THE MANAGEMENT OF THE ROYAL DOCKYARDS, 1796-1807. *Bull. of the Inst. of Hist. Res. [Great Britain] 1981 54(130): 226-240.* Discusses the achievements of Samuel Bentham, inspector general of naval works, 1796-1807, where he was responsible for improvements in the facilities and management of the royal dockyards at Deptford, Woolwich, Chatham, Sheerness, Portsmouth, and Plymouth. Examines the immediate impact of his work, particularly as it affected

the navy board and assesses the influence it had on dockyard management in the 19th century. Bentham did much to introduce the latest technological and administrative ideas, including his own concept of individual responsibility in government departments, and was a formative influence in public and naval administration. 80 notes. 1796-1807

Bentley, Thomas

575. Andrews, Gail C. THE DWIGHT AND LUCILLE BEESON COLLECTION OF WEDGWOOD IN THE BIRMINGHAM MUSEUM OF ART. *Mag. Antiques 1983 123(6): 1200-1209.* Discusses the careers and partnership of ceramic artists Josiah Wedgwood and Thomas Bentley from 1769 to 1780, and the Beeson collection of Wedgwood in the Birmingham Museum of Art. 1769-80

Benvenisti, Meron

576. Zureik, Elia T. BENVENISTI'S PALESTINE PROJECT. *Journal of Palestine Studies 1984 14(1): 91-105.* Meron Benvenisti became the administrator in charge of the Arab sections of East Jerusalem after the Israeli capture of them in 1967, and he has since written on the topic, defending his actions, and published data on such controversial matters as the demolition of Arab homes. While Benvenisti claims to be understanding of and sympathetic to the plight of the Palestinians, a careful review of his data and conclusions regarding land confiscation, the economy, and demographics reveals that his data are incomplete and biased. Benvenisti's conclusions, and the UN reports that promote them, are inaccurate and damaging to the Palestinian people. Based in part on UN reports and other primary and secondary sources; table, 25 notes. 1967-85

Benyovszky, Móric

577. Lugosi, Győző. BENYOVSZKY MÓRIC MADAGASZKÁRON—"AUTOLEGENDA" ÉS VALÓSÁG [Móric Benyovszky in Madagascar—autobiography and truth]. *Századok [Hungary] 1984 118(2): 361-390.* Investigates the career of Count Móric Benyovszky (1741-86), Hungarian adventurer, traveler, and writer. According to his *Memoirs and Travels* (1781-84), he claims to have colonized Madagascar on behalf of the French crown and was later sought by its inhabitants to be their king. The accomplishments claimed by Benyovszky, including his exploits in Madagascar, are clearly of a spurious nature. 82 notes. 1774-86

Beonio-Brocchieri, Vittorio

578. Colombo, Arturo. DALLA STORIA DELLE DOTTRINE POLITICHE ALLA DOTTRINA POLITICA DELLA STORIA [From the history of political doctrines to the political doctrine of history]. *Politico [Italy] 1979 44(2): 361-367.* Pays tribute to Vittorio Beonio Brocchieri (1902-79), emeritus professor of political science at the University of Pavia. At the age of 24 he was charged with the organization of a new academic discipline, the history of political theory. He thought the historical process could not be understood merely as a panorama of crimes and misfortunes but as the play of alternative factors dialectically opposed and at the same time dialectically necessary. 32 notes. 1902-79

Berchtold, Leopold

579. Wondrák, Eduard. LEOPOLD BERCHTOLD (1759-1809) UND DIE ANFÄNGE DER BERUFSHYGIENE UND UNFALLVERHÜTUNG [Leopold Berchtold (1759-1809) and the beginning of a system of worker's hygiene and accident prevention]. *Clio Medica [Netherlands] 1984 19(1-2): 73-80.* Graf Leopold Berchtold (1759-1809), born into great wealth in South Bohemia, traveled widely and studied medicine and hygiene with the aim of helping the lower classes. He wrote *A Handbook on Health Hazards for Craftsmen.* He converted his castle into a hospital and established a nearby cloth factory with excellent hygienic facilities to provide humble people with work in a good environment. For his good work he was referred to as the "philanthropist." 6 notes. 1780's-1809

Bereday, George

580. Brickman, William W. GEORGE ZYGMUNT FIJALKOWSKI BEREDAY, 1920-1983. *Slavic Rev. 1984 43(1): 182.* Provides an obituary of George Bereday, a leading historian of comparative education and Soviet education. 1920-83

Beresford, Maurice

581. Beresford, Maurice. FORTY YEARS IN THE FIELD. *Historian [Great Britain] 1985 (6): 3-8.* Autobiographical account by British geographer and historian Maurice Beresford of his work on medieval villages and agricultural practices, and of the significant part chance events played in this research. 13c-16c

Bergenheim, Edvard

582. Tiensuu, K. "Edvard Bergenheim: Tominta Koulumiehenä ja Arkkipiispana Vuoteen 1863" [Edvard Bergenheim: educator and archbishop (to 1863)]. Helsinki U. [Finland] 1985. 432 pp. *DAI-C 1986 47(1): 24; 47/116c.* 1820's-63

Berger, Johann Christoph

583. Nováková, Julie. DVA KOMENIOLOGICKÉ DODATKY [Two addenda to Comenius studies]. *Studia Comeniana et Historica [Czechoslovakia] 1984 14(28): 76-84.* 1632-67

For abstract see ***Comenius, John Amos***

Berger, Napoleon

584. Gamby, Erik. NAPOLEON BERGER ALIAS GUSTAF ÖBOM. *Swedish-American Hist. Q. 1983 34(1): 4-31.* Details the life of Napoleon Berger, a Swedish radical who was forced to leave his native country in the 1830's during the reign of Bernadotte. Although rumored to have died, Berger assumed the name of Öbom and wandered through Europe participating in Poland's futile war of liberation from Russia, and eventually settling in Switzerland. From 1839 to 1850, when he was forced to leave that country, Öbom was involved with the Workers' Association in Bern. Arriving in New York, he remained there until his death in 1881. He first published *Skandinaven i Amerika* (1851-53); 10 years later he started another newspaper, *Skandinavisk Post,* which lasted considerably longer. Based on archival materials of the Bern Workers' Association, Bern, Bundesarchiv: Justiz Flüchtlinge; 3 fig., 49 notes. 1834-81

Bergerac, Cyrano de

585. Nierenberg, W. A. CYRANO, PHYSICIST. *Proceedings of the American Philosophical Society 1986 130(3): 354-361.* A survey of the contributions of Cyrano de Bergerac (1619-54) in the area of physics. His was the first physics textbook in the French language, going through 17 editions; in his *Voyage to the Moon* there are certain understandings of the law of universal gravity, including the con-

cept of center; and his writings reveal a demonstration of understanding Newton's first law of motion. 9 fig. 1650-54

Bergius, John

586. Nischan, Bodo. JOHN BERGIUS: IRENICISM AND THE BEGINNING OF OFFICIAL RELIGIOUS TOLERATION IN BRANDENBURG-PRUSSIA. *Church Hist. 1982 51(4): 389-404.* John Bergius, a religious adviser to Brandenburg's first three Reformed electors, helped shape the political configuration of early modern Europe. Bergius spoke in favor of ecumenism and toleration among Protestant sects and, as a believer in irenicism, sought to surmount divisions between Lutherans and Calvinists by emphasizing their confessional and theological agreements and minimizing their differences. Since Bergius helped formulate both the Leipzig Protocol of 1631 and the Thorn Declaration of 1645, he played a leading role in defining the official position of Brandenburg's Reformed Church which contributed greatly to the development of European religious toleration. 59 notes. 1587-1658

Bergmann, Hugo

587. Sambursky, Miriam. ZIONIST UND PHILOSOPH: DAS HABILITIERUNGSPROBLEM DES JUNGEN HUGO BERGMANN [Zionist and philosopher: training of young Hugo Bergmann for university teaching]. *Bull. des Leo Baeck Inst. [Israel] 1981 (58): 16-40.* Describes the intellectual development of Hugo Bergmann (1883-1975) from his early years in Prague, where he first became interested in Zionism, studied philosophy at the German University of Prague (where he wrote a doctoral dissertation on the philosophical aspects of the history of the development of atomic theory), came under the influence of his friend and teacher Franz Clemens Brentano, and concluded by the time of the outbreak of World War I that the future for German Jews lay in Palestine. Excerpts from nine of Bergmann's letters; 28 notes. 1901-14

Bering, Vitus

588. Iakimenko, N. A. FLOTA KAPITAN VITUS BERING [Fleet captain Vitus Bering]. *Voprosy Istorii [USSR] 1981 (10): 171-175.* The Dane Vitus Bering came to Russia in 1703 and became an officer of the Russian Fleet, leading the 1725 expedition—the 1st Kamchatka Expedition—to the North Sea to explore the area between Asia and America. A second Kamchatka expedition in 1733 was also led by Bering, but he died in 1741 on an island later named after him before the conclusion of the expedition. Officially, the Bering expedition completed its work in 1743, but some continued working until 1748, producing extensive and detailed maps of the area. Primary sources; 40 notes. 1703-48

589. Projorenko, Eduard. BERING: UN PIONERO DEL POLO NORTE [Bering: a pioneer of the North Pole]. *Folia Humanística [Spain] 1982 20(237): 637-640.* Discusses the expeditions of Vitus Bering to the North Pole, and his contributions to exploration and discovery. 1703-41

Beritashvili, Ivan S.

590. Grigor'ian, Nora Andreevna. NOVYE SVIDETEL'STVA O ZHIZNI I TVORCHESTVE AKADEMIKA I. S. BERITASHVILI [New documentary evidence regarding the life and work of Academician I. S. Beritashvili]. *Voprosy Istorii Estestvoznaniia i Tekhniki [USSR] 1985 (1): 96-108.* The contents of 37 letters written to each other between 1911 and 1929 by Russian physiologists Nikolai Evgen'evich Vvedenski and Aleksandr Filippovich Samoilov and their pupil, physiologist and future Soviet Academy of Sciences member Ivan Solomonovich Beritashvili (Beritov) (1885-1974) revealed a long-lasting friendship between Beritashvili and Samoilov as well as a feud between Vvedenski and Beritashvili which influenced the latter's career. Beritashvili's 1911-12 research on strong galvanometry in Samoilov's Kazan' laboratory was the start of a long and friendly correspondence. Meanwhile, friction between Beritashvili and Vvedenski, caused in part by Beritashvili's refusal to espouse Vvedenski's concept of parabiosis, influenced Vvedenski to deny Beritashvili funding and prevent consideration of his doctoral thesis at Petersburg University in 1916. Archives, scientific papers, and secondary sources; 3 photos, 1 autograph, 3 notes, 13 ref. 1911-29

Berkeley, George

591. Meattini, Valerio. BERKELEY E L'ITALIA [Berkeley and Italy]. *Critica Storica [Italy] 1982 19(1): 3-21.* A volume of travel notes of the Irish archbishop and philosopher George Berkeley (1685-1753), recently published in Italy as *Viaggio in Italia* (1979), sheds light on his rich personality and on Italian affairs of the early 18th century. Berkeley traveled to Italy in 1714 as chaplain to the British envoy to the coronation of Amadeo II of Savoy as king of Sicily, and again in 1716-20 in the retinue of George Ashe, son of the bishop of Clogher and vice chancellor of the University of Dublin. 47 notes. 1714-20

592. Stewart, M. A. BERKELEY AND THE RANKENIAN CLUB. *Hermathena [Ireland] 1985 (139): 25-45.* Traces George Berkeley's (1685-1753) membership in the Edinburgh Rankenian Club, which initially consisted of young professional trainees and constituted a forum for radical new ideas in religion and politics; includes sketches of eight members of the club connected with Berkeley. 18c

Berlioz, Hector

593. Chailley, Jacques. BERLIOZ ET WAGNER [Berlioz and Wagner]. *U. of Ottawa Q. [Canada] 1982 52(3): 302-315.* Argues that the popular perception of the relationship between composers Hector Berlioz and Richard Wagner as one of unremittant churlish jealousy is based on a few acid phrases endlessly quoted out of context. Had not journalists, friends, women, and circumstances prevented it, the admiration that the two masters discovered for each other while conducting rival symphony orchestras in London might have had a chance to flourish. Berlioz's position as a music critic, his desire for success as an operatic composer, and the growing popularity of Wagner's "music of the future" created tensions which were exacerbated by individuals like Marie Recio, and which later biographers and critics have related at length. 16 caricatures. 1839-60

Bermúdez, José Francisco

594. Armas Chitty, J. A. de. JOSE FRANCISCO BERMUDEZ [José Francisco Bermúdez]. *Bol. de la Acad. Nac. de la Hist. [Venezuela] 1982 65(258): 325-330.* A speech delivered at the National Pantheon on the occasion of the bicentennial of the birth of General Bermúdez (1782-1831), who took part in many battles during the war of independence. His military activities and relations with the great liberator, Simón Bolívar, are recalled. 1815-31

595. Pérez Peñuela, Eleazar. DOS SIGLOS DEL NACIMIENTO DEL GENERAL BERMUDEZ [Two centuries since the birth of General Bermúdez]. *Rev. de la Soc. Bolivariana de Venezuela [Venezuela] 1982 39(133): 27-30.*

Presents a brief biography of José Francisco Bermúdez, hero of the Venezuelan War of Independence, and notes other studies that examine the general's life. 1780-1831

Bernácer, Germán

596. Almenar, Salvador. CONTRA LA CORRIENTE: GERMAN BERNACER (1883-1965) [Against the current: Germán Bernácer (1883-1965)]. *Rev. de Hist. Econ. [Spain] 1983 1(1): 153-159.* Bernácer was a teacher of physics and chemistry who in his late twenties resolved to devote himself to the study of economics and social problems. His studies on money and business crises were developed in confrontation with other theories and are said to have influenced economists like Keynes, Robertson, and others. Biblio. 1883-1965

Bernal Medina, Rafael

597. Ramírez Sánchez, Ignacio. RAFAEL BERNAL MEDINA, UNA LLAMA QUE PERDURA [Rafael Bernal Medina, a flame that endures]. *Bol. de Hist. y Antigüedades [Colombia] 1981 68(734): 823-827.* Tribute to the Colombian educator and historian Rafael Bernal Medina (1914-79). 1914-79

Bernanos, Georges

598. Lafaye, Jean-Jacques; Norris, Colin J., transl. STEFAN ZWEIG AND GEORGES BERNANOS IN THE NEW WORLD. *Cultures [France] 1982 8(1): 51-63.* Describes the differing exiles of Georges Bernanos and Stefan Zweig who met only once, at Bernano's home in Brazil. 1936-48

Bernard, Catherine

599. Plusquellec, Catherine. QUI ETAIT CATHERINE BERNARD? [Who was Catherine Bernard?]. *Revue d'Histoire Littéraire de la France [France] 1985 85(4): 667-669.* From the few surviving documents concerning the life of Catherine Bernard, a late 17th-century French writer, conjectures that she was born into a Protestant family in Rouen in the 1650's, converted to Catholicism as an adult, and may have died in 1712 after an honorable career in letters. 1650-1712

Bernard, James

600. Claeys, Gregory. A UTOPIAN TORY REVOLUTIONARY AT CAMBRIDGE: THE POLITICAL IDEAS AND SCHEMES OF JAMES BERNARD, 1834-1839. *Hist. J. [Great Britain] 1982 25(3): 583-603.* During the most public segment of his career, James Bernard (1785-1839) sought to destroy the influence of the financial and manufacturing classes in national life and to restore rule by a strong elective monarchy and landed aristocracy. Realizing that this could only succeed with the aid of the manufacturing working classes, he sought allies in Robert Owen and his followers and various London radicals. This unique appeal by the landed classes to the working class found some favor with the Owenites, both in allying classes to usher in their new moral world, and in reconciling the principles of aristocracy and democracy. The radical wing of the farmers' movement died with Bernard, but he remains interesting as an independent thinker trying to bridge the gap between Toryism and radicalism. Based on Bernard's writings, radical newspapers, and other printed sources; 65 notes. 1834-39

Bernardo Herrada, José

601. VanYoung, Eric. MILLENNIUM ON THE NORTHERN MARCHES: THE MAD MESSIAH OF DURANGO AND POPULAR REBELLION IN MEXICO, 1800-1815. *Comparative Studies in Society and History [Great Britain] 1986 28(3): 385-413.* The beliefs and activities of José Bernardo Herrada (also known as José Silvestre Sariñana), the mad messiah of Durango, 1800-01, played a role in the revolutionary movement of 1811-12 that led to eventual Mexican independence. His influence was especially prevalent among the Indians that supported the rebel forces of Father Miguel Hidalgo (1753-1811). Based on Mexican archival sources concerning the investigation and trial of Herrada; 59 notes. 1800-15

Bernáth, Aurél

602. Frank, János. THE AURÉL BERNÁTH EXHIBITION: COMMEMORATING A LIFE IN ART. *New Hungarian Quarterly [Hungary] 1985 26(100): 227-230.* The Ernst Museum in Budapest held a retrospective exhibition of the works of Aurél Bernáth (b. 1895) in 1985, on the occasion of the Hungarian artist's 90th birthday. 6 illus. 20c

Berneri, Camillo

603. Olivari, Michele. L'AZIONE POLITICA DI CAMILLO BERNERI NELLA GUERRA CIVILE SPAGNOLA [Camillo Berneri's political activity in the Spanish Civil War]. *Critica Storica [Italy] 1982 19(2): 214-242.* The noted anarchist theorist took an active part in the Spanish Civil War from July 1936 to May 1937, when he was assassinated. He had a significant role in the debates that divided the ranks of the republicans. Examines the positions he defended as a journalist in the ideological struggles of the war. 124 notes. 1936-37

Bernhardt, Sarah

604. Hibbert, Christopher. SARAH BERNHARDT'S PARIS. *Mankind 1982 7(1): 6-13, 37-43.* At age 18, Sarah Bernhardt began her acting career in Paris in an 1862 production of Jean Racine's *Iphigenie.* She soon gained a reputation as a temperamental actress with no particular talent. It was not until 1868 that she became a highly regarded performer. During her long, illustrious career she associated with numerous French political and cultural leaders including Prince Napoleon III, Leon Gambetta (who eventually became President of the Chamber of Deputies), novelist George Sand, Victor Hugo, and Gustave Flaubert. Bernhardt witnessed some of the most momentous events of French history: the Franco-Prussian War, the fall of Napoleon III, the Dreyfus affair, the Universal Exhibition of 1889 and the building of Gustave Eiffel's tower, and World War I. She performed almost until the day of her death, 26 May 1923. 9 photos, 9 illus. 1862-1923

605. Tumbleson, Treva Rose. "Three Female Hamlets: Charlotte Cushman, Sarah Bernhardt and Eva La Gallienne." U. of Oregon 1981. 343 pp. *DAI 1982 42(8): 3349-A.* 8201871 19c

Bernheim, Franz

606. Brugel, J. W. THE BERNHEIM PETITION: A CHALLENGE TO NAZI GERMANY IN 1933. *Patterns of Prejudice [Great Britain] 1983 17(3): 17-25.* Files of the German Foreign Ministry have recently disclosed that, in 1933, Franz Bernheim, a Jewish refugee from Germany, successfully sued the German government before the League of

Nations and was successful in gaining protection, until 1937, for 10,000 Jews in Upper Silesia from Hitler's anti-Semitic policies. 1933

Bernier, François

607. Auboyer, Jeannine. VOYAGE DANS L'INDE MOGHOLE [A voyage in Mogul India]. *Histoire [France] 1984 (70): 64-73.* Relates the voyage of François Bernier (1620-88), a Frenchman who was the guest and physician of Emperor 'Ālamgīr (1618-1707) and the precursor of orientalism. 1658-69

Bernini, Gianlorenzo

608. Soussloff, Catherine Maria. "Critical *Topoi* in the Sources on the Life of Gianlorenzo Bernini." Bryn Mawr Coll. 1982. 248 pp. *DAI 1983 44(1): 6-A.* DA8304639 1623-80

Bernis, François Joachim de Pierre de

609. Martin, Jacques. LE CARDINAL DE BERNIS, AMBASSADEUR [Cardinal de Bernis, ambassador]. *Rev. des Deux Mondes [France] 1982 (8): 350-363, (10): 28-40.* Parts 1-2. Discusses the career of Cardinal François Joachim de Pierre de Bernis (1704-94) to 1763 as a belletrist, member of the Académie Française, and ambassador under Louis XV. Bernis's *Mémoires* are a valuable account of the origin of the Austrian alliance and the beginnings of the Seven Years War. 1724-63

Bernoulli, Daniel

610. Grigor'ian, Ashot T. and Kovalev, Boris D. DANIIL BERNULLI [Daniel Bernoulli]. *Voprosy Istorii Estestvoznaniia i Tekhniki [USSR] 1982 (1): 108-112.* In 1725, Swiss mathematician Daniel Bernoulli was invited by Peter I to St. Petersburg to head the department of mathematics at the newly established Academy of Sciences. Fifteen of Bernoulli's 75 published works were written during his eight-year stay in Russia. These included the first draft of his *Hydrodynamica* (1738), which is preserved in the manuscript collection of the Academy of Sciences, USSR. 3 notes. 1700-82

611. Ozhigova, E. P. O PEREPISKE DANIILA BERNULLI S NIKOLAEM FUSSOM [Daniel Bernoulli's correspondence with Nikolaus Fuss]. *Voprosy Istorii Estestvoznaniia i Tekhniki [USSR] 1981 (1): 108-115.* 1773-78

*For abstract see **Fuss, Nikolaus***

Bernshtam, Aleksandr N.

612. Zadneprovski, Iuri A. and Podol'ski, A. G. ALEKSANDR NATANOVICH BERNSHTAM: K 70-LETIIU SO DNIA ROZHDENIIA [Aleksandr Natanovich Bernshtam on his 70th birthday]. *Narody Azii i Afriki [USSR] 1981 (2): 161-168.* Describes the life of Aleksandr N. Bernshtam, Turcologist, archaeologist, and ethnographer. A member of the Soviet Academy of Sciences since 1937, his greatest contribution to Soviet studies of the Turkish peoples was to introduce Marxist analysis in place of prerevolutionary Russian chauvinism. His main interests were ethnogenesis and socioeconomic orders. He was the first Soviet scholar to examine the role of the Huns in Central Asia. His 1935 candidate dissertation, "The Socioeconomic Structure of Ancient 7th- and 8th-century Turkic Society in Turkey and Mongolia," was a classic contribution. Tribute is paid to his personal qualities. Based on Bernshtam's works and secondary sources; 15 notes. 1937-81

Bernstein, Eduard

613. Fletcher, Roger. REVISION AND MILITARISM: WAR AND PEACE IN THE PRE-1914 THOUGHT OF EDUARD BERNSTEIN. *Militärgeschichtliche Mitteilungen [West Germany] 1982 (1): 23-36.* Eduard Bernstein (1850-1932) demonstrated clear tendencies toward pacifism, diminished considerably by his patriotism, social Darwinism, and belief in the stabilizing effects of industrialization. Thus his views of militarism—never defined by him prior to 1914—as a cause of war were modified by his support for universal conscription as a democratic institution, approval of colonial wars and opposition to the virulent antimilitarism of the left wing of the Social Democratic Party. Based on published sources; 106 notes. 1900-16

614. Pachter, Henry. THE AMBIGUOUS LEGACY OF EDUARD BERNSTEIN. *Dissent 1981 28(2): 203-216.* Discusses the life and political career of Eduard Bernstein (1850-1932) and his independent interpretation of socialist theory and contribution to the development of socialism in Western Europe, particularly Germany. 1850-1932

615. Tennstedt, Florian. ARBEITERBEWEGUNG UND FAMILIENGESCHICHTE BEI EDUARD BERNSTEIN UND IGNAZ ZADEK. HILFWISSENSCHAFTLICHE MITTEILUNGEN ZU PERSÖNLICHEN ASPEKTEN VON REVISIONISMUS UND SOZIALREFORM BEI DEUTSCHEN SOZIALDEMOKRATEN [The worker movement and the family history of Eduard Bernstein and Ignaz Zadek: auxiliary scientific information on personal aspects of revisionism and social reform of German Social Democrats]. *Internationale Wissenschaftliche Korrespondenz zur Geschichte der Deutschen Arbeiterbewegung [West Germany] 1982 18(4): 451-481.* Describes the lives and prints poems, family pictures, and family trees relating to the German Social Democrats Eduard Bernstein (1850-1932) and Ignaz Zadek (1858-1931). 1850's-1930's

Berry, Duc de

See Louis XVI

Berry, Walter

616. Edel, Leon. WALTER BERRY AND THE NOVELISTS: PROUST, JAMES, AND EDITH WHARTON. *Nineteenth-Century Fiction 1984 38(4): 514-529.* Describes the career of author Walter Berry, who became an expatriate living in Paris, the nature of his friendship with Edith Wharton, and his contacts with Marcel Proust and Henry James. 1914-27

Berth, Edouard

617. Hoffman, Robert L.; Rice-Maximin, Edward (commentary). WILD SWINGS, AND OTHER ODDITIES OF POLITICAL COMMITMENT. *Proceedings of the Annual Meeting of the Western Society for French History 1983 11: 361-369.* 1900-40

*For abstract see **Andreu, Pierre***

Berthier, Louis-Alexandre

618. Scott, Samuel F.; with commentary by Paret, Peter and Rowen, Herbert. MARSHALL LOUIS-ALEXANDRE BERTHIER. *Consortium on Revolutionary Europe, 1750-1850: Proceedings 1983: 62-73.* Berthier was one of Napoleon's least capable but best educated generals. He was appointed a Marshal of the French Empire in 1804. During most of the 1780's and 1790's Berthier had served as a staff

officer under various commanders. He was an industrious and well-organized person, but he was not suited for command. His training as an engineer and his many years as a staff officer made him excellent at working with maps and papers, but indecisive and uncomfortable in the field. Comments and discussion, pp. 98-116. 18 notes. 1780-1815

Berti, Giuseppe

619. Isola, Gianni. BIBLIOGRAFIA DEGLI SCRITTI DI GIUSEPPE BERTI CON UN SAGGIO INTRODUTTIVO "GIUSEPPE BERTI FRA MEMORIA E STORIA" [Bibliography of Giuseppe Berti's writing with an introductory essay on "Giuseppe Berti between memory and history"]. *Ann. dell'Istituto Giangiacomo Feltrinelli [Italy] 1982 22: 375-414.* Giuseppe Berti (d. 1979) was an important figure in the Italian Communist Party since its inception. He took part in some of the most important events of the history of the party and was its historian. Preceded by a biographical introduction, the author provides a bibliography of Berti's writings from 1920 to his death. 61 notes, biblio. 1920-79

Bertini, Giovanni

620. Magni, Cristina. MATERIALI PER UNA BIOGRAFIA DI GIOVANNI BERTINI [Material for a biography of Giovanni Bertini]. *Bollettino dell'Archivio per la Storia del Movimento Sociale Cattolico in Italia [Italy] 1985 20(1): 118-140.* Giovanni Bertini (1878-1949), one of the founders of the Italian Popular Party (PPI) in 1918, backed social and economic reforms to benefit farmers during his career in parliament, cut short by the advent of Fascism. Includes a list of the acts of Italy's 24th, 25th, and 26th parliamentary sessions, and a bibliography of writings by and about Giovanni Bertini. 1904-49

Bertolini, Stefano

621. Simoncelli Bianchi, Maria Luisa. PROFILI DI STEFANO BERTOLINI [Profiles of Stefano Bertolini]. *Arch. Storico per le Province Parmensi [Italy] 1981 33: 47-58.* Stefano Bertolini (1711-82), inspired by the Enlightenment and especially by Montesquieu, was a historian who worked in Florence and whose scholarship was excellent. ca 1740-82

Bertrand, André-N.

622. Bolle, Pierre. PARIS ÉTÉ 40: JOURNAL D'UN PASTEUR [Paris summer of 1940: diary of a pastor]. *Bull. de la Soc. de l'Hist. du Protestantisme Français [France] 1981 127(3): 457-496.* After the government had left Paris on 10 June, 1940, Pastor André-N. Bertrand (1876-1946) remained behind. As vice president of the national council of the French Reformed Church and of the Protestant Federation of France, he took charge of Protestant affairs in Paris. Bertrand kept a diary from 10 June to 18 August, 1940, here published, somewhat edited. The diary deals with the German occupation, efforts to keep Protestant churches open and free from requisition, efforts on behalf of French prisoners of war (especially Protestant ministers), attempts to keep the Protestant scouting and other youth movements free from Vichy control, and negotiations with Catholic authorities for joint action. Based on the diary in family archives; map, 73 notes. 1940

Bertucci, Francesco Antonio

623. Springer, Elisabeth. KAISER RUDOLF II., PAPST CLEMENS VIII. UND DIE BOSNISCHEN CHRISTEN: TATEN UND UNTATEN DES CAVALIERE FRANCESCO ANTONIO BERTUCCI IN KAISERLICHEN DIENSTEN IN DEN JAHREN 1594 BIS 1602 [Emperor Rudolf II, Pope Clement VIII, and the Christians of Bosnia: deeds and crimes of chevalier Francesco Antonio Bertucci during his years in the emperor's service, 1594-1602]. *Mitteilungen des Österreichischen Staatsarchivs [Austria] 1980 33: 77-105.* Francesco Antonio Bertucci, a knight of the Maltese Order from Dalmatia-Albania, tried during the latter part of the 16th century and early 17th century to interest European heads of state in his plans regarding southeastern Europe. This study explores Bertucci's involvement with Emperor Rudolf II and Pope Clement VIII in organizing Christians in a united front against the Turks, to deliver Albanians, Dalmatians, and Bosnians to take Fort Clissa, and reinstate Hungary's priorate to the Maltese Order. Bertucci first approached the emperor in 1594; in 1596 action was finally taken and joint Christian forces fought the Turks at Fort Clissa, where Bertucci was taken prisoner. Based on fascicle 356 of the Hungarian Dossiers of the Haus-, Hof- und Staatsarchiv in Vienna and other primary sources; 2 illus., map. 1594-1602

Bervi-Flerovski, Vasili Vasilevich

624. Grau, Conrad. VASILIJ VASIL'EVIČ BERVI-FLEROVSKIJ—EIN RUSSICHER UTOPISCHER SOZIALIST [Vasili Vasilevich Bervi-Flerovski—a Russian utopian socialist]. *Jahrbuch für Geschichte der Sozialistischen Länder Europas [East Germany] 1983 27: 201-217.* Vasili Vasilevich Bervi-Flerovski (1829-1918) came from a privileged family, his father being a professor at Kazan. Critical of the Tsarist regime, he concerned himself with agrarian problems in response to the evil conditions of serfdom, the 1848 revolutionary outbreak, and the writings of socialist intellectuals. Although he became acquainted with the writings of Marx in the 1860's and corresponded with him, Bervi remained more a utopian socialist who believed in the power of education and character development of individuals and leaders. Based on the writings of Bervi-Flerovski and other correspondents, and secondary sources; 60 notes. 1850's-1918

Berzin, Jan A.

625. Kaptelov, B. I. IA. A. BERZIN (K 100-LETIIU SO DNIA ROZHDENIIA) [J. A. Berzin: the centenary of his birth]. *Sovetskie Arkhivy [USSR] 1981 (5): 29-33.* Marks the centenary of the birth of the Latvian Communist Jan A. Berzin (1881-1938) with a short biography and texts of four documents illustrative of his revolutionary career from 1913 to 1934. Apart from his government and diplomatic activities, Berzin was also head of the Soviet Archive Administration from 1932 to 1937, when he evidently fell victim to Stalin's purges. Based on materials in the Soviet Central State Archive of the October Revolution (TsGAOR SSSR fond 3316, 5446, 5325, and DP fond 102); 8 notes. 1881-1938

Berzins-Ziemelis, Janis

626. Toman, B. A. IAN BERZIN-ZIEMELIS: REVOLIUTSIONER I ISTORIK PARTII [Janis Berzins-Ziemelis: revolutionary and Party historian]. *Voprosy Istorii KPSS [USSR] 1981 (10): 93-97.* In honor of the 100th anniversary of his birth, a study of the life and work of Janis Berzins-Ziemelis, activist of the Latvian and Russian revolutionary movements, Party and Soviet worker, diplomat, publicist, and Party historian. Starting with his birth in October 1881 into a Latvian peasant family, describes his education,

his early political activities and involvement with the Latvian Workers' Social Democratic oganization, his repeated arrests and exile for his beliefs, his relationship with V. I. Lenin, his work for and after the revolution in Russia, and continued efforts for the construction of socialism. Based on the works of Lenin and secondary works about Berzins-Ziemelis; 26 notes. 1900's-34

Besant, Annie

627. Mortimer, Joanne Stafford. ANNIE BESANT AND INDIA 1913-1917. *J. of Contemporary Hist. [Great Britain] 1983 18(1): 61-78.* Freethinker, champion of women's rights, socialist, and theosophist, Annie Besant worked for her social ideals in India from 1907 to 1913. Then she turned to politics, agitated for self-government, organized national movements, and finally in 1917 at age 70 was elected president of the Indian National Congress at Calcutta. Based on published primary and secondary sources; 45 notes. 1900-17

Beskrovnyi, Liubomir G.

628. Buganov, V. I. and Vodarski, Ia. E. LIUBOMIR GRIGOR'EVICH BESKROVNYI [Liubomir Grigorievich Beskrovnyi]. *Istoriia SSSR [USSR] 1981 (5): 150-156.* Obituary of the Soviet military historian Beskrovnyi (d. 1980), a teacher at the Frunze Military Academy and later head of various historical institutes attached to the Soviet Academy of Sciences. Beskrovnyi's published works include studies of the Russian army and fleet in the 18th and 19th centuries, Russian participation in the wars against Napoleon, studies of Kutuzov and Suvorov, and works of military historical geography on such topics as the Russo-Chinese frontier. 18c-19c

Bessarion

629. Bianca, Concetta. UNA NUOVA TESTIMONIANZA SUL NOME DI BATTESIMO DEL BESSARIONE [A new source for the baptismal name of Bessarion]. *Rivista di Storia della Chiesa in Italia [Italy] 1984 38(2): 428-436.* Discusses the problem of the baptismal name of the Greek monk and cardinal Bessarion of Trebizond (1403-72), with special reference to an autobiographical note discovered in a Plutarch manuscript by Stefano Borgia (d. 1804) and reported in 1777. This note suggests that Bessarion had been baptized as Johannes not as Basil. Nevertheless the author is still inclined to accept the latter name, which is documented in a reliable Bolognese source ca. 1450. Based on manuscript sources in the Vatican Library and in the Biblioteca Marciana, Venice, and secondary sources; 62 notes. 1450-1777

Bethlen, Gabriel

630. Barcza, József. BETHLEN GÁBOR REFORMÁTUS VALLÁSOSSÁGA [The religious attitude of Gabriel Bethlen within the Reformation]. *Theológiai Szemle [Hungary] 1981 24(1): 8-11.* Bethlen's daily life was surrounded by his religion. During battles his Latin Bible was always with him. He believed that although individuals are helpless to change their lives as predestined by God, they are still responsible for their attitudes toward others and themselves. He declined all personal honors and declared that all success and blessings come from God. 1613-29

631. Bitskey, István. BETHLEN, PÁZMÁNY ÉS A KÁLDI-BIBLIA [Bethlen, Pázmány, and the Káldi Bible]. *Századok [Hungary] 1981 115(4): 737-743.* Gabriel Bethlen and Péter Pázmány, the archbishop, were political adversaries who nonetheless deeply respected one another. Their correspondence between 1617 and 1627 shows how sincerely each of them believed in serving the true interest of Hungary, although they could not agree whether the best interest of the country would be achieved by joining the Habsburg or the Ottoman Empires. The greatness of Bethlen is shown by his ability to put aside religious differences and offer not only financial but also moral help to Káldi, the Jesuit translator of the Bible. 21 notes. 1617-27

632. Csohány, János. BETHLEN GÁBOR POLITIKAI KAPCSOLATAI A REFORMÁTUS EURÓPÁVAL [Gabriel Bethlen's political connection with the European reformation]. *Theológiai Szemle [Hungary] 1981 24(1): 12-15.* Threatened by the Habsburg and the Ottoman Empires, Bethlen decided to join with the Ottomans to keep Hungary out of the Thirty Years War. His marriage to Catherine of Brandenburg in 1626 opened the door to European politics and made it possible for Bethlen to join the anti-Habsburg association of the Hague. His participation in various battles delayed the entry of Habsburg absolutism into Hungary until 1671. 1619-71

633. Deac, Augustin; Bercan, Gheorghe; and Paul, Christian. A FAMOUS TRANSYLVANIAN RULING PRINCE BETHLEN GABRIEL. *Romania [Romania] 1981 6(2): 98-127.* Describes the career of Gabriel Bethlen, who ruled Transylvania, 1613-29, an era characterized by remarkable economic, political, and foreign relations achievements. 1613-29

634. Köpeczi, Béla. BETHLEN GÁBOR ÉS ÁLLAMA [The government of Gabriel Bethlen]. *Századok [Hungary] 1981 115(4): 664-672.* The absolutist ambitions of the Habsburg Empire and its attitude toward the Protestant minorities convinced Bethlen that Transylvania would be better off under Ottoman protection. The necessary political sacrifices were accepted by the nation and in 1620 he was elected King of Hungary. His plans for the future involved the acquisition of the crown of Poland in order to build a stronger Hungary, but he died before this could be accomplished. Under his rule, Transylvania became a prosperous state, while remaining apart from all foreign influence. 26 notes. 1613-29

635. Makkai, László. BETHLEN GÁBOR ÉS AZ EURÓPAI MŰVELŐDÉS [Gabriel Bethlen and European culture]. *Századok [Hungary] 1981 115(4): 673-697.* As Bethlen's own education was grounded in politics, his higher educational policy for Hungary stressed the importance of the courts and political attitudes. The pronounced distinction between Catholic and Protestant universities outside Hungary made it difficult to obtain appropriate teaching faculty for the young university established under Bethlen and to train promising young students abroad. 65 notes. 1597-1630

636. Makkai, László. BETHLEN GÁBOR ÉS A KÉSŐRENESZÁNSZ KULTÚRA [Gabriel Bethlen and late Renaissance culture]. *Magyar Tudomány [Hungary] 1981 26(7-8): 535-546.* Gabriel Bethlen (1580-1629), Calvinist ruler of Transylvania and king of Hungary, was a great patron of the arts. Though Transylvania was in ruins due to the Thirty Years' War, he recruited architects, musicians, performers, painters, and sculptors from all over Europe. He sent students on scholarship to Heidelberg and Marburg and when political events made that impossible, to Holland and England. He attempted to make Transylvania an international center of Calvinist culture. When, in 1628, the Calvinist University at Herborn went bankrupt, he invited its professors Gáspár Bojti Veres, Johann Heinrich Bisterfeld, and

Ludwig Philipp Piscator to establish a university at Gyulafehérvár. He and his court were tolerant of the then fashionable astrology, alchemy, hermetism, pansophism, and mannerism, as well as other religions. Bethlen did not subscribe to any of these philosophical movements, and remained firmly committed to Calvinism. 31 notes. 1600-28

637. Nagy, László. BETHLEN GÁBOR, A HADVEZÉR [Gabriel Bethlen, the commander]. *Hadtörténelmi Közlemények [Hungary] 1980 27(3): 379-404.* Analyzes Transylvanian prince Gabriel Bethlen's military leadership on and off the battlefield by noting his reputation among his contemporaries and posterity, examining the definition of a good military leader in Bethlen's time, identifying the sources of Bethlen's military knowledge and soldiering experience, and fixing the place of Bethlen among the military commanders of the Hungarian lands ruled by the Ottoman Empire. Bethlen's military leadership can be divided into the following periods: 1614-16, defensive war; 1616, an attempt to attack the Habsburg power; 1619, attack in alliance with Bohemia; 1620, the military campaign in Transdanubia; 1621, defensive and offensive battles; 1623, offensive war; and 1626, offensive war. Based on Bethlen's correspondence and contemporary military memoirs; 164 notes. 1614-26

638. Pach, Zsigmond Pál. BETHLEN GÁBORRÓL, SZÜLETÉSÉNEK 400. ÉVFORDULÓJÁN [Remembrance of Gabriel Bethlen on the 400th anniversary of his birth]. *Századok [Hungary] 1981 115(4): 659-663.* Bethlen's aim to unite Hungary and Transylvania demanded sharp statesmanship and diplomacy in foreign policy. Threatened by the Habsburg and Ottoman Empires, he used every diplomatic access available. His marriage to the daughter of Ferdinand II, which made him a relative of Gustav Adolph, the King of Sweden, served only one purpose, the consolidation of the Hungarian and Transylvanian governments. 1618-29

639. Péter, Katalin. BETHLEN GÁBOR EMLÉKEZETE A FEJEDELEM PÁLYAKEZDÉSE [Remembrance of Gabriel Bethlen: early beginning of the reigning prince's political life]. *Századok [Hungary] 1981 115(4): 744-749.* Bethlen's career began in Zsigmond Báthori's court where he was able to create a newly prosperous and peaceful Transylvania out of the upheaval that began after 1590. 23 notes. 1613-29

640. Takács, Béla. BETHLEN GÁBOR MŰVELŐDÉSPOLITIKÁJA ÉS MECÉNÁSI TEVÉKENYSÉGE [Gabriel Bethlen's cultural policy and his activity as patron of arts]. *Theológiai Szemle [Hungary] 1981 24(1): 15-17.* Although lacking formal education, Bethlen was the first Hungarian ruler to stimulate the desire of his nation for a higher cultural level. He promoted the education of promising students at foreign universities, modernization of school curricula, and the establishment of printing shops. 17c

641. Újváry, J. Zsuzsanna and Kalmár, János Miklós. NEMZETKÖZI TUDOMÁNYOS KONFERENCIA BETHLEN GÁBORRÓL DEBRECENBEN [International scientific conference in Debrecen on Gabriel Bethlen]. *Századok [Hungary] 1981 115(4): 750-753.* The conference that took place in 1980 to commemorate the 400th anniversary of Bethlen's birth featured 34 speakers and concluded with a public discussion about Bethlen and his influence on Transylvania during his reign. 1613-29

642. Zimányi, Vera. BETHLEN GÁBOR FEJEDELEM GAZDASÁGPOLITIKÁJA [Economic policy of Gabriel Bethlen, ruling prince]. *Századok [Hungary] 1981 115(4): 703-713.* During the 16th century, industry, commerce, and agriculture were greatly affected by the increasing population of western Europe. The 2% to 3% inflation spurred the Hungarian economy on to greater production. This upsurge suddenly came to a standstill during the first decades of the 17th century. This and the continuing wars put Bethlen in a difficult financial position. Taxes had to be greatly increased and prices regulated. At the same time mining and monopolistic production were encouraged. These steps greatly increased his government's income, which by 1626 had risen well above expectations. 16 notes. 1619-26

Bethlen, Kata

643. Németh, Katalin S. "SOK ÉS NAGY ERŐTLENSÉGEKKEL KÜSZKÖDŐ EMBER. . . ." BETHLEN KATA A KORTÁRSAK SZEMÉVEL ["A person weak and faint struggling against overwhelming difficulties. . . ." Kata Bethlen as seen by her contemporaries]. *Theologiai Szemle [Hungary] 1985 28(4): 233-237.* In her modesty Bethlen forbade all expressions of praise toward her person. Consequently there is very little literature or other authentic sources offering details to today's researcher. The article includes frequent quotations from her autobiography and short notes left by her protegé, Péter Bod. She was deeply religious and extremely supportive of all social and intellectual undertakings. The deaths of four of her children, the demise of both husbands, and her ill health left little room in her life for joy. She died at age 59 in 1759. 36 notes. 18c

Beurle, Carl

644. Tweraser, Kurt. CARL BEURLE AND THE TRIUMPH OF GERMAN NATIONALISM IN AUSTRIA. *German Studies Rev. 1981 4(3): 403-426.* Carl Beurle (1860-1919), like many of his educated middle-class contemporaries, revolted against the liberalism of his father in embracing social Darwinism and anti-Semitism. At first a disciple of Georg von Schönerer, Beurle later broke with him and adopted a more pragmatic stance, though he remained thoroughly anti-Semitic, as he became a potent force in Upper Austria and a major factor in the defeat of Austrian liberalism. 86 notes. 1874-1911

Bevan-Evans, Myrddyn John

645. Veysey, A. Geoffrey. MYRDDYN JOHN BEVAN-EVANS. *J. of the Soc. of Archivists [Great Britain] 1981 6(8): 536.* An obituary of Myrddyn John Bevan-Evans (1905-80), one of the first generation of county archivists, who was particularly interested in Flintshire, North Wales. 1905-80

Bevin, Ernest

646. Corbett, H. Vincent. PALESTINE: ERNEST BEVIN'S ROLE. *Journal of the Royal United Services Institute for Defence Studies [Great Britain] 1984 129(1): 52-54.* Although lacking in educational training, Ernest Bevin was probably the most admired foreign secretary of the century; his career as a labor negotiator made him a shrewd statesman. Because of Palestine's political and strategic value to Britain, and because of his sympathy for the impoverished Palestinians, Bevin's policies were attacked by the Zionist leadership. By drawing the United States into the Palestinian debate, many Arab states shifted their animosity from the British to the Americans. 1945-48

Bevis, John

647. Wallis, Ruth. JOHN BEVIS, M.D., F.R.S. (1695-1771), ASTRONOMER LOYAL. *Notes and Records of the Royal Soc. of London [Great Britain] 1982 36(2): 211-226.* Traces the life of John Bevis, the discoverer of the Crab Nebula in 1731. Bevis also published a star atlas and edited Edmund Halley's tables. 57 notes. 1720's-71

Beyle, Henri

See Stendhal

Beza, Theodore

648. Ménager, Daniel. THEODORE DE BEZE, BIOGRAPHE DE CALVIN [Theodore Beza, Calvin's biographer]. *Bibliothèque d'Humanisme et Renaissance [Switzerland] 1983 45(2): 231-255.* 1564-75

*For abstract see **Calvin, John***

Bezuidenhout, Pieter Lodewyk

649. Rautenbach, Cicero. VELDKORNET P. L. BEZUIDENHOUT VAN DIE EERSTE VRYHEIDSOORLOG WAS GEEN AFSTAMMELING VAN DIE BEZUIDENHOUTS VAN SLAGTERSNEK NIE [Field Cornet P. L. Bezuidenhout of the first Boer War was not a descendant of the Bezuidenhouts of Slagtersnek]. *Historia [South Africa] 1981 26(2): 110-118.* Traces the family and birthplace of Pieter Lodewyk Bezuidenhout (1837-1905), the sale of whose commodities in 1880 in Orange Free State led to the first Boer War. He was from the town of George in the Cape Colony and not descended, as is commonly supposed, from the Transvaal Bezuidenhout family from Slagtersnek, who achieved fame as rebels in 1815. Based on birth and baptism records. 1837-1905

Bharati, Subramania

650. Subrmanyam, Ka Naa. SUBRAMANIA BHARATI: A CENTENARY ESTIMATE. *Indian Horizons [India] 1982 31(3): 43-47.* Summarizes the brief life of the "morning star of the Tamil renaissance," Subramania Bharati (1882-1921). In his prose and poetry he demonstrated a love of the Tamils and their language and a deep hatred of the British. When he was not in exile in Pondicherry, he edited two newspapers for the nationalist cause. A follower of Lokmanya Tilak, Bharati preached revolution, which contrasted with his other moralistic poetic and prose pieces addressed to the young. ca 1900-21

Bhutto, Ali

651. Lodhi, Maleela. REFLECTIONS ON THE PAKISTANI DILEMMA—A REVIEW ARTICLE. *J. of Commonwealth and Comparative Pol. [Great Britain] 1982 20(1): 96-105.* Four recent books about Pakistan disagree about the influence of Islam on the nation, but agree that the Ali Bhutto period, 1971-77, was an important landmark in Pakistan's political history. Bhutto won an overwhelming victory in the 1970 elections and promised steps toward civilian democracy, but the war of the secession of Bangladesh interrupted the mood of optimism, and by 1977 urban protest brought Bhutto down, leading to the third military regime in Pakistan's history. Bhutto's personal leadership was a form of patrimonialism, a variety of autocracy; he refused to institutionalize his own Pakistan People's Party. Intent on preserving his own authority, he neglected the interests of the country. 1971-77

Bianchi, Leonard

652. Ciągwa, Józef. LEONARD BIANCHI 1923-1981 [Leonard Bianchi, 1923-81]. *Czasopismo Prawno-Historyczne [Poland] 1982 34(2): 253-255.* An obituary of the Vienna-born leading Slovak historian of law and jurist, Leonard Bianchi, 1923-81, known in Poland as a friend of Polish scholars. 1923-81

Bianchini, Giovanni

653. Rosińska, Grażyna. GIOVANNI BIANCHINI—MATEMATYK I ASTRONOM XV WIEKU [Giovanni Bianchini: 15th-century mathematician and astronomer]. *Kwartalnik Hist. Nauki i Techniki [Poland] 1981 26(3-4): 565-577.* Giovanni Bianchini (ca. 1385-1470) is a forgotten scholar. He lived through an era that had prepared the advent of the Copernican revolution and his decimal tables of trigonometric functions clearly contributed to the development of trigonometry which was, in turn, utilized by Copernicus. Yet, Bianchini is not even listed in the *Dictionary of Scientific Biography.* Based on secondary sources; 4 tables, 32 notes. Russian and English summaries. 14c-16c

Bianconi, Charles

654. Caffyn-Parsons, Una. CHARLES BIANCONI, PIONEER OF IRISH PUBLIC TRANSPORT. *Transport Hist. [Great Britain] 1981 12: 86-88.* A biography of Charles Bianconi (1786-1875), who organized public coach and horse-drawn wagon services in Ireland from 1815 until his death. 1815-75

Bichurin, Iakinf

655. Liščák, Vladimír. OTEC IAKINF [Father Iakinf]. *Nový Orient [Czechoslovakia] 1983 38(5): 146-147.* Remembers the life and work of Russian Orthodox priest Iakinf Bichurin (1777-1853), the author of more than 70 scholarly works about China. 19c

Bielawski, Józef

656. Czapkiewicz, Andrzej et al. JÓZEF BIELAWSKI [Józef Bielawski]. *Rocznik Orientalistyczny [Poland] 1984 43: 7-10.* Describes the lifework of Poland's foremost contemporary scholar in Islamic studies, Józef Bielawski, founder of the Department of Islamic Studies at the University of Warsaw and translator of the Koran. Introduces an issue of essays compiled in his honor. 20c

Bieliński, Aleksander

657. Wiśniewski, Stanisław. ALEKSANDER BIELIŃSKI (1818-1877) W LUBELSKIEJ KONSPIRACJI NIEPODLEGŁOŚCIOWEJ I NA ZESŁANIACH SYBERYJSKICH [Aleksander Bieliński (1818-77) in the underground liberation movement of the Lublin region]. *Annales Universitatis Mariae Curie-Skłodowska. Sectio F: Humaniora [Poland] 1982 37: 295-317.* A biography of Aleksander Bieliński, Polish landowner involved in the activities of the Union of Polish People of the Lublin region. Arrested in 1838, he was exiled to Siberia for 3 years. On return to his estate he became engaged in an anti-Russian conspiracy and was rearrested in 1843. His correspondence during the decade of exile contains descriptions of life in Siberia and the morale of Polish political prisoners. Based on sources from the Central Archive of Ancient Records; 63 notes. Russian and French summaries. 1830's-77

Bielke, Nils

658. Losman, Arne. KAROLINEN NILS BIELKE SOM KULTURPERSONLIGHET [Nils Bielke, soldier of Charles XII of Sweden: a leading personality in the world of culture]. *Karolinska Förbundets Årsbok [Sweden] 1983: 7-18.* The Swedish nobleman Nils Bielke (1644-1716) is generally considered to have had a poor character, but he exerted a tremendous cultural influence in Sweden and abroad. Bielke was the royal importer to the Swedish court of French luxury goods and the exporter of Swedish architectural know-how. He maintained close contact with Europe's leading intellectuals and scientists. His political career included positions at the Swedish and French courts and as governor general of Pomeria; he was made a count of the Holy Roman Empire and Sweden. In his military career he fought for the Swedish king, the Bavarian king, and later for the German emperor, advancing to field marshal. During his 10-year stay in Pomeria Bielke founded schools and was the chancellor of the Swedish university at Greifswald. His political leanings toward France severely strained his relations with the Swedish king, and after an accusation of participation in forgery and a seven-year prosecution, Bielke was banned from the capital and lost everything but his life. 1644-1716

Bier, August

659. Lochmann, Gerhard. AUGUST BIER—EINE HISTORISCH BEDEUTSAME CHIRURGENPERSÖNLICHKEIT [August Bier, a historically significant surgeon]. *Wissenschaftliche Zeitschrift der Ernst-Moritz-Arndt-Universität Greifswald. Gesellschafts- und Sprachwissenschaftliche Reihe [East Germany] 1982 31(4): 51-58.* Discusses the life of the surgeon, naval doctor, and University of Greifswald professor August Bier (1861-1949), who specialized in stomach surgery and amputations. 1861-1949

Bier, Johann Philip

660. Haynes, Emma Schwabenland. THE FATE OF A WEALTHY WARENBURG FAMILY. *J. of the Am. Hist. Soc. of Germans from Russia 1982 5(3): 12-15.* Describes the activities of several members of the family of Johann Philip Bier, a wealthy Volga German landowner, during the Russian Civil War and the survivors' emigration by 1922. 1890-1922

Biergans, Franz Theodor

661. Sergent, Pierre. FRANZ THEODOR BIERGANS, UN PUBLICISTE REVOLUTIONNAIRE ALLEMAND [Franz Theodor Biergans, a German revolutionary publicist]. *Annales Historiques de la Révolution Française [France] 1984 56(1-2): 88-102.* Biergans (1768-1842) was a Cologne journalist whose newspaper, published in 1795-96, defended the French Revolution. A pastor by training, he called for a new revolutionary order based on a deistic, rational religion and on human equality. 30 notes. 1790's-1842

Bilen, I.

662. Kuranov, I. N. KOMMUNIST, INTERNATSIONALIST, PATRIOT [Communist, internationalist, and patriot]. *Voprosy Istorii KPSS [USSR] 1982 (10): 109-112.* Commemorates the 80th birthday of I. Bilen (b. 1902), Secretary-General of the Communist Party of Turkey. Bilen's political life started in about 1920 in Istanbul, where he was working as a motor mechanic. He joined the groups of young men who were helping in the country's liberation struggle against the forces of the Entente and internal reaction. He became a member of the newly formed Communist Party in 1922 and a year later was sent to the USSR for training. Bilen was active in the Turkish labor movement in the 1930's and played a key role in the anti-imperialist front in World War II. He became Secretary-General of the Party in 1974 and since then has forcefully led Turkey's Communists in their fight against repression and for social justice. 18 notes. 1902-82

Biljoen, J. F. W. van Spaen van

663. Tromp, Heimerick, introd.; Newby, Evelyn, transl. A DUTCHMAN'S VISITS TO SOME ENGLISH GARDENS IN 1791: EXTRACTS FROM THE UNPUBLISHED JOURNAL OF BARON JOHAN FREDERIK WILLEM VAN SPAEN VAN BILJOEN, WITH A BIOGRAPHICAL INTRODUCTION BY HEIMERICK TROMP. *J. of Garden Hist. [Great Britain] 1982 2(1): 41-58.* The diary of Baron J. F. W. van Spaen van Biljoen (1746-1827) of the Netherlands contains observations of his trip to London and southern England in 1791 with his stepfather-in-law, Baron W. C. H. van Lynden van Blitterswijk, and describes a number of English gardens. 1770's-1791

Bing family

664. Loewengart, Stefan. AUS DER GESCHICHTE DER FAMILIE BING [From the history of the Bing family]. *Bull. des Leo Baeck Inst. [Israel] 1981 (59): 29-54.* The history of the Jewish family Bing beginning with Rabbi Abraham Bing (1752-1841) of Würzburg, a vehement opponent of the reform movement. His son Beer Abraham Bing (1780?-?1843) was a writer. Berthold Bing studied in France and was a magistrate of Nürnberg and a major promoter of the Diesel engine. He died in 1915. His son Rudolf Bing (1876-1963) emigrated to Israel. Based on secondary documents; 27 notes. 1757-1915

Binyon, Laurence

665. Atkinson, F. G. UNPUBLISHED LETTERS OF LAURENCE BINYON (I): THE YEARS OF STRUGGLE. *Notes and Queries [Great Britain] 1982 29(4): 335-339.* Reproduces texts of letters written by Laurence Binyon to Arthur Thomas Quiller-Couch, 1893-1900, that recount Binyon's two careers as poet and employee at the British Museum. Article to be continued. 1893-1900

Biondelli, Bernardino

666. Murru, Furio. BERNARDINO BIONDELLI E LA LINGUISTICA PREASCOLIANA [Bernardino Biondelli and linguistics before Ascoli]. *Critica Storica [Italy] 1982 19(1): 85-106.* Reviews Domenico Santamaria's book of the same title (1981). Besides containing biographical and bibliographical data on its subject, the book contains material to prove that there was no discontinuity in the work of Italian scholars in linguistics and philology in the first half of the 19th century. ca 1800-50

Birch, Thomas

667. Rousseau, G. S. "THE TORPEDO-ACT": PROSOPOGRAPHY AS BIOGRAPHY. *Annals of Science [Great Britain] 1985 42(4): 431-435.* Reviews A. E. Gunther's *An Introduction to the Life of the Rev. Thomas Birch, D.D., F.R.S., 1705-1766* (1984), a biography of the official historian of the Royal Society. This biography reveals facts about 18th-century English intellectual, religious, and social life, but fails to "interpret, interpolate and draw inferences" about Georgian society. Therefore, Gunther does not utilize his data to provide a collective biography of a given society, which

would reveal new aspects of English social history. Based on published documents and secondary sources; 3 notes. 1730's-66

Birck (Pürk), Wenzel

668. Stephanides, M. "Wenzel Birck (Pürk), 1718-1763: Leben und Werk eines Wiener Hofmusikers an der Wende vom Barock zur Klassic" [Wenzel Birck (Pürk), 1718-63: life and work of a Vienna court musician in the transition period from baroque to classical style]. U. of Vienna [Austria] 1982. 271 pp. *DAI-C 1984 45(3): 594; 9/2402c.* 1718-63

Biringuccio, Vanoccio

669. Fedorov, A. S. VANNOCHCHO BIRINGUCHHO [Vanoccio Biringuccio]. *Voprosy Istorii Estestvoznaniia i Tekhniki [USSR] 1981 (1): 137-140.* The 500th anniversary of the birth of the celebrated Italian chemist and metallurgist Vanoccio Biringuccio (1480-1539) was marked in 1980 throughout the world. Biringuccio, who was one of the most prominent scientists of the Renaissance, worked not only in his native Sienna, but also in Parma and Florence and, shortly before his death, in the Vatican. He was famous particularly for his work on the extraction of metal from ores; the casting of metal, especially to make bells; and the manufacture of gunpowder and firearms. His studies of these processes were the subject of his life work *De la Pirotechnia* [On pyrotechnics], which was published a year after his death and which was the main guide for the metals industry for more than 100 years. Secondary sources; illus. ca 1500-40

Biriuzov, Sergei S.

670. —. MARSHAL SOVETSKOGO SOIUZA S. S. BIRIUZOV [Marshal of the Soviet Union S. S. Biriuzov]. *Voenno-Istoricheskii Zhurnal [USSR] 1984 (8): 39-42.* Sergei S. Biriuzov (1904-64) was an outstanding military figure and a Party member from 1926. He fought on the southwestern front at the beginning of the Patriotic War, later commanding several armies, and took part in the Iaşi-Kishinev offensive of 1944 and the liberation of Bulgaria. He occupied a number of senior military positions after the war, rising to become a deputy minister of defense from 1962 until his death in a plane crash in October 1964. 1941-64

Birringer, Leopold

671. Brunner, Titu Stephanie. DAS TAGEBUCH DES LEOPOLD BIRRINGER AUS LANGENLOIS [The diary of Leopold Birringer from Langenlois]. *Unsere Heimat [Austria] 1984 55(4): 321-332.* Examines and analyzes the handwritten diaries of the vineyard owner Leopold Birringer (1836-1919), which were found in 1909 in his former house in Langenlois and spanned the period from 1864 to 1882. The main entries include details of his family and family events, as well as information about his land, vineyards, and properties. 1864-82

Biscoe, John

672. Savours, Ann. JOHN BISCOE, MASTER MARINER 1794-1843. *Polar Record [Great Britain] 1983 21(134): 485-491.* Reviews the life, career, voyages, explorations and contributions of Captain John Biscoe, an early circumnavigator of Antarctica. 1794-1843

Bishop, Maurice

673. Archer, Ewart. GAIRYISM, REVOLUTION AND REORGANIZATION: THREE DECADES OF TURBULENCE IN GRENADA. *Journal of Commonwealth & Comparative Politics [Great Britain] 1985 23(2): 91-111.* 1950's-84

*For abstract see **Gairy, Eric***

674. Nitoburg, E. L. GRENADA: BOL'SHAIA LOZH' I RAZBOI VASHINGTONA [Grenada: Washington's great treachery]. *Voprosy Istorii [USSR] 1985 (1): 107-119.* Views the circumstances leading to the assassination of Maurice Bishop and the overthrow of his government by the US invasion of the island of Grenada in 1983. In the period between Bishop's rise to power in 1979 and his death, the Central Intelligence Agency made several attempts on his life, while launching a disinformation campaign through the Voice of America radio station. Secondary sources; 81 notes. 1979-83

Bismarck, Otto von

675. Borejsza, Jerzy W. ÜBER BISMARCK UND DIE POLNISCHE FRAGE IN DER POLNISCHEN HISTORIOGRAPHIE [Concerning Bismarck and the Polish question in Polish historiography]. *Historische Zeitschrift [West Germany] 1985 241(3): 599-630.* For most Poles, Otto von Bismarck symbolizes the perpetual hostility of Germans to Poland. Historians recognize him as a conservative who wanted to preserve Poland under German dominance. Although Bismarck developed his ideas in reaction to the 1848 revolutions, he did not hesitate to arm Polish peasants against Polish aristocrats because he believed the aristocrats were the bearers of Polish nationalism. When he later believed that the peasants had replaced the aristocracy as bearers of Polish nationalism, his strategies changed. He believed that Polish nationalism was identified with revolution and overreacted against it. Based on works by Polish and German historians; 77 notes. 1863-98

676. Paur, Philip. THE CORPORATIST CHARACTER OF BISMARCK'S SOCIAL POLICY. *European Studies Rev. [Great Britain] 1981 11(4): 427-460.* Otto von Bismarck attempted to use social insurance legislation as a vehicle to subvert the power of the Reichstag from 1879 to 1884. He planned to circumvent the Reichstag's doctrinaire politics by organizing corporatist associations. Social insurance was to form the foundation of these vocational organizations. Bismarck abandoned corporatism after 1884 because the associations failed and a more conservative group was elected to the Reichstag. Secondary sources; 103 notes. 1879-84

677. Pinto Molina, María and Raya Rivas, Alejandro. BISMARCK Y EL EMPERADOR ALEMAN [Bismarck and the German emperor]. *Historia y Vida [Spain] 1984 17(195): 4-11.* Reviews the figure of Prince Otto von Bismarck, the Prussian chancellor responsible for the military and political expansion of Prussia at the end of the 19th century, and analyzes his relationship with the monarchs with whom he worked. 1862-90

678. Williamson, D. G. READING HISTORY: THE BISMARCK DEBATE. *History Today [Great Britain] 1984 34(Sept): 47-49.* Evaluates 20th-century historiography on Otto von Bismarck (1815-98), emphasizing his role in German unification and imperialism. 1850's-98

Bjørneboe, Jens

679. Garton, Janet. "A VISION OF A CONTINUAL BATTLE": JENS BJØRNEBOE AND THE THEATRE. *Scandinavica [Great Britain] 1984 23(2): 137-160.* Norwegian playwright Jens Bjørneboe described Norwegian theater as "the dictatorship of mediocrity." His first play, ***Før Hanen Galer***, was rejected and later rewritten as a novel. Bjørneboe was influenced by Bertolt Brecht's drama and felt the Norwegians misunderstood Brecht. He criticized Brecht and other playwrights who attempted to create an illusion of reality. Bjørneboe noted that the bombing of Hiroshima, 1945, changed reality. His three most successful plays were *Til Lykke med Dagen* (1965), *Fugleelskerne* (1966), and *Semmelweis* (1967). The three works reflect Bjørneboe's concern with authority. Based on letters, other primary, and secondary sources; 40 notes. 1965-68

Bjørnson, Bjørnstjerne

680. Rottem, Øystein. THE MULTIFARIOUS BJØRNSON. *Scandinavica [Great Britain] 1985 24(1): 59-64.* Reviews Bjørnstjerne Bjørnson's *Jeg velger mig april* (1982) and *De gode gjerninger redder verden* (1982), Philip Houm's *En mann forut vår tid* (1982), and *"Og nu vil jeg tale ut."—"men nu vil jeg ogsa tale ud." Brevvekslingen mellom Bjørnstjerne Bjørnson og Amalie Skram* (1982) edited by Øyvind Anker and Edvard Beyer. In 1982 the publisher Gyldendal Norsk Forlag marked the 150th anniversary of the birth of Bjørnstjerne Bjørnson by republishing his books. However, Bjørnson has not enjoyed recent popularity. He displayed solidarity toward his fellow writers and agitated for women's property rights and other political causes. Amalie Skram, a writer 40 years his junior, was an admirer of Bjørnson and their letters portray a friendship between two 19th-century Norwegian writers. 19c

Black, Henry

681. Morioka, Heinz and Sasaki, Miyoko. THE BLUE-EYED STORYTELLER: HENRY BLACK AND HIS RAKUGO CAREER. *Monumenta Nipponica [Japan] 1983 38(2): 133-162.* Henry Black (1858-1923) was a Westerner who played a unique role in Meiji Japan in his life-style and his career. He was an artist who made Japan his homeland, and spent his life there, earning his living on the stage as a public storyteller. As such, he became the first Westerner to successfully integrate himself with the common people of Japan, who admired his art and sincerity, although his family and countrymen looked down upon him. 1858-1923

Black, Joseph

682. Perrin, C. E. A RELUCTANT CATALYST: JOSEPH BLACK AND THE EDINBURGH RECEPTION OF LAVOISIER'S CHEMISTRY. *Ambix [Great Britain] 1982 29(3): 141-176.* Joseph Black (1728-99) is known to have supported Antoine Laurent Lavoisier's anti-Phlogiston theory toward the end of his life, but it is not known when he came to accept and support it. Attempts to identify the approximate date show that he was aware of the theory by the mid 1780's, mentioning it to his students but not accepting it then. He gradually moved over to acceptance in the later 1780's as a result of his following the controversy in general, analysis of experimental evidence, student theses. The public acceptance in 1790 is argued to have been from conviction, not pressure, and was the last in a long series of small steps. Mainly primary sources; 98 notes. 1780-90

Blackwell, Joseph

683. Kabdebo, Tamás. JOSEPH BLACKWELL ÉS A PESTI ANGOL KONZULÁTUS TERVE AZ 1840-ES ÉVEKBEN [Joseph Blackwell and the plan of the British consulate in Pest in the 1840's]. *Századok [Hungary] 1984 118(6): 1201-1214.* Joseph Blackwell, British businessman, writer, and diplomat, was active in promoting the creation of a British consulate in Pest in the 1840's. A staunch supporter of Hungary, he was convinced of the economic potential of the country, and he developed plans to make Hungary a major provider of wheat in the world market and also laid the financial groundwork for the development of a railroad from Fiume to Steinbrücke. As an official British observer at the Diet of Hungary in 1844, he became familiar with the reform-minded leaders of the country. The course of the revolution in 1848 prevented the immediate realization of his varied plans for the Hungarian nation. Based on the Blackwell papers and British Foreign Office records; 58 notes. 1840-50

684. Kabdebo, Thomas. JOSEPH BLACKWELL'S LAST HUNGARIAN MISSION, 1849. *East European Quarterly 1986 20(1): 55-73.* An account of the last days of free Hungary in 1849 based on the reports of a British agent, Joseph Blackwell. Blackwell, an Englishman who spent most of his life on the continent, served on four different occasions as an agent for the British Foreign Office. He provided political information and helped in the encouragement of trade on his early missions. His last mission was taken in 1849 at the request of Lord Palmerston in the hope that Britain could mediate the conflict in Hungary. It was too late, but Blackwell's reports offer a fascinating insight into the Hungarian situation and into British foreign policy. Based on manuscripts of Blackwell in the Hungarian Academy of Sciences and in the British Foreign Office Archives; 78 notes. 1843-50

Blackwood, Sam

685. Taylor, Godfrey. A PRELIMINARY LOOK AT SLIM AND SAM: JAMAICAN STREET SINGERS. *Jamaica J. [Jamaica] 1983 16(3): 39-45.* 1930's-40's
*For abstract see **Beckford, Slim***

Blackwood, William

686. Milne, Maurice. THE "VEILED EDITOR" UNVEILED. WILLIAM BLACKWOOD AND HIS MAGAZINE. *Publishing History [Great Britain] 1984 (16): 87-103.* Discusses the life of editor and publisher William Blackwood, who established *Blackwood's Magazine* in 1817. Blackwood realized early in the 19th century that a new periodical that incorporated short articles, reviews, and political commentary would prove popular among the British. In an effort to establish such a publication, Blackwood faced financial and literary difficulties. Nonetheless, he was able to gather a broad range of intellectual supporters and contributors who helped establish *Blackwood's Magazine* and maintain its quality until it ceased publication in 1980. Secondary sources; 7 notes. ca 1800-34

Blaga, Lucian

687. Barbulesco, Titus. LUCIAN BLAGA ET LA REVUE *GÂNDIREA* ("LA PENSÉE") [Lucian Blaga and the review *Gândirea* [Thought]]. *Rev. des Etudes Roumaines [France] 1981 16: 111-117.* Lucian Blaga, a doyen of 20th-century Romanian letters, was a founder of *Gândirea,* the influential and respected review published in Cluj and Bucharest from 1921 to 1944. Along with Nichifor Crainic, Ion Pillat, and Vasile Voiculescu, Blaga helped to shape a golden

age of Romanian letters in the interwar period. Tolerant of plural cultural styles and deeply involved in shaping a metaphysical construction, Blaga was indifferent to political contingencies. He filled *Gândirea* with his own poetry, drama, essays, philosophy, all eventually gathered coherently in his famous three trilogies—of knowledge, of culture, and of values. 9 notes. 1921-44

Blagoev, Dimitur

688. Jotov, Jordan. INTERNATIONALIST AND PATRIOT: ON THE OCCASION OF THE 125TH ANNIVERSARY OF DIMITÂR BLAGOEV'S BIRTH. *Bulgarian Hist. Rev. [Bulgaria] 1981 9(3): 5-10.* Sketches the political biography of Dimitur Blagoev, a Bulgarian revolutionary active in the 1910's-20's, who founded the Social Democratic Party, fought in World War I, and supported the Russian October Revolution. 1910's-20's

689. Kosynkina, V. P. SLAVNYI SYN BOLGARII [A glorious son of Bulgaria]. *Voprosy Istorii KPSS [USSR] 1981 (9): 139-142.* The 125th anniversary of the birth of the Bulgarian revolutionary Dimitur Blagoev was marked on 22 June 1981 by a conference in Moscow at the Institute of Marxism-Leninism sponsored by the Central Committee of the Communist Party of the Soviet Union. Those taking part included members of the Federation of Soviet Societies for Friendship and Cultural Links Abroad, the Soviet-Bulgarian Friendship Society, and the Bulgarian Ambassador in Moscow, Dimitur Zhulev. The main report was by the institute's director, A. G. Egorov, who noted Blagoev's contributions to philosophy, political economy, sociology, history, ethics, aesthetics, literature, and pedagogy. Other speakers were K. N. Briukhanova, who described Blagoev's reaction to the October Revolution; D. F. Markov, who spoke about Blagoev's teachings on culture; and M. A. Birman, who called for more study in the USSR of Blagoev's life and work. 7 notes. ca 1875-1920

Blagoeva, Vela

690. Tileva, V. DOBAVKI KUM MATERIALITE ZA BIOGRAFIIA NA VELA BLAGOEVA [Additional material on Vela Blagoeva's life]. *Izvestiia na Narodnata Biblioteka "Kiril i Metodii" [Bulgaria] 1983 18: 365-383.* Presents 20 documents, 1877-1900, on Vela Blagoeva's work as a teacher and journalist, her attitude to Macedonia, and her disapproval of contemporary Bulgarian politics. 1877-1900

Blagonravov, A. A.

691. Frolov, K. V. and Parkhomenko, A. A. ISTORIIA NAUKI I TEKHNIKI V TVORCHESKOM NASLEDII AKADEMIKA A. A. BLAGONRAVOVA (K 90-LETIIU SO DNIA ROZHDENIIA) [History of science and technology in the scholarly legacy of Academician A. A. Blagonravov on the 90th anniversary of his birth]. *Voprosy Istorii Estestvoznaniia i Tekhniki [USSR] 1984 (4): 95-103.* Recounts the academic and professional achievements of A. A. Blagonravov (1894-1975). After service in the Revolutionary Army in 1919, he graduated in military engineering, which he later taught at the Leningrad Academy of Artillery. During World War II he trained officer corps while carrying out research in antiaircraft artillery. He became a member of the Soviet Academy of Sciences in 1943. As the leading Soviet expert in ballistics, he was involved in space research programs in the 1960's and 1970's. Secondary sources; 22 notes. 1919-75

Blair, Eric Arthur

See Orwell, George

Blake, William

692. Bentley, G. E., Jr. THE WAY OF A PAPERMAKER WITH A POET: JOSHUA GILPIN, WILLIAM BLAKE, AND THE ARTS IN 1796. *Notes and Queries [Great Britain] 1986 33(1): 80-84.* Speculates on the possible relationship of Quaker papermaker Joshua Gilpin with William Blake, poet and engraver, as alluded to in his diary in 1796. 1765-1841

693. Cox, Stephen D. RECENT WORK ON BLAKE. *Eighteenth-Century Studies 1985 18(3): 391-405.* Reviews eight recent studies on William Blake (1757-1827), all of which rely heavily on previous research. 1780-1827

694. Greenberg, Mark L. THE ROSSETTIS' TRANSCRIPTION OF BLAKE'S NOTEBOOK. *Library [Great Britain] 1982 4(3): 249-272.* Dante Gabriel Rossetti's purchase of William Blake's notebook in 1847 and the subsequent incomplete transcription of portions of the contents is a notable event in the early career of Rossetti. A careful analysis of the Rossetti transcription reveals that he and his brother William Michael introduced many alterations, and the resulting text has been used as Blake source material. Alexander Gilchrist's *Life of William Blake* includes much of the Rossetti transcription, and other scholars have since relied on the Rossetti version. Based on Rossetti's transcription and Blake's notebook; 6 illus., 14 notes. 1847-80

695. Lucie-Smith, Edward. THE FIERY VISION OF WILLIAM BLAKE IS BURNING BRIGHT. *Smithsonian 1982 13(6): 50-59.* On the occasion of a 1982 exhibition of the work of William Blake entitled "William Blake: His Art and Times," presents a biography of Blake who was greatly influenced by his love for medieval art, by friends Henry Fuseli and John Flaxman, and by the French Revolution. 1780's-1800's

Blakiston, Noel

696. Curato, Federico. NOEL BLAKISTON [Noel Blakiston]. *Rassegna Storica del Risorgimento [Italy] 1985 72(2): 214-218.* Discusses the work of Noel Blakiston (1905-84), who graduated from Magdalene College, Cambridge, in modern history and entered the British Archives in 1928. Not only an archivist and historian of the Italian Risorgimento, Blakiston was also a novelist and published short stories in leading magazines of the time. In 1957, he organized the state archives for the new nation of Malaysia at Kuala Lumpur; as Honorary Fellow, he organized the enormous mass of documents and charters dating from the 15th century at Eton College. From 1953 to his death in 1984, he wrote and spoke on the archival sources for the Risorgimento and the political aid given by Great Britain to Italy in the 19th century. Based on secondary sources; 17 notes. 19c

Blanchard, Marie Madeleine

697. Schneider, Rachel R.; Johnson, Mary (commentary). STAR BALLOONIST OF EUROPE: THE CAREER OF MARIE-MADELEINE BLANCHARD. *Consortium on Revolutionary Europe 1750-1850: Proceedings 1983: 697-711.* Marie Madeleine Blanchard was the wife of Jean Pierre Blanchard, who was one of the most famous balloonists in Europe during the late 18th and early 19th centuries. When her husband was killed during an exhibition in 1809, he left her with many debts. Madame Blanchard was a resourceful and brave person, and she took over her husband's business. From 1809 to 1819 she was the most famous female balloonist in Europe. Napoleon was one of her most devoted patrons. Altogether

she made 67 ascents, until she herself was killed in an accident. Her career reveals the possibilities that were open to a woman in that era. Comments, pp. 712-718. Primary sources; 21 notes. 1809-19

Blanco, Eduardo

698. Lovera De-Sola, R. J. EDUARDO BLANCO EN SU CONTEXTO: A PROPOSITO DE LOS CIEN AÑOS DE *VENEZUELA HEROICA* [Eduardo Blanco in his context: a propos of the centenary of *Venezuela Heroica]. Bol. de la Acad. Nac. de la Hist. [Venezuela] 1982 65(258): 445-460.* Eduardo Blanco (1838-1912) was one of the principal romantic writers of Venezuela. His chief work, *Venezuela Heroica,* is a series of tableaux of the independence wars. Blanco was a significant figure in the politics, culture, and literature of Romanticism in Venezuela. 72 notes. 1838-1912

Blanco, José Félix

699. Sánchez Espejo, Carlos. JOSE FELIX BLANCO EN EL PANTEON NACIONAL [José Félix Blanco in the national pantheon]. *Bol. de la Acad. Nac. de la Hist. [Venezuela] 1982 65(260): 917-927.* José Félix Blanco (1782-1873) was a foundling who became a priest, military chaplain, and eventually military leader and politician during the troubled years of the independence struggle. His remains were transferred to the pantheon in 1896 and this article celebrates his memory on the 200th anniversary of his birth. 32 notes. 1782-1873

Blanco Fombona, Rufino

700. Castellanos, Rafael Ramón. RUFINO BLANCO FOMBONA Y LA EDITORIAL AMERICA [Rufino Blanco Fombona and the Editorial América publishing house]. *Bol. de la Acad. Nac. de la Hist. [Venezuela] 1982 65(257): 159-166.* The exiled Venezuelan writer Rufino Blanco Fombona (1874-1944) will be best remembered as founder of the Editorial América in Madrid, which published nearly 400 titles in many collections of literature, social science, and history. 1915-35

Blasius, Mathieu Frédéric

701. McCormick, Cathy L. MATHIEU-FREDERIC BLASIUS: A MUSICIAN'S LIFE IN THE MIDST OF REVOLUTION. *Michigan Academician 1985 17(2): 213-223.* A chronicle of the life of French composer and performer Mathieu Frédéric Blasius (1758-1829) during the French Revolution shows how the social role of music in revolutionary France changed as music and politics became intertwined. 1780-1816

Blaumanis, Rudolfs

702. Waack, Inara. RUDOLFS BLAUMANIS—EIN BEDEUTENDER REPRÄSENTANT DER LETTISCHEN REALISTISCHEN LITERATUR [Rudolfs Blaumanis—an important representative of Latvian realistic literature]. *Wiss. Zeits. der Wilhelm-Pieck-Universität Rostock. Gesellschafts- und Sprachwissenschaftliche Reihe [East Germany] 1981 30(3-4): 37-41.* Describes the life and work of the Latvian realist and portrays some of his writings' main characters. 1863-1908

Bleiweis, Janez

703. Borisov, Peter. DR. JANEZ BLEIWEIS—ZDRAVNIK IN ZDRAVSTVENI PROSVETITELJ [Dr. Janez Bleiweis: physician and public health enlightener]. *Zbornik za Zgodovino Naravoslovja in Tehnike [Yugoslavia] 1983 7: 157-180.* Janez Bleiweis (1808-81) distinguished himself by his activity in Carniola not only in the field of veterinary science, but also in the sphere of public health service. Particularly important were his articles about health published in *Novice* (The News); they were written in a way intelligible to the Slovene rural population. He was actively involved in preventive medicine as a member of medical councils and committees during the cholera epidemic. As a deputy of the provincial assembly, he contributed to the improvement of medical institutions in Ljubljana. 1840's-81

Blicher, Steen Steensen

704. Ingemann Jørgensen, Claus. STEEN STEENSEN BLICHER—EIN SCHRIFTSTELLERPORTRÄT [Steen Steensen Blicher—portrait of a writer]. *Nordeuropa [East Germany] 1984 18: 28-35.* Chronicles the Danish author Steen Steensen Blicher's (1782-1846) development from a romantic lyric poet to a realistic narrative writer, with particular attention paid to his political activities as a village priest and as a contributor to the democratic movement toward the advance of the middle class in Jutland. 1806-46

Bligh, William Russell

705. Townsend, Norma. MUTINY IN ARMIDALE: THE CASE OF W. R. BLIGH. *Historical Studies [Australia] 1985 21(85): 534-549.* Reinterprets the dismissal, in 1859, of William Russell Bligh as Clerk of Petty Sessions in Armidale, New South Wales. Previously seen as a victory for the "liberal" bourgeoisie against the conservative squatters, the case is viewed in the context of Armidale development as a town, and specific personal rivalries. Bligh had used the court to get revenge against a former friend, Dr. Thomas Markham, who was popular. As the town developed, solicitors set up in practice. With the decline of the gold rush, the town looked for a new role and became the center for a new district court. Bligh's position became anachronistic, "frontier values being replaced by new, professional standards." Based on New South Wales archives, newspapers, legislative proceedings, and monographs; 118 notes. 1840's-50's

Bloch, Charles

706. —. ZUM SECHZIGSTEN GEBURTSTAG VON CHARLES BLOCH [For the 60th birthday of Charles Bloch]. *Jahrbuch des Inst. für Deutsche Gesch. [Israel] 1981 10: 13-14.* Charles Bloch was born in Berlin in 1921. In his early years his parents moved to the British mandate of Palestine. His studies of Hebrew and modern French history were interrupted in 1944 but his dissertation at the Sorbonne on relations between France and Great Britain earned him a doctorate in 1954. Returning to Israel in 1955 he joined the newly organized University of Tel Aviv where he still is a professor. 1921-81

Bloch, Ernst

707. Abosch, Heinz. MYSTISCHER MARXIST: ERNST BLOCHS POLITISCHE THEOLOGIE [Mystical Marxist: Ernst Bloch's political ideology]. *Schweizer Monatshefte [Switzerland] 1985 65(10): 831-834.* Discusses the life and political beliefs of the German philosopher Ernst Bloch (1885-1977) who supported Marxism and Soviet Communism as a part of his philosophy of messianic hope and utopianism. 1918-77

708. Vranicki, Predrag. FILOZOFIJA NADE: DIJALEKTIČKO-HISTORIJSKI MATERIJALIZAM ERNSTA BLOCHA [The philosophy of hope: the dialectical material-

ism of Ernst Bloch]. *Rad Jugoslavenske Akad. Znanosti i Umjetnosti: Društvene Znanosti [Yugoslavia] 1981 393(20): 187-208.* The German philosopher Ernst Bloch (1885-1977) espoused a doctrine called the philosophy of hope. Despite the poverty of the Stalinist model, he did not hesitate to call it dialectical materialism. Bloch refused to concentrate on just one element of existence—the history of man. Rather he preferred to consider existence as a whole. Ernst Bloch, throughout his writings, never lost faith in the greatness of man; he believed that the root of history is the creative, working man who changes and overcomes the present. 43 notes. 1948-77

Bloch, Joseph

709. Fletcher, Roger A. A REVISIONIST DIALOGUE ON WILHELMINE WELTPOLITIK: JOSEPH BLOCH AND KURT EISNER 1907-1914. *Int. Wiss. Korrespondenz zur Gesch. der Deutschen Arbeiterbewegung [West Germany] 1980 16(4): 453-477.* Describes the lives, work and thought of Joseph Bloch, a revisionist, and Kurt Eisner, a Social Democrat, and shows the similarities of their influence on classical German Social Democracy despite the great differences between them. 1907-14

Bloch, Marc

710. Fink, Carole. MARC BLOCH: THE LIFE AND IDEAS OF A FRENCH PATRIOT. *Can. Rev. of Studies in Nationalism [Canada] 1983 10(2): 235-252.* Marc Bloch (1886-1944), historian, Sorbonne professor and founder of the *Annales* school of historiography, was born into a middle-class family of assimilated Jews. Bloch was much affected by World War I and became an ardent French patriot. He neither denied his Jewish background nor stressed it. Although he moved in Jewish academic circles, he did not pursue questions of Jewish history or take part in political activities. Yet the Vichy government stripped him of his teaching post in 1940 because of his Jewish background. He then served in the resistance, but was captured by the Germans and shot in 1944. Based on Bloch's papers and interviews with his colleagues; 56 notes. 1910's-44

711. Rutkoff, Peter M. and Scott, William B. LETTERS TO AMERICA: THE CORRESPONDENCE OF MARC BLOCH, 1940-41. *French Hist. Studies 1981 12(2): 277-303.* Correspondence of Marc Bloch with American academic and political representatives (July 1940-July 1941) aimed at securing an academic post in the United States for the distinguished French medievalist. After thirteen months of negotiations, Bloch decided to remain in occupied France rather than leave several members of his family behind. In June 1944 he was executed by the Gestapo for his activities in the Resistance. Archives of the New School for Social Research in New York City. 1940-44

712. Weber, Eugen. ABOUT MARC BLOCH. *Am. Scholar 1981-82 51(1): 73-82.* Marc Bloch (1866-1944) was a wide-ranging, multilingual, interdisciplinary scholar of the first half of the 20th century, who criticized the narrowness of many of his colleagues. He fought against the routine, unimaginative, and sterile mentality that characterized much of the education of his times. Captured by the Nazis in France in 1944, he was tortured and executed for resistance activities. 1900's-44

Bloch-Bauer, Adele

713. Grimberg, Salomon. ADELE. *Art & Antiques 1986 (Sum): 70-74, 90.* Tells of the secret romance between artist Gustav Klimt and Adele Bloch-Bauer in turn-of-the-century Vienna, which was finally detected in the artist's passionate portraits of his lover. These paintings became the objects of attention and protest. 1900-12

Blok, Aleksandr A.

714. Gippius, Vasili. SPOTKANIA Z BŁOKIEM [Encounters with Blok]. *Slavia Orientalis [Poland] 1983 32(3): 343-351.* A translation from Russian of the author's reminiscences of his personal acquaintance with the Russian poet Aleksandr A. Blok in the years 1903-14 with references to contemporary Russian literary critics and excerpts from Blok's poetry in Russian. 1903-14

715. Iezuitova, L. A. and Skvortsova, N. V. NOVOE OB UNIVERSITETSKOM OKRUZHENII A. BLOKA (A. A. BLOK I A. A. SMIRNOV) [A fresh look at the university circle of A. Blok: A. A. Blok and A. A. Smirnov]. *Vestnik Leningradskogo U.: Seriia Istorii, Iazyka i Literatury [USSR] 1981 (3): 49-58.* Aleksandr A. Blok (1880-1921) joined the history and philosophy faculty at St. Petersburg in 1901 and became a friend of Aleksandr A. Smirnov (1883-1962), a student of Celtic languages and literature, Shakespeare, and French and Spanish. He shared Blok's interest in symbolism. The article includes the text of A. Smirnov's 4 November 1904 letter to Blok in which he praised Blok's work and expressed his affection and a 1922 work of Smirnov analyzing Blok's lyrical work. The appendix includes publications and poems written by Smirnov at the university. Based on Blok's and Smirnov's works and Soviet research. 1901-22

716. Kruglova, M. A. K ISTORII RODA A. A. BLOKA [The history of A. A. Blok's family origins]. *Sovetskie Arkhivy [USSR] 1981 (5): 67-69.* Attempts to trace members of the family of the Russian poet Aleksandr A. Blok (1880-1921) from materials in Soviet archive collections. One of his ancestors was a Mecklenburg-Shverin who studied medicine in Rostock and Berlin in 1755. Documentary evidence also exists to fill out details of Blok's parents' lives. Based on the Soviet Leningrad State Historical Archives, collection no. 536; 24 notes. 18c-1870's

717. Simcic, Olga. BLOK E IL MESSIANISMO POPULISTA NELLA RUSSIA PRERIVOLUZIONARIA [Blok and populist messianism in prerevolutionary Russia]. *Studium [Italy] 1981 77(4): 423-441.* Traces the intellectual itinerary of the Russian symbolist poet Alexander Blok (1880-1921) in the light of his friendship with the peasant poet Nikolai Kliuev. An individualist jealous of his freedom and artistic creativity, Blok could not share his friend's convictions and certainties. 1905-17

Blom, Trudi

718. Woodward, Laura Lynn and Woodward, Ralph Lee, Jr. TRUDI BLOM AND THE LACANDON RAIN FOREST. *Environmental Review 1985 9(3): 226-236.* Reviews the work of Trudi Blom (b. 1901) to help maintain the quality of traditional Lacandón Maya Indian life in the middle and late 20th century and to protect their forest environment along the Usumacinta River at the border of Guatemala and Mexico. 1940-85

Blomefylde, Myles

719. Baker, Donald C. and Murphy, John L. MYLES BLOMEFYLDE, ELIZABETHAN PHYSICIAN, ALCHEMIST AND BOOK COLLECTOR. *Bodleian Lib. Record [Great Britain] 1982 11(1): 35-46.* Reviews the scholarship relating to William Blomfield and Myles Blomefylde, both of Bury St. Edmunds, who had long been treated as one person. Sketches the life of Myles Blomefylde, including travel to Venice, service as a juror in Essex, the charge against him of practicing magic, book collecting, and the disposition of his library. Based on manuscripts in University Library, Cambridge, and in Essex Records Office; 28 notes. 1525-1603

Blonski, Pavel P.

720. Kozulin, Alex. PETER BLONSKY AND RUSSIAN PROGRESSIVISM: THE EARLY YEARS. *Studies in Soviet Thought [Netherlands] 1982 24(1): 11-21.* Treats the career of Pavel Petrovich Blonski, one of the founders of Soviet psychology and Soviet educational theory, as a case study. Exemplifies the transformation of a prerevolutionary scholar into a believer and an ardent implementer of Soviet science. Discusses Blonski's adaptation to Soviet society of John Dewey's concepts. Based on the works of Blonski, Dewey, and William James; 26 notes. 1917-41

Blount, Michael

721. Manning, Roger B. THE PROSECUTION OF SIR MICHAEL BLOUNT, LIEUTENANT OF THE TOWER OF LONDON, 1595. *Bulletin of the Institute of Historical Research [Great Britain] 1984 57(136): 216-223.* Sir Michael Blount, lieutenant of the Tower of London, became involved in 1594 in a plot to support Edward Seymour, Earl of Hertford, the Suffolk claimant to the throne. The conspiracy was discovered and Blount removed from his position and imprisoned, but not tried for treason. Appendix of information by Edward Coke, attorney-general, and two other documents; 40 notes. 1594-95

Bloy, Léon

722. Legrand, Francine-Claire. HENRY DE GROUX—LEON BLOY ET LAUTREAMONT [Henry de Groux: Léon Bloy and Lautréamont]. *Rev. de l'U. de Bruxelles [Belgium] 1981 (3): 67-73.* Details the personal and professional relationships which developed between painter Henry de Groux and novelists Léon Bloy (1846-1917) and Isadore Ducasse, Comte de Lautréamont (1846-70). 1870-1910

Blum, Leon

723. Eldar, Isra'el. QAVIM LE-DMUTO HA-YEHUDIT ŠEL LY'ON BLUM [Features of Leon Blum's Jewish personality]. *Yalkut Moreshet Periodical [Israel] 1985 (40): 91-120.* Discusses aspects of Leon Blum's biography (1872-1950) that reveal the influence of his Jewish condition on his activities as a leader of the French socialist movement, as prime minister of France, and on his attitudes toward the Jewish and non-Jewish world, mainly during World War II, when he became a prisoner in a concentration camp. 1900's-50

Blume, Alberto

724. Gómez Rodríguez, Ramiro. EL PROFESOR ALBERTO BLUME [Professor Alberto Blume]. *Boletín de Historia y Antigüedades [Colombia] 1985 72(749): 471-497.* Alberto Blume came to Colombia in 1872 as part of a German pedagogical mission whose purpose was to aid in the expansion and modernization of public education. He was assigned to work in the state of Santander, where he headed the Escuela Normal de Institutores and was eventually named superintendent of public instruction. A skilled and dedicated teacher and humanist, he promoted improved educational methods and contributed to the general cultural development of the region. 25 notes. 1872-78

Blumenfeld, R. D.

725. Parisi, Frank Joseph, Jr. "From Main Street to Fleet Street: R. D. Blumenfeld and the London *Daily Express,* 1887-1932." George Washington U. 1985. 490 pp. *DAI 1985 46(5): 1382-A.* DA8514505 1887-1932

Blumfeldt, Evald

726. Koit, Jakob. EVALD BLUMFELDT: IN MEMORIAM [Evald Blumfeldt: in memoriam]. *Eesti Teadusliku Seltsi Rootsis. Aastaraamat [Sweden] 1980-84 9: 218-222.* Evald Blumfeldt (1902-81), an Estonian historian and librarian earned his master's and doctoral degrees at Tartu University. From 1936 to 1940 Blumfeldt was the head of the Estonian archive of cultural history and from 1940 to 1944 an assistant professor of history at Tartu University. Blumfeldt's research and writing centered around the agrarian problems of Estonia during the medieval period. Some of his publications discuss the period of Estonian national awakening in the late 19th century. In 1944 Blumfeldt fled to Germany and in 1945 settled in Sweden. Blumfeldt continued his archivist career in Sweden's state archive and served as head of the Estonian Learned Society of Sweden. 13c-19c

Blyden, Edward Wilmot

727. Neuberger, Benyamin. EARLY AFRICAN NATIONALISM, JUDAISM AND ZIONISM: EDWARD WILMOT BLYDEN. *Jewish Social Studies 1985 47(2): 151-166.* Describes and analyzes the attitude of Liberian statesman Edward Wilmot Blyden, an early black African nationalist, toward the Jews, the "Jewish Question," and Zionism. Blyden's upbringing in St. Thomas, where he had Jewish friends, likely influenced his philo-Semitic, pro-Zionist views. Based on Blyden's published writings and secondary sources; 86 notes. 1832-1908

Bo Gu

See Chin Bangxian

Bo Yang

See Guo Yidong

Bobrowski, Czesław

728. Jędrychowski, Stefan. MOJE KONTAKTY Z PROFESOREM CZESŁAWEM BOBROWSKIM [My contacts with Professor Czesław Bobrowski]. *Ekonomista [Poland] 1984 (1-2): 65-68.* The author describes his professional contacts with Czesław Bobrowski (b. 1904), a Polish economist who has been a member of the Commission for Economic Reform since 1980. 1930's-84

729. Kula, Małgorzata. KONSEKWENTNA LINIA ŻYCIA: SZKIC DO BIOGRAFII [A persistent line of life: sketch toward a biography]. *Ekonomista [Poland] 1984 (1-2): 9-23.* Outlines the professional biography of Czesław Bobrowski (b. 1904), a Polish economist who organized and presided over the Consultative Economic Council in 1982. 1920's-83

730. Sokołowski, Kazimierz. CZESŁAW BOBROWSKI I *GOSPODARKA NARODOWA:* PRZYCZYNEK DO HISTORII [Czesław Bobrowski and *Gospodarka Narodowa:* a historical sketch]. *Ekonomista [Poland] 1984 (1-2): 25-43.* Views the influence of the Polish economist Czesław Bobrowski (b. 1904) on the economic review journal *Gospodarka Narodowa* [National economy] appearing between 1931 and 1937, of which he was a cofounder and editor. 1931-37

Bobrzyński, Michał

731. Hetnal, Adam A. BOBRZYŃSKI—HISTORIAN AND STATESMAN. *Polish Review 1985 30(1): 99-103.* Reviews Waldemar Łazuga's *Michał Bobrzyński. Myśl Historyczna a Dziatalność Polityczna* [Michał Bobrzyński: historical thought and political activity] (1982). Łazuga studies the controversial Polish figure, both historian and politician, who favored an Austro-Polish solution during World War I. 2 notes. 1870's-1935

Bocher, Joan

732. Davis, John. JOAN OF KENT, LOLLARDY AND THE ENGLISH REFORMATION. *J. of Ecclesiastical Hist. [Great Britain] 1982 33(2): 225-233.* Traces the views of Joan Bocher, or Joan of Kent, who was burned for heresy in 1550. She first came to notice for Lollard beliefs in Essex, where Lollardy was interacting with Cambridge evangelism. About the time of her removal to Kent in 1543 she was expressing heretical views about the sacraments, and had some success in influencing ladies at court. By 1549 she had become an Anabaptist. The correlation between these developments and local examples of religious radicalism are brought out, and their significance for the Reformation is explained. Based on manuscripts in Lambeth Palace Library, Kent Record Office, Rochester Diocesan Registry, and national collections; 40 notes. 1528-50

Bocskai, István

733. Juhasz, István. BOCSKAI ISTVÁN AZ EGYKORÚ EGYHÁZI HAGYOMÁNY MEGVILÁGÍTÁSÁBAN [István Bocskai in contemporary church tradition]. *Theológiai Szemle [Hungary] 1981 24(1): 43-47.* Bocskai's main strength was his widely acclaimed belief that he was selected to be the ruler of his country by God and therefore all his decisions were decisions of the Lord. This helped the cause of his freedom fighters considerably. His outlook on life and government was extremely strict, regulated by contemporary Calvinistic attitudes. His main aim was to free his country from the aspirations of the Habsburg Empire. 41 notes. 1604-07

Bodianski, O. M.

734. Pashaeva, N. M. SLAVIANSKAIA BIBLIOTEKA O. M. BODIANSKOGO [The Slavic library of O. M. Bodianski]. *Sovetskoe Slavianovedenie [USSR] 1982 (1): 94-103.* Looks at the travels of O. M. Bodianski, which he undertook at the end of the 1830's and beginning of the 1840's through the Slavic countries. The collection of 2,349 volumes that he acquired formed the basis of a Slavic library, and are presently housed in the Department of Rare Books of the Science Library of Moscow University. 4 notes, biblio. 1835-42

Bodin, Jean

735. Boucher, Jacqueline. L'INCARCERATION DE JEAN BODIN PENDANT LA TROISIEME GUERRE DE RELIGION [The incarceration of Jean Bodin during the third war of religion]. *Nouvelle Revue du Seizième Siècle [France] 1983 1: 33-44.* Of those arrested in 1569 for religious heterodoxy, Jean Bodin (1530-96) was the only lawyer of the Parliament of Paris who had signed a "profession de foi" in 1562. His imprisonment seems not to have adversely affected his subsequent career, or his marriage in 1576 to Françoise Trouillart. Bodin later entered the service of the Duc d'Alençon, himself a friend of the Reformation movement. 57 notes. 1560-90

736. Horowitz, Maryanne Cline; Gosselin, Edward A. (commentary). BODIN'S RELIGION RECONSIDERED: THE MARRANO AS ROLE MODEL. *Proceedings of the Annual Meeting of the Western Society for French History 1983 11: 36-46.* Several recent authors have argued that the French writer Jean Bodin (1530-96) might have been born of a Jewish mother and that he converted from Catholicism to Judaism at some point in his career. An examination of his writings reveals, however, that the situation was more complex than scholars have realized. Although Bodin outwardly remained a Catholic, he gradually adopted a universal type of religion that did not correspond precisely to any existing creed. Comments, pp. 47-52. 43 notes. 1560's-70's

737. Horowitz, Maryanne Cline. JUDAISM IN JEAN BODIN. *Sixteenth Cent. J. 1982 13(3): 109-113.* Recent works by historian Paul Lawrence Rose provide evidence that Jean Bodin (1529/30-96) was heavily influenced by Judaism. Based on Bodin's works and secondary sources; 15 notes. 1560's-90's

Bodmer, Karl

738. Mann, Maybelle. KARL BODMER: FROM FRONTIER AMERICA TO THE BARBIZON WOODS. *Art & Antiques 1982 5(2): 52-61.* Biography of Swiss painter, Karl Bodmer, noted for the drawings and watercolors he did while on an expedition led by Alexander Philip Maximilian, Prince of Wied-Neuwied in Rhenish Prussia, resulting in *Travels in the Interior of North America, 1832-1834* and an accompanying *Atlas,* and most famous for his paintings of American Indians. Describes Bodmer's career in Paris, the later editions of *Travels,* and Bodmer's work in photography at Barbizon. 1822-93

Boemus, Johannes

739. Lebeau, Jean. *NOVUS ORBIS.* LES COSMOGRAPHES ALLEMANDS DU XVIe SIÈCLE ET LES GRANDES DECOUVERTES *[Novus Orbis:* German cosmographers of the 16th century and the great discoveries]. *Rev. d'Allemagne [France] 1981 13(2): 197-215.* The popularization of the great voyages of discovery and exploration of the late 15th and early 16th centuries was brought about in the Holy Roman Empire chiefly by four scholars, Johannes Boemus (1485-1535), Simon Grynaeus (1493-1541), Sebastian Franck (1499-1542), and Sebastian Münster (1489-1552). All deeply involved in religious issues, they turned to Protestantism and gradually secularized a branch of knowledge formerly subjected to the authority of the Catholic Church. Nevertheless, they saw a certain religious significance in the revelation of the rest of the planet. Their works also emphasized tolerance of other cultures and the empirical approach, thus heralding the advent of modern thought. 45 notes. 1520-50

Boesch, Gottfried

740. Häfliger, Alois. NACHRUF. PROFESSOR GOTTFRIED BOESCH 1915-1983. PRÄSIDENT DER AGGS 1965-1972 [Obituary: Professor Gottfried Boesch, 1915-83, president of the General Historical Society of Switzerland, 1965-72]. *Schweizerische Zeitschrift für Geschichte [Switzerland] 1984 34(2): 311-313.* Gottfried Boesch received his schooling at Catholic order schools in central Switzerland and studied at the universities of Zurich and Fribourg, where he earned his doctorate in 1943 with a dissertation on Sempach in the Middle Ages. His teaching career led him from the Lucerne cantonal school to the university of Fribourg, where he was professor of Swiss history from 1967 to 1980, when he retired for health reasons. Throughout his career Boesch was an active researcher and prolific publishing scholar on many aspects of the history of central Switzerland. In addition, he developed great skills in museum work. Lucerne recognized this by making him curator of Castle Heidegg, where he lived from 1951 to his death and where, as a further sideline, he became a professional rosegrower. Leadership duties at the head of several historical societies added to the burdens of this extraordinarily active historian. ca 15c-20c

Boettcher, Arthur

741. Anniko, Matti. ARTHUR BOETTCHER, KARL BOGISLAUS REICHERT AND ERNST REISSNER: 19TH CENTURY PIONEERS IN INNER EAR RESEARCH AT THE TARTU UNIVERSITY IN ESTONIA. *Eesti Teadusliku Seltsi Rootsis. Aastaraamat [Sweden] 1980-84 9: 145-159.* Karl Bogislaus Reichert (1811-83), Ernst Reissner (1824-78), and Arthur Boettcher (1831-89), scientists of the anatomy institution at the Tartu University focused their research on the structure and the function of the inner ear. Reichert, trained in Königsberg, started his career in the field of embryology and continued this work with his student Reissner in ear morphology. Several structures in the ear have been named after Reichert, e.g., Reichert's canal, Reichert's recess, and Reichert's cartilage. Boettcher focused his research on the organ of Corti. He argued that during the development of this hearing organ a greater and smaller epithelial ridge was formed before the organ of Corti differentiated. The greater ridge is named "Boettcher epithelial ridge." Secondary sources; 7 fig., 32 notes. 1830's-80's

Bogdan, Damian P.

742. Bălan, Constantin. LE PROFESSEUR DAMIAN P. BOGDAN LORS DE SON 75[e] ANNIVERSAIRE [Damian P. Bogdan on his 75th birthday]. *Rev. Roumaine d'Hist. [Romania] 1982 21(3-4): 462-464.* Laureate of the Romanian Academy, paleographer, and specialist in Slavic languages at the Bucharest State Archives, member of the Department of Letters and Philosophy and professor at the School of Maps in Bucharest, and vital contributor to the 22-volume *Documents Concernant l'Histoire de la Roumanie,* which appeared between 1950 and 1957, Damian P. Bogdan (b. 1907) has for more than half a century enriched the body of world knowledge on the Middle Ages, paleography, sigillography, filigranology, linguistics, and textual and documentary criticism, rightly deserving the international respect and recognition that he enjoys. Primary and secondary listings and bibliographies; 13 notes. 10c-18c

Bogdan, Ioan

743. Michelson, Paul E. THE BIRTH OF CRITICAL HISTORIOGRAPHY IN ROMANIA: THE CONTRIBUTIONS OF IOAN BOGDAN, DIMITRIE ONCIUL AND CONSTANTIN GIURESCU. *Analele U. București: Istorie [Romania] 1983 32: 59-76.* Describes the careers of Romanian historians Ioan Bogdan, Dimitrie Onciul, and Constantin Giurescu. These three pioneered a new trend in historiography in Romania in which research, methodology, and fact replaced romantic glorification of persons and events. The new critical approach paralleled similar developments in Western historiography and was spurred by *Junimea,* a Romanian cultural movement that criticized shoddy work in all cultural disciplines. 1884-1920

Bogdanov, N. P.

744. Zelov, N. S. IZ LICHNYKH FONDOV DELEGATOV I VSESOIUZNOGO S"EZDA SOVETOV [From the personal archives of the deputies of the 1st All-Union Congress of Soviets]. *Sovetskie Arkhivy [USSR] 1982 (6): 40-43.* Surveys the contents of the personal archives of the deputies to the 1st All-Union Congress of the Soviets in 1922, and the light they shed on the first years of the Soviet state. Among the 20 archives are those of N. P. Bogdanov, I. I. Lepse, and A. I. Sviderski; some contain newspaper cuttings, personal and group photographs of the deputies, and personal reminiscences. Based on materials in the Central State Archive of the October Revolution of the Russian Republic. 1920's

Bogomolov, Aleksei S.

745. —. A. S. BOGOMOLOV [A. S. Bogomolov]. *Voprosy Filosofii [USSR] 1983 (5): 170-171.* Obituary of the Soviet philosopher and historian Aleksei S. Bogomolov (1928-83) summarizing his publications and describing his academic career and his participation on the editorial board of *Voprosy Filosofii.* 1928-83

Bohmann, Alfred

746. —. DR. ALFRED BOHMANN (1906-1983) [Dr. Alfred Bohmann (1906-83)]. *Europa Ethnica [Austria] 1983 40(2): 87.* A tribute to the Austrian historian Alfred Bohmann (1906-83), with particular reference to his work on the history of national movements in Bohemia and the Sudetenland. 1906-83

Bohn, Reinhold

747. Karasek-Strzygowski, Hertha; Hieb, Selma Tieszen, transl. REINHOLD BOHN. *Journal of the American Historical Society of Germans from Russia 1986 9(1): 13-17.* Reminiscences of farmer Reinhold Bohn concerning German village life and experiences under Russian occupation in Volhynia from 1915 to the 1930's. 1915-30's

Bohn, Waldemar

748. Losey, Doris and Utecht, Rosie. WALDEMAR BOHN'S STORY. *J. of the Am. Hist. Soc. of Germans from Russia 1980 3(3): 26-33.* Personal narrative of Waldemar Bohn, a Russian German, covering repression in the Ukraine during the 1930's, the German invasion during World War II, immigration to Germany, and eventual settlement in New Jersey. 1930's-50's

Bohr, Niels

749. Marx, György. NIELS BOHR ÉS MODELLJEI [Niels Bohr and his models]. *Magyar Tudomány [Hungary] 1985 30(12): 883-888.* The strongest characteristic of physicist Niels Bohr's (1885-1962) work was the utilization of models. For example he likened the atomic nucleus to billiard balls in a dish. In 1939 when he learned of nuclear fission he answered the questions of how much energy is required to

split an atom, which can be split, and why atoms do not split on their own by comparing atoms to a trembling water droplet. Bohr was a titan of physics, who combined in his thinking classical and modern physics and who worked tirelessly for the acceptance of the cultural and human significance of the principles of quantum mechanics. Lecture given at the Magyar Tudományos Akadémia on 7 October 1985 marking the centenary of Bohr's birth. 1913-45

750. Minei, Nicolae. EVADAREA FIZICIANULUI DANEZ [Escape of a Danish physicist]. *Magazin Istoric [Romania] 1980 14(11): 16-18.* Outlines the career of the Danish nuclear physicist Niels Bohr (1885-1962). After taking the decision to leave German-occupied Denmark, he was evacuated in 1943 via Sweden to England and the United States. Portrait. 1900-60

751. Semenishchev, Iu. P. "ISCHEZNOVENIE" NIL'SA BORA V 1943 G. [The "disappearance" of Niels Bohr in 1943]. *Novaia i Noveishaia Istoriia [USSR] 1981 (4): 158-171.* Niels Bohr was one of the few physicists who understood the destructive potential of nuclear power. The US government was aware of his work, and in order to outpace the research under way in Nazi Germany they decided to bring Bohr to America. In 1943 the Germans ended civilian administration in Denmark and installed military rule. Bohr escaped to Sweden in order to avoid deportation to Germany. On 30 September he was transported to Great Britain at considerable risk and in December he arrived in the United States. Bohr was opposed to a monopoly of the fruit of nuclear research by one power only and wanted to share it with all nations, including the USSR. British and American press, secondary sources; 54 notes. 1938-45

752. Weisskopf, Victor. NIELS BOHR, THE QUANTUM, AND THE WORLD. *Social Research 1984 51(3): 583-608.* Describes the career of Danish physicist Niels Bohr (1885-1962) and prints his 9 June 1950 open letter to the UN pleading for free international exchange of information on nuclear technology. 1885-1962

Bok, Vladimir G.

753. Kakovkin, A. Ia. VLADIMIR GEORGIEVICH BOK [Vladimir Georgievich Bok]. *Narody Azii i Afriki [USSR] 1981 (6): 121-124.* The celebrated Russian art historian Vladimir G. Bok (1850-99) is best known for his role in the formation of the collection of relics of Coptic Egypt in the Hermitage Museum in St. Petersburg and study of the subject in Russia. After his art studies at St. Petersburg University, Bok was appointed custodian of the Hermitage's Medieval and Rennaissance Department. His imagination fired by the recent discovery of artistic relics in Egypt, Bok, together with an assistant, paid two visits to that country in the late 1880's and brought back a number of items, which formed the basis of the Hermitage's fine later collection of this period. Before his early death in 1899, Bok published several works on the subject and was recognized as Russia's leading Egyptologist. Secondary sources; 15 notes. 1880's-99

Boldizsár, Iván

754. Boldizsár, Iván; Molnár, Eszter, transl. FIVE BITTER-SWEET STORIES. *New Hungarian Quarterly [Hungary] 1986 27(102): 87-100.* The author, a Hungarian writer, journalist, and editor of the *New Hungarian Quarterly,* relates five experiences from his life in Hungary from the waning years of World War II to 1950. 1944-50

Boldú, Ramón

755. Martí Mayor, José. LABOR LITERARIA Y CULTURAL DEL P. RAMON BOLDU, O.F.M. [Literary and cultural work of Father Ramón Boldú, O.F.M.]. *Archivo Ibero-Americano [Spain] 1984 44(176): 429-453.* Discusses the writing and publishing accomplishments of the Spanish Franciscan Ramón Boldú (1815-89) in the years following his return to Spain from Italy in 1845. Serving in Barcelona, Boldú contributed to the novel *Las Ruinas de Mi Convento* [The ruins of my convent], directed several large historical and theological works, founded the journal *Revista Franciscana* [Franciscan Review], and campaigned for the beatification of Christopher Columbus. An accompanying bibliography lists 121 books, pamphlets, articles, and manuscripts written or edited by Boldú. Based on the writings of Boldú and secondary sources; 19 notes, biblio. 1845-89

Boldur, Alexandru

756. Andronic, Alexandru. ALEXANDRU BOLDUR [The late Alexandru Boldur]. *Anuarul Institutului de Istorie și Arheologie "A. D. Xenopol" [Romania] 1983 20: 635-637.* Alexandru Boldur (1886-1982) was born at Kishinev, studied at St. Petersburg, became a professor of law in the Crimea, and later legal expert in the Ministry of Foreign Trade, Moscow. He was repatriated in 1924 and, after working in Paris as an expert on Bessarabia, came to Iași. He was professor of history at Iași from 1943, but his main achievement was the reorganization of the A. D. Xenopol Institute of History as an independent body. Boldur himself specialized in the history of Moldavia in the Middle Ages and, in the 1970's, in Thracian problems. 1886-1982

757. Zub, Alexander. ALEXANDRU V. BOLDUR (MAR. 10 1886-NOV. 19 1982) [Alexandru V. Boldur, 1886-1982]. *Südost-Forschungen [West Germany] 1983 42: 301-302.* Provides an obituary of the Romanian historian A. V. Boldur. 4 notes, biblio. 1886-1982

Boleyn, Anne

758. Dowling, Maria. ANNE BOLEYN AND REFORM. *Journal of Ecclesiastical History [Great Britain] 1984 35(1): 30-46.* Using new or relatively unknown sources, shows that Anne Boleyn was committed to religious reform. Describes her education and intellectual accomplishments, her concern for the Bible in English, her benefactions to the universities, and her patronage of reformers. By introducing radical works to the king she undermined Wolsey's negotiations with Rome. Her protection and promotion of heretics strengthen the view that she took an active interest in reform. Based on manuscripts in the British Library and other repositories; 74 notes. 1514-36

759. Paget, Hugh. THE YOUTH OF ANNE BOLEYN. *Bull. of the Inst. of Hist. Res. [Great Britain] 1981 54(130): 162-170.* A. F. Pollard has maintained Anne Boleyn gained favor due entirely to Henry VIII's infatuation. The author suggests that she fulfilled two important requirements for a future consort: royal descent to strengthen the claim of a legitimate heir, and an exceptionally gifted and cultivated nature. It can be seen that Anne's education at the most cultured courts in Europe, including France, Austria, and the Low Countries endowed her with skills in French and music which may well have been decisive in commending Anne to Henry as a consort and the mother of the son upon which all his hopes rested. 45 notes. ca 1507-14

760. Warnicke, Retha M. ANNE BOLEYN'S CHILDHOOD AND ADOLESCENCE. *Historical Journal [Great Britain] 1985 28(4): 939-952.* Analyzes contemporary evidence to show that Anne Boleyn, second queen of Henry VIII, was born in 1507, not 1501 as some historians have supposed, and that she was the elder of Sir Thomas Boleyn's two daughters. Based on archival materials, including correspondence; 36 notes. 1507-34

Bolívar, Simón

761. Abrisqueta, Francisco de. RECONSTRUCCION VASCO-BOLIVARIANA [Basque-Bolívar reconstruction]. *Rev. de la Soc. Bolivariana de Venezuela [Venezuela] 1979 36(123): 11-25.* Discusses the connections and influence of the Basque people and land upon the early philosophies and political thought of Simón Bolívar. 1790-1815

762. Acosta Saignes, Miguel. COMO REPUDIA UNA CLASE SOCIAL A SU LIBERTADOR [How a social class repudiated its liberator]. *Casa de las Américas [Cuba] 1983 23(138): 99-103.* Simón Bolívar led his own landowning class, the Mantuanos, to power. They had sought independence to escape Spanish exploitation, but when Bolívar sought to abolish slavery and to fill his armies with freedmen, he thwarted the Mantuanos' economic interests and they repudiated him. Since the Mantuanos dominated the new governments, they removed Bolívar from his command. Bolívar, always loyal to his class, would not overthrow those governments and spent the last six years of his life in illness, aggrieved by the ostracism of his peers. In 1830, Bolívar died, waiting for a ship to take him into exile. 1810-30

763. Altuve Williams, Guillermo. EL BOLIVAR QUE NECESITAMOS [The Bolívar that we needed]. *Rev. de la Soc. Bolivariana de Venezuela [Venezuela] 1981 38(132): 60-70.* Reviews Simón Bolívar's life and concludes that his dreams, ideals, and visions remain important goals for today's struggles. 1799-1830

764. Arcay, Luis Augusto. VIDA Y PRESENCIA DE BOLIVAR EN MADRID [Bolívar's life and memory in Madrid]. *Bol. de la Acad. Nac. de la Hist. [Venezuela] 1983 66(264): 1094-1096.* Recalls Simón Bolívar's journey to Spain at the age of 16, his studies in the capital, the circumstances of his meeting Maria Teresa Rodríguez del Toro y Alaisa, whom he married in 1802, and her death soon after arrival in Venezuela. 1799-1802

765. Arroyave Calle, Julio César. BOLIVAR, GENIO DE AMERICA. [Bolívar, America's genius]. *Rev. de la Soc. Bolivariana de Venezuela [Venezuela] 1981 38(130): 36-42.* Simón Bolívar (1783-1830) was not only a military hero of the Americas but also a man of political vision and humanistic spirit. 1810-30

766. Barón Castro, Rodolfo. SIMÓN BOLÍVAR AND EDUCATION. *Cultures [France] 1985 (36): 152-158.* Discusses the influences of several educators and educational experiences on South American liberator Simón Bolívar (1783-1830) and reviews Bolívar's interest in and perceptions of the importance of education. 1783-1830

767. Beaujón, Oscar. LAS PREVISIONES DEL GENERAL MONTILLA [The foresight of General Montilla]. *Rev. de la Soc. Bolivariana de Venezuela [Venezuela] 1981 38(132): 30-33.* Reviews the role played by Mariano Montilla (1782-1851) in the last days of Simón Bolívar's life and the importance of his actions. 1830

768. Beaujón, Oscar. ALGO SOBRE LOS MAESTROS DEL LIBERTADOR [Something on the Liberator's teachers]. *Rev. de la Soc. Bolivariana de Venezuela [Venezuela] 1979 36(123): 29-42.* Details the various teachers of Simón Bolívar, and attempts to correct the misinformation of previous scholars and misleading anecdotes. 1790-1830

769. Belaúnde, Javier de. BOLIVAR CONSTITUCIONALISTA [Bolívar the constitutionalist]. *Rev. de la Soc. Bolivariana de Venezuela [Venezuela] 1979 36(122): 76-82.* Discusses the constitutional ideas of Simón Bolívar, his political vision, and remarks made to the Congress of Angostura. 1800-30

770. Bencomo Barrios, Héctor. CRONOLOGIA DE LOS DOS ULTIMOS VIAJES DEL LIBERTADOR [Chronology of the last two trips of the Liberator]. *Rev. de la Soc. Bolivariana de Venezuela [Venezuela] 1980 37(128): 95-109.* Briefly describes Simón Bolívar's whereabouts in 1812, details the journeys and battles of 1829 and 1830, and reproduces the first announcement of his death. 1812-30

771. Billy, Robert de. BOLIVAR: UN HOMME, UN DESTIN [Bolívar: a man, a destiny]. *Rev. des Deux Mondes [France] 1983 (8): 281-296.* An account of the life of Simón Bolívar, the great liberator of Venezuela and other South American countries. Article to be continued. 1783-1812

772. Billy, Robert de. BOLIVAR: UN HOMME, UN DESTIN [Bolívar: a man, a destiny]. *Rev. des Deux Mondes [France] 1983 (8) 281-296, (9): 554-566, (10): 26-35.* Parts 1-3. Provides an account of Simón Bolívar's struggles to free South America from Spanish colonialism. 1803-30

773. Bolinaga de Dúo, María B. EL AGUA Y EL LIBERTADOR [Water and the Liberator]. *Rev. de la Soc. Bolivariana de Venezuela [Venezuela] 1979 36(123): 78-92.* Discusses Simón Bolívar's attitudes toward water conservation, focusing upon two edicts he issued during the last five years of his life. 1820-30

774. Briceño Perozo, Mario. ¿COMO DESMITIFICAR A BOLIVAR? [How to demythologize Bolívar?]. *Boletin de la Academia Nacional de la Historia [Venezuela] 1984 67(267): 477-483.* On the occasion of the Bolívar bicentennial it has become fashionable to call for a demythologization of the Liberator. However, all the seemingly incredible things that are narrated about him, his narrow escapes, his visions, etc., are perfectly historical. Even stripped of the tinsel with which he is sometimes covered, Bolívar remains a rigorously authentic colossus and genius. 1783-1830

775. Bushnell, David. THE LAST DICTATORSHIP: BETRAYAL OR CONSUMMATION? *Hispanic Am. Hist. Rev. 1983 63(1): 65-105.* On 13 March 1828, Simón Bolívar declared a state of emergency in Gran Colombia and assumed dictatorial powers under the 1821 constitution. He decreed the revamping of the judicial system, elimination of the elected municipal councils, an easing of ecclesiastical reform, restoration of Indian tribute, the end of black slavery through manumission juntas, promotion of particular branches of production, encouragement of foreign trade, and higher tariffs.

He delegated regional authority to Antonio Páez in Venezuela, Juan José Flores in Ecuador, and Mariano Montilla on the coast. Bolívar was supported by the civil servants, the judiciary, the clergy, and the military, but following an assassination attempt on his life 25 September 1828, the regime became more repressive. Many opposition leaders went into exile. Unable to hold Gran Colombia together, Bolívar resigned in March 1830. Historians' views of Bolívar's dictatorship are discussed. Based on documents in the Archivo de Congreso and Archivo Histórico Nacional in Bogotá and on published laws and documents of the period; 144 notes. 1828-30

776. Chiossone, Tulio. LA PROBIDAD DE SIMON BOLIVAR, EL LIBERTADOR [The integrity of Simón Bolívar, the Liberator]. *Boletin de la Academia Nacional de la Historia [Venezuela] 1984 67(267): 511-520.* Bolívar's personal honesty was proverbial. Though sometimes accused of ambition, he never used public money for his private expenses, distributed generously the gifts he received, and lived in a permanent state of relative poverty. 15 notes. 1783-1830

777. Clemente Arráiz, Rafael. EL GENIO INAGOTABLE [The inexhaustible genius]. *Rev. de la Soc. Bolivariana de Venezuela [Venezuela] 1979 36(121): 63-66.* Attempts to correct the inaccuracies of Venezuelan history concerning the genius and character of Simón Bolívar, illustrating that he was an incredible human being. 1783-1830

778. DelCastillo Mathieu, Nicolás. BOLIVAR ¿LEGISLADOR? [Bolívar—legislator?] *Boletin de Historia y Antiguëdades [Colombia] 1983 70(742): 693-705.* As a political thinker with a strong sense of realism, Simón Bolívar stressed the need to adapt laws and institutions to the characteristics of Latin American society. In his own constitutional proposals, however, he often included highly impractical features. ca 1811-30

779. Dey, Susnigdha. BASES INTELECTUALES DE SIMÓN BOLÍVAR [The intellectual foundations of Simón Bolívar]. *Bol. de la Acad. Nac. de la Hist. [Venezuela] 1981 64(254): 431-435.* It is rare for a man of action to be also a man of thought but Bolívar was a mixture of both. His mind was trained in the reading of the classic and modern authors. He knew the 17th- and 18th-century French and English philosophers and was especially influenced by Rousseau. Several lists of the books in his library have been found. He was also interested in elementary and higher education. Speech delivered at a session of the Indian Council of Cultural Relations in honor of Simón Bolívar in New Delhi, India, 8 December 1980. 1783-1830

780. Díaz González, Joaquín. EL JURAMENTO DE SIMON BOLIVAR EN EL MONTE SACRO [The oath taken by Bolívar on Monte Sacro]. *Boletin de la Academia Nacional de la Historia [Venezuela] 1984 67(266): 291-301.* On 15 August 1805 the 22-year old Simón Bolívar took a solemn oath on a hill outside of Rome not to rest until he had broken the chains with which Spanish power oppressed his people. Describes the antecedents of the vow and its effects on Bolívar's life. 1805

781. Díaz González, Joaquín. ANÍBAL Y BOLÍVAR [Hannibal and Bolívar]. *Bol. de la Acad. Nac. de la Hist. [Venezuela] 1981 64(253): 83-86.* Among history's great military leaders, the Carthaginian Hannibal and the South American Simón Bolívar displayed some parallel traits, chief among which were their burning patriotism and the war to extinction that they declared on their enemies. In Hannibal's case, luck not lack of genius caused extinction to befall his own city. 2c BC

782. Díaz González, Joaquín. TRAYECTORIA ELÍPTICA DEL LIBERTADOR [The elliptic path of the Liberator]. *Bol. de la Acad. Nac. de la Hist. [Venezuela] 1981 64(254): 311-314.* The career of Simón Bolívar begins on the Monte Sacro in Rome, where in 1805 he swore not to rest until he had broken the chains that bound his people. An equestrian statue was erected in his honor 125 years later in Rome, thus completing the elliptic curve that links him to that city. The inspiration of that youthful oath and of the struggles of the Roman plebs remained alive in Bolívar's spirit. 1805-1930

783. Doerig, Johann Anton. SIMON BOLIVAR (1783-1830) [Simón Bolívar (1783-1830)]. *Civitas [Switzerland] 1983 38(7): 211-215.* Describes Bolívar's life, the events that shaped him into the liberator, and his actions and ideas. 1783-1830

784. Egea López, Antonio. EL MARQUES DE UZTARIZ, EJEMPLO PARA SIMON BOLIVAR [The Marquis of Uztáriz, a model for Simón Bolívar]. *Boletín de la Academia Nacional de la Historia [Venezuela] 1984 67(268): 753-788.* 1735-1809
*For abstract see **Uztáriz, Marquis of***

785. Ezquerra, Ramón. EL MATRIMONIO DE BOLIVAR [Bolívar's wedding]. *Rev. de Indias [Spain] 1983 43(172): 689-706.* The author publishes the marriage contract between Simón Bolívar and María Teresa Rodríguez de Toro, with introductory data on Bolívar's arrival and residence in Madrid, and in particular about the church in which he was married. Based on documents in the National Library and the Historical Archive of Notarial Documents in Madrid; 6 notes, appendix. 1799-1802

786. Felice Cardot, Carlos. BOLIVAR VUELVE A LAS TIERRAS DE SUS ANTEPASADOS GALLEGOS [Bolívar returns to the country of his Galician ancestors]. *Bol. de la Acad. Nac. de la Hist. [Venezuela] 1982 65(258): 289-292.* Bolívar was a descendant of various Galician families who had played an important role not only in the colonies but in Spain since the Middle Ages. These families, mingling with native strains in Latin America, produced a type with almost the same vigorous characteristics as the Spanish; with a deep attachment to the new soil and a love of liberty. A speech delivered at the inauguration of a monument to Bolívar in La Coruña, Spain. 1783-1830

787. Fuentes C., Rafael L. EL "AMABLE HECHIZO" DE SIMON BOLIVAR [The "amiable charm" of Simón Bolívar]. *Rev. de la Soc. Bolivariana de Venezuela [Venezuela] 1980 37(127): 7-22.* 1780-1830
*For abstract see **Rodríguez del Toro y Alaisa, María Teresa***

788. Fuguett G., Euclides. LAS GENEALOGIAS DE DON SIMON BOLIVAR A TRAVES DEL TIEMPO Y EL ESPACIO [Simón Bolívar's genealogies through time and space]. *Bol. de la Acad. Nac. de la Hist. [Venezuela] 1982 65(258): 431-444.* This is a historical survey of the biological, psychological, and temperamental as well as physical and other antecedents of the men who forged the nation of Venezuela, and especially of their leader, Simón Bolívar. These

men were heirs to long lines of adventurous hidalgos, in whom were crystallized certain characteristics that they transmitted to the new society. Ref. 16c-19c

789. Galich, Luis Fernando. BICENTENARIO DEL NACIMIENTO DE SIMON BOLIVAR [Bicentennial of the birth of Simón Bolívar]. *Anales de la Academia de Geografía e Historia de Guatemala [Guatemala] 1983 57: 245-252.* Provides brief laudatory notes on the biography, personality, and education of Simón Bolívar (1783-1830), noting Bolívar's vision of Pan-Americanism. Also describes the Central American Congress's adoption of his ideas on abolition (17 April 1823) and its decision to participate in the Congress of Panama (1826). Events since the 1830's show the wisdom of the Liberator's call for the union of Latin Americans as a way to strengthen their sovereignty and self-determination in the face of imperial powers. ca 1800-30

790. Gandia, Enrique de. BOLIVAR, SAN MARTIN Y LA UNION AMERICANA [Bolívar, San Martín and the American Union]. *Boletín de la Academia Nacional de la Historia [Venezuela] 1984 67(267): 521-531.* Bolívar and San Martín are often opposed as rivals and antagonists by a certain biased historiography. In fact they were animated by a common ideal. Both dreamed of a strong Latin American country capable of resisting the designs of the European Holy Alliance. Recently discovered documents reveal that, like Bolívar, San Martín also envisaged the union of Latin America into a single nation. ca 1800-50

791. García, Concepción Caro. BOLIVAR Y LA LIBERACION DE AMERICA [Bolívar and the liberation of America]. *Investigación Económica [Mexico] 1983 42(166): 343-361.* Presents a concise review of Simón Bolívar's (1783-1830) involvement in the independence wars in South America in the 19th century, particularly 1816-25, his social projects, and his dream of unity for the American continent. Mentions several documents written by Bolívar. 19c

792. García Bustillos, Gonzalo. BOLIVAR DE VERDAD VERDAD [The true and real Bolívar]. *Rev. de la Soc. Bolivariana de Venezuela [Venezuela] 1980 37(125): 21-26.* Presents an impressionistic image of the spiritually motivated Simón Bolívar, distinguishing the real man from the legend. 1808-30

793. González Paredes, Ramón. BOLIVAR, EDUCADOR DE PUEBLOS [Bolívar, educator of peoples]. *Boletín de la Academia Nacional de la Historia [Venezuela] 1985 68(269): 105-117.* Discusses Bolívar's capacities as a man of culture and educator and his many activities on behalf of education as a legislator, founder of institutions, thinker, and speaker. Biblio. 1800-30

794. Grigulevich, José. SIMON BOLIVAR, EL LIBERTADOR [Simón Bolívar, the Liberator]. *Casa de las Américas [Cuba] 1983 23(138): 10-19.* Bolívar's contribution to the struggle for Latin American independence was more than military, for he created many of the basic republican institutions of the Latin American countries. While Bolívar could win the war of independence, his goal of a united Spanish America has never been realized and Bolívar himself was to die ostracized by his own followers. Bolívar's aim was for national revolution, but not social reorganization. Bolívar was caught in the contradiction of all bourgeois revolutionaries—how to take power from those above you, but deny power to those beneath you. 1810-30

795. Hernández de Alba, Guillermo. BOLÍVAR, EDUCADOR DE PUEBLOS [Bolívar, educator of peoples]. *Bol. Cultural y Biblio. [Colombia] 1980 17: 16-23.* Popular education was for Simón Bolívar one of the chief duties of government. Bolívar's interest in the education of the citizens led him to prescribe texts for religious instruction. 1811-30

796. Hispano, Cornelio. ANITA LENOIT, UNA EXQUISITA AVENTURA DEL LIBERTADOR [Anita Lenoit, an exquisite adventure of the Liberator]. *Rev. de la Soc. Bolivariana de Venezuela [Venezuela] 1980 37(125): 37-42.* Details the relationship between Simón Bolívar and Anita Lenoit, daughter of a French emigré family. 1812-68

797. Laclé, Antonio. LA FALSA CICLOTIMIA DE BOLIVAR [The false cyclothymia of Bolívar]. *Rev. de la Soc. Bolivariana de Venezuela [Venezuela] 1979 36(121): 71-73.* Debates whether or not Simón Bolívar suffered from alternating states of mania and depression, and the causes for his mental depression. 1790-1830

798. Larin, E. A. BOLIVAR I PLANY OSVOBOZHDENIIA KUBY [Bolívar and prospects to liberate Cuba]. *Novaia i Noveishaia Istoriia [USSR] 1983 (4): 126-134.* Simón Bolívar, a Venezuelan (1783-1830), was a leader in the wars of independence in Latin America. In his efforts, he included Cuba, but the opposition of the United States and Great Britain prevented his success Based on secondary sources; 35 notes. 1810-27

799. Lee López, Alberto. TRES GRANADINOS EN LA VIDA DE BOLIVAR [Three New Granadans in the life of Bolívar]. *Boletin de Historia y Antiguëdades [Colombia] 1983 70(742): 672-682.* In his campaign for South American independence, Simón Bolívar received valuable assistance from three New Granadans. Camilo Torres, as leader of the United Provinces of New Granada in 1813, foresaw Bolívar's greatness and backed his reconquest of Venezuela. Francisco Antonio Zea subsequently helped Bolívar to create a patriotic government at Angostura. Lastly, Francisco de Paula Santander (after 1819) assumed control of the Colombian civil administration while Bolivar continued his military leadership. ca 1811-30

800. LeRiverend, Julio. BOLIVAR Y MARTI: DOS TIEMPOS, UNA HISTORIA [Bolívar and Martí: two moments, one history]. *Santiago [Cuba] 1984 (53): 27-58.* Compares the careers of two outstanding Latin Americans. The two men belong to the same historical wave and represent two crests in a single movement. The author examines some of the themes that were common to both historical figures. 51 notes. 19c

801. Lovera-DeSola, R. J. LAS ACTIVIDADES INTELECTUALES DEL LIBERTADOR [The intellectual activities of the Liberator]. *Boletín de la Academia Nacional de la Historia [Venezuela] 1984 67(268): 827-834.* Reviews Efraín Subero's *Bolívar Escritor* (1983) in which the author finds and describes in Simón Bolívar "all the characteristics of the Venezuelan writer." Although it is improper to treat Bolívar as a man of letters rather than as a political thinker, Subero's book is well researched and contains much useful information. Book review. 1783-1830

802. Luna, Félix. SAN MARTIN Y BOLIVAR, UNA POLEMICA SUPERADA [San Martín and Bolívar, an outdated polemic]. *Boletín de la Academia Nacional de la Historia [Venezuela] 1985 68(270): 508-510.* Even a few decades ago nationalist prejudices biased the discussion of the careers of the Argentine liberator José de San Martín and Simón Bolívar and especially the interpretation of their interview in Guayaquil in 1822. Today the subject is discussed more objectively, on a more strictly historical plane. 1822

803. Madrid-Malo, Néstor. BOLIVAR EN LA COSTA ATLANTICA [Bolívar on the Atlantic coast]. *Boletin de la Historia y Antiguëdades [Colombia] 1983 70(742): 706-718.* Reviews instances of Simón Bolívar's activity on the Caribbean coast of Colombia, 1812-30. 1812-30

804. Magallanes, Manuel Vicente. EL JOVEN MANTUANO DEL 19 DE ABRIL DE 1810 [The young man from Mantua of 19 April 1810]. *Rev. de la Soc. Bolivariana de Venezuela [Venezuela] 1981 38(129): 108-120.* Traces the early years of Simón Bolívar's activism and emphasizes the importance of 19 April 1810 on Bolivar's life and the revolutionary movement in general. 1810

805. Maldonado Michelena, Víctor. DE SAN JACINTO A SAN PEDRO ALEJANDRINO [From San Jacinto to San Pedro Alejandrino]. *Rev. Nac. de Cultura [Venezuela] 1983 44(250): 99-107.* Simón Bolívar was born on 24 July 1783 in the San Jacinto district of Caracas, Venezuela. For 20 years, Bolívar dedicated himself to the service of Venezuela and the South American republics, taking active leadership in their military struggle for independence from Spain and in their subsequent efforts to achieve and maintain political viability. He died on 17 December 1830, outside the city of Santa Marta on the San Pedro Alejandrino estate. 1783-1830

806. Mantilla R., Luis Carlos. BOLIVAR ANTES DE LA GLORIA [Bolívar before his glory]. *Boletín de Historia y Antigüedades [Colombia] 1985 72(749): 413-419. Biographie Etrangère ou Galerie Universelle,* Volume 1, published in Paris in 1817, included a brief but highly favorable biography of Simón Bolívar, written prior to his principal political-military triumphs. Note. 1817

807. Martínez Díaz, Nelson. SIMON BOLIVAR DESDE EL MUNDO ACTUAL [Simón Bolívar from a present-day perspective]. *Boletín de la Academia Nacional de la Historia [Venezuela] 1985 68(270): 491-495.* The ideas which guided Simón Bolívar's revolutionary practice continue to be of relevance today and to excite as much discussion as in his time. His most cherished ideals clashed with the human and geographical realities of his continent. His career exemplifies the dilemma which continues to confront Latin America: to reformulate and adapt to a new context ideas generated and applicable in other latitudes. 1810-30

808. Mörner, Magnus. SIMÓN BOLÍVAR 1783-1983 [Simón Bolívar, 1783-1983]. *Historielärarnas Förenings Årsskrift [Sweden] 1983-84: 9-14.* In conjunction with the 200th anniversary of the birth of Simón Bolívar (1783-1830) there is a renewed worldwide interest in this South American freedom fighter and statesman. Discusses the influences Bolívar received from his childhood in Venezuela through his nine-year-long education in Europe, his opposition to racism, and his role as a charismatic military commander, able statesman, and, above all, great leader. Based on Bolívar's letters and other primary sources; 5 notes. 1783-1830

809. Morón, Guillermo. REFLEXION HETERODOXA A PROPOSITO DE SIMON BOLIVAR [Heterodox reflection about Simón Bolívar]. *Rev. Nac. de Cultura [Venezuela] 1983 44(250): 121-133.* From a juridical perspective, Simón Bolívar had three nationalities: Spanish, from 24 July 1783 to 5 July 1811; Venezuelan, from 1811 to 17 December 1819; and Colombian, from 1819 to his death in 1830. Bolívar's writings express his obsessive preoccupation with the unity of the newly formed republics of South America. He wished to replace the colonial unity of the preindependence period which he had helped to destroy, with a new unity rooted in common history, culture, and destiny. 1783-1830

810. Mosquera, Jaime. PRESENTACION DEL LIBRO "MEMORIA SOBRE EL LIBERTADOR SIMON BOLIVAR" [Presentation of the book *Memoir on the Liberator Simón Bolívar]. Bol. de la Acad. Nac. de la Hist. [Venezuela] 1981 64(256): 996-1000.* The book, written by Tomás Cipriano de Mosquera, has already appeared in four editions, the first in 1853. The present fifth edition has corrected all the previous copyists' and printers' errors. Its author was the leader of the Colombian Liberal Party and one of the most controversial figures of the last century. As a result of the conservatives having claimed to be heirs of the Liberator, Mosquera's book was ignored and forgotten until revived in the 1940's-50's. 1783-1830

811. Mureşan, Camil. SIMÓN BOLIVAR ÎN REPLICĂ CU SFÎNTA ALIANŢĂ [Simón Bolívar replies to the Holy Alliance]. *Magazin Istoric [Romania] 1983 17(8): 17-20.* A summary of the final years of Bolivar's struggle against Spain in South America, down to 1825, taken from a work in preparation. 1800-25

812. Orbes Moreno, Camilo. CORRESPONDENCIA INEDITA DEL LIBERTADOR SIMON BOLIVAR [Unpublished correspondence of the liberator Simón Bolívar]. *Rev. de la Soc. Bolivariana de Venezuela [Venezuela] 1981 38(130): 58-69.* Describes some of the recently published letters between Simón Bolívar (1783-1830) and Juan José Flores, Ecuadorian soldier and politician, contained in *Correspondencia del Libertador con el General Juan José Flores* (1977). 1825-30

813. Ortiz, María Dolores. SIMON BOLIVAR Y LA EDUCACION DE LA NIÑEZ Y LA JUVENTUD [Simón Bolívar and the education of children and youth]. *Islas [Cuba] 1983 (76): 55-63.* Describes Simón Bolívar's extensive activity on behalf of a system of education based on equality of opportunity for all social classes and which he considered the best means to achieve democracy. 1819-29

814. Pabón Nuñez, Lucio. BOLIVAR Y SANTANDER [Bolívar and Santander]. *Bol. de la Acad. Nac. de la Hist. [Venezuela] 1981 64(256): 849-858.* Describes the relationship and mentalities of the two generals of the independence wars of New Granada. Simón Bolívar (1783-1830) embraced in his vision a much wider continental horizon than Francisco de Paula Santander (1792-1840). The article describes the history of their rivalry and the latter's ultimate victory, which was, however, only fleeting. The ideal of Bolívar's vision survives. ca 1800-20's

815. Pastrana Rodriguez, Eduardo. POETICA BOLIVARIANA [Bolivarian poetry]. *Revista de la Biblioteca Nacional José Martí [Cuba] 1984 26(1): 81-115.* The exploits of Simón Bolívar inspired many Latin American poets to make him the subject of their creative works. In the

19th century, many of these poems were heroic and nationalistic in tone. In the 20th century, a substantial number were political in nature. 25 notes. 19c-1983

816. Pérez Leiva, Jairo R. BOLIVAR: LEGISLADOR, ESTADISTA Y DIPLOMATICO [Bolívar: legislator, statesman, and diplomat]. *Rev. de la Soc. Bolivariana de Venezuela [Venezuela] 1979 36(124): 9-29.* Discusses Simón Bolívar in the light of 18th-century philosophies. 18c-1850

817. Pérez Tenreiro, Tomás. BOLIVAR Y CARACAS [Bolívar and Caracas]. *Bol. de la Acad. Nac. de la Hist. [Venezuela] 1982 65(259): 764-767.* Simón Bolívar was born in Caracas and he always retained a great affection for the city of his birth and for Venezuela. This speech, delivered on the occasion of the unveiling of a bust of the Liberator in one of the squares of the neighborhood where he lived until the age of 15, recalls some of the events of his childhood. 1783-98

818. Puyana García, Gabriel. "LA TRAGICA EXPIACION DE SU GRANDEZA" ["The tragic atonement for his greatness"]. *Boletín de Historia y Antigüedades [Colombia] 1984 71(744): 128-142.* The career of Simón Bolívar had a tragic ending as his strength failed and his political proposals were rejected. Eventually his native Venezuela led the way in dissolving Gran Colombia and ostracized its founder. Biblio. 1827-30

819. Ramírez, Carlos M. GRANDEZA E INFORTUNIOS DE BOLIVAR [Grandeur and misfortunes of Bolívar]. *Rev. de la Soc. Bolivariana de Venezuela [Venezuela] 1979 36(124): 51-62.* Discusses selected high points and low points—political and personal—of the life of Simón Bolívar. 1783-1830

820. Roca Castellanos, Manuel. BOLIVAR ES BOLIVAR [Bolívar is Bolívar]. *Boletín de Historia y Antigüedades [Colombia] 1984 71(746): 751-758.* Exalts the unique greatness of Simón Bolívar. 1783-1830

821. Rodríguez, Adolfo. LA TIERRA DEL GUARICO EN LA INFANCIA DE BOLIVAR [The region of Guárico in Bolívar's childhood]. *Rev. de la Soc. Bolivariana de Venezuela [Venezuela] 1981 38(130): 43-49.* The history of Simón Bolívar's childhood in Guárico, Venezuela suggests that this region and its people played an important role in the Liberator's later revolutionary ideals. 18c-1818

822. Rojas, Armando. BOLIVAR EN YARE [Bolívar at Yare]. *Bol. de la Acad. Nac. de la Hist. [Venezuela] 1982 65(257): 35-39.* Yare was one of Simón Bolívar's estates, where he lived for a while after his return from Spain in 1802 with his bride María Teresa and again, 1807-10. Discusses a speech given at the inauguration of the house in which he lived and which is now restored as a national monument. Mentions two letters written by Bolívar concerning financial and other affairs related to the property. 1802-10

823. Rojas Jiménez, Oscar. BOLIVAR, POETA [Bolívar, poet]. *Rev. de la Soc. Bolivariana de Venezuela [Venezuela] 1981 38(130): 19-21.* Simón Bolívar (1783-1830) was not only a soldier, statesman, and revolutionary but also an excellent poet who wrote on several topics and in a variety of styles. 1800-30

824. Romero Luengo, Adolfo. LA TRILOGIA INMORTAL [The immortal trilogy]. *Rev. de la Soc. Bolivariana de Venezuela [Venezuela] 1980 37(127): 74-91.* Details the joint and individual legacies left by Simón Bolívar, Antonio José de Sucre, and Rafael Urdaneta; describes contributions of and meetings among the three men. 1800-30

825. Sa Na. SOBRE: SIMON BOLIVAR Y SUS IDEAS POLITICAS [On Simón Bolívar and his political ideas]. *Bol. de la Acad. Nac. de la Hist. [Venezuela] 1982 65(258): 471-485.* Analyzes the revolutionary activities and political ideas of the Latin American liberator by using the method of historical materialism. The Latin American revolution of the 19th century, which sought to establish bourgeois power by doing away with colonial rule, was nevertheless a grandiose movement with an ample social base. Bolívar was the founder of Latin American democracy and republicanism. His revolutionary ideal could not be realized in a radical manner due to the feudal economic conditions of the time. Translation of an article first published in the review *Shijie Lishi* (World History) of the Institute of World History of the Chinese Academy of Social Sciences in Beijing [China] 1980 (2); 30 notes. 1800's-30

826. Salcedo Bastardo, J. L. LA PRIMERA BIOGRAFIA DE BOLIVAR [The first biography of Bolívar]. *Boletin de la Academia Nacional de la Historia [Venezuela] 1984 67(266): 267-271.* Reprints the text of the first biographical notice on Simón Bolívar ever published. It appeared in the 'Series of Lives and Portraits of Famous Personages of Recent Times,' vol. 3, Milan, 1818. It is a short resume of his life and military career. Reprinted from *El Nacional,* Caracas, 24 July 1983. 1818

827. Salcedo Bastardo, J. L. SIMON BOLIVAR VISIONARIO DE LA UNIDAD SUD-AMERICANA [Simón Bolívar visionary of South American unity]. *Boletín de la Academia Nacional de la Historia [Venezuela] 1985 68(269): 83-85.* Celebrates Bolívar as military leader, revolutionary thinker, democrat, and visionary of continental unity. Bolívar is the source of profound truths which continue to affect the destiny of the continent. Bicentennial essay reprinted from the *Crédit Suisse Bulletin* (1983). 1783-1830

828. Salcedo Bastardo, J. L. APERTURA DEL AÑO BICENTENARIO DE BOLIVAR EN EUROPA [Inauguration of Bolívar's bicentennial in Europe]. *Bol. de la Acad. Nac. de la Hist. [Venezuela] 1983 66(262): 291-297.* On the Aventine hill in Rome the young Simon Bolívar in 1805 vowed to fight for the freedom of his continent. In this speech opening the bicentennial commemorations of the Liberator's birth held at the Instituto Italo-Latinoamericano in Rome, the author recalls this date. Bolívar was again connected with Rome when in 1830, just before his death, the president of Bolivia appointed him chargé d'affaires and minister plenipotentiary at the Holy See, a post he was unable to assume. 1783-1830

829. Sánchez Negrón, José E. BOLIVAR, EL PODER MORAL Y EL ESTOICISMO [Bolívar, moral power, and stoicism]. *Rev. de la Soc. Bolivariana de Venezuela [Venezuela] 1979 36(123): 54-63.* Uses various scenes from the life of Simón Bolívar to indicate and emphasize the stoicism of his thought as well as his manipulation of moral power. 1793-1830

830. Shul'govski, A. BOR'BA ZA PEREDOVYE IDEALY I SOVREMENNOST' [The struggle for progressive ideals and the present]. *Mirovaia Ekonomika i Mezhdunarodnye Otnosheniia [USSR] 1983 (8): 102-111.* Describes the life and ideas of Simón Bolívar. He was the leader in the wars of independence in South America, and statesman who sought to bring about social reforms and the abolition of slavery. 1783-1830

831. Shul'govski, A. SIMON BOLIVAR—ZHIZN' VO IMIA BUDUSHCHEGO [Simón Bolívar: life in the name of the future]. *Mirovaia Ekonomika i Mezhdunarodnye Otnosheniia [USSR] 1981 (9): 129-137.* Describes the role of Simón Bolívar (1783-1830) in South American independence movements. 1783-1830

832. Tamayo Vargas, Augusto. REFERENCIAS TENDENCIOSAS SOBRE BOLIVAR EN ALGUNOS TEXTOS DE AQUI Y DE ALLA [Tendentious references about Bolívar in some texts]. *Rev. de la Soc. Bolivariana de Venezuela [Venezuela] 1979 36(121): 59-62.* Criticizes two works: *Bolívar,* by Raúl Urueta (1973) and *Historia General de los Peruanos,* edited by J. A. de la Puente Candano and C. D. Valcárcel. Both present false statements regarding Peru and Simón Bolívar. ca 1800-30

833. Torres, Mauro. BOLIVAR EN LUCHA CON LA MUERTE [Bolívar in a fight against death]. *Boletín de Historia y Antigüedades [Colombia] 1984 71(745): 427-435.* The decline of Simón Bolívar's health from the time of his first serious illness during the war for independence to his death in 1830 was repeatedly checked by his remarkable physiological and psychological strength, but in the end proved irresistible. 1818-30

834. Uslar Pietri, Arturo. ACERCARSE A BOLIVAR [Approaching Bolívar]. *Rev. de la Soc. Bolivariana de Venezuela [Venezuela] 1980 37(128): 7-21.* Studies Simón Bolívar's travel through South America, his influence on the people, and their reaction to him. 1783-1830

835. Vallenilla Lanz, Laureano. EL LIBERTADOR JUZGADO POR LOS MIOPES [The Liberator judged by the short-sighted]. *Rev. de la Soc. Bolivariana de Venezuela [Venezuela] 1979 36(121): 29-44.* Certain historians have presented inaccurate facts and impressions regarding Simón Bolívar; attacks some historians on the basis of their methodology. ca 1800-30

836. Velásquez, Ramón J. LA EDUCACION DE BOLIVAR [The education of Bolívar]. *Rev. de la Soc. Bolivariana de Venezuela [Venezuela] 1979 36(123): 43-53.* 1790-1830

837. Verna, Paul. THE LIBERATOR, SIMÓN BOLÍVAR: SYMBOL FOR THE THIRD WORLD. *Cultures [France] 1985 (36): 149-151.* Summarizes the accomplishments and legacy of South American revolutionary and liberator Simón Bolívar (1783-1830). 1816-89

838. Verna, Paúl. EL ENIGMA DE BOLIVAR EN SOREZ [The enigma of Bolívar in Sorèze]. *Rev. de la Soc. Bolivariana de Venezuela [Venezuela] 1979 36(121): 67-70.* Attempts to distinguish history from legend as it relates to Simón Bolívar; and to prove that Bolívar was not an alumnus of the College of Sorèze, France. ca 1800

839. Yarce Maya, William Fernando. LOS CABALLOS EN LA VIDA DEL LIBERTADOR [Horses in the life of the Liberator]. *Bol. del Arch. General de la Nación [Venezuela] 1980 70(238-239): 95-101.* Horses are intimately related to the life and career of Simón Bolívar. They played an essential role in the formation of his character, in his military campaigns, and extensive travels. 1812-30

840. Zeuske, Michael. SIMON BOLIVAR IN GESCHICHTE UND GEGENWART [Simón Bolívar in history and the present]. *Lateinamerika [East Germany] 1983 (Fall): 3-32.* Simón Bolívar's leadership of South America's revolutionary war for independence against Spanish colonial rule was characterized by his goals of establishing national sovereignty for South American nations such as Venezuela and Bolivia and to achieve a centralization and federation of these nations. Some of the issues of the revolution such as the overthrow of slavery and agricultural reform remained unresolved in the South American republics after liberation. Class conflicts developed between liberation army officers and high-ranking officials and the population in general, which Bolívar feared would lead to civil war. Bolívar's ideals of a unified South American nation were not fully realized, although South American nations gained their independence. Adapted version of a report given to the Intertional Bolívar Colloquium, 24-25 June 1982 in Rostock-Warnemünde; 79 notes. Spanish summary. 1808-20's

841. —. [GERMAN ARCINIEGAS SOBRE BOLIVAR] [Germán Arciniegas on Bolívar]. *Boletín de la Academia Nacional de la Historia [Venezuela] 1985 68(269): 91-103.*

Briceño Perozo, Mario. EL BOLIVAR DE ARCINIEGAS [Arciniegas's Bolivar], *pp. 91-97.*

Armas Chitty, J. A. De. LAS TRAVESURAS DE GERMAN ARCINIEGAS [Germán Arciniegas and his pranks], *pp. 97-98.*

Apuleyo Mendoza, Plinio. POLEMICA EN TORNO AL LIBRO DE ARCINIEGAS SOBRE BOLIVAR [Controversy regarding Arciniegas's book on Bolívar], *pp. 99-103.* Rebuts the view of Germán Arciniegas, in *Bolívar y la Revolución* (1984), that the Liberator was simply a military leader and no more. Emphasizes his activity as thinker, orator, writer and other aspects of his many-sided personality. 1810-30

842. —. SIMON BOLIVAR [Simón Bolívar]. *Bol. de la Acad. Colombiana [Colombia] 1982 32(138): 267-289.*

Echeverri Mejía, Oscar. SIMON BOLIVAR, EDUCADOR, ESCRITOR Y POETA [Simón Bolívar: educator, writer, and poet], *pp. 267-284.* Reviews the accomplishments and abilities of Simón Bolívar as reflected in the works and history of the man, and as recorded in a number of critical and historical works. It is difficult to place only one label on such a man.

Guzmán Esponda, Eduardo. RESPUESTA AL DISCURSO ANTERIOR [Response to the previous discourse], *pp. 285-289.* Describes the civilized persuasiveness and discursive style of Oscar Echeverri Mejía in his evaluation of Simón Bolívar. 1820-30

843. —. [SOBRE EL BOLIVAR DE GERMAN ARCINIEGAS] [On Germán Arciniegas's Bolívar]. *Boletín de la Academia Nacional de la Historia [Venezuela] 1985 68(270): 417-424.*

Pavón Núñez, Lucio. BOLIVAR, CABALLERO DE LA GLORIA Y DE LA LIBERTAD [Bolívar, knight of glory and of liberty], *pp. 417-418.* Briefly replies to Arciniegas's *Bolivar y la Revolución* (1984) in which he claims that the Liberator was a great military leader but neither law giver, thinker, statesman, nor educator.

Rumazo González, Alfonso. BOLIVAR AGRAVIADO [An affront to Bolívar], *pp. 419-422.* Arciniegas's book is an example of the thinking of a small group of Colombian writers who have taken up again the theme common among partisans of Bolívar's adversary, General Francisco de Paula Santander, who was banished in 1829.

Consuegra, José. BOLIVAR, SIEMPRE BOLIVAR [Bolívar, forever Bolívar], *pp. 423-424.* Whatever one may think of his many-sided personality, Bolívar remains great and is recognized as such by the world and history. 1810-30

Bolívar y Ponte, Maria de

844. Gabaldón, José Rafael. MUJERES DE AMERICA [Women of America]. *Bol. de la Acad. Nac. de la Hist. [Venezuela] 1983 66(261): 113-124.* 1792-1810

*For abstract see **Rodríguez del Toro y Alaisa, María Teresa***

845. Grisanti, Angel. IMPOSTERGABLE UNA BIOGRAFIA DE LA MADRE DEL LIBERTADOR [A biography of the mother of Bolívar not to be disregarded]. *Rev. de la Soc. Bolivariana de Venezuela [Venezuela] 1981 38(129): 78-80.* Comments on a book written by Simón Bolívar's mother in which she tells of the ways she administered the affairs of the family after the death of her husband. 1786-91

Bolla, Ilona G.

846. Sinkovics, István. IN MEMORIAM ILONA G. BOLLA 1927-1980 [In memoriam Ilona G. Bolla (1927-80)]. *Ann. U. Sci. Budapestinensis de Rolando Eötvös Nominatae: Sectio Hist. [Hungary] 1982 22: 310-313.* An obituary of Ilona G. Bolla (1927-80). She was among the historians concerned with the medieval origins of modern Hungarian social organization and social conditions. 13c-17c

Bolton, James

847. Watling, Roy and Seaward, Mark R. D. JAMES BOLTON: MYCOLOGICAL PIONEER. *Arch. of Natural Hist. [Great Britain] 1981 10(1): 89-110.* Attempts to piece together the life and activities of the enigmatic naturalist James Bolton (fl. 1750-99). He spent his entire life in Halifax, Yorkshire and wrote a history of fungi growing about Halifax whose first volume was published in 1786. He described 231 species; most of them were either new species or new British records. This number has recently been drastically reduced by synonomy. Map, 7 fig., 63 notes, 2 appendixes. 1750-99

Bolton, Nancy

848. Boulton, David J. WOMEN AND EARLY METHODISM. *Pro. of the Wesley Hist. Soc. [Great Britain] 1981 43(2): 13-17.* Traces the activities and great influence of three women of the 18th century, Hannah Ball, Patty Chapman, and Nancy Bolton, through the correspondence John Wesley had with all three, the correspondence among the three, and the evangelical work they did in their communities, thus advancing Methodism in its early stages of development. 18c

Bolton, William Jay

849. Clark, Willene B. GOTHIC REVIVAL STAINED GLASS OF WILLIAM JAY BOLTON: A PRESERVATION PROJECT AND CENSUS. *Nineteenth Cent. 1981 7(2): 30-34.* Gives a biography and describes the work of English-American stained-glass architect William Jay Bolton, who decorated several Episcopal churches in the United States and later served as a parish priest in the Church of England. 1839-48

Boltzmann, Ludwig

850. Broda, Engelbert. LUDWIG BOLTZMANN, ALBERT EINSTEIN UND FRANZ JOSEPH [Ludwig Boltzmann, Albert Einstein and Francis Joseph]. *Wiener Geschichtsblätter [Austria] 1983 38(3): 109-119.* The work and life of physicists Ludwig Boltzmann and Albert Einstein show that in Austria under Emperor Francis Joseph science was supported in order to support conservative social structures rather than to respond to scientists' needs for research. 1880's-1910's

851. Flamm, D.; Starostin, B. A., transl. ZHIZN' LIUDWIGA BOL'TSMANA I EGO MESTO V ISTORII KINETICHESKOI TEORII [The life of Ludwig Boltzmann and his place in the history of kinetic theory]. *Voprosy Istorii Estestvoznaniia i Tekhniki [USSR] 1984 (3): 116-123.* Prints a Russian translation of D. Flamm's (Boltzmann's grandson) English account of the life of the Austrian theoretical physicist Ludwig Boltzmann (1844-1906). He studied in Vienna, where he later taught at the Institute of Physics. In the 1870's he made the discovery of discrete levels of energy, which paved the way for the development of quantum mechanics. In 1876 he became director of the Graz Institute of Physics. He held posts at the Munich and Leipzig universities, but as his health suffered, he returned to Vienna in 1902. Impassioned arguments with his academic opponents, especially Max Planck, contributed to the decline of his health and suicide. 25 notes. 1870-1906

Bolzano, Bernhard

852. Berka, Karel. BERNARD BOL'TSANO—LOGIK, MATEMATIK, GUMANIST [Bernhard Bolzano: logician, mathematician, humanist]. *Voprosy Filosofii [USSR] 1981 (10): 118-126.* Briefly describes Bolzano's biography and gives the general characteristics of the era in which Bolzano lived and worked; discusses his contribution to the methodology of logic and mathematics, his works, and his social, political, and philosophical views. ca 1806-48

853. Haubelt, Josef. BOLZANŮV UČITEL JAN MARIAN MIKA [Bolzano's teacher, Johann Marian Mika]. *Sborník Hist. [Czechoslovakia] 1982 28: 159-203.* 1754-1816

*For abstract see **Mika, Johann Marian***

854. Winter, Eduard. BERNARD BOLZANO (1781-1848) [Bernhard Bolzano, 1781-1848]. *Jahrbuch für Gesch. der Sozialistischen Länder Europas [East Germany] 1982 25(2): 9-16.* Bernhard Bolzano, mathematician and humanist scholar, was both German and Czech in culture. He represents the reconciliation of these two often conflicting nationalisms. The author surveys the Bolzano centennials of 1881 and 1981. 19 notes. 19c-20c

Bonaparte, Louis

855. Kikkert, J. G. KONING LODEWIJK VAN HOLLAND [King Louis of Holland]. *Spiegel Hist. [Netherlands] 1981 16(12): 665-670.* Louis Napoleon who ruled Holland, 1806-10, acquired the title "the Good" during his brief reign, yet historians have consistently drawn an unfavorable portrait of the man. In truth, he was a brave and skillful soldier, talented in music and letters, diligent in his work, and sen-

sitive and loyal to the interests of his Dutch subjects. The Orange kings who followed him owed much to this first king of the Netherlands. Primary sources; 8 illus. 1806-10

Bonaparte, Maria Anna

856. Teychiné Stakenburg, A. J. EEN GALANT AVONTUUR VAN MARIA ANNA BONAPARTE [An amatory adventure of Maria Anna Bonaparte's]. *Spiegel Historiael [Netherlands] 1984 19(6): 266-271.* Investigates the facts behind an alleged romance in 1798 between Maria Anna Bonaparte (1777-1820) and the English navy captain Gardiner Henry Guion (1775-1832). 1798

Bonaparte family

857. Andone, Alecsenia and Spirodeanu, Mircea. DOCUMENTE ALE FAMILIEI BONAPARTE [Documents of the Bonaparte family]. *Rev. Arhivelor [Romania] 1980 42(1): 86-98.* Publishes 20 letters, mostly by or on behalf of the Bonaparte family, which give details of their family life. Letters from the Romanian State Archives, Bucharest, in French with Romanian translations. 1815-88

Bonatz, Karl and Paul

858. Durand de Bousingen, Denis. LES ARCHITECTES PAUL ET KARL BONATZ: UNE PREFACE ALSACIENNE A UNE CARRIERE EUROPEENNE [Architects Paul and Karl Bonatz: an Alsatian prelude to a European career]. *Revue d'Alsace [France] 1985 111(589): 157-168.* The brothers Paul and Karl Bonatz, later renowned architects, began their career together by designing clinics and hospitals in Strasbourg, 1903-18, before moving to Stuttgart and separating. 1903-18

Bond, Maurice

859. Lewis, Joan C. Lancaster. OBITUARY: MAURICE BOND, C.B., M.V.O., O.B.E., F.S.A. *Archives [Great Britain] 1984 16(72): 385-387.* Obituary of Maurice Bond (1916-83), archivist and late Clerk of the Records of the House of Lords, stressing his leadership in the British Records Association. 1940's-83

Bonekemper, Johannes

860. Bonekemper, Carl; Wenzlaff, Theodore C., transl. JOHANNES BONEKEMPER AND HIS FAMILY. *Heritage Review 1979 (24): 14-21.* A biography of Johannes Bonekemper, a minister from Basel, Switzerland sent to the village of Rohrback, a settlement in southern Russia, in 1824 to provide spiritual education to the German immigrants. 1795-1893

Bonhoeffer, Dietrich

861. Rosenbaum, Stanley R. DIETRICH BONHOEFFER: A JEWISH VIEW. *J. of Ecumenical Studies 1981 18(2): 301-307.* Dietrich Bonhoeffer, a Lutheran minister who helped Jews escape Nazi Germany during World War II, held a Christocentric theology that did not explain the relationship between Judaism and Christianity. The author lists passages in Bonhoeffer's writings which state the superiority of Christianity to Judaism. He did not work hard enough to protest actions taken against the Jews in the 1930's. He hoped that increasing numbers of Jews would become Christians. Like many Christian theologians of the time, Bonhoeffer suffered from anti-Judaism. 1930-45

Bonnet, Jules

862. Delteil, Frank. JULES BONNET PROFESSEUR DE LYCEE ET SECRETAIRE DE LA S.H.P.F. [Jules Bonnet, secondary school teacher and secretary of the SHPF (Société de l'Histoire du Protestantisme Français)]. *Bull. de la Soc. de l'Hist. du Protestantisme Français [France] 1983 129(4): 531-538.* Highlights the career of Jules Bonnet, teacher and secretary of the SHPF from 1865 to 1885. Emphasizes his acts of demonstration of his Protestant faith, such as purchasing, as president of the SHPF in 1880, the historical house of Laporte-Roland, last descendant of the Camisards (Calvinists who fought Louis XIV's armies in the Cévennes after the revocation of the Edict of Nantes in 1685). The owner of this house had become very poor and the residence was going to be pulled down. As a Protestant, Bonnet also preferred to give up his career rather than keep teaching history judged controversial or partial because it did not conform to the religious philosophy of the dominant Catholic creed. Based on the archives of the SHPF, the Archives Nationales, and other primary sources; 40 notes. ca 1840-85

Bonny, Pierre

863. Delarue, Jacques. LA BANDE BONNY-LAFONT [The Bonny and Lafont gang]. *Histoire [France] 1985 (80): 62-69.* An account of the actions of former police inspector Pierre Bonny and adventurer Henri Lafont (Henri Chamberlin), both former felons, at the service of the Gestapo along with their associates, whose schemes involved corruption, denouncements, robberies, murders, and other criminal acts committed during the German occupation of France, 1940-44. 1940-44

Bonó, Pedro Francisco

864. González, Raymundo. BONO, UN INTELECTUAL DE LOS POBRES [Bonó, a poor people's intellectual]. *Estudios Sociales [Dominican Republic] 1985 18(60): 65-77.* Discusses the ideological changes in the social thought of Dominican philosopher Pedro Francisco Bonó, distinguishing three different stages and focusing mostly on the second one. 1850-81

Bontempelli, Massimo

865. D'Amato, Juliana. BONTEMPELLI AND HIS *REALISMO MAGICO. Italian Q. 1981 22(84): 51-59.* Biography of Italian writer Massimo Bontempelli (1878-1960), who produced short stories, novels, and plays, and is best known for his *realismo magico,* which is often confused with surrealism but is actually more like a fusion of the real and the mystical. 1910's-60

Boodt, Anselmus Boëtius de

866. Boodt-Maselis, M. C. de. ANSELMUS BOËTIUS DE BOODT (1550-1632) [Anselmus Boëtius de Boodt (1550-1632)]. *Spiegel Hist. [Netherlands] 1982 17(6): 312-321.* A biography of Anselmus Boëtius de Boodt. A native of the Spanish Netherlands city of Bruges in a difficult but dynamic period in the region's history, Boodt emigrated to Prague where he served over 30 years as court physician to Emperor Rudolph II. He was a true Renaissance man: learned in law and medicine, accomplished in poetry and letters, music, painting, and engraving. His encyclopedic work on mineralogy (1609) has remained influential to modern times. Primary sources; 12 illus. 1570-1632

Booth, Catherine

867. Murdoch, Norman H. FEMALE MINISTRY IN THE THOUGHT OF CATHERINE BOOTH. *Church History 1984 53(3): 348-362.* Catherine Booth (1829-90), cofounder of the Salvation Army, introduced thousands of working-class women to the ranks of ordained clergy. Her ideas on the right of women to preach evolved gradually between 1850 and 1859. She began preaching herself in a Methodist church in 1860, influenced by the example of evangelist Phoebe Palmer. Discusses the progress made possible for women by the Salvation Army, a social reform and evangelicizing agency. Based on Catherine Booth's *Female Ministry: A Woman's Right to Preach the Gospel* (1859) and secondary sources; 49 notes. 1850's-90

Borah, Woodrow Wilson

868. Borah, Woodrow Wilson; Wilkie, James W. and Horn, Rebecca, interviewers. AN INTERVIEW WITH WOODROW BORAH. *Hispanic American Historical Review 1985 65(3): 401-441.* Retired professor Woodrow Wilson Borah discusses his early life and career as a teacher and Latin Americanist. Much of his career was in the history department of the University of California at Berkeley, where he retired in 1980. Borah, who did much of his writing in association with Latin Americanist Shelburne Cook, is most noted for his demographic studies of Central American Indians in which he gave far higher estimates of pre-Columbian populations than had been common prior to his studies. He attributes these results to the use of time-series statistical documentation combined with anthropological methods. Borah talks of the decline in the quality of students and connects this with today's affluence and the fact that students do not read wisely. Biblio. 1930-85

Borch, Michał Jan

869. Stradins, Janis. MICHAŁ JAN BORCH—POLSKI PRZYRODNIK XVIII W. [Michał Jan Borch: a Polish naturalist of the 18th century]. *Kwartalnik Hist. Nauki i Techniki [Poland] 1980 25(3): 481-499.* A biography of the Polish naturalist and mineralogist, Count Michał Jan Borch, (1753-1811) who traveled in Italy, France, Switzerland, and Saxony as well as other countries. His *Lithographie Sicilienne* described and classified minerals, discussed their evolution, and analyzed the role of heat, water, and volcanic material in the formation of minerals. 6 photos, 63 notes. 1753-1811

Borelli, Giovanni Alfonso

870. Breimer, Lars and Sourander, Patrick. ALPHONSO BORELLI AND CHRISTINA. *Clio Medica [Netherlands] 1983 18(1-4): 155-166.* Giovanni Alfonso Borelli (1608-79) studied in Rome under one of Galileo's disciples and became a professor of mathematics at Pisa and Messina, authoring *On the Causes of the Malignant Fevers in Sicily, 1647-48.* Borelli's chief interest was, however, in physiology. Working with Marcello Malpighi, the founder of microscopic anatomy, he collected material for his *De Mota Animalium* (1680-81). Borelli, who worked 20 years on this work, analyzed not only the motion of the human body but discussed aeronautics and submarines. Exiled to Rome for political reasons, Borelli found a patron in Queen Christina, the former regent of Protestant Sweden, and his posthumously published work was dedicated to her. 21 notes. 1660's-81

871. Sourander, Patrick. DROTTNING CHRISTINA OCH GIOVANNI ALFONSO BORELLI: TILL 300-ÅRS-MINNET AV KINESIOLOGINS FÖDELSE [Queen Christina and Giovanni Alfonso Borelli: in commemoration of the birth of kinesiology 300 years ago]. *Nordisk Medicinhistorisk Årsbok [Sweden] 1982: 56-65.* Alfonso Borelli (1608-79), was a versatile Italian savant, distinguished mathematician, and founder of the iatromechanical school in medicine, whose most esteemed work "De motu animalium" (On the movements of animals) was dedicated to Queen Christina. Through the application of the strict laws of physics—in the spirit of Galileo, Cartesius, and Boyle—to the movements of the animal and human body Borelli opened a new field of knowledge and originated the science of kinesiology. He had to flee from the University of Messina because of his liberal political ideas but was saved by Queen Christina, the former regent of Protestant Sweden who, after adopting the Catholic faith, became the most prominent benefactor of the arts and sciences in late 17th-century Rome. The Queen shared Borelli's interest in technical devices and defrayed the costs of the first edition of his magnum opus which was published posthumously in two volumes in 1680 and 1681. 1670's

Borelli Bey, Octave

872. Garcin, F. UN NOTABLE FRANÇAIS DU CAIRE À LA FIN DU XIXe SIÈCLE [A French notable in Cairo at the end of the 19th century]. *Rev. de l'Occident Musulman et de la Méditerranée [France] 1980 (30): 71-97.* At the beginning of the English occupation in the 1880's there were several thousand French in Egypt, including workers, petty tradesmen and merchants, political refugees, and civil servants. A representative figure was Octave Borelli Bey, whose family was from Marseilles. He was a lawyer, businessman, and official, who owned a newspaper, *Le Bosphore Egyptien,* which he used to express the ambiguous attitudes of French notables toward Egypt and Britain, supporting the idea of international control over Egypt, in which France would play a leading role. Includes a list of Borelli's writings. Based on Borelli family papers, newspapers, and other printed sources; 2 illus., 169 notes, 2 appendixes. 1878-1900

Borg, Walter

873. Bondestam, Anna. WALTER BORG (1870-1918): GROSSHANDLARE OCH REVOLUTIONÄR [Walter Borg (1870-1918): merchant and revolutionary]. *Hist. och Litteraturhistorisk Studier [Finland] 1982 57: 137-205.* A biographical sketch of the Finnish businessman and socialist, Walter Borg of Turku, Finland, together with excerpts from the journal he wrote while in exile in Petrograd in Soviet Russia, April-May 1918. Borg helped to edit the Swedish-language socialist newspaper in Turku, *Arbetet* [Labor] from 1909 through 1917. In early 1918 he served as bank director for the Red city administration. Based on Borg family records, interviews and secondary sources; photo, 12 notes. 1870-1918

Borges, Jorge Luis

874. Alifano, Roberto. JORGE LUIS BORGES: INTERVIEW. *Massachusetts Rev. 1983 24(3): 501-515.* An interview with Jorge Luis Borges, Argentine author, in which he describes his life and the conditions in Argentina that led to his becoming a writer. ca 1920's-83

875. Lagos, Ramona. "El Concepto de la Literatura en la Obra de Jorge Luis Borges: Nivel Teorico y Praxis Literaria" [The concept of literature in the work of Jorge Luis Borges: theoretical level and literary practice]. U. of Arizona 1982. 387 pp. *DAI 1982 43(3): 817-A.* DA8217499 1923-77

876. Matamoro, Blas. HISTORIA DE BORGES [Borges's history]. *Cuadernos Hispanoamericanos [Spain] 1985 (424): 129-148.* The Argentinian author Jorge Luis Borges (b. 1899)

seems to hold two opposing views of history: the first denies the reality of history and asserts that of myth, archetype, and eternity against the concrete present; the second indicates the valuation of history as a process common to all human beings, who are its constant but provisional synthesis. The turning point between these two views occurred around 1930, when half a century of stability ended in Argentina and the national model of the 1870's collapsed, giving way to a period of stagnation that favored Borges's inclination toward the first position on history. Photo. 1920's-60's

877. Rodríguez Monegal, Emir; Roberts, Anthony F., transl. VICTORIA OCAMPO, BORGES, AND *SUR* REVIEW: A SPECIAL RELATIONSHIP. *Cultures [France] 1982 8(2): 183-187.* 1925-31
*For abstract see **Ocampo, Victoria***

Borgese, Giuseppe Antonio

878. Goetz, Helmut. GIUSEPPE ANTONIO BORGESE UND DER FASCHISMUS [Giuseppe Antonio Borgese and Fascism]. *Quellen und Forschungen aus Italienischen Arch. und Bibliotheken [Italy] 1980 60: 523-534.* Comments on Fernando Mezzetti's *Borgese e il Fascismo* (1978). The complexity of Borgese's relations with Fascism is illustrated by his seeking Mussolini's personal help in his candidature for the Accademia d'Italia. Borgese made the application after his emigration to the United States without signing the required loyalty oath. Publishes a letter dated 18 May 1932 from Italy's Ambassador de Martino in Washington, D.C. to Foreign Minister Dino Grandi, which further reveals both Borgese's ambiguous attitude toward Fascism and the Italian government's awareness of it. Based on primary documents; 36 notes. Italian summary. 1918-50

Borgia, Alessandro

879. Petruzzi, Paolo. MONS. ALESSANDRO BORGIA, ARCIVESCOVO DI FERMO (1724-64) E LA CONTROVERSIA SULLA DIMINUZIONE DELLE FESTE DI PRECETTO [Alessandro Borgia, archbishop of Fermo, 1724-64, and the controversy concerning the reduction of holy days of obligation]. *Riv. di Storia della Chiesa in Italia [Italy] 1982 36(1): 80-104.* Discusses the reaction of Alessandro Borgia (1682-1764), archbishop of Fermo, to the proposal made in 1742 by Pope Benedict XIV (1675-1758) that the number of holy days of obligation to be celebrated in the liturgical calendar be reduced. Although the suggestion was promoted by economic considerations—the poor were thus impoverished still further—Borgia objected to the reduction on both theological and liturgical grounds. Based on State and Diocesan Archives and secondary sources; 91 notes. 1724-58

Borgia, Cesare

880. Eslava Galán, Juan. CESAR BORGIA [Cesare Borgia]. *Hist. y Vida [Spain] 1983 16(186): 78-94.* Cesare Borgia, member of the famous Borgia family and illegitimate son of Pope Alexander VI, is remembered as a great warrior who intended to restore the ancient glories of Rome; unfortunately he died at the age of 31. 1475-1507

Borgia family

881. Luján, Néstor. MITO Y REALIDAD DE LOS BORJA [The Borgia's myth and reality]. *Historia y Vida [Spain] 1984 17(197): 93-107.* Reviews the story of the infamous Borgia family, focusing on the lives of Popes Calixtus III and Alexander VI and defending Lucrezia Borgia's behavior in terms of 15th- and 16th-century Italian politics. 1450-1519

Borja y Aragón, Francisco de

See Esquilache, Marquis de

Borkenau, Franz

882. Woodcock, George. FRANZ BORKENAU AND THE GENERATIONS OF CULTURE. *Queen's Q. [Canada] 1983 90(2): 305-311.* Franz Borkenau, who died in 1956, had been noted mainly for his leftist critique in *The Spanish Cockpit* of the Spanish Civil War. Only in 1981 did a collection of his appear which showed his interest in the same historical questions that Spengler and Toynbee considered. 1930's-56

Bormann, Martin

883. Broszat, Martin. EMINENȚA CENUȘIE A LUI HITLER: MARTIN BORMANN ACAPAREAZĂ PUTEREA ÎN REICH [Hitler's gray eminence; Martin Bormann monopolizes power in the Reich]. *Magazin Istoric [Romania] 1980 14(8): 33-35.* Traces Bormann's career up to 1943. His contacts with the Nazis predate 1933, and family connections helped his steady rise to power. Based on the author's *Der Staat Hitlers. Grundlagung und Entwicklung Seiner Inneren Verfassung* (1969). 1933-43

Bormeister, Ferdinand

884. Hoffmann, Robert. VOM HANDWERKERSOHN ZUM MISSIONÄR: DIE LEBENSERINNERUNGEN DES HANDSCHUHMACHERS FERDINAND BORMEISTER [From artisan's son to missionary: the memoirs of glovemaker Ferdinand Bormeister]. *Jahrbuch der Gesellschaft für die Geschichte des Protestantismus in Österreich [Austria] 1984 100(1): 5-29.* Reproduces the memoirs of the German missionary Ferdinand Bormeister (b. 1785), which were written in 1818. Examines Bormeister's life and religious studies, particularly the time Bormeister spent in the parish of Wels, 1812-18, which formed the main part of his memoirs and which proved to be the turning point in Bormeister's life. These memoirs are important because they illustrate the life of a Protestant parish in Upper Austria in the early 19th century, and provide a social and historical study of the life of a young man searching for his own identity at a time of extreme political and social change. They reveal the importance of Pietism and the revivalist movement in early 19th-century Germany and show the Protestant missionaries' aims of putting their missionary theology into practice by establishing mission schools to educate young men such as Bormeister. In 1816, Bormeister went to study at the Basel Mission. Based on documents in the archives of the Basel Mission and secondary sources; 62 notes. 1812-18

Bornemisza, Péter

885. Hörcsik, Richärd. BORNEMISZA PÉTER 1535-1585 [Péter Bornemisza (1535-85)]. *Theologiai Szemle [Hungary] 1985 28(3): 173-175.* Bornemisza was born in Pest to affluent parents, who, however, died in 1541 during the Turkish occupation. He was raised in the strongly Protestant Upper Tisza region, educated in Germany, Austria, Italy, and finally in Hungary, and became bishop in 1573. He was unique in his outspoken criticism of social injustice, and his habit of naming exploiters of the poor, including the highly placed, created many enemies for Bornemisza. He retired to his estate in 1583. 24 notes. 1535-85

886. Mintz, Matityahu. BER BOROKHOV. *Studies in Zionism [Israel] 1982 (5): 33-53.* Presents a short biography and describes the contributions of the early Zionist-Socialist philosopher Ber Borochow. Borokhov is credited with successfully integrating Zionism and Marxism and with providing Zionism a theoretical basis from which to develop. Borochow maintained that Jews lacked a material base (sovereign territory), which led to an unwarranted hatred of the Jews, which in turn, led to the danger of extinction. Borochow's solution to the Zionist problem was "territorialism"—the acquisition of land permitting Jews to determine their own political destiny. Several reasons supporting Palestine as the ideal location for Zionist settlement are offered. Based primarily on excerpts from Borochow's *Works;* 4 notes. 1901-17

887. Piasecki, Henryk. BER BOROCHOW—ŻYCIE, DZIAŁALNOŚĆ I TWÓRCZOŚĆ [Ber Borochow: life, activity, and production]. *Biuletyn Żydowskiego Instytutu Historycznego w Polsce [Poland] 1985 (3-4): 41-65.* Ber Borochow was the founder of the Russian-Polish socialist-Zionist political party Poale Zion. Traces Borochow's leadership of the party, the major events in its growth, and its eventual split in its 1917 and 1920 congresses into left- and right-wing factions. 1900-20

Borodin, Mikhail

888. Gupta, Surendra K. *BORODIN: STALIN'S MAN IN CHINA. Issues & Studies [Taiwan] 1981 17(9): 74-80.* Reviews Dan N. Jacobs's *Borodin: Stalin's Man in China* (1981), tracing its account of Mikhail Borodin's (1884-1953) career in the United States, revolutionary Russia, and particularly as representative of the Comintern in China, 1923-27. 1917-27

889. McKay, Craig Graham. A GLIMPSE OF BORODIN... *Cahiers du Monde Russe et Soviétique [France] 1986 27(1): 107-110.* M. N. Roy has given an amusing portrait of Comintern agent Comrade Mikhail Borodin's arrival in Mexico in 1919. But what was Borodin doing prior to his mission to the New World with some of the Russian crown jewels? On the basis of Scandinavian police reports and some US diplomatic documents, the author supplies a piece of the puzzle and at the same time throws some light on the propaganda activities of the Bolsheviks. 1918-19

Borrás, Enrique

890. Blanch, Armando. ENRIQUE BORRAS [Enrique Borrás]. *Hist. y Vida [Spain] 1983 16(188): 100-111.* Borrás, one of Spain's and Catalonia's most celebrated actors, achieved international fame, particularly for his performances in the works of Angel Guimerà. 1863-1957

Borromeo, Saint Carlo

891. Agnoletto, Attilio. CARLO BORROMEO TRA PRASSI E ASCESI. UNA RILETTURA BIOGRAFICA DELL'ULTIMO ANNO DI VITA (NOVEMBRE 1583-NOVEMBRE 1584) [Carlo Borromeo through practice and asceticism: a biographical review of the last year of his life (November 1583-November 1584)]. *Acme [Italy] 1984 37(3): 5-15.* Cites 19th- and 20th-century hagiographers as well as letters written 1583-84 in order to establish the exact nature of Saint Carlo Borromeo's faith after he was appointed Archbishop of Milan in early 1583. 1583-84

Bortkiewicz, Ladislaus von

892. Gattei, Giorgio. LE CATTEDRE MANCATE DI LADISLAUS VON BORTKIEWICZ (CONTRIBUTO ALLA BIOGRAFIA) [The missed professorships of Ladislaus von Bortkiewicz: a contribution to his biography]. *Econ. e Storia [Italy] 1982 3(2): 204-218.* The Russian economist Vladislav Bortkevich, who later Germanized his name, began a correspondence with the Swiss economist Leon Walras when still a young man. The correspondence clearly demonstrates the intellectual debt of the Russian to his older colleague and also supplies data concerning his unsuccessful attempts to obtain the chair of economics first at Lausanne in 1893 and then at Geneva in 1897, which had been suggested to him by Vilfredo Pareto and Maffeo Pantaleoni respectively. Based on *Correspondence of Leon Walras and Related Papers,* 3 vol., William Jaffé, ed., Amsterdam (1965) and other secondary material; 64 notes. 1887-1911

Bosc, Louis-Augustin-Guillaume

894. Beale, Georgia Robison. BOSC AFOOT. *Pro. of the Ann. Meeting of the Western Soc. for French Hist. 1982 10: 130-140.* Presents a synopsis of the life of Louis-Augustin-Guillaume Bosc (1759-1828). At different times he served in the French postal service and was a vice-consul in the United States. He is, however, best known for his botanical collections and writings. Based on Bosc's papers in the Bibliothèque Historique de la Ville de Paris; 45 notes. 1750's-1820's

Bosch, Jan Willem

895. Feenstra, R. IN MEMORIAM J. W. BOSCH, 1890-1982 [In memoriam: J. W. Bosch, 1890-1982]. *Tijdschrift voor Rechtsgeschiedenis [Netherlands] 1983 51(3-4): 429-431.* Jan Willem Bosch of the editorial staff of *Tijdschrift voor Rechtsgeschiedenis* started his career in the civil service in 1921 and, after retirement in 1955 as public prosecutor in Breda, devoted himself to studies in the history of Dutch law and its connections with Belgian and French law. 1890-1982

Bosch, Robert

896. Mulert, Jürgen. ERFOLGSBETEILIGUNG UND VERMÖGENSBILDUNG DER ARBEITNEHMER BEI DER FIRMA ROBERT BOSCH ZWISCHEN 1886 UND 1945 [Profit-sharing and benefits for workers in the Robert Bosch Company, 1886-1945]. *Zeitschrift für Unternehmensgeschichte [West Germany] 1985 30(1): 1-29.* As a pioneer in the spark plug industry, Robert Bosch (1861-1942) developed a small electromechanics shop into a worldwide enterprise manufacturing electrical components of cars as well as an increasing variety of electrical appliances. During the rapid expansion phase between 1900 and 1914 his company enjoyed somewhat of a monopoly. Although in contact with socialist thought and voting social democratic, he never actually was a socialist, despite the epithet of "the red Bosch." According to his own confession he espoused a moderate "middle-of-the-road" philosophy which made him suspect to the dogmatic fringes on both sides of the political spectrum. He was, however, quite popular with his employees, who called him affectionately or reverently "father Bosch." Describes the various approaches to profit-sharing developed and employed by the Robert Bosch Company between 1886 and 1945. As a staunch individualist he was quite concerned about the economic freedom of his employees. Therefore, he deliberately chose comparatively high wages, inventor's and achievement bonuses, and disability insurance schemes as the most prominent tools of profit-sharing for his employees. The

rapid development of labor legislation after World War I and the complete control exercised after 1933 obliterated private initiatives in the field of social policy. 1886-1945

Bosgrave, James

897. Skwarczynski, Paul. ELSINORE 1580: JOHN ROGERS AND JAMES BOSGRAVE. *Recusant Hist. [Great Britain] 1982 16(1): 1-16.* Brief biographies of the Protestant lawyer and diplomat, Dr. John Rogers, and Jesuit friar, James Bosgrave, two Englishmen who met in 1580 in Elsinore, Denmark, a meeting that resulted in Bosgrave's arrest, trial, and imprisonment in the Tower of London until 1585 when he was banished. In 1585 he returned to Poland, where he had taught before 1580, and stirred up much public indignation there to the persecution of Catholics in England. 1580-85

Bosl, Karl

898. —. ZUM 75. GEBURTSTAG VON PROFESSOR DR. KARL BOSL [On Professor Karl Bosl's 75th birthday]. *Bohemia [West Germany] 1984 25(1): 124-131.*

Kiessling, Herbert. ZUR FEIER DES 75. GEBURTSTAGES VON PROFESSOR DR. KARL BOSL [On Professor Karl Bosl's 75th birthday celebration], *pp. 124-126.* Karl Bosl (b. 1908) not only excelled as a European historian, but contributed directly to Bavaria's educational reforms after World War II.

Seibt, Ferdinand. KARL BOSL 75 JAHRE [Karl Bosl 75 years old], *pp. 127-131.* In addition to his amazing productivity as a broad-gauged social historian, Bosl has played a leading role in the Collegium Carolinum and has become an authoritative voice for the history of the Bohemian lands. Speeches presented at a celebration held by the Collegium Carolinum at the Bavarian National Museum in Munich, 14 November 1983. 1908-83

Boswell, James

899. Finney, Brian. BOSWELL'S *HEBRIDEAN JOURNAL* AND THE ORDEAL OF DR. JOHNSON. *Biography 1982 5(4): 319-334.* Because Boswell allowed Johnson to read most of his *Journal of Tour to Hebrides* as it was being written, the form of this biography, unlike the *Life,* reflects the growth in their relationship. It also constitutes a secondary form of discourse between them, the resulting subtleties of which make it a unique contribution to the history of biography. 1773-84

900. Redford, Bruce B. BOSWELL AS CORRESPONDENT; BOSWELL AS LETTER-WRITER. *Yale U. Lib. Gazette 1982 56(3-4): 40-52.* Boswell's editors have approached his correspondence from a historical point of view blurring the distinction between the letter as "documentary source" and as "verbal contraption." The published and forthcoming volumes of the Yale edition attest to the range of Bosell's correspondents not only revealing a broad impression of late Augustan society but also the squalor of Boswell's personal life. It would seem that Boswell's letters are valuable biographical and historical documents but are not of notable literary merit. 40 notes. 1765-95

Botev, Khristo

901. Pavlovska, Tsvetana. ZA VZAIMNOTO VLIIANIE MEZHDU LEVSKI I BOTEV [On the reciprocal influences between Levski and Botev]. *Istoricheski Pregled [Bulgaria] 1982 38(4): 65-79.* Vasil Levski (1837-73) and Khristo Botev (1848-76) met in Bucharest not earlier than 7 September 1868. Their ideological, historical, and philosophical viewpoints were similar. Levski's death affected Botev. Their poetry had marked similarities, especially in the mother and struggle themes. They were the two great activists of the Bulgarian renaissance. Following Levski, Botev increased his revolutionary activity among the Bulgarian emigration in the External Revolutionary Opposition. Botev was the supporter and continuer of the Apostle Levski's historical message. Based on *Botev and the Memories of His Contemporaries* (1977); 141 notes. 1865-73

Boteva, Ivana

902. Peneva, N. DVE NEIZVESTNI PISMA NA IVANA BOTEVA PETKOVA DO NAIDEN GEROV [Two newly discovered letters from Ivana Boteva Petkova to Naiden Gerov]. *Izvestiia na Narodnata Biblioteka "Kiril i Metodii" [Bulgaria] 1983 18: 385-389.* 1871-74

*For abstract see **Gerov, Naiden***

Botkin, Vasily P.

903. Offord, D. C. VASILY PETROVICH BOTKIN (1810-69). *Oxford Slavonic Papers [Great Britain] 1983 16: 141-163.* The importance of V. P. Botkin to Russian intellectual life from 1835 to 1865 was much greater than has been generally conceded. He did as much to determine the dominant ideas and spirit of the age as those whose names are more readily known. His own shifting views reflected the intellectual developments of the time, culminating in the eventual crisis that occurred in the ranks of the Russian intelligentsia in the 1860's. Based on the writings of Botkin; 110 notes. 1835-69

Bottai, Giuseppe

904. Goldbrunner, Hermann. AUS DER BIBLIOTHEK EINES INTELLEKTUELLEN FASCHISTEN: GIUSEPPE BOTTAI [From the library of an intellectual Fascist, Giuseppe Bottai]. *Quellen und Forschungen aus Italienischen Arch. und Bibliotheken [Italy] 1980 60: 535-578.* Surveys that part of Giuseppe Bottai's (1895-1959) library which represents his political, economic, and educational interests and supplies its biographical and historical context. Containing few of his own works but many by contemporary admirers and opponents, Bottai's library reflects the wide reading of this great theorist and career opportunist on subjects connected with his ministries of corporations and of national education and on such themes of special interest as Italy's political history, Fascism, its relation to national socialism, Mussolini, and the race question in Italian schools. Primary sources; 251 notes. Italian summary. 1920's-48

Bottazzi, Mattia

905. Mainardi, Giuseppe. LA BIOGRAFIA E I LIBRI DI MATTIA BOTTAZZI (. . . -1481/1482). CONTRIBUTI PER UNA STORIA DELLA CULTURA CREMONESE NEL SECOLO XV [Life and books of Mattia Bottazzi (d. 1481/1482): contribution to cultural life in Cremona during the 15th century]. *Rivista di Storia della Chiesa in Italia [Italy] 1985 39(1): 1-56.* Reconstructs family background and ecclesiastical career of Mattia Bottazzi, who became the first presbyter of the newly erected Collegiate foundation of Monticelli d'Ongina (near Cremona) in 1471. The author describes his library, noting his conservative taste in canon law, theology, and the liberal arts. Based on departmental and ecclesiastical archives of the province of Cremona and secondary sources; 292 notes. 1430's-82

Böttger, Johann Friedrich

906. Pánková, Marcela. BÖTTGERŮV OBJEV PORCELÁNU [Böttger's discovery of porcelain]. *Umění a Řemesla [Czechoslovakia] 1982 (3): 10-12.* Remembers the 300th anniversary of the birth of Johann Friedrich Böttger (1682-1719), originator of Dresden china. 1682-1719

Botti, Ferruccio

907. Dall'Olio, Enrico. DON FERRUCCIO BOTTI (1905-1983) [Don Ferruccio Botti (1905-83)]. *Archivio Storico per le Province Parmensi [Italy] 1983 35: 50-55.* Reviews the life and work of Ferruccio Botti, who wrote many works on the history of art and sculpture, and gave special attention to the relationship between hagiography and art. 1930's-83

Botticelli

908. Barolsky, Paul. WALTER PATER AND THE POETRY OF NOTHINGNESS. *Antioch Rev. 1982 40(4): 469-478.* Discusses Walter Pater's *The Renaissance,* consisting of biographies of Pico, Botticelli, Della Robbia, Michelangelo, Giorgione, Leonardo, and Du Bellay, with particular emphasis on the poetic, abstract, and autobiographical nature of the work. 15c

Bouche, Madame

909. Bertier de Sauvigny, Guillaume de. DE LA CANEBIERE A SAINT-PETERSBOURG: MADAME BOUCHE, LA PROPHETESSE MARSEILLAISE [From the Canebière to St. Petersburg: Madame Bouche, the prophetess from Marseilles]. *Hist. Mag. [France] 1983 (43): 44-48.* Relates the adventures of Madame Bouche, a Frenchwoman of ill repute, a visionary and prophetess, stressing her intimacy with Russia's Alexander I (1777-1825), whom she guided "spiritually." 1819-28

Boucher, François

910. Hofstadter, Dan. FRANÇOIS BOUCHER: HE SUMMED UP THE LIVES OF ARISTOCRATS. *Smithsonian 1986 16(12): 98-109.* Reviews the life and work of French bourgeois painter François Boucher (1703-70), whose taste for highly decorative and artificial shapes and colors and for painting the female nude has confounded critics from his own era as well as those in the 1980's. Reviews a new Boucher exhibit mounted in 1986 at the New York Metropolitan Museum. 1703-70

911. Jacoby, Beverly Edith Schreiber. "François Boucher's Early Development as a Draughtsman: 1720-1734." Harvard U. 1983. 389 pp. *DAI 1983 44(2): 309-A.* DA8311914 1720-34

912. Owens, Iris. THE BOUCHER DREAM. *Art & Antiques 1986 (Apr): 76-80, 88.* Describes the twenty-year relationship between François Boucher (1702-65), a prodigious painter, and Madame de Pompadour, the art-crazed mistress of Louis XV of France. 1745-65

Bouillon, Duc de

913. Delteil, Frank. HENRI DE LA TOUR, DUC DE BOUILLON: RECHERCHE RECENTE ET COMPLEMENTS [Henri de La Tour, duc de Bouillon: recent research and additions]. *Bulletin de la Société de l'Histoire du Protestantisme Français [France] 1986 132(1): 79-98.* Reviews a thesis presented at Lyons in 1982 by Henri Zuber on the political and diplomatic activities of Henri de La Tour, vicomte of Turenne, 1573-1623, and duc de Bouillon after 1591. Born in Auvergne, he won his first victory at 20 in Montauban in 1575, converted to Protestantism, and became an ally of Henri de Navarre in the civil wars that divided southern France until the Treaty of Fleix was signed in 1580. In 1584, following a 3-year imprisonment in the Netherlands, he again joined forces with Navarre, then heir to the crown of France. When Navarre converted to Catholicism in 1589 in order to accede to the throne, Bouillon and the Huguenots felt betrayed, but in 1590, Bouillon rejoined Henry IV in Paris to defend France from the Spanish. Based on Bouillon's *Mémoires,* published in 1901 by Baguenault de Puchesse, Catherine de Medici's letters, Millau communal archives, Aubigné's 1876 *Histoire Universelle,* and other primary and secondary sources; 108 notes. 1573-90

Boulanger, Georges

914. Decaux, Alain. UN AMOUR DE LA FRANCE: BOULANGER [A love of France: Boulanger]. *Hist. Mag. [France] 1983 (45): 34-47.* Georges Boulanger (1837-91) fought in Algeria, Italy, China, and Tunisia, and become general in 1884. In 1880 he submitted a plan for the reorganization of the army, which was voted into law in 1889. In addition to his military reforms, he was active in politics until an accusation of conspiracy caused him to flee France and led to his suicide. 1855-91

Boulanger, Nadia

915. Walter, Teresa. "Nadia Boulanger, Musician and Teacher: Her Life, Concepts, and Influences." (Vol. 1-2) Peabody Inst., Johns Hopkins U. 1981. 389 pp. *DAI 1982 42(9): 3806-A.* DA8204156 20c

Boulton, Matthew

916. Hopkins, Eric. BOULTON BEFORE WATT: THE EARLIER CAREER RE-CONSIDERED. *Midland History [Great Britain] 1984 9: 43-58.* Few would dispute Matthew Boulton's contributions to the Industrial Revolution, but little attention has been paid to his earlier career before formation of his celebrated partnership with James Watt in 1775. In the early 1770's Boulton's diverse business interests frequently came perilously close to disaster and were never financially stable. Boulton's difficulties are attributable not to incompetence but to attempting to accomplish too much alone. Watt's steam engine seems to have rescued Boulton from the threat of bankruptcy, a fate overtaking many other ambitious 18th-century businessmen. Boulton's entrepreneurial record before 1775 must be regarded as flawed. Based on the business papers of Matthew Boulton (1728-1809) and the firm of Boulton & Fothergill in the Birmingham Reference Library; 66 notes. 1762-82

Bourbon, Charlotte de

917. Ridder-Symoens, Hilde de. VROUWEN ROND WILLEM VAN ORANJE [Women around William of Orange]. *Spiegel Historiael [Netherlands] 1984 19(4): 181-186.* 1533-84
For abstract see ***William the Silent***

Bourbon, Philip de

918. Balansó, Juan. LOS BORBONES DE PARMA, RETRATO DE FAMILIA [The Bourbons of Parma, a family portrait]. *Historia y Vida [Spain] 1984 17(200): 28-41.* Examines the life of the first duke of Parma, Philip de Bourbon (1720-65), son of Spanish king Philip V, and his descendents until the dissolution of the duchy in 1859. 18c-19c

Bourbon family

919. Goaillard, Philippe. ACTUALITE DES BOURBONS [The Bourbons today]. *Revue de Pau et du Béarn [France] 1984-85 12: 81-83.* Reviews a 1983 book on the descendants of Henry IV (Henry of Navarre), *L'Etat Présent de la Maison de Bourbon* and includes a partial family tree of the Bourbons. 16c-20c

Bourdé, Guy

920. Rebérioux, Madeleine. GUY BOURDE 1942-1982 [Guy Bourdé; 1942-82]. *Mouvement Social [France] 1982 (121): 3-6.* Obituary of Guy Bourdé (1940-82), highlighting his career as a professor and a scholar in labor and social issues. Bourdé was a contributor to *Mouvement Social* and had been involved in comprehensive research on Latin American industrialization and urbanization. 6 notes. 1942-82

Bourdillon, Violet

921. Pearce, R. D. VIOLET BOURDILLON: COLONIAL GOVERNOR'S WIFE. *African Affairs [Great Britain] 1983 82(327): 267-277.* The life of Violet Bourdillon (1886-1979), a woman described in 1935 as "the perfect Governor's wife," completely contradicts the stereotyped conception of British women in the colonies. As the wife of Bernard Henry Bourdillon, Governor of Nigeria, Violet Bourdillon charmed both British and Africans, treated the colonial peoples with graciousness and respect, and functioned less as a ruler than as a guide and partner. In her old age she believed that it was highly desirable that the British Empire had come to an end and that people in the former colonies were now governing themselves. 59 notes. 1935-79

Bourg, Marguerite de

922. Fontaine, Marie-Madeleine. "UN COEUR MIS EN GAGE" PONTUS DE TYARD, MARGUERITE DE BOURG ET LE MILIEU LYONNAIS DES ANNEES 1550 ["A Heart in Pawn": Pontus de Tyard, Marguerite de Bourg, and Lyons society of 1550]. *Nouvelle Revue du Seizième Siècle [France] 1984 2: 69-89.* Traces references in the work of Pontus de Tyard to Marguerite de Bourg, dame de Gage, whose name furnished a ready pun-metaphor for poetic reference since her name also means "pawn" or "pledge" in French. Mother-in-law to the Dauphin's royal treasurer, Marguerite de Bourg was the educated only child of a rich Lyons merchant with high church and state connections and figured prominently in the literary works and life of Lyons, as did her three daughters. Reviews other dedications to Marguerite, particularly Italian translator of Plutarch, Ridolfi, in whose work she appears as "Aretefila." Drawn from contemporary papers and archives; 31 notes, 3 appendixes. 1556-78

Bourguina, Anna

923. Emmons, Terence. ANNA MIKHAILOVNA BOURGUINA. *Russian Review 1983 42(3): 351-353.* An obituary of Russian historian Anna Bourguina. 1940's-83

Bournonville, August

924. Lilliestam, Åke. MARIE WESTBERG—EN SVENSK BOURNONVILLE-DANSÖS [Marie Westberg, a Swedish Bournonville dancer]. *Personhistorisk Tidskrift [Sweden] 1980 76(3): 8-14.* 1872-90
For abstract see ***Westberg, Marie***

Bouthoul, Gaston

925. J. F. P. HOMMAGE A GASTON BOUTHOUL [Homage to Gaston Bouthoul]. *Etudes Polémologiques [France] 1981 (24): 11-20.* A biographical sketch of the activities of the French sociologist of war, Gaston Bouthoul (1896-1980), founder of the French Institute of Polemology, followed by hitherto unpublished writings including a letter to an unknown addressee, some notes on the function of conflict in social history, and a project for an article on the subject of polemology—the sociology of war and peace, the science of which Bouthoul was a founder. He proposes the view that war is an ordinary social phenomenon that needs to be desacralized and treated as a subject of scientific inquiry so that it may be combated. All three manuscripts date from the early 1970's. 20c

926. —. [IN MEMORY OF GASTON BOUTHOUL] (French text). *Etudes Polémologiques [France] 1981 (24): 21-45.*

Carrère, René. GASTON BOUTHOUL, HOMME DE VERITE ET DE PAIX [Gaston Bouthoul, a man of truth and peace], *pp. 21-24.* Sketches the academic biography of the French sociologist Gaston Bouthoul (1896-1980), listing his writings and the awards he received.

Freund, Julien. GASTON BOUTHOUL, SOCIOLOGUE DE LA GUERRE ET DE LA PAIX: LE FOND DE LA PENSEE DE GASTON BOUTHOUL [Gaston Bouthoul, the sociologist of war and peace: the essence of his thought], *pp. 25-42.* Traces the directions in the original thought and research of the French sociologist of war, Gaston Bouthoul, assessing his disagreements with pacifists over the treatment of war. Stresses the value of his research.

I. F. P. OBJET, METHODE ET SPECIFICITE DE LA POLEMOLOGIE [The aim, the method, and the specificity of the study of war], *pp. 44-45.* Defines the discipline of polemology, treating war as a scientific subject. 20c

Bovio, Giovanni

927. Angelini, Giovanna. EDUCAZIONE E DEMOCRAZIA NEL GIORNALISMO POLITICO DI BOVIO [Education and democracy in Giovanni Bovio's political journalism]. *Politico [Italy] 1981 46(1-2): 209-222.* After a brief and tormented experience in failing to start a newspaper of his own, Giovanni Bovio's passion for journalism found its natural outlet in an assiduous collaboration, lasting over 30 years, with many progressive journals, such as *Rivista Repubblicana, La Lega, Il Fascio della Democrazia, Giordano Bruno, Roma, Rivista Popolare,* and *Cuore e Critica.* His personality as educator and journalist merged with the more complex aspects of his political thought in his ideal of a social republic, appealing primarily to the individual conscience. 1878-94

Bowen, Edward

928. Mangan, James A. PHILATHLETE EXTRAORDINARY: A PORTRAIT OF THE VICTORIAN MORALIST EDWARD BOWEN. *J. of Sport Hist. 1982 9(3): 23-40.* Victorian England saw the emergence of the athletic pedagog, a new kind of schoolmaster. One of the most zealous was Edward Bowen, assistant master at Harrow School from 1859 to 1901. He was not only a vigorous athlete, but also a poet who celebrated the delights of games. Although many of his views were considered radical by upper-class English society, he gained substantial respect in an upper-class school system. Leslie Stephen played the same role at the University of Cambridge. They considered playing fields to be the initial

location for the development of character. Based on published sources, including material written by Bowen; 71 notes. 1859-1901

Bowen, Elizabeth

929. Richardi, Janis Marie. "The Modern British *Bildungsroman* and the Woman Novelist: Dorothy Richardson, May Sinclair, Rosamond Lehmann, Elizabeth Bowen, and Doris Lessing." U. of North Carolina, Chapel Hill 1981. 245 pp. *DAI 1982 42(8): 3612-A.* 8200609 20c

Bowen, Emrys George

930. Jones, Glanville R. J. OBITUARY: EMRYS GEORGE BOWEN (1900-1983). *Welsh History Review [Great Britain] 1984 12(2): 246-248.* The Welsh historical geographer, Emrys George Bowen, died on 8 November 1983. His academic career was centered on Aberystwyth and his life's work was the history of settlement in Wales. 1900-83

Boyer, Abel

931. Gibbs, Graham C. ABEL BOYER GALLO-ANGLUS GLOSSOGRAPHUS ET HISTORICUS 1667-1729: FROM TUTOR TO AUTHOR, 1689-1699. *Proceedings of the Huguenot Society of London [Great Britain] 1983 24(1): 46-59.* Describes the literary beginnings of the French Huguenot Abel Boyer (1667-1729), who settled in Great Britain in 1689. The author notes Boyer's position as history tutor and his subsequent work on the French-English and English-French dictionaries, begun in 1694. 1689-99

Boyle, Robert

932. Shapin, Steven. PUMP AND CIRCUMSTANCE: ROBERT BOYLE'S LITERARY TECHNOLOGY. *Social Studies of Science [Great Britain] 1984 14(4): 481-520.* Inventor of the "air pump" in the 17th century, Robert Boyle also set out to establish that scientific "facts" must either be witnessed, replicated, or affirmed via a special style of scientific reporting that qualified the reader as a "witness" to the facts. 17c

Bozhenko, Vasyl N.

933. Bulkina, V. P. LEHENDARNY KOMBRIH (DO 110-RICHCHIA Z DNIA NARODZHENNIA V. N. BOZHENKA) [A legendary Communist leader: on the 110th anniversary of the birth of Vasyl N. Bozhenko]. *Ukrains'kyi Istorychnyi Zhurnal [USSR] 1981 (4): 131-134.* Vasyl Nazarovych Bozhenko, born on 21 April 1871 in the village of Berezhunka in the Kherson region of the Ukraine to a poor peasant family, had no opportunity to receive any education. He joined the army, and on leaving in 1896, he joined the Odessa-based Russian Social Democratic Workers Party, where he helped in political propaganda work and political agitation. He was arrested in 1907, and in 1917 he joined the Bolsheviks. During the Russian Revolution and in the period of the Civil War, he played an important role in acting against the Petlurites (Ukrainian nationalists) and against the Ukrainian Central Council. 1871-1919

Božić, Ivan

934. Spremić, Momčilo. IVAN BOŽIĆ (23.APRIL 1915-20.AVGUST 1977) [Ivan Božić (23 April 1915-20 August 1977)]. *Jugoslovenski Istorijski Časopis [Yugoslavia] 1979 18(3-4): 204-206.* Obituary of a former professor at Belgrade University and a noted specialist in the medieval history of the Yugoslav peoples. Božić was the author of monographs on 14th- and 15th-century Dubrovnik, 14th-century Serbia, 15th-century Montenegro, and a major contributor to the *History of the Peoples of Yugoslavia* (1953) and the *History of Yugoslavia* (1972). 1915-77

Bracken, Josephine Leopoldine

935. Quintos, Floy C. THE "SWEET STRANGER" BECOMES A FILIPINA. *Asian & Pacific Q. of Cultural and Social Affairs [South Korea] 1981 13(2): 86-89.* Celebrates the posthumous recognition given in 1977 to Josephine Leopoldine Bracken by the Bayaning Filipino Foundation and puts to rest several myths concerning Josephine and her common-law husband, Jose Rizal. Reprinted from "Panorama," Sunday Magazine of the Bulletin *Today.* 1890-1977

Bradford, John

936. Hughes, Celia. TWO SIXTEENTH-CENTURY NORTHERN PROTESTANTS: JOHN BRADFORD AND WILLIAM TURNER. *Bull. of the John Rylands U. Lib. of Manchester [Great Britain] 1983 66(1): 104-138.* Contains brief biographies of John Bradford (ca. 1510-55) of Manchester and William Turner (ca. 1510-68) of Morpeth, Northumberland. Both were ordained late in life, were zealous Protestants, and became involved in religious conflict. They were active preachers, writers, and translators. While Turner survived into Elizabeth's reign, Bradford was burned at the stake under Mary. Primary sources; 70 notes. 16c

Bradlaugh, Charles

937. D'Arcy, Fergus A. CHARLES BRADLAUGH AND THE ENGLISH REPUBLICAN MOVEMENT, 1868-1878. *Hist. J. [Great Britain] 1982 25(2): 367-383.* Examines the ambivalent role of Charles Bradlaugh (1833-91) in the largely unsuccessful attempts of English radicals to revive republicanism as a popular movement through the International Democratic Association and the National Republican Brotherhood. Bradlaugh refused to associate himself with the movement until he believed it had developed its own momentum, insisted that its agitation should be legal and gradualist, and disowned advocates of revolutionary socialism and defenders of the Paris Commune. His involvement in the republican movement first clearly revealed the limitations of his radicalism, while his quarrel with the First International withdrew popular support from the socialist movement without significantly benefiting republicanism. Based on the radical press, especially the *National Reformer,* Home Office correspondence, and secondary sources. 104 notes. 1868-78

Bradshaw, William

938. Thompson, F. Glenn. ASSISTANT SURGEON WILLIAM BRADSHAW, V.C. *Irish Sword [Ireland] 1981 14(56): 237-239.* A biographical account of William Bradshaw (1830-61) of County Tipperary, Ireland, who chose a medical career in the British army. 19 notes. 1830-61

Bragaldi, Jean-Damascène

939. Ceyssens, Lucien. AUTOUR DE LA BULLE *UNIGENITUS:* LE P. DAMASCENE BRAGALDI, CONVENTUEL (1665-1715) [Around the *Unigenitus* bull: the monk Damascène Bragaldi, 1665-1715]. *Bull. de l'Inst. Hist. Belge de Rome [Belgium] 1981 51: 147-165.* Discusses the life of the enigmatic Franciscan monk, Jean-Damascène Bragaldi, describing his involvement in drafting the bull of Clement XI, *Unigenitus,* which condemned his involvement in Jansenism and Quesnel's *Reflexiones Morales.* 1665-1715

Bragg, William Henry

940. Home, R. W. THE PROBLEM OF INTELLECTUAL ISOLATION IN SCIENTIFIC LIFE: W. H. BRAGG AND THE AUSTRALIAN SCIENTIFIC COMMUNITY, 1886-1909. *Historical Records of Australian Science [Australia] 1984 6(1): 19-30.* William Henry Bragg (1862-1942), a British scientist who received a Nobel prize in physics in 1915, taught at the University of Adelaide for over two decades before returning to England in 1909. Accounts of his life often imply that he was working in almost complete isolation during those years, but he had several ongoing contacts with other Australian scientists that significantly aided his development "from a raw young mathematics teacher... into a mature physicist." Based on Bragg papers, University of Adelaide archives, and other records of Australian science; 54 notes. 1886-1909

941. Jenkin, John G. THE APPOINTMENT OF W. H. BRAGG, F.R.S., TO THE UNIVERSITY OF ADELAIDE. *Notes and Records of the Royal Society of London [Great Britain] 1985 40(1): 75-99.* Outlines the accomplishments of W. H. Bragg, who replaced Horace Lamb at the University of Adelaide in mathematics and physics. The author illustrates the early years of academic life in Australia. Based on documents in the University of Adelaide Archives; 125 notes. 1870-90

Brahe, Tycho

942. DiBono, Mario. TYCHO BRAHE E L'ASTRONOMIA: PER UNA NUOVA VALUTAZIONE DELL'ASTRONOMO DANESE [Tycho Brahe and astronomy: a new evaluation of the Danish astronomer]. *Physis [Italy] 1982 24(2): 157-195.* 1560-1601

Brailoiu, Constantin

943. Aubert, Laurent. UNE IMPORTANTE REEDITION DE DISQUES: LA COLLECTION C. BRAILOIU DE MUSIQUE POPULAIRE SUISSE [An important rerelease of records: the C. Brailoiu collection of Swiss folk music]. *Musées de Genève [Switzerland] 1986 (266): 2-7.* Romanian ethnomusicologist Constantin Brailoiu made an exhaustive inventory of traditional Swiss music, children's songs, and religious music, 1927-51; the recordings he made were rerecorded and released in 1985 by the Musée d'Ethnographie of Geneva, supplemented by substantial explicatory notes and photographs. 1927-51

Bramsted, Ernest K.

944. Hooper, John. ERNEST K. BRAMSTED (1901-1978): A EUROPEAN HISTORIAN IN GERMANY, ENGLAND AND AUSTRALIA. *Australian Journal of Politics and History [Australia] 1985 31(3): 397-407.* A brief intellectual biography of Ernest K. Bramsted (Ernst Kohn-Bramstedt), who was of southern Bavarian Jewish background and took part in the November 1918 revolution in Germany as a schoolboy. He gained a doctorate under Friedrich Meinecke in Berlin and was a teacher until he lost his job under the Nazis. Migrating to Holland and then England, he received another doctorate at the London School of Economics and worked for the BBC in World War II. Work in the postwar Control Commission in Germany was followed by membership on the editorial board of the *Documents on German Foreign Policy* series from 1948 to 1952, when he went to the University of Sydney, where he taught European history until retirement in 1969. His main works are summarized. Based on Bramsted's works and interviews; photo, 35 notes. 15c-20c

Brâncoveanu, Constantin

945. Cernovodeanu, Paul. DIN CORESPONDENȚA DIPLOMATICĂ A LUI CONSTANTIN BRÂNCOVEANU (I) [Excerpts from the diplomatic correspondence of Constantin Brâncoveanu. Part 1]. *Revista Arhivelor [Romania] 1985 47(1): 78-84.* The letters of Constantin Brâncoveanu, exchequer of Wallachia, written in 1698-1713, reflect his knowledge of the political reality in his country and his preoccupation with securing peace for the principality. Article to be continued. 1698-1713

Brandt, Josef

946. Spielmann, Josef. EIN SIEBENBÜRGISCHER PIONIER DER NEPHREKTOMIE: JOSEF BRANDT (1838-1912) [A Transylvanian pioneer of nephrectomy: Josef Brandt (1838-1912)]. *Sudhoffs Archiv [West Germany] 1980 64(2): 151-162.* In 1874 Josef Brandt, professor of surgery at Cluj, established himself as a pioneer in kidney surgery. 1873

Brangwyn, Frank

947. Davis, Angela. FORGOTTEN ARTIST: SIR FRANK BRANGWYN, 1867-1956. *Manitoba History [Canada] 1984 (7): 10-13.* Frank Brangwyn, a native of Belgium, was an early student of the political and artistic ideas of William Morris. In 1885 he moved to the Kent coast and, in subsequent years, traveled to Algeria, Morocco, Asia Minor, Russia, Spain, Romania, South Africa, Malaya, and Japan. Influenced by Jules Bastien-Lepage and by Millet, he was more highly esteemed in North America and continental Europe than in England. His works included oils and minerals, water colors, wood, print, furniture, stained glass and architectural and interior design. He executed the mural at the entrance to Manitoba's legislative Chamber, and influenced two of the province's foremost artists, Lionel LeMoine Fitzgerald and Walter J. Phillips. Illus., 31 notes. 1867-1956

948. Lamb, Robert John. "Sir Frank Brangwyn and the Spirit of the Age." City U. of New York 1985. 384 pp. *DAI 1985 46(5): 1114-A.* DA8515640 1890's-1956

Branişte, Valeriu

949. Branişte, Valeriu. AMINTIRI DIN ZILE NEGRE [Memories of black days]. *Magazin Istoric [Romania] 1980 14(7): 41-45.* Valeriu Branişte, Romanian publicist and politician, whose activities spanned the years 1893 to 1926, was twice imprisoned, in 1893 and 1918: his experiences are described in letters and articles assembled in *Oameni, Fapte, Întîmplări* by his daughter Valeria Căliman and Ş. Polverejan, from which extracts are here given. 1893-1926

Brant, Sebastian

950. Halporn, Barbara. SEBASTIAN BRANT'S EDITION OF CLASSICAL AUTHORS. *Publishing History [Great Britain] 1984 (16): 33-41.* Explores the life and work of Sebastian Brant (1457-1521), German humanist and poet, noting his contribution to the publication of classical works in early 16th-century Germany. In verse prefaces to his editions of Virgil and Terence, Brant displayed his knowledge of the original texts and provided his own aesthetic views. Brant's classical editions helped further the ideals of early German humanism. Based on a paper presented at the 19th International Congress of Medieval Studies, Kalamazoo, 1984. Secondary sources, 17 notes. 1480's-1521

Brat, Zvi

951. Brat, Zvi. MUL GIV'AT ALEQSEYEVQAH: SIPURO ŠEL ḤAYAL YEHUDI BA-DIVIZIYAH HA-LIṬA'IT [Across from Alexeyevka Hill: story of a Jewish soldier in the Lithuanian Division]. *Yalkut Moreshet Periodical [Israel] 1983 (36): 97-100.* Recounts the author's experience as a Jewish member of the Lithuanian Division of the Soviet Army, particularly the attempt to capture a strategic hill which had been the target of numerous failed attacks. English summary. 1942-43

Brătianu, Gheorghe I.

952. Teodor, Pompiliu. GHEORGHE I. BRĂTIANU—ISTORICUL I. DIMENSIUNILE OPEREI [Gheorghe I. Brătianu: historian. Part 1: the scope of his work]. *Anuarul Institutului de Istorie şi Arheologie "A. D. Xenopol" [Romania] 1983 20: 233-247.* Brătianu's published work spanned the years from 1922 to 1944, and he was in some ways a successor to N. Iorga. He was a familiar figure between the wars at international conferences, a disciple of Pirenne and Bloch. Starting as a specialist in medieval Romanian history, he turned to wider issues, to a study of East and Southeast Europe, and almost his last work (1944) covered the Genoese in the Black Sea in the 13th century. 79 notes. Article to be continued. 1920-45

Braudel, Fernand

953. Hufton, Olwen. FERNAND BRAUDEL. *Past & Present [Great Britain] 1986 (112): 208-213.* The most influential historian of our time, Fernand Braudel, died on 11 November 1985 at the age of 83. He had a breadth of vision unique among 20th-century historians. His two classics *La Méditerranée et le Monde Méditerranéan à l'Époque de Philippe II* and *Civilisation Matérielle, Économie et Capitalisme* interpret history based on a consideration of physical and material constraints, rejecting the influence of the individual. History is unlikely to be the same again. 15c-20c

954. Johnson, Douglas. BRAUDEL, THE HISTORIAN AS DRAMATIST. *History Today [Great Britain] 1986 36(July): 51-54.* A tribute to Fernand Braudel (1902-85), the French historian noted for his contributions to the *Annales* school of historiography. Braudel was regarded as the "Victor Hugo of history." 1940's-85

955. Pitte, Jean-Robert. OBITUARY: FERNAND BRAUDEL, 1902-1985. *Journal of Historical Geography 1986 12(3): 307-308.* Reviews Fernand Braudel's scholarly achievements and the place of the discipline of geography in his historical writings. 1902-85

956. Tenenti, Alberto. FERNAND BRAUDEL ET L'HISTOIRE ECONOMIQUE ET SOCIALE [Fernand Braudel and economic and social history]. *Vierteljahrschrift für Sozial- und Wirtschaftsgeschichte [West Germany] 1986 73(3): 362-365.* A eulogy for Fernand Braudel (1902-85), historian of the French structuralists associated with the journal *Annales,* long-time president of VIe Section de l'Ecole Pratique des Hautes Etudes, and author of models of comprehensive social history. Influenced by his experiences in North Africa and Brazil, he advocated writing history in social science research "laboratories," encompassing all levels of human experience from basic material culture to long-term economic and demographic developments and short-term political events. 15c-18c

957. Wallerstein, Immanuel. FERNAND BRAUDEL, 1902-85. *Review (Fernand Braudel Center) 1986 9(3): 323-324.* Eulogizes the historical methodology of Fernand Braudel as one that took the narrow route between the "Scylla of ahistorical generalization and the Charybdis of rerunning the film of the events that are dust." 20c

958. —. FERNAND BRAUDEL (1902-1985) [Fernand Braudel, 1902-85]. *Annales: Economies, Sociétés, Civilisations [France] 1986 41(1): 3-6.* Discusses the significance of the work of French historian Fernand Braudel. Braudel was influenced early in his career by the project undertaken by *Annales* editors Marc Bloch and Lucien Febvre to expand the areas of historical research, especially in areas of social history. Underlying Braudel's books on Western history is the attempt to unify the social sciences by opening up history to the contributions of all social disciplines whose general aim is the understanding of humanity. From 1956 to 1969, Braudel was the director of *Annales.* Illus. 1930's-85

Braun, Eva (1912-1945)

959. Poncet, Henry. RACONTES 40 ANS APRES PAR LES DERNIERS TEMOINS, LE MARIAGE ET LE SUICIDE D'HITLER [Told 40 years later by the last witnesses, the marriage and suicide of Hitler]. *Historama [France] 1985 (14): 18-25.* Five survivors of the bunker where Adolf Hitler and Eva Braun hid out for the last 100 days of their lives are interviewed about the ambience of the bunker, the state of mind of the men and women who were living and working there, and Hitler's thoughts and actions as the Third Reich crumbled. Their comments describe Hitler's composed resignation to defeat and to death, the last-minute marriage to Eva Braun, their suicides on 30 April 1945, and the disposal of their bodies. 1945

Braun, Eva (1917-1945)

960. Hegedüs, Sándor. BRAUN ÉVA (1917-1945) [Eva Braun (1917-45)]. *Párttörténeti Közlemények [Hungary] 1980 26(4): 187-198.* Growing up in an intellectual middle-class family, fluent in German, French, and English, Eva Braun joined the Young Workers' Movement at a very early age. Her group was successful in disturbing and interrupting several Fascist meetings and distributing socialist literature. Arrested in 1940 and severely tortured, she did not divulge the names of others in her organization. At this stage her social orientation changed to communism. After regaining freedom she resumed her political activities with even greater devotion. In 1945 she was arrested in Budapest by a Fascist patrol. The Communist literature which was found on her person was considered sufficient evidence for immediate execution without a hearing or trial. She was killed by a firing squad two weeks before Budapest was liberated by the Russian army. 44 notes. 1917-49

Braun, Matyas Bernard

961. Werther, Betty. UN MAESTRO BOHEMIO DE LA ESCULTURA BARROCA [A Bohemian master of Baroque sculpture]. *Folia Humanística [Spain] 1985 23(265): 137-140.* The life and work of Bohemian artist Matyas Bernard Braun, whose sculptures are considered to be some of the best examples of the Bohemian Baroque. 18c

Braun, Otto

962. Titov, A. EIGHTY YEARS OF OTTO BRAUN'S BIRTH. *Far Eastern Affairs [USSR] 1980 (4): 141-147.* A biographical look at Otto Braun, a veteran of the German and international working-class movement, who fought fas-

cism, was a true friend of the Soviet Union, and took part in the Chinese people's struggle for national and social liberation. 1918-80

Braunthal, Julius

963. Shafir, Shlomo. JULIUS BRAUNTHAL AND HIS POSTWAR MEDIATION EFFORTS BETWEEN GERMAN AND ISRAELI SOCIALISTS. *Jewish Social Studies 1985 47(3-4): 267-280.* Julius Braunthal (1891-1972), an Austrian-born Jewish Socialist, played a pivotal mediating role between Israeli Socialists and the Socialist International in the wake of the Holocaust, and worked to further cooperation between German and Israeli Socialists once ties were reestablished in 1952. Braunthal never wavered in his support for Zionism albeit from a universalist perspective. Based on the Julius Braunthal papers and other primary sources; 44 notes. 1935-72

Bravo de Paredes, Alonso

964. Cisneros, Luis Jaime and Guibovich, Pedro. UNA BIBLIOTECA CUZQUEÑA DEL SIGLO XVII [A library in 17th-century Cuzco]. *Histórica [Peru] 1982 6(2): 141-171.* As a contribution to the study of the diffusion of books and ideas in colonial society, publishes the inventory of the library of Alonso Bravo de Paredes, doctor of philosophy and professor in the University of Cuzco in the 17th century. Also included is a brief notice on his life and works, a critical evaluation of the culture of the times, and a list of authors who appear in the library. 8 notes, biblio. 17c

Bray, Reginald Arthur

965. Brandon, P. F. A TWENTIETH-CENTURY SQUIRE IN HIS LANDSCAPE. *Southern Hist. [Great Britain] 1982 4: 191-220.* Describes the career of Reginald Arthur Bray (1869-1950) as squire of Shere, Surrey, as a progressive intellectual using his skills in estate management. 1869-1950

Brazza, Savorgnan de

966. Guerrand, Roger-Henri. LE REVE COLONIAL DE SAVORGNAN DE BRAZZA [Savorgnan de Brazza's colonial dream]. *Histoire [France] 1982 (50): 64-73.* Describes Brazza's exploration of the Congo, his dream of abolishing black slavery and establishing French civilization, and his failure to stop continuing European colonialism in Africa. 1852-1905

Brecht, Bertolt

967. Esslin, Martin. THE BITTER BREAD OF EXILE: BRECHT BETWEEN THE SOVIET UNION & THE USA. *Encounter [Great Britain] 1982 59(6): 9-24.* Discusses the plight of exiled German writers, especially Bertolt Brecht, in sinking new roots. 1930-54

968. Gilbert, Michael John Tyler. "Bertolt Brecht and Music: A Comprehensive Study." U. of Wisconsin, Madison 1985. 536 pp. *DAI 1985 46(4): 992-A.* DA8507244 1910's-56

Breguet, Abraham-Louis

969. Kurzweil, Allen. MAN OF MANY FACES: A WILY WIZARD AND HIS TIME MACHINES. *Smithsonian 1985 16(2): 92-96, 98, 100-101.* Reviews the life and times of French master watchmaker Abraham-Louis Breguet (1747-1823), whose late 18th- and early 19th-century timepieces Frenchmen valued for their precision, prestige, and artistry, and which still command a high price in museum and collectors' circles in the 1980's. 1785-1824

Brenner, Yosef Chaim

970. Gorni, Yosef. YOSEF HAIM BRENNER'S ATTITUDE TOWARD SOCIALISM AND THE WORKERS' MOVEMENT. *Studies in Zionism [Israel] 1982 (6): 185-210.* Attempts to enlarge the meager knowledge of Yosef Haim Brenner's life by examining his changing views toward socialism. Brenner showed an existential despair in most of his literary works. Although convinced of the ultimate futility of human labor, he nevertheless acknowledged that man must do something, and therefore favored the workers of Israel in their attempts to settle and develop Palestine. Although Brenner denied the existence of God, his writings nevertheless had a religious character to them, including a need for faith. His internal turmoil can be seen in his attitudes toward the various socialistic movements. He became involved in the Bund, then the Poalei Zion Party, and then reproached all socialists as hypocritical and misguided. A final act before his early death was to make possible the existence of the Histadrut Workers Organization. Based primarily on Brenner's writings, with points emphasized from his letters; 67 notes. 1898-1921

971. Gorny, Yosef. HOPE BORN OUT OF DESPAIR. *Jerusalem Q. [Israel] 1983 (26): 84-95.* In an era of collectivist labor ideology, Yosef Chaim Brenner became a strikingly individualistic writer in the Ukraine, in London and, from 1909, in Palestine, where he was murdered in 1921. 1899-1921

Brentano, Franz

972. Boboc, Alexandru. FORME TIMPURII ALE REALISMULUI: FRANZ BRENTANO (II) [Early forms of realism: Franz Brentano, part 2]. *Analele Universității București: Filosofie [Romania] 1982 31: 23-28.* Continued from a previous article. The work of German philosopher and Catholic priest Franz Brentano (1838-1917) is of interest today because he stood at the crossroads during the restructuring of modern thought in theoretical philosophy. 1860's-1910's

Brereton, William

973. Morrill, John. SIR WILLIAM BRERETON AND ENGLAND'S WARS OF RELIGION. *Journal of British Studies 1985 24(3): 311-332.* Examines the well-documented political career of Sir William Brereton (1604-61) of Cheshire, and uses it as a case study of political behavior during the Civil War. Brereton exemplifies the religiously-militant county gentry prepared to fight against Charles I in order to destroy Archbishop William Laud's "papist" reforms and purify the Anglican Church. These locally influential radical Puritans, well-represented in the Long Parliament, were neither regicides nor republicans. Only minimally interested in constitutional and political reform, they were disillusioned by failure to reach an acceptable religious settlement. Based on the Brereton Papers in the Cheshire Record Office and other British archives; 72 notes. 1640-46

Bresciani, Antonio

974. DiRicco, Alessandra. PADRE BRESCIANI: POPULISMO E REAZIONE [Padre Bresciani: populism and reaction]. *Studi Storici [Italy] 1981 22(4): 833-860.* Antonio Bresciani was a well-known Italian author who, from the 1840's to the 1860's, wrote anthropological studies as well as novels. In both types of writing he expressed both populist

and reactionary views. As a Jesuit Bresciani cooperated in the publication of the journal, *Civiltà Cattolica,* which reacted against Italian efforts for independence and unity. His populism was inconsistent: while he praised obedience and submissiveness among people, he also subscribed to the ideal of the noble savage who was young, energetic, and free. Primary sources; 106 notes. 1840-69

Bresciani-Turroni, Constantino

975. Talamona, Mario. COSTANTINO BRESCIANI-TURRONI: L'OPERA SCIENTIFICA E IL CONTRIBUTO ALLA RICOSTRUZIONE DELL'ECONOMIA ITALIANA [Constantino Bresciani-Turroni: scientific work and his participation in Italian reconstruction]. *Revue Internationale d'Histoire de la Banque [Switzerland] 1982 (24-25): 121-140.* As president of the Bank of Rome, executive director of the International Bank for Reconstruction and Development, and minister of foreign trade, Bresciani-Turroni was one of the most influential defenders of liberal policies in postwar Italy. His monetary policies—at odds with Keynesian policies—were based on his analysis of the hyperinflation in post-World War I Germany. Based on the writings of Bresciani-Turroni and secondary sources; 49 notes. 1920-60

Bretholz, Berthold

976. Brügel, Johann Wolfgang. BERTHOLD BRETHOLZ (1862-1936) [Berthold Bretholz (1862-1936)]. *Bohemia [West Germany] 1983 24(2): 369-379.* Berthold Bretholz was director of the Moravian Regional Archives, 1899-1926. His four-volume history of Bohemia and Moravia, published from 1921 to 1924, asserted the continuity of German settlement in Bohemia since Roman times, a controversial thesis that has been discarded. A Bretholz bibliography of 163 items, compiled by Rudolf Hemmerle, is appended. 1880's-1936

Brett, Arthur

977. Ferris, J. P. THE REAL ARTHUR BRETT. *Recusant History [Great Britain] 1986 18(1): 34-41.* Describes the career of Sir Arthur Brett (ca. 1595-1636), who was chosen by Charles I as an envoy (actually, a spy) to the Vatican and who died shortly before he was to leave for Rome. ca 1566-1636

Brett, Oswald L.

978. Brett, Oswald Longfield. MARINE ART: I COULDN'T TAKE MY EYES OFF COOK'S *ENDEAVOUR. Sea History 1984 (32): 36-39.* Provides an autobiographical account by the Australian marine artist of his early interest in the sea and art, inspired in part by John Allcot's painting, *Endeavor.* Describes Brett's subsequent voyages, education, and achievements from 1939 to the 1970's. 1930's-70's

Breuer, Marcel

979. Major, Maté. MARCEL BREUER AND HUNGARY. *New Hungarian Q. [Hungary] 1982 23(85): 179-183.* The Hungarian-born artist Marcel Breuer (1902-81) started his career in the Bauhaus, then worked in other parts of Europe before going to the United States, initially to Harvard and then to private practice in New York. His links with Hungary proved infrequent. Based partly on the author's contacts with Breuer; photo. 1920-81

Bréville, Jacques Onfroy de

980. Hodeir, Catherine. ET JOB MIT LA REPUBLIQUE EN BD [... And Job set the Republic in "images"]. *Histoire [France] 1985 (79): 78-80.* Jacques Onfroy de Bréville (1858-1931), who signed himself Job, was an illustrator of French history through images combined with text, who has left albums in which he interpreted and depicted France's historic past with a new vision of epic character. 1880-1930

Brezhnev, Leonid

981. Medvedev, Roy. BREZHNEV: A BUREAUCRAT'S PROFILE. *Dissent 1983 30(2): 224-233.* Leonid Brezhnev was personally vain, not extremely ambitious, limited in ability and energy, not vindictive, and a complete organization man. 1964-82

Brezoski, Velimir

982. Ivanovski, Vlado A. D-R VELIMIR BREZOSKI [Doctor Velimir Brezoski]. *Istorija [Yugoslavia] 1983 19(1): 367-369.* Doctor Velimir Brezoski (1924-83) worked at the Macedonian Historical Institute. He specialized in the history of the National Liberation War in Macedonia from 1941 to 1945, and in Yugoslavia's socialist revolution and development from 1945 to 1950. 1945-80

Briceño, Antonio Nicolás

983. Briceño Perozo, Mario. EN EL BICENTENARIO DEL NACIMIENTO DE ANTONIO NICOLAS BRICEÑO: EL EJEMPLO DEL DIABLO [On the second centenary of the birth of Antonio Nicolás Briceño: the example of El Diablo]. *Bol. de la Acad. Nac. de la Hist. [Venezuela] 1982 65(258): 293-300.* Antonio Nicolás Briceño (b. 1782) nicknamed *El Diablo* for his violent and arbitrary temper, was a physician and military man who took part in the early battles for Latin American independence. He was also a farmer, jurist, journalist, writer, and parliamentarian. Reviews some of the references of historians to his career and a recent series of lectures to commemorate his bicentennial. Secondary sources. 1802-13

984. Rojas, Armando. ANTONIO NICOLAS BRICEÑO [Antonio Nicolás Briceño]. *Bol. de la Acad. Nac. de la Hist. [Venezuela] 1982 65(258): 301-306.* Recalls Briceño's family background, his patriotism, his controversial career, and final martyrdom at the hands of the Spaniards in 1813. A speech was delivered on the occasion of the inauguration of Briceño's restored birthplace in Mendoza, Trujillo. 1802-13

Briceño, José de

985. Vegas Rolando, Nicolás. JOSE DE BRICEÑO, ABANDERADO EN CARABOBO [José de Briceño, enlisted at Carabobo]. *Boletín de la Academia Nacional de la Historia [Venezuela] 1985 68(270): 473-476.* José de Briceño (b. 1807), member of a noted Venezuelan family, was professor of anatomy and rector of the Central University of Venezuela, founder of the Academy of History and president of the Medical Society of Caracas. He was appointed president of the municipal council and governor of the Federal District. As a very young man he served in one of the battalions which fought in the historic battle of Carabobo in 1822. 4 notes. ca 1822-64

Briceño Iragorry, Mario

986. Gabaldón Márquez, Joaquín. MARIO BRICEÑO IRAGORRY [Mario Briceño Iragorry]. *Bol. de la Acad. Nac. de la Hist. [Venezuela] 1983 66(264): 947-961.* Personal and family reminiscences about the noted historian and educator and remarks on his early influences on his intellectual outlook on the 10th anniversary of Briceño's death. Speech delivered at the Central University of Venezuela. 1920's-73

Bridges, Robert

987. Hamilton, Lee Templin. "Robert Bridges: An Annotated Bibliography." Louisiana State U. and Agric. and Mechanical Coll. 1982. 308 pp. *DAI 1983 43(8): 2679-A.* DA8229501 1913-30

Bright, John

988. Quinault, Roland. JOHN BRIGHT AND JOSEPH CHAMBERLAIN. *Historical Journal [Great Britain] 1985 28(3): 623-646.* John Bright and Joseph Chamberlain (1836-1914) had much in common. They both grew up in a similar Liberal tradition and they both represented Birmingham in parliament. Chamberlain's views on parliamentary reform, education, and even in foreign and imperial policy owed much to Bright's example. Bright's Irish policy had a deep influence on Chamberlain's career. Bright was in many ways a father figure to Chamberlain. Nevertheless, Chamberlain developed his own line of policy. Based on the correspondence between Bright and Chamberlain; 173 notes. 1868-1914

Bright, Richard

989. Kark, R. M. and Moore, D. T. THE LIFE, WORK AND GEOLOGICAL COLLECTIONS OF RICHARD BRIGHT, M.D. (1789-1858); WITH A NOTE ON THE COLLECTIONS OF OTHER MEMBERS OF THE FAMILY. *Arch. of Natural Hist. [Great Britain] 1981 10(1): 119-151.* Investigates the geological career of Richard Bright and places it in the perspective of geology at that time. Bright was one of the six greatest physicians of all time and Bright's disease of the kidneys is named after him. His initial geological fieldwork was carried out around his native Bristol and he subsequently took part in a geological expedition to Iceland in 1810. In 1814-15 he traveled in Hungary, observing rock formations. Based on the published works of Richard Bright; 3 fig., 166 notes. 1789-1858

Britten, Benjamin

990. Breuer, János. ZOLTÁN KODÁLY AND BENJAMIN BRITTEN. *New Hungarian Q. [Hungary] 1982 23(88): 52-56.* Benjamin Britten's popularity in Hungary was established through the first performance of his *Peter Grimes* at the Budapest Opera House on 22 December 1947. Zoltán Kodály and Britten set to music the same Shakespearean verses from *The Merchant of Venice;* Kodály's chorus was written in 1959 and Britten's in 1961. Britten first met Kodály in the spring of 1964 and a friendly exchange of letters about mutual musical interests and information followed. Britten himself wrote the obituary for the BBC after Kodály's death on 7 March 1967. Based on published works and personal correspondence; 4 notes. 1947-67

Brockelmann, Carl

991. Sellheim, Rudolf, ed. AUTOBIOGRAPHISCHE AUFZEICHNUNGEN UND ERINNERUNGEN VON CARL BROCKELMANN [Autobiographic notes and memoirs of Carl Brockelmann]. *Oriens [Netherlands] 1981 27-28: 1-69.* The renowned orientalist Carl Brockelmann (1868-1956) completed this typescript in Halle, East Germany, in 1947 for his son without thought of publication. The text of the manuscript begins with a genealogy of the family, continues with a history of more recent Brockelmanns, then covers Brockelmann's youth, student years, and teaching career in Germany. Based on the manuscript in possession of Gertrud Brockelmann, Halle; 51 notes, biblio., portrait. 1868-1947

Brodski, Aleksandr I.

992. Volkov, V. A. and Trifonov, D. N. POLUCHENIE A. I. BRODSKIM PERVYKH LABORATORNYKH KOLICHESTV TIAZHELOI VODY (K 50-LETIIU NACHALA PROIZVODSTVA TIAZHELOI VODY V SSSR) [A. I. Brodski's first laboratory samples of heavy water: the 50th anniversary of the beginnings of production of heavy water in the USSR]. *Voprosy Istorii Estestvoznaniia i Tekhniki [USSR] 1984 (1): 75-78.* Describes the work of the Soviet chemist Aleksandr I. Brodski (1895-1969) leading to the production of heavy water on an industrial scale in the 1930's and after World War II. Prints a lecture by Brodski on the concentration of the deuterium isotope. Based on the Central Archives of the Academy of Sciences of the USSR; photo, 4 notes. 1930's-69

Broecke, Petrus Adrianus van de

993. Martels Dankern, Z. R. W. M. HET LEVEN EN WERK VAN PETRUS ADRIANUS VAN DE BROECKE (1619-1675), PUBLICUS PROFESSOR ELOQUENTIAE TE PISA [The life and work of Petrus Adrianus van de Broecke (1619-75), public professor of eloquence at Pisa]. *Bulletin de l'Institut Historique Belge de Rome [Belgium] 1983-84 53-54: 201-234.* Biography of a Flemish poet in the Latin language who, born in Dendermonde (Belgium), after studies in Belgium and Bologna, achieved a position of standing in Pisa, 1657-75, where his numerous neoclassical poems and his voluminous correspondence were published. Lists van de Broecke's poetical works and correspondents. 1640's-75

Broek, Antonius Johannes van den

994. Eliashevich, M. A. and Lisnevski, Ia. I. NEW MATERIALS ON THE LIFE AND SCIENTIFIC ACTIVITIES OF A. J. VAN DEN BROEK. *Janus [Netherlands] 1981 68(4): 241-279.* The Dutch scientist Antonius Johannes van den Broek (1870-1926) was a lawyer by formal education and a self-taught theoretical physicist. His greatest scientific achievements are his hypothesis and theoretical proof, both of 1913, that the electric charge of the atomic nucleus is identical to the ordinal number of the corresponding chemical element in the Mendeleev periodic system. Based on various notes and rough copies of published and unpublished papers recently discovered in Minsk in the main library of the Belorussian Academy of Sciences; 24 notes, 16 illus. 1870-1926

Broeksma, Cornelis

995. Ploeger, Jan. DIE OPTREDE VAN CORNELIS BROEKSMA (1863-1901) [The conduct of Cornelis Broeksma (1863-1901)]. *Africana Notes and News [South Africa] 1983 25(6): 211-217.* Cornelis Broeksma was a God-fearing and honorable man and former public prosecutor in Johan-

nesburg. After the British occupation of 1900 he was a leading member of the commission of Dutch churches providing aid for Boer women and children in the camps. Relations between the commission and the British authorities became extremely strained until the commission was forbidden to enter the camps at all. To publicize camp conditions as widely as possible, Broeksma set up a secret channel of communication with Dr. W. J. Leyds, ambassador extraordinary and minister plenipotentiary of the Transvaal Republic in Europe. This plot was discovered and Broeksma arrested. He was charged by a military court of various offenses, including breaking the oath of neutrality and high treason. Broeksma admitted guilt and was sentenced to death. 1880's-1901

Bromlei, Iu. V.

996. Okladnikov, Aleksei Pavlovich. AKADEMIK IULIAN VLADIMIROVICH BROMLEI (K 60-LETIIU SO DNIA ROZHDENIIA) [Academician Iulian Vladimirovich Bromlei: tribute on his 60th birthday]. *Istoriia SSSR [USSR] 1981 (1): 216-221.* Biography of this Soviet ethnographer and director of the Academy of Sciences' Institute of Ethnography, with a review of his major publications and theories on ethnic and ethno-social evolution. Cites over 40 of his studies, published mainly in the 1970's. 17 notes. 1950's-80

997. —. AKADEMIKU IU. V. BROMLEIU 60 LET [Academician Iu. V. Bromlei's 60th birthday]. *Novaia i Noveishaia Istoriia [USSR] 1981 (2): 202-204.* Biographical sketch of Soviet historian Iu. V. Bromlei. He has held many academic posts including Professor of History at Moscow State University and Director of the Institute of Ethnography of the Academy of Sciences. His main research interests are in the history of the Slavs in the Middle Ages, especially the 15th- and 16th-century Croatian peasant, and in ethnography. He has done much to popularize ethnography and has played an active role in forming the new discipline of contemporary ethnography. He has been a full member of the Academy of Sciences since 1976 and is also an honorary member of the Royal Anthropological Institute of Great Britain and Ireland. Photo, 9 notes. 1946-80

Bron, Michał

998. Bron, Michał. ZNÓW W MUNDURZE (ZE WSPOMNIEŃ DĄBROWSZCZAKA) [In uniform again: from the memoirs of a soldier of the Dąbrowski Brigade]. *Z Pola Walki [Poland] 1981 23[i.e., 24](2): 157-180.* Recalls the formation of the Dąbrowski Brigade, a unit of Polish soldiers in the USSR, 1943-45, dealings with the Soviet authorities, and conversations with General Karol Świerczewski. After his return to the newly independent Poland in 1945, the author worked for the security forces, of which he gives an account, until his promotion to the post of military attaché in the Polish Embassy in Yugoslavia. 1940's

Brons, Anna

999. Sprunger, Mary. ANNA BRONS AND LUDWIG KELLER. *Mennonite Life 1985 40(2): 10-16.* Anna Brons, a 19th-century Mennonite from East Friesland, in modern Germany, was the author of the first major history of the Mennonites tracing their roots to the Swiss Reformation. She produced her work as a labor of love, and with strong intentions of fostering unity among the Mennonites. She provided much moral, and some financial support to Ludwig Keller (1849-1915), a professional historian of the Anabaptists. Both were strongly interested in recovering the vitality of 16th-century religion, especially through reprints of literature related to the old "evangelical brotherhoods." Brons was also very much of a German nationalist, even violating Mennonite pacifist principles to this end. Based on Brons-Keller correspondence in the Mennonite Library and Archives, North Newton, Kansas, and their published works. ca 1880-1900

Brontë, Anne

1000. Costello. Priscilla H. "The Parson's Daughters: The Family Worlds of Charlotte, Emily, and Anne Bronte." Union for Experimenting Colleges and U. 1983. 397 pp. *DAI 1983 44(4): 1091-A.* DA8315757 1816-49

Brontë, Charlotte

1001. Fernández-Nistal, P. "The Influence of John Bunyan's *The Pilgrim's Progress* on the Life and Works of Charlotte Brontë" (Spanish text). U. of Valladolid [Spain] 1984. 444 pp. *DAI-C 1986 47(2): 285; 47/1375c. U. of Valladolid, publ.* 17c

Broomé, Bertil

1002. Brandell, Ulf. BERTIL BROOMÉ IN MEMORIAM [Bertil Broomé: in memoriam]. *Personhistorisk Tidskrift [Sweden] 1981 77(2-3): 41-45.* Commemorates professor Bertil Broomé (1913-80), former secretary and president of the Swedish Personhistoriska Samfundet, a society for historical biographical research. Broomé's childhood and academic career are reviewed as well as his performance as head of the military record office, a position he held for 20 years, and his contributions to organizations. His quite extensive research, the most important of which is a study entitled, "The collectors of Hand Scripts and the Swedish archives 1700-1950," is also discussed. 1913-80

Brough, John

1003. Wright, J. C. PROFESSOR JOHN BROUGH. *Journal of the Royal Asiatic Society of Great Britain and Ireland [Great Britain] 1984 (2): 259-263.* Obituary of John Brough (1917-83), British Sanskrit scholar and translator of classical poetry. His major works include *Selections from Classical Sanscrit Literature* (1951) and *Poems from Sanscrit* (1968). 1917-83

Brougham, Henry

1004. Ford, Trowbridge H. BROUGHAM AS A BARRISTER: COURTROOM DILEMMAS OF A NOTORIOUS RADICAL. *Journal of Legal History [Great Britain] 1984 5(3): 108-129.* Henry Brougham (1778-1868) could hardly be considered a typical member of the English bar during the Georgian Era. During his early career he was shunned by solicitors who feared his radicalism. A successful defense of John and Leigh Hunt against a charge of seditious libel in 1811 greatly enhanced his reputation, and Brougham went on to defend a group of British turncoats, "Manchester's 38," Queen Caroline, and other objects of Whig sympathy. Following this unconventional route, Brougham achieved both wealth and standing at the bar. Paper presented to the Sixth British Legal History Conference, Norwich, 12-15 July 1983. Based largely on primary sources; 88 notes. 1796-1823

1005. Ford, Trowbridge H. LORD BROUGHAM AMONG HIS CRITICS. *Tijdschrift voor Rechtsgeschiedenis [Netherlands] 1981 49(3-4): 389-410.* Assesses the importance of Henry Brougham (1778-1868) in the framework of institutions for the political, judicial, and social developments resulting in Victorian politics and legal change. Criticized for inconsistency by radicals, Whigs, and Tories, yet recognized during his life for his powerful influence, inside and outside of Parliament, on the abolition of slavery and on parliamentary, educational, and criminal law reform, Lord Brougham precipitously lost this reputation among historians after his death. Based on works by and about Brougham and parliamentary debates; 95 notes. 1804-50's

Broughton, Arthur

1006. Crane, M. D. ARTHUR BROUGHTON, A LATE EIGHTEENTH CENTURY BOTANIST IN BRISTOL AND JAMAICA. *Arch. of Natural Hist. [Great Britain] 1981 10(2): 317-330.* Arthur Broughton (ca. 1758-96) was born in Bristol, England, and studied at Edinburgh, returning to Bristol to be a physician. Ill health led him to settle in Jamaica in 1784, where he remained until his death. He published many works on the flora of the Bristol region and Jamaica. His most important works on Jamaica are *Hortus Eastensis* (1792) and *Herbarium Jamaicense.* Much of his botanical output was bequested to the Bristol Library Society in 1796. Based on a biographical essay on Broughton in Richard Smith's ms. *Bristol Infirmary Biographical Memoirs* in Bristol Archives Office; 51 notes, biblio. 1780's-96

Browett, Elizabeth

1007. Abel, Trudi. THE DIARY OF A POOR QUAKER SEAMSTRESS: NEEDLES AND PENURY IN NINETEENTH CENTURY LONDON. *Quaker History 1986 75(2): 102-114.* Elizabeth Browett (1788-1849), orphaned in 1833, settled that year in Ratcliff, near the Thames wharves in London's East End. When she could get needlework—perhaps half the year—she finished waistcoats, providing her own candles, thread, and trimmings. Earning only one or two shillings a week, and spending perhaps a shilling on rent, she survived through continuous relief from her Friends' meeting and individuals. She suffered from rheumatism, neuralgia, and failing sight. Her consolations were going to meeting, visiting Friends, borrowing and reading Quaker books, and writing letters. But it was a lonely life. Based on Browett's diary for 1833-34 and secondary sources; 51 notes. 1833-34

Brown, Ford Madox

1008. Secor, Robert. GREAT EXPECTATIONS: FORD MADOX BROWN'S LETTERS TO ALFRED HUNT. *Notes and Queries [Great Britain] 1982 29(4): 313-316.* Reproduces five unpublished letters, 1869-83, recounting Ford Madox Brown's withdrawal from candidacy for the Old Water-colour Society and his effort to gain the Slade Professorship at Cambridge. 1869-83

Brown, Samuel

1009. Day, Thomas. SAMUEL BROWN IN NORTHEAST SCOTLAND. *Industrial Archaeology Review [Great Britain] 1985 7(2): 154-170.* Outlines the career of the British engineer Samuel Brown (b. 1774) with special reference to four bridges he built in northeast Scotland from 1828 to 1832. ca 1820's-40's

Browne, Edward G.

1010. Chelkowski, Peter. EDWARD G. BROWNE'S TURKISH CONNEXION. *Bulletin of the School of Oriental and African Studies [Great Britain] 1986 49(1): 25-34.* Turkey, and especially Istanbul, played an important role in the work of the British orientalist Edward G. Browne, who did so much to promulgate understanding of Persian history and culture. His contacts with Turkey, which lasted from 1877 until his death in 1926, gave Browne access to the large Persian colony in Istanbul, many of them exiled politicians and social and cultural reformers, as well as to manuscript collections, scholarly and literary friends, and sources of diverse materials and information. Correspondence in private collections and secondary works; 25 notes. 1877-1926

Brožek, Josef

1011. Brožek, Josef. MULTIPHASIC PROFILE: A SELECTIVE AUTOBIOGRAPHY (1). *Revista de Historia de la Psicología [Spain] 1984 5(1-2): 13-40.* Josef Brožek (b. 1913) of Lehigh University, Bethlehem, Pennsylvania, introduces a *Festschrift* in his honor with reflections on his life in Warsaw, Siberia, Czechoslovakia, and the United States, and on the influence of language and culture on his work in the psychology of nutrition, behavior, aging, and fatigue, and in the history of psychology. 1913-83

1012. Hoskovec, Jiří. JOSEF BROŽEK AND PSYCHOLOGY IN CZECHOSLOVAKIA. *Revista de Historia de la Psicología [Spain] 1984 5(1-2): 173-182.* Josef Brožek (b. 1913) lived in Czechoslovakia from 1920 to 1939 and contributed to the development of psychology in that country and the publication of information about it abroad thereafter. 1955-82

Bruegel, J. W.

1013. Stern, J. Peter. DEFENDING THE STATE AGAINST THE NATIONS: THE WORK OF J. W. BRUEGEL. *Historical Journal [Great Britain] 1985 28(4): 1023-1027.* Discusses the works of historian J. W. Bruegel on history of the Sudeten Germans. Biblio. 1918-85

1014. Winters, Stanley B. EIGHTY EVENTFUL YEARS: J. W. BRUEGEL LOOKS BACK AND AHEAD. *East Central Europe 1985 12(1): 51-58.* J. W. Bruegel was born in Moravia in 1905. Educated as a lawyer, he became assistant to a leading Czech cabinet minister in the 1930's. After the Nazi takeover in 1939, Bruegel fled to France and then to England, where he fought during the war for an enlightened attitude on the part of both Czechoslovaks and the British toward Germans with democratic ideals, but with little success. He returned briefly to Czechoslovakia after the war, but chauvinistic attitudes toward Germans led him to return to England. There he made his living as a journalist and broadcaster. Bruegel has published important books on Central European history, especially on the Germans in the Czechoslovak state. Based on an interview with Bruegel. 1920-85

Bruegel, Pieter

1015. Onclincx, Georges. NOTE SUR UNE BIOGRAPHIE MANUSCRITE (XVIIIe S.) DE PIERRE BRUEGEL L'ANCIEN MENTIONNANT SON DECES ET SON INHUMATION [Note on a manuscript biography of Pieter Bruegel the Elder, mentioning his death and burial]. *Revue Belge de Philologie et d'Histoire [Belgium] 1985 63(4): 726-730.* Analyzes an eight-page manuscript biography of Bruegel found at the Belgian Ministry of Foreign Affairs' heraldic collection, dating it to 1770-80 and attributing possible authorship to J. A. J. Jaerens or C. J. Beydaels. 17 notes. ca 1530-69

Brukenthal, Samuel von

1016. Cernea, Elena. DIE SAMMLUNG EINES AUFGEKLÄRTEN GEISTES: DIE BRUKENTHAL-SAMMLUNG [The collections of an enlightened intellect: the Brukenthal collection]. *Rev. des Etudes Sud-Est Européennes [Romania] 1981 19(4): 763-770.* Gives a short biography of Samuel von Brukenthal, a Transylvanian politician and man of culture, and introduces and describes his collections of minerals, coins, paintings, and a library that became a focal point for people interested in science and contained bibliophilic rarities. The collection drew a certain interest from the rest of Europe, induced an exchange of European spiritual culture, and aided in creating cultural reform in Transylvania. Based on the Brukenthal family archives and government archives. 1750-1800

Brunet, Marguerite

1017. Rainey, Brian E. LA MONTANSIER (ABSTRACT). *Proceedings of the Annual Meeting of the Western Society for French History 1984 11: 130.* Marguerite Brunet (1730-1820), known better as La Montansier, had a career which spanned several regimes. Arriving in Paris from the provinces, she established herself first as a courtesan and used her influence to acquire the rights to several theaters, among them that of Versailles, thus becoming France's first woman theater director. Her shrewdness enabled her to survive the revolution, during which she created two theaters in Paris and interacted with the principal revolutionary figures. Her theatrical involvement continued through the empire and the restoration. A study of her is interesting in itself and also illuminates aspects of the entire period. Abstract only. 1740's-1820

Brunetti, Girolamo

1018. Venturi, Graziella Grandi. IL CARTEGGIO DI GIROLAMO BRUNETTI TRA I "FONDI SPECIALI" DELL'ARCHIGINNASIO [The correspondence of Girolamo Brunetti in the Special Collections of the Archiginnasio]. *Archiginnasio [Italy] 1980 75: 363-384.* Inventory of the correspondence of Girolamo Brunetti (1732-1817), civil servant and author from Modena, in the Special Collections of the Archiginnasio, Bologna. 10 notes. 1750's-1817

Brüning, Heinrich

1019. Holtfrerich, Carl-Ludwig. ALTERNATIVEN ZU BRÜNINGS WIRTSCHAFTSPOLITIK IN DER WELTWIRTSCHAFTSKRISE [Alternatives to Brüning's economic policy in the world economic crisis]. *Hist. Zeits. [West Germany] 1982 235(3): 605-631.* Reviews historical literature on Heinrich Brüning's economic policies during the early stages of the world economic crisis, 1929-39. Repudiates Knut Borchard's thesis that the Weimar economy was hopelessly flawed and the political system too weak to reform it. Brüning did have options that were recommended to him and that would have reduced unemployment and perhaps forestalled the rise of Hitler to power. Brüning persisted with his deflationist policy in order to consolidate public finance, to dismantle social welfare payments, and to get permanent relief from reparations demands. Based on Brüning's writings and published documents; 68 citations and notes. 1930-32

1020. Jaitner, Klaus. DEUTSCHLAND, BRÜNING UND DIE FORMULIERUNG DER BRITISCHEN AUSSENPOLITIK MAI 1930 BIS JUNI 1932 [Germany, Brüning, and the formulation of British foreign policy, May 1930 to June 1932]. *Vierteljahrshefte für Zeitgeschichte [West Germany] 1980 28(4): 440-486.* Initially impressed with Chancellor Heinrich Brüning's (1930-32) leadership and competence in economic affairs, the British government was increasingly annoyed by the aggressive German pursuit of an Austro-German customs union and Brüning's unwillingness to compromise on disarmament and end of reparations. While British banking and industry circles supported Brüning's call for an immediate end of reparations, the Foreign Office worked toward a political-economic solution with significant German political concessions in exchange for ending reparations. Based on Foreign Office, Cabinet, and Prime Ministerial records of the Public Record Office; 192 notes. 1930-32

Brunner, Otto

1021. Blickle, Peter. NEKROLOG: OTTO BRUNNER (1898-1982) [Obituary: Otto Brunner (1898-1982)]. *Hist. Zeits. [West Germany] 1983 236(3): 779-781.* Reviews the career of Otto Brunner as professor of medieval history at the universities of Vienna and Hamburg. His reexamination of the concepts of state and leadership reoriented the discussion of medieval political institutions. 1898-1982

1022. Wandruszka, Adam. OTTO BRUNNER (1898-1982) [Obituary of Otto Brunner (1898-1982)]. *Südostdeutsches Arch. [West Germany] 1981-82 24-25: 193-195.* Appreciation of the life and work of Otto Brunner, medievalist and specialist in the historical development of the Austrian territories. For many years active as professor at the Institute for Austrian Historical Research in Vienna, he accepted a chair in the University of Hamburg, whose development he also actively fostered as rector. 1898-1982

1023. Winter, Otto Friedrich. IN MEMORIAM OTTO BRUNNER *[In memoriam* Otto Brunner]. *Mitteilungen des Österreichischen Staatsarchivs [Austria] 1983 36: 557-563.* Otto Brunner (1898-1982) was an Austrian late-medieval history scholar. He began his career as an archivist in the Vienna House, Court, and State Archive researching Austrian nobility. In 1931 he became a history professor at the University of Vienna and held positions in the Austrian Institute for Historical Research. In 1942 he was inducted into the German Air Force and became a lecturer at the Air Force Flight School in Tulln-Langenlebarn, Lower Austria. After World War II he became a professor of modern history at the University of Hamburg where he retired in 1966. Biblio. 1898-1982

Brunner, Sebastian

1024. Novogoratz, H. "Sebastian Brunner und der Frühe Antisemitismus" [Sebastian Brunner and the early days of anti-Semitism]. U. of Vienna [Austria] 1979. 328 pp. *DAI-C 1983 44(2): 302; 8/1320c.* 1840's-93

Brunswick family

1025. Puzyrev, V. P. "KHOLMOGORSKAIA SEKRETNAIA KOMISSIIA" [The Kholmogory Secret Commission]. *Voprosy Istorii [USSR] 1984 (9): 180-184.* Describes the life of the deposed Brunswick family, sent in 1741 to the remote settlement of Kholmogory on orders of Russia's Empress Elizabeth Petrovna. They remained there until the death of most members of the family, with the likeliest claimant to the throne assassinated during Elizabeth's rule. By 1780, Catherine II allowed the few remaining survivors, including the illegitimate children of the count, to leave for Denmark. The guards and servants of Kholmogory were not permitted to leave the estate until the death in Denmark of the last Brunswick in 1807. Based on sources from the State Archive of the Arkhangelsk oblast; 28 notes. 1741-1807

Brunszvik, Teréz

1026. Gárdonyi, Klára (Mrs. Csapodi). BRUNSVIK TERÉZ: PESTALOZZI KÖVETŐJE [Teréz Brunszvik: a follower of Pestalozzi]. *Helikon Világirodalmi Figyelő [Hungary] 1984 30(2-4): 270-273.* Brunszvik (1775-1861), the first representative of women's emancipation in Hungary, accomplished her goals not by loud slogans or demands for equal rights but by working quietly, diligently, and enthusiastically. A student of Johann Heinrich Pestalozzi, she introduced kindergartens to Hungary. The first "Angyalkert" [angel garden] was opened in 1828, and 114 more followed during the next 30 years. She was invited to Austria and Germany to help in similar undertakings. Brunszvik was a close friend of Ludwig van Beethoven, and some of his biographers think that his letters to his "immortal love" were addressed to her, an unlikely assumption. 1800-61

Brutti, Bartolomeo

1027. Apostolescu, Virgil. UN AVENTURIER APUSEAN LA CURTEA LUI PETRU ŞCHIOPUL: BARTOLOMEO BRUTTI [An adventurer at the court of Peter the Lame: Bartolomeo Brutti]. *Anuarul Institutului de Istorie şi Arheologie "A. D. Xenopol" [Romania] 1981 18: 567-574.* Bartolomeo Brutti (d. 1592) was an Italian of Albanian origin, a Machiavellian type who is first mentioned about 1571 as a papal agent in Constantinople concerned with an exchange of prisoners. Subsequently he served Spain, and was then employed by Peter the Lame, voivode of Moldavia, in various capacities, military and later diplomatic. An ardent Catholic seeking to further Catholic interests in Moldavia, he was arrested and strangled by Peter's successor Aron in 1592. Primary sources; 105 notes. 1570-92

Bry, Theodore de

1028. Wallis, Helen. EMIGRE MAP-MAKERS OF THE LATE 16TH CENTURY AND THE PROTESTANT NEW WORLD. *Proceedings of the Huguenot Society of London [Great Britain] 1985 24(3): 210-220.* The expeditions of Francis Drake and Walter Raleigh to the New World in the 1580's were charted by Protestant emigres from France and Flanders, among them Theodore de Bry, who produced graphic documentation of Raleigh's discovery of Virginia, and M. Emmerie Mollineux, who sculpted silver globes depicting Drake's voyage around the world. 1580's-90's

Bryslawski, Józef

1029. García Font, J. PEQUEÑA HISTORIA DE GRANDES ENANOS [A small story of big dwarfs]. *Historia y Vida [Spain] 1984 17(199): 68-79.* 1c-19c
For abstract see ***Cornelius of Lithuania***

Bryusov, Valeri

1030. Grossman, Joan Delaney. RUSSIAN SYMBOLISM AND THE YEAR 1905: THE CASE OF VALERY BRYUSOV. *Slavonic and East European Rev. [Great Britain] 1983 61(3): 341-362.* The outstanding symbolist poet Valeri Briusov (1873-1924) espoused the Russian Revolution of 1905 and cooperated with the Bolsheviks after 1917. An analysis of his work and private life reveals personal and artistic motives rather than purely political ones. Patriotic disillusionment after the Russo-Japanese War, a significant love affair, and a crisis of creativity with attendant depression, all contributed to his revolutionary leanings. 71 notes. 1904-06

Brzóska, Stanislaus

1031. Halicz, Emanuel. KSIĄDZ BRZÓSKA (HIERARCHIA KOŚCIELNA A POWSTANIE STYCZNIOWE) [Father Brzóska: the Church hierarchy and the January Insurrection]. *Zeszyty Hist. [France] 1980 (54): 40-58.* The bishop of Podlasie in southwestern Poland issued a pastoral letter on 21 August 1865, condemning the insurgent priest Stanislaus Brzóska (?-1865), whom the Russian military had earlier accused of insulting the government and army in sermons. For this he served six months in prison. As a partisan in the insurrection he managed to elude the Russian forces until April 1865. Meanwhile, the Russian authorities, interpreting canon law in such cases for their own benefit, pressured the bishop to condemn the priest, who was executed in May. The government later liquidated the diocese. Based on archival sources and secondary material; 2 notes. 1861-65

Buarque de Holanda, Sérgio

1032. Graham, Richard. AN INTERVIEW WITH SÉRGIO BUARQUE DE HOLANDA. *Hispanic Am. Hist. Rev. 1982 62(1): 3-17.* Brazilian historian Sérgio Buarque de Holanda responds to questions about his life, works, and philosophy. Born in São Paulo, Brazil, in 1902, he moved to Río de Janeiro in 1921, where he attended law school. He taught history from 1936 to 1939 at the Universidade do Distrito Federal in Río, then worked as a journalist, returning to São Paulo in 1946 as head of the Museu Paulista. He left that post in 1957 to take a chair of History of Brazilian Civilization at Universidade de São Paulo. He discusses his publications and his modernist philosophy of history. Biblio. 1902-81

1033. Leonel, Maria Célia de Moraes. SERGIO BUARQUE DE HOLANDA NA LITERATURA DOS ANOS 20 [Sérgio Buarque de Holanda in the literature of the 1920's]. *Rev. do Inst. de Estudos Brasileiros [Brazil] 1982 24: 63-74.* The noted historian Sérgio Buarque de Holanda (b. 1902) was in his youth one of the most significant critics and propagators of the modernist movement in literature. This is a study of his contributions to the philosophy and criticism of modernism in its early days, as seen in his articles published in *Estetica* and other literary periodicals of the 1920's. 17 notes. 1921-27

1034. Morse, Richard M. SERGIO BUARQUE DE HOLANDA (1902-82). *Hispanic Am. Hist. Rev. 1983 63(1): 147-150.* Brazilian Sérgio Buarque de Holanda (1902-82) is best known for his book *Raízes do Brasil* first published in 1936. He also wrote literary criticism and edited the first seven volumes of *História Geral da Civilização Brasileira,* writing the seventh volume himself. He held various professorial posts in Brazil and in other countries and was director of the Museu Paulista in São Paulo 1946-57. In 1980 the União Brasileira dos Escritores named him Intellectual of the Year. He died in São Paulo 24 April 1982. 1902-82

Buber, Martin

1035. Silberstein, Laurence J. MARTIN BUBER: THE SOCIAL PARADIGM IN MODERN JEWISH THOUGHT. *J. of the Am. Acad. of Religion 1981 49(2): 211-223.* Traces the intellectual and religious pilgrimage of Martin Buber pointing to the influence of experiences, personalities, and movements—particularly Zionism—on his life and writings. Buber is presented as more than a theologian. His unusually broad background made it possible for him to blend together issues of Jewish existence with those common to humankind. 27 notes, biblio. ca 1924-65

1036. Vermes, Pamela. THE BUBER-LUKÁCS CORRESPONDENCE (1911-1921) *Leo Baeck Inst. Year Book [Great Britain] 1982 27: 369-378.* 1911-21
*For abstract see **Lukács, Georg***

Bubnov, Andrei S.

1037. Amiantov, Iu. N. and Peregudova, Z. I. PROLETARSKII REVOLIUTSIONER, ISTORIK PARTII [A proletarian revolutionary and Party historian]. *Voprosy Istorii KPSS [USSR] 1984 (4): 119-123.* Andrei S. Bubnov joined the Bolshevik Party in 1903. He advanced the revolutionary cause, joining the Moscow Party in March 1917. On 24 October 1917 he was appointed commissar of the Petrograd railway system where he ensured revolutionary order. He held a number of state, Party, and military jobs. His memoirs detail the Bolshevik path from 1903, and emphasize Marxist-Leninist purity, military preparedness, and the unity between the Party and the people. Based on Party documents and A. S. Bubnov's memoirs; 25 notes. 1903-37

Bucer, Martin

1038. Hobbs, R. Gerald. HOW FIRM A FOUNDATION: MARTIN BUCER'S HISTORICAL EXEGESIS OF THE PSALMS. *Church History 1984 53(4): 477-491.* Reviews the life of Martin Bucer, one-time Dominican and later evangelical pastor of the Strasbourg church, focusing on the circumstances of publication and interpretive foundation of his 1529 commentary on the Psalms. Bucer published his widely circulated commentary under the pseudonym of Aretius Felinus to dissociate his controversial background from the work. Bucer's aims were to reach the true meaning of the Psalms, within their historical context, to address the concerns of more sophisticated Christian readers, and to place Christian doctrine on a firm foundation through a solid exegesis that would render the Psalms' meaning intelligible in Bucer's own age. Neither Bucer's interpretations nor his philosophical or theological goals or assumptions were without precedent; Bucer's primary aim was not innovation but to strengthen the tradition of past exegesis. 56 notes. 1526-64

Buchan, John

1039. Kruse, Juanita Fern. "John Buchan and the Idea of Empire." Miami U. 1982. 237 pp. *DAI 1983 43(7): 2418-A.* DA8227802 1890's-1945

Buchez, Philippe Joseph Benjamin

1040. Guccione, Eugenio. PHILIPPE BUCHEZ: UNA BIOGRAFIA INTELLETTUALE [Philippe Buchez: an intellectual biography]. *Storia e Pol. [Italy] 1983 22(2): 215-289.* Philippe Joseph Benjamin Buchez (1796-1865) was a part of French social Catholicism in the first part of 19th century. His ideas failed because he kept himself equidistant between a complete adherence to Church policy and an enlightened laicism. Therefore Buchez was rejected by both Catholic and secular culture. He wrote a great number of books, among which the best known was *Histoire Parlamentaire de la Révolution Française,* 40 vol. (1834-38). Based on Buchez Papers in the Bibliothéque Historique de la Ville de Paris; 160 notes. 19c

Buchwitz, Otto

1041. Zimmermann, Fritz. "VEREINT SIND WIR AUF JEDEN FALL STÄRKER!" OTTO BUCHWITZ ["United we are in any case stronger!" Otto Buchwitz]. *Beiträge zur Gesch. der Arbeiterbewegung [East Germany] 1979 21(2): 266-276.* Traces the life and political activities of the German socialist Otto Buchwitz (1879-1964). His early schooling was sporadic, and in 1893 he began work as a metal presser. Examines Buchwitz's trade union activities, travels throughout Germany in search of work in 1896, membership in the Social Democratic Party (SPD) in 1898, political development and political activities, 1901-12, work as a trade union delegate, meeting with August Bebel in 1912, activities during World War I, work as secretary of an SPD local in 1919, and election to the Reichstag, 1924-33. In 1933 he left Germany and went to live in Denmark, where he continued his political activities. He was imprisoned, 1941-45. Describes Buchwitz's activities in the East German Socialist Unity Party after 1950. Secondary sources; 23 notes. 1879-1964

Buck, Peter

1042. Sorrenson, M. P. K. POLYNESIAN CORPUSCLES AND PACIFIC ANTHROPOLOGY: THE HOME-MADE ANTHROPOLOGY OF SIR APIRANA NGATA AND SIR PETER BUCK. *J. of the Polynesian Soc. [New Zealand] 1982 91(1): 7-27.* Apirana Ngata and Peter Buck's position that their aboriginal ancestry permitted them to be better Polynesian anthropologists than the Europeans may have been justified by their work from the 1920's to 1950. 1920's-50

Buckle, Matthew

1043. Thomas, E. G. CAPTAIN BUCKLE AND THE CAPTURE OF THE *GLORIOSO. Mariner's Mirror [Great Britain] 1982 68(1): 49-56.* After a brief biographic sketch of Captain Matthew Buckle's life (b. 1718), describes the action in which the *Glorioso* was captured. Details events of the aftermath, including problems of repairs and staffing, and the sale of the prize. 27 notes, from family papers in the West Sussex Records Office and elsewhere. 1747-50

Bucsánszky, Alajos

1044. Kovács, I. Gábor. BUCSÁNSZKY ALAJOS ÚTJA A KALENDÁRIUM- ÉS PONYVA-TÖMEGTERMELÉSHEZ [Alajos Bucsánszky and the mass production of almanacs and popular literature]. *Magyar Könyvszemle [Hungary] 1985 101(1): 1-17.* Alajos Bucsánszky was born in Eger in 1802. In 1831 he was a bookbinder in Pozsony. In 1847 he moved to Pest and began publishing Hungarian, Latin, and German textbooks, readers, books on geography, and Hungarian history. His *Magyarok Története a Vezérek és a Királyok Képeivel* [Hungarian history with pictures of the leaders and kings], published in 1848, was 130 pages interspersed with 46 woodcuts, and its popularity required a second printing that year. He also published almanacs and popular literature cheaply priced, which by 1870 absorbed half the national market. Based primarily on materials in the Budapest Föváros Levéltár [Budapest City Archives]; 61 notes. French summary. 1831-73

Buczek, Karol

1045. Sikora, Franciszek. KAROL BUCZEK (26 X 1902 - 6 VII 1983) [Karol Buczek, 26 October 1902*-6 July 1983]. *Studia Historyczne [Poland] 1984 27(3): 552-554.* Presents accomplishments of Karol Buczek, a historian of the Institute of History of the Polish Academy of Sciences, especially in medieval history and historical geography. Pays attention to his political activities in the Polish peasant movement from 1934 to 1947. Note. 1920's-83

Buczek, Marian

1046. Figura, Janusz and Marcickiewicz, Jerzy. MARIAN BUCZEK (1896-1939) [Marian Buczek (1896-1939)]. *Z Pola Walki [Poland] 1980 23(4): 97-109.* Tribute to Marian Buczek, a dedicated fighter for a socialist Poland. He spent 1929-31 in USSR and was killed by Germans on 10 September 1939. He was awarded a posthumous medal after World War II. Based on Polish archives and secondary sources; 58 notes. 1896-1939

1047. Malinowski, Marian. PAMIĘCI MARIANA BUCZKA (1896-1939) [In memory of Marian Buczek (1896-1939)]. *Nowe Drogi [Poland] 1979 (11): 96-103.* A biographical sketch of Marian Buczek, Communist Party activist in Poland between the two world wars. 1896-1939

Budd, Richard

1048. Gray, Madeleine. MR. AUDITOR'S MAN: THE CAREER OF RICHARD BUDD, ESTATE AGENT AND EXCHEQUER OFFICIAL. *Welsh History Review [Great Britain] 1985 12(3): 307-323.* Richard Budd was a specialist in estate transactions in the 16th and early 17th centuries whose career illustrates that although such men made modest profits in addition to their official incomes, they were able to foster the rise of small and middling estates. As an exchequer official he was in a good position to take the initiative in dealing in crown land, especially in south Wales. Based on documents in the Public Record Office, London, and the National Library of Wales, Aberystwyth; 59 notes. 16c-17c

Budënny, Semën

1049. Azovtsev, N. PROSLAVLENNYI GEROI GRAZHDANSKOI I VELIKOI OTECHESTVENNOI VOINY (K 100-LETIIU SO DNIA ROZHDENIIA MARSHALA SOVETSKOGO SOIIUZA S. M. BUDENNOGO) [The famed hero of the Civil War and World War II: on the 100th anniversary of the birth of Marshal of the Soviet Union S. M. Budënny]. *Voenno-Istoricheskii Zhurnal [USSR] 1983 (4): 47-53.* Semën Budënny was one of the most outstanding Soviet military commanders. During the Civil War he commanded the 1st Cavalry Army against Denikin and Vrangel'. Later he occupied a number of important military posts, including that of 1st Deputy of the USSR People's Commissariat of Defense, 1940. He was in charge of the Reserve front in 1941 and in 1943 became commander of cavalry. After World War II he was Cavalry Inspector, 1953-54, and then joined the group of inspectors general of the USSR Ministry of Defense. 11 notes, 3 photos. 1917-73

1050. Bugai, Nikolai. S. M. BUDJONNY: LEGENDÄRER REITERHELD DER SOWJETMACHT [S. M. Budënny: Legendary cavalry hero of Soviet power]. *Militärgeschichte [East Germany] 1983 22(2): 163-175.* On the occasion of the 100th birthday of Semën Budënny (1883-1973), provides a comprehensive picture of the activity of this great army leader of the Red and Soviet Armies. Devotes special attention to the clever actions and great successes of the 1st Cavalry Army led by Budënny during the Civil War, which allowed him to become a model for the defenders of socialism. 4 photos, 31 notes. 1883-1973

1051. Khmil', I. V. VIDOMYI RADIANS'KYI VIIS'KOVYI I DERZHAVNYI DIIACH: DO 100-RICHCHIA Z DNIA NARODZHENNIA S. M. BUDIONNOHO [An outstanding Soviet military leader and statesman: 100th birthday anniversary of S. M. Budënny]. *Ukrains'kyi Istorychnyi Zhurnal [USSR] 1983 (4): 137-139.* Semën Budënny was called up for military service in 1903 and served as a private in a Don Cossack regiment in the Russo-Japanese War. In World War I he showed exceptional bravery and won several decorations. After joining the Bolshevik Party in Minsk in 1917, he returned to the Don region and organized a small pro-Bolshevik cavalry unit that rapidly grew into a division. In 1919 he was appointed commander of the First Cavalry Army, which contributed a great deal to the rout of Wrangel, Denikin, and the Poles. Secondary sources; 12 notes. 1903-52

Buga, Kazimieras

1052. Buga, Kazimieras. HOW I BECAME THE EDITOR OF THIS DICTIONARY. *Lituanus 1981 27(4): 11-22.* A translation of the preface to the *Academic Dictionary of Lithuanian,* by the first editor, Kazimieras Buga (1879-1924). Relates his life history, how he came to be a linguist, and how he proceeded to compile and edit the first portion of the dictionary. 1879-1924

Bugatto, Giuseppe

1053. Santeusanio, Italo. L'ARCHIVIO BUGATTO DELLA CURIA ARCIVESCOVILE DI GORIZIA [The Bugatto archives in the Gorizia archdiocese curia]. *Bollettino dell'Archivio per la Storia del Movimento Sociale Cattolico in Italia [Italy] 1985 20(2): 338-342.* The statesman Giuseppe Bugatto (1873-1948) was a member of the Austrian Parliament, 1907-18, but moved to Rome in 1939; the contents of his library and personal files were donated to the archdiocese of Gorizia and classified under 27 subject headings, including Diet of Gorizia, the Church, speeches in Vienna, economic programs, the problems of Friuli province, Italian Church activity in Vienna, correspondence, etc. 1907-41

Bugenhagen, Johannes

1054. Haendler, Gert. DIE AUSBREITUNG DER REFORMATION IN DEM OSTSEERAUM UND JOHANNES BUGENHAGEN [The expansion of the Reformation in the Baltic area and Johannes Bugenhagen]. *Kyrkohistorisk Årsskrift [Sweden] 1983: 30-41.* Describes the efforts of the German reformer Johannes Bugenhagen (1485-1558) to establish Lutheranism in the western Baltic area. Bugenhagen was a Pomeranian humanist teacher who brought many of his associates from Treptow into Lutheranism around 1521. He helped to organize churches in Hamburg (1528-29), Flensburg (1529), Lübeck (1530-32), the duchy of Pomerania (1534-35), the Danish kingdom (1537), and the duchy of Schleswig (1542). Based on Bugenhagen's printed treatises and letters and on German monographs; 80 notes. 1485-1558

Bugge, Sophus

1055. Wasberg, Gunnar Christie. SOPHUS BUGGE [Sophus Bugge]. *Nordisk Tidskrift [Sweden] 1985 61(1): 37-50.* Discusses influences of childhood environment in Larvik, Norway, on the later career of the Norwegian philologist, Sophus Bugge (1833-1907). 1833-1907

Buigues, Vicente

1056. Brotóns Picó, José. DON VICENTE BUIGUES, UN HOMBRE PARA LA MAR [Vicente Buigues, a man for the sea]. *Rev. General de Marina [Spain] 1983 204(June): 957-962.* Vicente Buigues was born in 1891 to a seafaring family near Cape Palos, Spain. His father owned a coastal schooner, and the son grew up at sea helping mariners in distress. In 1933 he joined the fishery protection service of the Spanish Navy. In 1943 he rescued sailors from a torpedoed German vessel. Buigues expressed his love for the sea in poems, some of which are included. 1933-83

Buisson, Ferdinand

1057. Chase, George. FERDINAND BUISSON: MORALISTE LAIQUE. *Pro. of the Ann. Meeting of the Western Soc. for French Hist. 1982 10: 321-331.* Ferdinand Buisson (1841-1932) was an educational reformer whose ideas had a significant impact in French primary schools during the Third Republic. A liberal Protestant, Buisson advocated a moderate position that stood between that of Catholics and that of positivists. Buisson attempted to bring about the moral regeneration of France after the country's humiliating defeat by Prussia in 1870. He stressed reason and freedom of conscience. Based on documents in the Archives Nationales and published primary sources; 37 notes. 1870's-1920's

Bukharin, Nikolai

1058. Pitassio, Armando. SU BUCHARIN E LE ORIGINI DELLO STALINISMO: ALCUNI RECENTI STUDI APPARSI IN ITALIA [On Bukharin and the origins of Stalinism: some recent studies appearing in Italy]. *Pensiero Pol. [Italy] 1981 14(2): 302-309.* As long as the Russian archives remain closed, it will be difficult to compile information on the relationship between Nikolai Bukharin and Joseph Stalin. Bukharin, condemned to death in 1938 as an opponent of the industrial and agricultural policies of the Stalinist regime, was a decided advocate of Lenin's ideas and opponent of European fascism, and advanced the doctrine of a noble, humanistic communism. 1900-40

Bukowski, Jerzy

1059. Suchodolski, Bogdan and Olszewski, Eugenjusz. JERZY BUKOWSKI (1902-1982) [Jerzy Bukowski (1902-82)]. *Kwartalnik Hist. Nauki i Techniki [Poland] 1983 28(2): 455-457.* Obituary for the Polish scientist Jerzy Bukowski, noting his contributions to aerodynamics and the history of technology. 1957-82

Bulgakov, Mikhail

1060. Haber, Edythe C. THE LAMP WITH THE GREEN SHADE: MIKHAIL BULGAKOV AND HIS FATHER. *Russian Review 1985 44(4): 333-350.* Contrasts the thought and ideas of Mikhail Bulgakov in his work *The Master and Margarita* with the writings of his father Afanasi I. Bulgakov. The elder Bulgakov, a professor at the Kiev Ecclesiastical Academy, was a noted scholar who wrote on Western churches and Russian sectarianism. He died in 1907 when his son Mikhail was only 16. The image of the lamp with the green shade in the younger Bulgakov's early literary works was a reminder of his father and an association with his calm scholarly labor. An examination of *The Master and Margarita,* however, reveals a more extensive influence from Bulgakov's father. Close parallels exist between the father's religious tenets and judgments and the son's less orthodox position on Christianity. 66 notes. 1880-1930

1061. Natov, Nadine, comp. A BIBLIOGRAPHY OF WORKS BY AND ABOUT MIKHAIL A BULGAKOV. *Canadian-American Slavic Studies 1981 15(2-3): 457-461.* Provides an annotated bibliography of 15 works by Mikhail A. Bulgakov and 52 critical works about him in the period 1976-81. 1920's-81

Bull, Edvard

1062. Bull, Edvard. EDVARD BULLS DAGBOK FRA APRIL 1940 [Edvard Bull's diary, April 1940]. *Tidsskrift for Arbeiderbevegelsens Historie [Norway] 1985 (1): 155-164.* Written at the request of Håkon Meyer, leader of the Thursday Group, Edvard Bull's diary covers the early days of the German occupation, 9-24 April 1940. 1940

Bulla, Béla

1063. Székely, András. ACADEMICIAN BÉLA BULLA (1906-1962): APPRAISAL OF HIS SCIENTIFIC ACTIVITY ON THE 75TH ANNIVERSARY OF HIS BIRTH. *Annales Universitatis Scientiarum Budapestinensis de Rolando Eötvös Nominatae: Sectio Geographica [Hungary] 1981-82 16-17: 3-13.* Traces the education, research, teachings and publications of Hungarian geographer Béla Bulla, whose efforts contributed to the knowledge of Quaternary landscapes, periglacial landforms, and glaciomorphological processes. 1928-62

Bullock, William

1064. Alexander, Edward P. WILLIAM BULLOCK: LITTLE-REMEMBERED MUSEOLOGIST AND SHOWMAN. *Curator 1985 28(2): 117-147.* Reviews the life and work of William Bullock (ca. 1773-1849), English museum proprietor, traveler, educator, showman, and entrepreneur who did much to develop the museum as an element of popular education. 1795-1849

Bülow, Frieda Freiin von

1065. Warmbold, Joachim. GERMANIA IN AFRIKA—FRIEDA FREIIN VON BÜLOW (1857-1909). "SCHÖPFERIN DES DEUTSCHEN KOLONIALROMANS" [Germania in Africa—Frieda Freiin von Bülow (1857-1909): author of German colonial novels]. *Jahrbuch des Instituts für Deutsche Geschichte [Israel] 1986 15: 309-336.* Frieda Freiin von Bülow's career as an author of German romantic novels was inspired by her personal experiences in Africa and her love for Carl Peters, a German colonial official. Her characters were based on real life counterparts. Her stories glorified German colonial policies in Africa and praised their defenders. Frieda von Bülow's interest in Africa ended with the termination of her relationship with Carl Peters. Based on periodicals and secondary sources; 148 notes. 1870's-1902

Bunin, Ivan

1066. Fedoulova, Rosa. LETTRES D'IVAN BUNIN A MARK ALDANOV [Letters of Ivan Bunin to Mark Aldanov]. *Cahiers du Monde Russe et Soviétique [France] 1981 22(4): 471-488.* Covers the years 1941-47 and includes only the letters that throw most light on the life of Bunin and the genesis of his last book, a compilation of short stories *Temnye Allei* [Dark Lanes]. They contain a number of interesting opinions of Bunin's on L. Tolstoi, I. Turgenev, N. Leskov, F. Dostoevsky, and V. Nabokov. Furthermore, these letters contain precious information on the periodical *Novyi Zhurnal,* published in New York, and also on the literary life of the Russian emigration in France. 1941-47

Bunyan, John

1067. Beal, Rebecca S. "PULLING THE FLESH FROM MY BONES": BUNYAN IN PRISON, MINISTRY IN SUFFERING. *Christian History 1986 5(3): 14-15, 34-35.* John Bunyan's years of suffering in Bedford jail deepened his understanding of the Christian life, and his comfort in faith and scripture led to his famous books such as *Grace Abounding* and *Pilgrim's Progress.* 1660-72

1068. Greaves, Richard L. A TINKER'S DISSENT, A PILGRIM'S CONSCIENCE. *Christian History 1986 5(3): 8-13.* John Bunyan played down the education he had derived from acquaintances and wide reading in order to reach a greater audience and emphasize the role of the Holy Spirit in his preaching and writing. 1663-88

Buonaiuti, Ernesto

1069. Buonaiuti, Ernesto. DUE LETTERE INEDITE [Two unpublished letters]. *Ponte [Italy] 1981 37(7-8): 647-650.* These letters were written by Ernesto Buonaiuti (1881-1946) during the last year and a half of his life to a Swiss theologian of Lausanne; they mention his situation at the university. 1945-46

1070. Donini, Ambrogio. CHE COSA È STATO BUONAIUTI [What Buonaiuti was]. *Ponte [Italy] 1981 37(7-8): 639-646.* The author, a student and close friend of Ernesto Buonaiuti (1881-1946), describes Buonaiuti's influence as priest and professor at the University of Rome and an important figure in the religious and intellectual life of the first quarter of this century but suspect both to the Church and to the Fascist State. 1920's-30's

1071. Gonnet, Giovanni. IL CASO BUONAIUTI O IL BRACCIO SECOLARE IN ITALIA [The Buonaiuti case or the secular arm in Italy]. *Ponte [Italy] 1981 37(7-8): 651-654.* Father Ernesto Buonaiuti (1881-1946) was professor of the History of Christianity at the University of Rome; censured by the Vatican for his ideas, he lost his license to teach but retained his chair. In 1932 he lost the chair and his income for refusing to swear allegiance to the Fascist government. Comments on the Buonaiuti case in the context of Church-State relations in Italy. 1920's-40's

Buonarroti, Philippe

1072. Defranceschi, J. L'EXPERIENCE CORSE DE PHILIPPE BUONARROTI: LES STRUCTURES AGRAIRES DE LA CORSE AU DEBUT DE LA REVOLUTION FRANÇAISE [The Corsican experience of Philippe Buonarroti: the agrarian structures of Corsica at the beginning of the French Revolution]. *Annales Historiques de la Révolution Française [France] 1985 57(2): 236-258.* During his years in revolutionary Corsica, 1789-93, Buonarroti was at first a journalist and then an official responsible for the sale of nationalized land. In Corsica, land was held communally and only the usufruct assigned to individuals. This system exercised a great influence on the communistic ideas of the future theoretician of the Babouvist Conspiracy of Equals. Based on documents in Corsican departmental archives; 59 notes. 1789-93

Buondelmonti family

1073. Bizzocchi, Roberto. LA DISSOLUZIONE DI UN CLAN FAMILIARE: I BUONDELMONTI DI FIRENZE NEI SECOLI XV E XVI [The dissolution of a family clan: the Buondelmontis in Florence, 15th-16th centuries]. *Arch. Storico Italiano [Italy] 1982 140(1): 3-45.* Landowners from Elsa, Pisa, and Greve, the Buondelmontis moved to nearby Florence in the 12th century. The family began its dissolution in the 15th century, owing to the multiplication of hereditary partitions. Based on materials in state, Church, and private archives in Florence; 168 notes. 15c-16c

Burchett, Wilfred

1074. Morris, Stephen J. A SCANDALOUS JOURNALISTIC CAREER. *Commentary 1981 72(5): 69-77.* Reviews the career and autobiography of Australian journalist Wilfred Burchett and claims that Burchett's political reportage in various countries has consistently corresponded with the ideology of the Australian Communist Party. 1940-81

Burckhardt, Jakob

1075. Gilbert, Felix. JACOB BURCKHARDT'S STUDENT YEARS: THE ROAD TO CULTURAL HISTORY. *Journal of the History of Ideas 1986 47(2): 249-274.* While still a university student in 1842, Jakob Burckhardt admitted in a letter that his writings in history and poetry were always more successful when he dealt with the context and background rather than with the personalities of an era. Like many German intellectuals of the period who studied at Berlin, the young Burckhardt was drawn to historical studies by the twin influences of Ranke and Hegel. But he was not a German, also studied in the Rhineland, and was not primarily interested in political history. While hardly a radical, his historiographical interests began to diverge in the 1840's toward different aspects of the past. The two seminar papers Burckhardt prepared under Ranke show that he imbibed the careful methods of his master, yet he fell under the sway of August Boeckh and Kugler's social history of art. This helped direct him to find his life's work—the creation of Renaissance cultural history. 102 notes. 1840's

1076. Meyer-Herzog, Kurt. WANDLUNGEN DES BURCKHARDT-BILDES [Changes in the image of Burckhardt]. *Schweizer Monatshefte [Switzerland] 1984 64(11): 905-912.* Analyzes the image of the 19th-century Swiss historian Jakob Burckhardt, which has fluctuated between that of a late representative of a past epoch, a creative prophet, and Burckhardt's self-image as protector of the cultural heritage of Europe. 19c

1077. Stadler, Peter. DER ALTE BURCKHARDT: ZUM ABSCHLUSS DER BIOGRAPHIE WERNER KAEGIS [The old Burckhardt: the completion of Werner Kaegi's biography]. *Hist. Zeits. [West Germany] 1983 237(3): 623-640.* With the completion of the seventh volume in 1982, Werner Kaegi completed his massive biography of Jakob Burckhardt (1818-97), a task that he began in 1947. This is the most comprehensive biography of a historian in the German language. Based on volumes six and seven of Kaegi's biography of Burckhardt; 20 notes. 1818-97

1078. Trevor-Roper, Hugh. JACOB BURCKHARDT. *Proceedings of the British Academy [Great Britain] 1984 70: 359-378.* The 19th-century historian of Renaissance Italy, Jakob Burckhardt, was born in Basel, Switzerland, and studied in Berlin. His hostility to the events of 1848 caused him to return to Switzerland, to become professor of history in his native Basel in 1858. His most famous works are his guidebook to Italian art, *Der Cicerone* (1854), and *Die Kultur der Renaissance in Italiem* (1860), in which he puts forward the view that Italian Renaissance culture was based on competitive individualism. The rise of Bismarck led in 1868 to a series of lectures under the title *Weltgeschichtliche Betrachtungen* in which Burckhardt reflected pessimistically on the potential conflict between religion, the state, and culture. Master-Mind Lecture, read 11 December 1984. 1840's

Burdeau, Auguste

1079. Sirinelli, Jean-Francois. LITTERATURE ET POLITIQUE: LE CAS BURDEAU-BOUTEILLER [Literature and politics: the case of Burdeau-Bouteiller]. *Revue Historique [France] 1984 272(1): 91-111.* Auguste Burdeau (1851-94), an ambitious lycee professor in Nancy and Paris, is believed to have provided the living example for a character, Paul Bouteiller, in Maurice Barres's trilogy, *Roman de l'Energie nationale.* Born into a poor family and educated on scholarship, Burdeau was an opportunist who served as minister in two cabinets and president of the Chamber of Deputies. Barres, writing in the 1920's when outstanding scholarship students of a later generation were becoming nationally prominent, used Burdeau, fictionalized as Bouteiller, to express concerns about students educated to move above their natural social station. Based on personal papers and archival collections; 102 notes. 1851-1920's

Burdžović-Tršo, Rifat

1080. Ćulafić, Dobroslav. O RIFATU BURDŽOVIĆU-TRŠU [Rifat Burdžović-Tršo]. *Istorijski Zapisi [Yugoslavia] 1983 36(3-4): 55-68.* Describes the life of the Montenegrin revolutionary Rifat Burdžović-Tršo. He joined the Yugoslav Communist Party when he was a law student in Belgrade, headed the Belgrade regional committee of the Communist Party in 1941, and was appointed head of the Sandžak regional committee of the Party in October 1941. He helped organize the antifascist struggle in Yugoslavia in 1941 and 1942, and was killed on 2 October by a group of Draža Mihajlović's Chetniks. French summary. 1941-42

Buren, Anna van

1081. Ridder-Symoens, Hilde de. VROUWEN ROND WILLEM VAN ORANJE [Women around William of Orange]. *Spiegel Historiael [Netherlands] 1984 19(4): 181-186.* 1533-84

*For abstract see **William the Silent***

Burgers, Thomas François

1082. Appelgryn, M. S. DIE SIEKTETOESTAND EN LAASTE DAE VAN PRESIDENT T. F. BURGERS [The state of health and the last days of President T. F. Burgers]. *Kleio [South Africa] 1980 12(1-2): 18-31.* Thomas François Burgers became president of the South African Republic of the Transvaal in 1872 at the age of 38. There is no doubt that his ill-health critically affected the history of the Transvaal. By the time he retired in 1877, he was worn down by overwork, ill-health, and poverty. Although he managed to reestablish his family's fortunes, he never regained his health and died in December 1881. Based largely on contemporary sources, particularly the S. P. Engelbrecht collection of Burgers's correspondence; 66 notes. 1872-81

Burgmann, Ernest Henry

1083. Hempenstall, Peter. THE BUSH LEGEND AND THE RED BISHOP: THE AUTOBIOGRAPHY OF E. H. BURGMANN. *Hist. Studies [Australia] 1981 19(77): 567-591.* A short biography of Ernest Henry Burgmann (b. 1885), who became Anglican Bishop of Goulbourn (later Canberra and Goulbourn) in 1934. After a small farm upbringing, he won a scholarship to St. John's College, University of Sydney, and, after several ministries, was Warden of St. John's Theological College, Armidale, 1918-25. He pioneered the use of psychology in pastoral work and encouraged the labor movement. In 1944 he published *The Education of an Australian,* which glorified the bush background. Nineteen pages of excerpts from this pamphlet are reproduced. Based on Burgmann's papers in the National Library and published articles; 22 notes. 1910's-40's

1084. Hempenstall, P. J. "THIS TURBULENT PRIEST": E. H. BURGMANN DURING THE GREAT DEPRESSION. *Australian J. of Pol. and Hist. [Australia] 1981 27(3): 330-343.* An analysis of the economic and social ideas of Ernest Henry Burgmann as warden of the Anglican Theological College, Morpeth, near Newcastle, New South Wales, from 1926 to 1934, when he became Bishop of Canberra and Goulburn. Burgmann had a reputation as the Red Bishop. He was outspoken on social issues, argued that capitalism was not worthy of Christianity, praised the Soviet Union, allied himself with the Unemployed Workers Movement and the "double the dole" campaign. He believed the working classes held the key to the future and would lead a revolution if capitalism was not reformed. However, he was non-Marxian, a pragmatic thinker, deeply influenced by unemployment in the Newcastle region. He advocated national economic democracy, a policy of rationalization, which meant reconciliation between classes and collaboration. Though his rhetoric was radical, his goals were conservative. He believed Anglicans should move beyond charity to helping the workers in the overthrow of capitalism. Based on Anglican Church archives and periodicals; 51 notes. 1920's-30's

Burke, E. N.

1085. Brodber, Erna and Burke, E. N., interviewer. A LIFE OF SERVICE: THE REV. E. N. BURKE. *Jamaica Journal [Jamaica] 1984 17(2): 10-17.* Prints an interview with educator, author, pioneer in social work and Anglican minister E. N. Burke with candid insight concerning a life filled with service to others. 1909-84

Burke, Edmund

1086. Conniff, James. EDMUND BURKE'S REFLECTIONS ON THE COMING REVOLUTION IN IRELAND. *Journal of the History of Ideas 1986 47(1): 37-61.* While Edmund Burke is typically considered a staunch antirevolutionary by scholars today, contemporaries (including Tom Paine) expressed surprise at the vehemence of his reaction against the French Revolution in 1790. This was in part because of his earlier, albeit ambiguous, support of reforms in England and Ireland. Burke defended his apparent about-face as necessary to protect the moderate, "mixed" sort of regime he supported. Burke's attitudes, especially toward Irish political, religious, and even land affairs, show that he was no unthinking champion of the status quo. Indeed, Burke's antirevolutionary rhetoric and ideas during the French Revolution may have been only a temporary, pragmatic position. 86 notes. 1770's-90's

1087. Ljungberg, Carl Johan. BURKE: MÅNGSIDIG OCH MISSFÖRSTÅDD [Burke: many-sided and misunderstood]. *Svensk Tidskrift [Sweden] 1985 72(3): 151-155.* A review of *Edmund Burke: A Bibliography of Secondary Sources to 1982* (1983) that discusses the development of Burke's views and their impact from his time until the present. 18c-20c

1088. Reitan, E. A. EDMUND BURKE AND ECONOMICAL REFORM, 1779-83. *Studies in Eighteenth-Century Culture 1985 14: 129-158.* Scholars have neglected the years during which Edmund Burke was the leader of "economical reform" and held political office, yet they were a watershed in his career and thought. The purpose of his 1779-80 reform plan, with reduction and reorganization of the civil list as its core, was pruning of the constitution, not radical change. With the plan's failure, Burke decided that substantial reform could be achieved only with support of "the *executive* power of the Kingdom," a conclusion that required overthrowing Lord North. With Rockingham in office Burke's reform proposals were more modest but George III's dismissal of the coalition ministry in 1783 ended his role in economic reform. His 1780 plan was intensely partisan, but by 1783 economic reform had developed a momentum and consensus of its own. As spokesman for conservatism in the 1790's Burke drew important lessons from his years as a reformer, but his later views were closer to those he held when he left office than to those he held before assuming office. Based on works of Burke and other prominent 18th-century figures, *Parliamentary History,* and secondary sources; 136 notes. 1779-83

Burliuk, David

1089. Valkenier, Elizabeth Kridl. IL'IA REPIN AND DAVID BURLIUK. *Canadian-American Slavic Studies 1986 20(1-2): 55-62.* Ostensibly complete opposites, the Russian artists Il'ia Repin and David Burliuk actually had much in common. Though the old Realist, Repin, and the young Futurist, Burliuk represented markedly different schools of Russian art, Repin challenged neoclassicism in his youth no less vigorously than Burliuk challenged the Realists. The two enemies actually became friends just prior to World War I. 10 notes. 1870-1913

Burmov, Aleksandur

1090. Khadzhinikolov, Veselin. ALEKSANDUR BURMOV—UCHENIIAT I ORGANIZATORUT [Aleksandur Burmov: scholar and organizer]. *Istoricheski Pregled [Bulgaria] 1981 37(2): 39-51.* Reviews the life and career of Aleksandur Burmov (1911-66). Burmov studied Slavic philology and history at the universities in Sofia and Vienna. He was professor of history at the University of Sofia and corresponding member of the Bulgarian Academy of Sciences. His early works were on the Bulgarian liberation struggle of the 1860's and 1870's, but he also wrote articles and monographs on various topics of medieval and modern Bulgarian history. He contributed to the establishment of the Bulgarian Historical Society, the organization of the study of history at the university, and most importantly the founding and editing of *Istoricheski Pregled.* Based chiefly on secondary works; 6 notes. ca 1940-66

Burmov, Todor

1091. Akinfiev, A. TODOR BURMOV—BOLGARSKII OBSHCHESTVENNYI I POLITICHESKII DEIATEL' I PUBLITSIST [Todor Burmov: Bulgarian social and political thinker and journalist]. *Sovetskoe Slavianovedenie [USSR] 1984 (5): 106-112.* Views the political activities and journalism of Todor Burmov (1834-1906). His early writings advocated separation of the Bulgarian Church from the Greek Orthodox Church. His mature political stance was a cautious brand of conservatism. He was active in the establishment of the independent Bulgarian state in 1879, holding the brief of the Ministry of the Interior and heading the Council of Ministers. Based on material from the Central State Archives of History of the Ukrainian Soviet Republic; 26 notes. 1834-1906

Burmystenko, Mykhailo O.

1092. Zhuchenko, I. Ia. M. O. BURMYSTENKO [Mykhailo O. Burmystenko]. *Ukrains'kyi Istorychnyi Zhurnal [USSR] 1982 (11): 152-154.* Mykhailo Oleksiiovych Burmystenko was born in 1902 in Saratov province. As a young man he distinguished himself in the defense of Soviet rule, and he joined the Communist Party in 1919. In the 1920's he was an operative in the Cheka. After completing a military service term and graduating from a school of journalism, he worked as a Party leader in Kalmykia. From 1938, he was Second Secretary of the Ukraine CP Central Committee. From the first days of the German invasion in 1941 he concentrated on selecting people for clandestine work in the enemy's rear and in laying foundations for partisan operations in the occupied territories. He was killed in a battle with Germans near Poltava on 22 September 1941. 1919-41

Burne-Jones, Edward

1093. Kestner, Joseph. EDWARD BURNE-JONES AND NINETEENTH-CENTURY FEAR OF WOMEN. *Biography 1984 7(2): 95-122.* The painter Edward Burne-Jones (1833-1888) reveals in his art a preoccupation with a key manifestation of nineteenth-century culture, misogyny. This fear of women derives from several experiences, particulary his affair with Maria Zambaco during the late 1860's and early 1870's. His early stories and his association with Rossetti indicate tendencies that later were manifest in a narcissistic hatred of women that is most obvious in his *Perseus* cycle and in his paintings of women as *femmes fatales* such as the mermaid and Nimuë. The sesquicentennial of his birth is an appropriate time to reconsider his life vis-à-vis this cultural manifestation. 1860's-80's

Burns, Robert

1094. Douglas, Hugh. ROBERT BURNS. *British Heritage [Great Britain] 1982-83 4(1): 64-71.* A brief biography of Burns (1759-96). 1779-96

Burstyn, Gunther

1095. DiNardo, R. L. and Bay, Austin. THE FIRST MODERN TANK: GUNTHER BURSTYN AND HIS MOTORGESCHÜTZ. *Military Affairs 1986 50(1): 12-15.* Study of the role and influence of Gunther Burstyn of the Austro-Hungarian Army before World War I in developing an armored combat vehicle—the Motorgeschütz. In spite of a superior design and insights in how to use it, Burstyn's work contained some impractical aspects and high cost. He was misplaced by being in the Imperial Austro-Hungarian Army, no place for an officer with foresight. Primary sources; 2 appendixes, fig., 18 notes. 1906-12

Busby, John

1096. Johnson, Gerald D. JOHN BUSBY AND THE STATIONERS' TRADE, 1590-1612. *Library [Great Britain] 1985 7(1): 1-15.* John Busby (1561-1613) had the reputation of a pirate, copy-snatcher, and surreptitious printer. Few literary historians have attempted to rescue Busby's notorious achievements. Busby was linked to the dubious publication of three Shakespeare plays. But upon examination of his earlier career, Busby appears to have been instrumental in the production of several major first editions. From 1590 to 1608 Busby aided in the publication of several new works of literary significance. 59 notes. 1590-1612

Busia, Kofi Abrefa

1097. Danso-Boafo, Alex Kwaku. "The Political Biography of Dr. Kofi Abrefa Busia." Howard U. 1981. 343 pp. *DAI 1983 43(9): 3082-A. 3099-A.* DA8301366 1966-81

Buson, Yosa

1098. Morris, Mark. BUSON AND SHIKI. *Harvard Journal of Asiatic Studies 1984 44(2): 381-425; 1985 45(1): 255-321.* Part 1. Detailed analysis of the poetry of Japanese poet and painter Yosa Buson (1716-83) and discussion of his life and his involvement in Japanese art movements of his time. Buson was the second greatest master of the haiku 17-syllable verse genre after Basho (1644-94), but in his time he was best known as a landscape painter, and it was from painting that he made his living. Japan was developing a mass audience for art that freed artists from dependence on wealthy patrons, but also created conflict between artistic ideals and commercialization. Buson, who modeled himself on the Chinese gentleman scholar but who was not wealthy, felt this conflict acutely. Part 2. Masaoka Shiki (1867-1902) led a virtual cult of poets honoring and imitating Buson. Discusses the influence of western art and poetry on Shiki and his Buson revival. 168 notes, 6 fig., chronology. 1730's-84

Bustamante, Gladys

1099. Gloudon, Barbara. HON. LADY GLADYS BUSTAMANTE, O.J. INTERVIEWED. *Jamaica Journal [Jamaica] 1984-85 17(4): 24-31.* The widow of the former prime minister of Jamaica, Sir Alexander Bustamante, talks about her early childhood and her life with Sir Alexander. 1880's-1980's

Bustānī, Butrus al-

1100. Jandora, John W. BUTRUS AL-BUSTĀNĪ, ARAB CONSCIOUSNESS, AND ARABIC REVIVAL. *Muslim World 1984 74(2): 71-84.* The career of Butrus al- Bustānī and his attitude toward the Ottoman Empire are examined in relation to his efforts to install a sense of Arab consciousness and common purpose in the Syrian public. His concept of the ideal Syrian society was based on the principles of Arab consciousness, love of fatherland, secularism, and religious equality guaranteed by the Ottoman regime. Al-Bustānī was also one of the first Syrians to propose that language was the main determinant of group identity, with the corollary being that Arabic-speaking Christians were part of the Arab nations and shared with Muslims a common cultural heritage. Based on Butrus al-Bustani's works and contemporary sources; 30 notes. 1870-90's

Butashevich-Petrashevski, Mikhail V.

1101. Kuk, Zenon M. PETRASHEVSKII AND HIS CIRCLE. *Michigan Academician 1985 17(2): 287-296.* Chronicles the life of Russian utopian socialist Mikhail Vasil'evich Butashevich-Petrashevski, who held regular meetings with a circle of liberal intellectuals in his home in St. Petersburg to discuss reforms of Russian society, from 1845 until his arrest by Czarist police in 1849. 1821-66

Butenschön, Johann Friedrich

1102. Müller, Friedrich. JOHANN FRIEDRICH BUTENSCHÖN. EIN DEMOKRATISCHER PUBLIZIST ZWISCHEN FRANZÖSISCHER REVOLUTION UND DEUTSCHER RESTAURATION [Johann Friedrich Butenschön: a democratic journalist between the French Revolution and German restoration]. *Jahrbuch des Instituts für Deutsche Geschichte [Israel] 1986 15: 193-230.* Butenschön (1764-1842) was born in Holstein (Denmark) but spent much of his life in Strasbourg, where he worked as a journalist for a radical German-language newspaper, *Argos.* In his first article in *Argos* Butenschön expressed his deep concern with human rights. He explained his conviction that no man ought to be exploited by another being. He later fought on the side of the Jacobins in the French Vendée, approved of the execution of Louis XVI, and supported the liberal goals of the French Republic. While opposed to the institution of the church, Butenschön did not support its dechristianization. Butenschön resigned from political life when Napoleon seized power. Based on documents in Munich state archives and Speyer's local library, newspapers, periodicals, and secondary sources; 150 notes. 1764-1842

Butini, Gabriel

1103. Candaux, Jean-Daniel. GABRIEL BUTINI GENEVOIS (G.B.G. POUR LES INTIMES) [Gabriel Butini Genevois, known as G.B.G. by his intimate friends]. *Musées de Genève [Switzerland] 1984 (242): 16-21.* The history of Swiss historian and chronicler of Geneva, Gabriel Butini (1626-83), including his genealogy and accomplishments, stressing the research work made to identify him. 1626-83

Butler, Elizabeth

1104. Cieszkowski, Krzysztof Z. THE PALLAS OF PALL MALL: THE LIFE AND PAINTINGS OF LADY BUTLER. *Hist. Today [Great Britain] 1982 32(Feb): 30-35.* Biography of British painter Elizabeth Southerden Thompson (1844-1933), later Lady Elizabeth Butler, who became an overnight sensation when her painting *Calling the Roll after an Engagement, Crimea* was exhibited at the Royal Academy in 1874, focusing on her paintings which were mostly done to commemorate famous battles, processions, and military campaigns. 1874-1933

Butler, Richard Austen

1105. Stafford, Paul. POLITICAL AUTOBIOGRAPHY AND THE ART OF THE PLAUSIBLE: R. A. BUTLER AT THE FOREIGN OFFICE, 1938-1939. *Historical Journal [Great Britain] 1985 28(4): 901-922.* Details the activities of British undersecretary for foreign affairs Richard Austen Butler in the two years leading up to World War II. In his memoirs *The Art of the Possible* (1971), Butler downplayed his support for Prime Minister Neville Chamberlain's policy of appeasement. Based on diaries, correspondence, and government archives; 69 notes. 1938-39

Butler, Samuel

1106. Pauly, Philip J. SAMUEL BUTLER AND HIS DARWINIAN CRITICS. *Victorian Studies 1982 25(2): 161-180.* Originally a Darwinist, Samuel Butler gradually became a critic of certain of Darwin's ideas. He felt Darwin had failed to give sufficient credit to his intellectual predecessors and asserted that Darwinism was not a unified movement. This led many evolutionists to assail Butler's ideas as unscientific. Primary sources; 34 notes. 1878-86

Butler, Stuart Thomas

1107. Watson-Munro, C. N. STUART THOMAS BUTLER 1926-1982. *Historical Records of Australian Science [Australia] 1983 5(4): 83-88.* Stuart Thomas Butler (1926-82) was an Australian theoretical physicist and most recently director of the Australian Atomic Energy Commission Research Establishment in Lucas Heights. He was best known for his work on direct nuclear reactions (for which he won the Tom Bonner Prize in Nuclear Physics awarded by the American Physical Society), on the energy loss of particles in a plasma, and on atmospheric tides induced by absorption of solar radiation in the ozone layer. Based on personal recollections and primary sources; photo, biblio. 1926-82

Butler, Uriah

1108. Jha, J. C. THE 1937 DISTURBANCE IN TRINIDAD AND TOBAGO. *Quarterly Review of Historical Studies [India] 1984 24(2): 1-9.* Uriah Butler, a Grenadian of African origin who migrated to Trinidad in 1921, preached revolution to Trinidad's workers. His efforts, as well as the poor standard of living and other grievances that workers were subjected to, led to the Butler Riots of 1937, which encouraged revolutionary labor movements throughout Trinidad and Tobago. Based on *The People, Forster Report,* and secondary sources; 47 notes. 1937

Bykhovski, Bernard E.

1109. —. BERNARD EMMANUILOVICH BYKHOVSKII [Bernard Emmanuilovich Bykhovski]. *Voprosy Filosofii [USSR] 1980 (12): 174.* An obituary of the prominent Soviet historian of philosophy and philosopher Bernard E. Bykhovski (1901-80) providing notes on his academic career. 1920's-80

Bylney, Thomas

1110. Davis, John F. THE TRIALS OF THOMAS BYLNEY AND THE ENGLISH REFORMATION. *Hist. J. [Great Britain] 1981 24(4): 775-790.* Examination of the four trials for heresy of the preacher Thomas Bylney reveal that Bylney was in the forefront of the English Reformation, although he never overtly repudiated the papacy or denied the real presence in the eucharist. Bylney was an Evangelist and that Evangelism was the first stage of the English Reformation. Bylney's ideas strongly influenced reformers such as Hugh Latimer and Robert Barnes. Religious changes were occurring in England before Henry VIII. 46 notes. 1525-34

Byron, George Gordon

1111. Clubbe, John. BYRON AS AUTOBIOGRAPHER. *South Atlantic Q. 1983 82(3): 314-320.* Comments on the three major sources of the possible autobiography of Lord George Gordon Byron (1788-1824): his letters, journal, and poem *Don Juan.* 1810-24

Bzowski, Abraham

1112. Pater, Józef. ŻYCIE I TWÓRCZOŚĆ ABRAHAMA BZOWSKIEGO O.P. (1567-1637) [Life and literary output of Abraham Bzowski (1567-1637)]. *Nasza Przeszłość [Poland] 1979 (51): 55-87.* Assesses the achievements of Abraham Bzowski, historian and theologian. 1567-1637

C

Caballeria, Micer Alfonso de la

1113. Beinart, Haim. HA-IM HIT'AREV ALFONSO DI LA QABALERIAH LE-MINIAT GERUSH HAYEHUDIM ME-SFARAD? [Did Micer Alfonso de la Caballeria intervene against the expulsion of the Jews from Spain?]. *Zion [Israel] 1985 50: 265-276.* Micer Alfonso de la Caballeria, son of Pedro de la Caballeria (convert and author of *Zelus Christi Adversus Judaeos)* and grandson of Bonafos de la Caballeria, had close and diverse relations with Jews in Saragossa. He also managed to have his trial stopped through the intervention of King Ferdinand II, for whom he was vice chancellor in the kingdom of Aragon. A safe-conduct by Ferdinand II, reprinted in this article, absolved Micer Alfonso from any accusation of intervention on behalf of the Jews in order to revoke the order for their expulsion. Based on Inquisition documents; 41 notes. English summary, p. XVII. 1485-92

Caballero, José María

1114. Carrasquilla Botero, Juan. AVENTURAS CONYUGALES Y EXTRACONYUGALES DE JOSE MARIA CABALLERO [Conjugal and extraconjugal adventures of José María Caballero]. *Bol. de Hist. y Antigüedades [Colombia] 1980 67(730): 417-443.* Reconstructs little-known personal and family details in the life of José María Caballero (1776-1828), chronicler of Bogotá. Based on notarial records in the Archivo Histórico Nacional; 61 notes, 4 documentary appendixes. 1803-28

Caballero y Góngora, Antonio

1115. Bateman, Alfredo. LOS PERSONAJES DE LA EXPEDICION BOTANICA [Personages of the Botanical Expedition]. *Boletín de Historia y Antigüedades [Colombia] 1984 71(747): 907-964.* Biographical sketches of figures associated with the Botanical Expedition organized in 1782 to carry out a scientific survey of New Granadan botanical species. They included the Spanish-born priest and scientist José Celestino Mutis, director of the project; archbishop and viceroy Antonio Caballero y Góngora, who gave it his support; German scientist Alexander von Humboldt, who visited Mutis and his collaborators; a great many educated creoles of the late colonial period; and José Gerónimo Triana, whose interests in scientific study later in the 19th century led him to uncover and organize the papers of the Botanical Expedition in Madrid. Biblio. 18c-19c

Cabero, Alberto

1116. Gazmuri Riveros, Cristián. NOTAS SOBRE LA INFLUENCIA DEL RACISMO EN LA OBRA DE NICOLAS PALACIOS, FRANCISCO A. ENCINA Y ALBERTO CABERO [Notes on the influence of racism in the work of Nicolás Palacios, Francisco A. Encina, and Alberto Cabero]. *Historia [Chile] 1981 16: 225-247.* At the beginning of this century racist ideas became the ideological background of widely read social and historical writings. The extreme racism of the physician Palacios influenced the historian Encina, who filtered and softened it. In Cabero, racist ideas lose their biological foundation and take on a more cultural connotation. Although Palacios is no longer taken seriously, Encina's vision dominates the consciousness of the average Chilean, while the most thoughtful of the three, Cabero, is practically unknown today. 59 notes. 1904-35

Cabral, Amílcar

1117. Davidson, Basil. THE IMPORTANCE OF CABRAL. *African Affairs [Great Britain] 1984 83(330): 117-119.* Reviews Jock McCulloch's *In the Twilight of Revolution: The Political Theory of Amílcar Cabral* (1983) and Patrick Chabal's *Amílcar Cabral: Revolutionary Leadership and People's War* (1983), which describe the moral and political influence of Guinean revolutionary Amílcar Cabral (1924-73). Although both books contribute to the growing literature on Cabral's life and political theory, the reviewer challenges some of the facts presented by Chabal that misinterpret the historical record. 1960's-74

1118. Davidson, Basil. ON REVOLUTIONARY NATIONALISM: THE LEGACY OF CABRAL. *Latin American Perspectives 1984 11(2): 15-42.* Describes the achievements of African revolutionary and political theorist Amílcar Cabral (1924-73), emphasizing the importance of his writings on colonialism, class conflict, and political change. Cabral's work has been of theoretical and practical value to revolutionary movements throughout the Third World. In particular, his ideas did much to redefine Marxist theory in a modern and nonwestern context. Secondary sources; 4 notes, ref. 1950's-73

1119. Robinson, Cedric J. AMILCAR CABRAL AND THE DIALECTIC OF PORTUGUESE COLONIALISM. *Indian Pol. Sci. Rev. [India] 1982 16(2): 176-196.* In the early sixties, Amilcar Cabral (1924-73) emerged from the liberation struggle of Guinea-Bissau and Cape Verde as one of the foremost revolutionary theorists in the world. Unlike most other African liberation struggles, Cabral's movement was not simply an independence movement but a conscious revolutionary struggle. Describes the evolution of Cabral's revolutionary practice and theory, in the context of the postwar Portuguese colonial presence in Africa. 57 notes. 1956-73

1120. Robinson, Cedric J. AMILCAR CABRAL AND THE DIALECTIC OF PORTUGUESE COLONIALISM. *Radical Am. 1981 15(3): 39-57.* Amilcar Cabral's life and thought as a representative of the petit bourgeois native middle management in Portuguese Africa (Cape Verde, Angola, Mozambique, and Guinea-Bissau) led to his becoming a leader of the revolutionary struggle in Guinea-Bissau and a theorist who ranks with Fanon, Nyerere, Nkrumah, and Lumumba. Twenty years of work and 10 years of open struggle led to independence for Guinea-Bissau in 1972 and Cabral's assassination by Portuguese agents in 1973. 37 notes, 8 illus. 1953-73

1121. Roth, Kurth. EIN LEBEN FÜR DIE BEFREIUNG DER VÖLKER AFRIKAS. AMILCAR CABRAL [A life for the liberation of the African people: Amilcar Cabral]. *Beiträge zur Geschichte der Arbeiterbewegung [East Germany] 1985 27(4): 524-531.* Provides a brief biography of African revolutionary Amilcar Cabral (1924-73), a native of Guinea-Bissau who was educated in Lisbon and became a leading figure in the African independence movements against Portugal and the other European colonial powers. Leading the independence movement of Guinea-Bissau in the 1950's, Cabral realized that peaceful means had no chance of success and turned to armed conflict in which he displayed military as well as political leadership. Cabral developed the concept that the developed socialist countries should ally themselves with the national liberation struggles of African and other subject states. He was murdered by Portuguese agents in 1973. 21 notes. 1950's-73

Cáceres de Arismendi, Luisa

1122. Gabaldón, José Rafael. MUJERES DE AMERICA [Women of America]. *Bol. de la Acad. Nac. de la Hist. [Venezuela] 1983 66(261): 113-124.* 1792-1810
For abstract see ***Rodríguez del Toro y Alaisa, María Teresa***

Cacopardo, Salvatore

1123. Siino, Pietro. SALVATORE CACOPARDO: UN RETTORE QUASI SCONOSCIUTO NELLA SUA UNIVERSITA [Salvatore Cacopardo: a rector almost unknown in his own university]. *Rassegna Storica del Risorgimento [Italy] 1983 70(4): 410-424.* Salvatore Cacopardo (1815-91) was rector of the University of Palermo, secretary general of public education, and president of the faculty of medicine. Information about his career and his contributions to public education, including his views on education as expressed in his correspondence, is presented. Partly based on material in the Central State Archive and the archive of the University of Palermo; 35 notes. 1861-91

Cadalso y Vázquez, José de

1124. Embeita, Maria. CADALSO Y EL ACTO AUTOBIOGRAFICO [Cadalso and the autobiographical act]. *Cuadernos Hispanoamericanos [Spain] 1982 (389): 322-326.* In his *Apuntaciones Autobiográficas* [Autobiographical sketches], written circa 1781 but first published in 1967, José de Cadalso y Vázquez (1741-82) follows the main features of autobiography as a genre established by literary historians since the 1850's. Due to its shortcomings, however, Cadalso's autobiographical work could be also classified within the tradition of confessions. 13 notes. 1760's-82

Caetani, Leone

1125. Hasan, Reyazul. PRINCE LEONE CAETANI—A GREAT ITALIAN ORIENTALIST, (1869-1935). *Hamdard Islamicus [Pakistan] 1982 5(1): 45-81.* Discusses the life and work of Italian orientalist Prince Leone Caetani (1869-1935), especially his Marxist interpretation of Islam. 1894-1935

Caine, Sydney

1126. Petter, Martin. SIR SYDNEY AND THE COLONIAL OFFICE IN THE SECOND WORLD WAR: A CAREER IN THE MAKING. *Can. J. of Hist. [Canada] 1981 16(1): 67-85.* In 1939 Sir Sydney Caine was a Principal, by 1944 he had attained the title of Assistant Under Secretary and in 1947 he became Deputy Under Secretary. He entered the British Colonial Office in 1926 after attending the London School of Economics. Because of his expertise in economics he was able to relate colonial supervision to the task of war management. Primary sources; 51 notes. 1926-47

Cairnes, John Elliot

1127. Boylan, T. A. and Foley, T. P. JOHN ELLIOT CAIRNES, JOHN STUART MILL AND IRELAND: SOME PROBLEMS FOR POLITICAL ECONOMY. *Hermathena [Ireland] 1983 (135): 96-119.* Reviews John Elliot Cairnes's career as one of the first professional economists and his acknowledged contributions to the thinking of John Stuart Mill, many of which were derived from Cairnes's analyses of Irish society. 1856-72

Caitanya, Kṛṣṇa

1128. Stewart, Tony Kevin. "The Biographical Images of Kṛṣṇa-Caitanya: A Study in the Perception of Divinity." U. of Chicago 1985. *DAI 1986 46(9): 2721-A.* 16c

Çako, Liri

1129. Xhunga, Liri. "FERRI" NAZIST NUK NA MPOSHTI SEPSE KISHIM NË ZEMËR PARTINË, BESIMIN NË FITORENE REVOLUCIONIT [The Nazi "hell" did not defeat us because we had the Party in our hearts and faith in the victory of the revolution]. *Studime Historike [Albania] 1985 39(1): 177-184.* Excerpts from the diary of 17-year-old Liri Çako, describing her sufferings during 1944-45, when with other girls she was taken to various concentration camps in Greece, Austria, and Germany. Their resistance to the Nazi pressure was inspired by the Communists among them. The Soviet army saved and freed them just when they were going to be executed. 1944-45

Calasanz, Joseph

1130. Asiain, Miguel Angel. MOMENTOS IMPORTANTES DE LA VIDA DE CALASANZ VISTOS POR SUS HIJOS [Important moments in Saint Joseph Calasanz's life as seen by his children]. *Analecta Calasanctiana [Spain] 1981 23(45): 179-199.* Saint Joseph Calasanz, general and founder of the Escuelas Pias, was removed by Pope Urban VIII in 1643; the commotion thereby created—including several letters to Pope Innocence X—lasted until the saint's death in 1648 when most letters referring to him were favorable, although his detractors tried to paint him as authoritarian and even arbitrary. 1643-48

Calcagno, Juan Francisco

1131. Méndez Díaz, Pedro. JUAN FRANCISCO CALCAGNO: EN EL CIENTOCINCUENTA Y CINCO ANIVERSARIO DE SU NACIMIENTO [Juan Francisco Calcagno: the 150th anniversary of his birth]. *Rev. de la Biblioteca Nac. José Martí [Cuba] 1983 25(1): 181-210.* Juan Francisco Calcagno (1827-1903) was a noted Cuban writer whose works helped establish the intellectual acceptance of Cuban independence and revolution in 1895. Photo, 45 notes, appendix. 1850's-1903

Caldas, Francisco José de

1132. Paredes Pardo, Jaime. REPASO DEL SABIO CALDAS [A review of the wisdom of Caldas]. *Bol. Cultural y Biblio. [Colombia] 1983 20(1): 98-130.* Francisco José de Caldas, who dedicated his life to the study of science, was a great patriot during the struggle for independence. 1793-1816

Calil, Georges

1133. Hinds, Allister E. COLONIAL POLICY AND THE PROCESSING OF GROUNDNUTS: THE CASE OF GEORGES CALIL. *International Journal of African Historical Studies 1986 19(2): 261-273.* A history of the development of the 20th-century Nigerian groundnuts industry through the example of one Lebanese oil processor in Kano. Georges Calil spent years attempting to get permission to build processing facilities in Nigeria to supply the local demand for oil. His successes were small and slow in coming because the colonial administration tried to protect European based processors and the export profits of the Groundnuts Marketing Board. Based on documents in the Nigerian archives; 58 notes. 1940-52

Calmon, Pedro

1134. Barreto, Dalmo Freire. CINQUENTENARIO DA ELEIÇÃO DOS SOCIOS DR.S PEDRO CALMON E ALEXANDRE JOSE BARBOSA LIMA SOBRINHO [Fiftieth anniversary of the election of members Drs. Pedro Calmon and Alexandre José Barbosa Lima Sobrinho]. *Rev. do Inst. Hist. e Geog. Brasileiro [Brazil] 1981 (333): 71-92.* Reviews the careers and contributions of two noted members of the Brazilian Institute of History and Geography on the occasion of their 50th year of membership. Calmon is praised for his historical writings, especially his biographies of Brazilian Emperors Pedro I and Pedro II. A list of his other major works is included. Calmon's honors and his public career are also outlined. Lima Sobrinho is honored as a journalist and as a political, literary, and social commentator. His political career as a lawyer and judge is reviewed, as are his publications in that area. Article concludes with remarks by both honorees. 1921-81

1135. Montello, Josué. OS 80 ANOS INADEQUADOS [An unusual octogenarian]. *Revista do Instituto Histórico e Geográfico Brasileiro [Brazil] 1982 (337): 207-210.* This tribute to Pedro Calmon, president of the Brazilian Historical and Geographic Institute, rector of the University of Brazil and prolific speaker and writer, emphasizes his continuing and multifaceted activity. He is not one of those who at the age of 80 are afraid of the chill of the night or of new ideas. 1902-82

Calmon family

1136. Calmon, Pedro. CENTENARIO DE MIGUEL CALMON [Centenary of Miguel Calmon]. *Rev. do Inst. Hist. e Geog. Brasileiro [Brazil] 1981 (333): 39-51.* Reviews the career of Miguel Calmon and other members of the Calmon family, who have played a notable role in the history and culture of Brazil. The Calmons included several political leaders and administrators, naval commanders, scientists, writers, industrialists, and educators. The careers of many family members are described. 1823-1935

Calvert, George

1137. Coakley, Thomas M. GEORGE CALVERT, FIRST LORD BALTIMORE: FAMILY, STATUS, ARMS. *Maryland Historical Magazine 1984 79(3): 255-269.* The pedigree and arms of George Calvert have baffled historians, genealogists, and specialists on heraldry from his time to our own. The fragmentary character of the evidence has given rise to much fanciful speculation. Based only on the real and plausible record, it is fairly certain that Calvert descended in the paternal line from a North Riding Yorkshire family which had probably been in the county for centuries and had attained gentle status at least by his father's generation. His mother was likely a Crosland, of the West Riding Croslands, and may have been named Alicia or Alice. Calvert's arms bore no confirmation before his own generation, and he almost certainly had no connection with the Callewaert family of Flanders. From Maryland Historical Society archives, English primary materials, and secondary studies; 2 illus., 22 notes. 1567-1648

1138. Krugler, John D. THE CALVERT FAMILY, CATHOLICISM, AND COURT POLITICS IN EARLY SEVENTEENTH-CENTURY ENGLAND. *Historian 1981 43(3): 378-392.* The conversion of Sir George Calvert to Catholicism and subsequent fall from political power had little impact on his future economic interests in colonization. Their Catholicism did not influence how they viewed court politics or how they were viewed by certain members of the court. The Calverts used long-standing friendships with Protestants such as Wentworth and Cottington to further their colonization schemes. In Calvert's case, personal loyalty overrode religious differences. Primary sources; 24 notes. 1600-30

Calvin, John

1139. Blaisdell, Charmarie Jenkins. CALVIN'S LETTERS TO WOMEN: THE COURTING OF LADIES IN HIGH PLACES. *Sixteenth Cent. J. 1982 13(3): 67-84.* John Calvin wrote many letters to encourage French noble women to proclaim their Protestant faith. There was little spiritual encouragement and counseling in them; their purpose was more political than pastoral. He treated men and women in the same brusque, political way. Based on Calvin's letters, secondary sources; 54 notes. 1540's-64

1140. Ménager, Daniel. THEODORE DE BEZE, BIOGRAPHE DE CALVIN [Theodore Beza, Calvin's biographer]. *Bibliothèque d'Humanisme et Renaissance [Switzerland] 1983*

45(2): 231-255. In three editions (1564, 1565, 1575) of his biography of John Calvin, Theodore Beza (1519-1605) defends him against his detractors. Beza portrays Calvin as a servant of God's word on earth. Although the genre of biography in 16th-century France was evolving to include psychological dimensions, Beza remained traditional by presenting the facts of Calvin's life as signs of God's will. Based on Beza's works; 117 notes. 1564-75

1141. Unceín Tamayo, Luis Alberto. MIGUEL SERVET Y CALVINO: HISTORIA DOCUMENTADA DE GRANDES ODIOS [Michael Servetus and Calvin: documented history of a great hatred]. *Boletín de la Academia Nacional de la Historia [Venezuela] 1984 67(268): 817-821.* Describes the deadly enmity between two opposed reformers, John Calvin and the Spaniard Michael Servetus, which ended by the former burning his opponent at the stake in Geneva in 1553. The author finds the root of such hatred in the heresy that infected them both. 16c

Calvocoressi family

1142. Calvocoressi, Peter. FROM BYZANTIUM TO ETON: A MEMOIR OF EIGHT CENTURIES. *Encounter [Great Britain] 1981 57(6): 20-26.* Surveys the history of the author's family from its Greco-Genoese origins on the Aegean island of Chios, through the diaspora following the Turkish massacre of 1822, and finally to London in the latter 19th century. 1050-1965

Camargo de la Barrera, Rafael

1143. Camargo Pérez, Gabriel. FERMIN DE PIMENTEL Y VARGAS [Fermín de Pimentel y Vargas]. *Bol. de Hist. y Antigüedades [Colombia] 1983 70(742): 909-923.* The priest Rafael Camargo de la Barrera (1858-1926) portrayed the customs of 19th-century rural Colombia in *costumbrista* writings that he published under the pseudonym Fermín de Pimentel y Vargas. In addition, he held various governmental appointments as well. 1858-1926

Cambon, Paul

1144. Weiner, Robert I.; with commentary by Schmidt, Martin and Gordon, Bertram M. PAUL CAMBON AND THE MAKING OF THE ENTENTE CORDIALE. *Pro. of the Ann. Meeting of the Western Soc. for French Hist. 1980 8: 498-511.* Discusses the period 1898-1904, when Paul Cambon was French ambassador to Great Britain. From the beginning of his mission Cambon saw the necessity of an Anglo-French rapprochement. He helped to settle the Fashoda crisis and other problems between the two countries. The Anglo-French entente cordiale of 1904 was in many ways a personal success for him. Comments, pp. 515-521. Based on the private Cambon papers, foreign affairs archives, and other primary sources; 91 notes. 1898-1904

Camm, John

1145. Horle, Craig W. JOHN CAMM: PROFILE OF A QUAKER MINISTER DURING THE INTERREGNUM. *Quaker Hist. 1982 71(1): 3-15.* Continued from a previous article. Late in 1654, opposition increased and John Camm's health deteriorated. Oliver Cromwell removed the garrison from Bristol and ordered the castle demolished. Camm and his companion, John Audland, were accused of being Catholics, Royalists, and disturbers of the peace, and were attacked with "warrants, orders, and riots." Camm seems to have persevered near Bristol through much of 1655, with the psychological and physical sufferings common to other Quaker itinerants. In the spring of 1656 he retired to his Camsgill home, where he died on 10 January 1657. Based mainly on contemporary pamphlets and Quaker archives; 31 notes. 1654-57

1146. Horle, Craig W. JOHN CAMM: PROFILE OF A QUAKER MINISTER DURING THE INTERREGNUM. *Quaker Hist. 1981 70(2): 68-83.* From his conversion in 1652, John Camm traveled as a Quaker "publisher of truth" through the northern counties, interrrupted church services, and was beaten and distrained for tithes. In London by 1654, he and Francis Howgill failed to persuade Cromwell to annul the law against Quakers' interrupting the minister's sermon. For three years he joined the missionary team in the Bristol area, speaking to thousands with the sympathetic protection of the soldiers. 38 notes, mainly to contemporary pamphlets and Quaker archives. Article to be continued. 1652-57

Campana, Stanislao

1147. Tassoni, Giuseppina Allegri. IL PITTORE STANISLAO CAMPANA [The painter Stanislao Campana]. *Archivio Storico per le Province Parmensi [Italy] 1983 35: 261-270.* Stanislao Campana (1794-1864), of a wealthy landowning family, studied at the Parma Academy of Fine Arts, received many commissions from the Austrian Archduchess, Marie Louise, was nominated "Professor of the Academy," and served as Superintendant of Galleries and Schools. 1810's-64

Campbell, Alexander Duncombe

1148. Munjeri, Dawson Kundishora. VHUTA (ALEXANDER DUNCOMBE CAMPBELL). *Heritage [Zimbabwe] 1982 2: 43-48.* A study of the life of Alexander Duncombe Campbell with particular reference to his term in office as the first native commissioner of the Salisbury district of Rhodesia, and the Chimurenga risings which were in part a reaction to his administration. 1872-99

Campbell, John Douglas

1149. Johnson-Cousin, Danielle. UN AIR "ECOSSAIS" DANS LA VIE DE MADAME DE STAËL. EXTRAITS INEDITS DU "JOURNAL" DE LORD JOHN CAMPBELL [A Scottish air in the life of Madame de Staël: previously unpublished excerpts from the journal of Lord John Campbell]. *Rev. d'Hist. Littéraire de la France [France] 1983 83(1): 81-116.* Discusses the personal and literary relationships shared by Madame de Staël, Lord John Douglas Campbell, and Dr. Robert Robertson, explaining that Lord Campbell was the model for Oswald, Lord Nelvil in *Corinne* (1807), written by Madame de Staël. 1802-07

Campbell, Stella

1150. Peters, Margot. BERNARD SHAW AND STELLA PAT. *Biography 1986 9(1): 25-36.* Always eager to encourage sedition, George Bernard Shaw found raw material in Mrs. Patrick Campbell's daughter, Stella. Mrs. Campbell had brought up young Stella a lady; her daughter had dared the stage—and Shaw approved. Shaw ordered her to break loose, offered her parts; but she remained, frustratingly, until the end of their acquaintance, a perfect lady. 1907-44

Campbell family

1151. Cowan, Edward J. THE ANGUS CAMPBELLS AND THE ORIGIN OF THE CAMPBELL-OGILVIE FEUD. *Scottish Studies [Great Britain] 1981 25: 25-38.* An intricate web of family ties and personal fears and antipathies, stemming largely from the growing Campbell landholding presence in Angus during the 16th century, produced the long-standing Campbell-Ogilvie feud. Based on official documents; notes, genealogical table, biblio. 16c-17c

Campos, Francisco

1152. Monteiro, Norma de Góes. FRANCISCO CAMPOS: TRAJETORIA POLITICA [Francisco Campos: political trajectory]. *Rev. Brasileira de Estudos Pol. [Brazil] 1981 (53): 183-210.* Describes the life, career and thought of Francisco Campos, one of the major theorists and actors of the Brazilian revolution of 1930. His activities in the Provisional Government, 1930-1934, are described in detail, especially his work as Minister of Education and Public Health, and, after 1934, his work as Minister of Justice. Many of the ideas of the new 1934 constitution were his, as were many laws and interpretations following upon it. He resigned in 1942, and his effective power ended with the overthrow of President Vargas in 1945. He remained active and continued to teach until his death in 1968. 75 notes. 1930-68

Camus, Albert

1153. Montanari, Federico. ALBERT CAMUS [Albert Camus]. *Belfagor [Italy] 1986 41(1): 27-46.* Surveys the life, times, and writings of French philosopher Albert Camus, noting several biographical details that explain his theory about the human condition. 1942-60

Candelas, Luis

1154. Hernández Girbal, F. EL ULTIMO ROBO DE LUIS CANDELAS [The last robbery of Luis Candelas]. *Historia y Vida [Spain] 1985 18(203): 40-53.* Presents the story of Luis Candelas (ca. 1805-37), also known as "Madrid's bandit," the inventive and popular thief who never killed anyone, and who was arrested and sentenced to death a few months after he and his band robbed the Queen's seamstress's house. 1820-37

Candianu-Popescu, Alexandru

1155. Corbu, Constantin. ALEXANDRU CANDIANU-POPESCU—PARTICIPANT ŞI CRONICAR AL VIEŢII POLITICE DIN A DOUA JUMĂTATE A VEACULUI TRECUT [Alexandru Candianu-Popescu: a participant in and chronicler of political life in the second half of the last century]. *Rev. de Istorie [Romania] 1980 33(9): 1737-1763.* Surveys the life and achievements of Alexandru Candianu-Popescu (1841-1901), Romanian writer, politician, jurist, and hero, using both his published and forthcoming memoirs. As a participant in major developments in the formation of modern Romania, he worked for the 1859 unification of Moldavia and Wallachia, the installation of a foreign prince on the Romanian throne, and the unification of Transylvania with Moldavia and Wallachia. He distinguished himself politically and militarily in the War of Independence of 1877-78, which he also chronicled. He is seen as typifying the patriotic spirit following the 1848 uprising, nevertheless expressing it strictly within the bounds of the prevailing bourgeois and landowners' political regime. 127 notes. French summary. 1841-1901

Cañedo y Vigil, Alonso

1156. Goñi Gaztambide, José. EL OBISPO DE MALAGA, CAÑEDO, EN EL TRIENIO CONSTITUTIONAL [The bishop of Malaga, Cañedo, during the three years of the constitutional regime]. *Hispania Sacra [Spain] 1980 32(65-66): 193-227.* Alonso Cañedo y Vigil (1760-1829), bishop of Malaga and later archbishop of Burgos, was a member of the Cortes of Cádiz, responsible for the elaboration of a constitution under French occupation. During that time he revealed his strong royalist convictions. During the period which followed he was harassed by extortionists and his diocese of Malaga was deprived of much of its property. He died a poor man in Burgos and his funeral expenses were paid by charitable donations. Based partly on primary material in the archive of the cathedral of Malaga; 95 notes. 1808-12

Canetti, Elias

1157. Sontag, Susan. DE L'ESPRIT CONSIDERE COMME UNE PASSION [Mind as passion]. *Urbi [Belgium] 1982 (5): 3-14.* Discusses the works of 20th-century novelist Elias Canetti and relates the *bizarrerie* and tragedy in Canetti's own works to late 19th- and early 20th-century intellectual and political history. 19c-20c

Canning, George

1158. Crimmin, P. K. GEORGE CANNING AND THE BATTLE OF CAMPERDOWN. *Mariner's Mirror [Great Britain] 1981 67(4): 319-326.* Discusses letters, with brief quotations, from George Canning (1770-1827) to members of his family during the later 1790's when he was a new member of Parliament. 10 notes. 1795-1800

1159. Gash, Norman. THE TORTOISE AND THE HARE: LIVERPOOL AND CANNING. *Hist. Today [Great Britain] 1982 32(Mar): 12-19.* Compares and contrasts the lives and careers of Robert Banks Jenkinson, 2d Lord Liverpool (1770-1828), and George Canning (1770-1827), who both attended Christ Church, Oxford, and became successful and prominent politicians. Text of the Sir John Neale lecture delivered at University College, London on 7 December 1981. 1790's-1828

Cantemir, Dimitrie

1160. Georgescu, Valentin Al. RENOVATION DE VALEURS EUROPEENNES ET INNOVATIONS ROUMAINE CHEZ D. CANTEMIR: STATISTIQUE DESCRIPTIVE, ETHNOPSYCHOLOGIE, HISTOIRE DU DROIT, THEORIE DE L'IDEE IMPERIALE [Renewal of European values and Romanian innovations in D. Cantemir: descriptive statistics, ethnopsychology, history of law, and theory of the imperial idea]. *Rev. des Etudes Sud-Est Européennes [Romania] 1982 20(1): 3-23.* An analytic review of the personality, scholarship, and work of Dimitrie Cantemir (1673-1723), prince of Moldavia (1693; 1710-11). A pioneer in the cultural history of Moldavia, this famous historian left an important body of work dealing with history and various branches of the social and legal sciences. As the innovator behind the theory of "imperial principle," his thought and political actions were marked by a resistance to Ottoman authority. 60 notes. 1673-1723

1161. Gorovei, Ştefan S. MISCELLANEA GENEALOGICA 1. NOTE CANTEMIRIENE 2. GLOSSE ARHONDOLOGICE [Miscellaneous genealogical data: notes about Dimitrie Cantemir and *Arhondologia Moldovei*]. *Anuarul Institutului de Istorie şi Arheologie "A. D. Xenopol" [Romania] 1984 21: 489-496.* Discusses the life and works of Dimitrie Cantemir, mainly his birthdate, which is uncertain (1673 or 1676), and a lost work by Cantemir entitled *Liber Moldavicae Nobilitatis Genealogiae* about the genealogy of Moldavia's nobility. *Arhondologia Moldovei,* written by Constandin Sion (1795-1862), includes the genealogical trees of the noble families of Moldavia during the period 1840-57, and possibly since 1822. Secondary sources; 95 notes. 1673-1862

1162. Lozovan, E. DIMITRIE CANTEMIR FRANC-MACON? [Dimitrie Cantemir—a Freemason?]. *Rev. des Etudes Roumaines [France] 1981 16: 68-73.* In a 1975 article the author advanced the hypothesis that Moldavian prince, savant, and politician Dimitrie Cantemir, based on his writing of *La Lettre sur la Conscience* at Constantinople sometime in the period 1712 to 1714, might have had Masonic contacts, a fact which would help to explain his well-known anti-Islamic attitude. Further research strengthens such an idea, especially when one examines the Vienna lodge founded by Ignaz von Born and frequented by Mozart and Haydn in the 1780's, and considers the many parallels in theme, symbols, and tone between works such as The Magic Flute (1791) and the *Histoire Hieroglyphique,* written by Cantemir—in fact, the general "Egyptian atmosphere" of Cantemir's works as a whole. Critical objections by French specialist in Freemasonry Charles Pidoux conclude the study. 13 notes. 1711-91

Cantillon, Richard

1163. Murphy, Antoin E. RICHARD CANTILLON—BANKER AND ECONOMIST. *Journal of Libertarian Studies 1985 7(2): 185-215.* Examines in detail the life and work of Richard Cantillon, French-Irish banker, economist, and author of *Essai sur la Nature du Commerce en Général* (1755), called the first unified and general work in economics. 1650's-1750's

1164. Murphy, Antoin E. RICHARD CANTILLON—AN IRISH BANKER IN PARIS. *Hermathena [Ireland] 1983 (135): 45-74.* Reviews the career of Richard Cantillon and, in particular, the events which led to his *Essai sur la Nature du Commerce en Général* (1755), a theoretical explanation of the failure of a massive economic experiment engineered by his associate, John Law. 1714-55

Čapek, Karel

1165. Krásná, Věra and Sládek, Zdeněk. KORESPONDENCE KARLA ČAPKA A MILANA HODŽI NA PŘELOMU LET 1928-1929 [The correspondence of Karel Čapek and Milan Hodža, 1928-29]. *Historický Časopis [Czechoslovakia] 1986 34(3): 424-429.* Reprints and comments on some letters of Karel Čapek and Milan Hodža, written at the end of the 1920's. The letters uncover some features of the contradiction between Eduard Beneš and Hodža. They reflect certain disagreements within Czechoslovak government bourgeoisie and show Čapek's interest in the internal political development in the Czechoslovak Republic and his effort to contribute to the settlement of contradictions in the government. 1928-29

Capistrano de Abreu, João

1166. —. [CAPISTRANO DE ABREU, JOÃO (TRIBUTE)]. *Revista de Ciência Política [Brazil] 1985 28(1): 139-152.*

Castro Rebello, Edgardo de. CAPISTRANO DE ABREU [Capistrano de Abreu], *pp. 139-146.* Publishes a lecture delivered at the Brazilian Ministry of Education and Culture, 22 October 1953, commemorating the centennial of the birth of Brazilian historian João Capistrano de Abreu.

—. A SINTESE HISTORICA NA OBRA DE CAPISTRANO DE ABREU [Historical synthesis in the work of Capistrano de Abreu], *pp. 146-152.* Prints a lecture delivered at the Casa do Estudante do Brasil, 29 June 1956. 15c-19c

Capitini, Aldo

1167. Ranieri, Ruggero. UN'ESPERIENZA DIVERSA DELL'ANTIFASCISMO: L'OPPOSIZIONE DI ALDO CAPITINI [A varied anti-Fascist experience: Aldo Capitini's opposition]. *Ponte [Italy] 1986 42(1): 111-126.* Studies the blend of religious and political convictions that influenced Italian liberal socialist thinker Aldo Capitini in his opposition to fascism: a personal commitment to nonviolent struggle, inspired in part by the writings of Mahatma Gandhi, and his definition of himself as an independent leftist. 1936-48

Capito, Wolfgang Fabricius

1168. Scholl, Hans. WOLFGANG FABRICIUS CAPITOS REFORMATORISCHE EIGENART [Wolfgang Fabricius Capito's reformatory character]. *Zwingliana [Switzerland] 1983 16(2): 126-141.* Outlines Wolfgang Fabricius Capito's idiosyncratic career as reformer in regard to his position toward Luther, the Anabaptists, and Karlstadt. Throughout his life, Capito insisted that he followed only God and not any single man or man-made position. Based on Wolfgang Capito's writings and secondary sources; 42 notes. 1525-33

Caprariis, Vittorio de

1169. Agnelli, Arduino. VITTORIO DE CAPRARIIS STORICO DELLE IDEE [Vittorio de Caprariis, historian of ideas]. *Pensiero Politico [Italy] 1984 17(3): 352-367.* Discusses the influences of Benedetto Croce on the development of the ideas of the cultural historian Vittorio de Caprariis who worked on the problem of the Reformation as the main source of European liberalism and fought against the "tendentious historiography" that interpreted past events as forerunners of modern liberty. The rationale and the genesis of an empirically founded political science were important for his intentions of helping to secure democracy and to provide sane ideals for modern life. Based on the works of de Caprariis, Croce, and secondary sources; 39 notes. 1950-63

Caracciolo, Domenico

1170. Vardaro, Libero. DOMENICO CARACCIOLO, DIPLOMATICO, VICERE E MINISTRO [Domenico Caracciolo, diplomat, viceroy, and minister]. *Cahiers Int. d'Hist. Econ. et Sociale [Italy] 1981 13: 340-354.* Provides a brief description of the personality and career of Domenico Caracciolo, the Neapolitan ambassador, viceroy, and politician. 59 notes. 1715-89

Carageali-Costache, Nicolae

1171. Apostol, Mihai. UN DRAMATURG NECUNOSCUT: NICOLAE CARAGEALI-COSTACHE [Nicolae Carageali-Costache: an unknown playwright]. *Revista Arhivelor [Romania] 1985 47(2): 199-202.* Discusses the life and works of Nicolae Caragiali-Costache (1860-?), a cousin of Ion Luca Caragiale. 1860-99

Caravaggio, Michelangelo Merisi da

1172. Banks, Oliver. A COMMON MURDERER. *Art & Antiques 1985 (Mar): 76-80.* Contrasts the splendid paintings of Michelangelo Merisi da Caravaggio with the violent and brutish life that he led. 1592-1610

1173. Gardner, James. IS CARAVAGGIO OUR CONTEMPORARY? *Commentary 1985 79(6): 55-61.* Michelangelo Merisi da Caravaggio's lawless and dissolute life, the often shocking and grotesque subject matter and treatment of his paintings, and his rather poor technique make the painter seem 20th-century. 1590's-1610

Carbonell, Diego

1174. —. [EN EL CENTENARIO DE DIEGO CARBONELL] [On Diego Carbonell's birth centenary]. *Boletín de la Academia Nacional de la Historia [Venezuela] 1985 68(269): 27-82.*

Briceño Perozo, Mario. DIEGO CARBONELL, HISTORIADOR [Diego Carbonell, historian], *pp. 27-36.*

Valásquez, Ramón J. DIEGO CARBONELL: APUNTES PARA UNA BIOGRAFIA [Diego Carbonell: notes for a biography], *pp. 36-48.*

Pérez Tenreiro, Tomás. EL "TABLADO" DE DON DIEGO CARBONELL [Diego Carbonell's "platform"], *pp. 49-59.*

Alvarez, Pedro J. HOMENAJE AL DR DIEGO CARBONELL CON MOTIVO DE CUMPLIRSE 100 AÑOS DE SU NACIMIENTO [Tribute to Dr. Diego Carbonell on the centenary of his birth], *pp. 60-69.*

Tablante Garrido, P. N. DIEGO CARBONELL [Diego Carbonell], *pp. 69-82.* On the centenary of the birth of Diego Carbonell (1884-1945) these contributions celebrate his achievements as physician, university professor, and particularly as a historian. Biographical data are provided and an evaluation of his gifts as orator as exemplified by his many speeches. Ref. 1884-1945

Carbonell, José María

1175. Llano Isaza, Rodrigo. QUIEN ERA DON JOSE MARIA CARBONELL [Who was José María Carbonell?]. *Bol. de Hist. y Antigüedades [Colombia] 1982 69(739): 1039-1049.* Though often mentioned as a popular agitator in the first stage of the Colombian independence movement, José María Carbonell remains a little-studied figure. Born in 1779 in Bogotá, he was associated with the botanical expedition and related by marriage to Antonio Nariño, of whom he became a close collaborator in the government of independent Cundinamarca. He was executed in the Spanish reconquest. 1779-1816

Cardarelli, Vincenzo

1176. Caponigro, Maria Adelaide. LA ROMA DI VINCENZO CARDARELLI [The Rome of Vincenzo Cardarelli]. *Studi Romani [Italy] 1985 33(1-2): 70-77.* Quotes passages from the journals of Italian writer Vincenzo Cardarelli, who moved to Rome in 1907, when he was 19, and remained there until his death in 1959. 1907-59

Cárdenas, Alonso de

1177. Loomie, Albert J. ALONSO DE CÁRDENAS AND THE LONG PARLIAMENT, 1640-1648. *English Hist. Rev. [Great Britain] 1982 97(383): 289-307.* Describes the relationship between Alonso de Cárdenas, Spanish representative and ambassador to England, and members of the Long Parliament, 1640-48. His primary mission was to keep the king and Parliament from joining France against Spain. Mistrusted and suspected for a few years by both the king and Parliament, Cárdenas was later able to convince moderates and then the Independents that France was a danger to their trade. In return, he was granted licenses to recruit troops for Spanish service overseas. The Spanish council of state was convinced to collaborate with Protestant radicals on the anticipation of relief for the Catholics in England. Limited resources prevented Cárdenas from offering large bribes, but he was able to use small gifts to obtain reports of closed proceedings of selected committees. Based on papers in the British Library, the Archivo General de Simancas Estado, the Archives Generales in Brussels, and the Archives du Ministeres des Affairs Etrangères in Paris. 1638-48

Cárdenas, Lázaro

1178. Weston, Charles H., Jr. THE POLITICAL LEGACY OF LAZARO CARDENAS. *Americas (Acad. of Am. Franciscan Hist.) 1983 39(3): 383-405.* As president of Mexico from 1934 to 1940, Lázaro Cárdenas strove to revitalize the social reform programs of the Mexican Revolution and to achieve more equal distribution of wealth and greater participation of the working class in policy formation. He also reorganized the official revolutionary party, which he renamed Party of the Mexican Revolution (PRM). He gave to labor and peasant organizations a prominent place in the party, but in the longer term its corporatist structure has tended to work against their interests, particularly as Cárdenas himself at the end of his term assisted more moderate elements in gaining control of the revolutionary regime. 69 notes. 1934-70's

Cárdenas Bejarano, José María

1179. Mier, José María de. JOSE MARIA CARDENAS BEJARANO [José María Cardenas Bejarano]. *Boletín de Historia y Antigüedades [Colombia] 1985 72(748): 147-154.* José María Cárdenas Bejarano (1803-38) filled a succession of official positions of mostly secondary importance during his political career in Colombia. Reproduces three documents of appointment from the archive of the Academia Colombiana de Historia. 1820's-38

Cardwell, Edward

1180. Woodall, Robert. EDWARD CARDWELL AT THE WAR OFFICE. *Army Quarterly and Defence Journal [Great Britain] 1986 116(1): 63-69.* Edward Cardwell, 19th-century British war minister, made many far-reaching and necessary army reforms, constructing a military system that lasted, with modifications, until World War II. 1868-72

Cardyn, Joseph

1181. Walckiers, M. A. "Joseph Cardyn jusqu'avant la Fondation de la J.O.C.: Vicaire á Laeken 1912-1918, Directeur des Oeuvres Sociales á Bruxelles 1915-1927" [Joseph Cardyn before the foundation of the Christian Worker Youth (JOC): curate at Laeken, 1912-18, and director of social work at Brussels, 1915-27]. Catholic U. of Louvain [Belgium] 1981.465 pp. *DAI-C 1983 44(1):60; 8/314c.* 1912-27

Čarek, Jiří

1182. Holec, František. ŽIVOTNÍ JUBILEUM PHDR. JIŘÍHO ČARKA [75th birthday of Dr. Jiří Čarek]. *Archivní Časopis [Czechoslovakia] 1983 33(4): 227-230.* Jiří Čarek (b. 1908) became a disciple of V. Vojtíšek (1883-1977) and an archivist of the city of Prague. His early interest was in sphragistics, on which he started publishing while still a student. A major work was on the seals of the Přemyslide princes and kings. The Prague archives owe much to him: he was instrumental in saving valuable holdings during World War II, he introduced major organizational changes, and he fought hard, though in vain, to win new premises for the archives. Much of his work has been on the history of Prague, and his surviving excerpts from old records are invaluable, thanks to the loss by fire of many originals. He produced an early guide to the city and has written extensively on many aspects of its history and on collections in the Archive, and on the arms of Czech towns. Biobibliography mentioning Čarek's main works in chronology. 1908-77

Carême, Antonin

1183. Gilles-Mouton, Colette. ANTONIN CAREME, LE PATISSIER-ARCHITECTE [Antonin Carême: the pastry cook-architect]. *Histoire [France] 1984 (70): 89-91.* Relates the career of pastry chef and writer of culinary art works, Antonin Carême (1784-1833). ca 1820

Caritat, Marie-Jean

1184. Williams, David. BIOGRAPHY AND THE PHILOSOPHIC MISSION: CONDORCET'S *VIE DE VOLTAIRE. Eighteenth-Century Studies 1985 18(4): 494-502.* More a revolutionary manifesto than a biography, the Marquis de Condorcet's (1743-94) *Vie* made Voltaire (1694-1778) into a symbol of Enlightenment idealism and prepared the way for his secular canonization during the French Revolution. 11 notes. 1774-95

Carlile, Richard

1185. Belchem, John. THE SHOWMAN OF FREETHOUGHT. *Bulletin of the Society for the Study of Labour History [Great Britain] 1984 (48): 76-77.* Reviews Joel H. Wiener's ***Radicalism and Freethought in Nineteenth-Century Britain: The Life of Richard Carlile*** (1983), a standard biography of Carlile, who, according to the reviewer, was "quite the most challenging figure in early 19th-century radicalism." 19c

Carlisle, William

1186. Rae, Donald A. WILLIAM CARLISLE AND CHARLES GORDON. *Hist. J. [New Zealand] 1982 (41): 29-31.* Describes the missionary work of brothers-in-law William Carlisle, a teacher who arrived in New Zealand in 1816, and Charles Gordon, an agriculturalist, who arrived in 1817; both were members of the Church Missionary Society until around 1820. 1816-20

Carlos I

1187. Macedo, Roberto. O REI QUE NÃO VEIO [The king who did not come]. *Revista do Instituto Histórico e Geográfico Brasileiro [Brazil] 1982 (337): 193-195.* Carlos I (1863-1908), the penultimate king of Portugal, whose immediate predecessors had transferred their court to Rio de Janeiro, was preparing a visit to Brazil when he was assassinated by political enemies in 1908. This is a tribute to his memory. Reprinted from *Correio do Ribatejo,* Santarém, Portugal, 19 May 1973. 1863-1908

Carlotti, François

1188. Carlotti, François; Darnton, Robert, introd. *IN MEMORIAM:* A FRENCHMAN'S RECOLLECTIONS OF THE GREAT WAR (French text). *French Historical Studies 1984 13(4): 557-569.* In memoirs written in his sixties, a Frenchman recalls his childhood impressions of World War I, which began when he was seven. From the loss of a favorite horse confiscated by the army, through ministrations to wounded troops, to the reading of local casualty lists, he describes the national trauma created by the bloody conflict. 1913-18

Carlyle, Thomas

1189. DeBruyn, John R. THOMAS CARLYLE AND SIR ARTHUR HELPS: II. *Bull. of the John Rylands U. Lib. of Manchester [Great Britain] 1982 64(2): 407-432.* 1855-75

For abstract see ***Helps, Arthur***

1190. Seigel, Jules. CARLYLE AND PEEL: THE PROPHET'S SEARCH FOR A HEROIC POLITICIAN AND AN UNPUBLISHED FRAGMENT. *Victorian Studies 1983 26(2): 181-195.* During the 1840's Thomas Carlyle, usually full of contempt for contemporary political figures, developed a deep appreciation and respect for Sir Robert Peel. Peel's Irish policy, paternalism, industriousness, vision of empire, and self-reliance all attracted Carlyle's admiration. Includes an unpublished fragment from a book about Peel that Carlyle worked on . Based on Carlyle manuscripts in the collection in the National Library of Scotland, Carlyle's works, and other primary sources; 18 notes. 1848-50

Carmona, Elia

1191. Loewenthal, Robyn Kay. "Elia Carmona's Autobiography: Judeo-Spanish Popular Press and Novel Publishing Milieu in Constantinople, Ottoman Empire, circa 1860-1932." (Vol. 1-2) U. of Nebraska, Lincoln 1984. 644 pp. *DAI 1985 45(12): 3654-A.* DA8503434 1860-1932

Carne family

1192. Jenkins, Philip. OLD AND NEW CATHOLICS IN STUART WALES: THE CARNE FAMILY OF GLAMORGAN. *Recusant History [Great Britain] 1985 17(4): 362-373.* The history of the Carne family suggests that it was possible for a major landed family to remain as crypto-Catholics from 1650 to 1710 without official sanctions. 1650-1710

Carneiro, Ernesto Pereira

1193. Sousa, Luís de Castro. O CONDE PEREIRA CARNEIRO E A PREVIDÊNCIA SOCIAL NO BRASIL [Count Pereira Carneiro and social security in Brazil]. *Rev. do Inst. Hist. e Geog. Brasileiro [Brazil] 1979 (322): 268-273.* Ernesto Pereira Carneiro (1877-1954) was a businessman active in public welfare. Besides contributing to the foundation of maternity hospitals and sports clubs, he was a pioneer in workers' housing projects and founded the workers' town of Niteroi. Speech delivered at the Federation of Brazilian Academies of Letters on the centenary of Carneiro's birth, June 1977. ca 1900-54

Carnelley, Thomas

1194. Makarenia, A. A. and Kapustinskaia, K. A. O NAUCHNYKH SVIAZIAKH D. I. MENDELEYEVA I T. KARNELLI [The scientific contacts between D. I. Mendeleev and T. Carnelley]. *Voprosy Istorii Estestvoznaniia i Tekhniki [USSR] 1981 (2): 135-137.* 1875-90

For abstract see ***Mendeleev, Dmitri I.***

Carnero Checa, Genaro

1195. Luna Vegas, Ricardo. GENARO CARNERO CHECA: GRAN PERIODISTA, DISCIPULO DE MARIATEGUI [Genaro Carnero Checa, great journalist, disciple of Mariátegui]. *Casa de las Américas [Cuba] 1981 22(128): 104-107.* The Peruvian journalist Carnero Checa (1910-80) was a creative and revolutionary fighter in the struggles of his people and his time. 1935-80

Carnot, Lazare

1196. Giessmann, Ernst-Joachim. LAZARE CARNOT UND DIE PREUSSISCHEN MILITÄRREFORMER [Lazare Carnot and the Prussian military reformers]. *Militärgeschichte [East Germany] 1986 25(4): 310-319.* Sketches the activity of Carnot (1753-1823) in the French Revolutionary and Napoleonic period and his move to Magdeburg in 1816 and discusses the influence of his activities and writings on the Prussian army leadership in relation especially to schools and training and fortification. 3 illus., sketch, 61 notes. 1753-1823

Caroe, Olaf

1197. Chowdharay-Best, George. SIR OLAF CAROE (1892-1981): PART II. *Central Asian Survey [Great Britain] 1982-83 1(2-3): 91-102.* Continued from a previous article. Olaf Caroe, whose last post was governor of Peshawar before the India-Pakistan partition, was considered a fair and able administrator, but his removal became necessary to quell unrest that was instigated by political slander. After returning to England, he pursued a new career as an author and historian on Asian topics and contributed to many journals. 1946-81

1198. AChowdharay-Best, George. SIR OLAF CAROE (1892-1981). Part 1. *Central Asian Survey [Great Britain] 1982 1(1): 93-104.* This is a tribute to one of the most influential writers on Central Asia during the past century and a survey of his career as an army and political officer in India up to his appointment as governor of the North-West Frontier province, 1914-40's. Article is to be continued with a description of his activities as governor and after retirement. 10 notes. 1914-40's

Carpenter, Mary

1199. Selleck, R. J. W. MARY CARPENTER: A CONFIDENT AND CONTRADICTORY REFORMER. *History of Education [Great Britain] 1985 14(2): 101-115.* Discusses Mary Carpenter's work for the care of destitute, impoverished, and criminal children. She lobbied to establish three kinds of schools to substitute for prison terms: "ragged" schools for the poor, industrial schools for the borderline criminal, and reformatories for delinquents. Her great religious zeal was matched with a radicalism comparable to that of Friedrich Engels. 76 notes. 1820-60

Carpentier, Alejo

1200. Cairo, Ana. CARPENTIER, UN ENEMIGO DEL FASCISMO [Carpentier: enemy of fascism]. *Revista de la Biblioteca Nacional José Martí [Cuba] 1984 26(1): 119-139.* Alejo Carpentier (1904-80), Cuba's most famous novelist, spent considerable time in his writings attacking fascism. Much of Carpentier's works on this subject appeared in various Latin American newspapers when the Cuban worked as a journalist in Europe. Nevertheless, Carpentier's principal novels also touched upon the topic of fascism. 24 notes. 1904-80

1201. Fernández Retamar, Roberto. POLITICA Y LATINOAMERICANISMO EN ALEJO CARPENTIER [Politics and Latin Americanism in Alejo Carpentier]. *Casa de las Américas [Cuba] 1985 (149): 78-86.* Against charges of a French or European outlook on Latin American affairs in the work of Cuban writer Alejo Carpentier (1904-80) attempts to show the consistency between his life and literary production and the manner in which his political ideas and Latin Americanism were intimately linked in his artistic career. Carpentier was a revolutionary in politics from his adolescence, and he celebrated, without narrow exclusivism, the magic and marvel of the Latin American world. 1930's-70's

1202. García-Carranza, Araceli. DE LA COLECCION ALEJO CARPENTIER VALMONT: UN INMENSO Y CRECIENTE DONATIVO [Concerning the Alejo Carpentier collection: an immense and growing gift]. *Revista de la Biblioteca Nacional José Martí [Cuba] 1983[i.e., 1984] 26(2): 37-39.* Alejo Carpentier, Cuba's most famous writer in the 20th century, donated all his notes, manuscripts, and other memorabilia to the José Martí National Library in 1973. In the remaining years of his life, he continued to add to this collection, making it indispensable for any serious study of his life and literary activities. 1930's-83

1203. García-Carranza, Araceli. VIDA Y OBRA DE ALEJO CARPENTIER [The life and works of Alejo Carpentier]. *U. de La Habana [Cuba] 1981 (214): 152-169.* Presents a detailed chronology of the life and works of Alejo Carpentier. 1904-80

1204. Müller-Bergh, Klaus. CONVERSANDO CON CARPENTIER: PARIS 1974 [Conversation with Carpentier, Paris 1974]. *Casa de las Américas [Cuba] 1982 22(131): 117-122.* Presents a 1974 interview with writer Alejo Carpentier (1904-80), then Cuban ambassador in Paris. Carpentier talked about the genesis of some of his novels, the material that went into their creation, and their reception in various countries, including the problems of their translation. Note. 1960's-70's

Carr, E. H.

1205. Davies, R. W. EDWARD HALLETT CARR, 1892-1982. *Proceedings of the British Academy [Great Britain] 1983 69: 473-511.* The historian and political theorist, Edward Hallett Carr (1892-1982) was born in London and educated at Trinity College, Cambridge. Embarking upon a career in the Foreign Service, he worked in Russia and from 1930 to 1933 was Advisor on League of Nations Affairs. From 1936 to 1947 he was Woodrow Wilson Professor of International Politics at the University of Wales, Aberystwyth, and from 1955 onward Fellow of Trinity College, Cambridge. His most important work is the *History of Soviet Russia,* a project which he began in 1944. 1910's-82

1206. Deutscher, Tamara. E. H. CARR—A PERSONAL MEMOIR. *New Left Rev. [Great Britain] 1983 (137): 78-86.* Recounts the life and achievements of British historian E. H. Carr, whose *History of Soviet Russia* influenced the international study of the USSR; discusses problems in writing, critical and professional reaction to Carr, and the author's collaboration with Carr. 1920's-82

1207. Haslam, Jonathan. E. H. CARR AND THE HISTORY OF SOVIET RUSSIA. *Hist. J. [Great Britain] 1983 26(4): 1021-1027.* Outlines the life and work of British historian of the USSR E. H. Carr, and reviews his three last books: *The Russian Revolution from Lenin to Stalin 1917-1929* (1979), *From Napoleon to Stalin and Other Essays* (1980), and *The Twilight of Comintern 1930-35* (1982). 1917-82

1208. Palla, Marco. LA VIA ALLA STORIA DI EDWARD HALLETT CARR [Edward Hallett Carr's road to history]. *Passato e Presente [Italy] 1982 (1): 115-144.* Calls attention to aspects of the intellectual career of a historian, noted chiefly for his contributions to Soviet history. Discusses his experience and preparation at the British Foreign Office, his interest in and study of 19th-century Russian figures, his criticism of Karl Marx, and contribution to the scientific study of international affairs. 62 notes. 1916-81

Carracci, Lodovico

1209. Feigenbaum, Gail. "Lodovico Carracci: A Study of His Later Career and a Catalogue of His Paintings." Princeton U. 1984. 712 pp. *DAI 1984 45(1): 1-2-A.* DA8409122 1605-19

Carranza, Bartolomé

1210. Huerga, Alvaro. LA MUERTE DE CARRANZA [The death of Carranza]. *Cuadernos de Investigación Hist. [Spain] 1981 5: 15-27.* The letters of Bartolomé Galli (b. 1526), Cardinal of Comis and Secretary of State of Gregory XIII, cast light on the death of Bartolomé Carranza, archbishop of Toledo (1557-76). Carranza was seized by the Spanish Inquisition in 1559 on charges of heresy and was removed to Rome. Galli's account of Carranza's death indicates that he died of an inflammation of the prostate gland occurring during a pilgrimage ordered as a penance by the pope. The archbishop died completely reconciled to the Church and the pope. Contains an appendix of five of Galli's letters, dated April 1576 to January 1577. Utilizes material from the Archivo Secretto Vaticano; 45 notes, appendix. 1559-77

Carrera, Rafael

1211. Woodward, Ralph Lee, Jr. LA POLITICA CENTROAMERICANA DE UN CAUDILLO CONSERVADOR RAFAEL CARRERA, 1840-1865 [The Central American policy of conservative caudillo Rafael Carrera, 1840-65]. *Anuario de Estudios Centroamericanos [Costa Rica] 1983 9: 55-68.* The focus on the Rafael Carrera administration of Guatemala is on his foreign policy in Central America, where he set up friendly conservative regimes. Also noted are his efforts in ending William Walker's presence in Nicaragua and his relations with England over the Belize question. Although personal opportunism played a role in Carrera's behavior, his main intent was ideological; namely, the furtherance of nationalism and autonomy in the individual states—a legacy that still survives today. Based on Guatemalan government archives, the Taracena Flores Collection at the University of Texas, published government reports, newspapers, broadsides, contemporary historians, and secondary sources; 99 notes. 1840-65

Carrillo, Alfonso

1212. Meseguer Fernández, Juan. EL ARZOBISPO CARRILLO Y EL CARDENAL CISNEROS [Archbishop Carrillo and Cardinal Cisneros]. *Archivo Ibero-Americano [Spain] 1985 45(177-178): 167-187.* Discusses the careers and personalities of Archbishop Alfonso Carrillo (1412-82) and Cardinal Gonzalo Jiménez de Cisneros (1436-1517). These two great Spanish prelates clashed in the 1470's over who should occupy the office of archpriest of Uceda. Some historical accounts state that Archbishop Carrillo imprisoned the young Cisneros for several years because of this conflict, but it is more likely that the incarceration lasted only a matter of days. A politician and a warrior, Carrillo sometimes relegated his pastoral responsibilities to a secondary plane. Cisneros, on the other hand, achieved a better balance between his spiritual duties and his secular agendas. Accordingly, Cisneros has received fuller and more favorable treatment from students of Spanish political and religious history. Based on archival sources and secondary works; 34 notes. 1470's

Carro, Jean de

1213. Šubrtová, Alena. JEAN DE CARRO (1770-1857)—PŘÍSPĚVEK K BIOGRAFII [Jean de Carro (1770-1857): a biographical note]. *Časopis Národního Muzea [Czechoslovakia] 1980 149(1-2): 45-61.* Evaluates newly found letters of Jean de Carro, a distinguished Swiss surgeon and "discoverer" of the Carlsbad spa, who supported the Czech National Museum. 18c-19c

Carroll, Lewis

1214. Kolbe, Martha Emily. "Three Oxford Dons as Creators of other Worlds for Children: Lewis Carroll, C. S. Lewis, and J. R. Tolkien." U. of Virginia 1981. 285 pp. *DAI 1982 43(5): 1532-A.* DA8219062 1865-1950's

Cartwright, Thomas

1215. Beddard, R. A. BISHOP CARTWRIGHT'S DEATH-BED. *Bodleian Library Record [Great Britain] 1984 11(4): 220-230.* Thomas Cartwright, Dean of Ripon, was an ultra-Tory cleric whose support of the king's prerogative dismayed even the leaders of the Cavalier wing of the church of Charles II. James III made him Bishop of Chester, in which post Cartwright fully complied with the king's attempt to provide toleration for Roman Catholics. He followed James into exile, dying in Ireland in 1689. Rumors quickly spread that he had apostatized and become a Catholic, but a letter from an Anglican priest at his deathbed proves that he remained committed to the Church of England to the last. Based on a manuscript in Bodleian Library, Oxford University; 70 notes. 1676-89

Carulli, Ferdinando

1216. Long, Richard M. FERDINANDO CARULLI, THE CLASSICAL GUITAR, AND THE AGE OF REVOLUTION. *Consortium on Revolutionary Europe 1750-1850: Proceedings 1985 15: 179-198.* The classical guitar was a popular instrument in 18th-century France, made fashionable by Louis XIV and others. Despite this popularity, very little music of high quality existed for the instrument. Ferdinando Carulli (1770-1841) was an Italian who wrote over 500 works for the guitar during his life in France. He was a pioneer in the writing of program music, which consisted of a written narrative to which the music conformed. His music tended to extol the militaristic values of the neoclassical period. Secondary sources; 27 notes. 18c

Carus-Wilson, Eleanora

1217. Chibnall, Marjorie. ELEANORA MARY CARUS-WILSON, 1897-1977. *Pro. of the British Acad. [Great Britain] 1982 68: 503-520.* A tribute to Professor Eleanora Carus-Wilson (1897-1977), recounting her life and work. By the time she entered full-time academic life at the London School of Economics, following war service at the Ministry of Food, she had already worked and published extensively on late 15th-century economic history, particularly the trade and merchants of London and Bristol. Thereafter she worked extensively on medieval trade and the cloth industry and was a member of numerous committees, including the Council of the Economic History Society, and she persuaded the British Academy to revive the series of *Records of Social and Economic History,* for which her work as editor was exemplary. She was a pioneer in the tradition of economic history laid down by M. Postan, Eileen Power, and R. H. Tawney, and embodied the same Christian socialism as Tawney. Based on Carus-Wilson's published works and unpublished diaries and personal recollections by family and friends; 8 notes. 1897-1977

Carvalho, Carlos Delgado de

1218. Menezes, Euripedes Cardoso de. CARLOS DELGADO DE CARVALHO [Carlos Delgado de Carvalho]. *Rev. do Inst. Hist. e Geog. Brasileiro [Brazil] 1980 (329): 105-118.* Carlos Delgado de Carvalho (1884-1980) was born at the Brazilian legation in Paris and educated in England and Switzerland. Having fought in the French army during World War I, he lost his Brazilian citizenship, which he later recovered. He was an ardent patriot and historian and a professor of geography, sociology, and history. He was the author of many works on these subjects and an innovator in the teaching of Brazilian geography. Lecture delivered on the occasion of death in 1980. 1900's-80

Casares, María

1219. Rodrigo, Antonina. MARIA CASARES, ACTRIZ UNIVERSAL [María Casares: universal actress]. *Hist. y Vida [Spain] 1983 16(180): 106-115.* María Casares, a widely acclaimed dramatic actress, lived and worked most of her life in exile and returned to her native Spain only after Franco's death. 1922-77

Casasola, Agustín Victor

1220. Carty, Winthrop P. ICONS OF THE MEXICAN REVOLUTION. *Américas (Organization of American States) 1985 37(4): 2-9.* Provides a biography of pioneering press photographer Agustín Victor Casasola, who took photographs of the 1910-20 Mexican Revolution; includes some of his famous pictures. 1910-20's

Casement, Roger

1221. Edwards, Owen Dudley. DIVIDED TREASONS AND DIVIDED LOYALTIES: ROGER CASEMENT AND OTHERS. *Tr. of the Royal Hist. Soc. [Great Britain] 1982 32: 153-174.* Compares the trial of Arthur Lynch in 1903 with that of Roger Casement in 1916 and examines the latter case in detail to explore the ambivalent attitudes to the crime of treason where it involved Ireland and Irish defendants. Casement "did not have a fair trial, and its unfairness was inimical in the extreme to the high Irish expectations of British justice." Although the verdict was just, since Casement was indeed guilty of giving aid and comfort to the enemy, "the justice in the Casement case was, from the standpoint of British interests, tragic." 24 notes. 1903

Casey, Joseph-Gregoire

1222. Ireland, John de Courcy. MACKAU AND CASEY: TWO FRANCO-IRISH MINISTERS OF MARINE AND THE FRENCH NAVAL REVIVAL AFTER 1815. *Mariner's Mirror [Great Britain] 1982 68(2): 127-131.* The promotion, after the battle of Trafalgar, of junior officers of ability provided the French navy with senior officers of distinction by the mid-19th century. Sketches the careers of Armand de Mackau (1788-1855) and Joseph-Gregoire Casey (1787-1863), two mid-century ministers of the navy. Both had earlier served at sea with distinction during and after the Napoleonic regime. They were noted for efficiency and innovation and were involved in the introduction of steam warships to the French navy. Based on sources in the Archives Nationales and the archives of the French navy. 1815-65

Càsoli, Pier Biagio

1223. Berselli, Aldo. P. B. CASOLI, L'OPERA DEI CONGRESSI E LA DEMOCRAZIA CRISTIANA [P. B. Càsoli, the Opera dei Congressi, and Christian Democracy]. *Civitas [Italy] 1983 34(2): 79-94.* Chronicles the political activities of Pier Biagio Càsoli, a priest, who championed the causes of Catholic liberalism in Italy and provided support for the papacy in disputes over the prerogatives of church and state. 1871-1904

Cassin, René

1224. Agi, Marc. RENÉ CASSIN: LA PAIX PAR LES DROITS DE L'HOMME [René Cassin: peace and human rights]. *Int. Problems [Israel] 1981 20(1): 14-20.* Treats the theories of René Cassin, winner of the Nobel prize for peace (1968) and his influence on basic human rights precepts. 1914-69

Castaldi, Cornelio

1225. Mantovani, Gilda. ANCORA PER LA BIOGRAFIA DI CORNELIO CASTALDI: IL CONTRATTO DOTALE E QUALCHE "BRICIOLA" D'ARCHIVIO [More material for the biography of Cornelio Castaldi: the dowry contract and some "crumbs" from archives]. *Quaderni per la Storia dell'U. di Padova [Italy] 1981 14: 93-95.* The prenuptial contract of the jurist and poet Castaldi reveals the source of the 600 ducats he bequeathed to his wife: they had been her dowry at the time of their marriage. 1503

Castelão, Alfonso Rodríguez

1226. Rodríguez, Luis M. DIBUJOS DE CASTELAO [Sketches by Castelão]. *Islas [Cuba] 1981 (68): 47-70.* Alfonso Rodríguez Castelão (1884-1950) was a writer, painter, and politician born in Riajo, La Coruña, Spain. Twenty of his sketches of the Spanish Civil War, reminiscent of Goya's *Disasters of War,* are presented here with an introduction. 1910's-50

Castellina, Luciana

1227. Castellina, Luciana; Blackburn, Robin and Hoare, Quintin, interviewers. IL MANIFESTO AND ITALIAN COMMUNISM: AN INTERVIEW WITH LUCIANA CASTELLINA. *New Left Review [Great Britain] 1985 (151): 26-42.* Luciana Castellina, former member of the Italian parliament and the Communist Party, talks about his role in publishing *Il Manifesto,* a political magazine that prompted a socialist movement in 1970. 1964-82

Castello Branco, Humberto de Alencar

1228. Ciria, Alberto. THE INDIVIDUAL IN HISTORY: FIVE LATIN AMERICAN BIOGRAPHIES. *Latin American Research Review 1985 20(3): 247-267.* ca 1920-70
*For abstract see **Sandino, Augusto César***

Castelvetro, Giacomo

1229. Migliorato, Giuseppe. VICENDE E INFLUSSI CULTURALI DI GIACOMO CASTELVETRO (1546-1616) IN DANIMARCA [Fortunes and cultural influences of Giacomo Castelvetro (1546-1616) in Denmark]. *Critica Storica [Italy] 1982 19(2): 243-296.* Castelvetro was the nephew of the noted philologist Lodovico Castelvetri of Modena. In a period of intense religious and political activity he acted as a courtier attached to no orthodoxy, friend of Catholics and Protestants, interested in esoteric lore but also in philology and the natural sciences. A manuscript written by him and discovered in the Royal Library of Copenhagen has occasioned this inquiry into his career in Denmark, 1594-95. Based on primary material in various Italian and Scandinavian archives; 177 notes, 4 documents in appendix. 1594-95

Castilhos, Julio de

1230. Cachapuz de Medeiros, Antônio Paulo. PROJEÇÕES DO CASTILHISMO NA POLITICA AUTORITARIA BRASILEIRA [Influence of Julio de Castilhos's ideas on Brazilian authoritarian politics]. *Veritas [Brazil] 1981 26(104): 469-492.* Julio de Castilhos (1860-1903) was a journalist and politician and an early member of the republican movement in Rio Grande do Sul. His authoritarian character and wide personal power made him a very influential figure. His positivism influenced the development of authoritarian ideas among politicians and the military. This influence spread to the whole country, especially through Getulio Vargas, the revolution of 1930, and the Estado Novo of 1937-1945, and affecting the governments that came to power after the 1964 revolution. 33 notes. 19c-20c

Castilla, Luis de

1231. Andrés, Gregorio de. EL ARCEDIANO DE CUENCA D. LUIS DE CASTILLA (D. 1618) PROTECTOR DEL GRECO Y SU BIBLIOTECA MANUSCRITA [Luis de Castilla (d. 1618), archdeacon of Cuenca, protector of El Greco, and his manuscript library]. *Hispania Sacra [Spain] 1983 35(71): 87-141.* The discovery of the inventory of manuscripts belonging to the archdeacon at the time of his death, which is here reproduced together with his genealogy and testament, was the occasion of a search for documents concerning his eventful career. Don Luis was a descendant, by an illegitimate line, of King Pedro I of Castille and was entrusted with important missions during the reign of Philip II. His influential family was the supporter of the painter El Greco. Based on material in various Spanish archives; 115 notes. ca 1540-1618

Castilla Corbalán y Espino de Brito, Francisco de

1232. Fernández, David W. FRANCISCO DE CASTILLA CORBALAN Y ESPINO DE BRITO [Francisco de Castilla Corbalán y Espino de Brito]. *Bol. de la Acad. Nac. de la Hist. [Venezuela] 1982 65(260): 1009-1011.* Don Francisco de Castilla Corbalán y Espino de Brito, born in the Canary Islands, related to the royal family of Castille, was governor and captain general of Cumaná and Nueva Barcelona from 1653 to 1654 but not much is known of his activity in colonial government. Biblio. 1653-54

Castiñeiras, Pedro

1233. —. PEDRO CASTIÑEIRAS NOS HA DEJADO [Pedro Castiñeiras has left us]. *Rev. General de Marina [Spain] 1981 201(Sept): 207-209.* Notes the death of Lieutenant Commander Pedro Castiñeiras, Spanish Navy. He had served as secretary of the *Revista,* head of the Historical Service of the Spanish Navy, writer on naval history, and researcher with the Institute of Naval History and Culture. Photo. 1950's-81

Castro, Abraham

1234. Cohen, Amnon. HA-UMNAM NIVNU HOMOT YERUSHALAYIM AL YEDE AVRAHAM CASTRO? [Were the walls of Jerusalem built by Abraham Castro?]. *Zion [Israel] 1982 47(4): 407-418.* The person responsible for the construction of the city walls of Jerusalem ca. 1536-39 was an Ottoman official, Mohammed Zalbi al- Naqash, and not Abraham Castro, as claimed by Yosef Sambari. Castro was in Jerusalem, was deeply involved in the city's affairs, and was respected by government officials. He functioned temporarily as a tax collector for the sultan and may have converted to Islam toward the end of his life. Other Jews also served in senior administrative positions in 16th-century Jerusalem. Some possessed capital and real estate and were involved in the city's development. Based on documents in the archives of the Shari'a Court of Jerusalem; 20 notes, appendix. 1520-66

1235. Shochetman, Eliav. OD LIDMUTO ULEKOROTAV SHEL R. AVRAHAM KASTRO [Additional information on the life of Abraham Castro]. *Zion [Israel] 1983 48(4): 387-405.* Manuscript and printed sources on Rabbi Abraham Castro, one of the leading figures of Egyptian Jewry in the 16th century, attest to his preoccupation with studies of the Cabala and to his contacts with various sages on matters of Cabala and halakha. New documents demonstrate that Rabbi Jacob Castro was Abraham's son and cast doubt on the theory that Abraham Castro converted to Islam. A genizah document relating to the financial activity of Jacob Castro is published as an appendix. Based on manuscript and other sources; 70 notes, appendix. English summary. 1504-88

Castro, Fidel

1236. Mencía, Mario. FIDEL CASTRO EN EL "BOGOTAZO" (ABRIL 1948) [Fidel Castro in the Bogotazo (April 1948)]. *Bol. de Hist. y Antigüedades [Colombia] 1982 69 (736): 167-206.* Fidel Castro came to Bogotá in 1948, as a Cuban student leader already firmly committed to the anti-imperialist cause, in order to participate in a Latin American student conference held concurrently with the Ninth International Conference of American States. He had already attracted favorable attention from student delegates and had met the Colombian Liberal leader Jorge Eliécer Gaitán, whose assassination while the conference was in session sparked the outburst of urban rioting, known as the Bogotazo. Castro participated and observed the momentary success but eventual suppression of the uprising, enhancing his understanding of revolutionary strategy and tactics. Based on reminiscences of participants. 1948

1237. Robinson, Jean C. INSTITUTIONALIZING CHARISMA: LEADERSHIP, FAITH & RATIONALITY IN THREE SOCIETIES. *Polity 1985 43(2): 181-203.* Examines the ways in which the charismatic leaders Mao Zedong, Muammar Qadhafi, and Fidel Castro have handled the task of institutionalizing their leadership so that it could survive them. 1950's-76

1238. Welch, Richard E., Jr. HERBERT L. MATTHEWS AND THE CUBAN REVOLUTION. *Historian 1984 47(1): 1-18.* Herbert L. Matthews's advocacy of the Cuban revolution through the pages of the *New York Times* helped prepare its readers for the fall of Batista, while the criticism he inspired illustrated the evolving response of the American press to Castro and his revolution. Traces Matthews's initial contacts with Castro, his first interview in 1957, his writings in the *Times,* and the attacks on his opinions. The controversy Matthews generated and the manner in which that controversy evolved reflected the changing response of the American press and public to the Cuban revolution in the years 1958-62. 52 notes. 1957-62

Castro, Josuè de

1239. DiTaranto, Giuseppe. SOCIETÀ E SOTTOSVILUPPO NELL'OPERA DI JOSUÈ DE CASTRO [Society and underdevelopment in the work of Josuè de Castro]. *Cahiers Int. d'Hist. Écon. et Sociale [Italy] 1980 (12): 1-110.* Studies the life and works of the Brazilian economist and sociologist, Josuè de Castro (b. 1908). While developing a systematic doctrine, de Castro brought to the attention of the entire world the economically underdeveloped status of two-thirds of humanity in the period following World War II. He attributed this condition to the value put on maximizing economic returns regardless of the needs of indigenous populations in the underdeveloped countries. While de Castro shared some theories with neo-Marxist interpretive models, his views most closely reflected those of the UN's Economic Commission for Latin America. Based on primary sources; 2 tables, 112 notes, 2 bibliographies, appendix. 1945-80

Catena, Pietro

1240. Veronese Ceseracciu, Emilia. DOCUMENTI PER LA BIOGRAFIA DI PIETRO CATENA [Documents for the biography of Pietro Catena]. *Quaderni per la Storia dell'U. di Padova [Italy] 1982 15: 113-120.* Pietro Catena was professor of mathematics in Padua, 1547-76, and a singular personality, as well as one of the precursors of the modern scientific method. 1547-76

Catherine de Bourbon

1241. Tucoo-Chala, Pierre. CATHERINE DE BOURBON ET LES PAYS DE L'ADOUR [Catherine de Bourbon and the Adour country]. *Revue de Pau et du Béarn [France] 1984-85 12: 9-17.* Reviews volume one of *Catherine de Bourbon. La Soeur d'Henri IV* (1984), a biographical work begun in 1918 by Raymond Ritter that includes a rich description of religious controversy in the Adour valley of southwestern France, 1559-92. 1559-92

Catherine II

1242. Luján, Néstor. CATALINA DE RUSIA, QUE MURIO RIENDO [Catherine of Russia, who died laughing]. *Hist. y Vida [Spain] 1983 16(178): 104-113.* Catherine II of Russia, a patron of the arts with a strong personality and a somewhat scandalous reputation, according to legend died laughing. 1729-96

Cattaneo, Carlo

1243. Armani, Giuseppe. MAURO MACCHI NELL'EPISTOLARIO DI CARLO CATTANEO [Mauro Macchi in the letters of Carlo Cattaneo]. *Bol. della Domus Mazziniana [Italy] 1981 27(1): 175-188.* 1850-69
*For abstract see **Macchi, Mauro***

1244. Corona, Maria Corrias. CATTANEO E ASPRONI: L'INCONTRO DI DUE DEMOCRATICI [Cattaneo and Asproni: the meeting of two democrats]. *Politico [Italy] 1982 47(2): 387-402.* 1860-67
*For abstract see **Asproni, Giorgio***

Caudwell, Christopher

1245. Starr, William Frederic. "Christopher Caudwell." Columbia U. 1982. 204 pp. *DAI 1985 46(1): 280-A.* DA8506045 1930's

Caulk, Richard

1246. —. RICHARD ALAN CAULK 1936-1983. *Northeast African Studies 1983 5(2): 1-4.* The American Ethiopianist Richard Caulk made a number of significant contributions to Ethiopian historical studies before his death in September 1983. While teaching at Haile Selassie I University in Addis Ababa between 1966 and 1977, he introduced a number of Ethiopian students to critical methods of historical research. Caulk himself published over a dozen significant articles on modern Ethiopian history and left behind an important manuscript on the foreign policy of Menelik II. Based on personal knowledge and Caulk's publications; biblio. 1936-83

Causer, Tom

1247. Shipley, Stan. TOM CAUSER OF BERMONDSEY: A BOXER HERO OF THE 1890S. *Hist. Workshop J. [Great Britain] 1983 (15): 28-59.* Explores the transmission of working-class values through the career of Tom Causer. Although a British lightweight champion and later a prosperous saloon owner, Causer remained entrenched in his working-class neighborhood. Through the example of such local heroes, many proletarian boys were drawn to boxing, as both participants and spectators. But despite the professionalization of boxing during this time, the boxer-hero sought to shine within his own working-class community, not to escape it. The socially mobile golden boy is not so much a sporting phenomenon as a reflection of the decline of community in the face of consumerism. Based on interviews, newspapers, and the sporting press; 79 notes, 2 appendixes. 1890-1918

Cauwelaert, Frans Van

1248. DeSchryver, Reginald. KONING ALBERT EN FRANS VAN CAUWELAERT: EEN BRIEFWISSELING RONDOM DE VORMING VAN DE REGERING-BROQUEVILLE, DECEMBER 1932 [King Albert and Frans Van Cauwelaert: a correspondence on the formation of the Broqueville government, December 1932]. *Bulletin de la Commission Royale Histoire [Belgium] 1984 150: 475-487.* Publishes four letters containing King Albert of Belgium's invitation to Frans Van Cauwelaert to join the newly formed cabinet of Charles de Broqueville in 1932 as minister of industry and labor and Van Cauwelaert's refusal. An introduction discusses the 1932 parliamentary and municipal elections and their effects on the career of Van Cauwelaert, the leader of Antwerp's Catholics. Ousted as mayor of Antwerp by the Socialists, Van Cauwelaert remained the leader of the Catholic opposition, particularly on the issue of equality in Catholic and public education. He refused to join a cabinet in which he would be placed under the authority of the Liberal Party's minister of public education. Based on the correspondence in the Antwerp Archives for Flemish Culture; 15 notes. 1932

Cavalier, Jean

1249. Poujol, Jacques. JEAN CAVALIER [Jean Cavalier]. *Bull. de la Soc. de l'Hist. du Protestantisme Français [France] 1982 128(1): 93-99.* Jean Cavalier was a tainted hero of the Protestant uprising in the Cévennes. From 1701 to 1704 he led Protestant troops against the royal government, then attempted reconciliation with Louis XIV, and later fled abroad and became British governor of Jersey. Many parallels exist between the 18th-century Protestant uprising and the activities of the *maquis* in the same region, 1943-44: the same place names, impatient young leaders rising from obscurity, and divided families. Cavalier's parents abjured Protestantism and collaborated with the Catholic authorities. The elder Cavalier repudiated his son when he persisted in resistance. Based on memoirs; 9 notes. 1701-04

1250. Viallaneix, Paul. JEAN CAVALIER DE L'APOCALYPSE [Jean Cavalier of the Apocalypse]. *Bull. de la Soc. de l'Hist. du Protestantisme Français [France] 1982 128(1): 87-92.* Jean Cavalier was a Camisard leader whose reputation has been clouded by the fact that he negotiated a truce with Marshal de Villars and submitted a letter of submission to Louis XIV in 1704. Other leaders, such as Rolland, fought to the death. Cavalier went into exile, took service under the English government, and eventually became the governor of Jersey. Actually he did not betray his cause. His hope of obtaining immediate toleration for Protestants proved futile, but so did continued warfare. By choosing a more peaceful approach he acted according to Scripture, and the French government did become tolerant in the latter part of the century. Based on Cavalier's memoirs and secondary works; 10 notes. 1704

Cavendish, Margaret

1251. Sarasohn, Lisa T. A SCIENCE TURNED UPSIDE DOWN: FEMINISM AND THE NATURAL PHILOSOPHY OF MARGARET CAVENDISH. *Huntington Library Quarterly 1984 47(4): 289-307.* Margaret Cavendish (1623-1673), second wife of the Duke of Newcastle, expressed her feminism by developing philosophies contrary to the prevailing system. Based on Cavendish's works and other primary sources and secondary sources; 69 notes. 1623-73

Cavour, Conte di

1252. Romano, Sergio. CAVOUR AND THE RISORGIMENTO. *Journal of Modern History 1986 58(3): 669-677.* Reviews Denis Mack Smith's *Cavour* (1985) and Rosario Romeo's *Vita di Cavour* (1985). Both "tell substantially the same 'story'," but "their angles of vision diverge." Romeo explains away the unpleasant aspects of the life and actions of Camillo Benso, Conte di Cavour (1810-61), portraying him as a liberal. Mack Smith recognizes "Cavour's great qualities" but considers that he paid too high a "moral price" for what he achieved. 6 notes. 1810-61

Caxias, Duke of

See Alves de Lima e Silva, Luis

Ceauşescu, Nicolae

1253. Flers, René de. SOCIALISM IN ONE FAMILY. *Survey [Great Britain] 1984 28(4): 165-174.* Discusses nepotism on the part of Romanian president Nicolae Ceauşescu and lists known and suspected Ceauşescu family members and in-laws holding Romanian government positions. The president's wife Elena Ceauşescu rose during the 1970's to become the regime's second most powerful figure; his son, Nicolae Ceauşescu, became Romanian Communist Party Secretary General in 1984. At least four other family members were full members of the Romanian Communist Party's Central Committee in 1984, and another served on the Central Auditing Commission. Other Central Committee members were suspected of Ceauşescu family connections, although some known members were only peripherally involved in politics. Based on newspapers and secondary sources; 24 notes. 1918-84

1254. Ioniţă, Gheorghe I. O EPOCĂ DE MĂREŢE INFĂPTUIRI, LUMINATĂ DE GÎNDIREA ŞI ACŢIUNEA PATRIOTICĂ REVOLUŢIONARĂ A TOVARĂŞULUI NICOLAE CEAUŞESCU [An epoch of great achievements, enlightened by the patriotic, revolutionary thinking and action of Nicolae Ceauşescu]. *Revista de Istorie [Romania] 1985 38(6): 535-543.* The epoch of Nicolae Ceauşescu started in 1965, with the 9th Congress of the Romanian Communist Party, during which N. Ceauşescu was elected secretary general of the Party. Discusses Romania's development during the period 1965-84, as well as N. Ceauşescu's activities and achievements in the economic, social, political, and cultural fields. 7 notes. French summary. 1965-84

1255. Popişteanu, Cristian. NICOLAE CEAUŞESCU: MAN OF PEACE. *Romania [Romania] 1983 8(1): 108-127.* Describes Nicolae Ceauşescu's leadership in Romania since 1965 and efforts on behalf of world peace. 1965-80's

1256. Spălăţelu, Ion. AN EXAMPLE OF PATRIOTISM, REVOLUTIONARY FIGHT AND DEDICATION. *Romania [Romania] 1983 8(1): 6-39.* A life of Nicolae Ceauşescu, Romanian Communist Party chief since 1965. 1933-83

1257. Ştefan, Marin and Buduru, Valeriu. IN ROMANIAN HISTORICAL LAND. *Romania [Romania] 1983 8(1): 73-93.* Nicolae Ceauşescu has regularly toured Romanian historical sites commemorating the Romanian people, their achievements, and their past. 100 BC-20c

1258. Tismaneanu, Vladimir. BYZANTINE RITES, STALINIST FOLLIES: THE TWILIGHT OF DYNASTIC SOCIALISM IN ROMANIA. *Orbis 1986 30(1): 65-90.* Examines the rule of Nicolae Ceauşescu, the general secretary of the Romanian Communist Party and president of Romania from 1965 to the present. Pursuing an unorthodox foreign policy, Ceauşescu was able to obscure his internal repression until the economic situation worsened after 1975. As a result of economic failure, political repression has increased. Based on published sources; 61 notes. 1965-86

1259. —. PREŞEDINTELE NICOLAE CEAUŞESCU—PERSONALITATE PROEMINENTĂ A CONTEMPORANEITĂŢII [President Nicolae Ceauşescu: a prominent personality in the world today]. *Magazin Istoric [Romania] 1982 16(1): 2-4.* A score of worldwide tributes celebrated Ceauşescu's success since 1965 in organizing the well-being of 22 million Romanians, of whose historical antecedents his socialism takes full account. 1965-81

Cecil, Robert

1260. Vinogradov, K. B. and Naumenikov, O. A. NA SLUZHBE BRITANSKOGO KOLONIALIZMA (STRANITSY POLITICHESKOI BIOGRAFII LORDA SOLSBERI) [In the service of British colonialism (pages from the political biography of Lord Salisbury)]. *Novaia i Noveishaia Istoriia [USSR] 1981 (1): 125-136, (2): 122-138.* Part I. Biographical sketch of Robert Cecil, the 3d Marquess of Salisbury (1830-1903), covering his career up to 1885 when he was asked to form a minority government by Queen Victoria. Prior to that he had been head of the India Office and Minister of Foreign Affairs. He was on the right wing of the Conservative Party and actively opposed the passing of the second and third parliamentary reform bills while championing the policy of British advancement in the Middle East and Central Asia. Part II. Continues the biographical sketch of Robert Cecil, 3d Marquess of Salisbury, three times prime minister of Great Britain covering his career from 1885 until his death in 1903. In forming his first cabinet he took the unprecedented step of giving himself the portfolio of Minister of Foreign Affairs and thereafter showed little interest in domestic affairs. 129 notes. 1855-1903

1261. —. [LORD CECIL AND REARMAMENT]. *Hist. J. [Great Britain] 1982 25(4): 953-956.*

Roskill, Stephen. LORD CECIL AND THE HISTORIANS, *pp. 953-954.* Comments on an earlier article by J. A. Thompson, which totally ignores the bad long-term effects of the disarmament policy advocated by Lord Robert Cecil and the League of Nations Union in the 1920's. Cecil contributed substantially to British politicians being forced to negotiate with the dictators from weakness in the 1930's.

Thompson, J. A. LORD CECIL AND STEPHEN ROSKILL, *pp. 955-956.* Reiterates that Cecil never advocated unilateral disarmament and was less doctrinaire and more realistic than he has been portrayed by Roskill and other historians. 1919-39

Celan, Paul

1262. Felstiner, John. PAUL CELAN: THE STRAIN OF JEWISHNESS. *Commmentary 1985 79(4): 44-55.* A study of the life, work, and death by suicide of Paul Celan (1920-70), born Paul Antschel in Czernowitz, Romania (later Chernovtsy, Ukraine), who survived as a Jew in Romania in World War II and after the war made his way to France, where he wrote poetry in German, translated Osip Mandelstam, worked at a factory job, and at last threw himself into the Seine. 1940-70

1263. Greinert, Walter. PAUL CELANS VERHÄLTNIS ZU FRANKREICH [Paul Celan's relationship with France]. *Austriaca [France] 1984 10(19): 145-150.* Paul Celan (1920-70), poet and native of Czernowitz, Bukovina (now Chernovtsy in the USSR) expatriated himself to Paris in 1948. He continued to write in German, his first language, because this was a way of recovering the lost land of his birth, but as he became more completely integrated into French society and culture, German became an almost hieratic language for him. He translated works in six different languages, including Hebrew, Romanian, and Russian. 21 notes. 1948-70

Cellarius, Martin

1264. Williams, R. L. MARTIN CELLARIUS AND THE REFORMATION IN STRASBURG. *J. of Ecclesiastical Hist. [Great Britain] 1981 32(4): 477-497.* Martin Cellarius (1499-1564) moved in Reformation circles after taking his degree in 1521, and in 1526 came to Strasbourg, where he wrote a systematic theology of predestination, published in 1527 (in Latin), and here analyzed with quotations from a contemporary manuscript English translation. Although on the central theme of predestination he was aligned with the conservative reformers, on some points (e.g., the coming of Christ) the work was regarded as radical, and Bucer denounced him as sympathetic with the recent Anabaptist tumults in Strasbourg. By 1528 the disagreement was settled. Cellarius eventually migrated to Basle where he became professor of the Old Testament in the university. Based on contemporary and modern printed materials and a manuscript in the Reigate Parish Church library; 76 notes. 1499-1564

Cellini, Benvenuto

1265. Güntert, Georges. SKORPION UND SALAMANDER: EINE EMBLEMATISCHE DEUTUNG DER VITA DES BENVENUTO CELLINI [Scorpion and salamander: an emblematic interpretation of the *Autobiography* of Benvenuto Cellini]. *Schweizer Monatshefte [Switzerland] 1986 66(1): 51-70.* Discusses the mythological elements of the Italian goldsmith Benvenuto Cellini's *Autobiography,* written 1558-66, including his use of the symbol of fire in his workshop and his gift and Herculean strength. 16c

Celtes, Konrad

1266. Trenkler, Ernst. KONRAD CELTES, HUMANIST, DICHTER UND GELEHRTER [Konrad Celtes: humanist, author, and scholar]. *Biblos [Austria] 1981 30(3): 188-195.* After having founded the Danubian literary society at Vienna in 1494, Konrad Celtes (1459-1508) was called to the University of Vienna by Emperor Maximilian I in 1497, where he promoted the publication of classical authors. 1494-1508

Centurión Guerrero de Torres, Manuel

1267. González del Campo, María Isabel. UN GRAN GUBERNADOR ESPAÑOL EN AMERICA: MANUEL CENTURION [A great Spanish governor in America: Manuel Centurión]. *Cuadernos de Investigación Hist. [Spain] 1983 7: 171-186.* Manuel Centurión Guerrero de Torres, renowned in Venezuela, is hardly known in Spain. Born in Málaga in 1732, he entered military service and was appointed commander general of the province of Guyana, presently in Venezuela, in 1766. With limited resources, he organized the defense of the region against both the Portuguese and Dutch, and was tireless in attracting new settlers to the district. He effectively controlled smuggling in the area and urged the opening of free trade between America and Spain. He was also active in promoting missionary activity, gaining great favor with the Capuchin monks. He returned to Spain for reasons of health in 1777, and is a good example of the hundreds of active, perceptive, and talented functionaries who developed the New World in the name of Spain. Based on material in the Archivo General de la Nación, Caracas and other sources; 42 notes. 1732-77

Cepari, Virgilio

1268. Pignatelli, Antonio M. IL P. VIRGILIO CEPARI S.I.: LA FORMAZIONE E LA PRIMA ATTIVITA: 1582-1601 [Father Virgilio Cepari S.J.: formation and first activities: 1582-1601]. *Arch. Hist. Societatis Iesu [Italy] 1982 51(101): 3-44.* Cepari was a well-known spiritual writer and hagiographer of the Jesuit Order; he personally knew some of the holy persons about whose lives he wrote, including Aloysius Gonzaga, John Berchmanns, and Francis Borgia. 16c

Cepenkov, Marko

1269. Sazdov, Tomé. WORK OF MARKO TSEPENKOV. *Macedonian Rev. [Yugoslavia] 1983 13(1): 51-57.* Examines the life and work of Marko Cepenkov (1829-1920), collector of Macedonian folklore and poetry. 1850-1920

Cerdan, Marcel

1270. Amar, Marianne. L'IMPOSSIBLE HISTOIRE DE MARCEL CERDAN [The impossible story of Marcel Cerdan]. *Histoire [France] 1986 (87): 44-56.* A biography of French boxer Marcel Cerdan (born in Sidi-Bel-Abbès in 1916), which covers his romance with singer Edith Piaf and his tragic death in an airplane crash in 1949. 1938-49

Čermelj, Lavo

1271. Rybař, Miloš. V SPOMIN DR. LAVU ČERMELJU. NOVI PODATKI O DRUGEM TRŽAŠKEM PROCESU [In memory of Dr. Lavo Čermelj: new data on the second trial in Trieste]. *Kronika [Yugoslavia] 1980 28(3): 217-220.* Lavo Čermelj (1889-1980), physicist-mathematician and spokesman for Slovenes' national aspirations in Italy, was convicted in 1941 by the Fascist Special Court for the Protection of the State in Trieste. Despite intervention with Mussolini by Pope Pius II, only four of the nine defendants convicted were freed. Based on Vatican documents. 1941

Cervantes, Juan de

1272. Schwaller, John Frederick. TRES FAMILIAS MEXICANAS DEL SIGLO XVI [Three Mexican families of the 16th century]. *Hist. Mexicana [Mexico] 1981 31(2): 171-196.* Examines the history of the families of the conquistadores Geronimo Ruiz de la Mota, Juan de Cervantes and Juan Ochoa de Lejalde from their beginnings to the end of the 17th century to inquire into the manner in which the new wealth and privileges acquired during the conquest were transmitted to their descendants. Such families concentrated their wealth in a few descendants by means of institutions such as the right of primogeniture, ecclesiastical benefices, and convents. The study throws light on a topic of much interest to historians, namely the passage from the *encomienda* at the time of the conquest to the emergence of the *hacienda* in the colonial period. Based on primary material in Spanish and Mexican archives, bibliography, genealogical trees, 39 notes. 1508-1620

Ceva, Bianca

1273. Alfieri, Vittorio Enzo. BIANCA CEVA COMBATTENTE PER LA LIBERTA [Bianca Ceva, freedom fighter]. *Risorgimento [Italy] 1982 34(3): 165-171.* Bianca Ceva died in 1982 at the age of 85. She was the sister of Umberto Ceva, a leader of the movement Giustizia e Libertà, who died by his own hand in prison in 1930. From that time Bianca devoted her life to the fight against Fascism and became a liaison between that movement and other antifascist forces. After liberation she returned to teaching and was director of the Institute for the History of the Liberation Movement. 1930-82

Cézanne, Paul

1274. Areán, Carlos. DOS EXPOSICIONES MODELICAS: CEZANNE Y MUNCH [Two exemplary exhibitions: Cézanne and Munch]. *Cuadernos Hispanoamericanos [Spain] 1984 (409): 151-158.* After stressing biographical similarities and stylistic contrasts between Paul Cézanne (1839-1906) and Edvard Munch (1863-1944), the author comments briefly on the main features of their works as exhibited during 1984 in Madrid at the Museo Español de Arte Contemporáneo and the Salas "Pablo Ruíz Picasso." Photo. 1860's-1944

Chaadaev, Pëtr

1275. Kamenski, Z. A. UROK CHAADAEVA [The lesson of Chaadaev]. *Voprosy Filosofii [USSR] 1986 (1): 111-121.* Examines the ideas and the evolution of the views of Pëtr Chaadaev during his late period, 1840-50 and debates the view of conservative Russian historians that the well-known Russian thinker fell into a spiritual prostration, not developing progressively, even though he was participating in the intellectual life of Moscow at that time. 1840's

1276. McNally, Raymond. AGAINST A FRIENDLY ENEMY: IVAN KIREEVSKIJ. *Studies in Soviet Thought [Netherlands] 1986 32(4): 367-382.* Pëtr Chaadaev (1794-1852) worked out many of his ideas through polemics with his friendly enemy, Ivan Kireevski (1809-56). Newly discovered archival sources throw much light on the development of the controversy between Chaadaev and the Slavophiles, especially during the late 1840's and early 1850's. Based on Soviet archival sources; 50 notes. 1845-56

1277. McNally, Raymond. SIGNIFICANT REVELATIONS IN CHAADAEV'S LETTERS TO A. I. TURGENEV. *Studies in Soviet Thought [Netherlands] 1986 32(4): 321-339.* Pëtr Chaadaev's (1794-1856) correspondence with Aleksandr I. Turgenev (1794-1845) reveal many of Chaadaev's significant ideas. Turgenev, living in the West after 1825, became Chaadaev's contact with the literary and cultural circles there. Many of the letters, including some newly discovered, were often deliberately designed to circulate beyond Turgenev. The letters support the view that Chaadaev broke the bounds of narrow Russian nationalist sentiments and became a truly European thinker. Based on Soviet archival sources; 37 notes. 1820-45

1278. Tempest, Richard. CHAADAEV AND TIUTCHEV. *Studies in Soviet Thought [Netherlands] 1986 32(4): 383-395.* The friendship between Pëtr Chaadaev (1-794-1856) and Fëdor Tiutchev (1803-73) began in 1844 and lasted for the rest of Chaadaev's life. Although Tiutchev arrived late on the ideological scene, and represented more the pan-Slavist element in Slavophilism, the friendship between the two was genuine and deep, each representing the perfect counterpart to the other. 38 notes. 1844-56

Chadwick, James

1279. Goldhaber, Maurice. WITH CHADWICK AT THE CAVENDISH. *Bull. of the Atomic Sci. 1982 38(10): 12-13.* Personal reminiscences of working nuclear physics with James Chadwick (1891-1974) in the Cavendish Laboratory, Cambridge, England, 1934-35. 1934-35

1280. Oliphant, Mark. THE BEGINNING: CHADWICK AND THE NEUTRON. *Bull. of the Atomic Sci. 1982 38(10): 14-18.* Biography of James Chadwick (1891-1974) and discussion of his discovery of the neutron, his work at the Cavendish Laboratory at Cambridge and with Ernest Rutherford in nuclear physics, and his desire to have England share control of the atomic bomb. 1891-1974

Chagall, Marc

1281. Frost, Matthew. MARC CHAGALL AND THE JEWISH STATE CHAMBER THEATER. *Russian Hist. 1981 8(1-2): 90-107.* Marc Chagall pioneered in stage designs for the Yiddish-language theater in Moscow, 1919-22, using themes drawn from and extending his other painting. His work was used primarily to decorate the Jewish State Chamber Theater (murals and paintings), but he also designed stage sets and the costumes for three plays by Shalom Aleichem. Based on Chagall's autobiography and Soviet histories of the immediately post-revolutionary theater; 13 illus., 21 notes. 1911-22

1282. Wernick, Robert. IN HIS TENTH DECADE MARC CHAGALL'S BRUSH STILL DANCED. *Smithsonian 1985 16(2): 66-72, 74, 76-77.* Reviews the life and work of Russian-born painter and creator of stained-glass windows Marc Chagall (1889-1984) who lived most of his life in France and whose work contained the surreal and colorful. 11 illus. 1910's-84

Chaikovskaia, Madame

See Anastasia

Chaila, Abbé du

1283. Poujol, Robert. RECHERCHES SUR L'ABBÉ DU CHAILA: SON AFFRONTEMENT AVEC LES EX-PASTEURS DU CROS, DE ST-GERMAIN-DE-CALBERTE (1686-1702) [Research on Abbé du Chaila: his confrontation with the former pastors du Cros of St.-Germain-de-Calberte

(1686-1702)]. *Bull. de la Soc. de l'Hist. du Protestantisme Français [France] 1981 127(1): 107-124.* As special Catholic missionary assigned to convert Protestants after the revocation of the Edict of Nantes, Abbé du Chaila was the central figure of the Counter-Reformation in the Cévennes. He particularly sought the aid of two former Protestant ministers, Jean-Jacques du Cros and Pierre-André du Cros (father and son), who were nobles and had considerable influence in the region. However, he confiscated for his own use their family mansion. They never forgave him. Jean-Jacques fled to Switzerland and became a Protestant again. Foiled in his attempts to escape, Pierre-André remained to harass du Chaila. To placate the young man, du Chaila arranged his marriage with the Abbé's own niece, a young noblewoman with a large dowry and prospects of further inheritance. The bride promptly supported her husband in legal action against her uncle. They finally inherited the mansion on the Abbé's death. Based on public and private archives; 42 notes. 1686-1702

Chaillot, Claude

1284. Jeannin-Naltet, Paul. UN DRAGON D'ESPAGNE DIJONNAIS: CLAUDE CHAILLOT, MARECHAL DE CAMP, CHEVALIER DE L'EMPIRE [A Spanish dragoon from Dijon: Claude Chaillot, Maréchal de Camp, Chevalier de l'Empire]. *Annales de Bourgogne [France] 1984 56(2-3): 114-121.* Traces the military career of Claude Chaillot, who enlisted in the French Republican Army in 1792. He was promoted and awarded two titles for courageous service in the battle of Talavera, Spain; later appointed to command a garrison at Saint-Dizier, he served until Louis XVIII returned to power in 1815, when he retired in Auxerre. 1792-1815

Chaillu, Paul Du

1285. Bucher, Henry H., Jr. CANONIZATION BY REPETITION: PAUL DU CHAILLU IN HISTORIOGRAPHY. *Rev. Française d'Hist. d'Outre-mer [France] 1979 66(1-2): 15-32.* An examination of the career of French explorer Paul Du Chaillu (1831-1903), which challenges many of the generally accepted beliefs about him and examines the contemporary controversies surrounding his discoveries. Based on contemporary periodicals; illus., 95 notes. 1831-1903

Chaize, François de la

1286. Roudil, Pierre. LE PERE DE LA CHAIZE: UN TOMBEAU!: UN INCONNU AU NOM CELEBRE [Father de la Chaize: a tomb! An unknown with a famous name]. *Historama [France] 1985 (16): 68-72.* Examines the life of Jesuit priest François de la Chaize, the personal confessor of Louis XIV, discussing the difficulty of his job in view of the royal secrets he had to keep, the slander he suffered from his contemporaries, and his influence on the king. 1624-1709

Chałasiński, Józef

1287. Jakubczak, Franciszek. JÓZEF CHAŁASIŃSKI (1904-1979) [Józef Chałasiński (1904-79)]. *Kultura i Społeczeństwo [Poland] 1979 23(4): 4-9.* An obituary of Polish historian sociologist Józef Chałasiński, from 1935 till 1979 (with interruptions) the editor of *Przegląd Sociologiczny* [Sociological review], a professor, an honored expert on the sociology of rural Poland, and an author of a number of works, for example *Młode Pokolenie Chłopów* [The new generation of peasants] (1938), and *Pamiętnikarstwo XIX i XX Wieku Jako Świadectwo Przeobrażeń Narodu Polskiego* [Diary writing of the 19th and 20th centuries as evidence of changes within the Polish nation], his last completed work. 1904-79

1288. Nowacki, Witold and Szczepański, Jan. PRZEMÓWIENIA POŻEGNALNE W CZASIE CEREMONII POGRZEBU NA POWĄZKOWSKIM CMENTARZU KOMUNALNYM [Eulogies read at the solemn graveside ceremonies for Józef Chałasiński at the community cemetery in Warsaw]. *Kultura i Społeczeństwo [Poland] 1979 23(4): 10-12.* Eulogies of Józef Chałasiński, Polish historian, sociologist, educator, author, member of the Polish Academy of Sciences, an expert on and activist among the peasantry, and an honored scholar of the historical development of Poland. 1920's-79

Ch'aloyan, Vazgēn

1289. Arevshatyan, S. S. VAZGĒN CH'ALOYAN (TSNNDYAN 80-AMYAKI AṚT'IV) [Vazgēn Ch'aloyan (on the 80th anniversary of his birth)]. *Patma-Banasirakan Handes. Istoriko-Filologicheskii Zhurnal [USSR] 1985 (1): 95-98.* Vazgēn Ch'aloyan (1905-81) devoted most of his life to the history of Armenian philosophy, placing its study on a sound basis. Together with his students, he produced a number of monographs on Armenian philosophers from Eznik Koghbats'i (5th century) to Shahamir Shahamiryan (18th century). Of his numerous published studies, the principal work is *The History of Armenian Philosophy* (Yerevan, 1959 and Moscow, 1974), and the most controversial *Armenian Renaissance* (Yerevan, 1963). Photo. Russian summary. 1930-81

1290. Grigorian, G. H. V. K. CHALOYAN (MERELABANAKAN) [V. K. Chaloyan (Obituary)]. *Patma-Banasirakan Handes. Istoriko-Filologicheskii Zhurnal [USSR] 1981 (2): 307-308.* Obituary of Vazgen Karapet Chaloyan (1905-1981), who pioneered the history of Armenian philosophy, devoting 44 years to research in this field. He published books on Eznik Koghbatsi (5th century), Davit Anhaght (5th-6th centuries), and in 1959 his history of Armenian philosophy from the beginning to the end of the 18th century. He contributed articles to Soviet periodicals and encyclopedias. His book *East-West* on the relationship between Eastern and Western philosophies was published in 1968 and 1979. He was awarded state honors for his services. Primary sources. 1930's-81

Chamberlain, Joseph.

1291. Dutton, David. LIFE BEYOND THE POLITICAL GRAVE: JOSEPH CHAMBERLAIN, 1906-14. *History Today [Great Britain] 1984 34(May): 23-28.* Despite a crippling stroke in 1906, British statesman Joseph Chamberlain continued to exert an important influence on the Unionist Party and its policies. 1904-14

1292. Quinault, Roland. JOHN BRIGHT AND JOSEPH CHAMBERLAIN. *Historical Journal [Great Britain] 1985 28(3): 623-646.* 1868-1914
*For abstract see **Bright, John***

Chamberlain, Neville

1293. Stafford, Paul. THE CHAMBERLAIN-HALIFAX VISIT TO ROME: A REAPPRAISAL. *English Hist. Rev. [Great Britain] 1983 98(386): 61-100.* Examines the meeting among Neville Chamberlain, Lord Halifax, and Benito Mussolini in Rome in January 1939, its preparation, and its consequence. Chamberlain hoped his visit to Rome and meeting with Mussolini would convince the Italian leader to moderate Hitler's ambitions and promote an armistice in Spain. Had Chamberlain acted earlier on the advice given by Halifax and Cadogan and expressed himself more forcefully, Mussolini and Hitler would not have reached the conclusion that

Britain was apprehensive about the growing strength of the German-Italian Axis and was hence vulnerable and irresolute. Reluctant to guarantee France against attack by Italy, Chamberlain eventually consented to staff talks to explore defenses against Germany and Italy. Based upon printed diplomatic documents and archive material in London and Paris.
1938-39

Chamberlin, Henri

See Lafont, Henri

Champion, Henry Hyde

1294. Whitehead, Andrew. "QUORUM PARS FUI": THE AUTOBIOGRAPHY OF H. H. CHAMPION. *Bull. of the Soc. for the Study of Labour Hist. [Great Britain] 1983 (47): 17-35.* Discusses the career of the British socialist Henry Hyde Champion, with special reference to the 1880's and 1890's. Also reproduces his autobiography entitled "Quorum Pars Fui: An Unconventional Autobiography," which was first published in May 1908 in *The Trident,* a little-known Melbourne magazine that Champion edited.
1880's-90's

Champion, John

1295. Holt, T. G. AN EIGHTEENTH-CENTURY CHAPLAIN: JOHN CHAMPION AT SAWSTON HALL. *Recusant History [Great Britain] 1984 17(2): 181-187.* Studies letters and other documents relating to John Champion (1695-1776), who served as chaplain to the Huddleston family at their residence, Sawston Hall (near Cambridge), to learn about the daily life of priests of the Catholic Church working for private employers in 18th-century England. 1730's-76

Chancellor, Betty

1296. Abramson, Doris. TWO ACTRESSES: BETTY CHANCELLOR & CLAIRE NEUFELD. *Massachusetts Rev. 1983 24(1): 180-197.* Reports on interviews with two actresses, Betty Chancellor (b. 1910), Irish actress and former American faculty wife, and Claire Neufeld (b. 1895), Austro-German actress and American faculty wife. Chancellor's husband is William Denis Johnston (b. 1901), Irish playwright; Neufeld's is Walter Richard Volbach (b. 1897), German stage director. Chancellor describes her childhood, emphasizing the influences on her acting career and concludes with the observation that she is only half a person when not acting. Neufeld also summarizes her childhood in Vienna, emphasizing her love for music, stating that to be Viennese is to be musical. Based on an autobiography and interviews; illus. 2 photos, 11 notes. ca 1920-80

Chang Hen-shui

1297. Rupprecht, Hsiao-wei Wang. "Chang Hen-shui: His Life and Fictional Technique." U. of Wisconsin-Madison 1983. 393 pp. *DAI 1984 45(1): 187-A.* DA8402859
1919-67

Chantal, Jeanne-Françoise Fremyot de

1298. Bordes, Hélène. LA MERE DE CHANTAL, "MAÎTRESSE D'ORAISON" [Mother Chantal, "mistress of prayer"]. *Dix-Septième Siècle [France] 1984 36(3): 211-220.* Saint Jeanne-Françoise Fremyot de Chantal (1572-1641) was cofounder with St. Francis de Sales of the Congregation of the Visitation of Holy Mary. After the death of St. Francis, she not only governed the order but carried on an immense correspondence in which she acted as spiritual director and teacher of prayer to a large number of notable churchmen and many lay and religious men and women, to whom she taught the prayer of quiet abandonment to the will of God. 35 notes. 1572-1641

Chao Chih-Chien

1299. Bennett, Elizabeth Foard. "Chao Chih-Ch'ien (1829-1884), a Late Nineteenth Century Chinese Artist: His Life, Calligraphy and Painting." (Vol. 1-2). Yale U. 1984. 258 pp. *DAI 1984 45(2): 385-A.* DA8411508 1829-84

Chao I

1300. Priest, Quinton Gwynne. "Historiography and Statecraft in Eighteenth Century China: The Life and Times of Chao I (1727-1814)." U. of Arizona 1982. 473 pp. *DAI 1983 43(12): 4006-A.* DA8309038 1740's-1814

Chaplin, Charles

1301. Bodon, Jean-Richard Rene. "Andre Bazin's *Charlie Chaplin:* An Annotated Translation and Analysis of Text Based on Methods Derived from 'De la Politique des Auteurs'." Florida State U. 1985. 297 pp. *DAI 1985 46(4): 820-A.* DA8513358 20c

1302. Manning, Harold, and Lyons, Timothy J. CHARLIE CHAPLIN'S EARLY LIFE: FACT AND FICTION. *Hist. J. of Film, Radio and Television [Great Britain] 1983 3(1): 35-41.* Examines primary sources relating to the early life and ancestry of Charles Chaplin, which help to dispel the confusion surrounding these subjects in other published works on Charlie Chaplin. 1670-1912

1303. Morris, C. Brian. CHARLES CHAPLIN'S TRYST WITH SPAIN. *J. of Contemporary Hist. [Great Britain] 1983 18(3): 517-531.* Charles Chaplin's films were particularly appealing in Spain in the 20 years immediately preceding the Civil War. His private life was avidly followed. Serious writers used his name in poetry and essay as a reference comparable to Charlemagne or Hamlet. "As an actor transformed by Spanish writers into a literary character, his fame acquired new dimensions." 23 notes.
ca 1916-36

Chapman, Patty

1304. Boulton, David J. WOMEN AND EARLY METHODISM. *Pro. of the Wesley Hist. Soc. [Great Britain] 1981 43(2): 13-17.* 18c
*For abstract see **Bolton, Nancy***

Chardin, Jean

1305. Labib-Rahman, Laleh. SIR JEAN CHARDIN, THE GREAT TRAVELLER (1643-1712/13). *Pro. of the Huguenot Soc. of London [Great Britain] 1981 23(5): 309-318.* A biographical study of the wealthy Huguenot East India merchant, jeweler, antiquarian, and philologist, Sir Jean Chardin, with particular reference to his overland journeys from France to Persia and India in 1664-70 and 1671-80, and to his life in England after 1680. 1660's-1713

Charents, Eghishe

1306. Goshgarian, Geoffrey. EGHISHE CHARENTS AND THE "MODERNIZATION" OF SOVIET ARMENIAN LITERATURE. *Armenian Rev. 1983 36(1): 76-88.* Rejecting all antecedents, Eghishe Charents undertook the task of developing a new Soviet-Armenian poetry, a goal he never reached and the ambiguity of which led to his death. 1922-34

Charles, Archduke

1307. Rothenberg, Gunther; with commentary by Paret, Peter and Rowen, Herbert. THE CASE OF ARCHDUKE CHARLES. *Consortium on Revolutionary Europe, 1750-1850: Proceedings 1983: 74-80.* The Habsburg Archduke Charles (1771-1847) lacked any formal military education. He was the son of Leopold of Tuscany, who became Holy Roman Emperor in 1790. Charles received lessons in the art of warfare from Colonel Lindenau and Colonel Mack. Charles was one of the ablest military commanders to fight against revolutionary and Napoleonic France, but his training made him too methodical and unimaginative. Thus he was not the equal of Napoleon. Comments and discussion, pp. 98-116. 21 notes. 1796-1807

Charles I (1600-1649)

1308. Havran, Martin J. THE CHARACTER AND PRINCIPLES OF AN ENGLISH KING: THE CASE OF CHARLES I. *Catholic Hist. Rev. 1983 69(2): 169-208.* This reinterpretation of the English king first appeals to historians to balance the current fascination with social history by a renewed commitment to personality and character studies. Stresses the physical welfare, emotional environment, family relationships, education, and religious training of Charles I to demonstrate how his mature character and principles, as well as his appearance and stammer, reflected his childhood experiences. His historical reputation and the issue of his martyrdom also are discussed. Concludes with an assessment of his Arminian religion. 1600-49

1309. Russell, Conrad. WHY DID CHARLES I FIGHT THE CIVIL WAR? *History Today [Great Britain] 1984 34(June): 31-34.* Discusses the role that King Charles I played in the civil war between Scotland and England, which involved both religious and political issues. 1640-42

Charles I (1887-1922)

1310. Bruegel, J. W. KARL HABSBURG'S LAST ADVENTURES. *East Central Europe 1983 10(1-2): 151-154.* Charles I (1887-1922), the last Habsburg ruler, attempted to regain his throne twice in Hungary in 1921, traveling there from exile in Switzerland once by train on a false passport, once by rented plane. Habsburg apologists claim that the French Prime Minister Briand was favorable to the attempts, but there is no documentary evidence for this. Opposition to the restoration was general, and war seemed to threaten, even though Charles never came close to success. A British destroyer removed him from Hungary, and he died of pneumonia a few months later. Based on published primary sources; 7 notes. 1918-22

Charles V (1500-1558)

1311. Haas, Leonard. EL EMPERADOR CARLOS V Y NUESTRO TIEMPO [Emperor Charles V and our times]. *Folia Humanistica [Spain] 1981 19(222-223): 467-474.* Born at the peak of the Renaissance, Charles V was also born into an era of transition in which the Catholic Church was challenged on all sides, and the Holy Roman Empire had to contend with newly felt nationalisms and the threatening Ottoman Empire. The last of the feudal, universal emperors, he was also a forerunner of the modern absolutist monarchs. He believed deeply in religion as a force for peace and cohesion among peoples, and he fought division and dissolution on all fronts all his life, making war to achieve peace and unity for the western world. 1500-58

Charpentier, Adrien

1312. Terrier, Didier. UNE FAMILLE DE MARCHANDS AU DEBUT DU REGNE DE LOUIS XV: LES CHARPENTIER, DE SAINT-QUENTIN [A merchant family at the beginning of Louis XV's reign: the Charpentiers of Saint-Quentin]. *Revue du Nord [France] 1985 67(265): 391-412.* The Charpentier family took an active part in Saint-Quentin's bustling manufacturing life in the first half of the 18th century. Thanks to their business correspondence, deposited at the registry of the city's commercial court after their bankruptcy, it is possible to follow their activity between 1725 and 1746. The father, Adrien Charpentier, limited himself to the trading of batiste and linen, which he bought from *mulquiniers* scattered in villages of the Vermandois. He had no control over the marketing of linen thread or on textile production itself, nor did he control the bleaching operations. Once the linen cloth was collected and stiffened, he sent it all over Europe, yet with a marked predilection for the British Isles. His son and son-in-law succeeded him in 1730. Poor management rapidly led the house of the Charpentier into inextricable difficulties. 1725-46

Charretier, Mathurin

1313. Greengrass, Mark. MATHURIN CHARRETIER: THE CAREER OF A *POLITIQUE* DURING THE WARS OF RELIGION IN FRANCE. *Pro. of the Huguenot Soc. of London [Great Britain] 1981 23(5): 330-340.* Outlines the political career of Mathurin Charretier, secretary, financial manager, and political and diplomatic advisor to Henri de Montmorency-Damville, governor of Languedoc, 1570-77; the sieur de Bellegarde, Marquis of Saluzzo, 1577-79; the Duc d'Anjou, 1581-83; and the Comte d'Auvergne, 1588-95. ca 1569-97

Chateaubriand, François de

1314. Delhez-Sarlet, Claudette. CHATEAUBRIAND: SCISSIONS ET RASSEMBLEMENT DU MOI DANS L'HISTOIRE [Chateaubriand: splits and reintegration of the self in history]. *Rev. de l'Inst. de Sociol. [Belgium] 1982 (1-2): 193-208.* Describes the internal and external personalities of François de Chateaubriand, based mostly on his memoirs. This split exemplifies the larger divisions in society. 1797-1830

Chater, John

1315. Sell, Alan P. F. JOHN CHATER: FROM INDEPENDENT MINISTER TO SANDEMANIAN AUTHOR. *Baptist Quarterly [Great Britain] 1985 31(3): 100-117.* Reviews the career of John Chater, an English Baptist independent minister who became a Sandemanian, a member of an enthusiastic religious sect founded in Scotland by John Glas (1695-1773) and named for his son-in-law Robert Sandeman (1718-71). 18c

Chaudhuri, Sashi Bhusan

1316. Sen, Ranajit. DR. S. B. CHAUDHURI: AN OBITUARY. *Quarterly Review of Historical Studies [India] 1983 23(2): 56-60.* Prints an obituary of Sashi Bhusan Chaudhuri, historian of the great Indian revolt of 1857, of the pattern of settlement of various ethnic groups in India, and of Indian independence movements against the British Empire. Photo, 17 notes. 18c-19c

Chaunu, Pierre

1317. Winock, Michel. PIERRE CHAUNU, UN REACTIONNAIRE PROGRESSISTE? [Pierre Chaunu, a reactionary progressive?]. *Histoire [France] 1982 (44): 85-90.* Interview with historian Pierre Chaunu (b. 1923), a controversial figure who is regarded by some as a rightist, and focuses on the origin of his vocation, his detachment from political problems and emotions, and his mentors. 1950's-82

Chaves Pinheiro, Francisco Manuel

1318. Galvão, Alfredo. FRANCISCO MANUEL CHAVES PINHEIRO, UM GRANDE ESCULTOR DO SÉCULO XIX BRASILEIRO [Francisco Manuel Chaves Pinheiro, a great Brazilian sculptor of the 19th century]. *Rev. do Inst. Hist. e Geog. Brasileiro [Brazil] 1979 (324): 320-330.* Chaves Pinheiro (1822-84) was an important though little known Brazilian sculptor. His statues adorn many civic monuments and churches. 19c

Chekhov, Anton

1319. Fauconnet, M.-S. "Tchekhov et la Qualité de la Vie" [Chekhov and the quality of life]. U. of Dijon [France] 1980. 92 pp. *DAI-C 1982 43(1): 30; 7/204c.* ca 1884-1904

1320. Vidaver, Doris and Cohen, Maynard M. DR. A. P. CHEKHOV. *American Scholar 1986 55(2): 227-233.* Anton Chekhov's medical training shows up in his literary work in terms of humaneness, objectivity, and attention to detail. He wrote while attending medical school to support himself and his family, though two careers were hard on him. In 1890 he visited a penal colony on the island of Sakhalin off the Siberian coast to write a medical treatise on the prisoners. He was involved in many causes, including those of the Jews and the famine of 1891. 1880's-1904

Chen Duxiu

1321. Benton, Gregor. REVIEW ARTICLE: TWO PURGED LEADERS OF EARLY CHINESE COMMUNISM. *China Quarterly [Great Britain] 1985 (102): 317-328.* A review of *Memoirs du Peng Shuzhi: L'Envol du Communisme en Chine* by Claude Cadart and Cheng Yingxiang (Paris, 1983) and *Chen Duxiu: Founder of the Chinese Communist Party* by Lee Feigon (Princeton, 1983). The volume on Peng, essentially an autobiography, is seen as less reliable than the study on Chen. 1895-1980

1322. Kuhfus, Peter. CHEN DUXIU AND LEON TROTSKY: NEW LIGHT ON THEIR RELATIONSHIP. *China Quarterly [Great Britain] 1985 (102): 253-276.* Though Leon Trotsky and Chen Duxiu appear never to have met, their mutual involvement continued from 1927 to 1940. As a leader of the opposition Chen drew a theoretical basis for his stand from Trotsky while Trotsky saw Chen as a potentially important recruit for the Trotskyist opposition. Based on Chinese materials and the *Exile Papers of Leon Trotsky;* 128 notes. 1927-40

Chen Wangdao

1323. Richter, Harald. CHEN WANGDAO: EIN ABRISS SEINES LEBENS UND WERKES [Chen Wangdao: a synopsis of his life and work]. *Oriens Extremus [West Germany] 1980 27(1): 61-72.* Chen Wangdao (Ch'en Wang-tao) (1890-1977), late rector of Fudan University, Shanghai, was a pioneer of the Chinese Communist Party, having been active in the May Fourth Movement of 1919. He studied law, literature, and philosophy at several universities in China and Japan. He translated the Communist Manifesto into Chinese, but his main interests lay in political journalism and education. Based on Chen's own works and secondary sources; 100 notes. 1919-77

Chen Xitong

1324. —. ONE MAYOR AND THREE GOVERNORS. *Issues & Studies [Taiwan] 1983 19(7): 72-75.* A number of new local and provincial leaders were elected in China in 1983. Chen Xitong (Ch'en Hsi-t'ung), mayor of Beijing; Liang Buting (Liang Pu-t'ing), governor of Shandong (Shantung); Lin Zheng (Lin Cheng), governor of Hunan; and Zhao Zengyi (Chao Tseng-i), governor of Jiangsi (Kiangsi) all began to serve the Chinese Communist Party before they reached the age of 20. All were out of favor during the Cultural Revolution. 1937-83

Chen Xujing

1325. Cole, James H. "TOTAL WESTERNIZATION" IN KUOMINTANG CHINA: THE CASE OF CH'EN HSÜ-CHING. *Monumenta Serica [West Germany] 1979-80 34: 77-143.* Chen Xujing (Ch'en Hsü-ching, b. 1903), scholar, teacher, and author, was educated in China, the United States, and West Germany. Discusses the period 1928-38 and the implications of Chen's commitment to total Westernization, with a brief bibliography. Analyzes the reasoning behind his belief in Anglo-Americanization and examines these sentiments in two case studies, Chen's 1935 debates with Hu Shi and Wu Jingchao. Chen may be regarded as a Westernist nationalist, who emphasized the use of Western culture for the welfare of China as a nation. Based on Chen's writings and private letters. 1928-38

Cherepnin, Lev V.

1326. Gorski, A. D. PAMIATI AKADEMIKA L. V. CHEREPNINA [In memory of Academician L. V. Cherepnin]. *Voprosy Istorii [USSR] 1985 (5): 110-115.* Biography of Soviet historian Lev Vladimirovich Cherepnin (1905-77), describing his scientific and pedagogical career and reviewing his major publications. Of prime importance for historiography are his monographs on the socioeconomic and political history of feudal Russia in the 14th to 17th centuries and his application of Marxist theories to the understanding and analysis of historical problems. 9 notes. 14c-17c

1327. Nazarov, V. D. NAUCHNAIA KONFERENTSIIA PAMIATI AKADEMIKA L'VA VLADIMIROVICHA CHEREPNINA [Seminar in memory of Academician Lev Vladimirovich Cherepnin]. *Istoriia SSSR [USSR] 1981 (6): 208-210.* Discusses the proceedings at a seminar organized by the Academy of Sciences of the USSR and Moscow State University and held 26-28 November 1980 in memory of the Soviet historian Academician Lev Vladimirovich Cherepnin (1905-77). More than 120 historians from 38 academic organizations, universities, archival centers, museums, and journals from all over the USSR described Cherepnin's contribution to the study of the formation and development of the centralized Russian state. In his opening report, Academician V. T. Pashuto hailed Cherepnin's innovative work in the sphere of methodology, especially his comparative historical analysis. A. D. Gorskii reviewed Cherepnin's writing on the Russian state in the 14th to 16th centuries and the land councils from the 16th to 18th centuries. Other speakers included A. A. Preobrazhenski, who examined Cherepnin's study of the class struggle in the 17th to 18th centuries. 14c-18c

Cherniakhovski, Ivan

1328. Fontrodona, Mariano. EL MARISCAL CHERNIAKHOVSKI [Marshal Cherniakhovski]. *Hist. y Vida [Spain] 1983 16(185): 118-125.* The Russian Jew Ivan Cherniakhovski served under Stalin and became a hero fighting the Germans in World War II, but was killed before the war was over. 1939-45

Cherniakova, Felicia

1329. Shershevsky, Miriam. 'AL MIKTAVAH ŠEL FELIŞIYAH CHERNYAQOVAH LE-DR. A. BERMAN [About Felicia Cherniakova's letter to Dr. A. Berman]. *Gal-Ed: On the History of the Jews in Poland [Israel] 1985 7-8: 234-243.* Felicia Cherniakova, a teacher, participated in the public cultural life of Warsaw. After her husband's suicide on 23 July 1943, Felicia Cherniakova sent a letter to Dr. Adolf Berman, a respected public figure who later became the chairman of the Central Committee of Polish Jewry. She complained about the defamation of her husband's character and accomplishments as chairman of the Warsaw Judenrat. The author presents the original text of the letter and its Hebrew translation. Secondary sources; photo, 11 notes. 1942-44

Chernov, Samson

1330. Mitrović, Jeremija D. ZABORAVLJENI RATNI SLIKAR I SNIMATELJ SAMSON ČERNOV [The forgotten war painter and photographer Samson Chernov]. *Zbornik Istorijskog Muzeja Srbije [Yugoslavia] 1979 15-16: 75-80.* Describes the work of the Russian war painter and photographer Samson Chernov, who in 1912-16 accompanied Serbian troops at the front during the Balkan Wars and World War I. He was war correspondent of the French newspaper *Illustration* and won distinction for his action photographs and oil portraits. Exhibitions of his photography and paintings were mounted in Britain and other European countries, doing much to publicize the wartime sufferings of the Serbs. He also made war films. Chernov, a Jew, converted to the Orthodox Eastern faith. Despite his talent, Chernov became a forgotten man and details of his biography are sketchy. 7 notes, plate. 1912-16

Chernov, Victor

1331. Burbank, Jane. WAITING FOR THE PEOPLE'S REVOLUTION: MARTOV AND CHERNOV IN REVOLUTIONARY RUSSIA 1917-1923. *Cahiers du Monde Russe et Soviétique [France] 1985 26(3-4): 375-394.* In the chaotic and decisive years after the October Revolution, Julius Martov and Victor Chernov, leaders of the Mensheviks and Socialist Revolutionaries, were unwilling to give their full support either to the Bolsheviks or to popular rebellions against the new government. Explains their cautious and ultimately self-destructive positions as a consequence of the contradictions between their theories of revolution and their observations of mass behavior after 1917. In particular, the revolutionary years shook the confidence of the democratic Left in the national values of workers and peasants. Fearful of rebellions against the fragile state, yet repulsed by the authoritarian tactics of the Bolsheviks, Martov and Chernov could find no militant position consistent with their ideological commitments and retreated to their traditional, nonviolent stance of moral criticism. 1917-23

Chernyi, Ivan A.

1332. Blizniuk, A. "MY PERVYE DOLZHNY NACHAT' REVOLIUTSIIU..." ["We should be the first to start the revolution..."]. *Morskoi Sbornik [USSR] 1985 (12): 45-77.* A political biography of Ivan Aref'evich Chernyi (1877-1905), Russian sailor of peasant origin, whose letters to his father describing a future democratic Russia and his allegiance to the Bolshevik Party served as police evidence, leading to his trial and execution. 1900-05

Chernyshevski, Nikolai

1333. Ráb, Václav. N. G. ČERNYŠEVSKIJ—VELKÝ PŘEDSTAVITEL RUSKÉHO REVOLUČNÍHO DEMOKRATISMU [N. G. Chernyshevski: the outstanding representative of Russian revolutionary democratism]. *Acta U. Carolinae Phil. et Hist. [Czechoslovakia] 1979 (4): 7-16.* Remembers the 150th anniversary of Nikolai Chernyshevski's birth in evaluating his personality as an outstanding Russian philosopher, scientist, and literary critic, who was devoted to principles of revolutionary democratism. Chernyshevski, who mastered 16 foreign languages, created in 1855-62 more than 250 works dealing with the problems of foreign and domestic policy, philosophy, history, political economy, and the theory of literature. His strong opposition to government suppression of the peasants' riots caused his forced exile to Siberia for life. Chernyshevski was valued by Lenin as an early social democrat. Based on published works; 6 notes. 1828-79

1334. Troitski, N. A. CERNÎŞEVSKI ÎN DEPORTARE [Deportation of Chernishevski]. *Magazin Istoric [Romania] 1983 17(11): 23-27; 53.* Summarizes a Russian article from *Voprosy Istorii* which describes the fate of Nikolai G. Chernyshevski (1828-89), who was exiled for his political activities to Siberia by the tsarist government in 1864. 1862-75

1335. Volk, S. S. and Nikonenko, V. S. TEORETICHESKIE ISTOCHNIKI MIROVOZZRENIIA N. G. CHERNYSHEVSKOGO [Theoretical sources of Nikolai Chernyshevski's philosophy]. *Acta U. Carolinae Phil. et Hist. [Czechoslovakia] 1979 (4): 43-66.* The philosophical and political views of Nikolai Chernyshevski, a Russian democrat and writer of the 19th century, originated from Ludwig Feuerbach's and Georg Hegel's philosophy and were influenced by Alexander Herzen and Vissarion Belinski, Russian democrats, and the Comte de Saint-Simon and Robert Owen, utopian socialists. The discoveries in the natural sciences and the works of Adam Smith were also important for Chernyshevski's growth as a thinker. Based on the works of Chernyshevski; 44 notes. 1850's-89

Cherviakov, D. I.

1336. Ivannikov, I. G. RABOCHII, SOLDAT, KOMMUNIST: O ZNATNOM TOKARE-VETERANE VELIKOI OTECHESTVENNOI VOINY D. I. CHERVIAKOVE [Worker, soldier, Communist: D. I. Cherviakov, lathe operator and veteran of World War II]. *Voprosy Istorii KPSS [USSR] 1984 (10): 86-96.* Sketches the biography of Belorussian worker and World War II combatant D. I. Cherviakov (b. 1922), secretary of the party organization of the Minsk guild of lathe operators, awarded the title of the Hero of Socialist Labor in 1974. His wartime record included participation in the battle of Kharkov in 1941 and in the Slovak Rising of 1944. Secondary sources; 9 notes. 1922-84

Chesterton, G. K.

1337. McCarthy, John P. THE HISTORICAL VISION OF CHESTERBELLOC. *Modern Age 1982 26(2): 175-182.* 1900-40

*For abstract see **Belloc, Hilaire***

1338. Voorhees, Richard J. CHESTERTON THE ROMANTIC. *Queen's Quarterly [Canada] 1984 91(1): 17-26.* G. K. Chesterton's reputation has long outlasted most of the writers whose names were bracketed with his. Chivalry, championship of the poor, delicacy toward women, and interest in violence are some of the romantic attitudes and convictions that informed his life and the more than 100 books he wrote. He is not one of the greatest writers of his age, but he is one of the wisest, most cordial, and most invigorating. 1900-30

Chetty, G. Chevapathy

1339. Murphy, Eamon. LABOUR LEADERSHIP AND POLITICS IN INDIA: PROFILES OF THREE SOUTH INDIAN UNIONISTS. *South Asia [Australia] 1981 4(2): 79-93.* Sketches the careers of three union leaders active in the pre-1947 union movement in the cotton-milling industry in Tamilnad in South India, G. Chevapathy Chetty, N. G. Ramaswamy Naidu, and S. R. Varadarajulu Naidu. In their union and political activities, political interests and personal ambitions often interfered with their roles as union leaders. Interview materials; map, 61 notes. 1920's-50's

Chevalier, Michel

1340. Ueno, Takashi. FURANSU SANGYŌ KAKUMEI-KI NI OKERU SEISANRYOKU RONJA NO KŌTSU SEIDO RON: MICHEL CHEVALIER NO SHOSETSU O CHŪSHIN NI [Theories of a productivist railroad system in the industrial revolution in France: Michel Chevalier as the central figure]. *Shakaikeizaishigaku (Socio-Economic Hist.) [Japan] 1981 46(6): 1-23.* Examines government encouragement of the construction and development of railroads in France, in particular the activities and writings of Michel Chevalier (1809-79). 1823-48

Chevallier, Jean Jacques

1341. Ourliac, Paul. JEAN-JACQUES CHEVALLIER, HISTORIEN DE LA PENSEE POLITIQUE (A PROPOS D'UN OUVRAGE RECENT) [Jean Jacques Chevallier, historian of political thought: apropos of a recent work]. *Rev. Hist. de Droit Français et Etranger [France] 1981 59(4): 653-656.* Pays tribute to Jean Jacques Chevallier, jurist, political scientist, historian, and professor at the Institut des Idées Politiques and at the University of Paris; reviews his *Histoire de la Pensée Politique. Vol. 1: De la Cité-État à l'Apogée de l'État-Nation Monarchique. Vol. 2: L'État-Nation Monarchique: Vers le Déclin* (1979), in which Chevallier analyzes the evolution of the history of political thoughts and ideas; and comments on *Histoire des Idées et Idées sur l'Histoire. Etudes Offertes à Jean-Jacques Chevallier* (1977), in which political doctrines and ideas are oriented especially to history. 1977-79

Chevallier, Temple

1342. Klottrup, Alan. "... ASTRORUM ACERRIMUS INDAGATOR ... " TEMPLE CHEVALLIER AND DURHAM 1834-1873. *Durham University Journal [Great Britain] 1985 78(1): 11-21.* This biographical article on Temple Chevallier (1794-1873) catalogs the many achievements of the cleric astronomer and outlines the events of his life. Not only was Chevallier active in the church, holding various positions including those of Honorary and then Residentiary Canon of Durham Cathedral, but he was also the first (and last) Professor of Mathematics and Astronomy at Durham University from 1835 to 1871. Chevallier's chief monument is the observatory that he founded during the 1830's at the university where he also held a number of offices and posts, including those of registrar and sub-warden. Based on Chevallier Papers and other manuscript sources located in Durham and Newcastle; 196 notes, biblio. 1834-73

Chi Baishi

1343. Sun, Teresa Chi-Ching. A STUDY OF THE LITERARY QUOTATION OF CH'I PAI-SHIH'S SEAL INSCRIPTIONS AND SOME INSIGHTS INTO HIS OUTLOOK OF LIFE. *Asian Profile [Hong Kong] 1981 9(5): 415-421.* Chi Baishi (Ch'i Pai-shih, 1863-1957) was an influential artist in China from the 1920's forward. He was appointed honorary professor at the Central Art College of China and elected to the Presidential Board of the Chinese Literature and Arts Association in 1952 and awarded the title of People's Artist and elected chairman of the Chinese Artist's Association in 1953. He carved 170 inscription seals which reveal his philosophy of life. He was deeply influenced by Ch'an (Zen) Buddhism, believed in the Confucian virtue of industriousness, was loyal to his friends, disdainful of fame, and practical, but not without a certain romantic imagination. Secondary sources; ref., 14 notes. 1900-57

Chicherin, Georgi V.

1344. Grant, Ron. G. V. CHICHERIN AND THE RUSSIAN REVOLUTIONARY CAUSE IN GREAT BRITAIN. *Immigrants & Minorities [Great Britain] 1983 2(3): 117-138.* Reviews the World War I career of Georgi V. Chicherin as a revolutionary Russian exile in Great Britain. A man of tremendous energy, Chicherin organized several radical movements during a period when other revolutionary exiles were largely muted by British patriotic fervor. His most adventurous program was launched in opposition to military service by exiles, either with British or their homeland forces. He was eventually interned, but was released and returned to Russia following the revolution. There he became Soviet Russia's second commissar of Foreign Affairs. Based on the Bridges-Adams papers, Oxford University, British Foreign Office papers, and secondary sources. 1914-18

Chidley, William James

1345. Finnane, Mark. THE POPULAR DEFENCE OF CHIDLEY. *Labour Hist. [Australia] 1981 (41): 57-73.* William James Chidley, Australian advocate of sex reform, stimulated massive support from 1911 through 1916. Chidley's call for a return to the "simple life" involved 1) dressing in a light tunic, 2) diet of fresh fruit and nuts, and 3) educating the public about natural sexual coition. Chidley, persecuted for his public views, died in 1916 in Callan Park Asylum. He publicized his jailings to marshal support from defenders of the rights of free speech, those who desired to lessen the medical control over lunacy proceedings, laborers who sought changes in the policies of the New South Wales Labor Party, and women who challenged patriarchical society in their search for a new social order. Chidley's public discussion of sexuality and the inequitable distribution of power between the sexes threatened the fabric of Australian society. Based primarily on archival, manuscript, and newspaper sources; 59 notes. 1911-16

Chimochowski, W.

1346. Domi, M. IN MEMORIAM: PROF. W. CHIMOCHOWSKI (1912-1982) [In memoriam: professor W. Chimochowski (1912-82)]. *Studia Albanica [Albania] 1983 20(1): 191-192.* An obituary of the Polish academic W. Chimochowski, who was well-known for his work on the history of the Albanian language. 1912-82

Chin Bangxian

1347. Pantsov, A. LIFE GIVEN TO THE STRUGGLE FOR FREEDOM (SEVENTY-FIVE YEARS SINCE THE BIRTH OF BO GU). *Far Eastern Affairs [USSR] 1983 (1): 122-129.* After winning leadership of the Chinese Communists in 1934 at age 24, Bo Gu (Po Ku; real name Chin Bangxian—Ch'in Pang-hsien) organized the unified front against the Japanese invasion as the Communists' liaison officer in negotiations with the Nationalists. He died in a 1946 airplane accident. 1925-46

Chirac, Jacques

1348. Palewski, Gaston. PROPOS [Remarks]. *Rev. des Deux Mondes [France] 1983 (4): 128-136.* Personal notes and recollections on various personalities in the worlds of politics and literature, such as the widow of US financier Jay Gould, French public figure of the 1940's René Mayer, novelist Arthur Koestler (1905-83), and French politician Jacques Chirac. ca 1860-1983

Chirino, Pedro

1349. Jurado, Manuel Ruiz. FR. PEDRO CHIRINO, S. J., AND PHILIPPINE HISTORIOGRAPHY. *Philippine Studies [Philippines] 1981 29(3-4): 345-359.* Sketches the life of Pedro Chirino (1557-1635), the Spanish Jesuit missionary whose historical writings first provided Europe with reliable knowledge of the Philippines. Chirino's choleric temperament was an obstacle to his personal relations with fellow missionaries and native Filipinos, but he accomplished much despite his character defect. Based on Chirino's historical works and other primary and secondary sources. 1590-1635

Chkalov, V. P.

1350. Beliakov, A. CHEREZ SEVERNYI POLIUS AMERIKU [Across the North Pole to America]. *Voenno-Istoricheskii Zhurnal [USSR] 1981 23(5): 38-43.* 1937
*For abstract see **Baidukov, G. F.***

Chodasiewicz, Roberto Adolfo

1351. Warren, Harris Gaylord. ROBERTO ADOLFO CHODASIEWICZ: A POLISH SOLDIER OF FORTUNE IN THE PARAGUAYAN WAR. *Americas (Academy of American Franciscan History) 1985 41(3): 1-19.* Roberto Adolfo Chodasiewicz (1832-96), a Russian military officer of Polish descent, deserted to the British during the Crimean War. After further service in Europe and the United States, he offered his skills to Argentina in the War of the Triple Alliance against Paraguay. Serving as a military engineer, he used balloons and other techniques to accomplish mapping of enemy territory, assisted in fortification work, and gave technical advice to allied commanders. He subsequently worked as an engineer in Paraguay and in Argentina, where he returned to military service. Based on unpublished "Autobiografía" in the Argentine Archivo General de la Nación, other documents there and in the Archivo General Mitre, and published primary and secondary works; 76 notes. 1860's-96

Choibalsan, Khorloogiin

1352. Vinkovics, Judit and Balogh, Péter. ÉLETRAJZOK A MONGOL NÉPI FORRADALOM KORÁBÓL [Biographies from the time of the Mongol people's revolution]. *Világtörténet [Hungary] 1983 (2): 113-125.* Provides brief biographies of Jebtzun Damba, K. Choibalsan, and Roman Ungern von Sternberg. Jebtzun Damba (1869-1924) became the bodgo-gegen in 1874 of Ugra (now Ulan Bator) and was the last holder of that title. Until his death he remained the leader of the feudal classes and never ceased his struggle against the revolutionary forces. One month after his death the Republic of Mongolia was established. Choibalsan (1859-1952), one of the builders of Mongolian independence, was prime minister from 1939 to 1952 and instituted many economic and social changes. Roman Ungern von Sternberg (1886-1921), with White Russian troops, captured Ugra in February 1921. In June 1921, he was defeated by the Soviet Army, and on 10 July the people's revolutionary government was established. 2 notes, biblio. 1874-1952

1353. —. OUTSTANDING MONGOLIAN PARTY LEADER AND STATESMAN (THE 90TH ANNIVERSARY OF THE BIRTH OF H. CHOIBALSAN). *Far Eastern Affairs [USSR] 1985 (3): 131-134.* Discusses the life of Khorloogiin Choibalsan (1895-1952), cofounder of the Mongolian People's Revolutionary Party, and his work in promoting friendship between the Soviet and Mongolian peoples. 1919-52

Choiseul, Étienne-François de

1354. Scott, H. M. CHOISEUL: THE MAKING OF A DIPLOMAT. *Int. Hist. Rev. [Canada] 1982 4(3): 414-420.* Reviews Rohan Butler's *Choiseul, Volume 1: Father and Son, 1719-54* (1980). The Duc de Choiseul (1719-85) exercised an unusually high degree of control over French diplomacy, 1758-70, but began his career as a typical aristocratic amateur, through patronage. 13 notes. 1719-54

Choisy, François Timoléon de

1355. —. A BOURGES, POUR FAIRE LA BELLE TANT QU'IL LUI PLAIRA, L'ABBE DE CHOISY DEVIENT COMTESSE DES BARRES [At Bourges, to act the beauty as much as he pleased, the abbé de Choisy became the Comtesse des Barres]. *Hist. Mag. [France] 1983 (41): 76-82.* Describes François Timoléon de Choisy's convincing impersonation of a countess in late 17th-century France, and his continued transvestism even after having become an abbé and member of the Académie Française. 1666-1724

Chopin, Frédéric

1356. Lupack, Barbara T. CHOPIN: NEW BIOGRAPHICAL INSIGHTS. *Polish Rev. 1982 27(1-2): 141-149.* Reviews of two biographies on Frédéric Chopin (1810-49): William G. Atwood's *The Lioness and the Little One* (1980) and Adam Zamoyski's *Chopin: A New Biography* (1980). The latter provides a good overview of the composer's life while Atwood's book concentrates on his later years from his first meeting with George Sand. Both works "are excellent" and "are significant and compelling additions to Chopin scholarship." 1810-49

Chrimes, Stanley Bertram

1357. Knowles, C. H. OBITUARY: STANLEY BERTRAM CHRIMES. *Welsh History Review [Great Britain] 1985 12(3): 420-422.* Stanley Bertram Chrimes (1907-84) studied at King's College, London and Trinity College, Cambridge. He taught at these colleges and at the University of Glasgow before being appointed to the chair of history and head of the Department of History and acting head of the Department of the History of Wales at University College, Cardiff, in 1953. He specialized in constitutional history, especially of the 15th century, and published several works, beginning with *English Constitutional Ideas in the Fifteenth*

Century (1936). He did valued work for the Historical Association, the Glamorgan History Society, and the Glamorgan County History Trust. 1907-84

Christensen, Aksel E.

1358. Hørby, Kai. AKSEL E. CHRISTENSEN, 11.9.1906-15.12.1981 [Aksel E. Christensen (11 September 1906-15 December 1981)]. *Historisk Tidsskrift [Denmark] 1983 82(2): 334-342.* Aksel E. Christensen was a prominent medieval historian, a landmark in his career being his 1931 Gold Medal-winning dissertation on late medieval Scandinavian guilds. He held a professorship at Copenhagen from 1948 to 1976, distinguishing himself both academically and administratively, and showing great zeal in defense of causes dear to him. 1906-81

Christian VIII (Christian Frederick)

1359. Sjøqvist, Viggo. BIDRAG TIL EN KARAKTERISTIK AF CHRISTIAN VIII [Contribution to a character sketch of Christian VIII]. *Historie [Denmark] 1984 15(3): 453-475.* Christian Frederick (1786-1848), king of Norway during the revolutionary year of 1814, and as Christian VIII, king of Denmark 1839-48, has been misunderstood by historians. An outdoorsman of colossal vitality and endurance, modern in all but his political views (which were rooted in the 18th century), he was sincerely religious, remarkably humane, had a wide knowledge of the arts, sciences, and humanities, and was perhaps the most intelligent monarch ever to sit on the Danish throne. Yet he was too stiff and formal, an insatiable womanizer, alienated from his son and heir, lacked the common touch, and was unpopular with the populace and court alike. Based on Christian VIII's diaries and letters, and other primary sources; 49 notes. 1786-1848

Christina, Queen

1360. Puaux, Anne. CHRISTINE DE SUEDE AU PALAIS FARNESE [Christina of Sweden at the Farnese Palace]. *Rev. des Deux Mondes [France] 1983 (12): 608-612.* Describes the life of the queen in Italy and France following her abdication in 1654 and her founding of a renowned literary and artistic circle in 1656. 1654-86

1361. Sourander, Patrick. DROTTNING CHRISTINA OCH GIOVANNI ALFONSO BORELLI: TILL 300-ÅRSMINNET AV KINESIOLOGINS FÖDELSE [Queen Christina and Giovanni Alfonso Borelli: in commemoration of the birth of kinesiology 300 years ago]. *Nordisk Medicinhistorisk Årsbok [Sweden] 1982: 56-65.* 1670's
For abstract see ***Borelli, Giovanni Alfonso***

Chu Wu

1362. —. CH'U WU—VICE CHAIRMAN OF THE NATIONAL COMMITTEE OF THE CPPCC. *Issues & Studies [Taiwan] 1984 20(1): 98-104.* Chu Wu (Ch'u Wu, b. 1898) is a longtime member of the CCP who studied in Russia in the 1920's and 1930's. He has held many responsible political posts. In June 1983 he was made a vice chairman of the 6th National Committee of the Chinese People's Political Consultative Conference. 1920-83

Chubar, V. I.

1363. Kol'iak, T. M. VLAS IAKOVYCH CHUBAR (DO 90-RICHCHIA Z DNIA NARODZHENNIA) [Vlas Iakovych Chubar: his 90th birthday]. *Ukrains'kyi Istorychnyi Zhurnal [USSR] 1981 (2): 28-34.* V. I. Chubar (1891-1939), noted Communist Party and Soviet government worker, traveled the path from an ordinary worker to the chairman of the Council of People's Commissars in the Ukraine and the deputy head of the Soviet government. Official Party sources; 13 notes. 1910's-39

Chulkov, M. D.

1364. Bondareva, E. A. TVORCHESKII PUT' I PROSVETITEL'SKAIA DEIATEL'NOST' M. D. CHULKOVA [The creative path and the enlightenment activities of M. D. Chulkov]. *Istoricheskie Zapiski Akademii Nauk SSSR [USSR] 1984 (111): 201-237.* Traces the career of M. D. Chulkov (1740-92). In his 20 years of creative activity in literature, Chulkov developed a new genre, style, and language, and also made contributions as a dramatist, poet, and journalist. He stood first in the collection of folk songs. The author credits Chulkov with writing the first Russian novel, analyzes the works of Chulkov and his contemporary fellow writers, and discusses the social, economic, and political context in which they worked. Studying the life and creative works of Chulkov provides the opportunity to examine the problems of the nonnoble intelligentsia in the last half of the 18th century and its contributions to the cultural epoch of the enlightenment in Russia. Based on Central State Historical Archives, papers and writings of Chulkov's contemporaries, and secondary sources; 96 notes. 1760's-92

Churchill, Winston

1365. Baxter, Colin F. WINSTON CHURCHILL: MILITARY STRATEGIST? *Military Affairs 1983 47(1): 7-10.* Among the most controversial aspects of Winston Churchill's long and controversial career, none has aroused more dispute than his role as a strategist in World War II, with his strategic reputation seesawing between hero worship and scapegoat. Although possessing a romantic temperament, which showed clearly his devotion to such institutions as the Empire and monarchy, in the conduct of military strategy Churchill generally displayed a sense of realism and he must surely rank as one of Great Britain's most successful military strategists. Based on primary sources; 34 notes. 1939-45

1366. Cohen, Michael J. CHURCHILL AND THE JEWS: THE HOLOCAUST. *Modern Judaism 1986 6(1): 27-49.* Disputes the assertion that Prime Minister Winston Churchill did everything humanly possible to help European Jews during the Holocaust, but on the contrary holds Churchill personally responsible for much of Great Britain's documented callousness and indifference toward their plight. 1939-45

1367. Harriman, Pamela C. CHURCHILL'S DREAM. *Am. Heritage 1983 34(6): 84-87.* The daughter-in-law of Winston Churchill recounts an unpublished story Churchill wrote in 1947. In it, Churchill indicated the depth of his despair over his rejection by the British voters in 1945 and his concern for the state of the postwar world. Photo. 1940-47

1368. Jenkins, Roy. WINSTON CHURCHILL AND THE "NATURAL CAPTAIN OF THE WEST." *Am. Heritage 1982 33(6): 94-97.* A British assessment of the relationship between Franklin D. Roosevelt and Winston Churchill during World War II. Roosevelt was probably a better strategist than was Churchill, and since Churchill needed Roosevelt more than Roosevelt needed him, he accepted a secondary role to the "natural captain of the West." 3 photos. 1938-45

1369. Johnson, Paul. RECORDING COLOSSUS: ON WINSTON CHURCHILL. *Encounter [Great Britain] 1983 61(3): 67-70.* Assesses existing biographies of Winston Churchill (1874-1965) and the difficulties involved in trying to write a successful and adequate one. 1874-1965

1370. Rintala, Marvin. RENAMED ROSES: LLOYD GEORGE, CHURCHILL, AND THE HOUSE OF LORDS. *Biography 1985 8(3): 248-264.* Together, and predictably, David Lloyd George and Winston Churchill used the budget of 1909 to destroy the legislative power of the House of the Lords, the last instrument of power of the landed aristocrats who had ruled Great Britain for so long. Arnold Bennett's hypothesis that the continuing prestige of the House of Lords would attract even the most disdainful members of the House of Commons when they were defeated by advancing age is tested by the examples of Lloyd George and Churchill. 1890's-1955

1371. Sainsbury, Keith. CHURCHILL AND ROOSEVELT: UNEASY PARTNERS. *Journal of the Royal United Services Institute for Defence Studies [Great Britain] 1985 130(3): 59-60.* Reviews *Churchill and Roosevelt: The Complete Correspondence* (1984), edited by W. F. Kimball. The relationship during World War II between Franklin D. Roosevelt and Winston Churchill was not as amiable as it appeared to be in public. While Churchill argued for US and British involvement in the liberation of Eastern Europe in order to forestall Soviet expansionism, Roosevelt was suspicious of Churchill's motives. Churchill generally dominated the relationship during 1942-43, but as Britain's strength waned during 1944-45, Roosevelt asserted US leadership. 1941-45

1372. Smith, Charles Roger. "Winston Churchill and the Rise of Totalitarianism: Statesmanship and the Challenge of Modern Tyranny." Catholic U. of Am. 1983. 416 pp. *DAI 1983 43(10): 3409-A.* DA8304644 1930's-50's

1373. Tejchman, Miroslav. SOVĚTSKÁ POLITIKA VŮČI BALKÁNU V LETECH 1941-1944 OČIMA BRITSKÉ DIPLOMACIE [Soviet policy toward the Balkans in the years 1941-44 in the eyes of British diplomacy]. *Slovanský Přehled [Czechoslovakia] 1982 68(4): 316-326.* Winston Churchill's interest in the Balkans centered on the preservation of the British Empire and its interests. He wanted to invade Europe from that "soft underbelly" of Europe but was overridden by his American allies. Seeing the strength of the Communist opposition to fascism, in October 1944 he went to Moscow and there presented his scheme of shared influence in the Balkans to the Russians. No document in the Soviet archives supports the contention that Stalin and Churchill arrived at percentages. However, by the end of the war the Soviet Union had liberated most of the Balkans as independent states, rejecting an earlier British Foreign Office plan for a Balkan federation. 63 notes. 1941-44

1374. Wilson, K. M. THE FATE OF A YOUNG CHURCHILLIAN CONCEIT: "THE WAR ON THE NILE LETTERS" AND THE *MORNING POST. Victorian Periodicals Review 1985 18(4): 143-146.* Reprints and evaluates portions of the letters that Winston Churchill wrote to the *Morning Post,* a London newspaper, in 1898 on the Nile Expeditionary Force. The *Morning Post* edited these letters, much to the anger of Churchill, who later described the expedition in *The River War* (1899). 1898-99

Churchill family

1375. Quinault, Roland. THE CHURCHILL DYNASTY. *Hist. Today [Great Britain] 1983 33(Sept): 21-27.* Traces the sometimes unorthodox public activities of the Churchill family since the 1st Duke of Marlborough. 18c-20c

Chydenius, Anders

1376. Virrankoski, Pentti. ANDERS CHYDENIUKSEN PERSOONALLISUUS [The personality of Anders Chydenius]. *Hist. Aikakauskirja [Finland] 1982 80(1): 3-13.* Characterizes the personality of Finnish pastor, economist, and politician, Anders Chydenius (1729-1803). Very energetic with many skills, he was ambitious, self-confident, and aggressive. His activities were held back partly by circumstances in Swedish politics and partly by his commitment to pietistic humility. Based on Chydenius's published works and secondary sources; 22 notes. 1750-1803

Ciano, Galeazzo

1377. Mikhailenko, V. I. O DNEVNIKAKH CHIANO [On the Ciano diaries]. *Novaia i Noveishaia Istoriia [USSR] 1981 (5): 150-163.* The diaries of the Minister of Foreign Affairs of fascist Italy Galeazzo Ciano give an insight into the workings of the fascist regime and into Ciano's conversations with Benito Mussolini. When in prison, Ciano wrote that his diaries show that Adolf Hitler and Mussolini alone were responsible for drawing Italy into the war. Far from this, the diaries document the criminal essence of fascism. German and Anglo-American secret services attempted to capture the diaries, whose history is recounted here. Based on archival material and secondary sources; 68 notes. 1936-44

1378. Palla, Marco. LA FORTUNA DI UN DOCUMENTO: IL DIARIO DI CIANO [The fortune of a document: the diary of Ciano]. *Italia Contemporanea [Italy] 1981 33(142): 31-54.* The diary of Galeazzo Ciano for the years 1937 to 1943 bolsters the view that Benito Mussolini alone was responsible for Italy's entry into World War II and for its conduct during the war. Ciano, Italy's foreign minister under Mussolini and his son-in-law, revealed to a number of people including American diplomats that he was writing the diary. Ciano's wife, Edda, took the diary to Switzerland when she fled Italy, and sold it to the Chicago *Daily News,* April 1945. The diary, subsequently published by Doubleday in the United States, has now appeared in a new Italian edition, *Diario 1937-1943* (1980). Based on primary sources, including archival material from the National Archives, Washington, and the Public Record Office, London. 1937-45

Cibat, Antonio

1379. Riera Palmero, Juan. NOTA SOBRE ANTONIO CIBAT Y LA CATEDRA DE FISICA EXPERIMENTAL DE BARCELONA (UN PROYECTO DE 1807) [A note on Antonio Cibat and the chair of experimental physics in Barcelona: a project of 1807]. *Dynamis [Spain] 1982 2: 357-362.* Antonio Cibat was born in the diocese of Gerona in the mid-18th century. He graduated in medicine and surgery from the College of Surgery in Barcelona, where he later taught, among other subjects, experimental physics. He was a member of the Royal Academy of Sciences and Arts of Barcelona and assistant surgeon in the army. In 1807 he submitted to the Junta Particular de Comercio of Barcelona a project for the establishment of a chair of experimental physics at the College of Surgery, which came to nothing. The reason given was the forced absence of the author of the proposal for his army duties. Based on primary material in state archives; 10 notes. 18c-1812

Cíger-Hronský, Jozef

1380. Okál', Ján. ZO ŽIVOTA J. C. HRONSKÉHO V RÍME [Scenes from Jozef Cíger-Hronský's life in Rome]. *Kalendár Jednota 1986 89: 120-139.* After World War II, the Slovak writer J. C. Hronský (Jozef Cíger, 1896-1960) lived in Rome as a political refugee before settling in Argentina. 1946-47 -Hronský

1381. Petro, Peter. JOZEF CIGER-HRONSKÝ: A MAJOR SLOVAK NOVELIST. *Slovakia 1982-83 30(55-56): 142-152.* Although a relatively obscure writer until recently, Jozef Cíger-Hronský became known for his interwar Slovak village novels, but reached his peak with two lyric novels written in Argentina in 1948 and 1960. 1931-60 -Hronský

1382. Rudinsky, Norma L. JOZEF CIGER-HRONSKÝ: CHRONOLOGY AND PARTIAL BIBLIOGRAPHY. *Slovakia 1982-83 30(55-56): 128-141.* A chronology of the life of Slovak writer, Jozef Ciger-Hronský and a bibliography of 52 entries. 1896-1983

Čingrija, Pero

1383. Perić, Ivo. POLITIČKI PORTRET PERA ČINGRIJE [A political portrait of Pero Čingrija]. *Radovi: Inst. za Hrvatsku Povijest [Yugoslavia] 1979 12: 127-262.* The political activities and attitudes of the Dubrovnik liberal bourgeois politician Pero Čingrija (1837-1921) were influenced by the ideas of the Croatian Illyrian movement and the Italian Risorgimento that he discovered while studying law in Padua. The two political movements were similar in their strong anti-Austrian stance and their advocacy of a struggle to secure the national and political rights of peoples under Austro-Hungarian rule. As a delegate to the Dalmatian Parliament from the Dalmatian Popular Party and later the leader of the Popular Croatian Party, Pero Čingrija consistently fought for the unification of Dalmatia with Croatia. He was against the use of Italian and German as official languages. He supported political cooperation between Croats and Serbs as a precondition for successful resistance against the Austrian government and Italian aspirations in Dalmatia. Although dissatisfied with the organization of the Yugoslav state, he welcomed its formation in 1918 and protested strongly against the Italian occupation of Yugoslav territories. Based on documents from the Dubrovnik Historical Archives and secondary sources; 568 notes. 1860-1921

Cipariu, Timotei

1384. Duţu, Alexandru. UN STRĂLUCIT CĂRTURAR ŞI PATRIOT: TIMOTEI CIPARIU [A famous bookman and patriot: Timotei Cipariu]. *Magazin Istoric [Romania] 1980 14(4): 48-52.* Summarizes the life of the Transylvanian Romanian scholar and publicist Timotei Cipariu (1805-87), with special attention to his political activities in the Revolution of 1848. 1825-87

Cipriani, Leonetto

1385. Danelon Vasoli, Nidia. L'ARCHIVIO PRIVATO DI LEONETTO CIPRIANI [Leonetto Cipriani's private archive]. *Rassegna Storica Toscana [Italy] 1982 28(1): 133-161.* Describes Leonetto Cipriani's archives, which provide material for his biography. He was familiar with the Bonaparte family, was a member of the French expedition against Algeria, traveled in America, and took part in the Risorgimento campaign of 1848 and in government and diplomatic affairs. 96 notes. 1848-68

Circignani, Nicolò

1386. Nimmo, Mara. "L' ETA PERFETTA DELLA VIRILITA" DI NICOLO CIRCIGNANI DALLE POMARANCIE ["The perfect age of virility" of Nicolò Circignani of Pomerania]. *Studi Romani [Italy] 1984 32(3-4): 194-214.* Uses the Archives of San Luca and the Vatican to document the artistic career of Nicolò Circignani (ca. 1516-90), whose style was described by contemporaries as reflecting "the perfect age of virility." ca 1516-90

Ciriani, Marco

1387. Ziller, Paolo. MARCO CIRIANI: DALLA LEGA DEMOCRATICA NAZIONALE A "GIUSTIZIA E LIBERTA" [Marco Ciriani: from the National Democratic League to Giustizia e Libertà]. *Civitas [Italy] 1985 36(2): 19-32.* Analyzes the political itinerary of Friulian Catholic activist Marco Ciriani (1878-1944), who joined the Lega Democratica Nazionale [National Democratic League] in 1905 and stayed with them until the Italian Popular Party was formed in 1919; however, when the Popular Party was expelled from the Mussolini government in 1923, Ciriani was compelled to contact the clandestine organization Giustizia e Libertà, which in turn led to his capture in Spilimberg by Fascist authorities, his imprisonment, and his death in Milan in 1944. 1905-44

Cisneros, Gonzalo Jiménez de

1388. Meseguer Fernández, Juan. EL ARZOBISPO CARRILLO Y EL CARDENAL CISNEROS [Archbishop Carrillo and Cardinal Cisneros]. *Archivo Ibero-Americano [Spain] 1985 45(177-178): 167-187.* 1470's
*For abstract see **Carrillo, Alfonso***

Citroën, André

1389. Casteele-Schweitzer, Sylvie van de. ANDRE CITROEN: L'AVENTURIER DE L'INDUSTRIE [André Citroën: the industrialist adventurer]. *Histoire [France] 1983 (56): 8-20.* French engineer and industrialist André Citroën (1878-1935) established one of the most important French automobile factories, but he ended in bankruptcy in 1934. 1914-34

Čiurlionis, M. K.

1390. Plioplys, Audrius V. ČIURLIONIS AND ABSTRACTION—A DISSENTING OPINION. *Lituanus 1986 32(2): 58-68.* Contrary to the assertions of some critics, the Lithuanian artist M. K. Čiurlionis (1875-1911) was not the first abstract painter. Čiurlionis was not influenced by factors that stimulated the development of abstraction; these factors include the relation of art to music, Einstein's theory of relativity, the advent of psychology, and the popularity of theosophy. Furthermore, he neither theorized about abstraction nor practiced it in his own work to any significant degree. The most detrimental effect of criticism linking Čiurlionis with abstraction has been the diminution of his genuine artistic accomplishments. 31 notes. 1890's-1911

Clare, John

1391. Estermann, Barbara. "John Clare: An Annotated Primary and Secondary Bibliography." (Vol. 1-2) Louisiana State U. 1984. 459 pp. *DAI 1985 46(4): 988-A.* DA8511750 1810's-64

Clarín

See Alas, Leopoldo

Clark, Andrew

1392. Munson, James. ANDREW CLARK'S WAR DIARY, 1914-19. *Bodleian Library Record [Great Britain] 1985 12(1): 82-84.* Describes the diary kept by Andrew Clark, rector of Great Leighs in Essex, consisting of 92 volumes and including over three million words. Clark attempted to gather first-hand information from all sorts and classes of people. Based on the diary in the Bodleian Library, Oxford. 1914-19

Clark, E. Warren

1393. Métraux, Daniel Alfred. LIFE AND ADVENTURE IN JAPAN: E. WARREN CLARK'S EDUCATIONAL AND RELIGIOUS MISSION OF THE EARLY 1870S. *Asian Profile [Hong Kong] 1983 11(4): 357-364.* Reviews the career of E. Warren Clark—scholar, chemistry and physics teacher, and lay missionary—in Japan. The Japanese government had invited Clark for his skills as a teacher of modern science, but Clark took his role as a lay missionary just as seriously and organized Bible classes while he worked in the city of Shizuoka. Although Clark was critical of Japanese religious practices and considered the Japanese to be pagans and heathens, he was impressed by other aspects of their culture. Clark later left for Tokyo to become chairman of Tokyo Imperial University's chemistry department. He eventually returned to the United States in 1875. Not only did Clark play an important role in the modernization of Japan, but he also educated Americans about Japan, particularly Meiji Japan. Based mostly on E. W. Clark's *Life and Adventure in Japan* (1878); 18 notes. 1870's

Clark, George Norman

1394. Parker, Geoffrey. GEORGE NORMAN CLARK 1890-1979. *Pro. of the British Acad. [Great Britain] 1980 66: 407-425.* An obituary of the British historian George Norman Clark (1890-1979). Sir George Clark's chief intellectual interests lay in the field of early modern British and European history, but his 17 books and nearly 50 articles cover a phenomenally wide range. A former editor of the *English Historical Review,* he also masterminded three major series, the *Oxford History of England,* the Home University Library of Modern Knowledge, and the *New Cambridge Modern History.* Uses unpublished papers by G. N. Clark and privately communicated information; photo, 14 notes, biblio. 1890-1979

Clarke, Charlotte Cibber

1395. Courtoy, Ava DiAnn. "'A Little, Dirty Kind of War': The Life of Charlotte Cibber Clarke." Florida State U. 1982. 221 pp. *DAI 1983 43(10): 3322-A.* DA8306158 18c

Claude, George

1396. Pittman, Walter E., Jr. ENERGY FROM THE OCEANS: GEORGE CLAUDE'S MAGNIFICENT FAILURE. *Environmental Rev. 1982 6(1): 2-13.* French inventor George Claude experimented during 1924-34 with the Claude-Boucherot process, which depended on the natural temperature gradient in large bodies of water to produce electrical power, but Claude's work met with scant success and a cool reception from the scientific community. 1924-34

Claudel, Camille

1397. Andersen, Marguerite. UNE FEMME SCULPTEURE INTERDITE: CAMILLE CLAUDEL [A banished woman sculptor: Camille Claudel]. *Resources for Feminist Research [Canada] 1984 13(4): 7-11.* Discusses the life of French sculptor Camille Claudel who was committed to an insane asylum by her parents where she spent the last 30 years of her life, and examines accounts of her life and works including Anne Delbée's *Une Femme,* Anne Riviere's *L'Interdite,* and Reine-Marie Paris's *Camille Claudel.* Prints several excerpts of letters written by Claudel in the asylum to her brother Paul, letters by her mother to the directors of the asylum, and writings of critics praising her art. 1905-32

1398. Wernick, Robert. CAMILLE CLAUDEL'S TEMPESTUOUS LIFE OF ART AND PASSION. *Smithsonian 1985 16(6): 56-65.* Reviews the life and work of Camille Claudel (1864-1942), French sculptor as well as model, collaborator, and lover of Auguste Rodin (1840-1917). 1880-1935

Claudel, Paul

1399. Baumel, Joan Patricia. "Paul Claudel and the Jews: A Study in Ambivalence." Fordham U. 1985. 208 pp. *DAI 1986 46(8): 2289-A.* DA8521403 1890's-1955

Clausewitz, Karl von

1400. Aron, Raymond. CLAUSEWITZ: STRATEGE UND PATRIOT [Clausewitz: strategist and patriot]. *Hist. Zeits. [West Germany] 1982 234(2): 295-316.* Karl von Clausewitz evolved from Prussian patriot to an un-self-conscious German cultural nationalist in the confrontation with France during the Napoleonic wars. He also reflected the conditions of his lifetime in his military theories, the most important of which was absolute war. His special emphasis on defensive war and his belief that politics and military activity are not separate concepts reflected the conditions between 1805 and 1813 when his homeland was defeated and subordinated to France. Clausewitz may have been a liberal as far as society was concerned, but he saw no need for a German constitution or change in the state. 1790's-1831

1401. Kipp, Jacob W. LENIN AND CLAUSEWITZ: THE MILITARIZATION OF MARXISM, 1914-1921. *Military Affairs 1985 49(4): 184-191.* Examines the intellectual bond between the Prussian military officer Karl von Clausewitz and the Russian revolutionary V. I. Lenin in order to better understand the relationship between Soviet military science and Marxism-Leninism. Lenin's militarization of Marxism involved a substantial shift in the place of war in socialist ideology and Lenin used Clausewitz as a guide. Lenin emphasized the inevitability of wars among capitalist states in the age of imperialism and presented the armed struggle of the working class as the only path toward the eventual elimination of war. Based on Russian and other primary sources; 55 notes. 1914-21

1402. VanCreveld, Martin. THE ETERNAL CLAUSEWITZ. *Journal of Strategic Studies [Great Britain] 1986 9(2-3): 35-50.* Argues that Karl von Clausewitz's *On War* has always remained relevant precisely because of the author's refusal to fall into the trap that caught many military thinkers; namely, that of trying to discover the existence of constants in a field of human activity where no scientific laws can exist. Clausewitz approached the study of war as objectively and systematically as possible, but he also recognized that it always involves clashing purposes and free creative choices. Primary sources; 32 notes. ca 1800-31

Clemenceau, Georges

1403. Gurvich, S. N. BYL LI KLEMANSO CHLENOM PARTII RADIKALOV? [Was Clemenceau a member of the Radical Party?]. *Frantsuzskii Ezhegodnik [USSR] 1980: 142-153.* Examines the political career of French prime minister and political theorist Georges Clemenceau from 1901 to 1910 to establish Clemenceau's relationship with and membership in France's Radical Party. Clemenceau participated in the discussions about the program and tactics of the future party in the preparations for the first organizational congress of the Radical Party, which took place in Paris, 21-23 June 1901. In addition, he wrote articles for radical newspapers about the preparatory talks, thus making known his sympathies for this political trend, of which he had previously been an ideologist and apparently intended to remain one. He did not attend the organizational congress, however, thus showing his refusal to join the party. Indirect documentary evidence indicates, however, that Clemenceau joined the party in December 1908 or January 1909. 46 notes. French summary. 1901-10

1404. Peumery, Suzanne-Edith. CLEMENCEAU VU PAR SON VALET DE CHAMBRE [Clémenceau portrayed by his manservant]. *Historama [France] 1985 (18): 64-68.* On the basis of a conversation in 1984 with Albert Boulin, manservant and confidant of Georges Clémenceau (1841-1929) from 1919 to the latter's death, gives an anecdotal and intimate portrait of this famous journalist, editor, statesman, and twice premier of France. 1919-29

Clephane, John

1405. Jenkins, Philip. JOHN CLEPHANE: A NEW WELSH SOURCE FOR THE HISTORY OF THE ENLIGHTENMENT. *Natl. Lib. of Wales J. [Great Britain] 1982 22(4): 416-426.* Supplements biographical details on John Clephane, Scottish scholar, physician, and philosopher, by drawing attention to his cultural or educative importance as Grand Tour director, or "bear-leader," to several young noblemen and gentlemen, notably his friend the second Lord Mansell (d. 1774). Clephane provided invaluable political, diplomatic, literary, and artistic advice to his clients before he retired from touring to pursue his medical work and participate in British intellectual life. Based on Mansell's correspondence; 45 notes. 1739-46

Clerk, Astley

1406. Ryman, Cheryl. ASTLEY CLERK 1868-1944: PATRIOT AND CULTURAL PIONEER. *Jamaica Journal [Jamaica] 1985-86 18(4): 17-26.* Describes the patriotism Astley Clerk (1868-1944) expressed and encouraged toward Jamaica and his contributions to Jamaican culture in the areas of music, folklore, art, linguistics, poetry, and research and publishing. 1890's-1944

Cleve family

1407. Cleve, Nils. NIKLAS GLASSMÄSTARE OCH HANS ÄTTLINGAR [Niklas the glazier and his descendants]. *Historiska och Litteraturhistoriska Studier [Finland] 1984 59: 115-136.* Traces the biographies of Niklas Cleve, a glazier who migrated to Viipuri city in southeast Finland around 1679, his son Joachim Cleve (1681-1729), a pastor in eastern Finland, and Joachim's widow, Margareta Alopaeus Cleve (1705-65). Based on Finnish church archives and on printed sources in Finnish and Swedish; illus., biblio. 1679-1765

Clifford, Anne

1408. Hodgkin, Katharine. THE DIARY OF LADY ANNE CLIFFORD: A STUDY OF CLASS AND GENDER IN THE SEVENTEENTH CENTURY. *History Workshop Journal [Great Britain] 1985 (19): 148-161.* Lady Anne Clifford (1590-1676) spent the first half of her life in open conflict with both her husband and her uncle over her right to inherit her father's estate. In large part, her gender prevented her from obtaining her estate for nearly 30 years, until both her uncle and cousin died. For the last three decades of her life, however, she exerted (ironically) a sort of "patriarchal" authority in the administration of her estate as her class location came to take precedence over her gender. Based largely on Lady Anne Clifford's diary; 42 notes. 1617-76

Clifford, Hugh

1409. Cookey, S. J. S. SIR HUGH CLIFFORD AS GOVERNOR OF NIGERIA: AN EVALUATION. *African Affairs [Great Britain] 1980 79(317): 531-547.* Sir Hugh Clifford was governor of Nigeria, 1919-25, and was probably the greatest colonial ruler of that country. He criticized indirect rule and advocated a policy of allowing indigenous society to be permeated by Western ideas; he believed in the equality of Europeans and Africans and in a humane colonial administration. His introduction of the elective principle encouraged the spread of democratic ideals and the rise of party politics, which hastened the thought of independence and contributed to the transfer of power to Nigerians. Based on primary material in the Colonial Office archives; 52 notes. 1919-25

1410. Hunter, Allan. LETTERS FROM CONRAD. *Notes and Queries [Great Britain] 1985 32(3): 366-370, (4): 500-505.* Part 1. Prints five letters written by Joseph Conrad to author and British colonial administrator Hugh Clifford during Clifford's visit to England, 1901-03. Part 2. Introduces and prints eight letters dated between 23 December 1913 and 13 June 1924, written by Joseph Conrad to British diplomat Hugh Clifford, concerning politics, friendship, and family affairs. 1901-03

Clive, Robert

1411. Lenman, Bruce and Lawson, Philip. ROBERT CLIVE, THE "BLACK JAGIR," AND BRITISH POLITICS. *Hist. J. [Great Britain] 1983 26(4): 801-829.* Provides a political biography of Robert Clive (1725-74), emphasizing the nature of his financial interests, his role in British politics, and his successes and setbacks in the colonial government of India. His suicide in 1774 was the result of a mistaken belief that his family's fortunes and those of the British Empire were headed for inevitable disaster. 101 notes. 1743-74

Clorivière, Pierre de

1412. Morlot, François. CLORIVIERE ET L'AMERIQUE [Clorivière and America]. *Archivum Historicum Societatis Iesu [Italy] 1985 54(107): 149-178.* Reprints journal entries showing Jesuit Father Pierre de Clorivière's zealous pursuit of a missionary posting in North America and how his obedience to superiors prevented two attempts in 1765 and 1816 to travel to Maryland or Quebec. 1765-1816

Cluseret, Gustave-Paul

1413. McLynn, Pauline. GUSTAVE-PAUL CLUSERET, A SOCIALIST SOLDIER OF FORTUNE IN THE AGE OF CAPITAL. *Army Quarterly and Defence Journal [Great Britain] 1984 114(4): 443-454.* Discusses the international career of French-born journalist and soldier of fortune Gustave-Paul Cluseret (1823-1900). 1850-1900

Coates family

1414. Barr, J. M. THE COATES FAMILY OF THE KAIPARA: THE BACKGROUND HISTORY OF GORDON COATES, PRIME MINISTER 1925-28. *Auckland Waikato Hist. J. [New Zealand] 1981 (38): 11-13.* Traces the background of Gordon Coates, the first New Zealand-born prime minister, to 1866 when his father Edward and uncle Thomas left Herefordshire county to sail for Auckland, New Zealand. 1866-1930's

Cobb, Richard

1415. Assouline, Pierre. L'EXTRAVAGANT MISTER COBB [The extravagant Mister Cobb]. *Histoire [France] 1986 (89): 91-95.* A profile of British historian of the French Revolutionary and imperial periods, Richard Cobb, which quotes his outspoken and opinionated judgments to emphasize his individualistic approach to the study of political movements. 18c-20c

Cobbe, Frances Power

1416. Bauer, Carol and Ritt, Lawrence. "A HUSBAND IS A BEATING ANIMAL"—FRANCES POWER COBBE CONFRONTS THE WIFE-ABUSE PROBLEM IN VICTORIAN ENGLAND. *Int. J. of Women's Studies [Canada] 1983 6(2): 99-118.* Cobbe (1822-1904), a feminist, documented the extent of domestic violence and asserted that the fundamental cause was the British attitude that women were inferior; she roused public attention to the issue and secured the passage in Parliament of the Matrimonial Causes Act of 1878 to help protect women from abuse. 1878

Cobbett, William

1417. Belchem, John. COBBETT: THE BIOGRAPHY OF A WRITER. *Bull. of the Soc. for the Study of labour Hist. [Great Britain] 1983 (46): 30-31.* Reviews G. Spater's *William Cobbett: The Poor Man's Friend* (1982), 2 vols., which rejects the "Tory" interpretation of the career of the British radical, William Cobbett. ca 1800-30

1418. Osborne, John W. WILLIAM COBBETT'S ANTI-SEMITISM. *Historian 1984 47(1): 86-92.* George Spater's two-volume *William Cobbett: The Poor Man's Friend* (1982) adds to the enormous amount of literature on the life and career of English journalist William Cobbett (1763-1835). Well grounded in primary sources, Spater's work represents a generally approving picture of this controversial figure. Yet he ignores Cobbett's anti-Semitism. Given Cobbett's anti-Semitism, his hatred of blacks, Scots, and most foreigners, one wonders at the gulf between reality and the favorable way in which he has been viewed by so many historians. Cobbett's life is far from being, as Spater's subtitle suggests, a poor man's friend. 34 notes. 1780's-1835

1419. Wilson, David Alexander. "Tom Paine and William Cobbett: The Trans-Atlantic Connection, 1774-1819." Queen's U., Kingston [Canada] 1983. *DAI 1983 44(5): 1553-A.* 1774-1819

Cobianchi, Gaetano

1420. Garosci, Aldo. GAETANO COBIANCHI UN PO' AVVENTURIERO, MEZZO LIBERALE E MEZZO DIPLOMATICO [Gaetano Cobianchi, part adventurer, half liberal, and half diplomat]. *Rassegna Storica del Risorgimento [Italy] 1983 70(2): 131-140.* Reviews Mario Nagari's *Gaetano Cobianchi. Una Vicenda Risorgimentale (Intra 1794-Parigi 1866)* (1982). Cobianchi was born in a family of textile merchants, was a traveling salesman for a Paris commercial house and found himself involved in the 1821 revolution of the Carbonari, was wounded, and imprisoned. From then on his was a career of conspiracy and adventure, which Nagari's book has succeeded in reconstructing. 1821-66

Cockburn, John

1421. Whyte, Ian D. GEORGE DUNDAS OF DUNDAS. *Scottish Hist. Rev. [Great Britain] 1981 60(1): 1-13.* 1706-57

For abstract see ***Dundas, George***

Cockerill, John

1422. Fremdling, Rainer. JOHN COCKERILL: PIONIERUNTERNEHMER DER BELGISCH-NIEDERLÄNDISCHEN INDUSTRIALISIERUNG [John Cockerill: pioneer entrepreneur of Belgian-Dutch industrialization]. *Zeits. für Unternehmensgeschichte [West Germany] 1981 26(3): 179-193.* Evaluates the work of John Cockerill (1790-1840) in modernizing the iron industry of the Netherlands and Belgium through his Engineering and Iron Works in Seraing, Belgium. Cockerill, a technical and organizational entrepreneur of an originally English family of mechanical engineers, started the gradual modernization process in 1820 with his decision to combine the structure of his works with the manufacture of all iron products. His lack of commercial skills, however, several times brought his ironworks close to bankruptcy, from which he was rescued by the Dutch and Belgian governments. Primary sources; 104 notes. 1790-1840

Cocteau, Jean

1423. Herubel, Michel. LETTRES DE JEAN COCTEAU [Letters of Jean Cocteau]. *Rev. des Deux Mondes [France] 1983 (11): 338-345.* Recounts episodes in the life of the famed French author and filmmaker from 1949-56. 1949-56

Codazzi, Agustín

1424. Perazzo, Nicolás. LA MUERTE DE AGUSTIN CODAZZI [The death of Agustín Codazzi]. *Boletín de la Academia Nacional de la Historia [Venezuela] 1985 68(269): 87-90.* Agustín Codazzi was official geographer to the governments of Venezuela and Colombia in the middle of the 19th century. After mapping Venezuela he was engaged to do the same in Colombia. He died during a field expedition in 1859. This note recalls the circumstances of his death. Ref. 1859

Codelli, Anton III

1425. Južnič, Stanislav. ANTON III. BARON CODELLI—"IZUMITELJ" TELEVIZIJE? [Anton III, Baron Codelli: the inventor of television?]. *Kronika [Yugoslavia] 1982 30(1): 25-31.* Describes the contribution of Anton III Codelli to the development of the early technique of television in the light of contemporary research in the field. Codelli could not be more successful in this field because he did not use for his model a cathode-ray tube which is the essential part of television today. 1910's-30's

Codignola, Tristano

1426. Agnoletti, Enzo Enriques. TRISTANO CODIGNOLA E IL LIBERALSOCIALISMO [Tristano Codignola and liberal-socialism]. *Ponte [Italy] 1986 42(1): 5-15.* Discusses the political activities during and after the Fascist period in Italy of Tristano Codignola (1913-81), son of a prominent educational theorist, active in the Resistance group Giustizia e Libertà, and, after the war, a leading member of the Action Party, a political party which adopted a critical attitude toward both capitalism and socialism. 1930's-56

1427. Borgogni, Tiziano. LE CARTE CODIGNOLA: PRIME CONSIDERAZIONI [The Codignola letters: initial considerations]. *Ponte [Italy] 1986 42(1): 134-140.* Describes the content of the Tristano Codignola papers preserved at the Istituto Storico della Resistenza in Tuscany, Italy. Letters, 1936-47, relate to Codignola's activities as a member of the Italian liberal socialist resistance movements Giustizia e Libertà and the Action Party. Others, 1953-54, trace his seminal role in the formation of Unità Popolare, and his rapprochement in 1955-57 with Christian Democrat Nicola Pistelli. 1936-57

Codreanu, Corneliu

1428. Spălățelu, Ion. 20,000,000 MĂRCI PENTRU GARDA DE FIER [20,000,000 marks for the Iron Guard]. *Magazin Istoric [Romania] 1982 16(11): 33-35.* Corneliu Codreanu, before he perished in 1938, contributed substantially to the chaos in Romania as leader of the Iron Guard, heavily subsidized by the Nazis. 1922-40

Cohn, Tobias

1429. Allen, Nigel. ILLUSTRATIONS FROM THE WELLCOME INSTITUTE LIBRARY: A JEWISH PHYSICIAN IN THE SEVENTEENTH CENTURY. *Medical History [Great Britain] 1984 28(3): 324-328.* A biographical sketch of Tobias Cohn (1652-1729), a physician famed for the breadth of his knowledge. His reputation is largely due to his publication of *Ma"aśeh Ṭobiyah* (1708), which is largely devoted to medicine and one of the first works in Hebrew to contain scientific and medical illustrations. 5 illus., 24 notes. 1648-1729

Colajanni, Napoleone

1430. Tesoro, Marina. L'ATTIVITA POLITICA DI NAPOLEONE COLAJANNI NELL'EPOCA DI CRISPI E DI GIOLITTI [The political activity of Napoleone Colajanni in the era of Francesco Crispi and Giovanni Giolitti]. *Politico [Italy] 1982 47(4): 741-760.* Analyzes the political life of Colajanni: the difficult relations with Crispi at the time of the Sicilian Fasci; the obstructionism and defense of democratic institutions during the crisis of 1898; the proposal of an ample constitutional progressive coalition at the beginning of the new century; the support of Giolitti reformism, but at the same time the condemnation of his corrupt methods of government. 1880's-1910's

Colburn, Henry

1431. Sutherland, John. HENRY COLBURN PUBLISHER. *Publishing History [Great Britain] 1986 (19): 59-84.* Although personally reprehensible and professionally unscrupulous, Henry Colburn (d. 1855) was an innovative London publisher who anticipated many 20th-century practices. During his business career (1806-53), Colburn was noted for his "puffing" (high pressure advertising) and indifference to "gentlemanly" publishing codes. Colburn's preference for opportunistic business alliances over the family firm or partnership, and his insistence that books must be profitable also were ahead of his time. Although many of his books were potboilers, Colburn also published works by Edward Bulwer-Lytton, Benjamin Disraeli, and Frances Trollope, and the diaries of John Evelyn and Samuel Pepys. Based on published primary sources and memoirs; 63 notes. 1806-53

Cole, Margaret

1432. Saville, John. MARGARET COLE (1893-1980). *Bull. of the Soc. for the Study of Labour Hist. [Great Britain] 1980 (41): 10-11.* An obituary of the British historian Margaret Cole (1893-1980), who had a special interest in the labor movement. 1893-1980

Coleman, Melvyn

1433. Chertok, Haim. "MY HOME IS OVER JORDAN." *Midstream 1985 31(5): 41-44.* Relates the story of Melvyn Coleman's defection from the sect of some 1,500 American-born blacks known as the Black Hebrews resident in the Negev city of Dimona and describes the confusion among both government and townspeople about the sect and its purposes within Israel. 1971-84

Coleridge, Samuel Taylor

1434. Coffman, Ralph J., Jr. THE WORKING LIBRARY OF SAMUEL TAYLOR COLERIDGE. *Journal of Library History 1986 21(2): 277-299.* The informational problems of a reader on the fringes of both clerical and professional orders are seen in the reconstruction of Samuel Taylor Coleridge's (1772-1834) various working libraries. During the early 19th century, movement toward the democratization of the printed word existed side by side with established elitist institutions. Coleridge's lack of credentials excluded him from the latter, but his wide circle of friends (many with private libraries) helped give him access to an otherwise closed world. Based on Coleridge's notebooks and letters, and other primary sources; 3 tables, 86 notes. 1782-1834

1435. Flavin, James Patrick. "The Life and Opinions of Samuel Taylor Coleridge, Poet and Philosopher." Miami U. 1982. 311 pp. *DAI 1983 44(1): 174-A.* DA8311267 1817

1436. Jackson, H. J. COLERIDGE'S COLLABORATOR, JOSEPH HENRY GREEN. *Studies in Romanticism 1982 21(2): 161-179.* Contrary to some scholarly opinion, Joseph Henry Green, surgeon, lecturer, literary executor, and amanuensis was a close personal friend and intellectual companion of Samuel Taylor Coleridge, the English poet and critic, 1817-34, although Green acted more as a disciple in intellectual matters. Newly found letters help support this assessment. 1817-34

1437. Mays, J. C. C. COLERIDGE'S BORROWINGS FROM JESUS COLLEGE LIBRARY, 1791-94. *Transactions of the Cambridge Bibliographical Society [Great Britain] 1985 8(5): 557-581.* Lists the library borrowings of Samuel Taylor Coleridge as an undergraduate at Jesus College, Cambridge, between 1791 and 1794. Based on a mutilated register, the record of Coleridge's borrowings reflects his academic ambitions, their mutation and demise. The majority of his borrowings were conventional, connected directly with college and university commitments, but the conventionality of his reading does not mean he took it any less seriously, and there are several volumes that only he among the students borrowed. This was the first library that Coleridge came to know, and, as with all his reading, his subsequent work retained traces of his years there. Manuscript in Jesus College, Cambridge, and printed sources; 39 notes. 1791-94

1438. Tamplin, John Charles. "Samuel Taylor Coleridge: Anglican." Kent State U. 1981. 234 pp. *DAI 1982 42(12): 5132-A.* DA8209519 1790-1824

Coleridge, Sara

1439. Mudge, Bradford K. SARA COLERIDGE: A PORTRAIT FROM THE PAPERS. *Lib. Chronicle of the U. of Texas at Austin 1983 (23): 15-35.* Although she openly supported the prevailing view of women's subordinate role, there were many indications that Sara Coleridge would have thrived, could she have lived a less restrictive life. 1820's-50's

Coleridge-Taylor, Samuel

1440. Carter, Nathan M. "Samuel Coleridge-Taylor: His Life and Works." Johns Hopkins University 1984. 392 pp. *DAI 1984 45(6): 1566-A.* DA8417662 1890's-1912

1441. Thompson, Jewel Taylor. "Samuel Coleridge-Taylor: The Development of His Compositional Style." (Vol. 1-2) U. of Rochester, Eastman School of Music 1981. 694 pp. *DAI 1982 42(11): 4643-A.* DA8127761 1890's-1912

Colet, John

1442. Kaufman, Peter Iver. JOHN COLET'S *OPUS DE SACRAMENTIS* AND CLERICAL ANTICLERICALISM: THE LIMITATIONS OF "ORDINARY WAYES." *J. of British Studies 1982 22(1): 1-22.* The Catholic reformer John Colet (1467?-1519), although conventionally associated with merely polite criticism of the Church's worldliness, became increasingly subversive after he left his Oxford studies to assume the deanship of St. Paul's Cathedral, London. It is impossible to precisely reconstruct what Colet preached in London. However, his writings—particularly *Opus de Sacramentis Ecclesiae*—and what is known about his London friends and enemies suggest that Colet advanced well beyond the "idealistic anticlericalism" of Erasmus and Thomas More toward the "heritical anticlericalism" of the Lollards. Based on Colet's published writings and other published documents and writings of his time; 96 notes. 1504-19

Colette, Gabrielle Sidonie

1443. Luján, Néstor. COLETTE [Colette]. *Historia y Vida [Spain] 1984 17(196): 90-94.* A study of the contrast between the scandalous life of French writer Gabrielle Sidonie Colette (1875-1954) and the serenity and order of her novels. 1890's-1954

Collier family

1444. Hughes, Mary Joe. CHILD-REARING AND SOCIAL EXPECTATIONS IN EIGHTEENTH-CENTURY ENGLAND: THE CASE OF THE COLLIERS OF HASTINGS. *Studies in Eighteenth-Century Culture 1984 13: 79-100.* Presents a case study of the Collier family who lived in Hastings, Sussex, in the first half of the 18th century. They were a relatively modest provincial family, but attained connections in high places. The author provides a picture of family affairs, and examines child-rearing practices, the Colliers' relationship with their children. Eighteen children were born and seven survived infancy, two boys and five girls. Describes the children's education, with the emphasis on the need for social advantages, and the parents' affection and expectations for their children. The author argues that "the values and behaviour of the English family reflect no early-modern transformation but deep continuities." Based on documents in the Sayer manuscripts, East Sussex Record Office, Lewes, Sussex, and secondary sources; 95 notes. 1700-50

Collingridge, George

1445. Spate, O. H. K. GEORGE COLLINGRIDGE 1847-1931: FROM PAPAL ZOUAVE TO HERMIT OF BEROWRA (WITH A BIBLIOGRAPHY OF COLLINGRIDGE'S PUBLICATIONS). *J. of the Royal Australian Hist. Soc. [Australia] 1981 66(4): 258-272.* George Collingridge, whose career was extremely varied, used his linguistic and cartographic skills to perform a pioneering role in the debate over the priority of discovery of Australia. His writings during the late 19th century stressed the Portuguese discoveries some 80 years before those of the Dutch during the 17th century. But his views were not easily accepted in Australia, both because of weaknesses in the use of evidence and of the Eurocentric nature of his interpretation. Based mainly on Collingridge's publications, especially *The Discovery of Australia* (1895) and his papers in the Dixon Library; biblio., 18 notes. 16c-17c

Collingwood, Cuthbert

1446. Howard-Vyse, Victoria. VICE ADMIRAL, LORD COLLINGWOOD. *Mariner's Mirror [Great Britain] 1982 68(1): 43-48.* A brief biographic sketch of Cuthbert Collingwood (1748-1810). He entered the navy as a volunteer in 1761, was made midshipman, 1766; lieutenant, 1775; and received his first command ca. 1778. When the French Revolutionary wars broke out, he was appointed Flag Captain to Admiral Bowyer, later becoming Vice-Admiral to Nelson in 1805. He became admiral, commander-in-chief, of the Mediterranean fleet after Nelson's death, and died at sea. 8 notes. 1760-1810

Coltham, Stephen

1447. —. IN MEMORIAM: STEPHEN COLTHAM. *Bulletin of the Society for the Study of Labour History [Great Britain] 1984 (49): 4.* An obituary notice for the British teacher and labor historian Stephen Coltham (d. 1984), who is remembered for his history of the English working-class newspaper, the *Bee Hive.* 20c

Colum, Pádraic

1448. Murphy, Ann. PÁDRAIC COLUM (1881-1972), NATIONAL POET. *Éire-Ireland 1982 17(4): 128-147.* Presents a biographical appreciation of Pádraic Colum, for 70 years—in Ireland and the United States—a prolific poet, dramatist, novelist, essayist, critic, and folklorist. Colum saw himself as an authentic national poet because—unlike W. B. Yeats, Lady Gregory, George W. Russell (known as AE), and others—he came from the Catholic peasantry and sought to express realistically the peasant heritage. In his various literary forms, Colum celebrated the piety, quiet heroism, and natural poetic qualities of the Irish peasants with their awareness of mythology and folklore and inherited knowledge of ballads, legends, and historical tales. Based on unpublished documents at the National Library of Ireland and the New

York Public Library (Berg Collection), an interview with Colum, corressponsence with Irish writers, and the published works of Colum; 58 notes. 1902-72

Columbus, Christopher

1449. Gil, Juan. LAS CUENTAS DE CRISTOBAL COLON [The accounts of Christopher Columbus]. *Anuario de Estudios Americanos [Spain] 1984 41: 425-511.* Many historical accounts to the contrary, Christopher Columbus died a rich man, leaving many sources of wealth to his family to enjoy for decades to come. Columbus only appears impoverished when compared with the Grandees of Spain—a comparison that Columbus often made. Based on material at the Archivo General de Indias in Seville, Spain; 3 photos, 181 notes. 1490-1520

1450. Hamann, Günther. CHRISTOPH COLUMBUS ZWISCHEN MITTELALTER UND NEUZEIT: NACHFAHRE UND WEGWEISER [Transition from the Middle Ages to modern times: Christopher Columbus as descendant and pioneer]. *Wiener Beiträge zur Gesch. der Neuzeit [Austria] 1980 7: 15-38.* Portrays the Genoese adventurer Christopher Columbus (1451-1506) as a product of his time and its still medieval concepts of life, science, and religion, whose nautical errors in his exploratory efforts cannot detract from his seafaring accomplishments and his unfaltering dedication to discovery and purpose. Based on a lecture given on the 100th anniversary of the founding of the Historical Institute at the University of Vienna, 12 December 1972; lists selected sources and literature. 1490's-1510's

1451. Heers, Jacques. CHRISTOPHE COLOMB LE GÉNOIS [Christopher Columbus, the Genoese]. *Histoire [France] 1981 (36): 76-85.* Describes the life and achievements of Christopher Columbus, centering on the European response to the adventures that led to his discovery of the new world. 1492-1506

1452. Lequenne, Michel. DIN NOU DESPRE COLUMB... [Something new about Columbus]. *Magazin Istoric [Romania] 1982 16(11): 29-32.* Summarizes the critical years in the discovery of America, 1492-93, based on two volumes published in 1979 covering the available texts: Columbus's journal, Las Casas's history, and other contemporary sources. 1492-93

1453. Ramos, Demetrio. COLÓN Y EL ENFRENTAMIENTO DE LOS CABALLEROS: UN SERIO PROBLEMA DEL SEGUNDO VIAJE, QUE NUEVOS DOCUMENTOS PONEN AL DESCUBIERTO [Columbus and the opposition of the nobility: a serious problem of the second voyage revealed in new documents]. *Rev. de Indias [Spain] 1979 39(155-158): 9-87.* Before the mutiny led by Roldán during Christopher Columbus's second voyage to America, there was a conflict involving nobles sent on the expedition by the Catholic monarchs of Spain. Under the leadership of Pedro Margarit, the nobles returned to Spain where they initiated claims against the Columbus family. This was the first of the conflicts involving Columbus's authority over the newly discovered lands, and it changes our understanding of the results of this second voyage. Documentation from the General Archive of Simancas, Spain, and other published primary sources; 199 notes, 3 appendixes. 1493-95

1454. Torres, Mauro. PSICOLOGIA DE CRISTOBAL COLON [Psychology of Christopher Columbus]. *Bol. de Hist. y Antigüedades [Colombia] 1981 68(732): 185-201.* Comments on the genesis of Columbus's plan for his 1492 expedition. 1480's-92

Colville, Olivia

1455. Baker, Colin. NYASALAND 1905-1909: THE JOURNEYS OF MARY HALL, OLIVIA COLVILLE AND CHARLOTTE MANSFIELD. *Soc. of Malawi J. [Malawi] 1982 35(1): 11-29.* Compares the travel accounts of three English women in Nyasaland, 1905-09, then a British protectorate. The women traveled a common route between Chinde on the coast and Liwonde on the Shire; the writings reflect their distinct personalities and the differing health and transportation conditions encountered during this four-year period. 62 notes. 1905-09

Coman, Ghenută

1456. Teodor, Dan Gh. GHENUTĂ COMAN [Ghenută Coman]. *Anuarul Institutului de Istorie şi Arheologie "A. D. Xenopol" [Romania] 1981 18: 869-870.* Ghenută Coman (1914-81) was born near Vaslui, studied history at Iaşi, and from 1941 to 1975 taught or served as an inspector in various schools. For a time in 1945 he ran a newspaper. From 1956 to 1965 he organized an archaeological and historical museum in the Vaslui region. His interests lay in the study of settlement in Moldavia and the eastern Carpathians, on which he published several monographs. 15c-20c

Comenius, John Amos

1457. Floss, Pavel. VÝVOJ KOMENSKÉHO ASTRONOMICKÝCH NÁZORŮ [The development of Comenius's astronomical views]. *Studia Comeniana et Historica [Czechoslovakia] 1984 14(27): 40-57.* In the 1640's, the Moravian thinker and educator John Amos Comenius (Komenský, 1592-1670) revised his conservative astronomical views under the influence of Tycho Brahe's researches and thanks to his acquaintance with Johannes Hevelius. Nevertheless, he could not accept the Copernican system and probably lacked the mathematical preparation necessary for its full appropriation. Though he remained committed to Aristotelian physics and biblical geocentrism, his thought also reflected Renaissance Neo-Platonism: man, as the culmination of the created cosmos, should properly inhabit the center of it. Published primary sources; 52 notes. German summary. 1614-70

1458. Michel, Gerhard. JAN AMOS KOMENSKÝ (1592-1670), EIN AUFKLÄRER IM 17. JAHRHUNDERT [John Amos Comenius (1592-1670), a man of the Enlightenment in the 17th century]. *Studia Comeniana et Historica [Czechoslovakia] 1984 14(27): 24-39.* Though heavily indebted to earlier intellectual traditions, the Moravian thinker John Amos Comenius (Komenský) anticipated major postulates of the Enlightenment, such as the advancement of learning, the priority of reason, and an emphasis on the practical application of knowledge. His reforming program of a general illumination was tied to a grand design of political dialogue, international peace, and religious toleration. Based on a lecture delivered at the Hochschule Hildesheim, 13 December 1982. 28 notes. 1628-70

1459. Nováková, Julie. DVA KOMENIOLOGICKÉ DODATKY [Two addenda to Comenius studies]. *Studia Comeniana et Historica [Czechoslovakia] 1984 14(28): 76-84.* The Moravian thinker John Amos Comenius (Komenský, 1592-1670) was inspired to research on a *perpetuum mobile* by his fellow exile, Johann Christoph Berger (Pergar), who in the 1630's settled in England as an engineer and inventor. The second addendum notes that Comenius's published controversies with the Socinians in Amsterdam can now be dated more precisely; they extended past 1666. Primary sources; 25 notes. German summary. 1632-67

1460. Nováková, Julie. PROČ KOMENSKÉHO CLAMORES ELIAE ZŮSTALI JEN PRACOVNÍM TEXTEM [Why Comenius's *Clamores Eliae* remained merely a working draft]. *Studia Comeniana et Historica [Czechoslovakia] 1984 14(27): 3-23.* In 1665, the Moravian thinker John Amos Comenius (Komenský, 1592-1670) conceived a large-scale work to usher in a new age of enlightenment and reform. Titled *Clamores Eliae* [Calls of Elijah], it was intended for Louis XIV of France, whom Comenius expected to call a European council. By the autumn of 1666, the author realized that his hopes had been excessive and that propaganda on a smaller scale might be more effective. In *Clamores Eliae* he continued to make revisions, fill in blank spaces, and paste in addenda, but did not complete the manuscript for publication. Based on an analysis of the manuscript and on published sources; 27 notes. German summary. 1665-70

Commandino, Federico

1461. Piovan, Francesco. IL MATRIMONIO DI FEDERICO COMMANDINO [The marriage of Federico Commandino]. *Quaderni per la Storia dell'Università di Padova [Italy] 1984 17: 232-234.* A marriage by proxy recorded in the state archives of Padua suggests that the mathematician Francesco Commandino may have stayed there after 1537. 1534-46

Commerson, Philibert

1462. Guillot, Renée-Paule. LA VRAIE "BOUGAINVILLEE": LA PREMIERE FEMME QUI FIT LE TOUR DU MONDE [The real "Bougainvillée": the first woman to go around the world]. *Historama [France] 1984 (1): 36-40.* Supplements Fanny Deschamps's 1982 best-selling novel *La Bougainvillée* by narrating with a historical perspective the adventures of noted naturalist Philibert Commerson (1727-73) and his governess and companion, Jeanne Baret, disguised as a young man-servant, during his participation in the expedition of exploration, which joined the one directed by famous French navigator, Louis-Antoine de Bougainville (1729-1811). 1766-73

Compton, William

1463. Bernard, G. W. THE RISE OF SIR WILLIAM COMPTON, EARLY TUDOR COURTIER. *English Hist. Rev. [Great Britain] 1981 96(381): 754-777.* Describes the rise of Sir William Compton (1482-1528) from the son of a small country farmer to one of the wealthiest landed magnates in early Tudor England. As a ward of the crown, Compton was first a page of Prince Henry, then a groom of Henry VIII's chamber, and later the chief gentleman of the king's bedchamber. Using his position in the king's privy chamber to further personal ambition and profit rather than to influence public affairs, Compton amassed a fortune in manors, money, and plate. Grants from the crown lands; fees and sums from offices of steward, bailiff, keeper, or constable of manors, forests, or parks in possession of the crown; income from money lending; and whatever he could acquire from possible theft of crown jewels and embezzlement of cash contributed to an inheritance that helped his grandson achieve noble status. His local power and influence in the south Midlands and his political influence from being in regular and close proximity to the king enabled him to do favors for and receive gifts or compensation from a wide variety of clients, clergy, and nobles. Based upon papers in the Bedfordshire County Public records offices and *Letters and Papers, Foreign and Domestic, of the Reign of Henry VIII;* table, 142 notes. 1493-1528

Condorcanqui, José Gabriel

See Tupac Amaru II

Condorcet, Marquis de

See Caritat, Marie-Jean

Condorcet, Marquise de

See Grouchy, Sophie de

Conneau, Théophilus

1464. Mouser, Bruce L. THEOPHILUS CONNEAU: THE SAGA OF A TALE. *Hist. in Africa 1979 6: 97-107.* Reviews the literature generated by or about Théophilus Conneau (1804-60), an Italian French slaver who worked in West Africa, 1827-33 and 1839-50, and who retired after being shipped to Baltimore for trial. Under his professional name, Theodore Canot, he collaborated with journalist Brantz Mayer to produce *Captain Canot; or, Twenty Years of an African Slaver* (1854). There have been several American and European editions of that work, some of which claim to have removed Mayer's moralistic overlay. In 1976, the original 1854 manuscript was published, but there are many problems with that edition. 46 notes. 1827-54

Connelly, Pierce

1465. Paz, D. G. APOSTATE PRIESTS AND VICTORIAN RELIGIOUS TURMOIL: GAVAZZI, ACHILLI, CONNELLY. *Proceedings of the South Carolina Historical Association 1985: 57-69.* 1840's-60's
For abstract see ***Achilli, Giacinto***

Connolly, Cyril

1466. Adams, Robert M. CYRIL CONNOLLY AND THE MAN OF LETTERS. *American Scholar 1984-85 54(1): 99-105.* Cyril Connolly's (1903-74) self-image was that of a journalistic drudge. However, he was a lively and entertaining writer shaped by the educational system of Scotland. His best mood was elegiac, even nostalgic. 1920's-60's

Connolly, James

1467. Newsinger, John. JAMES CONNOLLY AND THE EASTER RISING. *Sci. & Soc. 1983 47(2): 152-177.* James Connolly (1868-1916), Irish martyr of the Easter Rebellion, developed a sharp critique of Irish republicanism from 1896 to 1902. He predicted that independence was only possible for Ireland in connection with socialism. Contrary to most of his biographers, however, Connolly abandoned his socialism in favor of nationalism by 1916, and his role in the Easter Rising dramatizes his break with his earlier beliefs. 59 notes. 1896-1916

1468. Zagladina, Khmaira Timofeevna. IRLANDSKII REVOLIUTSIONER DZHEIMS KONNOLI [The Irish revolutionary, James Connolly]. *Novaia i Noveishaia Istoriia [USSR] 1984 (1): 168-187.* Biography of the Irish patriot and labor leader, James Connolly. In 1903, he emigrated to America, where he founded the Irish Socialist Federation in 1907. Upon returning to Ireland in 1910, he continued to champion the cause of the workers and the Irish independence movement and opposed the British version of Home Rule. He was executed by the British in 1916 as a leader of the Easter Rebellion. His views on the danger of Irish religious infighting and the need to unify the British and Irish labor movements have not lost their validity even today. 80 notes. 1903-16

Connor, Bernard

1469. Dalitz, R. H. and Stone, G. C. DOCTOR BERNARD CONNOR: PHYSICIAN TO KING JAN III SOBIESKI AND AUTHOR OF *THE HISTORY OF POLAND,* 1698. *Oxford Slavonic Papers [Great Britain] 1981 14: 14-35.* Irish emigrant Bernard Connor (1665?-98) was briefly appointed personal physician to King Jan III Sobieski of Poland in 1674. After his return to England, Connor published in 1698 his *History of Poland.* This work, the first of its kind in England and an important source both for the bibliography of Slavonic studies in Great Britain and for the history of 17th-century Poland, has been neglected. Accounts of and sources for Connor's life are here examined to correct previous errors. 105 notes, appendix. 1665-98

Conolly, John

1470. Scull, Andrew. A BRILLIANT CAREER? JOHN CONOLLY AND VICTORIAN PSYCHIATRY. *Victorian Studies 1984 27(2): 203-235.* Discusses the evaluation of the work of John Conolly who has often been credited with the enlightened reform of insane asylums. Yet only at the beginning of his career did Conolly advocate nonrestraint in the treatment of the insane, who were generally impoverished. After his personal experience of running an asylum, he gave up the enlightened ideals of his youth. For nearly all of his contemporaries, his change of heart merely acknowledged the realities of medical science, as it then stood. Thus the concept of medical progress depends largely on a social context. Based on Victorian journals, Parliamentary Papers, Hanwell County Asylum Lunatic Visitors' Reports, and secondary sources; 78 notes. 1820's-70's

Conrad, Joseph

1471. Hunter, Allan. LETTERS FROM CONRAD. *Notes and Queries [Great Britain] 1985 32(3): 366-370, (4): 500-505.* 1901-03
*For abstract see **Clifford, Hugh***

1472. Knowles, Owen and Miskin, G. W. S. UNPUBLISHED CONRAD LETTERS: THE HQS *WELLINGTON* COLLECTION. *Notes and Queries [Great Britain] 1985 32(3): 370-376.* Reprints seven previously unpublished letters written by Joseph Conrad to a variety of recipients from 1896 to 1924. 1896-1924

1473. Stape, J. H. THE CHRONOLOGY OF CONRAD'S 1914 VISIT TO POLAND. *Polish Review 1984 29(3): 65-71.* Because of Joseph Conrad's (1857-1924) deliberate obfuscation of events in his life, all previous treatments of the chronology of his visit to Poland in 1914 have been inaccurate. A new chronology is provided based on primary accounts, unpublished documents and "a careful sifting of available evidence." This chronology permits a better appreciation of Conrad's treatment of events in "Poland Revisited" (1914). Secondary sources; 21 notes. 1914

Constable, John

1474. Bevilacqua, Vincent M. THE RHETORICAL THEORY OF JOHN CONSTABLE'S *REFLECTIONS UPON THE ACCURACY OF STYLE. Rhetorica 1984 2(1): 63-73.* History of John Constable's life and works, his stylistic rhetorical inheritance, and his ideal of nature, concentrating on *Reflections upon the Accuracy of Style,* which reveals Constable's classical or Ciceronian tradition of rhetoric. 1690's-1730's

Constable, John (1776-1837)

1475. Conrad, Barnaby, III. CONSTABLE COUNTRY. *Horizon 1983 26(2): 23-29.* Biography of John Constable (1776-1837), who painted the English countryside with a revolutionary realism as well as beauty. 1776-1837

Constant, Benjamin

1476. Courtney, C. P. BENJAMIN CONSTANT SEEN BY HIS FATHER: LETTERS FROM LOUIS-ARNOLD-JUSTE TO SAMUEL CONSTANT, 1780-96. *French Studies [Great Britain] 1985 39(3): 276-284.* Reviews the relationship between French writer Benjamin Constant and his father, Louis-Arnold-Juste de Constant (1726-1816), in the light of the latter's correspondence with his brother, François-Marc-Samuel Constant in the period 1780-96. 1780-96

1477. Pholien, Georges. "ADOLPHE" ET SON PUBLIC [*Adolphe* and its public]. *Revue d'Histoire Littéraire de la France [France] 1985 85(1): 18-25.* Surveys the response of French intellectuals to Benjamin Constant's (1767-1830) autobiographical novel written in 1807 and published in London in 1816. 1770's-1800's

1478. Raynaud, Philippe. UN ROMANTIQUE LIBERAL, BENJAMIN CONSTANT [A liberal romantic, Benjamin Constant]. *Esprit [France] 1983 (3): 49-66.* Describes the approach of early 19th-century French philosopher Benjamin Constant to the reconciliation of individual rights and the rights of societies and compares Constant's ideas to classical 18th-century views as well as to the republican sentiments of the French Revolution. 1750-1818

Constantine

1479. Kipp, Jacob W. and Kipp, Maia A. THE GRAND DUKE KONSTANTIN NIKOLAEVIČ: THE MAKING OF A TSARIST REFORMER, 1827-1853. *Jahrbücher für Geschichte Osteuropas [West Germany] 1986 34(1): 3-18.* Subjected to the shallow militarism of the court as a youth and deprived of the throne by primogeniture, Constantine bore a resentment to his father, Tsar Nicholas I, which later extended to his policies. From his tutor, the famed seaman and Arctic explorer Feodor Petrovič Litke (Friedrich Benjamin Lütke), Constantine acquired a sense of naval professionalism destined to prepare him for state service and his role as admiral of the Russian navy. Although decorated for bravery in the 1849 military campaign against Hungary, Constantine's experiences in the field reinforced his alienation and led him to conclude that the Russian government was pursuing flawed foreign and domestic policies. Joining other reform-minded individuals in the wake of the Revolution of 1848, the grand duke rejected blind reaction and leaned increasingly toward rational, bureaucratic development consonant with Russia's needs. His first independent assignment, the revision and codification of naval regulations (1850-53), marked the emergence of Constantine as reformer. Based on

Soviet archives, including the Central State Archives of the October Revolution, and the public library of Saltykov-Shchedrin; 78 notes. 1827-53

Constantinescu, Miron

1480. Tismaneanu, Vladimir. MIRON CONSTANTINESCU OR THE IMPOSSIBLE HERESY. *Survey [Great Britain] 1984 28(4): 175-187.* Describes the political career of Romanian historian, sociologist, and politician Miron Constantinescu (1917-74). As an intellectual and a proponent of Romanian intellectual liberalization and the occupant of many high posts in the anti-intellectual Romanian Communist Party, Miron Constantinescu had a turbulent and precarious career, finally sacrificing his standards of scholarship and his moral scruples for illusory political power. Expelled from the Romanian Communist Party Central Committee for his liberal views in 1958, he was rehabilitated in 1965 by then Romanian Communist Party Secretary-General Nicolae Ceauşescu and helped to legitimize Ceauşescu's regime. He attempted to effect an intellectual renaissance under the new regime, refusing to acknowledge the probability of its failure under a repressive political system from which he never dissociated himself. Achieving great nominal political power under Nicolae Ceauşescu, he nonetheless had vanished from Romanian histories by 1984. Secondary sources; 10 notes. 1932-74

Conti, Leonardo

1481. Kater, Michael H. DOCTOR LEONARDO CONTI AND HIS NEMESIS: THE FAILURE OF CENTRALIZED MEDICINE IN THE THIRD REICH. *Central European History 1985 18(3-4): 299-325.* One of the benefits which was supposed to result from totalitarian dictatorships was centralization of certain institutions to improve service and efficiency. One area in Weimar Germany which needed centralization was health services, and Dr. Leonardo Conti (an "Old Fighter") wanted to accomplish this. Although he served in important positions in the 1930's both in the government and in the party, he did not reach his goal of being the "Reich Health Leader" until 1939. Even then he was not given real authority to reorganize health services because duties remained dispersed among several offices. Not only were health services never centralized, but the intrigues of Conti to achieve the desired power "compounded structural weaknesses in the governmental fabric of the Nazi dictatorship as a whole." Based on contemporary publications and archival materials in the Berlin Documents Center, the Bundesarchiv Koblenz, and the University of Bremen. 1930-45

Conze, Werner

1482. Zorn, Wolfgang. WERNER CONZE ZUM GEDÄCHTNIS [In memory of Werner Conze]. *Vierteljahrschrift für Sozial- und Wirtschaftsgeschichte [West Germany] 1986 73(2): 153-157.* An obituary for German social historian Werner Conze (1910-86). A professor of history at Münster, 1952-57, and Heidelberg, 1957-79, Conze became the leading German proponent of the new social history as leader of the Arbeitskreis für Moderne Sozialgeschichte, as editor of the publication series *Industrielle Welt,* as co-editor of *Vierteljahrschrift für Sozial- und Wirtschaftsgeschichte* and of a six-volume historical lexicon on political-social language, and through his own many books and articles. ca 1800-1980

Cook, Albert Ruskin

1483. Ofcansky, Thomas P. THE LIFE AND TIMES OF SIR ALBERT RUSKIN COOK. *J. of the Hist. of Medicine and Allied Sci. 1982 37(2): 225-228.* Sir Albert Ruskin Cook (1870-1951) was sent by the Church Missionary Society to be a resident missionary doctor in Mengo, Uganda. In October of 1896, 12 missionaries including Cook and his future wife arrived at Mombasa, the gateway to East Africa, and went by caravan to Mengo, arriving there in February of 1897 after a difficult time with malaria and dysentery causing numerous delays. Within a month after his arrival, he was seeing 50 to 80 patients daily, performing operations. By the end of the first year, he had seen more than 17,000 patients and opened a hospital with a capacity for 28 patients. By the end of World War I, Cook had opened a new hospital, introduced an electrical system providing lighting and power for X-ray equipment, and started the Mengo Medical School (1917) to train African clinical assistants. Based on published sources including Cook's autobiography (1945); 12 notes. 1896-1917

Coolhaas, Willem Philippus

1484. Opstall, M. E. van. IN MEMORIAM PROFESSOR DR. W. PH. COOLHAAS [In memoriam: W. Ph. Coolhaas]. *Nederlands Archievenblad [Netherlands] 1982 86(1): 11-17.* Obituary and list of publications of Willem Philippus Coolhaas (1899-1981), a civil servant interested in native history in the Netherlands East Indies, 1917-1939, archivist for the regional archives in Batavia, 1946-50, after working for the Netherlands national archives and, since 1955, professor of history at Utrecht University. His main work is the publication in seven parts, of colonial governors' reports to the Dutch East India Company. 1899-1981

Cooper, Duff

1485. Charmley, John. DUFF COOPER AND WESTERN EUROPEAN UNION, 1944-47. *Review of International Studies [Great Britain] 1985 11(1): 53-64.* Describes the efforts of Duff Cooper (1890-1954), British author, diplomat, and Conservative politician, to establish a close relationship with the French Committee of National Liberation during World War II and to initiate an Anglo-French alliance following the war. 1944-47

Cooper, Jemima Champion

1486. Netboy, Anthony and Netboy, Elizabeth Silsby. THE HANDLEYS IN TASMANIA AND OREGON. *Oregon Historical Quarterly 1985 86(1): 80-93.* Jemima Champion Cooper (1778-1862) and family migrated from Devonshire to the penal colony of Hobart in Van Diemen's Land (later Tasmania) in 1833. Her daughter Sarah married an English sea captain, Charles Handley (1811-95), in 1839. Handley skippered brigs carrying convicts and cargo between Sydney and Hobart. In 1844, the Coopers took up a donation land claim in Oregon. The Handleys followed in 1850 and Captain Handley farmed near Dundee and served as Yamhill County assessor and surveyor. Based on records in the Tasmanian Archives, a Handley family history, and records at the Oregon Historical Society; 5 photos, 8 notes. 1833-95

Coornaert, Emile

1487. Craeybeckx, Jan. EMILE COORNAERT (HONDSCHOOTE, 31 AOÛT 1886-PARIS, 25 FEVRIER 1980) [Emile Coornaert (Hondschoote, 31 August 1886-Paris, 25 February 1980)]. *Rev. Belge de Philologie et d'Hist.*

[Belgium] 1981 59(4): 1043-1047. Obituary of a French labor historian who worked on the history of Flanders in northern France and in Belgium. 1886-1980

1488. Dubief, Henri. EMILE COORNAERT (1886-1980). *Rev. d'Hist. Moderne et Contemporaine [France] 1980 27(4): 686-688.* A scrupulously honest and prudent historian with a keen sense of anachronism, Emile Coornaert, French historian of the working class, was known for research on the cloth industry in the early modern period. A social Catholic *silloniste* before 1914 and resistant in World War II, Coornaert rejected a possible political career because of the rightward tendency of the Mouvement Republicain Populaire (MRP). He was a founder and president of the Syndîcat Général de l'Éducation Nationale (SGEN), the university teachers' union, a Christian Socialist, and a member of the French Academy of Inscriptions and Belles-Lettres. 1886-1980

Copeau, Jacques

1489. Gontard, Denis. JACQUES COPEAU ET LES PROBLEMES D'ECOLE [Jacques Copeau and the problems of a school]. *Rev. d'Hist. du Théâtre [France] 1983 35(1): 110-116.* Jacques Copeau (1879-1949), founder of the Vieux Colombier Theater company and eventually head of the Comédie Française, after several attempts to organize an acting school finally succeeded in founding the Ecole du Vieux Colombier in 1920. In 1924 he moved the school to Pernand, where exercises and performances were inspired by life in Burgundy. During 1928-29, the students, *les Copiaus,* wrote and performed two major spectacles of "total theater," works including the characteristics of the most exciting theater of the 1970's: mime, rhythm, music, and mask. One of 14 articles from the Copeau colloquim, University of Dijon, France, 25-26 May 1979. Based on correspondence, journals, lectures, record books, and other primary sources from Copeau and the Vieux Colombier; 18 notes. 1911-29

1490. Sicard, Claude. LE *JOURNAL* DE JACQUES COPEAU [Jacques Copeau's *Journal].* *Rev. D'Hist. du Théâtre [France] 1983 35(1): 129-138.* Comments briefly on the writer and theater director Jacques Copeau's (1879-1949) *Journal* (1983) with excerpts. One of 14 articles from the Copeau colloquium, University of Dijon, France, 25-26 May 1979. 1899-1945

1491. —. TEMOIGNAGES [Testimonials to Jacques Copeau]. *Rev. d'Hist. du Théâtre [France] 1983 35(1): 9-28.*

Copeau, Pascal. JACQUES COPEAU, LE PERE [Jacques Copeau, father], *pp. 9-16.*

Bing, Bernard. LE SOUVENIR DE SUZANNE BING [The memory of Suzanne Bing], *pp. 17-21.*

Dasté, Catherine. CATHERINE DASTE PARLE DE SON GRAND-PERE [Catherine Dasté speaks of her grandfather], *pp. 22-23.*

Bourgeon, L. L'AME CHRETIENNE DE JACQUES COPEAU [Jacques Copeau's Christian soul], *pp. 24-28.* Reminiscences of Jacques Copeau (1879-1949), renowned theater director, by family members and friends. Four of 14 presentations at the Copeau colloquium, University of Dijon, France, 25-26 May 1979. 1890's-1979

Copernicus, Nicolaus

1492. Wardęska, Zofia. NA TROPACH NIEZNANEGO LISTU MIKOŁAJA KOPERNIKA I INNYCH ŹRÓDEŁ DO JEGO BIOGRAFII [On the trail of an unknown letter of Nicolaus Copernicus and other sources for his biography]. *Kwartalnik Hist. Nauki i Techniki [Poland] 1980 25(3): 607-618.* Letters written by Copernicus were discovered by Tadeusz Czacki in 1802 in Königsberg. The letters entered the possession of the Prussian state following the Third Partition of Poland from the hands of the Swedes, who had confiscated them from the library of the bishop of Warmia in Lidzbark in 1626. The letters were between Copernicus and the bishop of Warmia and Chełmno during the years 1518-41. 60 notes. 1518-1802

Copp, Johann

1493. Nikula, Oscar. JOHANN COPP: EN HOVMEDIKUS OCH ASTROLOG I RENÄSSANSENS ÅBO [Johann Copp: a royal physician and astrologer in Åbo during the Renaissance]. *Historiska och Litteraturhistoriska Studier [Finland] 1985 60: 73-86.* Traces the career of Johann Copp (1490-1558), a Bavarian physician who served Emperor Ferdinand I (1503-64) of Austria in Prague during 1528-50 and King Gustavus Vasa (1496-1560) of Sweden during 1555-58. He died in Turku, Finland. Based on published sources in Swedish; 3 illus., 28 notes. 1490-1558

Corbett, Jim

1494. Casada, Jim. JIM CORBETT: JUNGLE KNYGHT. *Sporting Classics 1986 5(2): 20-27, 78-79.* Describes the hunting career of Jim Corbett in India, 1907-46, where he killed a dozen rogue, man-eating tigers, and the six books he wrote on jungle lore and adventure during the latter part of his life in Kenya, 1946-55. 1907-55

Corbett, Julian S.

1495. Dicks, Uwe. JULIAN S. CORBETT UND DIE BRITISCHE SEEKRIEGSFÜHRUNG 1914-18 [Julian S. Corbett and the British direction of the war at sea, 1914-18]. *Militärgeschichtliche Mitteilungen [West Germany] 1985 (1): 35-50.* The British naval historian Sir Julian Corbett (1854-1920) described modern naval strategy in the generation before World War I. Although his writings held little interest for the political and military leadership in Britain, the conduct of naval operations in the war generally coincided with his precepts. In particular, his theories of command of the sea, control of sea communications, and peripheral operations against continental opponents were all applied successfully. Secondary sources; 94 notes. 1907-18

Corbino, Epicarmo

1496. Ferrante, Ezio. EPICARMO CORBINO: UFFICIALE DI PORTO E STORICO NAVALE [Epicarmo Corbino: harbor master and naval historian]. *Rivista Marittima [Italy] 1983 116(6): 73-82.* Epicarmo Corbino, economist, political theorist, and military historian, and founder of the *Annali dell' Economica Italiana,* was also between 1911 and 1925 Italian Harbor Master—a position that influenced his study on the Battle of Jutland. English, French, German and Spanish summaries. 1911-43

Córdova, José María

1497. Moreno de Angel, Pilar. HOJA DE SERVICIOS DEL GENERAL DE DIVISION DON JOSE MARIA CORDOVA, HEROE DE AYACUCHO [Service records of General José María Córdova, hero of Ayacucho]. *Boletín de Historia y Antigüedades [Colombia] 1985 72(748): 137-145.* Reproduces a group of documents, mainly from Archivo Nacional de Colombia, communicating promotions and assignments of José María Córdova during the independence struggle, together with a table of his battles and campaigns. 1814-29

Cornelius of Lithuania

1498. García Font, J. PEQUEÑA HISTORIA DE GRANDES ENANOS [A small story of big dwarfs]. *Historia y Vida [Spain] 1984 17(199): 68-79.* Discusses the role of some of the most influential dwarfs in history and their relationships with their masters: Cornelius of Lithuania, dwarf of Charles V; Lord Minimus, dwarf of Maria Enriqueta (wife of Charles I); Vlasius Rauchmantel; Józef Boryslawski; the American Charles Sherwood Straton, known as Tom Thumb; and the dwarf of Roman Emperor Domitianus. 1c-19c

Cornies, Johann

1499. Prinz, A.; Bauer, Armand and Bauer, Elaine, transl. JOHANN CORNIES. *Heritage Rev. 1982 12(1): 28-33.* Describes the life of Johann Cornies, a German Mennonite who emigrated to southwest Russia, where he developed many innovative methods of farming. 1804-48

Cornthwaite, Robert

1500. Supple, Jennifer F. ROBERT CORNTHWAITE: A NEGLECTED NINETEENTH-CENTURY BISHOP. *Recusant History [Great Britain] 1985 17(4): 399-412.* Biography of the 19th-century Catholic bishop in Yorkshire, Robert Cornthwaite (1818-90), an able administrator and man of great spirituality. 1840's-90

Correia, Innocêncio Serzedelo

1501. Barata, Mario. INOCÊNCIO SERZEDELO CORREIA, ABOLICIONISTA, REPUBLICAN E HOMEM DE ESTADO [Innocêncio Serzedelo Correia, abolitionist, republican, and statesman]. *Rev. do Inst. Hist. e Geog. Brasileiro [Brazil] 1982 (335): 169-174.* Gives a brief biography of Correia, who was instrumental in the creation of the Brazilian Republic in 1889 and in the abolition of slavery in Brazil. He also served as governor and administrator in several Brazilian states and territories, in the 1890 Constituent Assembly, and in the Federal Congress on many occasions. He was also a member of several cabinets in many different ministries. Describes some of the important political and economic writings of Correia, one of the most modest but most important men of Brazil's history. 1858-1932

Corrigan, Dominic

1502. O'Brien, Eoin. SIR DOMINIC CORRIGAN (1802-1880): DOCTOR AND PARLIAMENTARIAN. *Studies [Ireland] 1984 73(290): 146-158.* A biographical sketch based on the letters, diaries, and speeches of Sir Dominic Corrigan, who excelled in the study and practice of medical science and championed Irish Catholic causes in the House of Commons as a Liberal member of Parliament. Hansard's Parliamentary Debates, 1871, 1872, volumes 204-214. 1830's-80

Corrozet, Gilles

1503. Freeman, M. J. GILLES CORROZET ET LES DEBUTS LITTERAIRES DE PIERRE DE LARIVEY [Gilles Corrozet and the literary beginnings of Pierre de Larivey]. *Bibliothèque d'Humanisme et Renaissance [Switzerland] 1986 48(2): 431-437.* 1567-68
*For abstract see **Larivey, Pierre de***

Cortazar, Julio

1504. Cruz, Julia Anne Garza. "Lo Neofantastico en Julio Cortazar" [The neofantastic in Julio Cortazar]. U. of Texas, Austin 1982. 260 pp. *DAI 1983 43(12): 3927-A.* DA8309132 20c

1505. Fernández Moreno, César. UN ARGENTINO IRREDUCTIBLE [An irreducible Argentine]. *Casa de las Américas [Cuba] 1984 25(145-146): 87-89.* The Argentine writer Julio Cortázar (1914-84) was born in Brussels, spent part of his childhood there, lived 30 years in Paris, and was granted a French passport. Nevertheless he never ceased to be an Argentine. His work reveals the tension in him between his two countries. 1930's-84

1506. Teitelboim, Volodia. JULIO CORTAZAR [Julio Cortázar]. *Casa de las Américas [Cuba] 1984 25(145-146): 47-58.* Evokes the youthful personality of this fanciful but extremely serious and rigorous writer. His playfulness was a way of uncovering the false, the commonplace, and the unexamined superficiality of everyday life. He was a model of intellectual consistency and achieved a perfect unity of art and life. 1930's-84

Corte-Real, Manuel Inácio

1507. Azevedo, Rafael Avila de. O CONDE DE SUBSERRA [The count of Subserra]. *Bolo. do Inst. Hist. da Ilha Terceira [Portugal] 1981 39: 5-245.* Describes the military and political career of Manuel Inácio Martins Pamplona Corte-Real, one of the more notable figures in early 19th-century Portuguese liberalism; extracts from his diary and correspondence are appended. 1790-1832

Cortés, Hernán

1508. Fernández Gaytán, José. DE COMO HERNAN CORTES NO QUEMO SUS NAVES [How Hernán Cortés did not burn his ships]. *Revista General de Marina [Spain] 1985 209(Dec): 635-652.* Contrary to the legend that Hernán Cortés burned his ships before his march to Mexico in 1519, he only abandoned unseaworthy ships for which he had insufficient crews. 1519

1509. Oviedo y Pérez de Tudela, M. del Rocío. LAS CARTAS DE RELACION Y EL "RENACER" LITERARIO [Hernán Cortés's letters and the literary "Renaissance"]. *Revista de Indias [Spain] 1984 44(174): 533-539.* Suggesting that the Renaissance was originally a literary revolution, the author examines the literary aspects of Cortés's letters to the king about the conquest of Mexico. Pays special attention to style, classical and medieval influences, religion, legal concepts and terminology, nature, and humor. 20 notes. 1519-26

Cosin, John

1510. Hoffmann, John G. JOHN COSIN, PREBENDARY OF DURHAM CATHEDRAL AND DEAN OF PETERBOROUGH, 1642-1643. *Durham University Journal [Great Britain] 1985 78(1): 1-10.* Describes and analyzes John Cosin's administrative contributions to the cathedrals in Durham and Peterborough from 1624 to 1643, with special emphasis on 1642-43. Cosin (1594-1672), later Bishop of Durham and also Master of Peterhouse, Cambridge for nine years, was a supporter of Charles I and was rewarded with the office of Dean of Peterborough, which he held simultaneously with his prebendary at Durham. He improved the efficiency of the bureaucracy at both cathedrals, largely by increasing their revenues and implementing the Laudian policy of "Thorough." Based on manuscript sources in Durham Cathedral Muniments and the University of Durham Library and other primary and secondary sources; 82 notes. 1624-43

1511. Lawes, Aidan H. COSIN'S POST-RESTORATION CORRESPONDENCE—A RE-ASSESSMENT. *Durham University Journal [Great Britain] 1985 77(2): 141-147.* This reassessment of the correspondence in Durham University Library of John Cosin (1594-1672), scholar, politician, businessman, and bishop of Durham, sheds new light on his manipulation of episcopal leases to pay for building projects, endowments, influence against local political opponents, and provision for his family. Explores the significance of letters between Cosin and Miles Stapylton, his secretary and auditor, that have been passed over by previous editors of Cosin's correspondence. Based on the Cosin Letter-books in Durham University Library; 30 notes. 1660-72

Cosío Villegas, Daniel

1512. Schmidt, Henry C. THE MEXICAN INTELLECTUAL AS POLITICAL PUNDIT, 1968-1976: THE CASE OF DANIEL COSIO VILLEGAS. *J. of Interamerican Studies and World Affairs 1982 24(1): 81-103.* Daniel Cosío Villegas's life's work spanned a wide variety of activity, from founding the Fonda de Cultura Economica, El Colegio de México and editing the multivolume *História Moderna de México* to public speaking, popular writing, journalism in *Excelsior,* and television script-writing. He played a key role in opening the debate on fundamental political issues and personalities in modern Mexico, but one should not overemphasize his independence. He retained close links to the elite and served in government posts for much of his life. Based on the printed works of Cosío Villegas, his associates and contemporary intellectuals; 10 notes, ref. 1968-76

Costa, Antonio

1513. Albi de la Cuesta, Julio and Piñiero, Leopoldo Stampa. EL CAPITAN DON ANTONIO COSTA: "UNA MUERTE ROMANTICA EN DINAMARCA" [Captain Antonio Costa: a romantic death in Denmark]. *Rev. de Hist. Militar [Spain] 1983 27(54): 37-49.* Recounts the life of Antonio Costa (1767-1808). His death by suicide in the face of an impossible military situation after a lifetime of service reflected the tumult and romantic fervor of the period. His death also marked a curious episode when Spanish troops served in Denmark as erstwhile allies and then opponents of the French Empire. Based on secondary sources; plate, biblio. 1767-1808

Costa, Franco

1514. DeCurtis, Italo. PER UNA BIOGRAFIA DI DON COSTA: LE RADICI (PRIMA PARTE) [For a biography of Don Costa: the roots (Part 1)]. *Studium [Italy] 1982 78(1): 85-98.* Describes the early family, social, and cultural environment in which Father Franco Costa, national chaplain of the Catholic University Federation from 1955 to 1963, received his spiritual formation. 1890's-1900's

1515. DeCurtis, Italo. PER UNA BIOGRAFIA DI DON COSTA: LE RADICI. SECONDA PARTE [Toward a biography of Don Costa: the roots. Part 2]. *Studium [Italy] 1982 78(2): 207-224.* Examines Franco Costa's childhood and adolescence and sheds light on the importance of the spiritual background of the young priest between 1909 and 1917. 1909-17

Costa, Jeronimo Nunes da

1516. Israel, Jonathan I. THE DIPLOMATIC CAREER OF JERONIMO NUNES DA COSTA: AN EPISODE IN DUTCH-PORTUGUESE RELATIONS OF THE SEVENTEENTH CENTURY. *Bijdragen en Mededelingen betreffende de Geschiedenis der Nederlanden [Netherlands] 1983 98(2): 167-190.* Jeronimo Nunes da Costa (1620-97) was the son of Duarte Nunes da Costa, a Lisbon New Christian merchant who fled from the Inquisition in Portugal ca. 1609. After some years in Madrid and Florence, the family settled in Amsterdam and later in Hamburg. Jeronimo returned to Amsterdam in 1642, where he became an influential member of the Portuguese Jewish community and a diplomatic agent for Portugal. For many years he played an important diplomatic role and was especially influential in the conclusion of the Dutch-Portuguese peace treaty of 1661. This treaty ended many years of colonial conflict between the Dutch Republic and Portugal and established a framework of peaceful relations between the countries for many years to come. 84 notes. 1642-97

Costa, José Hipólito da

1517. Lima, Nestor dos Santos. A TRANSCENDÊNCIA LATINO-AMERICANA DE HIPÓLITO DA COSTA E O *CORREIO BRAZILIENSE* [The Latin American significance of Hipólito da Costa and the *Correio Braziliense]. Rev. do Inst. Hist. e Geog. Brasileiro [Brazil] 1979 (323): 24-29.* The thought and career of the Brazilian José Hipólito da Costa reveal his kinship with the great Latin American leaders from Francisco de Miranda and Simón Bolívar to José Martí, Sandino, Cárdenas and Che Guevara in that he had a continental vision. He corresponded with Miranda and in his periodical *Correio Braziliense* reflected both his patriotic and continental outlook. 19c

Costa, Juliana Diaz da

1518. Waller, John H. THE LADY JULIANA. *Mankind 1981 6(11): 22-25, 28, 30.* Presents a biography of Juliana Diaz da Costa who was born in India circa 1645. Her Portuguese parents had been enslaved by a local shah. She eventually gained great influence in the region, rising to power as a devoted servant to Prince Shah Alam who had been imprisoned by his father, Shah Aurangzeb, in 1686. He was released and sent to Afghanistan in 1693, but, learning of his father's death, he returned to Mogul India in 1707. With Juliana at his side Alam defeated his brother at the Battle of Jajau on 18 June 1707. Alam became undisputed ruler of Mogul India and Juliana's power was assured. She served an important role as liaison to European powers until her death in about 1732. 4 illus., 2 notes, 15 ref. ca 1665-1732

Costa y Deu, Juan

1519. Tarín-Iglesias, José. JUAN COSTA Y DEU, FIGURA DEL PERIODISMO [Juan Costa y Deu, a figure in journalism]. *Historia y Vida [Spain] 1984 17(193): 98-112.* Remembers the popular Spanish journalist Juan Costa y Deu (1883-1938), who for more than 30 years wrote for the Catalan newspaper *La Veu de Catalunya,* his friendship with most of the Catalan politicians of the 1930's, and his death in Italy after two years of exile. 1900-38

Costa-Gavras, Constantin

1520. Grenier, Richard. THE CURIOUS CAREER OF COSTA-GAVRAS. *Commentary 1982 73(4): 61-71.* Discusses the anti-Americanism and pro-Communism of Greek-born French filmmaker Constantin Costa-Gavras since 1964, noting his inability to separate fact from fantasy in dealing with the US role in Latin America. 1964-82

Cotesworth, William

1521. Ellis, Joyce. A BOLD ADVENTURER: THE BUSINESS FORTUNES OF WILLIAM COTESWORTH, C. 1668-1726. *Northern Hist. [Great Britain] 1981 17: 117-132.* William Cotesworth rose from a humble apprentice to a substantial Newcastle businessman. Originally a merchant and tallow chandler, hard work and wise speculation enabled him to build a substantial fortune in the local coal and salt industries. His business fortunes peaked in 1719-20; thereafter failing health, personal enemies, and excessive speculation seriously depleted his estate. Based mainly on the Cotesworth Manuscripts at the Gateshead Public Library. 1668-1726

Cotrugli, Benedetto de

1522. Spremić, Momčilo. BENEDETTO DE COTRUGLI, UN RAGUSEO DEL SECOLO XV: MENTALITA E POTERE [Benedetto de Cotrugli, citizen of Ragusa, in the 15th century: mentality and power]. *Ann. della Facoltà di Sci. Pol.: Materiali di Storia [Italy] 1979-80 16(4): 191-199.* A historical account of the life of Benedetto de Cotrugli, businessman of Dubrovnik, whose power and influence extended through southern Italy, Sicily, and North Africa. 15c

Cotte, Robert de

1523. Neuman, Robert. ROBERT DE COTTE AND THE BAROQUE ECCLESIASTICAL FAÇADE IN FRANCE. *Journal of the Society of Architectural Historians 1985 44(3): 250-265.* The façade of St. Roch, Paris (erected 1736-38), the last major work by Robert de Cotte, is often viewed as anomalous in an oeuvre devoted almost exclusively to the design of secular buildings. However, the recent discovery in Paris of certain drawings and related documents from de Cotte's studio makes it clear that he confronted the problem of the Italianate ecclesiastical façade throughout his career, although only a few of the commissions were actually carried out. The various solutions, while rooted in French tradition, betray a strong interest in Italian church portals of the late Renaissance and Baroque. The notes and drawings made by the architect during his Italian sojourn of 1689-90 confirm this interest. A chronological review of the projects reveals that the design for the St. Roch portal was closely related to de Cotte's earlier experiments for church façades in Paris, Dijon, and Orléans. He relied particularly on precedents set by Jules Hardouin Mansart as well as on his own unexecuted project for St. Louis de Versailles in 1724. Based on drawings and documents in the Bibliothèque Nationale, Archives Nationales, and the Bibliothèque de l'Institut. 1730's

Coudenhove-Kalergi, Richard

1524. Chodorowski, Jerzy. RICHARD COUDENHOVE-KALERGI I JEGO DOKTRYNA ZJEDNOCZENIA EUROPY [Richard Coudenhove-Kalergi and his doctrine of a united Europe]. *Przegląd Zachodni [Poland] 1984 40(1): 1-25.* Discusses the political career of Richard Coudenhove-Kalergi (b. 1894), founder of the pan-European movement, which spread through Western Europe in the 1920's. The movement united Europe's intellectual and social elite, enlisted through Kalergi's aristocratic and Masonic connections. During World War II, Kalergi established the European Council in the United States. He reactivated the Pan-European Union in 1947, with its seat in Switzerland. It united intellectuals of the center left, but failed to attract members of the younger generation. Secondary sources; 55 notes. 1920's-50

Courbet, Amédée

1525. Taillemite, Etienne. COURBET ET SES HOMMES [Courbet and his associates]. *Revue Historique des Armées [France] 1985 (3): 15-26.* Amédée Courbet (1827-85) entered the French navy after graduating from the Polytechnic School. His many talents and exceptional competence brought him rapid promotion. His term as governor of New Caledonia, however, was sterile and frustrating even though several progressive changes were made there. As commander of the Tonkin naval force, he was engaged in the Min River campaign and in operations against the Chinese. Many of his associates later attained high office. 5 photos, 20 notes. 1848-85

Courbet, Gustave

1526. Wagner, Anne M. COURBET'S LANDSCAPES AND THEIR MARKET. *Art Hist. [Great Britain] 1981 4(4): 410-431.* Describes the artistic career of French painter Gustave Courbet (1819-77), especially the way in which his landscapes were influenced by the market he produced them for. 1844-77

Courier, Paul-Louis

1527. DeCesare, Raffaele. NOTE BIBLIOGRAFICHE SULLA FORTUNA ITALIANA DI PAUL-LOUIS COURIER NELLA PRIMA META DEL XIX SECOLO [Bibliographic notes from the first half of the 19th century on the career in Italy of Paul-Louis Courier]. *Aevum [Italy] 1983 57(3): 493-549.* Introduces an annotated bibliography citing criticism, articles, and references in correspondence to French pamphleteer and officer in the Napoleonic army, Paul-Louis Courier, and his influence in Italy. 1806-48

Court, John

1528. Wood, Margaret. A DAUGHTER OF JOHN COURT REMEMBERS.... *Hist. J. [New Zealand] 1982 (41): 14-16.* Recounts Court's life in Auckland beginning in 1889 when he and his family left London to settle in New Zealand where he opened a shop called John Court Limited, which was run by Court's four sons after his death in 1933. 1889-1933

Court, W. H. B.

1529. Cain, P. J. WILLIAM HENRY BASSANO COURT, 1904-1971. *Pro. of the British Acad. [Great Britain] 1982 68: 521-535.* After study at Cambridge and Harvard, including unpublished research on early New England, W. H. B. Court joined the University of Birmingham in 1930 and remained there for the rest of his career. His major work was on the Industrial Revolution in the Midlands, showing how its origins went back to Tudor times and how small-scale production was equally as important as large industry. After working on the section on coal in the official World War II history, he became Professor of Economic History at Birmingham in 1947 and published his *Concise Economic History of Britain, from 1750 to Recent Times* in 1954. He viewed economic and social history as one discipline, and, despite being well-versed in economic theory, always stressed that it was inadequate to take a simple economic view of human motivation. Based on Court's writings; 44 notes. 1904-71

Couthon, Georges

1530. Morineau, Michel. MORT D'UN TERRORISTE... PROLEGOMENES A L'ETUDE D'UN JUSTE: "ARISTIDE" (CIDEVANT GEORGES) COUTHON, PRECEDE D'UN COUP D'OEIL SUR SES BIBLIOTHEQUES [Death of a Terrorist... prolegomena to a study of a just man: "Aristide" (formerly, Georges) Couthon, preceded by a glance at his libraries]. *Ann. Hist. de la Révolution Française [France] 1983 55(2): 292-339.* Examines personal and political aspects of Georges Couthon's career. His personality and beliefs were related, and though he was an invalid he never lost his intellectual powers. Motivated by a desire to secure justice for the peasantry and save the revolution, he was a supporter of the Terror as a practical measure to defend the revolution against its enemies. Based on material in the Archives Nationales, Paris, and departmental archives of the Puy-de-Dôme; 112 notes. 1755-94

1531. Soboul, Albert. GEORGES COUTHON. [Georges Couthon]. *Ann. Hist. de la Révolution Française [France] 1983 55(2): 204-227.* Georges Couthon (1755-94) was born in Orcet, in the Auvergne, the son of a notary. A lawyer himself, he became a municipal official and judge in Clermont-Ferrand in 1789 and 1790, then a deputy to the National Assembly in 1791 and the Convention in 1792. He moved toward the Montagnard faction and became an associate of Robespierre and member of the Committee of Public Safety. He was sent on a mission to Lyon and was active in the radical phase of the revolution. He was responsible for the 1794 law which inaugurated the Great Terror with execution without trial, but he was later arrested and put to death. Throughout his life, he was guided by an almost religious zeal for the revolution and commitment to defending it from its enemies within and outside France. 2 notes. 1789-94

Couturier, Marie-Alain

1532. Carré, A.-M. LA VERITE BLESSEE [The harmed truth]. *Revue des Deux Mondes [France] 1984 (9): 600-605.* A biographical sketch of Marie-Alain Couturier (1897-1954) and a review with quotes of *La Vérité Blessée,* a collection of notes left by this Dominican priest and artist, who expressed deep thoughts and accomplished great actions such as the search for the active collaboration of the most outstanding contemporary artists who were unbelievers. ca 1925-53

Coverdale, Miles

1533. Hughes, Celia. COVERDALE'S ALTER EGO. *Bull. of the John Rylands U. Lib. of Manchester [Great Britain] 1982 65(1): 100-124.* Miles Coverdale played a significant role as a reformer as well as a Bible translator. First embracing Lutheran doctrines, he later shifted toward the Swiss reformers and finally ended up as a "proto-Puritan." His translations of religious writings were important in disseminating the ideas of continental reformers, and his integrity offered a powerful example to younger churchmen as he tried to bring about a gradual reformation of the English church. Based on Coverdale's works; 41 notes. 1520-69

Coward, Noel

1534. Catsiapis, Hélène. NOËL COWARD ET LA FRANCE [Noel Coward and France]. *Rev. d'Hist. du Théâtre [France] 1981 33(1): 83-96.* Sketches Coward's visits to France and the influence of France on his plays, especially *Private Lives* (1930). His knowledge of Paris was limited to the area of the Ritz, the Place Vendôme, the Rue de la Paix, and the Place de l'Opéra, with a little detour up the Rue Royale to Maxim's. His view of France, even during World War II, was of the luxury, pleasures, and parties of elegant Deauville and "gay Paris." 40 notes. 1920-50

Cox, David

1535. Wilcox, Scott Barnes. "David Cox: His Development as a Painter in Watercolors." (Text only) Yale U. 1984. 294 pp. *DAI 1985 46(5): 1115-A.* DA8514895 ca 1800-59

Cox, William

1536. Altholz, Josef L. MISTER SERJEANT COX, JOHN CROCKFORD, AND THE ORIGINS OF *CROCKFORD'S CLERICAL DIRECTORY. Victorian Periodicals Review [Canada] 1984 17(4): 153-158.* 1853-79
*For abstract see **Crockford, John***

Cragnolini, Anton

1537. Prelovšek, Damjan. LJUBLJANSKI STAVBNI MOJSTER ANTON CRAGNOLINI [The Ljubljana master builder Anton Cragnolini]. *Kronika [Yugoslavia] 1981 29(2): 96-102.* Italian builders played an important role in the building of Ljubljana, especially in the 18th and 19th centuries. Genoa-born Anton (Antonio) Cragnolini (1809-37) was one of them. He fininshed his studies of ornamental sculpture at the Venetian Art Academy and then worked for some years with his father Cristoforo who was a master builder in Celovec. At the beginning of the 1830's he set up some important buildings in Ljubljana and in Zagreb, displaying great skill and stylistic novelty. Focuses on Cragnolini's Ljubljana works and his role in the Slovene architecture of the first half of the 19th century. 1830's

Craig, Edward Gordon

1538. Rood, Arnold. E. GORDON CRAIG, DIRECTOR, SCHOOL FOR THE ART OF THE THEATRE. *Theatre Res. Int. [Great Britain] 1983 8(1): 1-17.* Describes English drama teacher Edward Gordon Craig's attempts to establish a school for dramatic art in London, 1903-04, in Paris, 1910, and in Moscow, 1909. Craig's School for the Art of the Theatre was finally started in Florence in 1913. 1903-41

Cranmer, Thomas

1539. Croft, R. D. ARCHBISHOP THOMAS CRANMER AND THE EDUCATION OF THE ENGLISH CLERGY. *Hist. of Educ. [Great Britain] 1982 11(3): 155-164.* Archbishop Thomas Cranmer saw education as the key to the reformation of the clergy. He sought to raise standards by influencing grammar schools, especially the refounded King's School, Canterbury, introducing Protestant preachers and teachers in the universities, and prescribing in-service training for existing clergy. In his own time his work was unsuccessful, but many of the ideas were taken up by the Elizabethan episcopate. 38 notes. 1533-53

Creech Jones, Arthur

1540. Scarr, Deryck. WHISPERS OF FANCY: WITH MR ARTHUR CREECH-JONES IN SEYCHELLES. *J. of Imperial and Commonwealth Hist. [Great Britain] 1983 11(3): 322-338.* Deals with the role of the Secretary of State for the Colonies Arthur Creech Jones (1891-1964) in Labour's first government after World War II and his relations with the Seychelles Islands. The Labour government approached colonial problems of graft and political corruption with high liberal expectations only to discover that the powers of government were limited, and that each colony presented different problems that London had to treat individually. Based on Colonial Office materials at the Public Record Office, London, materials in the Mauritius Archives, the National Archives of Seychelles, and secondary works; 47 notes. 1945-50

Creel, Enrique C.

1541. Wasserman, Mark. ENRIQUE C. CREEL: BUSINESS AND POLITICS IN MEXICO, 1880-1930. *Business History Review 1985 59(4): 645-662.* Enrique C. Creel was a prominent Mexican entrepreneur and politician during the era of Porfirio Diaz and the first two decades of the 20th-century revolution. Besides his landholdings and banking interests, Creel served as governor of Chihuahua and as Mexican ambassador to the United States. After a period of exile in Los Angeles during the early years of the revolution, he returned to Mexico and became a key financial adviser to the government of president Alvaro Obregón. Creel's career reflects the resiliency of the Mexican economic elite in this period and demonstrates the special nature of entrepreneurship there, a close alliance of business and political power. Based largely on Mexican archival materials and published works; 48 notes. 1880-1930

Cremonini, Cesare

1542. Stella, Aldo. CESARE CREMONINI (1550-1631): IL SUO PENSIERO E IL SUO TEMPO [Cesare Cremonini (1550-1631): his thought and his times]. *Quaderni per la Storia dell'Università di Padova [Italy] 1983 16: 192-194.* Reports on a conference held in Cento, the Aristotelian natural philosopher Cesare Cremonini's birthplace, which included papers by Maria Assunta del Torre (key-note), Werther Angelini, Gian Ludovico Masetti Zannini, Rosaria Campioni, Aldo Stella, Tullio Tomba, Massimo Campanini, Domenico Bosco, Ugo Montanari, and Marco Gallerani. 1550-1631

Creutz, Gustav Philip

1543. Häkli, Esko. GUSTAV PHILIP CREUTZ OCH HANS BIBLIOTEK [Gustav Philip Creutz and his library]. *Opusculum [Finland] 1984 4(1): 11-32.* Gustav Philip Creutz (1731-85) belonged to a prominent Finnish family. After completing his studies at the University of Turku, he entered into the service of the Swedish state. In 1763-64 he was the envoy of Sweden in Madrid, and then moved to Paris. During this period in Paris, Creutz gathered a large library collection, which after his death became the property of the Swedish state. The catalogue of the Creutz Library is an interesting document that reflects what Creutz was interested in and contemporary taste in general. 1763-83

Cristescu, Gheorghe

1544. Copoiu, Nicolae. OMUL ŞI MILITANTUI: GHEORGHE CRISTESCU [The man and the militant: Gheorghe Cristescu]. *Magazin Istoric [Romania] 1982 16(10): 18-19, 44.* Eulogizes Gheorghe Cristescu, first Secretary General of the Romanian Communist Party, who survived, aged 89, to attend the celebrations in 1971 of its first half century. 1882-1973

1545. Deac, Augustin and Toacă, Ion. GHEORGHE CRISTESCU (1882-1973) [Gheorghe Cristescu (1882-1973)]. *Anale de Istorie [Romania] 1982 28(5): 88-92.* Cristescu, from his earliest days a militant, concerned not only with the workers' movement in Romania but also with Romania's struggle to unite Romanian territories still beyond the frontiers, played a prominent part in Socialist Party congresses of 1907-15. He was secretary of the Socialist Party after World War I, and in 1921-24 he was Secretary General of the Romanian Communist Party. Portrait. 1900's-73

Croce, Benedetto

1546. Boulay, Charles. CROCE ET L'EUROPE [Croce and Europe]. *Rev. des Etudes Italiennes [France] 1982 28(1-2): 72-128.* Discusses the life of historian, philosopher, and statesman Benedetto Croce and the influence of his environment on his perceptions of history and his opinions on affairs of state. 1866-1952

1547. Caserta, Ernesto G. CROCE AND MARXISM. *J. of the Hist. of Ideas 1983 44(1): 141-149.* During 1895-1900, and before his discovery of Hegel, Benedetto Croce became interested in the work of Karl Marx and his followers. This interest was spurred by the suggestions of his former teacher Antonio Labriola. Yet despite several studies on Marxist ideas, Croce never became a convert and indeed found much to criticize about them, especially in the crudely scientistic and materialistic form they took in the writings of popularizers such as Loria. While the views of Vico and De Sanctis had more lasting and significant places in his intellectual development, Croce's encounter with Marx provoked him to crystallize notions of ethics, aesthetics, and history that would avoid what he saw as the reductionism inherent in the Marxist canon. 29 notes. 1890's-1900's

1548. Roberts, David D. BENEDETTO CROCE AND THE DILEMMAS OF LIBERAL RESTORATION. *Rev. of Pol. 1982 44(2): 214-241.* With the Fascist collapse in the 1940's, Italy's premier political philosopher Benedetto Croce was looked to as a formulator for a new Italian liberalism. Building on theory developed in the 1930's that questioned the very philosophical roots of liberalism, Croce promulgated a "neo-liberal" vision that stressed liberty at the expense of justice. He did not believe the traditional arguments over the relationship between the individual and the state were as important as reemphasizing liberal pluralism and tolerance. Croce defined his "religion of liberty," which sought to unite human freedom with the historical processes. Finally, he sought to free liberalism from the traditional connection with antistatism and laissez faire economics. Instead of uniting Italy's liberal factions, Croce's neo-liberalism disillusioned, alienated, and polarized the groups and their party leaders who wanted to pursue social justice reforms. Primary and secondary sources; 56 notes. 1930-45

Crockford, John

1549. Altholz, Josef L. MISTER SERJEANT COX, JOHN CROCKFORD, AND THE ORIGINS OF *CROCKFORD'S CLERICAL DIRECTORY. Victorian Periodicals Review [Canada] 1984 17(4): 153-158.* Discusses the roles of William Cox (1809-79) and John Crockford (1823-65), British entrepreneurs, in establishing *Crockford's Clerical Directory* as the official directory of the Church of England. 1853-79

Croizat, Ambroise

1550. Lacroix-Riz, Annie. UN MINISTRE COMMUNISTE FACE A LA QUESTION DES SALAIRES: L'ACTION D'AMBROISE CROIZAT DE NOVEMBRE A MAI 1947 [A Communist minister and the question of wages: Ambroise Croizat from November 1945 to May 1947]. *Mouvement Social [France] 1983 (123): 3-44.* Labour Secretary from November 1945, the General Secretary of the Metal Workers Federation of CGT, the Communist Ambroise Croizat strove to fulfill CGT objectives. But the majority wanted to keep wages blocked as the government negotiated a new US loan. Croizat then turned to administrative measures that roused employers' indignation and led them to seek protection from the government. These expedients met an unfavorable evolution of the balance of political forces. When the CGT sought a 25% wage increase in May-June 1946, Croizat's position was already weakened; bound by a renewed regulation in the fall, he lost any means to alleviate a very strict freeze. His dismissal emphasized the real difficulties of the CGT in the first months of 1947. 1945-47

Cromwell, Oliver

1551. Kross, Edith. OLIVER CROMWELL UND DIE NEW MODEL ARMY [Oliver Cromwell and the New Model Army]. *Militärgeschichte [East Germany] 1984 23(6): 530-539.* Oliver Cromwell (1599-1658) was a representative of the revolutionary-democratic wing of the Independents. He sought to establish a revolutionary army of peasants and other classes of the people as well as to dismiss incompetent Presbyterian officers. After victories by his New Model Army, it was influenced by the Levellers, but Cromwell supported constitutional monarchy and brought army democracy to an end. Following the execution of Charles I, Cromwell sought to stabilize the situation by using the army against radicals. Thus the army degenerated into an aggressive, mercenary army of expansive capitalism. Illus., 2 maps, sketch, 20 notes. 1643-58

1552. Matar, Nabil I. PETER STERRY, THE MILLENNIUM AND OLIVER CROMWELL. *J. of the United Reformed Church Hist. Soc. [Great Britain] 1982 2(10): 334-342.* Examines the relationship between Peter Sterry, private chaplain to Oliver Cromwell, and his patron; discusses the influence of the interplay between religion and politics on Sterry's thoughts and actions. 1649-58

Crone, Gerald R.

1553. —. GERALD ROE CRONE, 1899-1982. *Geog. J. [Great Britain] 1983 149(2): 270-273.* Gerald R. Crone, librarian and map curator for the Royal Geographical Society from 1945 to his retirement in 1966, died on 6 October 1982. He was presented the society's Victoria Medal in 1966 in recognition of the many outstanding contributions he made to the history of cartography and to the history of geographical thought. Prior to the early 1960's, most of his contributions were in article form, but in his later years he wrote several books for the general reader. One of his most popular books was *Maps and Their Makers: An Introduction to the History of Cartography,* which was first published in 1953 and later went through five editions. Photo. 1899-1982

Croneborg, Barbara

1554. Schoultz, Gösta von. ÖSTERRIKISKAN PÅ ÖSTANÅS: BARBARA CRONEBORG, F. VON GEYMÜLLER [The Austrian woman at Östanås: Barbara Croneborg, born von Geymüller]. *Rig [Sweden] 1982 65: 89-102.* Describes the life of Barbara Croneborg at the Östanås estate in the Swedish province of Värmland. She was born to a wealthy Austrian family, von Geymüller, in Vienna in 1799, married the secretary of the Swedish consulate in Vienna, Ulric Croneborg, in 1825 and moved to Sweden in 1827 where she spent the rest of her life. Much information comes from the 400 letters she wrote between her husband's death in 1844 and her own in 1866. Based on primary sources; photo, 6 plates, ref. 1799-1866

Crookes, William

1555. DeKosky, Robert K. WILLIAM CROOKES AND THE QUEST FOR ABSOLUTE VACUUM IN THE 1870S. *Ann. of Sci. [Great Britain] 1983 40(1): 1-18.* Examines the technical evolution and scientific context of William Crookes's effort to achieve an absolute vacuum in the 1870's. Prior to late 1876, along with interrogation of the radiometer effect, the quest for perfect vacuum was a major motive of his research program. At this time, no absolutely dependable method existed to determine exactly the pressures at extreme rarefactions. Crookes therefore employed changes in radiometric, viscous, and electrical effects with changing pressure in order to monitor the progress of exhaustion. After late 1876, his research priorities shifted because he had reached a plateau of technical accomplishment in the effort to attain extreme vacua and because observed effects in vacua—particularly electrical—assumed an importance in their own right, and as bases for elucidation and defense of his concept of a "fourth state of matter" at very low pressures. 1870's

Crowe, Eyre

1556. Corp, Edward T. THE PROBLEM OF PROMOTION IN THE CAREER OF SIR EYRE CROWE, 1905-1920. *Australian J. of Pol. and Hist. [Australia] 1982 28(2): 236-249.* Analyzes intrigue within the British Foreign Office to prevent Sir Eyre Crowe (1864-1925) from becoming permanent undersecretary. He finally achieved this in 1920 and served with distinction until he died in 1925, but from 1906, when he had emerged as a brilliant official, various attempts to block his progress were tried. These were partly the work of Sir Charles Hardinge, partly due to wartime agitations by suffragettes, who pointed to his German family connections, and partly the prejudice of Lloyd George at the end of the war. But Crowe distinguished himself by his reorganization of the registry in 1905, his paper on Germany in Europe in 1907, his creation of the Ministry of Blockade during the war, and his advocacy at the Supreme Council at Versailles. Based on Foreign Office archives and private papers. 1900-25

Crowley, Robert

1557. Martin, J. W. THE PUBLISHING CAREER OF ROBERT CROWLEY: A SIDELIGHT ON THE TUDOR BOOK TRADE. *Publishing History [Great Britain] 1983 (14): 85-98.* The English printer of the early Reformation, Robert Crowley (1518-88) was the first publisher of the 14th-century *Vision of Piers Plowman* and other landmark titles. After exile, he returned under Elizabeth I and wrote many tracts, although he never owned a press of his own. His works deal with religious controversy and social issues, but he also published other works concerning religious reform. Himself a cleric, he was described as "preacher of gods woord" by his contemporaries. Based on contemporary documents, later historical works, and catalogues; 50 notes. 1550-88

Crusafont i Pairó, Miquel

1558. Avila Granados, Jesús. MIQUEL CRUSAFONT [Miquel Crusafont]. *Historia y Vida [Spain] 1984 17(201): 113-118.* Remembers the Spanish paleontologist Miquel Crusafont i Pairó (1910-83), author of *Evolución y Ascensión* (1960) and *El Fenómeno Vital* (1967), in which he disclosed the results of his extensive research as director of the Museum of Paleontology of Sabadell, a center of intense activity where scientists from around the world come to study. 1930-83

Cruz, Juana Inés de la

1559. Perelmuter Pérez, Rosa. LOS CULTISMOS HERRERIANOS EN EL PRIMERO SUEÑO DE SOR JUANA INES DE LA CRUZ [Herrerian euphuisms in the Primero Sueño of Sister Juana Ines de la Cruz]. *Bull. Hispanique [France] 1981 83(3-4): 439-446.* Although the influence of Góngora on Sister Juana Ines de la Cruz (1651-95) and that of Fernando de Herrera (1534-97) on Góngora have been studied, overlooked has been the direct influence of Herrera on Sister Juana. The presence in Sister Juana's *Primero Sueño* of 800 euphuisms also found in Herrera's poetic vocabulary, but of which Góngora uses only slightly more than 300, points to a closer relationship between Sister Juana's work and that of Herrera than had previously been indicated. Primary sources; 13 notes. 16c-17c

1560. Sáinz, Luis. OCTAVIO PAZ Y SOR JUANA: HAGIOGRAFIA, HEREJIA Y EXEGESIS [Octavio Paz and Sister Juana: hagiography, heresy, and exegesis]. *Revista Mexicana de Ciencias Políticas y Sociales [Mexico] 1982 28(110): 139-156.* A review essay on Octavio Paz's *Sor Juana de la Cruz o las Trampas de la Fe* [Sister Juana de la Cruz or the snares of faith], a work in which many of the themes that have occupied the poet meet around the tragic figure of the 17th-century Mexican nun-poet. Recreates the cultural environment of 17th-century Mexico in which the nun lived. 17c

1561. Scott, Nina M. SOR JUANA INES DE LA CRUZ: "LET YOUR WOMEN KEEP SILENCE IN THE CHURCHES..." *Women's Studies International Forum 1985 8(5): 511-519.* Sister Juana Inés de la Cruz entered a Mexican convent because in her time the convent was the only environment which sanctioned a woman's desire for a life of study and meditation. However, she devoted a large part of her literary activities to secular topics, dared to criticize the male Catholic establishment, and questioned the Church's inconsistent treatment of women. 1669-93

Csáky, Emmerich

1562. Matsch, Erwin. SECHS AUSSENMINISTER, DIE AUS DEM ALTEN ÖSTERREICH KAMEN [Six ministers of foreign affairs from old Austria]. *Archiv für Kulturgeschichte [West Germany] 1982 64(1): 171-215.* Characterizes and traces the careers of six men who had posts in the Foreign Service Office of the Austro-Hungarian monarchy. Upon the dissolution of the monarchy, these men became ministers of foreign affairs and served their respective native countries between 1919 and 1938: four Hungarians, Dr. Josef Somssich (1864-1941), Emmerich Csáky (1882-1961), Dr. Gustav Gratz (1875-1946), and Koloman von Kánya (1869-1945); the Pole, Dr. Alexander Skrzyński (1882-1931); and the Austrian, Egon Berger von Waldenegg (1880-1960). Of particular interest is the question of national allegiance which these men faced as a result of serving under two different regimes. Of the four Hungarians, only Gratz remained loyal to his legitimate king; of all six, only Skrzyński broke radically with his past, thus to become an opponent of Gratz. Based on unpublished memoirs, personal conversations, and archives of Vienna and on secondary sources; 84 notes. 1919-38

Csoma de Koros, Alexander

1563. Kádár, László Antal. KŐRÖSI CSOMA SÁNDOR ÉLETCÉLJA ÉS MUNKÁSSÁGA [The activities and goals of Sándor Kőrösi Csoma]. *Földrajzi Közlemények [Hungary] 1984 32(4): 339-346.* Csoma (Alexander Csoma de Koros) dedicated his life to the discovery of the geographical location of the ancestors of the Hungarian race. As a linguist he felt that by discovering similarities between Hungarian and other languages, the origin of the Magyars could be pinpointed. During his travel he met William Moorcroft, who, in 1822, hired him to produce a Tibetan-English dictionary and a grammar. Both were published in Calcutta in 1834. Before he could establish his final theory about the origin of his nation, he died of malaria in 1842 at the age of 44. Kőrösi's very thorough geographical review of Tibet published in *Journal of the Asiatic Society* (1832) is included in the article. 9 notes. 1839-42

1564. Kara, György. SÁNDOR CSOMA DE KŐRÖS: 1784-1842. *New Hungarian Quarterly [Hungary] 1984 25(94): 55-70.* Prints a biography of Alexander Csoma de Koros (1784-1842), also known as Skendher bheg. Born in the Hungarian village of Kőrös in Háromszék, Transylvania, he studied philology and theology at Göttingen University. He spent his life from 1822 on in Tibet and India, studying Buddhism and Tibetan language, and producing the first Tibetan-English dictionary in 1834. He also studied Tibetan geography, history, and medicine. He died in 1842 en route between Calcutta and Lhasa. 3 illus., 2 plates, 5 notes. 1819-42

1565. Mukerjee, Hirendranath. CSOMA DE KOROS—A DEDICATED LIFE. *Bulletin of Tibetology [India] 1984 (1): 17-20.* Reprint of an article from the Calcutta *Presidency College Magazine,* 1926 18(1), celebrating the pioneer of Tibetan studies Alexander Csoma de Koros (1784-1842). 1820's-42

1566. Sinha, Nirmal C. THE UNIVERSAL MAN. *Bulletin of Tibetology [India] 1984 (1): 14-16.* Alexander Csoma de Koros (1784-1842) was the first non-Tibetan scholar to attempt a systematic probe into the vast canon, Kanjur and Tanjur. 1820's-42

Cuarteroni, Carlos

1567. Cruz Hermosilla, Emilio de la. CARLOS CUARTERONI, CAPITAN DE FRAGATA, PESCADOR DE PERLAS Y... OBISPO [Carlos Cuarteroni, lieutenant commander, pearl fisherman, and bishop]. *Rev. General de Marina [Spain] 1979 197(Aug-Sept): 159-164.* Describes the career of Carlos Cuarteroni (1816-80). Born in Cádiz to a family of Genoese origin, Cuarteroni joined the navy at age 13, sailed to the Philippines, acquired a ship of his own at age 33, went fishing for pearls off the coast of the Pacific islands, salvaged an English ship which had sunk with a cargo of silver, became a Trinitarian monk and then an Augustinian, and was finally appointed apostolio prefect of Labuan, in the Dutch East Indies. 1840-80

Cuffay, William

1568. Gossman, Norbert J. WILLIAM CUFFAY: LONDON'S BLACK CHARTIST. *Phylon 1983 44(1): 56-65.* William Cuffay, the son of a West Indian slave, was the only significant black Chartist in London. He was a member of the "physical force" party during the 1830's. He helped organize the Metropolitan Tailors Chartist Association in 1839, and from that his role expanded. In the 1840's, he led disruptive events in opposition to the upper classes. He was involved in demonstrations, riots, and conspiracies in 1848. He was transported to Tasmania in 1849 at age 61, where he lived until 1870. The government pardoned him in 1856. Notes. 1820-70

Culmer, Richard

1569. Greaves, Richard L. A PURITAN FIREBRAND: RICHARD CULMER OF CANTERBURY. *Hist. Mag. of the Protestant Episcopal Church 1981 50(4): 359-368.* The career of Richard Culmer (1597-1662) illustrates the depth of conflicting religious ideology and the bitter divisiveness within local communities during the English Civil War. Puritan, iconoclast, controversialist, pamphleteer, Culmer was an outspoken proponent of the parliamentary cause. In 1643 he was appointed by Parliament to demolish "all monuments of superstition" in Canterbury Cathedral, a task to which he devoted himself with notable zeal. His fulfilling this commission is described and traced to the harshness with which the Puritans had been suppressed in the 1630's. Based largely on the Domestic Calendar of State Papers of Charles I and Culmer's *A Parish Looking-Glasse;* illus., 43 notes. 1630-45

Culpeper Family

1570. Cleggett, David. FAMILIES OF AN ATLANTIC COMMUNITY. *Virginia Cavalcade 1983 32(3): 114-125.* History of the Culpeper and Fairfaxe families of England, some of whose members were associated with Virginia; provides a gallery of portraits. 16c-18c

Cumming, William Skeoch

1571. Greenwall, Ryno. WILLIAM SKEOCH CUMMING: SCOTTISH YEOMAN ARTIST. *Africana Notes and News [South Africa] 1984 26(3): 81-85.* Prints a biography of William Skeoch Cumming (1864-1929). Focuses on his military service in the Boer War as a background to several paintings. Plate, 18 notes. 1900-06

Cummings-John, Constance Agatha

1572. Denzer, LaRay. CONSTANCE A. CUMMINGS-JOHN OF SIERRA LEONE: HER EARLY POLITICAL CAREER. *Tarikh [Nigeria] 1981 7(1): 20-32.* Traces the early life and political career of Constance Agatha Cummings-John (née Horton), founder of the Sierra Leone Women's Movement, from her birth in 1918 in Freetown, Sierra Leone to the 1950's, focusing on her involvement in anticolonial and independence movements in West Africa and on her dealings with other African leaders, including I. T. A. Wallace-Johnson (1894-1965) and H. C. Bankole Bright (1883-1958). 1918-50's

Cunha, Euclides da

1573. Peregrino, Umberto. ALGUMAS ESPECIAIS QUALIFICAÇÕES DE *OS SERTÕES* [Some special characteristics of *Os Sertões]. Revista do Instituto Histórico e Geográfico Brasileiro [Brazil] 1983 (338): 109-132.* Euclides da Cunha (1866-?) was an engineer and war correspondent who reported on the military expedition against Antonio Conselheiro, leader of the Canudos revolution in Bahia, on which his book was based. *Os Sertões* (1902) was enormously popular when it first appeared, except with the army, and remains a great monument of Brazilian literature. Contains biographical, literary and historical notes on the author and his work. 6 notes. 1902

Cunhal, Alvaro

1574. Lakin, V. F. STOIKII PATRIOT-INTERNATSIONALIST (K 70-LETIIU SO DNIA ROZHDENIIA GENERAL'NOGO SEKRETARIA PORTUGAL'SKOI KOMPARTII (PKP) AL'VARO KUN'IALA) [A firm internationalist-patriot: the 70th anniversary of the birth of the general secretary of the Portuguese Communist Party (PCP), Alvaro Cunhal]. *Voprosy Istorii KPSS [USSR] 1983 (11): 108-112.* Alvaro Cunhal was born in October 1913, the son of a lawyer, and at an early age joined the struggle for the workers' cause. In 1935, he was elected general secretary of the Federation of Communist Youth of Portugal, and in the following year he became a member of the Party's Central Committee. In 1961, he became the Party's general secretary. Under his leadership the PCP made an important contribution to the April revolution of 1974. At the present moment, in spite of the slanderous campaign against the PCP and the attempts of reactionary forces to isolate it, the influence of the Communist Party on the masses is growing. In 1980, the Party numbered over 187,000 members. Secondary sources; 16 notes. 1930's-83

Cunitz, Maria

1575. Mühlpfordt, Günter. JOHANN HERBIN: DER ERSTE FRAUENRECHTLER DER DEUTSCHEN AUFKLÄRUNG [Johann Herbin: the first champion of women's rights of the German Enlightenment]. *Zeitschrift für Geschichtswissenschaft [East Germany] 1983 31(4): 325-338.* 1633-76

*For abstract see **Herbin, Johann***

Cuoco, Vincenzo

1576. Sbarra, Ugo. "Vincenzo Cuoco, Vita e Opere" [Vincenzo Cuoco: life and works]. McGill U. [Canada] 1983. *DAI 1983 44(5): 1471-A.* ca 1800-15

Curie, Marie

1577. Cabot, José Tomás. LA VIDA EJEMPLAR DE MARIE CURIE [The exemplary life of Marie Curie]. *Hist. y Vida [Spain] 1983 16(182): 118-124.* Marie Curie made great contributions to the fields of chemistry, physics, and medicine and led an exemplary personal and professional life. 1890's-1934

1578. Davoine, François. MARIE CURIE: UN GRAND EXEMPLE DE RIGUEUR SCIENTIFIQUE ET DE PERSEVERANCE [Marie Curie: a great example of scientific rigor and perseverance]. *Transactions of the Royal Society of Canada [Canada] 1984 22: 291-305.* Shortly after marrying Pierre Curie and determining to pursue her doctorate, Marie Curie learned of the discovery of Roentgen concerning the emissions of uranium. Thus, she embarked upon the research that she would communicate to the Academy of Science in 1898, postulating the discovery of polonium and radium. It was only on 28 March 1902 that the Curies were able to announce radium's atomic mass as 225.93. Subsequently it was discovered that radium was effective in the treatment of cancer. Declining the economic benefits of a patent, the Curies shared the 1903 Nobel Prize in physics with A. H.

Becquerel. After the death of Pierre in 1906, Marie was awarded a Nobel Prize in chemistry in 1911. One of her ambitions was achieved with the establishment of an Institute of Radium in July 1914, and much of the remainder of her life was spent in the promotion of medical research involving radioactivity. 6 illus. 1890's-1920's

1579. Kronen, Torleiv. MADAME CURIE OG ELLEN GLEDITSCH: ET VENNSKAP OG EN BREVVEKSLING [Madame Curie and Ellen Gleditsch: a friendship and a correspondence]. *Nordisk Tidskrift [Sweden] 1985 61(1): 24-36.* Describes the friendship between the Norwegian physicist, Ellen Gleditsch (1879-1968), and the Polish physicist, Marie Curie (1867-1934), as reflected in letters from 1907 to 1968, now deposited in the Curie Museum and the Bibliothèque Nationale in Paris. 1907-68

1580. Skrzypczak, Ewa. THE HOMELAND AND EARLY YEARS OF MARIA CURIE-SKLODOWSKA. *Transactions of the Royal Society of Canada [Canada] 1984 22: 283-290.* Marie Sklodowska Curie was born on 7 November 1867 in Warsaw. As a daughter of a family of middle-class landowners, she studied in Russian-dominated schools, but the educational futures of her brother and sister as well as herself were financially insecure. She eventually studied at the Sorbonne and selected mathematics and physics over literature and history in preparation for a teaching career. During World War I, she organized and administered x-ray equipment for medical services. Throughout her life she remained attached to her Polish homeland. 1867-1910's

1581. Yaffe, Leo. THE SCIENTIFIC LEGACY OF MARIE CURIE. *Transactions of the Royal Society of Canada [Canada] 1984 22: 307-316.* The discoveries of Marie Curie led to the creation of artificial radioactivity by Irène and Frédéric Joliot-Curie in 1934, providing a source of radioisotopes now routinely used in medicine, industry, agriculture and the physical and biological sciences. Four years later, nuclear fission was discovered by Enrico Fermi under the influence of Chadwick's discovery of the neutron and the work of the Joliot-Curies. Glenn T. Seaborg's work with the transuranic elements and the use of carbon-14 dating in archaeology and anthropology were also part of Curie's legacy. 1930's-80's

Curwen, John

1582. Leinster-Mackay, D. JOHN HULLAH, JOHN CURWEN AND SARAH GLOVER: A CLASSIC CASE OF "WHIGGERY" IN THE HISTORY OF MUSICAL EDUCATION? *British J. of Educ. Studies [Great Britain] 1981 29(2): 164-167.* Example of the distortions introduced by the Whig interpretation of educational history. The majority of current histories of education in Great Britain focus on John Hullah and his methods of teaching vocal music, when in fact these were largely replaced in the mid-1860's by the methods devised by Sarah Glover and disseminated by John Curwen. 16 notes. 1840's-60's

Curzon, George N.

1583. Bhatia, L. M. CURZON—A FRIEND OF INDIA. *Indo-British Review [India] 1985 11(2): 38-45.* Surveys efforts by George N. Curzon, 1st Baron and 1st Marquis Curzon of Kedleston (1859-1925), to improve the efficiency of the British colonial government in India as viceroy and governor-general. 1899-1905

1584. Dalal, J. A. F. CURZON IN INDIA. *J. of the United Service Inst. of India [India] 1980 110(459): 66-72.* After compiling a brilliant record as a student at Eton and Oxford, George Nathaniel Curzon (1859-1925) made a series of travels through Asia during the 1880's and 1890's and subsequently produced a number of publications on the subject. It was during one of these trips that he first became interested in India. In 1898, at the age of 39, he was named viceroy of India. He showed great energy in pressing reforms and in promoting British interests in the region. His second term was cut short when in 1905 he resigned due to political opposition. A review article of David Dilks's *Curzon in India,* 2 vol. (1969-70). 1880-1906

1585. Khalfin, Naftula Aronovich. LORD KERSON—IDEOLOG I POLITIK BRITANSKOGO IMPERIALIZMA [Lord Curzon: an ideologist and practitioner of British imperialism]. *Novaia i Noveishaia Istoriia [USSR] 1983 (1): 120-140.* Discusses George N. Curzon's contribution to the theory and practice of British imperial policy. Concentrates on Curzon's participation in the formulation of policy toward India, Afghanistan, the North-West frontier, and Turkestan. His ideas are still alive and kindle fires in the hearts of British and American imperialists of the contemporary era. Based on documents in the Indian National Archive, the State Archive of the Uzbek Soviet Socialist Republic (file I-2), published documents, memoirs, and secondary accounts in Russian and English; 94 notes. 1882-1925

Curzon, Grace

1586. Bryant, F. Russell. LADY CURZON, THE MARCHIONESS FROM DECATUR. *Alabama Hist. Q. 1982 44(3-4): 213-260.* A biography of Grace Hinds (1878-1958). Describes her early life and background in Decatur and Huntsville, Alabama, and her marriages and path to London society. In 1917 she married George N. Curzon, then a member of Lloyd George's War Cabinet. She became one of London's premier hostesses and with Curzon's elevation to marquess in 1921, Marchioness Curzon of Kedleston. 207 notes. 1906-58

Cushing, Harvey

1587. Teichman, Sam L. and Aldea, Peter A. PIONEERS IN PITUITARY PHYSIOLOGY: HARVEY CUSHING AND NICHOLAS PAULESCU. *Journal of the History of Medicine and Allied Sciences 1985 40(1): 68-72.* 1890's-1920's

*For abstract see **Paulescu, Nicholas C.***

Cutteridge, James Oliver

1588. Campbell, Carl C. EDUCATION AND BLACK CONSCIOUSNESS: THE AMAZING CAPTAIN J. O. CUTTERIDGE IN TRINIDAD AND TOBAGO, 1921-42. *Journal of Caribbean History [Barbados] 1984 18(1): 35-66.* Describes the career of the controversial Director of Education in Trinidad and Tobago, Captain James Oliver Cutteridge. The controversy resulted from his racist textbooks, especially *Nelson's West Indian Readers* (6 vols., 1927-31), widely used in British West Indian schools, but accused of being designed "to turn black and coloured children into fools." The criticism reflected the rising black consciousness in Trinidad and Tobago. Primary sources; 106 notes. 1921-39

Cuza, Alexandru Ioan

1589. Ploeşteanu, Grigore. ALEXANDER I. CUZA IM EXIL (1866-1873): INNERER NACHKLANG UND DIPLOMATISCHE IMPLIKATIONEN [Alexandru I. Cuza in exile, 1866-73: personal echoes and diplomatic implications]. *Rev. Roumaine d'Hist. [Romania] 1983 22(1): 47-58.* Following his overthrow on 23 February 1866 as ruler of Romania, Alexandru Ioan Cuza divided his time between Vienna, Warsaw, and Paris. His frequent meetings with foreign diplomatic personnel was duly noted by the Austrian police, suspicious of plots involving the exiled hospodar. Prince Carol, his successor on the throne in Bucharest, resisted all efforts to allow Cuza back into the country; new documentation supports the contention that France and Austria in particular supported the restoration of Cuza in order to disrupt what they saw as undue German influence in the Balkans. Based on archival correspondence, published documents, and secondary works; 53 notes. 1866-73

Cvetkova, Bistra Adreeva

1590. Kornrümpf, Hans-Jurg. BISTRA ADREEVA CVETKOVA (IN MEMORIAM) [Bistra Adreeva Cvetkova: in memory]. *Südost-Forschungen [West Germany] 1983 42: 299-300.* Provides an obituary of B. A. Cvetkova (1926-82), Bulgarian historian at the University of Sofia. 1926-82

Cyankiewicz, Andrzej

1591. Krukowski, Jan. ANDRZEJA CYANKIEWICZA PORTRET SKORYGOWANY [Andrzej Cyankiewicz and his corrected portrait]. *Kwartalnik Hist. Nauki i Techniki [Poland] 1981 26(3-4): 615-629.* Cyankiewicz was born ca. 1740 in Wadowice. He studied at the University of Cracow from 1759 and received his Bachelor's degree in philosophy 10 December 1763. He went on to receive his Master's and his PhD 12 October 1764. His further career was closely connected with academic and religious life. Cyankiewicz died on 13 May 1803 in Proszowice. He is known as a translator of several monumental works, such as Locke's *An Essay Concerning Human Understanding,* and many others. Based on published primary and secondary sources; photo, 68 notes. 1740-1803

Czapliński, Władysław

1592. Olszewski, Henryk. WŁADYSŁAW CZAPLIŃSKI 1905-1981 [Władysław Czapliński (1905-81)]. *Czasopismo Prawno-Historyczne [Poland] 1982 34(2): 249-251.* An obituary of Władysław Czaplinński, a Polish historian, also associated with legal history and a remarkable pedagogue. 1905-81

1593. Przyboś, Adam. WŁADYSŁAW CZAPLIŃSKI 1905-1981 [Władysław Czapliński (1905-81)]. *Studia Historyczne [Poland] 1984 27(2): 251-265.* Obituary of Władysław Czapliński, Polish historian with special interest in Silesia, Scandinavia, and the Vasa dynasty. Lists his academic and popular publications and distinctions. 11 notes. English summary. 1905-81

1594. Tazbir, Janusz. WŁADYSŁAW CZAPLIŃSKI (1905-1981) [Władysław Czapliński (1905-81)]. *Acta Poloniae Historica [Poland] 1982 (46): 285-286.* Władysław Czapliński graduated from the Jagiellonian University in Cracow in 1927, researched and taught in schools, conducted clandestine courses during the war, and in 1946 became a professor of modern history at Wrocław University until his retirement in 1976. He was a specialist in 17th-century politics and diplomacy, the Church, and the higher levels of society, publishing his main work on 17th-century Poland in Warsaw in 1966. He was, however, strongly drawn to Baltic studies and research, and scored a first with a work on Denmark and Poland from the 16th to the 20th centuries published in Wrocław in 1976. 1927-81

1595. Tazbir, Janusz. WŁADYSŁAW CZAPLIŃSKI (1905-1981) [Władysław Czapliński (1905-81)]. *Zapiski Hist. [Poland] 1982 47(3): 127-129.* Obituary of the Polish historian Władysław Czapliński, sketching his academic career and major publications, and listing the most eminent of his pupils. 20c

Czartoryski, Adam

1596. Ludwikowski, Rett R. ADAM CZARTORYSKI—"LIBERALNY" PRZYWÓDCA EMIGRACYJNEJ KONSERWY? [Adam Czartoryski: a "liberal" leader of the conservative camp in exile?]. *Studia Hist. [Poland] 1982 25(3-4): 387-402.* Discusses the political outlook of Prince Adam Czartoryski (1770-1861) and his close collaborators. Despite a vague liberal disposition in his youth, the prince became more and more conservative. The idea of strong government, capable of moderating excesses of laissez-faire, a concept of society as an organism, and emphasis on the role of the Church formed the basis of his conservative ideology. In 1845 Czartoryski realized the necessity of agrarian reform in order to secure the people's support in the event of national insurgency and to prevent social turmoil. He remained always a man of half measures. Based mainly on Czartoryski's speeches published in 1847; 51 notes. 1831-47

Czerniakow, Adam

1597. Fuks, Marian. W 40 ROCZNICĘ ŚMIERCI ADAMA CZERNIAKOWA [The 40th anniversary of the death of Adam Czerniakow]. *Biuletyn Żydowskiego Instytutu Hist. w Polsce [Poland] 1983 (1): 25-40.* On July 23, 1942, Engineer Adam Czerniakow, president of the Jewish Council (Judenrat) in the Warsaw ghetto, committed suicide after he lost hope of saving even a part of Warsaw's Jews from the concentration camps. He refused to sign the Nazi document of 22 July 1942 "concerning removal of the ghetto inhabitants eastwards;" when the Nazis left his office, he took poison. The author discusses the problem of Judenrats as well as living conditions in the Warsaw ghetto and gives the biography of Engineer Czerniakow, particularly his activities from the outbreak of war in September 1939 to his death. Based on Czerniakow's recently published diary and other primary sources. 1939-42

Czóbel, Béla

1598. Frank, János. THE CENTENARY OF BÉLA CZÓBEL, THE PAINTER. *New Hungarian Quarterly [Hungary] 1984 25(94): 173-176.* Evaluates the career of Paris-trained Hungarian painter Béla Czóbel (1883-1974). His introduction of *Les Fauves* influence into the Hungarian art world in 1906 was revolutionary. Notes Budapest commemorations of the centenary of his birth in 1983. 8 notes, 4 plates, 6 photos. 1903-76

D

Dąbrowski, Stefan

1599. Koberdowa, Irena. STEFAN DĄBROWSKI—ZAPOMNIANY DZIAŁACZ PPS LEWICY [Stefan Dąbrowski: a forgotten activist of the Polish Socialist Party—Left]. *Z Pola Walki [Poland] 1979 22(1): 147-160.* Stefan Dąbrowski was a Polish Socialist Party activist. He left school in Cracow in 1888 and went to the United States for two years, where he received American citizenship. He then arrived in Paris, where he came under the political influence of the Gierszyński family. In 1901, he joined the Polish branch of the Polish Socialist Party. He returned to Poland in about 1905 and continued his political work, mainly among Russian troops in the Warsaw region. He was arrested in 1909 and sent to Siberia. He continued his journalistic activities there and apparently escaped to the United States by 1914. Based on Dąbrowski's correspondence in the collections of the Historical-Literary Society in Paris and other documents held in archives in Warsaw; 39 notes, appendix. 1900-14

Daitz, Werner

1600. Herzstein, Robert E.; Becker, Peter and Barrett, Michael, commentary. FROM GREATER GERMAN REICH TO GREAT REGION ECONOMY: WERNER DAITZ AND NAZI POSTWAR PLANNING, 1939-1944. *Pro. of the South Carolina Hist. Assoc. 1981: 142-155.* Examines the career of Werner Daitz, who hoped to receive a high position in Nazi Germany with detailed plans for a postwar economy. Reaching his greatest influence in 1942, he was undermined by a combination of military defeat and the machinations of Martin Bormann two years later. Based primarily on German documents; 13 notes. Commentary, pp. 171-180. 1939-44

Dalin, Viktor

1601. —. VIKTOR MOISEEVICH DALIN [Viktor Moiseevich Dalin]. *Novaia i Noveishaia Istoriia [USSR] 1985 (6): 209-210.* An obituary for Viktor Dalin (1902-85), Soviet historian and consulting professor of the Institute of History of the Soviet Academy of Sciences who joined the Bolshevik Party in 1921. His lifelong interest in French utopianism and the labor movement yielded many publications, including a Russian language edition of the works of G. Babeuf. 1930-85

Dallas, Eneas Sweetland

1602. Taylor, Jenny. THE GAY SCIENCE: THE "HIDDEN SOUL" OF VICTORIAN CRITICISM. *Literature and History [Great Britain] 1984 10(2): 189-202.* Discusses the life and work of Eneas Sweetland Dallas, a little-known Victorian critic whose work, *The Gay Science* (1856), anticipates modern leftist and avant-garde literary criticism. Dallas's work can even be seen as revolutionary because it turns upside down the standard Victorian conception of art as morally purposeful. The basis of art, for Dallas, is pleasure, and he proceeds to attack poetic formalism, biographical criticism, and German idealism. For a psychological grounding, he elaborated a theory of the "hidden soul," which plays a key role in the relationship between conscious and unconscious thoughts in the creation and understanding of art. 50 notes. 1850's

Dalmases y Jordana, Cándido

1603. M. B. CÁNDIDO DE DALMASES Y JORDANA S.I.: BIBLIOGRAFIA [Cándido de Dalmases y Jordana, S.J.: bibliography]. *Arch. Hist. Societatis Iesu [Italy] 1981 50(100): 354-364.* Biographical sketch and bibliography of works by Father Cándido de Dalmases y Jordana, S.J. (b. 1906), member of the Instituto Histórico de la Compañía [Historical Institute of the Society]. 1939-81

Dálnoki Miklós, Béla

1604. Korom, Mihály. DÁLNOKI MIKLÓS BÉLA [Béla Dálnoki Miklós]. *Társadalmi Szemle [Hungary] 1982 37(11): 51-58.* Béla Dálnoki Miklós fought as a brigadier general on Hitler's side and was elected as the prime minister of Hungary by the first post-liberation parliament in 1944. Although his attempts to bring a large part of the Hungarian army under Russian jurisdiction did not work out, a year later, together with 12 other prominent individuals, he was honored with a lifetime membership in the parliament. His inability to adjust to the new and different political era eventually resulted in disgrace and his parliamentary membership was revoked. He died in 1948 and was buried without government honors. 1941-48

Dalrymple, John

1605. Donovan, Robert Kent. SIR JOHN DALRYMPLE AND THE ORIGINS OF ROMAN CATHOLIC RELIEF, 1775-1778. *Recusant History [Great Britain] 1984 17(2): 188-196.* Although himself a member of the Church of Scotland, Sir John Dalrymple (1726-1810), secretly worked for passage of the Roman Catholic Relief Act of 1778 in England and for similar limited religious liberty for members of the Catholic Church in Scotland in exchange for the inclusion of Catholics in military forces recruited to fight for the British Empire in the American Revolutionary War. His efforts were part of his support for a strong monarchy against the interests of Whig oligarchs. 1775-78

Dalton, John

1606. Cardwell, Donald and Mottram, Joan. FRESH LIGHT ON JOHN DALTON. *Notes and Records of the Royal Society of London [Great Britain] 1984 39(1): 29-40.* Recent discoveries of a bust of John Dalton and a letter from a contemporary shed new light on the career of the English scientist. 14 notes. 19c

Dalzel, Archibald

1607. Rawley, James A. FURTHER LIGHT ON ARCHIBALD DALZEL. *Int. J. of African Hist. Studies 1984 17(2): 317-323.* Provides data on the life of a famous British merchant and slaver in 18th-century West Africa. Based on British archives; 26 notes. 1763-1811

Damba, Jebtzun

1608. Vinkovics, Judit and Balogh, Péter. ÉLETRAJZOK A MONGOL NÉPI FORRADALOM KORÁBÓL [Biographies from the time of the Mongol people's revolution]. *Világtörténet [Hungary] 1983 (2): 113-125.* 1874-1952

For abstract see ***Choibalsan, Khorloogin***

Dancer, John Benjamin

1609. Prescott, Gertrude Mae. PUBLIC AND PRIVATE VISION: THE PHOTOGRAPHY OF JOHN BENJAMIN DANCER. *Lib. Chronicle of the U. of Texas at Austin 1982 (19): 52-77.* English optician, John Benjamin Dancer, was a self-taught pioneer in photography and developer of stereoscopic representation, but his career was marred by ill health and lack of recognition. 1839-70

Daneau, Lambert

1610. Desplat, Christian. LAMBERT DANEAU, L'ACADEMIE D'ORTHEZ ET LES SUPERSTITIONS [Lambert Daneau, the academy of Orthez, and superstition]. *Revue de Pau et du Béarn [France] 1984 12(Special Issue): 195-219.* Lambert Daneau was an educator at the Huguenot Académie de Béarn, Orthez, from 1583-91. Using the Bible and the church fathers as the sole criteria for matters of belief and ethics, he railed against sorcery, dancing, and games of chance as Satanic instruments leading straight to perdition. 1571-89

Daniels, Roland

1611. —. NOVYE MATERIALY O K. MARKSE [New sources on K. Marx]. *Voprosy Filosofii [USSR] 1983 (5): 100-126.* Outlines the life of Roland Daniels (1819-55) and reproduces with annotation his letters to Karl Marx in 1851. 19c

Danilov, Aleksandr I.

1612. —. ALEKSANDR IVANOVICH DANILOV (1916-1980) [Aleksandr Ivanovich Danilov, 1916-80]. *Srednie Veka [USSR] 1981 44: 406-409.* Obituary of the prominent Soviet historian, dean of the Medieval History Faculty of Moscow University, Minister of Education of the RSFSR and, since 1973, editor-in-chief of the journal *Srednie Veka.* Reviews his career and publications, particularly his Ph.D. thesis, "Problems of Early Medieval Agrarian History in Late 19th-Early 20th Century German Historiography," which formulated basic tenets of Marxist historiography and influenced subsequent Soviet historiography research. Photo. 1947-80

Danjila

1613. Veit, Veronika. GALDAN'S NEPHEW DANJILA (D. 1708): AN EXAMPLE OF THE K'ANG-HSI EMPEROR'S SUCCESSFUL POLICY TOWARDS THE MONGOLS. *Asian and African Studies [Israel] 1982 16(3): 345-356.* A biographical study of the nephew of Galdan, the last Mongol prince to give serious opposition to the Manchu conquerors of China. Based on Mongol and Manchu sources, especially the Mongol biographical handbook, *Iledkel Sastir;* 29 notes. 1684-1708

D'Annunzio, Gabriele

1614. Noether, Emiliana P. MUSSOLINI E D'ANNUNZIO: UNA STRANA AMICIZIA [Mussolini and D'Annunzio: a strange friendship]. *Rassegna degli Archivi di Stato [Italy] 1983 43(2-3): 297-319.* Traces the relationship of Benito Mussolini with Gabriele D'Annunzio from the early 20th century, when Mussolini accepted the writer's guidance, through the 1920's and '30's, when D'Annunzio had retreated from public participation and accepted financial support from the Fascist state. Fascism borrowed from D'Annunzio the ideas of the need of a superman who would surpass conventional bourgeois morality and of Italian greatness built upon aggressiveness. D'Annunzio's role in the seizure of Fiume provided a model of active leadership for Mussolini, but when Fiume was then lost, D'Annunzio's importance in Italian politics rapidly declined. Archival and printed primary sources; 82 notes. 1899-1938

1615. Pérez, Manuel Domingo. LA EMPRESA DE D'ANNUNZIO EN FIUME [D'Annunzio's undertaking in Fiume]. *Historia y Vida [Spain] 1984 17(191): 76-87.* The story of how Gabriele D'Annunzio, the Italian soldier and poet, conquered the city of Fiume (Rijeka) in September 1919 hoping for its annexation to Italy, and the subsequent problems created by his action. 1915-20

1616. Secrest, Meryle. D'ANNUNZIO'S LIFE, LIKE HIS HOUSE, HAD MANY MANSIONS. *Smithsonian 1983 14(4): 52-61.* The Italian author-lover-hero Gabriele D'Annunzio left a house as flamboyant in its design and contents as his life style. 1880's-1914

Danrit, Capitaine

See Driant, Emile

Dantas, Júlio

1617. Iria, Alberto. EVOCAÇÃO DE JÚLIO DANTAS NO 1º CENTENÁRIO DO SEU NASCIMENTO: DUAS RARIDADES BIBLIOGRÁFICAS DO MÉDICO MILITAR [Recollections of Júlio Dantas in the centenary of his birth: two bibliographical rarities of the military doctor]. *Anais da Acad. Portuguesa da Hist. [Portugal] 1979 25: 359-384.* Commemorates the illustrious career of Júlio Dantas who as a military doctor in the first decade of the 20th century reorganized Portuguese army medical facilities, instituted improved standards of hygiene, and contributed to better living conditions for the soldiers. The author reproduces two little-known reports by Dantas from 1907 and 1908 recommending ambulances and medical supplies vehicles. From 1912 he served as inspector of scholarly libraries and archives, and is also celebrated for his literary work. Read at a meeting of the Academia Portuguesa da História, May 1977; 3 illus., 26 notes. 1902-12

Dantiscus, Johannes

1618. Bogdan, Danuta. KORESPONDENCJA JANA DANTYSZKA Z HUMANISTAMI NIDERLANDZKIMI [Johannes Dantiscus's correspondence with humanists from the Netherlands]. *Komunikaty Mazursko-Warmińskie [Poland] 1980 (4): 583-590.* Reviews Henry de Vocht's *Johannes Dantiscus and His Netherlandish Friends*... (1961), where correspondence between Dantiscus, 16th-century Polish diplomat and poet, and his academic and diplomatic acquaintances in the Netherlands is quoted and discussed. His letters to Cornelius Schepper, Konrad Goclenius, Bartolomeus Gravius, and others reflect his varied interests and throw light on his private life; the work is the first attempt to gather material from scattered archival sources. Based on documents in the Olsztyn archive of the Warmia diocese; 27 notes. 16c

Darby, Abraham

1619. —. ABRAHAM DARBY, RICHARD REYNOLDS AND COALBROOKDALE. *Industrial Archaeology [Great Britain] 1983 17(2-4): 187-201.* Assesses the role and influence of Abraham Darby (1677-1717) and Richard Reynolds (1735-1816) and their families in the iron manufacturing industry at Coalbrookdale, 1709-1800. 1709-1800

Darío, Rubén

1620. Banberger, Ellen Lee. "Rubén Darío: El Hombre y Su Epoca" [Rubén Darío: the man and his time]. University of California, San Diego 1984. 147 pp. *DAI 1984 45(6): 1767-A.* DA8418279 1880's-1916

1621. Garciasol, Ramón de. RUBÉN DARÍO, ENVIADO ESPECIAL [Rubén Darío, special envoy]. *Cuadernos Hispanoamericanos [Spain] 1979 116(348): 562-588.* The Nicaraguan poet Rubén Darío (1867-1916), foremost exponent of Spanish American modernism, arrived in Spain in January 1899 as a correspondent for *La Nación* of Buenos Aires in order to record his impressions of the country in the aftermath of the Spanish-American War. The resulting articles, written between December 1898 and April 1900, were published in 1901 as *España Contemporánea,* and included such topics as poor education (widespread illiteracy, and the poverty of arts, letters, sciences, and public life), the royal family, the position of women and female employment, politics, economics, history, the causes of public indifference to the disastrous war, national decadence and decline, the aristocracy, theater, paucity of cultural journals and literary criticism, academicians and poets. Based on *España Contemporánea.* 1899-1900

1622. O'Brien, Miriam Therese. BUSCANDO A RUBEN DARIO EN MADRID [Looking for Rubén Darío in Madrid]. *Horizontes [Puerto Rico] 1981 24(48): 51-64.* During a visit to Madrid the author found mementos of the passage of Nicaraguan poet Rubén Darío. She visited hotels and restaurants frequented by him, rooms where he had lodged, the subway on which he traveled, the archive that preserves objects connected with his life, libraries that he used, and the granddaughter of the woman who was the poet's companion for many years. 12 notes, biblio. 1867-1916

Darling, Elizabeth

1623. Fletcher, Brian. ELIZABETH DARLING: COLONIAL BENEFACTRESS AND GOVERNOR'S LADY. *J. of the Royal Australian Hist. Soc. [Australia] 1982 67(4): 297-327.* Elizabeth Darling (*née* Dumaresq; 1798-1857), while seeking no public recognition and preoccupied with personal matters arising from her position as wife of the governor of New South Wales, proved important in the state's moral reform movement. She brought new ideas and schemes into the colony, thereby earning the title of "the greatest benefactress." Based mainly on the papers of the Dumaresq family in Sydney and Hobart and on British archives; 145 notes. 1818-57

Darvaris, Dimitrios

1624. Loukidou-Mavridou, Despina and Papadrianos, Ioannis. DIMITRIOS DARVARIS: SA CONTRIBUTION À L'ÉVOLUTION LITTÉRAIRE BULGARE [Dimitrios Darvaris and his contribution to the Bulgarian literary evolution]. *Pnevmatikes kai Politistikes Scheseis Ellēnōn kai Voulgarōn apo ta mesa tou 15 Eōs ta mesa tou 19 Aiōna. 1 Ellēnovoulgariko Symposio* (Salonika, Greece: Inst. for Balkan Studies, 1980): 211-226. Discusses the literary career of Dimitrios Darvaris (1757-1823), an important scholar and educator of the Greek diaspora whose work spread new Western teaching methods and ideas to the Balkans. Focuses on Darvaris' influence on Bulgarian Enlightenment intellectuals and on the development of modern educational theory in Bulgaria. 1780-1823

Darwin, Charles

1625. Browne, Janet. ESSAY REVIEW: NEW DEVELOPMENTS IN DARWIN STUDIES? *J. of the Hist. of Biology [Netherlands] 1982 15(2): 275-280.* Dov Ospovat's *The Development of Darwin's Theory: Natural History, Natural Theology, and Natural Selection, 1838-1859* (1981) is the departure for new studies because it reveals a Charles Darwin who changed several times before he began the *Origin.* 1838-59

1626. Bynum, W. F. [RECENT WORKS ON THE LIFE, WORK, AND TIMES OF CHARLES DARWIN]. *Medical Hist. [Great Britain] 1982 26(4): 462-466.* A review article of four recent works on Charles Darwin and his work. These volumes are principally concerned with the shift in British biology beginning in the 1830's from a functional to a structural orientation, and with a sociological evaluation of the scientific community in mid-Victorian London. 2 notes. 1830-80

1627. Colp, Ralph, Jr. THE RELATIONSHIP OF CHARLES DARWIN TO THE IDEAS OF HIS GRANDFATHER, DR. ERASMUS DARWIN. *Biography 1986 9(1): 1-24.* During his career as an evolutionary thinker Charles Darwin was first influenced by the evolutionary ideas of his grandfather, Erasmus Darwin, and then publicly called these ideas "erroneous." As an old man, he was stimulated by a German science writer to compose a short biography of his grandfather. Although in this biography Darwin avoided discussing his ideological relationship with grandfather, and although he was persuaded to excise some notable passages before publication, he produced a remarkably concise and vivid portrait of his grandfather as a scientist and man. 1790's-1880

1628. Colp, Ralph, Jr. THE PRE-BEAGLE MISERY OF CHARLES DARWIN. *Psychohistory Review 1984 13(1): 4-15.* Chronicles Charles Darwin's conflict with his father, Dr. Robert Darwin, as he struggled to decide, with the support of other family members, whether to take a position aboard the *Beagle,* which was about to leave on a voyage of discovery and exploration for purposes of scientific experiments and research. Quotes extensively from letters to friend and relative William Darwin Fox, other letters, and Darwin's autobiography. Primary sources; 87 notes. 1831

1629. Colp, Ralph, Jr. CHARLES DARWIN'S DREAM OF HIS DOUBLE EXECUTION. *Journal of Psychohistory 1986 13(3): 277-292.* In 1838 Charles Darwin recorded in his notebook that he had dreamed of being hung and then decapitated. At the time Darwin was contemplating marriage and was on the verge of formulating the ideas that he later published in his *Origin of Species* (1861). Darwin feared both that the obligation of marriage might end his scientific investigation and that his theory of evolution would offend the scientific community. Darwin, who identified with persecuted scientists, respected people who stood up for their ideas, and had fantasies of himself dying gloriously for a noble cause. His dream of double execution was thus tied to his ambivalence about marriage and his fear of being ostracized by his fellow scientists. 62 notes. ca 1830-59

1630. Colp, Ralph, Jr. NOTES ON CHARLES DARWIN'S AUTOBIOGRAPHY. *Journal of the History of Biology [Netherlands] 1985 18(3): 357-401.* Darwin had a lifelong interest in biography. After keeping records of his youth and a journal, telling his children stories about his past, and being encouraged by various scholars and journalists, he wrote his autobiography—"a prolonged family letter." Seeks to identify which parts of *Autobiography* are valid. For example, Darwin was candid regarding his own sense of intellectual inadequacy, but he did not discuss his extreme antipathy to the organized religion of his day. On balance, however, the genuine Darwin is in his *Autobiography.* 161 notes. 1809-82

1631. Colp, Ralph, Jr. CHARLES DARWIN: MAN AND SCIENTIST. *Centennial Rev. 1983 27(2): 96-110.* A biographical sketch of Charles Darwin (1809-82) and his career. Born to a wealthy family, Darwin attended Edinburgh University and Cambridge, but rejected proposed careers in medicine and the clergy. His interest in natural science led him to his five-year voyage on the *Beagle* and the gradual formulation of his theories on natural selection and evolution. The last 40 years of his life were spent in his country house at Down where he endured a prolonged illness and worked on his scientific research, gaining a reputation in geology and natural science. Hearing of the work of Alfred Wallace, Darwin finally published his own study on natural selection, *The Origin of Species.* A devoted family man, outwardly conventional, Darwin also wanted to defy society, which he did successfully with his publications on evolution. Published sources; 58 notes. 1809-82

1632. Porter, Roy. THE DESCENT OF GENIUS: CHARLES DARWIN'S BRILLIANT CAREER. *Hist. Today [Great Britain] 1982 32(July): 16-22.* Discusses the origins of Charles Darwin's genius, 1830's-82. 1830's-82

1633. Rudwick, Martin J. S. CHARLES DARWIN IN LONDON: THE INTEGRATION OF PUBLIC AND PRIVATE SCIENCE. *Isis 1982 73(267): 186-206.* The years 1837-42, when Darwin lived in London, were the period of his closest association with other scientists. He was especially active as a member, then secretary, of the Geological Society of London. Traces and discusses his activities during this public portion of his career and presents two diagrams to clarify the development and interrelationships of his ideas and activities and to suggest a model of potential utility in studies of other scientists. Based on the writings of Darwin, Charles Lyell, and other contemporaries, and secondary studies; 56 notes. 1837-42

1634. Sulloway, Frank J. DARWIN'S CONVERSION: THE *BEAGLE* VOYAGE AND ITS AFTERMATH. *J. of the Hist. of Biology 1982 15(3): 325-396.* In 1831, at the time of the *Beagle* voyage, Charles Darwin was not a finished naturalist, but later his theory of evolution emerged gradually in his mind, and others' writings helped in no small part to correct many misclassifications made during Darwin's now famous trip. Darwin's conversion was an ongoing process of both scientific and self-discovery. The instantaneous or dramatic insight is mere legend. 6 fig., 91 notes, 124 ref., 2 tables. 1831-59

Darwin, Erasmus

1635. Colp, Ralph, Jr. THE RELATIONSHIP OF CHARLES DARWIN TO THE IDEAS OF HIS GRANDFATHER, DR. ERASMUS DARWIN. *Biography 1986 9(1): 1-24.* 1790's-1880

For abstract see ***Darwin, Charles***

Dashkova, Ekaterina

1636. Mailloux, Luc. LA PRINCESSE DASCHKOFF ET LA FRANCE (1770-1781) [Princess Dashkova and France, 1770-81]. *Rev. d'Hist. Diplomatique [France] 1981 95(1): 5-25.* Princess Ekaterina Dashkova, one of the main architects of the palace revolution that placed Catherine the Great on the Russian throne in 1762, was strongly influenced by the ideas of the French Enlightenment and paid two visits to France in 1770 and 1781. On her first visit she met Diderot, but avoided other contacts; in 1781 she met Voltaire at Ferney. Strongly attached to the idea of a limited monarchy and an admirer of Montesquieu, her reading, education, and personal friendships led to her strong aversion for the French monarchy and aristocracy. Based on published sources; 47 notes. 1770-81

Datta, Kalikinkar

1637. Banerjee, Tarasankar. DR. KALIKINKAR DATTA. *Indo-British Review [India] 1983 10(2): 23-24.* Obituary of Indian historian Kalikinkar Datta (1905-82), whose works include major studies of the history of Bengal and of the early British imperial administration of India. 1905-82

1638. Jha, J. C. THE LIFE AND WORKS OF KALIKINKAR DATTA (1905-1982). *Journal of Indian History [India] 1982 60: 277-292.* Presents a brief summary of the life of Kalikinkar Datta, Indian historian. The essential aspects of Datta's life include a South Bihar background and an outstanding education at Calcutta University. His career, focused mainly at Patna College, was filled with teaching, writing, and administration. A prolific writer of over 30 books and 130 papers, his history took a descriptive approach largely devoid of analysis. 79 notes. 1905-82

Datta, Michael Madhusudan

1639. Mitra, Priti Kumar. "Dissent in Modern India (1815-1930): Concentrating on Two Rebel Poets—Michael Madhusudan Datta and Kazi Nazrul Islam." U. of Hawaii 1985. 644 pp. *DAI 1986 46(7): 2046-A.* DA8520318 1815-1930

Daumas, Maurice

1640. Gillispie, Charles C. MAURICE DAUMAS, 1910-1984. *Isis 1985 76(281): 72-74.* Maurice Daumas was trained at the University of Paris as a chemist, and after working for some time in this field moved gradually into the history of science and technology. Pursuit of this dual interest led him into pioneer work in urban history, such as the development of public transportation in Paris during the late 19th and early 20th centuries, and of French industrial architecture, especially in the 19th century. 19c-20c

1641. Herlea, Alexandre. MAURICE DAUMAS (1910-1984). *Technology and Culture 1985 26(3): 698-702.* After becoming head of the historical museum of the Paris Conservatoire des Arts et Métiers in 1960, Daumas—between 1962 and 1979—edited and wrote much of the monumental five-volume *Histoire Générale des Techniques,* which he conceived of as primarily a "technical history of technology." 15c-20c

Däumig, Ernst

1642. Morgan, David W. ERNST DÄUMIG AND THE GERMAN REVOLUTION OF 1918. *Central European Hist. 1982 15(4): 303-331.* Ernst Däumig played a central role in the German Revolution of 1918. He had been an editor of *Vorwärts* until the conservative central committee took control of the paper in 1916. He helped create the new Independent Social Democratic Party and served as its leader. He opposed cooperation with the majority socialists and eventually became a leader of the newly-organized Communist Party. He believed that councils were the new political organizations which would lead to true democracy. He became disillusioned with all his political activity early in 1922 and died shortly thereafter. Based on memoirs, secondary works, contemporary newspapers, and unpublished party material; 117 notes. 1916-22

Davanzati, Bernardo

1643. Parolini, M. Luisa. UN PRECURSORE DELLE TEORIE MONETARIE: BERNARDO DAVANZATI [A precursor of the monetarist theories: Bernardo Davanzati]. *Econ. e Storia [Italy] 1981 2(3): 299-332.* Davanzati was a noble banker and landlord of the Medicean age and represents Florentine culture well. As a student of economic affairs, he merits the title economist. Though his interests were confined to questions of land and money, his originality led him to anticipate some of the more recent problems and ideas in economics. 83 notes. 16c

David, Eduard

1644. Müller, Eckhard. ZUM POLITISCHEN WIRKEN DES REVISIONISTEN EDUARD DAVID IN DER DEUTSCHEN SOZIALDEMOKRATIE 1894-1907 [The political activities of the revisionist Eduard David in German Social Democracy, 1894-1907]. *Beiträge zur Gesch. der Arbeiterbewegung [East Germany] 1981 23(4): 569-582.* Traces the life and political development of the German revisionist Eduard David (b. 1863) between 1894 and 1907. He was a leading opportunist and wanted the Social Democratic Party to cooperate with the government and the bourgeois parties. Secondary sources; 53 notes. 1894-1907

David, Jacques-Louis

1645. Mellon, Stanley. JACQUES-LOUIS DAVID, REVOLUTIONARY: THE CASE REOPENED. *Consortium on Revolutionary Europe, 1750-1850: Proceedings 1983: 364-380.* The artist Jacques-Louis David was an important leader of the French Revolution in the years 1792-1794. His activities during these years were not merely an aberration or an interlude in his long career. He was a fanatical revolutionary, dedicated to the destruction of the clergy and the nobility. As a member of the Committee of General Security, he supported Robespierre and the Reign of Terror. His monumental statue named "Colossus" (designed but never executed) serves as a reminder of his dedication to the Revolution. 1792-95

1646. Rheims, Maurice. PREMIER PEINTRE ENGAGE: DAVID LE REGICIDE [The first "engagé" painter: David the regicide]. *Historama [France] 1985 (15): 84-91.* Gives an anecdotal account of the political career of Jacques-Louis David (1748-1825) and analyzes some of his works, which reflected the political turn of the opinions or actions of this famous painter, who, after being a protégé of Louis XVI, became a formidable revolutionist who voted to condemn the French king and was appointed Napoleon's official painter. 1793-1824

Davidson, Basil

1647. Hadjor, Kofi Buenor and Wallerstein, Immanuel. AN HISTORIC HISTORIAN: A 70TH BIRTHDAY TRIBUTE TO BASIL DAVIDSON. *Third World Book Review [Great Britain] 1985 1(3): 6-9.* An interview with Davidson and a bibliography on Davidson's 70th birthday, concentrating on his contribution to the study of African history. 1950-85

Davidson, Paul

1648. Feld, Hans. JEWS IN THE DEVELOPMENT OF THE GERMAN FILM INDUSTRY: NOTES FROM THE RECOLLECTIONS OF A BERLIN FILM CRITIC. *Leo Baeck Inst. Year Book [Great Britain] 1982 27: 337-365.* The author (b. 1902), who was an active participant in the German and European film industry, provides a survey of producers, actors, directors, distributors, and others in German filmmaking, beginning with Paul Davidson in 1905. Davidson was also involved in the founding of UFA in 1917 and in the inspiration of General Ludendorff's recognition of the possibilities of film as a propaganda weapon. 11 photos, biblio. 1910's-30's

Davies, Charles M.

1649. Costa, Thomas. CHARLES M. DAVIES [1828-1910]: THE BROAD CHURCHMAN AS JOURNALIST. *Victorian Periodicals Review [Canada] 1984 17(1-2): 29-33.* Charles M. Davies, London clergyman, scholar, novelist, and teacher, was also a journalist who wrote articles on religious topics, spiritualism, and Victorian daily life. 1850's-1910

Davies, Elinor

1650. Nelson, Beth. LADY ELINOR DAVIES: THE PROPHET AS PUBLISHER. *Women's Studies International Forum 1985 8(5): 403-409.* Lady Elinor Davies, who published between 1625 and 1652 more works than any other Englishwoman before her, believed herself to be the prophet of the apocalypse, divinely chosen to reveal that the apocalypses of Daniel and St. John would find their fulfillment in the events of the 17th century. Lady Elinor defied patriarchal authority in 1633 when she published prophecies attacking church and king, an act that brought her to trial and to prison. 1625-52

Davies, Emily

1651. Vicinus, Martha. VIVERE INSIEME: *COLLEGE WOMEN* INGLESI TRA FINE '800 E INIZIO '900 [Living together: English college women at the turn of the century]. *Memoria: Riv. di Storia delle Donne [Italy] 1982 (4): 45-58.* Women's friendships in Victorian England were looked upon as sentimental and overemotional but they had an important role in the development of that women's culture which had its beginning in the 19th century. Examines the friendships of several English women who pioneered women's higher education between 1870 and 1920, especially Constance Maynard (1849-1935), who founded Westfield College, Emily Davies, who founded Girton in 1869, Louisa Lumsden, and others. Partly based on Maynard's private papers; list of ref. 1870-1920

Davies, Joseph E.

1652. Mal'kov, V. L. MISSIIA DZH. DEVISA V MOSKVU V MAE 1943 G. [Joseph Davies's mission to Moscow in 1943]. *Novaia i Noveishaia Istoriia [USSR] 1985 (1): 91-105.* In 1942, Franklin D. Roosevelt invited Joseph Stalin to organize a summit meeting which would also include Winston Churchill. Stalin declined because he felt the situation in the USSR was too troubled for conducting summits. This prompted Roosevelt to dispatch to Moscow the former ambassador to the USSR, Joseph Davies. Davies, who had previously championed good relations with the Soviets, held meetings with Stalin and K. E. Voroshilov, persuading them of the advisability of arranging a summit meeting. As the printed excerpts of the Davies's diary show, the meetings were conducted in an atmosphere of hope for future international relations. Based on Library of Congress records; 34 notes. 1942-43

Davies, Scrope Berdmore

1653. Graham, Peter W. A DANDY IN AMBER: THE LIFE AND TIMES OF SCROPE BERDMORE DAVIES. *South Atlantic Q. 1982 81(4): 455-461.* Reviews T. A. J. Burnett's *The Rise and Fall of a Regency Dandy: The Life and Times of Scrope Berdmore Davies.* Davies (1782-1852) was a scholar, gambler, wit, and friend of Byron. He spent the last half of his life on the Continent, just a step ahead of creditors and financial ruin. He was a true dandy—that ornamental human air plant with no roots and no fruit. 1800's-52

Dávila Novoa, Pedro

1654. Plazas S., Francisco de Paula. DON PEDRO DAVILA NOVOA [Don Pedro Dávila Novoa]. *Bol. de Hist. y Antigüedades [Colombia] 1980 67(728): 151-157.* Brief biography of Pedro Dávila Novoa (1790-1870), a secondary political figure and rural landowner, born in Bogotá and later established in the province of Neiva. Presents a genealogy of his descendants. Parish and notarial archives of Neiva and Bogotá; biblio. 1815-20c

Davis, Edward Hughesdon

1655. Roderick, J. W. EDWARD HUGHESDON DAVIS 1920-1981. *Hist. Records of Australian Sci. [Australia] 1982 5(3): 109-114.* A biography of English-born Australian educator-engineer Edward Hughesdon Davis. Following training in England and service with the British army, he joined the faculty of the University of Sydney where he headed the Department of Engineering until his death. The author includes a list of Davis's research notes, papers, and books on soil mechanics. Biblio. 1940-81

Davis, Thomas

1656. Davis, Richard. THOMAS DAVIS AND THE INDIAN EMPIRE: THE LIBERALISM OF YOUNG IRELAND. *J. of Indian Hist. [India] 1980 58(1-3): 75-91.* Thomas Davis (1814-45) was the founder of the Young Ireland movement and its mouthpiece, the *Nation.* His poems and patriotic journalism advanced the policies of Daniel O'Connell in repeal of the Act of Union and the restoration of an Irish parliament. Davis sought to promote empathy with contemporary Indian problems, to use negative Indian experiences to assist the Irish cause, and to use England's problems in India to Ireland's advantage. His overall impact was negligible due to his extreme Celtic racism. 61 notes. 1841-45

Davy, Humphry

1657. Levere, Trevor H. HUMPHRY DAVY AND THE IDEA OF GLORY. *Tr. of the Royal Soc. of Can. [Canada] 1980 18: 247-261.* For Humphry Davy, true glory was to be achieved only through science. From youth, he brought to his experiments both poetic imagination and the philosopher's love of the law-abiding harmonies of nature. He typified the British empirical tradition in ignoring the philosophical idealism of contemporary Germany. While much of his work with the Royal Institution was utilitarian, his greatest contributions to chemistry were conceptual. His critique of Lavoisier's table of elements was based on 18th-century English philosophy, natural theology, patriotism, and a trace of German metaphysics as well as experiments with electricity. His discovery of the alkali metals in 1807 was exemplary in both logic and style. 47 notes. 1799-1817

1658. Yoshida, Akira. DAVY ET DULONG SUR LA THEORIE DES ACIDES AU DEBUT DU XIX[e] SIECLE [Davy and Dulong on the theory of acids at the beginning of the 19th century]. *Hist. Scientiarum [Japan] 1981 (21): 103-114.* Questions Humphry Davy's claim to the discovery of hydrogen. P. L. Dulong, on the basis of a note submitted to the Paris Academy of Sciences in 1815, should be accorded this honor. The note was never printed and has not been found in the archives of the academy, but its existence is supported by contemporary reports of its content. Primary sources; 39 notes. 1810-22

Davydov, Denis V.

1659. Iurganov, A. L. MATERIALY O VOENNOI SLUZHBE DENISA DAVYDOVA [Sources on the military service of Denis Davydov]. *Sovetskie Arkhivy [USSR] 1984 (4): 35-39.* Prints hitherto unpublished sources on the military career of the Russian poet Denis Davydov (1784-1839), who fought in the Russo-Turkish War of 1810. These include a certificate of his bravery in battle and a letter from the War Minister Baron Arakcheev awarding him the Order of St. Anne. Primary sources. 1810

1660. Popov, M. DENIS DAVYDOV: K 200-LETIIU SO DNIA ROZHDENIIA [Denis Davydov: the 200th anniversary of his birth]. *Voenno-Istoricheskii Zhurnal [USSR] 1984 (8): 63-66.* Denis V. Davydov (1784-1839) was a hero of the Patriotic War of 1812, distinguishing himself as a partisan, and later as a writer on military affairs. After entering the capital's cavalry guards regiment in 1801 he fought in all of Russia's wars in his lifetime. He was a free thinker but refused to join the Decembrist uprising in 1825. He appears in Leo Tolstoy's *War and Peace* as the partisan Vasili Denisov. 1801-39

Dawes, Charles

1661. Goedeken, Edward A. CHARLES DAWES AND THE MILITARY BOARD OF ALLIED SUPPLY. *Military Affairs 1986 50(1): 1-6.* Discusses the influence of Charles Dawes on the Military Board of Allied Supply (MBAS) during World War I. The MBAS reflects the importance military and civil leaders placed on supply during the war and the realization that military coordination was the key to Allied victory. Through his energy, Dawes transformed a small coordinating board into a far-reaching agency combing Europe for supplies. The lessons of supply coordination learned by the Allies during World War I would prove useful for fighting the next world war. Based on the Charles Dawes Papers and other primary sources; 39 notes. 1918

Dawes, Edwyn Sandys

1662. Henning, G. R. EDWYN SANDYS DAWES AND AUSTRALIAN MARITIME LABOR. *J. of Transport Hist. [Great Britain] 1982 3(2): 81-90.* Describes the life of Edwyn Sandys Dawes and his maritime career in the Pacific colonies of the British Empire. Provides his original statement on the need of sailors in the merchant marine of Australia to unionize for better working conditions. Concludes that Australian sailors received the highest rate of wages in the Asian world of mercantile trade during the 1890's. Based on published and primary sources. 1830-90

Dayal, Har

1663. Barooah, Nirode K. HAR DAYAL AND THE GERMAN CONNECTION. *Indian Historical Review [India] 1980-81 7(1-2): 185-211.* Har Dayal (1857-1939), undoubtedly the most prestigious Indian to be associated with the German war efforts, collaborated with the official Germans during two periods, first between September and October 1914 when he was associated with the Turco-German Afghan expedition, and secondly between January 1915 and January 1916 when he became a leading member of the Berlin India Committee. His first collaboration ended when he found himself relegated to a subordinate position in the exhibition avowedly planned to promote revolution against the British in India via Afghanistan. The termination of his second collaboration, which primarily involved propaganda, was forced upon him by the other members of the Berlin Committee who were antagonized by his intrigues and devious actions. 156 notes. 1914-19

Dayan, Moshe

1664. Falk, Avner. MOSHE DAYAN: NARCISSISM IN POLITICS. *Jerusalem Q. [Israel] 1984 (30): 113-124.* A psychoanalytic portrait of Moshe Dayan, whose narcissistic personality was evident in his actions and underlay his military and political achievements and failures. 1930's-81

1665. Falk, Avner. MOSHE DAYAN: THE INFANTILE ROOTS OF POLITICAL ACTION. *J. of Psychohistory 1983 11(2): 271-288.* An analysis of Moshe Dayan's life reveals that trauma and relationships experienced in the early stages of his life left a significant impression, often unconscious, which he later reenacted as an Israeli politician and military commander. Dayan's life reflects a case study of narcissistic personality involving his mother's father, his mother, and himself. 1915-73

D'Azeglio, Massimo

1666. Virlogeux, Georges. CONTRIBUTO ALLA BIBLIOGRAFIA DELLE LETTERE EDITE DI MASSIMO D'AZEGLIO [A contribution to the bibliography of the edited letters of Massimo d'Azeglio]. *Rassegna Storica del Risorgimento [Italy] 1982 69(4): 442-470. Based on primary sources; 23 notes.* 1842-66

Deák, Ferencz

1667. Sándor, Pál. A PÁLYAKEZDŐ DEÁK PORTRÉJÁHOZ [A portait of Deák at the beginning of his career]. *Századok [Hungary] 1981 115(3): 522-554.* Orphaned at five, Ferencz Deák was a shy and reserved child. He cared little about conventional values at 20. His appearance showed neglect. His speech was handicapped by mannerisms. After his election to the parliament he found it very disturbing that genuine liberal ideas were practically nonexistent. Illus., 92 notes. 1800-33

1668. Sándor, Pál; Vargyas, Katalin, transl. QUELQUES TRAITS DU PORTRAIT DE DEÁK AU DEBUT DE SA CARRIERE [Some traces of the picture of Deák at the start of his career]. *Acta Historica [Hungary] 1983 29(1): 3-34.* Prints details for a biography of the early career of Hungarian statesman Ferencz Deák (1803-76). Shows his place within the tradition of liberalism, his attitude toward militarism, and his concern with foreign policy of the great powers in central Europe. 73 notes. Russian summary. 1820-33

DeAmicis, Edmondo

1669. Bertone, Giorgio. "PARLARE AI BORGHESI": DE AMICIS, IL "PRIMO MAGGIO" E LA PROPAGANDA SOCIALISTA ["Talking bourgeois": De Amicis, the *Primo Maggio,* and socialist propaganda]. *Movimento Operaio e Socialista [Italy] 1980 3(2-3): 155-174.* Describes how respected and popular bourgeois writer Edmondo de Amicis was converted by Socialist Party leader Filippo Turati as a propagandist for socialist ideas. De Amicis wrote a novel *Primo Maggio* [May First] on the workers' demonstrations of 1890-91 in Turin which was not published until 1980 by Garzanti in Milan. 58 notes. 1891-1907

Déat, Marcel

1670. Sternhell, Zeev. DU SOCIALISME AU FASCISME, LE CAS MARCEL DEAT [From socialism to fascism; the case of Marcel Déat]. *Histoire [France] 1983 (53): 20-33.* A study, with illustrations, a biographical index, and a short bibliography, of the evolution toward fascism of some French socialist statesmen, focusing on Marcel Déat, member of the French Socialist Party, who founded the Rassemblement National Populaire (RNP) in 1940 and became an ardent collaborationist during the German occupation. 1930-44

DeBonis, Marco

1671. Nessi, Adolfo. P. MARCO DE BONIS DA OGGIONO, O.F.M. (1615-1671) [Father Marco De Bonis of Como, O.F.M., 1615-71]. *Arch. Franciscanum Hist. [Italy] 1983 76(1-3): 349-354.* Gives a brief biography of Franciscan superior Father Marco De Bonis, one of the most celebrated preachers of the Catholic Church in 17th-century Italy. 1632-71

Debré, Michel

1672. Rigaud, Jacques. LA MEMOIRE D'ETAT: D'EDGAR FAURE A MICHEL DEBRE [State memory: from Edgar Faure to Michel Debré]. *Revue des Deux Mondes [France] 1985 (2): 336-349.* Discusses recent French political history as portrayed in the memoirs of Michel Debré, Prime Minister in 1949 and 1962 and Finance Minister from 1966 to 1968, and Edgar Faure, Président du Conseil in 1952 and 1955. 1949-68

Decsy, Sámuel

1673. Busa, Margit. ADATOK A MAGYAR KURÍR SZERKESZTÉSÉNEK TÖRTÉNETÉHEZ [Information on the editing history of the *Magyar Kurír].* *Magyar Könyvszemle [Hungary] 1984 100(4): 354-359.* Prints two letters from József Márton and Sámuel Decsy to Ferenc Kazinczy regarding the problems of the editorship of the *Magyar Kurír.* In 1809 the editors of the journal were Decsy (1742-1816) and Dániel Pánczél (1759-1827). József Márton (1771-1840) wanted the editorship of the journal though he denies this in his letter. Márton and Pánczél denounced Decsy as a French sympathizer. Decsy won the case since he had stopped publication 19 December 1809 to 5 June 1810 rather than write about the French wars. Márton edited the journal only after Decsy's death. 15 notes. 1809-10

1674. Pintér, Márta Zsuzsanna. DECSY SÁMUEL SZERKESZTŐI MŰKÖDÉSÉHEZ (1807-1811) [Sámuel Decsy's editorial activities, 1807-11]. *Magyar Könyvszemle [Hungary] 1985 101(2): 154-158.* Contains the text of four letters written by Sámuel Decsy (d. 1816) between 1807 and 1811 to Elek Jordánszky (1765-1840), the archbishop's representative. Decsy was at this time coeditor with Dániel Pánczél (1760-1834) of the journal *Magyar Kurír* [Hungarian courier] and the letters not only show that Decsy translated two orations from the Latin for inclusion in the journal, but also give further proof of the rivalry that existed between the editors. 11 notes. 1807-11

Dedijer, Vladimir

1675. Dedijer, Vladimir. [DJILAS]. *Cross Currents 1985 4: 387-452.*
MY TWO COMRADES, *pp. 387-438.*
AN EXCHANGE OF LETTERS, *pp. 439-452.* 1936-67
For abstract see ***Djilas, Milovan***

Defferre, Gaston

1676. Kahn, Jean-François. GASTON DEFFERRE: 40 ANS BARRE A GAUCHE [Gaston Defferre: for 40 years tiller to the Left]. *Historama [France] 1984 (5): 68-71, 92-93.* Discusses Defferre's political career and French politics of the Left from 1940 to 1978. 1940-78

DeFilippo, Eduardo

1677. Mignone, Mario B. *Eduardo DeFilippo.* (Twayne World Authors Series, no. 733.) Boston: Twayne, 1984. 197 pp. 1920's-70's

Defoe, Daniel

1678. DeGalegno, Paul J. DANIEL DEFOE'S NEWGATE BIOGRAPHIES: AN ECONOMIC CRISIS. *Clio 1984 13(2): 157-170.* 1720's
For abstract see ***Sheppard, John***

1679. Labutina, T. L. DANIEL DEFO, AVTOR *ROBINZONA KRUZO:* EGO OBSHCHESTVENNO-POLITICHESKIE VOZZRENIIA [Daniel Defoe, author of *Robinson Crusoe:* his social and political views]. *Novaia i Noveishaia Istoriia [USSR] 1986 (1): 156-167.* Examines the social and political ideas of Daniel Defoe (1660-1731) against the background of his own checkered political career as Whig pamphleteer recruited by the Tory Speaker of the House of Commons Robert Harley to run his secret service. Defoe's work for Harley during the years 1704-14 involved extensive travel throughout the country and reporting on the popular moods, thus acquainting him with the seamy side of British society. The London underworld and the penal colony became a familiar setting of Defoe's fiction, although he did not use them to make any radical criticism of a society which generated both the criminals and the harsh laws to deal with them. Defoe's belief in the contractual nature of state went together with his bourgeois ideology of material self-betterment. Secondary sources; 80 notes. 1690-1731

DeGasperi, Alcide

1680. Durand, Jean-Dominique. ALCIDE DE GASPERI OVVERO LA POLITICA ISPIRATA [Alcide De Gasperi or inspired politics]. *Storia Contemporanea [Italy] 1984 15(4): 545-592.* Argues for a spiritual and prophetic reading of the life of Alcide De Gasperi (1881-1954), the Catholic political leader of Italy, 1945-53. Although faith and politics were indivisible for De Gasperi and were rooted in scripture, most studies of his life ignore the religious aspect of his career. He was a learned man, well versed in Dostoevski as well as Church doctrine, but he was a man of action who believed that Christianity impelled one to seek social justice and to honor the dignity of every person. His notion of a spiritual community of Europe led him to fight for a United States of Europe. Based on the published diaries and writings of Alcide De Gasperi and secondary sources; 229 notes. ca 1910's-53

DeGaulle, Charles

1681. Ashby, Molly Frances. A VISION OF GRANDEUR: CHARLES DEGAULLE'S FIFTH REPUBLIC FOREIGN POLICY. *Potomac Rev. 1982 (22-23): 1-30.* Examines the foreign policy of Charles de Gaulle. While seemingly irrational at times, de Gaulle's actions during the decade 1958-68 were consistently motivated by French self-interest. Discusses at length France's participation in the European community, especially NATO and the Common Market, and the agonizing conflict in Algeria. In these and other foreign policy questions, de Gaulle's steady vision of national grandeur guided his political decisions and helped restore French prestige. 23 notes. 1958-69

1682. Gambiez, Général. LE GÉNÉRAL DE GAULLE ET "L'EUROPE DE L'ATLANTIQUE À L'OURAL" [General de Gaulle and "Europe from the Atlantic to the Urals"]. *Nouvelle Rev. des Deux Mondes [France] 1981 (11): 289-300.* Reviews Charles de Gaulle's political attitudes and policies toward Europe, 1940-68. 1940-68

1683. Mauriac, Jean. LA BOISSERIE: CU ŞI FĂRĂ GENERAL DE GAULLE [La Boisserie: with and without General de Gaulle]. *Magazin Istoric [Romania] 1980 14(7): 23-28.* General de Gaulle died in 1970 at La Boisserie, a property at Colombey-les-Deux-Eglises, which he had bought in 1934. It was formerly a brewery; then converted to a private house, becoming famous as de Gaulle's family home, and now it is a museum. 1843-1979

1684. Pignol, Armand. L'IMAGE DE DEGAULLE DANS LES PAYS ARABES DU PROCHE-ORIENT: LA GENESE SOCIO-POLITIQUE D'UN STEREOTYPE [The image of de Gaulle in the Arab lands of the Near East: the sociopolitical genesis of a stereotype]. *Revue Historique [France] 1984 272(2): 403-420.* The widespread popularity of Charles de Gaulle among all classes in the Arab Near East provides an opportunity to analyze the origin of stereotyped public images. De Gaulle was regarded with suspicion upon his return to power in France in 1958. The Arab press lauded his independent posture in the Arab-Israeli war of 1967 "realistic," and Arab journalists and politicians began to cite de Gaulle as a model realist and friend of Gamal Abdel Nasser. Based on Arab press reports of the 1960's; 23 notes. 1958-60's

1685. Smirnov, V. P. DE GOLL I ZHIRO (K ISTORII SOZDANIIA FRANTSUZKOGO KOMITETA NATSIONALNOGO OSVOBOZHDENIIA) [De Gaulle and Giraud: a contribution to the history of the creation of the French Committee of National Liberation]. *Novaia i Noveishaia Istoriia [USSR] 1982 (1): 108-124, (2): 135-153.* Part 1. When Marshal Pétain made peace with the German invaders in 1940, Charles de Gaulle, recently promoted to the rank of general, flew to London and established the Free French. Contacts were established with the Resistance in France, where de Gaulle gained acceptance as a leader. Political and tactical considerations however led the Americans to favor General Henri Giraud, commander of Vichy French forces in North Africa under Admiral Darlan. De Gaulle's desire to undermine this was helped by the assassination of Darlan in December 1942. Part 2. De Gaulle suggested a meeting with Henri Giraud after the assassination of General Darlan. Giraud agreed, but wished de Gaulle to come to Algiers. At Casablanca (January 1943) a merger between Giraud's Algiers Imperial Council and de Gaulle's London-based National Committee for Fighting France was agreed to. On 31 May 1943 de Gaulle and Giraud met in Algiers, and de Gaulle assumed the dominant position in the resultant French Committee of National Liberation. This gave de Gaulle, and France, increased diplomatic importance. Based on US, British, and French documents. 1940-42

Deinard, Ephraim

1686. Kabakoff, Jacob. L'TOLDOT HAKHMEI YISRAEL B-RUSIA [Two autobiographies of Russian Jewish authors]. *Shvut [Israel] 1982 9: 99-101.* Ephraim Deinard, a book dealer, scholar, and Zionist, solicited autobiographies for a collection he planned to publish on the subject of Jewish scholarship in Russia. This article presents the autobiographies of Moshe Lieb Lilienblum (1843-1910) and Aryeh Leib Gordon (1845-1912), as well as a biography of Deinard. Based on selections from the Deinard Collection at the Jewish Theological Seminary of America; 15 notes. 1843-1912

Delany, Edward

1687. Vaughan, W. E. FARMER, GRAZIER AND GENTLEMAN: EDWARD DELANY OF WOODTOWN, 1851-99. *Irish Econ. and Social Hist. [Great Britain] 1982 9: 53-72.* The farming career of Edward Delany (1821-1901) of Woodtown, County Meath covered the famine, the post-famine prosperity, and the agrarian disasters of the late 1870's and mid-1880's. The author examines the fluctuating fortunes of Delany's family. Based on Edward Delany's farm account books in the National Library, Dublin, Manuscripts 19, 347, and 348; 3 tables, 42 notes. 1851-99

Delbrück, Max

1688. Kay, Lily E. CONCEPTUAL MODELS AND ANALYTICAL TOOLS: THE BIOLOGY OF PHYSICIST MAX DELBRÜCK. *Journal of the History of Biology [Netherlands] 1985 18(2): 207-246.* In 1931, Max Delbrück, a physicist, saw a conceptual link between physics and biology; during the remainder of a long and distinguished career, he applied the analytical tools of mathematical physics to problems of cell structure too minute for direct observation. The result was valuable information on genetic mechanisms. With his research rooted in modern physics and its philosophy, his work significantly contributed to the growth of molecular biology. During his career, scientific institutes and organizations such as Rockefeller Foundation provided money and resources. Although a noted individual, Delbrück worked well in group projects. His life, thought, and career are indicative of the shape of 20th-century science. 118 notes. 1931-81

Delčev, Goce

1689. Andonova, Nina. RAZKAZANO MI ZA GOTSEVIIA ROD [What I was told about Gotse's family]. *Istoricheski Pregled [Bulgaria] 1983 39(3): 119-123.* Nina Andonova recalls the stories she heard between 1920 and 1929 about Goce Delčev (Gotse Delchev), the Bulgarian revolutionary, and his family from her grandparents, parents, and others who inhabited Kukush, Delčev's native Bulgarian village. Kukush and many of its historical documents were destroyed in the Balkan War of 1913. Andonova describes not only the Delčev family's economic, social, and political positions but also Bulgaria's political and independence movement between 1872 and 1903. 1872-1903

1690. Andonov-Poljanski, Hristo. GOTSÉ DELCHEV *Macedonian Rev. [Yugoslavia] 1983 13(1): 5-37.* Discusses the work of the Macedonian revolutionary, Goce Delčev (1872-1903). 1872-1903

1691. Khristov, Khristo. GEORGI (GOTSE) DELCHEV—BELEZHIT BULGARSKI PATRIOT I REVOLIUTSIONER [Georgi (Goce) Delčev—a great Bulgarian patriot and revolutionary]. *Istoricheski Pregled [Bulgaria] 1982 38(3): 30-40.* Goce Delčev was imbued with the idea of Bulgarian liberation. In 1893 he formed the Secret Macedonian-Odrinsko Committee, which established a liberation organization. In 1897 Delčev became a member of the external revolutionary movement. In 1902 he organized important meetings for the SMOC on ideological matters and supported the SMOC's plans for the Ilinden Uprising, which took place in 1903. Delčev took part in the struggle and was killed by the Turks at Vanitsa on 19 April 1903. Based on biographies of Delčev, and on the works of T. Zhivkov; 18 notes. 1893-1903

1692. Pandev, Konstantin. GOTSE DELCHEV KATO ZADGRANICHEN PREDSTAVITEL NA VMORO [Gotse Delchev as a foreign representative of the Internal Macedonian Revolutionary Organization]. *Istoricheski Pregled [Bulgaria] 1983 39(3): 42-48.* A committed Bulgarian revolutionary, Gotse Delchev, a teacher by profession, became the Internal Macedonian Revolutionary Organization's foreign representative in 1896. Traveling in Macedonia, Bulgaria, Greece, and Yugoslavia he was a courier, propagandist, intermediary, and arms procurer for the organization from 1896 to 1903. 19 notes. 1896-1903

Delfosse, Guy

1693. Sicard, Etienne. TEMOIGNAGE: A PROPOS DE GUY DELFOSSE [A testimony: about Guy Delfosse]. *Revue Historique des Armées [France] 1985 (2): 58-61.* Highlights the brilliant military career of former "enfant de troupe" (child educated in a French military school) Guy Delfosse, which began in the Resistance in 1944 when he was 18 years old and ended with Delfosse as commander of the 5th "Gendarmerie" region in Lyons. He was shot on 27 March 1984 by a thief holding up a bank, while he resisted and was reasoning with the criminals. For his heroic action, General Delfosse was posthumously granted the Médaille de la Gendarmerie and decorated Grand Officier de la Légion d'Honneur. Based on an eyewitness account; 2 photos. 1925-84

Delgado, Juan José

1694. Sánchez Téllez, María del Carmen. JUAN JOSE DELGADO, S.J. (1697-1755). ANTROPOLOGO, MEDICO Y BOTICARIO EN FILIPINAS [Juan José Delgado, S.J. (1697-1755): anthropologist, physician, and druggist in the Philippines]. *Boletín de la Sociedad Española de Historia de la Farmacia [Spain] 1985 36(143): 155-165.* A brief biography of Jesuit missionary Juan José Delgado, born in Cadiz in 1697, and sent to Manila in 1719, where he wrote extensive works on Philippine geography, botany, zoology, ethnology, and, in particular, ethnopharmacology, or native Philippine medicine, while acting as a physician and pharmacist, although he had received no formal training. 1719-55

DeLisser, H. G.

1695. Cobham, Rhonda. THE LITERARY SIDE OF H. G. DE LISSER (1878-1944). *Jamaica Journal [Jamaica] 1984-85 17(4): 2-9.* Known primarily as the editor-in-chief of the *Gleaner,* H. G. de Lisser exerted considerable influence on Jamaican affairs between the wars, wrote several novels, and published a magazine called *Planters' Punch* between 1920 and 1944. 1879-1944

Della Robbia, Luca

1696. Barolsky, Paul. WALTER PATER AND THE POETRY OF NOTHINGNESS. *Antioch Rev. 1982 40(4): 469-478.* 15c
*For abstract see **Botticelli***

1697. Konečný, Luboš. LUCA DELLA ROBBIA—UMĚLEC I ŘEMESLNÍK [Luca della Robbia: artist and craftsman]. *Umění a Řemesla [Czechoslovakia] 1982 (3): 13-17.* Recalls the life and work of Florentine sculptor della Robbia (d. 1482) by examining items of his art in Czechoslovak collections. 1425-82

della Rocca, Raimondo Morozzo

1698. Tiepolo, Maria Francesca. RICORDO DI RAIMONDO MOROZZO DELLA ROCCA (1905-1980) [In remembrance of Raimondo Morozzo della Rocca (1905-80)]. *Rassegna degli Arch. di Stato [Italy] 1980 40(1-3): 172-175.* Historian and archivist Raimondo Morozzo della Rocca served as administrator of the state archives of Venice and authored many works on Venetian history. His research focused on Venetian relations with the Middle East and the study of chronology. Note, biblio. 1905-80

Delmonte, Domingo

1699. Montoya, Elsa. INFLUENCIA DE DOMINGO DELMONTE EN EL QUEHACER LITERARIO DE LA PRIMERA MITAD DEL SIGLO XIX CUBANO [Domingo Delmonte's influence in literary matters in the first half of the 19th-century in Cuba]. *Santiago [Cuba] 1981 (43): 185-196.* Domingo Delmonte (1804-53) was born in Venezuela and in 1808 was brought to Havana. He studied law and travelled widely. He spent the last 10 years of his life in Spain where he continued to be occupied with Cuban problems. In his letters and his novel *Francisco* he described the horrors of slavery. He inspired many to devote themselves to the task of education and he influenced the development of esthetic and literary taste in Cuba. 12 notes, biblio. 1804-53

Delp, Alfred

1700. Bleistein, Roman. ALFRED DELP: GLAUBENSZEUGNIS IM WIDERSTAND [Alfred Delp: testament of faith in revolt]. *Stimmen der Zeit [West Germany] 1984 202(4): 219-226.* Examines the questions surrounding Alfred Delp's participation in the assassination attempt on Adolf Hitler in 1944, his contributions to the Kreisauer circle, and his death sentence by the people's court, based on the fourth volume of Delp's works. 1944-45

Delpech, François

1701. Comte, Bernard. FRANÇOIS DELPECH (1935-1982) [François Delpech (1935-82)]. *Cahiers d'Hist. [France] 1982 27(1): 5-7.* François Delpech (1935-82), assistant professor at the University of Lyons and director of the U.E.R. des Sciences Historiques et Géographiques, Art et Environnement. Highlights the career of this noted French historian of religions, emphasizing his contribution to Jewish history and humanistic historical research. Note. 1935-82

DeMartino, Achille

1702. Saija, Marcello. UN PREFETTO NITTIANO DI FRONTE AL FASCISMO: ACHILLE DE MARTINO A BRESCIA NEL 1922 [A Nittian prefect confronted with Fascism: Achille DeMartino in Brescia in 1922]. *Italia Contemporanea [Italy] 1985 (159): 5-43.* The type of Italian nationalism supported by Francesco Nitti and poet Gabriel D'Annunzio in 1919 led to the formation of a coalition with Fascist elements on the national level, and it was in this climate of political instability that Nittian moderate Achille DeMartino was appointed prefect of Brescia in 1919. DeMartino, adopting a conciliatory attitude criticized by agricultural leaders Carol Bonardi and Antonio Bianchi, instituted electoral reforms in an attempt to curb Fascist terrorism in the province, but when Mussolini seized power after the March on Rome, DeMartino was replaced. Based on correspondence, newspaper articles in *Fiamma, La Sentinella,* and *La Provincia de Brescia,* and secondary sources; 154 notes. 1919-22

Demetrakopoulos, Mihail

1703. Spanos, Kōstas. ENNIA ANEKDOTA ENGRAFA TŌN OLYMPIŌN AGŌNISTŌN TOU 1821 I. D. MANAKOPOULOU KAI MIH. DĒMĒTRAKOPOULOU [Nine unpublished documents related to D. Manakopoulos and Mihail Demetrakopoulos, combatants of 1821, who were from the area of Olympia]. *Makedonika [Greece] 1984 24: 197-208.* Publishes nine previously unpublished documents concerning Ioannis Manakopoulos and Mihail Demetrakopoulos, two combatants of the Greek war of independence (1821-28), who came from the area of Olympia. These documents are in the National Library in Athens. Manakopoulos (b. 1810) fought at Naoussa in 1821, where the Turks took him prisoner and killed his father. The Turks released him in 1828. He rejoined the army and then served in the Greek national police force in the Cyclades. Injured in the line of duty he sued the government for a pension. Demetrakopoulos escaped the Turks after the defeat at Naoussa, joined revolutionary forces in the south, and settled in Athens after the war. ca 1821

Demidoff, Nicholas

1704. Borroni Salvadori, Fabia. I DEMIDOFF COLLEZIONISTI A FIRENZE [The Demidoffs, collectors in Florence]. *Ann. della Scuola Normale Superiore di Pisa: Classe di Lettere e Filosofia [Italy] 1981 11(3): 937-1003.* Traces the origins and the more salient events in the history of the family founded by the Russian gunsmith Nicholas Demidoff, who became a mineowner, art collector, and a well-known figure in the high society of Florence and other European capitals. 1822-1903

Demidov, Akinfi Nikitich

1705. Hudson, Hugh D., Jr. FREE ENTERPRISE AND THE STATE IN EIGHTEENTH-CENTURY RUSSIA: THE DEMIDOV METALLURGICAL EMPIRE. *Canadian Slavonic Papers [Canada] 1984 26(2-3): 182-200.* 1697-1745
*For abstract see **Demidov, Nikita Demidovich***

Demidov, Anatoly

1706. Preziosi, Alfonso. IL PRINCIPE DEMIDOFF E IL MUSEO NAPOLEONICO DI SAN MARTINO [Prince Demidov and the Napoleon Museum of San Martino]. *Rivista Italiana di Studi Napoleonici [Italy] 1984 21(1-2): 187-195.* The Russian Prince Anatoly Demidov, husband of Mathilde Bonaparte, daughter of Jerome Bonaparte, came to the island of Elba in 1851. He had masses celebrated for the commemoration of Napoleon I's birthday and distributed bread to the poor. He also built a gallery across from Napoleon's villa and instituted a cultural and historical museum. This project created jobs in the stagnant agricultural economy and also brought important visitors to Elba. Yet Demidov's motives were not entirely humanitarian; he may have been trying to prepare Elban public opinion for an eventual annexation with France. Based on the Archives of Portoferraio and secondary sources; 2 appendixes, 21 notes. 1851-80

Demidov, Nikita Demidovich

1707. Hudson, Hugh D., Jr. FREE ENTERPRISE AND THE STATE IN EIGHTEENTH-CENTURY RUSSIA: THE DEMIDOV METALLURGICAL EMPIRE. *Canadian Slavonic Papers [Canada] 1984 26(2-3): 182-200.* Nikita Demidovich Demidov (1656-1725) and his son Akinfi Nikitich (1678-1745) deserve to be ranked with the foremost entrepreneurs of any society in the initial stage of industrialization. They emerged from obscurity to sire a family industrial empire that by the mid-18th century provided Russia with more than 40% of its iron and propelled the country to the forefront of world iron production. The exploits of this metallurgical family during the Great Northern War require us to reevaluate conventional images of the role of the imperial state in the Russian economy. Here Peter I's intervention proved extremely successful. Table, 80 notes. 1697-1745

Demiéville, Paul

1708. Hervouet, Yves. PAUL DEMIEVILLE ET L'ECOLE FRANÇAISE D'EXTREME-ORIENT [Paul Demiéville and the L'Ecole Française d'Extrême-Orient]. *Bull. de l'École Française d'Extrême-Orient [France] 1981 69: 1-29.* Demiéville was from 1919 to 1924 a member of the École Française d'Extrême-Orient, studying Vietnamese, Vietnamese customs, and religious practices and specializing in Chinese Buddhist texts, particularly of the Milindapañha. In Beijing from 1921 to 1922 his first article (published in 1924) contains a translation of a Chinese public edict against suicide. Teaching in 1924 at the University of Amoy, he confided in a letter of 1925 "prejudices against Japan . . . and feeling ripe for conversion to Bolshevism." When Louis Finot became director of the École, replacing Leonard Aurousseau, Demiéville's article on the memory of previous existences was permitted to appear, bespeaking a closer relationship, which was not destined to continue with Finot's successor, Georges Coedès. Based on Demiéville's letters; 66 notes. 1919-69

Demina-Mikhailova, E.

1709. Demina-Mikhailova, E. PUT' CHEREZ VOINU [The path through the war]. *Morskoi Sbornik [USSR] 1985 (3): 69-71.* Personal account of a Soviet nurse who, despite her sex and youth, served aboard a Black Sea Fleet ship, where she remained until the end of World War II. 1941-45

Deng Lichun

1710. —. TENG LI-CH'ÜN—DIRECTOR OF THE POLICY RESEARCH OFFICE OF THE CCPCC SECRETARIAT. *Issues & Studies [Taiwan] 1981 17(10): 62-64.* Deng Lichun (Teng Li-ch'ün), of Hunan province, is a leading Communist writer and theoretician in China and has the confidence of those currently in power. Now in his sixties, Deng was active in the Party at least as early as 1935. He was purged during the Cultural Revolution. Since 1980 he has directed the Party Central Committee Research Office. 1980-81

Deng Tuo

1711. Cheek, Timothy. DENG TUO: CULTURE, LENINISM AND ALTERNATIVE MARXISM IN THE CHINESE COMMUNIST PARTY. *China Q. [Great Britain] 1981 (87): 470-492.* Deng Tuo (Deng Yunte), purged and driven to suicide during China's Cultural Revolution, suffered for his opposition to Mao Zedong. A long-time Communist Party member, Deng resisted Mao for the latter's non-Leninist willingness to place will above objective reality. Deng's current rehabilitation is a further indication of Mao's reduced place in contemporary Chinese hagiography. Based primarily on Deng's writings and other Chinese materials; 111 notes. 1927-80

1712. Zhelokhovtsev, A. DENG TUO'S POSTHUMOUS FATE. *Far Eastern Affairs [USSR] 1984 (4): 82-91.* Life history of Deng Tuo (1912-?), a controversial Chinese poet and journalist who was deeply involved with China historically and as a growing socialist country and who is now popular again after a period of suppression in the 1970's. 1930's-84

Deng Xiaoping

1713. Nethercut, Richard D. DENG AND THE GUN: PARTY-MILITARY RELATIONS IN THE PEOPLE'S REPUBLIC OF CHINA. *Asian Survey 1982 22(8): 691-704.* Deng Xiaoping's (Teng Hsiao-p'ing) appointment, at age 77, to head the Chinese Communist Party's Military Commission underscores the current importance and sensitivity of Party-military relations. Deng appears to be dedicated to consolidating Party and government control over the People's Liberation Army (PLA), curtailing its traditional role in politics, and eventually modernizing and reforming PLA forces. Objections have been raised to his plans, and he has had to make some concessions to the military opposition, but predictions are that he will be able to make progress toward his goals. Based on radio broadcasts, newspapers, and speeches. 1977-82

1714. Ng-Quinn, Michael. DENG XIAOPING'S POLITICAL REFORM AND POLITICAL ORDER. *Asian Survey 1982 22(12): 1187-1205.* The political reform led by Deng Xiaoping (Teng Hsiao-p'ing) has primarily aimed at instituting structural mechanisms to guard against overconcentration of power, and may not be possible to complete in the existing political order. The many conceivable sources of opposition can use many forms of resistance, both active and passive. Deng's demostrated willingness to compromise may improve the chances of success. Based on Chinese documents and speeches; 55 notes, 2 fig. 1978-81

1715. Walker, Tony. HALF EMPTY, HALF FULL. *Australian J. of Chinese Affairs [Australia] 1983 (9): 147-152.* Examines the political power of Deng Xiaoping to reorganize the government of China, and to relocate or diminish opposing political factions. 1982

1716. Wang, Nora. DENG XIAOPING: THE YEARS IN FRANCE. *China Q. [Great Britain] 1982 (92): 698-705.* Deng Xiaoping arrived in France in 1920 to combine work and study. Arrest and/or repatriation of the Chinese Communist Party leadership in 1925 brought the then 21-year-old Deng into the front ranks of the Party, but six months later he left France for the Soviet Union. There is little indication that he had any significant contact with French laborers or with the French Communist Party. Based primarily on French police records in the Archives Nationales; 47 notes. 1920-26

Deng Zhongxia

1717. Akatova, T. DENG ZHONGXIA: A LEADING FIGURE IN THE CHINESE WORKERS' MOVEMENT. *Far Eastern Affairs [USSR] 1982 (4): 77-88.* The author of *A Brief History of the Trade Union Movement in China,* Deng Zhongxia (Teng Chung-hsia) was instrumental in making much of this history between 1919 and his execution in 1933. 1919-33

Denny, Anthony

1718. Sil, Narasingha P. SIR ANTHONY DENNY: A TUDOR SERVANT IN OFFICE. *Renaissance and Reformation [Canada] 1984 8(3): 190-201.* Sir Anthony Denny had an uneventful, honest life and career. It reveals the importance of service by a principled person in Henry VIII's court in the midst of crooks and time-servers. The key to his modest success lies in his personal qualities of moderation and discretion. 73 notes. 1520's-49

Dérer, Ivan

1719. Horák, Jiří. REMEMBERING IVAN DÉRER. *East Central Europe 1985 12(1): 41-50.* Ivan Dérer (1884-1973), born in Slovakia, was a leading figure in the Czechoslovak government before World War II. A member of the Czechoslovak Social Democratic Party and active in the international Socialist movement, he was nevertheless hostile to Communism throughout his political career. Surviving arrest by the Gestapo and internment in a concentration camp, he headed his country's Supreme Court until the Communist coup in 1948 forced him from office. He reentered political life briefly in the Prague Spring in 1968, but after the Soviet intervention he was "derehabilitated." Stresses his importance as a statesman helping to create the democratic Czechoslovak state and also as a historian. 54 notes. 1918-68

DeRidder, Francis

1720. Campbell, Carl C. THE REBEL PRIEST: FRANCIS DERIDDER AND THE FIGHT FOR FREE COLOUREDS' RIGHTS IN TRINIDAD, 1825-32. *J. of Caribbean Hist. [Barbados] 1981 15: 20-40.* Francis DeRidder, a native of Demerara, fought actively for free colored rights in Trinidad between 1825 and 1832. This struggle was fought within and beyond the Catholic Church. As the only black clergyman on the island, he faced great opposition from white society, but he performed an important service in the struggle for civil rights for blacks. Primary sources; 78 notes. 1825-32

DeRijcke, Joos

1721. Paepe, Chr. A. J. R. de. JOOS DE RIJCKE (1498-1578?), EEN VLAAMSE ZENDELING IN ZUID-AMERIKA [Joos de Rijcke (1498-1578?), a Flemish missionary in South America]. *Spiegel Historiael [Netherlands] 1984 19(9): 398-403.* Comments on the Franciscan friar Joos de Rijcke's travels and missionary activities in South America from 1532 to the 1570's. 1532-70's

Deroin, Jeanne

1722. —. [PRATIQUE COOPÉRATIVE ET ASSOCIATIONS (1848-1851)] [Cooperative organization and associations, 1848-51]. *Communautés: Arch. de Sci. Sociales de la Coopération et du Développement [France] 1981 (55): 37-73.*

—. PRATIQUE COOPÉRATIVE ET ASSOCIATIONS (1848-1851) [Cooperative organization and associations, 1848-51], *pp. 36-58.* Describes the rise of labor organizations, 1848-51 and the end of the second republic; studies the various forms of association within the labor movement.

—. ANNEXE II: UN MÉMORIAL JEANNE DEROIN [Appendix II: In memory of Jeanne Deroin], *pp.59-73.* A tribute to the 19th-century feminist and socialist, which includes the reproduction of a commemorative report on Deroin's life and principles presented by A. Ranvier to the French Congress of Workers' Associations in 1900. 1848-1900

Descartes, René

1723. Shea, William R. DESCARTES AND THE FRENCH ARTISAN JEAN FERRIER. *Ann. dell'Istituto e Mus. di Storia della Sci. di Firenze [Italy] 1982 7(2): 145-160.* An account of the relations between René Descartes (1590-1650) and French artisan Jean Ferrier, who had been entrusted by the famous French philosopher and mathematician to construct hyperbolic lenses for an improved version of the telescope he had designed. Descartes's personality and his attitude on the practical implementation of scientific theories are herein illuminated. 1629-38

Deschamps, Hubert

1724. Salmon, P. HUBERT DESCHAMPS [Hubert Deschamps]. *Bull. des Séances de l'Acad. Royale des Sci. d'Outre-Mer [Belgium] 1981 27(1): 47-53.* Hubert Deschamps (1900-79) was not only a foreign service officer in Africa for many years, but a respected scholar as well. His research interests focused on Madagascar, where he spent some time for the French government. A Sorbonne professor and a prolific writer, Deschamps will be missed by those who knew him. Biblio. 1900-79

DeSerres, Charles Wilmot

1725. Schoeman, Karel. "THIS WELL-KNOWN AND ECCENTRIC INDIVIDUAL": DIE LEWE VAN CHARLES WILMOT DE SERRES ["This well-known and eccentric individual": the life of Charles Wilmot De Serres]. *Africana Notes and News [South Africa] 1985 26(6): 204-207.* Outlines what is known of the life of Charles Wilmot De Serres, an eccentric Englishman who emigrated to South Africa in 1854. After De Serres settled in Bloemfontein, he obtained employment as a schoolmaster, but soon gained local notoriety for his long walking tours throughout the region. In 1868, he mysteriously disappeared during the course of one of his journeys. Based on Bloemfontein newspaper accounts and secondary sources; 15 notes. English summary. 1854-68

Desloges, Marcelin

1726. Goblot, Jean-Jacques. UN "MYSTERIEUX REDACTEUR" DU *GLOBE:* MARCELIN DESLOGES [A "mysterious editor" of the *Globe:* Marcelin Desloges]. *Revue d'Histoire Littéraire de la France [France] 1985 85(2): 234-247.* Presents new material about the previously obscure Marcelin Desloges, one of the editors of the *Globe* between 1824 and 1830, who emerges as a disciple of Victor Cousin and active *carbonaro.* 1824-30

Dessauer, Friedrich

1727. Pohlit, Wolfgang. FRIEDRICH DESSAUER—NATURWISSENSCHAFTER, POLITIKER, PHILOSOPH [Friedrich Dessauer, scientist, politician, philosopher]. *Civitas [Switzerland] 1982 37(1-2): 38-44.* Memoir of Friedrich Dessauer (1881-1963) and his many interests and activities, including research in the field of aerosol-biophysics and x-rays as well as political and journalistic endeavors. 1881-1963

Detsi, João

1728. Onody, Oliver. UM CAPITÃO DO EXERCITO HUNGARIO NO BRASIL [A Hungarian army captain in Brazil]. *Rev. do Inst. Hist. e Geog. Brasileiro [Brazil] 1981 (331): 123-158.* Analyzes the documents, information, and career of João Detsi, a Hungarian of Greek origin who came to Brazil as a political refugee after the 1848 Revolution and became a naturalized citizen in 1856. Detsi's military career in Hungary is traced and documents relating to that career are discussed. Detsi held several public and private offices in Brazil, and fought in the 1866 war against Paraguay. His final activity was as founder and governor of several interior settlements in Brazil in the 1860's and 1870's. He died in 1881. Based on letters and documents from Brazilian and European archives and secondary sources; 2 photos, 4 plates, 102 notes. 1848-81

DeValera, Eamon

1729. Fitzpatrick, David. EAMON DE VALERA AT TRINITY COLLEGE. *Hermathena [Ireland] 1982 (133): 7-14.* Discusses Irish president Eamon de Valera's involvement with Trinity College, 1905-60. 1905-60

1730. MacQueen, Norman. ÉAMON DE VALÉRA, THE IRISH FREE STATE, AND THE LEAGUE OF NATIONS, 1919-46. *Éire-Ireland 1982 17(4): 110-127.* As president of the Dáil in 1919, Eamon de Valera endorsed the League of Nations. Under his successor, William T. Cosgrave, the Free State government exploited the League to establish the British dominions' sovereign independence. In power again in 1932, de Valera used the League Council presidency to forcefully enunciate the League's role as peacekeeper and protector of small nations. In opposition to profascist elements in the Dáil opposition, de Valera supported League sanctions against Italy in the Ethiopian crisis. By 1938, de Valera recognized that collective security under the League had failed, and instituted a foreign policy of isolation and neutrality. Based on Irish government and League of Nations documents, and press reports; 47 notes. 1919-46

1731. —. EAMON DE VALERA (1882-1975) [Eamon de Valera, 1882-1975]. *Europa Ethnica [Austria] 1982 39(4): 214.* A biography of Irish President Eamon de Valera (1882-1975). Pays particular attention to his activities during the Easter Uprising in Ireland in 1916 and to his work as president of the Irish Republic, 1932-59 and 1959-72. 1882-1975

Devès family

1732. Manchuelle, François. METIS ET COLONS: LA FAMILLE DEVES ET L'EMERGENCE POLITIQUE DES AFRICAINS AU SENEGAL, 1881-1897 [Mulattoes and settlers: the Devès family and the political emergence of Africans in Senegal, 1881-97]. *Cahiers d'Etudes Africaines [France] 1984 24(4): 477-504.* Describes politics and economic conditions in Senegal in the late 19th century by noting the role of the Creole Devès family, which cooperated with French colonists and became a dominant political elite. 1881-97

DeZoete, Beryl

1733. Ury, Marian. SOME NOTES TOWARD A LIFE OF BERYL DE ZOETE. *Journal of the Rutgers University Libraries 1986 48(1): 1-54.* Beryl Drusilla de Zoete (1879-1962) was an author, translator, dance critic, and researcher. For 44 years she was the companion and collaborator of Arthur Waley (1889-1966). All of her important work was written after she was 50 years of age. Her circle of acquaintances crossed national and artistic boundaries. She is best known for the three books she wrote on the dancing of South and Southeast Asia. Based primarily on books, manuscripts, letters, and cards that belonged to de Zoete and Waley in the Rutgers University Library; 98 notes. 1900-62

Diablo, El

See Briceño, Antonio Nicolás

Diad'kovski, Iustin

1734. Mikulinski, S. R. K 200-LETIIU SO DNIA ROZHDENIIA I. E. DIAD'KOVSKOGO [The bicentenary of the birth of I. E. Diad'kovski]. *Voprosy Istorii Estestvoznaniia i Tekhniki [USSR] 1984 (4): 58-71.* Biography of Iustin Diad'kovski (1784-1841), a Russian doctor who taught at the Moscow Medical Academy until expulsion in 1831 for atheism. His friendships with progressive intellectuals of the 1830's such as Vissarion Belinski and Nikolai Stankevich made him a popular figure in the capital despite lack of official position. Secondary sources; 23 notes. 1810-41

Diaghilev, Serge

1735. Hunkins, Rebecca. IGOR STRAVINSKY AND THE BALLETS RUSSES, 1910-1928. *Bull. of Biblio. 1983 40(3): 143-147.* Cites bibliographies, dissertations, monographs, and newspaper and periodical articles on composer Igor Stravinsky and impresario Serge Diaghilev of the Ballets Russes. 1910-28

Diamand, Bernard

1736. Brożek, Andrzej. MATERIAŁY DO BIOGRAFII BERNARDA DIAMANDA (1861-1921) [A contribution to the biography of Bernard Diamand (1861-1921)]. *Biuletyn Żydowskiego Instytutu Historycznego w Polsce [Poland] 1983 (4): 71-97.* Bernard Diamand was born in Lvov in the family of a rich Jewish merchant who was proud of his bond with Jewish tradition but was willing to accept the culture of the surrounding Polish environment. Bernard's brother, Herman (1860-1931) was a distinguished socialist activist. After graduation from the Technische Hochschule in Karlsruhe and obtaining the degree of doctor at the University of Bern in Switzerland, Bernard Diamand was first engaged as a chemist in Trzebinia (then under Austrian rule), and, in the years 1904-19, was simultaneously the director of three chemical plants near Katowice (then under Prussian rule). There he cooperated with the leading activists of the Polish movement such as Wojciech Korfanty (1874-1939). In 1919 the Commissioners of the Supreme People's Council in Poznań appointed him delegate for industrial affairs in Upper Silesia. Later he worked at the Ministry of the Former Prussian Province in Warsaw, on behalf of which he participated in international political and economic talks. In 1920 he served in the Ministry of Finance and then in the Ministry of Industry and Commerce in Warsaw. In London and Paris he negotiated important political and economic matters on behalf of the Polish government. He died in Warsaw. The article publishes two letters of W. Korfanty to B. Diamand, a message of Diamand to prime minister of the Polish government, Antoni Ponikowski, concerning the action in favor of Upper Silesia, and a message of the Ministry of Industry and Commerce in connection with that matter. Other documents concern the suggestion that the government allow special pecuniary aid to the desolated family of Diamand. The most extensive document is the letter of Władysław Diamand (1897-1972) giving a comprehensive sketch of the life and work of his father Bernard. 1890's-1921

Dianni, Jadwiga Stefania

1737. Wachułka, Adam and Pawlikowska-Brożek, Zofia. JADWIGA STEFANIA DIANNI (1886-1981) WE WSPOMNIENIACH HISTORYKÓW MATEMATYKI [Jadwiga Stefania Dianni (1886-1981) in the reminiscences of historians of mathematics]. *Kwartalnik Hist. Nauki i Techniki [Poland] 1982 27(1): 189-194.* 1886-1981

Díaz, José

1738. Meshcheriakov, Marklen Tikhonovich. KHOSE DIAS—VYDAIUSHCHIISIA RUKOVODITEL' ISPANSKIKH KOMMUNISTOV [José Díaz, eminent leader of Spanish Communists]. *Novaia i Noveishaia Istoriia [USSR] 1983 (3): 79-96.* José Díaz (1895-1942), an anarchist-syndicalist since 1917, joined the Spanish Communist Party in 1927, was elected its Secretary General in 1932, fought factionalism in trade unions and called for common endorsement of the Comintern's Anti-Fascist United Front. An antifascist workers' and peasants' militia was created by the Spanish Politbureau and a rigorous training program instituted by Díaz in the fall of 1934 in preparation for armed insurrection. Photo, 38 notes. Article to be continued. 1917-34

Díaz, Porfirio

1739. Conger, Robert D. "Porfirio Díaz and the Church Hierarchy, 1876-1911." U. of New Mexico 1985. 264 pp. *DAI 1986 46(9): 2786-A.* DA8523973 1876-1911

Díaz de Priego, Baltazar

1740. García del Pino, César. BALTASAR DIAZ DE PRIEGO: UN MATEMATICO SANTIAGUERO DEL SIGLO XVIII [Baltasar Díaz de Priego: an 18th-century mathematician from Santiago]. *Santiago [Cuba] 1982 (47): 115-149.* In 1764 a project to settle the port of Guantánamo was submitted to the minister of Charles III by a certain Baltasar Díaz de Priego, who called himself a native of the City of Cuba, though at the time domiciled in Cádiz, and had at one time occupied the chair of mathematics in the Royal University of La Habana. Summarizes the author's findings in archives about this unknown countryman who was a land surveyor and urbanist. Based on primary material in the Archivo General de Indias and Cuban archives; 5 appended documents, 117 notes. 1717-69

Díaz del Castillo, Bernal

1741. Scott, Nina M. BERNAL DIAZ, MEET JOHN SMITH. *Américas (Organization of Am. States) 1981 33(6-7): 32-39.* Compares and contrasts Bernal Díaz and John Smith in their roles as explorers and in their attitudes, as reflected in their journals, toward the Americas; finds Díaz representative of the Mexican tendency to be preoccupied with the past and Smith as representative of a future-oriented vision of the United States. 16c-17c

Díaz González, Joaquín

1742. —. [IN MEMORIAM: DR JOAQUIN DIAZ GONZALEZ] (Spanish text). *Boletín de la Academia Nacional de la Historia [Venezuela] 1985 68(269): 195-199.*

Romero Lobo, Francisco. DOCTOR JOAQUIN DIAZ GONZALEZ [Dr. Joaquín Díaz González], *pp. 195-197.*

González, Carlos Luis. JOAQUIN DIAZ GONZALEZ UN GRAN VENEZOLANO [Joaquín Díaz González, a great Venezuelan], *pp. 197-199.* On the occasion of his death in Rome (1984) pays tribute to an eminent physician, humanist, historian, diplomat, and member of the Academy of History. He was the founder of the chair of history of medicine in the University of the Andes and wrote many books on the subject. 1902-84

Díaz Sánchez, Ramón

1743. Pérez Tenreiro, Tomás. RAMON DIAZ SANCHEZ [Ramón Díaz Sánchez]. *Bol. de la Acad. Nac. de la Hist. [Venezuela] 1982 65(259): 603-613.* Díaz Sánchez was a writer of stories and novels, as well as of history, and a tireless investigator of his country's history and social reality. He was a member of the National Academy of History and was succeeded in his chair by the author. 1900's-30's

DiBreganze, Giovanni

1744. Brignoli, Marziano. PRELIMINARI DELLA NOSTRA GUERRA [Preliminaries to Italy's entry into World War I]. *Risorgimento [Italy] 1982 34(1): 1-35, (2): 120-148.* Reproduces the diary of Lieutenant Colonel Giovanni Di Breganze (1866-1931) who was military attaché at the Italian Embassy in Paris in 1914. Di Breganze dwells particularly on the industrial organization of the war, the Italian war plan, and inter-Allied cooperation in the conduct of the war. Text of diary preserved in the archive of the Comune di Milano; 30 notes. 1914-15

Dickens, Charles

1745. Kirkland, Carole Ann Bardella. "Charles Dickens: Educational Journalist." U. of Florida 1982. 252 pp. *DAI 1983 44(2): 328-329-A.* DA8313653 1880's-90's

Dickens, Charles (1812-1870)

1746. Decaux, Alain. L'HOMME QUI FIT PLEURER TOUTE L'ANGLETERRE: DICKENS [Dickens, the man who made all England weep]. *Historama [France] 1984 (2): 50-60.* Recounts the life of novelist Charles Dickens and Victorian England's reaction to his "realistic" novels. 1812-70

1747. Moss, Sidney P. THE AMERICAN EPISODE OF *MARTIN CHUZZLEWIT:* THE CULMINATION OF DICKENS' QUARREL WITH THE AMERICAN PRESS. *Studies in the American Renaissance 1983: 223-244.* When Charles Dickens visited America in January 1842 to prepare a travel book to be called *American Notes,* he was received as a conquering hero and praised as a defender of the people and as an example of entrepreneurial success. Yet when Dickens made statements about the need for an Anglo-American copyright law, and claimed to have been robbed by American publishing houses, the press turned against him. The polemics turned quite bitter and Dickens filled the *American Notes* and also the American chapters in *Martin Chuzzlewit* with anti-American prejudice. Even so, these two books of Dickens returned huge profits for American publishing houses. Based on the works of Dickens, American journals of the 1840's, and secondary sources; 50 notes. 1840's

1748. Shelden, Michael. DICKENS, "THE CHIMES," AND THE ANTI-CORN LAW LEAGUE. *Victorian Studies 1982 25(3): 328-353.* Critics have failed to realize that Charles Dickens's 1844 Christmas story, "The Chimes," is actually a plea for free trade radicalism. Dickens had become a firm supporter of the Anti-Corn Law League. His support for free trade gave him a social philosophy that explained the basic causes of mid-Victorian poverty and crime. Based on Dickens' works and letters; illus., 27 notes. 1840-50

Diderot, Denis

1749. Hermosa Andújar, Antonio. EL PROBLEMA DEL CONTROL DEL PODER EN EL PENSAMIENTO DE DIDEROT [The problem of control of power in the thought of Diderot]. *Revista de Estudios Políticos [Spain] 1984 (41): 131-159.* Examines Denis Diderot's views on democratic government, its nature and necessity, and the problems of legitimacy and power. His views, though in one sense forward-looking, are in another rooted in the past. He combines the principle of adequate representation of the various social strata with a strong ordering and balancing sovereign. 66 notes. 1713-84

1750. Lloyd, Caryl Ann Lefstad. "Denis Diderot and Authority, French and Italian." U. of Iowa 1981. 291 pp. *DAI 1982 42(11): 4841-A.* DA8210011 1738-84

1751. Luján, Néstor. DIDEROT Y LA ENCICLOPEDIA [Diderot and the *Encyclopédie]. Historia y Vida [Spain] 1984 17(191): 70-75.* Reviews the bohemian life of Denis Diderot, French intellectual encyclopedist. 1750-84

1752. Santucci, Antonio A. DIDEROT COLLABORATORE DI RAYNAL [Diderot: collaborator of Raynal]. *Studi Storici [Italy] 1982 23(2): 453-459.* 1770-90

For abstract see ***Raynal, Guillaume***

Dieckmann, Wilhelm

1753. Wegner-Korfes, Sigrid. REALPOLITISCHE HALTUNG BEI OFFIZIEREN DER FAMILIEN MERTZ VON QUIRNHEIM, KORFES UND DIECKMANN [Realistic political attitudes of officers from the Mertz von Quirnheim, Korfes, and Dieckmann families]. *Militärgeschichte [East Germany] 1986 25(3): 226-233.* 1920's-44

For abstract see ***Mertz von Quirnheim, Hermann***

Diego Paredes, Victoriano de

1754. —. [DON VICTORIANO DE DIEGO PAREDES]. *(Spanish text). Bol. de Hist. y Antigüedades [Colombia] 1981 68(732): 99-165.*

Paredes Gómez, Alberto. DON VICTORIANO DE DIEGO PAREDES [Victoriano de Diego Paredes], *pp. 99-102.* Sketches the life of the Colombian liberal politician, educator, and diplomat (1804-93).

Diego Paredes, Victoriano de. MEMORIAS DE DON VICTORIANO DE DIEGO PAREDES, DICTADAS POR EL A SU HIJA FRANCISCA PAREDES SERRANO Y MANUSCRITAS POR ESTA [Memoirs of Don Victoriano de Diego Paredes, dictated by him to his daughter, Francisca Paredes Serrano, and written by hand by the latter], *pp. 103-165.* 1824-93

Diesel, Rudolf

1755. Delorme, Roger. RUDOLF DIESEL—SINUCIDERE SAU ASASINAT? [Rudolf Diesel: suicide or murder?]. *Magazin Istoric [Romania] 1981 15(2): 51-54.* Examines the circumstances surrounding the mysterious death of the German inventor Rudolf Diesel (1858-1913), which took place on board the Antwerp-Harwich ferry. 1913

Dietl, Joseph

1756. Kucharz, Eugeniusz. THE LIFE AND ACHIEVEMENTS OF JOSEPH DIETL. *Clio Medica [Netherlands] 1981 16(1): 25-35.* Joseph Dietl (1804-78) studied medicine at the University of Vienna where he taught for several years. He accepted several positions from the Habsburg government, and distinguished himself in efforts to curb cholera and typhoid epidemics. As director of the New Hospital in Vienna he wrote a series of articles advocating morbid autopsy. After making a tour of Europe to study various hospitals, he accepted a position as head of the Medical Clinic in Cracow where he was an outstanding teacher and wrote works on balneology and the treatment of pneumonia. In 1861 he was appointed director of the Jagiellonian University. The Austrian government was opposed to his pro-Polish sympathies and forced him to retire in 1865. He was mayor of Cracow, 1866-75 and worked at improving medical and hygienic conditions. 27 notes. 1825-78

Dietrich, Baron de

1757. Perrin, Carleton E. A LOST IDENTITY: PHILIPPE FREDERIC, BARON DE DIETRICH (1748-1793). *Isis 1982 73(269): 545-551.* In a number of reference works, including the *Dictionary of Scientific Biography,* the French chemist and mineralogist Baron de Dietrich has been confused with Paul Henri Dietrich, Baron d'Holbach (1723-89), and the career of Holbach is presented as though the two were one person. The author presents here a biographical summary and bibliographical material concerning Baron de Dietrich. Based on a few of Dietrich's papers and several secondary works. 19 notes. 18c

Diez de Medina, Tadeo

1758. Klein, Herbert S.; Caravedo, Rocío, transl. ACUMULACION Y HERENCIA EN LA ELITE TERRATENIENTE DEL ALTO PERU: EL CASO DE DON TADEO DIEZ DE MEDINA [Accumulation and inheritance among the landowning elite of Upper Peru: the case of Don Tadeo Diez de Medina]. *Histórica [Peru] 1983 7(2): 179-213.* Describes the career of an hacendado of Upper Peru in the 18th and early 19th centuries. Contrary to current opinion, which regards this class as feudal and anticommercial, Tadeo Diez de Medina (1730-?1810), born into a landowning family, created a land-based empire, accumulated enormous wealth, and managed and transferred it. Based on primary material in several Latin American and Spanish archives; 3 tables, chart, 28 notes, biblio. 1750's-1800's

Digby, Alexander

1759. Mikhailova, M. B. ALEKSANDR DIGBI: ZODCHII KLASSITSIZMA NA IUGE ROSSII [Alexander Digby: a classicist architect in the south of Russia]. *Arkhitekturnoe Nasledstvo [USSR] 1980 28: 80-88.* Alexander Digby, a native of Tuscany, made important contributions to the architecture of Russian cities such as Astrakhan, Kerch, Odessa, and Kherson in the late 17th and early 18th centuries. 1689-18c

Digby, John

1760. Bandurraga, Peter L. JOHN DIGBY, A JACOBEAN COURTIER. *Halcyon 1982: 53-72.* John Digby, 1st Earl of Bristol (1580-1653), was educated at Oxford, and served as a courtier and diplomat for James I of England, during the 1620's. He sought to improve relations with Spain by attempting to arrange a marriage between the prince of Wales and the infanta of Spain. Despite his official status, he also championed individual rights in opposition to royal privilege. 1620's

Dike, K. O.

1761. Fage, J. D. K. O. DIKE: OBITUARY. *Africa [Great Britain] 1984 54(2): 96-98.* Provides an obituary of K. O. Dike (1917-83), one of the most prominent historians of Nigeria and an important figure in the development of African Studies in both Nigeria and the United States. 1917-83

Dill, John

1762. Danchev, Alex. A SPECIAL RELATIONSHIP: FIELD MARSHAL SIR JOHN DILL AND GENERAL GEORGE C. MARSHALL. *Journal of the Royal United Services Institute for Defence Studies [Great Britain] 1985 130(2): 56-61.* Describes instances in which British Field Marshal Sir John Dill and US General George C. Marshall established smooth working relations between Great Britain and the United States during World War II. In many cases, Dill and Marshall served as the "working interface" for Anglo-American wartime relations. Based on documents in the US National Archives, archives of Cambridge University, Marshall Research Library, the Public Record Office (London), and Franklin D. Roosevelt Library. 1941-50

Dillon, Robert

1763. VanBrock, François William. LE LIEUTENANT GENERAL ROBERT DILLON [Lieutenant-General Robert Dillon]. *Revue Historique des Armées [France] 1985 (1): 14-29.* A biographical account of the career of Robert Dillon, who acquired renown as colonel and second-in-command in the Duke of Lauzun Legion in America. Previously, he participated in campaigns in Senegal (1778-79) and England. In America during the Revolution, he fought with the Count de Rochambeau's corps at Yorktown and elsewhere. Accidental loss of his left hand ended his career in 1787. Based on Service Historique de l'Armée de Terre archives, records in the Archives Nationales, and other primary sources; 2 maps, 7 photos, 79 notes. 1760's-87

Dilthey, Wilhelm

1764. Jahnke, Ulrich. WILHELM DILTHEY UND DIE INSTITUTIONALISIERUNG DER PSYCHOLOGIE AN DER BERLINER UNIVERSITÄT [Wilhelm Dilthey and the institutionalization of psychology at the University of Berlin]. *Wissenschaftliche Zeitschrift der Humboldt-Universität zu Berlin. Gesellschaftswissenschaftliche Reihe [East Germany] 1984 33(1): 55-59.* Investigates Wilhelm Dilthey's (1833-1911) role in the institutionalization of psychology within the philosophy department at the University of Berlin through a detailed analysis of the genesis of Dilthey's thought process, his academic activities, and the scientific organization of these activities during his 23 years as professor at the University of Berlin. 1882-1905

Dimitrov, Andon

1765. Pandev, Konstantin. SPOMENI NA ANDON DIMITROV [The memoirs of Andon Dimitrov]. *Izvestiia na Instituta za Istoriia [Bulgaria] 1983 26: 260-301.* Deals with the life of Andon Dimitrov, one of the founding members of the Internal Macedonian Revolutionary Organization in 1893. Dimitrov was a teacher of Turkish in Salonika, but devoted his life to propagandizing and fighting for Macedonia's national liberation. Excerpts from Dimitrov's memoirs on his struggle are reproduced, describing the attitudes of the people and the authorities, political intrigues, and his hopes and fears. Based on Andon Dimitrov's memoirs; 47 notes. 1893-1912

Dimitrov, Georgi

1766. Amort, Čestmír. GEORGI DIMITROV V CHEKHOSLOVASHKATA ISTORIOGRAFIIA [Georgi Dimitrov in Czechoslovak historiography]. *Izvestiia na Inst. po Istoriia na BKP [Bulgaria] 1982 46: 290-303.* Reviews the great number of Georgi Dimitrov's works, articles about him, and books by Bulgarian and foreign authors dedicated to Dimitrov's life and Czechoslovak-Bulgarian friendship published in Czechoslovakia. 1920's-82

1767. Amort, Čestmír. JIŘÍ DIMITROV V ČESKOSLOVENSKÉ HISTORIOGRAFII [Georgi Dimitrov in Czech historiography]. *Slovanský Přehled [Czechoslovakia] 1982 68(3): 202-209.* Georgi Dimitrov has a secure place in Czech historiography. Interest in his life and activities first emerged at the time of the Leipzig trial regarding the Reichstag fire in 1933. The coverage of his courageous confrontation with Göring and documents from his earlier stay in Czechoslovakia are rich sources for historians today. His 90th birthday in 1972 was celebrated with a special issue of *Slovanský Přehled* and an international symposium. A number of Bulgarian biographies of his life have been translated into Czech and his contribution to the worldwide socialist revolution is far from forgotten. 67 notes. 1923-82

1768. Amort, Čestmír. G. DIMITROV A NÁRODNĚ OSVOBOZENECKÉ HNUTÍ ČECHŮ A SLOVÁKŮ [Georgi Dimitrov and the national liberation movement of Czechs and Slovaks]. *Hist. a Vojenství [Czechoslovakia] 1982 31(3): 111-127.* Discusses Dimitrov's role in the support of the Czechoslovak liberation movement during World War II. As Comintern secretary general Dimitrov stressed the basic duty of Czech Communists to create and lead the anti-Nazi resistance, and after 1941 he endeavored to unify the actions of Right and Left with the single goal of the defeat of Nazism. Dimitrov also organized special training for resistance fighters sent from abroad into occupied areas to lead the resistance of Czech and Slovak patriots. Based on writings of Dimitrov and some published items; 43 notes. 1939-48

1769. Amort, Čestmír. JIŘÍ DIMITROV A BOJ O JEDNOTNOU FRONTU V ČESKOSLOVENSKU V LETECH 1929-1933 [Georgi Dimitrov and the struggle for a united front in Czechoslovakia, 1929-33]. *Československý Časopis Hist. [Czechoslovakia] 1982 30(1): 35-57.* As leading functionary in the West European Bureau of the Comintern,

Georgi Dimitrov (1882-1949), participated in international Communist meetings, encouraged the actions of national Communist parties against unemployment, fascism, and war, and was instrumental in organizing the antiwar congress of 1932 in Amsterdam. From his Berlin headquarters Dimitrov followed the internal struggle in the Czechoslovak Communist Party and fully backed Klement Gottwald. In March 1933 the Nazi government arrested Dimitrov and liquidated his West European Bureau. Based on the press, some archival material, and several oral testimonies; 86 notes. Russian and German summaries. 1929-33

1770. Bachman, Kurt. GEORGI DIMITROV ZHIVEE V ISTORIIATA I NASTOIASHTETO [Georgi Dimitrov lives in history and in the present]. *Izvestiia na Inst. po Istoriia na BKP [Bulgaria] 1982 46: 317-327.* The Communist Party in West Germany has learned much from Georgi Dimitrov and his works and activities during the decades of struggle against fascism and reaction. 1920's-82

1771. Baev, Iordan. ROLIATA NA GEORGI DIMITROV ZA UKREPVANE NA MEZHDUNAROD-NOTO POLOZHENIE NA BULGARIA (NOEMVRI 1946-DEKEMVRI 1947) [Georgi Dimitrov's role in the strengthening of Bulgaria's international position, November 1946-December 1947]. *Izvestiia na Inst. po Istoriia na BKP [Bulgaria] 1982 46: 137-177.* Describes Georgi Dimitrov's administration of Bulgarian foreign policy as head of government after the Fatherland Front's 1946 electoral victory. 1946-47

1772. Baichinski, K. GEORGII DIMITROV O BOR'BE PROTIV FASHIZMA I ZNACHENII POBEDY SSSR V OTECHESTVENNOI VOINE [Georgi Dimitrov on the struggle against fascism and the importance of the Soviet victory in the Great Patriotic War]. *Voprosy Istorii KPSS [USSR] 1985 (7): 82-94.* Views Georgi Dimitrov's assessments of fascism in the 1930's and his support of international solidarity with the USSR throughout World War II. He warned against the dangers of nascent fascism at the 1935 Congress of the Comintern. During the war he directed from Moscow the activities of the Bulgarian Communist Party. Secondary sources; 28 notes. 1935-45

1773. Bajtschinski, Kostadin. GEORGI DIMITROFF UND DER AUFBAU DES SOZIALISMUS IN BULGARIEN [Georgi Dimitrov and the foundation of socialism in Bulgaria]. *Beiträge zur Gesch. der Arbeiterbewegung [East Germany] 1982 24(3): 323-333.* Assesses the important role played by the Bulgarian Communist leader Georgi Dimitrov (1882-1949) in establishing socialism in Bulgaria, and considers his contribution to the international Communist movement. Dimitrov's most important activities in Bulgaria were: to make the Bulgarian Communist Party into a Marxist-Leninist Party; and to unite the Bulgarian people in order to bring about the Socialist revolution which occurred 9 September 1944. In addition, as Bulgarian leader, Dimitrov established the foundations of the Bulgarian Socialist Republic. On an international level Dimitrov came to symbolize the cooperation of antifascist powers throughout the world as the result of his work as a theorist and strategist in the fight against fascism. Secondary sources; 9 notes. 1882-1949

1774. Birman, M. A. G. DIMITROV—RUKOVODITEL' REVOLIUTSIONNYKH PROFSOIUZOV BOLGARII 1904-1923 GG. [Georgi Dimitrov, a leader of revolutionary trade unions in Bulgaria, 1904-23]. *Études Balkaniques [Bulgaria] 1982 18(2): 21-32.* Georgi Dimitrov was elected secretary of the Bulgarian Revolutionary Trade Union Federation in 1904 and became its leader shortly thereafter. He participated in the creation of the Communist Party and worked at the Comintern. In 1923 he was one of the leaders of the uprising against the fascist regime. Based on works of Dimitrov; 57 notes. 1904-23

1775. Borsányi, György. GEORGI DIMITROV SZÜLETÉSÉNEK CENTENÁRIUMÁRA [For the centennial of the birth of Georgi Dimitrov]. *Társadalmi Szemle [Hungary] 1982 37(5): 72-82.* A biography of the Bulgarian revolutionary Georgi Dimitrov. Active from 1904, in 1913 he became a delegate of his party (later to become the Bulgarian Communist Party). Beginning in 1920, he was involved in international activities. Forced to emigrate in 1923, he lived abroad underground. Arrested in Germany in 1933 and accused of setting the Reichstag fire, he was found innocent. From 1934 to 1942, he was the head of the Communist International (Comintern). His state of health was poor by then. In 1945, he returned to liberated Bulgaria to become prime minister the following year. He died 2 July 1949 in a sanatorium near Moscow. 1903-49

1776. Borshani, Giorg. GEORGI DIMITROV I UNGARSKOTO RABOTNICHESKO DVIZHENIE [Georgi Dimitrov and the Hungarian workers' movement]. *Izvestiia na Inst. po Istoriia na BKP [Bulgaria] 1982 46: 271-289.* 1920's-40's

1777. Cherniavski, Georgi P. GEORGI DIMITROV V LENINGRADSKIIA PECHAT [Georgi Dimitrov in the Leningrad press]. *Istoricheski Pregled [Bulgaria] 1982 38(2): 113-118.* During the anti-Communist terror in Bulgaria following the 1925 Sofia church bombing, blamed on Communists, Dimitrov—in the USSR with the Comintern—presented his case in the Leningrad newspapers. On 24 December 1925 he published an article "When will Tsankov fall?"—hailed as prophetic of Tsankov's actual fall in January 1926. Based on Dimitrov's articles in *Leningradskaia Pravda,* and *Leningradskaia Gazeta;* 23 notes. 1925-26

1778. Cherniavski, G. I. NOVYE MATERIALY I ISSLEDOVANIIA O ZHIZNI I DEIATEL'NOSTI GEORGIIA DIMITROVA [New material and research on the life and activity of Georgi Dimitrov]. *Voprosy Istorii [USSR] 1983 (12): 155-162.* In recent years, historians of the Communist countries have undertaken a great deal of research on the life and revolutionary activity of Dimitrov and his contribution to the Bulgarian and international movement of the proletariat. A number of previously unknown documents and letters have been published and the main writings on the Bulgarian Communist published between 1981 and 1983 in Bulgaria, the USSR, East Germany, and Czechoslovakia are listed. Secondary sources; 55 notes. 1910's-49

1779. Čierny, Ján. JURAJ DIMITROV A KOMUNISTICKÁ STRANA ČESKOSLOVENSKA [Georgi Dimitrov and the Communist Party of Czechoslovakia]. *Hist. Časopis [Czechoslovakia] 1982 30(3): 369-376.* On the 100th anniversary of Dimitrov's birth, evaluates his connection with Czech Communists. In 1925 Dimitrov lived in exile in Prague. During the Reichstag fire trial in Leipzig in 1933, he became a hero of the international workers' movement. In Moscow during World War II, Dimitrov was able to help with some problems dealing with the future of Communists in liberated Czechoslovakia. His advice on the equality of Czech and Slovak populations later became law. 1882-1949

1780. Damianova, Echka. NAUCHNO SUBRANIE ZA DEINOSTTA NA GEORGI DIMITROV NA BALKANITE [An educational conference on the activities of Georgi Dimitrov in the Balkans]. *Istoricheski Pregled [Bulgaria] 1982 38(4): 153-156.* The Bulgarian Institute of Balkan Studies "Ludmila Zhivkova" held a conference on Georgi Dimitrov and the Balkan peoples 31 May 1982. The aim was to acquaint the participants with the latest studies on Dimitrov's works and life, especially his antifascist struggle. Professor Iordok Iotov, the editor of *Rabotnichesko delo,* described Dimitrov's work as head of the Balkan Communist Federation. All the speakers emphasized that Dimitrov first saw the danger of fascism, and formed a truly Leninist united front to counter it. 1925-45

1781. Dimov, Nencho. GEORGII DIMITROV I EVROPEISKOE KREST'IANSKOE DVIZHENIE (1923-1936) [Georgi Dimitrov and European peasant movements, 1923-36]. *Etudes Balkaniques [Bulgaria] 1982 18(3): 3-22.* Bulgarian Communist Georgi Dimitrov played a key role in the development of the international peasant movement from 1923 to 1936. Working through the Balkan Communist Federation and the Red Peasant International (Krestintern), he tried to unite peasants and the working class in their revolutionary struggle against capitalism and fascism. Based on the published works; 72 notes. 1923-36

1782. Dobrinov, Decho. GEORGI DIMITROV I VUTRESHNATA MAKEDONSKA REVOLIUTSIONNA ORGANIZATSIIA (OBEDINENA) (1925-1936 G.) [Georgi Dimitrov and the Internal Macedonian Revolutionary Organization (Unified), 1925-36]. *Istoricheski Pregled [Bulgaria] 1982 38(2): 89-97.* The Internal Macedonian Revolutionary Organization (Unified) was founded by decree of the Central Committee of the Bulgarian Communist Party in 1925. Georgi Dimitrov supported it although convinced that it could not proceed to true revolutionary activity. He saw it rather as a place to gather various factions, as both federalists and separatists. Dimitrov was able to preserve the organization's national liberation, Leninist character. Stalin disbanded it in 1936. Based on Bulgarian Communist Party Central Archives; 62 notes. 1925-36

1783. Dykhan, M. D. and Sokhan, P. S. H. DYMYTROV I BOLHARS'KA POLITYCHNA EMIHRATSIIA V ODESI: 1923-29 [G. Dimitrov and Bulgarian political emigres in Odessa, 1923-29]. *Ukrains'kyi Istorychnyi Zhurnal [USSR] 1983 (6): 51-57.* During his long stay in the USSR as a political emigre and later as a Soviet citizen, Georgi Dimitrov established close links with the Ukraine out of internationalist considerations and, secondly, because a large number of Bulgarian emigres lived in Odessa. He visited the city frequently to cool down political differences between various groups and to render his advice on the correct attitude toward the international Communist movement. USSR and UkrSSR State October Revolution Archives, Central Party Archives of the Bulgarian CP, and secondary sources; 31 notes. 1923-29

1784. Firsov, F. I. GEORGII DIMITROV—VYDAIUSHCHIISIA REVOLIUTSIONER-LENINETS [Georgi Dimitrov, outstanding Leninist and revolutionary]. *Novaia i Noveishaia Istoriia [USSR] 1982 (1): 75-92.* The Bulgarian Georgi Dimitrov (1882-1949), General Secretary of the Executive Committee of the Comintern in the 1930's, was born of working-class parents and became a Party activist at an early age and a leading figure in the revolutionary trade union movement in Bulgaria. In 1909 he was elected to the Party Central Committee. After the fascist coup of 1923 Dimitrov helped to organize an armed uprising, and after its failure fled the country, going to Moscow in 1924. 81 notes. Article to be continued. 1900-24

1785. Firsov, F. I. GEORGII DIMITROV—VYDAIUSHCHIISIA REVOLIUTSIONER-LENINETS [Georgi Dimitrov, an outstanding revolutionary Leninist]. *Novaia i Noveishaia Istoriia [USSR] 1982 (3): 73-91.* Describes three periods in Dimitrov's life as Comintern chief in the 1930's, in the Soviet Union during World War II, and as postwar leader of Bulgaria. 2 photos, 100 notes. 1934-49

1786. Gabrielian, Egnara G. GEORGI DIMITROV I RAZVITIETO NA SIALSKOSTOPANSKATA NAUKA V BULGARIIA [Georgi Dimitrov and the development of agricultural science in Bulgaria]. *Istoricheski Pregled [Bulgaria] 1982 38(2): 77-83.* Georgi Dimitrov had a positive attitude toward science, and early saw its potential in the cause of agriculture, whose importance he emphasized from 1945. His 1947 speech to the National Council was a landmark in scientific policy. Institutes of cattle breeding, soil science, and veterinary biology were opened in 1947, 1948, and 1950 respectively, with continuing cooperation from the USSR. In 1954 there were 5,035 specialist agricultural students in Bulgaria as against 1,246 in 1944. Based on Bulgarian agricultural and educational statistics; 34 notes. 1944-54

1787. Grishina, R. P. G. DIMITROV I LEIPTSIGSKII PROTSESS V MATERIALAKH NOVOI PUBLIKATSII DOKUMENTOV [G. Dimitrov and the Leipzig trial in the materials of newly published documents]. *Sovetskoe Slavianovedenie [USSR] 1982 (3): 97-102.* Georgi Dimitrov's role is clearly illustrated in new documents published in the USSR, East Germany, and Bulgaria under the title *The Reichstag Fire Trial and Georgi Dimitrov. Documents in 3 Volumes.* The situation after Hitler's 30 January 1933 power seizure, anti-Communist measures, and Hitler's use of the fire as a pretext for destroying actual and potential opposition are discussed. Dimitrov was a firm man, devoted to family, friends, comrades, and the revolutionary cause. 1933

1788. Grishina, R. P. GEORGII DIMITROV I BOR'BA KOMMUNISTOV ZA MIR, PROTIV VOINY I VOENNOI OPASNOSTI [Georgi Dimitrov and the Communists' struggle for peace and against war and the danger of war]. *Voprosy Istorii [USSR] 1982 (7): 43-54.* Discusses Dimitrov's activities in the Bulgarian antiwar movement, which unfolded under the impact of the Great October Socialist Revolution of 1917, and his antiwar activity in the Comintern. Pays particular attention to Dimitrov's role in the preparation of the Amsterdam antiwar congress held in 1932, in the elaboration by the 7th Comintern Congress of a new approach to the organization of the massive antiwar movement, and also to Dimitrov's antiwar activity aimed at undermining plans of fascist war-mongers. 1917-32

1789. Hegemann, Margot. ARMEE UND REVOLUTION IN BULGARIEN. ZUM 100. GEBURTSTAG GEORGI DIMITROFFS [Army and revolution in Bulgaria: on the 100th birthday of Georgi Dimitrov]. *Militärgeschichte [East Germany] 1982 21(2): 150-160.* Discusses the ideological and politically practical contribution of Georgi Dimitrov (1882-1949) to the organizing and leading of the military antifascist struggle of the masses of the Bulgarian people in 1923 and during World War II. Dimitrov used his military-political experience for the construction of the socialist Bulgarian People's Army and for the defense of socialism in Bulgaria. 5 illus.; 58 notes. 1923-49

1790. Isusov, Mito. GEORGI DIMITROV I POLITICHESKATA SISTEMA NA NARODNATA DEMOKRATSIIA V BULGARIIA [Georgi Dimitrov and the political system of people's democracy in Bulgaria]. *Istoricheski Pregled [Bulgaria] 1982 38(2): 27-58.* Georgi Dimitrov said that Soviet power and people's democracy, as seen in Bulgaria, were two forms of proletarian dictatorship, leading from capitalism to socialism. Each nation chooses the form appropriate to its historical experiences. Dimitrov argued that socialism cannot be created without a period of transitional proletarian dictatorship. People's democracy, the antithesis of monarcho-fascism, is not to be compared with bourgeois democracy. It is the unique union of the working class and other social forces and of the Communist Party and other political parties. Based on Dimitrov's speeches, and Party Archives in Bulgaria; 120 notes. 1945-49

1791. Kalbe, Ernstgert. HERVORRAGENDER LENINIST, REVOLUTIONÄR UND INTERNATIONALIST. GEORGI DIMITROFF [An outstanding Leninist, revolutionary and internationalist: Georgi Dimitrov]. *Beiträge zur Gesch. der Arbeiterbewegung [East Germany] 1982 24(3): 406-416.* Traces the life, career, and political activities of the Bulgarian Communist leader Georgi Dimitrov (1882-1949), his political activities in the 1890's and his involvement in the Bulgarian revolutionary movement in 1912. His meeting with V. I. Lenin in 1921 helped establish Dimitrov as a leading personality in the revolutionary working-class movement. He was instrumental in establishing the united antifascist front in 1923 and played an important part in the September 1923 uprising in Bulgaria and in the 1944 revolution, as well as establishing the People's Republic of Bulgaria in 1946. Secondary sources; 27 notes. 1882-1949

1792. Khadzhinikolov, Veselin. VELIK I CHOVECHEN CHERTI OT KHARAKTERA NA GEORGI DIMITROV [Great and humane character of Georgi Dimitrov]. *Istoricheski Pregled [Bulgaria] 1982 38(2): 3-26.* Reviews the life, accomplishments, and character of Georgi Dimitrov, a great Marxist-Leninist and a resolute antifascist. 1918-49

1793. Klejn, Zbigniew. W STULECIE URODZIN GEORGI DYMITROWA (1882-1949): IDEE PRZETWORZONE W CZYN [The centenary of the birth of Georgi Dimitrov (1882-1949): ideas transformed into action]. *Nowe Drogi [Poland] 1982 (6): 83-95.* Georgi Dimitrov, active in the Comintern and chairman of the Communist Party of Bulgaria, contributed to the solution of many problems posed by the theory and practice of socialism. ca 1900-49

1794. Kumanov, Milen. K VOPROSU O PUBLITSISTICHESKOM NASLEDII G. DIMITROVA I V. KOLAROVA [On the journalistic heritage of Georgi Dimitrov and Vasil Kolarov]. *Bulgarian Hist. Rev. [Bulgaria] 1981 9(3): 88-101.* Following the failure of the uprising of September 1923 the Bulgarian Communist leaders Georgi Dimitrov (1882-1949) and Vasil Kolarov fled to the USSR, where the Comintern conducted a thorough examination of the tactics and strategy which had led to the abortive rising. Dimitrov and Kolarov entered fully into the discussion through newspaper articles, speeches, and interviews. They also conducted a public campaign of agitation against the White Terror waged by the Bulgarian fascist regime in the aftermath of the rising. 1923-26

1795. Lewin, Erwin. BRIEFE DER FREUNDSCHAFT: WILHELM PIECK AN GEORGI DIMITROFF [Letters of friendship: Wilhelm Pieck to Georgi Dimitrov]. *Beiträge zur Gesch. der Arbeiterbewegung [East Germany] 1982 24(3): 370-376.* Reproduces a selection of letters written by the German Socialist Wilhelm Pieck to the Bulgarian Communist leader Georgi Dimitrov (1882-1949), 1945-48. These letters reveal Pieck's deep admiration and friendship for Dimitrov and provide an insight into the cooperation between the German and Bulgarian Communists. Based on Wilhelm Pieck's letters in the Institute for Marxism-Leninism, Berlin and secondary sources; 14 notes. 1945-48

1796. L'vunin, Iu. A. GEORGII DIMITROV V SSSR (20-E GODY) [Georgi Dimitrov in the USSR in the 1920's]. *Voprosy Istorii [USSR] 1982 (6): 180-184.* Georgi Mikhailovich Dimitrov was the leader of the revolutionary trade unions in Bulgaria. He played a major role in the Bulgarian uprising of 1923 and was subsequently elected an honorary member of the Moscow and Leningrad Soviets. He became special correspondent for the magazine *Gudok* and published works on Communism and Leninism. He attended many congresses in the USSR and worked on the executive and various other committees of the Comintern until he left in 1927 to work with the Bulgarian Communist Party in Vienna. Based on archives, personal reminiscences, and other sources; 31 notes. 1921-27

1797. L'vunin, Iu. A. G. DIMITROV V BOR'BE ZA SPLOCHENIE MASS PROTIV FASHIZMA I OPASNOSTI VOINY, ZA NASUSHCHNYE INTERESY TRUDIASHCHIKHSIA, 1929-1933 [Georgi Dimitrov in the struggle for rallying the masses against fascism and the danger of war, for the vital interests of workers, 1929-33]. *Vestnik Moskovskogo U., Seriia 8: Istoriia [USSR] 1982 (3): 3-20.* Dimitrov, leader of the Western European bureau of the Comintern from April 1929, tried to get international support for strikers in the Balkans. He erred in exaggerating the imminence of revolution and in seeing an identity between social fascism and opportunism. But he became convinced that the left position in German Communism was wrong and that the Communist movement erred. By 1931 he raised the question of a union of antifascist forces and in October 1932 called for a united front against fascism. Still, Hitler's victory was the result of the division of the working class because of the right-wing Socialist policy of cooperation with the bourgeoisie. Based on materials in the Central Party Archives, Institute of Marx-Lenin; 47 notes. 1929-34

1798. Mateev, Boris. GEORGI DIMITROV AND THE SOCIALIST RECONSTRUCTION OF AGRICULTURE IN BULGARIA. *Etudes Balkaniques [Bulgaria] 1982 18(3): 23-42.* Outlines the views of Georgi Dimitrov on the socialist reconstruction of agriculture in Bulgaria after the establishment in 1944 of people's democratic rule. He recommended an improvement in the cooperative system and the collectivization of agriculture simultaneous with socialist industrialization. These were accomplished through the cooperation of the Bulgarian Communist Party with the Bulgarian Agrarian People's Union during the 1940's and the 1950's. But Dimitrov's plans became fully realized in the 1970's with the establishment of agro-industrial complexes and the advent of an equal prosperity of urban and rural areas. 82 notes. 1945-79

1799. Mičev, Dobrin. GEORGI DIMITROV UND DIE INTERNATIONALE KOMMUNISTISCHE BEWEGUNG [Georgi Dimitrov and the international Communist movement]. *Bulgarian Historical Review [Bulgaria] 1982 10(2): 3-20.* Traces the life and career of the Bulgarian Communist leader Georgi Dimitrov (1882-1949) on the occasion of the centenary of his birth. The author examines his work and organizational activities for the Communist Party and trade union movement in Bulgaria, 1909-20, and emphasizes the development of his ideas and activities with the international communist movement, 1919-40's. During the 1920's and 1930's he paid many visits to Moscow where he met Lenin and travelled extensively throughout Europe where he undertook a great deal of work for the Communist International. Between 1932 and 1945 he helped to organize antifascist resistance in Europe and became famous for his alleged involvement in the burning of the Reichstag in Berlin in 1933, for which he was brought to trial and imprisoned by Hitler. The author also discusses Dimitrov's theories concerning the strategy and tactics of the international Communist movement. Secondary sources; biblio. 1882-1949

1800. Michev, Dobrin. GEORGI DIMITROV I BORBATA NA GERMANSKATA KOMUNISTICHESKA PARTIIA ZA SMUKVANE NA KHITLERISTSKATA DIKTATURA (1941-1945) [Georgi Dimitrov and the struggle of the German Communist Party to remove Hitler's dictatorship, 1941-45]. *Istoricheski Pregled [Bulgaria] 1982 38(2): 59-76.* After Germany's attack on the USSR, Georgi Dimitrov, together with Walter Ulbricht, organized resistance to Hitler, especially radio broadcasts. In 1945 Dimitrov helped the German Communists to organize an antifascist front and to eliminate fascist elements from German life and advised on the setting up of new trade unions and youth organizations. Based on Dimitrov's works, and on records of the German Socialist Unity Party; 112 notes. 1941-45

1801. Minchev, D. VIDNYI DEIATEL' BOLGARSKOGO I MEZHDUNARODNOGO KOMMUNISTICHESKOGO DVIZHENIIA (K 100-LETIIU SO DNIA ROZHDENIIA G. M. DIMITROVA) [A prominent member of the Bulgarian and international Communist movement: on the 100th anniversary of the birth of Georgi Dimitrov]. *Voenno-Istoricheskii Zhurnal [USSR] 1982 (6): 94-96.* Georgi M. Dimitrov was born in 1882 in the Bulgarian village of Kovachevitsy. He joined the Social Democratic Party (later renamed the Communist Party) in 1902, and two years later became a member of its central committee. After his acquittal in the Reichstag trial, he moved to the USSR, where he conducted agitational work during World War II. In 1945 he returned to Bulgaria, and in 1948, the year before his death, became the general secretary of the Bulgarian Communist Party. Secondary sources; note. 1882-1949

1802. Minei, Nicolae. PROCURORUL DIN BOXA ACUZAŢILOR [The prosecutor from the dock]. *Magazin Istoric [Romania] 1982 16(9): 19-24.* The centenary of Georgi Dimitrov's birth serves as occasion for an account of the Reichstag fire, February 1933, and the subsequent Leipzig trial. 1933

1803. Németh, István and Skáfár, Pál. TUDOMÁNYOS ÜLÉS GEORGI DIMITROV SZÜLETÉSÉNEK 100. ÉVFORDULÓJÁN [Scientific session on the 100th anniversary of Georgi Dimitrov's birth]. *Párttörténeti Közlemények [Hungary] 1982 28(3): 200-211.* The seven speakers expressed their appreciation of Georgi Dimitrov, who as a Comintern officer specialized in problems of Central and Eastern Europe and the Balkans. He was very active as a theorist and also participated in several revolutionary actions. 1982

1804. Panov, B. ZHIZN', OTDANNAIA BOR'BE (K 100-LETIIU SO DNIA ROZHDENIIA GEORGIIA DIMITROVA) [A life devoted to struggle: on the 100th anniversary of Georgi Dimitrov's birth]. *Mirovaia Ekonomika i Mezhdunarodnye Otnosheniia [USSR] 1982 (6): 12-22.* Georgi Dimitrov fought against fascism and war, devoted his life to defending the interests of all working people, and, proceeding from the historical experience of the Russian Revolution as well as the class struggle in Bulgaria and other countries, made an invaluable theoretical contribution to the elaboration of the political orientation of the international Communist and working-class movement. 1903-48

1805. Petrova, Dimitrina. GEORGI DIMITROV ZA EDINODEISTVIETO MEZHDU BKP I BZNS (1923-1944 G.) [Georgi Dimitrov on the joint action of the Bulgarian Communist Party and the Bulgarian Agrarian Popular Union, 1923-44]. *Izvestiia na Inst. po Istoriia na BKP [Bulgaria] 1982 46: 59-100.* Georgi Dimitrov strove to apply Leninist principles and strategy by attracting the Bulgarian Agrarian Popular Union as an ally against fascism in Bulgaria during the period 1923-44. 1923-44

1806. Petrushor, Vasile. ASPEKTI NA REVOLIUTSIONNATA DEINOST NA GEORGI DIMITROV, OTRAZENI V RUMUNSKATA ISTORIOGRAFIIA [Some aspects of Georgi Dimitrov's revolutionary activity as reflected in the historiography of Romania]. *Izvestiia na Inst. po Istoriia na BKP [Bulgaria] 1982 46: 304-316.* Lists articles and books published in Romania dealing with Georgi Dimitrov's activities, his personal contacts and visits to Romania, and his personal contribution to the development of durable Romanian-Bulgarian cooperation in the struggle for socialism. 1920's-82

1807. Rusakov, K. V. K 100-LETIIU SO DNIA ROZHDENIIA GEORGIIA DIMITROVA: VYDAIUSHCHIISIA BORETS ZA MIR I SOTSIALIZM [The 100th anniversary of the birth of Georgi Dimitrov: an outstanding fighter for peace and socialism]. *Voprosy Istorii KPSS [USSR] 1982 (7): 20-32.* Georgi Dimitrov (1882-1949) joined the Bulgarian Marxist party in 1902 and in 1909 became a member of the central committee of the Bulgarian Social Democratic Party. He rose to be general secretary of the Comintern by 1935. His conviction, organizational skill, and determination were put to the twin aims of achieving social change in Bulgaria and friendship with the USSR. He is renowned for his analysis of fascism, his demonstration of the link between proletarian internationalism and genuine patriotism, his stress on the importance of the USSR to the working people of the world, and his recognition of the anti-Soviet nature of Chinese politics. Based on speeches and secondary sources; 25 notes. 1900-49

1808. Savov, Nikolai. PRED STOGODISHNIIA IUBILEI NA GEORGI DIMITROV [In preparation for the hundredth anniversary of Georgi Dimitrov]. *Istoricheski Pregled [Bulgaria] 1982 38(2): 133-136.* Chronicles Dimitrov's revolutionary activity, his antifascist and propeace struggle, and his attacks on deviationist and bourgeois ideology. Cites academic and public celebrations of the centenary, including the National Museum of Georgi Dimitrov's republication of much of his work. 1918-49

1809. Sheptunov, Igor. ZA RABOTATA NA GEORGI DIMITROV NAD KNIGATA [On the literary work of Georgi Dimitrov]. *Istoricheski Pregled [Bulgaria] 1982 38(2): 106-112.* Georgi Dimitrov, a bibliophile, had an abiding interest in revolution and its theory and tactics. He wrote constantly, even during his imprisonment after the 1933 Leipzig trial. In 1944, while awaiting the overthrow of monarcho-fascism, he wrote on Bulgarian history, especially on religion and the Bulgarian Renaissance. His principle themes were religion in old Bulgaria, the French Revolution, Bulgarian national movements, and fascism. Based on Central Archives of the Bulgarian Communist Party and the works of Georgi Dimitrov; 22 notes. 1918-49

1810. Shevchenko, O. V. HEORHII DYMYTROV PRO KULTURNU REVOLIUTSIIU V NRB [Georgi Dimitrov on the cultural revolution in Bulgaria]. *Ukrains'kyi Istorychnyi Zhurnal [USSR] 1982 (6): 49-55.* Adhering to Lenin's precept that in every class-structured society there are two cultures, one to serve the rulers and the other the governed, Dimitrov constantly drummed into his countrymen that to bring an end to this anomaly was possible only through the joint effort of workers, peasants, and intellectuals in raising the cultural level of the working classes and educating them in a socialist spirit. 1944-48

1811. Shirinia, K. K. VYDAIUSHCHIISIA DEIATEL' MEZHDUNARODNOGO KOMMUNISTICHESKOGO DVIZHENIIA [A prominent figure in the international Communist movement]. *Voprosy Istorii KPSS [USSR] 1982 (6): 43-55.* Commemorates the centenary of the birth of the Bulgarian Communist leader Georgi Dimitrov (1882-1949). Particularly notes his role in placing the Bulgarian Social Democratic movement on the Leninist path, his leading role in the antifascist struggle between the wars, symbolized by his triumphant defense at the Reichstag Trial (1934), his contribution at the Comintern to the development of the strategy of the Popular Front, his role in leading Bulgarian resistance to fascism during World War II, and his ceaseless emphasis on the strengthening of the revolutionary party of the working class and on the role of the USSR within the international workers' movement. 1882-1949

1812. Sokhan, P. S. HEORHII DYMYTROV PRO MIZHNARODNE ZNACHENNIA LENINIZMU I DOSVIDU SOTSIALISTYCHNOHO BUDIVNYTSTVA V SRSR [Georgi Dimitrov on the international significance of Leninism and on the experience of socialist construction in the USSR]. *Ukrains'kyi Istorychnyi Zhurnal [USSR] 1982 (6): 39-48.* Almost from his initial revolutionary and trade union activities Dimitrov was governed in all organizational work by the directives formulated by Lenin. His brilliant knowledge of Lenin's heritage was especially vividly shown during the trial in Leipzig in 1934 when he, a defendant, acted as an accuser of Hitler and Nazism. A strict disciple of Leninism, he frequently added new and highly relevant elements to Communist tactics, especially after becoming chairman of the Comintern. His formulation of proletarian internationalism as "favoring the USSR and CPSU everywhere and at all times" still serves as a means to separate the friend from the foe. 1902-48

1813. Szokolay, Katalin. GEORGI DIMITROV ÉS A HÁBORÚ ELLENI HARC [Georgi Dimitrov and the struggle against war]. *Párttörténeti Közlemények [Hungary] 1982 28(2): 121-144.* Examines Dimitrov's work on the relationship of the working class and war. All imperialist wars can and should be avoided by the working masses. National wars, in which a nation fights for its right to exist, should be supported by labor and Communist organizations, even if the same war is endorsed by imperialist countries. However, advocating a defensive war should not include ideological solidarity with the bourgeois ruling class of that nation. 48 notes. 1920-36

1814. Vasilev, Liuben. GEORGI DIMITROV ZA POLOZHENIETO NA RABORNICHESKATA KLASA V BULGARIIA PRI KAPITALIZMA [Georgi Dimitrov on the condition of the working class in Bulgaria under capitalism]. *Izvestiia na Inst. po Istoriia na BKP [Bulgaria] 1982 46: 13-54.* Surveys Dimitrov's assessments on the Bulgarian working class from the beginning of the 20th century to his departure from the country in 1923. 1900-23

1815. Volokitina, T. GEORGII DIMITROV I NEKOTORYE VOPROSY RAZVITIIA OTECHESTVENNOGO FRONTA BOLGARII (1944-1948) [Georgi Dimitrov and the development of the Patriotic Front in Bulgaria, 1944-48]. *Sovetskoe Slavianovedenie [USSR] 1982 (4): 14-21.* The Patriotic Front, founded by Dimitrov in 1942, had behind it years of struggle to all the social classes and the military. Dimitrov, combining theory and practice in the fight against war, fascism, and internal tyranny, achieved success in September 1944, when his party took over the government. Dimitrov returned to Bulgaria in 1945 after 22 years in exile; elections were held in 1946, and by 1948 fusion of the various groups into one party was complete. Based on Bulgarian archival and secondary sources; 5 notes. 1942-48

1816. —. DOKUMENTY GEORGIIA DIMITROVA [Documents of Georgi Dimitrov]. *Voprosy Istorii KPSS [USSR] 1982 (6): 56-62.* Five statements by the Bulgarian Communist leader Georgi Dimitrov (1882-1949): an article on V. I. Lenin from *Bulletin der Balkankonföderation,* 1924; a speech to the graduates of the Lenin School, 1936; a comment on the Czech question at the Executive Committee of the Comintern, 1936; a letter to the Central Committee of the Bulgarian Communist Party, 1941; and a statement at the Executive Committee of the Comintern on the subject of the Nazi attack on the USSR in 1941. Notes. 1924-41

Dinesen, Isak

1817. Pelensky, Olga Anastasia. "Isak Dinesen: A Biographical Study of Her Artistic Imagination." Tufts U. 1983. 215 pp. *DAI 1983 44(3): 762-A.* DA8316860 20c

Dinev, Angel

1818. Kartov, Vladimir. MAKEDONSKATA PATRIOTSKA DEJNOST NA ANGEL DINEV VO INTERNACIJA I KONCENTRACIONITE LOGORI NA FASHISTICHKA BUGARIJA (1940-1944) [Angel Dinev's patriotic activity in internment in concentration camps in fascist Bulgaria, 1940-44]. *Istorija [Yugoslavia] 1981 17(2): 53-73.* Examines the activities of Angel Dinev (1891-1952), a prominent Macedonian revolutionary and journalist, during his internment in concentration camps in Bulgaria, 1940-44. His political and propaganda work helped to popularize the Macedonian revolutionary movement and its struggle for the recognition of the Macedonian national identity. 1940-44

Ding Ling

1819. Bertuccioli, Giuliano. DING LING: UNA SCRITTRICE RIVOLUZIONARIA [Ding Ling: a revolutionary writer]. *Mondo Cinese [Italy] 1985 13(1): 3-17.* Describes the career of the Chinese author Ding Ling, who abandoned bourgeois topics to write about Communist subjects in her fiction, but whose cultural background still led to her fall from favor under Mao. She has subsequently been "rehabilitated" and her works are again recognized for their revolutionary worth. 1920's-85

1820. Ding Ling; Terrinoni, Paoli, interviewer. INTERVISTA A DING LING [Interview with Ding Ling]. *Mondo Cinese [Italy] 1985 13(1): 18-27.* Chinese author Ding Ling describes aspects of her life and career. 1920's-84

1821. Feuerwerker, Yi-tsi Mei. IN QUEST OF THE WRITER DING LING. *Feminist Studies 1984 10(1): 65-83.* Recounts the political and literary life of the Chinese writer Ding Ling. She was born Jiang Bingzhi in the Hunan province in 1904. Acclaimed as a literary dissident who courageously stood for artistic independence in opposition to Party control, a closer interpretation by one who traveled with her shows her abiding commitment to China's revolution in spite of the hardships she endured because of political and ideological disfavor. Abridged from "In Quest of the Writer Ding Ling (In Quest of Myself)" in *Between Women: Biographers, Novelists, Critics, Teachers, and Artists...*; illus., photo, biblio. 1904-81

Dion, Roger

1822. Broc, Numa. ROGER DION (1896-1981) [Roger Dion, 1896-1981]. *Ann. de Géog. [France] 1982 91(504): 205-217.* Obituary of French geographer Roger Dion; includes a summary and appreciation of two major works by him: *Le Val de Loire* (1933) and *Histoire de la Vigne et du Vin en France des Origines au XIX*[e] *Siècle* (1959). 1896-1981

Dirac, Paul

1823. Kragh, Helge. COSMO-PHYSICS IN THE THIRTIES: TOWARDS A HISTORY OF THE DIRAC COSMOLOGY. *Hist. Studies in the Physical Sci. 1982 13(1): 69-108.* Maintains that Paul Dirac's (b. 1902) contributions to speculative cosmology, based on his large number hypothesis, rely heavily on quantum theory and not the astronomical-cosmological tradition. Edward Arthur Milne (1896-1950) and Arthur Stanley Eddington (1882-1944), the leading cosmophysicists of the 1930's, were important influences on Dirac's work. 113 notes. 1930-38

Disraeli, Benjamin

1824. Vincent, John. WAS DISRAELI A FAILURE? *Hist. Today [Great Britain] 1981 31(Oct): 5-8.* Presents examples of the political failures of Conservative Party leader Benjamin Disraeli, who became famous posthumously for lack of anyone else to glorify. 1830's-80's

Ditmar, A. B.

1825. —. A. B. DITMARU—70 LET [A. B. Ditmar is 70]. *Voprosy Istorii Estestvoznaniia i Tekhniki [USSR] 1981 (4): 152.* A brief biography of Ditmar, historian of geography and honorary member of the USSR Geographic Society. 1941-78

Djilas, Milovan

1826. Dedijer, Vladimir. [DJILAS]. *Cross Currents 1985 4: 387-452.*

MY TWO COMRADES, *pp. 387-438.* An account of 20 years of friendship with Milovan Djilas, culminating in Dedijer's defense of Djilas before the Yugoslavian Central Committee. The manuscript was written in 1957 and given to Eleanor Roosevelt for safekeeping.

AN EXCHANGE OF LETTERS, *pp. 439-452.* Letters exchanged between 1960 and 1967 between Milovan Djilas and Vladimir Dedijer. 1936-67

1827. Muravchik, Joshua. THE INTELLECTUAL ODYSSEY OF MILOVAN DJILAS. *World Affairs 1983 145(4): 323-346.* Yugoslavian Communist Milovan Djilas broke consecutively with Stalin, Tito, Lenin, and ultimately with Marx, and ended up as an "existential humanist," who saw ideologies—closed systems of thought and action—as the problem, where man sought political answers to questions that were more spiritual than political; his heresy led to dismissal from his offices in the Yugoslav government and imprisonment. 1919-82

Długosz, Jan

1828. Knoll, Paul W. JAN DŁUGOSZ, 1480-1980. *Polish Rev. 1982 27(1-2): 3-28.* A biographical sketch of the Polish priest Jan Długosz (1415-80), who is today regarded as one of the most important individuals in the history of Polish culture. Three elements justify his reputation: his diplomatic missions for the Polish Church and king; his patronage of the University of Cracow; and his work as a historian. His major work, the *Annales seu Cronicae Incliti Regni Poloniae,* represents a growing Polish national consciousness. His writings reveal Długosz as a protohumanist on the boundary between medieval tradition and a new era. A revised and expanded version of presentations made to the History Department Colloquium and the Polish Studies Association of the University of Southern California in November 1980 and March 1981. Published primary sources and secondary works; 86 notes. 1415-80

Dmitriev, S. S.

1829. Koval'chenko, I. D. and Tartakovskii, A. G. K 75-LETIIU S. S. DMITRIEVA [S. S. Dmitriev's 75th birthday]. *Istoriia SSSR [USSR] 1981 (4): 208-213.* A brief review of the life and work of Sergei Sergeevich Dmitriev (b. 1906), a renowned historian from Moscow University. His field of interest embraces Russian intellectual history and peasant crafts, journalism and source studies. His work covers the 18th and 19th centuries. Based on published works; 9 notes. 1981

Dobi, István

1830. Dancs, József. DOBI ISTVÁN [István Dobi]. *Társadalmi Szemle [Hungary] 1983 38(3): 80-88.* His farmer background helped Dobi to represent the oppressed agricultural laborer throughout his career. He was aligned with the Left and as president of the Smallholders Party always cooperated with the Communist Party in an effort to unify agricultural and factory workers. In 1948 he was appointed prime minister, a position at that time mostly symbolic. However, he stayed in politics to his death, always hoping to be able to help the country by looking after the interests of the peasant class. 1935-68

Dobiash-Rozhdestvenskaia, Ol'ga A.

1831. Kaganovich, B. S. O. A. DOBIASH-ROZHDESTVENSKAIA I EE NAUCHNOE NASLEDIE [O. A. Dobiash-Rozhdestvenskaia and her heritage]. *Frantsuzskii Ezhegodnik [USSR] 1982: 190-208.* Biography of the Russian historian Ol'ga Antonovna Dobiash-Rozhdestvenskaia (1874-1939), review of her published and unpublished studies, and discussion of the influence of Russian and French historians on her analysis of West European social and cultural history in the Middle Ages. Her reliance on original source material and ability to correlate data synthesized from diverse disciplines influenced, in turn, the development of Soviet historiography. Her eventual endorsement of a Marxist interpretation of history can be deduced from her statements in the late 1930's. 115 notes. French summary. 1900's-30's

Dobrogeanu-Gherea, Constantin

1832. Codreanu, Radu. CONSTANTIN DOBROGEANU-GHEREA ÎN FAMILIE ŞI CU PRIETENI [Constantin Dobrogeanu-Gherea with his family and friends]. *Magazin Istoric [Romania] 1981 15(1): 7-10.* Describes some of the family links and friendships of the Romanian politician Constantin Dobrogeanu-Gherea (1855-1920), with whom the author's family had close ties during the period 1906-16. 1906-16 -Gherea

1833. Ioniţă, Gh. I. C. DOBROGEANU-GHEREA—PROEMINENT GÎNDITOR SOCIALIST AL POPORULUI NOSTRU [C. Dobrogeanu-Gherea: a prominent socialist thinker of our people]. *Revista de Istorie [Romania] 1984 37(2): 185-189.* Discusses the works of Constantin Dobrogeanu-Gherea and his contribution to scientific analysis of economics, politics, and culture. Dobrogeanu-Gherea defined the socioeconomic and political situation in Romania, as well as the causes and necessity for the country's socialist transformation. 9 notes. 1883-1920 -Gherea

1834. Mamina, Ion. C. DOBROGEANU-GHEREA: 125 ANI DE LA NAŞTERE. UN PROEMINENT GÎNDITOR SOCIALIST [125th anniversary of the birth of Constantin Dobrogeanu-Gherea, a preeminent socialist thinker]. *Magazin Istoric [Romania] 1980 14(5): 55-57.* Surveys the political and economic writings of Constantin Dobrogeanu-Gherea (1855-1920) and evaluates his importance in Romanian politics. 1880's-1920

Dobrovolskas, Jonas

1835. Valikonyte, I. JONAS DOBROVOLSKAS [Jonas Dobrovolskas]. *Lietuvos Istorijos Metraštis [USSR] 1982: 159.* Obituary of Dobrovolskas (1935-82), who directed the department of Lithuanian history at the University of Vilnius from 1970 to 1976. He specialized in the history of World War II and of the Lithuanian SSR. 1935-82

Dobrowolski, Antoni Bolesław

1836. Michalski, Stanisław. ANTONIEGO BOLESŁAWA DOBROWOLSKIEGO ŻYCIE I DZIAŁALNOŚĆ NA TLE EPOKI [The life and work of Antoni Bolesław Dobrowolski against the background of his age]. *Kultura i Społeczeństwo [Poland] 1979 23(1-2): 3-33.* Antoni Dobrowolski, a prominent scholar in the natural sciences and the humanities, worked out a system of national education. Dobrowolski did not limit himself to the problems of his own specialty but had scientific and artistic interests as well as an immense optimism and faith in mankind. 1872-1954

Dobrowolski, Franciszek

1837. Kaminski, Ted M. FRANCISZEK DOBROWOLSKI (1830-1896), NEWSPAPERMAN AND POWER-BROKER IN PRUSSIAN POLAND. *Canadian Slavonic Papers [Canada] 1985 27(2): 140-157.* That the Poles survived the Germanization campaign of the Kulturkampf in Prussia's eastern provinces between 1886 and 1896 was a function of their total dedication to the preservation of their national consciousness against very imposing odds. One of the most influential leaders in this survival was the journalist and politician Franciszek Dobrowolski (1830-96), editor of the leading liberal and nationalist daily paper in Poznań, *Dziennik Poznański* for 25 years, secretary of the Central Electoral Committee of the Grand Duchy of Poznań, and chairman of the Poznań municipal Electoral Committee. A trusted servant of the landowner establishment, Dobrowolski was opposed by a populist secession party after 1888, which clouded his last years in politics. Primary materials from the Polish State Archives, Poznań, and secondary studies; 57 notes. 1885-96

Dobrowolski, Kazimierz

1838. Bieńkowski, Wiesław. SPOŁECZEŃSTWO I KULTURA W PROCESIE PRZEMIAN [The society and the culture in the process of change]. *Studia Historyczne [Poland] 1984 27(4): 695-697.* Presents the conference to celebrate the 90th birthday of the outstanding Polish sociologist and historian Professor Kazimierz Dobrowolski. After the short biography there is a list of papers given by Antonina Kłoskowska, Janusz Ziółkowski, Anna Kutrzeba-Pojnarowa, Hieronim Kubiak, Jerzy Józef Wiatr, Renata Siemieńska, Piotr Sztompka, and Jan Jerschina. 1920's-84

Dobson, William

1839. Money, Ernle. "THE ROYALISTS AT WAR": AN EXHIBITION OF THE WORK OF WILLIAM DOBSON AT THE NATIONAL PORTRAIT GALLERY, LONDON. *Contemporary Rev. [Great Britain] 1984 244(1416): 39-42.* Examines the life and work of the British portrait painter William Dobson (1610-46), who came to prominence as favorite painter of the Royal court during its brief sojourn at Oxford between 1642 and 1646 during the English Civil War. Reference is made to the National Portrait Gallery's exhibition of Dobson's work, which was open until early 1984. 1630-46

Dodd, William

1840. Barker, A. D. THE EARLY CAREER OF WILLIAM DODD. *Tr. of the Cambridge Biblio. Soc. [Great Britain] 1982 8(2): 217-235.* William Dodd, an English cleric and forger who was executed in 1777, had according to Samuel Johnson a "bad moral character." The author justifies Johnson's assessment by outlining the early life of Dodd. 98 notes. 1745-77

1841. Barker, A. D. SAMUEL JOHNSON AND THE CAMPAIGN TO SAVE WILLIAM DODD. *Harvard Lib. Bull. 1983 31(2): 147-180.* As much responsible as anyone for the popularizing of Shakespeare was William Dodd, a popular preacher and writer in the middle of the 18th century. He had written several widely-read poems and essays and had served as chaplain to George III. On 27 June 1777, Dodd was hanged after being convicted of criminal fraud, even though he had made restitution. Before the sentence was carried out an unsuccessful campaign was waged by a number of influential public men, including Samuel Johnson, seeking a pardon for Dodd. For several years after his death his fate was the subject of much public discussion. Quite likely the entire episode contributed to the eventual removal of capital punishment for conviction of theft and fraud. Based on primary sources and contemporary articles; 145 notes. 1752-91

Dodwell, George Benjamin

1842. Jones, Stephanie. GEORGE BENJAMIN DODWELL: A SHIPPING AGENT IN THE FAR EAST, 1872-1908. *Journal of Transport History [Great Britain] 1985 6(1): 23-40.* Notebooks kept by George Benjamin Dodwell (b. 1852) provide a detailed view of the activity of one of the most successful British shipping agents in the China-Japan trade. In his capacity as a middleman acting for owners or charterers of vessels, Dodwell was able to increase the profits of Adamson Bell & Co., to assist in the growth of the firm's Japanese trade, and to inaugurate steamship service between

Far Eastern ports and American and Canadian ports on the Pacific. After the demise of Adamson Bell in 1891, Dodwell's careful planning coupled with favorable political and economic events enabled his own firm Dodwell, Carlill & Co., to continue as a profitable and significant component of British maritime activity in the Far East. Based on Dodwell & Co., Ltd. documents and other primary sources; 4 tables, 38 notes. 1872-1908

Doeff, Hendrik

1843. Bossenbroek, M. EEN STRAATNAAM VOOR HENDRIK DOEFF [A street name for Hendrik Doeff]. *Spiegel Hist. [Netherlands] 1981 16(12): 646-652.* Hendrik Doeff (1777-1835), the "hero of Deshima," was instrumental in preserving the Dutch trading position in Japan while Holland was occupied by the armies of Revolutionary France. His diplomatic genius and fervent patriotism made him one of the most admired men of his time. His renown was subsequently diminished by unproven charges of corruption. Primary sources; 7 illus. 1799-1835

Dogel', Valentin A.

1844. Polianski, Iu. I. VALENTIN ALEKSANDROVICH DOGEL' (K STOLETIIU SO DNIA ROZHDENIIA) [Valentin A. Dogel': his 100th anniversary]. *Voprosy Istorii Estestvoznaniia i Tekhniki [USSR] 1982 (1): 72-78.* Examines the contributions of Soviet zoologist V. A. Dogel' in the areas of evolutionary morphology, histology, and parasitology. 1904-55

Dolci, Danilo

1845. Riggio, Eliana. FROM SICILY AND BACK: LOOKING FOR DANILO DOLCI. *Dissent 1985 32(3): 310-314.* In 1953 Danilo Dolci went to Sicily to battle the Mafia in his attempts to help the unemployed and illiterate through nonviolent civil disobedience; evaluated today, his success seems limited. 1953-85

Dombrovski, Aleksei V.

1846. Ianbulat, A. "SLUZHU TRUDOVOMU NARODU... " ["I serve the working people... "]. *Morskoi Sbornik [USSR] 1982 (1): 74-76.* Notes the 100th anniversary of the birth of Aleksei V. Dombrovski, a prominent lecturer in military naval sciences, who, during the October Revolution in Russia, joined the people's struggle for socialism and took part in many naval expeditions. 1904-52

Domínguez, Angel S.

1847. Domínguez, Luis Arturo. ANGEL S. DOMINGUEZ DE PERFIL Y DE FRENTE [Angel S. Domínguez in profile and full face]. *Bol. de la Acad. Nac. de la Hist. [Venezuela] 1981 64(254): 345-361.* Angel S. Domínguez (1895-1963) was a schoolteacher and poet. This is an article on his ancestry and career, his character, opinions, and final illness. 1895-1963

Domínguez Camargo, Hernando

1848. Perea Rodríguez, Jaime. HERNANDO DOMINGUEZ CAMARGO (1606-1659) [Hernando Domínguez Camargo, 1606-59]. *Boletín Cultural y Bibliográfico [Colombia] 1983 20(2): 89-106.* Recalls the adventurous life of the Colombian cleric Hernando Domínguez Camargo, one of the great Latin American poets and author of an unfinished epic poem on St. Ignatius of Loyola, excerpts of which are reproduced. 1606-59

Domínguez Ortiz, Antonio

1849. Cepeda Adán, José. EL PROFESOR ANTONIO DOMINGUEZ ORTIZ, DOCTOR HONORIS CAUSA [Professor Antonio Domínguez Ortiz, Doctor Honoris Causa]. *Cuadernos de Hist. Moderna y Contemporánea [Spain] 1980 1: 233-241.* Antonio Domínguez Ortiz (b. 1909) teaches at the University of Madrid and is a social historian. Among his works are: *La Sociedad Española en el Siglo XVII,* studies on housing, the decline of the village, internal colonization, slavery, the land problem, the converted Jews, and many other topics. 1909-80

1850. Domínguez Ortiz, Antonio; Bakewell, Peter, interviewer and transl. AN INTERVIEW WITH ANTONIO DOMÍNGUEZ ORTIZ. *Hispanic American Historical Review 1985 65(2): 189-202.* An interview with Spanish historian Antonio Domínguez Ortiz (b. 1909). Most of his teaching has been in secondary schools, and he advocates placing a greater importance on history in teaching. A graduate of the University of Seville, Domínguez Ortiz reminisces about some of his professors there, but he regards himself as a largely self-taught scholar. His primary interests are in the influence of Spanish America on the society and economy of Spain. He discusses the regional approach in history and the reciprocal influences of French and Spanish historians on each other. He comments on several of his books, and a select bibliography of his books is appended. Biblio. 1930's-85

Dominis, Marco Antonio de

1851. Bracewell, C. W. MARC'ANTONIO DE DOMINIS: THE MAKING OF A REFORMER. *Slovene Studies 1984 6(1-2): 165-176.* Bishop of the Catholic Church, Dalmatian Marc'Antonio de Dominis, sought unsuccessfully to reconcile the Church of England with Rome, and, eventually condemned by the Inquisition as a heretic for his inclusive ecumenism, he died in the custody of the Inquisition during his trial. His experiences with members of the Orthodox Eastern Church in Slovenia probably motivated his attack on the papacy and his desire for Christian unity. 1580's-1624

1852. Gamulin, Vesna. PRILOZI BIOGRAFIJI I DJELU MARKA ANTONIJA DE DOMINISA [Contributions to the biography and works of Marco Antonio de Dominis]. *Zbornik Zavoda za Povijesne Znanosti Istraživačkog Centra Jugoslavenske Akademije Znanosti i Umjetnosti [Yugoslavia] 1982 12: 41-48.* Marco Antonio de Dominis, the bishop of Split, quarreled with the Roman Catholic Church and its doctrine in about 1600 and went into exile in England from 1616 until 1622, when James I expelled him for suggesting union between the Roman Catholic Church and the Church of England. He returned to Rome and imprisonment until his death in 1624. Documents about and letters from de Dominis in the British Library and the Public Record Office in London are reproduced, illuminating aspects of de Dominis's life and theological activity during his highly productive exile in England. Based on documents in the British Library and Public Record Office in London; 28 notes. English summary. 1616-24

Domsaitis, Pranas

1853. Drunga, Mykolas. PRANAS DOMSAITIS: REDISCOVERED SCION OF EXPRESSIONISM. *Lituanus 1981 27(4): 23-29.* Briefly recounts the life of the Lithuanian expressionist painter Pranas Domsaitis (1880-1969). Important influences on his work were the German expressionists of the 1920's and 1930's and Lithuanian folk tradition. 5 illus. 1880-1969

Don, Johannes

1854. Vroom, Eppo. TER HERINNERING AAN JOHANNES DON, 21 MAART 1906-26 FEBRUARI 1982 [In memory of Johannes Don, 21 March 1906-26 February 1982]. *Nederlands Archievenblad [Netherlands] 1982 86(2-3): 173-175.* Obituary of Johannes Don, who was connected with the Kampen Municipal Archives since 1927 and their archivist 1946-71. 1906-82

Donald, Robert

1855. McEwen, J. M. LLOYD GEORGE'S ACQUISITION OF THE *DAILY CHRONICLE* IN 1918. *J. of British Studies 1983 22(1): 127-144.* The London *Daily Chronicle* was sold in October 1918—without precedent—by its private owner to agents of incumbent Prime Minister David Lloyd George. Robert Donald, the paper's editor dismissed after the takeover, had been critical of Lloyd George, had tried to arrange the paper's sale to Lloyd George's Liberal opponents, and may have sought an accommodation with Lord Beaverbrook. The latter, Lloyd George's information minister, wanted the *Chronicle* as part of a "newspaper empire" he was building. Although the actual takeover of the *Chronicle* surprised Donald, he was not the innocent victim sometimes depicted. Based on unpublished papers of Sir Robert Donald and Lord Beaverbrook; 47 notes. 1918

Donati, Giuseppe

1856. Bedeschi, Lorenzo. GIUSEPPE DONATI E LA POLIZIA FASCISTA [Giuseppe Donati and the Fascist police]. *Ponte [Italy] 1982 38(1-2): 97-108.* Giuseppe Donati (1889-1931) was director of *Il Popolo* (1923-25) and one of the leaders of the antifascist struggle. He was exiled in 1926 and died in destitution in Paris in 1931. Presents extracts from his letters to his wife which were intercepted by the fascist police, who also kept her under surveillance. 1925-31

1857. Vitale, Ignazio. L'ULTIMO ANNO DI DONATI IN ITALIA: DEL DELITTO MATTEOTTI ALLA DEPOSIZIONE CONTRO ITALO BALBO [Donati's last year in Italy: from the Matteotti murder to the deposition against Italo Balbo]. *Civitas [Italy] 1981 32(6): 5-28.* Reconstructs the essential events of Giuseppe Donati's last year in Italy, on the 50th anniversary of his death in exile (Paris, 1931), paying particular attention to the murder of Giacomo Matteotti (1924) and the polemics Donati printed in his newspaper *Il Popolo* against the Fascist regime. 1924-26

1858. Vitale, Ignazio. L'ULTIMO ANNO DI DONATI IN ITALIA [Donati's last year in Italy]. *Civitas [Italy] 1981 32(9): 5-27, 32(10): 35-53.* Part 2. LA DENUNCIA CONTRO DE BONO E I RAPPORTI CON I LIBERALI [The denunciation of De Bono and relations with the liberals]. Discusses the final attempt by Giuseppe Donati to forge a public and political alliance against Benito Mussolini, emphasizing his dealings with such liberal leaders as Giolitti and Gilardeni. Part 3. L'OPPOSIZIONE AL DISEGNO DI LEGGE ACERBO [The opposition to the projected Acerbo law]. Describes Donati's attitude toward the Acerbo bill, which introduced the Fascist electoral reform. He led a popular radical opposition against this law. 1923-24

Donche, Jacob

1859. Acker, K. G. van. JACOB DONCHE, RAADSHEER BIJ DE RAAD VAN VLAANDEREN, BALJUW VAN DENDERMONDE [Jacob Donche, councillor in the Council of Flanders, bailiff of Dendermonde]. *Handelingen der Maatschappij voor Geschiedenis en Oudheidkunde te Gent [Belgium] 1982 36: 91-102.* Records Jacob Donche's (1432-92) career and proves through contemporary manuscripts that the death date of 1473 had been assigned to him erroneously. Banned from Ghent 1451 for taking the side of Philip, Duke of Burgundy, Donche returned there in 1456 after the Duke's victory and, as his favorite, received several high positions in the Flanders Council until 1473. Although persecuted again by the people of Ghent in 1488, he remained loyal to the Burgundy dukes, acting as bailiff of Dendermonde, 1477-80 and 1485-86, where he was buried. Based on manuscript collections at Ghent and Yale universities; 67 notes. 1451-92

Doninelli, Aida

1860. Tribouillier de Schroeder, Pollyanna. AIDA DONINELLI: FROM GUATEMALA TO THE MET. *Américas (Organization of Am. States) 1982 34(4): 33-35.* Describes the career of Guatemalan soprano Aida Doninelli whose debut in the United States with the Metropolitan Opera Company in 1928 was only one of her many triumphs throughout the Americas. 20c

Dönitz, Karl

1861. Herzog, Bodo. DER KRIEGSVERBRECHER KARL DÖNITZ. LEGENDE UND WIRKLICHKEIT [The war criminal Karl Dönitz: legend and reality]. *Jahrbuch des Instituts für Deutsche Geschichte [Israel] 1986 15: 477-489.* Reviews Peter Padfield's *Dönitz—The Last Führer,* noting several omissions. Dönitz fully identified himself with the Nazis and regarded his encounter with Hitler as a memorable experience. He was not just an obedient soldier but also a brutal man. Despite the legend that Dönitz distanced his marines from the regime and knew nothing about the concentration camps, Dönitz hired inmates of the camps as dock laborers. The marines also transported the Norwegian Jews to Auschwitz and fought against the concentration camp inmates in Neustädt bay. In spite of ample evidence in the contrary, Padfield attempts to keep Dönitz's image intact. Based on military reports, documents in Bonn foreign service archive, and secondary sources; 47 notes. 1934-69

Donne, John

1862. Nicholls, David. DIVINE ANALOGY: THE THEOLOGICAL POLITICS OF JOHN DONNE. *Political Studies [Great Britain] 1984 32(4): 570-580.* English divine and poet John Donne (1572-1631) frequently used in his sermons analogies between the heavenly rule of God and earthly monarchy. However, unlike many religious and political thinkers who used this analogy, Donne did not believe that it justified a monolithic and arbitrary absolutism; rather, his trinitarianism made him see the divine model as advocating a pluralistic earthly society governed by law. 62 notes. 1572-1631

Dontsov, Dmytro

1863. Kelebay, Yarema Gregory. TOWARDS A BETTER UNDERSTANDING OF DMYTRO DONZOW. *Ukrainian Rev. [Great Britain] 1983 31(3): 56-63.* A biographical sketch of Dmytro Dontsov, Ukrainian writer-patriot whose works include *The Basis of Our Politics* (1921) and *National-*

ism (1926), based on Michael Sosnowski's Ukrainian-language *Dmytro Dontsov: A Political Portrait* (1974). Article to be continued. 1908-73

1864. Łobodowski, Józef. DMYTRO DONCOW: ŻYCIE I DZIAŁALNOŚĆ [Dmytro Dontsov: his life and activity]. *Zeszyty Hist. [France] 1981 (55): 144-166.* A review essay based on Mychajlo Sosnowskyj's *Dmytro Dontsov: A Political Portrait* (1974). During his university studies Dontsov (1883-1973) aligned himself with Ukrainian socialists who rejected the internationalist orientation. The tsarist police arrested him for his writings in 1907. After his conditional release he lived in Zakopane for two years, where he met Stanisław Brzozowski (1878-1911), who influenced his subsequent work. He completed a law degree in Lvov in 1917. In 1918 he lived in Kiev, from where civil war drove him out in 1919. He remained in Lvov in Poland from 1922 to World War II, then moved to Canada. 3 notes. 1905-73

Dorislaus, Isaac

1865. Maccioni, P. Allessandra and Mostert, Marco. ISAAC DORISLAUS (1595-1649); THE CAREER OF A DUTCH SCHOLAR IN ENGLAND. *Transactions of the Cambridge Bibliographical Society [Great Britain] 1984 8(4): 419-470.* Isaac Dorislaus first came to England in 1627 as first incumbent of the lectureship in history founded by Fulke Greville, Lord Brooke, at Cambridge, where his lectures (seemingly favoring republicanism over monarchy) were attacked by conservative faculty members who identified him with the growing Puritan faction at the university. In 1642 he became Advocate of the Army and was designated as one of the prosecutors at the trial of Charles I, though he never spoke. He was murdered by a royalist exile in The Hague in 1649 while on a diplomatic mission on behalf of Parliament, an event which soured Anglo-Dutch relations. Based on documents in the Gemeentearchief, Leiden, Cambridge University Library, and Bodleian Library, and secondary sources; 3 appendixes, 184 notes. 1627-49

Dorléans, Louis

1866. Gould, Robert Christie. "The Life and Political Writings of Louis Dorléans, Publicist of the French Catholic League." Bryn Mawr Coll. 1981. 279 pp. *DAI 1982 42(8): 3707-A.* 8202568 1580's

Dorval, Marie

1867. Schopp, Claude. LES AMOURS DE MARIE: DIX LETTRES INEDITES DE MARIE DORVAL A ALEXANDRE DUMAS [The loves of Marie: 10 unpublished letters from Marie Dorval to Alexandre Dumas]. *Revue d'Histoire Littéraire de la France [France] 1984 84(6): 918-934.* Prints letters from Marie Dorval dated 23 December 1833 to 20 April 1834 that describe her life as an actress and her love for Alexandre Dumas, as well as a copy of her contract at the Comédie Française. 1833-34

Dostoevski, Fëdor

1868. Rice, James L. DOSTOEVSKY'S MEDICAL HISTORY: DIAGNOSIS AND DIALECTIC. *Russian Rev. 1983 42(2): 131-161.* Traces Fëdor Dostoevski's medical history of epilepsy from its onset about 1846 to his death in 1881. Although Dostoevski claimed that his epilepsy had developed during his imprisonment from 1849 to 1854, it was of earlier origin and coincided on occasion with other psychiatric disturbances. He was often able to conceal his illness, but it became more severe in the late 1860's and was increasingly linked with postseizure psychic effects. Dostoevski portrayed the mental illnesses of his fictional characters with clinical accuracy, drawing from his own experience as well as wide reading on the subject. 93 notes. 1845-81

1869. Roazen, Paul. DOSTOEVSKY IN EXILE. *Virginia Quarterly Review 1985 61(3): 551-555.* Praises Joseph Frank's *Dostoevsky: The Years of Ordeal, 1850-59* (1983), the second volume of an intended four volumes on Dostoevski following *The Seeds of Revolt, 1821-49* (1976). In this second biography Frank details Dostoevski's imprisonment after his arrest in 1849. The ordeal led Dostoevski into believing the Russian peasantry to be a human embodiment of Christ. Covers Dostoevski's army life, first marriage, epilepsy, and devotion to Tsar Alexander II. 1850-59

1870. Sarkadi Nagy, Pál. "VALAKI KOPOG AZ AJTÓN..." DOSZTOJEVSZKIJ HALÁLÁNAK SZÁZADIK ÉVFORDULÓJÁRA ["Somebody is knocking at the door..." Remembrance of the 100th anniversary of Dostoevski's death]. *Theológiai Szemle [Hungary] 1981 24(2): 103-109.* Dostoevski died 28 January 1881. His first book, *Poor People,* was published in 1846. *Crime and Punishment* and *Brothers Karamazov* have established him as a second only to Tolstoy. With an unusually sharp sixth sense he was able to foresee changes that took place in his country during the years to follow. While he questioned the existence of God, he always professed to be a devoted servant of Christ, without whom he would consider his life completely pointless. 22 notes. 1846-81

1871. Ziegler, François de. DOSTOIEVSKI, NOTRE PROCHAIN [Dostoevski, our neighbor]. *Nouvelle Rev. des Deux Mondes [France] 1982 (1): 23-31, (2): 302-315.* A biographical sketch of Fëdor Mikhailovich Dostoevski (1821-81), highlighting his spiritual evolution, political commitments, and syncretic philosophy. 1841-81

Doucin, Louis

1872. Ceyssens, Lucien. AUTOUR DE LA BULLE UNIGENITUS: V. LE P. LOUIS DOUCIN, SJ (1652-1726) [Concerning the papal bull *Unigenitus:* 5. Father Louis Doucin, SJ (1652-1726)]. *Antonianum [Italy] 1983 58(2-3): 448-473.* Prints a biography of Louis Doucin, a French Jesuit historian of Nestorianism and inveterate foe of Jansenism, who studied in Rome, fought Jansenism in the Netherlands, and collaborated with Michel Le Tellier, confessor of King Louis XIV, in the production of the anti-Jansenist bull *Unigenitus* issued by Pope Clement XI. 1667-1726

Doufalík, Alois

1873. Kunz, Ludvík. BŘEZOVANÉ [Březová folk]. *Studia Comeniana et Historica [Czechoslovakia] 1984 14(27): 70-116.* Presents details of the life and writings of the eastern Moravian village teacher Alois Doufalík (1839-1918) and publishes an edition of his incomplete memoirs. Doufalík's perceptive sketches of the language, folklore and music making in his distinctive Slovak Moravian environment found some response among the Czech intelligentsia and attracted the attention of the composer Leoš Janáček to the region. Based on Moravian archival materials in Brno and Uherské Hradiště and on published sources; 3 illus., 68 notes. German summary. 1839-1918

Douglas, H. M.

1874. Ekechi, Felix K. PORTRAIT OF A COLONIZER: H. M. DOUGLAS IN COLONIAL NIGERIA, 1897-1920. *African Studies Rev. 1983 26(1): 25-50.* An examination of the harsh administration of H. M. Douglas in the Owerri district of Nigeria dispells the "misleading notion that European colonial administrators treated Africans with considerable kindness and tolerance." Based on fieldwork in Owerri and on British and Nigerian archives; 23 notes, biblio. 1897-1920

Douwes Dekker, Guido M. G.

1875. DeJong, C. LOTGEVALLEN VAN DRIE BROERS DOUWES DEKKER IN DE ANGLO-BOEREOORLOG 1899-1902. III: GUIDO M. G. DOUWES DEKKER, 1883-1959 [Adventures of the three brothers Douwes Dekker in the Anglo-Boer War 1899-1902. III: Guido M. G. Douwes Dekker, 1883-1959]. *Historia [South Africa] 1983 28(2): 14-26.* Considers the experiences in the Boer War of Guido Maximiliaan Gustaaf Douwes Dekker, youngest of three brothers from Batavia who volunteered on the Boer side, as reported by him in letters to the Javanese press (two reprinted here). Follows his life and career, as told by his son, in Batavia, as a prisoner-of-war in World War II, and in the Netherlands. Guido's letters describe his trip to the Transvaal in 1900, the battle of Dalmanutha and the Boers' retreat, relations between Boers and foreign volunteers, including the Dutch, and his return home the same year. Based on Guido's letters and family records; portrait, 9 notes. 1900-59

Dowding, Hugh

1876. Haslam, E. B. HOW LORD DOWDING CAME TO LEAVE FIGHTER COMMAND. *J. of Strategic Studies [Great Britain] 1981 4(2): 175-186.* Analyzes the reasons behind the removal of Air Marshal Sir Hugh Dowding as head of the Royal Air Force Fighter Command in November 1940, and the attitude of the Air Staff, the Secretary of State for Air, and the Prime Minister toward Dowding. He was no easy compromiser or politician and he often aroused opposition because of his style, but no one served his country more selflessly and courageously. He was removed because a number of influential people wanted a change at Bentley Priory. Primary sources; 6 notes. 1940

Downing, George

1877. Roseveare, Henry. "CRAFTY AND FAWNING": DOWNING OF DOWNING STREET. *History Today [Great Britain] 1984 34(July): 10-14.* George Downing (1623-84) had a long and varied career as a preacher, soldier, diplomat, and bureaucrat for which he earned great wealth but also an unsavory reputation for greed and duplicity among the English political elite. He is most noted for his innovations in public finance when he served in the Treasury. 1640's-84

Doyle, Arthur Conan

1878. Davidson, Apollon. KONAN DOIL'—OBLICHITEL' KOLONIALIZMA [Arthur Conan Doyle, exposer of colonialism]. *Aziia i Afrika Segodnia [USSR] 1986 (1): 54-57.* British author and physician Arthur Conan Doyle (1859-1930) denounced colonial atrocities in Africa, campaigning in particular against the South African Boers and King Leopold II of Belgium, whose mismanagement of the Congo (his personal possession from the mid-1880's to 1908) turned it into an "earthly hell." English summary. 1882-1910

Dracula (Vlad the Impaler)

1879. Dukes, Paul. DRACULA: FACT, LEGEND AND FICTION. *Hist. Today [Great Britain] 1982 32(July): 44-47.* Although the Dracula that we know today was the fictional creation of Bram Stoker in the 19th century, there is basis in fact for the legend. The real Dracula was the Romanian leader in the fight against the Turks, Vlad Ţepeş, or Vlad the Impaler, who became legendary only a few years after his death. 1456-1931

Dragićević, Risto

1880. Pejović, Dj. D. RISTO DRAGIĆEVIĆ (1901-1980) [Risto Dragićević (1901-80)]. *Istorijski Zapisi [Yugoslavia] 1981 34(1): 179-182.* The historian Risto Dragićević's works deal mainly with Montenegro and the Montenegrin people from the 15th century until modern times. 15c-20c

Dragović, Radovan

1881. Hasanagić, Edib. RADOVAN DRAGOVIĆ [Radovan Dragović]. *Zbornik Istorijskog Muzeja Srbije [Yugoslavia] 1979 15-16: 29-45.* Reviews the life and work of Radovan Dragović (1878-1906), secretary of the Serbian Social Democratic Party and one of the founders of the working-class movement in Serbia. Dragović came from a poor Serbian family and worked in his youth as a carpenter. He later spent three years in the Croatian capital, Zagreb, and in the Austrian town of Graz. There he became acquainted with the highly developed Austrian socialist movement. On his return he helped set up trade unions and served as secretary of the Serbian Social Democratic Party. Dragović also worked as a journalist before his premature death from tuberculosis at the age of 28. To accompany an exhibition mounted at the Museum of History of Serbia in Belgrade in 1978 to commemorate the 100th anniversary of the birth of Radovan Dragović; 13 notes, 2 plates. 1878-1906

Drake, Francis

1882. Villiers, Patrick. LES CORSAIRES ET LA GUERRE DE COURSE [Corsairs and their war on commerce]. *Histoire [France] 1981 (36): 26-34.* 16c-19c
*For abstract see **Bart, Jean***

Draye, Henri

1883. Nicolaisen, W. F. H. IN MEMORIAM: HENRI DRAYE (1911-1983). *Names 1984 32(1): 74-76.* An obituary of the Germanic philologist, Henri Draye, who taught at the University of Louvain, Belgium, and was Secretary-General of the International Committee of Onomastic Sciences. 1911-83

Drayton, Michael

1884. Duchemin, Parker. MICHAEL DRAYTON AND THE ART OF LANDSCAPE PAINTING. *University of Ottawa Quarterly [Canada] 1985 55(1): 109-117.* The English poet Michael Drayton (1563-1631) displayed an interest in the relationship between poetry and painting. In particular, Drayton's knowledge of landscape painting shaped his writing. His descriptive passages and colorful portraits indicated his familiarity with contemporary paintings and tapestries. Drayton's understanding of the principles of composition and the elements of landscape painting allowed him to make his poetry "a speaking picture" in depicting the English countryside. Based on Drayton's poetry and secondary sources; 17 notes. 1590's-1631

1885. Duchemin, Parker. BARBAROUS IGNORANCE AND BASE DETRACTION: THE STRUGGLES OF MICHAEL DRAYTON. *Albion 1982 14(2): 118-138.* Drayton viewed *Poly-Olbion* as his major work, though critics have generally denigrated the epic poem. Drayton's early intentions to write an epic led to productive years and royal patronage, but Part 1 of the poem was a critical failure. Drayton regarded his detractors as unpatriotic barbarians and completed Part 2, but he had trouble finding a willing publisher. Part 3 was unfinished and its author unappreciated at his death. 39 notes. 1590-1631

Dreher, Alfons

1886. Eitel, Peter. ALFONS DREHER (1896-1980) [Alfons Dreher, 1896-1980]. *Zeits. für Württembergische Landesgeschichte [West Germany] 1980 39: 303-304.* Alfons Dreher organized one of the best city archives in Ravensburg, Württemberg during his lifetime. 1910's-80

Driant, Emile

1887. David, Daniel. LES ANTICIPATIONS DU COMMANDANT DRIANT [What Commander Driant anticipated]. *Historama [France] 1985 (17): 80-82.* The writings of Emile Driant, an imaginative French officer who published under the pen name Capitaine Danrit, contain plans for steam-powered and airborne military vehicles, some of which came into existence long after he described them in his novels. 1894-1916

1888. David, Daniel. LE LIEUTENANT-COLONEL DRIANT: OFFICIER, JOURNALISTE, PARLEMENTAIRE, ECRIVAIN [Lieutenant-colonel Driant: officer, journalist, member of parliament, author]. *Revue Historique des Armées [France] 1985 (3): 84-95.* After a successful army career, which included service in North Africa and teaching at the St. Cyr military academy, Emile-Augustin-Cyprien Driant (1855-1916) resigned from the French army because political factors blocked further promotion. He became a political activist and organizer, a journalist, and an author, promoting military preparedness and the restoration of "national values" and "moral strength." Elected to the national assembly as a member of the Liberal Action Party from Nancy, he served on the army committee. He wrote more than 20 futuristic novels exalting patriotism and military virtues. With the outbreak of World War I, he volunteered for active duty and was given command of a light infantry groupment in the 72d Infantry Division near Verdun, where he was killed in action. 2 illus., 4 photos, 11 notes. 1875-1916

Drieu la Rochelle, Pierre

1889. Pereira, Paulette J. "The Impact of the German Occupation of France upon Four French Intellectuals: Charles Maurras, Pierre Drieu la Rochelle, Henry de Montherlant, and François Mauriac." Am. U. 1985. 221 pp. *DAI 1986 46(8): 2415-A.* DA8522268 1940-44

Drinov, Marin

1890. Gorina, L. V. ISTORICHESKIE VZGLIADY MARINA DRINOVA [Historical views of Marin Drinov]. *Vestnik Moskovskogo Universiteta, Seriia 8: Istoriia [USSR] 1985 (2): 55-64.* Marin Drinov (1838-1906) went first to the Kiev seminary and then Moscow University. He became professor in Slavic philology at Kharkov University. In addition, he played an active role in the creation of Bulgaria, serving as vice-governor in Sofia in 1878. The work of O. M. Bodianski and F. I. Buslaev influenced Drinov, who emphasized the intellectual or moral side of history. His work was influenced by positivism. 16 notes. 1860's-1906

1891. Gorina, L. LEKTSII PO ISTORII ZARUBEZHNYKH SLAVIANSKIKH NARODOV M. DRINOVA V KHAR'KOVSKOM UNIVERSITETE (1873-1906) [Lectures on the history of non-Russian Slavic peoples by M. Drinov at Kharkov University, 1873-1906]. *Sovetskoe Slavianovedenie [USSR] 1983 (6): 58-66.* A profile of Marin S. Drinov (1838-1906) that reviews his pedagogical career at the Slavonic faculty of Kharkov University. Drinov, a Bulgarian, came to Russia in 1858 to complete his education and after graduating from Moscow University was appointed lecturer at Kharkov University in 1873, where he stayed as a professor until his death, except for a two-year break in 1877-79 when he occupied a government post in Bulgaria during the Russo-Turkish war. His lectures and studies dealt primarily with medieval to 18th-century history, literature, and languages of Western and Southern Slavs. Note, biblio. 1873-1906

1892. Losievski, I. ALEKSANDR POTEBNIA I MARIN DRINOV (EPIZODY IZ ISTORII OTECHESTVENNOGO SLAVIANOVEDENIIA) [Aleksandr Potebnia and Marin Drinov: from the history of Russian Slavic studies]. *Sovetskoe Slavianovedenie [USSR] 1982 (6): 98-103.* Aleksandr Potebnia (1835-1891) and Marin Drinov (1838-1906), a Bulgarian, worked at the Kharkov University Historical Philology Department. When they met in 1873 they were both already fully formed, strong, individualistic personalities whose lives had strong similarities so that friendship and academic cooperation were natural. They worked together for the good of Slavic studies. 6 notes. 1873-1906

1893. Minkova, Liliana. PEREPISKA VIKENTIIA V. MAKUSHEVA S MARINOM DRINOVYM 1869-1878 GG. [Correspondence of Vikenti V. Makushev with Marin Drinov, 1869-78]. *Bulgarian Hist. Rev. [Bulgaria] 1981 9(1-2): 180-213.* In 1869 the Russian Slavist Makushev (1837-83) encountered the Bulgarian historian Drinov (1838-1906) in Naples, where Makushev was researching the history of the South Slavs. They subsequently exchanged some 40 letters, the texts of which are reproduced. They concern matters of academic and scholarly interest together with personal glimpses. 1869-78

Drobner, Bolesław

1894. Śliwa, Michał. BOLESŁAW DROBNER: SZKIC BIOGRAFII POLITYCZNEJ [Bolesław Drobner: outline of his political biography]. *Z Pola Walki [Poland] 1981 23[i.e., 24](2): 137-156.* Sketches the political biography of the Polish party activist and statesman Bolesław Drobner (1883-1968). Active in the left wing of the socialist movement, he was in close contact with Otto Bauer and Max Adler and was active in the 2d International. Arrested by the Soviets in 1940 and subsequently freed, he joined the Polish socialists in the USSR and, after World War II, held a number of high party posts in Poland. Only in his last years as party secretary in Cracow did he encounter popular criticism. Based on the Central Archives of the Central Committee of the Polish United Workers' Party and the Cracow Party Committee Archives; 84 notes. 1904-68

Drouyn de Lhuys, Edouard

1895. Spencer, Warren F. THE MAKING OF A REVOLUTIONARY NOTABLE: EDOUARD DROUYN DE LHUYS, 1844-48. *Consortium on Revolutionary Europe 1750-1850: Pro. 1982: 20-38.* Studies the public life of

Edouard Drouyn de Lhuys, who rose to positions of power under the Orleanist regime in France but finally helped to overthrow it. A wealthy man of aristocratic background, Drouyn was sensitive to the social injustice that faced the working class. His opposition to the crown's government grew from the knowledge that change was necessary to avert the chaos of a workers' revolt. He continued to serve as a public official throughout France's period of unrest. Based on Drouyn de Lhuys's personnel dossier AMAE, Fain papers and Dorn papers, Archives Nationales, and secondary sources. 1830-48

Druzhinin, Nikolai

1896. Dimitriev, S. S. and Nifontov, A. S. REDKOSTNYI IUBILEI SOVETSKOGO ISTORIKA (K 100-LETIIU AKAD. N. M. DRUZHININA) [An exceptional jubilee of a Soviet historian: on Nikolai M. Druzhinin's 100th birthday]. *Voprosy Istorii [USSR] 1985 (12): 21-33.* In January 1986 Academician Nikolai Druzhinin, one of the oldest Soviet scholars, will be 100. Surveys his life and scholarly activities, his work as an editor, his world outlook and teaching methods, and offers an assessment of his place in Soviet historical science. Discusses his major works on the Decembrists, the history of Moscow, higher educational establishments of 19th-century Russia, and his monographs *State-Owned Peasants and the Reform of Pavel Kiselyov* and *The Russian Village at the Turning-Point: 1861-1880.* 19c-20c

1897. Dmitriev, S. S. UCHENYI I NASTAVNIK NIKOLAI MIKHAILOVICH DRUZHININ (K95-LETIIU SO DNIA ROZHDENIIA) [Scholar and instructor Nikolai Mikhailovich Druzhinin: on the 95th anniversary of his birth]. *Vestnik Moskovskogo U., Seriia 8: Istoriia [USSR] 1981 (1): 27-39.* N. M. Druzhinin entered Moscow University in the autumn of 1904 and heard the lectures of Kliuchevski, Rozhkov, Liubavski, and Kizevetter. He worked for the Social Democratic Party in 1905 becoming librarian of the Moscow Committee of the party. He was arrested and exiled. He completed the history faculty in 1918 and then worked under Bogoslovsky. He was involved in museum work but began teaching at Moscow University in 1934. His work deals mainly with 19th-century Russia and the peasants. 16 notes. 1904-50's

1898. Druzhinin, N. M. BOL'SHEVISTSKUIU PRAVDU—ZASHCHITNIKAM REVOLIUTSII [For the defenders of the revolution—Bolshevik truth]. *Voprosy Istorii KPSS [USSR] 1981 (4): 117-122.* Memoirs by the Soviet historian Nikolai Druzhinin (b. 1886) on his service from 1919 to 1920 as head of the Lecture Section of the Political Education Section of the Red Army in Moscow. Druzhinin helped organize, arrange, and evaluate lectures on political and social topics. 1919-20

1899. Rybakov, B. A.; Koval'chenko, I.D.: and Kiniapina, N.S. NAUCHNO-PEDAGOGICHESKAIA DEIATEL'NOST' AKADEMIKA NIKOLAIA MIKHAILOVICHA DRUZHININA (K 100-LETIIU SO DNIA ROZHDENIIA) [Scholarly and pedagogical activities of Academician Nikolai M. Druzhinin: the centenary of his birth]. *Istoriia SSSR [USSR] 1986 (1): 69-76.* Outlines the academic biography of the Soviet historian Nikolai Druzhinin (b. 1886). After studies at Moscow University he joined the Red Army in 1919. His scholarly interests spanned the history of revolutionary movements, the laws of historical development, as well as geographically and historically circumscribed case studies in socioeconomic history. *Gosudarstvennye Krest'iane i Reforma P. D. Kiseleva,* [State serfs and P. D. Kiselev's reform] (2 vol., 1946, 1958) and *Russkaia Derevnia na Perelome (60- 70-e gody XIX v.)* [Russian village in crisis, the 1860's and 70's] (1978) are the most outstanding examples of the scope of his scholarship. After decades of representing Soviet academia in the international academic life, Druzhinin in the 1970's contributed to many academic debates in Soviet historical journals, including those on the formation of the Russian nation, M. Speranski's views on the peasant problem, and enlightened absolutism in Russia. Photo, 10 notes. 1914-86

1900. Štrom, František. TVÚRČÍ CESTA AKADEMIKA N. M. DRUŽININA [The life work of academician N. M. Druzhinin]. *Slovanský Přehled [Czechoslovakia] 1986 72(2): 164-168.* On 13 January 1986, Soviet historians commemorated the birth of N. M. Druzhinin in 1886. His historical research concentrated on the history of the 19th century, which had not been explored by bourgeois historians who considered it too contemporary. He promoted the study of that period in his teaching and as editor of a number of historical journals. 10 notes. 19c

1901. —. AKADEMIKU N. M. DRUZHININU 95 LET [Academician N. M. Druzhinin's 95th birthday]. *Novaia i Noveishaia Istoriia [USSR] 1981 (2): 196-199.* Biographical sketch of Soviet historian N. M. Druzhinin. His major research has been on the Decembrist movement, the position of the peasantry in 19th-century Russia, the Russian village and the revolutionary movement in Russia at the end of the 19th century. He has been awarded the Order of Lenin three times and was the recipient of the Lenin Prize in 1980. Photo, 12 notes. 1886-1981

Dryden, John

1902. Hammond, Paul. DRYDEN'S EMPLOYMENT BY CROMWELL'S GOVERNMENT. *Tr. of the Cambridge Biblio. Soc. [Great Britain] 1981 8(1): 130-136.* The handwriting on a receipt in the Public Record Office has made it possible to assert firmly that Dryden was employed by John Thurloe, Cromwell's secretary of state. This coincides with the opinion of Dryden's biographer James Osborn and contradicts Charles Ward. 7 notes, 4 reproductions. 1650-59

1903. Winn, James A. JOHN DRYDEN'S PICKERING ANCESTORS. *Notes and Queries [Great Britain] 1982 29(6): 506-510.* Presents a genealogy of John Dryden's maternal ancestors, tracing them from their first forebears to Dryden's own generation, and their location in Titchmarsh. 16c-17c

Držić, Marin

1904. Freidenberg, M. M. MARIN DRZHICH, KOMEDIOGRAF IZ DUBROVNIKA [Marin Držić, comedy writer from Dubrovnik]. *Sovetskoe Slavianovedenie [USSR] 1982 (3): 103-112.* Marin Držić, born circa 1508 in Dubrovnik, died in 1567 in Venice. He was a Reformation comedy writer whose language and themes have long fascinated scholars. The son of a merchant and a relative of the poet Djore Držić, Marin spent 1538-44 in Siena, returned to Dubrovnik to find the family business bankrupt, and became a paid companion to Count Kristof Rogendorf. In 1548 he presented his first, now lost, comedy, *Pomet.* He plotted secretly against the Turks to protect Dubrovnik. Based on Držić's works and studies of Soviet and Yugoslav critics; 13 notes. 1538-67

Duarte, José Napoleon

1905. García, José Z. EL SALVADOR: LEGITIMIZING THE GOVERNMENT. *Current History 1985 84(500): 101-104, 135-136.* President José Napoleón Duarte's negotiations with the Salvadoran rebels have been moderately successful, and he has made some progress in breaking the political impasse between moderates and rightists. 1983-84

DuBellay

1906. Barolsky, Paul. WALTER PATER AND THE POETRY OF NOTHINGNESS. *Antioch Rev. 1982 40(4): 469-478.* 15c
For abstract see ***Botticelli***

Dubnow, Simon

1907. Erlich, Victor; Levine, Burton, interviewer. INTERVIEW: VICTOR ERLICH. *Shmate 1986 (14): 25-28.* 1911-41
For abstract see ***Erlich, Victor***

1908. Levenberg, S. SIMON DUBNOV: HISTORIAN OF RUSSIAN JEWRY. *Soviet Jewish Affairs [Great Britain] 1982 12(1): 3-17.* Discusses the life and works of Russian-Jewish historian Simon Dubnow and his belief in the cultural and social durability of the Diaspora; examines Dubnow's historiography of Russian and East European Jews. 1880-1941

Dubois-Crancé, Edmond Louis Alexis

1909. History Club of the 3d Engineer Regiment. UN CERTAIN DUBOIS-CRANCE, CITOYEN DE CHARLEVILLE [Dubois-Crancé, citizen of Charleville]. *Rev. Hist. des Armées [France] 1982 (2): 34-43.* Edmond Louis Alexis Dubois-Crancé (1747-1814) began his political career with his election to the Estates-General. He was a member of the Constituent Assembly, the Committee on Public Safety, and the National Convention, specializing in military affairs and the modernization of the army. During this period, he also served as an army officer, rising to the rank of brigadier general. Minister of war in 1799, he retired in 1800 to his estate at Balham-sur-Aisne where he devoted his time to local government and the improvement of agriculture. 5 illus., appendix. 1789-1801

DuBois-Reymond, Emil

1910. Lübbe, Hermann. EMIL DU BOIS-REYMOND [Emil DuBois-Reymond]. *Schweizer Monatshefte [Switzerland] 1983 63(9): 697-711.* Reports on the family background and life of Emil DuBois-Reymond Bois-Reymond and highlights his contributions to the development of physiology. 1840's-96

Ducasse, Isadore

1911. Legrand, Francine-Claire. HENRY DE GROUX—LEON BLOY ET LAUTREAMONT [Henry de Groux: Léon Bloy and Lautréamont]. *Rev. de l'U. de Bruxelles [Belgium] 1981 (3): 67-73.* 1870-1910
For abstract see ***Bloy, Léon***

Dudley brothers

1912. McCoy, Richard C. FROM THE TOWER TO THE TILTYARD: ROBERT DUDLEY'S RETURN TO GLORY. *Historical Journal [Great Britain] 1984 27(2): 425-435.* Robert Dudley and his brothers, Ambrose and Henry, took part in a series of tournaments organized by King Philip in 1554 to reduce tensions between English and Spanish courtiers. A score check proves that Philip pursued a conciliatory policy in his tournaments. Robert Dudley, a leading figure in the tiltyard, and his brother Ambrose are prominently featured in an illustration of a College of Arms manuscript which describes the tournaments' rules. The manuscript is a record of the forms of Tudor chivalry and its illustration was intended to memorialize the Dudleys' performances shortly after they were released from the Tower of London. Based on College of Arms manuscript M. 6; fig., 33 notes. 1554-80

Duffield, Geoffrey

1913. Love, Rosaleen. SCIENCE AND GOVERNMENT IN AUSTRALIA 1905-14: GEOFFREY DUFFIELD AND THE FOUNDATION OF THE COMMONWEALTH SOLAR OBSERVATORY. *Historical Records of Australian Science [Australia] 1985 6(2): 171-188.* Geoffrey Duffield (1879-1929) was born in Australia, took graduate work in engineering and physics (especially spectroscopy) in England, and returned to Australia determined to secure the establishment of a solar physics observatory there. The creation of the Commonwealth Solar Observatory in 1923 was the culmination of years of work to develop support from scientists around the world and from the governments of Britain and Australia. Based on Duffield's papers; 128 notes. 1905-14

Dufour, R.

1914. Eerenbeemt, H. F. J. M. van den. EEN BELASTINGAMBTENAAR ALS PROPAGANDIST VAN DE MOERBEZIE IN ZIJDETEELT: R. DUFOUR IN HET UTRECHTSE, 1831-1843 [A tax official as propagandist for mulberry and silk cultivation: R. Dufour in Utrecht, 1831-43]. *Economisch- en Sociaal-Historisch Jaarboek [Netherlands] 1981 44: 191-210.* After the introduction of the mulberry tree in Holland in 1829, R. Dufour raised and sold thousands of the trees to Dutch growers. By 1837 he had convinced William I to join his association to advance the silk industry. Dufour, as first director of the association, cultivated mulberry trees, raised cocoons indoors all year, sold silkworm eggs, and developed the industry of silk weaving. His death in 1843, the loss of a government subsidy, and Javanese and French competition led to the eventual end of the association in 1851. 57 notes. 1831-51

Duguay-Trouin, René

1915. Villiers, Patrick. LES CORSAIRES ET LA GUERRE DE COURSE [Corsairs and their war on commerce]. *Histoire [France] 1981 (36): 26-34.* 16c-19c
For abstract see ***Bart, Jean***

Dugué, Perrine

1916. Charmelot, M. A. PERRINE DUGUE, LA "SAINTE AUX AILES TRICOLORES" [Perrine Dugué, the "saint with the tricolor wings"]. *Ann. Hist. de la Révolution Française [France] 1983 55(3): 454-465.* Perrine Dugué (1779-96) was a village girl from a republican family in Sainte-Suzanne who was killed during the Chouan rebellion. She was venerated, and a chapel was built to the memory of the revolutionary saint. 3 illus., 25 notes. 1779-96

Duke, H. E.

1917. O'Halpin, Eunan. HISTORICAL REVISION XX: H. E. DUKE AND THE IRISH ADMINISTRATION, 1916-18. *Irish Hist. Studies [Ireland] 1981 22(88): 362-376.* The tenure of H. E. Duke (later 1st Baron Merrivale) of Ireland was hampered by his unfamiliarity with the country and its problems, his failure to control political unrest, and his inability to deal with the Irish unionists. His position was further undermined by the London treasury's refusal to increase expenditure in Ireland and Lloyd George's decision to apply conscription in Ireland without consulting the Irish administration. Based on manuscripts in Public Record Office, London, House of Lords Record Office, and State Paper Office, Dublin; 88 notes. 1916-18

Dulac, Germaine

1918. Dozoretz, Wendy Harriet. "Germaine Dulac: Filmmaker, Polemicist, Theoretician." New York U. 1982. 368 pp. *DAI 1983 43(11): 3444-A.* DA8307822 1890's-1930's

Dullin, Charles

1919. Bonnat, Yves. CHARLES DULLIN ET SES DECORATEURS [Charles Dullin and his set designers]. *Revue d'Histoire du Théâtre [France] 1985 37(1): 28-32.* As director of the Théâtre de l'Atelier from 1923 to 1940, Charles Dullin encouraged innovation in set and costume design, demanding fresh ideas and techniques from artists André Masson, Jean Cocteau, Lucien Coutaud, Pierre Sonrel, Henri-Georges Adam, Louis Touchagues, Rodicq, Michel Duran, and André Barsacq; includes photographs of the work of each designer. 1923-40

1920. Romains, Jules. HOMMAGE A CHARLES DULLIN [A homage to Charles Dullin]. *Revue d'Histoire du Théâtre [France] 1985 37(1): 33-35.* An elegy to the wisdom, courtesy, talent, and humanity of French dramatist Charles Dullin, written two years after Dullin's death in 1948, and read at his Montmartre theater, the Théâtre de l'Atelier. 1928-48

Dumas, Alexandre

1921. Mabire, Jean. DUMAS GRAND-PERE, LE DIABLE NOIR [Grandfather Dumas, the black devil]. *Historama [France] 1984 (5): 32-37.* Recounts the colorful life of General Alexandre Dumas, father and grandfather of the famous writers, from 1775-1806, and his exploits while in the army of Napoleon. 1775-1806

Dumont, Henri Joseph

1922. Calle, Manuel Rivero de la. HENRY DUMONT PRECURSOR DE LOS ESTUDIOS ANTROPOLOGICOS EN CUBA [Henri Dumont, pioneer of anthropological studies in Cuba]. *Islas [Cuba] 1981 (68): 137-150.* Gives biographical and bibliographical data on Henri Joseph Dumont (1824-78), French physician and ethnographer who went to Cuba in 1864 and later wrote a *Comparative Anthropology and Pathology of Black Slaves* about that island. 1864-78

Dunand, Jean

1923. Bayer, Patricia. JEAN DUNAND: PREMIER CRAFTSMAN OF THE ART DECO STYLE. *Art & Antiques 1982 5(3): 56-63.* Biography of Swiss-born artist, John (later Jean) Dunand (1877-1942), who worked with a number of different materials but is best known for his works in metal and lacquer in the Art Deco style, including jewelry, vases and bowls, and lacquered wood panels, that made him well known in Europe and America during the 1920's and 1930's. 1877-1942

1924. Winter-Jensen, Anne. ART DECO: JEAN DUNAND, UN ARTISTE D'ORIGINE GENEVOISE [Art Deco: Jean Dunand, an artist of Genevan origin]. *Mus. de Genève [Switzerland] 1982 (226): 11-16.* Discusses the life and art of Jean Dunand, who played an important part in the Art Deco movement between 1920 and 1940, and examines a series of his pieces acquired by the Museum of Art and History in Geneva, including several vases and trays, a lacquered goblet, and two panels made for the steamboat *Normandie* in 1936. 1920-40

Dunant, David

1925. Mützenberg, Gabriel. DAVID DUNANT, ONCLE ET PRÉCURSEUR DU FONDATEUR DE LA CROIX-ROUGE [David Dunant, uncle and precursor of the founder of the Red Cross]. *Schweizerische Zeitschrift für Geschichte [Switzerland] 1980 30(3-4): 357-385.* David Dunant (1784-1872) was a member of an old Genevan middle-class family. As a student at the Collège of Geneva and in business as publisher and bookseller, he wrote diaries, notes, and pamphlets. These writings reveal him as a Genevan patriot who staunchly upheld the republican principles of the constitution of his beloved native city, an enlightened Christian, and a citizen whose sense of individual responsibility induced a strong commitment to work for the public welfare. Dunant's humanitarian and cosmopolitan interests foreshadowed the activities and achievements of his more famous nephew, Jean Henry Dunant, the founder of the Red Cross. Based mainly on manuscript materials in the Geneva state archives; 88 notes. 1780-1870

Duncan, Jonathan

1926. Rabitoy, Neil. JONATHAN DUNCAN—A LESSON IN ADMINISTRATIVE SURVIVAL. *Asian Profile [Hong Kong] 1979 7(5): 443-449.* Discusses the career of British colonial administrator Jonathan Duncan, who served as governor of the Bombay presidency, 1796-1811, and the importance of his tenure to the historiography of colonial Bengal. 24 notes, biblio. 1796-1811

Dundas, George

1927. Whyte, Ian D. GEORGE DUNDAS OF DUNDAS. *Scottish Hist. Rev. [Great Britain] 1981 60(1): 1-13.* The diary of George Dundas of Dundas (1706-57), landed proprietor, advocate, and member of Parliament, reveals insights into early Scottish agricultural improvements. He was not an innovator, but was in contact with the celebrated agricultural improver, John Cockburn. While Cockburn pursued improvements on his tenant's lands and planned a model village, Dundas improved his holdings and urged his tenants to do so as they could afford it. Dundas worked cautiously within the constraints of his age and while his achievements were not conspicuous, Cockburn overreached himself and was forced to sell his estate. Dundas represents an important transition stage in the development of Scottish agriculture. 37 notes. 1706-57

Dunn, Henry

1928. Bartle, G. F. HENRY DUNN AND THE SECRETARYSHIP OF THE BRITISH AND FOREIGN SCHOOL SOCIETY, 1830-1856. *Journal of Educational Administration and History [Great Britain] 1986 18(1): 13-22.* Describes the work and influence of Henry Dunn (1801-76) as general and foreign secretary of the society during this period, particularly the quarrel between Dunn and the Unitarians with regard to the principle of nonsectarian Biblical instruction in the society's schools, which contributed to Dunn's resignation as secretary of the society in 1856. 1830-56

Dunn, Matthias

1929. Sill, Michael. THE DIARY OF MATTHIAS DUNN, COLLIERY VIEWER, 1831-1836. *Local Historian [Great Britain] 1985 16(7): 418-424.* The diary of Matthias Dunn, a major figure in the development of the Northumberland and Durham coalfields during the first half of the 19th century, provides a management view of a period of industrial growth, with its attendant labor problems, which is of particular historical interest today. 1831-36

Dunston family

1930. Hurst, Veronica. BACKGROUND TO A COLLECTION: THE DUNSTON FAMILY. *Bodleian Library Record [Great Britain] 1986 12(3): 205-232.* Traces the family from the 18th century, with special reference to the large collection of books and ephemera they built. In 1983 these came by the will of the last member to Oxford University, together with a large sum of money to be devoted to research. Based on Dunston family documents in the Bodleian Library; 6 photos, 28 notes. 18c-20c

Dupetit-Thouars, Abel Aubert

1931. Ladrange, Paul. DUPETIT-THOUARS ET LA REINE POMARE [Dupetit-Thouars and Queen Pomare]. *Revue Historique des Armées [France] 1984 (4): 84-94.* An account of the turns of events leading to the setting up of a French protectorate over Tahiti by Abel Aubert Dupetit-Thouars (1793-1864). Centers on his vigorous and consequential interventions mainly brought by his political disputes with the Polynesian island ruler, Queen Pomare IV (1813-77). During his brief stays from 1838 to 1843, this French naval officer requested remedy against the queen's expulsion of two French Catholic missionaries two years earlier and intervened for the establishment of a French protectorate and later for the annexation of the island. Such annexation not being accepted by the French parliament, Tahiti returned to a protectorate in 1847. 5 photos, map. 1838-47

Dupin, Louis-Ellies

1932. Gres-Gayer, Jacques. UN THEOLOGIEN GALLICAN, TEMOIN DE SON TEMPS: LOUIS ELLIES DU PIN (1657-1719) [A Gallician theologian, witness to his age: Louis Ellies Dupin (1657-1719)]. *Revue d'Histoire de l'Eglise de France [France] 1986 72(188): 67-121.* An insufficiently known historian, teacher, and theologian in the age of Louis XIV, Dupin was accused of Gallicanism, of Jansenism, and of scholarship that, more remarkable for its energy than for its accuracy, gave comfort to heretics. Condemned by Bossuet, by Paris, and by Rome, he was distrusted by Jansenists and Jesuits alike. An effective polemicist against the bull *Unigenitus,* his relations with William Wake, Archbishop of Canterbury, led to accusations of an idealistic and impractical ecumenism. A close examination of his career reveals an underlying unity: his erudition served consistently the defense of Gallicanism and the undermining of papal authority over the French church. Based on manuscripts in the National Archives and in municipal archives, published correspondence, and secondary sources; 254 notes, genealogy. 1692-1719

Dupont-White, Charles

1933. Meoli, Umberto. CHARLES DUPONT-WHITE E L'EVOLUZIONE DELLA SUA CONCEZIONE ECONOMICO-SOCIALE [Charles Dupont-White and the evolution of his socioeconomic theories]. *Economia e Storia [Italy] 1984 5(1): 46-70.* Discusses Charles Dupont-White's life, his education in law at the Sorbonne, and his career as lawyer and political theorist. Dupont-White was the literary exponent of what historians of socialism have called "authoritarian" or "state" socialism, such as Napoleon III intended with regard to reforms. In Dupont-White's theory, the nation-state and its legal system took over the regal right of absolute kings. 81 notes. 19c

Dupuy, Trevor N.

1934. Brown, John Sloan. COLONEL TREVOR N. DUPUY AND THE MYTHOS OF WEHRMACHT SUPERIORITY: A RECONSIDERATION. *Military Affairs 1986 50(1): 16-20.* Because of the calculations and interpretations of Colonel Trevor N. Dupuy and others, the image of the German army during World War II is exaggerated when compared to the US Army. Reusing Dupuy's analysis, there is convincing evidence that US divisions of 1943-44 were more efficient than their German counterparts and that they won the war because they were tougher than their adversaries. Primary sources; 5 tables, 22 notes. 1943-44

Duracz, Teodor

1935. Komorowska, Żanna. TEODOR DURACZ (1883-1943). W STULECIE URODZIN [Teodor Duracz (1883-1943): the centenary of his birth]. *Nowe Drogi [Poland] 1983 (3): 113-122.* Teodor Duracz was a Polish Communist, a counsel for the defense of Polish Communist prisoners in 1920-39 and an active member of the underground Polish Workers Party during World War II. Based on materials in Duracz's file held at the Central Archives of the Polish United Workers Party, Warsaw and on a collection of Duracz's defense speeches; 34 notes. 1918-43

Durand, Marguerite

1936. Goliber, Sue Helder. MARGUERITE DURAND: A STUDY IN FRENCH FEMINISM. *Int. J. of Women's Studies [Canada] 1982 5(5): 402-412.* Biography of Marguerite Durand (1864-1936) including the story of the feminist newspaper *La Fronde* which Durand organized and edited, 1897-1905. 1897-1936

Durand, Mortimer

1937. Larsen, Peter. SIR MORTIMER DURAND IN WASHINGTON: A STUDY IN ANGLO-AMERICAN RELATIONS IN THE ERA OF THEODORE ROOSEVELT. *Mid-America 1984 66(2): 65-78.* Sir Mortimer Durand became British ambassador to Washington in 1903. He proved personally incompatable with President Theodore Roosevelt and he failed to report accurately US interest in the Far East and North Africa. Durand quickly became out of touch with the president, leaving the British embassy at a severe disadvantage in relation to other embassies in the United States. Durand was recalled in 1905. Based on the Theodore Roosevelt, Arthur James Balfour, and Mortimer Durand Papers, and on secondary sources; 40 notes. 1903-05

Duray, Miklós

1938. Samal, Mary Hrabik. THE CASE OF MIKLÓS DURAY. *Cross Currents 1985 4: 39-45.* Background on Miklós Duray (b. 1945), a member of the Hungarian minority in Czechoslovakia and human rights activist. 1945-85

Durchdenbach, Johann

1939. Irtenkauf, Wolfgang. JOHANN DURCHDENBACH, EIN PFARRERSLEBEN AM RANDE DER GEGENREFORMATION [Johann Durchdenbach, a pastor's life at the edge of the Counter-Reformation]. *Blätter für Württembergische Kirchengeschichte [West Germany] 1979 79: 169-180.* Traces Durchdenbach's trials and tribulations as he preached in Hungary, Austria, and Württemberg; includes extensive extracts from a marriage booklet and his autobiographical poem. 1583-1633

Dürer, Albrecht

1940. Conrad, Philippe. DÜRER OU LE CREPUSCULE DU MOYEN AGE [Dürer, or the twilight of the Middle Ages]. *Hist. Mag. [France] 1983 (37): 28-37.* Focuses on the career and works of German painter and engraver Albrecht Dürer (1471-1528), showing the gradual influence of the Italian Renaissance on Northern art. 1471-1528

Durkheim, Emile

1941. Knottnerus, J. David. EMILE DURKHEIM: HIS METHODOLOGY AND USES OF HISTORY. *Journal of the History of the Behavioral Sciences 1986 22(2): 128-139.* Despite a resurgence of interest in Durkheim, insufficient attention has been directed toward his social morphology. The result is an underestimation of the role of history in his sociology and conception of unified science. From the earliest stages of his intellectual career Durkheim displayed a sensitivity to the value of historical investigation for social explanation. This interest, reflecting various influences in the intellectual milieux of his time, varied among three distinct historical perspectives and methodological frameworks: the comparative, the evolutionary, and the developmental. Differentiating the three approaches counteracts the tendency among interpreters to collapse all three into the evolutionary framework alone. 1880's-1917

1942. Moore, Deborah Dash. DAVID EMILE DURKHEIM AND THE JEWISH RESPONSE TO MODERNITY. *Modern Judaism 1986 6(3): 287-300.* Emile Durkheim (1858-1917), the eminent French sociologist, was also an assimilated Jew whose scholarly publications, especially those on the nature of religion, reflect his Jewish background. 1890-1910

1943. Wu, Lien Chin. THE IMPACT OF MODERNIZATION ON TRADITIONAL RELIGION: THEORETICAL APPROACHES. *She Hui K'o Hsüeh Lun Ts'ung (Journal of Social Science) [Taiwan] 1984 32: 335-420.* A brief history of Karl Marx (1818-83), Emile Durkheim (1858-1917), and Max Weber's (1864-1920) thought on the relation of religion and social change and these thinkers' influence on the philosophies of social scientists from the mid 20th century to the present. Durkheimians see religion as evolving in response to societal change. Modernization theories, which have their intellectual roots in Marx and Weber, hypothesize that religion declines with secularization, industrialization, and urbanization. Based on the writings of Marx, Durkheim, and Weber; 39 notes, biblio. 1850's-20c

Durnovo, Peter N.

1944. Lieven, Dominic. BUREAUCRATIC AUTHORITARIANISM IN LATE IMPERIAL RUSSIA: THE PERSONALITY, CAREER AND OPINIONS OF P. N. DURNOVO. *Hist. J. [Great Britain] 1983 26(2): 391-402.* Examines the political thought and career of Peter N. Durnovo, interior minister under Nicholas II. Durnovo was a supporter of bureaucratic authoritarianism with a strong background in military training. A staunch supporter of imperialism, he was nevertheless humane in his dealings with political opponents. Durnovo firmly believed that only the educated, intelligent members of society should be allowed to make decisions for the good of all members of society. Primary sources; 69 notes. 1905-15

Durocher, Marie Josephine Mathilde

1945. Lobo, Francisco Bruno. DUAS PIONEIRAS—MADAME DUROCHER, RITA LOBATO [Two pioneering women: Madame Durocher and Rita Lobato]. *Rev. do Inst. Hist. e Geog. Brasileiro [Brazil] 1980 (328): 53-56.* At a time when Brazilian women were not allowed to enter the professions, Marie Josephine Mathilde Durocher (1809-93) and Rita Lobato Velho Lopes (b. 1867) were the first exceptions. The former was a midwife, author of many publications, and a leader in her profession. The latter was a physician, active though not prominent among her colleagues. Refs. 19c

Durova, Nadezhda

1946. Heldt, Barbara. NADEZHDA DUROVA: RUSSIA'S CAVALRY MAID. *Hist. Today [Great Britain] 1983 33(Feb): 24-27.* Describes how Russian novelist and memorialist Nadezhda Durova (1786-1866) masqueraded as a man and a soldier in the Russian army to escape the usual confining role reserved for women, and recounts events from contemporary Russian military campaigns. 1806-66

Duval, Marie

1947. Kunzle, David. MARIE DUVAL AND ALLY SLOPER. *History Workshop Journal [Great Britain] 1986 (21): 132-140.* Affirms the responsibility of Marie Duval, not her husband Charles Ross, for the development of the first regular, continuing comic strip and cartoon character, Ally Sloper. Examines the professional career of Marie Duval and accords her a primary place not only as a female caricaturist, but for her graphic experimentation and its wider influence on modern European art. 2 illus., 9 notes. 1867-76

Duverger, Jozef

1948. Schryver, A. de. IN MEMORIAM PROF. DR. JOZEF DUVERGER (1899-1979) [In memoriam: Jozef Duverger (1899-1979)]. *Handelingen der Maatschappij voor Geschiedenis en Oudheidkunde te Gent [Belgium] 1979 33: 1-2.* Obituary of the historical society's vice chairman for over 30 years and professor of art history at the Higher Institute for Art History and Archeology of the National University, Ghent, since 1932, who played an important role in the development of Belgian art history, opened hitherto unexploited source materials, and was active as an organizer of congresses and colloquia in his field. 1899-1979

Dvorník, Francis

1949. Němec, Ludvík. FRANCIS DVORNÍK—A MASTER OF HISTORICAL SYNTHESIS. *Kosmas 1985 4(2): 133-148.* Father Dvorník (1893-1975) brought from Czechoslovakia a brilliant background in Byzantino-Slavic studies, enhanced by his ecumenism and researches in church history. 1893-1975

Dwyer, Michael

1950. O'Dwyer, B. W. MICHAEL DWYER AND THE 1807 PLAN OF INSURRECTION. *J. of the Royal Australian Hist. Soc. [Australia] 1983 69(2): 73-82.* Michael Dwyer had taken part in Robert Emmet's failed revolution in Ireland, 23 July 1803. Since the British despaired of capturing him, he and his companions, Marin Burke, Hugh Byrne, Arthur Devlin, and John Mernagh, were given money and free transportation to Australia aboard the convict transport ship *Tellicherry,* which left Cobh, Cork Harbour, for Botany Bay on 31 August 1805. Describes the conflict between Dwyer and Governor William Bligh over Dwyer's efforts to foment an insurrection in Botany Bay. Bligh accused Dwyer of treason and Dwyer accused Bligh of persecuting him. Neither charge was true. 42 notes. 1803-08

Dyer, Reginald Edward Harry

1951. Bakshi, Z. C. GENERAL DYER AND THE PUNJAB DISTURBANCES OF 1919. *Army Q. and Defence J. [Great Britain] 1983 113(2): 168-175.* British Brigadier General Reginald Edward Harry Dyer was punished lightly for the massacre of defenseless and trapped civilians during civil disturbances in Amritsar, Punjab in 1919. 1919

Dzhinot, Yordan Hadzhikonstantinov

1952. Sazdov, Tomé. YORDAN HADZHIKONSTANTINOV DZHINOT—A LEADING LIGHT IN THE MACEDONIAN REVIVAL. *Macedonian Rev. [Yugoslavia] 1982 12(3): 249-251.* Briefly outlines the life of the Macedonian writer and educator Yordan Hadzhikonstantinov Dzhinot (b. 1821) and his role in the Macedonian national revival. 19c

Dzierżyńska, Zofia

1953. Muszkat, Marian. NA MARGINESIE PAMIĘTNIKÓW ZOFII DZIERŻYŃSKIEJ [A note on the memoirs of Zofia Dzierżyńska]. *Zeszyty Hist. [France] 1981 (57): 220-225.* Reviews the memoirs of Zofia Dzierżyńska, the wife of Felix Dzerzhinsky, the founder of the Soviet secret service. Describes her family circle and criticizes her silence on Stalin's liquidation of Polish Communists and Polish-Jewish Communists during the purges of the late 1930's. Zofia's husband during the Revolution saved many Poles in order to use them for a future Soviet Poland. The memoirs were first published in Russian in Moscow in 1975 but were later republished in Poland in Polish. 4 notes. 20c

E

Eberlein, Alfred

1954. Bahne, Siegfried. NACHRUF AUF ALFRED EBERLEIN [In memorian of Alfred Eberlein]. *Internationale Wissenschaftliche Korrespondenz zur Geschichte der Deutschen Arbeiterbewegung [West Germany] 1982 18(4): 590-592.* Describes the life of Alfred Eberlein (1916-82) who was the director of the library of the Institute for the History of the Worker Movement in Bochum, West Germany and prints a list of his publications. 1933-82

Ebert, Friedrich

1955. Vosske, Heinz. FÜR IMMER MIT DEM WERDEN UND WACHSEN DER DDR VERBUNDEN. FRIEDRICH EBERT [Forever linked with the creation and growth of the German Democratic Republic: Friedrich Ebert]. *Beiträge zur Gesch. der Arbeiterbewegung [East Germany] 1982 24(1): 104-113.* Traces the life, career, and political activities of the East German leader Friedrich Ebert (1894-1979). The author pays particular attention to his role in establishing and developing the Socialist Unity Party, strengthening its ideological unity, and establishing and strengthening the East German state, as well as his role in rebuilding Berlin. He also considers Ebert's contribution to establishing a socialist society in East Germany and his work for peace and international cooperation. Based on Ebert's writings and secondary sources; 23 notes. 1945-79

Eça de Queiroz, José Maria de

1956. Kandel, Boris. EÇA DE QUEIROZ IN RUSSIAN. *Luso-Brazilian Review 1985 22(2): 175-177.* Some of the works of José Maria de Eça de Queiroz (1845-1900), the greatest representative of critical realism in Portuguese literature, have been translated into Russian. The author provides a bibliography of these novels and stories and notes works dealing with Eça de Queiroz in contemporary Soviet literary criticism. ca 1900-76

Eckardt, Julius

1957. Garleff, Michael. JULIUS ECKARDT IN DEUTSCHLAND [Julius Eckardt in Germany]. *Zeitschrift für Ostforschung [West Germany] 1984 33(4): 534-550.* Analyzes life and the activity of German-Baltic political publicist, historian, and diplomat Julius Eckardt (1836-1908). He committed himself to the liberal reform movement in Riga in the 1860's, and later to a collective defensive fight against the beginning of Russification. He left his homeland in 1866, and, free from the pressure of censorship, advocated the recognition of the political and cultural peculiarities of the Baltic provinces as editor of G. Freytag's *Die Grenzboten* in Germany, but very soon recognized that Russian mistrust could increase in reaction to this; he changed the emphasis of his journalism to the presentation of Russia's domestic and foreign affairs. Eckardt went to Hamburg in 1870, where, as chief editor of *Der Hamburgische Correspondent* and as secretary of the senate, he participated in public activity in journalism and the civil service. In 1882, the incompatibility of these fields forced him to resume his travels. After a three-year term in ministries in Berlin, he spent his last two decades in the diplomatic service of the German Reich abroad. 1860's-1908

Eden, Anthony

1958. Rose, Norman. THE RESIGNATION OF ANTHONY EDEN. *Hist. J. [Great Britain] 1982 25(4): 911-931.* Anthony Eden's resignation as Foreign Secretary on 20 February 1938 has led to his being saddled with a romanticized reputation as a politician of strict principles. Detailed study of the circumstances of his disagreements with Neville Chamberlain over talks with Italy, recognition of the conquest of Abyssinia, and the withdrawal of Italian troops from Spain show a mixture of principle and personal whim and pride, coupled with resentment at Chamberlain's high-handed methods of conducting diplomacy. His reputation as a champion of antiappeasement grew later, and to contemporaries his behavior seemed confused and impractical. Based on documents in the Public Record Office, the Chamberlain papers in Birmingham University Library, and published sources; 118 notes. 1938

Edgeworth, Francis Ysidro

1959. Hicks, John. FRANCIS YSIDRO EDGEWORTH. *Hermathena [Ireland] 1983 (135): 157-174.* A biographical sketch of Francis Ysidro Edgeworth, an Irish professor of political economy at Oxford, which describes his approach to certain technical problems in economic theory. 1891-1926

Edmonds, James

1960. French, David. "OFFICIAL BUT NOT HISTORY"? SIR JAMES EDMONDS AND THE OFFICIAL HISTORY OF THE GREAT WAR. *Journal of the Royal United Services Institute for Defence Studies [Great Britain] 1986 131(1): 58-63.* The official British history of World War I, *History of the Great War* (1922-47), has often been criticized for lacking critical analysis of the performance of the British high command. Its author, Sir James Edmonds (1861-1956), was a military contemporary of many British leaders and evinced a personal distaste for criticizing his fellows and those in authority. He also needed, during his thirty years of work compiling the history, the cooperation of those very men he might have criticized. Edmonds' style was to distribute prepublication copies of the history's volumes for comment, which additionally served to tone down any controversial sections. To his credit, Edmonds did sort through massive amounts of material and put together a comprehensive, if generally uncritical, account of the war. Based on Edmonds' Memoirs, the Edmonds Papers, the Liddell Hart Papers, and other primary and secondary sources; 54 notes. 1920-50

Edward, Duke of Kent

1961. Bland, Olivia. THE DUKE OF KENT & KENSINGTON PALACE. *Hist. Today [Great Britain] 1982 32(Jan): 28-34.* Brief biography of Edward, Duke of Kent (1767-1820), son of King George III and Queen Charlotte and father of Queen Victoria, focusing on his financial mismanagement and his partial success in renovating his residence in the king's private apartments, Kensington Palace. 1790's-1820

Edward VIII

1962. Spruance, Sherril, comp. EDWARD VIII AND MRS SIMPSON: FIFTY YEARS LATER: REMEMBERING THE ABDICATION. *British Heritage 1986 7(5): 52-57.* Surveys, with photographs, the events of King Edward VIII's abdication and marriage to Mrs. Wallis Warfield Simpson in 1936-37. 1936-37

Efimov, Geronti V.

1963. —. G. V. EFIMOV. [G. V. Efimov]. *Novaia i Noveishaia Istoriia [USSR] 1981 (1): 220.* Obituary of Soviet historian G. V. Efimov. He finished his studies in Leningrad in 1935 and in 1941 became head of the department of Far Eastern Studies at Leningrad State University, a post he was to occupy for nearly 40 years. His main interests were the life of Sun Yat-Sen, the Chinese revolution of 1911-13, and Far Eastern international relations. He wrote *Ocherki Po Novoi i Noveishei Istorii Kitaia* [Studies in Modern Chinese History] and many textbooks on the Far East and had an active political life. 1935-80

1964. —. GERONTII VALENTINOVICH EFIMOV [Geronti Valentinovich Efimov]. *Vestnik Leningradskogo U.: Seriia Istorii, Iazyka i Literatury [USSR] 1981 (1): 123-124.* An obituary for the Soviet sinologist Geronti Valentinovich Efimov (1906-80) who was in charge of the Department of History of the Countries of the Far East of the Eastern Faculty of Leningrad University. Efimov was the author of around 140 works on modern and contemporary Chinese history, his best work being on the Sun Zhongshan (Sun Yatsen) period. 1906-80

Egalité, Philippe

See Louis-Philippe-Joseph

Egerton, George

1965. Stetz, Margaret Diane. "'George Egerton': Woman and Writer of the Eighteen-Nineties." Harvard U. 1982. 264 pp. *DAI 1982 43(5): 1558-A.* DA8222708 1884-1945

Egorov, Aleksandr I.

1966. Gusarevich, S. VOIN, POLKOVODETS, TEORETIK [Warrior, regimental commander, theoretician]. *Voenno-Istoricheskii Zhurnal [USSR] 1983 (10): 50-55.* A biography of Marshal of the Soviet Union Aleksandr I. Egorov (1883-1939), in connection with the centenary of his birth. Already a colonel at the end of the first world war, he joined the Bolsheviks and served brilliantly in the Red Army during the Civil War. In 1935 he was appointed marshal, and in 1938 commander of the Transcaucasian Military District. Based on published documents and secondary sources; photo, 14 notes. 1883-1939

Ehrenberg, Christian Gottfried

1967. Siesser, William G. CHRISTIAN GOTTFRIED EHRENBERG: FOUNDER OF MICROPALEONTOLOGY. *Centaurus [Denmark] 1981 25(3): 166-188.* Christian Gottfried Ehrenberg (1795-1876), a German, pioneered in virtually untouched fields; however, his interpretations resulting from these biological studies were often wrong. He maintained that microorganisms were animals and possessed complex internal organs. This, plus the high cost of his book, *Mikrogeologie* (1854), may explain why he was underestimated and overlooked by historians and yet warranted the title of founder of micropaleontology. 79 notes. 1818-76

Ehrenburg, Ilya

1968. Bérard-Zarzycka, Ewa. ILYA EHRENBOURG: JUIF, RUSSE ET EUROPEEN, 1891-1928 [Ilya Ehrenburg: Jew, Russian, and European, 1891-1928]. *Cahiers du Monde Russe et Soviètique [France] 1985 26(2): 219-242.* The first part of Ehrenburg's life was marked by two sojourns in the West, 1908-17 and 1921-40, and was for him a period of dilemmas and complex choices of a cultural identity: Jew, Russian, or European? Ehrenburg cut himself off from his Jewish roots, turning first to Catholicism, then to "Russianism." Later, he reverted to the Jewish heritage because it represented for him an essential element of challenge to Europe and to Russia, spiritually rent by war and revolution and dominated by the cult of progress, discipline, and collectivism. He contrasted this with the "Jewish spirit," which he defined as a quest for universalism, an eternal revolt, and loneliness. However, in Ehrenburg's view this "Jewish genius" can conceivably exist only within the framework of the diaspora and cultural osmosis. 1908-17

Eich, Günter

1969. Cuomo, Glenn Raymond. "A Study of Günter Eich's Life and Work between 1933 and 1945." Ohio State U. 1982. 265 pp. *DAI 1982 43(5): 1559-A.* DA8222071
1933-45

Eichholzer, Herbert

1970. Ecker, D. "Der Architekt Herbert Eichholzer (1903-1943)" [The architect Herbert Eichholzer (1903-1943)]. Graz Technical U. [Austria] *DAI-C 1986 47(1): 1; 47/2c.* 1927-37

Eikhenbaum, Boris

1971. Berard-Zarzycka, Ewa. LA GENESE DES TRAVAUX SUR LE *LITERATURNYJ BYT* D'APRES LE JOURNAL D'EJXENBAUM [The genesis of works on *literaturnyi byt* according to Eikhenbaum's journal]. *Revue des Etudes Slaves [France] 1985 57(1): 83-89.* Retraces the philosophical evolution of Soviet literary critic Boris Eikhenbaum (1886-1959) through observations on history and Soviet intellectual life of the late 1910's and early 1920's recorded in his personal journal (published in part in *Kontekst* 1981, M., 1982, pp. 263-302) to locate the genesis of Eikhenbaum's late-1920's works on the *literaturnyi byt* [literary way of life]. Frustrated and isolated by the 1920's official sanction of Marxist views on writers' and literature's historical and social roles, Eikhenbaum developed an ever more active concept of the writer's relationship with history, which he apparently viewed as part of the *literaturnyi byt.* His belief in both his own and a public need for biographical works on intellectuals written from a historical way of life perspective led to much work on *literaturnyi byt,* 1925-27. 14 notes. 1917-29

1972. Čudakova, Marietta O. SOTSIAL'NAIA PRAKTIKA I NAUCHNAIA REFLEKSIIA V TVORCHESKOI BIOGRAFII B. EIKHENBAUMA [Social practice and scientific reflection in the creative biography of Boris Eikhenbaum]. *Revue des Etudes Slaves [France] 1985 57(1): 27-43.* Discusses the alternation and eventual fusion of sociohistorical and theoretical viewpoints in the works of Soviet literary critic Boris Eikhenbaum (1886-1959). Eikhenbaum abandoned his original personality-centered world view in the late 1910's, when he became involved in the Formalist Opoiaz literary movement. By the mid-1920's, however, changes in the Soviet social structure (including the rise to power of the action-oriented and literature-despising revolutionary generation of Soviet youth) caused Eikhenbaum as well as his friends and fellow critics and Opoiaz members Viktor Shklovskii (1893-1984) and Iuri Tynianov to see a need for a sociology of literature. Eikhenbaum's solution, a fusion of historical and theoretical approaches and of literary and critical styles in his late-1920's work, displeased Tynianov and Shklovskii, who preferred to do purely literary work while dreaming of a return to Opoiaz-style collaboration on theoretical publications. Journal of Boris Mikhailovich Eikhenbaum, letters, and secondary sources; 16 notes.
1906-29

1973. Depretto-Genty, Catherine. B. M. EJXENBAUM ET JU. N. TYNJANOV [B. M. Eikhenbaum and Iu. N. Tynianov]. *Revue des Etudes Slaves [France] 1985 57(1): 62-72.* Analyzes personal and professional relations between Soviet literary critics Iurii N. Tynianov and Boris M. Eikhenbaum (1886-1959) and compares their styles of criticism. Eikhenbaum and Tynianov frequently published similar conclusions on the same topics at about the same time. Despite this tendency, which was particularly pronounced in some of their 1920-25 works on 19th- and 20th-century Russian poets, Tynianov's reductionist style was readily distinguished from Eikhenbaum's expansive, historical treatment of literature. Based on letters, journals, autobiographies, and secondary sources; 59 notes. 1916-41

1974. Depretto-Genty, Catherine. B. M. EIKHENBAUM: LA MEMOIRE DU SIECLE [B. M. Eikhenbaum: the memory of the century]. *Revue des Etudes Slaves [France] 1985 57(1): 7-9.* Reviews the achievements of Soviet literary critic Boris M. Eikhenbaum (1886-1959). A leading Russian Formalist and one of the most productive representatives of the Opoiaz literary movement during the 1920's, Eikhenbaum produced innovative studies of 19th- and 20th-century authors during the 1930's and 1940's. His accomplishments as a literary theorist include his early discovery of the German school of "auditory philology," which inspired his works on Russian verse. Eikhenbaum was not only an eminent textologist and a notable literary specialist, but also a diarist and the author of a historically valuable mass of correspondence. Secondary sources; 8 photos, 4 notes. 1910's-59

1975. Eikhenbaum, Ol'ga Borisovna. PIS'MA B. M. EIKHENBAUMA K RODITELIAM [Boris M. Eikhenbaum's letters to his parents]. *Revue des Etudes Slaves [France] 1985 57(1): 11-25.* Prints selections from and summaries of letters written between 6 September 1905 and 14 March 1911 by Boris Mikhailovich Eikhenbaum (1886-1959), then a student in St. Petersburg, to his parents in Voronezh. The letters record Eikhenbaum's feelings about his studies in music and medicine, which he abandoned for literary criticism, and the humanities; his impressions of the 1907 trial of his anarchist brother, Vsevolod Eikhenbaum (1882-1945), known by his pseudonym, Vs. Volin, and his relations with his future wife. 17 notes. 1905-11

Einaudi, Luigi

1976. Caffè, Federico. EINAUDI E I SUOI LIBRI [Einaudi and his books]. *Veltro [Italy] 1982 26(1-2): 41-48.* Discusses Italian publisher Luigi Einaudi's love for books and his exceptionally busy career, based on the eight-volume *Cronache Economiche e Politiche di un Trentennio* and the two-volume *Catalogo della Biblioteca di Luigi Einaudi.*
1910's-60's

Einstein, Albert

1977. Broda, Engelbert. LUDWIG BOLTZMANN, ALBERT EINSTEIN UND FRANZ JOSEPH [Ludwig Boltzmann, Albert Einstein and Francis Joseph]. *Wiener Geschichtsblätter [Austria] 1983 38(3): 109-119.*
1880's-1910's

For abstract see ***Boltzmann, Ludwig***

1978. Duffy, M. C. ESSAY REVIEW: COMMEMORATING EINSTEIN. *Ann. of Sci. [Great Britain] 1982 39(6): 593-603.* Reviews *The Impact of Modern Scientific Ideas on Society: In Commemoration of Einstein,* edited by C. M. Kinnon, A. N. Kholodkin, and J. G. Richardson (1981), papers presented at the UNESCO Symposium on the Impact of Modern Scientific Ideas on Society, Munich-Ulm, 18-20 September 1978, along with the addresses delivered on the occasion of UNESCO's celebration of the hundredth anniversary of Einstein's birth, Paris, 9 May 1979. The introduction and papers contain many exaggerated claims about Einstein's impact on society, and the impact of aesthetic physics on society. Many of the papers idolize Einstein and banalize science in general and physics in particular. Aesthetic physics is seen as superior to experimental and theoretical physics. Based on secondary sources; 12 notes. 20c

1979. Eamon, William. INVENTING THE WORLD: EINSTEIN AND THE GENERATION OF 1905. *Antioch Review 1985 43(3): 340-351.* Spurred on in part by a revolution in technology, there emerged in the early 20th century a number of individuals so innovative in their outlook on the world that their ideas constituted an intellectual revolution; pays particular attention to the role of Albert Einstein. 1900-33

1980. Feuer, Lewis S. EINSTEIN AND THE PRAGUE CIRCLE. *Midstream 1982 28(6): 36-39.* Examines Albert Einstein's (1879-1955) stay in Prague, 1911-13, focusing on the influence of religious and philosophical thinkers there, including Max Brod and Martin Buber; briefly compares Einstein's metaphysical views with those of Spinoza. 1911-13

1981. Gilbert, Felix. EINSTEIN UND DAS EUROPA SEINER ZEIT [Einstein and the Europe of his time]. *Hist. Zeits. [West Germany] 1981 233(1): 1-33.* Albert Einstein's career was exceptional in many ways. Aside from his scientific accomplishments, he also seemed to rise above forces of nationalism. Born in Ulm in 1879, he moved to Switzerland at age 15 and became a Swiss citizen. He refused to sign a prowar manifesto in 1914, although he permitted Germany to claim him as a citizen when he received the Nobel Prize in 1922. Einstein encouraged scientists and intellectuals to speak out against the forces that disrupted the international scientific community. After World War I, Einstein was the only German scientist with close ties to scientists in formerly enemy countries. He participated in an international commission of scientists for international cooperation. He became associated with Zionism and was deeply affected by the intensification of anti-Semitism in Germany. Based on Einstein's correspondence; 62 notes. 1879-1955

1982. Gribanov, D. P. OTNOSHENIE A. EINSHTEINA I IDEALISTICHESKOI FILOSOFII [The relationship of Albert Einstein and idealistic philosophy]. *Voprosy Filosofii [USSR] 1981 (7): 67-75.* Although Einstein's works contain passages which could be misconstrued as support for idealism, he supported the principles of materialism and dialectic and was a realist. 9 notes. 1920's-50's

1983. Grigorian, A. T. W STULECIE URODZIN EINSTEINA [On the occasion of the centenary of Einstein's birth]. *Kwartalnik Hist. Nauki i Techniki [Poland] 1979 24(4): 805-811.* Discusses the life of Albert Einstein from 1879 to 1935 and divides the subject into four parts: his youth in Germany up to 1900, his Swiss period to 1914, his German period in Berlin up to 1933, and lastly his American period at Princeton University to 1955. Concentrates on Einstein's attitude toward the history of science, particularly classical mechanics, and his criteria for assessing the value of physical theories. Photo, 10 notes. 1879-1955

1984. Klein, Martin J. ON UNIFIED BIOGRAPHIES. *Isis 1984 75(277): 377-379.* Reviews Abraham Pais's *"Subtle is the Lord...": The Science and the Life of Albert Einstein* (1982), criticizing its topical organization, but commending its "rich and rewarding... discussion of the intense, unremitting scientific work that was the essential activity of his [Einstein's] long life." 1879-1955

1985. Pyenson, Lewis. AUDACIOUS ENTERPRISE: THE EINSTEINS AND ELECTROTECHNOLOGY IN LATE NINETEENTH-CENTURY MUNICH. *Hist. Studies in the Physical Sci. 1982 12(2): 373-392.* Discusses how Albert Einstein's (1879-1955) uncle Jakob and father Hermann (1847-1902) fared as the owner-operators of an electrical apparatus factory in Munich, 1886-94. The failure of the business in 1894 impressed on young Albert the need to seek practical work and also left him with a sensitivity for physical instrumentation. Based on primary sources; 2 plates, 3 fig., 41 notes. 1886-94

Eisler, Gerhart

1986. Schebera, Jürgen. KOMMUNIST, PUBLIZIST, POLITIKER: GERHART EISLER [Communist, political writer, politician: Gerhart Eisler]. *Beiträge zur Gesch. der Arbeiterbewegung [East Germany] 1983 25(5): 724-736.* Traces the life, career, political and journalistic activities of the German political writer Gerhart Eisler (1897-1968). He was born in Leipzig, but his family moved to Vienna in 1901 and most of his education took place there. As a young man Eisler was deeply affected by the horrors of war and joined the Red Guard in Vienna in 1918. His journalistic career began in 1919 and in 1921 he went to Berlin to work as a political journalist for the German Communist Party (his sister was the Communist Ruth Fischer). His political activities continued, and in 1925 he became involved in the party's bureau of information. The author considers Eisler's career in the Communist Party, his extensive travels to the USSR, China, Sweden, Spain, France, and the United States. During World War II he worked as a political journalist in the United States and was imprisoned in 1948 for Communist activities and was deported to Germany in 1949. In Leipzig he continued his writings and political activities until his death in 1968. Secondary sources; 49 notes. 1918-68

Eisner, Kurt

1987. Fletcher, Roger A. A REVISIONIST DIALOGUE ON WILHELMINE WELTPOLITIK: JOSEPH BLOCH AND KURT EISNER 1907-1914. *Int. Wiss. Korrespondenz zur Gesch. der Deutschen Arbeiterbewegung [West Germany] 1980 16(4): 453-477.* 1907-14
*For abstract see **Bloch, Joseph.***

Ekonomides, Euthimios

1988. Natsiou, Dēmitri Th. SYMVOLĒ STĒN ISTORIA TOU TYPOU [A contribution to the history of the press]. *Ēpeirōtikē Hestia [Greece] 1981 30(347-348): 219-233.* Euthimios Ekonomides (d. 1888) was born in Trikala, Thessaly, studied in Germany, and taught in several Greek secondary schools in Europe. After sojourns in Trikala and Athens he settled in Lamia publishing a newspaper in which he advocated the liberation of Thessaly from the Ottoman Empire. In 1881, as a result of the Russo-Turkish War, Thessaly became part of Greece. Oekonomides returned to Trikala where he published the *Beacon of Olympia,* 1881-87, an excellent 4-page paper that commented on local politics, the activities of the Jewish community, and the educational institutions of the city. The archives of the paper are in the Benakeion Library; 196 notes. 1881-87

Ekzarkh, Alexander

1989. Voillery, Pierre; Voillery, Pierre and Peeva, Antonia, transl. RUSSOPHILIE OU FRANCOPHILIE DANS LA RENAISSANCE BULGARE? A PROPOS D'UN "ACTIVISTE DE LA RENAISSANCE BULGARE": L'AUTOBIOGRAPHIE D'ALEXANDRE EXARH, 1810-1891 [Russophilia or Francophilia in the Bulgarian revival? About an "activist of the Bulgarian revival": the autobiography of Alexander Ekzarkh, 1810-91]. *Cahiers du Monde Russe et Soviétique [France] 1981 22(4): 401-415.* Alexander Ekzarkh, born at the beginning of the 19th century in Stara

Zagora, was a central figure of the Bulgarian revival and one of the founders of independent Bulgaria. His manuscript autobiography, reproduced in its entirety here, offers a rare view of the life of a prominent Ottoman Christian and also sheds new light on events in Rumelia. 1810-91

Eldin, François

1990. Cornevin, Robert. A PROPOS DU PROTESTANTISME HAÏTIEN, UN PRECURSEUR: LE PASTEUR FRANÇOIS ELDIN [Regarding Haitian Protestantism, a precursor: Pastor François Eldin]. *Bull. de la Soc. de l'Hist. du Protestantisme Français [France] 1981 127(3): 385-396.* Pastor Eldin was the first French Protestant missionary in Haiti. A native of the Ardèche, Eldin was born in 1825. After entering the ministry and completing missionary training, he sailed for the West Indies in 1851. He spent several months on other islands but soon moved to Haiti, where he lived until 1864. Later he wrote a book describing Haiti and his experiences there. It contains much detail about Haitian society, geography, and religious practices. Based on François Eldin's *Haïti: 13 Ans de Séjour aux Antilles* (1878). 1851-64

Elekes, Lajos

1991. Kardos, József. ELEKES LAJOS (1914-1982) [Lajos Elekes, 1914-82]. *Levéltári Közlemények [Hungary] 1982 53(2): 329-332.* In 1947, Lajos Elekes joined the Lenin Institute as professor of history. Later in his capacity as the founder and director of the Pedagogical Research Center for Higher Education and the dean of his faculty he participated in many national and international conferences. His last appearance at the international historical congress in San Francisco brought him respect and stature and also strengthened the international position of Marxist ideology and history. 1940-82

Eliade, Mircea

1992. Cain, Seymour. MIRCEA ELIADE: CREATIVE EXILE. *Midstream 1982 28(6): 50-58.* Examines the career and scholarly pursuits of Mircea Eliade from 1928-78, focusing on Eliade's academic endeavors during his self-imposed exile in France after 1945, and on his place in 20th-century religious thought. 1928-78

Elias, Norbert

1993. —. TRE INTERVENTI SU NORBERT ELIAS [Three views on Norbert Elias]. *Rassegna Italiana di Sociologia [Italy] 1985 26(1): 100-128.*

Roversi, Antonio. STORIA E CIVILTA: COMMENTO A NORBERT ELIAS [History and civilization: commentary on Norbert Elias], *pp. 100-106.* Discusses the importance of Norbert Elias, a member of the Frankfurt School and a historian of civilization, whose three major books are : *La Società di Corte, La Civiltà delle Buone Maniere,* and *Potere e Civiltà.*

Rossetti, Carlo. LA SOCIOLOGIA DELLA STORIA DI NORBERT ELIAS [The sociology of history of Norbert Elias], *pp. 106-116.* Discusses the concepts of "figuration" and interdependence in the theory of civilization of Norbert Elias.

Bertelli, Sergio and Calvi, Giulia. RITUALE, CEREMONIALE ED ETICHETTA: UN COMMENTO AD ALCUNE CATEGORIE DI NORBERT ELIAS [Ritual, ceremony, and etiquette: a note on some categories of Norbert Elias], *pp. 116-128.* Discusses theoretical and historical oppositions in Elias. 1897-1983

Eliava, Shalva Z.

1994. Toidze, L. M. SLAVNYI BOETS LENINSKOI PARTII [A glorious warrior of the Leninist Party]. *Voprosy Istorii KPSS [USSR] 1984 (3): 129-132.* A brief political biography of Shalva Z. Eliava (1883-1937), a Georgian Communist who helped to establish Bolshevik control in Georgia in 1921. He became a revolutionary while studying in the Juridical Faculty at Petersburg University. As a Bolshevik he participated in the 1905 events in Tbilisi, was twice exiled, and after the 1917 Revolution became head of the VTsIK Commission on Turkestan. Later he was a Soviet diplomat in Turkey and Iran and an official in Moscow ministries. Based on archival material in the Central State Archive of the October Revolution and published accounts in Georgian and Russian; 16 notes. ca 1900-37

Eliot, George

1995. McCormick, Kathleen. GEORGE ELIOT'S EARLIEST PROSE: THE COVENTRY *HERALD* AND THE COVENTRY FICTION. *Victorian Periodicals Review 1986 19(2): 57-62.* Many of George Eliot's novels reflect the influence of her newspaper articles written during the 1840's for the *Coventry Herald and Observer.* Characters and plots in her Coventry novels depict topics and characters from the pages of the *Herald.* 1840's

1996. Rothblatt, Sheldon. GEORGE ELIOT AS A TYPE OF EUROPEAN INTELLECTUAL. *History of European Ideas [Great Britain] 1986 7(1): 47-65.* George Eliot (Mary Ann Evans; 1819-80) in some ways resembled the intellectual type in early Victorian England known as the clerisy. She was troubled by the disruptive consequences of egoism—seeking money, power, status, or position at the expense of others. She appeared to favor collectivity over self and believed in duty. She disliked class or sectarian conflict. She did not believe in trying to end injustice by overturning the social order. Yet unlike the anti-individualistic clerisy, Eliot remained loyal to Victorian liberal individualism. Perhaps she can best be characterized as a "woman of letters." Based on the works of Eliot and others; 49 notes. 1837-80

1997. Springer, Marlene. STOWE AND ELIOT: AN EPISTOLARY FRIENDSHIP. *Biography 1986 9(1): 59-81.* An examination of the personal correspondence between Harriet B. Stowe (whose letters remain unpublished) and George Eliot reveals much about the close connections formed by the important women writers of the period. Heretofore unexplained in depth by scholars, the correspondence discloses that they exchanged literary criticism, explored their religious positions with an attendant discussion of spiritualism and Stowe's conversation with Charlotte Brontë's spirit, shared their bond of womanhood and by extension their interest in women's rights, and even probed their private relations with husbands, siblings, children, and friends. 1869-80

Eliot, T. S.

1998. Blanshard, Brand. ELIOT AT OXFORD. *Southern Review 1985 21(4): 889-898.* Presents a classmate's memoir of T. S. Eliot as a student at Oxford, including personal anecdotes and a summary of Eliot's philosophical studies. 1914-15

1999. DuSautoy, Peter. T. S. ELIOT: PERSONAL REMINISCENCES. *Southern Review 1985 21(4): 947-956.* Prints the reminiscences of Peter du Sautoy, an associate of

T. S. Eliot at the London publishing house of Faber and Faber, where Eliot was a part-time director in 1945-65. 1945-65

Elisabeth de France

2000. Destremau, Noëlle. LA DOULEUR DE VIVRE DE MADAME ELISABETH [Madame Elisabeth's displeasure of living]. *Historama [France] 1985 (19): 50-51, 56-57.* An anecdotal and episodic account of the life of Elisabeth Philippine Marie Hélène, (Madame Elisabeth de France, 1764-94), who died on the scaffold during the French Revolution, focusing on her fortitude, altruism, and devotion to her brother, Louis XVI. 1789-94

Elizabeth I

2001. Haigh, Christopher. READING HISTORY: THE REIGN OF ELIZABETH I. *History Today [Great Britain] 1985 35(Aug): 53-55.* Reviews 20th-century historiography on the life and times of Elizabeth I of England, noting the political and religious conflicts of the 16th century that influenced Elizabeth's policies. 1558-1603

2002. Ives, Eric. QUEEN ELIZABETH I AND THE PEOPLE OF ENGLAND. *Historian [Great Britain] 1983 (1): 3-10.* Reviews the life and times of Elizabeth I with emphasis on her court and on the methods she used to keep England viable, united, and free from foreign invasion. 1558-1603

2003. Loades, David. ELISABETH IRE, LA REINE DE LA PROPAGANDE POLITIQUE [Elizabeth I: queen of political propaganda]. *Histoire [France] 1982 (43): 48-58.* Elizabeth's accession to the crown in 1558 prompted the development of a personality cult encouraged by the queen herself and her patriotic Protestant supporters; although unable to resolve the paralyzing financial problems of the crown, her success in achieving political and religious unity justify her reputation. 1553-1603

Elizabeth (Queen Mother)

2004. Lewis, Brenda Ralph. QUEEN ELIZABETH THE QUEEN MOTHER. *British Heritage 1984 5(4): 10-23.* Recounts the life of this beloved woman emphasizing her serenity and common sense attitudes in the six decades she's been in public view. 1920's-84

Elkaïm-Sartre, Arlette

2005. Charmé, Stuart. SARTRE'S JEWISH DAUGHTER: AN INTERVIEW WITH ARLETTE ELKAIM-SARTRE. *Midstream 1986 32(8): 24-28.* Arlette Elkaïm-Sartre, the adopted daughter of French writer Jean Paul Sartre, responds to questions about her evolving awareness of her Jewish identity and what her father thought about various Jewish issues. 1986

Ellis, Earl H.

2006. Ballendorf, Dirk Anthony. EARL HANCOCK ELLIS: THE MAN AND HIS MISSION. *US Naval Inst. Pro. 1983 109(11): 53-60.* Between 1911 and 1921 Marine Lt. Col. Earl H. Ellis gained recognition as a brilliant military planner. He was also an alcoholic. In 1921-23 Ellis undertook a secret intelligence reconnaissance of the Japanese-held Eastern Caroline Islands. His nephritis grew increasingly worse as he travelled through the islands and he died on Palau on 12 May 1923. The Japanese then confiscated his notes, charts, and code books. Based on archival sources; biblio., 5 notes. 1911-23

Ellis, Havelock

2007. Draznin, Yaffa. "The Olive Schreiner/Havelock Ellis Correspondence, February 24, 1884 through July 8, 1884: An Annotated Illustration of the Historical Editing of Private Letters." U. of Southern California 1985. *DAI 1985 46(5): 1376-A.* 1884

Eloy Valenzuela, Juan

2008. Otero D'Costa, Enrique. EL DR. JUAN ELOY VALENZUELA, SUBDIRECTOR DE LA EXPEDICION BOTANICA [Juan Eloy Valenzuela, deputy director of the botanical expedition]. *Bol. de Hist. y Antigüedades [Colombia] 1983 70(742): 787-834.* Juan Eloy Valenzuela (1756-1834) showed an early interest in natural science and collaborated with José Celestino Mutis in the botanical expedition of colonial New Granada. In 1786 he became parish priest of Bucaramanga, where, in addition to his ecclesiastical duties and civic service, he continued scientific studies. Though he has been called a patriot in the wars of independence, he actually was a royalist, and his influence helped make Bucaramanga and surrounding territory a loyalist stronghold. He ultimately reconciled himself to the patriots' victory and became an admirer of Simón Bolívar. In his final years he continued serving his parishioners and published articles of scientific, statistical, and generally edifying content. 8 notes. 1756-1834

Elpidin, Mikhail K.

2009. Senn, Alfred Erich. M. K. ELPIDIN: REVOLUTIONARY PUBLISHER. *Russian Rev. 1982 41(1): 11-23.* Mikhail K. Elpidin (1835-1908), sometime revolutionary and publisher, operated a radical Russian bookstore in Geneva and also worked for the tsarist secret police for a time. Elpidin fled to Switzerland in 1865 where he tried to establish himself as a publisher, provoking a split between the younger emigres and the older group led by Alexander Herzen. Elpidin's chief publishing achievement was printing Chernyshevski's novel *Chto delat'?* and although his publishing ventures were not a monetary success, his bookstore flourished. His political views were radical but ill-conceived and his fellow emigres did not take him seriously. His later connections with the tsarist secret police were well-known to the emigre community but apparently of little consequence in revealing secret information of any kind. 49 notes. 1865-1908

Elsener, Ferdinand

2010. Carlen, Louis. NEKROLOG: FERDINAND ELSENER [Obituary: Ferdinand Elsener]. *Hist. Jahrbuch [West Germany] 1983 103(2): 514-516.* Ferdinand Elsener (1912-82) was born in Rapperswil in the Swiss canton St. Gallen, attended a Benedictine secondary school, and studied law at the universities in Vienna and Zurich. At first he worked as an attorney in Rapperswil, but later became a professor of history of law and church history at the University of Tübingen in West Germany. He concentrated his studies on the reception of Roman law and Canon law. After his retirement he returned to his native Switzerland and continued his research in the history of Swiss law and customs. He published extensively. 1912-82

Elvert, Christian Friedrich d'

2011. Hadler, Frank. K MORAVSKÉMU KULTURNÍMU DĚJEPISECTVÍ 19. STOLETÍ [Moravian cultural historiography in the 19th century]. *Časopis Matice Moravské [Czechoslovakia] 1984 103(1-2): 19-28.* For 45 years Christian Friedrich d'Elvert (1803-96) presided over the Historical-Statistical Section (founded 1850) of the Moravian-Silesian Society of Agricultural, Natural, and Geographical Sciences. D'Elvert at first approached the material and intellectual culture of modern Moravia in the spirit of contemporary German *Kulturgeschichte,* but being a nationalist and mayor of predominantly German Brno, he could not view the Czech-German symbiosis objectively. By the 1880's his writings had become the tendentious "national" history that appealed to the German Moravian bourgeoisie. Primary sources; 28 notes. German summary. 1850-95

Emerit, Marcel

2012. Ştefănescu, Ştefan. MARCEL EMERIT, LORS DE SON 80e ANNIVERSAIRE [On the occasion of Marcel Emerit's 80th birthday]. *Analele U. Bucureşti: Istorie [Romania] 1979 28: 25-29.* The French scholar Marcel Emerit (b. 1899) went on a scholarship to the Institut Français de Hautes Etudes de Roumanie in Bucharest in 1923. He was subsequently professor at the universities of Bucharest, Lille, and Algiers. He is a corresponding member of the Institut de France. The problems of Romanian history have influenced his work as a historian. His Romanian studies deal with the social history of Romania and its relations with France during the period after the constitution of modern Romania. 13 notes. 1899-1979

Eminescu, Mihai

2013. Valmarin, Luisa. MIHAI EMINESCU: UNA PRESENTAZIONE [Mihai Eminescu: an introduction]. *Balcanica [Italy] 1983 2(4): 76-89.* Traces the career of Mihai Eminescu (1850-89), Romanian journalist and poet, focusing on his use of philosophy, folklore, and symbols from the noncanonical books of the Bible (especially 2 Enoch). 1860's-80's

Emmanuel Philibert

2014. Merlin, Pierpaolo. GIUSTIZIA, AMMINISTRAZIONE E POLITICA NEL PIEMONTE DI EMANUELE FILIBERTO. LA RIORGANIZZAZIONE DEL SENATO DI TORINO [Justice, administration, and politics in Piedmont under Emmanuel Philibert: reorganization of the senate in Turin]. *Bol. Storico-Bibliografico Subalpino [Italy] 1982 80(1): 35-94.* Describes the political achievements of Emmanuel Philibert, 10th Duke of Savoy, 1553-80, centering on his reorganization of the Turin senate and reform of the bench in Piedmont after the Cateau-Cambrésis peace treaty (1559). 1559-80

Emparán, Vicente de

2015. Leal, Idelfonso. DON VICENTE DE EMPARÁN: UN PERSONAJE POLÉMICO DEL 19 DE ABRIL DE 1810 [Vicente de Emparán: a controversial figure of 19 April 1810]. *Bol. de la Acad. Nac. de la Hist. [Venezuela] 1980 63(250): 343-346.* Points out the achievements of Vicente de Emparán (1747-1820), governor and field marshall of Cumaná and Barcelona (Venezuela). He built hospitals and schools, improved ports and farming, decorated temples at Cumaná, and provided Caracas with a new printing press in 1809. 1747-1820

Empson, Richard

2016. Horowitz, Mark R. RICHARD EMPSON, MINISTER OF HENRY VII. *Bull. of the Inst. of Hist. Res. [Great Britain] 1982 55(131): 35-49.* On 17 August 1510 Sir Richard Empson and Edmund Dudley, both former ministers to Henry VII, were executed on Tower Hill. Since that time English historians have "unceremoniously lumped together" the two ministers. This article—the first to be written on Empson—untangles reality from myth, points out that administrative documents, as opposed to chronicles, rarely contain only the names of Empson and Dudley without those of other councillors, and examines Empson's involvement in the indictments filed at king's bench. Richard Empson's separate identity is here restored. Based on manuscript sources in the Public Record Office and British Library, London, Westminister Abbey Muniments and Northamptonshire Record Office; 115 notes. 1473-1510

Emtage, J. E. R.

2017. Emtage, J. E. R. REMINISCENCES—NYASALAND 1925-1939. *Society of Malawi Journal [Malawi] 1984 37(2): 12-23.* Informal, personal reminiscences of the author's life in colonial Nyasaland. 6 photos. 1925-39

Encina, Francisco A.

2018. Gazmuri Riveros, Cristián. NOTAS SOBRE LA INFLUENCIA DEL RACISMO EN LA OBRA DE NICOLAS PALACIOS, FRANCISCO A. ENCINA Y ALBERTO CABERO [Notes on the influence of racism in the work of Nicolás Palacios, Francisco A. Encina, and Alberto Cabero]. *Historia [Chile] 1981 16: 225-247.* 1904-35
*For abstract see **Cabero, Alberto***

Enfant Sauvage

2019. Soda, Marcelle Marie. "Biography of the Wild Child." St. Louis U. 1982. 258 pp. *DAI 1982 43(5): 1504-A.* DA8223733 1800-11

Engelenburg, Frans V.

2020. Ploeger, Jan. DR. F. V. ENGELENBURG SE AANDEEL IN DIE LEIDSE STUDENTEMASKERADE VAN 1885: SY *LEIDEN TOT 1574* [Dr. F. V. Engelenburg's part in the Leiden student masquerade of 1885: his *Leiden tot 1574*]. *Africana Notes and News [South Africa] 1985 26(6): 238-246.* Dr. Frans Vredenrijk Engelenburg (1863-1938) is well-known in South Africa for his pioneering work in furthering the cause of Afrikaans as a founding member of the Zuid-Afrikaanse Akademie voor Taal, Letteren en Kunst, a journalist (he was editor and later owner of *De Volksstem* of Pretoria), and as a writer of South African historical biographies. However, these historical works had a forerunner dating back to his student days at the University of Leiden. Here he researched and wrote a history of the city entitled *Leiden tot 1574,* which was published in 1885 when the University of Leiden celebrated its 310th birthday with a masquerade depicting the history of the city up to 1575, when the university was founded. ca 1885

Engelmann, Paul

2021. Vincze, Edit S. ER STAMMTE AUS BEBELS HEROISCHER ARBEITERGENERATION: PAUL ENGELMANN [He came from Bebel's heroic generation of workers: Paul Engelmann]. *Beiträge zur Gesch. der Arbeiterbewegung [East Germany] 1981 23(5): 751-761.* Traces the life, career, and political activities of the Hungarian socialist Paul Engelmann (1854-1916), who became a member of the Hungarian

Social Democratic Workers' Party in 1874. As leader of the Hungarian working-class movement in the late 1880's he gained it recognition as part of the international working-class movement. Engelmann was also responsible for establishing the Hungarian Social Democratic Party in 1890 and for creating the modern trade union movement. In addition he played an important role in spreading social democratic ideas among the agricultural workers and small farmers. Based on documents held in archives in Budapest and Vienna and secondary sources; 52 notes. 1874-1916

Engelmann, T. W.

2022. Kamen, Martin D. ON CREATIVITY OF EYE AND EAR: A COMMENTARY ON THE CAREER OF T. W. ENGELMANN. *Proceedings of the American Philosophical Society 1986 130(2): 232-246.* T. W. Engelmann (1843-1909), a little-known pioneer in cell physiology, exhibited a creative urge to seek unity in a seeming diversity of nature. His creativity had unique qualities and took him into such diverse fields as physiology, optics, microbiology, and music (his friend Johannes Brahms dedicated a string quartet to him). His career produced a total of 245 publications. Based on Engelmann's publications; 7 fig., 42 notes. 1858-1909

Engels, Friedrich

2023. Claeys, Gregory. THE POLITICAL IDEAS OF THE YOUNG ENGELS, 1842-1845: OWENISM, CHARTISM, AND THE QUESTION OF VIOLENT REVOLUTION IN THE TRANSITION FROM "UTOPIAN" TO "SCIENTIFIC SOCIALISM." *History of Political Thought [Great Britain] 1985 6(3): 455-478.* Although Friedrich Engels manifested youthful revolutionary exuberance in his early writings upon arrival in England, he quickly moved toward the nonrevolutionary arguments of the Owenite socialists. In the early 1840's, Engels attacked Owenism and hoped to see it molded to Chartism. His *The Condition of the Working Class in England in 1844* (1844-45) critiqued Owenism from a Chartist viewpoint and manifested an impatience with the peaceful introduction to communism. The *German Ideology* (1846) was instrumental in converting Engels's concept of revolution and his rejection of Owenism. By the time of the *Manifesto,* Engels's communitarian sentiment had receded and he came to realize that Owenite moderation could not mitigate the ferocity inherent in the class struggle. 54 notes. 1840-50

2024. Hübl, Milan. GLI ULTIMI ANNI DI ENGELS A LA DEMOCRAZIA NEL PARTITO [The last years of Engels and democracy in the party]. *Studi Storici [Italy] 1982 23(2): 267-282.* The letters and other writings of Friedrich Engels from 1889 until his death on 5 August 1895 indicate his role in the socialist movement. While he never regarded himself as the "holy father" of the movement, he did express his views on issues important for the movement. These issues included the role of intellectuals in the party and the lack of theoretical preparation of the leaders of the German party. He regarded A. Bebel and E. Bernstein as his successors. Primary sources; 46 notes. 1889-95

2025. Mikhailov, M. I. KARL MARKS I FRIDRIKH ENGEL'S V KËL'NSKOM RABOCHEM SOIUZE [Marx and Engels in the Cologne workers' union]. *Novaia i Noveishaia Istoriia [USSR] 1985 (6): 19-33.* Highlights an important yet little studied episode in the activities of Karl Marx and Friedrich Engels during the Revolution of 1848 and disproves attempts by bourgeois and reformist historians to belittle this aspect of their activities in the struggle for general democratic reforms and an independent political party of the proletariat. 1848-49

2026. Mosolov, V. G. 160 LET SO DNIA ROZHDENIIA F. ENGEL'SA [The 160th anniversary of the birth of Engels]. *Voprosy Istorii KPSS [USSR] 1981 (2): 151-155.* Discusses the proceedings and papers presented at a conference held at the Institute of Marxism-Leninism in Moscow in honor of the 160th anniversary of the birth of Engels. The two major papers were by A. G. Egorov on the life and works of Engels and by N. Iu. Kolpinski on Engels and utopian socialism. Other papers dealt with Engels's letters on historical materialism and the ideological struggle that took place in Bohemia concerning the publication of Engels's *The Condition of the Working Classes in England.* 12 notes. 1820-95

2027. Vorob'eva, A. K.; Vorob'eva, O. B.; and Sinel'nikova, I. M. IZ PEREPISKI F. ENGEL'SA I CHLENOV SEM'I K. MARKSA [From the correspondence of F. Engels with members of K. Marx's family]. *Voprosy Istorii KPSS [USSR] 1980 (11): 55-71, (12): 80-87.* Part 1. Presents Russian translations of letters from Friedrich Engels to members of Karl Marx's family, including Jenny Marx, Paul Lafargue, and Jenny Long. The 13 letters span 20 years, 1869-1889, and were originally written in English, German, or French. Some are published for the first time. Part 2. Presents three letters written in 1889 and 1890 by Eleanor Marx Aveling to Friedrich Engels. 86 notes. 1869-90

Enghien, Louis, Duc d'

2028. Erlanger, Philippe. LE GRAND CONDE, CLEMENCE, ANNE, MARTHE ET LA GLOIRE [The Grand Condé, Clemence, Anne, Marthe, and the glory]. *Historama [France] 1985 (13): 10-17.* Recounts the loves of Louis, Duc d'Enghien, le Grand Condé, who grudgingly accepted marriage to Claire-Clémence de Maillé-Brézé, niece of Cardinal Richelieu, and the political ramifications of his love affair with Marthe du Vigean and his passionate affection for his sister Anne de Longueville. 1620-86

Englich, Józef

2029. Landau, Zbigniew. MINISTER SKARBU JÓZEF ENGLICH (PRÓBA BIOGRAFII) [Finance Minister Józef Englich: a biographical sketch]. *Śląski Kwartalnik Hist. Sobótka [Poland] 1979 34(1): 1-16.* Józef Englich (1874-1924), the finance minister of the Polish government, 1919-24, was more successful as a banker than as a statesman. 1919-24

Enrique y Tarancón, Vicente

2030. Cuenca Toribio, José M. A PROPOS DES MEMOIRES D'UN CARDINAL ESPAGNOL [Concerning the memoirs of a Spanish cardinal]. *Revue d'Histoire Ecclésiastique [Belgium] 1985 80(2): 467-470.* Lacking the high culture of French prelates, the Spanish clergy make poor memoirists. Vicente Enrique y Tarancón (b. 1907), cardinal and primate of Spain during the critical debate between Church and civil society of the 1970's, does bring out the personalities and movements of his early years in his otherwise leaden *Recuerdos de Juventud* (1984). 1928-45

Ensenada, Marqués de la

2031. Domínguez, Juan Blas. IDEAS POLITICOS Y DE GOBIERNO DEL MARQUES DE LA ENSENADA [Political and government ideas of the Marqués de la Ensenada]. *Rev. General de Marina [Spain] 1981 201(Dec): 555-562.* Reviews the historical appraisals of the political ideas of Zenón de Somodevilla, Marqués de la Ensenada (1702-81), minister in the reign of Ferdinand VI. Ensenada entered government service at age 18 and became a major reforming force out of a love for his country. He built up the Spanish armed forces, not out of any warlike motives, but because he longed for peace with honor. His policy embodied the Roman maxim: if you wish for peace, prepare for war. Illus. 1720's-81

2032. Salgado Alba, Jesús. LA PASION DE ESPAÑA Y DEL MAR EN LA POLITICA DEL MARQUES DE LA ENSENADA [The passion for Spain and the sea in the politics of the Marqués de la Ensenada]. *Rev. General de Marina [Spain] 1982 203(Aug-Sept): 5-18.* Zenón de Somodevilla, Marqués de la Ensenada, was a Spanish statesman whose rise to power in the service of Spain, at a time when his country was continuously challenged by Great Britain, was the product of his patriotism and administrative ability. By 1743 the power to direct the entire nation at war was in his hands. A tired and discouraged Spain gained a new direction with the Ensenada plan, implemented from 1747 to 1751. He established the political object of peace. He built up the navy, nationalized naval construction, and reformed the naval personnel system. He announced a policy to reoccupy Gibraltar. When he fell victim of political intrigue in 1754, there was rejoicing in London. 3 illus. 1719-54

Ensor, James

2033. Lesko, Diane Marion. "James Ensor's Transformations of Tradition: A Study of His Life and Art during the Creative Years 1877-1899." (Vol. 1-2) State U. of New York, Binghamton 1982. 538 pp. *DAI 1982 43(1): 2-A.* DA8210142 1877-99

Enver Pasha

2034. Rorlich, Azade-Ayşe. FELLOW TRAVELLERS: ENVER PASHA AND THE BOLSHEVIK GOVERNMENT 1918-1920. *Asian Affairs [Great Britain] 1982 13(3): 288-296.* Enver Pasha was the last war minister of the Ottoman Empire and he spent his final years in a futile effort to create a new state uniting all Turkic peoples, at times in cooperation with the Russian Bolsheviks. Secondary sources; 34 notes. 1918-20

2035. Swanson, Glen W. ENVER PASHA: THE FORMATIVE YEARS. *Middle Eastern Studies [Great Britain] 1980 16(3): 193-199.* Analyzes the formative years of Enver Pasha (1881-1922), who in 1908 became the hero of the Young Turks. While in the military academy, Enver experienced tyrannical actions of the regime of Sultan Abdul Hamid II. He detected a spy network, witnessed an undue punishment for disloyalty, and was himself confined for minor offenses. Resolving to eliminate tyranny, he became a revolutionary. Based on Turkish sources; 28 notes. 1881-1908

Erasmus, Desiderius

2036. Halkin, Léon-E. LA PIETE D'ERASME [The piety of Erasmus]. *Revue d'Histoire Ecclésiastique [Belgium] 1984 79(3-4): 671-708.* Beginning with Martin Luther and the Roman Index, five centuries of commentators offered contradictorily pejorative assessments of the prayer life and/or orthodoxy of Desiderius Erasmus (1469-1536). Close attention to his daily life, and close reading in his works of and about devotion reveal interior dispositions both devout and traditional. His piety was adamantly Christocentric, based on the Bible, the fathers, and teachings of the Church. Prayer was central. He rejected only formalism, credulity, and abuses not consonant with Tradition. 1469-1536

2037. Veltheer, W. ERASMUS, IN DE GROND NIET SO SLECHT [Erasmus: a more favorable postmortem]. *Spiegel Hist. [Netherlands] 1982 17(4): 190-196.* A discussion of the controversy surrounding the medical causes of the death of Erasmus engendered by the autopsy report of Professor A. Werthemann in 1928, which concluded that Erasmus died of syphilis. The evidence of his symptom complex, drawn from Erasmus's own observations along with the autopsy evidence, was analyzed in 1966 by the medical researcher A. Meijer. He found that the evidence can support other theories of the cause of death such as hyperparathyroid. Primary sources; 7 illus. 1480-1520

Erauso, Catalina de

2038. Iglehart, David. FROM CONVENT TO CONQUEST. *Américas (Organization of Am. States) 1982 34(1): 9-13.* Placed in a convent at four, the Basque Catalina de Erauso escaped and, disguised as a male, became a vagabond and warrior in Spain and Latin America. 17c

Erdei, Ferenc

2039. Huszár, Tibor. ERDEI FERENC [Ferenc Erdei]. *Társadalmi Szemle [Hungary] 1983 38(5): 86-94.* Ferenc Erdei's concern about the injustice suffered by the workers all over the world promoted his political views, which appeared in Hungarian newspapers from 1938 until his recent death. In 1949 he became minister of agriculture and later was elected as the chief secretary of the Hungarian Academy of Sciences. His articles, always concerned with the small landowner, showed occasional changes in political outlook over the years. In the last article before his death he realized that reality systems and principles are not necessarily compatible. He came to the conclusion that it is absolutely necessary for attitudes to change and to follow new developments. 20c

Eremenko, Andrei I.

2040. —. MARSHAL SOVETSKOGO SOIUZA A. I. EREMENKO [Marshal of the Soviet Union A. I. Eremenko]. *Voenno-Istoricheskii Zhurnal [USSR] 1982 (9): 58-61.* Biography of Marshal Andrei I. Eremenko (b. 1892) on the occasion of the 90th anniversary of his birth. Eremenko joined the Imperial Russian Army in 1914. After being wounded in action as a private early in the war, he became a cavalry officer and was sent to the Romanian front. He joined the Communist Party and the Red Army in 1918, and became a cavalry officer in 1929. His greatest achievements were in World War II, when as a Colonel General he commanded the forces of the southeast front in the battle of Stalingrad in 1942-43. After the war he was chief of a number of army districts before becoming General Inspector at the Soviet Defense Ministry. He later became a marshal of the Soviet Union and a member of the USSR Supreme Soviet. Note, 2 photos. 1892-1958

Erlander, Tage

2041. Heckscher, Gunnar. ERLANDERS 60-TAL [Erlander's 60's]. *Svensk Tidskrift [Sweden] 1982 69(8): 413-416.* Former Swedish Prime Minister Tage Erlander's memoirs of the 1960's *Tage Erlander: 1960-talet* [Tage Erlander: the 1960's] (1982) are a disappointment to nonsocialist readers. The book possesses a stridently Social Democratic line because it was published during the 1982 election campaign, therefore failing to show the good relations Erlander was able to build across party lines with nonsocialist public leaders. 1960's

2042. Ruin, Olof. TAGE ERLANDER: STATSMINISTER UNDER DET SVENSKA VÄLFÄRDSSAMHÄLLETS GYLLENE TID [Tage Erlander: prime minister in the golden years of the Swedish welfare society]. *Statsvetenskaplig Tidskrift [Sweden] 1984 87(3): 201-210.* Discusses the political style of Tage Erlander (b. 1901), prime minister of Sweden, 1946-69. Presented as a lecture at Stockholm University on 26 January 1984. English summary. 1946-69

Erlich, Alexander

2043. Haimson, Leopold H. OBITUARY: ALEXANDER ERLICH 1912-1985. *Russian Review 1985 44(3): 325-329.* Alexander Erlich was the son of Henryk Erlich, the dominant political figure of the Bund in St. Petersburg, and from him inherited a profound sense of political and moral duty. He also acquired early a deep commitment to socialist ideals and an interest in Marxist economic theory. In his academic career at Harvard and Columbia this heritage and his interests were combined. His *The Soviet Industrialization Debate 1924-1928* (1960) was a classic study touching on both the theoretical and political dynamics of the industrialization question and the broader historical perspective. 20c

Erlich, Henryk

2044. Erlich, Victor; Levine, Burton, interviewer. INTERVIEW: VICTOR ERLICH. *Shmate 1986 (14): 25-28.* Interview with Victor Erlich about his father, Henryk Erlich, and about his maternal grandfather, Simon Dubnow, about the Bund and non-Zionist Jewish nationalism in Germany, Poland, and Russia, their role in the Russian Revolution and in anti-Nazi movements during World War II. 1911-41

Ernst, Gideon

2045. Kunisch, Johannes. FELDMARSCHALL LOUDON ODER DAS SOLDATENGLÜCK [Field Marshall Loudon or soldier's luck]. *Hist. Zeits. [West Germany] 1983 236(1): 49-72.* Gideon Ernst, Baron von Loudon (1717-90) was a Baltic German in Austrian service who rose to the rank of field marshall in the Austrian army. Between 1744 and 1756 he served at junior officer rank but during the Seven Years' War he rose quickly to the second highest rank in Empress Maria Theresa's field army. Because of his record of combat victories Loudon had strong support in the imperial court to replace the unsuccessful Field Marshall Leopold Josef Graf Daun, but the empress supported Daun rather than the abler Loudon. The motives for this decision were related to Loudon's lesser nobility status, and his service with military units was unpopular with the Habsburg high command. Based on Austrian War Archives; 54 notes. 1744-90

Ershov, Leonid

2046. Białokozowicz, Bazyli. LEONID JERSZOW JAKO TEORETYK, HISTORYK I KRYTYK ROSYJSKIEJ LITERATURY RADZIECKIEJ (W SZEŚĆDZIESIĄTĄ ROCZNICĘ URODZIN) [Leonid Ershov as theoretician, historian, and critic of Soviet literature on his 60th birthday]. *Slavia Orientalis [Poland] 1984 33(2): 199-234.* Summarizes the academic achievements of the Soviet literary critic Leonid Ershov (b. 1924), author of several studies of Soviet satire of the 1920's and 1930's and works on socialist realism. 20c

Erskine, Robert

2047. Appleby, John H. ROBERT ERSKINE: SCOTTISH PIONEER OF RUSSIAN NATURAL HISTORY. *Arch. of Natural Hist. [Great Britain] 1982 10(3): 377-398.* Discusses the scientific and administrative achievements of the Scottish surgeon Robert Erskine at the court of Peter I of Russia. Erskine arrived in Moscow in the summer of 1704 to take up a post as house doctor to Peter's lieutenant, Prince Menshikov, and in January 1905 he became the tsar's chief physician. In 1706 he was appointed to the prestigious post of president of the Apothecaries Chancery. He had complete responsibility for all of Russian medicine and supervised apothecaries, botanical gardens, herbs, viticulture, and the collecting of natural history specimens. Erskine strongly influenced the tsar in the measures taken to develop Russian natural history. On his death in 1718 his library of over 2,500 books, 20% on natural history, was given to the Russian Academy of Sciences Library by the tsar. Based on documents in the Royal Society Archives and Archives of the Academy of Sciences of the USSR, Leningrad; fig., 29 notes, biblio. 1704-18

Escalada, José Manuel

2048. Martínez, Beatriz. EL PASO DE JOSE MANUEL ESCALADA POR EL SEMINARIO DE NOBLES DE MADRID (1787-1793) [José Manuel Escalada's time in the seminary for nobles, Madrid 1787-93]. *Bol. del Inst. de Hist. Argentina y Americana [Argentina] 1982 17(27): 221-237.* Escalada was a scion of one of the most important families in Río de la Plata engaged in import-export business. The author describes the exclusive institution where he was enrolled as a student, its organization, clientele, and financial costs as well as the regime of studies. After six years of training, José Manuel was given the following report: Talent and behavior fair; docile; application weak; external demeanor curious; inclined to the military state. Based on primary material in the National Historical Archive; 38 notes. 1787-93

Escalera y Domínguez, José Nícolas de

2049. Sánchez Martínez, Guillermo. UN PINTOR CUBANO DEL XVIII: JOSE NICOLAS DE ESCALERA Y DOMINGUEZ [An 18th-century Cuban painter: José Nícolas de Escalera y Domínguez]. *Rev. de la Biblioteca Nac. José Martí [Cuba] 1981 23(1): 143-152.* Escalera (1734-1804) is often considered the first Cuban painter. This claim has to be modified since there were certainly artists before him and he was undoubtedly influenced by Spanish painters in Seville. 11 notes, 3 appendixes. 18c

Escher, Hans Hartmann

2050. Bodmer, Jean-Pierre. VERA VIRTUS—VERA NOBILITAS: HANS HARTMANN ESCHER (1567-1623) UND SEIN STAMMBUCH [True virtue—true nobility: Hans Hartmann Escher (1567-1623) and his genealogical album]. *Zwingliana [Switzerland] 1983 16(1): 1-18.* Hans Hartmann Escher (1567-1623) was from one of the noblest houses in Zurich. His genealogical album *(Stammbuch)* reveals the wide range of his social and intellectual contacts. Although most of the entries are written in German, Escher obviously knew Latin and had some command of Greek. His primary interest was jurisprudence, but he represents the late humanism of the period. Based on sources in the Zentralbibliothek Zurich, Familienarchiv Escher, and secondary sources on *Stammbuchen;* 157 references to letters, 40 notes. 1580's-1623

Escobar, Vicente

2051. Rodríguez Bermúdez, Jorge. VICENTE ESCOBAR, NUESTRO PINTOR PRELIMINAR [Vicente Escobar: our early painter]. *Revista de la Biblioteca Nacional José Martí [Cuba] 1984 26(1): 141-151.* After José Nicolás de la Escalera (1734-1804), Vicente Escobar (1757-1834) was Cuba's principal painter at the end of the 18th and beginning of the 19th centuries. Although poorly trained and addicted to antiquarian subjects, Escobar specialized in portraits of Cuba's elite. Many of these paintings survive today. Secondary sources; 8 notes. 1757-1834

Escobar Huertas, Antonio

2052. Suero Roca, María Teresa. VIDA Y MUERTE DEL GENERAL ESCOBAR [Life and death of General Escobar]. *Historia y Vida [Spain] 1984 17(191): 110-123.* A short biography of the Spanish General Antonio Escobar Huertas and his role during the Spanish civil war (1936-39) in which he fought on the side of the Republic. 1936-40

Esenberlin, Iliyas

2053. Kocaoglu, Timur. ILIYAS ESENBERLIN, 1915-1983. *Central Asian Survey [Great Britain] 1983 2(3): 1-3.* Pays tribute to Kazakh writer Iliyas Esenberlin (1915-83), whose contributions to the development of Kazakh historical fiction were frequently interrupted by Soviet authorities. 8 notes. 15c-19c

Esenin, Sergei

2054. Azadovski, Konstantin. KLIUEV I ESENIN V OKTIABRE 1915 GODA (PO MATERIALAM DNEVNIKA F. F. FIDLERA) [Kliuev and Esenin in October 1915: from the dairy of F. F. Fidler]. *Cahiers du Monde Russe et Soviétique [France] 1985 26(3-4): 413-424.* Nikolai Kliuev and Sergei Esenin met for the first time at the beginning of October 1915 in Petrograd. Basing himself on archival documents and in particular on the *Diary* of F. F. Fidler, the author relates the first appearance in common of the two "peasant poets" in the intellectual society of the capital. 1915

2055. Davies, Jessie. DOCUMENTS ABOUT ESENIN. *Cahiers du Monde Russe et Soviétique [France] 1985 26(3-4): 445-477.* Presents, with an introduction, the "Autobiography" of Sergei Esenin's half-brother A. I. Razguliaev, natural son of Tat'iana Fedorovna, the poet's mother, together with three letters from his father. Analyzes the complicated relations between Esenin and his parents and some of the reasons for them. Traces the references in articles, correspondence, conversations, and interviews to Alexander Razguliaev. Explains the autobiography's relevance to the study of the poet. As a corollary to his mother's attitude to her husband as expressed in the "Autobiography," the three letters from Esenin's father testify to his genuine love and concern for his son. The anonymity of some living memoirists has been preserved. 1890's-1925

Esnault-Pelterie, Robert

2056. Vetrov, Georgi S. STRANITSY NAUCHNOI BIOGRAFII ROBERA ESNO-PEL'TRI (K 100-LETIIU SO DNIA ROZHDENIIA) [Highlights of the scientific biography of Robert Esnault-Pelterie: on the centennial of his birth]. *Voprosy Istorii Estestvoznaniia i Tekhniki [USSR] 1982 (1): 124-130.* Describes the aeronautic work in the 1900's of French engineer Robert Esnault-Pelterie (1881-1957) and his research in the 1920's-30's on liquid rocket propulsion. His theoretical and experimental work dealt with military aspects of rocketry and its use in space exploration. Though he doubted man's ability to withstand weightlessness in extraterrestrial flight, he urged France as early as 1928 to concentrate on rocketry research to counter Germany's ominous advances in this field and its threat to peace. 35 notes, 2 illus. 1900's-50's

Espartero, Baldomero

2057. Cepeda Gómez, José. EL GENERAL ESPARTERO DURANTE LA "DECADA OMINOSA" Y SU COLABORACION CON LA POLITICA REPRESIVA DE FERNANDO VII [General Espartero during the "ominous decade" and his collaboration with the repressive policy of Ferdinand VII]. *Cuadernos de Hist. Moderna y Contemporánea [Spain] 1981 2: 147-163.* General Baldomero Espartero (1793-1879) began as a seminarian but in 1809, as a result of the French invasion, joined the army and initiated a spectacular political and military career. In the years following the fall of Napoleon he fought in the American colonies and showed liberal leanings. Back in Spain, however, he acted as an informer on his former colleagues for King Ferdinand VII. Later in life he seems to have recovered his liberalism. Based on primary sources in the Spanish Military Historical archive; 34 notes. 1809-33

Espinosa Rodríguez, Manuel

2058. Espinosa Rodríguez, Manuel. MEMORIAS DE UN ALFEREZ DE NAVIO: EL CAÑONERO *LAURIA* [Memoirs of a naval ensign: the gunboat *Lauria]. Rev. General de Marina [Spain] 1982 202(Mar): 263-277.* The author describes his life as a Spanish naval officer, 1922-23, when he served on board the battleship *Alfonso XIII* and subsequently on the gunboat *Lauria* in operations along the Moroccan coast during the Rif War. 4 photos. 1922-23

2059. Espinosa Rodríguez, Manuel. MEMORIAS DE UN ALFEREZ DE NAVIO: EN EL GUARDACOSTAS *ARCILA* [Memoirs of a naval ensign: in the coast guard vessel *Arcila]. Rev. General de Marina [Spain] 1982 203(Nov): 377-391.* Anecdotal memoirs of life aboard the Spanish coast guard vessel *Arcila* during 1923-25. The ship was stationed in the waters of Spanish Morocco during the Rif War, operating out of Ceuta or Melilla. 3 illus. 1923-25

2060. Espinosa, Manuel. MEMORIAS DE UN GUARDIA MARINA: EN EL ACORAZADO *PELAYO* [Memoirs of a midshipman: in the battleship *Pelayo]. Rev. General de Marina [Spain] 1981 201(July): 21-30.* Recounts anecdotes of life as a midshipman in the Spanish Navy in 1920 training in the old battleship *Pelayo* and in the naval towns of El Ferrol and Vigo. 2 photos. 1920

2061. Espinosa, Manuel. MEMORIAS DE UN ALFEREZ DE NAVIO: EL DESEMBARCO EN ALHUCEMAS [Memoirs of a naval ensign: the landing at Alhucemas]. *Rev. General de Marina [Spain] 1983 204(Mar): 441-455.* Anecdotal memoirs of life in the Spanish Navy in 1925 during the Rif War. Espinosa was assigned to the old gunboat *Doña María de Molina,* which was undergoing repairs. In preparation for the projected Spanish-French amphibious operations at Alhucemas against the Rif rebels, Espinosa was reassigned to a group of 26 landing craft, built by Britain for the Dardanelles campaign of 1915 and purchased as surplus by Spain for the Rif War. The landing craft were slow, spartan, and suffered many mechanical problems. Nevertheless, from 8 September 1925 on, they landed 10,000 men and their supplies, and evacuated the 150 casualties. 2 illus. 1925

2062. Espinosa, Manuel. MEMORIAS DE UN GUARDIA MARINA [Memoirs of a midshipman]. *Rev. General de Marina [Spain] 1981 200(Apr): 451-464.* Experiences as a midshipman in the Spanish Navy, especially training cruises in 1918 on the old cruiser *Reina Regente* and later on the yacht *Giralda,* highlighted by a friendly visit by Alfonso XIII. 3 illus. 1918

Esquilache, Marquis de

2063. Kuethe, Allan J. and Blaisdell, Lowell. THE ESQUILACHE GOVERNMENT AND THE REFORMS OF CHARLES III IN CUBA. *Jahrbuch für Gesch. von Staat, Wirtschaft und Gesellschaft Lateinamerikas [West Germany] 1982 19: 117-136.* The Marquis de Esquilache, Franciso de Borja y Aragón (ca. 1557-1658), was not the only official shaping reform at the court of Charles III; many others also advocated reforms. However, Esquilache's modification of military regulations and the intendant system, and his tax and commercial reforms were continued after his departure by José de Gálvez. For these reasons Esquilache deserves more historical recognition, especially for the effect of his reforms on Cuba. Based upon documents from the Archivo General de Indias, Archives des Affaires Étrangères, the Archivo General de Simancas, and printed primary material; 55 notes. 1762-65

Esquiú, Mamerto

2064. Derisi, Octavio N. VIDA Y DOCTRINA DE FRAY MAMERTO ESQUIU: A LOS CIEN AÑOS DE SU MUERTE [Life and teaching of Fray Mamerto Esquiú: on the centenary of his death]. *Boletín de la Academia Argentina de Letras [Argentina] 1983 48(187-188): 11-24.* Fray Mamerto Esquiú (1826-83), Franciscan bishop of Córdoba, popular preacher and publicist, was known as the "orator of the Constitution" for the sermons he delivered 1853-54. He was a man of solid learning and traditional faith and a great advocate of constitutional progress for Argentina. 1826-83

Esquivel Obregón, Toribio

2065. —. [WRITINGS BY AND ABOUT TORIBIO ESQUIVEL OBREGON]. *Boletín del Archivo General de la Nación [Mexico] 1985 9(1): 5-62.*

Villegas Moreno, Gloria. INTRODUCCION [Introduction], *pp. 5-7.* Introduces the papers of Toribio Esquivel Obregón (1864-1946), a noted lawyer and writer from Nuevo Leon, whose personal archive is temporarily housed at the Archivo General de la Nación in Mexico City.

—. LOS PRIMEROS AÑOS [The early years], *pp. 8-11.* Reprints four letters and articles written by Toribio Esquivel Obregón as a young man. Illus., 3 photos.

—. VINCULO CON LA REVOLUCION [Tied to the revolution], *pp. 12-22.* Reprints seven articles and letters by and to Toribio Esquivel Obregón concerning the early years of the Mexican Revolution. Illus.

—. GESTION MINISTERIAL [Ministerial gestures], *pp. 23-29.* Reprints six notes, letters, and proposals by and to Toribio Esquivel Obregón while he served as secretary of the treasury in Mexico. 4 illus., 2 photos.

—. EXILIO EN NUEVA YORK [Exile in New York], *pp. 30-36.* Reprints seven letters by and to Toribio Esquivel Obregón while he was in political exile in New York. Illus., 2 photos.

—. REPATRIACION [Repatriation], *pp. 37-62.* Reprints 12 articles by and letters to Toribio Esquivel Obregón during the latter years of his life. 8 illus., 2 photos. 1893-1946

Estachería, José de

2066. Montiel Argüello, Alejandro. TRES DIGNITARIOS PROMOVIDOS DE NICARAGUA A GUATEMALA [Three dignitaries promoted from Nicaragua to Guatemala]. *Anales de la Acad. de Geog. e Hist. de Guatemala [Guatemala] 1981 55: 317-331.* Alonso Fernández de Heredia and José de Estachería were governors of Nicaragua before being promoted to the post of captain general. Juan Félix de Villegas was bishop in Nicaragua before being raised to the rank of archbishop in Guatemala. Based on documents in the Archivo General de Centro America; 130 notes. 1745-1801

Este family

2067. Pedriali, Pier Paulo. PER UNA STORIA DELLE ATTIVITA MARINARE DEGLI ESTENSI [Maritime activities of the Este family]. *Riv. Marittima [Italy] 1981 114(6): 47-55.* Comments on the seafaring activities of the Este family of Ferrara in the 16th century, with a detailed technical description of the frigate *Diamante.* 16c

Estigarribia, José Felix

2068. Pastore, Carlos. [EL MARISCAL JOSE FELIX ESTIGARRIBIA] [Marshal José Felix Estigarribia]. *Estudios Paraguayos [Paraguay] 1981 9(2): 105-132.*

ENTREVISTAS CON EL MCAL. ESTIGARRIBIA, *pp. 105-114.*

PROCLAMACION DE LA CANDIDATURA A LA PRESIDENCIA DE LA REPUBLICA DEL MARISCAL JOSE FELIX ESTIGARRIBIA, *pp. 115-132.* Marshal Estigarribia was the Paraguayan leader in the victory in the Chaco War against Bolivia in 1932-35. After a period of exile he was elected president of the republic for the four-year period 1939-43. The author, an officer on Estigarribia's general staff and later director of the Institute of Agrarian Reform, recounts his last interview with him, in which they discussed international, economic, political and administrative matters, and the events which led Estigarribia from the Chaco War through exile to the presidency. 8 notes, appendix. 1932-40

Estrée, Gabrielle d'

2069. Erlanger, Philippe. ELLE FAILLIT CHANGER LE DESTIN DE LA FRANCE: GABRIELLE, DITE "DUCHESSE D'ORDURE" [Gabrielle, nicknamed the obscene duchess, who nearly changed France's destiny]. *Historama [France] 1984 (4): 34-39.* A biographical sketch of Gabrielle d' Estrée (1573-99), the favorite of Henry IV (1553-1610), stressing her political influence on this French king, who would have made her queen of France if she had lived long enough. 1573-99

Etchepareborda, Roberto

2070. Dorn, Georgette M. OBITUARIES: ROBERTO ETCHEPAREBORDA (1923-85). *Hispanic American Historical Review 1985 65(3): 547-548.* Argentine historian Roberto Etchepareborda was born in Milan, Italy, the son of an Argentine diplomat. He was prominent in the Argentine Radical Party in the late 1950's and was active in Buenos Aires political life. Author of several books on Argentine history, he taught in universities in the United States and at the Universidad del Sur in Bahía Blanca, Argentina, where he was president, 1971-73. From 1979 until his death in Fairfax, Virginia on 9 April 1985 he served with the Organization of American States as director of their Department of Culture,

1979-84, and as coordinator of their program to celebrate the 500th anniversary of the discovery of America, 1984-85. 15c-20c

Etherege, George

2071. Pendleton, Mary Jo. "Sir George Etherege: A Pleasure More Noble." University of Southwestern Louisiana 1984. 176 pp. *DAI 1985 45(8): 2535-A.* DA8416779 ca 1660's-92

Ett, Henri Adolf

2072. Ruitenberg, G. M. W. and Leeuwen, H. W. van. IN MEMORIAM HENRI A. ETT [In memoriam Henri A. Ett]. *Nederlands Archievenblad [Netherlands] 1982 86(4): 281-284.* Obituary of Henri Adolf Ett (1908-82), lay archivist active in historical and literary research and in the registration of family archives commissioned by the Utrecht Historical Society. 1908-82

Eugene of Savoy

2073. Wernick, Robert. THE LITTLE PRINCE WHO GREW UP TO HAUNT LOUIS XIV. *Smithsonian 1985 15(10): 54-63.* French-born Prince Eugene of Savoy (1663-1736), turned down by King Louis XIV for a commission in the French army, enlisted in the army of Emperor Leopold I, proved himself to be a brilliant military strategist, became responsible for tripling the size of the Habsburg empire, and, as commander in chief of all the Austrian armies, collaborated with the Duke of Marlborough to defeat the French at Blenheim in 1704, thereby ruining the Sun King's imperial ambitions. 1683-1704

Euler, Leonhard

2074. Doerig, J. A. UN GRAN MATEMATICO EUROPEO, LEONARDO EULER (1707-1783) [A great European mathematician, Leonhard Euler (1707-83)]. *Folia Humanistica [Spain] 1984 22(254): 145-147.* Leonhard Euler, Swiss mathematician and physicist, served both Catherine the Great and Frederick the Great during his career and is most noted for his contributions to algebra and calculus, which had applications in optics, mechanics, and cartography. 1720's-83

2075. Greenberg, John L. A TRIBUTE TO LEONHARD EULER. *Ann. of Sci. [Great Britain] 1984 41(2): 171-177.* Reviews E. A. Fellmann's *Leonhard Euler 1707-1783: Beiträge zu Leben und Werk* [Leonhard Euler, 1707-83: on his life and work] (1983). Forces a reevaluation of Isaac Newton's importance in the development of European mathematics and mechanics, since continental mathematicians such as Euler contributed significantly to the Enlightenment as well. 18 notes. 18c

2076. Pach, János. A MEGTESTESÜLT ANALÍZIS—LEONHARD EULER [Incarnate analysis—Leonhard Euler]. *Magyar Tudomány [Hungary] 1984 29(3): 203-213.* Leonhard Euler (1707-83), Swiss mathematician, was born 15 April 1707 in Basel. At the age of 20 he went to St. Petersburg at the invitation of Catherine I, to become professor of physics, and in 1733 of mathematics. Frederick the Great invited him to Berlin in 1741, and he worked there for 25 years. In 1766, totally blind, he returned to St. Petersburg and Catherine. His many accomplishments include the discovery of the law of reciprocity, differential geometry, and the calculus of variations. His output was prodigious. The 1910 incomplete edition of his works numbered 866 citations. Primary sources; 2 plates, 27 notes. 1730-83

Evangelista, Cresanto

2077. Jose, Vivencio R. WORKERS' RESPONSE TO EARLY AMERICAN RULE, 1900-1935. *Philippine Social Sciences and Humanities Rev. [Philippines] 1981 45(1-4): 285-311.* Describes the struggles of the Philippine worker and peasant classes against the American-imposed regime in the Philippines. In particular, traces the career of Cresanto Evangelista who organized the Philippine working classes along radical socialist lines and used strikes and other disruptions to gain a voice in Philippine national affairs. 44 notes, 4 tables. 1900-35

Evans, Oswald Hardey

2078. Phillips, David Atlee. MY NOT-SO-GOLDEN NEWSPAPERING DAYS IN WILDEST CHILE. *Smithsonian 1983 14(3): 104-121.* 1949-54
*For abstract see **Phillips, David Atlee***

Evans-Pritchard, Edward Evan

2079. Burton, John W. THE GHOST OF MALINOWSKI IN THE SOUTHERN SUDAN: EVANS-PRITCHARD AND ETHNOGRAPHIC FIELDWORK. *Pro. of the Am. Phil. Soc. 1983 127(4): 278-289.* Assesses Edward Evan Evans-Pritchard's (1902-73) ethnographic contributions, underscoring the influence of Bronisław Malinowski's work on them. While Evans-Pritchard claimed in public to have loathed Malinowski, it is evident that the quality and breadth of his ethnographic labors, particularly in the Sudan, were in a significant way the direct manifestation of Malinowski's inspiration. Particularly, the studies he made of the Nuer closely resemble and reflect those Malinowski made of the Trobriand Islanders. Based largely on the publications of Evans-Pritchard; 6 notes, list of ref. 1926-73 -Pritchard

2080. Johnson, Douglas H. EVANS-PRITCHARD, THE NUER, AND THE SUDAN POLITICAL SERVICE. *African Affairs [Great Britain] 1982 81(323): 231-246.* A brief history and analysis of the experiences of anthropologist Edward Evan Evans-Pritchard with the Nuer peoples of the Sudan and the British colonial administrators. Revolt of the Nuer caused administrators to desire to learn more about them. Evans-Pritchard was selected for the job, which proved difficult because the aims, methods, and goals of anthropologist, administrators, and Nuer conflicted. The experience led Evans-Pritchard to later write and speak of the problem, to try to determine where the scientist's loyalties should lie, where the line should be drawn. These studies are very relevant in this age of foreign experts in Africa. Map, 56 notes. 1928-38

Evariste, Nguema Mba

2081. Świderski, Stanislaw. NGUEMA MBA EVARISTE, FONDATEUR DE LA COMMUNAUTE EGLISE ROMAINE DE SAINT PIERRE DE JERUSALEM [Nguema Mba Evariste, founder of the Church of St. Peter of Jerusalem]. *J. of Religion in Africa [Netherlands] 1983 14(1): 74-83.* Reports on the life, personality, and teachings of Evariste (1929-79), founder in 1966 of a small sect, mostly of family members, in Gabon. Evariste in a vision was commanded by St. Peter to reform spiritually indigenous religious beliefs and to purify the Catholic missions. He introduced Christian mysticism into the local religion and envisioned a society free of witchcraft and based on mutual respect and social justice. Based on Evariste's autobiographical writings; 3 illus., 4 notes. 1929-79

Evatt, H. V.

2082. Edwards, P. G. ON ASSESSING H. V. EVATT. *Historical Studies [Australia] 1984 21(83): 258-269.* Compares assessments by Paul Hasluck and Alan Renouf of H. V. Evatt, Australian Minister of External Affairs, 1941-49. Hasluck accepted that Evatt wished to assert an Australian voice but searched for a "good issue" on which to fight rather than examine the whole situation to discover what was vital to Australia. Renouf admits Evatt postured too much and overestimated threats to Australia, noting that the Canberra Pact was an error. Nonetheless, Evatt was guided by an ambition to see international affairs influenced more by principle and justice than by power. Based on memoirs and secondary sources; 47 notes. 1941-49

Eve, Paul Fitzsimmons

2083. Nelken, Halina. DR. PAUL FITZSIMMONS EVE (1806-1877) [Doctor Paul Fitzsimmons Eve (1806-77)]. *Zeszyty Hist. [France] 1982 (62): 26-52.* Sketches the life of Dr. Paul Fitzsimmons Eve, an American surgeon who gave his medical assistance to the wounded in the Polish uprising of 1830. As is evident from a letter of his to a friend, his sympathies for the Poles led him to a prolonged stay in the military hospital, where he carried out amputations and investigated the outbreak of cholera, which furnished him with material for his future research. Primary sources; 22 notes. 1830's

Everett, James

2084. Beckerlegge, Oliver A. JAMES EVERETT: 1784-1984. *Proceedings of the Wesley Historical Society [Great Britain] 1984 44(5): 135-144.* Pays tribute to English Methodist James Everett (1784-1872), a preacher forced to retire into the book trade by bronchitis, to whom Methodists owe a great debt despite their expelling him and other reformers from their fellowship in 1849. 1797-1872

Exter, Alexandra Alexandrovna

2085. Bowlt, John E. THE MARIONETTES OF ALEXANDRA EXTER. *Russian Hist. 1981 8(1-2): 219-232.* The Russian painter and designer Alexandra Alexandrovna Exter (1882-1949) created a set of marionettes in 1926 that reveal her notion that play and art should be related; the form her marionettes took show her dedication to abstract shapes. Based on memoirs and on Soviet histories of theater; 13 illus., 10 notes. 1916-26

Eyler, Leonard

2086. Ozhigova, E. P. O PEREPISKE DANIILA BERNULLI S NIKOLAEM FUSSOM [Daniel Bernoulli's correspondence with Nikolaus Fuss]. *Voprosy Istorii Estestvoznaniia i Tekhniki [USSR] 1981 (1): 108-115.* 1773-78

For abstract see ***Fuss, Nikolaus***

Eyles, Victor

2087. Torrens, H. S. OBITUARY: VICTOR EYLES, 10 OCTOBER 1895-8 MARCH 1978. *British J. for the Hist. of Sci. [Great Britain] 1980 13(3): 282-283.* Obituary of a founder of the British Society for the History of Science. Eyles was important as a geologist, especially of bauxite, and as a bibliophile. Based on the author's and Mrs. Eyles's recollections, and Eyles's writings; 6 notes. 1895-1978

F

Faber, Karl-Georg

2088. Dufraisse, Roger. NEKROLOG: KARL-GEORG FABER (1925-1982) [Obituary: Karl-Georg Faber (1925-82)]. *Francia [West Germany] 1983 11: 927-932.* Obituary of German historian Karl-Georg Faber (1925-82), whose interest in the history of France derived from the impact of the Napoleonic Wars on the local history of his native Palatinate. His work often focused on the legislation resulting from French military occupation of the area. He also contributed to the development of methodology and the history of historiography. 27 notes. 19c-20c

2089. Gollwitzer, Heinz. NEKROLOG: KARL-GEORG FABER [Obituary: Karl-Georg Faber]. *Hist. Zeits. [West Germany] 1983 236(3): 773-778.* Describes and evaluates the career of Karl-Georg Faber (1925-82), whose publications dealt authoritatively with regional history, German history, and historical theory, and whose activities involved public service concerning the university and society. 1927-82

Fabiani, Mario

2090. Mori, Giorgio. MARIO FABIANI [Mario Fabiani]. *Ponte [Italy] 1984 40(3): 32-55.* Prints a speech delivered on the 10th anniversary of the death of Italian Communist leader Mario Fabiani (1912-74), recalling his political activities from 1929 to 1956. 1929-56

Fabre, Henri

2091. Kobylianski, E. A. ANRI FABR—SOZDATEL' PERVOGO V MIRE GIDROSAMOLETA [Henri Fabre, inventor of world's first seaplane]. *Voprosy Istorii Estestvoznaniia i Tekhniki [USSR] 1984 (4): 128-130.* Recounts the professional activities of Henri Fabre (b.1882), French engineer and constructor of the first seaplane. Despite the original difficulties with launching the plane, attached to light pontoons, a successful flight took place in 1910. Two exhibition flights followed in 1911. Secondary sources; photo, 4 notes. 1910-11

Fabroni, Charles-Augustine

2092. Ceyssens, L. AUTOUR DE L'UNIGENITUS: LE CARDINAL CHARLES-AUGUSTIN FABRONI (1651-1727) [Concerning the papal bull *Unigenitus:* Cardinal Charles-Augustine Fabroni (1651-1727)]. *Bull. de l'Inst. Hist. Belge de Rome [Belgium] 1982 52: 31-82.* A study of the career and character of the powerful cardinal who was responsible for the notorious papal decree *Unigenitus* (1713) condemning Antoine de Quesnel's book *Reflexions Morales sur le Nouveau Testament* as being tainted with Jansenism. 1710's-27

Facius, Friedrich

2093. Patse, Hans. FRIEDRICH FACIUS ZUM GEDÄCHTNIS [Friedrich Facius: in memoriam]. *Blätter für Deutsche Landesgeschichte [West Germany] 1983 119: 173-175.* Obituary for Friedrich Facius (1907-83), a director of the state archives and scholar of Thuringian provincial history. A student of historian Willy Andreas at Heidelberg, Facius served in the state archives of Weimar and the provincial archives of Altenburg from 1933 through 1947. He joined the new federal archives in Coblenz (1952-61), served as principal state archivist in Ludwigsburg (1961-67), then directed the archives for southern Baden in Freiburg-im-Breisgau. Facius's scholarly published work concentrated on baroque gardens and parks, the military history of Thuringia from the 17th century to 1918, and the political history of Thuringia from 1818 to 1945. 1933-83

Fadeyev, Aleksandr

2094. Samoilenko, G. V. A. A. FADEEV I SLAVIANSKIE LITERATURY [A. A. Fadeyev and Slavic literatures]. *Sovetskoe Slavianovedenie [USSR] 1982 (3): 53-58.* Examines the works of Aleksandr Fadeyev (1901-56), a great Soviet writer and activist, whose love of Slavic cultures, especially Czech and Slovak, manifested itself in his devotion to their literatures. He knew all Slav literatures well, and, explaining Stur's linguistic reform work, interpreted Slovak development. He defended the Polish people during fascist occupation. During World War II he exhorted all Slavs to defend Slavdom, and he burned with indignation at the fascists' attempts to destroy Slav culture. He explained Socialist Realism, emphasizing its role in the defense of the working man. Based on a variety of Soviet, Czech, Slovak, Polish, and other Slavic sources. 1930-51

Fadrus, Viktor

2095. Weinhäupl, W. "Viktor Fadrus. Eine Darstellung Seines Lebens, Seines Beitrages zur Österreichischen Schulentwicklung und Seines Pädagogischen Denkens" [Viktor Fadrus: his life, his contribution to the development of Austrian education, and his pedagogical ideas]. U. of Salzburg [Austria] 1980. 245 pp. *DAI-C 1983 44(2): 255-256; 8/1125c.* 1919-33

Faduma, Orishatukeh

2096. Okonkwo, Rina L. ORISHATUKEH FADUMA: A MAN OF TWO WORLDS. *J. of Negro Hist. 1983 68(1): 24-36.* The Reverend Orishatukeh Faduma has been neglected by historians of pan-African movements. He played an important role in the African Movement, a back-to-Africa venture that took 38 Oklahoma blacks to the Gold Coast in 1914. Faduma worked as a teacher to improve American blacks' understanding of Africa and to teach Africans about American ideas. 83 notes. 1900-46

Faget family

2097. Lajeunie, Bernard. LES FAGET (XVIe-XVIIIe SIECLES): ASPECTS D'UNE ASCENSION SOCIALE [The Faget family (16th-18th centuries): aspects of social ascension]. *Revue de Pau et du Béarn [France] 1984-85 12: 131-175.* Because of a judicious conversion to Catholicism at the same time as Henri de Navarre and the dynamism of a son in the priesthood, the de Mont branch of the Faget family of Orthez, France, acquired letters of nobility more rapidly than two other branches of the same family of prosperous merchants. 16c-18c

Fahmī, Manṣūr

2098. Reid, Donald M. THE "SLEEPING PHILOSOPHER" OF NAGĪB MAḤFŪẒ'S *MIRRORS. Muslim World 1984 74(1): 1-11.* Although *Mirrors* is regarded as a work of fiction, this is denied by its author. Examines the life of the philosopher Manṣūr Fahmī, who forms the basis for the character Ibrāhīm 'Aql, though there are minor discrepancies in the fictionalized version. *Mirrors* also contains 53 other portraits that reveal much about the problems of 20th-century Egypt in terms of academic and political life. Based on Cairo University Archives and secondary sources; 31 notes. 1908-52

Faidherbe, Louis Léon César

2099. Hrbek, Ivan. GENERAL FAIDHERBE AND THE FRENCH COLONIAL POLICY IN WEST AFRICA. *Arch. Orientální [Czechoslovakia] 1981 49(1): 1-17.* Traces the life and military career of General Louis Léon César Faidherbe (1818-89), focusing on his relation with the imperial regime, 1852-70, of Napoleon III (1808-77) and on his life as a soldier, administrator, and apologist for French colonialism in Algeria, Senegal, and the Sudan. 1818-89

Fairfaxe Family

2100. Cleggett, David. FAMILIES OF AN ATLANTIC COMMUNITY. *Virginia Cavalcade 1983 32(3): 114-125.* 16c-18c

*For abstract see **Culpeper Family***

Falck, Anton Reinhard

2101. Horst, D. van der. "Het Leven van Anton Reinhard Falck tot Zijn Optreden als Secretaris van Stat in 1813" [The life of Anton Reinhard Falck until his appointment as secretary of state in 1813]. State U. of Leiden [Netherlands] 1983. 463 pp. *DAI-C 1986 47(1): 49; 47/235c.* 1777-1813

Falcón, Juan Crisóstomo

2102. Beaujón, Oscar. BOCETO PATOBIOGRAFICO DEL PRESIDENTE MARISCAL FALCON [Pathobiographical profile of President Falcón]. *Bol. de la Acad. Nac. de la Hist. [Venezuela] 1982 65(257): 25-34.* Draws a sketch of President Juan Crisóstomo Falcón (1820-70) in the context of a study by the Society for the History of Medicine on the health problems of the 19th-century presidents of Venezuela. For most of his life, Falcón enjoyed good health, with occasional headaches and skin rashes. His death was probably caused by cancer of the throat. 39 notes. 1820-70

Falconi, Juan de

2103. Ricard, Robert. FALCONI EN FRANCE. [Falconi in France]. *Bull. Hispanique [France] 1981 83(3-4): 433-437.* Juan de Falconi (1596-1638) was a Spanish religious scholar considered by French theologians Paul Dudon and Auguste Poulain to be a precursor of Quietism. The subsequent damage to his reputation appeared to have limited the translation and diffusion of his writings in France to one work, six editions of which were published 1668-91. However, studies published in 1955 and 1977 reveal that four other works had also been translated into French and widely disseminated from the year 1647, indicating a greater penetration of Falconi's influence in France than had previously been acknowledged. 4 notes. 1647-91

2104. Ricard, Robert. FALCONI EN FRANCE [Falconi in France]. *Bulletin Hispanique [France] 1982 84(3-4): 415-419.* Continued from a previous article. The Spanish theologian and ascetic writer Juan Falconi (1596-1638) was suspected of unorthodox views after his death because of a mistaken attribution of some of his writings to the French Quietist mystic Jeanne Guyon. 8 notes. 17c

Fallmerayer, Jakob P.

2105. Fey, Hilde. DEUTSCH-BULGARISCHE KULTURBEZIEHUNGEN: SPIRIDON PALAUZOV UND JAKOB PH. FALLMERAYER [German-Bulgarian cultural relations: Spiridon Palauzov and Jakob P. Fallmerayer]. *Bulgarian Hist. Rev. [Bulgaria] 1980 8(4): 71-74.* Describes the correspondence between Spiridon Palauzov, Bulgarian historian and Slavist, and Jakob P. Fallmerayer, German philologist and scholar, particularly in the 1840's. Provides a list of their mutual acquaintances and also cites recently-discovered documents pertaining to their friendship. Briefly describes the role of Dimitur Mutev (1818-64) in this cultural exchange. 1818-64

Faludi, Ferenc

2106. Szörényi, László. FERENC FALUDIS LITERARISCHE BEDEUTUNG [Ferenc Faludi's literary importance]. *Burgenländische Heimatblätter [Austria] 1979 41(4): 168-180.* Provides a brief summary of the life and literary career of Ferenc Faludi, examines the influence that the period he spent in Rome had on his writings, traces the evolution of his poems and writings, and assesses his important role as the creator of a modern Hungarian literature. 1720's-79

Falzone, Gaetano

2107. Curato, Federico. GAETANO FALZONE [Gaetano Falzone]. *Rassegna Storica del Risorgimento [Italy] 1985 72(1): 45-50.* Discusses the life and works of Gaetano Falzone (1912-84), who received a degree in Law in 1935, and who has himself described in a humorous fashion the years of his youth in Palermo. He wrote a courageous book, *Storia della Mafia* (1978), praised for its clarity and accurate research, which used sociological methodology and exposed the relations between the Mafia and political authorities. He also produced innumerable essays on the Risorgimento and on Sicily. 21 notes. 19c-20c

Fanfani, Amintore

2108. Fisichella, Domenico. FANFANI PRESIDENTE DEL CONSIGLIO: LA LINEA POLITICA E SOCIALE [Fanfani as prime minister: his political and social line]. *Storia e Pol. [Italy] 1982 21(4): 703-737.* Amintore Fanfani was secretary of the Christian Democratic Party from 1954 to 1959; in the same years he was much of the time head of government and had an important part in the passage from centrist to center-left politics. Secondary sources; 122 notes. 1954-62

Fanning, William

2109. Dyster, Barrie. THE RISE OF WILLIAM FANNING AND THE RUIN OF RICHARD JONES. *J. of the Royal Australian Hist. Soc. [Australia] 1982 67(4): 366-374.* An *Anonymous Day Book* was, in fact, written by William Fanning (1816-87). It covers 1841 and the period when Fanning went to Sydney, where his rise was accompanied by the fall of Richard Jones, hitherto Sydney's leading merchant. Based on the *Anonymous Day Book* in the Guildhall Library, London, and on the papers of Jardine Matheson & Co. at Cambridge University Library; 40 notes. ca 1841-80's

Fantis, Antonio de

2110. Acerbi, Antonio. ANTONIO DE FANTIS, EDITORE DELLA "VISIO ISAIE" [Antonio de Fantis, publisher of *Visio Isaiae]. Aevum [Italy] 1983 57(3): 396-415.* Traces the life and work of Renaissance scholar Antonio de Fantis (ca. 1465-1530), who studied under metaphysicist Ottaviano Scoto in 1515; later identified as an alchemist and cabalist, de Fantis also reprinted a 13th-century apocryphal text, *Visio Isaiae,* the source of which was in the Greek of Slavic tradition, and which was the subject of a 1981 study by E. Turdeanu. 1500-30

Fantner, Benedikt

2111. Exenberger, Herbert. BENEDIKT FANTNER (1893-1942): EIN ÖSTERREICHISCHER ARBEITERSCHRIFTSTELLER [Benedikt Fantner (1893-1942): an Austrian worker-author]. *Österreich in Geschichte und Literatur [Austria] 1982 26(4): 206-214.* Benedikt Fantner became a socialist at 18. In World War I he was captured by the Russians and fought in the Russian Revolution. The speech of Viktor Adler to the General Assembly of the Social Democratic Party (SPD) in November 1918 influenced him greatly. In February 1934 the SPD lost to the fascists and the trade unions went underground. As a writer Fantner became very important to the embattled socialists. He fought in the International Brigade in Spain in 1937. In 1941 he was interned in Dachau. In 1942 he was murdered near Linz. Based on documents of the Bundespolizeidirektion Wien; 35 notes. 1910's-42

Fantoni Labindo, Giovanni

2112. Melo, Paola. AUTORITRATTO DALLE LETTERE DI GIOVANNI FANTONI LABINDO [Autobiography in the letters of Giovanni Fantoni Labindo]. *Acme [Italy] 1984 37(3): 123-197; 1985 38(1): 75-128.* Part 1. Introduces and publishes 38 letters, some in verse, written between 1760 and 1800 by Italian poet Giovanni Fantoni Labindo (1755-1807) to family members, friends, and mistresses. Includes a brief chronology of his life and facsimiles of a letter he wrote as a child, a tract, and the title page of the first edition of his *Odi* (1782). Part 2. Publishes 22 letters, 1801-07, as well as a bibliography, an index of all 60 letters, errata from Part 1, facsimiles of two letters, and a plate showing Fantoni. 1760-1807

Farabundo Martí, Agustín

2113. Tsaregorodtsev, V. A. AGUSTIN FARABUNDO MARTI [Agustín Farabundo Martí]. *Voprosy Istorii [USSR] 1981 (8): 185-188.* Freedom fighter and Communist Agustín Farabundo Martí (1890-1932) was instrumental in inspiring and motivating the Farabundo Martí Front of National Liberation in El Salvador. Armed resistance to the Martínez dictatorship started in 1932, following Farabundo Martí's death by military tribunal decree. Maximiliano Martínez was finally removed in 1944, but the liberation struggle continued, directed by the Communist Party working in the underground. Active resistance by the liberation front continues to this day, with Agustín Farabundo Martí as its banner in the fight against internal reaction and US imperialism. Primary sources, 18 notes. 1930's-81

Faraday, Michael

2114. Porter, George. MICHAEL FARADAY—CHEMIST. *Pro. of the Royal Inst. of Great Britain [Great Britain] 1981 53: 90-99.* Surveys the career of Michael Faraday, whose studies covered three main areas: organic chemistry (1820-26), electrochemistry (1833-38), and magnetochemistry (1845-50). 1820-50

2115. Tsverava, G. K. FARADEI, GENRI, I OTKRYTIE INDUKTIROVANNYKH TOKOV [Faraday, Henry, and the discovery of electromagnetic induction]. *Voprosy Istorii Estestvoznaniia i Tekhniki [USSR] 1981 (3): 99-106.* The discovery of electromagnetic induction was made almost simultaneously, although independently, by Michael Faraday (1791-1876) and Joseph Henry (1797-1878), but historians have paid more attention to the former. Faraday's early results preceded those of Henry, but Henry was first in his use of the transformer principle. Henry's discovery of self-induction and his work on spiral conductors using a copper coil were made public in 1835, just before those of Faraday. Faraday benefited from his association with the Royal Society and the widespread publication of his works, while Henry carried out his experiments in relative isolation. The two men met in London in 1837. Based on publications by Faraday and Henry, and secondary historical sources; 3 photos, 20 notes. 1828-37

Farfán, Pedro

2116. Poole, Stafford. INSTITUTIONALIZED CORRUPTION IN THE LETRADO BUREAUCRACY: THE CASE OF PEDRO FARFÁN (1568-1588). *Americas (Acad. of Am. Franciscan Hist.) 1981 38(2): 149-171.* Pedro Farfán (1535-94) studied law at Salamanca as preparation for a career in Spanish imperial civil service. He reached New Spain in 1568 and served both as rector of the University of Mexico and judge of the Audiencia. In the latter capacity, especially, he exemplified the venality and favoritism that appear to have been typical of colonial administration. He made enemies as well, and as the result of an investigation of the Audiencia was eventually subjected to heavy fines and suspension from public office. The apparent failure to enforce the full terms of his sentence suggests that the crown itself regarded corruption as inevitable. Based on secondary works, printed documents, and materials in the Archivo General de Indias; 56 notes. 1568-88

Farhi family

2117. Philipp, Thomas. THE FARHI FAMILY AND THE CHANGING POSITION OF THE JEWS IN SYRIA, 1750-1860. *Middle Eastern Studies [Great Britain] 1984 20(4): 37-52.* The Farhi family was the most wealthy and influential Jewish family in Syria during this period, and its experience demonstrates the fundamental changes in the position of Jews during these years. They lost political and administrative power and wielded no power to match the Christians in the benefits accruing from economic progress, lacking the Christians' external support. Based on contemporary secondary sources; 57 notes. 1750-1860

Farkaš, Adam

2118. Šebjanič, Franc. ŠOLNIK IN DOMOLJUB ADAM FARKAŠ (1730-1786) [Schoolmaster and patriot Adam Farkaš (1730-86)]. *Zgodovinski Časopis [Yugoslavia] 1981 35(1-2): 121-141.* Among the representatives of the East Slovene Protestant movement a special place belongs to the pedagogue Adam Farkaš (1730-86). He was one of the most learned, distinguished, and influential Lutheran intellectuals in Prekmurje in the 18th century. 1758-86

Farkas, Imre

2119. Soltész, Zoltánné. A CSEPREGI FARKAS-NYOMDA ISMERETLEN KALENDÁRIUMA ÉS ÁRGIRUS-KIADÁSA [An unknown almanac and an edition of Árgirus from the Farkas printers at Csepreg]. *Magyar Könyvszemle [Hungary] 1984 100(3): 224-233.* Imre Farkas was a printer, first in Keresztúr and then in Csepreg, from 1608 to 1643. Until 1604 he was a helper at the Johann Manlius printing establishment, which he ran after Manlius's death. Farkas began his own work with the printing of an almanac for 1609. The newly discovered fragments of a 1631 almanac were his work, perhaps using Manlius's equipment. At the same time, a six-leaf fragment of a work entitled *Historia egy Árgirus Nevű Királyfiról és egy Tündér Szűzleányról,* printed by Farkas, was also discovered. In the text the letter "k" is replaced by the "c" and one type style is used throughout, both characteristics of Farkas's work. Primary sources; 7 plates, 24 notes. 1608-43

Farr, William

2120. Dupâquier, Michel. WILLIAM FARR, DEMOGRAPHE [William Farr, demographer]. *Population [France] 1984 39(2): 339-355.* Describes the life and work of British demographer William Farr (1807-83), who directed the General Register Office and introduced new methods of calculating population statistics. 1830's-83

Farrer, William

2121. Cawte, Mary. WILLIAM FARRER AND THE AUSTRALIAN RESPONSE TO MENDELISM. *Historical Records of Australian Science [Australia] 1984 6(1): 45-58.* William Farrer (1845-1906), Australia's most famous wheat breeder, began cross-breeding experimentation in 1886, trying to develop a strain resistant to rust. He has often been described as Mendelian in his approach. However, he did not learn of Mendel's work until the year before his death, and then his response to Mendelism was unenthusiastic. Based on Farrer's correspondence and other papers and several governmental reports; 149 notes. 1886-1906

Fauchard, Pierre

2122. Angot, Jean L. PIERRE FAUCHARD (1677-1761) EXPERT POUR LES DENTS, ET MAITRE CHIRUGIEN DE SAINTE-COME DE PARIS [Pierre Fauchard (1677-1761): qualified dentist and master surgeon from Sainte-Come Paris]. *Clio Medica [Netherlands] 1983 17(4): 207-222.* Paul Fauchard learned the rudiments of dentistry from a naval surgeon and at the age of 19 began his own practice, although he did not receive the degree of "dental expert" until 1708. He continued his studies, becoming a master surgeon in 1715 and eventually writing the *Dental Surgeon-Treatment of Teeth* (1728). In this treatise Fauchard not only suggested technical improvements but also attempted to elevate the practice of his profession. 11 notes, 6 illus. 1700-61

Fauchet, Claude

2123. Kates, Gary. PRIEST AND POLITICIAN: CLAUDE FAUCHET'S EPISCOPAL CAMPAIGN OF 1791. *Consortium on Revolutionary Europe 1750-1850: Pro. 1979: 140-147.* Concerns the career of Claude Fauchet, a prominent priest-politician in the early years of the French Revolution. Fauchet firmly believed that the ideals of the Revolution were compatible with Catholicism, and he supported the Civil Constitution of the Clergy. Most historians have portrayed him as a naive dreamer or a romantic revolutionary. The available evidence demonstrates, however, that he was a clever politician. This is exemplified by his successful campaign in April 1791 to become a bishop. Based on the departmental archives of the Seine and on printed primary sources; 32 notes. 1789-91

Faucit, Helen

2124. Carlisle, Carol J. PASSION FRAMED BY ART: HELEN FAUCIT'S JULIET. *Theatre Survey 1984 25(2): 177-192.* Describes the successful career of Helen Faucit, a British actress who portrayed Juliet in Shakespeare's *Romeo and Juliet* from 1833 until her last professional engagement in 1871. 1830's-70's

Faure, Edgar

2125. Rigaud, Jacques. LA MEMOIRE D'ETAT: D'EDGAR FAURE A MICHEL DEBRE [State memory: from Edgar Faure to Michel Debré]. *Revue des Deux Mondes [France] 1985 (2): 336-349.* 1949-68
For abstract see ***Debré, Michel***

Fauré, Gabriel

2126. Woldu, Gail Hilson. "Gabriel Fauré As Director of the Conservatoire National de Musique et de Déclamation, 1905-1920." Yale U. 1983. 304 pp. *DAI 1984 44(9): 2706-A.* DA8329295 1905-20

Fawcett, Benjamin

2127. Forster, Frank M. C. B. FAWCETT, A NINETEENTH-CENTURY AUSTRALIAN QUACK DOCTOR. *J. of the Royal Australian Hist. Soc. [Australia] 1981 67(3): 272-282.* Benjamin Fawcett (1817-90), a fraudulent physician, preyed on public gullibility. After working in the Australian goldfields, he moved to Bathhurst. His *Essay on Childbirth without Danger and Nearly Painless,* 2d ed. (1882) reflected the need for counsel and reassurance at a time of fears about the risks of childbirth. Based on the writings of Fawcett and the press; 52 notes. 1840's-90

Fawcett, Edward Douglas

2128. Temple, Robert K. G. E. DOUGLAS FAWCETT—THE ENGLISH JULES VERNE. *British Heritage 1985 6(2): 28-36, 46-47.* Biography of English novelist Edward Douglas Fawcett, who in the late 1800's and early 1900's wrote, as Jules Verne did, of inventions and events that wouldn't be realized until much later in the 20th century. 1890's-1940's

Fay, Francis

2129. Millett, Benignus. WHO WROTE THE *MARTYRIUM... CORNELII DOVENII,* COLOGNE, 1614? *Recusant History [Great Britain] 1985 17(4): 358-361.* A description of the 17th-century Irish Franciscan Francis Fay, who the author believes wrote the *Martyrium... Cornelii Dovenii* (Cologne, 1614), a *passio* of the martyred bishop of Down and Connor, Conor O'Devaney (ca. 1530-1612). 1614

Faymonville, Philip R.

2130. Mal'kov, V. L. SEKRETNYE DONESENIIA VOENNOGO ATASHE SSHA V MOSKVE NAKANUNE VTOROI MIROVOI VOINY [Secret reports of the American military attaché in Moscow on the eve of World War II]. *Novaia i Noveishaia Istoriia [USSR] 1982 (4): 101-117.* Philip R. Faymonville held the post of military attaché in Moscow from 1933 to 1938. In his secret reports he gave an objective analysis of the Soviet armed forces, the economy, and the policies of the Soviet government and military leadership. The balanced view of the USSR he presented led eventually to his recall. An appendix to this article publishes 14 of these reports covering the period 8 May 1937 to 15 September 1938. 1933-38

Fayod, Victor

2131. Monthoux, Olivier. L'ANNEE VICTOR FAYOD [The year of Victor Fayod]. *Musées de Génève [Switzerland] 1986 (261): 3-6.* Explains the life of Swiss mycologist Victor Fayod, the importance of his work and research, and the quality of his collections. 1860-1900

Febres-Cordero y Muñoz, Francisco

2132. Villacrés Moscoso, Jorge W. EL NUEVO SANTO ECUATORIANO HERMANO MIGUEL, TUVO ASCENDENCIA VENEZOLANA [The new Ecuadoran saint Brother Miguel was of Venezuelan descent]. *Boletín de la Academia Nacional de la Historia [Venezuela] 1984 67(268): 735-740.* Traces the genealogy of Francisco Febres-Cordero y Muñoz (d. 1910), known in religious life as Brother Miguel of the Society of Christian Brothers, who was raised to the honors of the altar by Pope John Paul II in October 1984. Brother Miguel, some of whose ancestors lived in Venezuela in the 18th century, was the author of many works on the Spanish language for the use of students and was a member of the Academy of the Spanish Language. 18c-1910 -Cordero

2133. —. [HOMENAJE AL HERMANO MIGUEL FEBRES-CORDERO] [Tribute to Brother Miguel Febres-Cordero]. *Boletín de la Academia Nacional de la Historia [Venezuela] 1985 68(270): 499-508.*

Felice Cardot, Carlos. EL HERMANO MIGUEL EN LA ACADEMIA DE LA HISTORIA [Brother Miguel in the Academy of History], *pp. 499-501.* Address at the unveiling of a portrait of Dr. Francisco Febres-Cordero y Muñoz, corresponding member, known as Brother Miguel, of the congregation of St. John the Baptist de la Salle, canonized by Pope John Paul II in October 1984.

Febres-Cordero Briceño, Rafael. DISCURSO EN HONOR A SAN MIGUEL FEBRES CORDERO [A tribute to Saint Michael Febres Cordero], *pp. 501-508.* Traces the career of the Ecuadoran educator, academician, and saint. 1854-1910

Fechenbach, Felix

2134. Schueler, H. K. "Felix Fechenbach, 1894-1933. Die Entwicklung eines Republikanischen Journalisten" [Felix Fechenbach, 1894-1933: the development of a republican journalist]. U. of Bonn [West Germany] 1980. 318 pp. *DAI-C 1983 44(1): 5; 8/21c.* 1894-1933

Fechin, Nicolai

2135. Schriever, George. NICOLAI FECHIN: RUSSIAN ARTIST IN THE AMERICAN WEST. *Am. West 1982 19(3): 34-42, 62-63.* Russian-born Nicolai Fechin (1881-1955) received formal art training at a regional academy and at the Imperial Academy of Art in St. Petersburg. He was soon winning awards, an instructorship, and invitations to show at international exhibitions. Beset by ill health, he emigrated to the United States in 1923. After four years' residence in New York where he earned high acclaim, Fechin settled in the West. His years in Taos, New Mexico, are generally regarded as his best. His virtuosity as a painter of portraits overshadowed his consummate mastery of line. If he had never painted a single picture he would still be hailed as a great artist because of his drawings. Despite his long and intimate association with the American Southwest, he remained Russian and his style owed nothing to his adopted land. 12 illus. 1900's-55

Fedenko, Panas

2136. Antonovych, Marko. PANAS FEDENKO (13. 12. 1893-10. 9. 1981). [Panas Fedenko, 13 December 1893-10 September 1981]. *Ukrains'kyi Istoryk 1982-83 19-20(3-4, 1): 151-153.* An obituary of the Ukrainian historian, novelist, journalist, and political activist Panas Fedenko, who spent most of his life abroad. Fedenko's works on the history of the Ukraine, ranging from the 17th to the 20th centuries, dealt chiefly with diplomatic, political, and social events. 1893-1981

Feierabend, Ladislav K.

2137. Feierabend, Ladislav. EXTRACT FROM MEMOIRS. *Kosmas 1982 1(1): 101-124, (2): 75-112; 1983 2(1): 99-118.* Ladislav K. Feierabend (1891-1969), Minister of Agriculture in Czechoslovakia before World War II and member of the Czechoslovak government-in-exile, published eight Czech memoir volumes under various titles in Washington from 1961 to 1968. Translated selections present his views of the Munich crisis and its aftermath, 1938-39, of Czechoslovak wartime politics in London, 1941-44, and of the Czechoslovak-Soviet alliance. 1938-44

Feijlbrief, Jan Koos

2138. Moor, W. de. "J. van Oudshoorn, Biografie van de Ambtenaarschrijver J. K. Feijlbrief (1876-1951)" [J. van Oudshoorn, a biography of the civil service clerk J. K. Feijlbrief (1876-1951)]. State U. of Leiden [Netherlands] 1982. 886 pp. *DAI-C 1986 47(1): 57; 47/282c.* ca 1900-51

Feliciano, Felice

2139. Welles, Elizabeth B. THE UNPUBLISHED ALCHEMICAL SONNETS OF FELICE FELICIANO: AN EPISODE IN SCIENCE AND HUMANISM IN 15TH CENTURY ITALY. *Ambix [Great Britain] 1982 29(1): 1-16.* Presents a letter and extracts from alchemical sonnets by Feliciano (also known as Antiquarius) (1433-79) following a brief biographical sketch. It is claimed that he practiced as an alchemist, as well as being a scribe, scholar, and Renaissance humanist. Most sonnets bewail what alchemy has cost him, it appears. Only translations are used in the text, but in an appendix, the original Italian is also given. Primary sources, documents in libraries such as the Vatican and Harvard University, and some contemporary books; much explicatory matter and many secondary sources; 34 notes. 1450-79

Felipe, León

2140. Gonzalez-Gerth, Miguel. LEON FELIPE COMES TO TEXAS. *Library Chronicle of the University of Texas at Austin 1984 (27): 105-113.* Gives a brief biography of Spanish poet León Felipe (1884-1968) and details a bequest of his books and letters to the Humanities Research Center at the University of Texas. 1919-68

Fell, Margaret

2141. Sharman, Cecil W. GEORGE FOX AND HIS FAMILY II. *Quaker History 1986 75(1): 1-11.* Many early Quakers were of the embryo business and professional class, with as much nonuniversity education as the age offered. Illustrative are Margaret Fell's children and their substantial merchant spouses. Their letters refer not only to religious affairs but to mundane matters, e.g. the purchase of clothing, provisions, and drink, coach hire, shortage of farm labor because so many Quakers were in prison, and the confiscation of letters and goods. Based on family correspondence; 25 notes. 1650's-70's

Felz, Hanns Jakob

2142. Allgäuer, Wolfgang. DIE LUFTEISENBAHNEN ÜBER DIE BREGENZER ACHE: 1871 BIS 1962 [The air train over the Bregenzer Ache, 1871-1962]. *Montfort [Austria] 1983 35(1): 67-70.* Describes the often unsuccessful attempts of Hanns Jakob Felz, a peasant, to invent, install, and run a ferry on cables over the Bregenzer Ache and subsequent problems and successes of the enterprise. 1855-1962

Feng Wenbin

2143. —. FENG WEN-PIN—VICE-PRESIDENT OF THE CCP CENTRAL PARTY SCHOOL. *Issues & Studies [Taiwan] 1982 18(9): 103-107.* Feng Wenbin (Feng Wen-pin, b. 1919), one of several cadres being promoted for their experience in the youth movement, has worked for the Party since 1931. Although he was removed from his post in the General Office of the Central Committee in 1982, he has remained Vice President of the Central Party School and holds office in units researching Party history. Based on Mainland media reports; 9 notes. 1927-82

Fenwick-Miller, Florence

2144. Vanarsdel, Rosemary T. MRS. FLORENCE FENWICK-MILLER AND *THE WOMAN'S SIGNAL,* 1895-1899. *Victorian Periodicals Rev. [Canada] 1982 15(3): 107-118.* Examines Florence Fenwick-Miller's career in journalism during her ownership of *The Woman's Signal,* a women's weekly newspaper dedicated to spreading information and promoting progress in the cause of "equal rights and the general advancement of women." 1895-99

Fényes, Samu

2145. Dandara, Livia. SAMU FÉNYES—UN ANTIREVIZIONIST CONDAMNAT LA MOARTE DE HORTHYIŞTI [Samu Fényes: an antirevisionist condemned to death by the supporters of Horthy]. *Magazin Istoric [Romania] 1982 16(11): 50-51.* Samu Fényes (1863-1937), Czech by birth and Hungarian by nationality, played a difficult role as an antirevisionist, in the troubled Transylvanian politics of the interwar period, and was executed by the Horthy government. 1920-37

Ferdinand II

2146. Maier, Konstantin. RESIDENZ, KOADJUTORIE ODER RESIGNATION: DER KAMPF ERZHERZOG FERDINANDS VON ÖSTERREICH UM DAS BISTUM KONSTANZ [Residence, coadjustorship, or resignation: Archduke Ferdinand of Austria's campaign for the bishopric of Constance]. *Zeitschrift für Kirchengeschichte [West Germany] 1985 96(3): 344-376.* Archduke Ferdinand II of Austria (1529-95) spent almost 15 years struggling with Cardinal Marcus Sitticus from Hohenems for control of the bishopric of Constance on behalf of his son, Andreas. Since Marcus Sitticus lived in a Roman palace far from Constance, the cathedral chapter was emboldened to oppose him for a variety of reasons. Archduke Ferdinand tried numerous stratagems to wrest Constance away from Marcus Sitticus, to no avail, until the cardinal resigned in 1589. Once in office, Cardinal Andreas proved much shrewder and more politically astute than had been suspected. He promulgated the Tridentine Church reforms by all means, thus ushering in a new epoch for his hard-won bishopric. Based on archival materials from the Vatican, Freiburg, Gallese, Innsbruck, Karlsruhe, Sigmaringen, and Stuttgart, and secondary sources; 212 notes. ca 1525-85

Ferenczi, Sándor

2147. Hermann, Imre. SÁNDOR FERENCZI THE MAN. *New Hungarian Quarterly [Hungary] 1984 25(95): 115-118.* Recalls the character and personality of the author's mentor and pioneer Hungarian psychologist, Sándor Ferenczi. Ferenczi is revealed as a kind, friendly, and modest man who displayed great empathy for his patients. Professionally, he was also volatile, frequently discarding his own theories soon after formulating them. A believer in self-analysis, he retained an objective curiosity about his own state of mind even throughout his lingering terminal illness. 1911-33

Ferguson, Samuel

2148. ÓDúill, Gréagóir. SAMUEL FERGUSON, AN STÁT AGUS AN LÉANN DÚCHAIS [Samuel Ferguson, the state and native learning]. *Studia Hibernica [Ireland] 1979 19: 102-117.* During his early twenties Ferguson (1810-86) became interested in the sources of Irish culture and by 1834 was appealing against the government's decision to diminish the Ordnance Survey and to cease financing the study of local history, arguing that this work had a uniting effect on the Irish. Interest in, and support for, native Irish learning remained his cultural philosophy to the end. In the 1840's he was in sympathy with Young Ireland. His call for Home Rule in 1848, however, was inspired more by a fear of the influence of Chartism and Benthamism on England than by any real desire for Irish independence. He moved away from support for Irish independence and by the 1860's was unionist in sympathy. In 1867 he applied for the post of Assistant Keeper in the newly established Public Records Office in Dublin, was acceptable to the conservative government and was appointed to the post. Subsequently he became even more definitely unionist. Based on private and public correspondence and secondary sources; 66 notes. 1830-86

Feringán, Sebastián

2149. Piñera y Rivas, Alvaro de la. EL INGENIERO MILITAR SEBASTIAN FERINGAN, CONSTRUCTOR DEL REAL ARSENAL DE CARTAGENA [Military engineer Sebastián Feringán, builder of the Royal Shipyard of Cartagena]. *Revista de Historia Naval [Spain] 1985 3(8): 111-139.* Sebastián Feringán y Cortés (1700-62) was appointed in 1728 to build a major dockyard for the Spanish navy at the Mediterranean port of Cartagena, with its spacious and well-protected natural harbor. Work began in 1733 and through the incessant efforts of Feringán continued for the rest of his life. His legacy includes the dockyard, drydocks, shipyard buildings, and a naval hospital, most of which still exist and serve the Spanish navy today. Based on the Archivo General de Simancas, the Servicio Histórico Militar, the Archivo Histórico de Marina, Cartagena, and the Archivo Histórico Ayuntamiento Cartagena; 12 illus., 71 notes. 1728-62

Fernández, Emilio

2150. Ellis, Kirk. STRANGER THAN FICTION: EMILIO FERNÁNDEZ' MEXICO. *J. of Popular Film and Television 1982 10(1): 27-36.* Brief biography of Emilio Fernández (b. 1904), Mexican film director of the 1940's. His films, criticized as portraying stereotypical images of Mexicans, were an accurate representation of aspects of Mexican reality. 1940's

Fernández, Macedonio

2151. Trigo, Xulio Ricardo. UNA CARTA DE MACEDONIO A JUAN RAMON (REPUBLICA ARGENTINA, 1948) [A letter from Macedonio to Juan Ramón (Argentina, 1948)]. *Cuadernos Hispanoamericanos [Spain] 1985 (416): 178-183.* 1948
*For abstract see **Jiménez, Juan Ramón***

Fernández Celis, José Miguel

2152. Lara Cagigas, Efraín. JOSE MIGUEL FERNANDEZ CELIS: UN ARTISTA HOY DESCONOCIDO [José Miguel Fernández Celis: an artist today unknown]. *Rev. de la Biblioteca Nac. José Martí [Cuba] 1982 24(1-2): 185-199.* Only a few paintings of Fernández Celis (1817-80) still exist. He was one of the few artists of distinction who worked in Santiago during the 19th century and his works were heavily influenced by Murillo and Zurbarán. 17 notes. ca 1840-80

Fernández de Heredia, Alonso

2153. Montiel Argüello, Alejandro. TRES DIGNITARIOS PROMOVIDOS DE NICARAGUA A GUATEMALA [Three dignitaries promoted from Nicaragua to Guatemala]. *Anales de la Acad. de Geog. e Hist. de Guatemala [Guatemala] 1981 55: 317-331.* 1745-1801
*For abstract see **Estachería, José de***

Fernández de Heredia, Gonzalo

2154. Cabre, María Dolores. EL ARZOBISPO DE TARRAGONA, GONZALO FERNÁNDEZ DE HEREDIA [The archbishop of Tarragona, Gonzalo Fernández de Heredia]. *Jerónimo Zurita. Cuadernos de Historia [Spain] 1983 (47-48): 299-321.* Provides a brief biography of the churchman and statesman Gonzalo Fernández de Heredia (ca. 1450-1511). Serving as ambassador of Fernando of Aragon in Rome and Naples 1475-1500, he was appointed bishop of Barcelona in 1479 and archbishop of Tarragona in 1490. He held these positions in absentia, taking up active administration of Tarragona only upon his return to Spain in 1500, and even then living in semi-seclusion in various castles of Tarragona until his death. The author discusses various diocesan affairs in Barcelona and Tarragona, the culture of the Renaissance in Tarragona, and the tapestry "La Bona Vida," brought by Heredia to the Cathedral of Tarragona. Based on documents from the Archivo Histórico Capitular de Tarragona, Archivo de la Corona de Aragón, and other archives; 104 notes, appendix. 1475-1511

Fernández de Moratín, Leandro

2155. Rien, H. "Leandro Fernández de Moratín: Versuch einer Historischsoziologischen Analyse des Autobiographischen, Literaturtheoretischen und Dramatischen Werks" [Leandro Fernández de Moratín: a historical and sociological analysis of his autobiographical and dramatic works and literary theory]. U. of Göttingen [West Germany] 1982. 215 pp. *DAI-C 1986 47(1): 18; 47/85c.* 1780's-1828

Fernández de Oviedo, Gonzalo

2156. Cobo Borda, Juan Gustavo. EL SUMARIO DE GONZALO FERNANDEZ DE OVIEDO [Gonzalo Fernández de Oviedo's *Sumario*]. *Cuadernos Hispanoamericanos [Spain] 1986 (429): 63-77.* Follows the life and travels of Spanish historian and colonial administrator Gonzalo Fernández de Oviedo through Europe and America. He sided against Bartolomeo de Las Casas and offered to European readers one of the most precise accounts of the American realities faced by the first wave of colonizers, in his *Sumario de la Natural y General Historia de las Indias* (1526). 25 notes. 1510-26

Fernández Duro, Cesáreo

2157. Salgado Alba, Jesús. FERNANDEZ DURO: LA ESPADA. LA PLUMA. EL ANCLA [Fernández Duro: the sword, the pen, the anchor]. *Rev. General de Marina [Spain] 1983 204[i.e., 205](Aug-Sept): 251-261.* Cesáreo Fernández Duro was the most prodigious Spanish naval officer and historian of the 19th century. He actively participated in four war campaigns, commanding two of them. He was awarded Spain's highest decoration for combat. He then became Spain's most famed, prolific, profound, and brilliant naval historian, holding six academic posts. 4 illus. 19c

Fernández Flórez, Wenceslao

2158. Echeverria Pazos, R. M. "Wenceslao Fernández Flórez, Periodista [Wenceslao Fernández Flórez, the journalist]. U. of Navarra [Spain] 1983. 593 pp. *DAI-C 1984 45(1): 3; 9/9c.* 1890's-1920's

Fernández Hall, Francisco

2159. Brañas, Cesar. CENTENARIO DEL NACIMIENTO DE D. FRANCISCO FERNANDEZ HALL [Centenary of the birth of Francisco Fernández Hall]. *Anales de la Academia de Geografía e Historia de Guatemala [Guatemala] 1983 57: 287-295.* Francisco Fernández Hall (1883-1941) was a charter member of the Academy of Geography and History of Guatemala and a prolific writer of short historical and literary pieces in Guatemalan newspapers, with longer works published in the *Anales.* This tribute contains a brief biography and a complete bibliography of this self-taught historian. Photo. 1883-1941

Fernández Larrain, Sergio

2160. Ramírez de Rivera, Hugo Rodolfo. EL DR SERGIO FERNANDEZ LARRAIN (1909-1983): HOMBRE PUBLICO E HISTORIADOR [Sergio Fernández Larrain (1909-83): public man and historian]. *Boletín de la Academia Nacional de la Historia [Venezuela] 1984 67(267): 611-618.* Sergio Fernández Larrain was a conservative member of both houses of the Chilean parliament, ambassador of Chile in Spain during Franco's regime, historian, bibliophile, and academic. As a politician he was active in the repression of Communist subversion. Among his historical works are biographies and collections of letters of Latin American writers. 3 notes. 1909-83

Ferran, Jaime

2161. Bornside, George H. JAIME FERRAN AND PREVENTIVE INOCULATION AGAINST CHOLERA. *Bull. of the Hist. of Medicine 1981 55(4): 516-532.* In 1885, Jaime Ferran (1852-1929), a Spanish physician, was first to use a vaccine to immunize against a bacterial disease in human beings, injecting broth cultures of living cholera vibrios into at least 30,000 Spaniards seeking protection against cholera. Analysis of the records indicates that significant protection was provided by the vaccine, although he received little credit at the time. He clearly deserves to be recognized as a pioneering medical microbiologist. Based on published records, including medical journals and government documents in Spanish and English; 41 notes, fig. 1881-90

Ferrandus, Thomas

2162. Rhodes, Dennis E. THE CAREER OF THOMAS FERRANDUS OF BRESCIA. *Bulletin of the John Rylands University Library of Manchester [Great Britain] 1984 67(1): 544-559.* Discusses the experimental printer Thomas Ferrandus, who was also a teacher, minor author, and priest. The 17 books that can be attributed to him are described, along with their present locations. Secondary sources; 2 appendixes, 20 notes. 15c

Ferrari, Giuseppe

2163. Monsagratti, Giuseppe. A PROPOSITO DI UNA RECENTE BIOGRAFIA DI G. FERRARI: VECCHIE TESI E NUOVE IPOTESI [Concerning a recent biography of G. Ferrari: old theses and new hypotheses]. *Rassegna Storica del Risorgimento [Italy] 1980 67(3): 259-296.* Reviews a biography of Giuseppe Ferrari (1812-76), philosopher and statesman, by Clara Lovett. There is an imaginative reconstruction of the post-1859 period, when Ferrari returned from France and stood for Parliament, of which he was for 16 years a member. Includes four new letters to Gaspare Gorresio, a Sanskrit scholar, on contemporary events. 19c

Ferrari, Mario

2164. Michelotti, Nicola. MARIO FERRARI (1918-1982) [Mario Ferrari (1918-82)]. *Archivio Storico per le Province Parmensi [Italy] 1983 35: 37-40.* Reviews the contributions to the understanding of contemporary politics, economics, and history made by the lawyer and writer for *Avanti,* Mario Ferrari. 1930's-82

Ferré, Léo

2165. Reid, Malcolm. FERRÉ. *Contemporary French Civilization 1982 6(3): 259-270.* Recounts the career of Léo Ferré, Spanish emigre, socialist, and composer now living in Quebec, and his link with the political and labor scene in France from the 1950's to the worker-student rebellion of May 1968. 1950-68

Ferreira de Vera, Alvaro

2166. Oliveira, António de. ALVARO FERREIRA DE VERA, ARBITRISTA [Alvaro Ferreira de Vera, planner]. *Rev. Portuguesa de Hist. [Portugal] 1981 19: 271-296.* Alvaro Ferreira de Vera, known for his historical and genealogical studies and writings on the nobility, was also a planner. In 1637 he proposed to the king of Portugal and Spain a plan relating to the insurance of ships sailing to India, which would save Portugal financially and obtain for himself a peerage and an office of state. Though the project was not then accepted, it influenced later legislation. Based on documents in Lisbon archives and secondary works; 56 notes, 3 appendixes. 1630-57

Ferreira Néri, Ana Justina

2167. Ipanema, Cybelle de. NO CENTENARIO DE MORTE DE DA. ANA JUSTINA FERREIRA NERI [The centenary of the death of Donna Ana Justina Ferreira Néri]. *Rev. do Inst. Hist. e. Geog. Brasileiro [Brazil] 1982 (334): 145-154.* Reviews the career of Ana Justina Ferreira Néri, who served as a volunteer nurse in the Paraguayan War in 1870 and who earned the title of "Mother of the Brazilians" by the troops. Writings about her, and excerpts from documents concerning her, are included, as are brief notices concerning her family, husband, children, and grandchildren, most of whom also had distinguished careers either in the military or in medicine. Based on archival collections in Brazil and secondary sources; 13 notes. 1880-1980

Ferrero, Guglielmo

2168. Goetz, Helmut. GUGLIELMO FERRERO: EIN EXEMPEL TOTALITÄRER VERFOLGUNG [Guglielmo Ferrero: an example of totalitarian persecution]. *Quellen und Forchungen aus Italienischen Arch. und Bibliotheken [Italy] 1981 61: 248-304.* Inquiry into the Fascists' persecution of Guglielmo Ferrero (1871-1942), critic, lawyer, sociologist, historian, novelist, and publicist. Discusses moral policy, the blind obedience of state employees, and the position of intellectuals in the Fascist regime in Italy. Mussolini personally played an important role in the persecution, which began in the early 1920's. This study focuses on the years 1926-29. The harassment included the control of visitors and correspondence and denial of a passport. Based on documents from the Central State Archive in Rome and the diaries of Ferrero's son. 1926-29

Ferrez, Marc

2169. Hoffenburg, H. L. MARC FERREZ. *Américas (Organization of American States) 1983 35(4): 12-17.* Outlines the life of the Brazilian photographer Marc Ferrez (b. 1843). In 1902 Ferrez was commissioned to record the birth of the Avenida Central, which was to cut through the alleys of colonial Rio de Janeiro. Ferrez photographed each architectural facade before it was destroyed, and some of his pictures are reproduced here. 1860's-1902

Ferrier, Jean

2170. Shea, William R. DESCARTES AND THE FRENCH ARTISAN JEAN FERRIER. *Ann. dell'Istituto e Mus. di Storia della Sci. di Firenze [Italy] 1982 7(2): 145-160.* 1629-38

*For abstract see **Descartes, René***

Ferrières-Sauvebeuf, Comte de

2171. Blanc, Olivier. LES "INDICS" DE LA REVOLUTION ["Squealers" during the French Revolution]. *Histoire [France] 1983 (62): 78-84.* The life and actions of the Comte de Ferrières-Sauvebeuf (1762-1814) who, during the Terror, gave information on the intrigues or other political actions of his fellow prisoners, and so regained his freedom, at least for a time. ca 1780-1814

Ferry, Jules

2172. Ch'en San-ching. JU FEI LI TI CHIH MIN SSU HSIANG CHI CH'I TUI HUA CHENG TS'E (1880-1885) [Jules Ferry's colonial doctrine and his policy toward China, 1880-85]. *Bull. of the Inst. of Modern Hist. Acad. Sinica [Taiwan] 1980 9: 269-289.* Jules Ferry (1832-93), twice premier of France, 1880-85, was one of the foremost European colonialists. Glory for France, commercial profit, and successful competition with England, were some of the goals of Ferry's colonial policy, which, however vigorous, did not extend to the conquest of China. Because of strong opposition from the French National Assembly and public opinion and British interference, Ferry was forced to be cautious and never fully integrated his policies and actions. Based on *Documents Diplomatiques Français* and contemporary writings; 69 notes. 1880-85

Fessler, Ignatius Aurelius

2173. Barton, P. "Fessler in Preussen" [Fessler in Prussia]. U. of Vienna [Austria] 1980. 1240 pp. *DAI-C 1984 45(3): 674; 9/2748c.* 1788-1809

2174. Rosenstrauch-Königsberg, Edith. IGNAZ AURELIUS FESSLERS LEBENSWEG. VOM KAPUZINER ZUM FREIMAURER, HISTORIKER UND PROTESTANTISCHEN BISCHOF [Ignatius Aurelius Fessler's path through life. From a Capuchin to a freemason, a historian, and a Protestant bishop]. *Jahrbuch des Instituts für Deutsche Geschichte [Israel] 1986 15: 465-476.* Reviews Peter F. Barton's four volume work *Ignatius Aurelius Fessler: From Baroque Catholicism to Enlightenment* and discusses Fessler's impact on the religious, political, and social institutions of his time. As a Capuchin monk, Fessler was instrumental in implementing Joseph II's 1771 reform, ending jailing of monks in the monasteries. As a historian, Fessler's writings revealed contemporary problems in historical disguise. As a freemason, Fessler uplifted the moral fiber of his brothers by fighting anti-Semitism and advocating humanitarianism. As a Protestant convert he served as bishop in Saratov, Russia, where he completed his favorite work, a history of his homeland Hungary. Barton's work is a valuable contribution to research on the Enlightenment. 6 notes. 1756-1839

Fest, Sándor

2175. Maller, Sándor. A PIONEER OF ANGLO-HUNGARIAN RELATIONS: IN MEMORIUM SÁNDOR FEST (1883-1944). *New Hungarian Quarterly [Hungary] 1984 25(95): 128-132.* A brief professional biography of Sándor Fest, the Hungarian educator whose life was dedicated to the introduction of English cultural themes into Hungarian education. He taught at Eötvös College, and later at the University of Debrecen where he fashioned curricula around the English classics and historic contacts between Englishmen and Hungarians. He was a member of the Hungarian Academy of Sciences. 1907-44

Fetzer, Jacob

2176. Fetzer, Jacob and Fetzer, Olga Ruff. THE JACOB AND OLGA RUFF FETZER STORY. *Journal of the American Historical Society of Germans from Russia 1985 8(1): 25-32.* Reminiscences by a married couple about life among the Germans in southern Russia, emigration to the United States, farming, working and raising a family in the Dakotas and Idaho. 1900's-70's

Feuchtersleben, Ernst von

2177. Laor, Nathaniel. SZASZ, FEUCHTERSLEBEN, AND THE HISTORY OF PSYCHIATRY. *Psychiatry 1982 45(4): 316-324.* Recounts the life and career of the 19th-century Viennese psychiatrist Ernst von Feuchtersleben (1805-49) and describes his views on mental illness. 1805-49

Ficino, Marsilio

2178. Fubini, Riccardo. FICINO E I MEDICI ALL'AVVENTO DI LORENZO IL MAGNIFICO [Ficino and the Medici to the advent of Lorenzo the Magnificent]. *Rinascimento [Italy] 1984 24: 3-52.* Challenges the traditional view of Marsilio Ficino (1433-99) that he was a close supporter of the Medici family and that his platonism was a justification of Medici political dominance. Despite Ficino's ties to the Medici, he nevertheless had intimate relationships with anti-Mediceans, including several who organized the Pazzi Conspiracy against the Medici in 1478. Ficino attempted to maintain at least minimal independence from all patrons. In his writing, Ficino advocated, in addition to his well-known eternal philosophy, social relationships of equal men who sought and shared knowledge. Based on printed works of Ficino and letters of Lorenzo de'Medici; 116 notes. 1450-93

Fidanova, Slavka

2179. Pachemska, Darinka. (A) SLAVKA FIDANOVA—PO POVOD 60-TIOT RODEN DEN: (B) BIBLIOGRAFIIA NA OBAVIENI TRUDOVI NA PROFESORSKATA SLAVKA FIDANOVA [Slavka Fidanova: on her 60th birthday with a bibliography of her published works]. *Istorija [Yugoslavia] 1980 16(1): 7-16.* Reviews the career of Slavka Fidanova (b. 1920), professor of history at the faculty of philosophy at the University of Skopje in Macedonia, in anticipation of her 60th birthday; includes a bibliography of 45 books and journal articles by Slavka Fidanova, published 1962-78. 1920-78

Fiderkiewicz, Alfred

2180. Dymek, Benon. ALFRED FIDERKIEWICZ (1886-1972) [Alfred Fiderkiewicz (1886-1972)]. *Z Pola Walki [Poland] 1979 22(2): 141-152.* Alfred Fiderkiewicz, a Polish political activist, first encountered socialist ideas at school. From 1904 to 1922 he was in the United States, working, studying, and conducting political work among Polish and American socialists. On his return to Poland, he joined the Polish People's Party but soon moved to the Communist Party of Poland. During World War II, he joined the new Polish Workers' Party. After the war, he organized Polish embassies abroad. He retired in 1956 and died in 1972. Based on A. Fiderkiewicz's autobiographical writings, documents in the Central Archives of the Central Committee of the Polish United Workers' Party in Warsaw, and eyewitness accounts; 33 notes. 1902-56

Field, Noel

2181. Gaster, Bertha. REMEMBERING NOEL. *New Hungarian Quarterly [Hungary] 1984 25(96): 53-56.* Reminiscences about Noel Field, an American who became a permanent resident of Hungary and editor of the *New Hungarian Quarterly.* At one time a US Foreign Service officer, Field, along with his wife Herta, became a convinced Communist at the time of the Spanish civil war, and although wrongfully imprisoned from 1949 to 1954, Field nevertheless retained his love for Hungary and remained there until his death. 1930's-70's

Fielden, John

2182. Weaver, Stewart Angas. "The Politics of Popular Radicalism: John Fielden and the Progress of Labor in Early Victorian England." Stanford U. 1985. 466 pp. *DAI 1985 46(6): 1717-A.* DA8511366 1832-47

Fielding, Henry

2183. Burling, William J. FIELDING, HIS PUBLISHERS, AND JOHN RICH IN 1730. *Theatre Survey 1985 26(1): 39-46.* Examines the first phase of Henry Fielding's theatrical career including the relationship between Fielding and his publishers—based upon the bibliographical history of his plays—and the question of why Fielding brought a revision of his play "Rape upon Rape" to producer John Rich for production in Rich's Lincoln's Inn Fields theater in view of their conflicting attitudes toward the pantomime. 1728-38

2184. Rizzo, Betty. NOTES ON THE WAR BETWEEN HENRY FIELDING AND JOHN HILL, 1752-53. *Library [Great Britain] 1985 7(4): 338-353.* The quarrel between John Hill (1716-75) and Henry Fielding (1707-54) was more serious than the mock war the two had in the pages of contemporary periodicals. Hill's column "The Inspector" in the *London Daily Advertiser* and Fielding's responses in the *Covent-Garden Journal* went deeper and lasted for two years. Originally begun by the two as a paper war to help boost circulation, their differences became more serious. Several other writers joined Fielding in the war with Hill. Primary sources; 39 notes. 1752-53

Fiévée, Joseph

2185. Popkin, Jeremy D. CONSERVATISM UNDER NAPOLEON: THE POLITICAL WRITINGS OF JOSEPH FIÉVÉE. *History of European Ideas [Great Britain] 1984 5(4): 385-400.* Joseph Fiévée (b. 1767), a contributor to the development of pragmatic conservatism before and during the Napoleonic era in France, initially welcomed the French Revolution but became disillusioned when Jacobins sacked his printshop in 1793. From 1802 to 1813 he had direct access to Napoleon (1769-1821) and enjoyed the confidence of leading royalists. He argued for the restoration of a hereditary privileged elite but accepted the revolution's abolition of its special legal status. He thus supported the notables, the dominant group in French politics down to 1848, rather than an aristocratic revival. Based on documents in the Archives Nationales and the Bibliothèque Historique de la Ville de Paris and printed primary sources; 50 notes. 1793-1813

Figueres, José

2186. Ciria, Alberto. THE INDIVIDUAL IN HISTORY: FIVE LATIN AMERICAN BIOGRAPHIES. *Latin American Research Review 1985 20(3): 247-267.* ca 1920-70
*For abstract see **Sandino, Augusto César***

Figueroa, Francisco de

2187. Maurer, Christopher Herman. "Francisco de Figueroa, *El Divino:* Estudio Biográfico y Edición de Sus Poemas" [Francisco de Figueroa, *El Divino:* biographical study and an edition of his poetry]. U. of Pennsylvania 1982. 376 pp. *DAI 1982 43(3): 820-A.* DA8217150 1559-89

Figueroa Marroquín, Horacio

2188. —. ENSAYO BIOGRAFICO SOBRE EL DOCTOR JOSE LUNA ARBIZU [A biographical essay about Dr. José Luna Arbizú]. *Anales de la Academia de Geografía e Historia de Guatemala [Guatemala] 1983 57: 225-242.*
Figueroa Marroquín, Horacio. *pp. 225-239.*
López Mayorical, Mariano. *pp. 240-242.* 1805-88
*For abstract see **Luna Arbizú, José***

Figurovski, N. A.

2189. —. N. A. FIGUROVSKOMU—80 LET [N. A. Figurovski is soon to be 80 years old]. *Voprosy Istorii Estestvoznaniia i Tekhniki [USSR] 1981 (4): 151.* Describes the career and publications of this prominent historian of chemistry. 1931-79

Filártiga family

2190. Claude, Richard Pierre. THE CASE OF JOELITO FILARTIGA AND THE CLINIC OF HOPE. *Human Rights Q. 1983 5(3): 275-301.* The humanitarian work of Dr. Joel Filártiga in Paraguay led to the torture-murder of his son Joelito at the hands of Paraguayan police; the Filártiga family successfully sued Américo Peña, the police inspector reponsible for Joelito's murder (who was residing in the United States), basing their suit on the alien tort provision of the Judiciary Act of 1789. 1976-83

Filatov, Ivan

2191. Minakov, V. SNAIPERSKII EKIPAZH [The sniper crew]. *Morskoi Sbornik [USSR] 1985 (3): 56-60.* Personal narrative of the bravery of Lieutenants Ivan Korzunov and Ivan Filatov of the 40th Air Regiment of the Soviet Black Sea Fleet during the German blockade of Sevastopol in 1941. 1941

Filch, William

2192. Mazouer, Charles. LA *VERITABLE ET MIRACULEUSE CONVERSION* DE BENOIT DE CANFIELD [The *True and Miraculous Conversion* of Benedict of Canfield]. *Revue d'Histoire Ecclésiastique [Belgium] 1985 80(1): 100-114.* William Filch or Fitch (1562-1610), an English Puritan, converted in 1585 from a life of dissipation to become "the most influential Capuchin mystic of seventeenth-century France." Although *The Rule of Perfection* is his major work, his 1596 autobiography *True and Miraculous Conversion* deserves critical analysis, not only for its unique elements (his personality, the Baroque era, the English and French settings), but also as part of the confessional genre, with literary themes and stereotypes that he both experienced and then wrote down. Based on published sources. 1562-1610

Filderman, Wilhelm

2193. Schlesinger, Wilhelm. A REAPPRAISAL OF THE "SHTADLAN" DURING THE HOLOCAUST: THE ACTIVITY AND CORRESPONDENCE OF DR. WILHELM FILDERMAN ON BEHALF OF ROUMANIA'S JEWS. *Centerpoint 1980 4(1): 113-121.* Discusses the key role played by Wilhelm Filderman, the leader of Romania's Jewish population during World War II, in saving large segments of that population by interceding directly with the anti-Semitic Marshal Antonescu, leader of the pro-Nazi Romanian government. 1940-44

Fildes, Paul

2194. Kohler, Robert E. BACTERIAL PHYSIOLOGY: THE MEDICAL CONTEXT. *Bulletin of the History of Medicine 1985 59(1): 54-74.* Patterns in the development of bacterial physiology can be seen in the career of Paul Fildes (1882-1971). After finishing medical school in London, Fildes became assistant to the pathologist William Bulloch. He followed the ideas of Bulloch, working at the London Hospital. Fildes's studies of influenza advanced the (wrong) view that there was a bacterial etiology for the disease. His work on tetanus from 1925 to 1928 also developed from traditional bacteriology to a more physiological mode. In 1939 and 1940, Fildes and Donald D. Woods discovered the mechanism of action of the sulfonamide antibiotics. The widespread use of antibiotics after the war destroyed the rationale for studying the complex physiology of the host-parasite relationship, and Fildes's long-range physiological program was set aside for the search for magic bullets. Based on published and manuscript material, including the records and correspondence of Fildes; 80 notes. 1900-45

Filelfo, Francesco

2195. Robin, Diana. A REASSESSMENT OF THE CHARACTER OF FRANCESCO FILELFO (1398-1481). *Renaissance Q. 1983 36(2): 202-224.* Notes that the last full length study of Francesco Filelfo was produced in 1808, and indicates that a new study is needed. A reevaluation of the Italian humanist's life suggests that the evidence that he was avaricious, immoral, quarrelsome, boastful, and obscene is incorrect. 78 notes. ca 1420-81

Filidoro, François

2196. Bourrier, Michel. FRANÇOIS FILIDORO, "LE CAPITAINE DU PORT DE L'ISLE D'ELBE" [François Filidoro, "the captain of the port of the island of Elba"]. *Riv. Italiana di Studi Napoleonici [Italy] 1983 20(1): 39-53.* Describes the fortunes of the corsair Filidoro of Porto Vecchio (1766-1851) whom Napoleon made captain of the port of Portoferraio during his first exile on the island. He took part in many Napoleonic campaigns, was decorated by the Emperor, and stayed with him even after his defeat. Napoleon in his testament left him 20,000 francs. 1790-1851

Filipovič, Filip

2197. Filipič, France. FILIP FILIPOVIČ IN ZAČETKI UVELJAVLJANJA KOMUNISTIČNEGA GIBANJA V SLOVENIJI [Filip Filipovič and the beginning of the Communist movement in Slovenia]. *Časopis za Zgodovino in Narodopisje [Yugoslavia] 1979 15(1-2): 404-429.* Describes the role of Filip Filipovič in organizing the Communist Party in Yugoslavia in 1919-20 and in bringing Slovene socialists into it. He influenced Slovene workers' class aims and opened them to the currents of the international class struggle and the achievements of revolutionary praxis, thereby enriching their social consciousness. 1919-20

2198. Sumarokova, M. M. PEDAGOGICHESKAIA I NAUCHNAIA DEIATEL'NOST' F. FILIPOVICHA V ROSSII (1904-1912) [The pedagogical and academic work of F. Filipović in Russia, 1904-12]. *Sovetskoe Slavianovedenie [USSR] 1982 (3): 23-34.* Filip Filipović (Boško Bošković), an activist in the Serbian, Yugoslav, and international worker and Communist movement and founding member of the Yugoslav Communist Party, studied in the St. Petersburg University physics and mathematics department from 1899 to 1904. He remained in Russia to teach. He joined the Social Democratic Party, was briefly imprisoned in 1905, and then from 1907 helped with educational reform. He helped organize the 1-5 June 1909 mathematics teaching congress. Between 1910 and 1912 he published articles, reviews, and annotations on mathematics teaching. He was a staunch supporter of the graph method because of its educational benefits. In 1912 he returned to Serbia. Based on Filipović's writings and Soviet and Yugoslav political and educational works; 26 notes. 1904-12

Filliozat, Jean

2199. Filliozat, Pierre-Sylvain. JEAN FILLIOZAT 1906-1982 [Jean Filliozat, 1906-82]. *Bulletin de l'Ecole Française d'Extrême-Orient [France] 1984 73: 1-30.* Jean Filliozat initially studied ophthalmology, but he also learned Sanskrit, Pali, Tibetan and Tamil, receiving certificates in Indian studies, history of religion, ethnology and oriental languages between 1932 and 1936. He considered the Société Asiatique as the institution (and Sylvain Lévi as the scholar) that influenced him most. In 1937-39 he taught Tamil at the Ecole Nationale de Langues Orientales Vivantes. In 1947 he negotiated the transfer of the Ecole Française d'Extrême-Orient from Hanoi to Paris, serving as its director, 1956-77. In 1955 he was involved in the establishment of a French Institute of Indology in Pondichéry. Filliozat strove to include all cultures of the globe in the horizon of the social sciences. His main achievements lay in new discoveries of Indian contributions to science in antiquity and aspects of Indian cultural influences throughout Asia. 1906-82

Filonov, Pavel

2200. Misler, Nicoletta. A TWO-WAY PERFORMANCE: PAVEL FILONOV AND HIS LENINGRAD PUBLIC. *Canadian-American Slavic Studies 1985 19(4): 511-520.* The career of Leningrad painter Pavel Filonov epitomizes the confrontation that developed between the artistic avant-garde and the Russian public. His participation in a 1927 production of Gogol's *Inspector General* generated much controversy, as did his proposed one-man exhibition in 1929. "The emergence of a Stalinist political culture rudely interrupted this dialogue and replaced it by a general, uniform, positive, and passive acceptance." 34 notes. 1927-33

Fina, Kurt

2201. Glaser, Hubert. NEKROLOG: KURT FINA [Obituary: Kurt Fina]. *Historisches Jahrbuch [West Germany] 1986 106(1): 236-239.* Kurt Fina (died 3 May 1983) was a most productive representative of didactics in history. After graduating from the university in Bamberg he spent his life as history teacher at the Siebold-Gymnasium in Würzburg. He introduced new teaching methods by using more object demonstrations and interpretation of original sources. 1922-83

Finaly, Gérald and Robert

2202. Kaspi, André. L'AFFAIRE DES ENFANTS FINALY [The Finaly children affair]. *Histoire [France] 1985 (76): 40-53.* Reexamines the story of the French Jewish children Robert and Gérald Finaly, who were placed in a Catholic convent after their parents had been executed by Nazis. Focuses on the conflict that resulted between the Church and the Jewish community following the war. 1942-53

Finder, Pawel

2203. Kołomejczyk, Norbert. WSPÓŁTWÓRCA POLSKIEJ PARTII ROBOTNICZEJ PAWEL FINDER (1904-1944) [Cofounder of the Polish Workers' Party, Pawel Finder (1904-44)]. *Nowe Drogi [Poland] 1979 (10): 73-83.* A biographical sketch of Pawel Finder. 1904-44

Fink, Karl August

2204. Diener, Hermann. KARL AUGUST FINK 1904-1983 [Karl August Fink, 1904-83]. *Quellen und Forschungen aus Italienischen Arch. und Bibliotheken [Italy] 1983 63: XXVII-XXXII.* Fink was born in Constance, and educated at Freiburg im Breisgau and Münster. The basic theme of all his work was Rome, the papacy, and Constance. His major efforts were the volumes of the *Repertorium Germanicum* for the pontificate of Martin V and *Das Vatikanische Archiv [The Vatican Archive]* (first ed. 1943, second 1951). From 1940 he was a professor of church history at Tübingen, and maintained close ties to the German Historical Institute in Rome. 1904-83

First, Ruth

2205. Marks, Shula. RUTH FIRST: A TRIBUTE. *J. of Southern African Studies [Great Britain] 1983 10(1): 123-128.* From her student days in Johannesburg in the 1940's to her assassination in 1982, Ruth First was a prominent South African Marxist radical and writer. Following her arrests and detentions in South Africa in the 1950's and 1960's, First went into exile and worked to topple the South African state from abroad and to build socialism in Mozambique under FRELIMO. Her many works included books on her imprisonment in South Africa, South-West Africa, Libya, ruling elites in independent Africa, and the life of Olive Schreiner. Based on Ruth First's writings; 16 notes. 1925-82

Fischer, Andreas

2206. Liechty, Daniel. ANDREAS FISCHER: A BRIEF BIOGRAPHICAL SKETCH. *Mennonite Q. Rev. 1984 58(2): 125-132.* Most studies of Andreas Fischer have been confined to his life in either Silesia or Slovakia. On the basis of these partial studies, projections had been made concerning the rest of his life. This short study of his whole life is to correct errors in those projections. Fischer is important for introducing Saturday worship to Anabaptists. Based on various sources; 39 notes. 1498-1541

2207. Liechty, Daniel. ANDREAS FISCHER: A CASE OF MISTAKEN IDENTITY. *Archiv für Reformationsgeschichte [West Germany] 1985 76: 299-304.* 1493-1540's

For abstract see ***Georgy, Andreas***

Fischer, Ernst

2208. Doll, Jürgen. DE L'EXPRESSIONISME AU STALINISME: ERNST FISCHER 1927-1934 [From expressionism to Stalinism: Ernst Fischer 1927-34]. *Austriaca [France] 1985 11(20): 51-63.* Ernst Fischer (1899-1972) supported expressionism at a time when the Austrian Social Democrats preferred classicism and rationalism. In Graz he worked toward a revolutionary theater in which the audience could participate in the action. Later, in Vienna, Fischer began to express more and more sympathy for the Russian Revolution and so moved to the left wing of the Social Democratic Party. His *Krise der Jugend* [Youth in Crisis], a critical polemic of Austrian Marxism and Social Democratic policy, made Fischer famous and led to the organization of the anti-fascist Youth Front. Because he was too abstract and too idealistic, Fischer failed to mobilize the Social Democratic working class. 38 notes. 1927-34

2209. Eisler-Fischer, Louise. INTERVIEW DE LOUISE EISLER-FISCHER, VIENNE, 6 MAI 1984 [An interview with Louise Eisler-Fischer, Vienna, 6 May 1984]. *Austriaca [France] 1985 11(20): 111-113.* Literature, especially poetry, was the first and foremost interest of Ernst Fischer (1899-1972), Austrian political leader. He was deeply influenced by expressionism, French poets, and Czech authors and philosophers. György Lukacs (1885-1971) and Hanns Eisler (1892-1962) were among his close friends. 1953-72

2210. Eisler-Fischer, Louise. ERNST FISCHER [Ernst Fischer]. *Austriaca [France] 1985 11(20): 25-28.* After a coronary occlusion forced Ernst Fischer (1899-1972) to retire from his elected office as a Communist member of parliament, he continued to write on literature and philosophy. His condemnation of the invasion of Czechoslovakia by Warsaw Pact forces led to his expulsion from the Austrian Communist Party and vehement attacks upon him by East Germany and the USSR. Based on the memoirs of Fischer's second wife; note. 1953-72

2211. Fischer-Kowalski, Marina. UNE FILLE A PROPOS DE SON PERE [A daughter's view of her father]. *Austriaca [France] 1985 11(20): 29-31.* The daughter of Ernst Fischer (1899-1972), Austrian political leader and intellectual, describes some of his physical traits and his habits as she remembers them from her childhood and adolescent years. Based on memoirs; 2 notes. 1947-62

2212. Hammer, Jean-Pierre. L'ITINERAIRE D'ERNST FISCHER [Ernst Fischer's route]. *Austriaca [France] 1985 11(20): 13-18.* After serving in the Austro-Hungarian army during World War I, Ernst Fischer (1899-1972) became a Social Democratic journalist. Later he saw in the USSR the only force capable of halting the spread of fascism. Returning to Austria from Moscow after World War II, he became a member of parliament and participated in the reconstruction of Austria. His accomplishments as journalist, essayist, poet, critic, and philosopher brought him world-wide acclaim. 6 notes. 1918-72

2213. Heer, Friedlich. L'AVENIR D'ERNST FISCHER APRES SON EXCLUSION DU P.C.A. LE 28.10.1969 [Ernst Fischer's future after his expulsion from the Austrian Communist Party, 28 October 1969]. *Austriaca [France] 1985 11(20): 103-105.* Ernst Fischer (1899-1972) was expelled from the Austrian Communist Party because he was opposed to human sacrifice, which he regarded as becoming ever more widespread "in our age of neocannibalism." The author suggests that this expulsion would only liberate Fischer's human potential for promoting progress and free him for political and intellectual activity. Article previously published in the "Neues Forum." 1969

2214. Hrdlicka, Alfred. INTERVIEW—17 FEVRIER 1984 [Interview—17 February 1984]. *Austriaca [France] 1985 11(20): 35-38.* Ernst Fischer (1899-1972) was the best known and most important leader of the Austrian Communist Party after World War II, but while he supported the Party line he also tolerated dissent. He was a persuasive speaker who might have been an outstanding university professor. Starting in 1956, he began to reject Stalinism and eventually he preferred art and literature to politics. Based on the memoirs of Alfred Hrdlicka; 2 notes. 1946-72

2215. Pelinka, Anton. UN EUROCOMMUNISTE DE LA PREMIERE HEURE? ERNST FISCHER, THEORICIEN POLITIQUE, 1945-1959 [A Eurocommunist from the start? Ernst Fischer, political theorist, 1945-59]. *Austriaca [France] 1985 11(20): 81-88.* Immediately after World War II, Ernst Fischer (1899-1972), the most prominent intellectual in the Austrian Communist Party, gave complete and unconditional support to the policies of the USSR. With the coming of the Cold War, Fischer remained within the Communist Party, but he continued to be committed to Austrian specificity, unity, and autonomy, which were the basis of the political thought of the great majority of the Austrian people. His condemnation of the Soviet invasion of Czechoslovakia resulted in his expulsion from the Communist Party. Because he saw liberty as the universal principle of politics, he concluded that pluralism is compatible with Marxism and freed himself from Stalinism and from the immediate goals of Soviet power. 33 notes. 1945-72

Fischer, Johann Bernhard

2216. Marauschek, Gerhard. FISCHER VON ERLACH UND DAS HAUS EGGENBERG [Fischer of Erlach and the house of the Eggenbergs]. *Blätter für Heimatkunde [Austria] 1982 56(4): 114-117.* Describes the artistic career of Johann Bernhard Fischer and the influence on his life of the artistic activity in Eggenberg. 1656-1718

Fisher, Warren

2217. O'Halpin, Eunan. SIR WARREN FISHER AND THE COALITION, 1919-1922. *Hist. J. [Great Britain] 1981 24(4): 907-927.* Discusses the reorganization of the British Treasury Department and Sir Warren Fisher's appointment as permanent secretary and effective head of the civil service in 1919. Fisher was an organizer, not a financial expert, and he largely succeeded in modernizing and unifying the civil service. In the process, however, Fisher became convinced that the civil service head should act as adviser to the prime minister on matters of general policy, but although David Lloyd George often took Fisher's advice on civil service appointments, Fisher was unable to play a part in the Irish problem, the major issue with which the coalition was faced. 103 notes. 1919-22

Fitzroy, Robert

2218. Ellis, Frederick E. SOME EARLY LETTERS OF ROBERT FITZROY. *Mariner's Mirror [Great Britain] 1982 68(4): 391-409.* Robert Fitzroy was captain of *HMS Beagle* during Darwin's voyage. Presents 10 letters, dated 12 October 1816, when Fitzroy was a schoolboy, to 6 April 1823, when he was a junior officer on *HMS Owen Glendower* in South American waters. Each letter is annotated with biographical and other relevant data. 4 reproductions of the letters. 1815-25

Flamel, Nicolas

2219. Halleux, Robert. LE MYTHE DE NICOLAS FLAMEL OU LES MECANISMES DE LA PSEUDEPIGRAPHIE ALCHIMIQUE [The myth of Nicolas Flamel or the workings of alchemical pseudoepigraphy]. *Archives Internationales d'Histoire des Sciences [Italy] 1983 33(111): 234-255.* Contrasts the romanticized and legendary life of Nicolas Flamel (1330-1418), who supposedly transformed base metals into gold, with the life as it appears in archival evidence. Flamel, it seems, became wealthy as a landlord, not as an alchemist. His writings have been the subject of scholarly debate since the 18th century, both as to the correctness of their ascription to Flamel and as to their sources. Although his works purport to be translations from ancient Latin books, his sources can be found in contemporary iconographical books of his period. Based on the works of Flamel and other original Renaissance sources and secondary sources; 142 notes. 1330-20c

Flatz, Gebhard

2220. Bertsch, Christoph. GEBHARD FLATZ: EIN VERTRETER DES KREISES UM FRIEDRICH OVERBECK IN ROM [Gebhard Flatz: a representative of the circle around Friedrich Overbeck in Rome]. *Montfort [Austria] 1981 33(3): 219-225.* In 1833 Gebhard Flatz (1800-81) arrived in Rome to join Friedrich Overbeck's Nazarene circle, painting numerous religious pictures, characterized by a naive, emotional, and individualist style. 1800-81

Flaubert, Gustave

2221. Mitzman, Arthur. THE UNSTRUNG ORPHEUS: FLAUBERT'S YOUTH AND THE PSYCHO-SOCIAL ORIGINS OF ART FOR ART'S SAKE. *Psychohistory Rev. 1983 12(1): 7-17.* Psychobiographical analysis of Gustave Flaubert's youth clarifies why he abandoned the bourgeois life of his parents in favor of the Bohemian, romantic life of the artist. Flaubert's complex relationship with his sister, Caroline, as revealed in correspondence, offers insight into his later life. Flaubert's romanticism was also a product of changing social attitudes toward families and social roles within families. 69 notes. 1790-1850

2222. Tondeur, Claire-Lise. FLAUBERT, LECTEUR DE ZOLA [Flaubert, reader of Zola]. *U. of Ottawa Q. [Canada] 1982 52(3): 431-435.* 1868-78
For abstract see ***Zola, Emile***

2223. Tondeur, Claire-Lise. "ECRIVAIN FEMELLE" OU "AMANT DU BEAU" ["Feminine writer" or "lover of the beautiful"]. *U. of Ottawa Q. [Canada] 1981 51(4): 675-682.* 1840-80
For abstract see ***Sainte-Beuve, Charles Agustin***

Fleck, Ludwik

2224. Gierasimiuk, Jerzy. SOCJOLOGIA POZNANIA NAUKOWEGO LUDWIKA FLECKA [Ludwik Fleck's cognitive sociology]. *Kwartalnik Hist. Nauki i Techniki [Poland] 1981 26(3-4): 533-547.* Ludwik Fleck (1886-1961) was a Polish physician and microbiologist who was also a sociologist. In 1935, Fleck published *Entstehung und Entwicklung einer Wissenschaftlichen Tatsache* [Genesis and development of a scientific fact], which appeared in Switzerland and did not attract much attention. But some 45 years later, Fleck's ideas are closely studied by the whole scientific community, and his book has been reprinted in the United States, West Germany, and Switzerland. 42 notes. Russian and English summaries. 1935-81

2225. Kielanowski, Tadeusz; Wiewiórkowski, Ludwik, transl. MY MEETINGS WITH LUDWIK FLECK IN LUBLIN DURING THE YEARS 1945-1950. *Kwartalnik Historii Nauki i Techniki [Poland] 1983 28(3-4): 583-587.* Recounts an acquaintance with Polish bacteriologist Ludwik Fleck (1896-1961) in the 1945-50 period, when he held the chair of medicine at Lublin University. Despite his wartime imprisonment in Auschwitz, he was able to resume both teaching and research, winning the esteem of colleagues and students. In the late 1940's he discovered a controversial phenomenon in hematology, which he called leukergy, concerning formations of white blood cells in sick and healthy organisms. Based on personal experience; photo. 1945-50

2226. Schnelle, Thomas. LUDWIK FLECK—A CLASSICAL SCHOLAR OF THE SOCIOLOGY OF SCIENCE AND OF EPISTEMOLOGY. *Kwartalnik Historii Nauki i Techniki [Poland] 1983 28(3-4): 524-543.* Outlines the life and works of Ludwik Fleck (1896-1961), Polish microbiologist and sociologist of science. After imprisonment in the Jewish ghetto of Lvov following the German invasion of the USSR, Fleck was moved to the Auschwitz concentration camp in 1943, where he was employed in diagnosing typhus and syphilis. Recognizing his abilities, the SS (Schutzstaffel) transferred him to their Institute of Hygiene at Buchenwald, where research on typhus vaccines was carried out. With Fleck's cooperation, quantities of ineffective vaccine were dispatched to the SS units, while the high quality vaccine was reserved for the laboratory staff. Fleck's main theoretical work, *Entstehung und Entwicklung einer Wissenschaftlicher Tatsache* (1935), was rediscovered in the 1970's. Based on personal acquaintance and sources in the Main Medical Library in Warsaw; 44 notes. 1930's-45

Fleischmann, Gizi

2227. Kless, Shlomo. HARAV VAYSMANDEL BIT-KUFAT HASHO'AH [Rabbi Weissmandel in the Holocaust period]. *Yalkut Moreshet Periodical [Israel] 1981 (32): 172-176.* In 1942, an illegal Jewish Committee for Rescue and Assistance was created in Slovakia, headed by Gizi Fleischmann. She and Rabbi Michael Dov Weissmandel of Bratislava were very active in this. They tried to secure funds to obtain the release of Jews through redemption payments to the German authorities. Excerpts of the letters written by the Rabbi in traditional Rabbinical Hebrew are reproduced. Based on books by Rabbi Weissmandel and some other secondary sources; 25 notes. 1942-44

Fleisser, Marieluise

2228. Meyer, Marsha Elizabeth. "Marieluise Fleisser: Her Life and Work." U. of Wisconsin, Madison 1983. 344 pp. *DAI 1984 44(12): 3702-A.* DA8400499 1920's-60's

Fleming, Alexander

2229. Hare, Ronald. NEW LIGHT ON THE HISTORY OF PENICILLIN. *Medical Hist. [Great Britain] 1982 26(1): 1-24.* Describes events preceding and following Alexander Fleming's discovery of penicillin in September 1928. Fleming's failure to recognize and advocate the development of penicillin as a therapeutic agent was the result of the behavior of penicillin in his laboratory tests, 1923-28. Based on the laboratory notebooks of Fleming and his assistant Stuart Craddock, other published articles, and the author's work in the same department; 8 tables, 5 fig., 72 notes. 1928

Fletcher, Joseph F., Jr.

2230. Fairbank, John K. JOSEPH F. FLETCHER, JR., 1934-1984. *Central Asian Survey [Great Britain] 1985 4(2): 129-133.* Reviews the accomplishments of Joseph F. Fletcher, Jr. (1934-84), late professor of Chinese and Central Asian History at Harvard University. An avid scholar of Inner Asian history, Fletcher sought to bring it into the mainstream of world history. To continue his work, the creation of a Joseph F. Fletcher, Jr. Fund for Inner Asian Studies is proposed. Primary sources. 1934-84

Fliedner, Theodor

2231. Carmel, Alex. DER MISSIONÄR THEODOR FLIEDNER ALS PIONIER DEUTSCHER PALÄSTINA-ARBEIT [Missionary Theodor Fliedner as pioneer of Palestinian work]. *Jahrbuch des Instituts für Deutsche Geschichte [Israel] 1985 14: 191-220.* Theodor Fliedner, a son of a Protestant minister, was born in Eppstein. He completed his secondary education in Idstein and studied theology in the Giessen and Göttingen universities. In 1851 Fliedner left for Jerusalem with the intention of establishing a hospital and a missionary school for all Christian sects. The hospital and the school, subsequently known as the Kuiserswerter establishment, initially consisted of two rooms: one for male and the other for female patients. Over the years it expanded into a network of health stations and training schools. By 1914 there were 30 active stations with 137 nurses in many cities including Istanbul, Smyrna, Cairo, Alexandria, Beirut, Aleppo, Haifa, and Bethlehem. Secondary sources; 55 notes. 1851-1914

Flinn, Michael W.

2232. Saul, S. B. PROFESSOR MICHAEL W. FLINN 1917-1983. *Econ. Hist. Rev. [Great Britain] 1984 37(1): v-vii.* Obituary of the economic historian. 1917-83

Flocker, Dr.

2233. McKale, Donald M.; Becker, Peter and Barrett, Michael, commentary. PURGING NAZIS: THE POSTWAR TRIALS OF FEMALE GERMAN DOCTORS AND NURSES. *Pro. of the South Carolina Hist. Assoc. 1981: 156-170.* Studies the careers of three women convicted of war crimes—physicians Oberherser and Flocker and a nurse named Huber. Concludes with some remarks about the war crimes trials in general. Based primarily on the records of the War Crimes Tribunal and German documents; 26 notes. Commentary, pp. 171-180. 1941-48

Florakis, Harilaos

2234. Shemenkov, K. A. PLAMENNYI REVOLIUTSIONER [An ardent revolutionary]. *Voprosy Istorii KPSS [USSR] 1984 (7): 110-114.* Tribute to Greek Communist Party General Secretary, Harilaos Florakis, on his 70th birthday. He joined the Party during the war in 1941 and led a unit of the Greek People's Liberation Army (ELAS) during the Civil War. He was sentenced in 1960 to a life term but was freed after popular protest, only to be jailed again under the colonels regime between 1967 and 1972. He became General Secretary in June 1972 and since the restoration of bourgeois democracy in June 1974 he has fought for the interests of the Greek people, peace, and friendship with the USSR. 1941-84

Flower, Francis

2235. Tighe, W. J. THE CAREER OF FRANCIS FLOWER. *Notes and Queries [Great Britain] 1985 32(4): 460-462.* Describes the career and character of Elizabethan courtier Francis Flower (d. 1597), who held a printing monopoly and worked as a tax collector and judge. 1568-98

Flower, Robin

2236. ÓLuing, Sean. ROBIN FLOWER (1881-1946). *Studies [Ireland] 1981 70(278[i.e., 278-279]): 121-134.* An appreciation of Robin Flower's Irish historical scholarship as folklorist, literary historian, poet and stylist. National Library Mss. Nos. 15091, 15077, and 11000 in Dublin and other letters of the subject; 35 notes. 1903-46

Fo, Dario

2237. Mignone, Mario B. DARIO FO, JESTER OF THE ITALIAN STAGE. *Italian Q. 1981 22(85): 47-62.* Biography of leading Italian militant playwright and showman, Dario Fo (b. 1926), whose life and work closely resemble the medieval *giullarata* of the 10th-13th centuries, entertainments that used laughter and satire as weapons against the ideological tyranny of the ruling classes and, especially, against the remaining forces of feudalism and the Catholic Church. 1950's-79

Fogel, Martin

2238. Huldén, Anders. MARTIN FOGELIUS: HAMBURGAREN SOM UPPTÄCKTE FENNOUGRISTIKEN [Martin Fogelius: the native of Hamburg who discovered Finno-Ugric studies]. *Historiska och Litteraturhistoriska Studier [Finland] 1985 60: 109-140.* Outlines the biography and Finno-Ugric research of the German comparative philologist and physician, Martin Fogel (1634-75), the first scholar to show with scientific proofs that the Finnish, Hungarian, and Lappish languages are related. Based on Fogel's papers in the provincial library at Hannover, Germany and on printed sources; 4 illus., biblio. 1650's-75

Fokker, Abraham Pieter

2239. Knecht-van Eekelen, A. de. ABRAHAM PIETER FOKKER (1840-1906) EN DE SERUMTHERAPIE BIJ DIFTERIE [Abraham Pieter Fokker (1840-1906) and the serum therapy for diphtheria]. *Tijdschrift voor de Geschiedenis der Geneeskunde, Natuurwetenschappen, Wiskunde en Techniek [Netherlands] 1984 7(4): 161-171.* A. P. Fokker was appointed professor of hygiene and pharmacology at Groningen University in 1877. He was a prolific writer and during more than two decades reported on new bacteriological findings in the medical journal *Nederlandsch Tijdschrift voor Geneeskunde.* He supported the doctrine of bacterial heterogenesis, the formation of bacteria from dead organic material. He opposed the "dogmatic" belief of "orthodox" bacteriologists in bacteria as specific elements in disease, and therefore mistrusted the value of the treatment of diphtheria with specific antitoxic serum as introduced by Behring and Roux (1894). Still, Fokker used this therapy because no better remedy for diphtheria was available. In 1899, the editor of the *Nederlandsch Tijdschrift voor Geneeskunde,* Manuel Straub (1858-1916), praised the results of the serum therapy and reproached Fokker for his disbelief in the antitoxic serum and bacteriological doctrine. The ensuing conflict led to the resignation of Fokker as a contributor to the journal. Fokker claimed that bacteriologists had no eye for new achievements such as the discovery of a viral disease, the tobacco mosaic virus desease, by Martinus Willem Beijerinck (1851-1931). 1894-1901

Fonseca, Carlos

2240. Grigulevich, I. R. KARLOS FONSEKA—RUKOVODITEL' SANDINISTSKOI REVOLIUTSII [Carlos Fonseca: leader of the Sandinista revolution]. *Novaia i Noveishaia Istoriia [USSR] 1983 (1): 100-119.* A political biography of Carlos Fonseca (1936-76), a leader of the Nicaraguan Sandinista rebellion forces. Like his inspirer Augusto César Sandino, Fonseca fought against the cruelties of American imperialism and the dictatorship of the Somozas. An intellectual from a poor background, he became a Marxist and visited Soviet Russia, even writing a book about his impressions. His later life was a round of arrests, imprisonments, and struggle. He was killed in a government ambush. Based on published works in Russian, Spanish and English; photos, 35 notes. 1936-76

Fonseca, Manuel Deodoro da

2241. Winz, Antonio Pimentel. MARECHAL DEODORO—UMA FIGURA HUMANA [Marshal Deodoro—a human figure]. *Rev. do Inst. Hist. e Geog. Brasileiro [Brazil] 1981 (331): 213-229.* Gives a brief biography and career outline of Manuel Deodoro da Fonseca, one of the most famous and important figures in Brazilian military history. His extensive military service is described, but the author concentrates on his role in the ending of the Brazilian monarchy and in establishing a republic in 1889. After that revolution, he became prime minister and presided over the enactment of many basic laws regarding civil rights, slavery, criminal law, and separation of church and state. His strong leadership did much to ensure the permanence and sovereignty of the new republic. Secondary sources. 19c

Forbáth, Imre

2242. Varga, Rózsa. FORBÁTH IMRE ANGLIAI EMIGRÁCIÓJÁRÓL [Imre Forbáth's emigration to England]. *Párttörténeti Közlemények [Hungary] 1985 31(1): 153-180.* While a medical student Forbáth was involved in the revolutionary movement of 1919. To avoid retributions he escaped to Prague, where in 1927 he received his medical degree. He joined the Communist Party in Czechoslovakia and in 1938 had to flee again. He settled eventually in England. In London Forbáth was actively involved in all Hungarian-Czechoslovakian political movements and had a romanticized vision of absolute cooperation between all central European countries after the war. In 1945 he returned to Czechoslovakia where he worked as a physician. Provides interesting insights into the lives during the war of intellectuals who escaped from Hungary during the national socialist regime. 72 notes. 1910's-40's

Forbes, Edward

2243. Browne, E. Janet. THE MAKING OF THE *MEMOIR* OF EDWARD FORBES, F.R.S. *Arch. of Natural Hist. [Great Britain] 1981 10(2): 205-219.* Discusses the creation of the *Memoir of Professor Edward Forbes F.R.S.*, a biography of Edward Forbes (1815-54), a naturalist and historian. The book, written by Archibald Geikle and George Wilson, was published in 1861. Wilson wrote the first six chapters before he died in 1859; the work was completed by Geikle after overcoming pressure by Forbes's widow to relinquish the task. The pressure was brought to bear in an effort to suppress a family scandal. Geikle himself perpetrated an elementary social gaffe by plainly outlining Forbes's grievances concerning the financial and administrative relations between the Geological Survey and the government. Based on documents in the Edinburgh University Archives and the Imperial College Archives, London; 31 notes, biblio. 1859-61

2244. Mills, Eric L. A VIEW OF EDWARD FORBES, NATURALIST. *Archives of Natural History [Great Britain] 1984 11(3): 365-393.* Examines the life and work of the British invertebrate zoologist, paleontologist and pioneer biogeographer Edward Forbes (1815-54). Considers Forbes's early life and student years in Edinburgh between 1831 and 1836, his work as a professional naturalist from 1836 to 1842, his career in London between 1842 and 1854, and his return to Edinburgh in May 1854, which was followed a few months later by his death. Assesses Forbes as a philosophical naturalist, the intellectual origins of his ideas on polarity, and the extent to which he was influenced by Samuel Taylor Coleridge. Based primarily on Forbes's works and secondary sources; 5 fig., 60 notes, biblio. 1830-54

Forbes, Eric Gray

2245. Meadows, Jack. OBITUARY: ERIC GRAY FORBES 1933-1984. *Annals of Science [Great Britain] 1985 42(6): 547-548.* Provides an obituary of Eric Gray Forbes, historian of astronomy, who taught at the University of Edinburgh. In addition to his interest in the history of science, he was an enthusiastic cricketer and a good linguist. 1950's-84

Forgách, Adam

2246. Némethy, Sándor. A DELEGATUM JUDICIUM EXTRAORDINARIUM POSONIENSE ANNO 1674 TÖRTÉNETE ÉS JOGÁSZI KRITIKÁJA [The history and legal criticism of the Delegatum Judicium Extraordinarium Posoniense, 1674]. *Theológiai Szemle [Hungary] 1981 24(4): 219-224, (5): 295-300; 1982 25(2): 99-105; 1983 26(1): 22-30, (4): 234-245, (5): 276-286.* 17c
For abstract see ***Kollonics, Lipót Károly***

Forssell, Gösta

2247. Nicou, Gunnel, comp. and Kock, Wolfram, ed. FRÅN GÖSTA FORSSELLS OCH DEN SVENSKA RÖNTGENOLOGIENS UNGDOMSTID [From the youth of Gösta Forssell and the early days of Swedish roentgenology]. *Nordisk Medicinhistorisk Årsbok [Sweden] 1984 (Supplement 10): 3-85.* Gösta Forssell (1876-1950) was the first professor of medical radiology in Sweden—with a personal chair from 1917, which became permanent in 1926. When the professorship was divided in 1936 into medical radiodiagnostics and medical radiotherapy, he represented the former until his retirement in 1941. According to the eulogy after his death by his student Elis Berven, his great achievement as a pioneer of medical radiology was that he succeeded in developing it into an independent branch of medicine on a par with other specialities. He also had the pleasure of seeing the Swedish radiological organization serve as a pattern for many countries. Publishes letters with linking text by Mrs. Nicou and the editor, which follow Gösta Forssell until 1907. They provide glimpses of the various environments in which he lived during his childhood and youth, his university years and the student world in Stockholm and Uppsala, his first contacts with the new branch of science and its predecessors, the genesis of Swedish radiology, and its first institutions. In addition they shed very interesting light on his character and on living conditions in Sweden. 1891-1907

Forssman, Alarik and Magnus

2248. DeJong, C. SWEEDSE IMMIGRANTE IN SUID-AFRIKA [Swedish immigrants in South Africa]. *Africana Notes and News [South Africa] 1984 26(1): 14-20, (3): 109-114.* Part 2. Alarik Forssman (1822-89), a Swedish immigrant, was a noted businessman and prospector. He was deeply involved in the economic development of the early Transvaal. Part 3. Alarik Forssman's elder brother Magnus Forssman (1820-74) arrived in South Africa in 1863 and as a qualified surveyor became government surveyor in the Transvaal republic in 1864 and head of the surveyors' office in 1866. He was responsible for a considerable amount of surveying work, including that of the Eastern Transvaal goldfields. To be continued. 1844-89

Forssman, Oscar

2249. deJong, C. SWEEDSE IMMIGRANTE IN SUID-AFRIKA [Swedish immigrants in South Africa]. *Africana Notes and News [South Africa] 1981 24(6): 213-220.* Scandinavian immigration to South Africa in the 19th century was a response to the ancient desire to travel to new lands, rather than dissatisfaction with conditions in the home countries. Such an emigrant was Oscar Forssman of Kalmar, Sweden, who sailed for Natal in 1844. After a few years in the incipient sugar industry there, he established himself in Potchefstroom as a general dealer, exporter-importer and property dealer. By 1863 he was taken up with the idea of bringing in Swedish immigrants and a shipload was dispatched on the *Octavia.* One of the passengers on the *Octavia* was Anna Ahlström whose diary provided material for the article by Dr. Trotzig on Forssman's expedition of colonization in South Africa which the present author has translated from Swedish. She gives vivid descriptions of the sea voyage, the arrival in Natal and the trek by ox-wagon to Forssman's farm called Scandinavia, which was intended to be the settlement, but the site was ill-chosen and was to be abandoned.

Forssman's immigration scheme failed but his family and his colonists made an important contribution to South Africa. 1844-89

Forster, E. M.

2250. Epstein, Joseph. ONE CHEER FOR E. M. FORSTER. *Commentary 1985 80(3): 48-57.* Eulogizes British author E. M. Forster, who produced little literature and claimed to be no great writer, whose main accomplishments were the rejection of Christianity and the acceptance of his own homosexuality, usually expressed in affairs transcending barriers of race and social class, thus realizing his ideals of liberalism. 1905-70

2251. Noble, R. W. "DEAREST FORSTER"-"DEAREST MASOOD": *AN EAST-WEST FRIENDSHIP. Encounter [Great Britain] 1981 56(6): 61-72.* Discusses the emotional and intellectual aspects of E. M. Forster's homosexual relationship with Syed Ross Masood from 1906 to 1937 as a possible influence in the British writer's works, particularly *A Passage to India* (1924). 1906-37

2252. Watt, Donald. THE UNCONCERNED HUMANIST: E. M. FORSTER IN THE PINK DECADE. *South Atlantic Q. 1982 81(3): 271-285.* During the mid-1930's the novelist E. M. Forster (1879-1970) saw eye to eye with Winston Churchill on the state of England and world affairs. That age threatened the collapse of all civilization. Both were prodded to make declarations bordering on the apocalyptic because of the disturbing course of recent history. Unlike most writers of his day, however, Forster would not abandon himself in involvement nor would he refuse to get lost—he would be concerned but not cornered by the events of the day. He mustered his own campaign against suppression, regimentation, and censorship, which were characteristic of the 1930's. He examined communism and questioned its ability to effect its program. He considered it preferable to fascism, which he despised. The stoical despair of one who sought alternatives to contemporary movements is traced in Forster's works. He urged the importance of literature as a force that transcends all institutions. Based on Forster's writings and studies on his life and literature; 50 notes. 1930's

Forster, Heinrich Gottfried

2253. Mohr, Jan. H. G. FORSTER: ZÁMEČNÍK POZDNÍHO BAROKA [H. G. Forster: locksmith of the late baroque period]. *Umění a Řemesla [Czechoslovakia] 1983 (3): 63-66.* Heinrich Gottfried Forster was a lock designer of great skill and artistry in Central and Eastern Europe in the late baroque period. 1700-60

Foscarini, Mario

2254. DeMas, Enrico. CRITICA DELLA RAGION DI STATO NELL'OPERA DI MARCO FOSCARINI [A critique of the reason of state in the work of Mario Foscarini]. *Pensiero Pol. [Italy] 1979 12(2): 330-333.* Politician, ambassador to Vienna, and official historian of Venice, Mario Foscarini died as the Doge in 1763. He was opposed to Renaissance theories of political expansionism and emphasized the value of Venice's political neutrality. Historical and moral reasons combine in his thought to assert that the state was too powerful at the expense of individual liberty. His political thought was assessed by Nicolas Amelot de la Houssaye (1634-1706), who compared Foscarini's view of the state to the jaundiced opinions of Tacitus. Based on papers delivered at a conference on "The Study of Man and the Study of Society in the 18th Century." 18c

Foscolo, Ugo

2255. Wis, Roberto. ISABELLA RONCIONI-BARTOLOMMEI NELLA REALTA [Isabella Roncioni-Bartolommei in reality]. *Aevum [Italy] 1981 55(3): 526-539.* Gives chronological data and other details on Ugo Foscolo's great passion for Isabella, whom he met in 1800 and to whom he addressed some of his most fervent poems. 1799-1824

Foster, William Charles

2256. Orlovich, Peter. OBITUARY: WILLIAM CHARLES FOSTER. *J. of the Royal Australian Hist. Soc. [Australia] 1981 67(1): 64-67.* Surveys the historical writings of William Charles Foster (1904-80) in the sphere of land settlement, including the definitive biography of Sir Thomas Mitchell, New South Wales surveyor-general, 1828-55, and works on municipal government and the early educational history of New South Wales. 19c

Foucauld, Charles Eugène

2257. Clark, Eleanor. A SAHARA SILHOUETTE. *Partisan Review 1984-85 51-52(4-1): 663-674.* Charles Eugène Foucauld was a French military officer who became a religious mystic living in North Africa and, later, a Trappist monk; a petition for beatification and canonization was made in 1979. His life was a peculiar mixture of secular politics and a desire for mystical sanctification. 1858-1916

Foucault, Michel

2258. Boisdeffre, Pierre de. VIE, MORT ET SURVIE DE MICHEL FOUCAULT [Life, death, and survival of Michel Foucault]. *Revue des Deux Mondes [France] 1984 (11): 362-369.* Highlights the life and career of Michel Foucault (1926-84) and comments on his philosophy. 19c-20c

Fowler, G. Herbert

2259. Deacon, Margaret B. G. HERBERT FOWLER (1861-1940): THE FORGOTTEN OCEANOGRAPHER. *Notes and Records of the Royal Society of London [Great Britain] 1984 38(2): 261-296.* G. Herbert Fowler was involved in the debate over midwater fauna and developed new approaches to plankton studies. A founder of the Challenger Society, a representative body for marine scientists, he was instrumental in policy formation for the Royal Navy on physical oceanography and national defense. Based on Fowler's letters and documents in the Public Record Office; 128 notes. 1880's-1940

Fox, Charles James

2260. Comalada Negre, Angel. DOS POLITICOS DEL XVIII: PITT Y FOX [Two politicians of the 18th century: Pitt and Fox]. *Historia y Vida [Spain] 1985 18(202): 22-32.* Examines the lives and careers of two English politicians during the troublesome reign of George III: William Pitt the Younger (1759-1806), a serious and conservative man who was prime minister for 17 years, and his principal political opponent Charles James Fox (1749-1806), a liberal who was against the war with the American rebels and an admirer of Napoleon. 1770-1806

Fox, George

2261. Gwyn, Douglas Phillip. "The Apocalyptic Word of God: The Life and Message of George Fox (1624-1691)." Drew U. 1982. 477 pp. *DAI 1983 43(9): 3033-A.* DA8302197 1647-91

2262. Sharman, Cecil W. GEORGE FOX AND HIS FAMILY. I. *Quaker History 1985 74(2): 1-19.* George Fox's father was a cloth merchant, and George himself had commercial training in the hurly-burly of markets and fairs. He was apprenticed to a stock dealer after he clashed with the local rector and was diverted from the university. The records reveal a courteous, considerate man who impressed fair-minded magistrates and the Fell family; an honest, straightforward, sensitive person with a sense of humor shining through the seriousness of his mission. He seemed always to have money to give alms and pay his way, usually traveled on horseback like a gentleman, and kept himself clean and neat. He invested mainly in foreign trade and had assets in 1685 worth 700 pounds. Based on Fox's *Journal,* letters from the Fell family of Swarthmore Hall, Ulverston, and a Swarthmore account book; 75 notes. Article to be continued. 1640-90

2263. Sharman, Cecil W. GEORGE FOX AND HIS FAMILY II. *Quaker History 1986 75(1): 1-11.* 1650's-70's

For abstract see ***Fell, Margaret***

Fox, William

2264. Blows, W. T. WILLIAM FOX (1813-1881), A NEGLECTED DINOSAUR COLLECTOR OF THE ISLE OF WIGHT. *Archives of Natural History [Great Britain] 1983 11(2): 229-313.* Outlines the contribution of the British natural scientist William Fox (1813-81) to the study of dinosaurs, whose fossils he collected throughout years of his residence on the Isle of Wight. His explorations of the coastal deposits yielded many remains, about which he corresponded with Richard Owen, then Superintendent of the British Museum's natural history section. Based on collections of the British Museum; 14 notes, biblio., appendix. 1813-81

Frachon, Benoit

2265. Drozdov, E. A. VIDNYI RUKOVODITEL' FRANTSUZSKOGO RABOCHEGO DVIZHENIIA: K 90-LETIIU SO DNIA ROZHDENIIA BENUA FRASHONA [A prominent leader of the French workers movement: on the 90th anniversary of the birth of Benoit Frachon]. *Voprosy Istorii KPSS [USSR] 1983 (5): 108-111.* Charts the career of working-class Communist Benoit Frachon and assesses his contribution to the French trades union movement, particularly during the events of 1968. 9 notes. 1920-68

Fraga Magaña, Gabino

2266. Carrillo Flores, Antonio. DOCTOR GABINO FRAGA MAGAÑA, FORJADOR DEL MODERNO DERECHO ADMINISTRATIVO MÉXICANO [Doctor Gabino Fraga Magaña, maker of modern Mexican administrative law]. *Memoria del Colegio Nac. [Mexico] 1982 10(1): 79-94.* Examines Gabino Fraga Magana's contribution to the development of Mexican administrative law. Text of a speech delivered at the National Institute of Public Administration, 7 September 1982. 1916-82

France, Anatole

2267. Dobiash-Rozhdestvenskaia, O. A. ANATOL' FRANS KAK ISTORIK [Anatole France as historian]. *Frantsuzskii Ezhegodnik [USSR] 1980: 220-225.* Written after Anatole France's death in 1924 by an eminent medievalist and paleographer, the article examines Anatole France's biography of Joan of Arc. Dobiash-Rozhdestvenskaia finds France's erudition irreproachable, his style brilliant, and the work a masterpiece of historiography. 17 notes. French summary. 1412-31

Francesco, Giorgio

2268. Pasquali, Giorgio. ICH, GIORGIO FEDERICO GUGLIELMO ERCOLE FRANCESCO, ROM DEZEMBER 1911: CON FOTO A GOTTINGA A CURA DI CARLO FERDINANDO RUSSO [I, Giorgio Federico Guglielmo Ercole Francesco, Rome, December 1911: with photographs at Göttingen, by Carlo Ferdinando Russo]. *Belfagor [Italy] 1984 39(6): 686-689.* Discusses autobiographical material and photographs of the Italian philologist Giorgio Francesco (b. 1885), who taught in Göttingen, Germany. 1911

Francia, José Rodríguez de

2269. Fontrodona, Mariano. EL DOCTOR FRANCIA, DICTADOR DEL PARAGUAY [Doctor Francia, Paraguay's dictator]. *Historia y Vida [Spain] 1984 17(199): 48-55.* Examines the figure of José Gaspar Rodríguez de Francia (1766-1840), Paraguay's dictator, comparing him to other autocratic figures. He achieved power though political intrigues and governed in a tyrannical manner, obsessed by possible plots against him. 1810-40

Francis I

2270. Carmona, Michel. LES DERNIERS JOURS DE FRANÇOIS Ier [Francis I's last days]. *Histoire [France] 1982 (49): 94-97.* A historical sketch, drawn from R. J. Knecht's *François Ier* (1982), which brings up the discredit suffered by Francis I toward the end of his life. 1515-47

2271. Castelot, André. "DIEU ME PUNIT PAR OU J'AI PECHE": LES DERNIERS JOURS DE FRANÇOIS Ier ["God has punished me where I have sinned": Francis I's last days]. *Hist. Mag. [France] 1983 (43): 50-55.* A historical account excerpted from a forthcoming biography of the last days of Francis I (1494-1547), whose death was probably caused by an abcess in the perineum brought about by chronic prostatitis due to venereal abuses. 1538-47

2272. Garrisson, Janine. FRANÇOIS Ier, SOUVERAIN ABSOLUTISTE [Francis I, absolutist monarch]. *Histoire [France] 1986 (90): 40-46.* In order to raise the money to wage four costly wars against Charles V of Spain, King Francis I of France, 1515-47, centralized the treasury in 1523, levied new taxes, and concentrated royal power in a small group which included Antoine Duprat, Charles de Bourbon, and Florimond Robertet, over whom he exercised absolute authority, divesting Charles de Bourbon of his lands in 1521 and condemning high-ranking courtiers Jacques de Beaune de Semblançay, Guillaume Poyet, and Philippe Chabot de Brion to the Bastille for life on suspicion of betrayal. 1515-47

2273. Lévis-Mirepoix, Duc de and François, Michel. FRANCISC I [Francis I]. *Magazin Istoric [Romania] 1980 14(2): 28-30.* The character of France's King Francis I (1494-1547) and a discussion of the battle of Marignano in 1515. 1494-1547

Francis of Assisi, Saint

2274. Pereira, Adelino. UMA BIOGRAFIA BARROCA DE SÃO FRANCISCO DE ASSIS: *EL MAYOR PEQUENO* [A baroque biography of Saint Francis of Assisi: "El Mayor Pequeño"]. *Arch. Ibero-Americano [Spain] 1982 42(165-168): 379-389.* The biography entitled *El Mayor Pequeño: Vida y Muerte del Serafín Humano Francisco de Assis* [The greatest little one: the life and death of the human seraph Francis of Assisi] was published in Rome in 1664. Its author was Francisco Manuel de Melo (1608-1666), a Portuguese writer who was equally at ease in Spanish. It is a good example of the "classical" view of St. Francis, emphasizing his stigmata, and of the baroque style of writing. 24 notes. 1664

Franck, Sebastian

2275. Lebeau, Jean. *NOVUS ORBIS.* LES COSMOGRAPHES ALLEMANDS DU XVIe SIÈCLE ET LES GRANDES DECOUVERTES *[Novus Orbis:* German cosmographers of the 16th century and the great discoveries]. *Rev. d'Allemagne [France] 1981 13(2): 197-215.* 1520-50
For abstract see ***Boemus, Johannes***

Franco, Afonso Arinos de Melo

2276. Alvarenga, Octávio Mello. AFONSO ARINOS E O RETRATO DE NOIVA [Afonso Arinos and the *Portrait of a Bride]. Rev. do Inst. Hist. e Geog. Brasileiro [Brazil] 1980 (326): 107-123.* Review of *Diario de Bolso, seguido de Retrato de Noiva* [Pocket diary, followed by Portrait of a Bride] (1979), a volume of personal notes from 1978 and letters to his fiancée, 1927-28, by Afonso Arinos de Melo Franco, Brazilian poet and politician. The letters reveal the passion and sensibility of his youth and the beginning of a lasting and tender union. 1927-28

Franco, Afrânio de Melo

2277. Aleixo, José Carlos Brandi. AFRÂNIO DE MELO FRANCO [Afrânio de Melo Franco]. *Revista de Ciência Política [Brazil] 1985 28(3): 12-25.* Presents a speech on the life and work of Brazilian politician Afrânio de Melo Franco from his graduation with a degree in law, 1891, to his death, 1943, delivered at the University of Brasília in 1985. 1891-1943

Franco, Francisco

2278. Preston, Paul. FRANCO: THE PATIENT DICTATOR. *History Today [Great Britain] 1985 35(Nov): 8-9.* Despite his recent benign treatment by the press, Spanish dictator Francisco Franco's early years in power were characterized by the kinds of brutality, corruption, and rampant terrorism associated with Hitler and Mussolini. 1930's-70's

2279. Weyl, Nathaniel. ISRAEL AND FRANCISCO FRANCO. *Midstream 1982 28(2): 11-16.* The little-known fact that Francisco Franco of Spain was descended from Spanish Jews was a major factor in his rescuing thousands of Jews from Nazi death camps during World War II, preserving the Jewish community in Spain during the war, and successfully stalling Hitler's 1940-41 plan of marching through Spain to take Gibraltar away from the British, which would have closed the Mediterranean to the Allies and allowed not only the German takeover of the entire Mediterranean region but also the extermination of the fragile Jewish settlements in Palestine. 1924-46

Franco, José Luciano

2280. LeRiverend, Julio. HOMENAJE A JOSE LUCIANO FRANCO [Tribute to José Luciano Franco]. *Santiago [Cuba] 1981 (44): 115-125.* This black Cuban historian's 89th birthday coincides with the centenary of the abolition of slavery in Cuba. He was an autodidact and eventually the author of several books of history and biography, notably on Spanish policy in the Caribbean and the clandestine slave trade. His three-volume biography of Antonio Maceo rehabilitated an important political figure of the 19th century. 1891-1981

Franco Bahamonde, Ramón

2281. Romañá, José Miguel. DE HEROE A VICTIMA. RAMON FRANCO [From hero to victim: Ramón Franco]. *Historia y Vida [Spain] 1984 17(198): 93-106.* Examines the life and the mysterious death of Ramón Franco Bahamonde (1896-1938), the brave Spanish aviator, Mason, leftist, and brother of Francisco Franco, the Spanish military dictator. 1920-38

Frank, Anne

2282. Barnes, Ian. ANNE FRANK, FORTY YEARS ON. *History Today [Great Britain] 1985 35(Mar): 48-50.* Outlines the life of Anne Frank during World War II and notes the impact of her *Diary* throughout the world. The author also describes the efforts of the Anne Frank Foundation, which was founded in Amsterdam in 1957, to counter anti-Semitism, discrimination, and other social problems. 1930's-85

Frank, Gustav

2283. Kishkin, L. S. CHESHKIE SVIAZI I. E. REPINA [Czech links with Il'ia E. Repin]. *Sovetskoe Slavianovedenie [USSR] 1982 (4): 98-109.* 1892-1904
For abstract see ***Repin, Il'ia E.***

Frank, Hans

2284. Frank, Hans. HANS FRANK NAPLÓJÁBÓL [From the diary of Hans Frank]. *Világtörténet [Hungary] 1979 (4): 132-143.* Excerpts from the 11,000-page personal diary of Hans Frank, German governor of occupied Poland during World War II. 3 notes. 1939-41

2285. Król, Eugeniusz C. RAPORTY ALBERTA HOFFMANA Z PODRÓŻY PO GENERALNEJ GUBERNI W 1942 ROKU [The reports of Albert Hoffman from travels in the General Government in 1942]. *Przegląd Hist. [Poland] 1981 72(4): 699-722.* As Hans Frank, the German governor of the General Government (the main part of German-occupied Poland during World War II) was at some odds with the SS and the police of the region, the commission to investigate the possibilities of transferring some Germans from the General Government administration to the front, instigated by Martin Bormann and headed by General Walter von Unruh, included "Bormann's man" Albert Hoffman, whose six reports were critical of Frank's administration as too lenient and corrupt, and included suggestions extreme even by Nazi standards. Frank kept his job. The German texts of the second and fifth reports are included. Based on primary and secondary sources; 25 notes. 1942

Frankl, Bela

2286. Györkei, Jenö. MÁTÉ ZALKA—PÁL LUKÁCS: REVOLUTIONÄR UND SOLDAT [Máté Zalka—Pál Lukács: revolutionary and soldier]. *Militärgeschichte [East Germany] 1984 23(1): 27-32.* Bela Frankl, who later took the name Máté Zalka, was born on 23 April 1896. An officer in World War I, he was wounded, taken prisoner, and transported to Siberia for recovery. Refused repatriation by Austria-Hungary, he remained in the USSR, joined in the civil war, and left the Red Army in 1921 for a two-year term in the Cheka before engaging in civilian occupations. In 1936, he completed the manuscript of his novel *Doberdó* and, taking the name Pál Lukács, became commander of the 12th International Brigade in Spain, where he participated in numerous battles before being killed on 11 June 1937. Only after the end of the Franco regime were his remains returned to his Hungarian homeland. Photo, 29 notes. 1914-37

Frankland, Edward

2287. Hamlin, Christopher. EDWARD FRANKLAND'S EARLY CAREER AS LONDON'S OFFICIAL WATER ANALYST, 1865-1880: THE CONTEXT OF "PREVIOUS SEWAGE CONTAMINATION." *Bull. of the Hist. of Medicine 1982 56(1): 56-76.* Edward Frankland (1825-99) was one of England's prominent chemists of the 19th century, and in 1865 he became government analyst of the Registrar General's Office, which required the analysis of a monthly water sample from each of the private water companies supplying London. Frankland believed that the water supply was unsafe, and he used his position to advocate alternate sources. He developed the concept of "previous sewage contamination" as indicative of the relative healthiness of the water supply, and publicized this during his tenure in office. When in the 1880's the companies began to use sand filters and their effectiveness was demonstrated by bacteriological studies, Frankland's criticism abated. Based on official records, including manuscripts; 95 notes, chart. 1865-90

Franklin, Jane

2288. Scott, J. M. AN EXPLORER'S WIFE: II. *Blackwood's Mag. [Great Britain] 1980 328(1982): 496-508.* Relates efforts by Lady Jane Franklin to locate the expedition headed by her husband, Sir John Franklin, which disappeared while searching for the Northwest Passage; not content with official efforts to locate her husband's party, Lady Jane embarked on a successful campaign in Great Britain to widen the rescue operations. 1845-59

Franklin, John

2289. Pelzer, John and Pelzer, Linda. ASSAULT ON THE ARCTIC. *British Heritage [Great Britain] 1983 4(3): 10-21.* Describes the travels and explorations of Sir John Franklin and others through the Arctic waters; also considers Franklin's mysterious disappearance. 1800-52

Franko, Ivan

2290. Prymak, Thomas M. IVAN FRANKO AND MASS UKRAINIAN EMIGRATION TO CANADA. *Canadian Slavonic Papers [Canada] 1984 26(4): 307-317.* Ivan Franko (1856-1916) is perhaps "the best known Ukrainian figure of modern times," widely acclaimed as a poet, writer, and scholar, and a political and social activist. One of his greatest concerns was for the oppressed Ukrainians of Austrian Galicia, more than 212,000 of whom emigrated to the Americas between 1890 and 1910. Along with Professor O. Oleskiv (1860-1903) and others, Franko in his public speeches and writings defended the peasants' right to emigrate and helped redirect the migration pattern from Asiatic Russia and Brazil to North America. Even before his death he became a cult figure among the Ukrainian Canadians through his work in the Galician Emigrant Aid Committee. 30 notes. 1890-1916

Frankowska, Maria

2291. Paradowska, Maria. PROFESOR DR MARIA FRANKOWSKA: JUBILEUSZ 50-LECIA PRACY NAUKOWEJ [Maria Frankowska: 50th jubilee of scholarly work]. *Etnografia Polska [Poland] 1981 25(1): 11-18.* The celebration of the achievements of the outstanding ethnologist, pedagog, and organizer of academic life, whose research interests lie mainly in the relgious and folk culture of South America, was organized in Poznań in conjunction with the Conference on Polish Ethnographic Research in the Third World. 1929-79

Franzos, Karl Emil

2292. Lim, J.-D. "The Life and Work of the Author Karl Emil Franzos." University of Vienna [Austria] 1981. 672 pp. *DAI-C 1984 45(4): 925; 9/3853c.* 19c

Frashëri, Sami

2293. Çollaku, Shaban. SAMI FRASHËRI SI KRIJUES DHE KRTIK LETRAR [Sami Frashëri: author and critic]. *Studime Filologjike [Albania] 1982 36(4): 151-175.* Sami Frashëri wrote in Turkish analyzing the aspirations of the common Albanian during the struggle for liberation. 59 notes. French summary. 1870-1904

2294. Çollaku, Shaban. ZIJA XHOLI "SAMI FRASHËRI—NGA JETA DHE VEPRA" SHTËPIA BOTUESE "8 NËNTORI," TIRANË, 1978, 185p. [Zija Xholi's *Sami Frashëri—His Life and Work* Shtëpia Botuese "8 Nentori," Tirana, 1978, 185 p.]. *Studia Albanica [Albania] 1983 20(2): 115-119.* A review article which examines Zija Xholi's *Sami Frashëri—His Life and Work* (1978). The work describes the life, political ideas and activities, and academic career of the 19th-century Albanian historian and philologist Sami Frashëri, and pays particular attention to his contribution to Albanian history, language, and culture. 19c

2295. Xholi, Zija. SAMI FRASHËRI—PATRIOTE, DEMOCRATE ET SCIENTIFIQUE EMINENT [Sami Frashëri—patriot, democrat, and eminent scientist]. *Studia Albanica [Albania] 1984 21(1): 19-42.* Assesses the life and career of the Albanian scholar and scientist Sami Frashëri (1850-1904) and considers his contribution to Albanian culture, language, geography, civilization, and science as well as his publications in Albanian, Turkish, and Arab. His early life and studies are described, together with his early political activities, which resulted in his deportation, 1874-76; his activities within and support for the Albanian liberation movement after 1878; his efforts to establish an Albanian national school, and his work as a teacher in the first school that was opened in 1887. In addition his role within the liberation movement, which included open resistance to Ottoman occupation after 1879, is examined, as well as the philosophical and political ideas reflected in some of his writings. 1850-1904

Frassati, Alfredo

2296. Thayer, John. ALFREDO FRASSATI IN THE HISTORY AND HISTORIOGRAPHY OF MODERN ITALY. *J. of Modern Hist. 1983 55(2): 285-296.* A review article on Luciana Frassati, *Un Uomo, un Giornale: Alfredo Frassati* (1978-80), Vol. 1 and 2 and to a certain extent, Vol. 3, which had not yet been published at the time the review was written. This biography is also a history of *La Stampa,* the newspaper, and a study of *giolittismo* (the movement named after Italian Premier Giovanni Giolitti, 1842-1928). Alfredo Frassati (d. 1961) was an Italian journalist and Luciana's father. His daughter's study "makes no claims to objectivity and shows no undue concern for professional monographic etiquette," but its "merely academic shortcomings do not detract from its importance for students of contemporary Italian history and historiography." Based on the author's personal interviews with Luciana Frassati as well as printed primary sources; 12 notes. 1895-1926

Frederick II

2297. Salmonowicz, Stanisław. FRIEDRICH DER GROSSE UND POLEN [Frederick the Great and Poland]. *Acta Poloniae Historica [Poland] 1982 (46): 73-95.* A recent German revival of interest in Frederick II (1712-1786) has paid little attention to Frederick's views on Poland, and there has not been much recognition of postwar work by Polish historians such as W. Konopczyński. Frederick's intense dislike of Poland, combined with his realization that Prussia's road to power could lie only across Poland, ended with his triumph in the First Partition of 1772. The twists and turns of Frederick's policy from the end of the Seven Years' War are examined in detail, and the excesses of his troops in Poland underlined. Based on published correspondence of Frederick the Great; 25 notes. 1760-80

2298. Salmonowicz, Stanlisław. FRYDERYK WIELKI WŁADCĄ OŚWIECONEGO ABSOLUTYZMU? [Frederick the Great, ruler of enlightened absolutism?]. *Przegląd Zachodni [Poland] 1980 36(4): 35-49.* The nature of Frederick's rule may be viewed as an interaction between his personality and ideas of natural philosophy of his time. He adhered to the Hobbesian social contract. Free people, fearing anarchy, passed all their rights to the State. In practice there was an exception, whenever the interests of the state and the junker class clashed, Frederick acceded to the Junkers. 18c

2299. Salmonowicz, Stanislaw. WAS FREDERICK THE GREAT AN ENLIGHTENED ABSOLUTE RULER? *Polish Western Affairs [Poland] 1981 22(1-2): 56-69.* Contradictions have been noted in the rule of Frederick II of Prussia. He was responsible for many reforms and also for unscrupulous aggression involving inhumane activities. An explanation of such behavior may lie in his concept of royal duty, which emphasized the well-being of his subjects. Although he understood and was sympathetic to Enlightenment views, he never allowed them to interfere with Prussian aggrandizement. 1740-87

2300. Schnitter, Helmut. KÖNIG FRIEDRICH II. VON PREUSSEN ALS FELDHERR UND MILITÄRTHEORETIKER [King Frederick II of Prussia as strategist and military theorist]. *Militärgeschichte [East Germany] 1986 25(3): 220-225.* Reviews the military strategy and theory of Frederick II of Prussia, indicating the influences on his thinking. Also notes the social and political conditions that affected the structure of the Prussian army in the 18th century. 22 notes. 1740-86

Frederick II, Landgrave (1720-1785)

2301. Ingrao, Charles; Vann, James Allen (commentary). LANDGRAVE FREDERICK II AND ENLIGHTENED ABSOLUTISM IN HESSE, 1760-1785. *Consortium on Revolutionary Europe 1750-1850: Pro. 1981: 68-75.* Portrays the reign of Landgrave Frederick II of Hesse-Cassel as well-intentioned but lacking in vision and creativity. Although his principal goals were the creation and conservation of national wealth, Frederick sympathized with the Enlightenment and instituted many of the reforms of other European countries. However, many of these proved inappropriate in a small state like Hesse. Comments, pp. 93-98. Based on Hessisches Staatsarchiv, Marburg-Lahn, and secondary sources; 35 notes. 1760-85

Frei, Eduardo

2302. Falcoff, Mark. EDUARDO FREI MONTALVA (1911-1982). *Rev. of Pol. 1982 44(3): 323-327.* Highlights the political career of Eduardo Frei, leader of Chile's Christian Democratic Party and president from 1964 to 1970. During his presidency, Frei promulgated reforms in agriculture, social services, education, and tax collection. A split within the Christian Democrats paved the way for the Allende victory in 1970. Frei's years after his term in office were largely spent in leading the Christian Democrats, now officially proscribed, against Communist and Socialist forces. 1964-82

Freitas, Augusto Texeira de

2303. Meira, Sílvio. O LEGADO CULTURAL DE TEIXEIRA DE FREITAS [The cultural legacy of Teixeira de Freitas]. *Revista do Instituto Histórico e Geográfico Brasileiro [Brazil] 1982 (337): 197-206.* Augusto Texeira de Freitas was a jurist who codified Portuguese colonial legislation in Brazil in 1858. He was also asked to draft a civil code, but the project was later abandoned by the imperial government and his earlier work was, in practice, the Brazilian civil code until 1917. In his compilation he criticized and avoided the influence of the Napoleonic code and showed the distinctive character of Portuguese law. Lecture read at the inaugural session of the National Congress of Economic Law, 1982. 1850's-60's

French, John D. P.

2304. Hammond, Keith. FRENCH: THE WASTE OF A TALENT. *Army Q. and Defence J. [Great Britain] 1981 111(2): 187-194.* Traces the military activities of Sir John D. P. French (1852-1925) during World War I, focusing on his troubled career in the British army from 1913 to 1921 and on aspects of his character that led to his downfall. 1913-21

Frere, Bartle

2305. Aiyar, S. P. and Pinto, Marina R. SIR BARTLE FRERE—THE MAN AND HIS WORK. *Indo-British Review [India] 1985 11(2): 46-56.* Reviews the career of Bartle Frere (1815-84) in the British colonial government in Bombay, of which he was governor, focusing on his respect for Indian religions despite his own firm Christianity and his performance during financial crisis and political pressure. 1834-67

2306. Emery, F. V. GEOGRAPHY AND IMPERIALISM: THE ROLE OF SIR BARTLE FRERE (1815-84). *Geographical Journal [Great Britain] 1984 150(3): 342-350.* Sir Bartle Frere's career as a proconsul of empire took him to the highest offices in Sind (1850-59), Bombay (1862-66), and South Africa (1877-80). After 1867 he played a leading part in the affairs of the Royal Geographical Society and the Royal Asiatic Society; he was elected Fellow of the Royal Society in 1877. From his many publications it is possible to reconstruct his ideas on the scope of geography and his views on the course of imperial expansion. To those who knew him Frere was a born geographer. He demonstrated it by his own field researches, especially during his early years in India; by his advocacy of geographical exploration, notably through his connection with Livingstone; by urging the educational value of geography; and by applying his expertise to such problems as famine in India. Besides his material accomplishments (for instance, the building of New Bombay), Frere's imperial ethos is illustrated through his interest in land reform; the innovative aspects of Christian missions; and the nature of frontiers, particularly in the South African context. From his work there also emerges evidence of a close relationship between the practice of geography and the policies of imperialism. 1815-84

Freud, Sigmund

2307. Bornemann, Ernest. SIGMUND FREUD UND SEIN HEIMATLAND [Sigmund Freud and his homeland]. *Frankfurter Hefte [West Germany] 1981 36(11): 37-44.* Explores the social and political circumstances of Austria prior to Freud's birth and throughout his life, especially emphasizing the reasons for the many negative social and scientific reactions to his work in psychoanalysis. 19c-1939

2308. Conway, Jeremiah P. THE RETREAT FROM HISTORY: A MARXIST ANALYSIS OF FREUD. *Studies in Soviet Thought [Netherlands] 1983 25(2): 101-112.* Expands on the relationship between Sigmund Freud and Karl Marx addressed by Paul Ricoeur in *Freud and Philosophy: An Essay on Interpretation* (1970). Analyzes the similarities and differences in the characterizations, methodologies, and antagonisms of Freud and Marx as illustrated by the newly published and previously untranslated work on this subject, including that of V. N. Voloshinov since 1927. 1900-82

2309. Diamond, Sigmund. SIGMUND FREUD, HIS JEWISHNESS, AND SCIENTIFIC METHOD: THE SEEN AND THE UNSEEN AS EVIDENCE. *J. of the Hist. of Ideas 1982 43(4): 613-634.* Reexamines Sigmund Freud's attitude toward his Jewishness through his written reactions to a novel by Guy Thorne, *When It Was Dark.* While the book touches in an imaginary way on the relevant sociopsychological theme of religious loyalties and motivations, it also has rather blatant anti-Semitic overtones. However, Freud's comments on the work fail to note this unsavory aspect. We know from a variety of sources and testimony that Freud remained somewhat ambivalent about his Judaic background and childhood and that he neither embraced it nor denied his familial connection to it. Yet he commended Herzl's Zionism and never showed cowardice in admitting his Jewish lineage. 36 notes. 1870's-1920's

2310. Homans, Peter. [INSIGHTS INTO FREUD AND JUNG]. *J. of the Hist. of the Behavioral Sci. 1983 19(3): 240-244.* Reviews Aldo Carotenuto's *A Secret Symmetry: Sabina Spielrein between Freud and Jung* (1982) which features a series of letters between Sabina Spielrein and both Sigmund Freud and Carl Jung. 1912-23

2311. Rice, James L. RUSSIAN STEREOTYPES IN THE FREUD-JUNG CORRESPONDENCE. *Slavic Rev. 1982 41(1): 19-34.* Discusses Sigmund Freud's ethnic biases and the extent and content of his actual experiences with Russians. Examines the Freud-Jung letters, of which there were 360 between 1906 and 1914, in light of the attempted emergence of a psychoanalytic movement in Russia and the experiences of Freud and Jung with Russian patients (Sabina Spielrein in Carl Jung's case and the Wolf Man in Freud's case). Primary sources; 53 notes. 1906-14

2312. Robinson, Paul. FREUD UNDER SIEGE. *Halcyon 1985 7: 1-15.* Critiques of Sigmund Freud fall into three general categories: the feminist critique, an assault on Freud's motives and research methods, and philosopher Adolf Grünbaum's painstakingly academic scrutiny; none of these attacks, however, has sufficient weight to dislodge Freud from his position as one of the most influential thinkers of the 20th century. 20c

2313. Schorske, Carl E. FREUD: LA PSYCHO-ARCHEOLOGIE DES VILLES [Freud: the psychoarchaeology of cities]. *Urbi [Belgium] 1982 (5): 15-22.* Focuses on the travels and works of Sigmund Freud from the 1870's to the early 1900's, particularly the symbolism of Rome as the center of Catholicism in his *Interpretation of Dreams.* 1870's-1902

2314. Schorske, Carl E. FREUD: THE PSYCHO-ARCHEOLOGY OF CIVILIZATIONS. *Massachusetts Hist. Soc. Pro. 1980 92: 52-67.* Sigmund Freud's lifelong fixation with Rome became a passion by the 1890's. His inability to visit Rome between 1895 and 1898 stemmed from personal inhibition and guilt feelings over his Jewish background and his identification of Rome with Catholicism. In his psycho-archaeological exhumations, Freud admitted to a Hannibal identification, a fixation he had from his youth which portrayed the Carthaginians as Semites in conflict with the Church; however, in the dreams he analyzed between 1896 and 1897, he viewed Rome as a rest stop for the weary Jewish traveller on pilgrimage. Freud conquered this fear and visited Rome in 1900, when he completed his self-analysis and the *Interpretation of Dreams.* Writing to his friend, Wilhelm Fliess, he expounded on a city of three layers: the modern edifice which he found suitable, a medieval Catholic city which he loathed, and the original, classical model which he worshipped. 25 notes. 1875-1902

2315. Zaretsky, Eli. EVOLUTIONARY BIOLOGY AND PSYCHOANALYSIS: A REVIEW ESSAY ON FRANK J. SULLOWAY'S *FREUD: BIOLOGIST OF THE MIND. Psychohistory Rev. 1981 10(2): 109-122.* Sulloway's book made Sigmund Freud a product of his times, less original than sometimes held, and a thinker who saw psychology as a product of evolutionary biology, not neurophysiology. Sulloway's hypothesis cannot account for the major focus of Freud's *The Interpretation of Dreams,* which develops themes relating to the centrality of wish and fantasy rather than drive and repression. While psychoanalysis has always been related to biology at any given time, evolutionary biology is not intrinsic to psychoanalytic thought. Sulloway does not appreciate the intellectual atmosphere in which Freud wrote. Rather than fashion a new branch of biology, Freud's biological understanding served only to aid in the creation of a theory that valued human subjectivity. Sulloway does not understand the history of biological and psychological thought and he seems to follow the sociobiological model in analyzing Freudian thought. Based on secondary sources; 15 notes. 1859-1981

Freyer, Hans

2316. Gielke, Ronald. HANS FREYER: VOM PRÄFASCHISTISCHEN SOZIOLOGEN ZUM THEORETIKER DER "INDUSTRIEGESELLSCHAFT" [Hans Freyer: from prefascist sociologist to theorist of industrial society]. *Zeits. für Geschichtswissenschaft [East Germany] 1981 29(7): 597-603.* Hans Freyer (1887-1969), German bourgeois sociologist, historian, and philosopher, analyzed and prepared the way to an understanding of the industrial society. He recapitulated his theories, which he modified and adapted to fit changing political situations, in his work *Theory on Today's Generation.* Industrial society eventually became an apologistic expression for an imperialistic policy. Since the 1960's, historians from the Marxist-Leninist camp have increasingly opposed Freyer's theories, while bourgeois sociologists and historiographers are divided in their views. 1930-65

Freytag, Gustav

2317. Langner, Ilse. DAS BRODELNDE JAHRHUNDERT: SOLL UND HABEN DES BÜRGERS [The seething century: debit and credit for the citizens]. *Frankfurter Hefte [West Germany] 1981 36(12): 49-60.* Describes the turbulence surrounding the Revolution of 1848 in Germany and its effects on science, philosophy, the economy, politics, and the life of liberal journalist Gustav Freytag, author of the novel *Soll und Haben.* 19c

Frick, Georg

2318. Getzner, Manfred A. GEORG FRICK (1805-1898): CHORREGENT, STÄDT. ADMINISTRATOR, MITBEGRÜNDER DER SPARKASSA UND DER MUSIKSCHULE IN FELDKIRCH [Georg Frick (1805-98): choir director, city administrator, and co-founder of the savings bank and music school in Feldkirch]. *Montfort [Austria] 1985 37(2-3): 131-146.* Georg Frick was active in civic affairs in the Vorarlberg city of Feldkirch as city treasurer, music and choir director, composer of church music, and co-founder of the city's voice school in 1888; prints a music manuscript, concert programs, and a list of his compositions. 1821-98

Frick, Philipp

2319. Dupper, Alexander. PHILIPP FRICK, A STOKER IN THE IMPERIAL RUSSIAN NAVY. *J. of the Am. Hist. Soc. of Germans from Russia 1982 5(4): 9-23.* Discusses the daily life and naval service of Philipp Frick, a Russian German cobbler who served in the Russo-Japanese War of 1904-05. 1878-1971

Fridman, Eva

2320. Fridman, Eva. A PERSONAL HISTORY OF LIFE UNDER THE NAZIS. *Centerpoint 1980 4(1): 74-78.* Narrates what it was like to be a Polish Jew during the Nazi occupation of Poland in 1941. 1941-44

Friedell, Egon

2321. Lorenz, Wolfgang. EGON FRIEDELL ODER: DAS ENDE DER TRAGÖDIE [Egon Friedell or the end of the tragedy]. *Civitas [Switzerland] 1983 38(9): 296-301.* Describes the life and philosophy of Austrian Egon Friedell, actor, theologian, dramatist, historian, translator, and philosopher, who killed himself upon being prosecuted by the Nazis. 1890's-1938

2322. Patterson, Gordon. RACE AND ANTI-SEMITISM IN THE LIFE AND WORK OF EGON FRIEDELL. *Jahrbuch des Inst. für Deutsche Gesch. [Israel] 1981 10: 319-339.* Egon Friedell (1878-1938), a leading member of Viennese coffee house society, was in his own mind and in his publisher's thinking a serious writer. A Jew, he failed to find a point of view that would permit him to be counted as a gentile. He was active in World War I, but in the postwar years he lost his fortune. Financial need compelled him to write two brilliant books, *Kulturgeschichte der Neuzeit* and *Kulturgeschichte des Altertums.* He committed suicide in March 1938. 65 notes. 1910's-30's

Friedman, Tuvia

2323. Friedman, Tuvia. RATSITI LIHYOT PARTIZAN [I wanted to be a partisan]. *Yalkut Moreshet Periodical [Israel] 1982 (33): 45-58.* Memoirs of the Radom ghetto, a stay in a Nazi slave labor camp, the search for partisans in the forested areas, rescue from the Germans, partisan life, and liberation. 1943-45

Fries, Jakob Friedrich

2324. Gregory, Frederick. REGULATIVE THERAPEUTICS IN THE GERMAN ROMANTIC ERA: THE CONTRIBUTION OF JAKOB FRIEDRICH FRIES (1773-1843). *Clio Medica [Netherlands] 1983 18(1-4): 179-190.* Jakob Friedrich Fries, a professor of medicine at Heidelberg and Jena, represented the Kantian school. Fries led the opposition to the romantic school of medicine whose chief exponent was Friedrich Wilhelm Joseph von Schelling. Schelling and his followers maintained that physicians had an exact knowledge of physiology and could base their treatment of patients on general hypotheses. Fries in his *Regulatives for Therapeutics Arranged according to Heuristic Propositions of Philosophy of Nature* (1803) argued that doctors should treat patients on the basis of examining the symptoms and not on *a priori* knowledge of the symptoms. 41 notes. 1800-40

2325. Hauschild, Jan-Christoph. "MEINE ABSICHT IST, SIE NOCH RECHT ARG ZU PLAGEN..." MITTEILUNGEN ÜBER DIE BISLANG UNBEACHTETE BEZIEHUNG JAKOB FRIEDRICH FRIES ZU DEM WEIMARISCHEN GYMNASIALPROFESSOR CARL LUDWIG ALBRECHT KUNZE (1805-1890) ["My intention is to bother you very much..." Information about the previously unobserved relationship of Jakob Friedrich Fries to the Weimar Gymnasium professor Carl Ludwig Albrecht Kunze (1805-90)]. *Archiv für Kulturgeschichte [West Germany] 1980-81 62-63: 417-424.* Describes the contents of the papers of Carl Ludwig Albrecht Kunze in the Goethe-Schiller Archives, Weimar, relating to Jakob Friedrich Fries. 39 notes. 1827-42

Frigyesi, Gusztáv

2326. Lukács, Lajos. FRIGYESY ÉS GARIBALDI 1866-67-BEN [Frigyesi and Garibaldi, 1866-67]. *Századok [Hungary] 1982 116(4): 689-714.* Gusztáv Frigyesi, who joined Giuseppe Garibaldi's forces in 1866 at the age of 32, was a devout follower of his general. Lost battles, internment, and imprisonment could not break his faith in the eventual liberation of Rome. He was happy to enter jail at the side of Garibaldi. When free, he tried secretly to recruit new members for the Hungarian Legion. By then Garibaldi's army was slowly fading away as more pressing social problems were facing the nation. The Italian government was not interested in Garibaldi's success but wanted an armistice and was prepared to accept any terms Napoleon III was willing to offer. Frigyesi died in 1878 at the age of 44 as a mental patient in an Italian hospital. 92 notes. 1866-67

Frisch, Ragnar

2327. Andvig, Jens Christopher. RAGNAR FRISCH AND BUSINESS CYCLE RESEARCH DURING THE INTERWAR YEARS. *Hist. of Pol. Econ. 1981 13(4): 695-725.* Ragnar Frisch was very influential in shaping the changes in the school of macroeconometric research in its early stages. The new school was able to supersede the old empirical business cycle research program. Frisch was not the only econometrician to bring about this new way of blending theoretical and empirical research in the field, but he was influential. Secondary sources; 19 notes, biblio. 1920-80

Frölich, Paul

2328. Klemm, Bernd. PAUL FRÖLICH (1884-1953). POLITISCHE ORIENTIERUNG UND THEORETISCHE REFLEXIONEN VON LINKSSOZIALISTEN NACH DEM ZWEITEN WELTKRIEG. SECHS BRIEFE PAUL FRÖLICHS AUS DER EMIGRATION (1946-1949) AN EHEMALIGE KPO-/SAP-MITGLIEDER IN BERLIN, DUISBURG, OFFENBACH, WESEL, LA HABANA/CUBA

UND STUTTGART [Paul Frölich (1884-1953): political orientation and theoretical reflections of Left Socialists after World War II: six letters of Paul Frölich from exile, 1946-49, to former German Communist Party Opposition (KPO) and German Socialist Workers' Party (SAP) members in Berlin, Duisburg, Offenbach, Wesel, Havana (Cuba), and Stuttgart]. *Internationale Wissenschaftliche Korrespondenz zur Geschichte der Deutschen Arbeiterbewegung [West Germany] 1983 19(2): 186-229.* Describes the life of and prints letters from Paul Frölich, cofounder of the German Communist Party, the KPO, and SAP to German socialists during his exile in the USA. 1946-49

Fronius, Robert

2329. Barton, Peter F., ed. DIE AUTOBIOGRAPHIE DES BADENER PFARRERS ROBERT FRONIUS [The autobiography of the Baden minister Robert Fronius]. *Jahrbuch der Gesellschaft für die Gesch. des Protestantismus in Österreich [Austria] 1981 97(1-4): 1-3.* Discusses the origins of the manuscript containing the unfinished autobiography (written in 1948), of the Austrian Protestant minister in Baden-bei-Wien Robert Fronius (1868-1952), one of the most influential theologians in the Protestant Church in this area in the late 19th and early 20th centuries. The autobiography is important because it provides an insight into the training of a theologian at the Protestant theological faculty in Vienna in the late 19th century. The work also describes Fronius's activities for the Protestant Church in Baden-bei-Wien. In addition, Fronius examines the dangers that faced the Protestant Church in Austria during the period 1933-45. Based on a manuscript in the archive of the Library of the Institute for Protestant Church History in Vienna; 5 notes. 1868-1945

2330. Fronius, Robert. AUS MEINEM LEBEN UND MEINER ARBEIT [From my life and work]. *Jahrbuch der Gesellschaft für die Gesch. des Protestantismus in Österreich [Austria] 1981 97(1-4): 4-108.* Reproduces in its entirety Robert Fronius's unfinished autobiography, which examines the following: the origins of the Fronius family name from the 12th century, the social standing and profession of the Fronius family, 12th-19th centuries; the author's place of birth in northern Transylvania and his early years there, 1868-79; his studies at Chernovtsy, 1879-88; his theological studies at the University of Vienna, 1888-91; his work as a private tutor and his admission as a minister of the church in 1893; his work as a church minister in Jozefów in Galicia, 1894-95; and his activities for the Protestant Church and the community in Baden-bei-Wien, 1895-1945. Based on a manuscript held in the archive of the Library of the Institute for Protestant Church History in Vienna; 35 notes. 1868-1952

Frunze, Mikhail

2331. Egorov, A. M. V. FRUNZE—REVOLIUTSIONER LENINSKOI SHKOLY [Mikhail Frunze, revolutionary of the Leninist school]. *Voenno-Istoricheskii Zhurnal [USSR] 1985 (3): 29-31.* Views the revolutionary activities of Mikhail Frunze (1885-1925), active in both the 1905-07 and the 1917 Revolutions. He led the 1905 strikes at the Ivanovo-Voznesensk factories and met V. I. Lenin during the 1906 Fourth Congress of the Russian Social Democratic Workers' Party. Arrested and deported in 1907, Frunze escaped and fought in the 1917 February Revolution, after which he returned to Ivanovo-Voznesensk as Party organizer. Based on a paper delivered at the 1985 Military Academic Conference of the Soviet Ministry of Defense and Central Political Command of Soviet Army and Navy. 1905-17

2332. Egorov, G. M. M. V. FRUNZE O VSENARODNOM KHARAKTERE ZASHCHITY SOTSIALISTICHESKOGO OTECHESTVA [Mikhail Frunze on the national character of the defense of the socialist fatherland]. *Voenno-Istoricheskii Zhurnal [USSR] 1985 (3): 45-46.* Views Mikhail Frunze's (1885-1925) involvement in the organization of Soviet civil defense, 1920-25. Together with S. Budennyi and K. Voroshilov, he founded the Military Scientific Society, which attracted large membership in the early 1920's. The society offered civil defense training to those exempt from military service. Based on a paper delivered at the 1985 Military Academic Conference of the Soviet Ministry of Defense and Central Political Command of Soviet Army and Navy. 1920-25

2333. Epishev, A. A. VOENNO-POLITICHESKAIA DEIATEL'NOST' M. V. FRUNZE [Military and political activities of Mikhail Frunze]. *Voenno-Istoricheskii Zhurnal [USSR] 1985 (3): 21-28.* Views the political aspects of Mikhail Frunze's (1885-1925) command of the Soviet Army during the 1918-22 civil war as well as his stance on civil defense and Soviet defense policy. His wartime command of the Eastern Front showed sensitivity to the local tribal issues. As a supporter of the Bolsheviks against the Trotskiist faction, he encouraged increased Bolshevik Party instruction for the troops. Based on a paper delivered at the Military Academic Conference of the Soviet Ministry of Defense and Central Political Command of Soviet Army and Navy in 1985. 1917-25

2334. Evseev, A. VOENNO-TEORETICHESKIE VZGLIADY M. V. FRUNZE [Military theoretical views of Mikhail V. Frunze]. *Voenno-Istoricheskii Zhurnal [USSR] 1985 (1): 53-63.* Views the contribution of the Soviet commander and cofounder of the Red Army Mikhail V. Frunze (1885-1925) to contemporary Soviet military doctrine. His seminal work on military theory, *Edinaia Voennaia Doktrina i Krasnaia Armiia* (1921) [Unified military doctrine and the Red Army], contains the Marxist formulation on the nature of class war. *Reguliarnaia armiia i militsiia* (1921) [Regular army and police force] deals with issues of military organization and education. Secondary sources; 29 notes. 1921

2335. Gusarevich, S. REVOLIUTSIONNAIA, PARTIINAIA I GOSUDARSTVENNAIA DEIATEL'NOST' M. V. FRUNZE [Activities of M. V. Frunze in the revolution, Party and the Soviet state]. *Voenno-Istoricheskii Zhurnal [USSR] 1984 (10): 33-41.* Outlines the political biography of Soviet revolutionary and military commander Mikhail Frunze (1885-1925). He organized and led the largest strike in Russia in the Ivanovo-Voznesensk region during the 1905 Revolution, was one of the founders of the Red Army in the first years of Bolshevik power, and having served in 1918-19 as Commander of the Eastern Front, he was appointed President of the Revolutionary Military Council [Revvoensovet] in 1924. Secondary sources; 4 photos, 13 notes. 1905-25

2336. Kurotkin, S. K. M. V. FRUNZE—VYDAIUSHCHIISIA POLKOVODETS I VOENNYI TEORETIK SOVETSKOGO GOSUDARSTVA (1885-1925) [Mikhail Frunze, the Soviet state's outstanding military leader and theoretician, 1885-1925]. *Voenno-Istoricheskii Zhurnal [USSR] 1985 (3): 13-20.* Views the military career and writings of Mikhail Frunze (1885-1925), who distinguished himself in the 1917 Revolution and the 1918-22 civil war. His command on the fronts of the civil war was characterized by the ability to analyze all the factors relevant to the outcome of a battle, thereby estimating the likeliest development. His understanding of armed conflict provided great perspicacity to his theoretical writings on military strategy and the character of future wars. Based on a paper delivered at the Military Academic Conference of the Soviet Ministry of Defense and Central Political Command of Soviet Army and Navy in 1985. 1917-25

2337. Losik, O. A. M. V. FRUNZE I SOVETSKAIA VOENNAIA NAUKA [Mikhail Frunze and Soviet military science]. *Voenno-Istoricheskii Zhurnal [USSR] 1985 (3): 37-40.* Mikhail Frunze (1885-1925), Soviet commander and one of the founders of the Soviet Army, believed in the need for a theoretical foundation of military science despite claims to the contrary from the Leon Trotsky faction. His military doctrine rested on the principle of Party leadership of the army. Based on a paper delivered at the 1985 Military Academic Conference of the Soviet Ministry of Defense and Central Political Command of Soviet Army and Navy; 6 notes. 1917-25

2338. Obaturov, G. I. VOENNO-PEDAGOGICHESKIE VZGLIADY M. V. FRUNZE [Mikhail Frunze's views on military training]. *Voenno-Istoricheskii Zhurnal [USSR] 1985 (3): 43-45.* Mikhail Frunze (1885-1925) laid the foundations of Soviet military training with the network of training centers established in 1921-23. As head of the Military Academy of the Red Army in 1924-25, he raised the level of ideological instruction and organized the training according to his own methodology. Based on a paper delivered at the 1985 Military Academic Conference of the Soviet Ministry of Defense and Central Political Command of Soviet Army and Navy; note. 1921-25

2339. Petrova, L. I. MIKHAIL VASIL'EVICH FRUNZE [Mikhail Vasil'evich Frunze]. *Prepodavanie Istorii v Shkole [USSR] 1985 (1): 7-13.* Outlines the revolutionary and military career of Mikhail Frunze (1885-1925), Soviet commander and author of the textbook of military theory *Edinaia Voennaia Doktrina i Krasnaia Armiia* [The single military doctrine and the Red Army] (1921). 1885-1925

2340. Volkovinski, S. N. IZ ISTORII BOEVOI DEIATEL'NOSTI M. V. FRUNZE PO LIKVIDATSII POLITICHESKOGO BANDITIZMA NA UKRAINE [From the history of the military activity of M. V. Frunze with regard to the liquidation of political banditry in the Ukraine]. *Istoriia SSSR [USSR] 1982 (2): 126-132.* In his capacity as commander of the armed forces of the Ukraine and deputy chairman of the Ukrainian Council of People's Commissars, Mikhail Frunze took the lead in the suppression of Ukrainian counterrevolution, in particular the movement of N. I. Makhno. This experience broadened Frunze's military views and facilitated his understanding of conditions in the Red Army during the transition from war to peace. Based on published and archival sources; 31 notes. 1920-21

2341. Volkovinski, V. N. DOKUMENTY M. V. FRUNZE V FONDAKH TSGAOR SSSR [Documents of Mikhail Frunze in the holdings of the Central State Archive of the October Revolution of the USSR]. *Sovetskie Arkhivy [USSR] 1985 (3): 47-50.* Surveys material concerning Mikhail Frunze (1885-1925), Soviet military commander and author of military manuals, during his stay in the Ukraine as head of the Revolutionary Military Council, 1920-24. Much has been found in the records of the All-Ukraine Central Executive Committee and the Council of People's Commissars (Sovnarkom). Based on material from the Central State Archive of the October Revolution of the Ukrainian Republic; 28 notes. 1920-24

2342. Volkovonski, V. UCHASTIE M. V. FRUNZE V ORGANIZATSII SHEFTSVA TRUDIASHCHIKHSIA UKRAINY NAD CHASTIAMI KRASNOI ARMII [The participation of M. V. Frunze in the organization of *sheftsvo* of Ukrainian workers of Red Army units]. *Voenno-Istoricheskii Zhurnal [USSR] 1983 (3): 75-78.* The widescale sponsorship *(sheftsvo)* of Ukrainian workers of Red Army units expressed the active concern of the Party and the people for the development of strong Soviet military forces. By the end of 1922, 165 units and formations of the Ukrainian military district had sponsors, and by 1924, when M. V. Frunze left the republic, all the military formations in the area were so provided. The Ukrainian government, the district command, and Frunze himself on several occasions praised the best sponsoring organizations and encouraged others to follow their example. Based on Soviet archival sources; 18 notes. 1920-24

2343. Volkovyns'kyi, V. M. M. V. FRUNZE—KOMMANDUIUCHYI ZBROINYMY SYLAMY UKRAINY I KRYMU (1920-1924 RR.) [M. V. Frunze, commander of the armed forces of the Ukraine and the Crimea, 1920-24]. *Ukrains'kyi Istorychnyi Zhurnal [USSR] 1981 (7): 48-56.* Mikhail V. Frunze, noted Soviet military leader, was commander-in-chief of the armed forces of the Ukraine and the Crimea from December 1920 to March 1924. His activities during that time are chronicled here. In this responsible post, Frunze successfully embodied and effected Leninist ideas about the military might of the world's first socialist state and laid the foundations of Soviet military science. Based on Soviet archives and Party literature; 42 notes. 1920-24

2344. Zhilin, P. A. M. V. FRUNZE O ZNACHENII VOENNOGO OPYTA DLIA TEORII I PRAKTIKI STROITEL'STVA SOVETSKIKH VOORUZHENNYKH SIL [Mikhail Frunze on the value of military experience in the theory and practice of the creation of Soviet armed forces]. *Voenno-Istoricheskii Zhurnal [USSR] 1985 (3): 47-49.* Mikhail Frunze (1885-1925), commander in the 1918-22 Civil War and cofounder of the Soviet Army, insisted on the value of past military experiences for training of the armed forces and for sustaining high morale. He advocated formation of informal discussion circles in the Soviet Army and Navy, where past conflicts and strategies would be used as main points of reference. Based on a paper delivered at the 1985 Military Academic Conference of the Soviet Ministry of Defense and Central Political Command of Soviet Army and Navy; 5 notes. 1917-25

Fry, Elizabeth

2345. Jackaman, Peter. BOOKS FOR BLOCKADE MEN: THE CONCERN OF MISTRESS FRY. *Lib. Rev. [Great Britain] 1982 (Sum): 111-120.* Recounts the efforts of Elizabeth Fry to provide libraries for the British Coast Guard, the Royal Navy, and the inmates of many continental penal systems during the early 19th century. Provides various appendixes showing contemporary book catalogs and costs of books. 1811-47

Fry, Roger

2346. Rosenbaum. S. P., interviewer. CONVERSATION WITH JULIAN FRY. *Modernist Studies [Canada] 1979 3(1-3): 126-135.* Julian Fry discusses his father, English art critic and member of the Bloomsbury Group, Roger Fry. 1890-1934

Fu Sinian

2347. Hsü Kuan-san. FU SSU-NIEN YÜ SHIH LIAO HSÜEH P'AI [Fu Ssu-nien and the historical source materials school]. *Hsiang Kang Chung Wen Ta Hsüeh Chung Kuo Wen Hua Yen Chiu So Hsüeh Pao. (The Journal of the Institute of Chinese Studies of the Chinese University of Hong Kong) [Hong Kong] 1984 15: 49-67.* Fu Sinian's (Fu Ssu-nien, 1896-1950) achievements in Chinese historiography exceeded those of his teacher Hu Shi (Hu Shih, 1891-1962). Drawing on both Western and Chinese scholarly traditions, Fu developed a scientific study of history that emphasized the importance of all types of evidence to the understanding of the past. The work of Fu and his subordinates at the Institute of History and Philology, Academia Sinica in the 1930's and 1940's has had immense influences on history, philology, and archaeology in China and Taiwan. Based on the writings of Fu and Hu; 67 notes. English summary. 1919-84

Fuchs, Walter

2348. Franke, Wolfgang. WALTER FUCHS IN MEMORIAM [In memoriam: Walter Fuchs]. *Oriens Extremus [West Germany] 1980 27(2): 141-150.* After graduating from Berlin University, the Sinologist Walter Fuchs (1902-79) became a lecturer at the Medical University of the the South Manchuria Railway in Mukden and traveled extensively in the Far East. Appointed professor at the Catholic Fujen University of Beijing in 1938, he reedited the Jesuit-compiled atlas of China and coedited the journal *Monumenta Serica.* He was the center of the German-speaking Sinologists in Beijing. In 1946, he received an honorary professorship at the Yenching University, but was repatriated to Germany in 1947 without his library of 10,000 books, the fate of which is unknown. Having been a Nazi, he found life difficult, but in 1956 was finally offered the *Extraordinariat* of Sinology at the Free University of Berlin. In 1960 he became Professor of Sinology at the University of Cologne. He was cofounder and coeditor of *Oriens Extremus* from 1953 until his death. Based on the author's and others' personal reminiscences; 10 notes. 1922-79

Fučík, Julius

2349. Korolev, G. I. and Filippov, V. N. IULIUS FUCHIK—ANTIFASHIST, PATRIOT, INTERNATSIONALIST [Julius Fučík—antifascist, patriot, internationalist]. *Novaia i Noveishaia Istoriia [USSR] 1983 (5): 94-109, (6): 97-118.* Part 1. Julius Fučík (1903-43) was only 18 when he joined the Communist Party of Czechoslovakia. In 1922 he began to contribute to various Communist and socialist publications and for six months served as editor of *Rudé Právo.* In addition to his journalistic work Fučík continued to take an active part in the workers' movement. Part 2. Before World War II Fučík took part in the labor movement in Czechoslovakia and made several trips to the USSR which convinced him of the invincibility of socialism. After Hitler's occupation of Czechoslovakia and the outbreak of the war he worked in the underground and assisted with the underground press of the Czech Communist Party. Fučík was arrested in 1942 and executed in September 1943. Secondary sources; 175 notes. 1921-43

2350. Marek, Jiří. BELETRISTICKÉ UMĚNÍ JULIA FUČÍKA [The literary art of Julius Fučík]. *Česká Literatura [Czechoslovakia] 1983 31(4): 298-314.* Julius Fučík (1903-42) was a cofounder of Czech socialist prose literature. There is also ample evidence of true literary talent in his journalistic and literary historical works, for which he is best known. 1929-40

Fuentes, Carlos

2351. Willar, Luis Manuel. "Carlos Fuentes: Literature and Society" [Spanish text]. U. of Wisconsin, Madison 1982. 453 pp. *DAI 1983 43(7): 2359-A.* DA8218052 1949-81

Fuentes y Guzman, Francisco Antonio de

2352. Sáenz de Santa María, Carmelo. EL ESCRITOR D. FRANCISCO ANTONIO DE FUENTES Y GUZMAN, CRIOLLO Y PATRIOTA [The writer Don Francisco Antonio de Fuentes y Guzman, Creole and patriot]. *Anales de la Soc. de Geog. e Hist. de Guatemala [Guatemala] 1980 53: 13-136.* Fuentes y Guzman (1642-99) belonged to a creole generation which was beginning to feel the tension between loyalty to the Spanish crown and ties to Guatemala. In his writings he tried to fashion a beautiful image of Guatemala. This book-length biography situates him in his historical setting and describes his career and literary works. 238 notes, biblio., appendix on Fuentes' literary style and on native terms in his vocabulary. 1642-99

Fuertes, Gloria

2353. Persin, Margaret H. GLORIA FUERTES AND (HER) FEMINIST READER. *Revista/Rev. Interamericana [Puerto Rico] 1982 12(1): 125-132.* Gloria Fuertes became a prominent poet during the 1950's and 1960's. Her work illustrates that the female voice in poetry is now equal to its male counterpart. 5 notes. 1940-81

Fülep, Lajos

2354. Bolyki, János. LUKÁCS GYÖRGY ÉS FÜLEP LAJOS KAPCSOLATÁRÓL [The association between Georg Lukács and Lajos Fülep]. *Theologiai Szemle [Hungary] 1985 28(5): 309-311.* Lukács and Fülep planned and edited *Szellem* [Spirit], a philosophical journal, from 1911 to 1912. They remained close until 1918, when Fülep was ordained as a clergyman of the Reformed Church and Lukács gained his reputation as a Marxist. Even after their lives followed different directions, they respected and defended each other. Based on the correspondence of Georg Lukács; 6 notes. 1910-50

2355. Szabó, Botond. FÜLEP LAJOS (1885-1970) [Lajos Fülep (1885-1970)]. *Theologiai Szemle [Hungary] 1985 28(5): 305-309.* Fülep, who spoke eight languages, spent most of his younger years traveling in England, France, and Germany, and stayed seven years in Italy. In 1911 he was the editor of *Szellem* [Spirit], a philosophical journal in the Hungarian language of the highest standards. His translations of Nietzsche and Papini into Hungarian were superb masterpieces. Fülep returned to Hungary and between 1920 and 1947 participated in many church activities as a clergyman of the Reformed Church. He was appointed a professor in Budapest in 1947 and retired from public life in 1962. Fülep was a very demanding and difficult person who would not accept even the slightest compromise. 37 notes. 1885-1970

2356. Timár, Árpád. LAJOS FÜLEP (1885-1970): A PROPHET IN HIS TIME. *New Hungarian Quarterly [Hungary] 1985 26(98): 165-172.* Hungarian journalist and art critic Lajos Fülep combatted historicism and academicism and supported schools of modern art in Hungarian painting. He lived in western Europe for several years, studying and writing on the theory of art. Discusses his contacts with other intellectuals in Hungary in the turbulent years following the outbreak of World War I. He studied Calvinist theology and taught art history before and after World War II. Plate, 4 photos. 1900's-70

Fuller, Andrew

2357. Young, Doyle L. ANDREW FULLER AND THE MODERN MISSION MOVEMENT. *Baptist Hist. and Heritage 1982 17(4): 17-27.* Describes Andrew Fuller's role in the foundation of the Baptist Missionary Society in England in 1792 and recounts the society's history to 1815. 1792-1815

Fuller, John Frederick Charles

2358. Klein, Robert Edward. "J. F. C. Fuller and the Tank." U. of Chicago 1983. *DAI 1983 44(4): 1174-A.* 1915-16

2359. Wyly, Michael D. J. F. C. FULLER: SOLDIER AND HISTORIAN. *Marine Corps Gazette 1984 68(12): 69-76.* Discusses the military career of British officer and historian John Frederick Charles Fuller (1878-1966), who proposed major changes in military doctrine and strategy. 1898-1968

Furniss, John Joseph

2360. Sharp, John. JUVENILE HOLINESS: CATHOLIC REVIVALISM AMONG CHILDREN IN VICTORIAN BRITAIN. *Journal of Ecclesiastical History [Great Britain] 1984 35(2): 220-238.* Traces the career of John Joseph Furniss (1809-65), English Redemptorist, with special reference to his revivalist work among children. Through his tracts and missions he touched the lives of thousands of adolescents, but at the same time he alienated his superiors by his sensationalism and the harshness of a teaching which attempted to frighten children into holiness. Based on Archives of the Redemptorist Fathers; 79 notes. 1850-65

Furuse, Denzō

2361. Nomoto, Kyoko. 1920-1930 NENDAI NO "NŌSON MONDAI" O MEGURU DŌKŌ NO ICHI-KŌSATSU: FURUSE DENZŌ NO KISEKI [Rural problems during the 1920's and 1930's: an analysis of Denzō Furuse's activities]. *Shigaku Zasshi [Japan] 1985 94(6): 67-90.* Traces activities of Denzō Furuse (1888-1959) to clarify the historical meaning of peasant movements after World War I. Furuse encouraged peasants to gain political power, so that Japan would have agrarian policies balanced with the commercial and industrial policies. He also emphasized the necessity of adapting the peasant economy to the capitalist system. He was one of the representatives responsible for establishing the Japanese Peasants' Union in 1922 and a founder of Nōgyōson Bunka Kyōkai [Cultural Society of Agriculture] in 1940. 104 notes. 1920-40

Fuss, Nikolaus

2362. Ozhigova, E. P. O PEREPISKE DANIILA BERNULLI S NIKOLAEM FUSSOM [Daniel Bernoulli's correspondence with Nikolaus Fuss]. *Voprosy Istorii Estestvoznaniia i Tekhniki [USSR] 1981 (1): 108-115.* The German mathematician and physicist Leonard Eyler, living in Russia, became almost completely blind after an eye operation in 1772. He wrote to his friend in Basle, Professor Daniel Bernoulli (1700-82), asking him to find a secretary and personal assistant. A young student, Nikolaus Fuss (1755-1826), was chosen. In the five years, 1773-78, that he spent in St. Petersburg, Fuss improved his knowledge of acoustics, optics, astronomy, statistics, mechanics, differential and integral calculus, and civil engineering. He exchanged with his old mentor, Daniel Bernoulli, some 10 letters on matters such as the pitch of organ pipes, the actuarial theory of life insurance, betting, the design of a bridge over the Neva, and the theory of numbers. Based on documents from the Leningrad Historical Archives and secondary sources; 10 notes. 1773-78

Fustel de Coulanges, Numa-Denis

2363. Mayeur, Françoise. FUSTEL DE COULANGES ET LES QUESTIONS D'ENSEIGNEMENT SUPERIEUR [Fustel de Coulanges and questions of higher education]. *Revue Historique [France] 1985 274(2): 387-408.* University reform in France after 1878 was influenced by the historian Numa-Denis Fustel de Coulanges. During his tenure as a lycee professor at Strassbourg he wrote critiques of the French secondary educational system. These were used by commissioners charged with the reform of education. On higher education he published a comparison of German and French universities. He stressed the advantages of the French system and parity of its conference techniques of instruction with the German seminar system. He analyzed the ecole Normal Superieur and made substantial recommendations. His prestige as a historian and public figure carried great authority in the educational reform procedure. Based on the works of Fustel de Coulanges; 74 notes. 1870's-80's

G

Gábor, Áron

2364. Kovássy, Zoltán. ADALÉKOK GÁBOR ÁRON ÉLETRAJZÁHOZ [Data for the biography of Áron Gábor]. *Hadtörténelmi Közlemények [Hungary] 1981 28(1): 117-124.* The archives of the Transylvanian village of Bereck, where Áron Gábor (1814-44), hero of the 1848-49 war was born, were burned during World War II. Family documents allow the reconstruction of his biography and details of his most famous feat, the founding of cannons for the Hungarian Army at Kézdivásárhely. Based on personal documents preserved by the Gábor family; 3 photos. 1848-49

2365. Papp, Kálmán. A KÖKÖSI HŐS [The hero of Kökös]. *Hadtörténelmi Közlemények [Hungary] 1984 31(4): 753-760.* Describes the life of Áron Gábor, the amateur gunsmith who forged cannons out of church-bells in Hungary's war of independence in 1848-49. Although his cannons had many faults and weaknesses, they still made a significant contribution to the initial Hungarian successes in the war. Gábor died in the battle of Kökös in July 1849. 3 plates, diagram. 1848-49

Gabrielli, Noemi

2366. Cavallari Murat, Augusto. NOEMI GABRIELLI (1901-1979) [Noemi Gabrielli 1901-79]. *Bol. Storico-Bibliografico Subalpino [Italy] 1982 80(1): 371-373.* Obituary of Noemi Gabrielli (1901-79), national associate member of the Deputazione Subalpina di Storia Patria and distinguished art historian. 1901-79

Gabrovski, Nikola

2367. Bratanov, Georgi. NIKOLA GABROVSKI [Nikola Gabrovski]. *Izvestiia na Instituta po Istoriia na BKP [Bulgaria] 1983 (49): 395-401.* Analyzes the second edition of Filip Ginev's biography of Nikola Gabrovski. Gabrovski, who lived between 1864 and 1925, was one of Bulgaria's greatest pioneers of scientific socialism. 1864-1925

Gagarin, Yuri

2368. Krivoruchenko, V. K. CHELOVEK IZ LEGENDY [A man from a legend]. *Voprosy Istorii KPSS [USSR] 1984 (3): 132-135.* Commemorates Yuri Gagarin's 50th anniversary. A short biography of the famous Soviet cosmonaut written by a man who met him. Shows how assiduous Gagarin was in educating Soviet youth about their moral and political role. He died on a training flight in 1968. 1950's-68

Gagern, Hans von

2369. Friesen, Gerhard. NEMESIS UND DAS GALAKLEID DER JAKOBINER: EINE POLITISCH-LITERARISCHE KONTROVERSE ZWISCHEN HANS VON GAGERN UND HEINRICH LUDEN [Nemesis and the Jacobins' party dress: a political and literary conflict between Hans von Gagern and Heinrich Luden]. *Jahrbuch des Inst. für Deutsche Gesch. [Israel] 1982 11: 91-125.* 1816-18

For abstract see ***Luden, Heinrich***

Gaideburov, P. A.

2370. Kanaeva, T. M. P. A. GAIDEBUROV—OBSHCHESTVENYI DEIATEL' I REDAKTOR "NEDELI" [P. A. Gaideburov: public figure and editor of *Nedelia* (The Week)]. *Vestnik Moskovskogo U. Seriia 8: Istoriia [USSR] 1982 (4): 28-37.* P. A. Gaideburov participated in radical student circles at St. Petersburg in 1861 and in groups associated with Land and Freedom. In 1869 he began to write for *Nedelia,* published by V. Genkel. Gaideburov wrote editorials defending peasant property, communes, and workers' associations. He called for government aid to peasants. He considered himself above partisanship. *Nedelia* had only 2,000 subscribers in 1871, but 7,500 in 1878. After 1881, subscriptions fell, but they rose to 15,000 in the mid-1890's. Institute of Russian Literature and Art, Central State Historical Archive, Central State Archive of October Revolution; 49 notes. 1860's-90's

Gainsford, Thomas

2371. Eccles, Mark. THOMAS GAINSFORD, "CAPTAIN PAMPHLET." *Huntington Lib. Q. 1982 45(4): 259-270.* His career as a military officer and his travels provided Thomas Gainsford (1566-1624) with material for his books, pamphlets, and newsbooks. His most popular book, *The Glory of England* (1618), compared England with other kingdoms. Based on primary sources; 37 notes. 1566-1624

Gairy, Eric

2372. Archer, Ewart. GAIRYISM, REVOLUTION AND REORGANIZATION: THREE DECADES OF TURBULENCE IN GRENADA. *Journal of Commonwealth & Comparative Politics [Great Britain] 1985 23(2): 91-111.* Describes political change in Grenada from the 1950's to 1984. Eric Gairy, who founded the Grenada People's Party in the 1950's, became the prime minister in 1967. He quickly acquired a reputation for corruption and repression. His subsequent security "crackdowns" only encouraged the political opposition and led to the establishment in 1973 of the New Jewel Movement (NJM). In 1979, a coup d'etat led by NJM cadres established the People's Revolutionary Government under Maurice Bishop. In turn, the new government quickly moved to crush all opposition, including the Catholic Church. By 1982, infighting within the political leadership over Grenada's direction led to Bishop losing authority and being assassinated in 1983, which initiated an American invasion. In 1984, Grenada held elections and the newly established New National Party under Herbert Blaize won 59% of the vote. Based on Grenadian newspapers and secondary sources; 2 tables, 35 notes. 1950's-84

Gaitan, Jorge Eliécer.

2373. Forero Benavides, Abelardo. LOS GRANDES HOMBRES QUE HE CONOCIDO [Great men I have known]. *Bol. de Hist. y Antigüedades [Colombia] 1981 68(734): 691-715.* 1920's-50's

For abstract see ***López, Alfonso***

2374. Sánchez Gómez, Gonzalo. EL GAITANISMO Y LA INSURRECCION DEL 9 DE ABRIL EN PROVINCIA [Gaitanism and the insurrection of 9 April in the provinces]. *Anuario Colombiano de Hist. Social y de la Cultura [Colombia] 1982 (10): 191-229.* Examines the role played by Jorge Eliécer Gaitán in the events preceding his assassination on 9 April 1948 and the subsequent wave of violence (the Bogotazo) and compares and contrasts the events in the principal Colombian cities with events in the provinces. The situation which led to the insurrection is reviewed and details of the actions in Bogotá, the western provinces, el Tolima, and Santander are described. Both the nature of the leadership and the characteristics of the rebellion varied greatly between the cities and the provinces, and this influenced the course of events in 1948 and in later years. Based on newspaper articles and primary sources; 39 notes. 1928-48

Gajdoš, Vševlad Jozef

2375. Zúbek, Teodorik J. MOJA KOREŠPONDENCIA S OTCOM V. J. GAJDOŠOM [My correspondence with Father Vševlad Jozef Gajdoš]. *Kalendár Jednota 1982 85: 146-154.* Despite severe persecution in Communist Czechoslovakia, Vševlad Gajdoš (1908-78) continued to work as librarian and historian and maintained contacts with a Slovak fellow Franciscan in America. 1949-78

Gal, Moshe

2376. Gal, Moshe. AL PENEY ARATSOT VEYAMIM: BEDEREKH LE'ERETS-YISRA'EL [Through land and sea: en route to Palestine]. *Yalkut Moreshet Periodical [Israel] 1981 (32): 71-100.* The outbreak of the war thwarted the author's plan to immigrate to Palestine in 1939 from Częstochowa, Poland. He fled to Lithuania where he stayed until 1941. Then, as the leader of a group of Jews, he started his trek toward Palestine, via Moscow, Teheran, Bombay, and Suez. The group ended up in the British detention camp of Atlit, Palestine. They were liberated in September 1942. Based on personal memoirs; note. 1939-42

Galaup, Jean-François de

2377. Taillemite, Etienne. LA GLOIRE TRAGIQUE DE LAPEROUSE [La Pérouse's tragic glory]. *Histoire [France] 1985 (83): 10-18.* Recalls the motives and itinerary of the French round-the-world expedition, 1785-88, under the command of navigator Jean-François de Galaup, Comte de La Pérouse (1741-88), and gives an account of his brilliant career and accomplishments, focusing on his professional competence, remarkable personality, and the noble traits he displayed during the expedition. 1759-88

Galdames, Luis

2378. González Novoa, Rafael. LUIS GALDAMES GALDAMES [Luis Galdames Galdames]. *Rev. Chilena de Hist. y Geog. [Chile] 1980 (148): 297-313.* A short biography of the activities of Luis Galdames, a prominent Chilean educator, intellectual, and political figure. 1910-41

Galich, Manuel

2379. Rodríguez, Mariano et al. MANUEL GALICH: IN MEMORIAM [Manuel Galich: in memoriam]. *Casa de las Américas [Cuba] 1985 25(148): 3-35.* Provides a series of tributes to and reminiscences of Manuel Galich (d. 1984), the Guatemalan statesman, diplomat, dramatist, and teacher. He served as minister of education under Juan José Arevalo and foreign minister and ambassador under Jacobo Arbenz. After the fall of the latter in 1954, he went into exile. In 1962 he was invited to Cuba where he contributed significantly to the cultural and academic life of the country. 1940's-84

Galileo

2380. Drake, Stillman A NEGLECTED GALILEAN LETTER. *Journal for the History of Astronomy [Great Britain] 1986 17(2): 99-108.* A five-page letter attributed to the Italian astronomer Galileo indicates that he was not a Platonist and provides details on his views of the work of astronomers Johannes Kepler and Tycho Brahe. 1577-1633

2381. Drake, Stillman. GALILEO'S EXPLORATIONS IN SCIENCE. *Dalhousie Rev. [Canada] 1981 61(2): 217-232.* Presents Galileo as making "explorations in science" and later making new "explorations of science" when opposition to his ideas forced him to examine the traditional view of the abstract and philosophical approach to nature. Based on a 1981 Killam Lecture delivered at Dalhousie University; 11 notes. 1590-1638

Galíndez de la Riba, Toribio

2382. Hampe Martínez, Teodoro. UN ERASMISTA PERULERO: TORIBIO GALINDEZ DE LA RIBA [A Peruvian Erasmist: Toribio Galíndez de la Riba]. *Cuadernos Hispanoamericanos [Spain] 1986 (431): 85-93.* Among the second wave of Spanish colonizers there were learned men like Toribio Galíndez de la Riba (Spain, d. 1554), who helped lay the administrative foundations of the colonial government. He was sentenced to death in 1554 for taking sides with the *encomenderos* against the royal representatives. The inventory of his books reveals a sharp secularist leaning toward Erasmist ideas and geographical and legal subjects. Based on sources from the Archivo General de Indias at Sevilla; 32 notes. 1530's-54

Galindo, Alejandro

2383. Mora, Carl J. ALEJANDRO GALINDO: PIONEER MEXICAN CINEAST. *Journal of Popular Culture 1984 18(1): 101-112.* Overview of the Mexican film industry and the contributions of Alejandro Galindo, pioneer cineast of the urban Mexican scene. Secondary sources; 3 fig., 26 notes. 1931-80

Gallacher, William

2384. Martynenko, A. K. IZ ZHIZNI I REVOLIUTSIONNOI DEIATEL'NOSTI UIL'IAMA GALLAKHERE (1881-1965) [The life and revolutionary activity of William Gallacher (1881-1965)]. *Novaia i Noveishaia Istoriia [USSR] 1983 (5): 74-93, (6): 78-96.* Part 1. William Gallacher began to take part in political life in the 1890's before the Labour Party was established, and during World War I became one of the most prominent organizers of the proletariat. Unlike such "workers' leaders" as James Macdonald, James Thomas, and Herbert Morrison, he stood by his principles and refused the temptations of a "brilliant career" in bourgeois society. His meeting with V. I. Lenin in 1920 took place at a time when he still subscribed to ultra-left ideas, and proved to be a watershed in his political development, helping him to grasp the significance of Marxist-Leninist teaching and the role and tasks of the Communist Party. Part 2. On his return to Britain after his meeting with Lenin at the 2d Congress of Comintern, Gallacher took an even more active role in the working class struggle and became one of the leaders of the British Communist Party. In 1935 he was elected to Parliament and served as a member for 15 years. He remained a firm believer in the ideas of Marxism-Leninism until his death. Secondary sources; 240 notes. 1890's-1965

Gallegos Freire, Rómulo

2385. Pinillos, María de las Nieves. ROMULO GALLEGOS: EN EL CENTENARIO DE SU NACIMIENTO [Rómulo Gallegos: the centennial of his birth]. *Cuadernos Hispanoamericanos [Spain] 1984 (409): 41-52.* Offers biographical data on Rómulo Gallegos Freire (1884-1969). As a writer, he was a creator of symbols and human and even geographical myths (the plain, the jungle, the river, etc.). As a politician, he always militated against dictatorship, barbarousness, and violence, favoring democracy, civilization, and education for his country. 1884-1969

Galler, L. M.

2386. Redanski, V. ADMIRAL L. M. GALLER (K 100 LETIIU SO DNIA ROZHDENIIA) [Admiral L. M. Galler (100th anniversary of his birth)]. *Voenno-Istoricheskii Zhurnal [USSR] 1983 (11): 92-94.* L. M. Galler (1883-1950) graduated from the Naval Cadet Corps in 1905 and by 1912 had his own command. After the October Revolution he joined the Bolsheviks immediately and in February 1921 was made chief of the general staff of the Baltic Fleet. In the 1920's he commanded a flotilla of battleships and in 1929-30 successfully brought them to the Black Sea from the Baltic. He joined the Party in 1932 and during World War II was made a deputy commissar for ship construction. After the war he was head of the Naval Academy of Ship Construction and Arming. Secondary sources; photo, 5 notes. 1905-48

Gallet, Louis

2387. Maier, Denise. LE SCULPTEUR LOUIS GALLET: 1873-1955 [The sculptor Louis Gallet: 1873-1955]. *Musées de Genève [Switzerland] 1985 (251): 15-21.* Retraces the life of Swiss sculptor Louis Gallet, discussing his development as an artist as well as the many marble and bronze statues he made of people and animals, and provides reproductions of photographs of several of his works. 1890's-1955

Galliffet, Marquis de

2388. Wartelle, Jean-Claude. UN MAUDIT DE L'HISTOIRE DE FRANCE: LE GENERAL DE GALLIFFET (1830-1909) [An accursed character in French history: General de Galliffet (1830-1909)]. *Revue Historique des Armées [France] 1984 (4): 95-108.* Highlights and comments on the personality and the brilliant military and political career of General Marquis de Galliffet (1830-1909). Condemned by the French left for his direct participation in the bloody suppression of the Commune in May 1871, Galliffet played an important role in French military and political history from the Franco-Prussian War of 1870, when he assumed a heroic attitude in Sedan, to the Dreyfus affair, when he became war minister in the Waldeck-Rousseau Republican cabinet of 1899. Based on French war ministry archives, Service Historique de l'Armée archives, and other archival sources; 7 photos, map, 37 notes. 1870's-99

Galpin, Ann I'Ons

2389. Yamey, C. L. THE WORK OF F. T. I'ONS' GRANDDAUGHTER ANN. *Africana Notes and News [South Africa] 1984 26(2): 52-54.* Prints a biography and describes the watercolor paintings of Ann I'Ons Galpin (1864-1919), granddaughter of the great South African artist Frederick Timpson I'Ons (d. 1887). 2 illus. 1880's-1919

Galton, Francis

2390. Fancher, Raymond E. BIOGRAPHICAL ORIGINS OF FRANCIS GALTON'S PSYCHOLOGY. *Isis 1983 74(272): 227-233.* Francis Galton (1822-1911) is said to have believed all his life in the high intelligence of those, like himself, with large heads. He also believed that high mental ability was almost completely determined by heredity and his own pedigree was impressive. Similarly his eugenic visions and his work in his anthropometrical laboratory are said to have been colored by a certain self-serving vanity. However, simple vanity is not the explanation of the biographical element in his theories. A keen sense of the limits of his own powers, as experienced in his formative years, seems to better explain his insistence on the biological basis of human capacities. 25 notes. 1869-93

Galvão, Alfredo

2391. Barata, Mário. PROFESSOR ALFREDO GALVÃO E A HISTÓRIA DA ARTE BRASILEIRA DO SÉCULO XIX [Alfredo Galvão and the history of Brazilian art in the 19th century]. *Rev. do Inst. Hist. e Geog. Brasileiro [Brazil] 1979 (324): 312-320.* A tribute to Alfredo Galvão on his induction as a member of the Institute of History and Geography. He was director of the Museum of Fine Arts and of the National School of Fine Arts, where he taught anatomical drawing. He is the author of many works on Brazilian artists and art history. 20c

Galvez, Bernardo de

2392. Fleming, Thomas. BERNARDO DE GALVEZ. *Am. Heritage 1982 33(3): 30-39.* Bernardo de Galvez, governor of the province of Louisiana during the American Revolution, provided much assistance to the US effort in the West. Through his efforts and his cooperation with US agent Oliver Pollock, the Mississippi River became a major supply route. Galvez's forces captured British posts at Manchac, Baton Rouge, Natchez, and Pensacola. After the war, Galvez was made captain general of Cuba and later viceroy of New Spain, where he died suddenly in 1786. 6 illus. 1777-86

Gálvez, Manuel

2393. Canal Feijóo, Bernardo. HOMENAJE A DON MANUEL GALVEZ [Tribute to Manuel Gálvez]. *Bol. de la Acad. Argentina de Letras [Argentina] 1982 47(185-186): 211-213.* Discusses the literary career of Manuel Gálvez (1882-1962), whose work reflected the turbulent times in which he lived. The author bequeathed his library and private papers to the Argentine Academy of Letters. A list of these materials is included. 1900's-62

Gama, Luís Gonzaga Pinto da

2394. Calmon, Pedro. LUIS GAMA [Luís Gama]. *Revista do Instituto Histórico e Geográfico Brasileiro [Brazil] 1982 (337): 179-184.* Luís Gonzaga Pinto da Gama (1830-82) was the son of a Portuguese father and an African woman. Sold into slavery by his father to pay a gambling debt, he became a literary figure and was prominent in the abolitionist movement. Speech delivered at a commemorative session. 1830-82

Gamanga, Kenewa

2395. Corby, Richard A. PROGRESSIVE CHIEFTAINCY IN SIERRA LEONE: KENEWA GAMANGA OF SIMBARU. *Tarikh [Nigeria] 1981 7(1): 57-64.* Examines the contributions of Kenewa Gamanga of the Simbaru Chiefdom in Sierra Leone to his region's economic, political, and agricultural development from his emergence as chief in 1941 to 1961 and discusses his role in Sierra Leone's independence movement. 1941-61

Gambetta, Léon

2396. Plantey, Alain. A PROPOS DE GAMBETTA [In connection with Gambetta]. *Revue des Deux Mondes [France] 1985 (11): 387-390.* The biographers of Léon Gambetta (1838-82) have asserted that he had no descendants, but the family archives reveal that he had a daughter named Berthe, whose mother's identity still remains a mystery. 1874

Games family

2397. Selwood, Ann M. THE GAMES FAMILY OF BODWIGIAD, PENDERYN, BRECONSHIRE. *National Library of Wales Journal [Great Britain] 1985 24(2): 214-221.* Traces the lineage of the Games family of Bodwigiad, Penderyn, Brecknockshire. The Gameses had owned land in the parishes of Ystradfellte and Penderyn since the days of Morgan ap Dafydd Gam, who is named in a deed dated 1448. The family had two branches, one being the family of John Games of Aberbrân and the other the family of Edward Games, who built the Elizabethan mansion of Newton. Richard Games, the son of John Games, supported the king during the Civil War and was made Commissioner of Array. By his marriage he had become connected to one of the most influential families of North Glamorgan, the Prichards of Llancaiach. He built up a considerable estate that remained in the hands of the family until 1667. Based on Games family documents and other primary sources; 32 notes. 15c-17c

Gammon, Philip

2398. Block, Joseph S. RELIGIOUS NONCONFORMITY AND SOCIAL CONFLICT: PHILIP GAMMON'S STAR CHAMBER STORY. *Albion 1981 13(4): 331-346.* Philip Gammon, shoemaker, was charged in 1536 by his Axminster neighbors with heresy and defiance of royal authority. Gammon, who denied the charges, was the defendant

in the only heresy trial brought before the Henrician Star Chamber. Labeled a Sacramentarian and a violent bully, Gammon's ordeal ended when one of the conspirators confessed that he and others had manufactured the evidence. Based on proceedings of the Star Chamber; 43 notes.
1536

Gandert, Otto Friedrich

2399. Müller, Adriaan von. OTTO-FRIEDRICH GANDERT ZUM GEDÄCHTNIS (8.8.1898-7.7.1983) [Otto Friedrich Gandert in memoriam (8 August 1898-7 July 1983)]. *Jahrbuch für die Gesch. Mittel- und Ostdeutschlands [West Germany] 1983 32: 271-273.* With the death of Otto Friedrich Gandert, archaeology has lost one of its last great generalists. Combining archaeology with natural science, Gandert was well prepared to assume the post of director of the Prehistory Division of the Mark Museum in Berlin in 1936, where he sponsored excavation, in particular of the Germanic settlement of Kablow in the district of Beeskow-Storkow. After the war he returned to Berlin, this time as curator of the State Museum for Pre- and Early History. Active in numerous museums, chairman of the Berlin Academy for Anthropology, Ethnology, and Prehistory, member of the German Archaeological Institute and the Historical Commission of Berlin, Gandert in his last years published a map of primitive Slavic archaeological sites in Mark Brandenburg. His work on the prehistory of Mark Brandenburg will be continued by his successors. 1898-1983

Gandhi, Indira

2400. Ahmad, Naveed. INDO-SOVIET RELATIONS SINCE MRS. GANDHI'S RE-ELECTION. *Pakistan Horizon [Pakistan] 1983 36(1): 73-100.* Since 1980, Indira Gandhi has shown an interest in expanding India's relations with Western nations, but has done nothing to alienate the USSR, although she no longer endorses its Afghan policy. 1980's

2401. Andersen, Walter K. INDIA IN 1981: STRONGER POLITICAL AUTHORITY AND SOCIAL TENSION. *Asian Survey 1982 22(2): 119-135.* Prime Minister Indira Gandhi maintained a firm hold on power during 1981. She tightened discipline in her ruling Congress (I) Party, but she did little to strengthen the party structure. She focused efforts on stimulating economic growth, attempting to revive lagging investments in such key areas as transportation, energy, and agriculture. Based on newspapers. 1981

2402. Kaushik, Devendra. INDIA-USSR AND EAST EUROPE: EMERGING TRENDS UNDER RAJIV GANDHI. *India Quarterly [India] 1985 41(1): 6-16.* Indicates the extent to which India's Prime Minister, Indira Gandhi, went to cultivate economic and technical cooperation with Eastern Europe, separate and independent of those with the Soviet Union. Kaushik asserts that Gandhi made deliberate use of her 1982 state visit to Moscow in both timing and content to underscore India's independent treatment of Eastern Europe and the Soviet Union. Little immediate change is seen as likely under Rajiv Gandhi. 10 notes. 1980's

2403. Sahgal, Nayantara. NEHRU'S QUIET DAUGHTER. *Wilson Q. 1982 6(5): 160-170.* Discusses Indira Gandhi's personality and political career since 1966.
1966-82

2404. Ul'ianovski, R. A. INDIRA GANDI. POLITICHESKII PORTRET [A political portrait of Indira Gandhi]. *Novaia i Noveishaia Istoriia [USSR] 1985 (5): 125-143.* A political biography of India's prime minister from 1966 to 1984, Indira Gandhi (1917-84). In 1964 she became Minister of Information and Radio Communication in the Nehru government. First elected as prime minister in 1966, Gandhi lost the office when power struggles within the Indian National Congress led to the party's defeat in the 1977 elections, but she was reelected as prime minister in 1980. During her years in office banking was nationalized, India's nonaligned policy was firmly established, and national unity was achieved. Secondary sources; 2 photos, 38 notes.
1940-84

Gandhi, Mahatma

2405. Arunachalam, K. MAHATMA GANDHI & COMPARATIVE RELIGION. *Political Science Review [India] 1983 22(4): 400-411.* Presents a review of K. R. Seshagiri's *Mahatma Gandhi and Comparative Religion.* Summarizes each chapter passing from Gandhi's childhood through his maturing beliefs to his concept of the Indian Freedom Movement. Gandhi's Hindu, Muslim, Buddhist, and Christian beliefs are examined from which emerges his support of education and his six creative principles of spirituality.
1880's-1947

2406. Cribb, R. B. THE EARLY POLITICAL PHILOSOPHY OF M. K. GANDHI, 1869-1893. *Asian Profile [Hong Kong] 1985 13(4): 353-360.* Views Gandhi's thought as evolving within a set of historical and social circumstances, with Gandhi's early ideas representing a core of belief around which his philosophy was later constructed, rather than a seed from which it grew. Gandhi's London years established a solid philosophical base from which he could begin extensive philosophical construction. He committed himself to truthfulness, temperance, chastity, and vegetarianism. But upon his return to India in 1891, his outlook remained parochial. His inability to make a living practicing law in India challenged his central principle that practicality and morality coincided. In 1893 he left for South Africa where he found a solution to this problem and developed the central concepts of his mature philosophy. Based on Gandhi's early writings and secondary sources; 16 notes. 1869-93

2407. Hay, Stephen. DIGGING UP GANDHI'S PSYCHOLOGICAL ROOTS. *Biography 1983 6(3): 209-219.* Based on scattered sources relating to Mahatma Gandhi's first 18 years, suggests that three character traits central in his adult years had their roots in his early interactions with his parents and playmates: his devotion to serving those in difficulty, his skill as a mediator, and his readiness to refuse to obey a law or command repugnant to his conscience.
1869-87

2408. Kripalani, Krishna. GANDHI AND TAGORE: TWO FACES OF MODERN INDIA. *Indian Horizons [India] 1980 29(4): 11-18.* Compares and contrasts the social and cultural backgrounds and the spiritual relationships of Rabindranath Tagore (1861-1941) and Mahatma Gandhi (1869-1947). The profound differences of their youths and the varying levels of self-disclosure in their respective poetical and political writings are explored. These diversities were offset by their agreement on Indian independence, the need for individual freedom, and ethics as the basis of social relationships. Their writings demonstrate their mutual respect. Based on a lecture presented under the auspices of the Japan-India Association, Tokyo, 31 May 1980.
1880's-1947

2409. Mukherjee, Prithwindra. L'AVENEMENT DE GANDHI. QUELQUES CONFRONTATIONS DOCTRINALES [The advent of Gandhi: some doctrinal confrontations]. *Défense Nationale [France] 1984 40(Feb): 61-77.* Seeks to distinguish between myth and reality in the career of Mahatma Gandhi (1869-1948) before and after 1945 by viewing it in historical and political context. 1890's-1948

2410. Naik, J. P. DEVELOPMENT AND GANDHIAN TRADITION IN INDIA. *Rev. of Pol. 1983 45(3): 345-365.* Gandhi's philosophy stressed harmony with nature, moderation, self-control, simplicity, and resourceful use of science and technology. It advocated decentralization of political and economic power, village self-sufficiency, nonviolence, compromise, and consensus. From 1920 to 1947, the Gandhian program took root, not only through Gandhi's individual effort and inspiration but by the development of voluntary movements and state power. However, with his assassination, the thrust of the movement withered. The Indian National Congress chose the West as the developmental model and the intellectuals ignored his reforms. Today, a Gandhian social transformation could only come about through selective application of his major reforms. 1920-47

2411. Pantham, Thomas. THINKING WITH MAHATMA GANDHI: BEYOND LIBERAL DEMOCRACY. *Pol. Theory 1983 11(2): 165-188.* By the 1920's, Mahatma Gandhi had decided that the fascist character of the Western democracies could be averted only by a total commitment to self-sacrifice and nonviolence. 1920's-48

2412. Switzer, Les. GANDHI IN SOUTH AFRICA: THE AMBIGUITIES OF SATYAGRAHA. *Journal of Ethnic Studies 1986 14(1): 122-128.* Mohandas Gandhi was sent to southern Africa in 1893 by an Indian law firm to adjudicate commercial suits in Durban and Pretoria, and stayed for 21 years. Here he perfected the strategy of *satyagraha* or soul (truth) force—passive resistance to Westerners. He founded the Natal Indian Congress and founded commonwealth cooperatives or *ashrams,* plus the newspaper *Indian Opinion* in 1903, which spearheaded the passive resistance campaigns from 1906 to 1913 in South Africa. After his departure, however, the Indian community was even worse off in terms of political and economic rights than before the struggle. Gandhi's attitude toward Africans was close to the paternalistic view of many colonial settlers, and Africans were not part of the *ashrams,* nor did Indians fight for African rights. 13 notes. 1893-1913

2413. Watson, Francis. GANDHI AS A "HUNGER STRIKER"?: ON THE MASTER OF THE FAST. *Encounter [Great Britain] 1981 57(5): 62-64.* Most of Mahatma Gandhi's fasts were taken for self-purification; even when political, they were not usually accompanied by threats to carry them to the point of death—with exceptions in 1932 and again in 1947. 1913-48

2414. Watson, Francis. GETTING GANDHI STRAIGHT. *Encounter [Great Britain] 1983 61(3): 80-87.* Provides personal memories of Mahatma Gandhi and a discussion of various views of his life and career. ca 1900-48

Gandhi, Rajiv

2415. Hurtig, Christiane. RAJIV GANDHI: LA DIFFICILE RECONVERSION D'UN HERITAGE [Rajiv Gandhi: the difficulties in recycling an inheritance]. *Etudes [France] 1986 364(3): 313-325.* Evaluates the difficulties facing Indian Prime Minister Rajiv Gandhi, who, although he benefited from the confidence inspired by his mother, Indira Gandhi, prior to her assassination, must contend with opposition, corruption, and a crisis in the Punjab region before completing plans for modernization, decentralization, and reform. 1975-86

Gandy, Joseph Michael

2416. Nachmani, Cynthia Wolk. "'Enrapt in a Cloud of Darkness . . .' Joseph Michael Gandy, Architecture, and the Romantic Imagination." New York U. 1984. 352 pp. *DAI 1985 46(1): 7-A.* DA8505520 1790's-1843

Ganges, Marquise de

2417. Héritier, Jean. LE SUPPLICE DE LA MARQUISE DE GANGES [The tortures suffered by the Marquise de Ganges]. *Historama [France] 1985 (15): 80-83.* An account of the torments suffered by the Marquise de Ganges caused by her husband's attempts to coax her into making a will in his favor, followed by her assassination by her brothers-in-law in 1667, a cause célèbre in which the guilt of the marquis was the object of a recent historical debate. 1667

Gansel, David

2418. Vigne, Randolph. DAVID GANSEL OF LEYTON GRANGE AND EAST DONYLAND HALL (1691-1753): A HUGUENOT ARCHITECT IN HIS SETTING. *Proceedings of the Huguenot Society of London [Great Britain] 1982 23(6): 358-375.* Views the family and professional fortunes of the Huguenot David Gansel (1691-1753), whose houses, Leyton Grange in Essex and East Donyland Hall near Colchester, bore marks of architectural improvements according to his own designs. 1691-1753

Ganshof, François L.

2419. Caenegem, R. C. van. IN MEMORIAM F. L. GANSHOF (1895-1980) [In memoriam F. L. Ganshof (1895-1980)]. *Tijdschrift voor Rechtsgeschiedenis [Netherlands] 1981 49(1-2): 4-12.* The obituary of François L. Ganshof, medievalist and historian of law at Ghent University, 1923-61, and since 1950 editorial consultant to *Tidschrift voor Rechtsgeschiedenis,* concentrates on and lists his publications in the judicial and institutional fields, as applied to Flemish, feudal, and Carolingian themes. Based on Ganshof's legal history publications; 39 notes. 1895-1980

Gao Gang

2420. Titov, A. 25 YEARS SINCE THE DEATH OF GAO GANG. *Far Eastern Affairs [USSR] 1981 (1): 139-150.* The Maoist leaders executed Gao Gang (Kao Kang, 1902-?54), a prominent figure in the Communist Party and in the People's Liberation Army, who helped organize the soviet area in the Border Region of Shaanxi-Gansu (Shensi-Kansu) during World War II. Gao worked to set up that revolutionary base with Soviet help and was a true Communist and internationalist. 1930's-50's

Garai, Carl

2421. Petrák, Katalin. GARAI KÁROLY (1899-1942) [Carl Garai (1899-1942)]. *Párttörténeti Közlemények [Hungary] 1982 28(4): 176-197.* Active during the Communist revolution, Garai had to flee Hungary, living in Vienna and later in Germany, 1920-29. In 1929 the Communist Party asked him to return to Hungary and supervise illegal propaganda. He was arrested the same year and sentenced to two and one-half years in prison. After his release he lived in the USSR and worked as the editor of the *Deutsche Zentralzeitung,* the very popular German-language daily produced in Moscow. He was arrested again in 1938. When he was freed the next year, his wife had disappeared, and his editorial job was not available. Working on occasional translations for Radio Moscow he was arrested for the third time in 1940 and died in 1942. 77 notes. 1899-1942

Garbolas family

2422. Kokkas, Panagiōtēs G. Ē OIKOGENEIA GKARPOLA KAI E PRŌTĒ HELLĒNIKĒ EPHĒMERIDA TĒS THESSALONIKĒS [The Garbolas family and the first Greek newspaper in Salonika]. *Makedonika [Greece] 1981 21: 222-251.* C. Garbolas (ca. 1790-1848) left Greece ca. 1800 for Vienna where he became a printer and then a publisher of Greek works. In 1837 he established a press in Athens specializing in academic literature. His three sons, Alexander, Miltiades and Sophocles, inherited the firm but soon dissolved it. Miltiades became a publisher in Salonika, and in 1875 Sophocles established the first Greek newspaper in Salonika, *Hermes* (later changed to *Pharos).* The paper originally was noted for its liberal views but became more conservative, particularly under the direction of Miltiades's sons, Alexander and Nicolas, who supported reform within the Ottoman Empire rather than Greek independence. Many Greeks accused the brothers of being Turkish agents, and the paper, having lost the bulk of its readership, ceased publication in 1912. 65 notes, French summary. 1800-1912

García, Antonio

2423. Arze Quintanilla, Oscar. ANTONIO GARCIA (1917-1982) [Antonio García 1917-82]. *Am. Indígena [Mexico] 1982 42(3): 523-526.* The Colombian social scientist was a dedicated defender of the rights of the indigenous populations of the Latin American continent. His work has made it possible to define the indigenist position and defend it against promoters of "hispanicism." Garcia was also influential among students of development problems in Latin America. He was one of the most brilliant Latin American economists and an expert in agrarian reform. List of his chief publications in the text. 1917-82

2424. Godoy, Ricardo, and Tiedemann, R. G. ANTONIO GARCIA: A MEXICAN PEASANT, POET AND REVOLUTIONARY. *J. of Peasant Studies [Great Britain] 1982 9(2): 241-251.* Reproduces a letter and poems written by Antonio Garcia Gonzales, Mexican peasant from Ixtlan. The letter was written in October 1971, shortly after his arrest for involvement in revolutionary activities in Mexico City, and the poems are from the early years of his imprisonment, between 1971 and 1973. An introduction gives some biographical remarks and a commentary sketches in the background of revolutionary organizations in Mexico, 1968-73. 6 notes. 1968-73

García Bacca, Juan David

2425. Bruni Celli, Blas. HOMENAJE AL PROFESOR JUAN DAVID GARCIA BACCA [Tribute to professor Juan David García Bacca]. *Bol. de la Acad. Nac. de la Hist. [Venezuela] 1982 65(258): 489-491.* A tribute to Juan David García Bacca, born in Spain in 1901, naturalized Venezuelan citizen, professor in many Latin American universities, most recently at the Central University of Venezuela. The author of many books on philosophy and mysticism, he has received many academic honors and decorations and is a member of the National Academy of History. 1920's-82

García Calderón, Francisco

2426. Rodríguez Monegal, Emir. AMERICA/UTOPIA: GARCIA CALDERON, EL DISCIPULO FAVORITO DE RODO [America/Utopia: García Calderón, the favorite disciple of Rodó]. *Cuadernos Hispanoamericanos [Spain] 1985 (417): 166-171.* Francisco García Calderón (1883-1953) accepted and improved enduring elements of José Enrique Rodó's (1871-1917) thought, such as critical accuracy in literary work, the view of culture as a heritage to be preserved and communicated, and, above all, the utopian vision of Latin America both as heir and shelter to the old Mediterranean culture and as essentially different from North America. 8 notes. 20c

García del Río, Juan

2427. Cacua Prada, Antonio. DON JUAN GARCIA DEL RIO, PERIODISTA INTERNACIONAL [Juan García del Río, international journalist]. *Bol. de Hist. y Antigüedades [Colombia] 1982 69(737): 499-519.* Born in Cartagena de Indias but educated in Spain, Juan García del Río (1794-1856) became definitely committed to the patriot cause only after his royalist father's death. He served his native Colombia and other South American republics in different official capacities, in America and Europe. He was a supporter of monarchy both in Peru, as collaborator of José de San Martín, and later in Gran Colombia with Simón Bolívar. Throughout his career he showed a special vocation for journalism. 1794-1856

García Herrera, Alvaro

2428. —. FALLECIMIENTO DEL ACADEMICO DE NUMERO DON ALVARO GARCIA HERRERA [Death of the academician Alvaro García Herrera]. *Bol. de Hist. y Antigüedades [Colombia] 1980 67(729): 161-202.* Biographical note, bibliography, and press notices concerning the Colombian diplomat, Liberal Party leader, and historian Alvaro García Herrera (1917-80). 1942-80

García Moreno, Gabriel

2429. Granata, Massimo. L'INTRANSIGENTISMO CATTOLICO ED IL MITO DI GARCIA MORENO [Catholic intransigence and the myth of García Moreno]. *Bollettino dell'Archivio per la Storia del Movimento Sociale Cattolico in Italia [Italy] 1984 19(1): 49-77.* Discusses the founding of the Catholic republic of Ecuador by Gabriel García Moreno (1821-75) and the mythification of his achievements by the conservative Catholic press, which interpreted his assassination as martyrdom. 1861-1925

Garcia Pérez, Alan

2430. Roett, Riordan. PERU: THE MESSAGE FROM GARCIA. *Foreign Affairs 1985-86 64(2): 274-286.* Discusses domestic and international measures undertaken in Peru, 1985, by newly elected president, Alan Garcia Pérez. Garcia, the first Peruvian president affiliated with the Aprista Party, devalued the national currency, cut interest rates, and raised gasoline prices. In response to domestic austerity plans imposed by the International Monetary Fund (IMF), Garcia threatened to abandon the IMF, and announced Peru would pay no more than 10% of its annual foreign exchange earnings toward outstanding debt, citing a choice between debt and democracy. Based on a speech, communiqué, and secondary source. 1980-85

García Rovira, Custodio

2431. Cacua Prada, Antonio. CUSTODIO GARCIA ROVIRA, EL ESTUDIANTE MARTIR [Custodio García Rovira, the student martyr]. *Bol. de Hist. y Antigüedades [Colombia] 1981 68(734): 652-660.* Born in Bucaramanga in 1780, the scholar and patriot Custodio García Rovira was executed in 1816 during the Spanish Reconquest. At the time he was president of the Provincias Unidas de la Nueva Granada and had just been married. 1780-1816

García Villoslada, Ricardo

2432. Aldea Vaquero, Quintín. EL HISTORIADOR RICARDO GARCIA VILLOSLADA EN SUS OCHENTA AÑOS DE EDAD [Historian Ricardo García Villoslada on his 80th birthday]. *Hispania Sacra [Spain] 1982 34(70): 689-701.* A tribute to Ricardo García Villoslada, Jesuit historian, professor of Church history in the Gregorian University from 1934 to 1975, and author of two important studies, one on the University of Paris when Francisco de Vitoria was a student there, and two volumes on Martin Luther, which are considered to be the most balanced view of the personality of the controversial reformer. 1930's-75

Gardey, Abel

2433. Bordes, Maurice. LE CONSEIL GENERAL DU GERS ET LA POLITIQUE FISCALE PENDANT L'ENTRE-DEUX GUERRES (1919-1939). [The Gers General Council and fiscal policy in the period between the wars, 1919-39]. *Information Historique [France] 1985 47(4): 158-166.* As chairman of the Gers Radical-Socialist delegation and cabinet member of several French governments of the Third Republic, Abel Gardey (1882-1957) was instrumental in changing his party's political orientation from left to right; although in 1919 he called for the imposition of a tax on income, he later contributed to the fall of Léon Blum's progressive socialist government in 1937 by supporting the policies of Edouard Daladier and Paul Reynaud. 1919-39

Gardner, Maria Louisa (Briar)

2434. Gardner, G. Louise. BRIAR GARDNER, 1879-1968. *Auckland Waikato Historical Journal [New Zealand] 1984 (44): 2-9.* An account of the life and work of pioneer potter Maria Louisa (Briar) Gardner as well as her family background. 1870's-1960's

Gárdos, Mariska

2435. Kende, János. GÁRDOS MARISKA (1885-1973) [Mariska Gárdos, 1885-1973]. *Párttörténeti Közlemények [Hungary] 1985 31(3): 202-216.* Hungarian labor leader Mariska Gárdos was 18 years old when she led the organization of women employees in the Union of Trade Workers. Later she founded the Hungarian Women Workers. In 1912 she made a trip to the United States, where she visited the industrial centers inhabited by Hungarians, made speeches, and took part in the editing of a socialist newspaper. After the downfall of the Hungarian Soviet Republic, she went into hiding in Budapest. Later she emigrated to Austria, where she worked with Hungarian Social Democratic emigres. After 1945 she helped in the development of the women's movement. Secondary sources; 22 notes. ca 1903-73

Garibaldi, Giuseppe

2436. Alatri, Paolo; Grasso, Vito; and Şerbănescu, Ana Maria. MARELE SI MODESTUL: GIUSEPPE GARIBALDI [The greatness and modesty of Giuseppe Garibaldi]. *Magazin Istoric [Romania] 1982 16(10): 22-28.* An address given by Professor Alatri, University of Perugia, to the Italian Institute in Bucharest on the centenary of Garibaldi's death, celebrating his achievements in the struggle for a united Italy. 1807-82

2437. Barbati, Vittorio. GARIBALDI UOMO DEL SUO TEMPO [Garibaldi, a man of his time]. *Riv. Marittima [Italy] 1982 115(12): 15-28.* Describes the development of Giuseppe Garibaldi personally and as a military leader through successive events of his life, from campaigns in South America to the conquest of the kingdom of the Two Sicilies. 1835-71

2438. Besler, Werner. GARIBALDI—VOLKSFÜHRER UND MILITÄR [Garibaldi: popular leader and military man]. *Militärgeschichte [East Germany] 1982 21(1): 43-53.* The emphasis of this biographical sketch of Giuseppe Garibaldi is on his military activity. Equally clear is the international attitude of the Italian national hero and popular leader who has become one of the significant personalities of the world revolutionary movement. 5 illus., map, 23 notes. 1830's-82

2439. Bourlanges, Angéline. GARIBALDI, L'AVENTURIER DE LA RESURRECTION ITALIENNE: INTERVIEW DE MAX GALLO [Garibaldi, the adventurer of Italy's resurgence: interview with Max Gallo]. *Hist. Mag. [France] 1983 (35): 20-26.* Focuses on Max Gallo's view of Giuseppe Garibaldi's role in the unification of Italy from 1848-70 and Garibaldi's role as a popular hero. 1848-70

2440. Bovio, Oreste. L'ARTE MILITARE DI GARIBALDI [Garibaldi's military art]. *Riv. Militare [Italy] 1982 105(1): 41-44.* Analyzes the personality, ideas, and military strategy of Giuseppe Garibaldi. ca 1860

2441. Caratti, Lorenzo. UN CURIOSO COLLEGAMENTO CHIAVARESE FRA LA FAMIGLIA DI GIUSEPPE GARIBALDI E QUELLA DI GIUSEPPE MAZZINI [A curious Chiavarese relationship between the family of Giuseppe Garibaldi and that of Giuseppe Mazzini]. *Rassegna Storica del Risorgimento [Italy] 1982 69(1): 8-14.* Studies the relationship between the ancestors of Giuseppe Garibaldi and those of Giuseppe Mazzini at Chiavari, Italy, 1736-76. Both families lived within the confines of St. John the Baptist Parish, Chiavari. The fathers of the two heroes may have known each other. Primary sources, including archival material from the archives of St. John the Baptist Parish, Chiavari; 6 notes, 3 appendixes. 1736-76

2442. Caratti, L. LA GENEALOGIA DI GIUSEPPE GARIBALDI [The genealogy of Giuseppe Garibaldi]. *Rassegna Storica del Risorgimento [Italy] 1979 66(4): 415-453.* Detailed study of the genealogy of Giuseppe Garibaldi. The first mention of the Garibaldis in Nice is the record of his parents' marriage, which occurred in 1794, in the parish of St. Martin's. The parish records of St. John the Baptist, in Chiavari near Genoa, contain records of Garibaldi's forebears from 1610 and shed light on family names, professions and status, and religious interests. Appendix with reproduction of relevant documents. 1610-1794

2443. Davis, John A. GARIBALDI AND ENGLAND. *Hist. Today [Great Britain] 1982 32(Dec): 21-26.* After his successes in South America, Italy, and France, Giuseppe Garibaldi became a hero in England for his idealism, liberalism, and humanism; above all he represented political change. 1860's

2444. Deas, Malcolm. GARIBALDI AND SOUTH AMERICA. *Hist. Today [Great Britain] 1982 32(Dec): 16-21.* Despite his lack of political sophistication, Giuseppe Garibaldi's flamboyance and elan were reflected in his 12 years of freedom fighting in South America that preceded his Italian campaigns. 1835-48

2445. DellaPeruta, Franco. GARIBALDI TRA MITO E POLITICA [Garbaldi between myth and politics]. *Studi Storici [Italy] 1982 23(1): 5-22.* Giuseppe Garibaldi had a more profound understanding of political forces in Italy than historians often credit him with. His political views became more clearly formulated after 1871. He supported universal suffrage for Italy, as well as decentralized administration, obligatory education for all children that was free and nonsectarian, fiscal reform, and the separation of Church and state. While members of the working class were not involved in his early efforts at unification, he came to see the importance of working-class living conditions. It was in this sense that he called himself a socialist. Primary sources; 59 notes. 1848-70

2446. Garrone, Alessandro Galante. GARIBALDI POLITICO E L'ITALIA GARIBALDINA [Garibaldi as politician and Garibaldian Italy]. *Rassegna degli Archivi de Stato [Italy] 1982 42(2-3): 225-239.* After the conquest of Sicily Garibaldi passed into legend, and many historians ignore his later career, but Garibaldi as a politician played an important role in the joining together of various democratic factions. From 1860 to his death in 1882, he was in contact with Italian and European leaders. His own political following in Italy was based largely in the cities, and Garibaldian politicians were influential after his death. Nevertheless, his political ideas were rudimentary, assuming that government should be by "honest people" and a "human and noble *[gentile]* dictator." Secondary sources; 15 notes. 1860-98

2447. LaSalvia, Sergio. LE "VITE" DI GARIBALDI [The "lives" of Garibaldi]. *Rassegna degli Archivi de Stato [Italy] 1982 42(2-3): 320-359.* Reviews the sources and historiographical works on Giuseppe Garibaldi, which have produced varied images of his life. Biblio. 1848-1932

2448. Luciolli, Mario. GARIBALDI: ENTRE LE SCYLLA DE L'IDEALISME ET LE CHARYBDE DES REALITES [Garibaldi: between the Scylla of idealism and the Charybdis of realities]. *Rev. des Deux Mondes [France] 1982 (10): 45-57.* Profiles the life, political ideologies, and accomplishments of Giuseppe Garibaldi; describes his influence on modern Italian politics. 19c-20c

2449. Nevler, V. E. DZHUZEPPE GARIBAL'DI—BORETS ZA SVOBODU NARODOV I MIR [Giuseppe Garibaldi—a great fighter for people's freedom and peace]. *Voprosy Istorii [USSR] 1983 (7): 96-106.* From his youth, Giuseppe Garibaldi was a consistent supporter of people's struggle for freedom and independence. He hated war and often said that had it not been for people's sufferings he would never have taken up arms. An ardent supporter of the 1st International, he emphasized the significance of its orientation toward friendship between peoples and against militarism. He exposed the predatory colonialist policy of the capitalist powers. 1830's-82

2450. Pozzani, Silvio. GARIBALDI E LA GRECIA MODERNA [Garibaldi and modern Greece]. *Risorgimento [Italy] 1982 34(3): 222-226.* Garibaldi came in contact with Greece as a young seaman when his merchant ship was captured by Greek pirates in 1827 and again in 1832. He was fascinated by the struggle of the Greeks against the Ottoman Empire and expressed his admiration for them on several occasions. Reprints some of his letters to Greek newspapers and associations. Text of 6 letters. 1827-32

2451. Ridley, Jasper. IL MITO DI GARIBALDI IN INGHILTERRA E LA VISITA DEL 1864 [The myth of Garibaldi in England and the 1864 visit]. *Rassegna degli Archivi de Stato [Italy] 1982 42(2-3): 270-284.* The contacts of Giuseppe Garibaldi with the British began when he was fighting with the Liberals of Uruguay, supported by Great Britain, against Argentina. His talents made a strong impression on the British naval command, but he did not gain notoriety in Great Britain until his defense of the Roman Republic in 1849 against French forces—over which British public opinion was split, hating the French and the papacy but fearing "socialism." In 1864, after his successful Sicilian expedition of 1860, Garibaldi visited Great Britain, invited by the Duke of Sutherland, and was feted by the nobility and government leaders. A meeting with exiled radicals, including Giuseppe Mazzini, was cancelled for "reasons of health," thus causing a rift with the Mazzinians. 1839-64

2452. Villari, Rosario. LA PREFIGURAZIONE POLITICA DEL GIUDIZIO STORICO SU GARIBALDI [The political prefiguration of the historical judgment on Garibaldi]. *Studi Storici [Italy] 1982 23(2): 261-266.* Giuseppe Garibaldi exercised significant political leadership in Italy in the decade following unification, 1861-70. His efforts to resist demobilization of his militia in 1861, his spectacular reception in London in 1864, and his work in the electoral campaign of 1867 indicate his political influence. He allied himself politically with the socialists, since he saw their efforts as enhancing prospects for democracy in Italy and in all Europe. 1861-70

2453. Vuilleumier, Marc. EN MARGE D'UN CENTENAIRE: GARIBALDI A GENEVE [On the 100th anniversary: Garibaldi in Geneva]. *Mus. de Genève [Switzerland] 1982 (230): 9-12.* Describes the impact of Giuseppe Garibaldi on Swiss nationalism from his arrival in Geneva in 1867 to his death in 1882, and his status as a popular hero. 1867-82

2454. Zancardi, Pietro. LE OPERAZIONI NAVALI DI GIUSEPPE GARIBALDI NEL SUD AMERICA [Garibaldi's naval operations in South America]. *Riv. Marittima [Italy] 1982 115(10): 15-38.* Recalls the period spent by Giuseppe Garibaldi in South America, particularly naval and military actions in service of Rio Grande do Sul and Uruguay. 1836-48

Garibaldi, Ricciotti

2455. Guida, Francesco. RICCIOTTI GARIBALDI E IL MOVIMENTO NAZIONALE ALBANESE [Ricciotti Garibaldi and the Albanian national movement]. *Arch. Storico Italiano [Italy] 1981 139(1): 97-138.* Ricciotti Garibaldi (1847-1924), Giuseppe's son, fought for the independence of the Balkans in 1867 in Crete, in 1897 in Greece, and in 1912 in Epirus. Manlio Bannici, an Italo-Albanian journalist, convinced him to join the movement for Albanian independence. Ricciotti Garibaldi was at the head of the Consiglio Albanese d'Italia [Italian Albanian Council] in 1904. He thought the cause of Albania was connected with that of the Italians still under the rule of Austria-Hungary. Ricciotti Garibaldi's activity was unsuccessful due to the antagonism of other groups of Italo-Albanians. Based on Ricciotti's papers in the Central Museum of the Risorgimento, Rome; 128 notes. 1867-1912

Garnett, Angelica

2456. Garnett, Angelica. LIFE AT CHARLESTON. *Southwest Review 1985 70(2): 160-172.* Angelica Garnett, daughter of Vanessa Bell, remembers her early life amidst the Bloomsbury literary circle at Charleston, the country home of Clive and Vanessa Bell (in Sussex, England), from the end of World War I to the beginning of World War II. 1909-85

Garth, Samuel

2457. Booth, C. C. SIR SAMUEL GARTH, F.R.S.: THE DISPENSARY POET. *Notes and Records of the Royal Society of London [Great Britain] 1986 40(2): 125-146.* Biographical sketch of the doctor who authored *The Dispensary* (1699), intended as a healing link between physicians and apothecaries. The satiric poem was an immediate success and established Garth as an unrivaled wit in late 17th-century London. A member of the Kit-Kat Club and ardent Whig, Garth was knighted by George I and made physician-in-ordinary to the king. He continued to write and translate until his death at age 59. 59 notes. 1680's-1719

Garvey, Marcus

2458. Ashdown, Peter. MARCUS GARVEY, THE UNIA AND THE BLACK CAUSE IN BRITISH HONDURAS, 1914-1949. *J. of Caribbean Hist. [Barbados] 1981 15: 41-55.* After 1914, owing in part to the influence of Marcus Garvey, race consciousness, especially on the part of black creoles, increased in British Honduras, now Belize. His Universal Negro Improvement Association (UNIA) Party was an important anti-British force in the colony in the 1920's. Eventually, however, it lost importance to the more popular multiethnic Peoples United Party (PUP). Primary sources; 80 notes. 1914-49

2459. Puig López, Zenaida and Torres Beltrán, Hilda. MARCUS GARVEY: PRIMER HEROE NACIONAL DE JAMAICA [Marcus Garvey: first national hero of Jamaica]. *U. de La Habana [Cuba] 1982 (217): 184-193.* Describes the life of Marcus Garvey and his struggles in the early 20th century to improve conditions for blacks in Jamaica and other parts of the world. 1887-1940

Garvin, James Louis

2460. Franke, Reiner. REVISION UND KRIEG: JAMES LOUIS GARVIN UND DER POLITISCHE JOURNALISMUS [Revisionism and war: James Louis Garvin and political journalism]. *Bohemia [West Germany] 1982 23(1): 126-138.* James Louis Garvin (1868-1947) edited the Liberal London journal *The Observer* between 1908 and 1942 and shaped its revisionist editorial policy during the interwar period. His conviction that the punitive character of the Paris peace treaties was encouraging future wars led him to an indulgent attitude toward German and even Nazi revisionism. Only after March 1939 did his disillusionment with Hitler allow him to give free rein to his antifascism. Based on *The Observer;* 52 notes. 1919-39

Gascoigne, George

2461. Shore, David R. WHYTHORNE'S *AUTOBIOGRAPHY* AND THE GENESIS OF GASCOIGNE'S *MASTER F.J.* *J. of Medieval and Renaissance Studies 1982 12(2): 159-178.* George Gascoigne's *Adventures of Master F.J.* which appeared in his *Hundreth Sundrie Flowres* (1573), and Thomas Whythorne's *Autobiography* (ca. 1576), were two collections of poems framed by narrative which marked a new age of psychological, autobiographical writing. Both works have been assessed by critics outside of their historical context, and are "inextricably interwoven with the fabric of day-to-day existence." Fascinated by the structure of personal experience, they tried to find coherence in the events of their lives. The similarities and differences of the two writings are compared, and they are related to the poetical and prose works of Edmund Spenser and Sir Philip Sidney, and to the autobiographical traditions in Italy, Germany, and the Low Countries. Based on the original writings and contemporary literary criticism; 43 notes. 1560-79

Gąsiorowska, Natalia

2462. Gąsiorowska, Natalia. WSPOMNIENIA Z OBOZU HITLEROWESKIEGO W BERLINIE I DROGI POWROTNEJ [Reminiscences about a Nazi camp in Berlin and the return journey]. *Kwartalnik Hist. [Poland] 1981 88(3): 753-760.* The late Natalia Gąsiorowska, professor of economic history in Poland, was deported to Berlin during the Warsaw Uprising in August 1944 and sent as a forced laborer to a factory. A fragment of her memoirs for April and May 1945 covers her return journey on foot with a small group of Polish women. The journey led them through burned or abandoned German villages toward the River Odra and Warsaw. 1945

Gaskoin, John Samuel

2463. Lingwood, P. F. and McMillan, N. F. THE CONCHOLOGIST JOHN SAMUEL GASKOIN (1790-1858)—HIS LIFE, WORK AND COLLECTIONS. *Arch. of Natural Hist. [Great Britain] 1981 10(2): 347-358.* A biography of the previously neglected English conchologist John Samuel Gaskoin (1790-1858) is presented, including details of his shell collection and its subequent dispersal by gift and purchase. Gaskoin lived during the golden age of shell collecting and was personally acquainted with many of its leading practitioners. He described more than 50 new species and varieties of marine and terrestrial gastropods. Table, 3 fig., 41 notes, biblio. 1790-1858

Gasperoni, Ermenegildo

2464. Gasperoni, Ermenegildo. V AVANGARDE BOR'BY TRUDIASHCHIKHSIA SAN'MARINO [In the vanguard of the struggle of the workers of San Marino]. *Voprosy Istorii KPSS [USSR] 1981 (8): 103-106.* Ermenegildo Gasperoni, President of the Communist Party of San Marino, recalls his own personal struggle as a Communist and the formation and development of his party. Gasperoni left San Marino in 1924 and spent the next 16 years in contact with Communist organizations throughout Europe, including a lengthy period with the international brigades during the Spanish civil war. He returned to San

Marino in 1940 with the intention of establishing a Communist Party there. A San Marino section of the Italian Communist Party had been set up in 1921, but it was not until after Gasperoni's return that an independent party was set up in the republic on 7 July 1941. The Party had 50 activists by 1944 and was the only political party in San Marino. It became legal in 1945, and by 1957 more than one in 10 of the republic's 14,000 population were members. The San Marino Communist Party became the party of government in the elections of 1978. 1924-78

Gassner, Andreas and Ferdinand

2465. Schallert, Elmar. PFARRER FERDINAND GASSNER VON NENZING: EIN BEITRAG ZUR PFARRGESCHICHTE IN DER MITTE DES 18. JAHRHUNDERTS [Pastor Ferdinand Gassner of Nenzing: a contribution to the history of pastors in the middle of the 18th century]. *Montfort [Austria] 1984 36(1): 46-55.* Chronicles the life and work of Pastor Ferdinand Gassner (1739-70), whose remains were discovered in 1982 under the floor of the St. Mauritius church in Nenzing during its renovation. Publishes information from the tax records of the community of Nenzing on the entire property and the financial position of Andreas Gassner, Ferdinand's father. 1749-70

Gast, John

2466. Linebaugh, Peter. LABOUR HISTORY WITHOUT THE LABOUR PROCESS: A NOTE ON JOHN GAST AND HIS TIMES. *Social Hist. [Great Britain] 1982 7(3): 319-328.* Comments on issues arising from Iorwerth Prothero's *Artisans and Politics in Early Nineteenth-Century London: John Gast and His Times* (1979), a biography of the Thames shipwright who was one of the most indefatigable trade unionists and organizer of artisans of his age. John Gast's career covers the period when revolutionary changes were introduced in the labor process of shipbuilding, and wages were imposed as the only form of workers' remuneration. His genius consisted not in opposing these measures, but in adapting appropriate forms of struggle for the new situation. His significance cannot therefore be understood without analyzing the labor process as the starting point of politics or through a social history separated from labor history. Based on printed sources and secondary works; biblio. 1800-37

Gates, John

2467. Prosad Sil, Narasingha. THE RISE AND FALL OF SIR JOHN GATES. *Hist. J. [Great Britain] 1981 24(4): 929-943.* A biographical sketch of Sir John Gates (1504-53). Gates trained as a lawyer at Lincoln's Inn and later moved to a minor position in Henry VII's household and was promoted to the king's privy chamber in 1542. Under Edward VI, Gates became a commissioner of the peace and a member of Parliament, as well as a privy councillor. He was mainly concerned with revenue work, and although he served the crown well in this role, he became a supporter of Lady Jane Grey in an attempt to prevent Mary Tudor's accession to the throne after Edward's death. Gates was executed in 1553. 89 notes. 1504-53

Gatti, Armand

2468. Pytlinski, Bonnie Laurie. "Armand Gatti and Political Trends in French Theater under De Gaulle (1958-1978)." U. of Florida 1982. 223 pp. *DAI 1983 44(2): 501-A.* DA8313677 1958-70's

Gaubert, Philippe

2469. Fischer, Penelope Ann Peterson. "Philippe Gaubert (1879-1941): His Life and Contributions as Flutist, Editor, Teacher, Conductor, and Composer." U. of Maryland 1982. 263 pp. *DAI 1984 44(8): 2286-A.* DA8323616 1893-1940

Gauguin, Paul

2470. Nantet, Bernard. GAUGUIN ET LE REVE TAHITIEN [Gauguin and the dream of Tahiti]. *Histoire [France] 1984 (64): 52-64.* Describes the career of the French painter Paul Gauguin, his journeys to the Antipodes and colonialism in Tahiti during the late 19th and early 20th centuries. 1860-1903

Gavazzi, Alessandro

2471. Paz, D. G. APOSTATE PRIESTS AND VICTORIAN RELIGIOUS TURMOIL: GAVAZZI, ACHILLI, CONNELLY. *Proceedings of the South Carolina Historical Association 1985: 57-69.* 1840's-60's
*For abstract see **Achilli, Giacinto***

Gavin, Hector

2472. Spriggs, Edmund Anthony. HECTOR GAVIN, MD, FRCSE (1815-1855)—HIS LIFE, HIS WORK FOR THE SANITARY MOVEMENT, AND HIS ACCIDENTAL DEATH IN THE CRIMEA. *Medical History [Great Britain] 1984 28(3): 283-292.* Educated at Edinburgh, Hector Gavin moved to London in 1838 and bought a medical practice. His fame comes from involvement in the sanitary movement of the 1840's. He wrote for and edited the *Journal of Public Health* and worked to get legislative action mandating sanitary improvements in London. When the General Board of Health was established in 1848, Gavin became its secretary. He was then appointed a medical commissioner to the British West Indies and sailed to Barbados in 1851. After much travel and work, he was recalled to England and worked at Newcastle and Dundee during the 1853 cholera epidemic. His next assignment was as sanitary commissioner in the Crimea, and his work, along with that of the other commissioners, won high praise from Florence Nightingale. Garvin was killed by the accidental discharge of a pistol in 1855. Based on contemporary publications and a biographical sketch written by Gavin's father; 40 notes. 1834-55

Gavrilenko, Alexander P.

2473. Tselikov, A. I. and Shinkarevich, Iu. P. OSNOVOPOLOZHNIK TEKHNOLOGICHESKOI SHKOLY MVTU (O PERVOM VYBORNOM DIREKTORE MVTU A.P. GAVRILENKO) [The founder of the study of technology at the Moscow Higher Technical College: A. P. Gavrilenko, the first elected director]. *Voprosy Istorii Estestvoznaniia i Tekhniki [USSR] 1984 (2): 85-94.* Describes the development of Russian engineering and the role in it of Alexander P. Gavrilenko (1861-1914), the founder of one of the best courses for engineers and the author of a major textbook on the subject. Gavrilenko taught at the Moscow Higher Technical College from 1888, and in 1905 was elected director. Secondary sources. 1890's-1914

Gay, Francisque

2474. Poupard, Paul. UN PIONNIER DU CATHOLICISME SOCIAL: FRANCISQUE GAY [Francisque Gay: a pioneer of social Catholicism]. *Revue des Deux Mondes [France] 1985 (8): 370-373.* Highlights the career achievements of Francisque Gay as publisher, editor, and statesman, and pays tribute to the religious thought of this militant advocate of social Catholicism. ca 1910-48

Gay-Lussac, Joseph Louis

2475. —. *Gay-Lussac: La Carrière et l'Oeuvre d'un Chimiste Français durant la Première Moitié du XIXe Siècle* [Joseph Louis Gay-Lussac: the career and work of a French chemist in the first half of the 19th century]. (Actes du Colloque Gay-Lussac, 11-13 Décembre 1978.) Palaiseau, France: Ecole Polytechnique, 1980. 290 pp. 1800-50

Gébelin, Antoine Court de

2476. Kirsop, Wallace. CULTURAL NETWORKS IN PRE-REVOLUTIONARY FRANCE: SOME REFLEXIONS ON THE CASE OF ANTOINE COURT DE GÉBELIN. *Australian J. of French Studies [Australia] 1981 18(3): 231-247.* Discusses the career of Antoine Court de Gébelin (1724?-84), scholar, buyer of books and user of libraries, founder of the Musée de Paris, freemason, and subscription publisher. 1750-84

Gellée, Claude

2477. Chanteloup, Lucien. LE LORRAIN: UN PEINTRE A LA DECOUVERTE DU SOLEIL [Lorrain: a painter discovering the sun]. *Hist. Mag. [France] 1983 (38): 82-88.* A narration, with illustrations, of the life and career of French painter, Claude Gellée, named "Le Lorrain" (1600-82), stressing this artist's great knowledge of solar lights and colors which made him the precursor of the romantic and impressionist painters. 17c

2478. Sylvestre, Michel. CLAUDE GELLEE ENTRE CHAMAGNE ET ROME: NOUVEAUX DOCUMENTS SUR LE PEINTRE ET SA FAMILLE D'APRES LES ARCHIVES LORRAINES [Claude Gellée between Chamagne and Rome: new documents concerning the painter and his family according to Lorraine archives]. *Mélanges de l'Ecole Française de Rome. Moyen Age-Temps Modernes [Italy] 1982 94(2): 929-947.* Describes the influence of customs and politics in Lorraine on the painting of Gellée; traces Gellée's genealogy; and discusses his work in Rome. 17c

Géminard, Théodore

2479. Géminard, Lucien and Robert, Daniel. SOUVENIRS DU PASTEUR THEODORE GEMINARD (1807-1854) [Memoirs of Pastor Théodore Géminard (1807-54)]. *Bull. de la Soc. de l'Hist. du Protestantisme Français [France] 1982 128(3): 371-388.* Théodore Géminard was born on 1 June 1807 near Saint-André de Valborgne and died on 15 July 1854 in Cassagnos, both in the Cévennes. The text of a memoir written by Pastor Géminard and provided by his great-grandson, Lucien Géminard, is sketchy, but contains some details of the pastor's travels, his education, his marriage, his relatives, the birth of his children, and the death of his wife. Some notes about his finances are included. Based on the memoir and notes; 70 notes, 2 maps, 5 appendixes. 1820's-54

Generalić, Ivan

2480. Zlydneva, N. TVORCHESTO IVANA GENERALICHA [Creativity of Ivan Generalić]. *Sovetskoe Slavianovedenie [USSR] 1982 (4): 71-81.* Ivan Generalić (b. 1914), a shepherd boy from the Croat village of Hlebine, was early influenced by another native artist of Hlebine, the famous Krsto Hegedušić. Generalić, a *naif,* has become during his long life the symbol and apostle of Yugoslav primitives; his village, like others later, became the center of an art based on the peasant and the village. Based on Soviet and Yugoslavian sources. 1930-60

Genet, Jean

2481. Sandarg, Robert. THE POLITICS OF JEAN GENET. *Res. Studies 1982 50(3-4): 111-118.* Describes French novelist, poet, and playwright Jean Genet's political activism from 1968-77 and his dream of destroying the Western establishment. 1968-77

Gennadios, Geōrgios

2482. Mougogiannēs, Giannēs G. GEŌRGIOS GENNADIOS [Geōrgios Gennadios]. *Ēpeirōtikē Hestia [Greece] 1984 (390-392): 511-513.* Geōrgios Gennadios (d. 1854) lost his father at an early age but with the help of his uncle and a patron obtained a good education, capped with two years at Leipzig, where he studied philology. After teaching in Greek communities in Bucharest and Odessa, he returned to Greece in the 1820's to take part in the revolution. After the war he was instrumental in helping to establish the country's educational system. 1800's-54

Gennep, Arnold van

2483. Zumwalt, Rosemary. ARNOLD VAN GENNEP: THE HERMIT OF BOURG-LA-REINE. *Am. Anthrop. 1982 84(2): 299-313.* Biography of French folklorist and ethnologist Arnold van Gennep (1873-1957), a prolific writer and activist in many professional organizations, who was never given the recognition he deserved by the French academic community. 1873-1957

Gennings, St. Edmund

2484. Rogers, David. A NOTE ON THE *LIFE* OF ST EDMUND GENNINGS. *Recusant History [Great Britain] 1984 17(1): 92-95.* Traces the literary history and the publication history of the biography of St. Edmund Gennings (d. 1591), a priest of the Catholic Church, martyred in London. 14 notes. 16c-1971

Gentz, Friedrich von

2485. Forsyth, Murray. FRIEDRICH VON GENTZ: AN ASSESSMENT. *Studies in Hist. and Pol. [Canada] 1981-82 2(2): 127-155.* Although Friedrich von Gentz (1764-1832) was a major critic of the French Revolution, he is not well known. He was also a political associate of Metternich at the Congress of Vienna and in post-Napoleonic era diplomacy. Although often called a mere publicist, Gentz was a serious political writer whose pen but not opinions could be hired. He was a capable political analyst and a keen observer of events. He was also one of the strongest early 19th-century advocates of a European point of view. Based on contemporary publications and memoirs; 53 notes. 1792-1832

George III

2486. Christie, Ian R. GEORGE III AND THE HISTORIANS—THIRTY YEARS ON. *History [Great Britain] 1986 71(232): 205-221.* Reappraises the state of historical scholarship relating to the early years of King George III's reign since the publication of G. Herbert Butterfield's *George III and the Historians* (London: Collins, 1957). What emerges from recent biographical writing is a portrait of a shrewd, cultivated, and well-meaning individual who was widely read and well informed about English history and constitutional law. He suffered not from insanity but from porphyria, a genetic illness which produces temporary mental disability in the form of delirium. Contrary to earlier findings, George III did not bend constitutional rules nor did he pursue policies leading to the subversion of British and colonial liberties. The kingship continued to function under George III very much in the same way as under his grandfather, George II. 45 notes. 1760-84

Georgy, Andreas

2487. Liechty, Daniel. ANDREAS FISCHER: A CASE OF MISTAKEN IDENTITY. *Archiv für Reformationsgeschichte [West Germany] 1985 76: 299-304.* Refutes Wacław Urban's identification of Andreas Georgy of Kremnitz, an early leader of the Reformation in Slovakia, with Andreas Fischer, between 1528 and 1540 an Anabaptist preacher in Silesia, Moravia, and Slovakia. Comparison of the handwriting of letters, signed in 1534 by "Andreas Vischer" and by "Andreas Cremniciensis" render their identity impossible. 41 notes. German summary. 1493-1540's

Géraldy, Paul

2488. Escoube, Pierre. PAUL GÉRALDY [Paul Géraldy]. *Rev. des Deux Mondes [France] 1983 (4): 113-116.* Reviews the work of French poet and playwright Paul Géraldy (1885-1983), a lucid and disenchanted moralist, who has remained well known for his poetic *Toi et Moi* (1913). ca 1908-83

Gérardot, Paul

2489. Christienne, Charles. UN CHEF D'ETAT-MAJOR GENERAL DE L'ARMEE DE L'AIR—LE GENERAL GERARDOT [General Gérardot: a chief of the air force general staff]. *Rev. Hist. des Armées [France] 1982 (3): 96-101.* Imbued with a life-long passion for aviation, General Paul Gérardot (1898-1980) served in the infantry in World War I. His air force career, begun in 1921, was noteworthy for a number of pioneering long-distance flights. In World War II, he headed the French section of the 13th US Air Tactical Command and then became commander of the 1st French Air Corps. After the war ended, he became chief of the air force general staff and later director of the air force training center. He was the author of numerous articles in which he upheld the strategic independence and primacy of the air force. Based partly on air force archives and personal acquaintance with General Gérardot; 5 photos. 1916-49

Gerdzhikov, Mikhail

2490. Bukovinova, Vida. MIKHAIL GERDZHIKOV I NATSIONALNOOSVOBODITELNOTO DVIZHENIE V ODRINSKA TRAKIIA (1902-1903 G.) [Mikhail Gerdzhikov and the national liberation movement in Adrianopolitan Thrace, 1902-03]. *Istoricheski Pregled [Bulgaria] 1983 39(3): 81-94.* Mikhail Gerdzhikov (1877-1947) was a friend of Gotse Delchev and a member of the Internal Macedonian Revolutionary Movement in the Adrianopolitan Thrace region. In April 1902 he hosted a meeting of the Central Committee of the organization in Plovdiv and undertook to popularize the organization with the masses, especially the young. He created an effective system of local committees. At a meeting of the organization in Plovdiv on 28 June 1903 he defended plans for the anti-Turkish uprising. After the failure of the uprising on 19 August 1903 he fled to Western Europe. Based on material on the 1903 uprising in the Bulgarian National Library and in the State Regional Archive in Burgas; 72 notes. 1902-03

Gerlach, Jan

2491. Pawlak, Marian. JAN GERLACH (1893-1983) [Jan Gerlach (1893-1983)]. *Zapiski Historyczne [Poland] 1983 48(4): 183-185.* An obituary of a Polish historian, teacher, and scholar, whose major works concern Polish peasants and assemblies in western Prussia, 15th-18th centuries. 1923-83

Gerov, Naiden

2492. Peneva, N. DVE NEIZVESTNI PISMA NA IVANA BOTEVA PETKOVA DO NAIDEN GEROV [Two newly discovered letters from Ivana Boteva Petkova to Naiden Gerov]. *Izvestiia na Narodnata Biblioteka "Kiril i Metodii" [Bulgaria] 1983 18: 385-389.* Presents two letters which Ivana Boteva Petkova wrote to Naiden Gerov, the Russian consul in Plovdiv, in 1871 and 1874. They show that Gerov and the recently deceased Bot'o Botev had been friends. 1871-74

Gervinus, Georg Gottfried

2493. Schmidt, Siegfried. GEORG GOTTFRIED GERVINUS NACH 1848/49: EINE DENKSCHRIFT VON 1851 ZU DEN SCHLUSSFOLGERUNGEN AUS DER REVOLUTION [Georg Gottfried Gervinus after 1848-49: a memorandum of 1851 on the consequences of the revolution]. *Zeitschrift für Geschichtswissenschaft [East Germany] 1984 32(8): 713-717.* Georg Gottfried Gervinus, a literary historian, founded the liberal newspaper *Deutsche Zeitung* and ran it until 1848, when he became a member of the Frankfurt parliament. After the Revolution of 1848 he abandoned his liberal principles and became a Republican, advocating union with petit bourgeois democracy. The memorandum shows the concerted efforts of the Left to organize political opposition to the government in the 1850's. Based on the Zentrales Staatsarchiv in Potsdam Nachlass Mathy no. 98 B1 245f.; 16 notes. 1840's-50's

Getman, Andrei L.

2494. Gusakovski, I. GENERAL ARMII A. L. GETMAN [Army General A. L. Getman]. *Voenno-Istoricheskii Zhurnal [USSR] 1983 (10): 94-96.* A brief biography of Soviet General Andrei L. Getman (b. 1903), detailing his career in the army. He joined in 1924 in his native Ukraine and rose to lead tank corps in World War II. During the 1970's he led the Soviet civil defense organization Voluntary Society for Cooperation with the Army, Air Force, and Navy (DOSAAF). Photo, note. 1903-83

Geva, Eli

2495. Morris, Benny. ELI GEVA—THE COLONEL WHO SAID "NO." *Present Tense 1984 11(2): 10-13.* A short biography of Eli Geva, who became a symbol for the widespread disaffection with the war when, as a colonel in the Israel Defense Forces, he preferred to be relieved of his command and fight as a private rather than go into the Lebanese capital with his troops. 1982

Ghalbūn family

2496. BinYunis, Mukhtar al-Hadi. ASAL AL-GHALĀBINAH WA-ĀTHĀRUHUM AL-'ILMĪYAH [The Ghalbūn family and their learned works]. *Majallat al-Buhūth al-Tārīkhīya [Libya] 1982 4(1): 7-37.* Shaykh Muhammad ibn Khalīl ibn Ghalbūn, the author of the first general history of Tripoli, *Al-Tadhkar,* in 1717, was a member of the Benī Sālim tribe, which settled in Libya in the 14th century. He was a learned religious jurist who founded a mosque school in Misurata. Two works on astronomy and inheritance law previously attributed to him were composed by his grandson Muhammad ibn Khalīl ibn Muhammad ibn Khalīl ibn Ghalbūn, jurist active in the 1790's. A third Muhammad ibn Ghalbūn ibn Khalīl, a 19th-century jurist, wrote various works, of which two verse compositions remain. The three manuscripts of *Al-Tadhkar,* which has been translated into Turkish and Italian, are compared. Manuscripts and original sources; fig., 43 notes. 18c-19c

Gheorghiu-Dej, Gheorghe

2497. Antoniuk, D. I. VIDNYI POLITICHESKII I GOSUDARSTVENNYI DEIATEL' RUMYNII [An eminent politician and statesman from Romania]. *Voprosy Istorii KPSS [USSR] 1981 (11): 89-92.* In honor of the 80th anniversary of the birth of Gheorghe Gheorghiu-Dej, describes his working career from the age of 11, the development of his political ideas, his involvement in the Communist Party, his activity during World War II and efforts in the postwar years, and his work for friendship and coordination with the USSR. 24 notes. 1901-76

Gherardi, Antonio

2498. Pickrel, Thomas Carl. "Antonio Gherardi, Painter and Architect of the Late Baroque in Rome." U. of Kansas 1981. 493 pp. *DAI 1982 42(7): 2912-A.* 8128790 17c

Ghica, Gheorghe

2499. Cernovodeanu, Paul. ŞTIRI PRIVITOARE LA GHEORGHE GHICA VODĂ AL MOLDOVEI (1658-1659) ŞI LA FAMILIA SA (II) [Information on Gheorghe Ghica, Voivode of Moldavia, 1658-59, and his family. Part 2]. *Anuarul Institutului de Istorie şi Arheologie "A. D. Xenopol" [Romania] 1983 20: 121-133.* Ruler of Moldavia in 1658, of Wallachia in 1659, Gheorghe Ghica was banished to Constantinople, where he died. He had married Ursu, daughter of a boyar in modest circumstances. Contemporary legal documents provide abundant information about the later history of the family. The direct line from Gheorghe died out, but through his son by an earlier liaison the family retained its prominence. Primary sources; 46 notes. 1658-1777

Ghose, Aurobindo

2500. Sahadat, John. A PARADIGM OF RELIGIOUS CONSCIOUSNESS IN INDIAN NATIONALISM. *Asian Profile [Hong Kong] 1982 10(5): 485-493.* Attempts to show how the Indian revolutionary-turned-philosopher and yogi Aurobindo Ghose (1872-1950) interpreted his religious experience and how he used religious symbolism to work out a paradigm of an organic society and to give new meaning and direction to Indian nationalism. Starting from the principle of the one indivisible divinity in every individual human being, he created a divine image of Mother India and transformed the struggle for political freedom into a religious sacrifice. 22 notes. 1890's-1950

Giannone, Pietro

2501. Stone, Harold. PIETRO GIANNONE. *American Scholar 1984-85 54(1): 111-118.* Pietro Giannone (1676-1748) was a lawyer in Naples when he wrote *Istoria Civile del Regno di Napoli,* which interpreted the influence of the Vatican on Neapolitan history in a way that angered the Catholic Church. Giannone was forced to flee Naples, and he spent the rest of his life writing further historical works in exile and, for the last 12 years of his life, in prison. 1690's-1748

Gibb, Margaret Hunter

2502. —. MARGARET HUNTER GIBB OBE. *Bulletin of the Society for the Study of Labour History [Great Britain] 1984 (49): 4.* An obituary notice for the British socialist Margaret Hunter Gibb (1893-1984) who was a stalwart of the North East Group of the Society for the Study of Labour History. 1893-1984

Gibbon, Charles

2503. Shepard, Douglas H. CHARLES GIBBON AND CHARLES OBBIGN: AN IDENTITY. *Bull. of Res. in the Humanities 1982 85(3): 352-360.* A comparison of some of their work and a review of the life of Victorian English novelist Charles Gibbon reveals that author Charles Obbign was the same man. 1862-90

Gibbon, Edward

2504. Turnbull, Paul. THE "SUPPOSED INFIDELITY" OF EDWARD GIBBON. *Hist. J. [Great Britain] 1982 25(1): 23-41.* Examines Edward Gibbon's youthful conversion to Catholicism in 1753, his later accounts of it, and other biographical information from the last years of his life, 1789-93, in order to show some of the complexity of his attitude to religion. The evidence shows him as critical of many traditional Christian beliefs and practices, but deeply attracted to certain spiritual elements of Christianity, and with ambivalent feelings about other traditional doctrines and rituals. The traditional assumption that Gibbon was a philosophical modern pagan is thoroughly unsettled by this material. Based on the Gibbon papers in the British Library Add. Mss., and printed sources; 72 notes. 1753-93

Gibbons, Grinling

2505. Loeber, Rolf. ARNOLD QUELLIN'S AND GRINLING GIBBONS'S MONUMENTS FOR ANGLO-IRISH PATRONS. *Studies [Ireland] 1983 72(285): 84-101.* Provides a detailed study of six funerary monuments erected for the 17th-century Anglo-Irish families by Arnold Quellin (1653-86), sculptor, and Grinling Gibbons, wood-carver (1648-1721). The article illuminates the obscure career of Quellin as tombmaker and Gibbons's flourishing practice in Ireland. Based on British Library manuscripts and secondary sources; 7 illus., table, 59 notes. 1670-85

Gibbons, Matthew John

2506. Adams, Michael. MATTHEW JOHN GIBBONS: PIONEER AND FIRST OWNER OF STANWELL PARK. *J. of the Royal Australian Hist. Soc. [Australia] 1983 68(4): 257-272.* Matthew John Gibbons (1765-1835) occupied Stanwell Park outside Sydney in 1824, and Governor Richard Bourke granted him title to the property in 1831. Prints a biography of Gibbons who migrated from England to Australia in 1791 as steward for Francis Gorse in the New South Wales Corps. The Gibbons family lived for some years in London, but returned to Australia. Stanwell Park was a reward for many years of minor service in the bureaucracy of the colony. 115 notes. 1792-1835

Gibbs, James

2507. Little, Bryan. JAMES GIBBS: ARCHITECT. *Hist. Today [Great Britain] 1982 32(Dec): 40-44.* James Gibbs, a Scottish architect with Jacobite sympathies, designed many public and college buildings as well as churches in 18th-century England despite political impediments to his career. 1709-54

Giddings, George

2508. Greene, David L. THE ENGLISH ORIGINS OF GEORGE GIDDINGS OF IPSWICH, MASSACHUSETTS. *New England Hist. and Geneal. Register 1981 135(Oct): 274-286.* The Giddings family genealogy, published in 1882 by Minot S. Giddings gave no clues to the origins of George Giddings who came to Ipswich in 1635 at age 25. A recent study of records in Bedfordshire, England has produced substantial evidence concerning his ancestry. The author makes a strong case for George Giddings, baptized at Clapham Parish, Bedford 24 September 1609, died at Ipswich 1 June 1676 being the same man. 16c-17c

Gide, André

2509. Braunstein, Philippe. CHARLES GIDE ET ANDRE GIDE: UN JEU DE REGARDS [Charles Gide and André Gide: a brief look]. *Communautés: Arch. de Sci. Sociales de la Coopération et du Développement* Describes the familial and literary ties between writer André Gide (1869-1951) and his uncle, economist Charles Gide (1847-1932). 1882-1951

2510. Grunewald, Michel, ed. ANDRE GIDE—KLAUS MANN: EIN BRIEFWECHSEL [André Gide-Klaus Mann: letters]. *Rev. d'Allemagne [France] 1982 14(4): 581-682.* 1926-49

*For abstract see **Mann, Klaus***

2511. Lottman, Herbert R. ANDRE GIDE'S RETURN: A CASE-STUDY IN LEFT-BANK POLITICS. *Encounter [Great Britain] 1982 58(1): 18-27.* Examines the changing attitude of André Gide (1869-1951) to the Bolshevik revolution in the USSR, focusing on his political and literary activities and travels during the 1930's and on his book dealing with the subject *Retour de l'URSS.* 1930's

2512. Marshall, W. J. ANDRE GIDE AND THE U.S.S.R.: A RE-APPRAISAL. *Australian J. of French Studies [Australia] 1983 20(1): 37-49.* Focuses on André Gide's Communist commitment during the 1930's and the questions he raised concerning the relationship between politics, society, the artist, the revolution, and dissent. 1930's

Gide, Charles

2513. Braunstein, Philippe. CHARLES GIDE ET ANDRE GIDE: UN JEU DE REGARDS [Charles Gide and André Gide: a brief look]. *Communautés: Arch. de Sci. Sociales de la Coopération et du Développement* 1882-1951

*For abstract see **Gide, André***

2514. Desroche, Henri. CHARLES GIDE ET SES TROIS CREATIVITES: COMMENTAIRES ADDITIFS [Charles Gide and his three areas of creativity: additional comments]. *Communautés: Arch. de Sci. Sociales de la Coopération et du Développement [France] 1982 (61): 27-45.* Recounts the visionary efforts of Charles Gide from 1882 to 1932 to unify and harmonize society both by cooperation among various socioeconomic strata and by religious ecumenism. 1882-1932

2515. Penin, Marc. LE CHAUD ET LE FROID: DEUX CHARLES GIDE [Hot and cold: two Charles Gides]. *Communautés: Arch. de Sci. Sociales de la Coopération et du Développement [France] 1982 (61): 8-26.* Describes the diverse qualities in the personality and writings of economist Charles Gide (1847-1932), which included, on the one hand, a pessimistic and stern moral outlook and, on the other, humor and a libertarian sense. 1847-1932

2516. Pénin, Marc. CHARLES GIDE, ECONOMISTE: POUR UN ACTION EN REHABILITATION [Charles Gide, economist: an effort in rehabilitation]. *Rev. d'Econ. Pol. [France] 1983 93(6): 816-846.* Reviews Gide's career as an economist from 1881-1932, and his pioneering work in social economics. 1881-1932

Gilbert, William Schwenck

2517. Holland, Diane Lynn. CELEBRATED, CULTIVATED, UNDERRATED? A PROFILE OF W. S. GILBERT. *British Heritage 1986 7(3): 67-74.* There is little substance to the myth that Sir William Schwenck Gilbert (1836-1911), the playwright and collaborator with Sir Arthur Sullivan, was a curmudgeon who disliked and was jealous of Sullivan. 1863-1906

Gillies, Thomas Bannatyne

2518. Gillies, Mary. THOMAS BANNATYNE GILLIES, 1828-1889. *Hist. J. [New Zealand] 1981 (39): 14-16.* Discusses the career of Thomas Bannatyne Gillies, cofounder of the Auckland Institute and Museum in New Zealand, superintendent of the province, and eventually judge on the Supreme Court. 1852-89

Gillman, Clement

2519. Hoyle, B. S. GILLMAN OF TANGANYIKA, 1882-1946: PIONEER GEOGRAPHER. *Geographical Journal [Great Britain] 1986 152(3): 354-366.* Clement Gillman (1882-1946) trained as an engineer and worked in German East Africa and in Tanganyika from 1905 to his death in 1946. He was distinguished not only as an engineer but also as a pioneer field scientist and advocate of modern geography. He was a constant traveler and a prolific writer. His numerous published papers and private diaries provide an insight into the foundations of East African geography and into the formative period when modern Tanzania was in the making. If, as is claimed, colonialism served primarily to reveal the problems of modern Africa rather than to solve them, Gillman was one of the instruments by which those problems were brought to light and first understood. 1905-46

Gilpin, Joshua

2520. Bentley, G. E., Jr. THE WAY OF A PAPERMAKER WITH A POET: JOSHUA GILPIN, WILLIAM BLAKE, AND THE ARTS IN 1796. *Notes and Queries [Great Britain] 1986 33(1): 80-84.* 1765-1841

*For abstract see **Blake, William***

Gindely, Antonín

2521. Polišenská, Milada. POČÁTKY ANTONÍNA GINDELYHO V ČESKÉM ZEMSKÉM ARCHIVU: VE SVĚTLE JEHO KORESPONDENCE [Antonín Gindely's early days at the Bohemian provincial archive in the light of his correspondence]. *Archivní Časopis [Czechoslovakia] 1982 32(1): 23-31.* Antonín Gindely's appointment as first director of the Bohemian archive in 1862 became the basis for his serious academic work, but his letters reveal how little he was interested in the post, aspiring instead to a university professorship. Based on letters and other sources; 36 notes. 1860-62

Ginsberg, Asher

See Haam, Achad

Ginzburg, Carlo

2522. Luria, Keith and Gandolfo, Romulo. CARLO GINZBURG: AN INTERVIEW. *Radical History Review 1986 (35): 89-111.* An interview with left-wing Italian historian Carlo Ginzburg. Ginzburg explores the cultural meanings in people's "private lives," including their fantasies and religious beliefs. In embracing contradictions, Ginzburg stresses reexamining the rules of evidence, rethinking methods, and questioning traditional attachment to "hierarchies of relevance." Discussed in the interview are his childhood and family persecution in Fascist Italy, early interest in art, development as a historian, relationship of culture and history, criticisms of his works, and his enjoyment in teaching modern European history. 11 notes. 1930's-85

2523. Luria, Keith. THE PARADOXICAL CARLO GINZBURG. *Radical History Review 1986 (35): 80-87.* Discusses the paradoxical meanings of Italian historian Carlo Ginzburg's most important books and articles. As an insider on the outside, Ginzburg "explores the culture and mentality of a vast majority of people through case studies of unusual individuals." In approaching popular culture through its elusive contacts with elite or learned culture, Ginzburg is not without his critics. Yet Ginzburg calls upon us to respect the entire past—"that which has disappeared as well as that which has survived." Based on secondary sources; 11 notes. 1980's

Ginzburg, Isaiah

2524. Ginzburg, Isaiah. A PHARMACIST IN TSARIST RUSSIA—A REMINISCENCE, 1892-1909. *Pharmacy in History 1985 27(3): 138-159.* The memoirs of Isaiah Ginzburg (1875-1951) provide a glimpse of the life of a pharmacist and the practice of pharmacy in late Tsarist Russia. Ginzburg details his period of apprenticeship, his education, and his professional career throughout Russia. Based on recollections dictated in the 1940's, 3 illus., 3 photos. 1892-1909

Ginzburg, Lidiia

2525. Maguire, Robert A. THE HISTORICAL CONTEXT OF LIDIIA GINZBURG'S THOUGHT. *Canadian-American Slavic Studies 1985 19(2): 128-134.* Attempts to place Lidiia Ginzburg's six decades of distinguished Soviet literary scholarship within its historical framework. She was heavily influenced by the formalists, especially her mentor, Tynianov, but perhaps even more so by the earlier critic, Belinskii. Ginzburg's writings have much to offer ". . . as we begin to climb out of the mire of ahistoricism and to recognize the sterilities of deconstructionism." 1926-84

Giorgione

2526. Barolsky, Paul. WALTER PATER AND THE POETRY OF NOTHINGNESS. *Antioch Rev. 1982 40(4): 469-478.* 15c

*For abstract see **Botticelli***

Giovanelli, Ronald Gordon

2527. Piddington, J. H. RONALD GORDON GIOVANELLI, 1915-84. *Historical Records of Australian Science [Australia] 1985 6(2): 223-235.* Giovanelli worked for over 30 years with the (Australian) Commonwealth Scientific and Industrial Research Organization. He established an international reputation as a solar physicist and helped develop an international community of specialists in this field. Based on professional articles, personal recollections, and interviews and correspondence; biblio. 1940's-84

Giovanni, Bertoldo di

2528. Draper, James David. "Bertoldo di Giovanni: His Life, His Art, His Influence." New York University 1984. 608 pp. *DAI 1984 45(6): 1558-A.* DA8421506 15c

Giquel, Prosper

2529. Leibo, Steven Andrew. "A French Adviser to Imperial China: The Dilemma of Prosper Giquel." Washington State U. 1982. 382 pp. *DAI 1983 43(9): 3083-A.* DA8301315 1850's-86

Girard, Françoise

2530. Spencer, Samia. THE FEMALE CABINET MEMBERS OF FRANCE AND QUEBEC: TOKEN WOMEN? *Contemporary French Civilization 1985 9(2): 166-191.* Discusses female cabinet members Lise Payette of Quebec and Françoise Girard of France in the context of the role of women in politics in general, and concludes that though there has been progress, there is still a need for more women in high offices. 1970's-84

Girardon, François

2531. Walker, Dean Crittenden, Jr. "The Early Career of François Girardon, 1628-1686: The History of a Sculptor to Louis XIV during the Superintendence of Jean-Baptiste Colbert." New York U. 1982. 351 pp. *DAI 1983 43(7): 2142-A.* DA8227242 1628-86

Giraud, Henri

2532. Kaspi, André. PETAIN, GIRAUD, DE GAULLE: LA "COMEDIE" D'ALGER [Pétain, Giraud, and de Gaulle: the "comedy" of Algiers]. *Histoire [France] 1986 (88): 50-58.* General Henri-Honoré Giraud was named military chief of French forces in North Africa in 1942 and received the support of Allied forces in spite of his opposition to General Charles de Gaulle and his collaboration with the Vichy regime of Henri Philippe Pétain. 1942-46

2533. Smirnov, V. P. DE GOLL I ZHIRO (K ISTORII SOZDANIIA FRANTSUZKOGO KOMITETA NATSIONALNOGO OSVOBOZHDENIIA) [De Gaulle and Giraud: a contribution to the history of the creation of the French Committee of National Liberation]. *Novaia i Noveishaia Istoriia [USSR] 1982 (1): 108-124, (2): 135-153.* 1940-42

*For abstract see **DeGaulle, Charles***

Giraudoux, Jean

2534. Barthélemy, Maurice. GIRAUDOUX BIBLIOPHILE [The bibliophile Giraudoux]. *Rev. d'Hist. Littéraire de la France [France] 1983 83(5-6): 764-772.* Jean Giraudoux (1882-1944) started collecting books very early in his life, but was not able to really indulge in it till he arrived in Paris in 1900. Examination of the Giraudoux library reveals much about this aspect of his life. 1900-44

2535. Dawson, Brett. DE HARVARD AU QUAI D'ORSAY (AVRIL 1908-JUIN 1910) [From Harvard to the Quai d'Orsay, April 1908-June 1910]. *Rev. d'Hist. Littéraire de la France [France] 1983 83(5-6): 711-724.* An account of one of the most unknown episodes of the life of Jean Giraudoux, which immediately precedes his diplomatic career. It covers the period from April 1908 to June 1910, part of which was spent as journalist for *Matin.* 1908-10

2536. Garguilo, René. GIRAUDOUX DEVANT LES PORTES DE LA GUERRE [Giraudoux before the gates of war]. *Rev. d'Hist. Littéraire de la France [France] 1983 83(5-6): 754-763.* For years Jean Giraudoux (1882-1944) stood guard at the gates of war so they would barely open. He loved both France and Germany. His work and life is the drama of a man caught between two spiritual homelands. 1914-41

Girouard, Percy

2537. Kirk-Greene, A. H. M. CANADA IN AFRICA: SIR PERCY GIROUARD, A NEGLECTED COLONIAL GOVERNOR. *African Affairs [Great Britain] 1984 83(331): 207-239.* Outlines the role of Percy Girouard, a Canadian who served in the British colonial service throughout Africa. Following military and engineering training in Canada, Girouard joined Herbert Kitchener in the Sudan during the 1890's and helped to establish the Sudan Military Railway. He next served in South Africa and (after the Boer War) accepted the post of commissioner of railways, which he held until 1904. In 1907 the British Colonial Office appointed Girouard governor of Northern Nigeria, where he introduced reforms in land policy, administration, and education and established the first railroads. In 1909 Girouard received a new appointment as governor of Kenya and served at the post until 1912, when he resigned over a dispute with the Colonial Office. Except for official positions during World War I, Girouard largely retired from public life following his colonial service. Based on the private collection of the Girouard Papers and secondary sources; 109 notes. 1890's-1932

Gisela, Josef

2538. Stern, Marcella. DER WIENER GENREMALER JOSEF GISELA [The Viennese genre painter Josef Gisela]. *Wiener Geschichtsblätter [Austria] 1985 40(1): 17-20.* Discusses the life of the Viennese painter Josef Gisela (1851-99), whose subject matter was scenes of everyday life. 1870's-99

Giuntini, Aldo

2539. Ghisalberti, Alberto M. UN BENMERITO DEL VITTORIANO [A person worthy of the Vittoriano]. *Rassegna Storica del Risorgimento [Italy] 1980 67(3): 346-348.* Examines the career of Aldo Giuntini (1884-1952), an engineer who was made superintendent of the Altare della Patria in Rome, commonly known as the Vittoriano, in 1911. Despite the fact that he was later employed by the Ministry of Public Works to look after other projects, Giuntini continued to take a special interest in this monument to the Risorgimento. Secondary works. 1884-1952

Giurescu, Constantin

2540. Michelson, Paul E. THE BIRTH OF CRITICAL HISTORIOGRAPHY IN ROMANIA: THE CONTRIBUTIONS OF IOAN BOGDAN, DIMITRIE ONCIUL AND CONSTANTIN GIURESCU. *Analele U. București: Istorie [Romania] 1983 32: 59-76.* 1884-1920
For abstract see ***Bogdan, Ioan***

2541. Zub, Alexandru. CONSTANTIN C. GIURESCU: PERSPECTIVĂ ISTORIOGRAFICĂ [Constantin C. Giurescu: an historiographical perspective]. *Anuarul Inst. de Istorie și Arheologie "A. D. Xenopol" [Romania] 1979 16: 489-500.* Traces the major historiographical influences on the Romanian historian Constantin C. Giurescu (1901-77), particularly his predecessors A. D. Xenopol and Nicolae Iorga, and notes how this is reflected in his works. Describes his education and the development of his career, his relations with his contemporaries, and the influence of his publications. 96 notes. 1901-77

Gladstone, William Ewart

2542. Beales, Derek. GLADSTONE AND HIS DIARY: "MYSELF, THE WORST OF ALL INTERLOCUTORS." *Hist. J. [Great Britain] 1982 25(2): 463-469.* Reviews the first six volumes for the years 1825-68 of the *Gladstone Diaries* (1968-78), M. R. D. Foot and H. C. G. Matthew, ed. Based on Gladstone's diaries in the Gladstone Papers, Hawarden Castle, Flintshire, and secondary sources; 32 notes. 1825-68

2543. Crosby, Travis L. GLADSTONE'S DECADE OF CRISIS: BIOGRAPHY AND THE LIFE-COURSE APPROACH. *J. of Pol. and Military Sociol. 1984 12(1): 9-22.* After reviewing briefly, and rejecting, a psycho-historical approach to the life of William Gladstone, the author utilizes life-course studies as a guide to Gladstone's career. Choosing a 10-year segment of Gladstone's life (the 1850's), the author suggests that the personal events of those years reveal age-linked stresses and coping mechanisms. These affected not only Gladstone's perceptions of political issues, but the politicians involved in them as well. The decade ends for Gladstone with a resolution of his difficulties and a consequent modified political behavior. 1850's

2544. Glasgow, Eric. GLADSTONE IN PERSON. *Contemporary Review [Great Britain] 1986 248(1440): 37-40.* Examines the personal attitudes and opinions of the British statesman William Ewart Gladstone (1809-98) in the years 1856-70 and 1890-96, as revealed in a new edition of Lionel A. Tollemache's *Talks with Mr. Gladstone* edited by Asa Briggs. 1856-96

2545. Ramm, Agatha. GLADSTONE'S RELIGION. *Historical Journal [Great Britain] 1985 28(2): 327-340.* William Ewart Gladstone (1809-98), British liberal politician, showed an overwhelming interest in religion throughout his life. His religious attitudes were influenced by his education, the Evangelical movement, and changing views of church and state. Although Gladstone supported the Church of England as the embodiment of religion for the nation, he also advocated religious freedom and equality. Gladstone's views reflected his classical education, liberal political philosophy, and broad understanding of Christianity. Based on documents in the British Library, Gladstone's published diaries and letters, and secondary sources; 48 notes. 1840's-98

2546. Schroeder, Paul W. GLADSTONE AS BISMARCK. *Can. J. of Hist. [Canada] 1980 15(2): 163-195.* William Ewart Gladstone, four times prime minister of Great Britain, envisioned and tried to create a European order based on cooperation rather than conflict and mutual trust instead of rivalry and suspicion; the rule of law was to supplant the reign of force and self-interest. This concept of a harmonious Gladstonian Concert of Europe opposed to and ultimately defeated by a Bismarckian system of manipulated alliances and antagonisms remains a prevalent interpretation of late 19th-century European history. Actually, Gladstone's foreign policy represents no idealistic alternative to Bismarckian Realpolitik, either functionally, in terms of its actual results and impact on the European system, or ideally, in terms of its basic conceptions and purposes. Based on correspondence, diaries, and other primary sources; 114 notes. 1880-85

Gladwin, Mary

2547. Harding, Priscilla M. A RED CROSS NURSE IN BELGRADE: MARY GLADWIN SAW WORLD WAR I FROM THE INSIDE OF A HOSPITAL. HER BATTLES WERE NO EASIER THAN THOSE OF THE SOLDIERS. *Am. Hist. Illus. 1982 17(1): 41-47.* Discusses Red Cross nurse Mary Gladwin's assignment during World War I at the American Military Hospital in Belgrade, Serbia; conditions were inhumane due to the fighting and the large number of wounded. 1914-15

Glaeser, Ernst

2548. McCown, Edna Carolyne. "Ernst Glaeser: Between the Fronts. A Study of His Work." State U. of New York, Stony Brook 1982. 208 pp. *DAI 1982 43(4): 1158-A.* DA8220366 1928-63

Glavar, Peter Pavel

2549. Gregorič, Jože. PISMA PETRA PAVLA GLAVARJA JOŽEFU TOMLJU 1761-1784 [The letters of Peter Pavel Glavar to Jožef Tomlj, 1761-84]. *Acta Ecclesiastica Sloveniae [Yugoslavia] 1982 4: 7-255.* The letters of Peter Paul Glavar written to Joseph Tomlj are a valuable contribution to the ecclesiastic, economic, and cultural history of Slovenia in the second half of the 18th century. They also help to reveal Glavar's personality. 1761-84

Gleditsch, Ellen

2550. Kronen, Torleiv. MADAME CURIE OG ELLEN GLEDITSCH: ET VENNSKAP OG EN BREVVEKSLING [Madame Curie and Ellen Gleditsch: a friendship and a correspondence]. *Nordisk Tidskrift [Sweden] 1985 61(1): 24-36.* 1907-68

*For abstract see **Curie, Marie***

Glöckel, Otto

2551. Buchegger, F. "Otto Glöckel als Regierungsmitglied 1980-1920" [Otto Glöckel's work in the government, 1918-20]. U. of Vienna 1981. 460 pp. *DAI-C 1984 45(3): 692; 9/2828c.* 1918-20

Gloray, Alix

2552. Skalski-Coignard, Jeanne. ALIX GLORAY, D'ANNONAY EN VIVARAIS, PRISONNIÈRE À LA TOUR DE CONSTANCE [Alix Gloray of Annonay: prisoner in the Tower of Constance]. *Bull. de la Soc. de l'Hist. du Protestantisme Français [France] 1981 127(2): 267-270.* Alix Gloray was born 6 January 1639 in Annonay, the daughter of a Protestant clothing merchant. For a year she was married to Jean Buet, but became a widow at the age of 27. On 1 March 1671 she married André Lombard, a widower and rather well-to-do landowner who raised his own grapes and sold the wine. They had seven children, only one of whom survived them. It is not clear why or when Alix was arrested. She was listed as a prisoner in the Tower of Constance 13 March 1692 and died there 28 April 1693. Her husband died in 1699, at which time he was listed as a relapsed heretic. Her daughter Marie had already succeeded in finding refuge in Geneva in 1688. Based on department archives of Ardèche; 17 notes. 1692-99

Glover, Sarah

2553. Leinster-Mackay, D. JOHN HULLAH, JOHN CURWEN AND SARAH GLOVER: A CLASSIC CASE OF "WHIGGERY" IN THE HISTORY OF MUSICAL EDUCATION? *British J. of Educ. Studies [Great Britain] 1981 29(2): 164-167.* 1840's-60's

*For abstract see **Curwen, John***

Glover, Thomas B.

2554. Sugiyama, Shinya. THOMAS B. GLOVER: A BRITISH MERCHANT IN JAPAN, 1861-70. *Business History [Great Britain] 1984 26(2): 115-138.* Scottish-born Thomas B. Glover arrived in Nagasaki, Japan in 1859. In 1861 he set himself up as commission agent and independent merchant (exporting tea and importing cotton and woolen manufactures, with financial help from Jardine, Matheson & Co. of Hong Kong). The years 1864-67 saw the development of Glover & Co. into the largest Western firm in Nagasaki, acting as agent for shipping and insurance companies, and selling ships and armament. From 1868 to its bankruptcy in 1870 the firm was hurt by financial and managerial overexpansion and changes in Japanese politics. Glover turned into an industrialist, constructing a patent ship dock and the Takashima coal mine. Uses Jardine Matheson Archive; 145 notes, 3 tables. 1860's

Glubb, John Bagot

2555. Lunt, J. D. "A GOOD MAN AND HIS HEART WAS SIMPLE." *Army Quarterly and Defence Journal [Great Britain] 1986 116(2): 154-157.* The address given in memory of Sir John Bagot Glubb, who served on the British mandatory administration in Iraq and was the British pasha in the Transjordan, 1930-56, where he transformed the Arab Legion into an exceptional army by enlisting Bedouin support. 1926-56

Gnägi family

2556. Yoder, Don. THE KÜNG-GNÄGI CONNECTION. *Pennsylvania Mennonite Heritage 1983 6(1): 2-6.* Discusses genealogical connections among the Küng, Gnägi, and Yoder families in Canton Bern, Switzerland in the 17h century as found in church records. 17c

Gnedin, Evgeni

2557. Pietrow, Bianka. JE. A. GNEDIN (1898-1983): EIN REPRÄSENTANT SOWJETISHCER AUSSENPOLITIK DER VORKRIEGSZEIT [Evgeni A. Gnedin (1898-1983): a representative of Soviet foreign policy in the prewar period]. *Osteuropa [West Germany] 1984 34(8): 593-595.* Describes the life of Evgeni A. Gnedin, a Russian diplomat in Berlin in the 1930's who was arrested and imprisoned under the Stalin regime. 1922-83

2558. Raymond, Paul D. REVOLUTIONARY IDEALIST TO POLITICAL DISSIDENT: THE LIFE OF EVGENII GNEDIN (PARVUS). *Soviet Union 1985 12(2): 185-212.* During his 80 years, Evgeni Gnedin, who died in 1983, experienced first-hand the evolution of the Soviet state. The son of the expatriate revolutionary and later (in Germany) successful financier and capitalist, Aleksandr Parvus, Gnedin was soon separated from his father by his parents' divorce. Welcoming the revolution, Gnedin joined the foreign affairs commissariat *(Narkomindel)* in 1922, before moving to the newspaper *Izvestiia* in 1931, and then back to the *Narkomindel* in 1935. He participated in secret negotiations leading up to the Nazi-Soviet Pact, but was arrested and remained imprisoned until 1955. Following rehabilitation, he worked with the literature magazine *Novy Mir* until 1970, becoming increasingly involved in dissident and later *samizdat* activities, resigning from the Communist Party of the Soviet Union in 1979. Gnedin sought to remain moral in a corrupt society where rewards frequently went to the opportunists and the expedient. Primary sources; 117 notes. 1898-1983

Gobineau, Joseph Arthur de

2559. Virtanen, Anna-Maija. GOBINEAUN ROTUOPPI JA GERMAANIEN IHANNOINTI [Gobineau's racial doctrine and the idealization of the Germanic peoples]. *Historiallinen Arkisto [Finland] 1985 (86): 53-68.* The French writer Joseph Arthur de Gobineau (1816-82) did not consider modern Germans to be a superior race. He did admire the ancient Germanic peoples as part of the broader Aryan race. He was a cultural pessimist because he considered modern races to have lost their purity. His ideas were revived in Germany by Richard Wagner (1813-83) and his associates. The Gobineau Society, founded in Germany in 1894, translated Gobineau's works into German but distorted his ideas by idealizing modern Germans as racially superior and stressing anti-Semitism. 72 notes. English summary. 1853-1914

Godard, Jean-Luc

2560. Mahieu, José Agustín. GODARD AHORA [Godard today]. *Cuadernos Hispanoamericanos [Spain] 1981 124(374): 373-383.* A review of 20 years of Jean-Luc Godard's work shows that he has remained consistently himself, questioning passionately the art of the cinema, and making no concessions to his individual way of seeing things and analyzing them. 4 notes, chronological list of Godard's productions. 1960-80

2561. Simmons, Steven Clyde. "'Modernisms' in Film: Essays on Jean-Luc Godard." Stanford U. 1982. 216 pp. *DAI 1982 43(4): 956-A.* DA8220542 1950's-80

Godwin family

2562. Greene, Betty. THE GODWINS OF LUGWARDINE, AND OTHER HEREFORD TILE MAKERS. *Industrial Archaeol. Rev. [Great Britain] 1981 5(3): 241-252.* The Godwin family began to make clay products at Lugwardine, near Hereford, in 1850, and soon specialized in the manufacture of inlaid tiles which were much in demand for church floors throughout the Victorian Gothic period. Godwin tiles were used by Sir George Gilbert Scott in his restoration of Hereford cathedral in 1857. Successors to the Godwins are still engaged in tilemaking, which remains an important industry in the Hereford area. 9 plates, table, 26 ref., 3 appendixes. 1850-20c

Goering, Reinhard

2563. Davis, Robert Chapin. "Final Mutiny: Reinhard Goering, His Life and Art." Stanford U. 1982. 474 pp. *DAI 1982 43(4): 1157-A.* DA8220447 1912-36

Goethe, Johann Wolfgang von

2564. Avetisian, V. A. I. V. GETE I KUL'TURA DREVNEGO VOSTOKA [Johann Wolfgang von Goethe and the culture of the ancient East]. *Narody Azii i Afriki [USSR] 1982 (3): 115-120.* It is thought that Goethe's great interest in the culture of the ancient Orient established the beginning of a new stage in the development of literature—its internationalization. He turned his attention to the Old Testament of the Bible, which inspired him to create some of his best known works, such as the second part of *Faust.* Later on, Goethe's concept of the East widened when he became acquainted with the artistic treasures of India and China. He viewed the ancient East and its culture against a background of constant comparison with Western civilization. Goethe also studied the culture of pre-Islamic times and considered Mohammed a destroyer of the colorful and original culture of the ancient Arabs. He also acquired a thorough knowledge of ancient Persian culture. 1770's-1832

2565. Ayrault, Roger. LES SONNETS DE GOETHE (1800-1802; 1807-1808) [Goethe's sonnets 1800-02 and 1807-08]. *Rev. d'Allemagne [France] 1981 13(2): 281-298.* Johann Wolfgang von Goethe (1749-1832) participated in the romantic restoration of the sonnet when, influenced by August Wilhelm von Schlegel (1767-1845) and Ludwig Tieck (1773-1853), he wrote a series of three sonnets on the relation of art and nature. Several years later, while he was associating with Zacharias Werner (1768-1823), he wrote a structured series of 16 love sonnets which were inspired by his relations with Elisabeth Brentano (1785-1859) and Minna Herzlieb. 4 notes. 1800-08

2566. Barner, Wilfried. 150 JAHRE NACH SEINEM TOD: GOETHE UND DIE JUDEN [150 years after his death: Goethe and the Jews]. *Bulletin des Leo Baeck Instituts [Israel] 1982 (63): 75-82.* Evaluates Johann Wolfgang von Goethe's image of Jews in his literary works. The author examines how and why Goethe's attitude to Judaism developed and what value it had in the history of the Germans and Jews. The author specifically discusses: Goethe's religious estimation of the Jews in the light of the Christian environment in which he grew up; his visits to the Jewish ghetto in Frankfurt; his desire to learn Hebrew and his study of the Old Testament; his use of Jewish religion and philosophy and his portrayal of life in the ghettos in his literary works; and how Goethe distanced himself from denominational Christianity and believed in "world piety." Unlike many of his contemporaries Goethe never publicly denounced the Jews and refrained from using the image of the Jew as a comic character to be mocked in his world. In 1825, a Jewish almanac translated a poem by Goethe into Hebrew and throughout the 19th century other works were translated. The spread of Goethe's importance among Jews throughout the world since the 19th century is also discussed. 18c-19c

2567. Hennig, John. GOETHES KENNTNIS DES BALTISCHEN SCHRIFTTUMS [Goethe's knowledge of Baltic literature]. *Zeits. für Religions- und Geistesgeschichte [West Germany] 1982 34(1): 18-27.* Discusses Johann Wolfgang von Goethe's knowledge of the literature of the East Baltic provinces. The only book on this topic, written by Otto von Petersen of the Herder Institute in Riga in 1930, views the relationship in terms of the Baltic provinces' acquaintance with Goethe rather than the other way around. It does not touch on information obtained by Goethe through literature written by non-Balts. With the intention to supplement Petersen's book, the author lists the Baltic literature known to Goethe. Each entry gives the author's name, the approximate time Goethe became familiar with it, and a few comments, some of which are taken from Goethe's letters. Mentions some of the persons who aided in keeping him abreast of events in the provinces. Secondary sources. 1770-1832

2568. Kemp, Friedhelm. SE VOIR DANS L'HISTOIRE. LES ECRITS AUTOBIOGRAPHIQUES DE GOETHE [Seeing oneself in history: Goethe's autobiographical writings]. *Rev. de l'Inst. de Sociol. [Belgium] 1982 (1-2): 143-155.* Goethe's autobiographical works are legitimate historical sources for his period. 1779-1832

2569. Šamberger, Zdeněk. GOETHE A ČECHY V DOBĚ OBROZENÍ (K 150.VYRICI JEHO UMRTI) [Goethe and Bohemia in the national period: the 150th anniversary of his death]. *Slovanský Přehled [Czechoslovakia] 1982 68(5): 353-363.* Goethe gained firsthand knowledge of the Bohemian countryside and of the Czech national reawakening through his visits to Carlsbad (Karlovy Vary) and Marienbad (Mariánské Lázně) over a period of 10 years. There he met with many influential Czech nobles, showed a keen interest in the Czech national question, read the Bohemian Museum journal, and met with men like Dobrovský. Goethe's work also attracted Czech intellectuals, most especially Ladislav Čelakovský who formed a Goethe literary circle. Goethe's interest in Czech culture was so great that he promoted the museum journal in Germany. 70 notes. 1790-1820

2570. Yip, Terry Siu-Han. "Goethe in China: A Study of Reception and Influence." U. of Illinois, Urbana-Champaign 1985. 352 pp. *DAI 1985 46(4): 974-A.* DA8511694 1920's-30's

2571. —. [GOETHE: THE RELUCTANT BOURGEOIS]. *New Left Rev. [Great Britain] 1982 (133): 67-94.*

Livingston, Rodney. INTRODUCTION TO BENJAMIN, *pp. 67-68.* Walter Benjamin's study of Johann Wolfgang von Goethe, "The Reluctant Bourgeois," was commissioned for the Great Soviet Encyclopaedia and is one of his rare departures from classical German literature.

Benjamin, Walter; Livingston, Rodney, transl. GOETHE: THE RELUCTANT BOURGEOIS, *pp. 69-93.* A comprehensive biographical essay and interpretation of Goethe's life and works, which points out his early inability to make a political commitment, and his later life, which is understandable only in the context of the political position he created. Discusses Goethe's resistance to bourgeois ideas. 1749-1832

Goga, Octavian

2572. Teiuş, Sabina. OCTAVIAN GOGA—IL POETA DELL'UNITÀ NAZIONALE RUMENA [Octavian Goga—the poet of national Romanian unity]. *Balcanica [Italy] 1984 3(3): 33-39.* Translates into Italian selected poems of the Romanian Octavian Goga (1881-1938) and places them in the context of the Romanian nationalist movement and the vision of a return to nature. ca 1900-38

Gogh, Vincent van

2573. Porter, Roger J. LET THE REST BE DARK: VAN GOGH IN HIS LETTERS. *Biography 1982 5(1): 53-65.* For Van Gogh, the letter, usually to his brother Theo, was as essential to him as the painting, and indeed often the painting was not complete until he could meditate upon it in a letter. His correspondence suggests a range of moods and self-dramatizations that mirrors those of his self-portraits, not only of the tormented outsider but of the domestic man yearning for peace. 1879-90

2574. Schiff, Bennett. TRIUMPH AND TRAGEDY IN THE LAND OF "BLUE TONES AND GAY COLORS." *Smithsonian 1984 15(7): 76-89.* Recounts the last few years in the life of Vincent van Gogh (1853-90), focusing on the period from February 1888 to May 1889 when he lived in Arles in the south of France. 1886-90

2575. Whitney, Charles A. THE SKIES OF VINCENT VAN GOGH. *Art History [Great Britain] 1986 9(3): 351-362.* Vincent van Gogh's (1853-90) night sky paintings and his letters indicate that the artist had an educated astronomical eye and a symbolic affinity for the stars. In his letters van Gogh discusses the colors of stars in *Café Terrace at Night* (1888) describing color not readily visible to the eye, but observable in modern color photography. The composite view in *Starry Night on the Rhône* (1888) pictures an accurately placed stellar constellation. The celestial composite of *Starry Night* (1889) depicts a spiral nebula while *Road with Men Walking, Carriage, Cypress, Star and Crescent Moon* (1890) is a rendering of the twilight sky van Gogh would have seen in April 1890. Based on van Gogh's paintings and letters and meteorological data for 1888-90 in the Bureau Climatologique Interrégional de Sud-Est, Aix-en-Provence; 2 charts, 7 photos, 13 notes. 1888-90

Gogol, Nikolai

2576. Shapiro, Gavriel. NIKOLAI GOGOL AND THE BAROQUE HERITAGE. *Slavic Review 1986 45(1): 95-104.* Traces the influence of baroque cultural, historical and literary sources on the writings of Nikolai Gogol. His Ukrainian upbringing was replete with baroque traditions, e.g., literature, architecture, and painting. As a mature writer, Gogol continued to be inspired by the baroque heritage. 51 notes. 1821-43

Gökalp, Ziya

2577. Fadeeva, I. L. KONTSEPTSIIA KUL'TURY I TSIVILIZATSII TURETSKOGO FILOSOFA ZII GEK ALPA [The concept of culture and civilization of the Turkish philosopher Zia Gökalp]. *Narody Azii i Afriki [USSR] 1982 (2): 106-114.* After the revolution in Turkey, led by Kemal Atatürk from 1919 to 1923, much attention was paid to the development of national culture. Many of the principles of Kemalism were based on the writings of the prominent Turkish philosopher and sociologist Ziya Gökalp (1875-1924). Gökalp's work helped Atatürk to formulate his policy of Europeanization, nationalism, etatism, and secularism. Zia Gökalp was particularly exercised by the question of how Turks could embrace European civilization while still preserving Islam. He argued that there need be no conflict: culture, which is the product of one nation, can be maintained; while civilization is a desirable amalgam of the social life of many nations, which retain separate identities. Secondary sources; 24 notes. 1900-24

Golder, Frank A.

2578. Wachhold, Allen Glen. "Frank A. Golder: An Adventure in Russian History." U. of California, Santa Barbara 1984. 415 pp. *DAI 1985 46(5): 1383-A.* DA8509458 1899-1920's

Goldmann, Lucien

2579. Cohen, Mitchell Stuart. "Lucien Goldmann and the Wager of Marxist Humanism." Columbia U. 1982. 242 pp. *DAI 1982 43(5): 1666-A.* DA8222369 1938-70

Goldschmidt, Alfons

2580. Kiessling, Wolfgang. ... DENN ER WAR MARXIST. ALFONS GOLDSCHMIDT [Then he was a Marxist: Alfons Goldschmidt]. *Beiträge zur Geschichte der Arbeiterbewegung [East Germany] 1984 26(3): 376-387.* Alfons Goldschmidt (1879-1940) was devoted to Marxism and the interests of the working class, particularly after his travel to Moscow, USSR, in 1920. A native of Germany, he taught economics in Argentina, Mexico, Chile, and the United States, in and out of colleges and universities. 23 notes. 1900-40

Golimbievski, Anatoli L.

2581. Sinegubov, V. MUZHESTVO CHEREZ VSIU ZHIZN' [Courage throughout life]. *Morskoi Sbornik [USSR] 1982 (5): 56-58.* Anatoli L. Golimbievski, a heroic fighter in World War II was seriously wounded but conquered all difficulties to remain a useful citizen, a shining example of Soviet patriotism. Based on the life of A. L. Golimbievski; 2 photos, note. 1939-82

Golitsyn, Dmitri

2582. DeMadariaga, Isabel. PORTRAIT OF AN EIGHTEENTH-CENTURY RUSSIAN STATESMAN: PRINCE DMITRY MIKHAYLOVICH GOLITSYN. *Slavonic and East European Rev. [Great Britain] 1984 62(1): 36-60.* Prince Dmitri Golitsyn (1663-1737), Privy Councillor in the Russian Empire, was an outstanding representative of the politically sophisticated higher nobility. He led an aristocratic attempt in 1730 to limit the autocratic power of the new empress Anna by a signed instrument subjecting any major political decisions to the Privy Council's approval. As the lower nobility rallied to the empress, the attempt failed; Golitsyn lost his influence and was arrested in 1737. Despite his enlightened political background, his plan of 1730 lacked a sound constitutional basis and was grounded in oligarchical, corporate conceptions of the Old Regime. 72 notes. 1689-1737

Gollancz, Marguerite

2583. Robinson, David. MARGUERITE GOLLANCZ. *J. of the Soc. of Archivists [Great Britain] 1981 6(8): 532-533.* An obituary of the British archivist Marguerite Gollancz (1911-81), one of the generation of archivists who founded and developed County Record Offices in the period of expansion after World War II. 1936-81

Goller, Christian

2584. Dornberg, John. THE MILLION-DOLLAR SAINT. *Art & Antiques 1985 (Feb): 78-80.* Discusses the life and work of Christian Goller, a master forger of old paintings, examining some of his painting techniques and describing the type of clientele that commissioned him. 1966-77

Gómez, Laureano

2585. Forero Benavides, Abelardo. LOS GRANDES HOMBRES QUE HE CONOCIDO [Great men I have known]. *Bol. de Hist. y Antigüedades [Colombia] 1981 68(734): 691-715.* 1920's-50's

*For abstract see **López, Alfonso***

Gómez Carrillo, Enrique

2586. Horwinski, Linda Jean. "Enrique Gómez Carrillo, Connoisseur of *La Belle Epoque:* His Prose Works, 1892-1927." U. of California, Los Angeles 1981. 396 pp. *DAI 1982 42(8): 3620-A.* 8201106 1892-1927

Gómez de Avellaneda, Gertrudis

2587. Harter, Hugh A. *Gertrudis Gómez de Avellaneda.* (Twayne World Authors Series, no. 599: Spain.) Boston: Twayne, 1981. 182 pp. 1839-73

Gomez de Cervantes family

2588. Ganster, Paul. LA FAMILIA GOMEZ DE CERVANTES: LINAJE Y SOCIEDAD EN EL MEXICO COLONIAL [The Gomez de Cervantes family: ancestry and society in colonial Mexico]. *Hist. Mexicana [Mexico] 1981 31(2): 197-232.* Examines the biographies of two 18th-century members of the family to show how the family succeeded in retaining its fortune and position in society over many generations. Given the fluctuations of the economy and the uncertainty of male children arriving at adult age, it was unusual for the descendants of the conquistadores to maintain their economic and social privileges for long. The Gomez de Cervantes however arrived in Mexico at the time of the conquest and remained prominent to the beginning of the 19th century. Based on primary material in the Archivo General de Indias, Seville, and the national archive of Mexico; genealogical tree, 40 notes, biblio. 1524-1759

Gómez Ortega, Casimiro

2589. Bueno, A. G. and Ruíz Ochayta, M. LA INTRODUCCION DE LA FILOSOFIA LINNEANA EN LA BOTANICA ESPAÑOLA: ACTITUD DE C. GOMEZ ORTEGA (1741-1818) [The introduction of Linnaean philosophy in Spanish botany: attitude of C. Gómez Ortega (1741-1818)]. *Boletín de la Sociedad Española de Historia de la Farmacia [Spain] 1985 36(141-142): 15-39.* Notes the influence on Spanish botany of Casimiro Gómez Ortega (1741-1818), who was trained by Linnaeus's students Giuseppe and Caetano Lorenzo Monti in Bologna, Italy, lists his works in Spanish, and prints letters written to Carolus Linnaeus. 1760-1800

Gómez-Caamaño, José Luis

2590. Carmona Cornet, Ana María and Esteva de Sagrera, Juan. EN MEMORIA DE NUESTRO MAESTRO: JOSE LUIS GOMEZ-CAAMAÑO (1909-1984) [In memory of our professor: José Luis Gómez-Caamaño (1909-84)]. *Boletín de la Sociedad Española de Historia de la Farmacia [Spain] 1984 35(137): 1-22.* Discusses the life and work of the Spanish professor of pharmacy José Luis Gómez-Caamaño (1909-84) and of the history of pharmacy, mentioning the critical talent that he stimulated and his reflections on the science of pharmaceuticals and its complicated ethics. 1930's-84

Gomułka, Władysław

2591. Barcikowski, Kazimierz and Log-Sowiński, Ignacy. PAMIĘCI WŁADYSŁAWA GOMUŁKI "WIESŁAWA": 1905-1982 [In memory of Władysław Gomułka (pseud. Wiesław), 1905-82]. *Nowe Drogi [Poland] 1982 (9): 5-11.* Speeches in memory of Władysław Gomułka (1905-82), summarizing his activities as Polish party leader and international statesman. 1920's-82

2592. Gomułka, Władysław. Z PISM I PRZEMÓWIEŃ WŁADYSŁAWA GOMUŁKI: 1943-1948 [From the letters and speeches of Władysław Gomułka, 1943-48]. *Nowe Drogi [Poland] 1982 (9): 12-62.* A selection of Władysław Gomułka's speeches and open letters, 1943-48, among them a letter to the Sikorski government, an excerpt from the Polish Workers' Party Manifesto, a speech at an open meeting in Warsaw, and others. 1943-48

2593. —. WŁADYSŁAW GOMUŁKA [Władysław Gomułka]. *Z Pola Walki [Poland] 1983 26(2): 49-104.* The full authorized text of a discussion of the political career of Władysław Gomułka, the First Secretary of the Polish United Workers' Party from 1956 to 1970. The discussion took place

on 6 December 1982 and was organized by the editorial board of the journal *Z Pola Walki*. The participants were Gomułka's former friends and colleagues, historians, and politicians: Bogdan Brzeziński, Ignacy Loga-Sowiński, Włodzimierz Lechowicz, Jerzy Albrecht, Marian Wojciechowski, Lucjan Motyka, Antoni Korzycki, Czesław Bobrowski, Edward Ochab, Bolesław Jaszczuk, Władysław Machejek, Franciszek Szlachcic, Stefan Jędrychowski, Izolda Kowalska-Kiryluk, and Mieczysław Jaworski. 2 notes.
1943-70

Gonçalves, Bento

2594. Iastrzhembski, S. V. BENTO GONSALVESH—VIDNYI ORGANIZATOR PORTUGAL'SKOI KOMMUNISTICHESKOI PARTII [Bento Gonçalves, prominent organizer of the Portuguese Communist Party]. *Novaia i Noveishaia Istoriia [USSR] 1986 (1): 97-109.* A political biography of Bento Gonçalves (1902-42), cofounder of the Portuguese Communist Party and its Secretary General, 1929-35. In 1935 he took part in the 7th Congress of the Comintern. On return from Moscow, he and the rest of the Portuguese delegation were arrested. Gonçalves was sentenced to an ever-extended term in the Tarrafal labor camp, where he died despite appeals of his friends and family to free him. Based on the author's personal archives; 40 notes.
1929-42

Góngora, Mario

2595. Collier, Simon. AN INTERVIEW WITH MARIO GONGORA. *Hispanic Am. Hist. Rev. 1983 63(4): 663-675.* Chilean historian Mario Góngora worked for more than 30 years in the University of Chile before taking up his present appointment in the Catholic University of Chile (Santiago). He established his reputation in the field of Spanish American colonial history, later turning his attention to the history of ideas and the national period of Chilean history. Biblio.
1915-82

Gonne, Maud

2596. Pratt, Linda Ray. MAUD GONNE: "STRANGE HARMONIES AMID DISCORD." *Biography 1983 6(3): 189-208.* The nature of Maud Gonne's personality and historical significance is difficult to assess because of Yeats's poetic myth, Irish romanticism, and Gonne's efforts to create a legend for herself. Recent biographical study indicates some measure of her accomplishments, the centrality of William Butler Yeats to her life, and the damage to her credibility from feminine stereotypes. 1890's-1953

Gonzague, Marie de

2597. Ribardière, Diane. PENDANT 50 ANS, DEUX FRANÇAISES REINES DE POLOGNE [For 50 years, two French queens of Poland]. *Historama [France] 1985 (16): 48-54, (17): 62-68.* 1640's-83
For abstract see ***Arquien, Marie d'***

González, Florentino

2598. —. CARTAS DE FLORENTINO GONZALEZ AL GENERAL PEDRO ALCANTARA HERRAN [Letters of Florentino González to General Pedro Alcántara Herrán]. *Bol. de Hist. y Antigüedades [Colombia] 1981 68(734): 725-757.* Presents 17 letters of the mid-19th-century Colombian statesman Florentino González and one of his wife Bernardina Ibáñez, to Pedro A. Herrán. The letters are from 1839 to 1860, writen from Bogotá or other Colombian cities and from Lima, where González was fulfilling a diplomatic assignment. They concern Colombian politics and foreign relations, including relations with the United States where Herrán was located much of the time, and the proposal for construction of an interoceanic canal over the Atrato River route. Based on material in the Academia Colombiana de Historia.
1839-60

González Dávila, Gil

2599. García Regueiro, Ovidio. ORO Y DESCUBRIMIENTO: LA EXPEDICION DE GIL GONZALEZ DAVILA [Gold and discovery: the expedition of Gil González Dávila]. *Cuadernos Hispanoamericanos [Spain] 1985 (418): 4-30.* Discovery of new lands and quest for gold went inseparably together in the European tradition after the 1450's. The expedition that took Gil González Dávila (ca. 1480-1543) to the Pacific coasts of Costa Rica and Nicaragua in 1519-24 fits into the pattern. In his account and related documents, the geopolitical factor, Christianization, and economic results are given strictly equal treatment. The net profit of the expedition ranged between 800-1,000% of the total amount invested. Based on published sources from the Archivo de Indias at Simancas (Valladolid) and secondary sources; 5 tables, 43 notes. 1519-24

González de Posada, Carlos

2600. Benavides, Manuel. DOS ILUSTRADOS ASTURIANOS: RUBIN DE CELIS Y GONZALEZ DE POSADA [Two enlightened ones from Asturias: Rubín de Celis and González de Posada]. *Cuadernos Hispanoamericanos [Spain] 1985 (418): 158-161.* Reviews Inmaculada Urzainqui and Alvaro Ruíz de la Peña's *Periodismo e Ilustración en Manuel Rubín de Celis* (1983) and Jorge Demerson's *Carlos González de Posada: Aproximación a su Biografía* (1984). These works are a clear instance of the increasing attention given by Spanish historiography both to the 18th century at the local and regional level and to the biography of secondary figures who throw new light on the main topics of the century. 18c

González Flores, Jesús María

2601. Salinas Cantú, Hernán. BIOGRAFIA DEL DR. JESUS MA. GONZALEZ FLORES [Biography of Dr. Jesús Ma. González Flores]. *Humanitas [Mexico] 1981 22: 201-212.* Detailed biography of Dr. Jesús María González Flores (1857-1947), one of the professionals responsible for the introduction and use of ether and chemical antiseptics to Mexico. 1880-1947

González Pérez, José

See Gris, Juan

González Suárez, Federico

2602. Davidson, Russ. FEDERICO GONZALEZ SUAREZ: BIO-BIBLIOGRAPHICAL NOTES. *Inter-American Rev. of Biblio. 1983 33(1): 13-20.* Federico González Suárez (1844-1917), born in Quito, Ecuador, was the most important of the many churchmen who played a leading role in the political and intellectual life of Latin America. Besides holding high ecclesiastical office and wielding decisive political power, González Suarez was the author of many works on history, archaeology and ethnology, literature, and politico-ecclesiastical matters. Biblio., 9 notes. 1870's-1917

Goodlatte, Clare

2603. Cartwright, M. F. OVER THE WALL INTO POLITICS. *Q. Bull. of the South African Lib. [South Africa] 1981 35(4): 150-153.* Sketches the life of Sister Clare Goodlatte (1866-1942). Irish by birth and educated in London, Goodlatte went to South Africa around 1886 to teach. After teaching at Port Elizabeth and Grahamstown, she retired to Woodstock in 1921, where she engaged in social work among the poor. Becoming interested in communism and its potential for resolving racial frictions, she left her social work to devote her time to this new cause. Later, she became disenchanted with communism because of the course of that movement in Stalinist Russia. Based on Goodlatte's letters and secondary sources; illus., 6 notes. 1886-1940

Goodwin, John

2604. More, Ellen. JOHN GOODWIN AND THE ORIGINS OF THE NEW ARMINIANISM. *J. of British Studies 1982 22(1): 50-70.* Discusses the emergence of a "radical" Arminian critique of Calvinism within English Nonconformity. John Goodwin (1595-1666), its chief exponent, was a pivotal link between the predestinarianism of the early 17th century and the rational latitudinarianism of the Restoration. Goodwin began his clerical career in the 1620's as a covenant Puritan, but by the mid-1640's had been deeply influenced by Arminian redemptionist theology and Protestant rationalism. By 1648 Goodwin was asserting that Scripture must be read in the light of reason and that toleration is essential as religious truths are subject to progressive revelation. Based on the published writings of John Goodwin and other mid-17th-century religious writers; 86 notes. ca 1625-51

Googe, Barnabe

2605. Eccles, Mark. BARNABE GOOGE IN ENGLAND, SPAIN, AND IRELAND. *English Literary Renaissance 1985 15(3): 353-370.* Barnabe Googe journeyed to Madrid in 1562 "for knowledge sake" and borrowed from Montemayor and Garcilaso when he published eclogues and lyrics in 1563. Sir William Cecil arranged for his young kinsman Barnabe to sit in Parliament in 1571, to write newsletters from Ireland in 1574, and to serve as provost marshal of Connaught from 1582 to 1585. Googe dedicated translations to Cecil, Elizabeth I, and Sir William Fitzwilliam, who had been Lord Deputy of Ireland. 1562-85

Gorbachev, Mikhail

2606. Gustafson, Thane and Mann, Dawn. GORBACHËV'S FIRST YEAR: BUILDING POWER AND AUTHORITY. *Problems of Communism 1986 35(3): 1-19.* After one year as General Secretary of the Communist Party of the Soviet Union, Mikhail Gorbachev (b. 1931) has restored much of the power of his office, especially through a heavy turnover of cadres. His power now needs to be reinforced by authority, which is contingent upon a viable program. Gorbachev's economic blueprint for the USSR contains some serious inherent contradictions. Their resolution will need hard choices that will test Gorbachev's ability to build both power and authority. Based on *Pravda, Izvestiia,* and research materials from Radio Free Europe/Radio Liberty; fig., table, 3 photos, and 94 notes. 1985-86

2607. Hough, Jerry F. GORBACHEV'S STRATEGY. *Foreign Affairs 1985 64(1): 33-55.* Provides a brief biographical background of Mikhail Gorbachev's rise to power in the USSR and analyzes his actions since assuming power in March 1985 in the context of Soviet economic conditions and the past leadership of the USSR since Khrushchev. 10 notes. 1970's-85

2608. Reid, Carl. GORBACHEV THE EFFICIENT? *International Perspectives [Canada] 1985 (May-June): 10-13.* Mikhail S. Gorbachev built his career on managing collective and state farms and has long advocated a more efficient agro-industrial complex through the use of the brigade contracting system and the integration of farms, scientific institutes, and the chemical fertilizer industry. Nevertheless, he has not challenged the historic role of the Party as the ideological and economic regulator of the Soviet Union, a necessity if reform is to be implemented. Although he has the aura of the reformer about him, some of his actions contradict his words, and he is not likely to offend conservative elements in the Party by decentralizing authority. Illus. 1976-85

2609. Schneider, Eberhard. MICHAIL SERGEJEWITSCH GORBATSCHOW [Mikhail Sergeevich Gorbachov]. *Osteuropa [West Germany] 1985 35(6): 396-405.* Discusses the life, education, and political career of Mikhail Gorbachev (b. 1931) who was elected as General Secretary of the Communist Party in the USSR in 1985. 1955-85

Gorchakov, Aleksandr

2610. Czövek, István. ARCKÉPEK A 19. SZÁZADI OROSZ POLITIKA MŰHELYÉBŐL. (A. M. GORCSAKOV (1798-1883) ÉS D. A. MILJUTYIN (1816-1912)) [Portraits from the workshop of 19th-century Russian policy: A. M. Gorchakov (1798-1883) and D. A. Miliutin (1816-1912)]. *Századok [Hungary] 1984 118(4): 709-729.* Following the defeat in the Crimean War, the necessity to introduce reforms in Russia led to the rise of some able, ambitious politicians who were successful in enhancing their country's European position. Depicts the careers of Prince Aleksandr Gorchakov, a moderate, reforming chancellor, and Dmitri A. Miliutin, who managed to hold office as minister of war for more than 20 years, despite his often criticized liberal proclivities. Based mainly on secondary sources, but also using the Central State Archives of the October Revolution; 71 notes. 1820-81

Gordimer, Nadine

2611. Green, Robert. NADINE GORDIMER: A BIBLIOGRAPHY OF WORKS AND CRITICISM. *Bulletin of Bibliography 1985 42(1): 5-11.* Biography of, and bibliography of works by and about, Nadine Gordimer, 20th-century South African novelist. 1923-84

Gordon, Aryeh Leib

2612. Kabakoff, Jacob. L'TOLDOT HAKHMEI YISRAEL B-RUSIA [Two autobiographies of Russian Jewish authors]. *Shvut [Israel] 1982 9: 99-101.* 1843-1912
*For abstract see **Deinard, Ephraim***

Gordon, Charles

2613. Rae, Donald A. WILLIAM CARLISLE AND CHARLES GORDON. *Hist. J. [New Zealand] 1982 (41): 29-31.* 1816-20
*For abstract see **Carlisle, William***

Gordon, Charles George

2614. Judd, Denis. GORDON OF KHARTOUM: THE MAKING OF AN IMPERIAL MARTYR. *History Today [Great Britain] 1985 35(Jan): 19-25.* To the British public, the murder of General Charles George Gordon by the Mahdi's troops in Khartoum in 1885 represented the conflict between Western values and the forces of darkness. In truth,

Gordon's mission was the result of a confused British foreign policy. Moreover, Gordon's death was due to his own miscalculations, arrogance, and incompetence. 1882-85

2615. Plaut, Fred. GENERAL GORDON'S MAP OF PARADISE: THE "SECRET" OF THE SEYCHELLES. *Encounter [Great Britain] 1982 58-59(6-1): 20-32.* Describes the life and career of Charles George Gordon (1833-85), his religious beliefs, and his attempt to identify Praslin, one of the Seychelles, as the site of the Garden of Eden; reproduces the map he drew of the area and provides a history of attempts by Christian cartographers to locate Paradise, beginning with Cosmas Indico Pleustes, a 6th-century monk, and ending with European maps of the 18th century. 6c-18c

Gordon, David

2616. Salmon, Joseph. DAVID GORDON VE'ITON HAMAGID: HILUFE EMDOT LELEUMIYUT HAYEHUDIT 1860-1882 [David Gordon and the periodical *Ha-Maggid*]. *Zion [Israel] 1982 47(2): 145-164.* David Gordon was one of the most important national-Zionist thinkers from the 1860's to the 1880's. Gordon joined *Ha-Maggid* in 1858, having already developed a critical attitude toward aspects of traditional Jewish society following his encounter with liberal Judaism. He did not reject all that was new or innovative, but rather searched for a synthetic approach that would maintain the traditional yearning for redemption while at the same time embracing the modernizing tendencies of a moderate *maskil* [intellectual]. Gordon's program developed in reaction to the events of his day. In the 1870's, following the 1863 Polish uprising, three Reform synods, and a growing crisis in Eastern Europe, he supported various initiatives aimed at enhancing Jewish settlement in Palestine. Later he based his national philosophy on the failure of emancipation and made his periodical the organ of the *Hibbat Zion* movement. Based on *Ha-Maggid* and other sources; 108 notes. 1860-82

Gordon, Robert

2617. Stone, Jeffrey C. ROBERT GORDON OF STRALOCH: CARTOGRAPHER OR CHOROGRAPHER? *Northern Scotland [Great Britain] 1981 4(1-2): 7-22.* Disputes previous accounts which merely describes Gordon as a cartographer and elaborates upon the various cultural and academic activities he pursued, concluding that even his basic cartographical pursuits became important contributions to other related disciplines. Secondary sources. 1580-1661

Gorky, Maxim

2618. Belousov, S. R. PERVAIA BIOGRAFIIA A. M. GOR'KOGO V KITAE [China's first biography of Maxim Gorky]. *Narody Azii i Afriki [USSR] 1981 (6): 106-111.* 1930's-44

For abstract see ***Zou Daofen***

2619. Wolf, M. "Kindheits- und Jugenddarstellung in den Autobiographischen Romanen von Lev N. Tolstoj, Aleksej N. Tolstoj und Maksim Gor'kij" [Description of childhood and adolescence in the autobiographical novels of Leo Tolstoy, Aleksei Tolstoy, and Maxim Gorky]. U. of Vienna [Austria] 1980. 148 pp. *DAI-C 1982 43(3): 423; 7/2993c.* 1912-22

Gorozhankin, Ivan N.

2620. Alekseev, L. V. IVAN NIKOLAEVICH GOROZHANKIN V UNIVERSITETE I V ZHIZNI [Ivan Nikolaevich Gorozhankin's academic and personal life]. *Voprosy Istorii Estestvoznaniia i Tekhniki [USSR] 1984 (4): 112-119.* Biography of Ivan N. Gorozhankin (1848-1904), botanist and founder of Russian comparative morphology. He studied at Moscow University, where he remained as teacher and researcher. He participated in Moscow's intellectual life and counted eminent Russian writers Ivan Turgenev, Nikolai Leskov, and Leo Tolstoy among his acquaintances. An unhappy personal life after an early death of his first wife diminished his academic output. Secondary sources; 13 notes. 1870's-1904

Gorrie, John

2621. Brereton, Bridget. SIR JOHN GORRIE: A RADICAL CHIEF JUSTICE OF TRINIDAD (1885-1892). *J. of Caribbean Hist. [Barbados] 1980 13: 44-72.* During his tenure as chief justice, Sir John Gorrie (1829-92) was at the center of Trinidad politics. He was a career colonial official who was also a political radical with a strong belief in equal justice for all, believing that the law was the only means by which the exploitation of labor could be partially checked. He reformed judicial proceedings, instigated a long series of cases against the planters, and outside the courts took a prominent part in politics, promoting social reform, including the lowering of import duties, and promoting a people's bank and a crop advance and discount company. This earned him the hatred of "respectable" inhabitants and the respect of poor blacks and Indians. Based on Colonial Office documents and Trinidad newspapers; 89 notes. 1885-92

Gorshkov, Sergei G.

2622. Broadwin, John A. RUSSIA'S TOP ADMIRAL. *Contemporary Rev. [Great Britain] 1984 245(1424): 135-139.* A biography of Sergei G. Gorshkov (b. 1910), the architect of the modern Soviet Navy, and one of the great naval administrators of the 20th century. 1910-84

2623. Rohwer, Jürgen. DAS ENDE DER ÄRA GORSCHKOW [End of the Gorshkov era]. *Marine-Rundschau [West Germany] 1986 83(2): 88-97.* Chronicles the career of recently replaced commander-in-chief of the Soviet navy Sergei G. Gorshkov, youngest Soviet admiral in 1941 at the age of 31, and a guiding force behind the modernization and expansion of the Soviet fleet since the 1950's. 1940's-85

Gosselman, Carl August

2624. Mier, José M. de. UN VIAJERO, UN CONFERENCISTA Y DOS RAREZAS BIBLIOGRAFICAS [A traveller, a lecturer, and two bibliographic rarities]. *Bol. Cultural y Biblio. [Colombia] 1982 19(2): 215-236.* Discusses the life and writings of Swedish traveller, Carl August Gosselman, and selected 19th-century editions of his *Viaje por Colombia en los Años de 1825 y 1826;* describes the proceedings of an 1888 conference, which were published in a pamphlet, *Colombia hace 60 Años,* and which discussed Gosselman's work at length. 19c

Got'e, Iuri V.

2625. Got'e, Iu. V. UNIVERSITET (IZ ZAPISOK AKADEMIKA IU. V. GOT'E) [University: from the notes of Academician Iuri V. Got'e]. *Vestnik Moskovskogo U. Seriia 8: Istoriia [USSR] 1982 (4): 13-27.* The son of a bookseller, Got'e (1873-1943) entered Moscow University in 1891. As a student in history, he heard lectures and attended seminars of

V. I. Ger'e, P. G. Vinogradov, V. O. Kliuchevski and others. His most important teacher was P. N. Miliukov, under whom he wrote a work on the defense of the southern border of the Moscow state in the 16th and 17th centuries; he graduated in 1905. 2 notes. 1891-1905

Gotō Fumio

2626. Weiner, Susan Beth. "Bureaucracy and Politics in the 1930's: The Career of Gotō Fumio." Harvard University 1984. 214 pp. *DAI 1984 45(6): 1839-A.* DA8419461 1930's

Gotovac, Vlado

2627. Kolb, Charles E. M. THE CRIMINAL TRIAL OF YUGOSLAV POET VLADO GOTOVAC: AN EYEWITNESS ACCOUNT. *Human Rights Q. 1982 4(2): 184-211.* In 1981, the courageous Croatian writer and poet Vlado Gotovac was charged and convicted of disseminating hostile propaganda for having granted interviews to foreign journalists, in a trial whose outcome was determined in advance. 1981

Gottschalk, Joachim

2628. Brandt, Hans-Jürgen. ERINNERUNGEN AN DIE TRAGÖDIE EINER KÜNSTLEREHE: MELA UND JOACHIM GOTTSCHALK [Memories of the tragedy of an artist's marriage: Mela and Joachim Gottschalk]. *Frankfurter Hefte [West Germany] 1982 37(1): 5-8.* When the German actor Joachim Gottschalk was prevented from continuing to act because he was married to a Jewish woman, he and his wife committed suicide, 6 November 1941. 1940-41

Gottschall, Benjamin

2629. Caplan, Sophie. PSYCHOLOGICAL AND SPIRITUAL RESISTANCE IN NAZI CONCENTRATION CAMPS: THE EXAMPLE OF RABBI BENJAMIN GOTTSCHALL. *Australian Journal of Politics and History [Australia] 1985 31(1): 109-127.* Describes the acts of religious resistance of Rabbi Benjamin Gottschall (1914-78), former rabbi at Louny, in the Czech province of Bohemia, who was an inmate at Theresienstadt and Auschwitz, 1942-44, and probably survived only because he was sent to a labor camp near Dresden. In the concentration camps Gottschall conducted secret religious services in an attic, conducted burial rites over the dead in the mortuary, issued Sabbath greetings, obtained a prayer book, baked unleavened bread for the Passover seder, and circulated a Hebrew calendar on cement-bag fragments. After the war he ministered to synagogues in Prague and, after 1950, in Newcastle, New South Wales, Wellington, New Zealand, Brisbane, and Sydney. Based on recorded oral testimonies, the *Encyclopaedia Judaica,* and monographs; 99 notes. 1942-78

Gottwald, Klement

2630. Cesar, Jaroslav and Krempa, Ivan. K VÝRIČÍ KLEMENTA GOTTWALDA [On Klement Gottwald's anniversary]. *Československý Časopis Historický [Czechoslovakia] 1986 34(5): 641-657.* Klement Gottwald (1896-1953) led the Communist Party of Czechoslovakia after the historic 5th Party Congress of 1929, when the Party adopted the Bolshevik line he had advocated. In his wartime exile in Moscow and in the early postwar years, when he became premier, he secured Czechoslovakia's new Soviet orientation and presided over the Communist victory of February 1948. His premature death deprived socialism and Czechoslovakia of a major fighter and statesman. 16 notes. Russian and German summaries. 1920's-53

2631. Hájek, Jiří. KLEMENT GOTTWALD A SOCIALISTICKÁ KULTURNÍ REVOLUCE [Klement Gottwald and the socialist cultural revolution]. *Česká Literatura [Czechoslovakia] 1982 30(3): 204-207.* Whatever the subsequent perversions, it was Klement Gottwald and his formulation of principles for a cultural policy that provided a valid starting point for cultural political activity. 1948-49

2632. Heřtová, Jaroslava. ZDENĚK NEJEDLÝ A NÁSTUP GOTTWALDOVSKÉHO VEDENÍ KSČ [Zdeněk Nejedlý and the advent of the Gottwald leadership of the Communist Party of Czechoslovakia]. *Česká Literatura [Czechoslovakia] 1982 30(3): 214-216.* Nejedlý and Klement Gottwald had always shared the same ideals, but the arrival of Gottwald at the head of the Communist Party was a turning point for Nejedlý, who joined the Party and came to influence the young generation of Marxist critics and to inspire later writers. 1920's-30's

2633. Krempa, Ivan. REVOLUČNÍ ODKAZ KLEMENTA GOTTWALDA [Klement Gottwald's revolutionary legacy]. *Československý Časopis Hist. [Czechoslovakia] 1982 30(2): 161-172.* As the Communist Party of Czechoslovakia has emerged victoriously from the dangerous attempts at disintegration in the 1960's, the Leninist leadership of Klement Gottwald (1896-1953), both before and after World War II, is being once more duly appreciated. 20 notes. 1921-53

2634. Snítil, Zdeněk. DAS REVOLUTIONÄRE VERMÄCHTNIS KLEMENT GOTTWALDS—LEBENDIGER BESTANDTEIL DER SECHZIGJÄHRIGEN GESCHICHTE DER KPTSCH [The revolutionary legacy of Klement Gottwald: a lively component of the 60-year history of the Czechoslovak Communist Party]. *Beiträge zur Gesch. der Arbeiterbewegung [East Germany] 1981 23(3): 339-344.* Assesses the Czechoslovak Communist leader Klement Gottwald's (1896-1953) importance in establishing the Communist Party in Czechoslovakia, and considers his role within the Party, particularly as its leader, 1948-53. Under his leadership the Czechoslovak Communist Party established close links with the USSR and other socialist states including East Germany. Gottwald—revolutionary, politician, and statesman—began his political activities in 1917, joined the Czechoslovak Communist Party in 1921, gained a reputation as a politician during the 1920's and 1930's, was active in Moscow during World War II continuing the work of the Party, participated in the Slovak uprising of 1945, was nominated as Party chairman in 1946, and served as president of the Czechoslovak Republic, 1948-53. 1917-53

2635. Truhlář, Břetislav. KLEMENT GOTTWALD A JEHO VZŤAH K SLOVENSKEJ KULTÚRE V DVADSIATYCH ROKOCH [Klement Gottwald and his attitude toward Slovak culture in the 1920's]. *Česká Literatura [Czechoslovakia] 1982 30(3): 208-210.* Arriving in Banská Bystrica in 1921, Gottwald became administrator of *Hlas L'udu,* where as in *Spartakus,* which he founded and edited, he provided a forum for many important Slovak socialist writers. 1921-29

2636. Vávra, Vlastimil and Drška, Pavel. K VOJENSKOPOLITICKÉMU ODKAZU KLEMENTA GOTTWALDA [Military and political legacy of Klement Gottwald]. *Hist. a Vojenství [Czechoslovakia] 1981 30(5): 33-42.* Klement Gottwald, a leading personality in the history of the Czech Communist movement, struggled against fascism in all of its mutations. This struggle was led first from the platform of the Czech Parliament and the Communist Party press. After the Munich disaster, Gottwald escaped to Moscow to continue the fight. After liberation, his participation in the development of a modern socialist army made it a dependable tool in the hands of workers and peasants in the socialist state. Based on Gottwald's writings; 12 notes. 1922-53

Goutte, Jean de la

2637. Reites, James W. JEAN DE LA GOUTTE—SLAVE OF THE TURK. *Arch. Hist. Societatis Iesu [Italy] 1982 51(102): 300-313.* The story of the French Jesuit, who spent the last two years of his life as a captive of the Turks, reveals not only his heroism but also a facet of the first Jesuit general's personality, his deep concern and care for his charges. 1554-56

Govorukhin, Orest

2638. Al'tman, I. A. RUSSKII REVOLIUTSIONER V BOLGARII—OREST GEORGIEV-GOVORUKHIN [A Russian revolutionary in Bulgaria—Orest Georgiev-Govorukhin]. *Bulgarian Hist. Rev. [Bulgarian] 1982 10(4): 84-91.* Orest Makarovich Govorukhin, known as Orest Georgiev during his stay in Bulgaria, was a Russian revolutionary, friend of Lenin's elder brother, and a teacher. He entered Bulgaria in 1894 after political exile in Zurich and at first taught chemistry and Russian in Plovdiv. He came to Sofia in 1897 and from 1911 taught Russian language and literature at the University of Sofia. Orest Govorukhin left Bulgaria for the USSR in 1925 because of fascist terror. During his stay in Bulgaria he was active in the Bulgarian Communist movement. Based on the works of Bulgarian historians; 55 notes. 1894-1925

Goytisolo, Juan

2639. Gorokhoff, Claude. LES PARIS DE L'EXIL: PARIS DANS *LE TROPIQUE DU CANCER* D'HENRI MILLER ET DANS *PIÈCES D'IDENTITÉ* DE JUAN GOYTISOLO [The exile's Paris: Paris in *Tropic of Cancer* by Henry Miller and in *Señas de Identidad* by Juan Goytisolo]. *Rev. Belge de Philologie et d'Hist. [Belgium] 1981 59(3): 597-619.* Describes the reactions of two famous literary exiles (Miller in the 1930's and Goytisolo in the 1950's) in Paris. Although limited to the quarters inhabited by foreigners and appalled at ugliness and coldness, both men came to appreciate Paris as a link to the past and to their own countries. Based on an exegesis of the texts and the literature of literary criticism; 131 notes. 1931-66

Gradić, Stjepan

2640. Krasić, Stjepan. STJEPAN GRADIĆ AND CULTURAL CONDITIONS IN SEVENTEENTH CENTURY DUBROVNIK. *East European Q. 1982 16(1): 17-31.* Describes the professional activities of "one of the great men" of Dubrovnik (Ragusa). Gradić (1613-83) was an aristocrat who received a good education both in his home city and in Italy. He was a diplomat for both Dubrovnik and the papacy. He was an outstanding speaker, who twice delivered addresses to conclaves before the pope was chosen. He was a scientist, a poet, and a librarian as well, concluding his career as the Head Vatican Librarian. Based on published material and unpublished Vatican sources; 52 notes. 1613-83

Gräffer, Franz

2641. Roth, B. "Franz Gräffer, 1785-1852: Leben, Werk und Wirkung" [Franz Gräffer (1785-1852): life, work, and influence]. U. of Vienna [Austria] 1979. 304 pp. *DAI-C 1984 45(3): 681; 9/2781c.* 1815-52

Graham, Shardalow Lee Tucker

2642. Sinclair, W. A. G. S. L. TUCKER, 1924-80. *Australian Econ. Hist. Rev. [Australia] 1981 21(1): 1-5.* A tribute to the Australian economic historian, Graham Shardalow Lee Tucker (1924-80). He made significant contributions to the study of economic thought and demographic history. He was considered a world authority on Ricardian thought. Lists Tucker's publications. 1924-80

Graliński, Zygmunt

2643. Borkowski, Jan. ZYGMUNT GRALIŃSKI—MIESZCZAŃSKI POLITYK W RUCHU LUDOWYM [Zygmunt Graliński—a bourgeois politician in the people's movement]. *Kultura i Społeczeństwo [Poland] 1979 23(4): 119-130.* Zygmunt Gralinski (1897-1940), born a bourgeois, exposed to both radical and Masonic influences while studying in France, joined the people's movement in Poland as a member of the Polskie Stronnictwo Ludowe—"Wyzwolenie" [Polish People's Party—Liberation], later Stronnictwo Ludowe [People's Party]. A member of the legislature and the Ministry of Foreign Affairs from 1928, he was a strong antifascist, a democrat, an advocate of an alliance with democratic Western Europe, and a supporter of unity in the peasant movement. However, he failed the movement by not supporting active opposition to the dictatorial tendencies of the Polish government in the 1930's. Based on archival and other primary and secondary sources; 24 notes. 1920's-40

Grameno, Mihal

2644. Xega, Franklin. MIHAL GRAMENOJA LUFTËTAR PËR LIRINË E ATDHEUT [Mihal Grameno as a fighter for his country's freedom]. *Studime Filologjike [Albania] 1981 35(1): 25-29.* Describes the part played by Mihal Grameno (1871-1931) in the Albanian nationalist struggle between 1907 and 1909. 1907-09

Gramsci, Antonio

2645. Gramsci, Antonio. FROM ANTONIO GRAMSCI *LETTERE DAL CARCERE. Italian Quarterly 1984 25(97-98): 189-204.* Publishes 10 of Antonio Gramsci's letters written during his imprisonment and previously unpublished in English. 1927-33

2646. Rosengarten, Frank. THREE ESSAYS ON ANTONIO GRAMSCI'S *LETTERS FROM PRISON. Italian Quarterly 1984 25(97-98): 7-40.* Antonio Gramsci's correspondence with his mother, his wife, and his sister-in-law provides insight into his character and his thoughts on imprisonment, education, religion, and women. Also surveys the several editions of *Letters from Prison* published in Italian and foreign languages, citing editors and translators. 1926-37

2647. Szabó, Tibor. GRAMSCI POLITIKAI FILOZÓFIÁJA: EGY MARXISTA POLITIKUS-FILOZÓFUS ARCKÉPÉHEZ/ [Gramsci's political philosophy: portrait of a Marxist political philosopher]. *Társadalmi Szemle [Hungary] 1981 36(1): 67-75.* Reviews the life and work of Antonio Gramsci (1918-47). 1918-47

2648. Tusa, Vincenzo. GRAMSCI A USTICA [Gramsci in Ustica]. *Ponte [Italy] 1981 37(6): 509-512.* Antonio Gramsci was sentenced to confinement for five years on the island of Ustica, province of Palermo, Sicily, but remained there only 43 days, from 7 December 1926 to 20 January

1927; nevertheless he speaks of the island in many of his letters as a haven of peace and quiet after his stay in the prison of Regina Coeli. 20c

Grandi, Dino

2649. DeFelice, Renzo. I DIARI, LE MEMORIE E LE CARTE DI DINO GRANDI [The diary, the memoirs, and the letters of Dino Grandi]. *Rassegna degli Archivi di Stato [Italy] 1983 43(2-3): 371-379.* Also published in Italian with English translation following in *Italian Quarterly* 1983 24(93). 1922-45

Granger, John

2650. Hattaway, R. GRANGER'S WHITFORD BRICK AND TILE WORKS. *Auckland Waikato Historical Journal [New Zealand] 1984 (44): 21-24.* John Granger founded factories to produce bricks and tiles at what would become Whitford, New Zealand. 1865-1981

Granlund, Johan

2651. Bringéus, Nils-Arvid. JOHAN GRANLUND (1901-1982): ETNOLOG OCH KULTURHISTORIKER [Johan Granlund (1901-1982): ethnologist and cultural historian]. *Rig [Sweden] 1983 66: 65-71.* An obituary for Johan Granlund, professor of ethnology at Stockholm University, who also published research in Swedish cultural history. Includes a bibliography of his works for 1972-83 which supplements the bibliography of 1929-76 publications issued by the Nordic Museum, Stockholm, in 1976. 1929-83

Granö, Johannes Gabriel

2652. Mereste, U. I. G. GRANE I TEORETICHESKAIA GEOGRAFIIA [J. G. Granö and theoretical geography]. *Skandinavskii Sbornik [USSR] 1983 28: 121-131.* Outlines the academic achievements of Johannes Gabriel Granö (1882-1956), who formulated principles of theoretical geography and methodology of geographic research while teaching at the Tartu University. Secondary sources; 15 notes. Swedish summary. 1882-1956

Granovski, Timofei

2653. Vlček, Rudomír. KE 130. VÝROČÍ ÚMRTÍ T. N. GRANOVSKÉHO [Honoring the 130th anniversary of the death of T. N. Granovski]. *Slovanský Přehled [Czechoslovakia] 1985 71(6): 519-526.* Timofei N. Granovski (1813-55), one of the foremost Westernizers among the Russians of the 1840's, was instrumental in the investigation and study of Western history, especially the medieval period, in Russia. In addition to being a historian, he was a political scientist who saw the ideal state in the British style constitutional monarchy. It was his study of the West that brought him into the liberal Western camp and made him a critic of Russian autocracy. 21 notes. 1840's-55

Grant, James Augustus

2654. Cunningham, I. C. THE JAMES GRANT PAPERS IN THE NATIONAL LIBRARY OF SCOTLAND. *Hist. in Africa 1980 7: 333-336.* Announcement of the acquisition by the National Library of Scotland of the papers of James Augustus Grant (1827-92). Lists the various papers by categories, including family correspondence, letters from explorers and others relating to Africa, Grant's journals, sketches, maps, newspaper clippings, and assorted papers. Material available for perusal by qualified students. 1846-92

Grassman, Sven

2655. Siven, Claes-Henrik. SVEN GRASSMAN: EN UDDA RÖST [Sven Grassman: a different voice]. *Svensk Tidskrift [Sweden] 1982 69(1): 41-46.* Reviews Sven Grassman's *Det tyste riket* [The quiet kingdom] (1981). Grassman is unique among Swedish economists because he criticized the Social Democratic government's policies from an entirely different perspective than most economists. Unlike others he also contended that Sweden's *Riksbank* [National Bank] presented inaccurate information regarding Sweden's balance of payments and foreign debt. Sweden's economic growth was therefore much less than it could have been. But he also interprets the negative connection between production and average production costs improperly. Moreover, his account of his departure from the Institut för internationell ekonomi [Institute of International Economics] differs from the author's investigation of the incident. 1970-81

Gratius, Ortwin

2656. Mehl, James V. ORTWIN GRATIUS' *ORATIONES QUODLIBETICAE:* HUMANIST APOLOGY IN SCHOLASTIC FORM. *J. of Medieval and Renaissance Studies 1981 11(1): 57-69.* Gratius has often been characterized satirically as "a ridiculous ally of harebrained scholastics and demented monks." The author attempts a rehabilitation by discussing Gratius's work as a humanist teacher and editor in Germany's most conservative university at Cologne, 1501-07. Analyzes Gratius's disputations based on the surviving texts and contemporary comments. Topics include the construction of propositions, quotation of classical authors, and the art of rhetoric. Gratius's appeal for humanistic learning at the University of Cologne was not successful, yet his work had an impact on his colleagues as they came to tolerate preparatory courses in the humanities. 51 notes. 1501-07

Gratz, Gustav

2657. Matsch, Erwin. SECHS AUSSENMINISTER, DIE AUS DEM ALTEN ÖSTERREICH KAMEN [Six ministers of foreign affairs from old Austria]. *Archiv für Kulturgeschichte [West Germany] 1982 64(1): 171-215.* 1919-38

For abstract see ***Csáky, Emmerich***

Graves, Robert

2658. Vajda, Miklós. ROBERT GRAVES AND HIS HUNGARIAN PRIZE. *New Hungarian Quarterly [Hungary] 1985 26(100): 188-191.* With royalites gained from the publication and translation of his works in Hungary, the British writer Robert Graves endowed an ongoing prize in 1968 for outstanding Hungarian poetry. 1968-84

Gray, John

2659. Temple, Ruth Z. THE OTHER CHOICE: THE WORLDS OF JOHN GRAY, POET AND PRIEST. *Bull. of Res. in the Humanities 1981 84(1): 16-64.* Discusses the career of English writer and priest John Gray including his decadent period in the 1890's, and his conversion to Roman Catholicism in 1900, with special attention to his relationships with his contemporaries. 1890-1934

Graziadei, Antonio

2660. Colombo, Arturo. L'ATTIVITÀ PARLAMENTARE DI ANTONIO GRAZIADEI [The parliamentary activity of Antonio Graziadei]. *Politico [Italy] 1981 46(4): 633-654.* A member of Parliament from 1910 to 1926, when he was dismissed along with others of the Aventine secession,

Antonio Graziadei was a leading Socialist and then a founder of the Italian Communist Party. Traces Graziadei's parliamentary activity from his constant opposition to Giolittian policy through his neutralism in World War I to his split with the Socialist Party in the difficult postwar period and his analysis of Fascism as essentially restorationist and to the detriment of the popular classes. 1910-26

2661. Tesoro, Marina. ANTONIO GRAZIADEI: IL POLITICO E L'ECONOMISTA [Antonio Graziadei, politician and economist]. *Politico [Italy] 1981 46(4): 629-632.* Graziadei was a dissenter in the ranks first of the Socialist and then the Communist Party. His principal aim was to combat "the unfounded portions of Marx's thought, especially the doctrine on value which he had borrowed from Ricardo." He often disagreed with Antonio Gramsci and with Amadeo Bordiga. He was finally expelled from the Communist Party but to the end he was convinced he had been faithful to the *Communist Manifesto.* His thought remains an important contribution to the present discussions for a revision of Marxist thought. 1900-20's

Grażynski, Michał

2662. Marszałek, Leon. MICHAŁ GRAŻYNSKI [Michał Grażynski]. *Zeszyty Hist. [Poland] 1983 (64): 91-131.* Michał Grażynski (1890-1965), Polish political activist of the Józef Piłsudski camp, participated in the third Silesian rising, organizing opposition to the Germans. In independent Poland under Piłsudski's government he worked briefly in the Ministry for Agricultural Reform. After the May 1926 coup he became the chief organizer of the youth movement. Mistrusted by the Polish government in exile after 1939, he was interned by the British authorities until 1943. He remained in Great Britain until his death. Central Military Archives; 78 notes. 1890-1965

Greatrakes, Valentine

2663. Kaplan, Barbara Beigun. GREATRAKES THE STROKER: THE INTERPRETATIONS OF HIS CONTEMPORARIES. *Isis 1982 73(267): 178-185.* In 1666 Valentine Greatrakes, an Irish healer, visited England where his ministrations aroused widespread interest among the scientific and intellectual community. Many were convinced that his healing powers were genuine; several tried to explain how his "cures" were effected; and a few denounced him as a quack. Their numerous writings reflect a considerable range of attitudes toward healing and healers in 17th century England. Based mainly on English writings of the 1660's-70's; 17 notes. 1660's-70's

Greaves family

2664. Stunt, Timothy C. F. THE GREAVES FAMILY: SOME CLARIFICATIONS. *Notes and Queries [Great Britain] 1981 28(5): 405-408.* Identifies the members of the extensive Greaves family, active in early 19th-century British Evangelicalism, and their religious activities. 19c

Grechko, Andrei A.

2665. Ivanov, S. P. POLKOVODETS SOVETSKOI SHKOLY [A military leader of the Soviet school]. *Voenno-Istoricheskii Zhurnal [USSR] 1983 (10): 55-60.* A military biography of Marshal of the Soviet Union Andrei A. Grechko (b. 1903), on the occasion of his 80th birthday. Emphasizes his rise to military greatness during World War II and his elevation to minister of defense. 4 photos, 3 notes. 1903-83

Greco, El

2666. Canaday, John. THE GREEK WHO BORE GREAT GIFTS TO ALL MANKIND. *Smithsonian 1982 13(4): 48-61.* Describes the art and career of El Greco. 1560's-1614

2667. Miller, Hope Ridings. A MAN FOR HIS TIME. *Horizon 1982 25(5): 48-55.* On the occasion of an international tour of an exhibition of El Greco's works, discusses evidence that refutes El Greco's reputation as a mad, partially blind visionary and suggests that his style was "... deliberately developed... to draw attention to his work as a forceful expression of Counter Reformation theology." 1580's-1610's

Green, E. R. R.

2668. Black, R. D. Collinson. E. R. R. GREEN 1920-1981. *Irish Econ. and Social Hist. [Great Britain] 1981 8: 5-7.* An obituary for Professor E. R. R. Green (1920-81), the first director of the Institute of Irish Studies at Queen's University in Belfast. Green was best known for his work in Irish economic history in the 19th century and Ulster's industrial archaeology. 2 notes. 1920-81

Green, Joseph Henry

2669. Jackson, H. J. COLERIDGE'S COLLABORATOR, JOSEPH HENRY GREEN. *Studies in Romanticism 1982 21(2): 161-179.* 1817-34
*For abstract see **Coleridge, Samuel Taylor***

Green, T. H.

2670. Nicholson, Peter P. T. H. GREEN AND STATE ACTION: LIQUOR LEGISLATION. *History of Political Thought [Great Britain] 1985 6(3): 517-550.* British political philosopher T. H. Green was active in the temperance movement, joined the United Kingdom Alliance in 1872, and advocated extremely stringent regulations on licensing and tavern hours. Green believed that too much liquor and too many licensed premises contributed to drunkenness and that drunkenness was detrimental to the individual and society. Green accepted Kant's notion of the common good as the moral criterion for state action and argued that the state should interfere whenever it can produce conditions favorable to the moral action of its citizens. Green's moral theory was not expedient but his reform proposals were knowledgeable, rational, and consistent with his political philosophy. 129 notes. 1870-1900

Greene, Graham

2671. Stannard, Martin. IN SEARCH OF HIMSELVES: THE AUTOBIOGRAPHICAL WRITINGS OF GRAHAM GREENE. *Prose Studies [Great Britain] 1985 8(2): 139-155.* Graham Greene's belief in a split between the private or dream world and the public "real" world led him to present his "I" as a plurality of selves which he was reluctant to unite or clarify. 20c

Greenwood, James

2672. Diamond, B. I. and Baylen, J. P. JAMES GREENWOOD'S LONDON: A PRECURSOR OF CHARLES BOOTH. *Victorian Periodicals Review [Canada] 1984 17(1-2): 34-43.* During his career in journalism, James Greenwood (1831-1927) always displayed a concern for the working-class poor. From 1869 to 1874, he wrote a series of notable articles on the social problems of Victorian London, which influenced members of the Fabian Society. 1840's-96

Gregorovius, Ferdinand

2673. Miltenburg, A. P. J. FERDINAND GREGOROVIUS, GESCHIEDSCHRIJVER VAN ROME [Ferdinand Gregorovius, historian of Rome]. *Spiegel Hist. [Netherlands] 1982 17(9): 438-444.* An overview of the life and work of the German historian Ferdinand Gregorovius (ca. 1831-91). His journey to Italy in 1852 took him to Rome where he lived until 1874 and where he produced his life work, *The History of the City of Rome in the Middle Ages.* Primary sources; 8 illus. 1831-91

Gregory, John W.

2674. Branagan, David and Lim, Elaine. J. W. GREGORY, TRAVELLER IN THE DEAD HEART. *Historical Records of Australian Science [Australia] 1984 6(1): 71-84.* John W. Gregory (1864-1932), a British geologist, was professor of geology and mineralogy at the University of Melbourne from 1900 to 1904, when he accepted a similar position at the University of Glasgow. He wrote several articles while in Australia, and his best known book, *The Dead Heart of Australia* (1906), is an account of an expedition that he led into central Australia in 1901-02. The article summarizes his Australian activities, emphasizing the Dead Heart Expedition, and evaluates his writings. Based on Gregory's writings, archives of the University of Melbourne, and other reports; 2 photos, map, 84 notes. 1900-06

Greig, Aleksei S.

2675. Kriuchkov, Iuri S. ADMIRAL A. S. GREIG—UCHENYI I KORABLESTROITEL' [Admiral A. S. Greig, scholar and fleet builder]. *Voprosy Istorii Estestvoznaniia i Tekhniki [USSR] 1982 (2): 80-88.* Admiral Aleksei S. Greig (1775-1845), astronomer and mathematician, is best remembered for the innovations he introduced in the design, construction, and diversity of warships as commander-in-chief of the Black Sea Fleet, 1816-30. He greatly expanded the size of the fleet, improved the seaworthiness, maneuverability, and armament of vessels, and modernized shipbuilding techniques by using steam-operated machinery. With prophetic foresight he recognized the potential of steamships and added five steam warships to his revamped fleet. 38 notes, 3 illus. 1816-30

Greive, Hermann

2676. Ehrlich, Ernst Ludwig. HERMANN GREIVE ZUM GEDENKEN [In memory of Hermann Greive]. *Judaica [Switzerland] 1984 40(3): 129-131.* Obituary of Hermann Greive (d. 1984), historian of relations between Catholicism and Judaism and anti-Semitism in Germany and Austria. 19c-20c

Grekov, Boris D.

2677. Bromlei, Iu. V. and Naumov, E. P. AKADEMIK B. D. GREKOV I RAZVITIE SOVETSKOI ISTORICHESKOI NAUKI (K 100-LETIIU SO DNIA ROZHDENIIA) [Academician B. D. Grekov and the development of Soviet historical science: on the 100th anniversary of his birth]. *Novaia i Noveishaia Istoriia [USSR] 1982 (2): 202-210.* Boris D. Grekov was born 22 April 1882 in Mirgorod. He entered Warsaw University historical philological faculty in 1901, Moscow University in 1905, and published his first work in 1908. A convinced Marxist interested in the development of the historical process and a great pedagogue, he studied the social conditions and the legislation of 16th- and 17th-century Russia. He was a member of the Slavic section of the Soviet Academy of Sciences as well as a deputy both of the Supreme Soviet of the RSFSR and of the Supreme Soviet of the USSR. He was decorated with two Orders of Lenin, and the Order of the Labor Red Banner. 38 notes. 1882-1982

2678. Gorskaia, N. A. PAMIATI AKADEMIKA B. D. GREKOVA [B. D. Grekov: in memoriam]. *Voprosy Istorii [USSR] 1982 (4): 109-116.* Review article of the major historical works of Boris D. Grekov (1882-1953). His studies, published 1912-52, deal with Russian feudalism, serfdom, socioeconomic development, and legal status of peasants, mainly 15th-17th centuries. His work shows his gradual endorsement of Marxism. 30 notes. 1912-52

Grenville, George

2679. Galgano, Michael J. GEORGE GRENVILLE AND THE ENGLISH CONSTITUTION. *J. of the West Virginia Hist. Assoc. 1981 5(1): 7-17.* Discusses the political career of George Grenville, who entered the English Parliament and served from 1741 until his death in 1770, and especially his role as a staunch defender of Great Britain's Constitution. 1741-70

Grepp, Kyrre

2680. Petrick, Fritz. ER WIRD BEIM PROLETARIAT UNVERGESSEN BLEIBEN: KYRRE GREPP [He will never be forgotten by the proletariat: Kyrre Grepp]. *Beiträge zur Gesch. der Arbeiterbewegung [East Germany] 1980 22(1): 109-115.* Provides a summary of the life and political activities of Kyrre Grepp (1879-1922), one of the pioneers of the Communist movement in Norway. Discusses his early life and education, his marriage to Rachel Helland in 1904, his ill health, and his activities, particularly as editor of the socialist weekly *Our Time* from 1908. Grepp was a member of the Social Democratic Youth League which was on the left of the Norwegian working class movement, and the author shows how Grepp worked to safeguard the aims of this movement. He also became a committee member of the Norwegian Workers Party (DNA) and was a member of the executive committee of the Comintern. Based on papers belonging to the Norwegian Workers Party and the Communist Internationale and secondary sources; 30 notes. 1904-22

Greville, Frances

2681. Bell, Susan Groag. LADY WARWICK: ARISTOCRAT, SOCIALIST, GARDENER. *San José Studies 1982 8(1): 38-61.* A biography of Frances, Countess of Warwick (1861-1938), born Frances Evelyn Maynard Greville and known to her friends as "Daisy." She was a noted aristocrat, socialist reformer, author of a book about her garden at Easton Lodge, Essex, and lover of Edward VII from 1889 to 1897. 1861-1938

Grew, Nehemiah

2682. Sakula, Alex. DOCTOR NEHEMIAH GREW (1641-1712) AND THE EPSOM SALTS. *Clio Medica [Netherlands] 1984 19(1-2): 1-22.* Dr. Nehemiah Grew (1641-1712), a distinguished botanist, attempted to promote the internal use of mineral water for the cure of an assortment of maladies. Grew analyzed the water from the Epsom source, discovered in 1618, and in 1679 presented three papers to the Royal Society of Surgeons on the therapeutic values of Epsom water. In 1695 he published a Latin treatise on the subject. Partly as a result of Grew's writing, Epsom, 15 miles outside of London, became a popular spa for the English aristocracy. Grew discovered a source similar to Epsom water near London, and hoped to become rich from it, but failed to do so. Two brothers, George and Francis Moult, apothecaries, discovered another source near London, borrowed ideas from Grew's works, and made a fortune selling bottled mineral water. 59 notes. 1660's-1712

Grey, Jane

2683. Prochaska, Frank. THE MANY FACES OF LADY JANE GREY. *History Today [Great Britain] 1985 35(Oct): 34-40.* Reviews the short life and turbulent times of Lady Jane Grey (1537-54), who served as queen of England, 9-19 July 1553. Notes the portrayal of Jane in subsequent works of art and literature and in 20th-century films. 16c-20c

Grey family

2684. Bernard, G. W. THE FORTUNES OF THE GREYS, EARLS OF KENT, IN THE EARLY SIXTEENTH CENTURY. *Hist. J. [Great Britain] 1982 25(3): 671-685.* Describes the financial misfortunes of the Grey family, 1503-35, in order to show how a prominent baronial family could fall from power. Richard Grey, third earl of Kent (d. 1524), managed to alienate or sell most of the lands he inherited in 1503 and put himself at the mercy of grasping courtiers. But Henry VII's efforts to get these lands for return to Grey show his desire to maintain a strong and well-endowed nobility. Richard's successor, Sir Henry Grey, tried by a variety of legal devices to recover his lands but only made things worse and ended up as a minor Midlands gentleman. Based on documents in the Public Record Office, the Bedfordshire County Record Office, and published sources; 96 notes. 1503-35

Greysing, Martin

2685. Schuster, Laurenz O. Praem. ABT MARTIN GREYSING (1592-1665) [Abbot Martin Greysing (1592-1665)]. *Montfort [Austria] 1981 33(3): 197-218.* In 1657, abbot Martin Greysing from Mellau in Vorarlberg managed to establish the Schlägl monastery in Upper Austria as an abbey, which guaranteed the survival of that establishment after the damages of the Thirty Years War. 1592-1665

Grieve, Christopher Murray

See MacDiarmid, Hugh

Griffith, Arthur

2686. Glandon, Virginia E. ARTHUR GRIFFITH AND THE IDEAL IRISH STATE. *Studies [Ireland] 1984 73(289): 26-36.* The author suggests that a reassessment of the role of Arthur Griffith, nationalist propagandist, economic theorist, diplomat, and statesman from 1900 to 1922 is long overdue. Three questions are raised in this paper: Was Griffith a Republican? Where did he stand on physical force as a method for winning Irish independence? Why did he sign the Anglo-Irish Treaty of 6 December 1921 without further reference to Dublin? To answer them the author read all the available literature relating to Griffith and the period and conducted interviews from 1971 to 1973 with several of Griffith's contemporaries, such as Liam O'Briain, Ernest Blyth, and Dr. Michael Hayes. Based on tapes and transcripts of interviews with Griffith's contemporaries and Richard Mulcahy's Papers at University College, Dublin; 22 notes. 1900-22

Griffith, Samuel Walker

2687. Joyce, R. B. THE MAITLAND YEARS OF SIR SAMUEL WALKER GRIFFITH. *Australian J. of Pol. and Hist. [Australia] 1983 29(2): 262-276.* Provides the biography of Sir Samuel Walker Griffith, who served as Premier of Queensland, 1890-93. The author examines his boyhood years at Maitland between 1856 and 1860. After outlining Griffith's family background, he discusses the boy's schooling and argues that divergences from family piety began before Griffith arrived at Maitland and were accentuated by experiences there and his later student years at the University of Sydney and overseas. Based on Griffith's papers and contemporary newspapers; 47 notes. 1856-93

2688. Shaw, George. ROGER BILBROUGH JOYCE 1924-84. *Australian Journal of Politics and History [Australia] 1984 30(3): 324-326.* 1870's-1920
For abstract see ***Joyce, Roger***

Griffith, William

2689. Barton, David A. WILLIAM GRIFFITH (1806-83): THE "HERCULES OF THE REFORM MOVEMENT." *Pro. of the Wesley Hist. Soc. [Great Britain] 1982 43(6, part 2): 165-170.* William Griffith was born in London and at the age of 12 was converted as the result of a revival that swept through the school he attended. He became a preacher but did not take his final examination for the Wesleyan ministry. His radical views became more extreme as he grew older, and in 1849 the Wesleyan Conference expelled him because he refused to sign a declaration stating that he had had nothing to do with the anonymous writings that attacked important people in the church and urged constitutional reform of the Methodist Church. In 1855 he became permanent pastor of the Derby Reform Church and in 1857 of their new chapel in Becket Street, from which position he retired in 1877. ca 1818-83

Grigorenko, Petro G.

2690. Gaius, Marius. MAJOR GENERAL PYOTR GRIGORENKO—SOVIET HERETIC. *Military Rev. 1982 62(10): 2-14.* The case of General Petro G. Grigorenko illustrates the fate of the dissenter within the Soviet military and societal structure. He served 34 years in the military with superior ratings, but when he expressed ideas that he hoped could bring about meaningful changes in Soviet society and politics, he was stripped of his post, sent to a psychiatric hospital, and eventually exiled. Although dissenters rarely have come from the ranks of the military, Grigorenko's moral courage motivated him to speak out against military inefficiency, the suppression of Czechoslovakia in 1968, and for the establishment of a Tatar national homeland. Photo, 52 notes. 1940's-80

Grigor'ev, V. A.

2691. —. GEROI BITVY POD MOSKVOI [Heroes of the battle of Moscow]. *Voenno-Istoricheskii Zhurnal [USSR] 1982 (1): 48-53.* Describes the actions of certain Communists and Komsomol members who performed feats of bravery during the Battle of Moscow, 1941-42. First Lieutenant I. S. Shevliakov sacrificed his life to ensure success in the attack on Novo-Kobelevo; Sergeant V. A. Grigor'ev destroyed over 15 enemy tanks. In December 1941 Lieutenant N. F. Kretov destroyed 10 tanks and was responsible for heavy enemy casualties during a tank-ambush. Based on archives of TsAMO SSSR; 9 notes. 1941-42

Grigulevich, Iosif R.

2692. —. CHLENU-KORRESPONDENTU AN SSSR I. R. GRIGULEVICHU 70 LET [Corresponding member of the USSR Academy of Sciences, I. R. Grigulevich is 70 years old]. *Novaia i Noveishaia Istoriia [USSR] 1983 (3): 206-210.* Tribute to historian Iosif R. Grigulevich, whose writings on Latin America include 26 monographs and some 300 shorter works. Of particular interest are his studies on the role played by the Catholic Church in Latin American politics and Church ties to ruling oligarchies, bibliographies of 19th- and 20th-century freedom fighters, and his outstanding monograph *Kul'turnaia Revoliutsiia na Kube* [The Cuban cultural revolution] (1965). Photo, 21 notes. 1957-82

Grimarest, Jean Léonor Le Gallois de

2693. —. [AUTOUR DU TRAITÉ DU RÉCITATIF DE GRIMAREST] [Author of the *Traité du Récitatif* by Grimarest]. *Dix-Septième Siècle [France] 1981 33(3): 303-317.*

France, Peter. PRÉCEPTES ET PROBLÈMES [Precepts and problems], *pp. 303-310.*

McGowan, Margaret. DE LA DÉCLAMATION EXPRESSIVE [The expressive statement], *pp. 310-317.* Jean-Léonor Le Gallois de Grimarest (1659-1713), a mediocre writer, is best known for his biography of Molière published in 1705. A severe critic, Grimarest developed the idea that contemporary actors were incapable of expressing emotion either in gestures or words; he suggested they study rhetoric. 53 notes. 17c-18c

Grimm, Jacob and Wilhelm

2694. Reiher, Ruth. DIE BRÜDER GRIMM IN IHREM VERHÄLTNIS ZUR NATIONALEN TRADITION [The Grimm brothers and their attitude toward the national tradition]. *Wissenschaftliche Zeitschrift der Humboldt-Universität zu Berlin. Gesellschaftswissenschaftliche Reihe [East Germany] 1984 33(5): 515-517.* Examines Jacob and Wilhelm Grimm's concept of *Volk* [people of a nation] and the characteristics of the German nation as a reaction to the tumultuous sociopolitical situation in Germany during the early 19th century. Notes how these concepts affected their work. 19c

Gris, Juan

2695. Green, Christopher. PURITY, POETRY AND THE PAINTING OF JUAN GRIS. *Art Hist. [Great Britain] 1982 5(2): 180-204.* Juan Gris's paintings and his theory of the synthetic process, which permitted aesthetic purity apart from realism, 1917-19, were influenced by his friendship with French poets such as Pierre Reverdy. 1917-19

2696. Silver, Kenneth. EMINENCE GRIS. *Art in America 1984 72(5): 153-161.* Reviews the life and work of José Victoriano Carmelo Carlos González Pérez (pseud. Juan Gris), who emigrated from Spain to France in 1906 and from 1910 to 1917 participated in the development of cubism, continuing in the tradition until his death in 1927. 1910-27

Grogan, Ewart Scott

2697. Ofcansky, Thomas P. A BIO-BIBLIOGRAPHY OF E. S. GROGAN. *History in Africa 1983 10: 239-245.* Following his remarkable two-year walk from the Cape Colony to Cairo, Ewart Scott Grogan settled in Britain's East Africa Protectorate, where he remained as one of the leaders of Kenya's European community for over 50 years. Grogan's prolific writings on a wide variety of economic, political, and social issues are of great importance for historians of Kenya's colonial era. Based on Grogan's writings and secondary sources; biblio. 1900-67

Grojanowski, Jacob

2698. Shaul, Elisheva. GVIYAT-'EDUT ME-QABRAN-KEFIYAH YA'AQOV GROYANOVSQI: IZVIṢAH—QOLO—ḤELMNO [Eyewitness account of forced gravedigger Jacob Grojanowski: Izbica-Koło-Chełmno]. *Yalkut Moreshet Periodical [Israel] 1983 (35): 101-122.* Jacob Grojanowski was the first man to escape from the Chełmno extermination camp where over 300,000 people were exterminated in gas-vans. One of a selected number of forced gravediggers, Jacob Grojanowski witnessed the first stage in the plan for total annihilation of the Jews by gas. He escaped and provided a detailed account for Dr. Emmanuel Ringelblum's underground Warsaw Ghetto Archives in the hope that he would be able to warn Jews of the fate awaiting them. Based on materials in the Ringelblum Archives, Warsaw. English summary. 1941-42

Gromov, Konstantin Grigorevich

2699. —. GEROI BITVY ZA BERLIN [Heroes of the battle for Berlin]. *Voenno-Istoricheskii Zhurnal [USSR] 1981 23(5): 33-37.* 1945

*For abstract see **Bavaev, Tadzhiali***

Groot, Willem de

2700. Ahsmann, Margreet. WILLEM DE GROOT (1597-1662) EN ZIJN STUDIE TE LEIDEN IN HET LICHT VAN BRIEVEN VAN ZIJN BROER HUGO [Willem de Groot (1597-1662) and his studies and Leiden as seen through his brother Hugo's letters]. *Tijdschrift voor Rechtsgeschiedenis [Netherlands] 1982 50(4): 371-401.* Covers the life and works of Willem de Groot, the little-known younger brother of Hugo Grotius (1583-1643). Willem studied law and received his doctorate at Leiden University, 1614-16, and then became an advocate at The Hague in 1618 and for the Dutch East India Company in 1639, when he was prevented by the political situation from studying Dutch law with his brother. Hugo's letters to Willem, 1614-16, (Willem's to Hugo are lost) discuss questions of natural law and the theses of legal disputations. Based on Hugo Grotius's correspondence; 235 notes. 1614-16

Gropius, Walter Adolph

2701. Khait, V. L. SOTSIAL'NO-UTOPICHESKIE TENDENTSII V ARKHITEKTURNOM SOZNANII ZAPADA XX VEKA [Utopian social tendencies in the 20th-century architectural consciousness of the West]. *Voprosy Filosofii [USSR] 1982 (6): 124-131.* From the 1920's onward, utopian architects in Western nations, such as Frank Lloyd Wright, Walter Adolph Gropius, and Le Corbusier, have been motivated by social and aesthetic concerns, overestimating their own importance as engineers of social transformation, and giving way to a new conservatism in architecture. 1920's-70's

Grosman, Ladislav

2702. Grosman, Ladislav. MEMORIES OF MY SERVICE IN A LABOR BATTALION. *Yad Vashem Studies on the European Jewish Catastrophe and Resistance [Israel] 1981 14: 287-302.* Recalls the years served in the Sixth Labor Battalion in Slovakia during World War II. Though the military regimen was rigorous, life in a labor battalion was preferable to being deported to a Nazi death-camp, the fate of the vast majority of Slovakian Jews. In a postscript to his memoir, the author of *The Shop On Main Street* tells how he returned to his home town, now without Jews, to make the film based on the popular book. 1941-44

Grosser, Bronisław

2703. Grinberg, Maria. BRONISŁAW GROSSER (1883-1912). W SETNĄ ROCZNICĘ URODZIN [Bronisław Grosser (1883-1912): on the hundredth anniversary of his birth]. *Biuletyn Żydowskiego Instytutu Historycznego w Polsce [Poland] 1983 (2-3): 97-109.* Provides a brief biography of the Polish Jew Bronisław Grosser, who became a member of the Jewish Bund (Allgemeiner Yiddisher Arbeiterbund in Lite, Poilen, un Russland) at an early age. He studied law in Switzerland, where he edited the *Głos Bundu* [Bund's voice], returning to Warsaw in 1905 where he was active during the revolution in Russia. He became a member of the Bund's central committee shortly before dying of an illness in 1912. 1900's-12

Grosso, Alfonso

2704. Merin, Maritza Hartman. "Alfonso Grosso y el Realismo Social" [Alfonso Grosso and Social Realism]. Wayne State U. 1983. 315 pp. *DAI 1983 44(3): 767-A.* DA8315612 1940's-50's

Grotewohl, Otto

2705. Fosske, Heinz. OTTO GROTEVOL': ODIN IZ OSNOVATELEI SEPG, PERVYI PREM'ER-MINISTR NEMETSKOGO GOSUDARSTVA RABOCHNIKH I KREST'IAN [Otto Grotewohl: one of the founders of the Socialist Unity Party, first prime minister of the German workers' and peasants' state]. *Novaia i Noveishaia Istoriia [USSR] 1981 (3): 82-107.* Traces the career of Otto Grotewohl (1894-1964). He became a printer in his home town of Brunswick, joined the Social Democratic Party, saw military service, was a member of the Landtag, was arrested and imprisoned, 1938-39, and emerged in 1945 as proponent of unity with the Communists. By 1949 he was president of the Council of Ministers of East Germany. 4 illus., 39 notes. 1910-64

Grotius, Hugo

2706. Azcárraga, José Luis de. ANTE EL CUARTO CENTENARIO DE HUGO GROCIO, EL "SEDICENTE" APOSTOL DE LA LIBERTAD DE LOS MARES [With respect to the fourth centenary of Hugo Grotius, the "supposed" apostle of the freedom of the seas]. *Rev. General de Marina [Spain] 1983 204(Mar): 371-376.* Reviews the life of the Dutch legal scholar Hugo Grotius, 1583-1645. Grotius, a child prodigy, wrote poems and histories, became Syndic of Rotterdam, was imprisoned due to a political coup and his Arminian religion, escaped to become the Swedish ambassador in Paris, and died as an aftermath of a shipwreck. Among the legal principles for which he is justly famed is that of the freedom of the seas. This principle was developed in a number of his studies beginning in 1604. The principle lives today in the Charter of the United Nations and in the work of the Third Law of the Sea Conference, completed in December 1982. Illus. 1583-1645

2707. Bots, Hans and Leroy, Pierre. HUGO GROTIUS ET LA REUNION DES CHRETIENS: ENTRE LE SAVOIR ET L'INQUIETUDE [Hugo Grotius and the reunion of Christians: between knowledge and anxiety]. *Dix-Septième Siècle [France] 1983 35(4): 451-469.* During the last five years of his life, eminent Dutch jurist and scholar Hugo Grotius (1583-1645) suffered from a change of mood and a condition of anxiety brought about partly by family problems, partly by failure in his diplomatic mission entrusted by Sweden, but mainly by his dominating concern in the question of the reunion of all Christian religions including the Catholic Church. He was insistent on formulating again and more explicitly what might help establish a religious peace in Europe. His works reflect such concern, particularly the *Votum pro Pace Ecclesiastica* (1644), which deals with a debate with theologian André Rivet. Based on Grotius's letters and other correspondence from scholars of the time; 76 notes. 1640-45

2708. Butkevich, V. G. POLITIKO-PRAVOVYE VZGLIADY GUGO GROTSIIA [Political and juridical views of Hugo Grotius]. *Sovetskoe Gosudarstvo i Pravo [USSR] 1984 (9): 80-87.* Assesses the conflict between Christian belief and scientific knowledge in the political and juridical thought of Hugo Grotius (1583-1645), Dutch diplomat and jurist, founder of international law. 1583-1645

2709. Eyffinger, E. HUGO DE GROOT [Hugo Grotius]. *Spiegel Hist. [Netherlands] 1983 18(5): 279-286.* An account of the life and character of Hugo Grotius on the 400th anniversary of his birth. Molded by the same upheavals that gave birth to the Dutch Republic, Grotius became one of its greatest intellectuals and its most famous political exile. Based on primary sources; 10 illus. 1583-1645

2710. Higgins, Rosalyn. GROTIUS AND THE UNITED NATIONS. *International Social Science Journal [France] 1985 37(1): 119-127.* Reviews the career of Hugo Grotius (1583-1645) and reflects on the application of his ideas to the workings of the UN, especially in its making of international law. 1945-82

2711. Zuber, Roger. LA TRIPLE JEUNESSE DE HUGO GROTIUS [Hugo Grotius's triple youth]. *Dix-Septième Siècle [France] 1983 35(4): 437-450.* A biographical sketch of Hugo Grotius (1583-1645), divided into three chronological parts, each one filled with different scholarly or political activities, but all characterized by the particular traits of youth. This eminent Dutch jurist, who had been a child prodigy, at 20 already had a great experience of life. From 1615 to 1625, he acquired an independence of judgment, advocated free-will doctrines, and wrote masterpieces of Church history. He was imprisoned by the Dutch government in 1618, escaped in 1621, and took refuge in France. Still active during this last period, he was more a historian and poet than a jurist and became a diplomat in the service of Sweden. Based on a general presentation of Grotius and his work; 37 notes. 1583-1645

Grouchy, Sophie de

2712. Chaussinand-Nogaret, Guy. LA MARQUISE DE CONDORCET, LA REVOLUTION ET LA REPUBLIQUE [The Marquise de Condorcet, the revolution and the republic]. *Histoire [France] 1984 (71): 30-38.* A biography of the political role played by Sophie de Grouchy, Marquise de Condorcet, who was an ardent advocate of the principles which guided the French Revolution and held a famous salon. 1789-1822

Grounds, Roy

2713. Frankel, O. H. SIR ROY GROUNDS, 1905-1981. *Hist. Records of Australian Sci. [Australia] 1982 5(3): 89-91.* Reviews the professional career of Australian architect Sir Roy Grounds. Trained in a Melbourne architectural firm, Grounds's aptitude won him the opportunity to study in the United States and England. His first major commission was the headquarters of the Australian Academy of Science, a project that gained national recognition. Succeeding achievements brought professional honors and knighthood. He was also a conservationist, and his final major work was the privately-accomplished reclamation of an abused forest area for a game refuge. 1939-81

Groussac, Paul

2714. Lagmanovich, David. PAUL GROUSSAC, ENSAYISTA DEL 80 [Paul Groussac, essayist of the generation of 1880]. *Inter-American Rev. of Biblio. 1982 32(1): 28-46.* Paul Groussac (1848-1929), educator, historian, and librarian, was born in France but spent his adult life in Argentina. The author focuses on Groussac as an essayist. Groussac combined his historical knowledge with romanticism to contribute to the development of the essay as a genre in Argentina. Time and travel are widely used themes in his essays. His *Los Que Pasaban* [Those who pass by] illustrates his ability as a biographer to give a picture of minor literary figures and of himself as well as the major Argentine literary figures discussed. Groussac served as a bridge between the different generations of Argentine literature, but he is best seen as a man of the generation of 1880. Based on an examination of Groussac's works; 48 notes. 1880-1929

Groux, Henry de

2715. Legrand, Francine-Claire. HENRY DE GROUX—LEON BLOY ET LAUTREAMONT [Henry de Groux: Léon Bloy and Lautréamont]. *Rev. de l'U. de Bruxelles [Belgium] 1981 (3): 67-73.* 1870-1910
*For abstract see **Bloy, Léon***

Grove, William Robert

2716. Cooper, M. L. and Hall, V. M. D. WILLIAM ROBERT GROVE AND THE LONDON INSTITUTION, 1841-1845. *Ann. of Sci. [Great Britain] 1982 39(3): 229-254.* From March 1841 until the end of 1845, W. R. Grove was professor of experimental philosophy at the London Institution. No previous study of the institution has dealt in detail with the period of Grove's tenure of this, the first professorship. Here, by reference to the various manuscripts and publications of the institution, and to Grove's papers and correspondence, it is possible to describe the background to Grove's appointment and the achievements of his term of office. 1841-45

Groza, Petru

2717. Csatári, Dániel. PETRU GROZA EMLÉKEZETE [In memory of Petru Groza]. *Párttörténeti Közlemények [Hungary] 1985 31(1): 181-193.* Groza (1884-1958) attended the universities in Budapest, Berlin, and Leipzig, settling in Bucharest where he joined Marshall Avarescu's party. He was appointed by the king as prime minister of Romania in 1920, was out of office in 1922, but was prime minister again in 1926-27, when Avarescu regained his popularity. His attempts to fight corruption were unsuccessful. In 1945 Groza was appointed for the third time as prime minister to establish the first democratic cabinet in Romania, and he and his family spent a month in the Soviet Union as Stalin's guest. 15 notes. 1910's-58

2718. Lipcsey, Ildikó. PETRU GROZA—THEORY AND PRACTICE IN MINORITY RIGHTS. *New Hungarian Quarterly [Hungary] 1985 26(99): 99-104.* Petru Groza, prime minister of Romania, 1945-52, and head of state, 1952-58, was an experienced politician and expert in issues dealing with minorities. Sympathetic toward the plight of the ethnic Hungarians of Transylvania, he also favored close cooperation with postwar Hungary. 1945-49

2719. Marcu, Paraschiv. OBSERVANCES: DR. PETRU GROZA (1884-1958). *Romania [Romania] 1983 8(2): 73-79.* Prints a biography of Petru Groza, former prime minister of Romania and chairman of the Presidium of the Grand National Assembly. 1919-58

2720. Sheviakov, A. A. VYDAIUSHCHIISIA POLITICHESKII I GOSUDARSTVENNYI DEIATEL' NOVOI RUMYNII [An outstanding politician and statesman of the new Romania]. *Voprosy Istorii [USSR] 1984 (11): 110-122.* Sketches the biography of Romanian politician Petru Groza (1884-1958). Imprisoned by the wartime government in 1943, he returned to active politics and served as prime minister, 1945-52. Secondary sources; 56 notes. 1940's-58

2721. —. DR. PETRU GROZA (1884-1958) [Dr. Petru Groza (1884-1958)]. *Anale de Istorie [Romania] 1984 30(6): 79-83.* Petru Groza was born on 7 December 1884 in Băcia. After obtaining his high-school diploma in 1903, he studied law at the universities of Budapest, Berlin, and Leipzig. In 1907 he became a doctor of juridical sciences, Magna cum Laude. Groza served as deputy in the Romanian parliament, minister of resident nationalities, and minister of communications and public works. In 1945, he became the leader of the first revolutionary-democratic government. He was an intellectual, a politician, a patriot, and progressive militant who contributed to the creation of modern Romania, the consolidation of its independence, and its prestige among the nations. 1910's-58

Gruenwald, Maria Dorotea

2722. Kauffman, Harold D. A MOTHER'S QUEST FOR A BETTER LIFE. *Journal of the American Historical Society of Germans from Russia 1986 9(1): 33-38.* Describes the life of Maria Dorotea Gruenwald, descendant of Rhenish German settlers who moved to the Saratov area near the Volga River in the 18th century, from her marriage in 1877, through her emigration to America in 1907, to her death in 1938. 18c-1938

Gruev, Damian

2723. Bozhinov, Voin. DAMIAN GRUEV I BULGARSKATA PROSVETA V MAKEDONIIA [Damian Gruev and Bulgarian education in Macedonia]. *Istoricheski Pregled [Bulgaria] 1983 39(3): 68-72.* Damian Gruev, (1871-1906), who helped found the Internal Macedonian Revolutionary Organization in 1893, worked for the Bulgarian patriarchy for 10 years. He taught in Smilevo from 1891 to 1892, in Prilep from 1892 to 1893 and in Shtip from 1894 to 1895. The Patriarchy appointed him as a teacher at the Bulgarian school in Bitol from 1899 to 1900. Throughout his career he inculcated Macedonian and Bulgarian nationalism and ideas of liberation in his students. Based on material in the Bulgarian Central State Historical Archive; 15 notes. 1891-1900

2724. Eldurov, Svetlozar. DAMIAN GRUEV I CHUZHDITE PROPAGANDI V MAKEDONIIA [Damian Gruev and foreign propaganda in Macedonia]. *Istoricheski Pregled [Bulgaria] 1983 39(3): 49-57.* Damian Gruev (1871-1906), who taught at the Bulgarian school in Macedonia, was subjected to Serbian anti-Bulgarian propaganda from 1887. He became a member of the Macedonian liberation movement in 1893, and helped organize Macedonian national resistance to Turkey and Serbia. He exposed the lies told about Macedonia and its history by Serbian, Turkish and Greek propagandists, and emphasized Macedonia's close connection with Bulgaria. His murder on 10 December 1906 by a Turkish soldier is believed to have resulted from Serbian and Turkish collusion. Based on material in Bulgaria's Central State Historical Archive; 36 notes. 1887-1906

2725. Lape, Ljuben. KON ŽIVOTOT I DELOTO NA DAME GRUEV [The life and work of Damian Gruev]. *Istorija [Yugoslavia] 1981 17(2): 21-23.* In 1893 Damian Gruev founded the Macedonian National Liberation and Revolutionary Movement and acted as its chief ideolog. He died in December 1906. 1893-1906

2726. Lapé, Liuben. THE LIFE AND WORK OF DAMÉ GRUEV. *Macedonian Review [Yugoslavia] 1984 14(1): 48-49.* Describes briefly the life and work of Damian Gruev (1871-1906), the founder, ideologist, and principal organizer of the Internal Macedonian Revolutionary Organization. 1871-1906

2727. Petrov, Todor and Ianakiev, Nikolai. VOENNO-REVOLIUTSIONNI VUZGLEDI I DEINOST NA DAMIAN GRUEV [Damian Gruev's revolutionary ideas and activities]. *Istoricheski Pregled [Bulgaria] 1983 39(3): 58-67.* Describes the revolutionary activities of Damian Gruev (1871-1906), who, while teaching in Macedonia, helped found the Internal Macedonian Revolutionary Organization in 1893 and prepare the Ilinden Uprising of 1903. He obtained arms for the revolutionary struggle and spent three years in prison for his activities. He was convinced that Bulgaria must fight for independence and that Macedonia must belong to a free Greater Bulgaria. These convictions led him to support and train revolutionaries for sabotage, assassination, and acts of terrorism. Based on material from the Central State Historical Archive of Bulgaria; 46 notes. 1893-1903

Grundtvig, Nikolai Frederik

2728. Burrows, John. GRUNDTVIG: PIONEER OF MODERN DENMARK. *History Today [Great Britain] 1984 34(Apr): supplement.* Nikolai Frederik Grundtvig (1783-1872), an educational reformer, was responsible for establishing folk high schools for working-class adults in Denmark. 1820's-72

2729. Christoffersen, Svein Aage. GRUNDTVIG: LITTERATUR [Grundtvig: literature]. *Norsk Teologisk Tidsskrift [Norway] 1984 85(3): 175-189.* Reviews nine new Danish books on the life and work of the Danish writer, theologian, and teacher Nikolai Frederik Severin Grundtvig (1783-1872), and comments briefly on a number of Grundtvig's own works republished in 1983. Biblio. 1783-1872

Grynaeus, Simon

2730. Lebeau, Jean. *NOVUS ORBIS.* LES COSMOGRAPHES ALLEMANDS DU XVIe SIÈCLE ET LES GRANDES DECOUVERTES [*Novus Orbis:* German cosmographers of the 16th century and the great discoveries]. *Rev. d'Allemagne [France] 1981 13(2): 197-215.* 1520-50
*For abstract see **Boemus, Johannes***

Gu Jiegang

2731. Richter, Ursula. GU JIEGANG: HIS LAST THIRTY YEARS. *China Q. [Great Britain] 1982 (90): 286-295.* Though Gu Jiegang (Ku Chieh-kang) made the required self-criticism and denunciations of former colleagues, he remained true to his historical methodology and theories. Rehabilitated after the fall of the Gang of Four, he died in December 1980. Based on Gu's works and meeting with him and his assistants in the spring of 1980; selected biblio. of Gu's post-1977 publications, 33 notes. 1950-80

Gu Yanwu

2732. Guy, R. Kent. THE DEVELOPMENT OF THE EVIDENTIAL RESEARCH MOVEMENT: KU YEN-WU AND THE SSU-K'U CH'UAN-SHU. *Tsing Hua Journal of Chinese Studies [Taiwan] 1984 16(1-2): 97-118.* The assertion that the Manchu throne ordered the editors of *Siku Quanshu (Ssu k'u ch'üan shu;* SQ), an annotated catalog of extant literature commissioned by the Chinese government in 1772, to distort the image of Gu Yanwu (Ku Yen-wu; 1613-83) in the SQ and to slight his role as founder of modern evidential scholarship is mistaken. Throughout the 18th and 19th centuries, scholars had diverse views of Gu and his work. His image in the SQ, while including criticism, is generally favorable and reflects the thinking of the dominant intellectuals of the time, not the coercion of the Qing dynasty. Based on Gu's writings and those of 18th- through early 20th-century writers about him and his works; 61 notes. Chinese summary. 17c-20c

Gual, Adrià

2733. Blanch, Armando. ADRIA GUAL [Adrià Gual]. *Historia y Vida [Spain] 1985 18(202): 62-72.* Remembers Adrià Gual (1872-1943), the Catalan playwright whose most important work, besides his own dramatic productions, was the creation of institutions known as "the intimate theater," and the Catalan School for Dramatic Art, both dedicated to the task of promoting theater arts. 1900-43

Gual, Pedro

2734. Lee López, Alberto. DON PEDRO GUAL [Pedro Gual]. *Bol. de Hist. y Antigüedades [Colombia] 1983 70(740): 271-277.* The Venezuelan-born Pedro Gual (1783-1862) was an active figure in the movement for independence and subsequently filled important political and diplomatic posts in Gran Colombia, Ecuador, and Venezuela. He worked at all times to promote justice among nations. 1783-1862

2735. Polanco Alcántara, Tomás. EL CENTENARIO DE DON PEDRO GUAL [The centenary of Don Pedro Gual]. *Bol. de la Acad. Nac. de la Hist. [Venezuela] 1983 66(261): 1-18.* Pedro Gual (1783-1862) was Bolivar's trusted friend and collaborator. He was the first minister of foreign affairs of Gran Colombia. He was also a man of progressive ideas. He was concerned with popular education, the promotion of the arts and sciences and the growth of the economies of the nascent republics. Speech at the Academia Nacional de la Historia to commemorate the bicentennial of Gual's birth; 37 notes. 1783-1862

Guardia y Oya, Alberto de la

2736. Moreno de Alborán, Salvador. LOS CONTRALMIRANTES A TITULO POSTUMO, DON RICARDO MINGUEZ SUAREZ-INCLAN Y DON ALBERTO DE LA GUARDIA Y OYA [The posthumous rear admirals Ricardo Minguez Suarez-Inclan and Alberto de la Guardia y Oya]. *Rev. General de Marina [Spain] 1979 197(Aug-Sept): 133-140.* A classmate of the naval officers posthumously promoted to the rank of rear admiral pays tribute to their memory and recalls the main events of their careers. 20c

Guardini, Romano

2737. Chauvin, Charles. ROMANO GUARDINI: UN PHILOSOPHE DU PARADOXE CHRETIEN [Romano Guardini: a philosopher of the Christian paradox]. *Documents [France] 1985 40(2): 90-101.* A biographical essay of Romano Guardini (1885-1968), focusing on the character of the philosophy of this German theologian, born in Italy, who embodied the Christian paradox. 1885-1968

Guarini, Guarino

2738. Meek, H. "Guarino Guarini and His Architecture." Queen's U. [Northern Ireland] 1985. 263 pp. *DAI-C 1986 47(2): 271; 47/1322c.* 1640's-83

Guber, Aleksandr A.

2739. Gavrilov, Iu. N. AKADEMIK ALEKSANDR ANDREEVICH GUBER (K 80-LETIIU SO DNIA ROZHDENIIA) [Academician Aleksandr Andreevich Guber on his 80th birthday]. *Narody Azii i Afriki [USSR] 1982 (3): 78-82.* Aleksandr A. Guber, one of the older generation of Soviet scholars, is a talented Orientalist, historian, and social researcher; he founded the Soviet School of Southeast Asian Studies. He is an Academician and Doctor Honoris Causa of the University of Cambridge, and his name is connected with training of Orientalists at Moscow University. His first scientific publication appeared in 1925. In 1932 he published a detailed study of Indonesia, the first of its kind based on Marxist analysis. In 1960 he published a collection of articles entitled *Lenin and the Orient* with emphasis on problems of national liberation and Communist movements. Guber's qualities as an observant scholar and fighter for the interests of the working class make his assessments valid in the 1980's and are a valuable contribution to modern Oriental research. 1925-82

Guerrazzi, Francesco Domenico

2740. Bruzzone, Gian Luigi. FRANCESCO DOMENICO GUERRAZZI E BACCIO EMANUELE MAINERI. PROFILO DI UN' AMICIZIA [Francesco Domenico Guerrazzi and Baccio Emanuele Maineri: profile of a friendship]. *Rassegna Storica del Risorgimento [Italy] 1984 71(4): 438-467.* The reputation of the republican writer Francesco Domenico Guerrazzi was, during his lifetime, enormous, but quickly suffered an eclipse. Only recently have historians attempted to establish an impartial view of his political life and his writings. His historical novel, *The Siege of Florence* (1836), made a great impression on Maineri, who would later be his correspondent. Guerrazzi's letters reveal, in an informal and vigorous style, his interests and his ideas about the Italian writers and musicians who were the subjects of published works. Based on the Maineri archives and secondary sources; 163 notes, appendix of 27 letters. 1860-73

2741. Timpanaro, M. A. Morelli. GLI STUDI SUL GUERRAZZI DAL CONVEGNO DI LIVORNO DEL 1973 ALL'EDIZIONE DEL CATALOGO DELLE LETTERE NEL 1978 [Studies on Guerrazzi from the conference in Leghorn in 1973 to the edition of the catalog of letters of 1978]. *Rassegna degli Arch. di Stato [Italy] 1979 39(1-3); 161-166.* Surveys recent studies on Francesco Domenico Guerrazzi (1804-73) and notes the publication of the proceedings of the conference in Leghorn entitled *Francesco Domenico Guerrazzi nella Storia Politica e Culturale del Risorgimento* in 1975. Of central importance in understanding Guerrazzi are his approximately 8,000 letters that have now received the critical attention of Lucha Toschi in his *L'Epistolario di F. D. Guerrazzi con il Catalogo delle Lettere Edite e Inedite.* 2 notes. 1804-1978

Guerrero, Práxedis

2742. —. PRAXEDIS GUERRERO: EARLY REVOLUTIONARY. *Monthly Review 1985 37(7): 41-47.*

Devis, Rey. REVOLUTION IS BEAUTIFUL, *pp. 41-42.* A brief description of Práxedis Guerrero, a hero of the Mexican revolution.

Ortiz, Bobbye. FORERUNNER OF FEMINISM, *pp. 43-47.* Describes Práxedis Guerrero's concern for women's oppression; includes an abridged version of "La Mujer," a talk given in Los Angeles in 1910. 1900-10

Guetti, Lorenzo

2743. Zalin, Giovanni. L'ECONOMIA VALLIGIANA E LA SOCIETA CONTADINA NEGLI SCRITTI DI UN PROTAGONISTA DELL'OTTOCENTO TRENTINO: DON LORENZO GUETTI [The valley economy and peasant society in the writings of a 19th-century author from Trentino: Don Lorenzo Guetti]. *Econ. e Storia [Italy] 1981 2(3): 365-376.* With reference to a recent edition of the works of Don Lorenzo, illustrates his original contribution to the development of the valley economy of Trentino in the 19th century. This Italian priest, endowed with a profound knowledge of the physical environment and the psychology of the country people, was the initiator of the cooperative movement in the Trentino valley. 30 notes. 1880's-90's

Guibert, Jacques Antoine Hippolyte de

2744. Charnay, Jean-Paul. GUIBERT ET LE POUVOIR [Guibert and power]. *Rev. Hist. des Armées [France] 1982 (1): 12-15.* The evidence that Jacques Antoine Hippolyte de Guibert (1743-90) was the author of *Lettres d'un Habitant de la Campagne à un Habitant de la Capitale,* in which Jacques Necker (1732-1804) is praised for his financial administration but criticized for his military policy, is partly internal. The *Lettres* reflect Guibert's logical method and his views on politics, economics, and public administration. This evidence was recently reinforced by the discovery of a set of documents, of which one appears to be in Guibert's handwriting and two are letters dealing with the publication of the *Lettres.* Evidence linking Necker with Guibert's election to the French Academy strengthens this attribution. 3 illus., 12 notes. 1760's-90

2745. Charnay, Jean-Paul. GUIBERT... AMBIGUITES ET AVENIR D'UN SOLDAT PHILOSOPHE [Guibert... a controversial and influential military theorist]. *Rev. Hist. des Armées [France] 1982 (1): 4-11.* After a brief but brilliant career as a troop commander, Jacques Antoine Hippolyte de Guibert (1743-90) turned his attention to reforming and modernizing the French army. The changes he promoted brought down upon him the wrath of those with vested interests in the past. He was the leading military theoretician of the Enlightenment, searching for the optimum social, political, and economic conditions of war, studying war in relation to all the empirical data of the period, and expanding the psychological and philosophical dimensions of grand strategy. 4 illus., diagram, 4 notes. 1766-90

Guidi, Filippo Maria

2746. Horst, Ulrich. KARDINALERZBISCHOF FILIPPO MARIA GUIDI O.P.—EIN FILIUS ILLEGITIMUS PIUS' IX.? [Cardinal Archbishop Filippo Maria Guidi: an illegitimate son of Pope Pius IX?]. *Riv. di Storia della Chiesa in Italia [Italy] 1980 34(2): 513-517.* Takes issue with August Bernhard Hasler's claim, on the basis of a statement by a contemporary Polish diplomat during Vatican Council I, that the Dominican cardinal and Archbishop of Bologna, Filippo Maria Guidi (1815-79), may have been the illegitimate son of Pope Pius IX, showing that the baptismal register of the parish church of San Biagio d'Argenta, diocese of Ferrara, contains full details of Guidi's birth and parentage and that the state of the register permits no later interpolation or forgery. Based on baptismal register of the parish church of San Biagio d'Argenta; plate, 13 notes. 1815-79

Guillard, Charlotte

2747. Beech, Beatrice. CHARLOTTE GUILLARD: A SIXTEENTH-CENTURY BUSINESS WOMAN. *Renaissance Q. 1983 36(3): 345-367.* Reviews the life and career of Charlotte Guillard who was a printer and publisher during the early and mid-16th century in Paris. Married twice to printer-publishers, she took over their businesses and managed them effectively under her own name. For the most part, she published theological and legal texts. 117 notes. 1520's-50's

Guillaumin, Gilbert-Urbain

2748. Levan-Lemesle, Lucette. GUILLAUMIN, EDITEUR D'ECONOMIE POLITIQUE 1801-1864 [Guillaumin, publisher of political economy (1801-64)]. *Revue d'Economie Politique [France] 1985 95(2): 134-149.* Assesses the career of publisher Gilbert-Urbain Guillaumin, one of the first disseminators of liberal economic literature in France. 1801-64

Guillén, Julio

2749. Landín Carrasco, Amancio. JULIO GUILLEN, DE CERCA [Julio Guillén, up close]. *Rev. General de Marina [Spain] 1982 203(Nov): 357-365.* Anecdotal personal memoir of Rear Admiral Julio Guillén of the Spanish Navy, historian, director of the Naval Museum, editor of the *Revista General de Marina,* member of the Spanish Royal Academy, and artist. He died in 1972. 3 illus. 1943-72

Guillén, Nicolás

2750. García-Carranza, Josefina. SINTESIS BIO-BIBLIOGRAFICA DE NICOLAS GUILLEN [The biobibliographical synthesis of Nicolás Guillén]. *U. de La Habana [Cuba] 1982 (216): 55-121.* Brief chronology of Nicolás Guillén's life, including dates of his publications from 1902 to 1981, a chronological index of his publications, 1930-80, a chronological index of works in which he collaborated, 1922-77, and an index of titles. 1902-81

2751. Márquez, Roberto. RACISM, CULTURE AND REVOLUTION: IDEOLOGY AND POLITICS IN THE PROSE OF NICOLAS GUILLEN. *Latin Am. Res. Rev. 1982 17(1): 43-68.* Nicolás Guillén's relatively unknown prose complements his poetry, often sharing identical themes. He was spokesman of the proletariat and gave himself totally to the struggle of the people. His prose persistently addressed three subjects: the condition of blacks, the Cuban cultural experience, and the overthrow of an unjust sociopolitical system. He fused a revolutionary spirit with art of enduring quality. Based on published and unpublished writings of Guillén; 27 notes. 1920-65

Guion, Gardiner Henry

2752. Teychiné Stakenburg, A. J. EEN GALANT AVONTUUR VAN MARIA ANNA BONAPARTE [An amatory adventure of Maria Anna Bonaparte's]. *Spiegel Historiael [Netherlands] 1984 19(6): 266-271.* 1798
For abstract see ***Bonaparte, Maria Anna***

Güiraldes, Ricardo

2753. Blasi, Alberto. RICARDO GÜIRALDES Y *PROA* [Ricardo Güiraldes and *Proa]. Cuadernos Hispanoamericanos [Spain] 1986 (432): 29-38.* The avant-garde movement in Argentina developed around the *Martín Fierro* and *Proa* ventures. The publishing history, 1924-25, of the latter periodical confirms the view that Ricardo Güiraldes (1886-1927) was not only one of its editors but also the very sponsor and kernel, since the life of *Proa* and Güiraldes's own biography clearly run apace. Based on letters from the Fonds Larbaud and secondary sources; 23 notes. 1924-25

Guirior, Manuel de

2754. Zudaire Huarte, Eulogio. DON MANUEL DE GUIRIOR, TENIENTE GENERAL DE LA REAL ARMADA [Manuel de Guirior, lieutenant general of the Royal Navy]. *Revista de Historia Naval [Spain] 1984 2(4): 47-66.* Traces the life and career of the Spanish naval officer Manuel de Guirior (1708-88). As a young officer he fought against North African and British pirates, then served in Spanish warships in Spanish and American waters against Britain, escorted members of the royal family, and finally was appointed Viceroy of New Granada in 1771 and of Peru in 1775. Based on the General Archives of the Indies, the Bazan archives, the National Historical Archive, and other archives; 2 illus., 28 notes. 1708-88

Guiscard, Antoine de

2755. Jones, Peter. ANTOINE DE GUISCARD, "ABBÉ DE LA BOURLIE," "MARQUIS DE GUISCARD." *British Lib. J. [Great Britain] 1982 8(1): 94-113.* Examines the life and career of the Huguenot refugee Antoine de Guiscard (1658-1711) and his unsuccessful plans for an invasion of France in 1706. Describes Guiscard's early life, his work for the Camisard cause in France, 1705-10, his attempted murder of Robert Harley, and his death in Newgate prison, London in 1711. Based on documents relating to Antoine de Guiscard in the Blenheim Papers at the British Library, London and secondary sources; 2 fig., 58 notes. 1658-1711

Guizot, François

2756. Comalada Negre, Angel. HISTORIADORES Y POLITICOS DEL SIGLO XIX: THIERS Y GUIZOT [Historians and politicians of the 19th century: Thiers and Guizot]. *Hist. y Vida [Spain] 1983 16(181): 78-88.* Reviews the careers of Adolphe Thiers and François Guizot and points out the important roles they played as historians and in the politics of 19th-century France. 19c

2757. Roels, Jean. LA THEORIE DOCTRINAIRE DE LA REPRESENTATION POLITIQUE: GUIZOT [The doctrinaire theory of political representation: Guizot]. *Annali della Facoltà di Scienze Politiche: Materiali di Storia [Italy] 1982-83 19(7 part 2): 539-556.* Analyzes the theory of political representation and the concept of power in a parliamentary monarchy in the works of François Guizot (1787-1874), a moderate-conservative monarchist, French Premier (1847), and historian. 1820's-74

Gullan, Marjorie

2758. Shields, Ronald Eugene. "Marjorie Gullan: Speech Teacher, Lecturer, Public Reader, and Pioneer in Choral Speaking." Louisiana State U. and Agric. and Mechanical Coll. 1983. 293 pp. *DAI 1984 44(9): 2624-2625-A.* DA8400140 1910's-50's

Guo Lianghui

2759. Lancashire, Edel. *THE LOCK OF THE HEART CONTROVERSY IN TAIWAN, 1962-63: A QUESTION OF ARTISTIC FREEDOM AND A WRITER'S SOCIAL RESPONSIBILITY.* *China Quarterly [Great Britain] 1985 (103): 462-488.* In 1962 Guo Lianghui began the serialized publication of her 16th novel, *Xin Suo* [The lock of the heart]. Following this, two editions of the book sold well and a third was undertaken when the author came under heavy criticism for the obscenity of the work. The book was banned, increasing its sales, and Guo was dismissed from both the China Association of Literature and Art and the Taiwan Women Writers' Association. Though she had some supporters, for many the supposed threat to the state found in her book justified the denial of her freedom of expression. 111 notes. 1962-63

Guo Yidong

2760. Lancashire, Edel. POPEYE AND THE CASE OF GUO YIDONG, ALIAS BO YANG. *China Q. [Great Britain] 1982 (92): 667-686.* Having fled to Taiwan in 1949, the writer Guo Yidong (pen name, Bo Yang) continued to produce anti-Communist works but did not hesitate to criticize aspects of Chinese culture. Having earned the enmity of the government he was arrested for insulting the Head of State as a result of translating the comic strip Popeye into Chinese and was sentenced to 18 years imprisonment. Pardoned after nine years, Bo Yang resumed writing. Based on Chinese materials; 116 notes. 1949-77

Gurakuqi, Luigj

2761. Çami, Muin. PIRO TAKO, LUIGJ GURAKUQI, JETA DHE VEPRA [Piro Tako on Luigj Gurakuqi, his life and works]. *Studime Hist. [Albania] 1981 35(3): 245-250.* Reviews Piro Tako's biography (1980) of the Albanian patriot and democrat Luigj Gurakuqi. 1902-24

Gurvitch, Georges

2762. Swedberg, Richard. GEORGES GURVITCH: THE UNHAPPY POSITIVIST. *J. of the Hist. of Sociol. 1982 4(1): 66-93.* Traces the life and work of the Russian-born sociologist, Georges Gurvitch, relatively unknown in the United States because much of his work has not been translated into English. His life falls into the following periods: early life in Russia, 1894-1920; voluntary exile, spent in Czechoslovakia and Germany, 1920-25; life in France, 1925-40; to the United States, 1940-45; and 1945 to his death in 1965. 1894-1965

Gusarov, Fedor V.

2763. Trushin, N. I. POD KLICHKOI "BOBROV" [Under the pseudonym Bobrov]. *Voprosy Istorii [USSR] 1985 (8): 171-176.* Views the political activities of Fedor V. Gusarov (1875-1920; pseud. Bobrov), active in the Military Organization of the Russian Social Democratic Workers' Party, which he joined in 1900. Political agitation among soldiers stationed at Kronstadt during the Revolution of 1905 led to his arrest in 1906 and trial *in camera,* followed by exile. Based on sources from the Central State Archive of the October Revolution and Central State Archive of Military History; 42 notes. 1900-06

Gusev, K. V.

2764. Koval'chenko, I. D. and Naumov, V. P. K 60-LETIIU K. V. GUSEVA [On the 60th birthday of K. V. Gusev]. *Istoriia SSSR [USSR] 1983 (1): 218-219.* A specialist in Soviet history, K. V. Gusev has published many books and articles on the period of the Russian Revolution and Civil War with especial emphasis on the history of the Party of Socialist Revolutionaries. Gusev has served for many years on the editorial board of *Istoriia SSSR* and occupies numerous important political and academic positions. 20c

Gustav I

2765. Svanström, Ragnar and Palmstierna, Carl-Frederic. GUSTAV I VASA [Gustavus I Vasa]. *Magazin Istoric [Romania] 1980 14(11): 13-15, 33.* Summarizes the main events of the reign of Gustav Eriksson (1496-1560) who as Gustavus I expelled the Danes and established Sweden's independence. 1523-60

Gustav II Adolph

2766. Karner, Ágoston. GUSTAV ADOLF: MEGEMLÉKEZÉS HALÁLÁNAK 350 ÉVES ÉVFORDULÓJÁN [Gustav II Adolph: remembrance on the 350th anniversary of his death]. *Theológiai Szemle [Hungary] 1982 25(5): 288-290.* As one of the most progressive kings of Sweden, Gustav II Adolph was able to successfully combine the art of politics and warfare and at the same time uphold the tenets of the Protestant faith. A lifetime enemy of the Catholic Habsburg dynasty, he was instrumental in helping the unification of Protestant Germany. He died in 1632 in the battle of Lützen. 1611-32

2767. Petersen, E. Ladewig. GUSTAV II ADOLF: EN OVERSIGT OVER NYERE FORSKNING [Gustav II Adolf: a survey of recent research]. *Hist. Tidsskrift [Denmark] 1983 83(1-2): 195-206.* Discusses two studies of Swedish King Gustavus Adolphus (1594-1632): Günter Barudio, *Gustav Adolf—der Grosse. Eine Politische Biographie* [Gustavus Adolphus, the great: a political biography] (1982) and *Gustav II Adolf—350 år efter Lützen* [Gustavus Adolphus, 350 years after Lützen] (1982), edited by Gudrun Ekstrand and Katarina af Sillén for the Royal Armory in Stockholm. 27 notes. 1611-32

Gustav III

2768. Artéus, Gunnar. THE MILITARY LEADERSHIP OF GUSTAVUS III. *Militärhistorisk Tidskrift [Sweden] 1982 186: 9-18.* Evaluates Gustavus III's personality and abilities as a military leader on the basis of the role which a Swedish monarch ought to fulfill in wartime. The king possessed personal qualities that were desirable in a military leader, but lacked the necessary military training and education to become an outstanding general in a technical sense. Based on a paper presented at the International Conference of Military Historians in Washington, DC, 1982; 11 notes. 1788-90

2769. Oakley, Stewart. GUSTAVUS III OF SWEDEN. *Studies in History and Politics [Canada] 1985 4: 71-88.* In 1772, Gustav III seized control of Sweden's government in what he presented as the action of a "patriot king" standing above party strife. He embarked on a series of enlightened reforms but soon lost popularity with aristocrats because he reduced their influence and with the middle and farming classes because of economic policies to which they objected. Personal problems agitated the already restless monarch, and when the Diet was called in 1786 the opposition was ready to challenge his authority. Settling economic grievances that required no constitutional change, the king looked for external glory but failed in an attack on Russia. He was, however, able to use the involvement of Russia's ally Denmark to rouse Swedish support against an old foe. When he again rode roughshod over the Diet in 1791, he was assassinated by an ex-guards captain who was the agent of a conspiracy. Secondary sources; 75 notes. 1772-91

Gustav VI Adolph

2770. Palmstierna, Carl-Fredrik. KING GUSTAF VI ADOLF AND QUEEN LOUISE OF SWEDEN: A PERSONAL MEMOIR. *Contemporary Rev. [Great Britain] 1982 240(1397): 313-318.* Personal memories of King Gustav VI Adolph of Sweden (1882-1973) and his second wife Queen Louise (1889-1965) by the king's private secretary and librarian between 1951 and 1973. 1951-73

Gusti, Dimitri

2771. Păunescu, Emil. DIMITRIE GUSTI ŞI COOPERAREA INTELECTUALĂ INTERNAŢIONALĂ [Dimitri Gusti and international intellectual cooperation]. *Anuarul Inst. de Istorie şi Arheologie "A. D. Xenopol" [Romania] 1982 19: 565-573.* Dimitri Gusti (1880-1955) was a scholar, educator, sociologist, and patriot whose works, the last appearing about 1947, have regrettably received attention again only in the last 15 years. Early in his career he founded the Romanian Institute of Social Affairs in 1918, was active on behalf of the League of Nations until 1946, and played a part in international organizations concerned with scientific and social studies, including UNESCO. 74 notes. 1918-55

Gutierrez de Ulloa, Antonio

2772. Castañeda Delgado, Paulino and Hernández Aparicio, Pilar. LA VISITA DE RUIZ DE PRADO AL TRIBUNAL DEL SANTO OFICIO DE LIMA [The visit of Ruiz de Prado to the court of the Holy Office in Lima]. *Anuario de Estudios Americanos [Spain] 1984 41: 1-53.* Although the most famous Inquisitor in 16th-century Peru was Antonio Gutierrez de Ulloa, Juan Ruiz de Prado also played a significant role in the viceroyalty. In addition to forcing Ulloa out of office, Ruiz de Prado wrote an extremely valuable report on the activities of the Holy Inquisition in Peru. Based on documents in the Archivo General de Indias in Seville and the Archivo Histórico Nacional in Madrid; 150 notes. 1571-97

Gutiérrez González, Gregorio

2773. Botero Restrepo, Juan. EL POETA Y POLITICO DON GREGORIO GUTIERREZ GONZALEZ [The poet and politician Gregorio Gutiérrez González]. *Bol. de Hist. y Antigüedades [Colombia] 1981 68(734): 803-812.* Though better known as a poet who evoked the life and traditions of Antioquia, Gregorio Gutiérrez González (1826-72) is even more notable for his record of public service, particularly as a collaborator of Antioquia's conservative governor Pedro Justo Berrío. 1826-72

Gutiérrez-Ponce, María

2774. Ortega Ricaurte, Carmen. APUNTES SOBRE LA VIDA, LA OBRA Y LA EPOCA DE LA COMPOSITORA MARIA GUTIERREZ-PONCE [Notes on the life, work, and times of the composer María Gutiérrez-Ponce]. *Boletín de Historia y Antigüedades [Colombia] 1985 72(749): 293-322.* María Gutiérrez-Ponce, born in Paris in 1880 to the family of a Colombian diplomat, spent her life in Europe, sharing the social and other activities of her father's career. She also studied and composed music, classical and popular, attaining considerable success as a composer of popular dance music. In the 1930's, she wrote Colombian folkloric compositions as well. 1900-51

Gutschow, Konstanty

2775. Diefendorf, Jeffry M. KONSTANTY GUTSCHOW AND THE RECONSTRUCTION OF HAMBURG. *Central European History 1985 18(2): 143-169.* An account of the professional life of Konstanty Gutschow, a prominent German city planner, who was particularly important during the Nazi period. He became the winner of a competition for the redesigning of Hamburg sponsored by Hitler, and, as a result, became for all practical purposes the city planner for Hamburg in January 1939 where he eventually had a staff of 250. His work was well received professionally, and, although he lost his position during the denazification process, he claimed (and was supported by witnesses) that his job and his approach to it were nonpolitical. Whatever the political judgment, "he made a constructive contribution to the history of Hamburg and to the planning of the reconstruction of Germany's cities that must not be overlooked." Based on the Hamburg archives and the private papers of Gutschow; 58 notes. 1929-49

Guyon, Richard

2776. Deák, István. GUYON RICHÁRD DÉLVIDÉKI HADJÁRATA A SZABADSÁGHARC UTOLSÓ HETEIBEN EGY KIADATLAN HADTEST-NAPLÓ TÜKRÉBEN (1849. JÚNIUS 26-JÚLIUS 30) [The South Hungarian campaign of Richard Guyon during the last weeks of the war of independence as shown in an unpublished corps diary (26 June to 30 July 1849)]. *Századok [Hungary] 1981 115(3): 557-586.* Born in Scotland in 1812 Guyon married the daughter of a Hungarian noble. The author provides a day by day description of his life as a general between 26 June and 30 July 1849, based on the diary of an unknown officer in Guyon's army who spoke and wrote in German only. Still the writer was a great patriot and showed deep feelings toward the Hungarian cause. The complete diary translated into Hungarian is included in the article. Based on documents in the Hungarian National Archives; 24 notes. 1849

Guzmán, Antonio Leocadio

2777. Lovera De-Sola, R. J. A UN SIGLO DE ANTONIO LEOCADIO GUZMAN [A century after Antonio Leocadio Guzmán]. *Boletín de la Academia Nacional de la Historia [Venezuela] 1985 68(270): 477-490.* Describes the career of Antonio Leocadio Guzmán (1801-84), one of the most important politicians of the early decades of Venezuelan independence. He was one of the initiators of the democratic process in his country. He initiated a powerful political movement, which, however, was unable to bring him to the presidency. 45 notes. 1824-84

Guzmán, Pantaleón

2778. Vargas, Francisco Alejandro. CORONEL PANTALEON GUZMAN [Colonel Pantaleón Guzmán]. *Bol. de la Acad. Nac. de la Hist. [Venezuela] 1982 65(257): 109-112.* Pantaleón Guzmán (ca. 1777-1831) was one of the heroes of the war of independence. He took part in campaigns between 1811 and 1814 and in 1816 attended the famous assembly of San Diego de Cabrutica. He died in 1831 in a battle in defense of Gran Colombia, in which he took part not knowing that he who had conceived of Gran Colombia, Simón

Bolívar, was already dead. Based on primary material in the General Archive and the Archivo del Libertador; 21 notes. ca 1777-1831

Guzmán Esponda, Eduardo

2779. Pérez Silva, Vicente. ANTONIO JOSE RESTREPO Y EDUARDO GUZMAN ESPONDA [Antonio José Restrepo and Eduardo Guzmán Esponda]. *Bol. Cultural y Biblio. [Colombia] 1982 19(3): 116-144.* Compares the life and writings of Colombian writers Antonio José Restrepo and Eduardo Guzmán Esponda, focusing on a 1932 exchange of letters on Spanish grammar between them, provoked by Guzmán Esponda's *Bajo el Sol del Brasil* (1931). 1931-32

Guzmán y Pimental, Gaspar de

2780. Bradbury, Ian. OLIVARES. *Teaching History [Great Britain] 1985 (43): 9-11.* Gaspar de Guzmán y Pimental, Conde de Olivares (1587-1645) as prime minister, 1621-43, attempted a series of reforms designed to return Spain to the dominant position it had occupied in the mid-16th century. 1621-43

Gwatkin, Henry Melvill

2781. Slee, Peter. THE H. M. GWATKIN PAPERS. *Tr. of the Cambridge Biblio. Soc. [Great Britain] 1982 8(2): 279-283.* Traces the career of Henry Melvill Gwatkin (1844-1916) as a student and professor of theology at Cambridge University. The author provides a catalogue of manuscripts, letters, pamphlets, reviews, and papers by Gwatkin. 1844-1916

Gwyn, Francis

2782. Jenkins, Philip. FRANCIS GWYN AND THE BIRTH OF THE TORY PARTY. *Welsh Hist. Rev. [Great Britain] 1983 11(3): 283-301.* Investigates the career of Francis Gwyn (1648-1734) who was an important Welsh contributor to the development of party ideologies in Britain. Gwyn mediated between the hostile wings of Toryism represented by the High Church royalism of Lord Rochester on the one hand and the country dissenters led by Harley and Mansell. Gwyn's family connections enabled him to count on royalist support and he entered Parliament in 1673. He consolidated his position as a result of the Exclusion Crisis, becoming clerk to the Privy Council in 1679. On the accession of William of Orange he served on the Commission of Accounts and remained an MP with an increasingly powerful base in the West Country. By the early 1690's Gwyn was in close contact with rebel Whigs who were as alienated by the political revolution as the old Tories. His role in cementing the coalition cannot be definitely proved but there is strong evidence of his activity. Likewise, he was probably a key figure in reforming the Tory-Harleyite alliance of 1710 after the factionalism of Jacobin unrest. Gwyn's career was ruined only with the Hanoverian succession, but the party he had helped to create was to survive. Based on manuscript sources; 78 notes. 1673-1714

Gwynn Jones, T.

2783. Lloyd, D. Tecwyn. T. GWYNN JONES FEL CYNGHORWR LLENYDDOL [T. Gwynn Jones as literary adviser]. *Natl. Lib. of Wales J. [Great Britain] 1981 22(1): 103-25.* Professor T. Gwynn Jones (1871-1949) was proofreader and literary adviser to the Welsh publishers Hughes a'i Fab of Wrexham. Prewar Welsh literary activity and standards are reflected here, together with the practical difficulties of Welsh publishing. Details are given of several important Welsh literary figures, including an account of the Welsh novelist Meirion Lloyd Jones (1896-1937) sent to Gwynn Jones by Lloyd Jones's sister. Transcripts of letters, reports, and Lloyd Jones's biography; 23 notes. 1938

Gwynne, Nell

2784. Rawling, Gerald. PRETTY WITTY NELL. *British Heritage [Great Britain] 1982 3(3): 26-31.* Biography of the legendary mistress of Charles II, Nell Gwynne (1650-87), a Cockney fish hawker who met the king at the beginning of her stage career and remained his mistress for 17 years, bearing him two sons, Charles, Duke of St. Albans, and James, Lord Beauclerk. 1660's-87

Gyokudo

2785. Covell, Jon Carter. JAPAN'S TROUBADOUR OF NATURE LED A LONELY LIFE. *Asian & Pacific Quarterly of Cultural and Social Affairs [South Korea] 1984 16(3): 40-45.* Gyokudo (1745-1820) resembles the Western master Vincent Van Gogh. He had few friends, and his paintings were not appreciated by his contemporaries. Today his paintings are highly prized. Gyokudo was a samurai who served a feudal master until the master died, after which Gyokudo and his two sons wandered about Japan. Often Gyokudo exchanged his landscape paintings for food and lodging for himself and his sons. His poverty forced him to use carbon ink; vegetable tints were all he could afford to use for colors, and because paper was expensive, his works were generally less than a foot square. Photos. 1745-1820

Gyp

See Martel de Janville, Sibylle de

Gyurjian, Hakob

2786. Ghazarian, M. M. HAKOB GYURJIAN (TSĚNĚNDYAN 100-AMYAKI ARTIV) [Hakob Gyurjian on the centenary of his birth]. *Patma-Banasirakan Handes. Istoriko-Filologicheskii Zhurnal [USSR] 1982 (1): 3-13.* The history of 20th-century art acknowledges Hakob Gyurjian (1881-1948) as a great Armenian sculptor of the French school. Describes his development and his works, including heads of Beethoven, Tchopanian, Gorky, Rachmaninov, Catholicos Hovsepian, and Tolstoy, animal sculptures, and historical and mythological figures. In Moscow, 1917-21, he made sketches for postrevolution monuments and memorial plaques. Exhibited in many capitals, part of his work is in Musée d'Art Décoratif (Paris) but most he bequeathed to the Erevan State Gallery. Primary sources; 3 illus., photo, 16 notes. 1900-48

H

Haam, Achad

2787. Reinharz, Jehuda. ACHAD HAAM UND DER DEUTSCHE ZIONISM [Achad Haam and German Zionism]. *Bull. des Leo Baeck Inst. [Israel] 1982 (61): 3-27.* Achad Haam, known as AH, was the pseudonym of Asher Ginsberg, a Ukrainian Jew. He was the first East European Jewish intellectual to begin discussions with Western Jews. His most devoted supporter was Martin Buber; Kurt Blumenfeld was another follower. AH looked upon life in Palestine as a personal matter. Buber's view was more romantic but he began to learn Hebrew and to encourage others to do likewise. 81 notes. 1890's-1914

Haan, Jacob Israël de

2788. Giebels, Ludy. JACOB ISRAËL DE HAAN IN PALESTINA [Jacob Israël de Haan in Palestine]. *Studia Rosenthaliana [Netherlands] 1980 14(1): 44-78; 1981 15(1): 111-142, 15(2): 188-216.* Parts I-III. Describes the life of Jacob Israël de Haan, who went to Palestine in 1919 and from 1919 to 1924 changed from a sincere Zionist to a forceful adversary of that same Zionism and was killed by a Zionist commando in 1924; due to his anti-Zionist stand, this poet-jurist was profoundly isolated in every sphere in which he excelled. English summary. 1919-24

Haase, Hugo

2789. Keller, Elke. "ES GEHT NICHT UM IHRE GUTEN VORSÄTZE". (W. I. LENIN) VOM REVOLUTIONÄREN SOZIAL-DEMOKRATEN ZUM ZENTRISTEN. HUGO HAASE ["It's not a question of their good intentions" (V. I. Lenin): from revolutionary Social Democrat to centrist—Hugo Haase]. *Beiträge zur Gesch. der Arbeiterbewegung [East Germany] 1981 23(4): 583-596.* Traces the life and political career of the German Social Democrat Hugo Haase (1863-1919), paying particular attention to his activities and influence within the Social Democratic Party, 1894-1919, his opposition to World War I, and his work as a lawyer to defend many German revolutionaries, including Ernst Toller in 1919. Haase was assassinated in 1919. Based on documents of the German Social Democratic Party in Berlin and secondary sources; 75 notes. 1894-1919

Haberler, Gottfried

2790. Baldwin, Robert E. GOTTFRIED HABERLER'S CONTRIBUTION TO INTERNATIONAL TRADE THEORY AND POLICY. *Q. J. of Econ. 1982 97(1): 141-148.* A summary of Gottfried Haberler's contributions in theoretical international economics from 1929 to 1979, during which time he has added substantially to the economic theory of comparative costs as well as contributing his production-possibilities framework. 1920's-70's

Habermas, Jürgen

2791. Habermas, Jürgen; Anderson, Perry and Dews, Peter, interviewers. A PHILOSOPHICO-POLITICAL PROFILE. *New Left Review [Great Britain] 1985 (151): 75-105.* Philosopher and sociologist, Jürgen Habermas, discusses the development of his theories from 1949-85 in an interview with the *New Left Review.* Habermas applies his theories to political and sociological trends in Europe and the United States. 1949-85

2792. Smith, A. Anthony. HABERMAS ON THE UNIVERSITY: *BILDUNG* IN THE AGE OF TECHNOLOGY. *Vitae Scholasticae 1984 4[i.e., 3](2): 297-308.* Jurgen Habermas of the University of Frankfurt, has been considered the leading contemporary representative of the school of thought referred to as critical theory or Frankfurt School. Critical theory analyzes society by evaluating data and judging whether it furthers human emancipation. Habermas applied critical theory to the role of the university in society by using the classical German humanist notion of *Bildung* in which officials of the state were to act in a responsible manner. In the university, Habermas argued that the study of one's speciality should be pushed until the student is forced to reflect on the social consequences of the research. The author concludes by considering objections to Habermas's proposal. 18 notes. 1929-74

Habsburgo-Loreno y de Borbón, Carlos de

2793. Heras Borrero, F. Manuel de las. EL ARCHIDUQUE CARLOS DE HABSBURGO-LORENO Y DE BORBON [Archduke Carlos de Habsburgo-Loreno y de Borbón]. *Hist. y Vida [Spain] 1983 16(180): 26-35.* Describes the complexities of the struggle for succession to the Spanish throne after 1931 and focuses on one of the pretenders. 1931-53

Hackert, Jakob Philipp

2794. Kuhn, Brigitte. PHILIPP HACKERT (1737-1807) ALS ZEICHNER DER ITALIENISCHEN LANDSCHAFT. ZU EINIGEN ZEICHNUNGEN IM KUPFERSTICHKABINETT IN DER WIENER AKADEMIE DER BILDENDEN KÜNSTE [Philipp Hackert (1737-1807) as a drawer of the Italian landscape: based on drawings in the Engravings Collection in the Vienna Academy of Fine Arts]. *Römische Historische Mitteilungen [Austria] 1983 25: 273-303.* Provides a detailed stylistic analysis of seven landscape drawings by the German landscape artist Jakob Philipp Hackert (1737-1807). Brief details of Hackert's life and artistic career are included, and particular reference is made to his lengthy sojourn in Italy, especially his travels to Naples, his contacts with the court there, and his nomination as court painter to Ferdinand IV in 1786. Special attention is paid to Hackert's artistic development, the observation of nature present in his work, and his panoramas. The two main elements of realism that influenced his landscapes were the 17th-century Dutch school and his own artistic studies in Paris. Based on drawings in the Engravings Collection in the Vienna Academy of Fine Arts; 99 notes, 12 illus. 1737-1807

Hackhofer, Johann Cyriak

2795. Hutz, Ferdinand. JOHANN CYRIAK HACKHOFERS KINDER [Johann Cyriak Hackhofer's children]. *Blätter für Heimatkunde [Austria] 1982 56(4): 117-120.* Describes the fate of the children of Johann Cyriak Hackhofer, the Austrian baroque painter. 1704-94

2796. Hutz, Ferdinand. J. C. HACKHOFERS HANDZEICHNUNGEN [The paintings of Johann Cyriak Hackhofer]. *Blätter für Heimatkunde [Austria] 1982 56(1): 18-23.* Describes the work of Styrian fresco painter Hackhofer (1675-1731). 1675-1731

Haden, Francis Seymour

2797. Dodier, Virginia. HADEN, PHOTOGRAPHY AND SALMON FISHING. *Print Quarterly [Great Britain] 1986 3(1): 34-50.* Similarity between certain etchings done between 1859 and 1865 by Francis Seymour Haden to photographs by British aristocrat Lady Hawarden (1822-65) indicates that the artists shared models, motifs, and subjects. Examples of the closely associated work include Haden's *A River in Ireland,* 1864, and Hawarden's *Multeen River, Dundrum,* ca. 1860-64. Although Haden made no direct references to Lady Hawarden, his letters to art critic Philippe Burty mention Dundrum, the Hawarden family estate in Ireland. Haden's description of Dundrum as a salmon fishing area suggests that he and the Hawardens may have met through Haden's and Viscount Hawarden's interest in salmon fishing. Based on Haden-Burty correspondence, catalogues; 17 illus., 81 notes. 1859-65

Hadfield, Robert Abbott

2798. Tweedale, Geoffrey. SIR ROBERT ABBOTT HADFIELD, F.R.S. (1858-1940), AND THE DISCOVERY OF MANGANESE STEEL. *Notes and Records of the Royal Society of London [Great Britain] 1985 40(1): 63-74.* Biographical sketch of Robert Abbott Hadfield, a British metallurgist who developed a new steel in 1883 that was greeted with indifference for 15 years until an American firm poured the first manganese steel in 1892. 37 notes. 1858-1900

Haenke, Thaddaeus

2799. Polišenský, Josef. TADEÁŠ HAENKE A KRIZE ŠPANĚLSKÉ KOLONIÁLNÍ AMERIKY [Thaddaeus Haenke and the crisis of Spanish colonial America]. *Sborník Národního Muzea v Praze. Řada C: Literární Hist. [Czechoslovakia] 1980 25(3-4): 49-76.* Born in northern Bohemia and trained in Prague and Vienna, Thaddaeus Haenke (1761-1816) became an explorer and naturalist in the Spanish royal service. After participating in the Malaspina expedition to the Pacific, he settled in the Cochabamba area in Upper Peru, now Bolivia. Haenke recognized the interaction of nature and society and opposed exploitation of the native peoples. During the early revolutionary campaigns he was in an awkward position as a royal employee with friends among the insurgents and with enlightened sympathies. Based on several Bohemian archives, and archives in Montevideo, Santiago, London, and Bloomington, Indiana; 87 notes. Russian and English summaries. 1782-1816

Hagemeister, L.

2800. Berezhnoi, A. S. KRUGOSVETNYI MOREPLAVATEL' L. A. GAGEMEISTER [The circumnavigator and seafarer L. Hagemeister]. *Latvijas PSR Zinātņu Akadēmijas Vēstis [USSR] 1984 (8): 48-59.* A biography of the seafarer and circumnavigator L. Hagemeister (Russian name Leonti Andrianovich Gagemeister), born on 27 June 1780 in the Latvian village of Drostenhof of German Baltic descent, who served in the Russian navy and died on 3 November 1834. Primary sources; 8 notes, biblio. 1800-34

Hagen, Kaspar

2801. Lingenhöle, Walter. KASPAR HAGEN—NEUES ZUM DICHTERISCHEN NACHLASS: IM HUNDERTSTEN TODESJAHR DES BREGENZER MUNDARTDICHTERS [Kaspar Hagen—new data on his poetic heritage: the 100th anniversary of the death of the Bregenz dialect poet]. *Montfort [Austria] 1985 37(4): 316-331.* Discusses the life and prints pictures, poems, and a family tree of Kaspar Hagen (1820-85), a poet of the Vorarlberg region of Austria who wrote poems in the local dialect. Attempts to trace his literary remains, which were mostly destroyed in a fire in 1945. 1840's-85

Hagen, Kuno Friedrich von der

2802. Eckert, Helmut Alexander. BILDNIS UND LEBENSGANG EINES FRIDERIZIANISCHEN OFFIZIERS KUNO FRIEDRICH VON DER HAGEN [Image and life of an officer during the reign of Frederick the Great: Kuno Friedrich von der Hagen]. *Zeitschrift für Heereskunde [West Germany] 1982 46(302-303): 115-117.* Describes the career of Kuno Friedrich von der Hagen (1733-62), son of a Prussian captain who became a captain himself, served with distinction in the Prussian army, and died in an attack on an Austrian force near Burkersdorf. 1754-62

Hager, Carl Otto

2803. Hofmeyr, S. M. CARL OTTO HAGER, NEGENTIENDE EEUSE KERKARGITEK [Carl Otto Hager, a 19th-century church architect]. *Q. Bull. of the South African Lib. [South Africa] 1982 37(1): 167-176.* Describes the distinctive neo-Gothic architecture of the Low German Reformed churches in the Cape of Good Hope province and the Orange Free State which were designed or built by Carl Otto Hager (1813-1898). A German immigrant, he settled in Stellenbosch. Originally a Lutheran, he achieved fame for his neo-Gothic Reformed churches. Based on memoirs in the Dutch Reformed Church Archives, Cape Town; 50 notes. 1838-98

Haggard, Rider

2804. Schultz, John A. FINDING HOMES FIT FOR HEROES: THE GREAT WAR AND EMPIRE SETTLEMENT. *Can. J. of Hist. [Canada] 1983 18(1): 99-110.* World War I reinvigorated British imperialist sentiment. Patriots, such as novelist Rider Haggard, hoped to strengthen the Empire as a bastion of British ideals and a bulwark of democracy through government-aided colonization, especially the free relocation of ex-servicemen. During the war, Haggard and his fellows at the Royal Colonial Institute waged an effective campaign to persuade government officials that "the Empire would provide fitting homes for the heroes of Flanders and Gallipoli," culminating in the Empire Settlement Act of 1922. Based on Colonial Office records, the Empire Land Settlement papers, diaries, and secondary sources; 72 notes. 1914-22

Hahn, Kurt

2805. Richards, Anthony. "Kurt Hahn: The Midwife of Educational Ideas." U. of Colorado, Boulder 1981. 225 pp. *DAI 1982 42(8): 3471-A.* 8200819 20c

Hahn, Philipp Matthäus

2806. Brecht, Martin. HAHN UND HERDER [Hahn and Herder]. *Zeitschrift für Württembergische Landesgeschichte [West Germany] 1982 41: 364-387.* Describes the relationship between the German Pietist minister Philipp Matthäus Hahn (1739-90) and Johann Gottfried Herder (1744-1803). Even though the latter mentioned Hahn in his works only rarely, numerous references to Herder in the extant diary and letters of Hahn reveal a mutually respectful regard for each other. Hahn regarded Herder as a thinker midway between his own Pietist views and the rationalistic theology that sprang from the Enlightenment, against which Hahn struggled all of his life. Reprints numerous excerpts of Hahn's diary and letters. 25 notes. 1770's-80's

2807. Prawitt, Leo. PHILIPP MATTHÄUS HAHN: EIN VERZEICHNIS DER SEKUNDÄRLITERATUR ZU LEBEN UND WERK [Philipp Matthäus Hahn: an index of the secondary literature on his life and work]. *Blätter für Württembergische Kirchengeschichte [West Germany] 1980-81 80-81: 175-203.* An extensive bibliography in chronological order, which would serve as the basis for a Hahn archive. 1770-1980

Haig, Douglas

2808. DeGroot, Gerard J. EDUCATED SOLDIER OR CAVALRY OFFICER? CONTRADICTIONS IN THE PRE-1914 CAREER OF DOUGLAS HAIG *War & Society [Australia] 1986 4(2): 51-69.* Despite studies asserting that Douglas Haig was a "complete" or an "educated" soldier, the British field marshall remained mired in his cavalry heritage. Haig was receptive to administrative reform, which accounts for his recent reputation as something of a progressive, but any change in cavalry doctrine was anathema for him. To the end of his life he lauded the cavalry's manly and moral prowess. Even four years of modern combat in World War I did not appreciably complete Haig's military education.

Based on the Haig papers, documents in the National Army Museum and Public Record Office, and on secondary sources; 56 notes. 1897-1918

2809. French, David. SIR DOUGLAS HAIG'S REPUTATION, 1918-1928: A NOTE. *Historical Journal [Great Britain] 1985 28(4): 953-960.* Though World War I British Field-Marshal Sir Douglas Haig's biographers often portrayed him as unconcerned about postwar accusations that his rigid and unimaginative strategy resulted in thousands of unnecessary British deaths, and though he never publicly defended himself, he was active from the end of the war to his death in 1928 in privately defending his war policy and convincing others to do so on his behalf. Based on diaries and correspondence; 30 notes. 1914-28

2810. Hammond, Keith. HAIG—A SUITABLE CASE FOR TREATMENT? *Army Q. and Defence J. [Great Britain] 1982 112(3): 324-329.* The British supreme commander during World War I, Field Marshal Douglas Haig was unfeeling, unimaginative, and, finally, incompetent, because of his controversial military strategy of attrition and heavy battle casualties. 1914-18

Haigh, John George

2811. Villafranca, Justo. JOHN GEORGE HAIGH, EL FALSO VAMPIRO [John George Haigh, the false vampire]. *Historia y Vida [Spain] 1984 17(191): 61-66.* The case of John George Haigh, the British murderer who after his arrest confessed his crimes in detail and based his defense on alleged vampiristic tendencies. 1945-49

Haignere, Daniel

2812. Hilaire, Yves-Marie. DANIEL HAIGNERE ET LES PRETRES ERUDITS DU BOULONNAIS ET DE L'ARTOIS ENTRE 1850 ET 1890 [Daniel Haignere and the learned priests of Boulonnais and Artois between 1850 and 1890]. *Revue d'Histoire de l'Eglise de France [France] 1985 71(186): 65-71.* After the conclusion of the revolutionary period in France, there was only a very gradual development of an interest in learning among the clergy in the area of Boulogne and Artois, but it was stimulated by the strong personality of Daniel Haignere (1824-93). Although the diocesan almanacs do not show an increase of learned clergy during the period 1864-89 the writings of Haignere constituted one third of all the works produced, during the 25 years. From 1850 there had been a considerable expansion of scholarly interest in the area; largely instrumental in this development was the influence of Haignere, who not only studied archives and wrote historical works, but was also a journalist, in which capacity he came under the discipline of his bishop for his social and political views. Yet despite such difficulties he continued to write, producing important works dealing with the history of the area of Boulogne and Artois. 1850-90

Haile Selassie

2813. Kapuscinski, Ryszard. THE EMPEROR. *Dissent 1983 30(1): 49-55.* Presents excerpts from the author's *The Emperor* (1983), which recounts the career of Haile Selassie, emperor of Ethiopia, 1932-74. 1932-74

Haiman, Hugó

2814. Fenyvesi, István. A KNER-KIADÓ OROSZ ÉS SZOVJET KÖNYVEI A 20-AS ÉVEKBEN: AZ "ISMERETLEN FORDÍTÓ," HAIMAN HUGÓ CENTENÁRIUMÁRA [Russian and Soviet books of the Kner Publishing House in the 1920's: the "unknown translator," Hugó Haiman's centenary]. *Magyar Könyvszemle [Hungary] 1981 97(1-2): 95-107.* Outlines the activities of the Kner Publishers of Gyoma and the life and work of Hugó Haiman, translator for that firm in the 1920's. Kner Publishers produced the *Monumenta Literarum,* a series of translations of Russian classical and Soviet works, the first of which was a Tolstoy novella translated by Hugó Haiman. Haiman was born in Nizsna on 20 November 1881. In 1914 he was taken prisoner and thus perfected his knowledge of Russian in Siberia. After his return he translated Russian works for Imre Kner and other publishers. Besides Tolstoy he translated the works of Ilya Ehrenburg, Ivan Bunin, and Fedor Gladkov. Haiman died 22 February 1932. Based primarily on the correspondence of Imre Kner and Hugó Haiman housed in the Békés Megyei Levéltár at Gyula; 51 notes. French summary. 1930-32

Hájek, Thaddeus

2815. Müller-Jahnke, Wolf-Dieter. ZUM PRIORITÄTENSTREIT UM DIE MELOSKOPIE: HÁJEK CONTRA CARDANO [The priority struggle over meloscopy: Hájek vs. Cardano]. *Sudhoffs Archiv [West Germany] 1982 66(1): 79-84.* Thaddeus Hájek in the 1560's was accused by various German and Italian humanists to have copied his work on meloscopy (the "science" of being able to predict based on a combination of planetary movements and human facial features) from Girolamo Cardano. 1560's

Haldane, R. B.

2816. Parker, Danny Michael. "R. B. Haldane: Labour's First Lord Chancellor." Auburn U. 1983. 140 pp. *DAI 1983 44(1): 261-262-A.* DA8313406 1923

Halévy, Elie

2817. Stansky, Peter. REVIEW ESSAY: ELIE HALEVY. *Hist. and Theory 1982 21(1): 143-149.* Critically reviews Myrna Chase's *Elie Halévy: An Intellectual Biography* (1980). While Halévy's goal of writing a full interpretation of 19th-century England remained incomplete insofar as he never finished his book on the 1852-95 era, his stress on the intellectual and cultural accounting for England's Victorian liberty and stability remains relevant. He is especially remembered for the "Halévy thesis" concerning the socioeconomic implications of Methodism. His last writings reveal a fear that the growth of state power might endanger the English democratic tradition. 1870-1937

Halkin, Léon-E

2818. Halkin, Léon-E. QUARANTE ANS APRES. REFLEXIONS CRITIQUES D'UN HISTORIEN DEPORTE [40 years later: critical reflections of a deported historian]. *Cahiers de Clio [Belgium] 1985 (82-83): 133-144.* Presents the methodological reflections and personal reminiscences of the author, a Belgian historian forced out of his country during World War II, on the 40th anniversary of the liberation of the concentration camps. 1938-45

Hall, Mary

2819. Baker, Colin. NYASALAND 1905-1909: THE JOURNEYS OF MARY HALL, OLIVIA COLVILLE AND CHARLOTTE MANSFIELD. *Soc. of Malawi J. [Malawi] 1982 35(1): 11-29.* 1905-09
*For abstract see **Colville, Olivia***

Halley, Edmund

2820. Cohen, Edward H. and Ross, John S. THE COMMONPLACE BOOK OF EDMOND HALLEY. *Notes and Records of the Royal Society of London [Great Britain] 1985 40(1): 1-40.* Discusses the youthful notes of Edmund (or Edmond) Halley (1656-1742), describes the manuscript and the register it contains, and prints the text of his "Observations and Maximes." 16 notes. 17c

2821. Cotter, Charles H. CAPTAIN EDMOND HALLEY, R.N., F.R.S. *Notes and Records of the Royal Soc. of London [Great Britain] 1981 36(1): 61-78.* Edmund Halley's contributions to maritime science were made at a crucial time in British history. He made the first map of the southern sky from St. Helena in the south Atlantic and became interested in terrestrial magnetism, publishing several tables of variations for finding longitude. He became interested in tidal science and hydrographic surveying, making a sea chart of the mouth of the Thames and the English Channel. He made the first chart of the trade winds and published astronomical tables. 43 notes. 1677-1742

2822. Paul, Norma Joan. THE COMET MAN: EDMUND HALLEY. *British Heritage 1985-86 7(1): 36-45.* Sketches the career of the English astronomer Edmund Halley (1656-1742), for whom Halley's Comet was named after he identified it, calculated its orbit, and predicted the time of its return. 1670's-1742

Hambro, Carl Joachim

2823. Seip, Helge. PORTRETT AV EN STATSMAN OG IT MENNESKE [Portrait of a statesman and a human being]. *Nordisk Tidskrift [Sweden] 1985 61(3): 263-267.* Discusses the public and personal life of the Norwegian politician, Carl Joachim Hambro (1885-1964), as described by his son, Johan Hambro, in a biography, *C. J. Hambro: Liv og Drøm* [C. J. Hambro: life and dream] (1984). 1885-1964

Hamerton, Philip Gilbert

2824. Czach, Marie. "Philip Gilbert Hamerton: Victorian Art Critic." U. of Illinois, Urbana-Champaign 1985. 532 pp. *DAI 1986 46(7): 1762-A.* DA8521749 1860's-94

Hamilton, James

2825. Knox, R. Buick. JAMES HAMILTON AND ENGLISH PRESBYTERIANISM. *J. of the United Reformed Church Hist. Soc. [Great Britain] 1982 2(9): 286-307.* Discusses the life of James Hamilton (1814-67), minister of National Scotch Church in Regent Square, London. 1839-67

Hamilton, William Rowan

2826. O'Donnell, Seán. WILLIAM ROWAN HAMILTON, 1805-1865. *Éire-Ireland 1983 18(4): 132-135.* Besides being a pioneering and prophetically visionary mathematician, whose theories foreshadowed Einstein's, William Rowan Hamilton had scholarly interests in many other intellectual fields. Hamilton's meticulous care in documenting his ideas and achievements enables modern scholars to reconstruct the extraordinary scope of his career. A study of Hamilton by Seán O'Donnell is the second in the Boole Press of Dublin's new series, *Profiles of Genius.* 1805-65

2827. Schweber, Silvan S. HAMILTONIAN TRANSFORM. *Isis 1982 73(266): 107-109.* Reviews Thomas L. Hankins's *Sir William Rowan Hamilton* (1980). This "erudite" and "gracefully written" biography of the inventor of quaternions deals ably with the subject's life, his mathematics and physics, and the cultural influences of the early 19th century. 1825-65

Hammarskjöld, Dag

2828. Trachtenberg, L. S. DAG HAMMARSKJÖLD AS A LEADER: A PROBLEM OF DEFINITION. *Int. J. [Canada] 1982 37(4): 613-635.* Dag Hammarskjöld, secretary general of the UN from 1953 to 1961, fulfilled a leadership role above and beyond his constitutionally mandated administrative duties. His involvement in various international crises demonstrated a strong moral and philosophical vision of the role of the UN in the global community. He evidenced great skill in gaining support for his actions. Through his friendships and secret correspondence with national leaders he was able to build a tacit basis of support before acting on important issues. He sought to amplify the powers of the organization and his own office in order to be more politically effective. These ideas were applauded among many of the small and new states but resisted by those of the Security Council. Based on the correspondence of Dag Hammarskjöld. 1953-61

Hammarstrom, Ingrid

2829. Stave, Bruce M. A CONVERSATION WITH INGRID HAMMARSTROM: URBAN HISTORY IN SWEDEN. *J. of Urban Hist. 1983 9(4): 473-500.* Covers Ingrid Hammarstrom's personal background, education, and career as urban historian, as well as the growth of urban history in Sweden. Hammarstrom's historical studies cover such topics as building cycles, urbanization, and the role of transportation. 20 notes, biblio. 1500-1900

Hammerstein, William, Freiherr von

2830. Wolff-Metternich, Hermann von. FELDMARSCHALL-LEUTNANT VON HAMMERSTEIN: EIN BINDEGLIED ZWISCHEN WESTDEUTSCHLAND UND ÖSTERREICH IM 19. JAHRHUNDERT [Field Marshall-Lieutenant von Hammerstein: a bridge between western Germany and Austria in the 19th century]. *Zeitschrift für Heereskunde [West Germany] 1984 48(316): 156-157.* Describes the career of William, Freiherr von Hammerstein, whose wide-ranging military involvements, including service in the armies of Hannover, Westphalia, and Austria, led him to reflect the strong urge for German unity that arose in the 19th century. ca 1800-61

Hammond, N.

2831. Hammond, N. MEMORIES OF A BRITISH OFFICER SERVING IN SPECIAL OPERATIONS EXECUTIVE IN GREECE, 1941. *Balkan Studies [Greece] 1982 23(1): 127-155.* The author, a historian of ancient Macedonia and Epirus, was a wartime soldier whose familiarity with prewar Greece and with the Greek language brought him into the Greek theater of operations in 1941. He enjoyed unusual freedom of movement and a wide range of experience, because he was attached first to the Special Operations Executive in Athens and then to its paranaval branch in Crete. 1941

Hamsun, Knut

2832. Lewko, Marian. "ZGRUCHOTANA WIELKOŚĆ": WOKÓŁ TEATRU KNUTA HAMSUNA ["A shattered greatness": around the theater of Knut Hamsun]. *Roczniki Humanistyczne [Poland] 1981 29(5): 5-39.* Knut Hamsun, Norwegian modernist novelist, poet, and playwright, won the Nobel Prize in 1920. He was a controversial artist, but most Polish critics have rated him highly. His works were translated into Polish in the early 1900's. His plays were first staged in Poland in 1901 and throughout the 1910's, but are now forgotten. Hamsun seems to have had considerable influence on the development of his contemporary Polish comedy playwright, Tadeusz Rittner. Based on Hamsun's novels, poems, and plays, contemporary Polish press articles, and reviews of theatrical performances; 157 notes. French summary. 1901-18

Han Peixin

2833. —. FOUR SECRETARIES OF THE CCP PROVINCIAL-LEVEL COMMITTEES. *Issues & Studies [Taiwan] 1983 19(6): 97-100.* Among recently appointed secretaries of CCP Provincial Committees are Wang Fang of Zhejiang (Chekiang) and Su Yiran (Su I-jan) of Shandong (Shantung), both of whom have had public security experience and have served the regime from its early years. Han Peixin (Han P'ei-hsin) of Jiangsu (Kiangsu) and Li Lian (Li Li-an) of Heilongjiang (Heilungkiang) have been politically active since the Cultural Revolution. Han has light industry experience and Li has held a variety of Party posts.
1960's-83

Hanauer, Charles-Auguste

2834. Oberlé, Roland. LE PERE DE L'HISTOIRE ECONOMIQUE DE L'ALSACE, L'ABBE HANAUER [Abbé Hanauer, the father of economic history in Alsace]. *Rev. D'Alsace [France] 1982 108: 155-164.* Recounts the career of Charles-Auguste Hanauer (1828-1908), educator, librarian of the city of Haguenau, and author of *Alsatian Peasants in the Middle Ages* and *Economic Studies of Ancient and Modern Alsace,* which is still valid for the economic history of Alsace-Lorraine of that period. 1850's-1908

Handel, George Frederick

2835. Fredell, Tom. HANDEL IN ASCENDANCY DUBLIN. *Éire-Ireland 1985 20(4): 6-14.* George Frederick Handel's visit to Dublin in 1741-42 had significant results for both the composer and Ireland. Handel presented many of his works in Dublin—including the premiere of his oratorio, the *Messiah,* at a charity concert. Invigorated by the receptive Dublin audiences, Handel—at a low point in his career—underwent an artistic reorientation and resolved to focus his energies on developing the oratorio as a musical form. The visit also speeded the integration of secular and religious music in Ireland and increased the effectiveness of Irish philanthropy through the charity concert medium. Secondary sources; 30 notes. 1741-42

2836. Gallois, Jean. GEORG FRIEDRICH HAENDEL: UN ITINERAIRE MUSICAL ET SPIRITUEL [George Frederick Handel: a musical and spiritual itinerary]. *Etudes [France] 1985 363(1-2): 55-63.* Discusses Handel's passion for life, intellectual curiosity, and Christian faith, and relates the progression of his music to his spiritual development.
1703-51

2837. Lockwood, Allison. HANDEL: MASTER AMONG MASTERS. *British Heritage 1985 6(6): 35-41.* Sketches the career of the German composer George Frederick Handel (1685-1759), a resident of Great Britain for 47 years.
1707-59

2838. Luján, Néstor. HAENDEL [Handel]. *Historia y Vida [Spain] 1985 18(203): 54-58.* A remembrance of George Frederick Handel (1685-1759), the German-born baroque composer who in 1726 became an English citizen and who fought tenaciously to regain his health after an attack of hemiplegia in 1737. 1700-59

Handley family

2839. Netboy, Anthony and Netboy, Elizabeth Silsby. THE HANDLEYS IN TASMANIA AND OREGON. *Oregon Historical Quarterly 1985 86(1): 80-93.* 1833-95
For abstract see ***Cooper, Jemima Champion***

Hang Shiqun

2840. Henrickson, George. CH'ÜAN TSU-WANG (1705-1755) AND HANG SHIH-CHÜN (1696-1773): THE CONTROVERSIAL RELATIONSHIP. *Papers on Far Eastern Hist. [Australia] 1981 (24): 63-82.* Discusses the relationship between the Chinese scholars Quan Zuwang (Ch'üan Tsu-wang) and Hang Shiqun (Hang Shih-chün), 1722-55, which was ostensibly friendly, but which was tinged with professional jealousy and pettiness. Also attempts to unravel the mystery surrounding Hang's scurrilous preface to Quan's collected works, *Jiqi Ting Ji (Chi-ch'i t'ing chi).* Hang was asked to write an epitaph to Quan after the latter's death in 1755, but this was never written, and Hang kept the manuscript of Quan's collected works until just before his death in 1773, although a former student of Quan's, Dong Bingchun (Tung Ping-ch'un) was anxious to publish his former mentor's work. 45 notes. 1722-73

Hanneman, Adriaen

2841. Kuile, O. ter. ADRIAEN HANNEMAN, 1604-1671 [Adriaen Hanneman, 1604-71]. *Spiegel Hist. [Netherlands] 1981 16(10): 527-533.* An account of the life of the Dutch portrait painter Adriaen Hanneman. He was born in the Hague, where he studied and lived most of his life. From 1626 to 1638 he lived in London, where he may have worked as an assistant to Anthony VanDyke. His work is much influenced by VanDyke and some paintings credited to VanDyke may be the work of Hanneman. Primary sources; 13 illus. 1604-71

Hannibal

2842. Díaz González, Joaquín. ANÍBAL Y BOLÍVAR [Hannibal and Bolívar]. *Bol. de la Acad. Nac. de la Hist. [Venezuela] 1981 64(253): 83-86.* 2c BC
For abstract see ***Bolívar, Simón***

Hanotaux, Gabriel

2843. Hanotaux, Gabriel. LA SOCIETE DES NATIONS (1920-1924) [The League of Nations, 1920-24]. *Rev. d'Hist. Diplomatique [France] 1980 94(1-3): 111-229.* Presents extracts from the notebooks of Gabriel Hanotaux, relating to his activities as one of the French representatives at the League of Nations, 1920-24. He describes his personal interventions and reactions to them, the results of his efforts, and gives his opinions on affairs in general and on the other people involved. Hanotaux thought that the purpose of participation in the League was to restore and maintain French power, and saw Britain as his principal adversary. The notebooks show a growing disillusionment and Hanotaux's personal conservatism. 225 notes. 1920-24

Hansen, H. C.

2844. Rasmussen, Erik. H. C. HANSEN, J. O. KRAG OG UDENRIGSMINISTERIET: KOMMENTARER OMKRING EFTERKRIGSTIDENS SOCIALDEMOKRATISKE LEDERSKIKKELSER [H. C. Hansen, J. O. Krag, and the Foreign Ministry: comments on leading figures among postwar Social Democrats]. *Historie [Denmark] 1982 14(3): 381-419.* In the new dictionary of Danish national biography, *Dansk Biografisk Leksikon,* Vagn Dybdahl has written the biographies of several Social Democratic prime ministers of the years since 1945. These articles do not have the balance desirable in a standard reference work. Dybdahl has underrated H. C. Hansen (1906-60) and overrated Jens Otto Krag (1914-78), whom Hansen was reluctant to appoint as foreign minister. Dybdahl suggests a political line running from Hans Hedtoft (1903-55) to Krag and fails to appreciate the tradition linking Vilhelm Buhl (1881-1954) to Hansen and subsequently to Viggo Kampmann (1910-76). Based on interviews, memoirs, and other primary and secondary sources; 119 notes. 1945-78

Hantsch, Hugo

2845. Posch, Fritz. GEDENKEN AN HUGO HANTSCH [Memories of Hugo Hantsch]. *Zeits. des Hist. Vereines für Steiermark [Austria] 1982 73: 153-159.* A tribute to the Austrian historian Hugo Hantsch (1895-1972). The author examines his life and academic career, and considers his work on the history of Syria, as well as his writings on the general history of Austria and nationality problems. 1895-1972

Hao Jianxiu

2846. —. HAO CHIEN-HSIU—SECRETARY OF THE CCPCC'S SECRETARIAT. *Issues & Studies [Taiwan] 1985 21(10): 141-145.* Hao Jianxiu (Hao Chien-hsiu) (b. 1935) is a third generation Chinese Communist Party cadre, that is, she was promoted to significant party posts after 1949. An impoverished textile worker, Hao was educated at Party expense and became a member of the Party in 1953. She was subsequently given responsible posts and became Minister of the State Council Ministry of Textile Industry in 1981 and, in 1982, was appointed alternate secretary of the Party's Central Committee Secretariat. 1949-85

Happer, Andrew P.

2847. Crabtree, Loren W. ANDREW P. HAPPER AND THE PRESBYTERIAN MISSIONS IN CHINA, 1844-1891. *J. of Presbyterian Hist. 1984 62(1): 19-34.* The career of Andrew P. Happer as pioneer missionary, Sinologist, and founder of Christian higher education in China helps to illuminate the dramatic changes China and Presbyterian missions underwent in the 19th century. His consuming passions were education and evangelism. As an evangelical, he believed his call was to convert individual Chinese to Christ and then to Christianize Chinese society through education. His attempts to interpret Chinese culture for western audiences in China and the United States mark him as an important contributor to Sino-American relations. Based on documents and reports of the Presbyterian Church, and letters and articles by Happer; photo, 51 notes. 1844-94

Harand, Irene

2848. Haag, John. A WOMAN'S STRUGGLE AGAINST NAZISM: IRENE HARAND AND *GERECHTIGKEIT* 1933-38. *Wiener Lib. Bull. [Great Britain] 1981 34(53-54): 64-72.* Irene Harand (1900-75) courageously fought Nazism in her native Austria in the 1930's. Her humanitarianism was rooted in her Christian values. In speaking and writing, Harand attacked anti-Semitic myths, exposed Nazi barbarities, and defended the Austrian regime. After the Anschluss, Irene Harand lived out her life in the United States. She deserves to be remembered for her struggle to make human sympathy and toleration prevail over national and racial hatreds. Based mainly on primary sources; 57 notes. 1933-38

Harapi, Zef

2849. Kongoli, Bestar. TË DHENA PËR JETËN DHE VEPRIMTARINË LETRARE TË ZEF M. HARAPIT (1891-1946) [The life and literary activity of Zef M. Harapi (1891-1946)]. *Studime Filologjike [Albania] 1983 37(1): 145-157.* A brief biography of Zef Harapi and review of his work as a playwright and educator. 16 notes. French summary. 1891-1946

Haraszthy, Ágoston

2850. Schoenman, Theodore. ÁGOSTON HARASZTHY, THE FATHER OF CALIFORNIAN VITICULTURE. *New Hungarian Q. [Hungary] 1983 24(89): 141-146.* Describes the earlier days of Ágoston Haraszthy, before he became instrumental in the founding of California's wine industry. Of aristocratic Hungarian birth, he was a member of the elite Royal Hungarian Bodyguard of Austria's Emperor Francis I. After Haraszthy's Western, liberal values led to his fall from favor at court, he undertook a prolonged visit to the United States. The visit led to settlement in Wisconsin, where he founded Sauk City before moving on to California. 1830-48

Harcourt, Edward

2851. Brister, Louis E. COLONEL EDUARD HARKORT: A GERMAN SOLDIER OF FORTUNE IN MEXICO AND TEXAS, 1832-1836. *Southwestern Historical Quarterly 1985 88(3): 229-246.* Eduard Harkort, better known in Texas history as Edward Harcourt, served as chief engineer in the Texas army during 28 March-11 August 1836. Harcourt was a German immigrant who reached Texas via New Orleans after spending nearly a decade in Mexico. During that time, he served four years in the Mexican army and supported the federalists. Opposition to Antonio López de Santa Anna's centralist government caused his deportation in November 1835. His experience in mining, cartography, and the military prompted General Sam Houston to appoint Harcourt to the Texas army as captain of engineers. His first task was to construct Fort Travis on the eastern shore of Galveston Island and to fortify Velasco, but he died before that work was completed. Illus., 51 notes. 1832-36

Hardy, Frederick

2852. Harfield, A. G. NARRATIVE OF MAJOR GENERAL FREDERICK HARDY, CB, 84TH REGIMENT. *J. of the Soc. for Army Hist. Res. [Great Britain] 1983-84 61(248): 228-245.* Reviews the general's military career with specific emphasis on his service in India during the Mutiny of 1857, using discussions with his son and his journal as the primary sources of information. 1830-1916

Hardy, Thomas

2853. Buckler, William E. THE HARDY-MOULE AFFAIR WITH A READING OF FOUR HARDY POEMS. *Biography 1982 5(2): 136-142.* The relationship between the young Thomas Hardy and Horace Moule, whose blighted life ended in suicide in September 1873, has long been shadowed in mystery. Though considerably older than Hardy, Moule was unusually attentive, serving as tutor, literary counselor, and psychological reinforcer during some of the most stressful phases of Hardy's efforts to shape his maturity and realize his ambitions as a writer. Based on the known biographical facts and on a reading of four Hardy poems, this essay suggests that the relationship had a strong, if one-sided, erotic component which was the source of much personal anxiety to Hardy, but which he gradually dealt with in poems that, though very oblique, are impeccably honest. 1866-73

2854. Steinberg, Alan G.; Pendleton, Gayle Trusdell (commentary). THOMAS HARDY AND THE LONDON CORRESPONDING SOCIETY: THE REVOLUTION THAT NEVER WAS. *Consortium on Revolutionary Europe 1750-1850: Proceedings 1983: 399-417.* Thomas Hardy and several other English shopkeepers, artisans, and laborers founded the London Corresponding Society in January 1792. The chief goal of the group was parliamentary reform, especially universal manhood suffrage. The society did not espouse violent revolution, but it did support most of the events of the French Revolution. The society's rise to prominence was short-lived. In 1793 it opposed the war against France. Hardy and other leaders were acquitted of charges of treason in 1794, but by that time their group already was in decline. England was not yet ready for the kinds of reforms that Hardy and his associates advocated. Comments, pp. 442-447. Based on materials in the British Library and on published primary sources; 45 notes. 1792-94

Harmsworth, Alfred

2855. McEwen, J. M. NORTHCLIFFE AND LLOYD GEORGE AT WAR, 1914-1918. *Hist. J. [Great Britain] 1981 24(3): 651-672.* 1914-18

*For abstract see **Lloyd George, David***

Harnack, Arvid

2856. Zechlin, Egmont. ERINNERUNG AN ARVID UND MILDRED HARNACK [Remembering Arvid and Mildred Harnack]. *Geschichte in Wissenschaft und Unterricht [West Germany] 1982 33(7): 395-404.* Arvid Harnack believed since the 1930's (when he and the author were friends in Marburg) that Germany would have to choose between the socialist East and capitalist West. He chose the USSR. On 23 December 1942 the Nazis executed him. 1930's-42

Harpe, Frédéric César de la

2857. Dragunov, G. P. PEREPISKA LAGARPA S ALEKSANDROM I [Correspondence between de la Harpe and Alexander I]. *Istoriia SSSR [USSR] 1983 (4): 184-187.* 1783-1824

*For abstract see **Alexander I***

Harris, Wilson

2858. Abaray, Michael J. WILSON HARRIS: A BIBLIOGRAPHY. *Bull. of Biblio. 1981 38(4): 189-193, 208.* Brief biography of contemporary novelist and poet Wilson Harris (b. 1921), born in Guyana and now living in London, followed by a bibliography of primary and secondary sources published from 1949 to 1980. 1949-80

Harrison, Eddie

2859. Heath, John E. A BUS CONDUCTOR BETWEEN THE WARS. *Transport Hist. [Great Britain] 1981 12: 89-91.* Recounts the memories of Eddie Harrison (b. 1911) who spent almost his entire working life as a conductor on the buses in the Ilkeston-Nottingham area of Great Britain. 1928-40

Hart, Simon

2860. —. ZAANDAM 24 MAART 1911-AMSTERDAM 27 SEPTEMBER 1981 (OBITUARY) [Zaandam 24 March 1911-Amsterdam 27 September 1981: obituary]. *Economisch-en Sociaal-Historisch Jaarboek [Netherlands] 1982 45: 293-297.* Simon Hart began working at the Amsterdam Municipal Archives in 1929 and was director from 1974 to 1976. He was also chief archivist of the Evangelical Lutheran Church since 1934. His research speciality was American Lutheran church history. As archivist he headed the effort to catalog all birth, death, and marriage registers before 1811. A brief addendum lists several publications. 1929-81

Hart, William

2861. Hudson, Pat and Hunter, Lynette, ed. THE AUTOBIOGRAPHY OF WILLIAM HART, COOPER 1776-1857: A RESPECTABLE ARTISAN IN THE INDUSTRIAL REVOLUTION. *London J. [Great Britain] 1981 7(2): 144-160.* Presents, with a brief introduction and commentary, the first half of the autobiography of William Hart (1776-1857), a cooper who came to work in London in the late 1790's. It is an unusual contribution to literature of the industrial revolution and provides insights into working-class attitudes and experiences that must have been typical of the artisan class of the time. Hart describes his standard of living, particularly the fluctuation in his fortunes, his religious development, his work, and his opinions on contemporary social and industrial affairs. Primary sources; 25 notes. Article to be continued. 1790's-1857

2862. Hudson, Pat and Hunter, Lynette, ed. THE AUTOBIOGRAPHY OF WILLIAM HART, COOPER, 1776-1857: A RESPECTABLE ARTISAN OF THE INDUSTRIAL REVOLUTION. PART II. *London J. [Great Britain] 1982 8(1): 63-75.* The second part of Hart's autobiography covers his employment in the West India Docks, his marriage, and his religious education and experience. He often seems preoccupied with the difficulty of reconciling rationalization and conscious effort with reliance upon divine providence. 10 introductory notes, 15 notes to the autobiography. 1804-51

Hartner, Willy

2863. North, J. D. IN MEMORIAM: WILLY HARTNER, 1905-1981. *Arch. Int. d'Hist. des Sci. [Italy] 1981 31(107): 439-442.* Willy Hartner (1905-1981), twice elected president of the Académie Internationale d'Histoire des Sciences was born in Germany where he studied chemistry, astronomy, and the history of mathematics. His broad linguistic and cultural interests made him an effective historical scholar. He was a visiting professor at Harvard from 1935 to 1937 and then returned to Germany, where he held the positions of professor, dean, and rector of the University of Frankfurt. 1930-81

Hartung, Fritz

2864. Schochow, Werner. EIN HISTORIKER IN DER ZEIT: VERSUCH ÜBER FRITZ HARTUNG (1883-1967) [A historian in time: a study of Fritz Hartung (1883-1967)]. *Jahrbuch für die Gesch. Mittel- und Ostdeutschlands [West Germany] 1983 32: 219-250.* The life and work of Fritz Hartung is permeated by a firm commitment to conservative, national, and monarchical views, gained through heritage and tradition, and held by the majority of the scholars of his generation. In the shifting political climate of his times, Hartung was prepared to compromise on political issues but faced confrontation to maintain professional and academic integrity. Member of the Prussian Academy of Sciences, professor at the University of Berlin, and prolific author, Hartung enjoyed a distinguished academic career. In the political arena, however, he was less successful. His attempt to activate an all-German republic of letters in the post-World War II period was doomed to failure. Relations among scholars in divided Germany could not be better than internal or international politics permitted. Based on the papers of Fritz Hartung in the Staatsbibliothek Preussischer Kulturbesitz (West Berlin), the papers of Richard Fester in the Bundesarchiv (Koblenz), and the letters of Friedrich Meinecke in the Geh. Staatsarchiv (West Berlin); 57 notes. 1910's-60's

Harty, Oliver

2865. Brock, F. W. van. MAJOR GENERAL OLIVER HARTY IN BRITTANY, 1799-1800. *Irish Sword [Ireland] 1981 14(57): 287-315.* Oliver Harty, a native of County Limerick, Ireland, was an officer in the French service from 1762 until 1800. In 1799 he was assigned to Brittany to put down an uprising of Chouans who were led by Major General Georges Cadoudal. Harty was outnumbered, in a hostile country, and surrounded by uncooperative civilian authorities. In spite of these difficulties he defeated Cadoudal and the Chouans at the battle of Grand Champ in January 1800. Based on records of the Service Historique de l'Armée de Terre, Archives Nationales, Paris; 5 maps, table, 126 notes. 1799-1800

Harwood, Busick

2866. Williamson, Raymond. SIR BUSICK HARWOOD: A REAPPRAISAL. *Medical Hist. [Great Britain] 1983 27(4): 423-433.* Attempts to rehabilitate the reputation of Sir Busick Harwood (1745-1814) as an academic reformer. After service in India, Harwood returned to England and began teaching at Cambridge where he remained until his death. Holding chairs of both anatomy and medicine, Harwood developed thorough and up-to-date courses based on personal experimentation. He also made a large collection of specimens, which the university bought after his death. His poor reputation is undeserved and based on repeated error in earlier accounts. Based on Harwood's works and secondary sources; 32 notes. 1785-1814

Hasanagić, Edib

2867. Ladjević, Gojko. BIOGRAFIJA EDIBA HASANAGIĆA [Edib Hasanagić: a biography]. *Zbornik Istorijskog Muzeja Srbije [Yugoslavia] 1981 17-18: 5-9.* Traces the life and work of Edib Hasanagić, who was director of the Serbian Museum of History in Belgrade from its establishment in 1963 until his retirement in 1980. He was born in Priboj in 1914. After attending grammar school in Skopje, Hasanagić graduated in law from Belgrade University. After a distinguished record in World War II, he became in 1953 Director of the Institute of Social Studies in Belgrade. As head of the Serbian Museum of History, Hasanagić distinguished himself through his numerous books and monographs on the theory and administration of museums and on the popularization of history. 1914-80

Hašek, Jaroslav

2868. Klevanski, Aleksandr Kharitonovich. RUSSKAIA EPOPEIA IAROSLAVA GASHEKA [The Russian epic of Jaroslav Hašek]. *Novaia i Noveishaia Istoriia [USSR] 1983 (2): 126-148.* The five years spent in Russia by Hašek helped crystallize the salient traits of the protagonist of his satirical series of novels, *The Good Soldier Schweik* (1920-23). A corporal in the Austrian army, Hašek surrendered to the Russians in September 1915, enlisted there in the newly formed Czech national corps, joined the Czech Social Democratic Party and, in 1918, was appointed to the political sector of the 5th Red Army while continuing his activity as journalist and propagandist. After repeated demands by the Czech delegation to the II International, he was finally permitted to return to Czechoslovakia for political agitation in 1920. Based in part on Soviet and Czech Party archives; photo, 88 notes. 1915-20

2869. Köttner-Benigni, Klara. EIN UNESCO-JUBILAR: JAROSLAV HAŠEK, DER SCHÖPFER DES "SCHWEJK" [A UNESCO jubilee celebration: Jaroslav Hašek, the creator of "Schweik"]. *Burgenländische Heimatblätter [Austria] 1983 45(2): 49-52.* Traces the life and career of the Czech writer Jaroslav Hašek (1883-1923) on the occasion of the centenary of his birth. Pays particular attention to his book *Good Soldier Schweik,* which revealed Hašek's attitude toward the Austro-Hungarian monarchy. 1883-1923

Haslam, John

2870. Schiller, Francis. HASLAM OF "BEDLAM," KITCHINER OF THE "ORACLES": TWO DOCTORS UNDER MAD KING GEORGE III, AND THEIR FRIENDSHIP. *Medical Hist. [Great Britain] 1984 28(2): 189-201.* John Haslam (1764-1844) was a pioneer in the study of connections between physiological brain disorders and insanity, especially paralytic dementia. He was removed from his position at Bethlem Hospital for cruelty to a patient. He seems to have been a scapegoat for the mid-18th-century drive for reform. Haslam turned to private practice and writing to gain his living, and published two satirical reviews of books by his friend William Kitchiner (1775?-1827), who wrote widely but idiosyncratically about diet and health. Although Haslam has been accused of baiting his friend to observe his reaction, he seems in fact merely to have been trying to produce material that would sell. Although personally annoyed, Kitchiner suffered no loss, for his books continued to sell very well. Based on the writings of Haslam and Kitchiner; 2 fig., 44 notes. 1789-1821

Hasselberg, Gösta

2871. Jägerskiöld, Stig. GÖSTA HASSELBERG [Gösta Hasselberg]. *Karolinska Förbundets Årsbok [Sweden] 1979-80: 9-10.* Obituary of Gösta Hasselberg, longstanding member of the board of the Swedish Carolinian Association, whose activities included studies of Eastern European legal history. His doctoral thesis dealt with the city laws of Visby on the island of Gothland; he was eventually appointed to the professorship for the history of law at the juridical faculty at Uppsala University. 1940-79

Hastings, Warren

2872. Turnbull, Patrick. WARREN HASTINGS. *British Heritage [Great Britain] 1982 3(6): 38-51.* Discusses the life, career, and achievements of Warren Hastings, appointed governor of Bengal in 1771. 1771-85

Hatalkar, V. G.

2873. Kenny, L. B. [V. G. HATALKAR (1905-84)]. *Quarterly Review of Historical Studies [India] 1984 23(4): 54-55.* Recounts the career of Indian scholar and academic V. G. Hatalkar, Professor of French at the University of Bombay, and a founding member of the Institute of Historical Studies (Calcutta). He was the author of two books on the history of the French in India in the 18th century: *Relations of the French with Marathas* and *Relations of the French with the Kingdom of Mysore.* Photo. 1932-79

Haton, Claude

2874. Simonin, Michel. RONSARD, CLAUDE HATON ET CATHERINE DE MEDICIS: UN DOCUMENT INEDIT SUR *LE DISCOURS DES MISERES DE CE TEMPS* [Ronsard, Claude Haton, and Catherine de Médicis: an unpublished document on the *Discourse on the Troubles of Today]. Nouvelle Revue du Seizième Siècle [France] 1984 2: 55-67.* The chronicler and priest Claude Haton bequeathed his *Memoirs* to the world, thanks to a 1018-page manuscript dated 1601 and acquired by the Royal Library in 1834. Although its existence had been known before, not until Félix Bourquelot published his edition for the Unpublished Documents of French History series did it become available to scholars and the reading public. Addressed to Queen Catherine, the document, in verse, purported to reproduce a poem by the troubadour Pierre de Ronsard about the contemporary miseries of his France, inflicted by God upon the French in return for their bad rulers. Haton claimed to be relaying the words of "a messenger," and quotes Nostradamus to authenticate his claim. It is uncertain whether Haton was the victim of a fraud or fraudulent himself, and if so, why. Based on the text of the *Memoirs,* which is quoted here, and numerous related studies, texts, and documents; 56 notes. ca 1601

Haubach, Theodor

2875. Beck, Dorothea. THEODOR HAUBACH, JULIUS LEBER, CARLO MIERENDORFF, KURT SCHUMACHER: ZUM SELBSTVERSTÄNDNIS DER "MILITANTEN SOZIALISTEN" IN DER WEIMARER REPUBLIK [Theodor Haubach, Julius Leber, Carlo Mierendorff, Kurt Schumacher: toward an understanding of the "militant socialists" in the Weimar Republic]. *Archiv für Sozialgeschichte [West Germany] 1986 26: 87-123.* Traces the common development of the political theory of Haubach, Leber, Mierendorff, and Schumacher, four young academics of almost the same age who were profoundly marked by the experience of the front during the First World War. Estranged from Marxist ideology, they recognized a bond between social democracy and the idea of the nation, acknowledged the republic as a form of government, and approved of the state's exercise of power with the use of armed force. They criticized the party's lethargic decisionmaking structure and supported an emotive, charismatic political style. Schumacher survived almost the whole Nazi period in a concentration camp; the others all died as members of the wartime resistance. Their ideas survived in postwar Social Democratic Party programs. 1919-33

Haupt, Georges

2876. Labrousse, Ernest. GEORGES HAUPT, A NEMZETKÖZI SZOCIALIZMUS FRANCIA TÖRTÉNETÍRÓJA [Georges Haupt, the French historiographer of international socialism]. *Világtörténet [Hungary] 1979 (2): 93-97.* In his youth (1949-58) Haupt published in Romanian. In 1958, he emigrated to France and began to publish in French. 1949-72

Hausdorff, Felix

2877. Asser, Günter. FELIX HAUSDORFF UND DER BEGINN DER MENGENTHEORETISCH ORIENTIERTEN MATHEMATIK [Felix Hausdorff and the beginning of number theory-oriented mathematics]. *Wissenschaftliche Zeitschrift der Ernst-Moritz-Arndt-Universität Greifswald. Gesellschafts- und Sprachwissenschaftliche Reihe [East Germany] 1982 31(4): 29-36.* Discusses the life and prints reminiscences of the German mathematics professor Felix Hausdorff (1868-1942) and his contributions to mathematical theory and topology in the context of the development of modern mathematics. 19c-20c

Hausenstein, Wilhelm

2878. Frank, Paul. WILHELM HAUSENSTEIN, DIPLOMATE [Wilhelm Hausenstein, diplomat]. *Documents [France] 1982 37(2): 114-123.* Retraces the career of Wilhelm Hausenstein, the first West German representative to Paris, examining the difficulties he encountered in France in the early 1950's and his efforts toward reconciliation between the two countries. 1950-55

Hauser, Johann

2879. Sakrausky, Oskar. JOHANN HAUSER—PFARRHERR UND DIENER AM EVANGELIO AUS VILLACH [Johann Hauser—preacher and minister of the gospel in Villach]. *Carinthia I [Austria] 1981 171: 51-81.* Traces the life and religious work of the Protestant preacher and minister Johann Hauser (b. 1521) in Villach, 1566-94. 1566-94

Hauser, Kaspar

2880. Mistler, Jean. GASPARD HAUSER, FILS DE PERSONNE [Kaspar Hauser, son of nobody]. *Hist. Mag. [France] 1984 (47): 24-31.* Tells the story of the life of Kaspar Hauser (1812-33), an abandoned child who, as an adolescent, was discovered in 1828 in Nürnberg and whose enigmatic life has been the subject of several legends on his reputed noble origin. 1828-33

Hausmann, Raoul

2881. Benson, Timothy O. "Raoul Hausmann: The Dada Years." (Vol. 1-2) U. of Iowa 1985. 617 pp. *DAI 1986 46(8): 2108-A.* DA8518806 ca 1900-20

Haussmann, Georges

2882. Gaillard, Jeanne. UN BOURGEOIS CONQUÉRANT: LE BARON HAUSSMANN [A bourgeois conqueror: Baron Haussmann]. *Histoire [France] 1981 (37): 34-43.* While describing the career of Georges Haussmann, whose name remains synonymous with the urban rebuilding of Paris during the Second Empire in France, the author also shows Haussmann's intense Bonapartism and his symbolism of the rising middle classes. 1830-91

Havel, Václav

2883. Gillar, Jaroslav. OHNE ANGST LEBEN—DER MITBÜRGER VÁCLAV HAVEL [Living without fear—fellow citizen Václav Havel]. *Schweizer Monatshefte [Switzerland] 1984 64(9): 719-727.* Discusses the release from prison in 1983 of the Czechoslovakian dramatist and dissident Václav Havel (b. 1936) and prints excerpts from his works. 1983-84

Haviaras, Stratis

2884. Georgakas, Dan. AN INTERVIEW WITH STRATIS HAVIARAS. *J. of the Hellenic Diaspora 1981 8(4): 73-82.* Discusses the literary career of Greek poet and American novelist Stratis Haviaras, especially his novel *When the Tree Sings* (1979), how he made the transition from Greek to American writer, and his future writing plans. 1920-80

Havlíček, Karel

2885. Nálepková, Olga. KAREL HAVLÍČEK BOROVSKÝ—PŘEDSTAVITEL ČESKÉHO BURŽOAZNÍHO LIBERALISMU [Karel Havlíček Borovský—a representative of Czech bourgeois liberalism]. *Časopis Matice Moravské [Czechoslovakia] 1986 105(1-2): 91-116.* The outstanding Czech journalist Karel Havlíček (1821-56) was closely associated with two other Czech national leaders, František Palacký and František Ladislav Rieger. Together they represented the strengths and weaknesses of the Czech liberal bourgeoisie, an immature class lacking in capital and political self-confidence. In 1848, they demanded a constitutional monarchy and a federal system for the Habsburg Empire, but shrank from republicanism, national independence, and social revolution. What enshrined Havlíček in the national memory was his democratic, populist tendency and his exceptional courage. To the Czech public he bequeathed a distinctly reformist way of thinking. Based on Havlíček's articles; 66 notes. German summary. 1846-51

2886. Špét, Jiří. KAREL HAVLÍČEK A NÁRODNÍ MUZEUM [Karel Havlíček and the National Museum]. *Časopis Národního Muzea [Czechoslovakia] 1981 150(3-4): 191-205.* Reflects on close contacts of Czech nationalist journalist Karel Havlíček (1821-56) to the National Museum of Prague he viewed as the center of Czech cultural life. 1821-56

2887. Weltsch, Ruben. FROM BATELOV HEIGHT TO SPARROW HILLS: AN EPISODE IN THE MATURING OF KAREL HAVLÍČEK'S NATIONALISM, 1842-44. *East Central Europe 1985 12(2): 127-145.* Karel Havlíček (1821-56), cherished by Czechs of varied political persuasions, was a unifying force in Czech society. In the 1840's, he spent two years in Russia as a tutor. Hoping that Russia would aid the cause of pan-Slavism, he was disappointed by what he felt was a Russian lack of interest in the smaller Slavic peoples, or even a willingness to use these peoples for their own selfish purposes. But his stay in Russia allowed him to overcome his provincialism, and his reading and writing while there helped shape him as a professional author who used his talents for the cause of Czech nationalism. Based mainly on Czech sources; 46 notes. 1842-44

Hawranek, Franciszek

2888. Brożek, Andrzej. FRANCISZEK HAWRANEK (9 III 1919-17 IX 1981) [Franciszek Hawranek, 9 March 1919-17 September 1981]. *Kwartalnik Hist. [Poland] 1982 89(2-3): 534-536.* Franciszek Hawranek began his work as a teacher in an elementary school in 1945 and received his doctorate in 1964. He took a particular interest in the history of the workers' movement in Upper Silesia, but also contributed other studies on this region and other neighboring territories. He was an excellent popularizer and his list of publications includes around 300 items. He also helped organize research projects by serving as director of the historical section of the Silesian Institute since 1970 and as vice director of the institute since 1975. 1919-81

Hawtrey, Stephen

2889. Cowie, Evelyn E. STEPHEN HAWTREY AND A WORKING-CLASS ETON. *Hist. of Educ. [Great Britain] 1982 11(2): 71-86.* Stephen Hawtrey (1808-86) founded St. Mark's School, Windsor, in 1844 to work out his ideas on a liberal education for working-class boys. Hawtrey turned his school into a sort of working-class Eton, expressing his philosophy that a good education was the same for all classes. He included Latin, music, and mathematics in the curriculum, plus sports and other character-building exercises. He was one of a group of educators who argued that a merely practical education prevented social mobility for able pupils. 63 notes. 1844-86

Haya de la Torre, Víctor Raúl

2890. Salisbury, Robert V. THE MIDDLE AMERICAN EXILE OF VICTOR RAUL HAYA DE LA TORRE. *Americas (Acad. of Am. Franciscan Hist.) 1983 40(1): 1-15.* Deported from Peru in 1923, Víctor Raúl Haya de la Torre took asylum first in Mexico, then traveled in Europe, and returned to Latin America in 1927. He hoped to lead a revolutionary movement in Peru but in the meantime traveled through Mexico and Central America, lecturing and laying plans. In Central American countries he was repeatedly harassed by local authorities and US diplomats. This gave his anti-imperialist and revolutionary message more notoriety than it would have had otherwise. Based on published sources and records in US and Mexican diplomatic archives; 55 notes. 1923-28

Hayek, Friedrich von

2891. Manin, Bernard. FRIEDRICH-AUGUST HAYEK ET LA QUESTION DU LIBERALISME [Friedrich von Hayek and the question of liberalism]. *Rev. Française de Sci. Pol. [France] 1983 33(1): 41-65.* Discusses Friedrich von Hayek's formulation of liberal principles in law and political economy and its historical antecedents. 1920's-70's

Hayford, Adelaide Casely

2892. Okonkwo, Rina. ADELAIDE CASELY HAYFORD: CULTURAL NATIONALIST AND FEMINIST. *Phylon 1981 42(1): 41-51.* Adelaide Casely Hayford (1868-1960) was a prominent cultural nationalist and feminist on the Gold Coast of West Africa. She organized a technical training school for girls, headed the Ladies' Division of the Universal Negro Improvement Association, and traveled and spoke to refute the stereotype of African barbarism. She combined feminism and cultural nationalism to improve the lives of African women. 1868-1960

Hayford, Mark Christian

2893. Haliburton, G. M. MARK CHRISTIAN HAYFORD: A NON-SUCCESS STORY. *J. of Religion in Africa [Netherlands] 1981 12(1): 20-37.* A biography of Mark Christian Hayford (1864-1935), the brother of Joseph Ephraim Casely Hayford, one of the founders of modern Ghana, examining his family and social background, his evangelism and fund raising, his relationship with the Prophet William Wade Harris and his movement, a fund raising scandal in Europe, and his death in London. Based on archives of the Ivory Coast, Senegal, London, and personal letters, conversations, and secondary sources. 1864-1945

Haygood, Laura A.

2894. Papageorge, Linda Madson. FEMINISM AND METHODIST MISSIONARY ACTIVITY IN CHINA: THE EXPERIENCE OF ATLANTA'S LAURA HAYGOOD, 1884-1900. *West Georgia Coll. Studies in the Social Sci. 1983 22: 71-77.* A devout Christian and a feminist, Laura A. Haygood became a missionary in China and participated in feminist reforms of the missionary administration. 1884-1900

2895. Papageorge, Linda Madson. "THE HAND THAT ROCKS THE CRADLE RULES THE WORLD": LAURA ASKEW HAYGOOD AND METHODIST EDUCATION IN CHINA, 1884-1899. *Pro. and Papers of the Georgia Assoc. of Hist. 1982: 123-132.* Georgian Laura Askew Haygood worked for the Women's Missionary Society of the Methodist Episcopal Church, South. The movement of women missionaries constituted a form of American Protestant feminism. Tells of Haygood's work at the McTyeire School for upper-class Chinese girls in Shanghai. 44 notes. 1884-1900

Hayman, Frederick

2896. Harasymiw, Bohdan. FREDERICK G. HEYMANN (1900-1983). *Canadian Slavonic Papers [Canada] 1984 26(1): 121-122.* The death of Frederick Heymann, editor, journalist, and outstanding historian of Czechoslovakia is a great loss to Slavic and historical scholarship. Professor at the University of Calgary since 1959, he published works such as *Poland and Czechoslovakia* (1966) and two volumes on the Hussites and the Bohemian Reformation, *John Zizka and the Hussite Revolution* (1955), and *George of Bohemia: King of Heretics* (1965). 1900-83

Hayter, George

2897. Alexander, David. GEORGE HAYTER (1792-1871): A PRINTMAKER OF THE 1820'S. *Print Quarterly [Great Britain] 1985 2(3): 218-229.* A 1982 exhibition at Morton Morris and Company in London entitled "Drawings by Sir George Hayter and John Hayter" has drawn attention to the considerable abilities of George Hayter. Best known as a portraitist, Hayter produced over 60 etchings between 1815 and 1829, exhibiting his interest in technique and enjoyment of experimentation. Although he produced very few prints after 1833, toward the end of his life he put together several albums of his early works to present to the British Museum. A checklist of Hayter's prints is given. Primary sources. 1815-33

Hayward, Max

2898. Katkov, George and Schapiro, Leonard. REMEMBERING MAX HAYWARD: THE GENIUS OF A TRANSLATOR. *Encounter [Great Britain] 1980 54(3): 86-92.* Max Hayward is best known as a translator of the works of Boris Pasternak and Alexander Solzhenitsyn but was also one who drew attention to spiritual qualities in the USSR. 1948-79

Haywood, Eliza

2899. Schofield, Mary Anne. EXPOSE OF THE POPULAR HEROINE: THE FEMALE PROTAGONISTS OF ELIZA HAYWOOD. *Studies in Eighteenth-Century Culture 1983 12: 93-103.* Popular, though minor, women novelists of the 18th century, such as the English writer Eliza Haywood, have not been adequately examined by critics and scholars. Haywood was the first popular novelist to deal extensively with the feminist milieu and, more important, with a woman's concept of self. Study of her heroines provides us with a comprehensive treatment of the "woman question" in the period. In her appeal to a growing female readership, Haywood created four distinct heroine types: the supporter of the conservative *status quo,* the independent female, the character who merged these two types and, the character who offered patterns of socially acceptable female behavior. Haywood's novels register the social and moral tensions of their age. She was not just an author of titillating romances, but an aggressive writer commenting effectively on the position and role of 18th-century women. Based on Haywood's published writings and secondary sources; 12 notes. 1719-51

Hazai, Samul

2900. Tepperberg, Christoph. DER K. U. K. CHEF DES ERSATZWESENS UND SEIN ARCHIV [The Habsburg chief of reserves and his archives]. *Scrinium [Austria] 1983 (28): 354-360.* Samul Hazai was appointed chief of Austrian army reserves in 1917 and the official documents of his department became part of the Austrian War Archive after World War I. 1917-18

Heaviside, Oliver

2901. Buchwald, Jed Z. OLIVER HEAVISIDE, MAXWELL'S APOSTLE AND MAXWELLIAN APOSTATE. *Centaurus [Denmark] 1985 28(3-4): 288-330.* The last autodidact to have significant impact on the development of physics, Oliver Heaviside (1850-1929), based his concepts of electromagnetism on a reformation of Maxwellian theory. Although his emphasis on energy captured the essence of British dynamical reasoning, Heaviside's highly compressed discussions, novel vector symbolism, and studied avoidance of Lagrangian analytical methods isolated him intellectually from his Maxwellian contemporaries. Primary sources; 13 notes, biblio. 1873-95

Heberden, William

2902. Heberden, Ernest. WILLIAM HEBERDEN THE ELDER (1710-1801): ASPECTS OF HIS LONDON PRACTICE. *Medical History [Great Britain] 1986 30(3): 303-321.* William Heberden, although from a family of little means, was able to get a Cambridge education and open a successful London practice in 1748. He was a popular lecturer who took pleasure in raising questions about authorities. Heberden had numerous prominent patients and often relied on natural cures—such as pure air and spa waters—in treating them. In 1783, Samuel Johnson became Heberden's patient, and the year before he had been one of five doctors consulted by mail in connection with Benjamin Franklin's bladder stones. Even after he had formally retired, Heberden was invited to consult in the cases of George III and Sir Joshua Reynolds. Despite his wealth and fame, Heberden was also willing to help the poor and always treated patients as individuals as well as clinical studies. Based on the Heberden Letters in the British Library; 95 notes. 1738-92

2903. Heberden, Ernest. CORRESPONDENCE OF WILLIAM HEBERDEN, F.R.S. WITH THE REVEREND STEPHEN HALES AND SIR CHARLES BLAGDEN. *Notes and Records of the Royal Society of London [Great Britain] 1985 39(2): 179-190.* Transcription of 18th-century letters found in Countway Library, Boston and the archives of the Royal Society from William Heberden (1710-1801), physician, to Stephen Hales (1677-1761), clergyman and physiologist, and Charles Blagden (1748-1820), physician. 39 notes. 18c

Heckscher, Eli

2904. Flakierski, Grzegorz. RÖTTER: DEN JUDISKA FRÅGAN I BREVVÄXLINGEN MELLAN HUGO VALENTIN OCH ELI HECKSCHER [Roots: the Jewish question in the correspondence between Hugo Valentin and Eli Heckscher]. *Hist. Tidskrift [Sweden] 1982 (2): 177-201.* Eli Heckscher and Hugo Valentin were both historians, conservatives, approximately the same age, and from Swedish-Jewish families. Their correspondence shows, however, that they differed greatly regarding the nature of Judaism, assimilation, the causes and nature of anti-Semitism, Zionism, nationalism, and the nature of culture. Based on the correspondence preserved in the Eli Heckscher papers, Royal Library, Stockholm; 106 notes. English summary. 1919-48

Hedāyat, Sadeq

2905. Komissarov, D. IRAN: OBLICHITEL' ZLA I NESPRAVEDLIVOSTI [Iran: exposer of evil and injustice]. *Aziia i Afrika Segodnia [USSR] 1983 (11): 51-53.* Provides biographical information on Iranian writer Sadeq Hedāyat (1903-51) who introduced the genre of the modern short story into contemporary Persian literature. 1903-51

Heeren, Arnold Hermann Ludwig

2906. Rutto, Giuseppe. IL GIOVANE HEEREN IN ITALIA: LA CORRISPONDENZA CON IL CARDINALE GIUSEPPE GARAMPI [The young Heeren in Italy: his correspondence with Cardinal Giuseppe Garampi]. *Quellen und Forschungen aus Italienischen Arch. und Bibliotheken [Italy] 1981 61: 380-392.* Describes the early education of Göttingen historian, Arnold Hermann Ludwig Heeren. Five letters exchanged between him and Cardinal Garampi, diplomat and prefect of the Vatican Secret Archive, written in 1786-88 and preserved in the same archive, throw some light on the humanistic influence received by the future historian of classical antiquity during a journey to Italy. 58 notes. 18c

Hegel, Georg

2907. Chang, Ko-chuan. HEGEL TSAO NIEN TI CHE-HSÜEH SSU-HSIANG [The philosophical ideas of the early Hegel]. *Kuo-li Taiwan Ta-hsüeh Wên-Shih Chê-hsüeh Pao (Bull. of the Coll. of Liberal Arts, Natl. Taiwan U.) [Taiwan] 1980 29: 175-233.* The philosophical ideas of the early Georg Hegel can be divided into four periods: 1) the middle-school period, 1784-88, 2) the university period, 1788-93, 3) the Switzerland period, 1793-96, and 4) the Frankfurt period, 1797-1800. During the first period, Hegel voiced his optimism about the eventual union of the Christian churches and expounded on "pragmatic history." During the university period, Hegel focused on moral philosophy, insisting that reason and instinct form the foundation of moral behavior. From Switzerland, Hegel spoke against the idea of original sin and advocated religious tolerance. While at Frankfurt, he insisted that political education and democratic elections were essential for the political improvement of society. He explained that the true Christian spirit was based on love and that the old and new Christian churches should reunite. Based on Hegel's works; 313 notes, biblio. 1784-1800

2908. Mörike, Hans-Jürgen. HEGELS ÜBERGANG NACH PREUSSEN. PHILOSOPHIE DER REFORM—REFORM DURCH PHILOSOPHIE? [Hegel's move to Prussia. Philosophy of reform—reform through philosophy?]. *Wissenschaftliche Zeitschrift der Humboldt-Universität zu Berlin. Gesellschaftswissenschaftliche Reihe [East Germany] 1984 33(1): 11-14.* Analyzes biographical and contemporaneous documents concerning Georg Hegel's move from the University of Heidelberg to the University of Berlin in an attempt to explain the reasons for Hegel's move and their significance for the discussion of Hegel's philosophy of justice, which tended to support the spirit of the Prussian restoration. 1817-20

Heilmann, Ernst

2909. Lösche, Peter. ERNST HEILMANN—SOZIALDEMOKRATISCHER PARLAMENTARISCHER FÜHRER IM PREUSSEN DER WEIMAR REPUBLIK [Ernst Heilmann: Social Democratic parliamentary leader in Prussia of the Weimar Republic]. *Geschichte in Wissenschaft und Unterricht [West Germany] 1982 33(7): 420-432.* Ernst Heilmann (1881-1940) was chairman of the Social Democratic Party in the Prussian state parliament from 1921 to 1933. He refused to leave fascist Germany in 1933, was arrested and subsequently murdered in Buchenwald. He contributed much to the stability of the Prussian state parliament and recognized that feudalism in Prussia had to make way for parliamentary democracy. He believed in the Weimar republican constitution and underrated the fascists. Social Democrats were so concerned about their own party that they never believed there could be a threat to democracy itself. 47 notes. 1920's-30's

2910. Möller, Horst. ERNST HEILMANN: EIN SOZIALDEMOKRAT IN DER WEIMARER REPUBLIK [Ernst Heilmann: a Social Democrat in the Weimar Republic]. *Jahrbuch des Inst. für Deutsche Gesch. [Israel] 1982 11: 261-294.* Ernst Heilmann (1881-1940) was one of the leading Social Democrats who refused to emigrate after the National Socialist seizure of power in 1933, despite the fact that he was marked as a leading enemy of the Nazis. Heilmann, of Jewish birth, had entered the Social Democratic Party as a student and worked as a parliamentary expert for the party before entering the Prussian Landtag in 1919 and the Reichstag in 1928. As a principal of the right wing of the Social Democrats he led the delegation in the Landtag. He was often criticized for his bohemian personal life. He was a severe critic of Nazism. His refusal to leave Germany after Hitler came to power was consistent with his sense of responsibility to his followers and his party. He died by an injection ordered by the leadership of the SS in a concentration camp in 1940. Based on parliamentary papers and memoirs, and some materials in the Friedrich-Ebert-Stiftung, Bonn; 99 notes. Hebrew summary. 1919-40

Heimpel, Hermann

2911. Heimpel, Hermann. TRAUM IM NOVEMBER [November Dream]. *Gesch. in Wiss. und Unterricht [West Germany] 1981 32(9): 521-525.* On the occasion of Heimpel's 80th birthday, reprints his 1961 account of Hitler's first attempt to take power, in the Munich Beer Hall Putsch of 8-9 November 1923. Heimpel's ironic description of the events of that night mixes reality and dream with the key symbolic image of the flaming torches burning the library with the author's historical sources. 1923

Heine, Heinrich

2912. Escoffier, Françoise. HENRI HEINE ET "LA REVUE DES DEUX MONDES" [Heinrich Heine and *Revue des Deux Mondes*]. *Rev. des Deux Mondes [France] 1982 (10): 130-137.* Describes Heinrich Heine's life in Paris, contributions to *Revue des Deux Mondes,* and various contemporaries. 1831-56

Heinemann, Gustav W.

2913. Camphausen, Axel von. STAAT, KIRCHE UND GESELLSCHAFT BEI GUSTAV W. HEINEMANN [State, church, and society in the papers of Gustav W. Heinemann]. *Geschichte in Wissenschaft und Unterricht [West Germany] 1981 32(1): 1-23.* Analyzes three published volumes of the collected works of Gustav Heinemann (1899-1976), a key figure in 20th-century German Protestant and political life, with special reference to his views on the proper relationship of church and state in modern society. Heinemann always insisted on the independence of the German Evangelical Church, but he also emphasized in his numerous essays and speeches the political responsibilities of Christians and the Church. His political career bore witness to a belief that "Christians belong in the political battle." One of the founders of the Christian Democratic Party after World War II, he later switched to the Social Democratic Party and served as president of the Federal Republic, 1969-74. 155 notes. 1945-76

Heinricher, Kurt

2914. —. DR. KURT HEINRICHER (1911-1982) [Dr. Kurt Heinricher (1911-82)]. *Europa Ethnica [Austria] 1983 40(2): 89-90.* A tribute to the Austrian lawyer and historian Kurt Heinricher (1911-82), paying particular attention to his work concerning the problems of the Southern Tirol and Italian nationalism, 1939-45. 1911-82

Heitler, Walter

2915. Rasche, Günther. LAUDATIO AUF PROFESSOR WALTER HEITLER [A laudation of Professor Walter Heitler]. *Arch. Int. d'Hist. des Sci. [Italy] 1980 30(105): 162-166.* This tribute was given in May 1977 in Zurich, when Walter Heitler received the Golden Medal of the Humboldt Society for outstanding achievements in physics. Best known are Heitler's achievements in the areas of theoretic chemistry, quantum electrodynamics, and the Meson-Nucleon reactions, which brought him into cooperation with many renowned researchers in different countries. A refugee from Germany in 1933, Heitler has pursued his research work and lectures abroad since then. 1922-79

Heliade-Rădulescu, Ioan

2916. Vulcan, Iosif; Lăcustă, I., ed. PANTEONUL ROMÂN [Romanian pantheon]. *Magazin Istoric [Romania] 1981 15(5): 17-19, 61.* Reprints three biographical sketches, of Ioan Heliade-Rădulescu (1802-72), Mihail Kogălniceanu (1817-91) and Avram Iancu (1824-72) from a series on prominent Romanians first published in the Budapest magazine *Familia,* 1865-68. 1802-68

Heller, Frank

2917. Hedman, D. "Eleganta Eskapader: Frank Hellers Författarskap till och med *Kejsarens Gamla Kläder*" [Elegant adventures: Frank Heller's authorship until *The Emperor's Old Clothes*]. Uppsala U. [Sweden] 1985. 448 pp. *DAI-C 1986 47(2): 285; 47/1379c. Bokförlaget Settern, publ.* 1906-18

Helps, Arthur

2918. DeBruyn, John R. THOMAS CARLYLE AND SIR ARTHUR HELPS: II. *Bull. of the John Rylands U. Lib. of Manchester [Great Britain] 1982 64(2): 407-432.* Contains correspondence between the two concerning Helps's historical and literary writings. The friendship grew close and, although differences existed between them, there was a basic compatibility that kept them friends. Helps especially expressed gratitude for Carlyle's influence on his work. Based on their correspondence; 72 notes. 1855-75

2919. DeBruyn, John R. SIR ARTHUR HELPS, GLADSTONE AND DISRAELI. *Bulletin of the John Rylands University Library of Manchester [Great Britain] 1985 68(1): 76-114.* Arthur Helps was a master of the art of letter writing, and his correspondence as Clerk of the Privy Council with the two prime ministers provides invaluable information. Excerpts from various letters illustrate his opinion of the two, and they also clarify his relationship with each. Most of the letters excerpted are unpublished and of historical and biographical interest. Based on the correspondence; 139 notes. 1813-75

Helvétius, Claude Adrien

2920. Silber, Gordon R. IN SEARCH OF HELVETIUS' EARLY CAREER AS A FREEMASON. *Eighteenth-Century Studies 1982 15(4): 421-441.* Traces Claude Adrien Helvétius's role as founder of the Loge des Sciences, planner of the Loge des Neuf-Soers, and as principal leader of Freemasonry in Paris by 1750. 36 notes, 2 appendixes. 1720-70

Henao, José Tomás

2921. Botero G., Néstor. APUNTES HISTORICO-GENEALOGICOS EN TORNO A UN PARROCO DE ALDEA [Historical and genealogical notes about a parish priest of a small town]. *Revista de la Academia Colombiana de Historia Eclesiástica [Colombia] 1980 14(38): 5-18.* Traces the ancestry of José Tomás Henao, the Catholic parish priest of the Colombian village of Sonsón from 1810 until his death in 1852. 15c-19c

Henao Monjaraz, Gabriel de

2922. Goldberg, Rita. NUEVOS DATOS SOBRE EL POETA DON GABRIEL DE HENAO MONJARAZ [New information concerning the poet Gabriel de Henao Monjaraz]. *Bol. de la Biblioteca Menéndez Pelayo [Spain] 1982 58: 155-173.* Presents biographical data concerning Gabriel de Henao Monjaraz (1589-1637), a minor poet, and some of his immediate descendants, particularly his natural son, Gabriel de Henao (1612-1704), the Jesuit historian and theologian. The elder Henao was a native of Valladolid but maintained a residence in Madrid. He collected sizable libraries in both cities, that of Madrid eventually passing to the Royal Library. The text of his poem "Avisos para la Muerte" demonstrates his pedestrian poetic gifts. Utilizes material from the Archivo Histórico Nacional, Archivo General de Simancas, and others; 23 notes. 1589-1704

Henderson, Nevile

2923. Biber, Dušan. SIR NEVILE HENDERSON O POLITIKI KRALJA ALEKSANDRA DO NACISTIČNE NEMČIJE [Sir Nevile Henderson on the policy of King Alexander I toward Nazi Germany]. *Prispevki za Zgodovino Delavskega Gibanja [Yugoslavia] 1980 20(1-2): 23-29.* Cites the assessment of British Ambassador Henderson of the policy of rapprochement between the kingdom of Yugoslavia and the Third Reich. King Alexander did not try to conceal his

sympathy toward Hitler and did not oppose the Anschluss. He looked upon Germany as a counterbalance to the expansionism of Italy and expected German supremacy in Central Europe. He considered Russia, whether Bolshevist or other, the greatest danger for the Balkans. He advocated the independence of Yugoslavia. Henderson anticipated that in spite of the alliance with France, Yugoslavia would arrive at an agreement with Italy, then Germany, and finally also with Russia. From a paper delivered to a conference on the Germans, Poland, and Europe, 1871-1971, Poznán, 1979.
1932-34

Heneage, Thomas

2924. Sil, Narasingha P. "JENTELL MR. HENEAGE": A FORGOTTEN TUDOR SERVANT. *Notes and Queries [Great Britain] 1984 31(2): 169-172.* Describes the role of Thomas Heneage, one of the least known of Henry VIII's intimate servants. In addition to serving Henry, he held an important role in Edward VI's household as well.
ca 1500-53

Henningsen, Sven

2925. Due-Nielsen, Carsten. SVEN HENNINGSEN 2.2.1910-24.1.1982 [Sven Henningsen, 2 February 1910-24 January 1982]. *Hist. Tidsskrift [Denmark] 1983 83(1-2): 211-222.* Describes and comments on the work of Sven Henningsen (1910-82), professor of Modern History and Social Science at the University of Copenhagen and a leader in introducing American social science methods to the study of contemporary history and international relations. Based on monographs, interviews, and personal acquaintance.
1936-82

Henríquez Ureña, Pedro

2926. Gutiérrez Girardot, Rafael. LA HISTORIOGRAFIA LITERARIA DE PEDRO HENRIQUEZ UREÑA: PROMESA Y DESAFIO [The literary historiography of Pedro Henríquez Ureña: promise and challenge]. *Casa de las Américas [Cuba] 1984 (144): 3-14.* Pedro Henríquez Ureña (1884-1946), critic and historian of literature, was born in the Dominican Republic and spent his youth in Cuba, which he considered his second mother country. He taught in the United States and Buenos Aires. In his work he outlined a model of explanation for a social history of Latin American literature as a search for self-expression and self-constitution, which remains as a challenge for future scholars. 14 notes.
1884-1946

2927. Orfila Reynal, Arnaldo. RECUERDO DE PEDRO HENRIQUEZ UREÑA [Remembrance of Pedro Henríquez Ureña]. *Casa de las Américas [Cuba] 1984 (144): 15-17.* Recalls meeting the Dominican scholar Pedro Henríquez Ureña (1884-1946) at an international students congress in Mexico City and the subsequent friendship which resulted. The author was instrumental in finding employment in Argentina for Ureña, then teaching in Minnesota. He remembers especially his warm and sociable personality.
1921-46

2928. Rodríguez Feo, José. MIS RECUERDOS DE PEDRO HENRIQUEZ UREÑA [My reminiscences of Pedro Henríquez Ureña]. *Casa de las Américas [Cuba] 1984 (144): 21-27.* Recalls a friendship which began when the author was an undergraduate at Harvard College and the Dominican professor Pedro Henríquez Ureña (1884-1946) was giving the Charles Eliot Norton lectures on Spanish-American literary currents in 1940-41. Remembers especially Henríquez Ureña's extraordinary erudition, his genius as a teacher and director of the young, and his humanistic ideals. 3 notes.
1940-46

Henry, Denis

2929. McDonnell, A. D. "The 1918 General Election in Ulster, and the Biography of a Candidate, Denis Henry." Queen's U. of Belfast 1983. 493 pp. *DAI-C 1984 45(3): 689; 9/2816c.*
1918

Henry, Françoise

2930. Allen, Máirín. FRANÇOISE HENRY, 1902-1982. *Éire-Ireland 1985 20(1): 133-139.* Sketches the professional career of Françoise Henry, archaeologist and art historian. Born and educated in France and writing many of her works in French, Henry was employed at Irish academic institutions after 1934. In addition to studies in the general history of European painting, Henry was an authority on Ireland's early Christian art. She was also a key figure in the development of Irish archaeological studies.
5c-15c

2931. O'Grady, John N. FRANÇOISE HENRY—AN APPRECIATION. *Studies [Ireland] 1982 71(281): 24-26.* A personal appreciation of Ireland's notable scholar of Early Christian art and founder of art historical studies at University College, Dublin.
1982

Henry, Joseph

2932. Tsverava, G. K. FARADEI, GENRI, I OTKRYTIE INDUKTIROVANNYKH TOKOV [Faraday, Henry, and the discovery of electromagnetic induction]. *Voprosy Istorii Estestvoznaniia i Tekhniki [USSR] 1981 (3): 99-106.*
1828-37

For abstract see ***Faraday, Michael***

Henry Frederick, Prince of Wales

2933. Strong, Roy. HENRY, PRINCE OF WALES: ENGLAND'S LOST STUART KING. *History Today [Great Britain] 1986 36(May): 16-23.* Discusses the brief life of Henry Frederick (1594-1612), son of James I and Prince of Wales, who was noted for his "quickie wittie answers and pryncely carriage" as well as his reverend behavior. The boy who would be king died of typhoid fever and was succeeded by Charles I (1600-49).
1594-1612

Henry IV

2934. Garrisson-Estèbe, Janine. HENRI IV, "LE ROI PARISIEN" [Henry IV, the "Parisian king"]. *Histoire [France] 1982 (49): 52-61.* Describes the reign of Henry IV from 1589 to 1610.
1589-1610

2935. Love, Ronald S.; Martin, Ronald (commentary). HENRY IV AND IVRY REVISITED: THE KING AS A MILITARY LEADER. *Proceedings of the Annual Meeting of the Western Society for French History 1983 11: 65-77.* Historians have generally recognized that Henry IV of France (ruled 1589-1610) was a good field commander, but they have criticized his skills as a military strategist. An examination of the battle of Ivry (March 1590), however, reveals that Henry was a master at both tactics and strategy. He needed a spectacular victory over the Catholic League in order to consolidate his hold on the throne. By clever ruses he picked the time and place, and he forced the Duke of Mayenne into battle. During the fight Henry skillfully used infantry, cavalry, and artillery. Comments, pp. 88-90. Based on documents in the Bibliothèque Nationale and the French foreign affairs ministry; 32 notes.

Henry the Younger

2936. Petri, Franz. HERZOG HEINRICH DER JÜNGERE VON BRAUNSCHWEIG-WOLFENBÜTTEL: EIN NIEDERDEUTSCHER TERRITORIALFÜRST IM ZEITALTER LUTHERS UND KARLS V [Duke Henry the Younger of Brunswick-Wolfenbüttel: a lower German prince during the time of Luther and Charles V]. *Archiv für Reformationsgeschichte [West Germany] 1981 72: 122-158.* Examines the historical and political background of the controversy between Duke Henry the Younger of Brunswick-Wolfenbüttel (1489-1568) and the Schmalkaldians, as portrayed in contemporary political sources and in characterizations of the duke's personality given by controversial writings of his time. The emphasis is on: 1) the insight gained from documents taken as booty by the Schmalkaldians and from other contemporary correspondence, 2) Duke Henry's relationship to Charles V, going back to the beginning of the emperor's regency and the reasons for his failure to support the duke in his controversy with the Schmalkaldians, and 3) the period following his reinstatement to his principality by the emperor at the end of the Schmalkaldian war, it being particularly important to come to a complete judgment of Henry's personality. Based on a lecture held by a study group at the University of Göttingen in 1980 on "Luther and the Literary Controversy over Duke Henry the Younger of Brunswick-Wolfenbüttel." 16c

Henry VII

2937. Kar, Jasoabanta. HENRY VII: THE DYNASTIC STRUGGLE. *Q. Rev. of Hist. Studies [India] 1981-82 21(1): 12-21.* Upon his accession to the English throne in 1485 as a result of his victory at Bosworth Field, Henry VII was aware that his claim to the monarchy was based more on circumstances than on the principle of hereditary succession. Due to the impact of political difficulties of the 14th and 15th centuries on succession, there were others in 1485 who had more substantial and valid claims to the throne. Henry VII eliminated the opposition and expended considerable energies in establishing the legitimacy of his dynasty primarily through marriage alliances. 74 notes. 1485-1509

Henry VIII

2938. Cressy, David. SPECTACLE AND POWER: APOLLO AND SOLOMON AT THE COURT OF HENRY VIII. *Hist. Today [Great Britain] 1982 32(Oct): 16-22.* The transition of Henry VIII from Renaissance monarch (the youthful Apollo) to Reformation patriarch (the aging Solomon) can be traced through the graphics and visual images displayed in his court, festivals, and kingdom. 1509-47

Hensel, Fanny Mendelssohn

2939. Quin, Carol Lynelle. "Fanny Mendelssohn Hensel: Her Contributions to Nineteenth-Century Musical Life." U. of Kentucky 1981. 314 pp. *DAI 1982 42(7): 2929-A.* 8129758 1825-47

Henshaw, Thomas

2940. Pasmore, Stephen. THOMAS HENSHAW, F.R.S. (1618-1700). *Notes and Records of the Royal Soc. of London [Great Britain] 1982 36(2): 177-188.* Thomas Henshaw, an active and prolific member of the Royal Society, wrote much on natural phenomena and other topics such as the spirals of nut trees, freezing, heartburn, the making of counterfeit pearls, tooth replacement, and flying. He also accompanied the Duke of Richmond in 1672 to Denmark where he met with Danish scientists. 14 notes. 1640's-1700

Henslowe, Philip

2941. Cerasano, S. P. REVISING PHILIP HENSLOWE'S BIOGRAPHY. *Notes and Queries [Great Britain] 1985 32(1): 66-72.* Presents additional material on the life of Philip Henslowe, a courtier to Elizabeth I and James I, and a prominent figure in English Renaissance theater, who lived from approximately 1559-1616. 1559-1616

Hentig, Werner Otto von

2942. Hauner, M. L. WERNER OTTO VON HENTIG, 1886-1984. *Central Asian Survey [Great Britain] 1984 3(2): 138-141.* Diplomat Werner Otto von Hentig (1886-1984) was the last surviving German player in the international politics of Central Asia and the Middle East. He entered the German diplomatic service in 1911 and during World War I undertook a daring mission in which he traveled across enemy lines to Afghanistan to offer the ruler of Afghanistan, Amir Habibullah, a treaty with Germany in which for the first time a major foreign power recognized Afghanistan's independence and full sovereignty, in return for Afghanistan's joining the Central Powers in the war against the British Empire. During World War II, he attempted to foment a coup in Kabul in order to return to power the exiled King Amanullah and thus gain leverage against the British army in India. Hentig could have been the "German Lawrence," but his actions, including his support for the political emancipation of Turkic peoples, lost him vital support in Berlin. 1911-84

Herbert, William

2943. Sil, Narasingha P. SIR WILLIAM HERBERT IN TUDOR POLITICS, 1547-53. *Biography 1982 5(4): 297-318.* Herbert is usually seen as a schemer loyal to none but himself. This paper attempts to penetrate behind the generally recognized Machiavellian facade of his character. It reveals what may be considered the most plausible character of the man: ambitious, artful, but not altogether a monster of avarice without redeeming features. 1547-53

2944. Sil, Narasingha P. THE EARL OF PEMBROKE AND THE CRISIS IN QUEEN MARY'S REIGN, 1553-58. *Renaissance and Reformation [Canada] 1986 10(2): 159-179.* Reexamines the Earl of Pembroke's career to demonstrate that his preeminence during the mid-1550's was earned. During Queen Mary's reign, Pembroke became a wealthier man, demonstrated military ability, served as a competent administrator, and gained recognition as the most influential nobleman in England. 111 notes. 1553-58

2945. Sil, Narasingha P. SIR WILLIAM HERBERT, EARL OF PEMBROKE (C. 1507-70): IN SEARCH OF A PERSONALITY. *Welsh Hist. Rev. [Great Britain] 1982 11(1): 92-107.* Sir William Herbert does not deserve the reputation for wickedness with which Aubrey and others have saddled him. He was a pragmatist, "neither a paragon of virtue nor a monster of vices." He was not totally illiterate, having a good command of the Welsh language and an interest in scholarship. He might be classified as an Erastian who kept his conscience to himself, patronizing Catholics as well as Protestants. Pembroke amassed a fortune but spent generously on others as well as himself. In political life he adjusted to changes in the Tudor court with a discretion which was indicative of a moderate man anxious to survive. 94 notes. 1507-70

Herbin, Johann (Herbinius)

2946. Mühlpfordt, Günter. JOHANN HERBIN: DER ERSTE FRAUENRECHTLER DER DEUTSCHEN AUFKLÄRUNG [Johann Herbin: the first champion of women's rights of the German Enlightenment]. *Zeitschrift für Geschichtswissenschaft [East Germany] 1983 31(4): 325-338.* There had been a tradition of women's rights at Wittenberg since Luther. Johann Herbin (Herbinius, 1633-76) was well traveled and had befriended many women in Germany and abroad. He wrote a thesis on the role of women in intellectual history, including in it "plebeian" and "illustrious" women from antiquity to the present. His inspiration was Maria Cunitz (d. 1664), a gifted linguist and scientist, who reedited Kepler's astronomical tables. His work was a beacon for 19th-century women. Secondary works; 68 notes. 1633-76

Herder, Johann Gottfried

2947. Brecht, Martin. HAHN UND HERDER [Hahn and Herder]. *Zeitschrift für Württembergische Landesgeschichte [West Germany] 1982 41: 364-387.* 1770's-80's

*For abstract see **Hahn, Philipp Matthäus***

2948. Broce, Gerald. HERDER AND ETHNOGRAPHY. *Journal of the History of the Behavioral Sciences 1986 22(2): 150-170.* The source and nature of the ethnography of the important 18th-century thinker Johann Gottfried Herder can in large part be understood through his relationship to his own society and especially through his part in the German cultural nationalist movement of the day. Herder's long involvement with the literature of travel led him to an understanding of many ideas now associated with cultural anthropology; he often recounted ethnographic information in a plain and impartial way. He also gave frequent moral judgments of native cultures. These judgments, often favorable and occasionally negative, may be traced to his announced political sympathies. 1760's-90's

Heredia, José María

2949. Barnet, Miguel. YO, HEREDIA, ERRANTE Y PROSCRIPTO [I, Heredia, wandering and exiled]. *Santiago [Cuba] 1984 (54): 23-33.* This tribute to the Cuban poet José Heredia (1803-39), written in the form of an autobiographical text, recalls his short life and many wanderings, his restless search for freedom and nostalgia for his motherland. 1803-39

2950. Larin, E. A. ZHIZN', TVORCHESTVO I BOR'BA KHOSE MARIA EREDIA [The life, work, and struggles of José Maria Heredia]. *Novaia i Noveishaia Istoriia [USSR] 1985 (3): 122-133.* José Maria Heredia (1803-39) was one of Latin America's greatest romantic poets. His life was bound up with the struggles of Spain's New World colonies for independence, and following the failure of the 1823 uprising in his native Cuba he fled to the United States. His work is suffused with a romantic patriotism and longing for the liberation of his homeland, but his return to Havana in 1836 was accompanied by accusations of capitulation to the governing power. 1823-39

2951. Portuondo, José Antonio. VIGENCIA DEL POETA HEREDIA [Actuality of the poet Heredia]. *Santiago [Cuba] 1984 (54): 13-21.* José María Heredia (1803-39) was a poet, internationalist conspirator, and political exile. In his poems he sang of liberty, nature, and women. He is considered the first Cuban revolutionary poet, who provided his country with the symbols for its struggle for freedom. 1803-39

Herlea, Alexander

2952. Gaudemet, J. IN MEMORIAM: ALEXANDRE HERLEA (1907-1979) [In memoriam: Alexander Herlea (1907-79)]. *Rev. Hist. de Droit Français et Etranger [France] 1980 58(1): 169.* A tribute to the Romanian historian of law, Alexander Herlea. His main interest was in the legal institutions of Romania, particularly Transylvania, but he also studied the influence of the French civil code on the Romanian civil code and questions of the unification of law. In 1976 he founded the Association for the Comparative History of Institutions and Law of the Socialist Republic of Romania. 1907-79

Herman, Ottó

2953. Felkai, László. HERMAN OTTÓ TUDOMÁNYPOLITIKAI NÉZETEI [Ottó Herman's views on the politics of science]. *Magyar Tudomány [Hungary] 1985 30(12): 948-954.* Ottó Herman (1835-1914), natural scientist, ethnographer, and politician, founded the National Animal Protection Association, the Hungarian Folk Art Center and its journal *Aquila* and was president for a time of the Hungarian Ethnography Association. He worked for the evolution of a Hungarian scientific language as evidenced in his works on spiders, birds, and fishing. He believed that scientific works should be made understandable to lay persons and should have the goal of easing man's labors. Herman denounced bureaucracy which interfered with scientific endeavor, even criticizing the Magyar Tudományos Akadémia (Hungarian Academy of Sciences). The separation of Church from scientific endeavors was also essential to scientific research. Based primarily on Ottó Herman's *Diary;* 17 notes. 1867-1914

Herrera, Abraham Cohen

2954. Altmann, Alexander. LURIANIC KABBALA IN A PLATONIC KEY: ABRAHAM COHEN HERRERA'S *PUERTA DEL CIELO. Hebrew Union Coll. Ann. 1982 53: 317-355.* Abraham Cohen Herrera (d. 1635) grew up in Florence where he received both a Hebrew and a classical education. Committed to the Platonic tradition, Herrera attempted to reconcile Lurianic Cabala with Italian Renaissance philosophy. 168 notes. ca 1570-1635

Herrera, Juan de

2955. Cervera Vera, Luis. LIBROS RELIGIOSOS EN LA BIBLIOTECA DE JUAN DE HERRERA [Religious books in the library of Juan de Herrera]. *Hispania Sacra [Spain] 1982 34(70): 521-548.* Juan de Herrera (1530-97) was Philip II's architect and creator of the Escorial. He was an assiduous reader of the works of Raymond Lull but did not neglect common devotional literature and other contemporary religious works. Includes an annotated list of 38 titles of religious books in Juan de Herrera's possession at the time of his death; 131 notes. 1530-97

Herriot, Edouard

2956. Malafeev, Konstantin Andreevich. EDUARD ERRIO: STRANITSY ZHIZNI I DEIATEL'NOSTI [Edouard Herriot: his life and activity]. *Novaia i Noveishaia Istoriia [USSR] 1984 (4): 163-188.* Deals primarily with the political career of the French socialist statesman Edouard Herriot (1872-1957) between the two world wars as leader of the Radical Socialist Party. Disillusioned by the imperialist bend of the Versailles Treaty, he sought a stable international peace in rapprochement with the USSR to stem the rising German revanchist movement, especially after Hitler's coup d'etat, January 1933. Arrested in September 1942 for refusing to collaborate with the Vichy government, he was deported to Germany in August 1944 and liberated by Soviet troops in April 1945. Based on Soviet and French primary and secondary sources; photo, 170 notes. 1920's-40's

Herschel, William

2957. Gingerich, Owen. WILLIAM HERSCHEL'S 1784 AUTOBIOGRAPHY. *Harvard Library Bulletin 1984 32(1): 73-82.* Describes the life and accomplishments of German immigrant William Herschel (1738-1822), who settled in England in 1759 and became a musician, natural philosopher, and noted astronomer. Herschel built his own telescope and with it discovered the planet Uranus in 1781. His brief autobiographical sketch written in 1784 indicated that Herschel intended to continue his studies of astronomy. He subsequently discovered "new satellites of Uranus and Saturn, the direction of solar motion, infrared radiation, hundreds of double stars and their binary nature, and thousands of nebulae," as well as the form of the Milky Way. Based on Herschel's autobiographical manuscript in the Houghton Library, Harvard University, the Herschel Archives in the Royal Astronomical Society, and on secondary sources; 15 notes. 1750's-89

Hersent, Hildevert

2958. Barjot, D. HILDEVERT HERSENT, INGENIEUR-ENTREPRENEUR DU XIX[e] SIECLE [Hildevert Hersent, 19th-century engineer and entrepreneur]. *Information Historique [France] 1985 47(5): 177-180.* A brief biography of Hildevert Hersent (1827-1903), who became a successful and innovative construction engineer and participated in many great international construction projects, 1875-1903, overcoming his modest beginnings in Normandy. 1856-1903

Herter, Ernst

2959. Hüfler, B. "Ernst Herter, 1846-1917: Werk und Porträt eines Berliner Bildhauers" [Ernst Herter (1846-1917): work and portrait of a Berlin sculptor]. Berlin Free U. [West Germany] 1978. 132 pp. *DAI-C 1984 45(4): 895; 9/3701c.* 1860's-1917

Hertzog, J. B. M.

2960. 'Molotsi, Peter H. GENERAL J. B. M. HERTZOG, 1866-1942: ARCHITECT OF APARTHEID. *J. of Ethnic Studies 1983 11(1): 23-43.* J. B. M. Hertzog, a defeated Afrikaner general, seized the chance for renewal offered to South Africa by the Union of 1910 and "paved the way for his people's older republican sense of history and ideology to dominate modern South Africa." Arguing against the conventional interpretation of Hertzog's "great and selfless career" dedicated to the "two stream policy" of race relations, 'Molotsi names the general as the source of apartheid in the form of legislation which moved segregation from its unevenly practiced customary base to a new statutory foundation. He thus frustrated any hopes for the evolution of a multiracial community and excluded Africans from all but the lower echelons of South Africa's modernization process. British and Foreign state papers and secondary works; 76 notes. 1907-42

Hervelt, Jacob van

2961. Eis, J. H. van. JACOB VAN HERVELT, EEN ONBEKEND MEDICUS UIT DE 17[e] EEUW [Jacob van Hervelt: an unknown physician from the 17th century]. *Tijdschrift voor de Geschiedenis der Geneeskunde, Natuurwetenschappen, Wiskunde en Techniek [Netherlands] 1985 8(1): 15-26.* A contribution to the biography of Jacob van Hervelt, who drew the attention of his contemporaries through his book *Geneeskundige Aanmerkingen* [Medical case-histories]. This book offers a good opportunity to learn something about the daily practice of a medical doctor outside the major towns of the Dutch Republic. For a while his polemics with Stephan Blankaart won him a place on the national scene of 17th-century Dutch medicine. 1668-93

Herzberg, Wilhelm

2962. Michael, Reuven. DR. WILHEIM HERZBERG (1827-1897): EINE LÜCKENHAFTE BIOGRAPHIE [Dr. Wilhelm Herzberg (1827-97): an incomplete biography]. *Bulletin des Leo Baeck Instituts [Israel] 1983 (65): 53-85.* Asseses the life and career of the Polish-born Jewish writer Wilhelm Herzberg (1827-97), but reveals that very little is known of his early life and personal friendships. In 1868 his *Jüdische Familienpapier: Briefe eines Missionärs* appeared and the success of this book ensured his renown. The author describes the book, which examined the moral superiority of the Jewish teachings over Christian teachings. Herzberg wrote the book in the 1860's and many of the characters typify Jewish society of the period. In addition Herzberg's ideas on Jewish education are also discussed as are his thoughts on contemporary society. In addition, he wrote several novels and in 1877, he was nominated as director of an agricultural school in Palestine. He published his thoughts on the fate and future of the Jewish people in the 1880's, including his opposition to the immigration of Jews to Palestine. Despite criticism of Herzberg in the Jewish press, he continued as an educator in Jerusalem. Based on documents in the Zionist Central Archives in Jerusalem and on secondary sources; 62 notes. 1827-97

Herzen, Alexander

2963. Bannour, Wanda. ALEXANDRE IVANOVITCH HERZEN: UN DEMI-SIECLE D'HISTOIRE EUROPEENNE [Alexander Ivanovich Herzen: a half century of European history]. *Rev. de l'Inst. de Sociol. [Belgium] 1982 (1-2): 157-162.* Recounts the life of Alexander Herzen (1812-70) in relation to the social problems of 19th-century tsarist Russia, based on Herzen's autobiography for the years 1852-68. 1852-68

Herzen, Natalie A.

2964. Zimmerman, Judith E. NATALIE HERZEN AND THE EARLY INTELLIGENTSIA. *Russian Rev. 1982 41(3): 249-273.* Recounts the life of Natalie A. Herzen (1817-52), wife of Alexander Herzen. Born an illegitimate child of Herzen's uncle, Natalie was taken in as ward to a wealthy Moscow matron. A remarkably self-possessed young girl, Natalie was also romantic, deeply religious, and intensely alienated from the values of her social surroundings. Married to Herzen in 1838, Natalie underwent severe strain and illness from mid-1841 to late-1843 during the period of her husband's exile in Novgorod when she lost three infant children. Her strong, resilient spirit recovered and her best years were spent first in a close circle of St. Petersburg friends and later during the initial years of their life in Western Europe. Natalie played an important role in development of the group that coalesced around Herzen and remained committed to her own ideals of social justice. 72 notes. 1817-52

Herzfeld, Hans

2965. Berges, Wilhelm. REDEN ZUM 70. UND 80. GEBURTSTAG VON HANS HERZFELD. AUS DEM NACHLASS HERAUSGEGEBEN VON DIETRICH KURZE [Addresses commemorating the 70th and 80th birthdays of Hans Herzfeld: edited by Dietrich Kurze from the written legacy of Hans Herzfeld]. *Jahrbuch für die Gesch. Mittel- und Ostdeutschlands [West Germany] 1983 32: 93-107.* The phases of Hans Herzfeld's life (1892-1917, 1917-33, 1933-45, and post-1945) coincide with and reflect epochal periods in German history. Finding meaning for the political and social shifts of his times, Hans Herzfeld did not despair but recorded and assessed them. He labored well into the post-World War II period to reevaluate his earlier findings on bourgeois liberalism, on questions relating to World War I, and on issues of militarism and democracy. Tolerant of the opinions of others, beloved teacher, prolific author, researcher, and administrator, Hans Herzfeld continued his numerous pursuits well after retirement, easing the way for many both at home and abroad who found his work exemplary and worthy of emulation. Based on the writings of Hans Herzfeld; 15 notes. 1892-1982

2966. Kouri, Erkki. HANS HERZFELD SAKSALAISESSA HISTORIOGRAFIASSA [Hans Herzfeld in German historiography]. *Hist. Aikakauskirja [Finland] 1982 80(4): 343-356.* Describes the academic career of the German historian Hans Herzfeld (1892-1982), a specialist in German diplomatic and political history. After wartime imprisonment by the Nazis, Herzfeld was appointed professor at Freiburg, and then at the Free University of Berlin. Through his organizational and scholarly leadership he helped to reestablish historical studies in West Germany. His moderate conservative and nationalist views were expressed in polemics with many contemporary historians. 42 notes. 1892-1982

2967. Ritter, Gerhard A. HANS HERZFELD—PERSÖNLICHKEIT UND WERK [Hans Herzfeld—personality and work]. *Jahrbuch für die Gesch. Mittel- und Ostdeutschlands [West Germany] 1983 32: 13-91.* In an overview of Hans Herzfeld's life and work one can detect considerable change in his political views, with the essence of his character untouched in his desire to influence his times both as academician and scholar. Although his historical studies focused on both state and nation, Herzfeld's main concern was man. He identified as the primary cause of the 20th-century German catastrophe the crystallization of the idea of the modern German state, which placed too little emphasis on the freedom and rights of the individual. Closely affiliated after 1950 with the International Textbook Institute in Braunschweig, Herzfeld promoted a revision of school textbooks that would advance historical truth and move away from a prejudicial national interpretation of events, seeing this as essential in the reconciliation of Germany with its neighbors. Based on the published works of Hans Herzfeld and on letters from, to, and about him in the papers of Fritz Hartung, Siegfried August Kaehler, Eduard Spranger, Richard Fester, Friedrich Thimme, Gerhard Ritter, and Heinrich Ritter von Srbik; 2 illus., 221 notes. 1892-1982

Herzl, Theodor

2968. Kornberg, Jacques. THEODOR HERZL: THE ZIONIST AS AUSTRIAN LIBERAL. *Jerusalem Quarterly [Israel] 1984 (31): 107-117.* Reviews Alex Bein's biography of Theodor Herzl, especially his conversion from Viennese *litterateur* to Jewish Zionist statesman as a reaction to conservatism and anti-Semitism in Europe. 1880's-1904

2969. Toury, Jacob. HERZL'S NEWSPAPERS: THE CREATION OF *DIE WELT*. *Zionism [Israel] 1980 1(2): 159-172.* Describes Theodor Herzl's efforts to organize, fund, and publish a modern, liberal, politically independent newspaper that would serve Zionism in an Austria that was turning steadily more anti-Semitic. Some of the factors militating against Herzl's success included government inaction, infighting with other daily newspapers (both Jewish and non-Jewish), and an inability to raise enough money for publication. The first issue of *Die Welt* appeared 4 June 1897, and ceased publication at the beginning of World War I, some years after Herzl's death. Based on Herzl's diaries. 1895-1902

Hess, Moses

2970. Penkower, Monty N. MOSES HESS. *Midstream 1984 30(7): 14-17.* Reviews the life and work of the German socialist Moses Hess, including the reawakening of his Jewish roots. 1812-75

Heuraet, Hendrik van

2971. Maanen, Jan A. van. HENDRIK VAN HEURAET (1634-1660?): HIS LIFE AND MATHEMATICAL WORK. *Centaurus [Denmark] 1984 27(3-4): 218-279.* Presents new biographical data and surveys the mathematical work of Hendrik van Heuraet (1634-1660?). Correspondence between van Heuraet and other mathematicians, especially Christiaan Huygens, (1629-95), dealing with the properties of curves and the theories of hyperbolas and parabolas, and van Heuraet's own publications reveals an innovative theorist whose work was respected by his contemporaries. Based on letters and other primary sources; 33 fig., biblio., 118 notes. 1657-60

Heureaux, Ulises

2972. Domínguez, Jaime de Jesús. LA DICTADURA DE HEUREAUX [The dictatorship of Heureaux]. *Estudios Sociales [Dominican Republic] 1985 18(61): 9-28.* Explains how the Dominican dictator Ulises Heureaux, remained in power despite the overwhelming problems of his country, focusing on the political, economic, and military aspects of the dictator's government and on his personal style. 1886-99

Heuss, Alfred

2973. Meier, Christian. LAUDATIO AUF ALFRED HEUSS [Commendation for Alfred Heuss]. *Historische Zeitschrift [West Germany] 1984 239(1): 1-10.* An address delivered in 1983 at the presentation of the first Historical Collegium Prize of the Bavarian Academy of Sciences to Alfred Heuss. Heuss has addressed fundamental issues of ancient history, applied modern techniques of comparative history, explored relationships between anthropology and history, exposed the dilemma of history as memory versus research, and enriched the entire field of historical scholarship. 1930's-83

Heuss, Theodor

2974. Hess, Jürgen C. "MACHTLOS INMITTEN DES MÄCHTESPIELS DER ANDEREN . . ." THEODOR HEUSS UND DIE DEUTSCHE FRAGE 1945-1949 ["Powerless in the midst of power games of others . . .": Theodor Heuss and the German question, 1945-49]. *Vierteljahrshefte für Zeitgeschichte [West Germany] 1985 33(1): 88-135.* Theodor Heuss (1884-1963), first president of West Germany 1949-59, opposed German orientation to either West or East in the first postwar years. As a prominent liberal of the 1920's, he remained strongly attached to the ideal of a unified, free German nation. But this realistic assessment of German powerlessness after the war led him to stress an intelligent internal policy as a first priority and to accept a West German state by early 1948. In contrast to his centralism and nationalism in the 1920's, he now favored a federal republic open to reconciliation with France and integration in Europe. Based on Heuss's papers at the Bundesarchiv, Archiv des Deutschen Liberalismus, and the Württemberg State Archive and Library; 279 notes. 1945-49

Hevelius, Johannes

2975. —. [Hevelius: scholar and artist?]. (Polish text). *Kwartalnik Hist. Nauki i Techniki [Poland] 1981 26(3-4): 693-702.*

Grzybkowska, Teresa. CZY HEWELIUSZ BYŁ ARTYSTĄ? [Was Hevelius an artist?], *pp. 693-698. Jan Heweliusz: Scholar—Artist* by Karolina Targosz (1979) seeks to show that Johannes Hevelius (1611-87) was not only a scholar and astronomer, but also an artist. The reviewer rejects this claim. 8 notes.

Targosz, Karolina. A JEDNAK UCZONY-ARTYSTA [And yet: a scholar and artist], *pp. 698-702.* The author defends her conclusion and points out that the reviewer's attempt to separate science and art is untenable. Secondary sources; 6 notes. 1636-87

Hewins, George

2976. Hewins, Angela. THE MAKING OF A WORKING CLASS AUTOBIOGRAPHY: "THE DILLEN." *Hist. Workshop J. [Great Britain] 1982 (14): 138-142.* Relates how the author taped and edited the reminiscences of George Hewins for publication as *The Dillen,* a kaleidoscope of scenes, stories, and songs from the lower depths of Stratford-upon-Avon, principally during the Edwardian period. Hewins was a born storyteller, and the book presents a direct statement about childhood, work, and the effects of poverty and the Poor Law on the family before 1914. It is probably unique in being the memories of a semiliterate but exceptionally articulate laboring man who remained within the poverty circle (due to disablement in World War I) and lived within the same few square miles until his death in 1977. Illus. 1879-1914

Heydrich, Richard

2977. Kárný, Miroslav. K OTÁZCE SOCIÁLNÍ DEMAGOGIE V HEYDRICHOVĚ PROTEKTORÁTNÍ POLITICE [On social demagoguery in Heydrich's protectorate policy]. *Slezský Sborník [Czechoslovakia] 1984 82(1): 1-23.* In recent biographies of Richard Heydrich based on German archives, much credit is given to Heydrich for raising the standard of living in the Protectorate, especially Moravia. However, closer examination of the reports sent to the Third Reich clearly shows double bookkeeping and false reporting that masked the real conditions, such as an actual rise in prices of most consumer goods and a number of strikes swiftly and brutally put down by the Gestapo. 13 notes. 1939-42

Heyl, James Bell

2978. Franke, Norman H. JAMES BELL HEYL: BERMUDA'S PHARMACIST-PHOTOGRAPHER. *Pharmacy in Hist. 1982 24(3): 117-119.* Biography of Anglo-American pharmacist-photographer James Bell Heyl. Following the family tradition, Heyl studied pharmacy in the 1840's at Charity Hospital in New Orleans. He later moved to Hamilton, Bermuda, where he practiced pharmacy for over 50 years at the Apothecary's Hall. He pursued his interest in photography, such that he is a recognized early photographer of Bermuda. Primary sources; photo, 20 notes. 1840's-90's

Heymann, Frederick G.

2979. Harasymiw, Bohdan. FREDERICK G. HEYMANN, 1900-1983. *Slavic Rev. 1984 43(1): 183-184.* Obituary of historian Frederick G. Heymann, whose special field of study was Czechoslovakia. 1900-83

Heywood, Jasper

2980. Flynn, Dennis. THE ENGLISH MISSION OF JASPER HEYWOOD, S.J. *Archivum Historicum Societatis Iesu [Italy] 1985 54(107): 45-76.* Shows the differences between Jasper Heywood's interpretation of his Jesuit mission in Elizabethan England, which ended with his imprisonment and exile, and the account of the matter given by his superiors, especially Robert Persons, in his letters to Jesuit Father General Claudio Acquaviva and other Jesuit officials. 1574-98

Hickey, Thomas

2981. Breeze, George. THOMAS HICKEY AND IRELAND. *Studies [Ireland] 1983 72(286): 156-169.* Thomas Hickey (1741-1824), Irish portraitist, is chiefly remembered for his work in India and China, when he accompanied British diplomats as official painter—notably on Lord Macartney's embassy to China (1792-94). The author delineates Hickey's movements, but mainly concentrates on his early work in Ireland from 1758. 6 illus., 23 notes. 1758-1824

Hieb, Jacob

2982. Hieb, Jacob. MY RETURN TO RUSSIA. *J. of the Am. Hist. Soc. of Germans from Russia 1982 5(2): 5-9, (3): 16-20.* Part 1. The author traveled to the USSR in 1928 to determine why relief parcels sent to friends and relatives by the South Dakota famine relief organization had not been received. Part 2. Recounts the author's experiences and encounters on his way by railroad and sleigh to the Ukraine. Article to be continued. 1928

Higgs, John

2983. Havinden, Michael. OBITUARY: SIR JOHN HIGGS, KCVO, FSA (1923-86). *Agricultural History Review [Great Britain] 1986 34(2): 204-205.* After a career which embraced a number of interests both foreign and domestic, Sir John Higgs, the first secretary and one of the original organizers of the British Agricultural History Society, was at his death the Secretary and Keeper of the Records to the Duchy of Cornwall. 1923-86

Hill, Howard

2984. —. HOWARD HILL. *Bull. of the Soc. for the Study of Labour Hist. [Great Britain] 1980 (41): 12.* An obituary of the British labor historian Howard Hill (d. 1980). 20c

Hill, John

2985. Rizzo, Betty. NOTES ON THE WAR BETWEEN HENRY FIELDING AND JOHN HILL, 1752-53. *Library [Great Britain] 1985 7(4): 338-353.* 1752-53
*For abstract see **Fielding, Henry***

2986. —. THE LETTERS AND PAPERS OF SIR JOHN HILL, 1714-75. *Annals of Science [Great Britain] 1986 43(2): 175-178.*

Rousseau, G. S. *pp. 175-177.* Responds to a review article by Claude E. Dolman on the author's edition of *The Letters and Papers of Sir John Hill, 1714-75* (1982).

Suggests that the review is a "show of irrelevant pedantry" and that many of the points can be refuted. John Hill was more than an 18th-century scientific dilettante.

Rizzo, Betty. *pp. 177-178.* Also disagrees with Dolman's assessment of Rousseau's book and suggests that more is to be learned about John Hill, the botanist who introduced the Linnaean taxonomic system to England. 18c

Hill, Rowland

2987. Daunton, M. J. ROWLAND HILL & THE PENNY POST. *History Today [Great Britain] 1985 35(Aug): 31-37.* Reviews the life and career of Rowland Hill (1795-1879), a civil servant who led the reform of the British postal system from the 1830's to the 1860's and introduced one-penny postage in Great Britain. Hill's ruthless dedication to the single theme of postal reform caused him to lose the support of several politicians. 1830's-60's

Hillel, Daniel

2988. Hillel, Daniel. KADDISH'L. *Midstream 1985 31(7): 29-33.* Reminiscences of a scientist about his pious grandfather, who had emigrated from Poland to Charleston, South Carolina, and thence to Palestine, where the author—then a child—and his family joined him in the 1930's. The grandfather often referred to the boy as "mein Kaddish'l" (the one who would recite the prayer in remembrance of the old man's death). 1930's-74

Hindle, Johann

2989. Planyavsky, Alfred. JOHANN HINDLE (1792-1862): EIN REISENDER BASSGEIGER DES BIEDERMEIER [Johann Hindle (1792-1862): a traveling bass-violinist of the Biedermeier era]. *Jahrbuch des Vereins für Geschichte der Stadt Wien [Austria] 1984 40: 89-121.* Illuminates the life and work of the Viennese traveling bass-violin virtuoso Johann Hindle during the 19th century. 1810-62

Hinds, Grace

See Curzon, Grace

Hinger, Anton

2990. Wiest, Stephan. OBERLEHRER ANTON HINGER AUS HOHENZOLLERN—EIN ORGANISATOR UND FÖRDERER DES SCHULWESENS IM FÜRSTENTUM LIECHTENSTEIN 1857-1895 [Oberlehrer Anton Hinger from Hohenzollern—an organizer and promoter of the school system of the principality of Liechtenstein 1857-95]. *Jahrbuch des Historischen Vereins für das Fürstentum Liechtenstein [Liechtenstein] 1983 83: 151-196.* Anton Hinger was a pioneer in the field of education at a time when mandatory school attendance was still met with resistance by parents who depended on their children's help in the fields, and when the teacher's training was not uniformly good and their pay pitifully low. He became a model teacher who especially enjoyed the teaching of music and the sciences—horticulture in particular. He wrote the statutes for the school system, developed a curriculum for the whole region, introduced better textbooks and became a leader in the field of teacher training. His work affected almost all aspects of education in Liechtenstein. Based on departmental archives of Liechtenstein, private family records, and secondary sources; table of contents, map, group portrait, obituary, 77 notes. 19c

Hinks, Arthur Robert

2991. Steers, J. A. A. R. HINKS AND THE ROYAL GEOGRAPHICAL SOCIETY. *Geog. J. [Great Britain] 1982 148(1): 1-7.* Describes the life of Arthur Robert Hinks, who was Secretary of the Royal Geographical Society, 1915-45, and editor of its journal, *The Geographical Journal.* Although trained as an astronomer and geodesist, he distinguished himself in cartography in an era when geography was a new discipline in British universities. His tenure with the journal parallels the period when human geography was new to many. Due to his academic background, some writers of human geography experienced difficulty in having their articles accepted for publication. Based on correspondence with those acquainted with A. R. Hinks. 1873-1945

Hippius, Zinaida

2992. Pachmuss, Temira. IZ ARKHIVA MEREZHKOVSKIH: PIS'MA Z. N. HIPPIUS K M. V. VISHNIAKU [Excerpts from the Merezhkovski Archives: letters of Zinaida Hippius to M. V. Vishniak]. *Cahiers du Monde Russe et Soviétique [France] 1982 23(3-4): 417-467.* Hippius's letters to Vishniak recreate vividly the atmosphere of Russian Paris in the 1920's and 1930's. They reveal the complex interrelationships of Russian emigres in strained financial circumstances. The letters portray emigre activities, the appearance of Russian journals, newspapers, and almanacs, and they discuss various ideological conflicts and disagreements among the emigres. The letters also convey Hippius's sense of humor and her keen observation. Moreover, they reveal her personality, as well as her complex Weltanschauung. Vishniak wrote, "Hippius's letters are extremely interesting. In them, she discussed topics that were invariably important. Besides, she was an excellent stylist, always writing in a perfect and picturesque Russian..." Her letters "characterize her as a person and a 'politician'." Hippius's correspondence also enables the reader to observe the personality of Vishniak and his role as editor of an influential Russian publication in Western Europe. 1920's-30's

Hirn, Marta

2993. —. FIL DR. H. C. MARTA HIRN 80 ÅR [Dr. Marta Hirn on her 80th birthday]. *Finskt Museum [Finland] 1984 91: 5-15.*

Tamminen, Markett. *p. 5.* A biographical note on Marta Hirn (1903-), director of the historical picture archives at the Finnish National Museum in Helsinki from 1949 to 1970.

MARTA HIRNS LITTERÄRA PRODUKTION [Marta Hirn's literary production], *pp. 6-11.* A bibliography of publications from 1932 through 1982.

Hirn, Marta. AKTNING FÖR BILDEN [Attention to the picture], *pp. 12-15.* An essay on the importance of well-used pictures for historical publications. Originally published in 1957. 1903-82

Hirohito

2994. Storry, Richard. KINJO TENNO: EMPEROR OF JAPAN. *Hist. Today [Great Britain] 1982 32(Jan): 5-9.* Biography of Hirohito, (b. 1901) the 124th emperor of Japan, now Kinjō Tennō (the "present emperor," reign name Shōwa), who has been on the throne for 65 years. Focuses on his imperial life. 1901-81

Hirsch, Samson Raphael

2995. Liberles, Robert. CHAMPION OF ORTHODOXY: THE EMERGENCE OF SAMSON RAPHAEL HIRSCH AS RELIGIOUS LEADER. *AJS Rev. 1981 6: 43-60.* Samson Raphael Hirsch's childhood in Hamburg, when correlated with excerpts from his writings, particularly symbolic references to Horeb, Elijah and Phinehas, reveal much about the forces behind his puzzling personality. 47 notes. 1833-88

Hitler, Adolf

2996. Hartmann, Jacques. 30 JANVIER 1933: HITLER CHANCELIER DU REICH [30 January 1933: Hitler is Reich Chancellor]. *Hist. Mag. [France] 1983 (36): 80-85.* Focuses on the rise of the Nazi Party in Germany from 1929 to 1933. 1929-33

2997. Kater, Michael H. HITLER IN A SOCIAL CONTEXT. *Central European Hist. 1981 14(3): 243-272.* The literature on Adolf Hitler has "failed to classify Hitler properly from a sociological or sociohistorical perspective." In his attempt to increase understanding of Hitler's "personality and preeminence by analyzing the social conditions that surrounded his adolescence and supported his rise to and stay in power," the author discusses his classlessness, his antipathy for certain social groups, his reading habits, and his charisma. Based primarily on secondary works; 58 notes, biblio. 1919-80

2998. Poncet, Henry. RACONTES 40 ANS APRES PAR LES DERNIERS TEMOINS, LE MARIAGE ET LE SUICIDE D'HITLER [Told 40 years later by the last witnesses, the marriage and suicide of Hitler]. *Historama [France] 1985 (14): 18-25.* 1945
For abstract see ***Braun, Eva***

2999. Stephenson, Jill. WAR AND SOCIETY IN WÜRTTEMBERG, 1939-1945: BEATING THE SYSTEM. *German Studies Review 1985 8(1): 89-105.* Discusses Adolf Hitler's desire during the second world war to avert civilian discontent and reviews and evaluates the means by which, for the most part, he successfully accomplished this goal. Hitler believed that the Second Reich had fallen largely because of domestic food shortages during the years 1916-18; hence he developed plans to avoid such crises. Through increased food production during the 1930's, a propaganda program designed to encourage thrift and curtail waste, the exploitation of occupied countries' resources, occasional rationing, and other measures, the Nazi regime satisfied many civilians. An analysis of civilian life in wartime Württenberg, however, shows how Hitler's measures led to disaffection and alienation from the Nazi regime, owing to widespread attempts to beat the system. Primary sources; 69 notes. 1936-45

3000. Tallgren, V. A. L. "Hitler und die Helden; Heroismus und Weltanschauung" [Adolph Hitler and heroes: heroism and ideology]. Helsinki U. [Finland] 1981. 278 pp. *DAI-C 1983 44(1): 59; 8/311c.* ca 1914-45

3001. Weinberg, Gerhard L. HITLER AND ENGLAND, 1933-1945: PRETENSE AND REALITY. *German Studies Review 1985 8(2): 299-309.* Examines and dismisses the thesis that Adolf Hitler and his government desired a good relationship with Great Britain and did not desire war. Examines the Anglo-German Naval Agreement of 1935, the mission of Joachim von Ribbentrop to London in 1936, the so-called alliance offer to England in 1936, and Hitler's learning of Britain's intentions to declare war in 1939, all of which scholars have claimed were evidence of Hitler's wish to avoid war with Britain; these events actually show that Hitler had no such expectations, desires, or intentions. Based on secondary sources; 30 notes. 1933-45

Ho Chi Minh

3002. Anh, Nguyen The. HOW DID HO CHI MINH BECOME A PROLETARIAN? *Asian Affairs [Great Britain] 1985 16(2): 163-169.* Traces the changes in politics and names of the greatest Communist leader of Vietnam in the first half of the 20th century. Nguyen Tat Thanh, Nguyen Ai Quoc, and Ly Thuy were names used by Ho Chi Minh, who originally sought a career in the French Indochina colonial service. There are many undocumented legends about his poor working-class years from 1912 to 1919. It is now well proven, however, that he frequented the intellectual salons of the privileged as well. He was sponsored early in his efforts by Communist intellectuals Phan Van Truong and Phan Chu Trinh. In 1920, when the French Communist Party was founded, Ho Chi Minh became an agent for the Comintern specializing in colonial affairs. In 1923, he went to the Soviet Union and later became a full-time agent of the Southeast Asian branch of the Far Eastern Comintern. Based on an article in the bilingual periodical *Duong Moi* (Paris) adapted and translated with the assistance of Dennis Duncanson. Based on secondary sources; 10 notes. 1911-24

3003. Glazunov, E. P. ZHIZN', POSVIASHCHENNAIA BOR'BE ZA SCHAST'E NARODA (K 95-LETIIU SO DNIA ROZHDENIIA KHO SHI MINA) [A life devoted to a fight for the happiness of a people: tribute to Ho Chi Minh on the 95th anniversary of his birth]. *Voprosy Istorii KPSS [USSR] 1985 (5): 121-124.* Biographical sketch of the Vietnamese Communist leader Ho Chi Minh (1890-1969) depicting his lifelong struggle to liberate his native land from colonial oppression. His revolutionary fervor, true patriotism, activism as co-founder of the French Communist Party, participation in Comintern and Soviet Congresses, lengthy sojourn in the USSR in the 1920's, and close adherence to Lenin's philosophy made him an undisputed leader in Vietnam's anticolonial war of liberation. Based on Ho Chi Minh's writings; 23 notes. 1920's-69

3004. Kobelev, E. KHO SHI MIN [Ho Chi Minh]. *Aziia i Afrika Segodnia [USSR] 1985 (5): 30-33.* Pays tribute to the personality and political achievements of Vietnamese Communist leader Ho Chi Minh (1890-1969). 1920's-69

3005. Kobelev, E. HO CHI MINH: PATRIOT, COMMUNIST AND HUMAN BEING (ON THE 90TH ANNIVERSARY OF HIS BIRTH). *Far Eastern Affairs [USSR] 1980 (2): 167-179.* Describes the life and work of Ho Chi Minh (1890-1969), who led the Vietnamese national liberation movement, the Communist Party of Vietnam, and the independent Vietnamese state for over half a century. 1920's-70's

3006. Viktorov, A. V. OSNOVATEL' KOMMUNISTICHESKOI PARTII V'ETNAMA [Founder of the Communist Party of Vietnam]. *Voprosy Istorii KPSS [USSR] 1985 (7): 144-148.* Sketches the political biography of Ho Chi Minh (1890-1969). During the 1920's and 30's he was a frequent visitor to Moscow. In 1920 he joined the French Communist Party. He fought for the liberation of Indochina from colonial oppression. After Vietnam's independence in 1945 he founded its Communist Party. During the US invasion he was chairman of the Defense Council. Secondary sources. 1920's-69

Hŏ Kyun

3007. So, Jae-yung. THE LIFE OF HŎ KYUN AND THE FEATURES OF HIS LITERARY WORKS. *J. of Social Sci. and Humanities [South Korea] 1980 (52): 1-17.* A review and critique of the life and works of Korean writer Hŏ Kyun. Covers his unhappy childhood, political career, cut short by scandals, and his long period of exile. The latter period caused him to turn to writing as a means of fighting boredom. Hŏ Kyun's poems, stories, and biographies express several moods, but the dominant theme, interpolated from his own experiences, was raillery against a social system that prevented persons of humble birth from rising to positions of power regardless of abilities. 45 notes. ca 1569-1630

Hobbes, Thomas

3008. Ball, Terence. HOBBES' LINGUISTIC TURN. *Polity 1985 42(4): 739-760.* Thomas Hobbes has often been regarded as a "protopositivist" precursor of the scientific study of politics. The author suggests that it may be more appropriate to consider him as a thinker acutely aware that social and political reality is linguistically made. However, Hobbes was inclined to treat the distortion or breakdown of communication as a technical problem to be met by the sovereign's imposition of "shared" meanings. 1629-79

3009. Harrison, Kevin. THOMAS HOBBES: DURING THE CIVIL WAR AND COMMONWEALTH HOBBES UPHELD THE DANGEROUS PRINCIPLE THAT SOVEREIGNTY LAY WITH THE KING. *British Heritage 1983 4(4): 30-39.* Traces the life, teaching career and writings of the English philosopher Thomas Hobbes (1588-1679), and pays particular attention to the ideas Hobbes expressed in his most famous work *Leviathan* in which he upheld the principle that sovereignty lay with the king, attacked the Civil War, rebellion, and the universal pretensions of the Roman Catholic Church. 17c

3010. Pearlstein, Richard M. OF FEAR, UNCERTAINTY, AND BOLDNESS: THE LIFE AND THOUGHT OF THOMAS HOBBES. *Journal of Psychohistory 1986 13(3): 309-324.* Thomas Hobbes (1588-1679) argued in *Leviathan* (1651) that man is motivated by fear and greed and that society needs a strong paternal figure, a king with great power to regulate society. His thinking was shaped by the political turmoil of 17th-century England as well as by his own difficult childhood. 58 notes. 17c

3011. Shulman, George Mark. "The Lamb and the Dragon: Gerrard Winstanley and Thomas Hobbes in the English Revolution." U. of California, Berkeley 1982. 754 pp. *DAI 1983 43(8): 2781-A.* DA8300655 1640-60

3012. Wright, George Herbert. "The Protestant Hobbes." U. of California, Berkeley 1985. 493 pp. *DAI 1986 46(9): 2723-A.* DA8525163 17c

Hobley, Charles William

3013. Matson, A. T. and Ofcansky, Thomas P. A BIO-BIBLIOGRAPHY OF C. W. HOBLEY. *Hist. in Africa 1981 8: 253-260.* The career of Charles William Hobley in East Africa is outlined. From 1890 until his death in 1947 Hobley worked for British settlement and became involved with the people and environment of East Africa. Primary sources; biblio. 1890-1947

Hobsbawm, Eric J.

3014. Wrigley, Chris. ERIC HOBSBAWM: AN APPRECIATION. *Bulletin of the Society for the Study of Labour History [Great Britain] 1984 (48): 2.* A tribute to the British labor historian, Eric Hobsbawm, who retired from full-time teaching at Birkbeck College, University of London, in the summer of 1982. The author outlines the achievements of Hobsbawm's distinguished career from 1946 to 1982. 1946-82

Hodgkin, Thomas

3015. Summers, Anne. THOMAS HODGKIN (1910-1982). *Hist. Workshop J. [Great Britain] 1982 (14): 180-182.* An obituary of Thomas Lionel Hodgkin, outlining his varied career and assessing his achievement. As a civil servant in Palestine in the 1930's he became an anti-imperialist and Communist. He later joined the Oxford Extra-Mural Delegacy in North Staffs and then in Africa. Resigning his position, he devoted himself to the study of African and Third World history and politics, and later wrote a history of Vietnam, *Vietnam: The Revolutionary Path* (1981). The serious study of African history owes much to his scholarship, which he undertook despite the uncertainty of assuming different positions in order to pursue his interest in the unfashionable and the invisible. 1930's-82

Hodgkin, Thomas Lionel

3016. Crowder, Michael. THOMAS LIONEL HODGKIN: A TRIBUTE. *African Res. and Documentation [Great Britain] 1982 (30): 1-2.* Discusses the scholarly contributions of Thomas Lionel Hodgkin to the field of Africanist literature, and his contribution to African university education. 1950's-82

Hodgson, Margaret Violet Livingstone

See Ballinger, Margaret

Hoernle, Edwin

3017. Anikeev, A. A. EDVIN GEMLE: UCHENYI KOMMUNIST I ANTIFASHIST, 1883-1952 [Edwin Hoernle: Communist scholar and antifascist, 1883-1952]. *Novaia i Noveishaia Istoriia [USSR] 1985 (4): 96-108.* Edwin Hoernle (1883-1952) was born in Württemberg, a gifted student who entered the church, but left in 1910. He was a major figure in the Spartacus League from 1916 and a leader of the Communist Party of Germany in the interwar years. His major interests were peasant affairs and after Hitler's coming to power he worked with the Comintern in the struggle against fascism from his exile in Moscow. He prepared the agrarian reform after the liberation of eastern Germany in 1945 and supported the 1952 decision to build socialism in the German Democratic Republic. 1910's-52

Hoff, Bert van 't

3018. Fox, J. IN MEMORIAM MR. B. VAN 'T HOFF 1900-1979 [In memoriam: Bert van 't Hoff (1900-79)]. *Nederlands Archievenblad [Netherlands] 1979 83(4): 273-278.* Obituary of Bert van 't Hoff, who, after getting his archivist diploma at the General National Archives, The Hague, in 1930, became librarian of the Atheneum Library, Deventer, and in 1946 national archivist in charge of Holland and West Frisian archives, and is best known for his 1950 inventory of the Heinsius Archives, his 1951 edition of Heinsius's correspondence with John Churchill, and for his expertise in historical cartography. 1925-79

Hoff, Jacobus Henricus van 't

3019. Snelders, H. A. M. J. H. VAN'T HOFF'S RESEARCH SCHOOL IN AMSTERDAM (1877-1895) *Janus [Netherlands] 1984 71(1-4): 1-30.* Jacobus Henricus van 't Hoff (1852-1911) obtained his doctorate at Utrecht in 1874 and was appointed lecturer in chemistry at the University of Amsterdam in 1877. In 1884 he published his epoch-making book on chemical dynamics, and then the following year his most important contribution to physical chemistry, the theory of dilute solutions. In 1895 he resigned and subsequently went to Berlin. At Amsterdam he had been instrumental in founding physical chemistry as an independent discipline. The students who had studied under him played a leading role in academic education for the next 25 years. Based on the publications of J. H. van 't Hoff and his students; 6 tables, 104 notes. 1877-95

Hoffmann, Alfred

3020. Kellenbenz, Hermann. NACHRUF: ALFRED HOFFMANN (1904-1983) [Obituary: Alfred Hoffmann (1904-83)]. *Vierteljahrschrift für Sozial- und Wirtschaftsgeschichte [West Germany] 1983 70(4): 602-605.* Outlines the career of Austrian economic historian Alfred Hoffmann, longtime archivist in Linz and after 1961 professor of economic and social history at the University of Vienna. He wrote a number of books and articles on the economic, social, and institutional history of medieval and early modern Austria, including the first volume of the standard economic history of Upper Austria. He served as president of the International Commission for Metrology and was a member of the Austrian Academy of Sciences from 1957. 1920's-83

3021. Mayrhofer, Fritz. IN MEMORIAM ALFRED HOFFMANN 1904-1983 [In memoriam: Alfred Hoffmann (1904-83)]. *Hist. Jahrbuch der Stadt Linz [Austria] 1982: 309-311.* Prints an obituary recounting the contributions of Austrian historian Alfred Hoffmann (1904-83) to the local history of Linz. 16c

Hoffmann, John Baptist

3022. Tete, P. "A Missionary Social Worker in India: J. B. Hoffmann, the Chota Nagpur Tenancy Act and the Catholic Co-operatives 1893-1928." Pontifical Gregorian U. [Vatican] 1984. *DAI-C 1985 46(4): 896; 46/4325c.* 1893-1928

Hofmannsthal, Hugo von

3023. LaFerté, Etienne de. UN MOMENT DANS LA VIE DE HUGO VON HOFMANNSTHAL: JUIN 1895. II [A moment in the life of Hugo von Hofmannsthal: June, 1895. Part 2]. *Rev. des Deux Mondes [France] 1983 (5): 319-324.* Describes letters and poems to friends which provide biographical information as well as illuminate the author's state of mind during one of his most creative periods. 1895

3024. Thomas, Sarah Elizabeth. "Hugo von Hofmannsthal and Anton Kippenberg of the Insel-Verlag: A Case Study of Author-Publisher Relations." Johns Hopkins U. 1982. 377 pp. *DAI 1982 43(1): 175-A.* DA8213435 1914-29

Hogan, J. J.

3025. Nevin, Thomas. JEREMIAH HOGAN AND UNIVERSITY COLLEGE DUBLIN. *Studies [Ireland] 1985 74(295): 325-335.* An appreciation of the administrative and academic work of Dr. J. J. Hogan, fourth president of University College Dublin, 1964-72. 1919-72

Hogarth, William

3026. Mayer, Yvonne. W. HOGARTH. *British Heritage 1982 3(6): 8-18; 1982-83 4(1): 54-63; 1983 4(2): 20-24, 26-33.* Part 3. Discusses the marriage of British painter and engraver William Hogarth to Jane Thornhill in 1729, the impetus of the marriage to force Hogarth to increase his production, and the reflection of his own life in his works. Examines the *Harlot's Progress* series of paintings and prints in detail. Part 4. Hogarth went on holiday with four friends, initiated what became the Engravers' Act of 1735, called Hogarth's Act, and published the series of prints, *Harlot's Progress* (1732) and *Rake's Progress.* Includes drawings and paintings. Part 5. Recounts Hogarth's career from the 1730's to his death in 1764, and describes the status and style of English art during this period. 1729-64

3027. AMayer, Yvonne. W. HOGARTH. *British Heritage [Great Britain] 1982 3(4): 14-21, (5): 10-20.* Part 1. A biography of the life of William Hogarth (b. 1697), beginning with his early work as an engraver and academic drawing student. Part 2. Describes Hogarth's paintings illustrating scenes from *The Beggar's Opera* and *Falstaff Examining His Recruits,* and a sketch for *A Committee of the House of Commons,* 1728-32. 1697-1732

Hogendorp, Dirk van

3028. Macedo, Roberto. CRONOLOGIA DO GENERAL DE NAPOLEÃO, CONDE DIRK VAN HOGENDORP [Chronology of Napoleon's general, Count Dirk van Hogendorp]. *Revista do Instituto Histórico e Geográfico Brasileiro [Brazil] 1983 (341): 21-25.* Van Hogendorp (1761-1822) was a Dutchman who served first in the Prussian army and then in the Dutch navy and colonies, with a short stay in India. He occupied important posts in the Netherlands after it was annexed by Napoleon, and in many other parts of the latter's European empire. In 1817 he arrived in Rio de Janeiro and died there in 1822, just when it was rumored that he might be appointed minister of foreign affairs. Table. 1780's-1822

Hohenems family

3029. Strnad, Alfred A. KARDINAL MARCUS SITTICUS VON HOHENEMS UND DIE HOHENEMSER IN ITALIEN [Cardinal Marcus Sitticus von Hohenems and the Hohenemses in Italy]. *Montfort [Austria] 1985 37(1): 18-36.* Chronicles the way in which the knightly Hohenems family became part of the Pope's Court and could make use of prestige, wealth, and influence as papal nepotist family, beginning with the marriage between Wolf Dietrich von Ems and the Italian woman Chiara de'Medici, to whom Mark Sittich III, later Cardinal Marcus Sitticus von Hohenems, was born. 16c

Höijer, Theodor

3030. Viljo, E. "Theodor Höijer: En Arkitekt under den Moderna Storstadsarkitekturens Genombrottstid i Finland från 1870 till Sekelskiftet" [Theodor Höijer: an architect from the first period of modern urban building in Finland from 1870 to the turn of the century]. Helsinki U. [Finland] 1985. 229 pp. *DAI-C 1986 47(1): 3; 47/9c. Suomen Muinaismuistdyhdistys, publ.* 1870-1910

Holden, Isaac

3031. Jennings, Elizabeth. SIR ISAAC HOLDEN, BART. (1807-97): HIS PLACE IN THE WESLEYAN CONNEXION. *Pro. of the Wesley Hist. Soc. [Great Britain] 1982 43(5): 117-126.* Of humble origins, Isaac Holden's predilections for the Methodist society and textile technology led to his success in both fields in Great Britain and in France. Article to be continued. 1824-97

Holles, John

3032. Stirens, Michael Wagner. "First Earl of Clare—John Holles." U. of Minnesota 1985. 136 pp. *DAI 1986 46(7): 2048-A.* DA8519344 1580's-1637

Hollis, Thomas

3033. Marshall, P. D. THOMAS HOLLIS (1720-74): THE BIBLIOPHILE AS LIBERTARIAN. *Bulletin of the John Rylands University Library of Manchester [Great Britain] 1984 66(2): 246-263.* Thomas Hollis, born into an established British mercantile family, undertook to encourage political reform by reprinting and circulating tracts dealing with civil and religious liberty. He collected books himself, encouraged others to do so, and contributed thousands of them to colonial American libraries. His concern for American liberty was eventually overwhelmed by his obsessive fears of Catholicism. Primary sources; 42 notes. 1740's-74

Hollmerus, Ragnar

3034. Dahlström, Fabian. RAGNAR HOLLMERUS OCH MUSIKEN [Ragnar Hollmerus and music]. *Hist. och Litteraturhistorisk Studier [Finland] 1982 57: 53-80.* Describes the activity of the Finnish music teacher, Ragnar Hollmerus (1886-1954), as a choir director in Helsinki, Finland, from 1912 to 1921 and as a composer of vocal music. Based on private archives; 34 notes, appendix listing Hollmerus's major compositions. 1900-54

Holloway, Thomas

3035. Bingham, Caroline. "DOING SOMETHING FOR WOMEN": MATTHEW VASSAR & THOMAS HOLLOWAY. *History Today [Great Britain] 1986 36(June): 46-51.* Outlines the lives of two Victorian businessmen, Matthew Vassar and Thomas Holloway, who used their wealth to found colleges for women in Poughkeepsie, New York and London, England. 19c

Hollý, Ján

3036. Sojková, Zdenka. PODOBIZNA JÁNA HOLLÉHO [A portrait of Ján Hollý]. *Česká Literatura [Czechoslovakia] 1984 32(6): 545-552.* Ján Hollý (1785-1849), a Slovak poet of the second generation of the Slovak national revival, was the subject of a number of embryonic literary portraits by Czech writers even before the birth centenary article by Jan Neruda (1834-91) that accompanied a portrait of Hollý reproduced in Josef Vilímek's *Humoristické Listy.* 1823-98

Holman, May

3037. White, Kate. MAY HOLMAN: "AUSTRALIAN LABOR'S PIONEER WOMAN PARLIAMENTARIAN." *Labour Hist. [Australia] 1981 (41): 110-117.* May Holman, the first Labor woman to serve in the Western Australian Assembly, won six terms from 1925 to 1939. Holman assumed the seat for Forrest when her father died in 1925. She traveled extensively in her district to retain close contact with her supporters. She often defended the interests of the timber industry which dominated her district. Although not a strong feminist, May did rely upon the Labor Women's Organization as her political base. The combination of a trip to the League of Nations in Geneva, economic depression in Forrest, and a protracted illness convinced May to become more vocal in advocating the importance of women in politics. May's vocalness eroded union support for her during the 1930's, yet she is remembered as a capable female labor parliamentarian who served and represented her district well. Based primarily on newspaper accounts, some governmental and Labor records; 32 notes. 1925-39

Holmès, Augusta

3038. Theeman, Nancy Sarah. "The Life and Songs of Augusta Holmès." U. of Maryland 1983. 285 pp. *DAI 1984 45(2): 340-A.* DA8412064 1860's-1903

Holstein, Friedrich von

3039. Vinogradov, K. B. and Gostenkov, A. V. DNI I DELA FRIDRIKHA GOL'SHTEINA [The life and work of Friedrich von Holstein]. *Novaia i Noveishaia Istoriia [USSR] 1984 (2): 147-165.* A detailed account of the life of German diplomat Baron Friedrich von Holstein (1831-1909), who was relatively little known during his lifetime. Discusses his political and diplomatic activity within a sociopolitical framework. Primary and secondary sources; 85 notes. 1860's-1909

Holt, Laurence James

3040. Bassett, Michael and Dalziel, Raewyn. JIM HOLT, 1939-1983. *New Zealand J. of Hist. [New Zealand] 1983 17(2): 101-102.* An obituary for Laurence James Holt, who taught history at the University of Auckland, New Zealand, from 1964 until he resigned in 1983 to take up the post of chief historian of the New Zealand Historical Publications office. 1939-83

Holzer, Wolfgang

3041. Perger, Richard. WOLFGANG HOLZER: AUFSTIEG UND FALL EINES WIENER POLITIKERS IM 15. JAHRHUNDERT [Wolfgang Holzer: the rise and fall of a Viennese politician in the 15th century]. *Jahrbuch des Vereins für Geschichte der Stadt Wien [Austria] 1985 41: 7-61.* Discusses the life and family history of the Viennese mayor Wolfgang Holzer (ca. 1424-63), who was executed for his opposition to Albrecht VI in the Austrian civil war of 1462-63. 15c

Holzträger, Hans

3042. Holzträger, Hans. A GERMAN EVANGELICAL MINISTER'S REMINISCENCES OF HIS YOUTH IN NORTH TRANSYLVANIA. *Yad Vashem Studies on the European Jewish Catastrophe and Resistance [Israel] 1981 14: 269-286.* From earliest childhood to his service in the German Youth Movement, a minister recounts his experiences with Jews in a small Transylvania village. Describes how an outward tolerance of various nationalities deteriorated as the Nazis directed their corrosive propaganda at the unsophisticated villagers. Admits his own anti-Semitic prejudices as a youth, which he explains as the result of exposure to a narrow interpretation of Christian scripture. Later on, he witnessed several anti-Semitic incidents that befell his Jewish neighbors, and then realized that terrible crimes could be perpetrated against a vulnerable minority, when the hearts and minds of the people were indoctrinated with hate. 1930-45

Homan, Ernest Edward

3043. Smith, R. Cherer. ERNEST EDWARD HOMAN. *Heritage [Zimbabwe] 1983 3: 54-56.* Outlines the business career and public role of Ernest Edward Homan in Salisbury. 1891-1921

Homberger, Heinrich

3044. Winterberger, Gerhard. HEINRICH HOMBERGER ZUM GEDÄCHTNIS [In memory of Heinrich Homberger]. *Schweizer Monatshefte [Switzerland] 1985 65(4): 309-313.* Commemorates the life and work of the late delegate of the headquarters for the Swiss Commercial and Industrial Union, Heinrich Homberger (1896-1985), with emphasis on Homberger's participation in the politically significant economic negotiations during World War II. 1922-76

Honecker, Erich

3045. Masich, V. F. VERNYI SYN NEMETSKOGO RABOCHEGO KLASSA: K 70-LETIIU SO DNIA ROZHDENIIA GENERAL'NOGO SEKRETARIA TSK SEPG ERIKHA KHONEKKERA [A true son of the German working class: on the 70th birthday of Erich Honecker, general secretary of the Socialist Unity Party of East Germany]. *Voprosy Istorii KPSS [USSR] 1982 (8): 86-89.* Erich Honecker was born on 25 August 1912 into a workers' family, and early knew deprivation. He entered the Young Communist League in 1926 and the German Communist Party in 1927. From 1930 to 1933 he studied in Moscow. He was imprisoned in Germany in 1935 and freed by the Soviet army in 1945. He performed signal services for the Socialist Unity Party of Germany, becoming its general secretary in 1971. He has been chief of East Germany's defense committee since 1971. He combats imperialism. He fights for peace and progress and is a true friend and ally of the USSR. Based on *Protocols of the Activities of the 10th Party Congress of the Socialist Unity Party of Germany,* Berlin, 1981; 12 notes. 1912-82

Hong Chengzhou

3046. Wang, Chen-main. "The Life and Career of Hung Ch'eng-Ch'ou (1593-1665): Public Service in a Time of Dynastic Change." University of Arizona 1984. 259 pp. *DAI 1984 45(6): 1839-A.* DA8421986 1620's-65

Hongi Hika

3047. Parsonson, G. S. THE LIFE AND TIMES OF HONGI HIKA. *Hist. News [New Zealand] 1982 (44): 1-8.* Biography of early Maori leader, Hongi Hika (ca. 1768-1828), a minor chief of the Ngai Te Wake, a clan of the Ngapuhi of the Kerikeri-Waimate district in New Zealand, who was a friend of the British missionaries of the Church Missionary Society there but did not espouse Christianity, focusing on the Maori means of keeping law and order. 1768-1828

Honywood, Michael

3048. Linnell, Naomi. MICHAEL HONYWOOD AND LINCOLN CATHEDRAL LIBRARY. *Library [Great Britain] 1983 5(2): 126-139.* Michael Honywood (1597-1681) was Dean of Lincoln from 1660 to 1681. Honywood was forced into exile at Utrecht in 1643 during the English Civil War. He returned in 1660 as Dean at Lincoln with an admirable personal library. Honywood not only donated his library to the Cathedral but helped to build the gallery that housed his collection. Based on manuscripts in the Lincolnshire Archives Office; 18 notes. 1660-81

Hookes, Ellis

3049. Honeyman, David J. ELLIS HOOKES (1635-1681): FIRST RECORDING CLERK OF THE SOCIETY OF FRIENDS. *Quaker Hist. 1983 72(1): 43-54.* Evaluates the success of Ellis Hookes in gaining adherents to the Society of Friends in England during the 17th century. Based on primary sources; 20 notes. 17c

Hope, Alexander

3050. Ward, S. G. P. GENERAL THE HONORABLE SIR ALEXANDER HOPE. *Journal of the Society for Army Historical Research [Great Britain] 1984 62(249): 1-12.* Describes the career of Alexander Hope (1769-1837), his interest in improving the British Army, service in Europe, Scotland, and Ireland, and his accumulative instinct for papers, letters, and appointments. 1790's-37

Hopla, Judson

3051. Ackley, C. S. THE SPANISH SEVERSKY. *Am. Aviation Hist. Soc. J. 1981 26(1): 60-67.* 1920's-39
For abstract see ***Seversky, Alexander Procofieff de***

Hopley, Frederick John van der Byl

3052. Kimberley, Michael J. FREDERICK JOHN VAN DER BYL HOPLEY 1883-1951. *Heritage [Zimbabwe] 1981 (1): 32-36.* Hopley was a distinguished sportsman who took up farming after World War I, became Director of Physical Education briefly in Salisbury, 1949-51, and is commemorated by the John Hopley Trophy awarded to the best amateur sportsman in Zimbabwe. 1883-1951

Horák, Jiří

3053. Urban, Zdeněk. U ISTOKOV SOTRUDNICHESTVA CHEKHOSLOVATSKIKH I SOVETSKIKH UCHENYKH [Early collaboration between Czechoslovak and Soviet scholars]. *Voprosy Istorii Estestvoznaniia i Tekhniki [USSR] 1982 (2): 116-119.* While compiling a bibliography of the works of the folklorist and literary historian Jiří Horák (1884-1975), the author came across Horák's articles about his trip to Russia in the early 1920's. His reportage on his 17-day stay in Petrograd includes a description of his meeting with the Russian geographer and geologist Aleksandr E. Fersman (1883-1945), reprinted here in a slightly abridged translation. Note, illus. 1921

Hore-Belisha, Leslie

3054. Trythall, A. J. THE DOWNFALL OF LESLIE HORE-BELISHA. *J. of Contemporary Hist. [Great Britain] 1981 16(3): 391-411.* Isaac Leslie Hore-Belisha, of Sephardic Jewish ancestry, educated in law at Oxford, and experienced in several government ministries, was made Secretary of State in 1937, but dismissed in 1940. Although talented, he was excessively flamboyant and unconventional. He ruthlessly changed army commanders when he felt it necessary, and undoubtedly his dismissal was brought about by those who feared that he intended to replace the senior officers of the British Expeditionary Forces (BEF) in Europe. Other reasons, however, continue to be alleged: that his general administrative changes were unpopular, that he had made an indiscreet remark to the effect that there were not enough pill boxes from the end of the Maginot line at Givet to the coast, or that he was the victim of anti-Semitism. Primary sources; 93 notes. 1937-40

Horkheimer, Max

3055. Shaw, Brian J. REASON, NOSTALGIA, AND ESCHATOLOGY IN THE CRITICAL THEORY OF MAX HORKHEIMER. *Journal of Politics 1985 47(1): 160-181.* Max Horkheimer (1895-1973), as director of Frankfurt's Institut für Sozialforschung, was a major influence on such Critical Theorists as Theodor Adorno, Herbert Marcuse, Erich Fromm and Jürgen Habermas. His philosophy of history was informed by both wide reading and emphasis on the freeing of the critical imagination. His stance against modernity, often seen as a transition from radical Marxism in the 1930's to a pessimistic Jewish transcendentalism, remained consistent throughout his career. His self-indulgent, masochistic philosophy arose from his recognition of the ultimate futility of his chiliastic impulses. In his later years, Horkheimer opposed birth control, feminism, and criticism of American intervention in Vietnam. Despair and resignation, rather than resistance, are the only appropriate responses to absolute evil. 15 notes, biblio. 1930's-73

Horner, Leonard

3056. Brown, Colin M. LEONARD HORNER, 1785-1864: HIS CONTRIBUTION TO EDUCATION. *Journal of Educational Administration and History [Great Britain] 1985 17(1): 1-10.* Discusses Leonard Horner's significant contribution to education in Scotland in the context of educational innovation and in the light of the research of some 20th-century writers. 1785-1864

Horney, Karen

3057. Garrison, Dee. KAREN HORNEY AND FEMINISM. *Signs 1981 6(4): 672-691.* Karen Horney (1885-1952), the German psychiatrist and critic of Freud, discovered that "men are afraid of women," and this set the stage for her feminism. Well-respected by her colleagues, she began her controversial writing in 1922 by declaring that primary penis-envy is to be expected in normal girls, and she hinted a feminine libido existed. After Freud published his speculative theories on women, Horney broke with Freud, declaring that women's problems are fundamentally questions of male-dominated socialization. Personally disliking confrontation, she withdrew from controversial issues after she lost her debate with Freud in 1931. Based on the published writings of Horney and Freud; 62 notes. 1920-35

Horoviş, Šemu'el Šmelke ben Şvi Hirš ha-Levi

3058. Nosek, Bedřich. SHEMUEL SHMELKE BEN TSVI HIRSH HA-LEVI HOROVITS: LEGEND AND REALITY. *Judaica Bohemiae [Czechoslovakia] 1985 21(2): 75-94.* Discusses the genealogy, life, and ideology of Hasidism, emphasizing ethics and pietism, of Rabbi Šemu'el Šmelke ben Şvi Hirš ha-Levi Horoviş, a descendant of the Moravian Jewish Hořovský family, who returned from Poland in 1773 to teach in the Moravian town of Mikulov (Nikolsburg) and who became provincial rabbi of all Moravia in 1775. 16c-18c

Horst, Ferdinand

3059. Horst, Ferdinand and Semmler, Willimena Lagge. MEMORIES OF CHILDHOOD IN WORMS, RUSSIA. *Journal of the American Historical Society of Germans from Russia 1985 8(4): 1-11.* Ferdinand Horst (born 1899, emigrated to Nebraska in 1909) and Willimena Lagge Semmler (born 1893, emigrated to South Dakota in 1905) recount their memories of daily life, agriculture, education, and holidays in their native German-Russian settlement of Worms, South Russia. 1893-1909

Horthy, Miklós

3060. Pushkash, A. I. DIPLOMATICHESKIE MANEVRY KHORTISTOV V OKTIABRE 1944 G. [Horthyist diplomatic maneuvers in October 1944]. *Voprosy Istorii [USSR] 1981 (11): 100-108.* At the end of August 1944, with the Soviet army approaching the borders of Hungary and the Allies opening the second front in Europe, the Hungarian dictator and ally of Hitler, Miklós Horthy, attempted to salvage the remnants of his regime and spare his country the ravages of war. Horthy and his clique staked their hopes on Winston Churchill's plan to reach Hungary before the Soviet troops, but these hopes were entirely illusory. The Horthyists sought several times to conclude a separate peace with the United States and Great Britain by using Hungarian diplomats in neutral countries. In letters to the Allies, Horthy pleaded that the Soviets be prevented from entering Hungarian territory. The Allies preferred not to complicate relations with their Soviet ally. Simultaneously Horthy approached the Soviets, offering them generous conditions for a separate cessation of hostilities, but rejected Moscow's demand that Hungary declare war on Germany. Horthy chose to resign and seek asylum in Germany. 1944

3061. Sakmyster, Thomas. FROM HABSBURG ADMIRAL TO HUNGARIAN REGENT: THE POLITICAL METAMORPHOSIS OF MIKLOS HORTHY, 1918-1921. *East European Q. 1983 17(2): 129-148.* Describes the transformation of the staunch legitimist, Admiral Miklós Horthy, into "a new kind of political creature, a kind of link between the two basic varieties of right-wing ideology," traditional conservatism and radical, anti-Semitic rightism. Provides a clear description of Horthy's transformation and his relationship to the leaders of the radical right. Based largely on secondary works and memoirs; 58 notes. 1918-21

Hørup, Viggo

3062. Thorborg, Karsten. VIGGO HØRUP: EN AF DET MODERNE GENNEMBRUDS MAEND [Viggo Hørup: one of the pioneers of modern times]. *Historisk Tidsskrift [Denmark] 1981 81(1): 123-176.* Viggo Hørup (1841-1902) was a leading radical, democratic politician in the constitutional struggle that took place in 19th-century Denmark. He was a member of *Folketinget* from 1876-92 and just before his death became a minister in the first Liberal government. He is also regarded as Denmark's greatest journalist. From 1873-83 he wrote in the liberal national newspaper *Morgen-bladet* and, in 1885, with the support of the Brandesians, he founded *Politiken.* Although many biographies have been written about him, very little has been said about the origins of his attitude to life and his political ideas. His lectures, poems and a single philosophical work are analyzed with the intent to grasp the development of his understanding of himself and his times during the formative years, 1860-73. As sources of inspiration for this, Kristian Arentzen, his teacher of Danish at the Metropolitan School, and the works of Søren Kierkegaard and Heinrich Heine are mentioned. Hørup's attitude to life is characterized as Socratic/existential, and it is shown how this attitude lay behind his futile election campaign in 1872 and his attack on the Copenhagen educational hegemony in *Morgen-bladet* the following year. Based on Karsten Thorborg's *Hørup in Letters and Poems* (1981). 1860-1902

Horvat, Ignac

3063. Hajszan, R. "Ignac Horvat: Leben und Wirken eines Burgenländischkroatischen Priesters und Schriftstellers" [Ignac Horvat: life and work of a Burgenland Croatian priest and writer]. U. of Vienna [Austria] 1979. *DAI-C 1983 44(3): 470; 8/2140c.* 20c

Horváth, Ödön von

3064. Huder, Walter. EXIL ALS TODESFALLE. EINE SENTIMENTAL-HEROISCHE FATALIÄ: DER GESCHICHTE EXEMPEL ÖDÖN VON HORVÁTH [Exile as an occasion of death: a sentimental-heroic death, Ödön von Horváth as an example of history]. *Austriaca [France] 1984 10(19): 133-144.* When Ödön von Horváth (1901-38), one of Europe's most talented theatrical writers, was accidentally killed in Paris where he had fled from the Nazis, the shock caused his friends and fellow exiles to speculate on the metaphysical significance of his death. Tracing his actions on the last day of his life led some to question if his death was truly accidental, since so many of the exiles had committed suicide. Since he died as a fugitive from German fascism, his death is seen also as an act of heroism. 1938

3065. Kadrnoska, Franz. DIE SPÄTEN ROMANE ÖDÖN VON HORVÁTHS: EXILLITERATUR UND VERGANGENHEITSBEWÄLTIGUNG [The late novels of Ödön von Horváth: exile literature and clearing up the past]. *Österreich in Geschichte und Literatur [Austria] 1982 26(2): 81-109.* Ödön von Horváth (1901-38) was born and educated in Budapest, where he became involved in revolutionary politics in the late 1910's. By 1924 he was an acknowledged dramatist in Berlin. In 1931 he first encountered Nazism as an eyewitness in the Saalschlacht trial. After various travels he returned to Berlin in 1934 to study Nazism as the subject of a play. In 1936 the authorities withdrew his permission to remain in Germany, and he died in 1937. His two late novels *Jugend ohne Gott* (where the plot develops from state indoctrination) and *Ein Kind Unserer Zeit* (dealing with the unemployed between the wars) reveal his confrontation with the Nazis, 1936-37. Secondary sources; 124 notes. 1930's

3066. Müller, Karl. ÖDÖN VON HORVÁTHS WEG NACH INNEN [Ödön von Horváth's introspectiveness]. *Österreich in Geschichte und Literatur [Austria] 1982 26(5): 285-297.* Three views prevail about Ödön von Horváth: that he was an uncompromising antifascist (though the official East German view regards him as a failure), that he wrote popular literature, and that he was a metaphysical writer. From 1933 he became more introspective. This was part of his guilt fixation connected with a problematic relationship with his own and his father's generation. The fascist disregard of human rights disturbed his contact with people. Secondary sources; 42 notes. 1930's

Hosemann, Theodor

3067. Becker, I. "Theodor Hosemann (1807-1875). Ansichten des Berliner Biedermeier" [Theodor Hoseman (1807-75): Views of the Berlin Biedermeier period]. Free University of Berlin [West Germany] 1980. 342 pp. *DAI-C 1985 46(3): 572; 46/2700c.* 1820's-40's

Hostinský, Otakar

3068. Jůzl, Miloš. VZÁJEMNÝ VZTAH ZDEŇKA NEJEDLÉHO A OTAKARA HOSTINSKÉHO [Friendship between Zdeněk Nejedlý and Otakar Hostinský]. *Acta U. Carolinae Phil. et Hist. [Czechoslovakia] 1980 (1): 99-114.* Otakar Hostinský, professor of aesthetics at the Prague University, and his student Zdeněk Nejedlý, placed Bedřich Smetana's musical compositions above those of Dvořák. The disagreement among music critics at the beginning of the 20th century resulted in a distorted picture of Hostinský. Details of this controversy are explained with the use of correspondence between Hostinský and Nejedlý. Based on Hostinský-Nejedlý correspondence; note. 19c-20c

Hostos, Eugenio María de

3069. Maldonado-Denis, Manuel. INTRODUCCION AL PENSAMIENTO SOCIAL DE EUGENIO MARIA DE HOSTOS [Introduction to the social thought of Eugenio María de Hostos]. *Casa de las Américas [Cuba] 1981 21(124): 51-66.* Within the limitations of his time and particular circumstances the Puerto Rican writer Eugenio María de Hostos (1839-1903) was a revolutionary. He fought for the independence of Cuba and Puerto Rico, and in his work as sociologist, moralist, and teacher he remains one of the great figures of 19th-century Caribbean society. 10 notes. 19c

3070. Oraá, Luis M. ETAPAS DE LA "PEREGRINACION" DE HOSTOS [Stages in the "travels" of Hostos]. *Estudios Sociales [Dominican Republic] 1979 12(47): 151-179.* Traces the career of Eugenio María de Hostos (1839-1903), Puerto Rican intellectual, educator, and liberal political activist, whose travels took him to Spain, Colombia, Peru, the Dominican Republic, Chile, and the United States. 1850's-1903

Houghton, William J.

3071. Macey, Muriel. WILLIAM J. HOUGHTON AND THE *COMET*. *Africana Notes and News [South Africa] 1981 24(8): 261-264.* William J. Houghton founded the *Comet,* an irregularly issued newspaper, in Cape Colony in 1881. It continued to appear into the 1890's from various locations in the colony as a gadfly publication attacking perceived corruption in railroad construction, the British royal family, and other matters. 10 notes. 1881-90's

Hourmouziou, Stylianos

3072. Papadopoullou, Charalampous. TO MOUSIKON ERGON TOU STYLIANOU CHOURMOUZIOU KAI VIOGRAPHIKAI SĒMEIŌSEIS AUTOU [The musical work of Stylianos Hourmouziou and biographical notes]. *Kypriakai Spoudai [Cyprus] 1980 44: 153-181.* Describes the accomplishments of Stylianos Hourmouzios, a Cypriot scholar of Byzantine liturgical music, primarily during 1897-1901. 1897-1901

Houying, Dai

3073. Yang, Gladys. RESEARCH NOTE: WOMEN WRITERS. *China Quarterly [Great Britain] 1985 (103): 510-517.* 1957-83
For abstract see ***Anyi, Wang***

Hovhannissian, Abgar

3074. Grigorian, V. R. ABGAR HOVHANNISSIAN [Abgar Hovhannissian]. *Patma-Banasirakan Handes. Istoriko-Filologicheskii Zhurnal [USSR] 1983 (4): 212-215.* Tribute on the 75th birthday of historian Abgar Hovhannissian, vice-president of the Armenian Academy of Sciences and pro-rector of Erevan University. His works have mainly been on French revolutionary movements, 1789-94 and 1840-41, and their utopian communist ideologies, and Armenian history during the second half of the 18th century dealing with liberation movements against Turkish and Persian domination, Russian policy with regard to Transcaucasia, and international relations at the beginning of the 19th century. Primary sources; photo. 1933-83

Howard, Catherine

3075. Erlanger, Philippe. HENRY VIII ET CATHERINE HOWARD, SA QUATRIEME EPOUSE [Henry VIII and Catherine Howard, his fourth wife]. *Rev. des Deux Mondes [France] 1982 (9): 579-590.* Describes the opposition of Henry VIII's fifth queen, Catherine Howard, to the Reformation and her indiscreet liaisons with factious and subversive members of court, including Lady Rochford and Francis Dereham, which led ultimately to her execution in 1543. 1520-43

Howard, George (Viscount Morpeth)

3076. Mandler, Peter. CAIN AND ABEL: TWO ARISTOCRATS AND THE EARLY VICTORIAN FACTORY ACTS. *Historical Journal [Great Britain] 1984 27(1): 83-109.* The views and careers of Lord Ashley (later the 7th Earl of Shaftesbury) and George Howard, Viscount Morpeth (later the Earl of Carlisle), provide evidence on the nature of aristocratic politics in early Victorian England. The pair, who had been friends at Oxford University, entered Parliament in 1826 as representatives of different political parties: Ashley was a Tory; Morpeth was a Whig. The two aristocrats, although both were social reformers, clashed during the 1830's-50's over factory legislation that sought to improve working conditions in the textile industry. Over the years, their positions altered over the factory reforms, reflecting changes in their political attitudes and those of their parties. Based on documents in Castle Howard and the British Library; 119 notes. 1820's-50's

Howard, Henry

3077. Levy Peck, Linda. THE EARL OF NORTHAMPTON, MERCHANT GRIEVANCES, AND THE ADDLED PARLIAMENT OF 1614. *Hist. J. [Great Britain] 1981 24(3): 533-552.* Reassesses the reputation of Henry Howard, 1st Earl of Northampton, among some of his contemporaries and later historians as the bête noire of the House of Commons. Analyzes the two major incidents on which this reputation is built—his speech on merchant grievances and royal prerogative, made in 1607, and his handling of the second Addled Parliament of James I of 1614—and from them draws a very different picture of Northampton's role in Parliament. Reconsidering Northampton's activities sheds interesting light on the Jacobean privy councillor in Parliament, the question of consensus, faction, and the relationships between the Houses of Lords and Commons in England. 79 notes. 1607-14

Howard, Michael

3078. Skaggs, David Curtis. OF HAWKS, DOVES, AND OWLS: MICHAEL HOWARD AND STRATEGIC POLICY. *Armed Forces & Society 1985 11(4): 609-626.* Michael Howard, Regius professor of modern history at Oxford University, has become an outspoken commentator on contemporary strategic policy. An analysis of his writings reveals he advocates a strategic approach to international relations that: emphasizes the complexities facing nation-states which endeavor to maintain stability while guarding their value systems; adopts a historical approach to the causes of war that stresses the importance of "bellicism" as a causal factor; examines the dimensions of strategy that deplore the neglect of social factors; and seeks to avoid conflict through reliance on both the nuclear and conventional aspects of deterrence. His trenchant criticisms have brought the wrath of modern hawks and doves, while he has sought an "owl" position between the two camps. 1945-84

Howard, Philip Thomas

3079. DeClercq, Carlo. LE CARDINAL PHILIPPE-THOMAS HOWARD ET SES ACTIVITES ROMAINES [Cardinal Philip Thomas Howard and his Roman activities]. *Bull. de l'Inst. Hist. Belge de Rome [Belgium] 1981 51: 167-196.* A biography of Cardinal Philip Thomas Howard (1629-94) including the events that led up to his cardinalship and his religious activities in Rome; provides black and white plates of portraits of himself and his family. 1615-94

Hoxha, Enver

3080. Alia, Ramiz. ENVER HOXHA—FLAMUR I LUFTËS PËR LIRI E SOCIALIZËM [Enver Hoxha: the flag for freedom and socialism]. *Studime Historike [Albania] 1985 39(4): 3-7.* A eulogy of Enver Hoxha by the First Secretary of the Albanian Party of Labor, stressing Hoxha's contribution to history. As a Marxist-Leninist, Hoxha was a man of the people. He knew how to formulate the people's wishes and bring them to practical implementation. Like Scanderbeg, who dominated the history of Albania for five centuries, Hoxha will be the teacher and example to follow in the future history of the Albanians. 1940's-85

3081. Boriçi, Hamit. VEPRIMTARIA E SHOKUT ENVER HOXHA NË FUSHËN E SHTYPIT DHE TË PUBLICISTIKËS [Comrade Enver Hoxha's activities in the press and journalism]. *Studime Filologjike [Albania] 1985 39(2): 197-212.* Enver Hoxha started his journalistic work at *l'Humanité* in Paris in 1930, established and wrote for the revolutionary press in Albania, and maintained a continuing interest in its technical aspects. Based on Enver Hoxha's works; 33 notes. French summary. 1930-84

3082. Çami, Foto. LE CAMARADE ENVER HOXHA—FONDATEUR, ORGANISATEUR ET DIRIGEANT DE NOTRE GLORIEUX PARTI [Comrade Enver Hoxha: founder, organizer, and leader of our glorious Party]. *Studia Albanica [Albania] 1985 22(1): 3-8.* Traces the importance and influence of Enver Hoxha, particularly with reference to his activities in the Albanian Communist Party (renamed the Party of Labor in 1948) and for Albania since 1941. Examines Hoxha's political ideology, his writings, his revolutionary program for national liberation, his organization and direction of the struggle against fascism during World War II, and the realization of his revolutionary aims. 1940's-84

3083. Çollaku, Gaqo. MËSIMET E SHOKUT ENVER HOXHA PËR PËRGATITJEN DHE EDUKIMIN E INTELIGJENCIES SË RE SOCIALIST [Comrade Enver Hoxha's teaching on the training and education of the new socialist intelligentsia]. *Studime Historike [Albania] 1985 39(3): 57-72.* Faced with a lack of educated cadres and general ignorance, Enver Hoxha understood that the masses needed an intelligentsia to lead them to socialism. He encouraged the use of existing cadres after retraining them in Marxism-Leninism. In 1945 he launched an educational reform to create a working class intelligentsia; he encouraged the foundation of high schools, a university, and an academy. According to Marxism-Leninism the intelligentsia should be involved in actual production. That is how today the working class and peasantry have their own intelligentsia. Based on Hoxha's work and Ramiz Alia's reports; 35 notes. French summary; 4 notes. 1945-85

3084. Frashëri, Xhemil; Gjipali, Koço; and Dezhgiu, Muharrem. KUJTIME—ASPEKTE TË FIGURËS DHE TË VEPRIMTARISË TË SHOKUT ENVER HOXHA SIMBAS KUJTIMEVE TË BASHKËKOHESVE [Recollections: views of the person and activities of Comrade Enver Hoxha as seen by his contemporaries]. *Studime Historike [Albania] 1985 39(2): 189-213.* Brief recollections on Enver Hoxha and his work by his contemporaries. Note. 1930-84

3085. Gjipali, Koço. ASPEKTE TË FIGURËS DHE TË VEPRIMTARISË SË SHOKUT ENVER HOXHA PËRMES KUJTIMEVE TË BASHKËKOHËSVE [Aspects of the personality and activity of comrade Enver Hoxha as seen by his contemporaries]. *Studime Historike [Albania] 1985 39(3): 187-208.* The recollection of ordinary people, who met Enver Hoxha from the late 1930's to the late 1950's in Gjinokastër, Korçë, and elsewhere, where he initially worked clandestinely in the fight against fascism, and later openly as the leader of the people. These memoirs underline Hoxha's ability to communicate with ordinary people, to show an interest in their lives, and to provide encouragement and knowledgeable advice. 2 notes. 1935-58

3086. Omari, Luan. LE ROLE DU PCA ET DU CAMARADE ENVER HOXHA POUR LA CREATION DU POUVOIR POPULAIRE DURANT LA LUTTE ANTIFASCISTE DE LIBERATION NATIONALE [The role of the Albanian Communist Party and comrade Enver Hoxha in creating popular power during the antifascist struggle for national liberation]. *Studia Albanica [Albania] 1984 21(2): 3-17.* Discusses the strategy and tactics adopted by the Albanian Communist Party and Enver Hoxha to create popular power between April 1939 and November 1944. Particular attention is paid to the struggle against the occupation of Albania by Italian fascists during this period and to the foundation of the Albanian Communist Party, which played a major role in the struggle. In addition, the author examines the development of and theoretical ideas of Enver Hoxha and the Party concerning the characteristics and organization of popular power. These ideas were formulated at the 2d Conference of National Liberation at Labinot in September 1943 and ratified at the Congress of Përmeti in May 1944, which resulted in the creation of the Albanian state. Based on Albanian Communist Party documents and documents in the Public Record Office, London and secondary sources; 14 notes. 1939-44

3087. Pollo, Stefanaq. KONTRIBUTI I SHQUAR I SHOKUT ENVER HOXHA NË HISTORIOGRAFINË TONË TË RE [Comrade Enver Hoxha's distinguished contribution to our new historiography]. *Studime Historike [Albania] 1985 39(2): 3-22.* Enver Hoxha's contribution to Albanian historiography cannot be overestimated. He concentrated on the role of the people. As a scientific historian, he formulated principles and lessons to be followed by the historians of various periods and did not hesitate to castigate those abandoning the Marxist-Leninist scientific approach. The 40,000 pages he wrote provide not only the facts but also the right explanation. Based on Enver Hoxha's writings; 17 notes. French summary. 1944-84

3088. —. DOKUMENTE DHE MATERIALE—SHOKU ENVER HOXHA MBI HISTORINË DHE SHKENCËN HISTORIKE SHQIPTARE [Documents and materials: Comrade Enver Hoxha on the history and scientific historiography of Albania]. *Studime Historike [Albania] 1985 39(2): 143-187.* Excerpts from writings and comments of Enver Hoxha on Albanian history and historiography. 4 notes. 1941-84

Hozjusz, Stanisław

3089. Bogdan, Danuta. LEGACJA KARDYNAŁA STANISŁAWA HOZJUSZA NA SOBÓR TRYDENCKI [The legation of Cardinal Stanisław Hozjusz at the Council of Trent]. *Komunikaty Mazursko-Warmińskie [Poland] 1981 (2-4): 429-436.* A review article of Henryk Damian Wojtyska's *Cardinal Hosius: Legate to the Council of Trent* (1967) dealing with the activities of the Polish cardinal and bishop of Ermeland during the second phase of the Council of Trent, utilizing correspondence and arriving at a middle ground in the appraisal of Hozjusz. Based on secondary sources; 15 notes. 1561-63

Hrechukha, Mykhailo S.

3090. Doroshenko, V. S. M. S. HRECHUKHA [M. S. Hrechukha]. *Ukrains'kyi Istorychnyi Zhurnal [USSR] 1982 (9): 122-124.* Mykhailo S. Hrechukha (1902-76), an outstanding Ukrainian Party leader and statesman, was born into a peasant family. From an early age he worked in Ukrainian sugar refineries before joining the Communist Party in 1926. As a Party member he was devoted to the cause of socialist transformation of the countryside and took an active part in the struggle against the kulaks. He held various local Party and administrative posts, and in 1939 was elected chairman of the Ukrainian Supreme Soviet Presidium, a position that he held for 15 years. 1926-76

Hronský, J. C.

See Cíger-Hronský, Jozef

Hrushevsky, Mikhail S.

3091. Antonovych, M[arko]. SPRAVA HRUSHEVS'KOHO [The Hrushevs'kyi case]. *Ukrains'kyi Istoryk 1985 22(1-4): 200-211.* Appends 12 documents, dating from 1916 to 1918, pertaining to the case of the renowned Ukrainian historian Mikhail S. Hrushevsky (1866-1934), who was accused of publishing anti-Austrian statements in the Russian newspaper *Rech'* on 25 October 1915. Based on Innenministerium records of the Allgemeines Verwaltungsarchiv in the Österreichisches Staatsarchiv of Vienna; 44 notes. 1916-18

3092. Hrushevsky, Mikhail S. IAK IA BUV KOLYS BELETRYSTOM? [How I was once a prose writer]. *Ukrains'kyi Istoryk 1980 17(1-4): 89-94.* At the age of 19 Mikhail S. Hrushevsky decided that he could serve the Ukrainian cause best as a writer. He describes his attempts at short story writing and gradual acquisition of the storyteller's skills. He soon came to be regarded by well-known Ukrainian writers as a promising beginner. But a graduation scandal in which he was indirectly involved turned him into a humble and restrained person whose soul no longer had room for literary ambitions. Instead he devoted his energy to historical research. 1885-88

3093. Hrushevsky, Mikhail S. IAK MENE SPROVADZHENO DO L'VOVA [How I came to Lvov]. *Ukrains'kyi Istoryk 1984 21(1-4): 230-235.* Reprints a letter written in 1898 to the editor of the Lvov newspaper *Dilo* describing the circumstances that led to Hrushevsky's appointment as professor of history at the University of Lvov in 1894 and justifying the newly-set goals of the Shevchenko Scientific Society, of which Hrushevsky became the head in 1897. The letter also reveals that serious conflicts had developed between Mikhail S. Hrushevsky (1866-1934), a leading Ukrainian historian, and Oleksander Barvins'kyi (1847-1926), a noted Ukrainian teacher, historian, and political leader. 13 notes. 1891-98

3094. Korduba, Myron. MYKHAILO HRUSHEVS'KYI IAK UCHENYI [Mikhail S. Hrushevsky as a scholar]. *Ukrains'kyi Istoryk 1984 21(1-4): 33-47.* Sketches a biography and discusses the scholarly contributions of the renowned Ukrainian historian Mikhail S. Hrushevsky (1866-1934), concentrating on his multi-volume *Istoriia Ukrainy-Rusy* [History of Ukraine-Rus], a monumental work characterized by originality, objectivity, and sound source analysis. Myron Korduba (1876-1947), a student of Hrushevsky at the University of Lvov, evaluates his professor's scholarship very highly; he stood head and shoulders above his contemporaries, both Ukrainian historians and all those who labored in the field of Slavic history. Originally published in Polish in *Przegląd Historyczny* 1935 32(12): 389-406. Ukrainian translation by Vasyl Iashchun. 29 notes. 1866-1934

3095. Lentsyk, Vasyl. [Lencyk, W.] MYKHAILO HRUSHEVS'KYI V OTSINTSI SVOIKH STUDENTIV [Mikhail S. Hrushevsky in the evaluation of his students]. *Ukrains'kyi Istoryk 1984 21(1-4): 123-131.* Reveals that the students of the historian Mikhail S. Hrushevsky (1866-1934) evaluated their professor highly as a teacher and a scholar. While teaching at the University of Lvov from 1894 to 1914, Hrushevsky insisted on lofty standards of historical scholarship. Many of his students—Ivan Kryp'iakevych (1886-1967), Stepan Tomashivs'kyi (1875-1930), and Myron Korduba (1876-1947), among others—made significant contributions to Ukrainian historiography. Secondary sources; 20 notes. 1894-1914

3096. Stepanyshyna, O. OSTANNI ROKY ZHYTTIA MYKHAILA HRUSHEVSKOHO [The final years of Michael Hrushevsky's life]. *Ukrains'kyi Istoryk 1981 18(1-4): 174-179.* After the first arrests in the Historical Section of the Ukrainian Academy of Sciences, Hrushevsky was advised by the authorities to move to Moscow, which he initially refused to do. Under increasing pressure, he left Kiev and traveled to Moscow where the NKVD put him into a prison. One of his relatives, then close to Stalin, intervened on his behalf and he was released. In 1934, ill and exhausted, he went to the Caucasus where he was stricken by a rare disease. He died 24 November 1934. 1931-34

3097. Wynar, Lubomyr. AVTOBIOHRAFIIA (1926) [Autobiography, 1926]. *Ukrains'kyi Istoryk 1980 17(1-4): 71-88.* Introduces Mikhail S. Hrushevsky's account of his attempts to initiate various Ukrainian societies and publications in Galicia in the face of vigorous Polish opposition, to radicalize the Ukrainian Populist Party, and to modernize Ukrainian political thinking in Galicia and in the Russian Ukraine. His organizational skills were also devoted to building a solid base under the Shevchenko Scientific Society and to popularizing the Ukrainian cause in lectures for young people. 1895-1925

3098. Wynar, Lubomyr. MATERIALY DO BIOHRAFII MYKHAILA HRUSHEVS'KOHO [Materials for the biography of Mykhailo Hrushevs'kyi]. *Ukrains'kyi Istoryk 1982 19(1-2): 65-75.* Publishes five letters which provide information concerning the life and scholarship of the renowned Ukrainian historian Mykhailo Hrushevs'kyi (1866-1934): one letter each from Nikolai Voiakovs'kyi, Kost' Pan'kivs'kyi (1894-1974), and Mykola Chubatyi (1889-1975), and two from Mykhailo Ieremiiv. 19 notes. 1866-1934

3099. [Wynar, Lubomyr R.]. BIBLIOHRAFIIA PRATS' PRO MYKHAILA HRUSHEVS'KOHO. [Bibliography of publications on Mikhail S. Hrushevsky]. *Ukrains'kyi Istoryk 1984 21(1-4): 291-319.* A partially annotated bibliography of publications pertaining to the renowned Ukrainian historian Mikhail S. Hrushevsky (1866-1934), prepared to commemorate the 50th anniversary of his death. Containing 399 entries, the bibliography comprises five parts: bibliography of bibliographies, articles and books, encyclopedic entries, special serial issues, and published primary sources. 1866-1934

Hryhorenko, Petro

3100. Hryhorenko, Petro. SPOHADY [Recollections]. *Sučasnist [West Germany] 1981 (2): 45-60.* Excerpts from memoirs of World War I in the Ukraine and his activities in the human and national rights movement in the Soviet Ukraine in the 1960's. 1914-70

Hu Hanmin

3101. Barrett, David P. THE ROLE OF HU HANMIN IN THE "FIRST UNITED FRONT": 1922-27. *China Q. [Great Britain] 1982 (89): 34-64.* Critical of the Chinese Communists since the Shanghai meeting of 1924, Hu Hanmin returned from a winter in Moscow, 1925-26, prepared to work against continued Guomindang-Communist cooperation. Though impressed with the strength of the Soviet Union, Hu saw the Comintern as a front for Russian imperialism. A nationalist above all else, he turned against the Communists to save China and the revolutionary ideals of Sun Zhongshan (Sun Yat-sen). Based on Chinese and Russian materials; 143 notes. 1922-27

Hu Jintao

3102. —. SOME NEW FACES ON THE 12TH CCP CENTRAL COMMITTEE. *Issues & Studies [Taiwan] 1983 19(2): 72-77, (3): 79-83.* Part 1. Brief biographies of five new Central Committee members who are scientific and technical specialists, several of whom were victims of the Cultural Revolution: mining engineer Yu Hongen (Yü Hung-en); nuclear engineers Jiang Xinxiong (Chiang Hsin-hsiung) and Peng Shilu (P'eng Shih-lu); petroleum engineer Zhao Zongnai (Chao Tsung-nai); and radio specialist Li Huifen. Part 2. Four new members of the CCP Central Committee are representative of current party policy to promote competent younger cadres. Automobile plant technician Wang Zhaoguo (Wang Chao-kuo, b. 1941); Hu Jintao (Hu Chin-t'ao, b. 1943), a graduate of Tsinghua University; Yang Di (Yang Ti, b. 1923), with a background in public security, and educator Xing Zhikang (Hsing Chih-k'ang, b. 1931) all rose to prominence since the late 1970's. Based on Mainland media reports; 11 notes. 1976-82

Hu Sheng

3103. —. HU SHENG—PRESIDENT OF THE ACADEMY OF SOCIAL SCIENCES. *Issues & Studies [Taiwan] 1985 21(12): 111-117.* A brief history of the Chinese Academy of Social Sciences and a biography of its new president, Hu Sheng, who was appointed in 1985. Hu (b. 1918) has been active in the CCP since the Sino-Japanese conflict. Educated as a philosopher, he has written an important work on politics and held journalism and propaganda assignments. His experience indicates an ideological emphasis in his appointment. Based on Chinese publications; 5 notes. 1937-85

Hu Shi

3104. Hu Shih. THE REMINISCENCES OF DR. HU SHIH.

THE REMINISCENCES OF DR. HU SHIH, PART 2. *Chinese Studies in Hist. 1981 14(3): 70-101.* Hu Shi's reliance upon critical, historical, and comparative methodological analysis got him into trouble with Chinese Marxists, who mistakenly believed that his method was a ploy to attack Marxist socialism. The very same approach to learning greatly aided Hu in his reinterpretation of China's cultural heritage and especially on his revisionist work on Chan (Zen) Buddhism.

HISTORICAL RESEARCH IN THE POPULAR NOVELS (1922-1933), *Chinese Studies in Hist. 1982 15(3-4): 156-168.* Details Hu Shi's progress in studying Chinese vernacular literature and his application of critical and scientific methods of literary research (textual criticism, higher criticism, and critical historical study) to determine the best texts of these novels as well as to discover biographical information on the authors.

SOME CONCLUDING REMARKS ON THE PROGRESS AND SETBACKS OF THE CHINESE RENAISSANCE MOVEMENT, *Chinese Studies in Hist. 1982 15(3-4): 169-188.* Clarifies reflections on the influence of Buddhism, Confucianism, and Lao Tzu on Chinese religious and intellectual life. Also contains the author's observations on the Neo-Confucian movement, the dual development of Chinese literature, and the medieval barbarization of the Chinese language. 3c-20c

Hu Yaobang

3105. Lee Tsung-ying. EASTERN DIARY. *Eastern Horizon [Hong Kong] 1981 20(8): 1-6.* 1981
*For abstract see **Hua Guofeng***

3106. Ts'ai Yu-ch'en. HU YAO-PANG: HIS CAREER AND PROSPECTS. *Issues & Studies [Taiwan] 1981 17(11): 8-21.* Hu Yaobang (Hu Yao-pang, b. 1915) has been active in the Communist Party since his early teens. Since his post-Cultural Revolution rehabilitation, he has contributed to high-level Party actions, including the de-Maofication campaign. In June 1981 he was appointed Party Chairman. Hu's chances to succeed Deng Xiaoping (Teng Hsiao-p'ing) depend on whether Deng and his followers can improve the Chinese economy. 1920's-81

Hu Zhi

3107. Taylor, Rodney L. JOURNEY INTO SELF: THE AUTOBIOGRAPHICAL REFLECTIONS OF HU CHIH. *Hist. of Religions 1982 21(4): 321-338.* Hu Zhi (Hu Chih) (1517-85) was a thinker of the Ming Dynasty, a follower of Wang Yangming in search of self-cultivation and sagehood according to the Confucian tradition. The autobiography of Hu Zhi, *Kun Xue Ji (K'un Hsueh Chi),* or *Recollections of the Toils of Learning,* details the events of his interior religious life, with little attention to the positions he occupied during the years of his autobiographical record. After committing himself to sagehood, he at first embraced Confucianism, but soon became interested in Buddhism. While studying the latter, and practicing a Buddhist form of meditation, he had two enlightenment experiences. After the second experience, he became convinced of the superiority of the Confucian ethic over Buddhism and readopted this way of thinking, which stresses calmness of mind along with compassion and service to humanity rather than Buddhist detachment. Later in life, after several earlier attempts, he passed the highest examination and experienced a correspondence between his inner and outer life. 119 notes. 1542-85

Hua Guofeng

3108. Fontana, Dorothy Grouse. BACKGROUND TO THE FALL OF HUA GUOFENG. *Asian Survey 1982 22(3): 237-260.* In 1976 when Hua Guofeng emerged triumphant after the death of Mao Zedong and the arrest of the Gang of Four, few would have predicted his downfall by the end of 1978 with a political resurgence by twice-purged Deng Xiaoping. Hua rose to power on the strength of his alliances with the Whateverists and the Northern Military Leaders, while his own power base was far more limited. Although he had many apparent advantages, he was outmaneuvered and gradually forced back by Deng and his Southern allies. Based on radio broadcasts and newspapers; 56 notes, 2 fig. 1976-78

3109. Lee Tsung-ying. EASTERN DIARY. *Eastern Horizon [Hong Kong] 1981 20(8): 1-6.* Examines the substitution of Hu Yaobang for Hua Guofeng as the Chairman of the Communist Party of China, detailing Hua's political career and the reasons for his fall from power, and analyzes the resolution that disposed of Hua and discussed Mao Zedong's role in Chinese history and the impact of the Cultural Revolution. 1981

Huang, Zongxi

3110. Fisher, Tom. LOYALIST ALTERNATIVES IN THE EARLY CH'ING. *Harvard Journal of Asiatic Studies 1984 44(1): 83-122.* Huang Zongxi (Huang Tsung-hsi, 1610-95) and Lü Liuliang (Lü Liu-liang, 1629-83), both notable 17th-century Chinese scholars, enjoyed a friendship of respect and shared a common interest in neo-Confucianism. However, their friendship ended due to personal, philosophical and political issues, particularly their divergent interpretations of neo-Confucian dynastic legalism. Though both were Ming loyalists, Huang finally accommodated to the Qing government after an initial period of fierce resistance. Lü, after an initial period of accommodation, became extremist in his resistance and critical of Huang's cooperation with the new regime. However, the record of events leading to the rupture of their friendship will never be fully known due to the poor scholarship of one of their contemporaries, Quan Zuwang (Ch'üan Tsu-wang). Secondary sources; 143 notes. 1635-70

Huang Yanpei

3111. Kabayashi, Yoshifumi. KŌ EN-BAI TO SHOKUGYŌ KYŌIKU UNDŌ [Huang Yanpei (Huang Yen-p'ei) and the movement for vocational education]. *Tōyōshi Kenkyū [Japan] 1981 39(4): 1-32.* Reveals the historical implications and limits of the movement for vocational education, which developed in the 1910's and declined in the early 1930's. Huang Yanpei played the central role therein with his educational thoughts and practices. He tried to do away with the abuses of China's traditional aesthetic education by advocating vocational education. He was strongly influenced by the idea of pragmatism. His demand for pragmatic education initially obtained strong approval. Meanwhile, due to the poor educational environment under warlord rule and Huang's indifference to the revolutionary movements, Huang lost the suppport of the middle classes, who were expecting an increase of ideal workers, and of students advocating nationalism. Based mainly on *Chiao-yü Tsa-chih Hsin-chiao-yü, Tung-fang Tsa-chih,* and *Shih-pao;* 136 notes, 5 tables. 1904-37

Hubatsch, Walther

3112. Salewski, Michael. WALTHER HUBATSCH ZUM GEDENKEN: 17. MAI 1915-29. DEZEMBER 1984 [In memory of Walther Hubatsch: 17 May 1915-29 December 1984]. *Zeitschrift für Religions- und Geistesgeschichte [West Germany] 1986 38(2): 186-189.* Walther Hubatsch was a prolific conservative German historian. He was one of the first to write in defense of Prussia against the collective condemnation, focusing his research on Prussian reforms in the early 19th century and especially on the personality of Count Friedrich Karl vom Stein (1757-1831). His investigations of the Prussian system of administration have opened new vistas of awareness and inquiry. 3 notes. 19c

Hubay, Miklós

3113. Kabdebó, Lóránt. ABROAD FOR THE DURATION: MIKLÓS HUBAY ON THE EARLY FORTIES. *New Hungarian Q. [Hungary] 1982 (85): 95-108.* Interviews Hungarian playwright Miklós Hubay, with special reference to his wartime stay in Switzerland, his work for *La Nouvelle Revue de Hongrie,* contact with Hungarian diplomats, life in a neutral country during World War II, and the propagation of Hungarian literature. Transcript of an interview conducted in September 1980. 1940's

Huber, George

3114. Huber, George; Reeb, Paul, interviewer. GEORGE HUBER: AN INTERVIEW. *Heritage Review 1984 14(3): 35-44.* Interview with George Huber, who because of his German ancestry was sent to Siberia for 15 years by the Soviet Russians after World War II. 1944-82

Huber, Nurse

3115. McKale, Donald M.; Becker, Peter and Barrett, Michael, commentary. PURGING NAZIS: THE POSTWAR TRIALS OF FEMALE GERMAN DOCTORS AND NURSES. *Pro. of the South Carolina Hist. Assoc. 1981: 156-170.* 1941-48

For abstract see ***Flocker, Dr.***

Hübner, Alexander von

3116. Austensen, Roy A. ALEXANDER VON HÜBNER AND THE REVOLUTION OF 1848: A REASSESSMENT. *Consortium on Revolutionary Europe 1750-1850: Proceedings 1985 15: 282-301.* Alexander von Hübner was an important Austrian diplomat, author, and protege of Metternich. He served as an envoy in a number of capitals before his retirement in 1871. His latter years were spent writing travel narratives and accounts of his diplomatic service. His published diary's account of the Revolution of 1848 made him an important source for early historians of the period. The discovery of a major portion of the original diary has yielded more information on his life, and has revealed differences between the published and the unpublished versions of the document. The changes that he made prior to publication tended to justify his actions, as well as those of his mentor, Metternich. Based on materials in the Institute of Medieval and Modern History of the University of Padua; 44 notes. 1848

Hudson, Michael

3117. Sanderson, John B. MICHAEL HUDSON AND THE IMPLICATIONS OF ORDER. *Durham University Journal [Great Britain] 1985 77(2): 179-185.* Michael Hudson (1605-48), cleric, scholar, and soldier, was the former tutor and a staunch defender of King Charles I during the English Civil War. Hudson attacked Parliamentarians by claiming that God, a God of order, had not left it to man to choose the form of government he wished to be ruled under. Primary sources; 76 notes. 1647-49

Huggins, Godfrey

3118. Gann, L. H. LORD MALVERN (SIR GODFREY HUGGINS): A REAPPRAISAL. *Journal of Modern African Studies [Great Britain] 1985 23(4): 723-728.* Sir Godfrey Huggins played a key role in the history of British Central Africa, as Prime Minister of Southern Rhodesia from 1933 to 1953 and then as Prime Minister of the Federation of Rhodesia and Nyasaland until 1956. Huggins was a British immigrant to Rhodesia, who had served in the medical service during World War I and remained a late-Victorian moderate Tory throughout his long political career. Although overtaken by events in Rhodesia and cast into oblivion or ill repute by later African nationalists, Huggins ruled Rhodesia peacefully for many years and sought to uplift both Europeans and Africans through economic, medical, and educational advances. 1933-56

Hughes, Herbert

3119. Browne, John Paddy. HERBERT HUGHES (1882-1937), HIS IRISH COUNTRY SONGS. *Éire-Ireland 1982 17(3): 103-112.* Herbert Hughes, an arranger of Irish music for concerts, broadcasts, recordings, and motion pictures, recovered over 400 fragments and complete tunes of Irish country songs. Many of these were obtained from workhouse inmates in County Donegal, as Percy Grainger, Ralph Vaughan Williams, and other collectors had done in similar English institutions. Through the phonograph record, many old songs collected by Hughes were reintroduced to later generations in Ireland. Based on Hughes's unpublished papers, his published music collections, and interviews; 24 notes. 1902-36

Hughes, Hugh Price

3120. King, William McGuire. HUGH PRICE HUGHES AND THE BRITISH "SOCIAL GOSPEL." *Journal of Religious History [Australia] 1984 13(1): 66-82.* Assesses the contributions of Wesleyan Methodist minister Hugh Price Hughes (1847-1902) to the British, or Victorian, Nonconformity movement of the 1880's and 1890's. Past attempts to appraise Hughes's success as a leader have failed to separate Hughes's activity as an advocate of social or responsible Christianity from his role as leader of the controversial Forward Movement, a ministry-led crusade for social reform accused by many of being either over-radical or too concerned with personal power. All controversy over the Forward Movement aside, Hughes's importance was in his skill and success as a popularizer of the social gospel. Based in part on articles in the *Methodist Times* and other primary and secondary sources; 94 notes. 1880-1905

Hughes, John

3121. Connor, Charles P. ARCHBISHOP HUGHES AND THE QUESTION OF IRELAND, 1829-1862. *Records of the American Catholic Historical Society of Philadelphia 1984 95(1-4): 15-26.* As an Irish immigrant and bishop to New York's largely Irish-Catholic population, Archbishop John Hughes was unavoidably involved in "the Irish question"—Irish independence from British rule. Hughes supported Daniel O'Connell's Catholic emancipation movement in Ireland, but rejected such radical and violent societies as the Young Irelanders and the National Brotherhood. Hughes also disapproved of American-Irish radical fringe groups, urging immigrants to assimilate themselves into American life while remaining patriotic to Ireland "only individually." In Hughes's view, a large-scale movement to form Irish settlements in the western United States was too isolationist and ultimately detrimental to immigrants' success in the New World. From an address delivered at the Catholic Historical Association meeting, Villanova University, April 1984. Based on the Hughes Papers and secondary sources; 54 notes. 1829-62

Hugo, Adèle

3122. Dufresne, Claude. ETRE MADAME VICTOR HUGO, HELAS! [To be Madame Victor Hugo, alas!]. *Historama [France] 1985 (15): 50-56.* Evokes the intimate and romantic portrait of Adèle Hugo, wife of Victor Hugo (1802-85), who, in spite of her life with a difficult, selfish, and unfaithful husband and her own weaknesses, always remained a friend of the French writer and kept intact their conjugal relationship. 1819-68

Hugo, Léopold

3123. Decaux, Alain. LEOPOLD HUGO AU PIEGE DE SOPHIE TREBUCHET [Léopold Hugo in the snare of Sophie Trébuchet]. *Historama [France] 1984 (10): 28-36.* The ancestry, lives, and careers of Léopold Hugo and his wife Sophie Trébuchet were rather more pedestrian than their son, Victor, and they themselves portrayed them. Léopold's republican exploits as a battalion chief were overstated by Victor Hugo, a treatment he also accorded his mother's personal qualities. 1707-1825

3124. Ricaumont, Jacques de. LE ROMAN DE SOPHIE TREBUCHET [The romance of Sophie Trebuchet]. *Rev. des Deux Mondes [France] 1983 (10): 111-114.* 1772-1821
For abstract see ***Trebuchet, Sophie***

Huidobro, Vicente

3125. Araya, Guillermo. EN TORNO A VICENTE HUIDOBRO [Vicente Huidobro]. *Bull. Hispanique [France] 1981 83(1-2): 163-174.* Reviews the special edition of *Revista Iberoamericana* issued in 1979, number 106-107, and dedicated to the Chilean poet Vicente Huidobro. Huidobro opted early in his career to seek to be a universal poet, with no ties to a particular country. To accomplish this ambition, he became a self-exiled writer with Paris as his home. Huidobro based the essential aspect of his poetic doctrine, creationism, on rebellion against nature, preferring the production of new forms to the imitation of conventional natural beings. Between 1920 and 1930, Huidobro anticipated the linguistic revolution that would begin with Noam Chomsky's *Syntactic Structures* in 1954. 18 notes. 1920-30

Hulak, Mykola

3126. Marchenko, Valerii. MYKOLA HULAK [Mykola Hulak]. *Sučasnist [West Germany] 1982 (4-5): 117-136.* Born into a rich Ukrainian family, Mykola Hulak received an excellent education; wrote several works in German and French; and joined the antitsarist Brotherhood of Cyril and Methodius. He was imprisoned in 1847 and released two decades later. 1822-81

Hulewicz, Jan

3127. Dutkowa, Renata. JAN HULEWICZ (19 V 1907-7 X 1980) [Jan Hulewicz, 1907-80]. *Kwartalnik Hist. [Poland] 1982 89(4): 759-762.* Jan Hulewicz as a historian of learning and education left a permanent mark through his research, editorial work, and teacher training. Under the influence of Stanisław Kot, he turned to the history of education and culture and established life-long contact with the peasant movement. During the war he served in the government-in-exile. After the war he taught at the University of Cracow. Contrary to the reigning methodology, he emphasized the role of the individual in history rather than impersonal forces. He made a great contribution as editor of the National Library series published by the Ossolineum Press. 4 notes. 1907-80

Hullah, John

3128. Leinster-Mackay, D. JOHN HULLAH, JOHN CURWEN AND SARAH GLOVER: A CLASSIC CASE OF "WHIGGERY" IN THE HISTORY OF MUSICAL EDUCATION? *British J. of Educ. Studies [Great Britain] 1981 29(2): 164-167.* 1840's-60's
For abstract see ***Curwen, John***

Hulme, Thomas E.

3129. Csengeri, Karen Elaine. "The Life and Work of T. E. Hulme." U. of Michigan 1985. 351 pp. *DAI 1985 46(4): 977-A.* DA8512392 ca 1900-17

Humbert, Georges

3130. Humbert, Jacques. LE GENERAL GEORGES HUMBERT GOUVERNEUR DE STRASBOURG 1919-1921 [General Georges Humbert, governor of Strasbourg 1919-21]. *Rev. Hist. des Armées [France] 1981 (3): 116-130.* After an outstanding career, General Georges Humbert (1862-1921) was appointed military governor of Strasbourg and commandant of the territory of Alsace. In this capacity his main tasks were to participate in numerous patriotic ceremonies, military reviews, and receptions for notable visitors, and to establish cordial relations between the troops and the civilian population. As a member of the superior war council, he initiated a study of the strategic utilization of Alsace. Based on personal recollections of the author; 8 photos. 1919-21

Humboldt, Alexander von

3131. Bateman, Alfredo. LOS PERSONAJES DE LA EXPEDICION BOTANICA [Personages of the Botanical Expedition]. *Boletín de Historia y Antigüedades [Colombia] 1984 71(747): 907-964.* 18c-19c
For abstract see ***Caballero y Góngora, Antonio***

3132. Honigmann, Peter. ALEXANDER VON HUMBOLDTS BEZIEHUNGEN ZUR UNIVERSITAT DORPAT [Alexander von Humboldt's relationship to the University of Dorpat]. *Jahrbuch für Gesch. der Sozialistischen Länder Europas [East Germany] 1982 26(1): 151-168.* Alexander von Humboldt's relationship to the University of Dorpat is examined in the context of his association with Russia. Throughout his long life, Humboldt conducted many research enterprises in Russia. The high point of his Russian experiences came in the summer months of 1829 when he visited the Urals, the Altai, and the Caspian Sea. Humboldt writings in East German and Leningrad archives, and secondary sources; a letter from Humboldt to S. S. Uvarov on 18 May 1842, and a list of 35 students and professors with whom Humboldt corresponded; 107 notes. 1792-1859

Humboldt, Wilhelm von

3133. Petronijević, Božinka. WILHELM VON HUMBOLDT IN DER SPRACHWISSENSCHAFTLICHEN LITERATUR AUF DEM SERBOKROATISCHEN SPRACHGEBIET [Wilhelm von Humboldt in the Serbocroatian philological literature]. *Wissenschaftliche Zeitschrift der Humboldt-Universität zu Berlin. Gesellschaftswissenschaftliche Reihe [East Germany] 1984 33(5): 505-508.* Discusses the treatment of Wilhelm von Humboldt as philosopher of language and as founder of universal linguistics. Also notes morphological linguistic typology in Serbocroatian philological research from 1858-83. 19c

Humphreys, R. A.

3134. Collier, Simon. AN INTERVIEW WITH R. A. HUMPHREYS. *Hispanic Am. Hist. Rev. 1982 62(2): 180-192.* R. A. Humphreys, the English Latin American historian, studied at Cambridge and the University of Michigan before accepting a teaching position at University College, London. He remained there from 1932 until his retirement in 1974. He has been a key figure in the establishment of Latin American studies in Great Britain and is now completing a two-volume work, *Latin America and the Second World War.* He discusses his life and his philosophy of history in this interview. Based on an interview conducted in Humphrey's home in Cantonbury, London, 14 July 1981; biblio. 1930's-81

Hunnius, Anton Christian

3135. Weisert, John J. DR. ANTHONY HUNN: FROM STORM AND STRESS TO TEMPEST AND SUNSHINE. *Filson Club Hist. Q. 1982 56(2): 211-224.* A biographical sketch of Anton Christian Hunnius. Born in Weimar, Germany, he spent his early adult years trying to achieve fame as a poet, actor, and dramatist. His most successful play was a comedy, *Der Taubstumme.* Dissatisfied with the lifestyle of theater, Hunnius prepared a rigorous personal study program in medical school. Soon after he graduated, he immigrated to Kentucky where he immediately established a successful medical practice. Shortening his name to Hunn, the new American also became a newspaper editor who was involved in disputes with Henry Clay and American nativists. In 1829, Hunn published *The Medical Friend of the People* which was a newspaper about his experiences as a doctor. He died in Kentucky in 1834. Secondary materials in German and contemporary Kentucky newspapers; 30 notes. 1765-1834

Hunt, Henry

3136. Belchem, John. "ORATOR" HUNT, 1773-1835: A BRITISH RADICAL REASSESSED. *History Today [Great Britain] 1985 35(Mar): 21-27.* Considers the career of political orator Henry Hunt (1773-1835), pointing out his important contributions to the development of British working-class radicalism. 1815-35

Hunter, John (1728-1793)

3137. Jacyna, L. S. IMAGES OF JOHN HUNTER IN THE NINETEENTH CENTURY. *Hist. of Sci. [Great Britain] 1983 21(1): 85-108.* The history of science has generally been a study of the lives and careers of great men. Like Newton and Cuvier, John Hunter (1728-93) was seen as a "catastrophic" figure whose career marked a turning point. The conventional view is that he brought science and medicine firmly into alliance, demonstrated the relevance of physiology to pathology and therapeutics, and showed that the world could be ordered into a "natural system" based on the correlation of structure with function. The architects of this image were the early Hunterian orators at the Royal College of Surgeons. Contemporary surgeons wished to burnish Hunter's image so that they could aspire to the rank of gentlemen. They wished to stress the intellectual significance of surgery and assert that they were a learned profession. Examination of Hunter's own writings is needed to determine his true contribution as opposed to a reputation based on a conscription of his name for polemical purposes. Based on primary sources; 76 notes. 18c-19c

Hunter, John (1754-1809)

3138. Wilkinson, Lise. "THE OTHER" JOHN HUNTER, M.D., F.R.S. (1754-1809): HIS CONTRIBUTIONS TO THE MEDICAL LITERATURE, AND TO THE INTRODUCTION OF ANIMAL EXPERIMENTS INTO INFECTIOUS DISEASE RESEARCH. *Notes and Records of the Royal Soc. of London [Great Britain] 1982 36(2): 227-242.* The lesser known John Hunter does not deserve the neglect of historians. He wrote extensively on disease in Jamaica, typhus in London, and on a post-mortem abnormality. He has been eclipsed by the scientist and researcher also named John Hunter, a contemporary and colleague in the Royal Society. 77 notes. 1770's-1809

Hunter, Joseph

3139. Godfrey, Peter B. JOSEPH HUNTER, 1783-1861. *Tr. of the Unitarian Hist. Soc. [Great Britain] 1984 18(2): 17-23.* Briefly recounts the life of the Unitarian scholar and antiquary, Joseph Hunter (1783-1861). 1783-1861

Hunter, Robert

3140. Lustig, Mary Lou. "Eboracensis: The Public Career of Robert Hunter (1666-1734)." Syracuse U. 1982. 516 pp. *DAI 1983 43(8): 2766-A.* DA8228996 1691-1734

Hunter, William

3141. Porter, Roy. WILLIAM HUNTER, SURGEON. *Hist. Today [Great Britain] 1983 33(Sept): 50-52.* William Hunter, a prominent Scottish physician in London, instituted university training for surgeons and initiated the field of obstetrics in formal medicine. 1740's-60's

Hurtado, Osvaldo

3142. Needler, Martin C. THE PRESIDENT OF ECUADOR. *Contemporary Rev. [Great Britain] 1984 244(1417): 57-61.* Outlines both the career of Osvaldo Hurtado, the president of Ecuador, and Ecuador's socioeconomic and political history ca. 1945-81. Also considers the problems now facing the country. ca 1945-83

Husa, Karel

3143. McLaurin, Donald Malcolm. "The Life and Works of Karel Husa with Emphasis on the Significance of His Contribution to the Wind Band." Florida State U. 1985. 241 pp. *DAI 1985 46(4): 834-A.* DA8513387 1940's-82

Husák, Gustáv

3144. Barnovský, Michal. GUSTÁV HUSÁK A NAŠA CESTA K FEBRUÁRU 1948 [Gustáv Husák and our way toward February 1948]. *Hist. Časopis [Czechoslovakia] 1983 31(1): 3-13.* Uses the anniversary of Communist coup of February 1948 in Czechoslovakia to evaluate the political and organizational work of Czech President Gustáv Husák. From 1944 to 1948, Husák was able to unite and coordinate revolutionary demands of different groups of working people and cope with reactionary intrigues of the defeated bourgeoisie. In this way he enhanced the political influence of the Communists in Slovakia and throughout the whole state. Based on published sources; 16 notes. 1944-48

3145. Ivanov, S. I. GUSTAV GUSAK: K 70-LETIIU SO DNIA ROZHDENIIA [Gustav Husák: in commemoration of the 70th anniversary of his birth]. *Voprosy Istorii KPSS [USSR] 1983 (1): 117-121.* Husák joined the Communist Party in 1933 when a student at Bratislav University. During the war he fought with the underground and was one of the leaders of the Slovak national uprising in 1944. Arrested in 1951, he was released in 1960 and reinstated into the Party in 1963. In 1971 he became General Secretary of the Central Committee of the Czecholsovakian Communist Party. Husák has always been a close adherent to Marxism-Leninism and a supporter of friendship with the Soviet Union. Czechoslovakian Communist Party and secondary sources; 7 notes. 1929-81

3146. Plevza, Viliam. GUSTÁV HUSÁK A SPOLOČENSKÉ VEDY (K 70. NARODENINÁM) [Gustáv Husák and the social sciences: on his 70th birthday]. *Československý Časopis Hist. [Czechoslovakia] 1983 31(1): 1-23.* Gustáv Husák (b. 1913), First Secretary of the Communist Party of Czechoslovakia, became a Party member in 1933, while attending the University of Bratislava. Aside from his leading role in the resistance during World War II, his leadership in postwar Slovakia, and his solution of the Czechoslovak troubles in the 1960's, he maintained a lively interest in history and the social sciences. The current Czechoslovak emphasis on Marxist-Leninist methodology owes something to his direction. 56 notes. Russian and German summaries. 1933-83

Husarski, Julian

3147. Roszkowski, Wojciech. JULIAN HUSARSKI—PIONIER KAPITALIZMU PAŃSTWOWEGO W POLSCE [Julian Husarski, a pioneer of state capitalism in Poland]. *Przegląd Hist. [Poland] 1981 72(3): 447-459.* Julian Husarski (1878-1930), a Polish engineer and amateur economist (influenced by Thorstein B. Veblen), despite personal capitalist successes in earlier life, became a proponent of the nationalization of large capital. Although he held certain economic posts in the Polish administration between the Wars, Husarski's views, sometimes hard to interpret and clarify, never gained a wider acceptance. Based on primary and secondary sources; 41 notes. Russian and French summaries. 1920's

Husrev Paşa

3148. Bacqué-Grammont, Jean-Louis. NOTES ET DOCUMENTS SUR DIVÂNE HÜSREV PAŞA [Notes and documents on Husrev Paşa the Mad]. *Rocznik Orientalistyczny [Poland] 1979 41(1): 21-55.* A reconstruction of the career of Husrev Paşa the Mad (Intrepid) who, from 1521 to his death (ca. 1545) served Suleiman I (the Magnificent) both in the field and as governor of important provinces such as Egypt and Anatolia. Based on documents in Topkapi Palace Museum, Istanbul; 2 photos, 105 notes. 1520-50

Huss, Magnus

3149. Bernard, Henri. ALCOOLISME ET ANTIALCOOLISME EN FRANCE AU XIXe SIECLE: AUTOUR DE MAGNUS HUSS [Alcoholism and antialcoholism in France in the 19th century: in relation to Magnus Huss]. *Histoire, Economie et Société [France] 1984 3(4): 609-628.* Examines the consumption of alcohol in France during the 19th century, with attention to the social and political repercussions of its excessive use. Focuses attention on the fight against alcoholism undertaken by Magnus Huss (1807-90), a Swede who became medical director of a clinic in Séraphins, and whose direct influence and publications contributed greatly to the understanding of chronic alcoholism. The author discusses his contributions to French medicine, and to the fight by the French medical establishment against alcoholism. 2 illus., 84 notes. 19c

Hussein, Saddam

3150. Baram, Amazia. SADDĀM HUSSEIN: A POLITICAL PROFILE. *Jerusalem Q. [Israel] 1980 (17): 115-144.* Gives a political biography of Saddām Hussein al-Tikrītī, the president of the Iraqi Republic and a significant political leader whose actions affect the stability and peace of the Middle East. 1937-80

3151. Bengio, Ofra. SADDAM HUSAYN'S QUEST FOR POWER AND SURVIVAL. *Asian and African Studies [Israel] 1981 15(3): 323-341.* Saddam Hussein has survived as ruler of Iraq through a skillful balancing act that has been based on his control of the Baath Party, the armed forces, and a large internal security apparatus. Based on Iraqi sources; 30 notes. 1979-82

Husseini, Amin al-

3152. Carpi, David. THE MUFTI OF JERUSALEM, AMIN EL-HUSSEINI, AND HIS DIPLOMATIC ACTIVITY DURING WORLD WAR II (OCTOBER 1941-JULY 1943). *Studies in Zionism [Israel] 1983 (7): 101-132.* Muhammad Amin al- Husseini spent the late 1930's in various Middle Eastern capitals after his exile from Jerusalem. In 1941, Italian ambassador Mellini was sent to Teheran to bring Husseini to Italy, where he could live in safety. Once in Italy, the Mufti began a political and diplomatic effort to focus popular Arab support toward helping the Axis. Mussolini lent his support for Arab control of Palestine and suggested that the Mufti and Adolf Hitler speak as well. This discussion was less successful; Hitler did not endorse Arab control over any part of the region. In 1942 the Mufti and Iraq's Rashid 'Ali el-Kilani vied for recognition as the leaders of the Arab movement. This struggle lessened the impact of both of their philosophies on their Italian hosts. By mid-1943 the Axis already had lost North Africa and all of the Mufti's hopes were dashed. He remained in Germany until the war ended. Based on archives of the Italian Foreign Office. 1941-43

3153. Jbara, Taysir Yunes. "Al-Hajj Muhammad Amīn Al-Husaynī, Muftī of Jerusalem, the Palestine Years 1921-1937." New York U. 1982. 292 pp. *DAI 1983 43(11): 3676-A.* DA8307832 1921-37

Husserl, Edmund

3154. Baron, Lawrence. DISCIPLESHIP AND DISSENT: THEODOR LESSING AND EDMUND HUSSERL. *Pro. of the Am. Phil. Soc. 1983 127(1): 32-49.* 1890-1910
*For abstract see **Lessing, Theodor***

3155. Jaegerschmid, Adelgundis. DIE LETZTEN JAHRE EDMUND HUSSERLS (1936-1938) [The last years of Edmund Husserl, 1936-38]. *Stimmen der Zeit [West Germany] 1981 199(2): 129-138.* Describes the last years of the philosopher Husserl, during which he suffered from the Nazi persecution of Jews and illness. 1936-38

Hutchings, Frederick George Baxendale

3156. Bebbington, John. COMRADE AND CAPTAIN. *Library Review [Great Britain] 1985 34(Spr): 10-13.* The deputy librarian at Leeds describes the personality and management style of Frederick George Baxendale Hutchings (1902-78), librarian there, 1946-49. 1943-71

3157. Craven, A. B. CITY LIBRARIAN. *Library Review [Great Britain] 1985 34(Spr): 7-9.* Frederick George Baxendale Hutchings (1902-78) succeeded R. J. Gordon as chief librarian of Leeds, 1946-1963, and proceeded to take on the development of branch libraries, renovate the central library, extend services to hospitals and encourage his staff to exercise their talents. 1946-63

3158. Nichols, Harold. CRAFTSMAN AND CLYDESIDER. *Library Review [Great Britain] 1985 34(Spr): 14-17.* Prints reminiscences about Frederick George Baxendale Hutchings (1902-78): his early life as an assistant librarian in the 1930's, innovations at the library at Leeds, his work in Kuala Lumpur, and his lecturing responsibilities. 1930-77

Hutchinson, R. C.

3159. Green, Robert. PAIFORCE: THE NOVELIST AS A MILITARY HISTORIAN. *Army Quarterly and Defence Journal [Great Britain] 1985 115(2): 187-191.* Shows how the English novelist R. C. Hutchinson brought narrative fiction techniques to military history. The British War Office commissioned him to write about the Paiforce (Persian and Iraq Forces) campaign, Britain's defense of Allied oil supplies in the Middle East against German attack in World War II. 1941-46

Hutton, James

3160. Jones, Jean. JAMES HUTTON: EXPLORATION AND OCEANOGRAPHY. *Ann. of Sci. [Great Britain] 1983 40(1): 81-94.* James Hutton is known to have regarded exploration as an important source of geological knowledge and to have studied the accounts of travelers with close attention. Unpublished letters in the Fitzwilliam Museum, Cambridge, however, show that he was more actively involved in exploration than had been previously supposed. During the preparation for Cook's second voyage, he gave advice about both geological and marine research. He advised Banks against making a major voyage to Arctic regions on the grounds that it would be unprofitable geologically. He encouraged Banks and other friends to measure sea and air temperatures on their voyages, and there are indications that he himself took part in marine experiments. His interest in oceanography, which has not been discussed before, is found to complement his work in meteorology. 1770's

3161. Jones, Jean. JAMES HUTTON'S AGRICULTURAL RESEARCH AND HIS LIFE AS A FARMER. *Annals of Science [Great Britain] 1985 42(6): 573-601.* By bringing together information in published and unpublished works of the 18th and early 19th centuries, notably Hutton's unpublished manuscript the "Elements of Agriculture," it is possible to augment our meager knowledge of Hutton's agricultural activities. His decision to farm is discussed, as are his time as a student of agriculture in East Anglia and on the continent (1752-54), his life as a farmer at Slighhouses in Berwickshire (1754-67), his research after he returned to Edinburgh (1767-97), and his opinions on the role of government in agricultural affairs. The section on Slighhouses deals not only with Hutton's agricultural experiments and improvements, but also with his personal life, travel, and scientific studies. Investigation shows that his interest in agriculture gave impetus to his studies in other disciplines, and that his years as a farmer were ones of great intellectual activity which laid the foundation for many of his future achievements, particularly in geology. 1752-97

3162. Jones, Jean. JAMES HUTTON AND THE FORTH AND CLYDE CANAL. *Ann. of Sci. [Great Britain] 1982 39(3): 255-263.* James Hutton held shares in the company that built the Forth and Clyde Canal, and was closely involved in its construction. For seven years he attended meetings on and off the site, helping to decide on the route, the supply of building stone, and other problems. As far as we know it is the only occasion on which he used his geological knowledge in a public enterprise. 1767-88

Huxham, John

3163. Schupbach, William. THE FAME AND NOTORIETY OF DR. JOHN HUXHAM. *Medical Hist. [Great Britain] 1981 25(4): 415-421.* John Huxham was an English physician and the author of numerous treatises, principally on fevers, diphtheria, and smallpox. However, the respect these brought him throughout Europe contrasts with his poor reputation among his Devonshire patients. Huxham's notoriety is here examined in relation to a portrait (ca. 1758-88) of a certain "Miss Irons," defaced by the painting of a mezzotint engraving of an unidentified man. The article questions traditional assumptions regarding the history of the painting, and suggests that Thomas Rennell was the original artist and author of the defacement and that John Huxham was the subject of the mezzotint. Based on memoirs and contemporary records; 4 fig., 22 notes. 1692-1788

Hyde, Edward

3164. Brownley, Martine Watson. THE WOMEN IN CLARENDON'S LIFE AND WORKS. *Eighteenth Cent.: Theory and Interpretation 1981 22(2): 153-174.* Women played prominent roles in the 1st Earl of Clarendon's life, and his attitudes toward them show some of the strengths and weaknesses in his character that molded his public career and his literary practice. He expected little from women, doubted their stability, and believed that their proper sphere was the home. Although he was forced in retrospect to recognize women's increased political participation in the period from Buckingham's assassination to the Restoration, he never reconciled himself to it. Primary sources; 66 notes. 1609-74

3165. Green, Ian. THE PUBLICATION OF CLARENDON'S AUTOBIOGRAPHY AND THE ACQUISITION OF HIS PAPERS BY THE BODLEIAN LIBRARY. *Bodleian Lib. Record [Great Britain] 1982 10(6): 349-367.* Traces the history of the manuscripts of Edward Hyde, 1st Earl of Clarendon's *History of the Rebellion* (1702-04) and of his autobiographical *Life of Edward Earl of Clarendon* (1759), and of their publication. The author's descendants probably gave the manuscript of the latter to the Bodleian Library in order to forestall charges that the text had been tampered with. The gift prompted the creation in the Bodleian of the large collection of Clarendon papers. Based on Clarendon manuscripts and related documents in Bodleian Library, and Chancery papers in Public Record Office, London; 70 notes. 1702-90

I

Iakobi, Pavel

3166. Liubovich, N. A. NOVOE O PAVLE IAKOBI [New information on Pavel Iakobi]. *Novaia i Noveishaia Istoriia [USSR] 1981 (1): 153-157.* Discusses aspects of Russian emigré revolutionary Pavel Iakobi's (1842-1913) activities as an insurgent in the Polish uprising of 1863-64 and, later, as a doctor in Garibaldi's army in France. Based on Aleksandra Iakobi's notebooks, in the Central State Archive of the Literature and Art of the USSR; 12 notes. 1860-71

Iakovlev, Aleksei I.

3167. Dushinov, S. M. LICHNYI FOND A. I. IAKOVLEVA V ARKHIVE AKADEMII NAUK SSSR [Aleksei I. Iakovlev's personal file in the archives of the USSR Academy of Sciences]. *Sovetskie Arkhivy [USSR] 1981 (5): 48-52.* Aleksei Ivanovich Iakovlev (1878-1951) was a renowned Soviet archivist and lecturer on bibliographical and archive matters. The article presents a brief analysis of Iakovlev's large personal archive, now deposited in the Soviet Academy of Sciences Archive. It contains numerous unpublished works and the manuscript of his published work on slavery in 17th-century Muscovy. Three hundred forty five files contain his letters and those of many famous people, including A. M. Kollontai and V. O. Kliuchevski. There are many copies of documents about 18th-century gentry landholding, the church, and published materials about many personalities, including M. N. Speranski. The Archive also contains materials about Iakovlev in other persons' files. Based on the USSR Academy of Sciences Archives, collection no. 665, and a few published works; 42 notes. 17c-18c

Iakubovich, Aleksandr I.

3168. Klibanov, A. I. ALEKSANDR IVANOVICH IAKUBOVICH: DEISTVITEL'NOST' I LEGENDA [Aleksandr Ivanovich Iakubovich: the reality and the legend]. *Istoricheskie Zapiski Akad. Nauk SSSR [USSR] 1981 (106): 205-270.* The Decembrist Aleksandr I. Iakubovich (1792-1845) was contradictory, even for his contemporaries. His 1818-45 letters, especially to O. A. Leporskii, I. D. Kazimirskii, and V. L. Davydov, show that the 1812 war was a lesson in patriotism for him. Between 1820 and 1824 he fought in three wars. Patriotism and realization that the tsarist government was unable to provide good government led him to join the Decembrist movement. After the crushing of the Decembrist revolt he was tried and exiled. This he bore with courage and fortitude, although his family's refusal to communicate with him in exile adversely affected his mental health. 225 notes. 1815-45

Iakubovski, I.

3169. Batov, P. MARSHAL SOVETSKOGO SOIUZA I. I. IAKUBOVSKI (K 70-LETIIU SO DNIA ROZHDENIIA) [Marshal of the Soviet Union I. I. Iakubovski: on the 70th anniversary of his birth]. *Voenno-Istoricheskii Zhurnal [USSR] 1982 24(1): 62-64.* I. I. Iakubovski was born 7 January 1912 in the village of Zaitsevo, Mogilevski district. After graduation from Leningrad armored tank courses he participated in the liberation of the Western Ukraine in 1939 and in the Soviet Finnish war, 1939-40. His military talent was displayed most fully in World War II as commander of a tank brigade and later as deputy commander of the 6th and 7th Tank Guards Corps he took part in many operations including the Stalingrad, Kiev, Silesian, and Berlin campaigns. After the war he was deputy minister of defense and from 1967 to his death in 1976 was commander in chief of the Warsaw Pact Troops. Secondary sources; note, 2 photos. 1912-76

3170. Zinchenko, Iu. I. UCHAST' I. H. IAKUBOVS'KOHO V BOIAKH ZA VYZVOLENNIA UKRAINY VID FASHYSTS'KYKH ZAHARBNYKIV (DO 70-RICHCHIA Z DNIA NARODZHENNIA) [The participation of I. H. Iakubovs'kyi in the war for the liberation of Ukraine from fascist marauders: on the 70th anniversary of his birth]. *Ukrains'kyi Istorychnyi Zhurnal [USSR] 1982 (1): 119-120.* Ivan H. Iakubovs'kyi (1912-76), born of a peasant family, aspired to a military career after training in Leningrad during the 1930's. In World War II he distinguished himself in the tank division and was later awarded the Golden Star and was twice decorated as Hero of the Soviet Union. Note. 1930's-40's

Iakutin, Efrem Vasil'evich

3171. Poletaev, O. GEROI GRAZHDANSKOI VOINY [Heroes of the Civil War]. *Voenno-Istoricheskii Zhurnal [USSR] 1981 23(5): 48-51.* Considers eight of the Heroes of the Civil War: Boris Leonidovich Ostrovski, Nikolai Nikolaevich Petrov, Ivan Fedorovich Rossiiski, Pantelei Alekseevich Surov, Vasili Spiridonovich Taranov, Petr Semenovich Terent'ev, Avgust Andreevich Tsinit, and Efrem Vasil'evich Iakutin. Gives a brief account of the life, career, and present status of each man, with particular reference to his activity during the Civil War and World War II, and subsequent career, quoting at length the honors they received for heroism and service to their country. 4 notes. 1917-22

Iancu, Avram

3172. Vulcan, Iosif; Lăcustă, I., ed. PANTEONUL ROMÂN [Romanian pantheon]. *Magazin Istoric [Romania] 1981 15(5): 17-19, 61.* 1802-68
For abstract see ***Heliade-Rădulescu, Ioan***

Ianin, Valentin L.

3173. Khoroshev, A. S. UCHENYI, PEDAGOG, GRAZHDANIN (K PRISVOENII CHL.-KOR. AN SSSR, PROF. V. L. IANINU LENINSKOI PREMII) [Scholar, pedagogue, citizen: on conferment of the Lenin Prize on professor V. L. Ianin, corresponding member of the Soviet Academy of Sciences]. *Vestnik Moskovskogo Universiteta, Seriia 8: Istoriia [USSR] 1984 (5): 3-7.* Outlines the academic achievements of Valentin L. Ianin, Soviet archeologist at the Moscow State University, awarded the Lenin Prize in 1984. His best known works, dealing with the political history of medieval Novgorod, are *Novgorodskie Posadniki* [The Novgorod Posadniki] (1963) and *Novgorodskaia Feodal'naia Votchina,* [Novgorod Feudal Patrimony] (1981). 1984

Iavornyts'kyi, Dmytro I

3174. Hapusenko, I. M. D. I. IAVORNYTS'KYI IAK ISTORYK (DO 125-RICHCHIA Z DNIA NARODZHENNIA) [D. I. Iavornyts'kyi as a historian (on the 125th anniversary of his birth)]. *Ukrains'kyi Istorychnyi Zhurnal [USSR] 1980 (12): 131-133.* Describes the life and work of Dmytro I. Iavornyts'kyi (1855-1940), a noted Ukrainian historian, archaeologist, and ethnographer, who devoted his scholarly work to the study of the Zaporozhian Cossacks. 9 notes. 1870-1940

Ibáñez, Bernardina and Nicolasa

3175. Roca Castellanos, Manuel. LAS IBAÑEZ ENAMORADAS DE LA LIBERTAD [The Ibáñezes in love with liberty]. *Bol. de Hist. y Antigüedades [Colombia] 1982 69(738): 747-774.* Evokes the memory of Bernardina and Nicolasa Ibáñez, sisters who were linked romantically with Simón Bolívar and Francisco de Paula Santander during the struggle for Colombian independence, and comments on the sources concerning their lives. 1813-35

Ibañez, Carlos

3176. Ramírez Rivera, Hugo Rodolfo. EL PRESIDENTE IBAÑEZ Y LA MASONERIA [President Carlos Ibañez and Freemasonry]. *Historia [Chile] 1981 16: 343-366.* Reproduces, with an introduction, two documents of the Chilean Grand Lodge relating to the second presidential term, 1952-58, of General Carlos Ibañez del Campo. One is the annual message read before the members of the lodge in 1957. In it the Grand Master reveals his apprehensions regarding the weaknesses of the political constitution of Chile, the concentration of power in the hands of the president, and the citizens' indifference to public affairs. The other document contains the texts of two interviews with President Ibañez in which members of the lodge seem to wish to warn him against possible dictatorial tendencies. Texts of documents preserved in private archives; 43 notes. 1952-58

Ibn Saud

3177. Goldberg, Jacob. ABD AL-AZIZ IBN SA'UD V'HADOKTRINA HA'VAHABIT: HIRHURIM AL PARADOKHS [Ibn Saud and the Wahhabi ideology: a paradox]. *Hamizrah Hehadash [Israel] 1981 30(1-4): 107-112.* Ibn Saud is described as an unusual Saudi. He was candid, open-minded, and a great deal more worldly than other Saudi diplomats of his time. His cosmopolitan demeanor is attributed to his childhood in Kuwait, which exposed him to new ideas and customs during his family's exile. Ibn Saud's worldliness caused him to be more temperate than his predecessors in pursuit of Wahhabian ideology, which calls for unlimited expansion of the Saudi domain. Such recognition of the reality of 20th-century politics created opposition to him on the part of traditional Ikhwan backers, culminating in the 1929 Ikhwan rebellion. 25 notes. 1910-29

Ibuse Masuji

3178. Treat, John Whittier. "The Literature of Ibuse Masuji." Yale U. 1982. 413 pp. *DAI 1983 43(12): 3916-A.* DA8310526 1920's-66

Ichikawa Fusae

3179. Takeda, Kiyoko. ICHIKAWA FUSAE: PIONEER FOR WOMEN'S RIGHTS IN JAPAN. *Japan Quarterly [Japan] 1984 31(4): 410-415.* Ichikawa Fusae (1893-1980) served before the war in the uphill struggle to secure women's rights to express their political thoughts, and after the war she led the campaign to educate women in the use of their newly-won suffrage. A thinker and an activist as well as an excellent organizer, she was committed to parliamentary government and universal suffrage; she rejected socialism and was an enemy of political corruption. 1930's-80

Ideville, Henri D'

3180. Guyon, Edouard-Félix. UN SECRÉTAIRE D'AMBASSADE SOUS LE SECOND EMPIRE: HENRI D'IDEVILLE [An embassy secretary under the Second Empire: Henri D'Ideville]. *Rev. d'Hist. Diplomatique [France] 1980 94(4): 352-375.* Henri-Amédée Le Lorgne D'Ideville's *Journal d'un Diplomate,* published in 1872, contains an account of his activities as a secretary at the French embassies in Turin, Rome, Athens, and finally Dresden from 1859 to 1869. He wrote of political affairs and also of the daily life of a diplomat and his impressions of the cities where he was posted. The journal contains details about French policy toward Italian unification and the Roman question in the 1860's, the Cretan revolt of 1867, and the political position of Saxony in 1869. D'Ideville's personal testimony illuminates the relatively small official and diplomatic world of the four capitals and records his impressions of sovereigns and ministers, most notably Cavour and Pius IX. 2 notes. 1859-69

Idris family

3181. Reissner, Johannes. DIE IDRISIDEN IN ASIR: EIN HISTORISCHER ÜBERBLICK [The Idrisids in Asir: a historical overview]. *Welt des Islams [Netherlands] 1981 21(1-4): 164-192.* Ahmad ibn Idris (1760-1837), a sufi teacher from Morocco, brought the sufi order he had founded to Sabya, Asir about 1830. His great-grandson, Mohammed ibn Ali al- Idrisi (1876-1923) began a mission of religious reform here in 1906, which led him into confrontation with the Ottoman rulers and the imam of Yemen. In 1913 he became the first Arab ruler to conclude an alliance with Great Britain against the Ottoman Empire. After his death, Asir became a protectorate of the Saudis, who annexed it in 1930. The new Saudi-Yemeni boundary was formalized in 1936. Based on three published works, 1975-77, of John Baldry and other secondary sources; 28 notes, biblio. ca 1830-1936

Iefremov, Serhii

3182. Holubenko, Petro. NA VARTI UKRAINS'KOHO VIDRODZHENNIA—SERHII IEFREMOV IAK PUBLITSYST [A watch on the Ukrainian national revival: Serhii Iefremov as a publicist]. *Sučasnist [West Germany] 1983 (6): 36-48.* An analysis of Serhii Iefremov's work as a journalist and details of his other political activities and views in the Ukraine, providing references and accounts of the newspapers and periodicals to which he contributed. Between 1896 and 1919 he wrote more than 3,000 articles. Some of the topics included the awakening of Ukrainian political consciousness, a regular analysis of Ukrainian political and social development, the Jewish question in the Ukraine, the treatment of the Ukraine by Russia, and the influence of Dmytro Dontsov. A paper first presented to the Ukrainian Academy in the United States in 1976; based on primary sources. 1896-1919

Ignatieff, Natalie and Paul

3183. Ignatieff, Michael. FAMILY ALBUM. *Hist. Workshop J. [Great Britain] 1982 (14): 92-105.* Episodes from the lives of the author's paternal grandparents, Paul and Natalie Ignatieff, between 1873 and their deaths in 1945. Paul Ignatieff was a Ukrainian landowner who became minister of education in 1915 as "the last liberal in the czar's government." The family emigrated in 1919, first to England, where they failed to make a go of farming in Sussex, and then to Canada. Particular memories concern Natalie's childhood and marriage in 1903; anti-Jewish riots in Kiev, 1905; the tsar's government in 1915-16; the Revolution and Civil War in southern Russia; and the lingering influence of Russian memories on the family's subsequent life. Based on family documents; 3 illus. 1873-1945

Ignatiev family

3184. Ignatieff, Michael. THE FAMILY ALBUM. *Queen's Q. [Canada] 1982 89(1): 54-70.* A second-generation Canadian member of the Russian family of the last liberal minister in the Czarist government describes the family history of the various relatives who fled Russia. 1900-50's

Ignatius of Loyola, Saint

3185. Elizalde, Ignacio. LUIS VIVES E IGNACIO DE LOYOLA [Luis Vives and Ignatius of Loyola]. *Hispania Sacra [Spain] 1981 33(68): 541-547.* Juan Luis Vives (1492-1540) "the most European Spaniard who ever existed," was a contemporary of Saint Ignatius of Loyola. Both lived in Burgos, 1528-30, and possibly knew each other. Their aquaintance and exchange of views is suggested by similar passages in the *Spiritual Exercises* (1524) of the founder of the Jesuits and the *Dialogues* (1522) of Vives, and an examination of their other writings, 1522-29. 15 notes. 1522-30

Ike Taiga

3186. Takeuchi, Melinda. IKE TAIGA: A BIOGRAPHICAL STUDY. *Harvard J. of Asiatic Studies 1983 43(1): 141-186.* Prints a biography of Japanese painter Ike Taiga (1723-76), who was a central figure in the indigenization and popularization of the Chinese-inspired *Nanga* (literati) school of painting. He expanded the range of acceptable subjects for painting to include Japanese folklore, Buddhist and Taoist subjects, Japanese scenes, and illustrations of literature. He also expanded the range of techniques to include various washes, brushes, and even finger painting. Based on primary sources; 3 plates, 48 notes, 4 appendixes. 1730's-76

Illeritski, Vladimir E.

3187. —. VLADIMIR EVGENEVICH ILLERITSKII [Vladimir Evgenevich Illeritski]. *Voprosy Istorii [USSR] 1981 (3): 188.* Obituary of Vladimir E. Illeritski (1912-80), a doctor of historical sciences, professor of the Moscow State Historical Archive Institute, and author of over 100 scholarly works, on the history of Russian revolutionary historical thought. 1912-80

Illésházy, István

3188. Ötvös, Péter. ILLÉSHÁZY ISTVÁN AZ EMIGRÁCIÓBAN LEVELEK A "BUJDOSÁS" IDEJÉBŐL [István Illésházy abroad; letters from "exile"]. *Századok [Hungary] 1983 117(3): 609-625.* The presentation of selected sections of 159 letters of the correspondence between Baron István Illésházy (1541?-1609) and his wife in the Austrian National Library. Illésházy, greatly distressed, instructs his wife several times to give up her efforts to obtain clemency from the emperor and join him in his exile. 26 notes. 1593-1605

Illyés, Gyula

3189. George, Emery. IN MEMORIAM GYULA ILLYÉS (1902-1983). *Cross Currents 1984 3: 321-332.* Traces the life, literature, and politics of Hungarian author Gyula Illyés and prints English translations of five of his poems. 1920-83

Immerseele, Jan van

3190. Mees, Krista. KOOPMAN IN TROEBELE TIJDEN: JAN VAN IMMERSEELE (1550-1612) [A merchant in troublesome times: Jan van Immerseele, 1550-1612]. *Spiegel Historiael [Netherlands] 1984 19(12): 544-551.* Presents in the Antwerp merchant Jan van Immerseele the model of an entrepreneur whose capabilities and managerial skills kept his trade in textile dyes largely free from the political, economic, and religious turbulence of his times. 1570's-1612

Inchbald, Elizabeth

3191. Macheski, Cecilia. "A Feeling Mind: The Early Literary Career of Elizabeth Inchbald (1753-1821)." City University of New York 1984. 257 pp. *DAI 1985 45(11): 3354-A.* DA8501154 1770's-1821

Ingen-Housz, Jan

3192. Snelders, H. A. M. THE AMSTERDAM PHARMACIST WILLEM VAN BARNEVELD (1747-1826) AND THE DISCOVERY OF PHOTOSYNTHESIS (1778). *Janus [Netherlands] 1981 68(1-3): 1-14.* 1770's-80's
For abstract see ***Barneveld, Willem van***

Inglés, Vicente

3193. Abad Pérez, Antolin. FR. VICENTE INGLES, UN RESTAURADOR DE LAS MISIONES EN EL SIGLO XVIII [Friar Vicente Inglés, a restorer of the missions in the 18th century]. *Missionalia Hispanica [Spain] 1983 40(117): 131-159.* A member of the important missionary expedition that set out from Spain in 1695 was the Franciscan Vicente Inglés (1670-1739), who arrived at Manila in 1696. His apostolic and administrative activity in various important offices in the Philippines is summarized. Based on published sources and secondary works from the Madrid National Library; 54 notes, appendix. 1695-1739

Ingres, Jean-Auguste-Dominique

3194. Rifkin, Adrian D. INGRES AND THE ACADEMIC DICTIONARY: AN ESSAY ON IDEOLOGY AND STUPEFACTION IN THE SOCIAL FORMATION OF THE "ARTIST." *Art Hist. [Great Britain] 1983 6(2): 153-170.* Explores the relationship of French painter Jean-Auguste-Dominique Ingres (1780-1867) to art history seen by his biographers. 1789-1850

Innes, Emily

3195. Gulick, John M. EMILY INNES 1843-1924. *J. of the Malaysian Branch of the Royal Asiatic Soc. [Malaysia] 1982 55(2): 87-115.* Emily Innes was author of *The Chersonese with the Gilding Off,* an account of seven years, 1875-82, as the wife of a minor British official in Malaya. Her life and experiences in the region are recounted including her relationships with Malay Rajas and villagers and her associations with other British, particularly Isabella Bird, Bloomfield Douglas, and Hugh Low. Based on newspapers, public records, the Robertson and Innes letters, and secondary sources; 4 photos. 1875-1924

Inoue Enryō

3196. Staggs, Kathleen M. "DEFEND THE NATION AND LOVE THE TRUTH": INOUE ENRYŌ AND THE REVIVAL OF MEIJI BUDDHISM. *Monumenta Nipponica [Japan] 1983 38(3): 251-282.* Inoue Enryō (1858-1919), Japanese philosopher, employed Western learning to reinvigorate Japanese Buddhism at a time when that religion faced a major crisis—the need to adapt itself to the modern age and to compete with Western thought. He proved Buddhism's intellectual respectability by linking it to Western philosophy and to Western scientific principles and by clearing up internal contradictions. He also pointed out that Buddhism and Japan were mutually dependent, and that Buddhism was useful to modern Japan. The slogan he coined, "Defend the nation—love the truth," were merely two aspects of the same thing. Religion was to be coupled with patriotism. 1880's-90's

Ioffe, Abram F.

3197. Grigorian, A. T. ABRAM FIODOROWICZ JOFFE (1880-1960) [Abram Fedorovich Ioffe (1880-1960)]. *Kwartalnik Hist. Nauki i Techniki [Poland] 1981 26(2): 453-458.* Abram F. Ioffe was educated in St. Petersburg and Germany and taught all his life in the USSR, at the Russian Physical-Chemical Society and the University of St. Petersburg before 1917, during the revolution at the State Radar and Radiological Institute in Petrograd, and later at the State Institute of Physical Technology. There, in 1929, he became director. He researched into the physics of metals and the conductivity of electric crystals. He was the author of *The Physics of Semiconductors* (1957) and *Basic Concepts in Contemporary Physics* (1949). 1910-60

3198. —. IZ NASLEDIIA AKADEMIKA A. F. IOFFE [From the heritage of academician A. F. Ioffe]. *Voprosy Filosofii [USSR] 1980 (12): 135-147.* Publishes 25 letters and other documents relating to the life and career of the famous Russian physicist, A. F. Ioffe, for the period 1906-79, paying tribute to his talents and his role in Soviet science. Based on archives of the Academy of Sciences and secondary sources; 27 notes. 1906-79

Ionescu, Take

3199. Netea, Vasile. UN MILITANT POUR L'UNITE NATIONALE ROUMAINE: TAKE IONESCU [A militant for Romanian national unity: Take Ionescu]. *Rev. Roumaine d'Hist. [Romania] 1981 20(4): 745-752.* Take Ionescu's entrance into the Romanian government in 1912 was the beginning of sustained diplomatic activity lasting throughout the two Balkan wars which followed and opposing Romanian alignment with the Central Powers during World War I. An opponent of the enforced separate peace of Bucharest, his attempts in London and Paris to reveal the true character of Romania's position were crucial in achieving a climate of sentiment in the West favorable to Romanian national goals. His leadership of the Romanian emigration produced the National Council of Romanian Unity in 1918, which proved a significant force in acquiring Transylvania. Contemporary writings, secondary studies; 12 notes. 1893-1918

Iordăchescu, Teodor

3200. —. TEODOR IORDĂCHESCU (1884-1958) [Teodor Iordăchescu (1884-1958)]. *Anale de Istorie [Romania] 1984 30(5): 115-118.* Teodor Iordăchescu was born on 1 August 1884 in Galați. He obtained his high school diploma in Constanța where he became active in the workers movement. In 1908, he came to Bucharest, and while working for the administration of civil hospitals he continued to be active in socialist propaganda and organized workers in unions. He published many articles in socialist press organs and participated in the congresses of the Workers' Party in 1912 and 1914. In 1918, he was elected to the Executive Committee of the Romanian Socialist Party. Iordăchescu was one of the first socialist militants who supported the transformation of the Socialist Party into the Communist Party and devoted his life to his country and the workers' movement. 1908-58

Iorga, Nicolae

3201. Ceaușescu, Ilie and Talpeș, Ioan. INDEPENDENȚA NAȚIONALĂ ȘI INTEGRITEA TERITORIALĂ A PATRIEI ÎN OPERA ȘI ACTIVITATEA LUI NICOLAE IORGA [National independence and the territorial integrity of the country in the work and activity of Nicolae Iorga]. *Magazin Istoric [Romania] 1980 14(11): 26-29.* A tribute to Nicolae Iorga (1871-1940), President of the Romanian Council, on the 40th anniversary of his assassination by the Iron Guard. Historian, patriot, and politician, he championed the freedom of Romania and the smaller powers. 3 illus. 1900-40

3202. Florescu, Gh. I. N. IORGA. ÎNCEPUTURILE ACTIVITĂȚII PARLAMENTARE (1907-1911) (I) [N. Iorga: parliamentary beginnings, 1907-11. Part 1]. *Anuarul Institutului de Istorie și Arheologie "A. D. Xenopol" [Romania] 1981 18: 457-473.* Peasant riots early in 1907 led to new Romanian parliamentary elections and the return of Nicolae Iorga as Liberal deputy for Iași. He had stood as a champion of agrarian reform and of Greater Romania. His maiden speech to the chamber on 12 June 1907, which is discussed in detail, marked the true start of Iorga's political career. Primary sources; 88 notes. Article to be continued. 1907-11

3203. Florescu, G. I. CU PRIVIRE LA EDITAREA DISCURSURILOR PARLAMENTARE ALE LUI N. IORGA [Publication of the parliamentary speeches of N. Iorga]. *Anuarul Inst. de Istorie și Arheologie "A. D. Xenopol" [Romania] 1982 19: 637-652.* Nicolae Iorga's political career began in 1907 as deputy for Iași and with only brief interruptions lasted until 1940; he held office as deputy, senator, president of the Chamber of Deputies, president of the Senate, and prime minister. His parliamentary speeches, 1907-17 (during part of which time he was deputy for Prahova), were edited by Ion Constantinescu and published in Bucharest in 1981. 73 notes. 1907-17

3204. Kirileanu, G. T. NICOLAE IORGA AȘA CUM I-AM CUNOSCUT [Nicolae Iorga as I knew him]. *Magazin Istoric [Romania] 1982 16(3): 44-48.* Recollections of Romanian historian and statesman Nicolae Iorga, 1911-14, from a personal diary among the unpublished papers of G. T. Kirileanu, who from 1906 to 1930 was in charge of the Royal Library, Bucharest, and a close friend of Iorga's. 1911-14

3205. Marinescu, Beatrice. NICOLAE IORGA AND ENGLAND. *Rev. Roumaine d'Hist. [Romania] 1982 21(1): 135-146.* A substantial part of Nicolae Iorga's work was devoted to the strengthening of relations between the British and Romanian peoples. He first visited Great Britain in 1892 to complete research on his doctoral thesis; he returned in 1914 to speak at the International Congress of History and in 1930 to receive an honorary doctorate from Oxford. He formed warm and lasting friendships with British scholars such as Horatio F. Brown, W. G. East, and especially R. W. Seton-Watson. His writings in *Neamul Românesc* sought to acquaint Romanians with the history of Great Britain, which he praised for its goals and efforts in World War I. Based on Iorga's memoirs and secondary sources; 47 notes. 1892-1940

Iqbal, Muhammad

3206. Ahmad, Ziauddin. IQBAL'S CONCEPT OF ISLAMIC POLITY. *Pakistan Horizon [Pakistan] 1981 34(2): 44-58.* Discusses the life of Moslem leader Muhammad Iqbal, the spiritual founder of modern Pakistan, especially his presidential address to the All India Muslim League in 1930, his legal philosophy, and political thought. ca 1900-38

3207. Justyński, Janusz. NARÓD I PAŃSTWO W DOKTRYNIE INDYJSKICH REPREZENTANTÓW ODRODZENIA MUZUŁMAŃSKIEGO [The nation and the state in the doctrine of Indian representatives of the Muslim revival]. *Czasopismo Prawno-Historyczne [Poland] 1983 35(1): 119-134.* 1833-1940's
*For abstract see **Abdul Latif***

Irving, Henry

3208. Scherer, Barrymore. SIR HENRY IRVING. *British Heritage 1983 4(2): 48-59.* Recounts Sir Henry Irving's career as an actor and theater manager, and describes Victorian stagecraft. 1857-1905

Irwin, Raymond

3209. Staveley, Ronald. FROM LANCASHIRE TO UNIVERSITY COLLEGE: RAYMOND IRWIN AND PROFESSIONAL LEADERSHIP. *Library Review [Great Britain] 1985 34(Aut): 153-159.* During his library career, Raymond Irwin championed rural county libraries, contributed to postwar planning by the Library Association, and served as director of the University College London School of Library, Archive, and Information Studies (UCL School) until he retired in 1968. 1925-68

Isaac, David ben

3210. Zimmer, Eric. R. DAVID B. ISAAC OF FULDA: THE TRIALS AND TRIBULATIONS OF A SIXTEENTH CENTURY GERMAN RABBI. *Jewish Social Studies 1983 45(3-4): 217-232.* The life and works of Rabbi David ben Isaac of Fulda (ca. 1540-1607) shed light on the position of the rabbi and his relations with his community in 16th-century Germany, as well as on the study of mysticism and methods of teaching Talmud during this period. Based on manuscript and other sources; 60 notes. 16c

Isaac, J. M.

3211. Auster, Louis. JULES MARX ISAAC: AN UNSUNG HERO. *Midstream 1984 30(2): 30-32.* An account of the life and research of the humanist and scholar J. M. Isaac (1877-1963), who was Inspector General of Education in France to 1940. Isaac focused attention on the development of Christian-Jewish relations and inspired positive reactions from the Protestant World Council of Churches and the Vatican Council. 15c-20c

Isaacs, Isaac

3212. Lee, Godfrey S. THE BATTLE OF THE SCHOLARS—THE DEBATE BETWEEN SIR ISAAC ISAACS AND JULIUS STONE OVER ZIONISM DURING WORLD WAR II. *Australian Journal of Politics and History [Australia] 1985 31(1): 128-134.* Contrasts the approach to Zionism of Sir Isaac Isaacs, a Melbourne-born Jew who identified with Australia's British traditions and became Governor-General in 1931, with that of Julius Stone, an English-born Jew, who became Challis Professor of International Law and Jurisprudence at Sydney. Isaacs opposed the idea of a Jewish national home in Palestine and supported British attempts to restrict immigration. Stone, and most Australian Zionists, campaigned to persuade the British to permit migration to Palestine. The two men conducted their debates in the *Hebrew Standard* and pamphlets. Based on newspapers and pamphlets; 29 notes. 1939-47

Isabella II

3213. Keene, Judith Winifred. "A Very Royal Upbringing: A Study of the Influences on the Development and Education of Isabella II of Spain from 1830-1847." U. of California, San Diego 1983. 292 pp. *DAI 1983 44(3): 839-A.* DA8315175 1830-47

Isola, Agostino

3214. Sturrock, June. WORDSWORTH'S ITALIAN TEACHER. *Bulletin of the John Rylands University Library of Manchester [Great Britain] 1985 67(2): 797-812.* Discusses Agostino Isola, the man who taught William Wordsworth Italian and Spanish at Cambridge, and who stimulated his interest in the Italian Romantic epic. Exiled for his "political tendencies," he became a teacher of Italian and Spanish at Cambridge in 1724. He was a first-rate teacher, loved by his pupils. Primary sources; 47 notes. 1713-97

Istrati, Panaït

3215. Souvarine, Boris. PANAIT ISTRATI—PORTRAIT OF A REBEL. *Dissent 1982 29(3): 342-351.* Discusses political ideologies of Romanians Panaït Istrati and Christian Rakovski as reflected in their careers and written works. 1925-82

Itard, Jean

3216. Caveing, M.; Rashed, R.; and Taton, R.; Charbonneau, Louis, transl. ELOGE: JEAN ITARD (1902-1979). *Historia Mathematica 1985 12(1): 1-5.* Prints an English translation of an abridgement of an obituary, "Nécrologie Jean Itard (1902-1979)," *Revue d'Histoire des Sciences* 1979 32: 345-350 honoring French historian of mathematics Jean Itard, including a bibliography. 1902-79

Iturbide, Agustín de

3217. Anna, Timothy E. THE RULE OF AGUSTIN DE ITURBIDE: A REAPPRAISAL. *Journal of Latin American Studies [Great Britain] 1985 17(1): 79-110.* Agustín de Iturbide's unfavorable historical reputation originated soon after his abdication as emperor of Mexico. As the man who led Mexico to independence, Iturbide originally enjoyed immense prestige. This and his Mexican birth led many Mexicans to implore him to assume the throne, and when he did so few opposed the act. His empire failed because of overspending, an inability to provide employment and rewards, a lack of public services and increased crime, taxation and salary discounts for civil and military employees, limitations on freedom of the press, and the arrest of some congressmen and the dissolution of Congress. Although he abdicated in the face of the Plan of Casa Mata, the plan had not called for his overthrow. Iturbide abdicated because he was unwilling to pay the political price of staying on the throne. Based on primary sources in the Library of the National Institute of Anthropology and History (Mexico City) and the Benson Latin American Collection (University of Texas); 100 notes. 1821-22

Iuskevych, Artem

3218. Soldatov, Serhii. ARTEM IUSKEVYCH: 1930-82 PAMIATI BORTSIA-UKRAINTSIA ZA VOLIU NARODIV [Artem Iuskevych, 1930-82: in memory of the Ukrainian fighter for the liberty of peoples]. *Sučasnist [West Germany] 1982 (4-5): 112-116.* A Ukrainian member of the CPSU, secretary of a local Party committee, trusted official of the establishment, Artem Iuskevych abruptly withdrew his loyalty to the system in 1974 and declared his readiness for bringing down Soviet rule in Estonia. Arrested the same year, he died in 1982. 1974-82

Ivan IV

3219. Ostrowski, Donald. YET ANOTHER "REFUTATION" OF THE KEENAN THESIS. *Russian Hist. 1982 9(1): 121-126.* Niels Rossing and Birgit Rønne's *Apocryphal—Not Apocryphal? A Critical Analysis of the Discussion concerning the Correspondence between Tsar Ivan IV Groznyi and Prince Andrej Kurbskij* (1980) fails to give equal consideration to arguments for and against Edward Keenan's theory that the Kurbski-Grozny correspondence is apocryphal. Among other things, the authors do not understand the use of watermarks. Their opposition to the theory prevents their taking the case on its merits. 8 notes. 1564-1630's

3220. Shepard, Jonathan. [REVIEW OF RUSLAN G. SKRYNNIKOV, *IVAN THE TERRIBLE,* AND FRANCIS CARR, *IVAN THE TERRIBLE*]. *Hist. J. [Great Britain] 1982 25(2): 513-517.* Discusses various controversial aspects of Ivan IV's reign, notably his conduct of the Livonian War, his fear of aristocratic conspiracy, and the rationality of his political conduct after 1565. Reviews Rusland G. Skrynnikov's *Ivan the Terrible* (1981) and Francis Carr's *Ivan the Terrible* (1981). Note. 1530-84

3221. Szvák, Gyula. OT KARAMZINA DO SOLOV'EVA: K VOPROSU EVOLIUTSII OBRAZA IVANA IV V RUSSKOI ISTORIOGRAFII [From Karamzin to Soloviëv: on the evolution of the image of Ivan IV in Russian historiography]. *Ann. U. Sci. Budapestinensis de Rolando Eötvös Nominatae: Sectio Hist. [Hungary] 1981 21: 219-236.* Karamzin's biography, based on Kurbski's research, was the first scientific study of Ivan, praising his intelligence, energy, and assiduity, and concluding that, vitiated by his wife's faults, he committed excesses. Karamzin, supporting Tsarist absolutism and not being a progressive thinker, was unreliable. N. Artsybashev supported Karamzin saying Ivan was not a natural tyrant but had to resist the boyars. The Decembrists condemned him as a tyrant. Belinski concurred with Karamzin. The sixth volume of Soloviëv's *History of Russia* elevates the state's role, praising Ivan for resolutely counteracting problems threatening the state. His critique is rational and synthesizes Ivan's qualities. The 1850's thus saw two views on Ivan, one that he was a natural tyrant, the other that he was forced unwillingly to tyrannical measures. Based on works of Kurbski, Karamzin and others; 72 notes. 1830-60

Izbiński, Leszek

3222. Popiołek, Stefan. LESZEK IZBIŃSKI (5 V 1939-5 VI 1980) [Leszek Izbiński, 5 May 1939—5 June 1980]. *Archeion [Poland] 1982 (73): 335-337.* Obituary of Leszek Izbiński (1939-80), director of the State Regional Archives in Brzeg. He published works on the history of Polish resistance in Brzeg during World War II, Polish labor in Germany, and the Brzeg political prison. Secondary sources; biblio. 1939-80

Izotov, Nikita A.

3223. Kuzmenko, M. M. 50-RICHCHIA IZOTOVSKOHO RUKHU [The 50th anniversary of the Izotov movement]. *Ukrains'kyi Istorychnyi Zhurnal [USSR] 1982 (6): 125-127.* Nikita A. Izotov (1902-51), a miner, published an article in *Pravda* in May 1932 telling the reader about his method of overfulfilling his daily production norms. The article became a discussion topic at general meetings of miners at numerous collieries. Soon afterwards, Izotov undertook to instruct young miners on how to emulate his method. He was given a separate pit which became a "school." Thus, a new labor movement came into being which rapidly spread to all collieries of the Donets basin and then into other economic branches. 1932-37

J

Jabłoński, Zbigniew

3224. Bieńkowski, Wiesław. ZBIGNIEW JABŁONSKI (17 V 1926-7 X 1984) [Zbigniew Jabłoński (1926-84)]. *Studia Historyczne [Poland] 1985 28(1): 150-153.* Presents the life of Zbigniew Jabłoński, a historian and the head of the Library of the Polish Academy of Sciences, Cracow. Firstly he was interested in the history of Western Pomerania in the 15th and 16th centuries. Then he concentrated his research on the cultural and intellectual life in Cracow during the 18th and 19th centuries, with the stress put on the history of theater. 15c-19c

Jabotinsky, Vladimir

3225. Shavit, Yaakov. FIRE AND WATER: ZE'EV JABOTINSKY AND THE REVISIONIST MOVEMENT. *Studies in Zionism [Israel] 1981 (4): 215-236.* Describes Jabotinsky's role as leader of the Zionist Revisionist movement. Members of the movement saw Jabotinsky as a man of destiny for whom they would give their lives. Political opponents considered Jabotinsky a misguided man who caused others to err. Explores the belief that Jabotinsky was the personification of the movement, and concludes that, although he held a large, perhaps crucial role, to accept fully Jabotinsky's priority to the movement is to accept a grossly oversimplified view of the Zionist movement. Based on some of Jabotinsky's papers from the Jabotinsky Institute, and numerous secondary sources. 24 notes. 1905-45

3226. —. [VLADIMIR JABOTINSKY]. *Jerusalem Q. [Israel] 1980 (16): 3-39.*

Avineri, Schlomo. THE POLITICAL THOUGHT OF VLADIMIR JABOTINSKY, *pp. 3-26.* Discusses the life and political thought of Vladimir Jabotinsky and his impact on the growth of Zionism and the establishment of Israel.

Eldad, Israel. JABOTINSKY DISTORTED, *pp. 27-39.* Counters Avineri's view of Jabotinsky as a totalitarian and reaffirms the nationalist political goals of this leader of world Zionism. 1900's-40

Jaccoud, Pierre

3227. Oudin, Bernard. 25 ANS APRES, PIERRE JACCOUD CRIE TOUJOURS SON INNOCENCE [25 years later Pierre Jaccoud still pleads innocent]. *Hist. Mag. [France] 1983 (42): 44-48.* Recounts the sensational 1960 trial of Geneva lawyer Pierre Jaccoud for murder and Jaccoud's attempts to clear his name following his release from prison. 1958-83

Jacini, Filippo

3228. Cabella, Enrico. AMICI SCOMPARSI: FILIPPO JACINI E GIUSEPPE OSNAGO [Departed friends: Filippo Jacini and Giuseppe Osnago]. *Risorgimento [Italy] 1984 36(1): 1-3.* Discusses the career of Filippo Jacini, who wrote a thesis for his law degree on agrarian contracts in the upper Milanese area, worked as a lawyer, and was involved in Italian political life. Along with Benedetto Croce, he was part of the liberal resistance to Fascism, doing relief work for the resistance movement. He represented the Italian Liberal Party and worked for charity organizations for the last 20 years of his life. Also lamented is the passing of Giuseppe Osnago, accountant and secretary-treasurer of the Milanese Committee of the Institute for the History of the Italian Risorgimento. 20c

Jackson, Hamlet

3229. Smith, Robert Michael. CHRISTIAN JUDAIZERS IN EARLY STUART ENGLAND. *Hist. Mag. of the Protestant Episcopal Church 1983 52(2): 125-133.* Around 1618 Hamlet Jackson left England with his wife and settled in Amsterdam where both converted to Judaism. In the most precise sense of the word they became Christian Judaizers, later called Traskites after John Traske. They were persecuted by the Stuarts, but related to the Puritans of the 17th century and influenced the Evangelicals of the 19th century, especially in their emphasis on sabbatarianism and election. Based on Ephraim Pagitt's *Heresiography;* 40 notes. 1618-1700

Jackson, Humphrey

3230. Appleby, John H. HUMPHREY JACKSON, F.R.S., 1717-1801: A PIONEERING CHEMIST. *Notes and Records of the Royal Society of London [Great Britain] 1986 40(2): 147-168.* Defends the analytical chemist Humphrey Jackson as a versatile and ingenious innovator. Jackson experimented with tar water, fever powder, food adulteration, wood preservatives, brewing, and isinglass. 63 notes. 1730's-1801

Jackson, Peter

3231. Wiggins, David K. PETER JACKSON AND THE ELUSIVE HEAVYWEIGHT CHAMPIONSHIP: A BLACK ATHLETE'S STRUGGLE AGAINST THE LATE NINETEENTH CENTURY COLOR-LINE. *Journal of Sport History 1985 12(2): 143-168.* Peter Jackson (1861-1901) was the most famous black athlete in the late 19th century. Although a gifted prizefighter, he was denied a chance for the world heavyweight title, as he could not transcend the increasing American intolerance for interracial sport. In 1886, Jackson, a native of the Virgin Islands who moved with his family to Australia, won the Australian championship by defeating Tom Lees. With no one to fight in Australia, in 1888 he sailed for San Francisco hoping to fight John L. Sullivan for the world title. Although the sporting public clamored for a contest between Sullivan and Jackson, Sullivan refused all offers to fight the black fighter. Sullivan's manager later wrote that he had kept Sullivan from fighting because he wanted to protect his boxer from the humiliation of losing to a black. Based on newspapers and other published sources; 60 notes, illus. 1880-1901

Jacobs, Hubert

3232. Manion, Fred. FR. HUBERT JACOBS, S.J. *Archivum Historicum Societatis Iesu [Italy] 1985 54(108): 497-507.* A tribute to Jesuit historian Hubert Jacobs, born in the Netherlands in 1909, and editor of texts in Portuguese, Spanish, Italian, and Latin, followed by a partial bibliography. 16c-17c

Jacobs, Marjorie

3233. —. [TRIBUTE TO MARJORIE JACOBS]. *South Asia [Australia] 1982 5(2): i-ii.* Ward, John M. PREFACE FOR FESTSCHRIFT IN HONOUR OF EMERITUS PROFESSOR MARJORIE JACOBS, *pp. i-ii.* Sketches the academic achievements of Marjorie Jacobs, professor of history at the University of Sydney. Bridge, Carl and Masselos, Jim. *p. ii.* Describes Marjorie Jacobs' pioneering work in teaching Indian history at Australian universities. 1950's-80

Jacquin, Nikolaus J.

3234. Stafleu, Franz. NIKOLAUS FREIHERR VON JACQUIN UND DIE SYSTEMATISCHE BOTANIK SEINER ZEIT [The Baron Nikolaus J. Jacquin and the systematic botany of his time]. *Anzeiger der Österreichischen Akad. der Wiss. Philosophische-Historische Klasse [Austria] 1980 117(1-10): 284-310.* Describes the education, life, and work of Jacquin, a famous biologist of French ancestry and European spirit. 1727-1817

Jaeger, Evgen

3235. Glaser, Edvard. ZDRAVNIK, HUMANIST: DR. EVGEN JAEGER, RAZISKOVALEC IN PRIRODOSLOVEC [Physician, humanist: Dr. Evgen Jaeger, researcher and natural scientist]. *Zbornik za Zgodovino Naravoslovja in Tehnike [Yugoslavia] 1985 8: 139-146.* Biography of the physician and entomologist Evgen Jaeger (1892-1959) of Podčetrtek, Slovenia. 1892-1959

Jaeger, Frans Maurits

3236. Hogardi, C. L. FRANS MAURITS JAEGER: EEN CHEMICUS ALS HISTORICUS [Frans Maurits Jaeger: a chemist as a historian]. *Tijdschrift voor de Geschiedenis der Geneeskunde, Natuurwetenschappen, Wiskunde en Techniek [Netherlands] 1984 7(4): 183-195.* F. M. Jaeger (1877-1945) worked from 1908 until his death as a professor of inorganic chemistry at Groningen University. Around 1918 he showed a great interest in the history of chemistry and produced a number of publications on this subject, which show all the characteristics of Jaeger's approach to science. He was a positivist scientist, who stressed the importance of experimentation. He used important contemporary developments in chemistry, especially the theory of atomic structure and the elements, to assess the merits of past chemists. Although he claimed to rate every historical period at its true value, he was in fact exalting the chemistry of his own time. 1908-45

Jaeger, John Conrad

3237. Paterson, M. S. JOHN CONRAD JAEGER 1907-1979. *Hist. Records of Australian Sci. [Australia] 1982 5(3): 65-88.* A brief biography of Australian scientist-educator John Conrad Jaeger who was trained in Australia and at Cambridge University. His teaching career was spent at the University of Tasmania and the Australian National University but he is most noted for his research. He was interested in many topics but made his most significant contributions in applied mathematics, geology, and engineering. His best-known published work is *Conduction of Heat in Solids.* 1907-79

Jaffe, William

3238. Walker, Donald A. WILLIAM JAFFE, HISTORIAN OF ECONOMIC THOUGHT, 1898-1980. *Am. Econ. Rev. 1981 71(5): 1012-1019.* In this biographical essay, Jaffe's career is judged successful particularly in his efforts to explain Leon Walras' concepts to the academic community. Jaffe's scholarly work was not restricted to the study of one economist; in his scholarship and writing he was a major historian of economic theory. 4 notes, biblio. 1898-1980

Jagodyński, Stanisław Serafin

3239. Iakovenko, N. N. NOVYE DANNYE K BIOGRAFII S. S. IAGODYN'SKOGO [New data for the biography of S. S. Jagodyński]. *Sovetskoe Slavianovedenie [USSR] 1981 (1): 93-96.* Very little is known about the later career of Stanisław Serafin Jagodyński, a leading figure in the Polish Renaissance, translator of Petrarch, and writer of satirical verse. He was a student in Cracow and Padua, and travelled in Italy and elsewhere with King Władysław in 1624-25. Evidently he was also in the service of the Radziwill family, 1625-26. Primary sources, including a document in the L'vov Scientific Library of the Academy of Sciences, Ukraine; reproduction, 10 notes. 17c

Jaguaribe de Matos, Francisco

3240. Rodrigues, José Honório. GENERAL FRANCISCO JAGUARIBE DE MATOS [General Francisco Jaguaribe de Matos]. *Revista do Instituto Histórico e Geográfico Brasileiro [Brazil] 1983 (339): 105-112.* Prints a biobibliography of General Francisco Jaguaribe de Matos (1881-1974), chief of the technical secretariat of the Rondon Commission which mapped and studied central Brazil from the ethnological, zoological, botanical, and mineralogical points of view. His principal work consisted in the exhaustive study of the state of Mato Grosso and neighboring regions. 1907-74

Jahandar Shah

3241. Nigam, S. B. P. THE JAHANDARNAMAH OF NUR-UD-DIN. *Journal of Indian History [India] 1983 61(1-3): 93-116.* A synopsis of a 17th-century chronicle of the reign of Indian Mogul emperor Jahandar Shah written by a contemporary soldier-turned-historian, Nur-ud-din. 68 notes. 1659-1713

Jahn, Friedrich Ludwig

3242. Sprenger, Reinhard K. ZUR JAHNREZEPTION IN DER WEIMARER REPUBLIK [The reception of Jahn in the Weimar Republic]. *Stadion [West Germany] 1982-83 8-9: 169-192.* Examines how Friedrich Ludwig Jahn (1778-1852), founder of the German gymnastics movement, was perceived in educational magazines during the Weimar Republic. Disillusionment over the lost world war, the revolution, the Versailles Peace Treaty, problems with the new parliamentary system, and the German crisis of identity led to the perception of Jahn's idea of the German *Volkstum* [nationhood] as a welcome continuity in German history that could lead to a national rebirth. A patriotic leader whose mission was to improve the morals of youth by gymnastics, his aspiration for national unity through gymnastics was interpreted as a model for the national state and incorporated the concepts of duty and obligation. Jahn's influence during the Weimar Republic weakened the first German republic and was used as a justification for National Socialism. Based on contemporary periodicals and secondary sources; 109 notes. 1919-33

Jakóbiec, Marian

3243. Sielicki, Franciszek. W SIEDEMDZIESIĘCIOLECIE URODZIN PROFESORA MARIANA JAKÓBCA [On the 70th birthday of Professor Marian Jakóbiec]. *Slavia Orientalis [Poland] 1980 29(3): 295-300.* A biographical sketch of Professor Marian Jakóbiec, who wrote about the influence of Russian literature on Polish, Russo-Polish literary relations, Ukrainian literature, and Polish-Ukrainian literary contacts, as well as about Yugoslav literature. 20c

Jakšić, Jakov

3244. Vasić, Pavle. JAKOV JAKŠIĆ PANCIRLIJA U SRBIJI [Jakov Jakšić Pancirlija in Serbia]. *Zbornik Istorijskog Muzeja Srbije [Yugoslavia] 1981 17-18: 85-105.* Traces the career and writings of Jakov Jakšić, known as Pancirlija, an officer who took part in the Serbian uprisings at the beginning of the 19th century. He was at one time aide-de-camp to the Serbian army's drillmaster-in-chief, and one of his best-known writings was *Srbski Vojeni Ustav, 1813* [The Serbian military constitution of 1813], which is in fact a drillbook based on that used by the Russian Imperial Army. Jakšić also wrote a diary, which describes the Serbian uprisings, and poetry, much of it about Napoleon's campaign in Russia. Later in life, Jakov Jakšić became head of the Serbian Printing Office. He died in 1848. Includes photocopies of Jakšić's manuscripts, including illustrations from his military drillbook; portrait, 45 notes. ca 1804-48

Jakšić, Stojan

3245. Jovanović-Jakšić, Ivanka. IZ USPOMENA STOJANA JAKŠIĆA [From the memoirs of Stojan Jakšić]. *Zbornik za Istoriju [Yugoslavia] 1981 (23): 177-204.* The memoirs of Stojan Jakšić (1883-1955) consist of three major segments: his autobiography; his memories of his brothers Milutin and Vasa; and his recollections of work and colleagues on the Kikinda *Srpski Glas,* a newspaper that he helped found and edit during the years just prior to World War I. All three of the Jakšić brothers were leaders of the fledgling Democratic Party of the Hungarian Serbs, struggling for the revival of a positive nationalist movement among the masses, which had grown accustomed to political and cultural passivity in the face of Magyar oppression. 16 notes. 1883-1920

Jamal-ud-Din al-Afghani

3246. Abdulla, Ahmed. SYED JAMALUDDIN AFGHANI'S IDEAS BLAZE THE TRAIL. *Pakistan Horizon [Pakistan] 1981 34(2): 35-43.* Discusses the life of 19th-century Moslem leader Syed Jamal-ud-Din al-Afghani, who attempted to unite Moslems throughout the world. 1850-97

James, Henry

3247. Field, Mary Lee. "NERVOUS ANGLO-SAXON APPREHENSIONS": HENRY JAMES AND THE FRENCH. *French-American Rev. 1981 5(1): 1-13.* In his early writings on French literature, while James evidenced admiration for the art of French writers, he was clearly offended by the vulgarity of the subject matter. Later, he more freely admitted great admiration for French artistic powers and, finally, he concentrated totally on technique while ignoring the possible vulgarity of the subjects. After 1900, James no longer reviewed new novels and rarely commented on minor writers. Complex, thoughtful, literary, and critical reflections on Balzac, Zola, and Flaubert written at this time indicate that he had reconciled himself on aesthetic grounds to the indecency of the French novel. He formulated critical theories which encompassed vulgarity as well as the art of French literature. 51 notes. 1880-1905

3248. Panichas, George A. HENRY JAMES AND PARADIGMS OF CHARACTER. *Modern Age 1982 26(1): 2-7.* In his published writings and personal letters, Henry James discloses paradigms of character by which we may measure and judge our own approximation of civilized life. During his lifetime, James never received popular or critical acclaim. Nevertheless, James remained a master of control, form, and phrase, and was challenged by a need to master the dramatic form itself. Both his life and work disclosed virtues which can guide our taste and our human hierarchy of values. Based on the letters of Henry James; 14 notes. 1883-95

3249. Varner, Jeanine Baker. "Henry James and Gustave Flaubert: The Creative Relationship." U. of Tennessee 1981. 146 pp. *DAI 1982 42(9): 3992-A.* DA8203873 1874-1902

James I

3250. Duchein, Michel. PREMIER ROI D'ANGLETERRE ET D'ECOSSE: LE FILS DE MARIE STUART [The first king of England and Scotland: Mary Stuart's son]. *Historama [France] 1985 (18): 86-90.* A biography of James Stuart (1566-1625), James VI of Scotland and James I of Great Britain. 1603-25

3251. Shriver, Frederick. HAMPTON COURT RE-VISITED: JAMES I AND THE PURITANS. *J. of Ecclesiastical Hist. [Great Britain] 1982 33(1): 48-71.* Reexamines the Hampton Court Conference in 1604 with special reference to the role of the king. Although James demonstrated considerable independence of the bishops, he was persuaded to modify some of his earlier intentions which were in accord with Puritan hopes, and to consent to a draft proclamation, which did not relax the Anglican Church's rules against the Puritans. Describes the proceedings of the conference, and summarizes the efforts of the bishops to carry out its decisions. James I was determined to maintain the established church under royal supremacy, eager to punish Puritan troublemakers, but not intent on persecuting Puritans who remained quiet. Based on manuscripts in Public Record Office and British Library; 74 notes. 1603-04

James II

3252. Whitworth, R. H. 1685—JAMES II, THE ARMY AND THE HUGUENOTS. *Journal of the Society for Army Historical Research [Great Britain] 1985 63(255): 130-137.* Describes the life of King James II, particularly his military accomplishments and failures and contributions to British military history, including his employment of Huguenots in his army. 1650's-90

Jameson, Anna

3253. Holcomb, Adele M. ANNA JAMESON: THE FIRST PROFESSIONAL ENGLISH ART HISTORIAN. *Art Hist. [Great Britain] 1983 6(2): 171-187.* Born in Ireland and self-educated, English author Anna Jameson's first work was published about 1825 and by the 1840's she had become specialized in art. 1825-50's

Jamin, Philip

3254. Fulpius, Lucien. PHILIP JAMIN (1848-1918) GRAVEUR, HISTORIEN ET MYCOLOGUE [Philip Jamin (1848-1918): engraver, historian, and mycologist]. *Mus. de Genève [Switzerland] 1982 (227): 5-7.* Recounts the life and career of Philip Jamin of Geneva and his original contributions, especially to the field of mycology. 1868-1918

Janet, Pierre

3255. Laffey, John F. SOCIETY, ECONOMY, AND PSYCHE: THE CASE OF PIERRE JANET. *Hist. Reflections [Canada] 1983 10(2): 269-294.* Pierre Janet (1859-1947) used numerous images of work, capital, and other economic concepts in his discussions of psychology. He was a product of 19th-century bourgeois capitalism and an academic mandarin of the French Third Republic. He believed social and economic pressures contributed to certain kinds of mental illness. More empirical and less theoretical than Freud's studies, Janet's work has, by comparison, been relegated to secondary stature. 112 notes. 1890-1940

Jansen, Hubertus H. P.

3256. Kossmann, Johanna. IN MEMORIAM HUBERTUS P. H. JANSEN. AMSTERDAM 4-7-1928-LEIDEN 9-6-1985. [In memoriam Hubertus P. H. Jansen (1928-85)]. *Bijdragen en Mededelingen betreffende de Geschiedenis der Nederlanden [Netherlands] 1985 100(3): 462-464.* Professor Hubertus H. P. Jansen was a stimulating teacher and productive scholar with versatile interests at the University of Leiden. Among his major works are *Jacoba van Beieren, Emo tussen angst en ambitie* [Emo between fear and ambition], and *Levend verleden* [A living past]. 1950's-85

Jaque de los Rios Mancanedo, Miguel de

3257. Clavijo, Ramón. VIAJE A LAS INDIAS ORIENTALES Y OCCIDENTALES [Travels to the East and West Indies]. *Historia y Vida [Spain] 1984 17(197): 28-35.* Examines a manuscript in the Public Library of Jerez de la Frontera by Miguel de Jaque de los Rios Mancanedo a late 16th- and early 17th-century Spanish sailor who chronicled his exotic travels to the Far East and the New World in his "Viaje a las Yndias Orientales y Occidentales" (1606). 1590's-1606

Jaruzelski, Wojciech

3258. Smirnov, A. F. VOITSEKH IARUZEL'SKII [Wojciech Jaruzelski]. *Voprosy Istorii KPSS [USSR] 1983 (7): 131-133.* Briefly surveys the life of Poland's military leader, Wojciech Jaruzelski, on the occasion of his 60th birthday. Born the son of a teacher in 1923 he was among the first Poles to serve in units under the Red Army in 1943. By 1960, he was head of the Polish Army's Political Department, and by 1962 Deputy Minister of National Defense. In the 1970's he was in the Polish United Workers' Party Politburo and subsequently became prime minister of Poland. He was awarded the Order of Lenin for his services to the Soviet state. Based on newspaper reports in Russian and Polish; 10 notes. 1923-83

Jasieński, Feliks

3259. Gałęcka, Krystyna. FELIKS JASIEŃSKI W ŚRODOWISKU WARSZAWY, LWOWA I KRAKOWA [Feliks Jasieński in the circles of Warsaw, Lvov, and Cracow]. *Roczniki Humanistyczne [Poland] 1979 27(4): 21-38.* Describes the life of Feliks Jasieński (1861-1929), art collector, critic, and exhibition organizer. After traveling widely abroad,

Jasieński settled down in Cracow, where he organized a salon for young writers and artists. In 1920, he donated his collection, about 15,000 items, to the National Museum in Cracow. 6 photos, 105 notes. 1880's-1929

Jasinski, René

3260. Robichez, Jacques. RENE JASINSKI [René Jasinski]. *Revue d'Histoire Littéraire de la France [France] 1985 85(6): 1091-1092.* Regrets the passing of René Jasinski (1898-1985), recalling his contributions to the study of French literature, particularly that of the 17th century, as a critic, historian, and editor; he also wrote poetry of his own. ca 17c

Jaśko, Stanisław

3261. Kosowski, Stanisław. STANISŁAW JAŚKO—RZEŹBIARZ SAMOUK [Stanisław Jaśko: self-taught sculptor]. *Nasza Przeszłość [Poland] 1979 (51): 141-145.* Provides a biographical sketch of Stanisław Jaśko, sculptor in many churches in Trzebinia, 1864-1911. 1864-1911

Jaspers, Karl

3262. Sternberger, Dolf. KARL JASPERS: A PERSONAL PORTRAIT. *Encounter [Great Britain] 1983 61(4): 33-37.* Discusses the relationship between the life and the existential philosophy of Karl Jaspers (1883-1969). ca 1910-69

Jászi, Oszkár

3263. Hanák, Péter. DER DONAUPATRIOTISMUS VON OSKÁR JÁSZI [The Danube patriotism of Oszkár Jászi]. *Österreichische Osthefte [Austria] 1983 25(3): 324-337.* Traces the life and career of the Hungarian political thinker, sociologist, and politician Oszkár Jászi, paying particular attention to his political philosophy, his concept of the historic role of the Habsburg monarchy, and his idea for a confederation of the Danube peoples. ca 1900-48

3264. Jeszenszky, Géza. THE CORRESPONDENCE OF OSZKÁR JÁSZI AND R. W. SETON-WATSON BEFORE WORLD WAR I. *Acta Hist. [Hungary] 1980 26(3-4): 437-454.* Analyzes the correspondence between R. W. Seton-Watson, or Scotus Viator, the pseudonym under which he was known in Hungary, and Oszkár Jászi (1875-1957), editor of the progressive periodical *Huszadik Század* (Twentieth Century). Seton-Watson's *Racial Problems in Hungary* (1908) was widely condemned in Hungary as being anti-Hungarian and pro-Slav. Oszkár Jászi defended Seton-Watson as a fair observer of the political and racial situation and continued to accept articles from him for his periodical. World War I suspended contact between the two. Based on 16 letters in the Department of Manuscripts, National Széchényi Library; 73 notes. 1908-14

3265. Váradi Sternberg, János. JÁSZI OSZKÁR LEVELEZÉSE NYIKOLAJ RUBAKINNAL [Oszkár Jászi's correspondence with Nikolai Rubakin]. *Magyar Könyvszemle [Hungary] 1983 99(4): 393-396.* 1917-18
*For abstract see **Rubakin, Nikolai A.***

Jedin, Hubert

3266. DeLuca, Giuseppe. L'OPERA STORICA DELLO JEDIN [The historical work of Hubert Jedin]. *Riv. di Storia della Chiesa in Italia [Italy] 1980 34(1): 3-6.* On the occasion of his 80th birthday, surveys the contribution of German ecclesiastical historian, Hubert Jedin (1900-80), to historical research on the Counterreformation, especially the Council of Trent. Secondary sources. 1900-80

3267. Maccarrone, Michele. JEDIN IL COSTRUTTORE [Jedin the builder]. *Studium [Italy] 1981 77(2): 219-224.* A tribute to Monsignor Hubert Jedin (1900-80), distinguished historian, professor at Rome, Bonn, and Breslau, and author of many important works on Church history, who died in Rome in July 1980. 1900-80

3268. Repgen, Konrad. HUBERT JEDIN (1900-1980) [Hubert Jedin (1900-80)]. *Hist. Jahrbuch [West Germany] 1981 101(2): 325-340.* A biographical survey of the life and works of the theologian and historian Hubert Jedin. Jedin was born in 1900 in Silesia and studied theology and Church history at the University in Breslau. Exiled by the Nazi regime, he spent the years 1933-49 in Rome at the Campo Santo Teutonico, where he conducted research on the Council of Trent. From 1949 until his death in 1980 he was professor of medieval Church history at the University in Bonn and was active in several other scholarly institutes. His main publications are the multivolume *History of the Council of Trent,* a biography of the Augustinian theologian Giralomo Seripando, and his multivolume *Handbook of Church History.* Based on an address at the General Meeting of the Görres Society on October 7, 1980 in Aachen. 1933-80

Jeffes, Anthony

3269. Cerasano, S. P. ANTHONY JEFFES, PLAYER AND BREWER. *Notes and Queries [Great Britain] 1984 31(2): 221-225.* Discusses documents about the life of actor and brewer Anthony Jeffes. 1597-1648

Jegado, Hélène

3270. Baroche, Jacques. LES 36 CRIMES D'HELENE JEGADO [The 36 crimes of Hélène Jegado]. *Historama [France] 1984 (8): 76-80.* Hélène Jegado was a French serving woman who between the years 1833 and 1850 poisoned 36 individuals, apparently because it helped her fill a need to care for those in distress. When she was finally brought to trial, her lawyer attempted a plea of insanity, but it was rejected and Hélène sentenced to death. 1833-51

Jejeebhoy, Jamshetjee

3271. Siddiqi, Asiya. THE BUSINESS WORLD OF JAMSHETJEE JEJEEBHOY. *Indian Econ. and Social Hist. Rev. [India] 1982 19(3-4): 301-324.* Jamshetjee Jejeebhoy was a Parsee merchant of Bombay who amassed a fortune in trade during the Napoleonic wars and who had both entrepreneurial ability and capital to devote to trade in the following years. He was more specialized than many of his fellow merchants. Opium was his main export; the profit was modest, but his volume was high. After 1832, Jejeebhoy and the other Bombay merchants began to encounter increased difficulties in competing for shares of international commerce because the adoption of free trade opened their protected markets to invasion by outsiders. Based on memoirs and records of the Bombay merchants and secondary works; 121 notes. 1800-60

Jekyll, Gertrude

3272. Hinge, David. GERTRUDE JEKYLL: 1843-1932. A BIBLIOGRAPHY OF HER WRITINGS. *J. of Garden Hist. [Great Britain] 1982 2(3): 285-292.* Biobibliography of garden writer Gertrude Jekyll including her books, translations, and contributions to books and periodicals. 1843-1937

Jelinek, Ivan

3273. Jelinek, Ivan. THE WHITE MOUNTAIN. *Kosmas 1983 2(2): 99-124.* Presents autobiographical reminiscences of a Czech soldier returning to Czechoslovakia with the Allies in 1945 and finding himself confronted with the historic problem of Czech subservience. 1945

Jellinek, Oskar

3274. Alvarez-Péreyre, Jeanine. OSKAR JELLINEK TRANSITE PAR FRANCE [Oskar Jellinek's journey through France]. *Austriaca [France] 1984 10(19): 33-47.* The first part of a previously unpublished letter of Oskar Jellinek (1886-1949), native of Brünn and Austrian poet and novelist, describes how the author and his wife escaped from the Nazis by fleeing first to Czechoslovakia and later to Paris. After having been interned at Villemalard near Blois, Jellinek was released and succeeded in obtaining passage to the United States. 18 notes; biblio. note. 1938-40

Jemolo, Arturo Carlo

3275. Morghen, Raffaello. ARTURO CARLO JEMOLO, STORICO DELLO STATO E DELLA CHIESA, NELLA CRISI TRA DUE ETA [Arturo Carlo Jemolo, historian of church and state, in the crisis of two ages]. *Riv. di Storia della Chiesa in Italia [Italy] 1982 36(1): 49-60.* Reviews the life and work of the Italian historian Arturo Carlo Jemolo (1891-1981) and examines the significance of his work on the history of church-state relations in the Italian peninsula, Jansenism, and ecclesiastical problems during the revolutionary period in the light of his political and intellectual experiences and the changing historical perspective of the later 20th century. Based on secondary sources; 10 notes. 1891-1981

Jensen, Sigurd

3276. Bagge, Povl and Skrubbeltang, Fridlev. NEKROLOG: SIGURD JENSEN 4.1.1912-2.10.1981 [Obituary: Sigurd Jensen, 4 January 1912-2 October 1981]. *Hist. Tidsskrift [Denmark] 1982 82(1): 163-169.* Sigurd Jensen was archivist at the Danish Record Office from 1939 and keeper of the local archives of Copenhagen, 1956-79. His approach was characterized by thoroughness, impartiality, and clarity. Whenever possible, he placed his subject in its historical context. His early work was on Danish agricultural reform in the 18th and 19th centuries, his later work on the history of Copenhagen and of Denmark, 1900-45. 9 ref. 1912-81

Jĕrbashian, Edward

3277. Sarinian, S. N. EDWARD JĔRBASHIAN [Edward Jĕrbashian]. *Patma-Banasirakan Handes. Istoriko-Filologicheskii Zhurnal [USSR] 1983 (4): 216-219.* Tribute on the 60th birthday of Edward Jĕrbashian, literary theorist and critic, lecturer at Erevan University, and director of the Abeghian Literature Institute. His works deal mainly with the theory of literature, aesthetics methodology, and the history of literary genres. In addition to his studies of the works of Armenian poets, he has examined the history of modern Armenian poetry. Notable among his works are *Language and Versification* and *History of Modern Armenian Literature.* Primary sources; photo. 1953-83

Jerrold, Douglas

3278. White, Bruce A. DOUGLAS JERROLD'S "Q" PAPERS IN *PUNCH. Victorian Periodicals Rev. [Canada] 1982 15(4): 131-137.* In the 1840's, Douglas Jerrold became the rival of Dickens and Thackeray as a social commentator and critic for *Punch* with his articles signed "Q." 1841-45

Jerzmanowski, Stanisław

3279. Jerzmanowski, Stanisław. W POTRZASKU (PRZYCZYNEK DO DZIEJÓW LIKWIDACJI NIEPODLEGŁOŚCI W POLSCE W 1945 ROKU PRZEZ SOWIECKICH OKUPANTÓW). [Trapped: A contribution to the history of the liquidation of independence in Poland in 1945 by the Soviet invaders]. *Zeszyty Hist. [France] 1980 (54): 71-97.* Memoirs of Zbyszek Jerzmanowski, a 19-year-old Polish Home Army soldier whose unit disbanded in 1944, as the Soviet army stalled at Warsaw. He then joined the Berling Army's 31st Infantry Regiment. The Soviets interned the unit in November. He escaped with some friends in March 1945. Local peasants hid them until they joined the active Home Army unit of Orlik. Zbyszek died in one of its raids on 17 June 1945. 1944-45

Jespersen, Knud

3280. Carlsen, A.-V. KNUD ESPERSEN—SYN TRUDOVOI DANII [Knud Jespersen—son of laboring Denmark]. *Novaia i Noveishaia Istoriia [USSR] 1984 (6): 88-114.* Outlines the biography of Knud Jespersen (1926-77), chairman of the Communist Party of Denmark in 1958-77 and member of Parliament in 1973-77. His childhood experience of unemployment and the German occupation of Denmark during World War II inclined him to support Communist causes. After his release from a Nazi concentration camp Jespersen joined the Communist Party and began a lifelong career of trade union activism opposing unemployment. Within the party, Jespersen opposed the revisionist faction which threatened to splinter it in 1956-57. Based on private interviews and secondary sources; 3 photos, 121 notes. 1940's-77

3281. Carlsen, A.-V. "KRASNYI KNUD"—VERNYI SYN TRUDOVOI DANII ["Red Knud," the faithful son of workers' Denmark]. *Skandinavskii Sbornik [USSR] 1983 28: 26-37.* Outlines the political biography of Knud Jespersen (1926-77), Danish Communist activist and member of the Danish Communist Party's Central Committee in 1952-77. During World War II he fought against the Nazi occupation of Denmark. In the postwar years he was active in the trade union movement and as a spokesman against unemployment. Secondary sources; 25 notes. Swedish summary. 1940's-77

Jessel, George

3282. O'Keefe, David. SIR GEORGE JESSEL AND THE UNION OF JUDICATURE. *Am. J. of Legal Hist. 1982 26(3): 227-251.* The Judicature Acts of 1873 and 1875 consolidated the English courts of law and equity into a Supreme Court of Judicature, and judges Lord Calmont Cairns, Lord Chancellor Selborne, and Sir George Jessel were the guiding figures in the drafting of the legislation. This brief biographical sketch outlines Jessel's piloting the first bills through the House of Commons and his judicial decisions later based on the legislation. Using mostly printed reports, the author assesses Jessel's ideas on principles and procedure, the injunction jurisdiction, the assignment of acquired property, equitable rules, and the case of *Walsh* v. *Lonsdale* (1881) where a common law claim was met with an equitable defense. It has long been held that the Judicature Acts made little change in the workings of English law. The inconsistencies that existed prior to the acts continued after them; the work of Sir George Jessel illustrates this. Based on acts, journals, and law reports; 90 notes. 1870-81

Jesudason, G.

3283. Zimmerman, E. C. A LETTER FROM INDIA. *Concordia Hist. Inst. Q. 1981 54(4): 163-171.* With a brief introduction and postscript, reprints the letter written by the Reverend G. Jesudason (1872-1955), the first national Indian to become a pastor in the Missouri Evangelical Lutheran India Mission (MELIM), in 1950, to the Reverend Professor E. C. Zimmerman of Concordia Seminary, explaining to Zimmerman about his missionary work, his life, and his family, so Zimmerman could report to his students who were preparing for missionary work in India. 1900's-50

Jesús María, Nicolás de

3284. Martínez Rosales, Alfonso. FRAY NICOLÁS DE JESÚS MARÍA, UN CARMELITA DEL SIGLO XVIII [Friar Nicolas de Jesus Maria, an 18th-century Carmelite]. *Historia Mexicana [Mexico] 1983 32(3): 299-348.* Biographical and critical examination of Friar Nicolás de Jesús María, a Carmelite priest in New Spain during the first half of the 18th century. 79 notes, biblio. 1709-67

Jevons, William Stanley

3285. Mazlish, Bruce. JEVONS' SCIENCE AND HIS "SECOND NATURE." *Journal of the History of the Behavioral Sciences 1986 22(2): 140-149.* William Stanley Jevons contributed to a second "revolution" in economics (Adam Smith's being the first), hoping to make it an "exact" science by mathematizing the subject and substituting marginal utility theory for the labor theory of value. Yet he also conceived of economics as a moral science, and tried to defend this claim on Utilitarian grounds. An examination of his personal, or "second," life, however, shows a deeper aspect to his aspirations, where he extrapolates from his own struggles a prescription for human behavior in the economic realm and then treats that prescriptive behavior as based on "natural" and "assumptive" principles. 1850's-82

Jewsbury, Maria Jane

3286. Fryckstedt, Monica C. THE HIDDEN RILL: THE LIFE AND CAREER OF MARIA JANE JEWSBURY, I. *Bulletin of the John Rylands University Library of Manchester [Great Britain] 1984 66(2): 177-203.* While considered a minor figure today, Maria Jane Jewsbury had a keen sense of humor and expressed a deep concern for the position of women. Her early writings caught the attention of William Wordsworth who promoted her career. She was a major contributor to the annual volumes of art and literature that flourished between the 1820's and 1850's in Great Britain. Primary sources; 63 notes. Article to be continued. 1800-33

Jiang Qing

3287. Harris, Lillian Craig. COMRADE DOWAGER CHIANG CH'ING. *Asian Affairs: An Am. Rev. 1982 9(3): 163-173.* Examines the life of Jiang Qing (Chiang Ch'ing), wife and widow of Mao Tse-tung, as a product of her era and social environment. Based largely on secondary sources; 37 notes. 1914-81

Jiang Xinxiong

3288. —. SOME NEW FACES ON THE 12TH CCP CENTRAL COMMITTEE. *Issues & Studies [Taiwan] 1983 19(2): 72-77, (3): 79-83.* 1976-82
For abstract see ***Hu Jintao***

Jie, Zhang

3289. Yang, Gladys. RESEARCH NOTE: WOMEN WRITERS. *China Quarterly [Great Britain] 1985 (103): 510-517.* 1957-83
For abstract see ***Anyi, Wang***

Jiménez, Juan Ramón

3290. Cardwell, Richard A. JUAN RAMÓN JIMÉNEZ—AN INTRODUCTION. *Renaissance and Modern Studies [Great Britain] 1981 25: 1-23.* An introductory survey of the literary achievement of the Spanish poet Juan Ramón Jiménez (1881-1958), presenting something of his character and work and the cultural environment in which he worked. 1890's-1958

3291. Escolar, Hipólito. LA EDICION EN LA EPOCA DE JUAN RAMON JIMENEZ [Publishing in the age of Juan Ramón Jiménez]. *Cuadernos Hispanoamericanos [Spain] 1984 (408): 75-96.* Analyzes, from a typographical point of view, the first editions of Juan Ramón Jiménez's (1881-1957) works from 1900 until 1936, and offers a detailed account of the publishing ventures engaged in by Juan Ramón Jiménez during the same period in Spain. Jiménez was always most concerned with the technical and artistic phase of book production: publishing policies, editorial specifications, cover designs, paper quality, binding, etc. Illus., 66 notes. 1900-36

3292. Trigo, Xulio Ricardo. UNA CARTA DE MACEDONIO A JUAN RAMON (REPUBLICA ARGENTINA, 1948) [A letter from Macedonio to Juan Ramón (Argentina, 1948)]. *Cuadernos Hispanoamericanos [Spain] 1985 (416): 178-183.* The 1948 trip of the Spanish poet Juan Ramón Jiménez (1881-1958) to Argentina was of the greatest importance both for the Argentinian literary scene and the poet himself. His meeting with Macedonio Fernández (1874-1952) increased their mutual esteem and artistic appreciation, as a 1948 letter from Macedonio to Juan Ramón clearly shows. Photo, 17 notes. 1948

Jimenez Murillo, Manuel

3293. Alegre Pérez, Maria Esther and González García, Manuela. ESTUDIO DE LA VIDA Y OBRA CIENTIFICA DE D. MANUEL JIMENEZ MURILLO [A study of the life and scientific works of Manuel Jimenez Murillo]. *Bol. de la Soc. Española de Hist. de la Farmacia [Spain] 1983 34(136): 185-201.* Traces the training and career of Jimenez Murillo, who was competent in various subfields of pharmacy, published prolifically, and raised the status of the profession. 1784-1859

Jinā'ī, Yūsuf bin 'Īsā al-

3294. Hawana, Samir A. SHEIKH YUSSIF BIN ISSA AL-QINA'I: A PIONEER KUWAITI EDUCATOR. *Vitae Scholasticae 1983 2(1): 60-72.* In 1902 Sheikh Yūsuf bin 'Īsā al- Jinā'ī (1876-1973) left his family's business in Kuwait to pursue "knowledge." His quest led him to study in Arabia, Iran, and Iraq. In 1911, he opened a school in Kuwait on a modern model, but still emphasizing Islam and Muslim history. He opened a second school in 1921 and, despite the Depression, the Emir formed a Bureau of Education in 1936. 22 notes. Arabic summary. 1902-36

Jinnah, Mohamed Ali

3295. Justyński, Janusz. NARÓD I PAŃSTWO W DOKTRYNIE INDYJSKICH REPREZENTANTÓW ODRODZENIA MUZUŁMAŃSKIEGO [The nation and the state in the doctrine of Indian representatives of the Muslim revival]. *Czasopismo Prawno-Historyczne [Poland] 1983 35(1): 119-134.* 1833-1940's
*For abstract see **Abdul Latif***

3296. Moore, R. J. JINNAH AND THE PAKISTAN DEMAND. *Modern Asian Studies [Great Britain] 1983 17(4): 529-561.* Traces the role of Mohamed Ali Jinnah (1876-1948) in the Muslim League after 1937 through its demand in 1940 for an independent Muslim nation to its achievement in 1947 of the partition of India. Jinnah worked for Muslim independence movements, regardless of their conflicting political theory. 138 notes. 1935-47

3297. Mujahid, Sharif al. QUAID-I-AZAM JINNAH AND WORLD MUSLIM UNITY: AN INTERPRETATION. *Pakistan Horizon [Pakistan] 1981 34(1): 16-28.* Surveys the political career and beliefs of Mohamed Ali Jinnah, the founder of Pakistan and an early champion of international Moslem unity. 1906-48

3298. Unterberger, Betty Miller. AMERICAN VIEWS OF MOHAMMAD ALI JINNAH AND THE PAKISTAN LIBERATION MOVEMENT. *Diplomatic Hist. 1981 5(4): 313-336.* Mohammed Ali Jinnah (1876-1948), leader of the Moslem League and founder of Pakistan, was little known in the United States prior to World War II; the few reports that existed were ill-formed and reflected a pro-Congress bias. During the war, Jinnah's support of the Allied cause and a better understanding by Americans of the situation in India led American journalists and diplomats to recognize him as a great statesman and to realize that partition was the only viable solution to the political, cultural, and religious problems of the subcontinent. Based on US State Department records, contemporary news accounts, and other primary sources; 89 notes. 1930-48

Jinsai, Itō

3299. Yamashita, Samuel Hideo. "Compasses and Carpenter's Squares: A Study of Itō Jinsai (1627-1705) and Ogyū Sorai (1666-1728)." U. of Michigan 1981. 360 pp. *DAI 1983 43(11): 3678-A.* DA8306712 1662-1728

Jiun Sonja

3300. Watt, Paul Brooks. "Jiun Sonja (1718-1804): Life and Thought." Columbia U. 1982. 225 pp. *DAI 1983 43(11): 3626-A.* DA8307634 1750's-1804

Joan of Kent

See Bocher, Joan

Job

See Bréville, Jacques Onfroy de

Jobim, José Martins da Cruz

3301. Fernandes, Reginaldo. JOSE MARTINS DA CRUZ JOBIM, UM FUNDADOR DA ACADEMIA NACIONAL DE MEDICINA [José Martins da Cruz Jobim, one of the founders of the National Academy of Medicine]. *Rev. do Inst. Hist. e Geog. Brasileiro [Brazil] 1980 (327): 247-268.* Recalls some aspects of the personality and career of the man who significantly contributed to the practice and teaching of medicine in Brazil. Besides being a founder of the National Academy of Medicine, he was responsible for the establishment of the medical faculties of Bahia and Rio de Janeiro and director of the latter. He was a pioneer in the field of tropical medicine. Secondary material; biblio. 1802-78

Jochmann, Rosa

3302. Pasteur, Paul. ROSA JOCHMANN: RESISTANTE AUTRICHIENNE A RAVENSBRÜCK [Rosa Jochmann, Austrian Resistance fighter at Ravensbrück]. *Austriaca [France] 1983 9(17): 103-113.* Rosa Jochmann (b. 1901), a leading Social Democratic activist, was arrested several times for her opposition to "Austrofascism." After the Nazi annexation of Austria, her clandestine support of the Resistance led to her detention at Ravensbrück. There her courageous leadership helped her fellow political prisoners to survive. She strengthened the national solidarity of the Austrian prisoners and after liberation she assisted in their repatriation. Later she led a movement in parliament to provide aid for the victims of fascism. Based partly on archives of the Austrian Resistance and letters of Rosa Jochmann; 13 notes, biblio. 1932-45

Joffre, Joseph

3303. Blondel, Jean. JOFFRE RACONTE PAR LUI-MÊME [Joffre described in his own words]. *Revue Historique des Armées [France] 1984 (1): 30-41.* Marshal Joseph Joffre's (1852-1931) various writings reveal him as a highly dedicated, skilled professional officer but one who could not abide the intrusion of politicians in technical military matters. As a military leader, he inspired confidence and high morale. Personally, he remained calm and logical in crisis, valued his privacy, and maintained an optimistic determination to succeed. He was a devoted husband. As a member of the French mission to the United States, he worked effectively with American officals. Based partly on personal archives; illus., 6 photos. 1870-1931

3304. Conte, Arthur. JOSEPH JACQUES CESAIRE JOFFRE, CATALAN ET MARECHAL DE FRANCE [Joseph Jacques Césaire Joffre, Catalonian and marshal of France]. *Revue Historique des Armées [France] 1984 (1): 4-9.* Joseph Joffre (1852-1931), a native of Rivesaltes in Roussillon, had a laconic and imperturbable personality. After graduating from the Polytechnic Institute, he became an officer in the corps of engineers and served in the Franco-Prussian War. This was followed by service in the Far East, Central Africa, and Madagascar. He became a director of the corps of engineers in the ministry of war, next a division and a corps commander, chief of the army general staff, and finally, commander of the Northeastern Army Group. The forces under his command turned back the German offensive in the Battle of the Marne, after which he was relieved and promoted to the rank of marshal. 6 photos. 1870-1918

3305. —. DOCUMENTS OU INEDITS [Unpublished documents]. *Revue Historique des Armées [France] 1984 (1): 46-53.* Facsimiles of five unpublished documents relating to the career of Marshal Joseph Joffre (1852-1931) provide evidence of his professional competence, leadership ability, and coolness in crisis. From the archives of the Army Historical Service; photo. 1874-1914

Jogiches, Leo

3306. Mason, Tim. COMRADE AND LOVER: ROSA LUXEMBURG'S LETTERS TO LEO JOGICHES. *Hist. Workshop J. [Great Britain] 1982 (13): 94-109.* 1890-1907

*For abstract see **Luxemburg, Rosa***

Johansen, Frederik Hjalmar

3307. Hinchliffe, Ian. FREDERIK HJALMAR JOHANSEN, POLAR EXPLORER 1867-1913. *Polar Record [Great Britain] 1983 21(135): 591-595.* A brief biography of Frederik Hjalmar Johansen, a capable Norwegian polar explorer whose fame was cut short by bad luck, alcoholism, and a vendetta with Roald Amundsen. 1892-1913

Johansen, Paul

3308. —. GEDENKEN ZUM 80. GEBURTSTAG VON PAUL JOHANSEN [A memorial celebration on Paul Johansen's 80th birthday]. *Zeits für Ostforschung [West Germany] 1982 31(4): 559-592.*

Angermann, Norbert. PAUL JOHANSEN ALS HISTORIKER DES ALTEN LIVLAND [Paul Johansen as historian of old Livonia], *pp. 561-573.* Lectures at the celebration 1981 of what would have been the 80th birthday of Paul Johansen (1901-65), born of Danish parents in Reval (now Tallinn), Estonia and its municipal archivist until 1939; from 1940 professor of Hanseatic and Eastern European history at Hamburg University and director, 1959-65, of its Finno-Ugrian Seminar. A tribute to Johansen's work as archivist and historian of medieval and 16th-17th-century Reval and Estonia—then known, with Latvia, as Livonia—its agrarian and cultural history, colonization, and foreign relations.

Weczerka, Hugo. PAUL JOHANSEN ALS HOCHSCHULLEHRER UND HANSEHISTORIKER [Paul Johansen as university teacher and Hanseatic historian], *pp. 573-579.* A former student and assistant pays tribute to Johansen's teaching methods and relations with students at Hamburg University and discusses his works on Eastern European and Hanseatic history and his activities on behalf of the Hanseatic History Society.

Veenker, Wolfgang. PAUL JOHANSEN UND DIE GRÜNDUNG DES FINNISCH-UGRISCHEN SEMINARS DER UNIVERSITÄT HAMBURG [Paul Johansen and the establishment of the Finno-Ugrian Seminar at Hamburg University], *pp. 579-588.* Discusses the history of Finno-Ugrian studies since the 17th century and the efforts of several scholars to establish the interdisciplinary Finno-Ugrian Seminar at Hamburg University. Paul Johansen directed the seminar from 1959 to his death.

Weczerka, Hugo. VERZEICHNIS DER VERÖFFENTLICHUNGEN PAUL JOHANSENS SEIT 1962 (MIT NACHTRÄGEN) UND DER IHM GEWIDMETEN BEITRÄGE [A list of Paul Johansen's publications since 1962 (with addenda) and of contributions dedicated to him]. *pp. 589-592.* Supplements Paul Johansen's bibliography to 1961, compiled by F.-K. Proehl. Based on Johansen's life and works; notes, biblio. 10c-17c

John III Sobieski

3309. Matwijowski, Krystyn. JAN III SOBIESKI JAKO MĄŻ STANU [John III Sobieski as a statesman]. *Śląski Kwartalnik Hist. Sobótka [Poland] 1980 35(2): 201-209.* Assesses John III Sobieski's doctrines and his foreign policies, including his interest in the friendly relations with Sweden and Russia, and his domestic policy of national unity. 1674-96

3310. Przyboś, Adam. JAN SOBIESKI W OBOZIE MALKONTENTÓW [Jan Sobieski in the opposition camp]. *Śląski Kwartalnik Hist. Sobótka [Poland] 1980 35(2): 191-200.* Surveys John III Sobieski's political loyalty to the French court before his ascension to the Polish throne. 1670's

3311. Szczygieł, Ryszard. JAN III SOBIESKI A ZAMOŚĆ [John III Sobieski and Zamość]. *Śląski Kwartalnik Hist. Sobótka [Poland] 1980 35(2): 283-291.* Surveys the relations between Sobieski and the magnate Marcin Zamoyski, owner of the town fortress of Zamość on the eastern frontier of Poland, thus of strategic importance in the 17th century. 1670's-96

3312. Wimmer, Jan. TRADYCJE WOJSKOWE RODU SOBIESKICH [Military tradition in the Sobieski family]. *Śląski Kwartalnik Hist. Sobótka [Poland] 1980 35(2): 149-161.* Views the military traditions in the Sobieski family, the activities of its members and the military apprenticeship of the future king of Poland, John III Sobieski. 16c-17c

3313. Wojcik, Zbigniew. JEAN SOBIESKI—DU POLITICIEN À L'HOMME D'ÉTAT [Jan Sobieski, from politician to statesman]. *Acta Poloniae Historica [Poland] 1983 (47): 5-31.* Reconsiders the political career and strategy of John III Sobieski (1629-96) both before and after his election as king of Poland in 1674. He consistently wished to strengthen the power of the crown, which led him before 1674 to be most of the time a member of the "pro-French" party. As king he wished to create a hereditary monarchy and strengthen its authority, but could not overcome the opposition of the nobility. Similarly, his foreign policy, based first on trying to strengthen Poland on the Baltic at the expense of Brandenburg, and then on extending Polish influence towards the Balkans and the Crimea, was a failure. He had a realistic view of the strategies necessary to strengthen Poland, but he was a very bad tactician. Printed sources and secondary works; 24 notes. 1629-96

John of Austria

3314. Pferschy, Gerhard. WER WAR ERZHERZOG JOHANN? EIN VERSUCH [Who was Archduke John? An investigation]. *Blätter für Heimatkunde [Austria] 1982 56(1): 2-8.* Explores background, development, ideas, and actions of Archduke John of Austria (1782-1859). 1782-20c

John the Russian, Saint

3315. Heyer, Friedrich. DER HEILIGE JOHANNIS HO ROSOS IN PROKOPION AUF EUBÖA [St. Iōannēs ho Rhōssos in Prokopion on Euboea]. *Ostkirchliche Studien [West Germany] 1985 34(1): 23-28.* Summarizes the life of St. John the Russian (ca. 1690-1730), a wonderworker born in the Ukraine, who lived half his life as one of the prisoners of war captured from the army of Peter the Great by the Ottoman Empire. Traces his cult in the Cappadocian village of Prokopion, transplanted by refugees to the Greek island of Euboea in 1924. 1711-1924

John the Steadfast, Elector

3316. Wright, William J. PERSONALITY PROFILES OF FOUR LEADERS OF THE GERMAN LUTHERAN REFORMATION. *Psychohistory Review 1985 14(1): 12-22.* Examines Martin Luther, Philip Melanchthon, Landgrave Philip of Hesse, and Elector John of Saxony as leaders of the German Lutheran Reformation, using Raymond B. Cartell's personality theory. None of the leaders were found to be consistently neurotic and all had common personality patterns by present-day standards. The personality traits seem to have played an important role in group performance. Secondary sources; 52 notes, 4 tables. 16c

John XXIII

3317. Piquer, Jordi. JUAN XXIII Y KRUSCHEV [John XXIII and Khrushchev]. *Historia y Vida [Spain] 1984 17(193): 58-69.* Examines the curious diplomatic relations between Pope John XXIII and Soviet leader Nikita Khrushchev, focusing on the pope's style, his role in the Cuban missile crisis of 1962 and in the liberation of Ukrainian Cardinal Joseph Slipyj, and his audience with Khrushchev's daughter and son-in-law. 1945-63

Johnson, Pamela Hansford

3318. Franks, Mildred Miles. PAMELA HANSFORD JOHNSON: SECONDARY SOURCES, 1934-1981. *Bull. of Biblio. 1983 40(2): 73-82.* Bibliography of biographical and critical studies and book reviews of English novelist Pamela Hansford Johnson and her works. 1934-81

Johnson, Samuel

3319. Brownley, M. W. SAMUEL JOHNSON AND THE PRINTING CAREER OF HESTER LYNCH PIOZZI. *Bulletin of the John Rylands University Library of Manchester [Great Britain] 1985 67(2): 623-640.* 18c
For abstract see ***Piozzi, Hester Lynch***

3320. Chadwick, Owen. THE RELIGION OF SAMUEL JOHNSON. *Yale University Library Gazette 1986 60(3-4): 119-136.* There was no higher study for Samuel Johnson than theology. Although he was a stable Christian layman well-versed in religion, he was not an ardent churchgoer. Johnson wrote some fifty-odd sermons, although his name did not appear on any of them. At times of crisis he composed collects for moral reassurance even though he shunned formalism and was not a man of the Psalter. At heart a theologian who wrote no theology, he was the epitome of the moral man possessed of a skeptical intelligence who was still unquestioning in his faith. Based on a lecture to the Johnsonians, Yale University, September 1984; 32 notes. 1744-84

3321. Finney, Brian. BOSWELL'S *HEBRIDEAN JOURNAL* AND THE ORDEAL OF DR. JOHNSON. *Biography 1982 5(4): 319-334.* 1773-84
For abstract see ***Boswell, James***

3322. Greene, Donald. THE GREAT HIGHBROW: SAMUEL JOHNSON AFTER TWO CENTURIES. *South Atlantic Quarterly 1985 84(3): 264-279.* Attacks the ersatz life portraits of Samuel Johnson (1709-84) painted by James Boswell and Thomas Babington Macaulay. Extols his powerful intellect, his wide-ranging interests, his profound concern for the problems of the human condition, his unmatched artistry with words—all of which Boswell and Macaulay tended to deny or disdain. Their biographies of Johnson presented nothing more than fiction. Based on literary criticism and other articles on Samuel Johnson; 31 notes. 1730's-84

3323. Honan, Park. DR. JOHNSON AND BIOGRAPHY. *Contemporary Review [Great Britain] 1984 245(1427): 304-310.* An exhibition was held in London by the Arts Council, 19 July-14 September 1984, to mark the bicentenary of Dr. Samuel Johnson's (1709-84) death. Traces the life and career of Dr. Johnson as a poet, a critic, and a lexicographer, and examines his work as a biographer, particularly his *Lives of the English Poets* which he wrote in 1777. 1709-84

3324. Lipking, Lawrence. THE DEATH AND LIFE OF SAMUEL JOHNSON. *Wilson Quarterly 1984 8(5): 140-151.* The final days of Samuel Johnson (1709-84) attracted the morbid fascination of the English public who wanted to see how the great man of letters approached death. Although the accounts of the actual death scene vary considerably, all agree that Johnson had no choice but to die well. 1784

3325. Lockwood, Allison. SAMUEL JOHNSON. *British Heritage 1984 5(4): 62-73.* Recounts Samuel Johnson's life on the occasion of his bicentenary celebrated by the Johnson Society of London and Lichfield, his birthplace. 1709-84

3326. Luján, Néstor. SAMUEL JOHNSON [Samuel Johnson]. *Historia y Vida [Spain] 1984 17(194): 88-95.* Discusses the life of 18th-century English writer Samuel Johnson, whose greatest accomplishment was the writing of his English dictionary, and reveals a very different personality than the one James Boswell described in his biography. 1730-84

3327. McEllhenney, John G. JOHN WESLEY AND SAMUEL JOHNSON: A TALE OF THREE COINCIDENCES. *Methodist Hist. 1983 21(3): 143-155.* 1738-77
For abstract see ***Wesley, John***

3328. Porter, Roy. "MAD ALL MY LIFE": THE DARK SIDE OF SAMUEL JOHNSON. *History Today [Great Britain] 1984 34(Dec): 43-46.* Throughout his life, Samuel Johnson (1709-84), English author and intellectual, displayed signs of mental illness that reflect his intense spiritual struggle. 18c

3329. Rogers, J. P. W. SAMUEL JOHNSON'S GOUT. *Medical History [Great Britain] 1986 30(2): 133-144.* Samuel Johnson, who was familiar with the popular works on the disease, believed that he suffered from gout periodically from 1775 until his death in 1784. In the 18th century, however, gout was not clearly distinguished from various types of arthritis. Although a diagnosis of gout is not excluded by Johnson's medical history and symptoms, other diseases of the joints are equally indicated. Pain attributed to gout was common in the 18th century and generally accepted as an unfortunate but unavoidable affliction. Secondary sources; 38 notes. 18c

3330. Shenker, Israel. A SAMUEL JOHNSON CELEBRATION RECALLS HIS WIT AND WISDOM. *Smithsonian 1984 15(9): 60-68.* Describes the life and writings of Samuel Johnson (1709-84), English conversationalist and author of moralistic essays, philosophical verse and, under the patronage of the Earl of Chesterfield, the two-volume English lexicon, *Dictionary* (1755). ca 1740-84

3331. Vance, John. SAMUEL JOHNSON AND THOMAS WARTON. *Biography 1986 9(2): 95-111.* Few of Samuel Johnson's relationships have been as misunderstood and little appreciated as his friendship with Thomas Warton. The evidence suggests that the relationship was among the most emotional of Johnson's life and that what lessened the spirit of the friendship after the mid-1750's was not a difference in personality or literary taste, as had been commonly thought, but rather it was Johnson's realization that his emotional stake in the relationship had been too high. 1750's-80's

Johnston, Denis

3332. Abramson, Doris. A TRIBUTE TO DENIS JOHNSTON. *Massachusetts Rev. 1982 23(3): 389-409.* Interview with William Denis Johnston (b. 1901), Irish playwright, lawyer, war correspondent, professor, and director for stage, film, and television, with a biographical sketch and excerpts from his diary. Reminisces about his associations with George Bernard Shaw and Samuel Beckett (b. 1906). Based on Johnston diary, reminiscences, and interview; illus., portrait, 6 notes. ca 1920-82

Johnston, Tom

3333. Douds, Gerard. TOM JOHNSTON IN INDIA. *Journal of the Scottish Labour History Society [Great Britain] 1984 (19): 6-21.* Discusses the imperial activities and beliefs of Tom Johnston (1882-1965), who was active in the labor movement, was a Labour Member of Parliament, 1922-31, and was subsequently Lord Privy Seal and Secretary of State for Scotland. Particular attention is paid to his tour of India in 1925. 1920's

Joliot-Curie, Frédéric

3334. Yaffe, Leo. THE SCIENTIFIC LEGACY OF MARIE CURIE. *Transactions of the Royal Society of Canada [Canada] 1984 22: 307-316.* 1930's-80's
*For abstract see **Curie, Marie***

Jomini, Antoine-Henri

3335. Alger, John I.; Gallaher, John (commentary). JOMINI: A MAN OF PRINCIPLE. *Consortium on Revolutionary Europe 1750-1850: Pro. 1980 1: 142-148.* Concerns the career and the writings of Antoine-Henri Jomini (1779-1869). Jomini was born in Switzerland, served in Napoleon's army from 1804 to 1813, and then joined the army of Tsar Alexander I. He helped to revolutionize warfare through his publications that appeared from 1807 to 1834. He established the immutable principle that "to be superior to the enemy at the decisive point is the key to victory." Comments, pp. 150-151. Based on printed primary sources; 14 notes. 1807-34

3336. Hirzel, Werner. ANTOINE-HENRI JOMINI (1779-1869) [Antoine-Henri Jomini (1779-1869)]. *Zeits für Heereskunde [West Germany] 1980 44(292): 154-157.* Reports on writings and life of the Swiss adventurer and military adviser and his career at the court of Napoleon. 1779-1869

Jones, Evan

3337. Tanna, Laura. EVAN JONES: MAN OF TWO WORLDS. *Jamaica Journal [Jamaica] 1985-86 18(4): 38-45.* Evan Jones (b. 1927), born in Jamaica and a resident of England, discusses growing up in Jamaica, his education in the United States and England, the development of his career as a writer, and the production of his television screenplays and filmscripts. 1930's-85

Jones, Noah

3338. Sell, Alan P. F. RETIREMENT DENIED: THE LIFE AND MINISTRY OF NOAH JONES (1725-1785). *Tr. of the Unitarian Hist. Soc. [Great Britain] 1984 18(2): 24-38.* Outlines the career of the Unitarian minister Noah Jones (1725-85), with particular reference to his ministry in Walsall and the divisions of the church there. 1725-85

Jones, Richard

3339. Dyster, Barrie. THE RISE OF WILLIAM FANNING AND THE RUIN OF RICHARD JONES. *J. of the Royal Australian Hist. Soc. [Australia] 1982 67(4): 366-374.* ca 1841-80's
*For abstract see **Fanning, William***

Jones, Stanley

3340. Deminger, S. "Evangelist på Indiska Villkor. Stanley Jones och den Indiska Renässansen, 1918-1930" [Evangelist on Indian terms: Stanley Jones and the Indian Renaissance, 1918-30]. Uppsala U. [Sweden] 1985. 224 pp. *DAI-C 1986 47(2): 293; 47/1410c.* 1918-30

Jones, William

3341. Dasgupta, R. K. SIR WILLIAM JONES. *Indian Horizons [India] 1984 33(3-4): 17-28.* Offers an evocative bibliographic essay on the life and works of Sir William Jones (1746-94), an Oriental scholar and English judge of outstanding reputation. As a great master of Graeco-Latin learning and scholar of Sanskrit, Arabic, and Persian, Jones initiated the introduction of Oriental literature to the Western world. 1760's-94

Jórczak, Jan

3342. Gudziński, Eugeniusz. JAN JÓRCZAK (1905-1983) [Jan Jórczak (1905-83)]. *Kwartalnik Historii Ruchu Zawodowego [Poland] 1984 23(1-2): 168-169.* An obituary of an activist of the Polish labor movement from the 1920's to the 1950's. 1920's-80

Jordan, Denis Oswald

3343. Coates, J. H. DENIS OSWALD JORDAN, 1914-82. *Historical Records of Australian Science [Australia] 1985 6(2): 237-246.* A specialist in the physical chemistry of nucleic acids and in macromolecular science, Jordan moved in 1954 from his native England to Australia. He was soon prominent as a faculty member and administrator at the University of Adelaide and in the wider community of Australian scientists. Based on author's personal knowledge; 4 notes, biblio. 1940's-82

Jordán, František

3344. Čerešňák, Bedřich and Malíř, Jiří. NAD DÍLEM FRANTIŠKA JORDÁNA [The life work of František Jordán]. *Sborník Prací Filosofické Fakulty Brněnské U.: Řada Hist. [Czechoslovakia] 1981 30(28): 7-29.* František Jordán (1921-79) was a major Moravian historian, university teacher, and member of the Czechoslovak Academy of Sciences, whose untimely death deprived his country and university of a leading expert on the history of Moravia, especially its capital, Brno, and its labor movement, and on the history of Czech-Yugoslav relations. Includes bibliography of Jordán's works. 1921-79

Jordan, Johann Peter

3345. Grabski, Andrzej F. KTO BYŁ TŁUMACZEM JOACHIM LELEWELA? POMYŁKA FRYDERYKA ENGELSA [Who translated Joachim Lelewel? Friedrich Engels's error]. *Kwartalnik Historii Nauki i Techniki [Poland] 1985 30(1): 93-110.* In an 1848 newspaper article, Friedrich Engels erroneously identified Wilhelm Jordan as the translator of Joachim Lelewel's *Histoire de Pologne* [History of Poland] from French into German. Annotations in later Polish editions of the book indicate that the translator was Johann Peter Jordan, a Slavicist and an activist in the Serbian national movement. Discusses J. P. Jordan's involvement in popularizing Polish literature and history in 19th-century Germany. Based on published primary and secondary Polish, German, and Serbian sources; 58 notes. Russian and German summaries. 19c

Joris, David

3346. Stayer, James M. DAVID JORIS: A PROLEGOMENON TO FURTHER RESEARCH. *Mennonite Quarterly Review 1985 59(4): 350-361.* David Joris (1501-56) was considered by some contemporaries the major Anabaptist leader. The author provides a provisional biographical summary and an assessment of Joris's 16th-century interpreters. He also reviews the significant writings on Joris and suggests directions for future research. 77 notes. 16c

Joseph II

3347. Tizian, Karl. "JOSEPH II. UND SEINE ZEIT" IN MELK: BEMERKUNGEN ZU EINER NIEDERÖSTERREICHISCHEN AUSSTELLUNG AUS VORARLBERGER SICHT ["Joseph II and His Time" at Melk: remarks on a Lower Austrian exhibition as seen from Vorarlberg]. *Montfort [Austria] 1981 33(2): 159-163.* The exhibition "Joseph II and His Time" at Melk lacked a discussion of the Habsburg emperor's policies toward Vorarlberg, especially his attempts to create a separate Feldkirch diocese, which met with strong opposition from the bishop of Augsburg. 1780-90

Joseph Karl Ludwig, Archduke

3348. Kutlík-Garudo, Igor E. ZUR 150. WIEDERKEHR DES GEBURTSTAGES VON JOSEF HABSBURG, DEM VERKANNTEN GROSSEN ROMANI-SPRACHFORSCHER [On the 150th birthday of Joseph Habsburg, the misunderstood great Romany philologist]. *Anzeiger der Österreichischen Akad. der Wiss. Philosophisch-Historische Klasse [Austria] 1982 119(1-10): 158-174.* Prints a biography of Archduke Joseph Karl Ludwig Habsburg (b. 1833), focusing on his contributions to the study of the linguistics of Romany, the language of European Gypsies, which he published under the pseudonym of József Főherczeg. 1864-1902

Jouvenel, Bertrand de

3349. Braun, John Ronald. *"Une Fidélité* Difficile: The Early Life and Ideas of Bertrand de Jouvenel, 1903-1945." U. of Waterloo [Canada] 1985. *DAI 1985 46(5): 1381-A.* 1903-45

Jovellanos, Gaspar Melchor de

3350. Diaz, Nidia A. "El Anticlericalismo de Jovellanos" [Jovellanos's anticlericalism]. U. of New York 1983. 290 pp. *DAI 1983 44(1): 183-A.* DA8312341 1770-1811

Joyce, James

3351. Cunard, Nancy. ON JAMES JOYCE—FOR PROFESSOR ELLMANN. *Lib. Chronicle of the U. of Texas at Austin 1982 (20-21): 82-89.* 1930-37
For abstract see ***Cunard, Nancy***

3352. Fitch, Nancy Elizabeth. "History in a Nightmare: A Study of the Exilic in the Life and Work of James Joyce, V. S. Naipaul and Edna O'Brien." U. of Michigan 1981. 156 pp. *DAI 1982 42(9): 4104-A.* DA8204648 20c

3353. Herr, Cheryl. QUOTING WITH AN ACCENT: BLOOMSDAY IN ROME. *Midwest Q. 1983 25(1): 34-46.* Describes the life and experiences of James Joyce during the six months that he spent in Rome, a period when *Ulysses* was gestating in his mind. Before this period, Joyce was drifting and in a state of flux concerning his work. The experience of Rome's culture and daily life helped Joyce fix his goals and give shape to the ideas that would become *Ulysses.* Biblio. 1906-07

Joyce, Jeremiah

3354. Seed, John. JEREMIAH JOYCE, UNITARIANISM AND THE VICISSITUDES OF THE RADICAL INTELLIGENTSIA IN THE 1790S. *Tr. of the Unitarian Hist. Soc. [Great Britain] 1981 17(3): 97-108.* Discusses the experiences and perceptions of Jeremiah Joyce, Unitarian minister, writer, and activist in the radical Society for Constitutional Information, in relation to Unitarianism, the social and political changes in England in the 1790's, and the collapse of radicalism among English Unitarians. 1790-1816

Joyce, Lucia

3355. Hayman, David. SHADOW OF HIS MIND: THE PAPERS OF LUCIA JOYCE. *Lib. Chronicle of the U. of Texas at Austin 1982 (20-21): 64-79.* A review of the papers of Lucia Joyce (b. 1907), the daughter of James Joyce, composed over four years, 1958-61, when Lucia was responding well to treatments for schizophrenia. 1958-61

Joyce, Roger

3356. Lemon, Andrew and Wheeler, Doreen. OBITUARY—ROGER JOYCE. *Archives and Manuscripts [Australia] 1985 13(1): 7-9.* Provides an obituary of Roger Joyce (1924-84), who served as professor of history at La Trobe University and was an important member of the Australian Society of Archivists. 1940's-84

3357. Shaw, George. ROGER BILBROUGH JOYCE 1924-84. *Australian Journal of Politics and History [Australia] 1984 30(3): 324-326.* Roger Joyce died a few weeks after the publication of his *Samuel Walker Griffith* (1984), a biography of the Queensland politician and later chief justice. Reviews this work and provides a tribute to Joyce. A product of the post-World War II Sydney school, Joyce was "strong on the analysis of particular documents and events, and cautious to the point of understatement in interpreting evidence." 1870's-1920

Józewski, Henryk

3358. Józewski, Henryk. ZAMIAST PAMIĘTNIKA [Instead of a diary]. *Zeszyty Hist. [France] 1982 (59): 3-163, (60): 65-157.* Part 1. Part of a larger, unpublished work *Opowieść o Istnieniu* [A story of existence], of a Pole, Henryk Józewski (1892-1981), includes his early pro-Polish activity in Kiev, participation in the Kiev branch of the Polska Organizacja Wojskowa [Polish Military Organization], activity during the Russo-Polish War of 1920, involvement in the Polish government between the world wars, tenure as the governor of Volhynia, conciliatory actions in the Polish-Ukrainian controversy, positive appraisal of Joseph Pilsudski, resistance activity during World War II, imprisonment by the Communist forces after the war, and his regaining of freedom in 1957. Part 2. The old Polish-Ukrainian issue had always been complicated by the lack of an independent Eastern Orthodox Church in Poland and the resulting representation of the Ukrainians' religion by Moscow. This was rectified in the period between the world wars. In Volhynia beween 1928 and 1938 great strides were made in Polish-Ukrainian cooperation within the Polish state. This was opposed by Polish Nationalists, and Ukrainian extremists, and the Soviets. 1892-1960

József, Attila

3359. Tasi, József. JÓZSEF ATTILA ELŐÖRS-KORSZAKA [Attila József's *Előörs* period]. *Magyar Könyvszemle [Hungary] 1981 97(4): 332-337.* The liberal poet Attila József was not accepted for publication by the leading periodicals of his time. When he became a member of the Miklós Bartha Society, a Transylvanian organization founded in 1925, he was accepted by the periodical *Előörs* [Avant-Garde]. His poem *Akácokhoz!* appeared in the 26 October 1929 issue. The poem dealt with the peasants' attempts at organization. When Endre Bajcsy-Zsilinszky (1886-1944), editor of *Előörs,* broke with the society because of its leftist leanings, József had to leave the periodical. Eventually he aligned himself with the then illegal Communist movement. Primary sources; 40 notes. 1929-32

Juan, Prince

3360. Azcona, Tarsicio de. EL PRINCIPE DON JUAN, HEREDERO DE LOS REYES CATOLICOS EN EL V CENTENARIO DE SU NACIMIENTO (1478-1497) [Prince Juan, heir of the Catholic monarchs, on the occasion of the 5th centenary of his birth, 1478-97]. *Cuadernos de Investigación Hist. [Spain] 1983 7: 219-243.* Using account books and other documentary sources profiles the life and activities of Juan, Prince of Asturias, and heir to Ferdinand and Isabel (1478-97). Suggests that the cause of his death was a long-term weakness of constitution rather than sexual excess, as has been traditionally held. Contrary to the suggestion of some historians, the Austrian Succession was not an unalloyed benefit to Spain. Had Juan lived and a national dynasty continued, the history of Spain would have been much different and perhaps happier. Provides texts of six documents, 1475-96. Text of an address to the Fundación Universitaria Española, 29 November 1978. Based on documents from the Archivo General de Simancas, Archivo Histórico Nacional, and other archives; biblio., appendix. 1478-97

Juan y Santacilia, Jorge

3361. Díez Davó, Remigio. SEMBLANZA DE JORGE JUAN [Biographical sketch of Jorge Juan]. *Rev. General de Marina [Spain] 1981 201(Oct): 281-291.* Jorge Juan y Santacilia (1713-1773) was an extraordinary Spanish naval officer. Scientist, engineer, writer, diplomat, administrator, and scholar, he utilized his great talents and energy in the service of Spain and knowledge. He made scientific expeditions to the Americas and published a number of works on geography, astronomy, and naval science. For his scholarship he was named to the French, British, and Prussian academies of science. He directed the building of Spanish dockyards and dry docks. He reorganized the Spanish naval academy. He founded the Spanish mint. He served as ambassador to Morocco to carry through sensitive negotiations. With reason he was known as the Spanish sage. 3 illus., biblio. 1713-73

3362. O'Dogherty, Pascual. JORGE JUAN, MARINO Y CIENTIFICO [Jorge Juan, sailor and scientist]. *Rev. General de Marina [Spain] 1981 201(Aug): 11-21.* The life of Jorge Juan (1713-73) combined distinguished qualities of active and heroic naval service, scientific and mathematical investigations and publications, and construction of naval vessels. 4 illus., biblio. 1713-73

Juel, Niels

3363. Jespersen, Knud J. V. ANMELDELSER: NIELS JUEL [Reviews: Niels Juel]. *Hist. Tidsskrift [Denmark] 1980 80(2): 543-549.* Reviews Jørgen H. Barfod's *Niels Juel. Liv og Gerning i den Danske Søetat* (1977), Jørgen H. Barfod's *Niels Juel. A Danish Admiral of the 17th Century* (1977), and Hans Chr. Bjerg's *Slaget i Køge Bugt l. Juli 1677. Forudsaetninger, Forløb og Følger* (1977), which commemorate the 300th anniversary of the Battle of Køge Bight, 1677, and are in honor of the memory of Niels Juel (1629-97). 1629-97

Jugan, Jeanne

3364. Langlois, Claude. "JE SUIS JEANNE JUGAN": DEPENDANCE SOCIALE, CONDITION FEMININE ET FONDATION RELIGIEUSE ["I am Jeanne Jugan": social dependence, the status of women, and religious foundation]. *Archives de Sciences Sociales des Religions [France] 1981 52(1): 21-35.* The role of Jeanne Jugan as founder of the Little Sisters of the Poor at Saint-Servan in Brittany in 1839 was until 1947 ignored in official histories of the order, which attributed the foundation to the *abbé* Le Pailleur, vicar of Saint-Servan, and his young protegée Marie Jamet. The deliberate falsification arose from the institutionalization of the order and its integration into the respectable world of ultramontane religious congregations during the late 19th century, when an old servant woman would not have been seen as a suitable founder. But the expansion and success of the Sisters in providing hospices for the aged owed much to the example of Jeanne Jugan, especially in reviving the idea of direct begging for goods for the poor. Printed sources and secondary works; 42 notes. 19c

Jumblatt, Kamal

3365. Fëdorov, A. EGO NAZYVALI UCHITEL' [They called him the teacher]. *Aziia i Afrika Segodnia [USSR] 1985 (12): 15-17.* Describes the life and achievements of Lebanese scholar, writer, and statesman Kamal Jumblatt (1917-77), who strove to free Lebanon from the ethno-religious chauvinism crippling its political system and from economic dependence on the United States. English summary. 1920's-77

Jung, Carl

3366. Homans, Peter. [INSIGHTS INTO FREUD AND JUNG]. *J. of the Hist. of the Behavioral Sci. 1983 19(3): 240-244.* 1912-23
For abstract see ***Freud, Sigmund***

3367. Rice, James L. RUSSIAN STEREOTYPES IN THE FREUD-JUNG CORRESPONDENCE. *Slavic Rev. 1982 41(1): 19-34.* 1906-14
For abstract see ***Freud, Sigmund***

Jünger, Enrst

3368. Evans, Arthur R., Jr. ASSIGNMENT TO ARMAGEDDON: ERNST JÜNGER AND CURZIO MALAPARTE ON THE RUSSIAN FRONT, 1941-43. *Central European Hist. 1981 14(4): 295-321.* Describes and compares the lives of Ernst Jünger, and Curzio Malaparte. Analyzes specifically the written works of each about trips to the Russian front on the Axis side during World War II. Malaparte reported as a journalist on the war at its beginning from Romania and southern Russia in 1941 as the Army Group South moved toward Kiev and later in 1942 from Finland where he observed the siege of Leningrad. Jünger's tour as an army observer of the north Caucasus took place in 1942 and early 1943. Both writers dealt with the activities of the German soldiers and the reaction of the Russians. 66 notes.
1920-45

Júnior, Almeida

3369. Mello Júnior, Donato. O PINTOR ALMEIDA JUNIOR E O IMPERADOR D. PEDRO II [The painter Almeida Júnior and Emperor Pedro II]. *Revista do Instituto Histórico e Geográfico Brasileiro [Brazil] 1982 (337): 185-192.* There are many versions of the relations between Pedro II and the Brazilian painter Almeida Júnior (1850-99), but what is certain is that an imperial subsidy enabled the artist to pursue his studies in Europe. The emperor also owned several of the painter's works. Based on primary material in the Fine Arts school and museum archives; 19 notes.
1850-99

Juras, Francis M.

3370. Laučka, Isabelle T. THE MONSIGNOR AND HIS ARCHIVES. *Lituanus 1982 28(4): 48-54.* Located in Putnam, Connecticut, the American Lithuanian Cultural Archive (ALKA) serves as a repository for Lithuanian artifacts which have been collected since 1922. It was formed by Monsignor Francis M. Juras (1891-1980) to preserve the Lithuanian national heritage. Father Juras, a native-born Lithuanian who came to the United States in 1912, worked ceaselessly on behalf of Lithuanian organizations and activities in this country. Now under the Lithuanian Catholic Academy of Sciences, the ALKA functions as an archive on the history of Lithuanian parishes. As a museum its holdings include Lithuanian books (some rare), periodicals, photographs, paintings, crosses, tapestries, folk art, and agricultural implements. Photo. 1912-80

Jürgen, Otsa

3371. Arens, Ilmar. OTSA JÜRGEN, LÄÄNIGA AUTASUSTATUD ROOTSI ARMEESPIOON TARTUS 1656-1657 [Otsa Jürgen's honorary vassalage for his espionage services to the Swedish army in Tartu, 1656-57]. *Eesti Teadusliku Seltsi Rootsis. Aastaraamat [Sweden] 1980-84 9: 85-97.* In 1662, King Charles XI of Sweden granted to an Estonian peasant Otsa Jürgen and to his wife personal freedom and the usage of some tax free land in return for his faithful service to the Swedish crown. Otsa Jürgen had served as a military courier delivering secret letters and messages to the king and the crown during the "Muscovy War" (1656-61) as the Russians were besieging the town of Tartu. In 1680 Otsa Jürgen informed King Charles XI that his rights were being violated by the local authorities and petitioned the king to reconfirm his liberties. His request was honored by the General Gouvernor Jakob John Hästler, who informed Otsa Jürgen that his status as the king's vassal was inviolable. Secondary sources; 2 illus., 48 notes. English summary, p. 5.
1656-80

K

Kabris, Joseph

3372. Terrell, Jennifer. JOSEPH KABRIS AND HIS NOTES ON THE MARQUESAS. *J. of Pacific Hist. [Australia] 1982 17(2): 101-112.* Of three Europeans who lived in the Marquesas Islands in the South Pacific between 1796 and 1806, the Frenchman Joseph Kabris came closer than any to the Marquesan culture. He arrived on an English whaler around 1796 and was eventually completely absorbed into a local tribe. Following his involuntary return to Europe in 1804 he wrote a number of booklets on his experiences, one of which is included in English translation. This account of Marquesan life is straightforward, neither romantic nor sensational, and provides unique but apparently authentic early ethnographic observations on the area and its culture. Based mostly on primary sources; 55 notes. 1795-1817

Kaczmarczyk, Zdzisław

3373. Wąsicki, Jan. PROF. DR. ZDZISŁAW KACZMARCZYK (1911-1980) [Zdzisław Kaczmarczyk (1911-80)]. *Przegląd Zachodni [Poland] 1981 37(1-2): 1-8.* Born in 1911 in Cracow, Zdzisław Kaczmarczyk attended Karol Marcinkowski High School in Poznań and in 1929 enrolled in the law school of Poznań University. After graduation in 1933 he became assistant to Zygmunt Wojciechowski, leader in studies of Polish-German relations. Kaczmarczyk's master's thesis was entitled "Economic Immunities in Church Lands in Polonia Minor in the 12th Century." His doctoral and habilitation theses were also historical. After World War II Dr. Kaczmarczyk returned to Poznań and together with Dr. Wojciechowski formed the Instytut Zachodni. Dr. Kaczmarczyk's curriculum included teaching, publication, and organizational efforts to promote the study of the history of provinces that were once under Prussian rule. 1911-80

Kádár, János

3374. Fedoseev, P. N. VYDAIUSHCHIISIA RUKOVODITEL' NARODNOI VENGRII (K 70-LETIIU SO DNIA ROZHDENIIA IANOSHA KADARA) [The outstanding leader of People's Hungary: on the 70th birthday of János Kádár]. *Voprosy Istorii KPSS [USSR] 1982 (5): 107-111.* János Kádár was born 26 May 1912 into a worker's family and early knew the harsh conditions of capitalism. He joined the Communist Party in 1931 and was arrested many times. After the war he was elected to many political functions. He was arrested and imprisoned on false charges in 1951 and rehabilitated in 1954. He was elected to the Politburo in 1956. After the attempt at counterrevolution in 1956, Kadar became First Secretary of the Central Committee of the Hungarian Socialist Workers' Party and began the consolidation of socialism. He introduced successful reforms in industry and agriculture. Brezhnev and Kadar meet regularly. He is a staunch Marxist-Leninist, a great leader of his people, and a true friend of the USSR. Based on Kadar's works, *Pravda,* and other Soviet sources; 12 notes. 1912-82

3375. Száraz, György. AZ Ő TITKA—MEG A MIÉNK, JEGYZETEK EGY KÁDÁR-KÉPHEZ [His secret—and ours: notes on a portrait of Kádár]. *Társadalmi Szemle [Hungary] 1982 37(6): 79-85.* Marginalia on a book by László Gyurkó about János Kádár, with a survey of the latter's historical role in the past decades. He played no part in the László Rajk trial. 1949-80

Kadłubowski, Karol

3376. Gadomski, Bogdan and Jędrzejewska, Lucyna. DZIAŁACZE ZWIĄZKOWI—UCZESTNICY REWOLUCJI PAŹDZIERNIKOWEJ [Trade union activists who participated in the October Revolution]. *Kwartalnik Hist. Ruchu Zawodowego [Poland] 1979 18(1): 69-77, (3): 57-68.* Part 4. Surveys participation in the 1917 Russian Revolution of the following Polish trade unionists: Karol Kadłubowski, Feliks Kapłan, Ignacy Kaźmierczak, Kazimierz Kiełczewski, Izaak Kobryner, Karol Kocemba, Jan Kopczynski, Jan Leśniewski, with biographical sketches. Part 5. Surveys the participation of Bogdan Łapiński, Tomasz Magrzyk, Aleksander Majewski, Aleksander Makutynowicz, Roman Markowiak, Roman Markowski, Bronisław Marks, Balbina Matuszewska, and Wincenty Matuszewski, with biographical sketches. 1917

Kaempfer, Engelbert

3377. Lazar, M. "Engelbert Kaempfer als Kartograph und Geograph" [Engelbert Kaempfer as cartographer and geographer]. U. of Vienna [Austria] 1980. 306 pp. *DAI-C 1984 45(3): 684; 9/2793c.* 17c

Kâfi, Hasan

3378. İpşirli, Mehmet. HASAN KÂFÎ EL-AKHİSARÎ VE DEVLET DÜZENİNE AİT ESERİ USÛLÜ'L-HİKEM FÎ NÎZAMÎ'L-ÂLEM [Hasan Kâfî el-Akhisarî and his work on the organization of the state, *Usûlü'l-Hikem fî Nizâmi'l-Âlem]. Tarih Enstitüsü Dergisi [Turkey] 1979-80 10-11: 239-278.* Hasan Kâfî (1544-1616) was born in Akhisar (now Prusac, Yugoslavia), and during a long career in Ottoman service composed 17 works of philology, law, philosophy, theology, history, and politics. His *Usûlü'l-Hikem fî Nizâmi'l-Âlem* (Principles of Wisdom in the Order of the World), composed in 1596, marks him as an early and perceptive observer of Ottoman decline. The text is reproduced in full in the modern Turkish alphabet. 1544-1616

Kafka, Franz

3379. Cohen, Arthur A. KAFKA'S PRAGUE. *Partisan Rev. 1981 48(4): 552-563.* This biographical sketch explores the varied cultural impacts of being a Jew, a German, and a Czech on Franz Kafka's fiction and his view of reality. Prague was Kafka's world, defining both his biography and his craft. The two were often the one in his mind. The classic example of alienation, Kafka spent his life trying to relate to *le vrai,* the pedestrian flow of days. Lacking the warm intimacy of family, Kafka saw his writing as a fatal necessity. Kafka's life was in Prague but his art was universal in significance. 1883-1924

3380. Golomb, Jacob. KAFKA'S EXISTENTIAL METAMORPHOSIS: FROM KIERKEGAARD TO NIETZSCHE AND BEYOND. *Clio 1985 14(3): 271-286.* As a German Jew in the early 20th century struggling for identity, Franz Kafka identified on a personal level with Søren Kierkegaard's existential anxieties and guilt feelings. But his spiritual father and most important influence on his theological development was Friedrich Nietzsche, who emphasized an "absurd and irrational reality." Based on translations of Kafka's literary works and private papers and secondary sources; 60 notes. 1900's-24

3381. Steinhauer, Harry. FRANZ KAFKA: A WORLD BUILT ON A LIE. *Antioch Rev. 1983 41(4): 390-408.* A short biography of Franz Kafka and interpretations of five of his parables: *Before the Law, The Knock at the Manor Gate, An Everyday Heroism, A Little Fable,* and *A Commentary* (also known as *Give It Up).* The last parable reinforces the conclusion reached by the man from the country in *Before the Law* that the world is built on a lie. 1914-20

3382. Wexelblatt, Robert. KLEIST, KIERKEGAARD, KAFKA AND MARRIAGE. *San José Studies 1983 9(1): 6-15.* These three literary and philosophical figures shared a similar negative attitude toward marriage because of their intellectual perspectives on the human condition. 19c-20c

Kagame, Alexis

3383. Harroy, Jean-Paul. ALEXIS KAGAME [Alexis Kagame—obituary]. *Bulletin des Séances de l'Académie des Sciences d'Outre Mer [Belgium] 1982 28(1): 66-78.* Alexis Kagame (1912-81) was an important Rwandan scholar, folklorist, teacher, and religious figure. A prolific writer, he was also editor-in-chief of the Catholic periodical *Kinyamateka.* His political involvement caused him occasional problems with the local Catholic hierarchy after World War II. His doctoral dissertation (1955) on the indigenous Rwandan philosophy of being is but one example of his abiding interest in the culture and thought of his country and people. 1912-81

Kaggwa, Apolo

3384. Balezin, A. S. PERVYE UGANDIISKIE PROSVETITELI [The first Ugandan educators]. *Narody Azii i Afriki [USSR] 1981 (4): 129-138.* The first schools in Uganda were run by European missionaries (1877-1900's), providing education primarily for children of the local elite. From this generation, however, there emerged several pure Ugandan intellectuals and politicans, who did much to establish a national system of education and give their people a sense of identity through their historico-ethnographical writings. Among the most prominent of these were Apolo Kaggwa, Daudi Kasagama and John Nyakatura, whose lives and works are described in detail. Table, 42 notes. 1870's-1920's

Kahlo, Frida

3385. Herrera, Hayden. "Frida Kahlo: Her Life, Her Art." City U. of New York 1981. 1016 pp. *DAI 1985 46(2): 286-A.* DA8501138 1930's-54

Kainar, Josef

3386. Blahynka, Milan. JOSEF KAINAR ZA PROTEKTORÁTU [Josef Kainar (1917-72) during the Protectorate]. *Česká Literatura [Czechoslovakia] 1982 30(1): 30-41.* One collection of Kainar's verse, *Dvůr,* was banned by the censor during the war and has never been found, although certain items from it are included in later compilations. Another collection *Osudy,* concerning fear within man, does survive, as does his considerable wartime output of blues lyrics. Based on private correspondence and secondary sources; 13 notes. 1937-47

Kajii Motojirō

3387. Ulmer, Robert Allan. "The Private World of Kajii Motojirō." Yale U. 1982. 367 pp. *DAI 1982 43(5): 1550-A.* DA8221759 1920-32

Kakungulu, Semei

3388. Twaddle, Michael. THE NINE LIVES OF SEMEI KAKUNGULU. *History in Africa 1985 12: 325-333.* Semei Kakungulu was a prominent figure in Ugandan politics and religious life in the late 19th and early 20th centuries. During his long career, Kakungulu was noted as a hunter, Ganda chief, border warlord, British ally, near founder of a new kingdom in Busoga, and separatist sect leader. Nine major accounts of his life survive in the Ganda vernacular. Kakungulu appealed to many Ganda writers whose new literacy and conversion to Christianity prompted them to view him as a heroic figure. Apart from this, Kakungulu features prominently in Ganda oral traditions, and many Ugandans had a vested interest in the land allocations he made as a chief, as well as determining his clan-derived pedigree to rule. Based on Ugandan manuscripts and field research; 8 notes. 1890's-1945

Kalabiński, Stanisław

3389. Karwacki, Władyslaw Lech. STANISŁAW KALABIŃSKI (1923-1980) [Stanisław Kalabiński (1923-80)]. *Acta Poloniae Historica [Poland] 1982 (45): 298-300.* Stansław Kalabiński's earliest studies were clandestine, and after the Warsaw Uprising, in which he took part, he was a prisoner of war. After taking his doctorate at Leningrad he went in 1954 to the Institute of History at the Polish Academy of Sciences, where he remained until his premature death. His life study was the Polish working class in the 19th and 20th centuries, which he covered in detail in the volumes published between 1970 and 1980. He was convinced that this was the essential groundwork for any proper study of Polish society. 1923-80

Kalamba IV Mangole

3390. Biaya, T. K. KALAMBA IV MANGOLE ET NKWEMBE: HISTOIRE, IDEOLOGIE ET POLITIQUE [Kalamba IV Mangole and Nkwembe: history, ideology, and politics]. *Canadian Journal of African Studies [Canada] 1984 18(1): 66-69.* Traces the career of Kalamba IV Mangole, king of the Luluwa of western Kasai, Zaire, and the role of traditional ideology (Nkwembe) in his rise and downfall; analyzes the determining influence of the religious factor in traditional political and social action. The supernatural is not an isolated element but the true expression of local power and action. References in text. 1961-82

K'alant'ar, Ashkharhbēk

3391. Aṛak'elian, B. N. ASHKHARHBĒK K'ALANT'AR (TSNNDYAN 100-AMYAKI AṚT'IV) [Ashkharhbēk K'alant'ar (on the 100th anniversary of his birth)]. *Patma-Banasirakan Handes. Istoriko-Filologicheskii Zhurnal [USSR] 1984 (3): 3-6.* Ashkharhbēk K'alant'ar (1884-1942) studied under Nicholas Marr at the University of St. Petersburg and graduated in 1911. He took part in the excavations at Ani. From 1921 to 1937 he lectured in history at the University of Yerevan, the title of professor being conferred on him in 1929. He was a member of the Committee for the Preservation of Antiquities from its inception in 1923. His work was interrupted permanently in 1937. Photo, 6 notes. Russian summary. 1884-1942

Kalecki, Michal

3392. López G., Julio. MICHAL KALECKI [Michal Kalecki]. *Investigación Económica [Mexico] 1983 42(166): 11-18.* Discusses books and articles written by economist Michal Kalecki, particularly his monograph, *An Essay on the Theory of the Economic Cycle* (1933). 1930-80's

Kalinin, Mikhail

3393. Novikov, A. N. BESEDY KALINYCHA [Conversations with Kalinych]. *Voprosy Istorii [USSR] 1982 (3): 173-177.* The prominent Soviet political figure Mikhail Kalinin wrote a regular column in the *Zhurnal Sel'skoi Molodezhi* [Journal of rural youth]. His articles exerted considerable influence on young people in the villages, especially in the period of collectivization. Kalinin advocated literacy and vocational training and exposed the anti-Party activity of Trotsky and Zinoviev. Based on government archives and secondary sources; 32 notes. 1925-35

3394. Slamikhin, N. A. "LICHNOGO SCHAST'IA VNE BOR'BY NET": K 110-LETIIU SO DNIA ROZHDENIIA M. I. KALININA ["No personal happiness outside the struggle": 110 years since the birth of M. I. Kalinin]. *Voprosy Istorii KPSS [USSR] 1985 (11): 130-137.* In March 1919 the Bolshevik party and the young Soviet republic suffered a heavy loss with the death of Iakov Mikhailovich Sverdlov. His demise raised the question of who would replace him as president of the All-Russian Central Executive Committee. Lenin recommended Mikhail Kalinin for his appropriate background. Discusses Kalinin's biography from his birth of 7 November 1875 in a village near Tver (now Kalinin). His Party career and position regarding Stalin are not analyzed. Also discusses his position in the Presidium of the USSR and his talent as a Party propagandist. Other topics include an examination of contemporary comments on Kalinin. Draws on Kalinin's selected works; 31 notes. 1875-1946

Kalinowski, Władysław

3395. Ankudowicz, Maria Anna. TRZY NIE ZNANE LISTY FELIKSA NOWOWIEJSKIEGO DO PROFESORA WILEŃSKIEGO KONSERWATORIUM WŁADYSŁAWA KALINOWSKIEGO [Three unknown letters of Feliks Nowowiejski to Władysław Kalinowski, professor at the Conservatory of Arts in Vilnius]. *Komunikaty Mazursko-Warmińskie [Poland] 1979 (1): 83-89.* Władysław Kalinowski was born in Vilnius on 8 October 1880. He studied music in Vilnius and Bavaria and became an organist. On his return to Vilnius in 1910, Kalinowski served as an organist and choir conductor for 35 years. His letters to Nowowiejski, another musician, dated 7 July 1931, 21 March 1933, and 20 September 1934, all deal with musical matters. 32 notes. German summary. 1880-1934

Kalischer, Zevi Hirsch

3396. Myers, Jody Elizabeth. "Seeking Zion: The Messianic Ideology of Zevi Hirsch Kalischer, 1795-1874." U. of California, Los Angeles 1985. 314 pp. *DAI 1986 46(7): 1977-A.* DA8519133 1795-1874

Kállai, Gyula

3397. Kállai, Gyula. THE AWAKENING OF BUDAPEST. *New Hungarian Quarterly [Hungary] 1985 26(97): 70-74.* Publishes an excerpt from the second volume of Gyula Kállai's memoirs, *On the Border of Two Worlds* (1984), which describes the devastation and liberation of Budapest in 1945. Gyula Kállai in his youth belonged to the illegal Communist Party, worked on Social Democrat newspapers and for antifascist causes, served after the war as undersecretary of the prime minister and as foreign minister, was imprisoned in 1951, and was rehabilitated in 1954, becoming, finally, prime minister. 1945

Kallay, Benjamin

3398. Bozhilova, Rumiana. BENIAMIN KALAI ZA BULGARSKOTO NATSIONALNOOSVOBODITELNO DVIZHENIE V NAVECHERIETO NA IZTOCHNATA KRIZA [Benjamin Kallay on the Bulgarian national liberation movement on the eve of the Eastern Crisis]. *Istoricheski Pregled [Bulgaria] 1981 37(1): 91-104.* An analysis of the diary of Benjamin Kallay (1839-1903), Austro-Hungarian general consul in Belgrade, 1868-75. During his tenure as consul Kallay addressed the Bulgarian question and gained experience on Balkan issues which furthered his career. In 1878 he was a member of the delegation of the Habsburg Empire at the Congress of Berlin and influenced the decisions concerning Bulgaria there. Later he served on the international commission in Eastern Rumelia and as governor of Bosnia and Herzegovina. Based chiefly on *Dnevnik Beniamina Kalaja (1868-1875)* [The diary of Benjamin Kallay (1868-1875)], Andrija Radenikv, ed. (1976); 124 notes. 1868-75

Kálnoky, László

3399. Lengyel, Balázs. WOUNDED BY EXISTENCE: LÁSZLÓ KÁLNOKY, 1912-1985. *New Hungarian Quarterly [Hungary] 1986 27(102): 73-78.* Discusses the life and works of László Kálnoky (1912-85), Hungarian poet and translator. 1912-85

Kamenev, Sergei

3400. Drobot, B. and Nagaev, I. SOVETSKII POLKOVODETS S. S. KAMENEV [The Soviet military leader S. S. Kamenev]. *Voenno-Istoricheskii Zhurnal [USSR] 1981 23(4): 42-45.* Publishes one document based on a speech delivered by S. S. Kamenev (1881-1936) at a session of the USSR Revolutionary Soviet in 1931 and outlines his military and political career. Sergei Kamenev became chief of staff of the 3d Russian Army during World War I. He then volunteered to join the Red Army, becoming commander of the Eastern Front where he subsequently became embroiled in disagreements on how to conduct the campaign against Kolchak's White Army. After the civil war he played a part in the building up of the Red Army and had an active political life. Based on a document in the Central State Archive of the Soviet Army; photo, 11 notes. 1914-36

Kamiński, Adam

3401. Palarczykowa, Anna. ADAM KAMIŃSKI (5 XI 1905-18 XI 1981) [Adam Kamiński (5 November 1905-18 November 1981)]. *Archeion [Poland] 1983 (76): 323-330.* An obituary of a historian and an archivist in Cracow archives between 1929 and 1971. His main interest was in the history of southern Polish towns and cities between the 16th and 18th centuries. He published many articles, reviews, dictionary entries, and reports between 1932 and 1980. Bibliography of A. Kamiński's works. 16c-18c

Kamo

3402. Gharibjanian, G. B. KAMOYI HĒGHAPOKHAKAN GORTSUNĒUTYUNNĒRĒ ARTASAHMANUM 1911-1912 TT.: TSĒNĒNDYAN 100-AMYAKI ARTIV [Kamo's revolutionary activities abroad, in 1911-12: on his birth centenary]. *Patma-Banasirakan Handes. Istoriko-Filologicheskii Zhurnal [USSR] 1982 (2): 14-21.* Kamo (Simon A. Ter Petrosian, 1882-1922) carried out legendary exploits for the Bolshevik revolution: he robbed the tsarist treasury, escaped from prisons, simulated madness to avoid questioning in Berlin, established underground press and homes for revolutionaries in various countries, visiting 19 countries during 1906-12 and sending weapons and literature to revolutionaries in Russia and the Caucasus. Visiting centers of Russian dissidents abroad, Kamo organized their revolutionary activities. V. I. Lenin paid tribute to Kamo's "exceptional devotion, energy, and bravery." Primary sources; photo, 20 notes. 1911-12

3403. Gharibjanian, G. B. V. I. LENINI HAY ZINAKITSNĒRN U ASHAKĒRTNĒRĒ [V. I. Lenin's Armenian comrades-in-arms and disciples]. *Patma-Banasirakan Handes. Istoriko-Filologicheskii Zhurnal [USSR] 1980 (1): 13-20.* ca 1890-1917
*For abstract see **Avanesov***

Kandinsky, Wassily

3404. Carmean, E. A., Jr. KANDINSKY'S CODES. *Horizon 1981 24(7-8): 66-69.* Brief biography of Russian painter Wassily Kandinsky, focusing on his *Improvisations,* a series of abstract paintings, the majority of which have religious themes, painted during his Munich period, 1909-14. 1909-14

3405. Guignard, Elise. WASSILY KANDINSKY: ÜBERLEGUNGEN ZU SEINEN SCHRIFTEN ANLÄSSLICH DER AUSSTELLUNG IM KUNSTHAUS ZÜRICH [Wassily Kandinsky: contemplations on his writings apropos the exhibit in the Zurich art museum]. *Schweizer Monatshefte [Switzerland] 1984 64(7-8): 580-587.* Discusses the Russian artist Wassily Kandinsky's (1866-1944) perspectives on his career as an artist and his aesthetic theories based on his writings from 1915-33 with consideration of two French authors, Paul Valery and Guillaume Apollinaire, whose thoughts on art during the first two decades of the 20th century parallel Kandinsky's. 1912-21

Kandyba, Ivan

3406. Kandyba, Ivan. THE KANDYBA DECLARATION (PART 2). *Ukrainian Rev. [Great Britain] 1981 29(2): 19-36.* Ukrainian activist Ivan Kandyba recounts his experiences of surveillance and persecution by the Soviet Committee of State Security (KGB) during the 1970's. 1976-78

3407. Kandyba, Ivan; Matla-Rychtycka, Zena, transl. KANDYBA DECLARATION (PART 3). *Ukrainian Rev. [Great Britain] 1981 29(3): 63-80.* Kandyba contrasts his treatment by the authorities of the USSR with the rights provided for in the Soviet constitution and the Universal Declaration of Human Rights. 1970's

Kandyba-Ol'zhych, Oleh

3408. Antonovych, M[arko]. DR. OLEH KANDYBA [Dr. Oleh Kandyba]. *Ukrains'kyi Istoryk 1985 22(1-4): 46-48.* A general introduction preceding a series of articles in the journal devoted to the Ukrainian poet, archaeologist, writer, and political activist Oleh Kandyba-Ol'zhych (1907-44). 1907-44 -Ol'zhych

3409. Antonovych-Rudnytska, M. IZ SPOMYNIV PRO OL'ZHYCHA [From my recollections about Ol'zhych]. *Ukrains'kyi Istoryk 1985 22(1-4): 101-111.* Reminiscences of personal contacts in the 1920's and 1930's with the Ukrainian poet Oleh Kandyba-Ol'zhych (1907-44) in Berlin and

Prague, including a commentary on his poetic creativity and cultural work within the Ukrainian community. 2 notes.
1920's-30's -Ol'zhych

3410. Shtohryn, Dmytro. OLEH KANDYBA-OL'ZHYCH [Oleh Kandyba-Ol'zhych]. *Ukrains'kyi Istoryk 1985 22(1-4): 167-183.* An extensive bibliography illustrating the vigor of Oleh Kandyba-Ol'zhych (1907-44) as a poet, writer, scholar, and political activist. This compilation consists of six parts: 1) materials for a biography of Kandyba-Ol'zhych, 2) titles of his literary works and literary criticism, 3) his poetry in translation (English, German, Polish, and Russian), 4) reviews of his literary works, 5) evaluations of his poetic creativity, and 6) references to him in books pertaining to Ukrainian literature. Based on "Poetychna Tvorchist' Oleha Kandyby-Ol'zhycha" [Poetic creativity of Oleh Kandyba-Ol'zhych], the author's M.A. thesis at the University of Ottawa (1968), and additional research. Article to be continued.
1907-83 -Ol'zhych

3411. Wynar, Liubomyr. NAUKOVA DIIAL'NIST D-RA OLEHA KANDYBY [Scholarly activities of Dr. Oleh Kandyba]. *Ukrains'kyi Istoryk 1985 22(1-4): 49-74.* Analyzes the scholarly work of Oleh Kandyba-Ol'zhych (1907-44) in three periods: 1) 1925-30: university studies in Prague, doctorate from Charles University in 1930, and beginning of archaeological work; 2) 1931-40: intensive scholarly activities, which included, among others, publishing of various works, contacts with Harvard University and organization of the Ukrainian Scientific Institute in America; and 3) 1941-44: diminished scholarly pursuits, largely due to his political activism within the Ukrainian territories occupied by the Nazis. Concentrates on the first period in this article, revealing valuable information about source materials. Based on sources in the archives of Charles University (Prague), letters of many persons written to the author, as well as published primary and secondary sources; 2 photos, 54 notes, appendix. Article to be continued.
1925-30 -Ol'zhych

3412. —. [CORRESPONDENCE FROM, TO AND ABOUT OLEH KANDYBA-OL'ZHYCH]. *Ukrains'kyi Istoryk 1985 22(1-4): 141-164.*

Antonovych, M[arko]. LYSTY O. KANDYBY DO IE. ONATS'KOHO [Letters of O. Kandyba to Ie. Onats'kyi], *pp. 141-148.* Introduces and appends texts of six letters and one postcard written between 1938 and 1940, by the Ukrainian poet, archaeologist, publicist, and political activist Oleh Kandyba-Ol'zhych (1907-44) to the Ukrainian journalist, political activist, and scholar Ievhen Onats'kyi (1894-1979), pertaining chiefly to the publication of the *Zbirnyk Ukrains'koho Naukovoho Instytutu v Ameritsi* [The collection of the Ukrainian Scientific Institute in America].

—. LYSTIVKA O. KANDYBY DO MARYNY I MARKA ANTONOVYCHIV [O. Kandyba's postcard to Maryna and Marko Antonovych], *pp. 147-148.* A postcard, written on 7 October 1933, during one of O. Kandyba-Ol'zhych's archaeological trips.

Vynar, Liubomyr. LYSTY IE. ONATS'KOHO DO O. KANDYBY [Letters of Ie. Onats'kyi to O. Kandyba], *pp. 149-155.* Introduces and appends texts of four letters, written in 1939, concerning mainly the *Zbirnyk.*

Shtohryn, Dmytro. LYSTY PRO O. KANDYBY-OL'ZHYCHA [Letters concerning O. Kandyba-Ol'zhych], *pp. 156-162.* Introduces and appends texts of six letters, written to the author in 1956-66, by the following persons: M. Mykhalevych, Ie. Onats'kyi, O. Nepryts'kyi-Hranovs'kyi, Iu. Rusov, M. Hlobenko, and D. Dontsov.

—. OSTAP HRYTSAI I MYKOLA KAPUSTIANS'KYI PRO OL'ZHYCHA [Ostap Hrytsai and Mykola Kapustians'kyi on Ol'zhych], *pp. 163-164.* An introduction and texts of two letters, written in 1952 to Liubomyr Vynar, concerning O. Kandyba-Ol'zhych, by O. Hrytsai (1881-1954) and M. Kapustians'kyi (1894-1969).
1933-66

Kaneko, Kentarō

3413. Kanda, James. THE KANEKO CORRESPONDENCE. *Monumenta Nipponica [Japan] 1982 37(1): 41-76, (2): 223-256.* Part 1. Kentarō Kaneko (1852-1942) was a recognized diplomat, scholar, statesman, and Japanese jurist, and one of the foremost Japanese authorities on the United States. A graduate of the Harvard Law School of 1878, he was a close personal friend of Oliver Wendell Holmes, Jr., John Chipman Gray, and James Bradley Thayer. His 130 personal letters to various American friends present a valuable legacy of a man of the Meiji era with close American connections. Reproduces a number of his letters in this article. Part 2. Covers Kaneko's letters and career as a statesman who worked on the draft of the Meiji constitution, Privy Councillor, and advisor to the Portsmouth Peace Conference in 1905. Included are his observations on the Russo-Japanese War, on immigration difficulties between Japan and the United States, and other political issues.
1878-1905

3414. Kanda, James. THE KANEKO CORRESPONDENCE (PART THREE). *Monumenta Nipponica [Japan] 1982 37(3): 289-316.* Continued from a previous article. Kaneko Kentarō, a diplomat, statesman, scholar, jurist, participant in the drafting of the Meji Constitution, and Privy Councilor (appointed in 1906), continued his correspondence during the period 1908-24 with his eminent friends in the United States such as Oliver Wendell Holmes, John Chipman Gray, and James Bradley Thayer, a correspondence he began upon his graduation from Harvard Law School in 1878.
1908-24

Kang Youwei

3415. T'ang Chih-chün. KUAN YÜ K'ANG YU-WEI Y'Ü WU HSÜ PIEN FA CHU WEN T'I [Problems relating to the 1898 reform and K'ang Yu-wei]. *Journal of the Institute of Chinese Studies of the Chinese University of Hong Kong [Hong Kong] 1985 16: 31-41.* Some views on Kang Youwei's (K'ang Yu-wei, 1858-1927) thoughts and actions at the time of China's 1898 reform movement. Although a new text proponent, Kang had an early interest in advocating the Duke of Zhou (Chou, 12th century B.C.) as a model for 19th-century officialdom. Kang tampered with the texts of two imperial edicts issued just prior to the 1898 reform, and the visit of pro-reformist Prince Ito Hirobumi (1841-1909) played a part in precipitating the Empress Dowager's (1835-1908) overthrow of the Guangxu emperor (Kuang-hsü, 1871-1908). Based on the Kang's writings and other contemporary documents; 30 notes. English summary.
1886-98

Kann, Robert A.

3416. Winters, Stanley B. DAS WERDEN EINES HISTORIKERS: ROBERT A. KANN IN AMERIKA 1939-1976 [The becoming of a historian: Robert A. Kann in America, 1939-76]. *Österreich in Geschichte und Literatur [Austria] 1985 29(1): 1-19.* Robert A. Kann emigrated from Austria to the United States in 1939 to escape Nazi persecution at the age of 33. He studied history at Columbia University and taught at Rutgers University. Kann's main work *The Multinational Empire* (1950) dealt with the final stages of the

Habsburg and German empires in the 19th and early 20th centuries and praised the cultural achievements of Slavic countries during this period. Kann resumed residency in Vienna in 1976. 72 notes. 1939-76

Kant, Immanuel

3417. Meisels, Henry R. IMMANUEL KANT AND THE ROYAL CASTLE LIBRARY IN KOENIGSBERG. *J. of Lib. Hist. 1981 16(3): 517-522.* In 1776 Immanuel Kant was appointed assistant librarian at the Royal Library, a post for which he had petitioned the king, Fredrick II. However, in 1772, after having been made professor of logic and metaphysics in 1770, Kant resigned the post. He apparently had taken the position mainly to add to his income and found several aspects of library work to be distasteful. Based on Kant's letters; 5 notes. 1766-72

Kantorowicz, Ernst H.

3418. Giesey, Ralph E. ERNST H. KANTOROWICZ: SCHOLARLY TRIUMPHS AND ACADEMIC TRAVAILS IN WEIMAR GERMANY AND THE UNITED STATES. *Leo Baeck Institute. Year Book [Great Britain] 1985 30: 191-202.* Ernst H. Kantorowicz (1895-1963) was a renowned German-Jewish intellectual historian specializing in medieval studies. After the great critical and popular success of his biography of Frederick II (1926), Kantorowicz was offered a teaching post at the University of Frankfurt. He terminated this prestigious position in 1933 when he refused to implement anti-Semitic classroom regulations imposed by the Nazis. After arriving in the United States, Professor Kantorowicz became involved in the loyalty oath issue that rocked the Berkeley campus of the University of California in the late 1940's and early 1950's. Whether in exile or in his native land, Ernst Kantorowicz was respected for his scholarship and was a consistent defender of academic freedom. Based mainly on primary sources, including Ernst Kantorowicz's published and unpublished writings, and interviews; 2 photos, 25 notes. 1918-63

Kánya, Koloman von

3419. Matsch, Erwin. SECHS AUSSENMINISTER, DIE AUS DEM ALTEN ÖSTERREICH KAMEN [Six ministers of foreign affairs from old Austria]. *Archiv für Kulturgeschichte [West Germany] 1982 64(1): 171-215.* 1919-38

*For abstract see **Csáky, Emmerich***

Kaplan, Yosef

3420. Ma'ayan, Shmuel. QIVIM LA-DMUTO ŠEL LOḤEM [Hopes for the image of a fighter]. *Yalkut Moreshet Periodical [Israel] 1982 (34): 16-30.* Yosef Kaplan was one of the leaders of the Jewish underground in the Warsaw ghetto, and an important member of Hechalutz and Hashomer Hatzair. Eyewitness accounts, articles, and documents describe his home and childhood, his involvement in the youth movement of Hashomer Hatzair in Kalisz, Poland, and his work as a member of the executive committee in Warsaw. 29 notes. English summary. 1914-42

Kaplíř, Kaspar Zdenko

3421. Macek, Jaroslav. KASPAR ZDENKO KAPLÍŘ VON SULLOWITZ (1611-1686) [Kaspar Zdenko Kaplíř von Sullowitz, 1611-86]. *Jahrbuch des Vereins für Gesch. der Stadt Wien [Austria] 1983 39: 7-68.* Provides an overview of the life of Kaspar Zdenko Kaplíř, a Habsburg military leader, emphasizing his role in the Thirty Years War and the siege of Vienna. 1630's-86

Kappeler family

3422. Bachmann-Dick, Fritz. THE RELATIONSHIP BETWEEN THE FAMILY OF JOHANN JAKOB KAPPELER AND THE BACHMANN FAMILIES AT THUNDORF AND STETTFURT. *Swiss American Historical Society Newsletter 1984 20(2): 21-47.* 14c-19c

*For abstract see **Bachmann family***

Karabchevski, N. P.

3423. Smoliarchuk, V. I. N. P. KARABCHEVSKII—RUSSKII SUDEBNYI ORATOR I PISATEL' [N. P. Karabchevski—Russian legal orator and writer]. *Sovetskoe Gosudarstvo i Pravo [USSR] 1983 (8): 115-121.* Charts the professional career of the outstanding Russian lawyer, N. P. Karabchevski (1852-1925), providing details of his most famous cases. Secondary sources; 34 notes. 1870's-1925

Karácsony, Sándor

3424. Lendvai, Ferenc L. ÚJ SZÁNTÁS: KARÁCSONY SÁNDOR ÉS KÖRE A FELSZABADULÁS UTÁNI POLITIKAI ÉLETBEN [Uj Szantas: the political life of Sándor Karácsony and his circle after the liberation]. *Társadalmi Szemle [Hungary] 1981 36(7): 66-73.* The aim of Sándor Karácsony, editor of *Új Szántás* [New Ploughing], was to disregard all extremes of the right as well as the left. This worked very well when he disagreed with rightist policies, but it also made it difficult for him to accept Marxist policies and cultural trends without reserve. His support of the regime was deemed insufficient, and after two years of publication his paper was banned in 1948. There is a possibility that Karácsony could have been a useful member of the proletarian dictatorship. 13 notes. 1946-48

Karageorgiades family

3425. Koudounarēs, A. L. OIKOGENEIA MOUROUZĒ [The Mourouzes family]. *Kypriakaí Spoudaí [Cyprus] 1981 45: 161-170.* 1204-1980

*For abstract see **Mourouzes family***

Karakeev, K. K.

3426. Mints, I. I.; Samsonov, A. M.; and Poliakov, Iu. A. 70-LETIE CHLENA-KORRESPONDENTA AN SSSR K. K. KARAKEEVA [The 70th birthday of Corresponding Member of the Academy of Sciences of the USSR K. K. Karakeev]. *Istoriia SSSR [USSR] 1983 (6): 207-209.* Reviews the career of Corresponding Member of the Academy of Sciences of the USSR K. K. Karakeev on the occasion of his 70th birthday. A specialist on the history of Soviet Kirgizstan, Karakeev has published numerous books and articles on the history of Kirgizia and has translated many of the classics of Marxism-Leninism into the Kirgiz language. In addition, he is a member of the Communist Party of Kirghizia, holds several important posts in the Kirghiz Academy of Sciences and has been awarded numerous orders and medals by both the USSR and the Kirghiz SSR. 1940's-83

Karal, Enver Ziya

3427. Dimitrov, Strašimir. NECROLOGIE: LE PROFESSEUR DR. ENVER ZIYA KARAL [Enver Ziya Karal]. *Etudes Balkaniques [Bulgaria] 1982 18(2): 133-135.* Obituary of Enver Ziya Karal (1906-82), president of the Turkish Historians' Association, former professor of modern and contemporary history at the University of Ankara, and director of the Institute of the History of Revolution. His career was marked by historical research on the modernization of the Ottoman Empire and its struggle against medieval obscurantism, the reforms of Kemal Atatürk, the editing and coediting several volumes of *The History of the Ottoman Empire* (particularly the period between 1856 and the 1908 Turkish revolution), and the promotion of friendly relations between Turkey and Bulgaria. 16c-20c

3428. Kansu, Şevket Aziz. KARAL İÇİN [For Karal]. *Belleten [Turkey] 1982 46(182): 245.* Tribute sent to the Turkish Historical Association on the death of Professor Enver Ziya Karal (1906-82), who served in the University of İstanbul and on the Turkish Constitutional Commission. 1940's-82

3429. Uğurlu, M. Cemil TARİHÇİ VE DÜŞÜNÜR ENVER ZİYA KARAL (1906-1982) [Enver Ziya Karal (1906-82): historian and thinker]. *Belleten [Turkey] 1982 46(184): 839-844.* Enver Ziya Karal (1906-82) had a distinguished academic career as professor, dean, and university rector. In addition he gave his time to the *History of Turkey,* on volume 9 of which he was working at his death, and to his study of Atatürk, the second half of which he was completing. He also served in 1961 as head of the Constitutional Commission. Beyond his contribution to education, historical research, and politics, he is to be remembered as "the teacher of teachers," for whom education was not merely learning to read and write, but acquiring freedom to think. Plate, 9 notes. 20c

Karamanlis, Constantine

3430. Gorce, Paul-Marie de la. CONSTANTIN CARAMANLIS [Constantine Karamanlis]. *Rev. des Deux Mondes [France] 1982 (8): 345-349.* Recounts Karamanlis's role in the postwar economic and political integration of Greece into the European system, his eight-year tenure as prime minister and his reemergence in 1974 as president of a democratic regime after seven years of exile. 1944-82

Karamatjević, Prvoslav

3431. Šuica, Nada. PIVO KARAMATIJEVIĆ, UMETNIK I BORAC [Pivo Karamatijević, artist and fighter]. *Zbornik Istorijskog Muzeja Srbije [Yugoslavia] 1981 17-18: 211-216.* Traces the life and work of the Serbian artist Prvoslav (Pivo) Karamatijević (1912-63). He rose to prominence in the 1930's with paintings depicting the life of the peasant in the Sandžak (Novi Pazar) region of southern Serbia. When World War II broke out in Yugoslavia in 1941 he joined the partisans in Zlatar. In 1942 he took part in the famous battles against the German forces on the Neretva and Sutjeska rivers in Bosnia, and later spent a short time at a partisan base in southern Italy. Throughout the war he kept a graphic record of what he saw through a collection of line drawings, which have since been widely exhibited. He was a prolific contributor to the partisan press. 7 plates, 11 notes, bibliography listing 13 books, journal articles and exhibition catalogues. 1912-63

Karapēt, Ivan

3432. Ananian, Zh. A. NOVYE DOKUMENTY O IVANE KARAPETE (IZ ISTORII ARMIANO-RUSSKIKH TORGOVO-EKONOMICHESKIKH OTNOSHENII PERVOI TRETI XVIII V.) [New documents on Ivan Karapēt: from the history of Armeno-Russian commercial and economic relations, 1700-30]. *Patma-Banasirakan Handes. Istoriko-Filologicheskii Zhurnal [USSR] 1982 (3): 200-226.* A number of documents shed some light on Ivan Karapēt's biography, which is not yet fully known. Karapēt was a prominent political worker as well as an important merchant who had working connections with famous government officials in Russia. The new materials reflect various features of Armenian-Russian commercial and economic relations during the early 18th century. Primary sources. Armenian summary. 1700-30

Karaszewicz-Tokarzeski, Michał

3433. Trojanowska, Maria. NIEUDANA WYPRAWA KURIERSKA I JEJ SKUTKI [An unsuccessful courier expedition and its results]. *Zeszyty Hist. [France] 1981 (56): 157-181.* Reminisces about the attempt to smuggle General Michał Karaszewicz-Tokarzeski, the early head of the underground in German-occupied Poland during World War II, into Soviet-occupied eastern Poland. The author, along with the rest of the general's party, was arrested by the Soviets and spent time in the Soviet penal system until the formation of the Polish Army in the Soviet Union. 1940-41

Karavelov, Lyuben

3434. Zaharia, Edgar Anthony. "Liuben Karavelov: Bulgarian Apostle of Balkan Federation." U. of Arizona 1984. 348 pp. *DAI 1985 46(1): 242-A.* DA8504762 1867-79

Kardelj, Edvard

3435. Bilandžić, Dušan. OD "SNAGA NARODNIH MASA" DO "PLURALIZMA SAMOUPRAVNIH INTERESA" IN MEMORIAM EDVARDU KARDELJU [From "The strength of the popular masses" to "The pluralism of self-management interests": Edvard Kardelj, in memoriam]. *Politička Misao [Yugoslavia] 1979 16(2): 199-213.* Traces the development of the political thought of the Yugoslav leader Edvard Kardelj (d. 1977), parallel with the development of Yugoslav postwar history, from his article "Snaga Narodnih Masa" [The strength of the popular masses], published in 1945, to the publication in 1977 of his magnum opus, *Pravci Razvoja Političkog Sistema Socijalističkog Samoupravljanja* [The development of the political system of socialist self-management], in which he introduced the phrase "pluralizam samoupravnih interesa" ("the pluralism of self-management interests"). 1945-77

3436. Rogel, Carole. EDVARD KARDELJ'S NATIONALITY THEORY AND YUGOSLAV SOCIALISM. *Canadian Review of Studies in Nationalism [Canada] 1985 12(2): 343-357.* Edvard Kardelj was a longtime associate of Tito and an important figure in Yugoslavia's government until his death in 1979. He was also the main theoretician of the socialist regime, working out the ideological framework for Yugoslavia's economic self-management and its independent foreign policy. Kardelj formulated a theory of Yugoslav nationalism predicated on the integration of the country's different cultures. 51 notes. 1930-79

Kardos, Lajos

3437. Pataki, Ferenc. KARDOS LAJOS (1899-1985) [Lajos Kardos (1899-1985)]. *Magyar Tudomány [Hungary] 1985 30(12): 944-947.* Lajos Kardos (1899-1985), eminent psychologist, died in London on 12 July 1985. He was born in Rákospalota and educated in Vienna where he received his doctorate in 1929. In 1985 he was elected corresponding member of the Magyar Tudományos Akadémia (Hungarian Academy of Sciences). Photo. 1925-85

Karg von Bebenburg, Johann Friedrich

3438. Blacha, R. E. "Johann Friedrich Karg von Bebenburg: ein Diplomat der Kurfürsten Joseph Clemens von Köln und Max Emanuel von Bayern 1688-1694" [Johann Friedrich Karg von Bebenburg: a diplomat of the electorate princes Joseph Clemens of Cologne and Max Emmanuel of Bavaria, 1688-94]. University of Bonn [West Germany] 1983. 291 pp. *DAI-C 1985 46(3): 615; 46/2956c.* 1688-94

Karl Eugen

3439. Uhland, Robert. GERHARD STORZ ÜBER HERZOG KARL EUGEN [Duke Karl Eugen as seen by Gerhard Storz]. *Zeitschrift für Württembergische Landesgeschichte [West Germany] 1983 42: 328-335.* Reviews Gerhard Storz's *Karl Eugen—Der Fürst und das Alte Gute Recht* (1981). The young Karl Eugen grew up in a military environment. By 1743 he was the leader of a regiment and was strongly influenced by the Prussian approach toward military matters. He was greatly impressed by Frederick II, who looked after him during his stay in Berlin. In his middle years, Karl was involved with theatrical arts and music at his newly built court in Ludwigsburg. A description of his great love affair with Franziska von Leutrum, his second wife, can be found in her detailed diary. Between 1783 and 1789, his "new passion" for traveling took up most of his time. He died from uremia and not from "spiritual illness." Note. 18c

Karlstadt, Andreas Bodenstein von

3440. Bubenheimer, Ulrich. GELASSENHEIT UND ABLÖSUNG: EINE PSYCHOHISTORISCHE STUDIE ÜBER ANDREAS BODENSTEIN VON KARLSTADT UND SEINEN KONFLIKT MIT MARTIN LUTHER [Resignation and detachment: a psychohistorical study of Andreas Bodenstein von Karlstadt and his conflict with Martin Luther]. *Zeits. für Kirchengeschichte [West Germany] 1981 92(2-3): 250-268.* Andreas Bodenstein von Karlstadt (ca. 1480-1541) possessed, on the one hand, an anxious depressive personality, on the other, an active externalized love of life. The inner, psychic drives, which, for Karlstadt, were much stronger than external drives, reveal an attachment to his mother that corresponded to a conservative attitude toward the Pope, just as his subsequent "resignation" from the Mother Church paralleled the leaving of home and mother. Karlstadt's spiritual renewal of October 1520 connects an inner spiritual renewal with a positive evaluation of his mother. The final break with Luther in 1524 was the result of an intense sibling rivalry with the younger Reformer. Luther's treatment of Karlstadt reveals symptoms of rationalization, projection, and scapegoating. Based on Karlstadt's writings; 58 notes. 1520-50

Karner, Charles

3441. Veöreös, Imre. KARNER KÁROLY—TUDÓS AZ EGYHÁZ SZOLGÁLATÁBAN [Charles Karner—a scholar in the service of the church]. *Theologiai Szemle [Hungary] 1985 28(3): 155-158.* Karner, the renowned professor of the Lutheran Theological Academy in Sopron, offered many contributions to religious literature, including his translation into Hungarian of the "Gospel According to St. Matthew" in 1935. He was also the founder and editor of the journal *Keresztyén Igazság* [Christian truth] published in 1934-44. 20c

Károlyi, Mihály

3442. Károlyi, Catherine. THE RAJK TRIAL AND MIHÁLY KÁROLYI. *New Hungarian Quarterly [Hungary] 1985 26(99): 104-109.* Mihály Károlyi, president of the Hungarian Republic in 1919 and ambassador to France from 1947 to 1949, was a supporter of László Rajk, who played a crucial role in the Hungarian Communist Party after World War II and served as foreign minister from 1948 to 1949. Károlyi believed that Rajk was unjustly accused of treason and executed. 1947-49

Karpinski, A. P.

3443. Zhukov, V. A. NAUCHNYE SVIAZI AKADEMIKA A. P. KARPINSKOGO S UCHENYMI S.SH.A. [The scientific contacts between A. P. Karpinski and American scientists]. *Voprosy Istorii Estestvoznaniia i Tekhniki [USSR] 1981 (2): 138-141.* The celebrated Soviet geologist A. P. Karpinski did much to promote scientific contacts between Russia and the United States. As director of the geological committee of Russia in the late 1880's, Karpinski started a correspondence with American geologists, paleontologists, and zoologists which was to last some 50 years. In the early period his exchange of papers with scientists such as the American professor of geology at Cambridge University, the director of the New York State Museum, and the director of the Geological Institute of Missouri helped to develop an American interest in Russian geology. After the 1917 Revolution, Karpinski became president of the Soviet Academy of Sciences. Documents from the Archives of the Academy of Sciences of the USSR and secondary sources. ca 1885-1936

Karschin, Anna Luise

3444. Singer, Heidi Mari. "Leben und Zeit der Dichterin A. L. Karschin" [The life and times of poetess Anna Luise Karschin]. City U. of New York 1983. 289 pp. *DAI 1984 44(10): 3076-A.* DA8401957 1730's-91

Kartosuwiryo

3445. Soebardi, S. KARTOSUWIRYO AND THE DARUL ISLAM REBELLION IN INDONESIA. *J. of Southeast Asian Studies [Singapore] 1983 14(1): 109-133.* Kartosuwiryo's political career began when he was a medical student in 1923, and ended with his execution in 1962. His career portrays Indonesia's struggle for independence from the Dutch, both before and after World War II, from the Japanese during the war, and during the factional struggle to define the new nation's characteristics. He participated in many of these efforts, always leaning toward an Islamic state, culminating in the Darul Islam movement which opposed the development of a more secular state. Darul Islam was a religious and political movement that, in its last days, became an Islamic warrior group determined to overthrow a compromised state. 55 notes. 1923-62

Kasagama, Daudi

3446. Balezin, A. S. PERVYE UGANDIISKIE PROSVETITELI [The first Ugandan educators]. *Narody Azii i Afriki [USSR] 1981 (4): 129-138.* 1870's-1920's
For abstract see ***Kaggwa, Apolo***

Kasian

3447. Gharibjanian, G. B. V. I. LENINI HAY ZINAKIT-SNĒRN U ASHAKĒRTNĒRĚ [V. I. Lenin's Armenian comrades-in-arms and disciples]. *Patma-Banasirakan Handes. Istoriko-Filologicheskii Zhurnal [USSR] 1980 (1): 13-20.* ca 1890-1917

For abstract see ***Avanesov***

Kasparyants

3448. Gharibjanian, G. B. V. I. LENINI HAY ZINAKIT-SNĒRN U ASHAKĒRTNĒRĚ [V. I. Lenin's Armenian comrades-in-arms and disciples]. *Patma-Banasirakan Handes. Istoriko-Filologicheskii Zhurnal [USSR] 1980 (1): 13-20.* ca 1890-1917

For abstract see ***Avanesov***

Kastein, Josef

3449. Dreyer, Alfred. JOSEF KASTEIN—SCHÖPFERISCHE JAHRE IN DER SCHWEIZ [Josef Kastein—the creative years in Switzerland]. *Bull. des Leo Baeck Inst. [Israel] 1981 (60): 21-50.* Describes the literary activities of writer Dr. Julius Katzenstein (Josef Kastein), a Jewish attorney from Bremen. Between 1927 and 1935 he lived in Ascona, Switzerland, where he wrote important monographs on Sabbatai Zevi and Uriel da Costa, and a history of the Jews, books in German on Jews, and a number of novels. In 1953 he emigrated to Palestine. 100 notes. 1927-35

Katayama, Sen

3450. Kuznetsov, Iu. D. VYDAIUSHCHIISIA INTERNATSIONALIST (K 125-LETIIU SO DNIA ROZHDENIIA SEN KATAIAMY) [An outstanding internationalist: on the 125th anniversary of the birth of Sen Katayama]. *Voprosy Istorii KPSS [USSR] 1984 (12): 124-127.* Assesses the contribution to international Communist movement made by Sen Katayama (1859-1933), Japanese-born Communist active in the United States, Tokyo, and Moscow. He was one of the founders of the US Communist Party in 1919, and the Communist Party of Japan in 1922. During his Moscow period in the 1920's he was active in the Comintern. He was honored with burial within the Kremlin. Secondary sources; 15 notes. 1859-1933

3451. Senatorov, A. I. SEN KATAIAMA: STRANITSY ZHIZNI I DEIATEL'NOSTI [Sen Katayama: pages of his life and activities]. *Novaia i Noveishaia Istoriia [USSR] 1983 (1): 71-91.* A study of the life and work of Sen Katayama (1859-1933), a Japanese revolutionary and founder of the Japanese Communist Party, now buried by the Kremlin walls in Moscow. Follows his early years, his wanderings in the United States, including time at Yale, his radical work in late 19th-century Japan, conversion to Marxism at the turn of the century, and brilliant history as an early Communist agitator and organizer. Much of his time in the early 1920's was spent in America and Mexico. Based on published works in Russian, Japanese, and French; photo, 45 notes. Article to be continued. 1890's-1920

3452. Hartmann, Rudolf. JAPANISCHER REVOLUTIONÄR UND PROLETARISCHER INTERNATIONALIST. SEN KATAYAMA [Japanese revolutionary and proletarian internationalist: Katayama Sen]. *Beiträge zur Geschichte der Arbeiterbewegung [East Germany] 1984 26(2): 238-246.* Katayama Sen (1859-1933) studied in the United States and in Germany, where he was influenced by the labor movement. He was a leader of communist parties and movements in Japan. He opposed militarism and imperialism as well as capitalism. 20 notes. 1884-1933

Katsnel'son, I. S.

3453. —. PAMIATI I. S. KATSNEL'SONA (1910-1981) [In memory of I. S. Katsnel'son (1910-81)]. *Narody Azii i Afriki [USSR] 1981 (5): 245-246.* Obituary of I. S. Katsnel'son, a leading Soviet Egyptologist and specialist on the history of the ancient Sudan. At his initiative a center for ancient Sudanese studies was established in 1970 at the Hermitage, Leningrad, and nine conferences were held in subsequent years. He was also an expert on ancient Egyptian literature, and on the history of Russo-Ethiopian relations in the latter half of the 19th century. Some of his numerous publications are listed. 1910-81

Katzenelson, Yitzhak

3454. Szeintuch, Yechiel. THE WORK OF YITZHAK KATZENELSON IN THE WARSAW GHETTO. *Jerusalem Q. [Israel] 1983 (26): 46-74.* Living in the Warsaw ghetto and aware of the Jewish fate there, poet Yitzhak Katzenelson wrote and was active in the underground until it collapsed in 1943, whereupon he was able to escape to France. 1939-43

Kaufmann, Felix

3455. Saurugg, H. "Felix Kaufmann (1895-1949)—Interpretation und Kritik Seines Rechtsphilosophischen Systems" [Felix Kaufmann (1895-1949): interpretation and critique of his system of legal philosophy]. U. of Graz [Austria] 1983. 290 pp. *DAI-C 1985 46(4): 865; 46/4160c.* 1910's-49

Kaul, Kamala

3456. Marshall, Elizabeth Hulsey. THE CONVERSION OF THE NEHRU WOMEN TO GANDHIAN FREEDOM-FIGHTING. *Proceedings and Papers of the Georgia Association of Historians 1984 5: 70-82.* Traces the roles of Jawaharlal Nehru's mother (Swarup Rani), sister (Vijaya Lakshmi Pandit), and wife (Kamala Kaul) as Gandhian freedom fighters. Each eventually succumbed to Mahatma Gandhi's charisma and became important figures in India's struggle for independence. Each exemplified a different category of Indian women: Swarup Rani—older women, Vijaya—educated women, and Kamala—the average Indian woman. Their activities enhanced the status of women in Indian politics. Based on the memoirs (published) of Vijaya Lakshmi Pandit, Krishna Nehru Hutheesing, and Jawaharlal Nehru as well as secondary sources; 55 notes. 1914-48

Kaupowicz, Franciszek

3457. Martuszewski, Edward. KS. FRANCISZEK KAUPOWICZ ORAZ DZIAŁALNOŚĆ OŚWIATOWA I NARODOWA W BRĄSWAŁDZIE W POŁOWIE XIX WIEKU [Franciszek Kaupowicz and educational and nationalist activity in Brąswałd in the mid-19th century]. *Komunikaty Mazursko-Warmińskie [Poland] 1980 (3): 397-411.* Biography of Franciszek Kaupowicz, a Pole from Lithuania who was a Catholic vicar in the Brąswałd district of Warmia, East Prussia, from 1845 to 1871. Kaupowicz was active in obtaining prayer books, books for religious instruction and theological books in Polish and German as well as Polish novels, poetry, and historical books. He was active in opposing the Prussian government's attempts to Germanize the Polish population. 2 tables. 1845-71

Kautsky, Karl

3458. Bronner, Stephen Eric. KARL KAUTSKY AND THE TWILIGHT OF ORTHODOXY. *Pol. Theory 1982 10(4): 580-605.* A friend of Marx and Engels and once the foremost Marxist theorist, Karl Kautsky disappeared from the Marxist stage, probably because he was not radical enough. 1875-1938

3459. Kas'ianenko, V. I. IZ ISTORII BOR'BY V. I. LENINA, RKP(B) PROTIV KAUTSKIANSTVA [V. I. Lenin's struggle with Kautskyism]. *Voprosy Istorii KPSS [USSR] 1985 (2): 81-96.* Studies V. I. Lenin's critique of Karl Kautsky's anti-Soviet stance, 1917-20. Unlike such German Communists as Franz Mehring and Klara Zetkin, Kautsky supported the Menshevik faction, viewing Leninism as a deviation from Marxist orthodoxy. Lenin saw Kautsky's support for Noi Zhordaniia's Menshevik government of Georgia as further proof of his essentially bourgeois loyalties. Secondary sources; 77 notes. 1917-20

Kavelin, Konstantin D.

3460. Smoliarchuk, V. I. K. D. KAVELIN: ISTORIK RUSSKOGO PRAVA, PRAVOVED [K. D. Kavelin, historian of Russian law and jurist]. *Sovetskoe Gosudarstvo i Pravo [USSR] 1984 (7): 113-121.* Outlines the academic contribution and political profile of Konstantin D. Kavelin (1818-85), Russian jurist and Westernizing liberal with an interest in the development of ancient Russian law and ethical and psychological aspects of jurisprudence. 1830's-85

Kay, John

3461. Neelov, Vladimir Ivanovich. TRAGEDIIA IZOBRETATELIA I TRIUMF IZOBRATENIIA. PERVYE SHAGI PROMYSHLENNOI REVOLIUTSII XVIII V. (K 250-LETIIU IZOBRETENIIA DZHONOM KEEM CHELNOKA-SAMOLËTA) [The tragedy of the inventor and the triumph of the invention: first steps in the Industrial Revolution (in honor of the 250th anniversary of John Kay's invention of the flying shuttle)]. *Voprosy Istorii Estestvoznaniia i Tekhniki [USSR] 1985 (1): 124-129.* Describes the career of British inventor John Kay (1704-64). Due to British weavers' refusal to respect his patent rights and the indifference of the British Parliament on the subject, his 1733 invention of the flying shuttle nearly bankrupted John Kay, who moved to France for economic reasons in 1747. For the rest of his life he designed and marketed his inventions in France, periodically returning to England to fight for remuneration from the users of his flying shuttle. Use of this shuttle, which approximately doubled the rate of cloth production, spread throughout Great Britain by the 1780's and eventually, throughout the world. Secondary sources; 4 photos, sketch, 5 notes, 8 ref. 1704-64

Kay-Shuttleworth, James

3462. Paz, D. G. SIR JAMES KAY-SHUTTLEWORTH: THE MAN BEHIND THE MYTH. *History of Education [Great Britain] 1985 14(3): 185-198.* Emphasizes public health and education reformer Sir James Kay-Shuttleworth's literary career, failed marriage, medical ambitions, political interests, and social life, demonstrating the social mobility possible through marriage in Victorian England. 105 notes. 1820-80

Kazakov, Konstantin P.

3463. Batitski, P. MARSHAL ARTILLERII K. P. KAZAKOV [Artillery Marshal K. P. Kazakov]. *Voenno-Istoricheskii Zhurnal [USSR] 1982 (10): 92-94.* Biography of Artillery Marshal Konstantin P. Kazakov (b. 1902) on his 80th birthday. After joining the Communist Party in 1920, Kazakov entered a military school, graduating in 1923. He immediately entered an artillery regiment in the Red Army, rising within a few years to commander of a division. When World War II broke out, Kazakov was head of an artillery regiment in the Kiev region. In a distinguished war career, he commanded the artillery of the southwest front, took part in the battle of Stalingrad, and fought on the Leningrad front. After the war, he rose to the rank of military inspector in the defense ministry. Note, 6 photos. 1920-82

Kazakov, Mikhail

3464. Krasovski, S. GENERAL ARMII M. I. KAZAKOV (K 80-LETIIU SO DNIA ROZHDENIIA) [General Mikhail Kazakov: the 80th anniversary of his birth]. *Voenno-Istoricheskii Zhurnal [USSR] 1981 23(10): 89-91.* Outlines the military career of Soviet General Mikhail Il'ich Kazakov (1901-79). Kazakov joined the Red Army in 1920 and by 1931 he was in command of the 5th Cavalry Regiment. Although a quiet and self-effacing man he played a major part in World War II, commanding armies and fronts at Briansk and Voronezh. He remained in uniform after the war and also had an active political life, becoming a candidate member of the Central Committee of the CPSU and a deputy to the Supreme Soviet of the USSR. He was the recipient of many honors, including two Orders of Lenin, and was made a Hero of the Soviet Union. 2 photos, note. 1901-79

Kazbunda, Karel

3465. Šamberger, Zdeněk. PAMÁTCE DOCENTA KARLA KAZBUNDY [In memory of Karel Kazbunda]. *Arch. Časopis [Czechoslovakia] 1983 33(2): 86-91.* Karel Kazbunda (1888-1982) was a leading Czech historian, archivist, and a teacher at Charles University, Prague, and the State School of Archives. Wounded in World War I, he was sent to work at the Austrian High Command in Vienna, where he met many Austrian historians and archivists. He stayed on in Vienna at the Czechoslovak diplomatic mission, eventually becoming archivist to the Czechoslovak Foreign Ministry. In Vienna he not only found many documents relevant to 1848 (his main interest, with its significance for the Czech question), but also salvaged for Czechoslovakia many valuable records, including many in which Horthy's Hungary was interested. His posthumous papers are now at the National Museum in Prague and include his copies of many Viennese documents, of which the originals have since been destroyed. 5 notes. 1888-1982

3466. Winters, Stanley B. KAREL KAZBUNDA 1888-1982. *Austrian Hist. Y. 1981-82 17-18: 581-582.* Discusses the academic career of Karel Kazbunda (1888-1982), the influential Czech historian. His major interests included the revolutions of 1848, imperial foreign policy, and internal Bohemian politics during the Austrian constitutional era. Although he published numerous books and articles, he never rose above the rank of *docent* because of the politics of the day. 1910's-82

Kazi Nazrul Islam

3467. Mitra, Priti Kumar. "Dissent in Modern India (1815-1930): Concentrating on Two Rebel Poets—Michael Madhusudan Datta and Kazi Nazrul Islam." U. of Hawaii 1985. 644 pp. *DAI 1986 46(7): 2046-A.* DA8520318 1815-1930

Kazinczy, Ferenc

3468. Wéber, Antal. KAZINCZY PÉLDÁJA [The example of Kazinczy]. *Magyar Tudomány [Hungary] 1982 27(10): 735-741.* Ferenc Kazinczy (1759-1831) worked all his life to develop the Hungarian language, literature, and culture stressing that the death of the language is the death of the people. He was and remained all his life a classicist. In the years he spent in prison, 1794-1801, the political and social situations in the country changed. His attempts to change literary tastes were limited not because of his style, but because classicism had passed. Yet his contributions to Hungarian culture, his translations from German and French classics, and his continual improvements of the Hungarian literary language were and remain significant. 1809-23

Keats, John

3469. Brugière, Bernard. KEATS AND PROUST: A STUDY IN AFFINITIES. *Hist. of European Ideas [Great Britain] 1981 1(2): 143-160.* John Keats (1795-1821) and Marcel Proust (1871-1922) had a "fundamental, subterranean kinship." Their childhoods were similar, resulting in both writers being fascinated by images of childhood security. They were both absorbed in images of the present rather than the past. Both associated aesthetics with the theme of illusion. Based on original sources; 22 notes. 1795-1821

3470. Marquess, William Henry. "Lives of the Poet; the First Century of Keats Biography." Harvard U. 1983. 244 pp. *DAI 1983 44(6): 1801-A.* DA8322407 1848-1925

Kędrzycki, Julian Belina

3471. Orłowski, Jan. JULIAN BELINA KĘDRZYCKI JAKO TŁUMACZ LERMONTOWA [Julian Belina Kędrzycki as a translator of Lermontov]. *Slavia Orientalis [Poland] 1979 28(4): 463-467.* Discusses Kędrzycki as a translator of Lermontov and as a poet. He was a private tutor and later a lecturer in Polish literature at the University of Kiev. After 1863 he was sentenced to work in the mines of Siberia for nearly 20 years. He translated poems by Lermontov into Polish and as a poet was influenced by Lermontov's works. 1830's-60's

Kekkonen, Urho

3472. Komissarov, Iu. LINIIA DRUZHBY, DOVERIIA I SOTRUDNICHESTVA [Course of friendship, trust, and cooperation]. *Mirovaia Ekonomika i Mezhdunarodnye Otnosheniia [USSR] 1985 (9): 14-20.* On the occasion of Urho Kekkonen's 85th birthday, asserts that the wisdom and internationalism of the former Finnish leader's policies are what is needed to secure and maintain world peace. 1945-85

3473. Palm, Thede. DEN GAMLE PÅ EKUDDEN [The old man of Ekudden]. *Svensk Tidskrift [Sweden] 1981 68(10): 496-500.* Reflects upon President Urho Kekkonen's influence on Finnish foreign policy in light of his recent resignation from office and the publication of *Ekudden,* extracts from Kekkonen's speeches and notes. Kekkonen wisely opposed changes in Finland's Treaty of Friendship and Mutual Aid with the USSR because it would invite Russian efforts to do the same. His proposals for a nuclear-free North indicate the impact of frequent Finnish-Russian "consultations" on his foreign policy. The Finnish president was also responsible for the tight rein exercised upon criticism of Russia by the Finnish media. 1948-81

3474. Uino, Ari. URHO KEKKONEN JA TULENKANTAJAT [Urho Kekkonen and the Torchbearer group]. *Hist. Aikakauskirja [Finland] 1982 80(3): 208-214.* Clarifies the relationship between Urho Kaleva Kekkonen (1900-), who later became president of Finland, and the group of liberal nationalist Finnish authors around the cultural journal *Tulenkantajat* [Torchbearers], published 1928-30. As a young lawyer, Kekkonen helped his friends in the conservative fennocist student organization, the Academic Karelian Society, when they took control of the journal in 1930. He was not sympathetic with the liberal authors who had founded the journal. Based on the archives of *Tulenkantajat* and of President Kekkonen, on periodical files and memoirs; 34 notes. 1928-34

3475. Uino, A. "Nuori Urho Kekkonen: Yhteiskunnallisen ja Poliittisen Kasvun Vuodet (1900-1936)" [The young Urho Kekkonen: years of social and political growth, 1900-36]. Jyväskylä U. [Finland] 1985. 475 pp. *DAI-C 1986 47(1): 47; 47/223c.* 1900-36

Keliuotis, Juozas

3476. Keliuotis, Juozas; Naujokaitis, Sigita, transl. PERSECUTION OF AN INTELLECTUAL—MEMOIRS BY JUOZAS KELIUOTIS. *Lituanus 1985 31(3): 5-27.* Juozas Keliuotis (1902-83) was a Lithuanian intellectual whose memoirs are about to be published in book form in the United States. Presents excerpts translated into English that deal with Keliuotis's arrest and deportation to a forced labor camp following the second Soviet occupation of Lithuania near the end of World War II. Appendix, photo. 1944-45

Keller, Gisela C.

3477. Keller, Gisela C. REFUGEES—ONE OF MANY. *Heritage Rev. 1981 11(4): 7-21.* Recalls the experiences of the author, a German bureaucrat, who fled from the advancing Soviet army during World War II. Article to be continued. 1938-45

Keller, Jindřich

3478. Poštolka, Milan. JINDŘICH KELLER (4.6. 1939, STRAKONICE-22.10 1981, PRAHA) [Jindřich Keller (4 June 1939-22 October 1981)]. *Časopis Národního Muzea [Czechoslovakia] 1981 150(3-4): 229.* Examines in memoriam the life and work of distinguished Czech music historian and curator of the State Collection of Musical Instruments. 1939-81

Kelly, David

3479. Bucher, Erwin. PILET-GOLAZ IM URTEIL DES ENGLISCHEN GESANDTEN [Pilet-Golaz in the opinion of the English envoy]. *Schweizerische Zeits. für Gesch. [Switzerland] 1981 31(4): 492-494.* 1940
For abstract see ***Pilet-Golaz, Marcel***

Kelly, Ned

3480. Souter, Gavin. BIZARRE FOLK HERO STILL BROODS OVER THE AUSTRALIAN BUSH. *Smithsonian 1983 14(3): 40-49.* Recounts the short and bloody life of Ned Kelly, a 19th-century Australian bushranger who killed three policemen, and discusses contemporary tributes to him, including the paintings of Sidney Nolan. 1854-80

Kelly, Petra

3481. Legner, Johann. PETRA KELLY, DISCIPLE DE GANDHI? [Petra Kelly, disciple of Gandhi?]. *Documents [France] 38(2): 76, 78, 80.* Discusses Petra Kelly, West German political activist and writer, who has vigorously worked for an alternative movement based on nonviolence, inspired by Mahatma Gandhi. She is a feminist, but is opposed to incorporating women in the military. She works closely with the Greens. 1970's-83

Kemp, William

3482. Boaden, Ann and Youngberg, Karin. KEMP'S NINE DAIES WONDER. *British Heritage [Great Britain] 1983 4(3): 38-43.* Outlines the life and career of William Kemp, an Elizabethan entertainer who flourished from 1585-1603; focuses on a nine-day dance that Kemp performed from London to Norwich. 1585-1603

Kemp family

3483. Armstrong, Max. THE KEMP FAMILY OF KERIKERI. *Hist. J. [New Zealand] 1981 (39): 1-5.* Provides a history of the Kemp family in Kerikeri, New Zealand, beginning with James Kemp and his wife Charlotte, who established a mission station there in 1819. 1819-74

Kennedy, Ildephonse

3484. Forbes, Eric G. ILDEPHONSE KENNEDY, OSB (1722-1804) AND THE BAVARIAN ACADEMY OF SCIENCES. *Innes Rev. [Great Britain] 1981 32(2): 93-99.* The Scottish-born Benedictine monk Ildephonse Kennedy joined the Bavarian Academy of Sciences in 1759, the year it received its charter, and two years later he became its secretary. His activities as an officeholder of the academy are outlined here. Based on secondary sources, including the writings of Lorenz Westenrieder; 33 notes. 1759-99

Kenny, Elizabeth

3485. Cohn, Victor. SISTER KENNY'S FIERCE FIGHT FOR BETTER POLIO CARE. *Smithsonian 1981 12(8): 180-200.* Australian-born nurse Elizabeth Kenny (1880-1952) was undeterred by her own lack of medical training and the opposition of doctors and the establishment in implementing her revolutionary ideas for treating poliomyelitis before discovery of the polio vaccine. 1911-52

Kent, Nathaniel

3486. Horn, Pamela. AN EIGHTEENTH-CENTURY LAND AGENT: THE CAREER OF NATHANIEL KENT (1737-1810). *Agric. Hist. Rev. [Great Britain] 1982 30(1): 1-16.* A biographical outline of the career of Nathaniel Kent, important agrarian reformer. From a humble beginning as a secretary on the fringes of government service, Kent had established a major land agency business by the 1790's. In 1775 he published his influential *Hints to Gentlemen of Landed Property,* which described his management methods and philosophy. The pinnacle of his career was the management of the royal estates at Windsor and Richmond. 78 notes. 1775-1810

Kent, Tyler

3487. Kimball, Warren F. and Bartlett, Bruce. ROOSEVELT AND PREWAR COMMITMENTS TO CHURCHILL: THE TYLER KENT AFFAIR. *Diplomatic Hist. 1981 5(4): 291-311.* The secrecy surrounding the 1940 arrest and imprisonment of Tyler Kent, an anti-Semitic and anti-Roosevelt code clerk at the American embassy in London who passed confidential documents to Axis agents, fueled revisionist speculation that the affair concealed evidence of a Churchill-Roosevelt conspiracy to involve the United States in the war. The evidence, released in 1972, does not support a conspiracy thesis. While the papers conveyed by Kent indicate Anglo-American naval cooperation, they also show Franklin D. Roosevelt's reluctance to become more involved without congressional and public approval. Their release in 1940 would have merely embarrassed Prime Minister Winston Churchill and the president. Based on US State Department records and other primary sources; 46 notes. 1940

Ker, Neil Ripley

3488. —. OBITUARY: NEIL KER, C.B.E., F.B.A. *Library [Great Britain] 1983 5(2): 171-173.* Neil Ripley Ker (1908-82) was a palaeographic scholar who labored at Oxford for his entire academic career as a lecturer, reader, fellow, and librarian. *Great Britain: A Handlist of Surviving Books* (1941) is his best known work. He did a great deal for bibliographic scholarship during his career. Ker was also a vice-president of the Bibliographic Society of London. 1908-82

Kerekes, Ferenc

3489. Tóth, Béla. EGY KÜLFÖLDÖN TANULÓ MAGYAR DIÁK, KEREKES FERENC KÖNYVEI [The books of Ferenc Kerekes, a Hungarian student studying abroad]. *Magyar Könyvszemle [Hungary] 1984 100(4): 359-363.* Gives a biographical sketch of Ferenc Kerekes, a professor at the Kollégium of Debrecen and a bibliography of his library. Kerekes was born in Erdőhegy on 29 June 1784. He studied philosophy and theology at the Kollégium, at the Georgikon in Keszthely and later in Vienna. After accepting a professorship at the Kollégium in 1815 he traveled widely in Europe. He died 29 July 1850 in Balatonfüred. His library of 113 titles and numerous volumes attests to his broad interests in chemistry, mining, agriculture, forestry, history, linguistics and literature. 2 notes, biblio. 1815-50

Keresztury, Dezső

3490. Kiss, Irén. DEZSŐ KERESZTURY AT EIGHTY—TEACHER, WRITER, POET. *New Hungarian Quarterly [Hungary] 1984 25(96): 95-103.* An interview with Dezső Keresztury (b. 1904), an eminent Hungarian poet, essayist, and educator, which reveals his background, education, intellectual and spiritual development, and political view. 1914-84

Kérillis, Henri de

3491. Jeanneney, Jean-Noël. LA SOLITUDE D'HENRI DE KÉRILLIS [The isolation of Henri de Kérillis]. *Histoire [France] 1983 (58): 78-84.* Analyzes the career and the evolution of the political attitudes of French rightist deputy Henri de Kérillis, who was the sole deputy of his party to vote against the Chamber of Deputies' approval of the Munich Agreement (1938). 1930's

Kéroualle, Louise de

3492. Castelbajac, Bernadette de. UNE AIEULE DE LADY "DI": LOUISE DE KEROUALLE, ESPIONNE ET PRESQUE REINE [An ancestor of Lady "Di": Louise de Kéroualle, lady spy and almost queen]. *Hist. Mag. [France] 1983 (44): 50-55.* Recounts the life of Louise de Kéroualle, who became the Duchess of Portsmouth, at the court of Charles II from 1670-85, and describes political and familial ties between France and England during this period. 1670-85

Kerr, James

3493. Gelbier, Stanley and Randall, Sheila. CHARLES EDWARD WALLIS AND THE RISE OF LONDON'S SCHOOL DENTAL SERVICE. *Medical Hist. [Great Britain] 1982 26(4): 395-404.* 1905-11
For abstract see ***Wallis, Charles Edward***

Kerr, Philip

3494. Bosco, Andrea. LORD LOTHIAN E LA NASCITA DI "FEDERAL UNION" (1939-1940) [Lord Lothian and the creation of the Federal Union, 1939-40]. *Politico [Italy] 1983 48(2): 271-304.* Discusses the political and diplomatic career of the 11th Marquess of Lothian (1882-1940), emphasizing his efforts to establish a movement for European federation known as the Federal Union. 1939-40

3495. Pinder, John. PROPHET NOT WITHOUT HONOUR: LOTHIAN AND THE FEDERAL IDEA. *Round Table [Great Britain] 1983 (286): 207-220.* Philip Kerr, Lord Lothian, was a student of Alexander Hamilton's *Federalist Papers* and a lifetime proponent of federations, particularly federations of anglophones, but never foresaw a European federation that included Britain without the United States. 1905-40

Kersten, Adam

3496. Matwijowski, Krystyn. ADAM KERSTEN 1930-1983 [Adam Kersten, 1930-83]. *Acta Poloniae Historica [Poland] 1984 (49): 341-342.* Obituary of Adam Kersten, one of the foremost historians of 17th-century Poland and of Scandinavia. Reviews his career and publications. 16c-18c

3497. Wasilewski, Tadeusz. ADAM KERSTEN (26 IV 1930-11 I 1983) [Adam Kersten: 26 April 1930-11 January 1983]. *Kwartalnik Historyczny [Poland] 1983 90(4): 1011-1013.* An obituary of a Polish historian and social activist, Adam Kersten (1930-83). 1930-83

Kersten, Fritz

3498. —. NACHRUF FRITZ KERSTEN [Obituary for Fritz Kersten]. *Zeitschrift für Heereskunde [West Germany] 1986 50(325): 91.* Obituary for Fritz Kersten, historian and illustrator of military uniforms and regular contributor to *Zeitschrift für Heereskunde* since 1965. 20c

Kertész, André

3499. Phillips, Sandra Sammataro. "The Photographic Work of André Kertész in France, 1925-1936: A Critical Essay and Catalogue." City U. of New York 1985. 1994 pp. *DAI 1985 46(6): 1426-A.* DA8515650 1925-36

Kessel, Eberhard

3500. Baumgart, Winfried. NEKROLOG: EBERHARD KESSEL 1. 4. 1907—17. 1. 1986 [Obituary: Eberhard Kessel 1 April 1907-17 January 1986]. *Historische Zeitschrift [West Germany] 1986 243(1): 211-215.* Summarizes the career of Eberhard Kessel, emeritus professor of medieval, modern, and recent history at Mainz. A prolific writer on Prussian military history, Kessel expanded his interests after returning to Germany in 1946 from captivity as a prisoner of war in the United States. He wrote analytical studies on the philosophy of historicism and the role of the individual in historical interpretation. He also edited the collected works of Friedrich Meinecke. Based on Kessel's works and personal knowledge of his life. 1907-86

Ketteler, Wilhelm Emmanuel

3501. Bolten, Analouise Clissold. "Watch—Pray—Fight: Wilhelm Emmanuel Ketteler as Priest-Politician." George Washington U. 1983. 393 pp. *DAI 1983 44(5): 1544-A.* DA8320038 1848-77

Key, Ellen

3502. Register, Cheri. MOTHERHOOD AT CENTER: ELLEN KEY'S SOCIAL VISION. *Women's Studies Int. Forum 1982 5(6): 599-610.* Misrepresented as an antifeminist romantic, Swedish essayist Ellen Key was a central figure in feminism. 1896-1906

Keyes, Roger John Brownlow

3503. Barclay, Glen St. J. "BUTCHER AND BOLT": ADMIRAL ROGER KEYES AND BRITISH COMBINED OPERATIONS, 1940-1941. *Naval War Coll. Rev. 1982 35(2): 18-29.* The emphasis of Admiral of the Fleet Sir Roger John Brownlow Keyes on amphibious operations and combined operations dates back to his participation in the unsuccessful assault on Gallipoli in 1915 and his command of the great seaborne raid on Zeebrugge in 1918. When Winston Churchill appointed Keyes to be Director of Combined Operations, it allowed a greater emphasis on the development of a British raiding capacity against Nazi advances in Europe and Africa. Yet Keyes went out of his way to offend or intrigue against other British military leaders, which made effective combined operations impractical under his leadership. Churchill was forced to relieve him from command on 4 October 1941, replacing him with Louis Mountbatten. 55 notes. 1940-41

Keynes, Geoffrey

3504. D. J. M. SIR GEOFFREY KEYNES. *Tr. of the Cambridge Biblio. Soc. [Great Britain] 1982 8(2): 139-140.* Obituary of physician and biographer Geoffrey Keynes, who died on 5 July 1982. He had been president of the Cambridge Bibliographical Society from 1958 to 1971. He wrote biographies of Donne, William Blake, Sir Thomas Browne, John Evelyn, and Bishop Berkeley. His book *Blood Transfusion* reveals his view of the relationship of the history of a subject to modern practice. 1958-72

Keynes, John Maynard

3505. Colander, David. WAS KEYNES A KEYNESIAN OR A LERNERIAN? *Journal of Economic Literature 1984 22(4): 1572-1575.* Discusses Abba Lerner's influence on John Maynard Keynes, who was more of a realist than Lerner, and who developed only those theoretical issues relevant to the question at hand. 1941-83

3506. Skidelsky, Robert. THE ECONOMIST AS PRINCE: J. M. KEYNES. *Hist. Today [Great Britain] 1983 33(July): 11-20.* A biographical sketch of John Maynard Keynes (1883-1946) examining his upbringing, education, academic and government careers, marriage, and the importance of his thought to world economics from World War I to the present. 1902-83

3507. Wolfson, Murray. A WORLD GONE MAD: THE DEPRESSION YEARS. *Australian Quarterly [Australia] 1984 56(4): 417-427.* Views the economic thought of John Maynard Keynes in historical perspective as embodying the preconceptions of the years of the Great Depression. 1929-36

Keyserling, Hermann

3508. Stephenson, Gunther. DAS LEBENSWERK GRAF KEYSERLINGS AUS HEUTIGER SICHT [The life's work of Count Keyserling in retrospect]. *Zeits. für Religions- und Geistesgeschichte [West Germany] 1981 33(1): 32-41.* The Estonian count Hermann Keyserling, founder of the Darmstadt School of Wisdom, was one of the leading philosophers during the first half of the 20th century. He injected new impulses in the battle of cultural, moral, political, and spiritual decay through writings marked by extreme subjectivity. Keyserling's idealistic goals, his self-willed personality, a lack of concrete programs and guidelines, and contradictory and underdeveloped thoughts caused his philosophy to find little resonance and be of short duration. 1910-35

Khachin, Georgii Andreevich

3509. —. GEROI STALINGRADSKOI BITVY [Heroes of the battle of Stalingrad]. *Voenno-Istoricheskii Zhurnal [USSR] 1982 (9): 42-45.* 1942-43
*For abstract see **Bashkirov, Viacheslav Filippovich***

Khaletski, I. A.

3510. Popov, N. KOMANDARM 2 RANGA I. A. KHALETSKII (K 90-LETIIU SO DNIA ROZHDENIIA) [Army Commander 2d Class I. A. Khaletski on his 90th birthday]. *Voenno-Istoricheskii Zhurnal [USSR] 1983 (7): 94-96.* Innokenti Andreevich Khaletski (b. 1893), the son of a Siberian tailor, became a telegrapher in Krasnoyarsk and a member of the Post and Telegraph Operatives Union. In 1918 he joined the Bolshevik Party, fought in the Civil War, helped to develop modern communications in the Red Army, and in 1937 was elevated to the rank of People's Commissar for Communications of the USSR. Note. 1893-1983

Khama, Seretse

3511. Harragin, Walter. REPORT OF THE JUDICIAL ENQUIRY RE SERETSE KHAMA OF THE BAMANGWATO TRIBE. *Botswana Notes and Records [Botswana] 1985 17: 53-64.* A sensational political crisis developed in colonial Botswana from the marriage in London in September 1948 of the heir to the Bamangwato chieftainship, Seretse Khama, and an Englishwoman, Ruth Williams. Their marriage took place without approval by the indigenous authorities, including the regent Tshekedi Khama, Seretse's uncle, or the British administration. Local assemblies meeting in Serowe during 1948-49 at first condemned the marriage and removed Seretse from the succession, but then reinstated him and drove his unpopular uncle from office. The British referred the dispute to an official committee of inquiry, which in late 1949 took evidence from both sides and recommended that Seretse be kept from assuming his chieftainship so long as his succession was opposed by the South African government and threatened disruption among the Bamangwato. Based on oral testimony. 1921-49

Khama, Tshekedi

3512. Crowder, Michael. TSHEKEDI KHAMA AND OPPOSITION TO THE BRITISH ADMINISTRATION OF THE BECHUANALAND PROTECTORATE, 1926-1936. *Journal of African History [Great Britain] 1985 26(2-3): 193-214.* Tshekedi Khama, ruler of the Ngwato of Bechuanaland from 1926 to 1950, despite his conflict with the British colonial government, was not deposed. Although most African leaders who refused to collaborate were deposed, Tshekedi employed both traditional and modern resources to retain his authority. An analysis of the period from 1926 to 1936 indicates that the Western-educated Ngwato leader, while accepting colonialism, sought to retain the political integrity of his land and the welfare of his people. He mobilized the press, Parliament, and public opinion in Great Britain in support of his goals. The British authorities were confronted by the fact that there was no other indigenous leader in the region who would be accepted as a legitimate alternative or would be as competent as Tshekedi. Thus, the British were forced to collaborate with Tshekedi, who successfully manipulated the colonial administration. Based on documents in the Botswana National Archives; fig., 80 notes. 1926-36

Khan, Hakim Ajmal

3513. Metcalf, Barbara D. NATIONALIST MUSLIMS IN BRITISH INDIA: THE CASE OF HAKIM AJMAL KHAN. *Modern Asian Studies [Great Britain] 1985 19(1): 1-28.* The term nationalist Muslim concealed a great diversity among Indian Islamic political and religious orientations. The religious and political reforms undertaken by the Muslim physician Hakim Ajmal Khan (1863-1928) reflected this diversity of orientation, which ranged from personal religious responsibility to shared national culture and included cosmopolitan and symbolic communal elements. 67 notes. 1897-1925

Khan, Liaquat Ali

3514. Long, Roger Douglas. "Liaquat Ali Khan: From National Agriculturist Party to Muslim League." U. of California, Los Angeles 1985. 428 pp. *DAI 1986 46(9): 2783-A.* DA8525859 1926-51

Kharitonov, Vasili G.

3515. Dukhin, Ia. K. BLAGOEVETS VASILI KHARITONOV [Blagoev follower Vasili Kharitonov]. *Voprosy Istorii [USSR] 1981 (12): 172-175.* In 1881 Vasili Grigor'evich Kharitonov, a pioneer of Russian social democracy and follower of Dimitri Blagoev, was expelled from the Troitska medical college for his political activities. The group of which he was a member produced many social democrats. He entered the St. Petersburg mathematics faculty in 1882, and in 1883 entered the law faculty, becoming more deeply involved in clandestine social democratic politics. At the end of 1884 the newspaper *Rabochi* was founded, with Kharitonov as editor. On 23 January 1886 he was arrested and later, after the police discovered incriminating material at his home, admitted his membership in the Social Democratic Workers' Party. He hoped for an open trial where he could have denounced the system, but he was sentenced to administrative exile. Based on the history of the Russian Social Democratic Party; 34 notes. 1881-86

Kharlamov, Nikolai

3516. Zakharov, S. E. TRUDNUIU MISSIIU VYPOLNIL S CHESTIIU (K 80-LETIIU ADMIRALA N. KHARLAMOVA) [He accomplished a difficult mission honorably: on Admiral N. Kharlamov's 80th birthday]. *Morskoi Sbornik [USSR] 1985 (12): 53-54.* Outlines the military career of Admiral Nikolai Kharlamov (b. 1905), deputy chief of staff of the Soviet navy during World War II, distinguished during the 1945 war with Japan. 1930-85

Khataievich, Mendel M.

3517. Shevchuk, I. M. DO 90-RICHCHIA Z DNIA NARODZHENNIA M. M. KHATAIEVYCHA [On the 90th birthday anniversary of M. M. Khataievich]. *Ukrains'kyi Istorychnyi Zhurnal [USSR] 1983 (3): 122-124.* Mendel M. Khataievich was born in Gomel in 1893 in the family of a petty tradesman. He joined the Russian Social Democratic Workers' Party in 1913, at once showing exceptional skills in distributing Bolshevik literature. After the October Revolution he played a prominent role in organizing Soviet forces in Belorussia. In 1924 he was called to Moscow to work in the Party's central apparatus. From 1932 he was the Party's leading figure in the Ukraine, holding two posts simultaneously, First Secretary of the Dnepropetrovsk Oblast Party Committee and Second Secretary of the Ukrainian Communist Party Central Committee. Based on the Party Archives of the Party History Institute attached to the Ukrainian CP Central Committee and secondary sources; 8 notes. 1913-37

Khesin, S. S.

3518. Khesin, S. S. VOENNAIA MOLODOST' ISTORIKA [A historian's military youth]. *Voprosy Istorii [USSR] 1985 (6): 71-83.* Reminiscence of the author's experience of the German invasion of the USSR in 1941 and his political work in the Soviet Army until 1945. In the midst of final exams at Leningrad University in 1941, he fought alongside fellow graduate volunteers in the artillery regiment, with a brief spell of work on the Leningrad radio station. After transfer to army political education later that year, he taught Soviet history to Baltic Fleet crews and wrote for several army and navy publications. Wartime experiences shaped his research interests and gave him an opportunity to participate in historic events. Personal narrative; 17 notes. 1941-45

Khetagurov, G. I.

3519. Beloborodov, A. GENERAL ARMII G. I. KHETAGUROV (K 80-LETIIU SO DNIA ROZHDENIIA) [Army General G. I. Khetagurov: on the 80th anniversary of his birth]. *Voenno-Istoricheskii Zhurnal [USSR] 1983 (4): 92-94.* G. I. Khetagurov (1903-75), an Ossetian by birth, fought in the Civil War in a partisan detachment, graduated from military college in 1926, and served in the Soviet Far East. At the outbreak of World War II he held the rank of colonel and was serving as head of artillery of the 21st Mechanized Corps. He fought at Moscow and Stalingrad, and as commander of the 29th Rifle Corps took part in the Berlin operation. In the postwar period he held various posts in the northern group of armies and with the troops of the Baltic States district. Note, 2 photos. 1910's-75

Khevenhüller-Metsch, Georg

3520. Neumann, W. PROF. H. C. GEORG GRAF KHEVENHÜLLER-METSCH (1891-1980) [Professor Count Georg Khevenhüller-Metsch (1891-1980)]. *Carinthia I [Austria] 1980 170: 269.* An obituary of the Austrian count, historian, and academic Georg Khevenhüller-Metsch (1891-1980) examines his work on the history of his family and his efforts to preserve Carinthian archives. 1891-1980 -Metsch

3521. Piccottini, G. GEORG GRAF KHEVENHÜLLER-METSCH UND SEINE VERDIENSTE UM DIE AUSGRABUNGEN AUF DEM MAGDALENSBERG [Count Georg Khevenhüller-Metsch and the excavations on the Magdalensberg]. *Carinthia I [Austria] 1980 170: 270.* Pays tribute to the Austrian historian and academic Count Georg Khevenhüller-Metsch (1891-1980), particularly for his archaeological work concerning the excavation on the Magdalensberg in Carinthia, 1948-80. 1948-80

Khmaladze, Semën Adamovich

3522. —. GEROI GRAZHDANSKOI VOINY [Heroes of the Civil War]. *Voenno-Istoricheskii Zhurnal [USSR] 1982 (8): 57-60.* 1917-69
*For abstract see **Appar, Petr Andreevich***

Khmelnitsky, Bogdan

3523. Shevchenko, F. P. KYIV U ZHYTTI TA DIIAL'NOSTI BOHDANA KHMEL'NYTS'KOHO [Kiev in the life and activities of Bogdan Khmelnitsky]. *Ukrains'kyi Istorychnyi Zhurnal [USSR] 1981 (2): 35-48.* On the occasion of the coming 1,500th anniversary of Kiev, views the life and work of one of the outstanding leaders of the Ukrainian people, Hetman Bogdan Khmelnitsky, in connection with Kiev, the importance of which for the Ukraine and its history he understood and so strengthened its defense capacity. 93 notes. 1648-57

Khomiakov, A. S.

3524. Plank, Peter. PARALIPOMENA ZUR EKKLESIOLOGIE A. S. CHOMJAKOVS [Paralipomena on A. S. Khomiakov's ecclesiology]. *Ostkirchliche Studien [West Germany] 1980 29(1): 3-29.* The Russian theologian, landowner, historian, poet, and inventor A. S. Khomiakov (1804-60) strongly influenced Russian theology of the 20th century with his works on the role of the church council and infallibility, the hierarchy of priests, and the sacraments. 19c-20c

Khrulev, Andrei V.

3525. Kurotkin, S. GENERAL ARMII A. V. KHRULEV [Army General A. V. Khrulev]. *Voenno-Istoricheskii Zhurnal [USSR] 1982 (9): 94-96.* Gives a biography of Army General Andrei V. Khrulev (1892-1962) on the 90th anniversary of his birth. As a young Red Guard Khrulev took part in the storming of the Winter Palace in St. Petersburg in 1917. A year later he was sent to Mogilev to help establish Soviet rule, and in the same year he was admitted to the Communist Party. In 1919 he went to the southern front to join the campaign to mop up Denikin's forces. After distinguished service between the world wars, Khrulev was put in charge of the Red Army's supplies in 1939. His skill at organization was an important factor in the Soviet Union's eventual victory. He died in 1962 and was buried in the Kremlin wall. 2 notes, 2 photos. 1917-62

Khrushchev, Nikita

3526. Rooke, Margaret. KHRUSHCHEV. *Contemporary Rev. [Great Britain] 1982 240(1396): 251-255.* A brief survey of Nikita Khrushchev's achievements in power, 1956-64. 1956-64

Khurrubi, Muhammad Ali al-

3527. Al-Hasnawi, Habib Wada'a. ABŪ 'ABD ALLĀH MUHAMMAD 'ALĪ AL-KHURRŪBĪ AL-FAQĪH AL-SŪFĪ: HAYĀTUHU WA-NASHĀTĀTUHU AL-FIKRIYAH WA-AL-SŪFIYAH [Abu 'Abdallah Muhammad Ali al- Khurrubi, Sufi religious jurist: his life and intellectual and Sufi activities]. *Majallat Al-Buhūth Al-Tārīkihiya [Libya] 1981 3(2): 273-297.* Sheikh Muhammad was born in Qarqash near Tripoli in the late 15th century and died in Algiers in 1556. He was an important figure in the cultural history of Libya, a learned religious jurist and notable Sufi of the Shadili order. The incursions of Christian imperialist Spain and Portugal into North Africa drew the religious establishment into politics. Al-Khurrubi left Tripoli at the Spanish invasion of 1514 and settled at the courts of the Maghreb where his fame drew many students. Based on his own works and contemporary sources; 30 notes. ca 1500-56

Khvostov, Vladimir

3528. Narochinski, A. L. and Voznesenski, V. D. AKADEMIK V. M. KHVOSTOV—UCHENYI, ORGANIZATOR NAUKI, OBSHCHESTVENNYI DEIATEL' [Academician Vladimir Khvostov—scholar, organizer of scholarship, social activist]. *Novaia i Noveishaia Istoriia [USSR] 1985 (5): 162-172.* Profile of Vladimir Khvostov (1905-72), Soviet historian and academician. After studies at Kazan and Moscow universities, he remained at Moscow University. He coedited *Istoriia Diplomatii* (vol. 1 in 1941, vol. 2 in 1945). During World War II he volunteered to serve in the Soviet Army, joining the Communist Party in 1943. He became director of the Institute of History of the Soviet Academy of Sciences in 1959. He took an active part in international academic life and in Party affairs. Among his distinctions were two Orders of Lenin. 22 notes. 1930-72

3529. Poliakov, Iu. A. SHTRIKHI PORTRETA UCHENOGO (O VLADIMIRE MIKHAILOVICHE KHVOSTOVE) [Features of a scholar's portrait: Vladimir Mikhailovich Khvostov]. *Novaia i Noveishaia Istoriia [USSR] 1985 (6): 105-112.* Discusses the academic and personal qualities of Vladimir Khvostov (1905-72), Soviet historian and academician. Among his major achievements are *Istoriia Diplomatii* (vol. 1 in 1941, vol. 2 in 1945), of which he was the coeditor, and his *Istoriia SSSR. Epokha Sotsializma* (1957), reprinted several times and used as a university textbook. His erudition and organizational skills made him uniquely suited for the post of director of the Institute of History of the Soviet Academy of Sciences, a post he held from 1959 to 1972. 1940-72

Kielland, Alexander L.

3530. Lindberger, Örjan. KIELLAND PERSONLIGEN [Kielland personally]. *Nordisk Tidskrift [Sweden] 1985 61(1): 7-15.* Discusses information about the Norwegian author Alexander L. Kielland (1849-1906) revealed in his letters, edited by Johannes Lunde as *Alexander L. Kielland: Brev 1869-1906* [Alexander L. Kielland: letters 1869-1906] (1978-81) and in autobiographical notes edited by Öyvind Anker as *Agerhöns med Champagne* [Partridge with champagne] (1983). 1872-88

Kienzl, Wilhelm

3531. Samlicki-Hagen, I. "Die Lehr- und Wanderjahre Wilhelm Kienzls (1874-1897)" [Wilhelm Kienzl's years of learning and wandering, 1874-97]. U. of Vienna [Austria] 1979. 518 pp. *DAI-C 1984 45(3): 593-594; 9/2401c.* 1874-97

Kierkegaard, Søren

3532. Malik, Habib Charles. "Receiving Søren Kierkegaard: A History of the Early Transmission and Impact of His Thought, 1855-1925." Harvard U. 1985. 613 pp. *DAI 1986 46(7): 2047-A.* DA8520243 1855-1925

3533. Pojman, Louis P. CHRISTIANITY AND PHILOSOPHY IN KIERKEGAARD'S EARLY PAPERS. *J. of the Hist. of Ideas 1983 44(1): 131-140.* From 1835 to 1840, Søren Kierkegaard struggled with his relationship with the Christian religion. Initially, he was antagonistic toward the dehumanizing effects of conformist, bourgeois religiosity. Gradually he came to appreciate Christianity in a rather Hegelian manner as anthropomorphic symbolism. The decisive switch in his attitude may have been triggered by his reading of Hamann who portrays the limitations of reason and the sublimity of arational belief. Contact with Scleiermacher's personalist philosophical theology seems to have been the final catalyst in his Christian conversion. Primary sources; 12 notes. 1835-40

3534. Veisland, Jorgen Steen. "Kierkegaard and the Dialectics of Modernism." U. of Washington 1982. 254 pp. *DAI 1982 42(12): 5113-5114-A.* DA8212643 20c

3535. Wexelblatt, Robert. KLEIST, KIERKEGAARD, KAFKA AND MARRIAGE. *San José Studies 1983 9(1): 6-15.* 19c-20c
*For abstract see **Kafka, Franz***

Kim, M. P.

3536. Piotrovski, B. B.; Samsonov, A. M.; and Borisov, Iu. S. K 75-LETIIU AKADEMIKA M. P. KIMA [The 75th birthday of Academician M. P. Kim]. *Istoriia SSSR [USSR] 1983 (3): 218-221.* Describes the life and work of M. P. Kim, Soviet Academician and historian, born in 1908. He has studied the history of the USSR and of socialist economies. Presently, he teaches in the Soviet Academy of Social Sciences. 1908-83

3537. Rybakov, Boris Aleksandrovich and Kukushkin, Iu. S. 75-LETIE AKADEMIKA M. P. KIMA [Academician M. P. Kim, 75 years old]. *Voprosy Istorii [USSR] 1983 (5): 102-104.* Provides a tribute to Maksim Pavlovich Kim, born 1908 in Maritime Province. A graduate of the Moscow Institute of History, Philosophy, and Literature, he was appointed professor at the Academy of Social Sciences of the CC CPSU in 1947, was editor-in-chief of the journal *Istoriia SSSR* (History of the USSR), 1957-60, and currently heads the Academy of Sciences' Department of History of Soviet Society and the Scientific Council on the "History of Socialist and Communist Construction in the USSR." He has published about 300 studies on Leninism and Soviet political and cultural history. 1930's-83

Kim Chong-il

3538. Kang, Induk. KIM CHONG-IL'S GUIDANCE ACTIVITIES AS MIRRORED IN THE RECENT NORTH KOREAN PRESS. *J. of Northeast Asian Studies 1982 1(4): 91-99.* As reported by the North Korean media, Kim Jong-il, the probable successor of his father Kim Il-sung, has provided theoretical and practical direction for North Korea in the fields of politics, ideology, economics, education, industry, and culture from 1960 to 1982, all in line with his father's thought. 1960-82

3539. Lee, Chong-Sik. EVOLUTION OF THE KOREAN WORKERS' PARTY AND THE RISE OF KIM CHŎNG-IL. *Asian Survey 1982 22(5): 434-448.* In October 1980 the Sixth Congress of the Korean Workers' Party (KWP) officially confirmed Kim Chŏng-il as the successor to his father, President Kim Il-sung who has led the party for the past three and a half decades. Kim Il-sung's selection of his son as successor was his attempt to prolong the KWP's role as the mainstay of ideological revolution in the face of strong currents of modernization that might smother the revolutionary spirit. He may have delivered onerous and overwhelming burdens to his son, for the Communist movement frowns on the concentration of power in the hands of individuals, preferring a trend toward pluralism and rational decisionmaking. Based on documents. 1970-80

3540. Park, Kwon-sang. NORTH KOREA UNDER KIM CHONG-IL. *J. of Northeast Asian Studies 1982 1(2): 57-78.* Discusses the history and current status of government in North Korea under Kim Il-sung and the likely changes in the next decade if Kim Il-sung dies or steps down in favor of his son Kim Chong-il. 1970-82

Kim Hong-do

3541. Kim, Kumja Paik. "Kim Hong-do (1745-before 1818), a Late Yi Dynasty Painter." Stanford U. 1982. 333 pp. *DAI 1982 43(5): 1327-A.* DA8220485 1760-1818

Kim Il-sung

3542. Koh, Byung Chul. POLITICAL SUCCESSION IN NORTH KOREA. *Korea & World Affairs [South Korea] 1984 8(3): 557-574.* Analyzes personal and political factors in North Korean head of state Kim Il-sung's choice of his son Kim Jong-il (born 1942) as his successor after the 1972 abandonment of supposed efforts to groom his brother Kim Yong-ju. 1966-84

3543. Park, Kwon-sang. NORTH KOREA UNDER KIM CHONG-IL. *J. of Northeast Asian Studies 1982 1(2): 57-78.* 1970-82
*For abstract see **Kim Chong-il***

3544. —. KIM IR SEN (CU PRILEJUL ANIVERSĂRII A 70 DE ANI DE LA NAŞTERE) [Kim Il Sung on the 70th anniversary of his birth]. *Anale de Istorie [Romania] 1982 28(3): 115-118.* Kim Il-Sung, from 1948 president of the Central Committee of the Korean Workers Party, was in charge of North Korea since it came into being on the defeat of the Japanese in August 1945. Kim (b. 1912) was a leader in the struggle for independence waged by various revolutionary groups during the Japanese occupation. He continued to inspire the modernization and industrialization of his country. 1930's-82

Kim Jong-il

3545. Koh, Byung Chul. POLITICAL SUCCESSION IN NORTH KOREA. *Korea & World Affairs [South Korea] 1984 8(3): 557-574.* 1966-84
*For abstract see **Kim Il-sung***

Kim Phyon Mok

3546. Harada, Tamaki. CHŌSEN NO SAKOKU-JŌI-RON: KIN HEIMOKU WO CHŪSHIN NI [Seclusionism and exclusionism in Korea: Kim Phyon Mok]. *Shichō [Japan] 1984 (15): 65-84.* Concentrates on Kim Phyon Mok, a Korean Confucian who advocated seclusionism and exclusionism against China, Japan, and the West in 1866-82. Kim Phyon Mok's faction had a great influence while Taewŏn-gun was in power. However, after the Min family, who favored a more open foreign policy, had taken Taewŏn-gun's place and the coup d'etat of 1882 attempted by Taewŏn-gun's supporters had failed, Kim Phyon Mok lost his influential power. Based on primary sources; 38 notes. 1866-82

King, James

3547. Jack, R. Ian and Liston, Carol A. A SCOTTISH IMMIGRANT IN NEW SOUTH WALES: JAMES KING OF IRRAWANG. *J. of the Royal Australian Hist. Soc. [Australia] 1982 68(2): 92-106.* James King typified the entrepreneurial qualities of educated Scottish immigrants to Australia after 1820. King, a Sydney glassware merchant in 1826 later turned pastoralist, silicone exporter, and glass manufacturer. He pioneered viticulture in the Hunter Valley, and by manufacturing glazed pottery vessels for storing and transporting wine contributed significantly to a stable local wine industry. He exhibited prize wines at Paris in 1855. His widow endowed a traveling scholarship at Sydney University. Based on excavation files, University of Sydney Archaelogical Society; King Papers, Mitchell Library (Sydney), New South Wales Colonial Office Records (Sydney); colonial newspapers; 124 notes. 1826-57

King, John

3548. Endelman, Todd M. THE CHECKERED CAREER OF "JEW" KING: A STUDY IN ANGLO-JEWISH SOCIAL HISTORY. *AJS Rev. 1982-83 78: 69-100.* Recounts the career of John King (born Jacob Rey and known popularly as "Jew" King), who was not part of the elite, but was one of the most well-known Jews in London between 1780 and 1820. He tried to integrate himself into non-Jewish spheres of activity. King was a notorious moneylender, an ambitious upstart, and a radical critic of the established political order. He abandoned traditional Jewish practices early in life, but could not successfully cast off his Jewish origins. Late in life he returned to the Sephardi community and took up the defense of Judaism in the face of Christian missionary attacks. 1780-1820

King, Truby

3549. Olssen, Erik. TRUBY KING AND THE PLUNKET SOCIETY: AN ANALYSIS OF A PRESCRIPTIVE IDEOLOGY. *New Zealand J. of Hist. [New Zealand] 1981 15(1): 3-23.* As the founder of the Society for Promoting the Health of Women and Children (1907), Truby King, a medical doctor, campaigned successfully for a strict regimen of child-rearing practices. In time, New Zealand infant mortality rates declined substantially. But King had a much larger purpose. Reflecting Victorian concepts of family and motherhood, he espoused a middle-class ideology emphasizing control, discipline, regularity, and order. His ideas were thus important in the modernization of colonial life. Based on manuscripts, published documents and reports, unpublished theses, and secondary accounts; table, 84 notes. 1858-1946

Kingsley, Charles

3550. Wright, C. J. "MY DARLING BABY": CHARLES KINGSLEY'S LETTERS TO HIS WIFE. *British Library Journal [Great Britain] 1984 10(2): 147-157.* Collates the letters of English clergyman and novelist Charles Kingsley to his wife Frances Grenfell Kingsley, using references made by Susan Chitty in her biography of Kingsley, *The Beast and the Monk* (1974) and the Kingsley collection in the British Library. A brief, prefatory biographical sketch explains the sexually explicit nature of these letters and their drawings in light of Kingsley's intensely emotional nature. Based on the British Library collection of the letters of Charles Kingsley (Add. MSS. 62552-62557); 2 photos, 32 notes. 1844-75

Kinkoku, Yokoi

3551. Fister, Patricia Jean. "Yokoi Kinkoku: The Life and Painting of a Mountain Ascetic." (Vol. 1-3) U. of Kansas 1983. 517 pp. *DAI 1983 44(5): 1228-A.* DA8317879 ca 1790-1832

Kino, Eusebio Francisco

3552. Burrus, Ernest J. REVIEW ESSAY: *RIM OF CHRISTENDOM: A BIOGRAPHY OF EUSEBIO FRANCISCO KINO, PACIFIC COAST PIONEER* BY HEBERT [I.E., HERBERT] EUGENE BOLTON... *Hispanic American Historical Review 1985 65(3): 553-558.* Reviews the third edition of *Rim of Christendom: A Biography of Eusebio Francisco Kino, Pacific Coast Pioneer* (1984) by Herbert E. Bolton. Eusebio Francisco Kino (1645-1711) was a Jesuit missionary in Lower California, 1681-1711. This edition has a foreword by John L. Kessell that includes a select bibliography of pertinent items published since the first edition in 1936. Cites sections of the book that need revision. 21 notes. 1660's-1711

Kipling, Rudyard

3553. Reid, Fred and Washbrook, David. KIPLING, KIM AND IMPERIALISM. *Hist. Today [Great Britain] 1982 32(Aug): 14-20.* Discusses author Rudyard Kipling's views of British imperialism which are popularly thought to be expansionist, racist, and jingoist. In his novel, *Kim,* Kipling's views do not fit the stereotype. 1892-1901

Kippenberg, Anton

3554. Thomas, Sarah Elizabeth. "Hugo von Hofmannsthal and Anton Kippenberg of the Insel-Verlag: A Case Study of Author-Publisher Relations." Johns Hopkins U. 1982. 377 pp. *DAI 1982 43(1): 175-A.* DA8213435 1914-29

Kipuros, Dimitrios

3555. Kipuros, Dimitrios. FÜR DIE BEFREIUNG GRIECHENLANDS VON DEN FASCHISTISCHEN OKKUPANTEN [For the liberation of Greece from the occupation]. *Militärgeschichte [East Germany] 1985 24(1): 63-72.* Memoirs of a participant in the partisan opposition to Italian and German occupation of Greece during World War II. Map, 7 notes. 1940-45

Kireevski, Ivan

3556. McNally, Raymond. AGAINST A FRIENDLY ENEMY: IVAN KIREEVSKIJ. *Studies in Soviet Thought [Netherlands] 1986 32(4): 367-382.* 1845-56
*For abstract see **Chaadaev, Pëtr***

Kirileanu, Gheorghe Teodorescu

3557. Burlacu, Ioana. DIN CORESPONDENŢA LUI GHEORGHE TEODORESCU KIRILEANU CU CONSTANTIN MEISSNER (II) [From the correspondence between Gheorghe Teodorescu Kirileanu and Constantin Meissner. Part 2]. *Revista Arhivelor [Romania] 1983 45(3): 309-314.* A second installment of six letters from the Bucharest State Archives, from Kirileanu to his teacher Constantin Meissner, dated 1902-05, dealing with literary, social, and career matters. 1902-05

Kirke, Walter

3558. St. George, Brian. GENERAL SIR WALTER KIRKE. *Army Quarterly and Defence Journal [Great Britain] 1985 115(4):442-451, 1986 116(1): 52-62.* PART 1: SUBALTERN TO MAJOR—1896-1914. Covers Walter Kirke's early career in the British army, which took him to India and Burma. PART 2: 1914 TO 1933—HALF PAY AND ODD JOBS. Covers Walter Kirke's career as he advanced up the military ladder, including his mission to Finland, 1924, and long periods of half pay, culminating in his appointment as a general. Article to be continued. 1896-1933

Kirlova, Vasil

3559. Kamarianou-Tsioran, Ariadnēs; Giapana, Charlampou, transl.; and Kyrri, Kōsta P., commentary. DIAPREPEIS LOGIOI APO TĒN KYPRO DROUN STĒ ROUMANIA KYPRIAKES KATAGOGES HO MEGALOS ROUMANOS POIĒTĒS VASIL KIRLOVA (1803-1839) [Distinguished scholars from Cyprus active in Romania: Cypriot origins of the great Romanian poet, Vasil Kirlova (1803-39)]. *Kypriakos Logos [Cyprus] 1980 12(67-68): 233-240.* Chronologically relates the sources and the biographical details of Cypriot scholars in Romania, 16th to 19th centuries, with emphasis on the Romanian poet, Vasil Kirlova. Greek translation of an article appearing in *Magazin Istoric,* 1978 12/3 (132): 59-62. 1582-1839

Kisch, Egon Erwin

3560. Kronberger, J. "Egon Erwin Kisch: Seine Politische und Publizistische Entwicklung vom Bürgerlischen Journalisten zum Schöpfer der Literarischen Sozialistischen Reportage" [Egon Erwin Kisch: his political and journalistic development from a bourgeois journalist to the creator of literary socialist reportage]. U. of Vienna [Austria] 1979. *DAI-C 1982 43(3): 407; 7/2924c.* 1910-48

Kiselev, Pavel D.

3561. Thurston, Gary. P. D. KISELEV AND THE DEVELOPMENT OF A RUSSIAN LEGAL CONSCIOUSNESS. *Canadian-American Slavic Studies 1985 19(1): 1-27.* The administrative career of Pavel D. Kiselev (1788-1872) illustrates one individual's efforts to restructure Russian society through education, civil rights, and the creation of a coherent legal consciousness. A well-read student of the Enlightenment, Kiselev is remembered primarily for his tenure as Minister of State Domains. He worked creatively to alleviate the plight of the state peasantry and, though not always effective, his efforts to bridge the gulf between the gentry and the masses suggest that not all advocates of change were radicals intent on overturning the tsarist establishment. 94 notes. 1819-55

Kishida Ginkō

3562. Reynolds, Douglas R. BEFORE IMPERIALISM: KISHIDA GINKŌ PIONEERS THE CHINA MARKET FOR JAPAN. *Proceedings and Papers of the Georgia Association of Historians 1984 5: 114-120.* Traces the career of Chinese entrepreneur Kishida Ginkō and concludes that he was an important pioneer of modern Sino-Japanese relations who has been neglected by historians. During his second visit to China in 1868, he recognized the potential of the China trade when he initiated sales of Japanese eyewash. Later

(1878), he made a substantial profit by printing pocket editions of Chinese classics that could be sneaked into civil service examination halls. Because of his efforts in pioneering the China market for Japan, Kishida was recognized as the "father of the *tairiku ronin* [Chinese adventurers]." 33 notes. 1833-1905

Kiss, Károly

3563. Ács, Tibor. AZ ELFELEJTETT ELSŐ KATONA AKADÉMIKUS—KISS KÁROLY (1793-1866) [The forgotten first soldier-academician: Károly Kiss (1793-1866)]. *Hadtörténelmi Közlemények [Hungary] 1982 29(1): 26-58.* Elected as a corresponding member in 1831 and as a regular member in 1840, Kiss had great merits in developing Hungarian military terminology and military science in general. He joined the army in 1809 and was stationed in many countries. He started writing poetry in 1813; later also short stories, plays, and translations. As a colonel, he was active in organizing the army in the Revolution of 1848-49. He helped keep the ideals of national independence alive as a historian during absolutism. Based on original documents; 3 reproductions, 154 notes. Russian and German summaries. 1809-66

Kitanchev, Traiko

3564. Stoianov, Luchezar. TRAIKO KITANCHEV—ZHIVOT I DEINOST [Traiko Kitanchev—his life and activity]. *Istoricheski Pregled [Bulgaria] 1983 39(3): 110-118.* Traiko Kitanchev was born in 1858 in Podnochani, Resensko, and attended the Bulgarian school in Fener. Between 1882 and 1891, he taught in Solun, Gabrov, and the Bulgarian grammar school in Sofia. He was imprisoned from 1891 to 1894 for his revolutionary activities. In 1895 he opposed Eastern Rumelia's paying tax to Turkey. His life as poet, teacher and freedom fighter is justly famous, and his death in 1895 was a great loss to the Bulgarian revolutionary movement. Based on biographies of Traiko Kitanchev; 39 notes. 1880's-95

Kitchener, Horatio Herbert

3565. Rawling, Gerald. LORD KITCHENER. *British Heritage [Great Britain] 1982 3(5): 30-43.* Biography of British knight and peer whose titles are too numerous to mention, Lord Horatio Herbert Kitchener (1850-1916), ambitious, self-made military man who served in the Boer War, ruled India for four years, and headed the War Office for two years before he was killed when the British cruiser HMS *Hampshire* hit a mine laid by a German U-75 submarine. 1850-1916

Kitsos, George

3566. Mitakē, Dionysos. GEŌRGIOS KITSOS [George Kitsos]. *Ēpeirōtikē Hestia [Greece] 1980 29(344-345): 977-995.* George Kitsos (ca. 1790-1841) served as an officer in the army of his brother-in-law, Ali Pasha, the tyrant of Jannina. When Jannina fell to the Turks in 1821, Kitsos fled to Greece where he became a leader in the Greek War of Independence. The Turks captured his brother and sister at Jannina and later took his wife and children. While serving as an officer in the Greek army and rendering valuable service to the Greeks he was trying to raise money to ransom his family. He was in charge of the defense of Messolonghi, 1826, when Turkish prisoners escaped from that fortress. His enemies falsely accused him of having allowed the Turks to escape as part of an agreement to recover his family. Based on documents from the Greek national archives. Article to be continued. 1820-26

3567. Mitake, Dion. GEŌRGIOS KITSOS [George Kitsos]. *Ēpeirōtikē Hestia [Greece] 1981 30(347-348): 207-218.* George Kitsos (d. 1841) was a wealthy man in a position of privilege at the court of Ali Pasha of Epirus. In the Greek war of independence he put his wealth at the disposal of Greece and fled his native Epirus. As a result he lost his fortune, and during the war several members of his family were killed. He served as a general in the Greek army and fought with distinction in several major battles. After the war, despite repeated efforts to obtain a pension, he did not receive one and died in poverty. Based on the file on Kitsos in the Greek National Library; 4 reproductions of letters, 23 notes. 1820-41

Kittner, Patrizius

3568. Hofmann, Richard A. DIE NIKOLSBURGER JAHRE DES PORTRÄTISTEN PATRIZIUS KITTNER [The Nikolsburg years of the portraitist Patrizius Kittner]. *Bohemia [West Germany] 1982 23(1): 113-125.* After retiring from the civil service in Brno, Patrizius Kittner (1809-1900) moved with his family to Mikulov (Nikolsburg) in southern Moravia. This period, 1869-76, before his move to Vienna, has been ignored in bibliographical accounts. A self-taught miniaturist, Kittner produced hundreds of excellent portraits in the style of the 19th-century Vienna school. Though most of these passed into private hands, exhibitions took place in Brno in 1909 and 1970. 12 illus., 56 notes. 1869-76

Kiwrchyan, Melk'on

3569. Sargsyan, Gr. A. MELK'ON KIWRCHYAN [Melk'on Kiwrchyan]. *Patma-Banasirakan Handes. Istoriko-Filologicheskii Zhurnal [USSR] 1985 (2): 93-102.* Evaluates the work of the Armenian realist writer Melk'on Kiwrchyan (1859-1915), whose writings were published in the periodical press of Constantinople under the pen name Hrand. He was arrested in 1898 and exiled to Kastamuni where he continued to write. Returning in 1908, he was imprisoned in April 1915 and murdered. His notable works include *From the Life of an Exile,* the lyrical *Memories of New Year's Eve,* a collection of short stories entitled *Khonarh Khaveru mēj* [Amongst the humble layers of society], and the short story *On Four Wheels.* 11 notes. Russian summary. 1859-1915

Kjöllerström, Sven

3570. Österlin, Lars. SVEN KJÖLLERSTRÖM IN MEMORIAM [Sven Kjöllerström: in memoriam]. *Kyrkohistorisk Årsskrift [Sweden] 1981: 197-200.* This brief memorial bibliography of Sven Kjöllerström (1901-81), professor of theology and juris doctor honoris cause, outlines the main themes and thoughts in his research, which spanned most of Sweden's 1,000 years of church history. 1935-81

Klaar, Adalbert

3571. Feigl, Helmuth. IN MEMORIAM ADALBERT KLAAR [In memory of Adalbert Klaar]. *Unsere Heimat [Austria] 1981 52(3): 210-214.* Obituary for the Austrian historian Adalbert Klaar (1900-81). 1900-81

Klaić, Miho

3572. Macan, Trpimir. GLEDIŠTA MIHA KLAIĆA NA BOSANSKO-HERCEGOVAČKU PROBLEMATIKU OD 1874. DO 1890 [Miho Klaić's views on the problem of Bosnia and Herzegovina, 1874-90]. *Radovi: Inst. za Hrvatsku Povijest [Yugoslavia] 1980 13(1): 33-49.* Miho Klaić (1829-96), leader of the Dalmatian National Party, was deeply committed to the solution of the problem of Bosnia and Herzegovina and its liberation from Turkish rule. He was very active in the drive to mobilize support for the 1875 rebellion in Bosnia and Herzegovina against the Turks. His views coincided with those of the circle of the pan-Slavist Josip Juraj Štrosmajer (1815-1905), which advocated the establishment of a south Slav association that would include Bosnia and Herzegovina. His views on the region's immediate future were not so clearly defined. They ranged from advocacy of total independence to a union of Bosnia and Herzegovina with either Serbia or Montenegro. Although he had some reservations about the Austro-Hungarian annexation of the region, Klaić viewed it as a further step toward the strengthening of the south Slav groups within the monarchy. Secondary sources; 12 notes. 1874-90

Klee, Paul

3573. Mandalari, Maria Teresa. WALTER BENJAMIN: L'AMICIZIA CON GERSHOM SCHOLEM E L'ANGELO DI KLEE [Walter Benjamin: his friendship with Gershom Scholem and Klee's angel]. *Belfagor [Italy] 1982 37(1): 55-73.* 1920's-30's
For abstract see ***Benjamin, Walter***

Kleist, Heinrich von

3574. Roudil, Pierre. LES NOCES DE MORT DE VON KLEIST [Kleist's wedding with death]. *Hist. Mag. [France] 1983 (40): 40-44.* Recounts the life of the German Romantic playwright and novelist Heinrich von Kleist from 1797 until his suicide in 1811 and describes contemporary hostility to the author's works. 1797-1811

3575. Wexelblatt, Robert. KLEIST, KIERKEGAARD, KAFKA AND MARRIAGE. *San José Studies 1983 9(1): 6-15.* 19c-20c
For abstract see ***Kafka, Franz***

Klemenčič, Milan

3576. Kambič, Mirko. MILAN KLEMENČIČ KOT FOTOGRAF [Milan Klemenčič as photographer]. *Kronika [Yugoslavia] 1985 33(1): 71-75.* Milan Klemenčič (1875-1959), an amateur photographer, left a carefully documented collection. For the period 1899-1910 alone over 2,000 photographs remain preserved, some in color dating back to 1907. His pictures of landscapes of western Slovenia and of people in various activities represent a valuable interdisciplinary source. Illus. 1899-1959

Klimt, Gustav

3577. Grimberg, Salomon. ADELE. *Art & Antiques 1986 (Sum): 70-74, 90.* 1900-12
For abstract see ***Bloch-Bauer, Adele***

3578. Schorske, Carl E. MAHLER AND KLIMT: SOCIAL EXPERIENCE AND ARTISTIC EVOLUTION. *Daedalus 1982 111(3): 29-50.* Compares the life and aesthetics of Gustav Mahler and Gustav Klimt, as well as their friendship. 1870-1907

Kliuev, Nikolai

3579. Azadovski, Konstantin. KLIUEV I ESENIN V OKTIABRE 1915 GODA (PO MATERIALAM DNEVNIKA F. F. FIDLERA) [Kliuev and Esenin in October 1915: from the dairy of F. F. Fidler]. *Cahiers du Monde Russe et Soviétique [France] 1985 26(3-4): 413-424.* 1915
For abstract see ***Esenin, Sergei***

3580. McVay, Gordon. UNPUBLISHED TEXTS OF NIKOLAY KLYUYEV. *Slavonic and East European Review [Great Britain] 1985 63(4): 560-566.* Nikolai Kliuev (1884-1937), one of the Russian "peasant poets" of the first third of the 20th century, played a significant part in Russian literary life before and after the October Revolution. Attacked as a *kulak,* arrested and exiled in the 1930's, he is regaining limited acceptance in the USSR. Some of his letters and inscriptions are presented, with commentary. Based on manuscript holdings of Moscow and Leningrad libraries; 39 notes. 1912-27

3581. Simcic, Olga. BLOK E IL MESSIANISMO POPULISTA NELLA RUSSIA PRERIVOLUZIONARIA [Blok and populist messianism in prerevolutionary Russia]. *Studium [Italy] 1981 77(4): 423-441.* 1905-17
For abstract see ***Blok, Alexander***

Klobučarić, Ivan

3582. Peloza, Makso. IVAN KLOBUČARIĆ—ARCHITETTO E CARTOGRAFO [Ivan Klobučarić, architect and cartographer]. *Balcanica [Italy] 1982 1(1): 62-66.* Describes the career and the main contributions to cartography and architecture of the Croatian Augustinian monk Klobučarić (1545-1606). 1545-1606

Kloepfer, Hans

3583. Oswald, H. "Beiträge zu einer Kloepfer-Monographie unter Besonderer Berücksichtigung des Epischen Werkes" [Contributions to a Kloepfer biography with special regard to his epic work]. Vienna U. of Commerce [Austria] 1982. 241 pp. *DAI-C 1984 45(2): 307-308; 9/1215c.* 1890's-1940's

Klymenko, Ivan Ie.

3584. Motiienko, A. P. DO 90-RICHCHIA Z DNIA NARODZHENNIA I. IE. KLYMENKA (1891-1942) [The 90th anniversary of the birth of Ivan Ie. Klymenko (1891-1942)]. *Ukrains'kyi Istorychnyi Zhurnal [USSR] 1981 (9): 94-96.* Ivan Ievdokymovych Klymenko was born into a large peasant family in the village of Rivchak in the Chernogov district of the Ukraine. Traces his course from his departure for Kiev in 1905 to become an apprentice printer with a military establishment and his metoric rise as a Party member. Details of his activities, positions held, and congresses and conferences attended. 1905-42

Kmet', Andrej

3585. Senčík, Štefan. ANDREJ KMET', KŇAZ A NÁRODOVEC: K 75. VÝROČIU JEHO SMRTI [Andrej Kmet', priest and patriot: on the 75th anniversary of his death]. *Kalendár Jednota 1984 87: 136-146.* Typical of the best in the Slovak national movement, Andrej Kmet' (1841-1908), as an educator and botanist, set an example of selfless labor and patriotic consciousness. 1841-1908

Kminek-Szedlo, Giovanni

3586. Vachala, Břetislav. GIOVANNI KMINEK-SZEDLO, DER ERSTE TSCHECHISCHE ÄGYPTOLOGE [Giovanni Kminek-Szedlo, the first Czechoslovakian Egyptologist]. *Archív Orientální [Czechoslovakia] 1986 54(1): 89-91.* Jan Kminek-Szedlo (1828-96) was born in Prague and studied at the University of Prague in 1847-48. He was inducted into the Imperial army and transferred to Italy as a cavalry officer. After leaving the army, he took up residence in Bologna, changed his first name to Giovanni, and studied philosophy and languages, becoming interested in Egyptology. He was appointed a lecturer in Egyptology at the University of Bologna in 1878. In the early 1890's he was appointed museum inspector at the Bologna Museum, where he cataloged the museum's collection of Egyptian objects. He published the resulting catalog in 1895. His other works included *Il Grande Sarcofago* (1876) and *Saggio Filologico* (1877). 12 notes. 1847-77

Knežević, Tripko

3587. Vuković, Dragutin. TRIPKO GURIŠ-KNEŽEVIĆ—PRADJED KARADJORDJEV [Tripko Guriš-Knežević, Karadjordje's great-grandfather]. *Zbornik Istorijskog Muzeja Srbije [Yugoslavia] 1979 15-16: 71-74.* Tripko Knežević, nicknamed Guriš (hunchback) because of his stoop, lived in the village of Velje Duboko in northern Montenegro in the late 17th century. Knežević, who according to traditional stories and epic songs is the grandfather of the great Serbian leader Karadjordje, distinguished himself in battles against the Turkish occupiers. After clashes in which he and his brothers killed many Turks and stole their cattle, Knežević was forced to settle near the town of Nikšić. There he was killed by the Turks during a battle in which he was flag-bearer for a Montenegrin regiment. Note. 17c

Knight, Anne

3588. Malmgreen, Gail. ANNE KNIGHT AND THE RADICAL SUBCULTURE. *Quaker Hist. 1982 71(2): 100-113.* Educated, unmarried Anne Knight (1786-1862), an Englishwoman of means, was an indefatigable correspondent who sent letters, broadsides, and tracts to relatives, friends, enemies, and strangers alike. She espoused Garrisonian abolition and, when the 1840 London convention barred women, feminism. Moving to Paris about 1848, she traveled as a tourist, radical observer, and Quaker missionary in Western France and Switzerland, and retired to die in J. F. Oberlin's native Waldersbach. She was acquainted with contemporary Nonconformist and communitarian socialist thought and developed a vigorous, undisciplined, millenialist style. She sustained her independent, left-wing politics—colored and restrained by her religion—within the loosely organized radical network. Based mainly on family manuscripts; 38 notes. 1824-48

Knight, Richard

3589. Hunt, Leslie B. and Buchanan, Peta D. RICHARD KNIGHT (1768-1844): A FORGOTTEN CHEMIST AND APPARATUS DESIGNER. *Ambix [Great Britain] 1984 31(2): 57-67.* Richard Knight was educated at a dissenting academy prior to apprenticeship to his grandfather and later his father. He became a partner in the family business (of which a brief history is given), inheriting it in 1799. There is some evidence that he knew and was a laboratory assistant to Joseph Priestley. Later experimentation enabled him to publish in 1800 a method for rendering platinum malleable. His other research is commented on, as is his development of his business. His membership in scientific societies is noted. 45 notes. 1785-1840

Knorre, Georgi F.

3590. Styrikovich, M. A. and Khvostov, V. I. GEORGII FEDOROVICH KNORRE (1891-1962) [Georgi Fedorovich Knorre (1891-1962)]. *Voprosy Istorii Estestvoznaniia i Tekhniki [USSR] 1983 (2): 132-136.* Biography of Georgi F. Knorre, professor at Moscow's N. E. Bauman Higher Technical School, author of numerous theoretical and applied studies on combustion and boiler-heating techniques. His major achievement was the development of a high-temperature cyclone furnace for efficient and economical gasification of fuels and gas purification. Note, biblio. 1930's-62

Knox, John

3591. Frankforter, A. Daniel. CORRESPONDENCE WITH WOMEN: THE CASE OF JOHN KNOX. *Journal of the Rocky Mountain Medieval and Renaissance Association 1985 6: 159-172.* Analyzes letters from John Knox to Anne Locke and Elizabeth Bowes to show the place of two women in the life of the leader of the Scottish Reformation. 1551-62

Knox, Robert Buick

3592. Mayor, Stephen. ROBERT BUICK KNOX. *Journal of the United Reformed Church History Society [Great Britain] 1985 3(6): 191-194.* Retirement tribute to Robert Buick Knox, Presbyterian Church historian of the British Isles, in whose honor this issue is dedicated. 16c-20c

Knox, Ronald

3593. Walsh, M. "Ronald Knox as Apologist." Pontifical Gregorian U. [Vatican] 1985. 488 pp. *DAI-C 1986 47(2): 299; 47/1437c.* 1910's-57

Knunyants

3594. Gharibjanian, G. B. V. I. LENINI HAY ZINAKITSNĒRN U ASHAKĒRTNĒRĒ [V. I. Lenin's Armenian comrades-in-arms and disciples]. *Patma-Banasirakan Handes. Istoriko-Filologicheskii Zhurnal [USSR] 1980 (1): 13-20.* ca 1890-1917

*For abstract see **Avanesov***

Köbis, Albin

3595. Sinegubov, V. REVOLIUTSIONNYM MATROSAM POSVIASHCHENO... [Dedicated to revolutionary sailors...]. *Morskoi Sbornik [USSR] 1982 (11): 71-74.* Albin Köbis (1892-1917), a revolutionary socialist German sailor who participated in the August 1917 Wilhelmshafen uprising, was shot by the Kaiser's military. 1917

Kocbek, Edvard

3596. Grafenauer, Bogo. NEKAJ OPOMB K NASTAJANJU IN BIBLIOGRAFIJI DEJANJA [Remarks on the beginning and the bibliography of *Dejanje*]. *Zgodovinski Časopis [Yugoslavia] 1982 36(4): 355-362.* Describes the life of Edvard Kocbek, focusing on his role in the founding and editorial direction of the periodical *Dejanje* [The deed]. 1936-41

Kočevar, Štefan

3597. Hribovšek, Avgust and Pertl, Eman. DR. ŠTEFAN KOČEVAR, DELAVEC NA SLOVENSKI NARODNI IN ZDRAVSTVENI LEDINI [Dr. Štefan Kočevar: pioneer in the field of Slovenian national and medical research]. *Zbornik za Zgodovino Naravoslovja in Tehnike [Yugoslavia] 1985 8: 101-113.* Reviews the life and work of the Slovene physician, initiator of national renaissance, politician, and writer Štefan Kočevar and his book *Slovenska Mati* [Slovene mother]. 1834-83

Koch, Jobst Heinrich

3598. Steinmüller, Karl. WIEN 1683: EIN BERICHT VON JOBST HEINRICH KOCH [Vienna, 1683: an account by Jobst Heinrich Koch]. *Wiener Geschichtsblätter [Austria] 1979 34(4): 176-187.* A biographical sketch of J. H. Koch (born between 1644 and 1648), who became *Hofpfalzgraf* in 1697, and a complete version of his account from Regensburg, dated 23 December 1683, of what happened to him and his family during the Turkish siege of Vienna from July till the end of 1683, as well as his accompanying letter from Wels, dated 6 February 1684, to his uncle Christian Leisner, a deacon in Plauen. 1683-84

Koch, Richard

3599. Koch, Richard. SCHWENINGER'S SEMINAR. *Journal of Contemporary History [Great Britain] 1985 20(4): 757-779.* Naomi B. Laqueur here publishes an abridged version of a chapter of the autobiography of her father, Richard Koch (1882-1949), who taught history and philosophy of medicine at the University of Frankfurt am Main until he was dismissed in 1933. He maintained a friendship with Ernst Schweninger (1850-1924), personal physician to Bismarck and other famous personages in public life. Schweninger, deemed a charlatan, was convinced of his calling to destroy conservative medicine and replace it with his "natural way of healing." His Socratic seminar in 1907, described by Koch, was full of common sense remedies and psychological insights. 1907

Koch, Richert Gerard Halfred von

3600. Sollinger, Gunther. G. H. VON KOCHS FOTOGRAFISKA SAMLING [G. H. von Koch's photographic collection]. *Arbetarhistoria [Sweden] 1985 9(35): 12-15.* Outlines the work of Richert Gerard Halfred von Koch (1872-1948), an upper-class Swede active in social welfare and reform, whose collection of photographs is now deposited in the archive of the Swedish Labor Movement in Stockholm. Illus.; 8 notes. 1897-1938

Kochanowski, Jan

3601. Müldner-Nieckowski, Piotr. UWAGI W SPRAWIE ZDROWIA, CHORÓB I PRZYCZYN ŚMIERCI JANA KOCHANOWSKIEGO (1530-1584) [Remarks on the health, illnesses, and causes of death of Jan Kochanowski (1530-84)]. *Archiwum Historii Medycyny [Poland] 1985 48(1): 51-62.* Unhealthy diet and excessive drinking were the likeliest causes of the hardening of arteries that appears to have caused the death of Polish poet and humanist Jan Kochanowski (1530-84). 1550-84

3602. Ulewicz, Tadeusz. THE PORTRAIT OF JAN KOCHANOWSKI IN THE ENCYCLOPAEDIAS OF NON-SLAVIC COUNTRIES. A CRITICAL SURVEY. *Polish Rev. 1982 27(3-4): 3-16.* Jan Kochanowski's (1530-84) name is "a symbol for the cultural achievement of the Polish language and literature." The *New Encyclopedia Britannica* (1974) continues this encyclopedia's tradition of neglecting non-Russian Slavic literature. The "shameful" article on Kochanowski is short and factually inaccurate. Similarly, the short article in the Spanish-American *Enciclopedia Universal Illustrada Europeo-Americana* consists of blunders and "assorted nonsense." A lengthier and reliable article may be found in the *Encyclopedia Americana* (1977). Since the 19th century French and, to a lesser extent, German encyclopedias have favorably treated Polish matters with generally accurate articles. The best non-Slavic encyclopedia articles on Kochanowski and Polish culture in general may be found in the *Enciclopedia Italiana.* Based on encyclopedia articles; 16 notes. 1550's-84

Kočić, Peter

3603. Butler, Thomas. BETWEEN EAST AND WEST: THREE BOSNIAN WRITER-REBELS. *Cross Currents 1984 3: 339-357.* 1878-82
*For abstract see **Andrić, Ivo***

Kodály, Zoltán

3604. Breuer, János. ZOLTÁN KODÁLY AND BENJAMIN BRITTEN. *New Hungarian Q. [Hungary] 1982 23(88): 52-56.* 1947-67
*For abstract see **Britten, Benjamin***

3605. Ujfalussy, József. KODÁLY ZOLTÁN ÖRÖKSÉGE [The heritage of Zoltán Kodály]. *Társadalmi Szemle [Hungary] 1982 37(11): 42-48.* Together with Béla Bartók, Zoltán Kodály was rediscovering his own musical reason for existence in the music of his country's people. The development of a democratic music, music which belongs to everyone, was his main aim. After World War II, his approach to music education was accepted by the government and standardized across the country. 1907-80

3606. Vargyas, Lajos. ZOLTÁN KODÁLY: A CENTENARY TRIBUTE. *New Hungarian Q. [Hungary] 1982 23(88): 39-45.* Zoltán Kodály (1882-1967), as artist, educator, and musician, saw in the living folk tradition, the richness of the popular mind, and the wealth of folk music a vital force. For him folk music meant not just a musical inspiration but the center, the goal of his composing. His effort to create a national musical language led him to the ancient dances of Hungary. Kodály had a particularly isolated career among his contemporaries. The closest to him was Béla Bartók, who closely associated with Kodály through Hungarian folk music. But Kodály appears as a highly individual figure, a genius of his nation. 1882-1967

Koenig, Alma Johanna

3607. Raynaud, Franziska. ALMA JOHANNA KOENIG (1887-1942?): LEBEN UND DICHTEN EINER WIENERIN [Alma Johanna Koenig (1887-?1942): the life and poems of a Viennese woman]. *Bulletin des Leo Baeck Instituts [Israel] 1983 (64): 29-54.* Discusses the life and literary career of the Czechoslovakian-born Jewish writer Alma Johanna Koenig. She was born in Prague but spent her childhood and early youth in Vienna. The author examines her upbringing and the influence of her parents on her. There were three important stages in Alma Koenig's creative development: 1911-20, 1922-32, and 1938-42. In the first period her main intellectual influences were the dramatist Josef Kainz and the poet Rainer Maria Rilke, and she belonged to a circle of literary and artistic people in Vienna. In 1921 she married Bernhard von Ehrenfels, 11 years her junior, but the marriage was unsuccessful and she was divorced in 1936. Between 1922 and 1932 Alma Koenig was very prolific, writing many poems, novels, and plays. However, no publisher would publish her works because she was Jewish, and by 1933 she was living in poverty. After the annexation of Austria in 1938 she made plans to leave but never did. In May 1942 she was arrested by the Nazis and taken to Minsk and was never heard of again. Secondary sources; 69 notes, biblio. 1887-1942

3608. Tauschinski, Oskar Jan. DOKUMENTATION. ALMA JOHANNA KOENIG: BRIEFE AN HELENE LAHR [Documents: Alma Johanna Koenig: letters to Helene Lahr]. *Zeitgeschichte [Austria] 1981 8(7): 260-291.* Alma Johanna Koenig (1887-1942) was an Austrian Jewish writer and poet. Her letters to Helene Lahr—the only complete series of letters discovered so far—reflect her vivid, warm, and human spirit, the combination of many cultures and languages in Vienna, and the growing hardship of Jews in Vienna. Alma Johanna Koenig, daughter of the Captain Karl Koenig of the former imperial army, was deported in 1942. She continued to write to the very end, even though her books were among those burnt in 1933 and she was prohibited from publishing after 1938. 1887-1942

Koenig, General

3609. Gromand, Roger. LE MARECHAL KOENIG, COMMANDANT-EN-CHEF FRANÇAIS EN ALLEMAGNE; 1945-49 [Marshal Koenig, French commander-in-chief in Germany]. *Revue des Deux Mondes [France] 1985 (8): 374-379.* Highlights the military career of General Koenig (1898-1970), French commander-in-chief in Germany from 1945 to 1949, focusing on the diplomatic qualities he displayed in his relations with the allies, his policies toward the German population, and his relations with the French government. 1945-49

Koestler, Arthur

3610. Palewski, Gaston. PROPOS [Remarks]. *Rev. des Deux Mondes [France] 1983 (4): 128-136.* ca 1860-1983
*For abstract see **Chirac, Jacques***

3611. Valiani, Leo. KOESTLER THE MILITANT. A LAST TRIBUTE. *Encounter [Great Britain] 1984 63(2): 68-72.* A personal memoir of Arthur Koestler, concentrating on his role during World War II. 1939-46

3612. —. THE LIFE & DEATH OF ARTHUR KOESTLER. *Encounter [Great Britain] 1983 61(1): 8-37.*

Raymond, Aron. A WRITER'S GREATNESS, *pp. 8-12.* Surveys the literary career and influence of Arthur Koestler.

Hook, Sidney. COLD WARRIOR, *pp. 12-16.* Discusses Koestler's most celebrated work, *Darkness at Noon,* an expose of the Moscow Trials.

Cranston, Maurice. IN THE TRADITION OF DANIEL DEFOE, *pp. 16-18.* An appreciation of Koestler's literary influence, particularly the impact of *Darkness at Noon, The Gladiators,* and *The Sleepwalkers.*

Hamilton, Iain. BIOGRAPHEE, *pp. 18-22.* Discusses Hamilton's writing of Koestler's biography, especially Koestler's attempts to censor portions of the manuscript, although he had contractually relinquished all censorial rights.

Harris, Harold. AUTHOR, *pp. 23-25.* A publisher and editor of Koestler's work reminisces on their friendship.

Pryce-Jones, David. CHESS MAN, *pp. 25-28.* Relates the adventures of Koestler and Pryce-Jones in their trip to Iceland as journalists to cover the Spassky-Fischer chess championship of 1972.

Beloff, John. PSYCHOLOGIST, *pp. 28-31.* Discusses Koestler's interest in psychology, the popular nature of his work in this field, and his interest in parapsychology.

Astor, David. CRUSADER, *pp. 31-33.* Discusses Astor's friendship with Koestler, the latter's role in the movement against capital punishment in Britain, and the establishment of the Koestler Awards to encourage literary work in British prisons.

Benson, Mary. "ANGEL," *pp. 33-36.* Discusses the relationship of Arthur and Cynthia Koestler.

Mikes, George. HUNGARIAN, *pp. 36-37.* An appreciation by a Hungarian friend. Further contributions will appear in a later issue. 1905-83

Kogălniceanu, Mihail

3613. Vulcan, Iosif; Lăcustă, I., ed. PANTEONUL ROMÂN [Romanian pantheon]. *Magazin Istoric [Romania] 1981 15(5): 17-19, 61.* 1802-68
*For abstract see **Heliade-Rădulescu, Ioan***

Kogălniceanu, Vasile M.

3614. Kogălniceanu, Ion M. VASILE M. KOGĂLNICEANU: UN DEMN URMAŞ AL TATĂLUI SĂU [Vasile M. Kogălniceanu: a worthy successor to his father]. *Magazin Istoric [Romania] 1981 15(4): 22-23, 54.* Surveys the life and work of the Romanian historian Vasile Kogălniceanu, 1863-1942, fourth son of the Wallachian statesman Mihail Kogălniceanu, 1817-91, whose official correspondence was published in 1893. 1893-1942

Kogan, Moisei

3615. —. MOISEI ALEKSANDROVICH KOGAN 1907-1982 [Moisei Aleksandrovich Kogan, 1907-82]. *Skandinavskii Sbornik [USSR] 1983 28: 215-216.* Obituary of Moisei Kogan (1907-82), Soviet Scandinavian historian. His main research area focused on the Viking routes. He was a noted pedagogue and promoter of good relations between students and staff. Photo. Swedish summary. 1907-82

Kohl, Helmut

3616. Brigouleix, Bernard. HELMUT KOHL: LA FORCE TRANQUILLE [Helmut Kohl: the quiet force]. *Documents [France] 1983 38(1): 31-35.* Highlights the career of Helmut Kohl (b. 1930), his rise to power, and the political attitudes of the newly elected West German chancellor. 1982

Koizumi, Chikahiko

3617. Tsuneishi, Kei-ichi. C. KOIZUMI: AS A PROMOTER OF THE MINISTRY OF HEALTH AND WELFARE AND AN ORIGINATOR OF THE BCW RESEARCH PROGRAM. *Historia Scientiarum [Japan] 1984 (26): 95-113.* Summarizes two aspects of the career of Chikahiko Koizumi (1884-1945), Japanese biochemist and military officer. He studied gas warfare in Europe and in his own laboratory during the first world war. As surgeon general, he attempted to reverse the physical decline in the population (as revealed in the examination of army recruits) through the promotion of a public health movement. He also founded a program of research and development in biological-chemical warfare (BCW). 3 graphs, 37 notes. 1914-45

Kokorev, V. A.

3618. Lieberman, Paula Lynn. "V. A. Kokorev: An Industrial Entrepreneur in Nineteenth-Century Russia. Yale U. 1981. 269 pp. *DAI 1983 43(7): 2422-A.* DA8210394 19c

Kolańczyk, Kazimierz

3619. Rozwadowski, Władysław. KAZIMIERZ KOLAŃCZYK 1915-1982 [Kazimierz Kolańczyk (1915-82)]. *Czasopismo Prawno-Historyczne [Poland] 1983 35(2): 237-240.* Obituary of Kazimierz Kolańczyk (1915-82), Polish legal historian at the University of Poznań, who published works on Roman law, communal land ownership in medieval Poland, and West German cultural policy in higher education. His major work was *O Pochodzeniu i Stanowisku Społecznym Prawników Rzymskich* [On the social origins and status of Roman lawyers]. Secondary sources; 14 notes. 1940's-82

Kolarov, Vasil

3620. Cherniavski, Georgi I. VASIL KOLAROV—REVOLIUTSIONER-INTERNATSIONALIST [Vasil Kolarov, revolutionary and internationalist]. *Novaia i Noveishaia Istoriia [USSR] 1985 (2): 92-112.* Biography of the Bulgarian Social Democrat and later Communist activist, V. Kolarov (1877-1950). He met Lenin during the Zimmerwald Conference in 1915 but did not fully endorse the Bolshevik program until after the October 1917 Revolution. In 1922, Kolarov became Secretary General of Comintern's Executive Committee, headed together with Georgi Dimitrov (1882-1949) the September 1923 uprising in Bulgaria, and participated in the Comintern's war on fascism in the 1930's. A leader of Bulgarian political exiles in the USSR during World War II, Kolarov was elected chairman of the Bulgarian People's Assembly in December 1945 and chairman of the Council of Ministers in July 1949. Based on the Central Party Archives of the Institute of Marxism-Leninism (USSR) and other primary and secondary sources; 104 notes. 1915-49

3621. Kumanov, Milen. K VOPROSU O PUBLITSISTICHESKOM NASLEDII G. DIMITROVA I V. KOLAROVA [On the journalistic heritage of Georgi Dimitrov and Vasil Kolarov]. *Bulgarian Hist. Rev. [Bulgaria] 1981 9(3): 88-101.* 1923-26
For abstract see ***Dimitrov, Georgi***

Kolben, Emil

3622. Kolben, Heinz. DR. H. C. ING. EMIL KOLBEN ZUM GEDÄCHTNIS [In memory of Dr. Emil Kolben]. *Bohemia [West Germany] 1985 26(1): 111-121.* Emil Kolben (1862-1943), an outstanding electrical engineer from Bohemia, spent the years 1888-92 in America, where he worked with Thomas A. Edison and learned from Nikola Tesla. He became a leading advocate of alternating current and in 1896 founded a successful electrotechnical firm, which in 1921-27 merged with two other enterprises to establish one of Czechoslovakia's major machine-building concerns, Českomoravská Kolben-Daněk. Honored in Austria-Hungary and Czechoslovakia, he died in the Nazi concentration camp at Terezín (Theresienstadt). Based on family memoirs and publications; diagram. 1862-1943

Kolchak, Aleksandr

3623. Barr, William. ALEKSANDR VASIL'YEVICH KOLCHAK: ARCTIC SCIENTIST AND EXPLORER. *Polar Record [Great Britain] 1981 20(129): 507-524.* Biography of Aleksandr Kolchak (1873-1920), focusing on his participation in two Arctic expeditions and his planning of a third expedition before he was executed by a Bolshevik firing squad. 1873-1920

Kolejka, Josef

3624. Kočí, Josef. ŽIVOTNÍ JUBILEUM DOC. PHDR. JOSEFA KOLEJKY, CSC. [Birthday anniversary of Josef Kolejka]. *Slovanský Přehled [Czechoslovakia] 1984 90[i.e., 70](2): 158-160.* A tribute to Josef Kolejka, a Czech historian, on his 60th birthday. His primary interest of study and teaching has been the history of Moravia and Silesia. A professor of history in Brno since 1953, he has been active in many professional organizations and the editor of a number of scholarly journals. 1924-84

Kollár, Adam František

3625. Tibenský, Ján. ADAM FRANTIŠEK KOLLÁR—HISTORIAN OF ENLIGHTENMENT. *Studia Historica Slovaca [Czechoslovakia] 1984 13: 137-164.* Adam František Kollár (1718?-83) was educated by the Jesuits and served as court librarian and historian for the Habsburg Empire. He advocated religious tolerance, the supremacy of the monarchy in relations between church and state, educational reform, and the improvement of living conditions for peasants and the middle classes. He earned the enmity of the ruling classes by denouncing rebellions by the Hungarian nobility and suggesting they should pay military taxes. He demonstrated the indigenous character of the Slavic peoples and developed Samuel Timon's concept of the contractual participation of Slavs in the development of the Hungarian state. 62 notes. 9c-17c

Kollonics, Lipót Károly

3626. Némethy, Sándor. A DELEGATUM JUDICIUM EXTRAORDINARIUM POSONIENSE ANNO 1674 TÖRTÉNETE ÉS JOGÁSZI KRITIKÁJA [The history and legal criticism of the Delegatum Judicium Extraordinarium Posoniense, 1674]. *Theológiai Szemle [Hungary] 1981 24(4): 219-224, (5): 295-300; 1982 25(2): 99-105; 1983 26(1): 22-30, (4): 234-245, (5): 276-286.* Part 4. Archbishop György Szelepcsényi was an essential figure in the preparation of anti-Protestant trials in Bratislava. They were to be treated as rebels, not as heretics. Two incriminating letters, reprinted here, were forged in the name of the former preacher István Wittnyédi de Muzsaj and produced at the trial. Part 5. Presents arguments disputing the authenticity of the Wittnyédi letters. They were first declared forgeries by one of the alleged recipients, Count Miklós Bethlen, in 1675. Part 6. On the role of György Szelepcsényi in the preparation of the trials in Pozsony (Bratislava). The incriminating letters by Wittnyédy were forgeries, as was shown by philological analysis. Wittnyédy's (1612-70) character was impeccable. Part 7. In 1621, at the age of 20, Adam Forgách was appointed lord-lieutenant of Nograd County. Six years later he married the daughter of one of the richest widows in the country. From there on his career continued in the most unsavory manner. His vain, boastful, proud attitude and money-grabbing, cowardly character were easily recognized. He broke the most solemn oaths and was completely devoid of any feeling of responsibility; he willingly took any position that would serve his selfish interests, even if he ended up as a traitor to his country. (8) KOLLEGRÁDI GRÓF KOLLONICS LIPÓT KÁROLY OSZTRÁK ÁLLAMFÉRFI, BÍBOROS, ESZTERGOMI ERSEK-PRÍMÁS JELLEMZÉSE [Part 8. Characterization of Count Lipót Károly Kollonics of Kollegrád, Austrian statesman, cardinal, and primate of Esztergom]. The talented, hard-working Kollonics, who reached the highest positions in the Austrian court and in the Catholic hierarchy, was completely devoid of even the minimal human decencies. He was full of hatred, rudeness, and greed. He was also a liar, a cheat, and a thief. As a ferocious enemy of Hungary and all non-Catholic churches, he was well received by the Habsburgs. His character is well-mirrored in his motto: "I will make Hungarians beggars, prisoners, and finally Catholics." He lived up to his creed by killing, jailing, and torturing people he knew to be innocent, increasing his own wealth considerably in the process. (9) SZÉCHENYI GYÖRGY ESZTERGOMI ÉRSEK-PRÍMÁS JELLEMZÉSE [Part 9. Characterization of György Széchenyi, Archbishop of Esztergom]. Although the *Hungarian Catholic Lexicon* speaks very highly of Széchenyi, the truth is different. A child of poor parents, he reached the rank of archbishop through political machinations. He was completely devoid of all moral feelings. As an archbishop, he did not fulfill his ecclesiastical obligations; he was insensitive to the suffering of others, and as a judge he sentenced to death people he knew were innocent. His only concern was the accumulation of money, although he spent very little on himself or on his relatives, probably out of stinginess. The only redeeming characteristic of Széchenyi was his love for Hungary. Based mainly on primary sources; 352 notes. 17c

Kollontai, Aleksandra

3627. Mullaney, Marie Marmo. GENDER AND THE SOCIALIST REVOLUTIONARY ROLE, 1871-1921: A GENERAL THEORY OF THE FEMALE REVOLUTIONARY PERSONALITY. *Historical Reflections [Canada] 1984 11(2): 99-151.* 1871-1921
*For abstract see **Balabanoff, Angelica***

3628. Sheinis, Z. S. ALEKSANDRA KOLLONTAI: SOVETSKII DIPLOMAT [The Soviet diplomat Aleksandra Kollontai]. *Novaia i Noveishaia Istoriia [USSR] 1985 (4): 83-95.* Aleksandra Mikhailovna Kollontai joined the Soviet diplomatic corps in April 1922 following a spiritual crisis provoked by her break with Pavel Efimovich Dybenko and the Workers' Opposition. She was probably the first woman diplomat in contemporary history. During her 30 years of service abroad in Norway, Mexico, and Sweden she loyally followed the state and Party line. She helped establish trade links with these countries and played a leading role in Scandinavia during World War II. 1922-52

Kolmakov, Petr K.

3629. —. PETR KIRIAKOVICH KOLMAKOV [Petr Kiriakovich Kolmakov]. *Skandinavskii Sbornik [USSR] 1980 25: 243-244.* Provides an obituary of the Soviet historian, linguist, and bibliographer, Petr K. Kolmakov (1898-1980). Kolmakov will be best remembered for his phenomenal linguistic skill—he knew more than 30 languages—and for his contribution to the science of librarianship and bibliography in the USSR. From 1920-35 he worked as a librarian before starting a career as editor of several bibliographical publications and as an adviser on librarianship and bibliography in the Academy of Sciences of the USSR. During his career he wrote more than 500 books, brochures, articles, and reviews. He also published the definitive Soviet bibliography on Asia and Africa and prepared several bibliographies on Soviet history. Photo. 1898-1980

Kolobov, L. A.

3630. Rakitski, A. ISKUSSTVO KOMDIVA [The military art of the division commander]. *Voenno-Istoricheskii Zhurnal [USSR] 1982 (6): 23-26.* In spring 1942, L. A. Kolobov took command of the 389th Rifle Division. He displayed his military talents in the night attack on the city of Armavir on 23 January 1943, in the capture of Berdichev in January 1944, and in the forced crossing of the river Vistula, for which he was awarded the title of Hero of the Soviet Union. After the war he was the vice-president of the Lenin Military-Political Academy. At present Lieutenant General Kolobov is retired and involved in the patriotic education of young people. Based on government archives and secondary sources; 7 notes. 1942-44

Kolski, Witold

3631. Kormanowa, Żanna. WITOLD KOLSKI (1902-1943) [Witold Kolski (1902-43)]. *Z Pola Walki [Poland] 1979 22(3): 121-138.* A personal account of the life and work of Witold Kolski by a former friend. W. Kolski was a prominent member of the Communist Party of Poland from 1924, when he joined as a student at the Jagiellonian University. He was imprisoned from 1936 to 1939 for his political activities and then he moved to the Russian-occupied Lvov. On 22 June 1941 he joined the Red Army and was killed on a mission in 1943. Based on documents in the Central Archives of the Central Committee of the Polish United Workers' Party and at the Archives of the Ministry of Internal Affairs, eyewitness accounts, and W. Kolski's own writings; 80 notes. 1924-43

Kol'tsov, Mikhail Yefimovitz

3632. Alcofar Nassaes, José Luis. EL PERIODISTA KOLTSOV Y LA GUERRA DE ESPAÑA [The Russian journalist Kol'tsov and the Spanish civil war]. *Historia y Vida [Spain] 1984 17(197): 116-125.* Mikhail Kol'tsov (1898-1939) went to Spain in 1936 to chronicle the civil war for the Soviet newspaper *Pravda,* and in 1938 he published his *Ispanskii Dnevnik* [Spanish diary], a page of which is included in this article. 1917-39

3633. Levavi (Babitski), Ya'acov. MICHAEL YEFIMOVITZ KOLTSOV (1898-1942) [Michael Yefimovitz Koltsov (1898-1942)]. *Shvut [Israel] 1980 7: 91-93.* Koltsov, a talented Bolshevik and valued member of the Soviet regime, coauthored a brochure that proposed resettling Russian Jews into agricultural work near the Black Sea. He was arrested in 1938 as an "enemy of the people," but was rehabilitated after Stalin's death. Portrait, 28 notes. 1924-42

Komenský

See Comenius, John Amos

Kommodov, Nikolai V.

3634. Sidorenko, N. T. N. V. KOMMODOV—VETERAN SOVETSKOI ADVOKATURY (V SVIAZI SO 100-LETIEM SO DNIA ROZHDENIIA) [Nikolai Kommodov, veteran Soviet lawyer, on the centenary of his birth]. *Sovetskoe Gosudarstvo i Pravo [USSR] 1985 (3): 117-122.* Outlines the legal achievements of Nikolai V. Kommodov (b. 1884), a Soviet lawyer famous for his adept psychological interpretations of crime. 1920's-60's

Konan, Naito

3635. Fogel, Joshua A. TO REFORM CHINA: NAITO KONAN'S FORMATIVE YEARS IN THE MEIJI PRESS. *Modern Asian Studies [Great Britain] 1982 16(3): 353-395.* In his journalistic writing between 1894 and 1899 Naito Konan (1866-1934) worked on ideas which he kept later on as Japan's leading authority on Chinese history and contemporary affairs. Strongly influenced by Chinese political theory, he tried to ascertain how it could be applied by Japan at the time of the Sino-Japanese War in 1894-95 and again in Taiwan in 1897-98. He favored the use of force by Japan to impose reform in China, but by 1899 had come to propose Sino-Japanese cultural contact and the Meiji restoration as a model for reform in China. 97 notes. 1894-99

Kondrat'ev, Aleksandr A.

3636. Arkhipenko, V. KOMANDIR "ZARI SVOBODY" [Commander of the *Zaria Svobody*]. *Voenno-Istoricheskii Zhurnal [USSR] 1982 (9): 46-53.* ca 1910-30
*For abstract see **Lavrenev, Boris***

Koni, A. F.

3637. Smoliarchuk, V. I. A. F. KONI: LICHNOST', DEIATEL'NOST', TVORCHESKOE NASLEDIE [A. F. Koni: personality, activity, and legacy]. *Sovetskoe Gosudarstvo i Pravo [USSR] 1981 (2): 133-139.* Discusses Russian jurist, public figure, writer, academician A. F. Koni (1844-1927). 1860's-1927

Koniecpolski, Stanisław

3638. Wielebska, Zofia. STANISŁAW KONIECPOLSKI HETMAN WIELKI KORONNY W LATACH 1632-1646 [Stanisław Koniecpolski, Great Crown Hetman in the years 1632-46]. *Studia Historyczne [Poland] 1985 28(3): 337-361.* Presents activities of Stanisław Koniecpolski (1591-1646), Great Crown Hetman, the highest military officer then in Poland, in 1632-46. He was a close, though not always agreeable, advisor to the Polish King Władysław IV Vasa (Ladislas IV). Engaged in policies toward Turkey and the Tatars, he aimed at increasing the number of regular troops and subordinating the Cossacks. He was an effective statesman and one of the most eminent military leaders of prepartition Poland. Based on primary, mainly archival, and secondary sources; 81 notes. English summary. 1632-46

Koning, Bernardus

3639. Stolp, Annie. HET LEVENSWERK VAN DE UITVINDER DS. BERNARDUS KONING, ZIJN GASLICHT- EN ZIJN GASMOTOR-EXPERIMENTEN (1778-1828) [The life and work of inventor Bernardus Koning, his gaslight and gasmotor experiments (1778-1828)]. *Economisch- en Sociaal-Historisch Jaarboek [Netherlands] 1980 43: 64-104.* The experiments of Bernardus Koning dealt with the "hydrophoor," a device to explode the hydrogen gas in water in order to increase the efficiency of the steam engine. Continuous experiments and much financial support did not result in an efficient model. Koning was instrumental in developing a gas lighting system for the Binnenhof. In the process numerous patents were obtained. The use of gas motors was greatly boosted by the inventions and experiments of Koning. 140 notes. 1778-1828

Köning, Wolfgang

3640. —. VOL'FGANG KENING [Wolfgang Köning]. *Sovetskaia Etnografiia [USSR] 1981 (1): 186-187.* Announces the death of Marxist ethnographer Wolfgang Köning (1925-81) of East Germany. 1925-81

Konrad, Kurt

3641. Charvát, Jaroslav. O KURTU KONRADOVI [Kurt Konrad]. *Acta Universitatis Carolinae Philosophica et Historica [Czechoslovakia] 1982 (2): 23-33.* Kurt Konrad (Kurt Beer, 1908-41) broke with his Moravian-Jewish milieu and gave up his medical studies to devote himself to the Czech working class. Effective as a Communist publicist, he contributed valuable historical studies on revolutions in Spain and on Hussitism as an authentic late medieval revolutionary movement. Some of this work was left unfinished, as Konrad was arrested for illegal resistance against the Nazi occupation of Czechoslovakia. He died in a German prison. Russian and Spanish summaries. 1908-41

Kons'kyi, Oleksander

3642. Antonovych, M[arko]. O. KONYS'KYI I M. HRUSHEVS'KYI [Oleksander Konys'kyi and Mikhail S. Hrushevsky]. *Ukrains'kyi Istoryk 1984 21(1-4): 48-63.* Oleksander Kons'kyi (1836-1900) became a renowned representative of Ukrainian realistic prose, which exhibited populist ideological tendencies, as well as a leading figure in the Ukrainian national movement. Konys'kyi knew and influenced Mikhail Hrushevsky (1866-1934), who was rising into prominence as a historian in the 1880's and 1890's. Additional sources for this topic may be provided by the manuscript collections of archives and libraries in the Soviet Ukraine. 77 notes. 1886-1900

Konstantinov, Antip

3643. Filatov, N. F. ANTIP KONSTANTINOV—KAMENNYKH DEL PODMASTER'E XVII V. [Antip Konstantinov: apprentice mason of the 17th century]. *Arkhitekturnoe Nasledstvo [USSR] 1980 28: 65-70.* Antip Konstantinov received his early training in stonemasonry from his stepfather, Lavrenti Vozoulin, and later became one of the best known builders of tent-roofed churches in Nizhni Novgorod, Moscow, and the Moscow suburbs. 17c

Konstantinov, Boris P.

3644. Zel'dovich, Ia. B. PAMIATI DRUGA [In memory of a friend]. *Voprosy Istorii Estestvoznaniia i Tekhniki [USSR] 1984 (2): 71-75.* Boris Pavlovich Konstantinov (1-910-69) had a wide range of interests in various fields of physics. He helped organize the Leningrad Institute of Nuclear Physics which now bears his name, and from 1966 to his death he was the vice-chairman of the USSR Academy of Sciences. His character is described by his friend from 1932 Ia. B. Zel'dovich in an extract from an anthology devoted to Konstantinov's life. 1932-69

Kook, Abraham Isaac

3645. Mamlak, Gershon. ABRAHAM ISAAC KOOK: THE SACRED ELEMENT IN ZIONISM. *Midstream 1985 31(10): 21-26.* Evaluates the spiritual legacy of Abraham Isaac Kook by examining his uniqueness and his "all-embracing world view, completely anchored in Judaism." 1904-35

Kopecki, Kazimierz

3646. Nowak, Zygfryd. KAZIMIERZ KOPECKI—TWÓRCA POLSKIEJ SZKOŁY ENERGETYKI KOMPLEKSOWEJ [Kazimierz Kopecki, the founder of the Polish school of complex energetics]. *Nauka Polska [Poland] 1984 32(5-6): 131-137.* An academic biography of Kazimierz Kopecki, Polish physicist, one of the founders of the Gdańsk Polytechnic in 1945, and author of the Energy in Crisis report of 1982, which suggested some underlying causes of Poland's economic impasse. 1945-82

Köpeczi, Béla

3647. Bodnár, György, interviewer. KOLOZSVÁR, PARIS, BUDAPEST: BÉLA KÖPECZI TALKS ABOUT HIS LIFE AND CAREER. *New Hungarian Q. [Hungary] 1980 21(78): 132-138.* Conversation with Béla Köpeczi, historian, member of the Hungarian Academy of Sciences, editor of *Helikon,* and professor of French at Eötvös Loránd University of Budapest, focusing on the significance of his Transylvanian background, study at Eötvös College, and his academic and publishing career. His research interests include

Ferenc Rákóczi's war of independence for Hungary, and he has fostered the study of the Enlightenment in Eastern Europe. 18c

Kopitar, Jernej

3648. Fried, István. JERNEJ KOPITAR UND DIE UNGARISCHE KULTUR [Jernej Kopitar and Hungarian culture]. *Österreichische Osthefte [Austria] 1980 22(4): 295-301.* Assess the life and work of the Hungarian writer Jernej Kopitar (1780-1844) and examines his place within Hungarian culture, 1800-40's. 1800-40's

Koplenig, Johann

3649. Koplenig, Hilde. DOKUMENTATION. JOHANN KOPLENIG. DER BEGINN 1891-1927 [Document: Johann Koplenig, the beginning, 1891-1927]. *Zeitgeschichte [Austria] 1981 8(8): 303-322.* Johann Koplenig was one of the founders and the driving force behind the Austrian Communist Party in the twenties. He was the son of a laborer in the Steiermark backwoods, and was very early active in the trade union movement—organizing shoemakers—and in the Socialist Party. As a POW in Russia in World War I he participated in the Bolshevik revolution. Subsequently, he organized the return of the Austrian POW's and himself came back in 1920. His work made it possible for the Communist Party to take root in Austria despite the violent opposition of the Austrian Social Democrats and numerous internal factional divisions. Based on personal recollections, the Koplenig papers, and newspapers; 79 notes. 1891-1927

Korais, Adamantios

3650. Clogg, Richard. KORAIS AND THE MOVEMENT FOR GREEK INDEPENDENCE. *Hist. Today [Great Britain] 1983 33(Oct): 10-14.* Adamantios Korais (1748-1833), a classical scholar and physician, was born in Smyrna but spent most of his life in Paris where he advanced the ideal of a free Greece with his political pamphlets and his translations of the Greek classics. Korais' major contribution to the Greek cause consisted in articulating the aspirations of the Greek national movement and in determining the cultural orientation of the fledgling Greek state. 1788-1833

Korczak, Janusz

3651. Bereday, George Z. F. JANUSZ KORCZAK: IN MEMORY OF THE HERO OF POLISH CHILDREN'S LITERATURE. *Polish Rev. 1979 24(1): 27-32.* A tribute to the Polish Jewish educator, philosopher, and physician, Janusz Korczak. His respect for the talents and innate abilities of children led him to espouse a progressive system of education. He was a staunch advocate of children's rights and brought the Children's Charter into being. He accompanied the children of the orphanage he administered to one of Hitler's concentration camps and died with them. 1930's-40's

3652. Gross, Feliks. A MAN OF TWO CULTURES. *Polish Rev. 1979 24(1): 24-26.* A tribute to the Polish-Jewish physician Janusz Korczak, educator and educational philosopher. A staunch advocate of children's rights, in the orphanage that he administered he gave children responsibilities and duties that might seem beyond their years. He accompanied his children to one of Hitler's concentration camps and perished with them. 1930's-40's

3653. Sakowska, Ruta. W SETNĄ ROCZNICĘ URODZIN JANUSZA KORCZAKA [100th anniversary of the birth of Janusz Korczak]. *Biuletyn Żydowskiego Instytutu Hist. w Polsce [Poland] 1979 (2): 93-96.* Report of a UNESCO conference, Janusz Korczak—His Life and Work, in Warsaw, 12-15 October 1978, attended by scholars from 15 countries. 1978

Korfes, Otto

3654. Wegner-Korfes, Sigrid. REALPOLITISCHE HALTUNG BEI OFFIZIEREN DER FAMILIEN MERTZ VON QUIRNHEIM, KORFES UND DIECKMANN [Realistic political attitudes of officers from the Mertz von Quirnheim, Korfes, and Dieckmann families]. *Militärgeschichte [East Germany] 1986 25(3): 226-233.* 1920's-44
*For abstract see **Mertz von Quirnheim, Hermann***

Kormanowa, Żanna

3655. Kawecka, Krystyna; Żarnowska, Anna; and Piber, Andrzej. 80-LECIE URODZIN PROF. ŻANNY KORMANOWEJ; BIBLIOGRAFIA PRAC PROF. DR. ŻANNY KORMANOWEJ [Tribute to Professor Żanna Kormanowa and her bibliography]. *Z Pola Walki [Poland] 1980 23(4): 196-216.* Professor Żanna Kormanowa celebrated her 80th birthday 11 August 1980. Her bibliography covers over 50 years of steady and fruitful work focused on the history of the working class. Professor Kormanowa was the first to offer in 1948 a university seminar on the topic at the Institute of History, University of Warsaw. In addition to her own scholarly production, Professor Kormanowa is also known as an outstanding pedagogue; she has been the director of 29 doctoral dissertations and many masters' theses. Based on Kormanowa's bibliography, 1925-80. 1925-80

Kornalewski, Joachim

3656. Skrobacki, Andrzej and Völker, Arina. LEKARZ OLSZTYŃSKI, JOACHIM KORNALEWSKI I JEGO ROZPRAWA O KOLTUNIE Z 1897 ROKU [Joachim Kornalewski, an Olsztyn physician and his debate over plica in 1897]. *Komunikaty Mazursko-Warmińskie [Poland] 1980 (2): 155-167.* Gives account of Joachim Kornalewski's theory of 1897 regarding plica, a hair disease. The debate involved Polish and German physicians from the 16th century onward but was finally solved when a Pomeranian doctor, Władysław Neumann, wrote in 1904 that the disease was connected with nervous conditions. Kornalewski, a Germanized Pole from Olsztyn in East Prussia claimed that its cause was due to a lack of personal hygiene and that its origins were Polish. His theory was based not on medical factors but on socio-ethnic prejudices. 1897-1904

Korniiets, Leonid R.

3657. Holubova, H. H. VIDOMYI DIIACH KOMUNISTYCHNOI PARTII I RADIANS'KOI DERZHAVY (DO 80-RICHCHIA Z DNIA NARODZHENNIA L. R. KORNIITSIA) [A renowned activist of the Communist Party and the Soviet nation: dedicated to the 80th anniversary of the birth of L. R. Korniiets]. *Ukrains'kyi Istorychnyi Zhurnal [USSR] 1981 (8): 119-121.* Chronologically presents details of the life of Leonid R. Korniiets (1901-69), born in the Kherson region (now Kirovograd) of the Ukraine. Focuses on his work for the Communist Party, his positions and awards. 1901-69

Korol, Akim Kononovich

3658. —. GEROI GRAZHDANSKOI VOINY [Heroes of the Civil War]. *Voenno-Istoricheskii Zhurnal [USSR] 1982 (8): 57-60.* 1917-69
*For abstract see **Appar, Petr Andreevich***

Korolev, S. P.

3659. Belotserkovski, O. M. O NAUCHNOM TVORCHESTVE S. P. KOROLEVA (K 75-LETIIU SO DNIA ROZHDENIIA) [On the scientific work of S. P. Korolev on the 75th anniversary of his birth]. *Voprosy Istorii Estestvoznaniia i Tekhniki [USSR] 1982 (4): 54-62.* S. P. Korolev (1907-66) began his brilliant career as an aircraft designer in 1931 when he and F. A. Tsander created the Group for Research into Jet Propulsion. In 1946 he was appointed chief constructor of intercontinental ballistic missiles and by 1948 had built the first Soviet rocket. During the first decade of the space era, Soviet scientists under his leadership solved such fundamental problems as the attainment of the first and second cosmic speeds and the orientation of space vessels. In the course of his life he supervised more than 150 aviation, rocket, and space projects. 1907-66

Koroliuk, Vladimir D.

3660. Floria, B. N. NAUCHNAIA DEIATEL'NOST' V. D. KOROLIUKA [Scholarly activities of V. D. Koroliuk]. *Sovetskoe Slavianovedenie [USSR] 1984 (4): 62-66.* Views the academic record of the Soviet historian Vladimir Koroliuk, specialist in history of the Western Slavs. His major contribution as the first Marxist historian of Poland include large sections of *Istoriia Pol'shy* [History of Poland] (1952), including chapters on the relations between Poland, Russia, and Lithuania. Secondary sources. 6c-20c

Korostovtsev, Mikhail A.

3661. —. PAMIATI MIKHAILA ALEKSANDROVICHA KOROSTOVTSEVA [To the memory of Mikhail Aleksandrovich Korostovtsev]. *Narody Azii i Afriki [USSR] 1981 (2): 248.* Mikhail A. Korostovtsev was born on 21 April 1900 and died on 21 October 1981. After navy service he defended his candidate dissertation in 1943, and was Telegraph Agency of the Soviet Union (TASS) correspondent and Academy of Sciences representative in Cairo in 1944. A philologist, textologist, and historian, he contributed greatly to the study of the ancient Egyptian language and slavery in ancient Egypt, especially in his *Slavery in Ancient Egypt of the New Kingdom.* He was head of the department of the ancient East in the Institute of Eastern Studies in the Soviet Academy of Sciences. Based on Korostovtsev's works. 1940's-81

Korsch, Karl

3662. Dingel, Frank. DAS SYMPOSIUM ÜBER KARL KORSCH VOM 20. BIS 21. JUNI 1980 AN DER UNIVERSITÄT FRANKFURT/M: EIN TAGUNGSBERICHT [The symposium on Karl Korsch, 20-21 June 1980 at the university in Frankfurt: a report]. *Int. Wiss. Korrespondenz zur Gesch. der Deutschen Arbeiterbewegung [West Germany] 1980 16(3): 404-412.* Describes the work and thought of Karl Korsch, a critical Marxist theorist, and reports papers presented at a conference in Frankfurt in 1980. 1924-82

Korzunov, Ivan

3663. Minakov, V. SNAIPERSKII EKIPAZH [The sniper crew]. *Morskoi Sbornik [USSR] 1985 (3): 56-60.* 1941

*For abstract see **Filatov, Ivan***

Kos, Franc

3664. Šumrada, Janez. GOSPODARJENJE NEKE SLOVENSKE DRUŽINE KONEC 19. IN V ZAČETKU 20. STOLETJA [Housekeeping of a Slovene family at the turn of the 20th century]. *Zgodovinski Časopis [Yugoslavia] 1984 38(3): 171-177.* Describes housekeeping arrangements of the family of the well-known Slovene historian Franc Kos (1853-1924) based on his accounts diaries of 1891-1911. 1891-1911

Kos, Milko

3665. Grafenauer, Bogo. GOVOR DR. BOGA GRAFENAUERJA OB 90-LETNICI ROJSTVA IN 10.-OBLETNICI SMRTI DR. MILKA KOSA [The speech by Dr. Bogo Grafenauer on the 90th birthday and the 10th anniversary of death of Dr. Milko Kos]. *Zgodovinski Časopis [Yugoslavia] 1984 38(1-2): 133-138.* A biography of Milko Kos (1892-1972). His work in the medieval history of the Slovene territory included editing of source materials. 1892-1972

Kosach-Borysova, Isydora Petrivna

3666. —. [ISYDORA PETRIVNA KOSACH-BORYSOVA AND LESYA UKRAINKA]. *Sučasnist [West Germany] 1983 (11): 25-38.*

Odarchenko, Petro. ISYDORA PETRIVNA KOSACH-BORYSOVA [Isydora Petrivna Kosach-Borysova], *pp. 25-29.* A biographical sketch emphasizing the Soviet treatment of Lesya Ukrainka's younger sister, Isydora. Despite the Kosach family's progressive convictions and the elevation of Lesya Ukrainka to the status of a classic poet and a revolutionary, Isydora and her husband were arrested by the NKVD in 1937. Her husband perished in a labor camp, but she herself was released in response to the demands of the progressive Ukrainian writer from Bukovina, Olha Kobylians'ka. Isydora died in Canada in 1980.

Kosach-Borysova, Isydora. BIOHRAFICHNI POVISTI PRO LESIU UKRAINKU [Biographical novels about Lesya Ukrainka], *pp. 30-38.* Reproduces in full the contents of a paper delivered at a meeting in Washington in 1968 by a younger sister of Lesya Ukrainka, accusing two Soviet Ukrainian writers, L. Smilians'kyi and K. Hranat, of distorting her sister's views, convictions, and actions in their novels. 1890's-1980

Košar, Jože

3667. Hartman, Bruno. JOŽE KOŠAR, 1908-1982 [Jože Košar, 1908-1982]. *Časopis za Zgodovino in Narodopisje [Yugoslavia] 1983 19(1-2): 6-8.* Obituary of Jože Košar (1908-82), Slovene historian, educator and publishing executive. 1908-82

Kosáry, Domokos

3668. Dippold, Péter. KOSÁRY DOMOKOS MŰVEINEK BIBLIOGRÁFIÁJA [Bibliography of the works of Domokos Kosáry]. *Történelmi Szemle [Hungary] 1983 26(3-4): 510-519.* Lists the scholarly production of the 70-year-old widely respected Hungarian historian. 18c-1918

Kosciusko, Thaddeus

3669. Cizauskas, Albert C. THE UNUSUAL STORY OF THADDEUS KOSCIUSKO. *Lituanus 1986 32(1): 47-66.* Tadeusz Kościuszko (Thaddeus Kosciusko) is usually remembered as a Pole who fought for American independence. In fact, Kosciusko came from a Lithuanian-Ruthenian family, and his devotion to political freedom was not limited to the cause of the North American colonies. He also played a leading role in the resistance of the Polish-Lithuanian commonwealth to foreign invasion and domination in the 1790's. Kosciusko's life bears testimony to his liberal and humanitarian beliefs. 4 notes. 1746-1817

Kosev, Dimitur

3670. Todorov, Nikolai. AKADEMIKU DIMITRU KOSEVU 80 LET [Academician Dimitr Kosev's 80th birthday]. *Etudes Balkaniques [Bulgaria] 1984 20(1): 148-150.* Prints a tribute to historian Dimitur Kosev (b. 1904) of the Bulgarian Academy of Sciences, including a political and professional biography. He has contributed scientific methodology to the study of the history of the Communist Party. Presented at a conference in honor of Dimitur Kosev's 80th birthday, Sofia, 5 January 1984. 1923-83

Kosmowska, Irena

3671. Mioduchowska, Maria. IRENA KOSMOWSKA—W STULECIE URODZIN [On the centennial of Irena Kosmowska's birth]. *Kultura i Społeczeństwo [Poland] 1979 23(4): 111-117.* Irena Kosmowska (1879-1945) was born to a family of progressive landowners. From 1907 she dedicated herself to the people's movement, especially through work for the radical publication *Zarań [The Dawn]* and in the Polskie Stronnictwo Ludowe [Polish People's Party]. An advocate of democracy and land reform, she became an object of government persecution around 1930. Continuing her active opposition to the government and writing for *Nowe Tory [New Paths],* she joined the underground movement after the German invasion of 1939 and died a German prisoner. 4 notes. 1907-45

Kosoko

3672. Oguntomisin, G. O. KOSOKO AND THE CHIEFTAINCY DISPUTE IN LAGOS (1834-1851). *Nigeria Mag. [Nigeria] 1980 (130-131): 17-26.* King Kosoko, after being denied the throne for a decade through the manipulation of succession rules, reigned for six years over Lagos before being deposed by the British for slave trading. 1834-51

Kossuth, Louis

3673. Haraszti, Éva. KOSSUTH AS AN ENGLISH JOURNALIST. *New Hungarian Quarterly [Hungary] 1985 26(98): 136-145.* During his 1855 stay in England, Hungarian patriot Louis Kossuth wrote columns for two weeklies, the liberal *Sunday Times* and the radical *Atlas.* He criticized British foreign and domestic policies. Public opinion and later the British press itself resented the foreign exile's perceived interference in British affairs and criticized his sometimes imperfect English writing style. Primary sources. 1855-56

Kostomarov, Mykola

3674. Hrushevsky, Mikhail S. KOSTOMAROV I NOVITNAIA UKRAINA [Kostomarov and the new Ukraine]. *Ukrains'kyi Istoryk 1984 21(1-4): 148-170.* Discusses the achievements of Mykola Kostomarov (1817-85), a historian, ethnographer, publicist, and political activist. Citing extensively from Kostomarov's publications, concludes that, despite some drawbacks, Kostomarov made immense contributions to Ukrainian historiography and the Ukrainian national movement. 20 notes. Reprinted from *Ukraina* 1925 3. 1840's-85

Kosztolányi, Dezső

3675. Vargha, Balázs. DEZSŐ KOSZTOLÁNYI 1885-1936: VISITOR TO AN ENCHANTED COUNTRY. *New Hungarian Quarterly [Hungary] 1985 26(98): 34-44.* Literary biography of Hungarian poet Dezső Kosztolányi (1885-1936). His childhood in the small town of Szabadka was reflected in later stories and novels, including short stories by his cousin József Brenner (pseudonym Géza Csáth), *The Magician's Garden.* In the 1900's, he participated in rivalry among other young poets, including Mihály Babits and Gyula Juhász, at once his friends and his critics. He created the character Kornél Esti in his poem *Esti Kornél Éneke* [The song of Kornél Esti] as his alter ego, the naughty hero of a cycle of short stories. He contributed regular features to newspapers and wrote many novels and poems expressing the sadness in his family life and disappointment with his son, a victim of mental illness. 3 notes, plate and 6 photos between pp. 40 and 41. 1900's-36

Kotnis, Dwarakanath Shantaram

3676. —. DR. DWARAKANATH SHANTARAM KOTNIS: A BIOGRAPHY. *China Report [India] 1981 17(2): 75-96.* Publication of an abridged version of the officially-sanctioned Chinese biography of Dr. Dwarakanath Shantaram Kotnis, an Indian physician who served with the Chinese Communist forces. This version concentrates on Kotnis's sociopolitical activities and covers the Japanese invasion of China, the ill-starred union of Communist and Guomindang forces, Chinese counteroffensives, and especially the training and increasing effectiveness of the Communist forces. 1937-42

Kotovski, Grigori I.

3677. Musiienko, V. V. LEHENDARNYI HEROI HROMADIANS'KOI VIINY (DO 100-RICHCHIA Z DNIA NARODZHENNIA H. I. KOTOVS'KOHO) [The legendary Civil War hero: on the centenary of the birth of G. I. Kotovski]. *Ukrains'kyi Istorychnyi Zhurnal [USSR] 1981 (6): 127-131.* Reviews the life and military exploits of Grigori I. Kotovski (1881-1925), hero of the Russian Civil War. Chronicles Kotovski's major battles against the White Russian forces of Denikin and their foreign allies, Ukrainian anti-Soviet forces led by Petliura and his associates, and against Polish forces. 23 notes. 1918-25

3678. Roitman, B. ROL' KAVBRIGADY G. I. KOTOVSKOGO V RAZGROME ANTONOVSHCHINY [The role of Grigori I. Kotovski's cavalry brigade in the destruction of Antonovism]. *Voenno-Istoricheskii Zhurnal [USSR] 1981 23(6): 71-74.* In recognition of the 100th anniversary of his birth, a short account of the life and career of Grigori Ivanovich Kotovski from his birth in Moldavia in 1881 to his return to the Ukraine in 1921. Considers his early life and education, his activity in the years leading to the Great October Russian Revolution, his political agitation in the army during World War I, his subsequent participation in the struggle for the establishment of Soviet power in Moldavia, his activity during the Civil War, and important work as a member of the Communist Party. Gives a detailed account of his involvement with the A. S. Antonov faction in the Civil War. Based on Soviet military archival material and personal documents of Kotovski; 12 notes. 1881-1925

Kováts, Mihály

3679. Zachar, József. A KOVÁTS MIHÁLY POROSZ SZABADCSAPATVEZÉR ELLENI BÉCSI ELJÁRÁS IRATANYAGA 1761/62-BŐL [The files of the Viennese legal procedures against the Prussian free corps commander

Mihály Kováts, 1761-62]. *Hadtörténelmi Közlemények [Hungary] 1982 29(1): 71-92.* Captain Mihály Kováts (who died a hero's death in 1779 in the United States) served in the Prussian army, 1752-61. Disappointed, he wanted to join the Hungarian unit of the French army in 1761, traveling via Poland and Hungary. On 10 May 1761, he was arrested by the Viennese authorities. Documents concerning the legal proceedings against him are published here. Serving in the enemy army was not punishable in itself; this followed from the mercenary system. In July 1762, Kováts was released. Primary documents; 41 notes. 1761-62

Kowalski, Max

3680. Gradenwitz, Peter. MAX KOWALSKI (1882-1956): RECHTSANWALT UND FEINSINNIGER MUSIKER [Max Kowalski (1882-1956) attorney and subtle musician]. *Bull. des Leo Baeck Inst. [Israel] 1981 (58): 41-51.* Max Kowalski was trained for the law, but for the whole of his life he made music as a composer, a singer, and a promoter of the new music of the 1930's. He was a friend of Arnold Schönberg, and the two often wrote similar pieces of music. But unlike Schönberg, Kowalski was a late romanticist. Both had to flee from Germany in the 1930's, Schönberg to the United States and Kowalski to England. 8 notes. 1882-1956

Kozachenko, P. K.

3681. Poplyko, F. GEROI BITVA ZA KAVKAZ [Heroes of the battle for the Caucasus]. *Voenno-Istoricheskii Zhurnal [USSR] 1983 (3): 57-60.* Publishes material on the soldiers and officers of the Soviet Army who received the title of Hero of the Soviet Union for military actions against German troops in the Caucasus during World War II. Commander of the 249th Fighter Regiment, P. K. Kozachenko was seriously wounded in an air battle but went on to shoot down two enemy planes and bring his group safely back to the airfield. Lieutenant Colonel V. Ia. Petrov of the 256th Tank Battalion, wounded in battle, refused to leave his post and continued to command his men. Based on Soviet military archival sources; 9 notes, 5 photos. 1942-43

Kozma, Lajos

3682. Vadas, József. LAJOS KOZMA AND LE CORBUSIER. *New Hungarian Q. [Hungary] 1984 25(94): 189-192.* Lajos Kozma (1888-1948) began his career in architecture, interior design, and book illustration in the spirit of *art nouveau.* Traces his career in the context of Hungarian economic conditions, social conditions, and political change. Relates his work to that of Le Corbusier in France. 1914-47

Krachkovski, I. Iu.

3683. Bogoliubov, M. N. and Frolova, O. B. 100 LET SO DNIA ROZHDENIIA AKADEMIKA I. IU. KRACHKOVSKOGO [The 100th anniversary of the birth of academician I. Iu. Krachkovski]. *Vestnik Leningradskogo U.: Seriia Istorii, Iazyka i Literatury [USSR] 1983 (4): 127-128.* After graduation in 1910, I. Iu. Krachkovski was offered a teaching post at the University of St. Petersburg. In the post-revolutionary period he lectured at the Oriental faculty of Leningrad University and was the founder of courses on Arab philology and the history of Arab literature. In 1921 he was elected to the USSR Academy of Sciences and in subsequent years was awarded a number of Soviet orders and medals for his academic and pedagogical work. 1883-1951

3684. Khalidov, A. B. AKADEMIK IGNATII IULIANOVICH KRACHKOVSKII (K. 100-LETIIU SO DNIA ROZHDENIIA) [Academician Ignati Iulianovich Krachkovski (100th anniversary of his birth)]. *Narody Azii i Afriki [USSR] 1983 (4): 83-89.* The prominent Arabic scholar I. Iu. Krachkovski, (1883-1951), was educated at St. Petersburg University and was awarded his master's degree before the first world war, after publishing a series of articles. In the period after the Russian Revolution his scholastic talents flowered, and in 1921 he was elected to the Academy of Sciences. His published works include studies in Arabic languages, literary criticism, and literary history. Apart from his research and pedagogical work, he was an able academic administrator. Secondary sources; 6 notes. 1901-51

Král, Václav

3685. Nedorezov, A. I. VATSLAV KRAL [Vatslav Kral]. *Sovetskoe Slavianovedenie [USSR] 1984 (6): 123-124.* In his 47 monographs and over 100 articles Vatslav Kral (1926-83), the great Czechoslovak historian, dealt with the modern history of Czechoslovakia, Soviet-Czechoslovak and international relations, and the worker and national-liberation movements. His major work dealt with the social and economic developments in Czechoslovakia between 1938-45. From 1963 he held several directorial posts under the Czechoslovak Academy of Sciences and he helped develop academic contacts between Czechoslovakia and the USSR. 1926-83

3686. —. PROF. DR. VÁCLAV KRÁL, DR.SC. 9.2.1926-12.12.1983 [Václav Král, 1926-83]. *Slovanský Přehled [Czechoslovakia] 1984 90[i.e., 70](1): 1.* Prints an obituary of the editor-in-chief of *Slovanský Přehled,* Václav Král. He was a beloved teacher of sociology and history and a highly respected scholar. He wrote extensively on a number of subjects, but is best known for his interest in Czechoslovak-Soviet relations, and most recently in Marxist historiography. In all his writing, Král furthered the progress of socialism under the leadership of the Czechoslovak Communist Party. 1926-83

Krämer, F. J. L.

3687. Dorsman, L. J. F. J. L. KRÄMER: LERAAR, HOOGLERAAR, ARCHIVARIS (1850-1928) [F. J. L. Krämer: teacher, professor, archivist, 1850-1928]. *Nederlands Archievenblad [Netherlands] 1983 87(3): 219-225.* Controversially appointed to a chair at Utrecht University, Krämer was noted for his works on Mary Stuart, Dutch-Spanish diplomatic relations, and the editing of the final editions of the correspondence of the house of Orange-Nassau. 1850-1928

Kramers, Hendrik Anthony

3688. Radder, Hans. BETWEEN BOHR'S ATOMIC THEORY AND HEISENBERG'S MATRIX MECHANICS. A STUDY OF THE ROLE OF THE DUTCH PHYSICIST H. A. KRAMERS. *Janus [Netherlands] 1982 69(3-4): 223-252.* In the transition period from Niels Bohr's atomic theory to Werner Heisenberg's matrix mechanics, the scientific work in the years 1916-25 of the Dutch physicist Hendrik Anthony Kramers (1894-1952) played a crucial role. His role regarding the acausal character of the Bohr-Kramers-Slater theory is analyzed in detail, as is his theory of optical dispersion, which is generally recognized as an important precursor of Heisenberg's matrix theory and the most important achievement of Kramers in the period under consideration. Based on the unpublished correspondence between Jan

Romein and Kramers and other sources; appendix of cited passages (in Dutch) from the Kramers-Romein correspondence; 78 notes. 1916-25

Krammer, Josef

3689. Szabó, János. JOSEF KRAMMER, DER ERSTE DIREKTOR DER BÜRGERSCHULE EISENSTADT [Josef Krammer, the first headmaster of the secondary school at Eisenstadt]. *Burgenländische Heimatblätter [Austria] 1981 43(2): 71-77.* As headmaster of the secondary school at Eisenstadt, 1881-1906, Josef Krammer (1858-1936) carefully carried through a program of Magyarization in constant conflict with the central school authorities. 1881-1906

Kranc, Remigiusz

3690. Kranc, Remigiusz. BYŁEM SKAZANY NA 10 LAT SYBERII (I) [I was sentenced to 10 years in Siberia. Part 1]. *Zeszyty Historyczne [France] 1984 (67): 188-202.* Memoirs of a Polish Capuchin provide an account of the Soviet penal system; describes his arrest and transfer from Magadan to Kolyma. Article to be continued. 1945-47

Krasnobaev, Boris I.

3691. —. PAMIATI BORISA IL'ICHA KRASNOBAEVA (1923-1983) [In memory of Boris Il'ich Krasnobaev (1923-83)]. *Vestnik Moskovskogo Universiteta, Seriia 8: Istoriia [USSR] 1984 (4): 87-89.* Obituary of Boris I. Krasnobaev (1923-83), Soviet historian of the 18th century. His major work, *Ocherki Russkoi Kul'tury XVIII V.* [Outline of Russian culture in the 18th century] (1972) won him a prominent place in Soviet historiography. He was coauthor of several primary and secondary school textbooks. Secondary sources; biblio. 18c

3692. —. PAMIATI BORISA IL'ICHA KRASNOBAEVA [In memory of Boris Il'ich Krasnobaev]. *Istoriia SSSR [USSR] 1984 (2): 217-218.* Provides an obituary of Boris Il'ich Krasnobaev (1923-83). Krasnobaev, a noted Soviet scholar in the development of culture in 18th-century Russia, was a member of the Communist Party and a prominent member of the Moscow University. In addition to his many scholarly studies, he was an editor of *Istoriia SSSR* and wrote for *Prepodavanie Istorii v Shkole.* 1923-83

Krasnov, Georgi

3693. Białokozowicz, Bazyli. GIEORGIJ KRASNOW (W SZEŚĆDZIESIĄTĄ ROCZNICĘ URODZIN) [Georgi Krasnov: on the 60th anniversary of his birthday]. *Slavia Orientalis [Poland] 1981 30(4): 433-445.* G. Krasnov, a professor at Gorki University in the USSR, is a leading scholar of 19th-century Russian literature, and is particularly known for his work on Leo Tolstoy. 1945-81

Kratochvíl, Jaroslav

3694. Pytlík, Radko. CESTY SOCIALISTICKÉHO ROMÁNU: K 100. VÝROČÍ NAROZENÍ JAROSLAVA KRATOCHVÍLA [Pathways of the socialist novel: to mark the centenary of the birth of Jaroslav Kratochvíl]. *Česká Literatura [Czechoslovakia] 1985 33(3): 193-205.* The modest but largely overlooked Moravian writer of historical novels and short stories, Jaroslav Kratochvíl (1885-1945), has a logical place in the evolution of the Czech novel, and his approach to reality in socialist realist synthetic novels remains relevant to the contemporary "progressive" novel. 1911-45

Kraus, Franz Xaver

3695. Weber, Christoph. FRANZ XAVER KRAUS UND ITALIEN [Franz Xaver Kraus and Italy]. *Quellen und Forschungen aus Italienischen Arch. und Bibliotheken [Italy] 1981 61: 168-190.* Franz Xaver Kraus, church historian, priest, politician, and patron of the arts, was born a German in Trieste in 1840. From 1870, the year he chose to settle in Italy, to his death in 1901, he devoted his time to the moral, cultural, and political regeneration and renewal of Italy. He became the promoter of modernistic groups in both Italy and Germany and joined the liberal Catholics that grouped themselves around the periodical *Rassegna Nazionale* and engaged in constant polemics with the conservative periodical *Civiltà Cattolica.* The author explores Kraus's involvement in and opinions on cultural, religious, and political activities and discussions of that period and the impact he exercised on his contemporaries. Based on Kraus's diaries and other writings by Kraus. 1870-1901

Kraus, Greta

3696. Hathaway, Thomas. GRETA KRAUS: "A CRAZY CAREER—UPSIDE DOWN FROM A TO Z." *Queen's Q. [Canada] 1982 89(1): 127-136, (2): 280-289.* Part 1. Greta Kraus, known for years primarily as a harpsichordist, explains how and why she now regularly accompanies singers at German *Lieder* recitals. A great deal of her insight comes from her youthful suffering in Europe at the hands of a number of incompetent piano teachers. Part 2. LOIS MARSHALL AND GRETA KRAUS ON MUSIC-MAKING. Interview with the German *Lieder* singer Lois Marshall and her accompanist Greta Kraus. For the singer, the secret of a good performance in this unique art is to mean what you sing; for the accompanist, the secret is to be totally committed to the score. 1920's-70's

Kraus, Karl

3697. John, Harry. THE STATURE OF KARL KRAUS. *Midstream 1986 32(3): 42-48.* Reviews the life of Austrian satirist Karl Kraus (1874-1936), his *Die Fackel* [The Torch] (from 1899), his satirical writing directed at corruption and the press, and public readings of his own and others' works. 1892-1936

3698. Matamoro, Blas. KRAUSIANA [Krausiana]. *Cuadernos Hispanoamericanos [Spain] 1986 (431): 19-44.* The biography of Karl Kraus (1874-1936), commenting on his activities in the literary and artistic scene of fin-de-siècle Vienna, his contributions to theater through cabaret techniques, and his views on Zionism, language, and sexual issues. 2 illus., biblio. 1910's-36

3699. Zohn, Harry. THE VITRIOLIC VIENNESE: AN INTRODUCTION TO KARL KRAUS. *Cross Currents 1984 3: 285-295.* Surveys the political satire of Karl Kraus (1874-1936), a Bohemian-born Austrian Jew (a Catholic, 1911-22), who used the German language to such effect that his writing is virtually untranslatable. 1899-1936

Krempelj, Anton

3700. Rihtarič, Ivan. PRISPEVKI K ŽIVLJENJU IN DELU ANTONA KREMPLJA [A contribution on the life and work of Anton Krempelj]. *Kronika [Yugoslavia] 1984 32(1): 57-79.* Text of a recently discovered 19th-century handwritten biobibliography of the Slovene historian Anton Krempelj (1790-1844). 48 notes. 1790-1844

Kreps, Evgenii M.

3701. Kreps, E. M. O PROZHITOM I PEREZHITOM (GLAVY IZ KNIGI) [Life and experiences: a chapter from a book]. *Voprosy Istorii Estestvoznaniia i Tekhniki [USSR] 1984 (2): 100-107.* This chapter from the memoirs of E. M. Kreps deals with his work on physiology and his responsibilities for equipment procurement at the Military-Medical Academy (VMA), 1925-80. He describes in detail his six-month business trip to Britain in 1930, where he worked with Professor A. V. Hill at University College London and at the marine biology center at Port Erin near Plymouth. 1925-30

3702. Kreps, E. M. O PROZHITOM I PEREZHITOM (GLAVY IZ KNIGI) [Life and events: chapters excerpted from memoirs]. *Voprosy Istorii Estestvoznaniia i Tekhniki [USSR] 1983 (3): 132-145.* This renowned Soviet physiologist and biochemist (b. 1899) reminisces about his school years in Petersburg, enrollment in the Military Medical Academy in 1917, and trip, in 1918, to Chelyabinsk where he was drafted into the White Army. He deserted to the Red Army, was mistakenly arrested as spy, and eventually cleared by a Bolshevik security guard who knew his brother. The author returned to Petrograd in August 1919, was readmitted to the Academy, and began work in the physiological laboratory of Ivan Petrovich Pavlov (1849-1936). Article to be continued. 1909-19

Kresz, Géza

3703. Király, Péter. GÉZA KRESZ—A LIFE IN MUSIC (1882-1959). *New Hungarian Quarterly [Hungary] 1984 25(94): 213-217.* Prints a biography of Hungarian-Canadian chamber musician and music educator Géza Kresz (1882-1959). Includes a facsimile of a letter to Kresz from Maurice Ravel. Illus. 1903-47

Kretov, N. F.

3704. —. GEROI BITVY POD MOSKVOI [Heroes of the battle of Moscow]. *Voenno-Istoricheskii Zhurnal [USSR] 1982 (1): 48-53.* 1941-42

*For abstract see **Grigor'ev, V. A.***

Kretzenbacher, Leopold

3705. Koren, Hanns. GRUSS UND GLÜCKWUNSCH [Greetings and congratulations]. *Blätter für Heimatkunde [Austria] 1982 56(4): 98-100.* Describes the life and work of Leopold Kretzenbacher, Austrian historian, in honor of his 70th birthday. 1912-82

Kreuger, Ivar

3706. Lindgren, Håkan. THE KREUGER CRASH OF 1932: IN MEMORY OF A FINANCIAL GENIUS, OR WAS HE A SIMPLE SWINDLER? *Scandinavian Econ. Hist. Rev. [Finland] 1982 30(3): 189-206.* The Swedish "match king," Ivar Kreuger, built an empire between 1908 and 1932 that embraced not only the production and distribution of matches but also other manufacturing interests, real estate, banking, and international credit operations. His companies controlled 62% of world match production in 1930-31, and during 1927-30 the loan agreements of the Kreuger Group accounted for 4% of the total net capital exports of the world. But the empire could only survive on the expansion of credit and when market values fell during the Depression, Kreuger experienced difficulty getting his short-term credits renewed. Kreuger was also unable to realize his ambition to control the world match output and thus fix prices. The industry proved impossible to monopolize. His industrial sense was limited. Based on published and unpublished Swedish business histories which have examined private archives; 27 notes. 1908-32

Križanić, Juraj

3707. Colarieti, Mirella. JURAJ KRIŽANIĆ—UN SIMPOSIO/DIBATTITO SULLA SUA VITA, LE SUE OPERE, LA SUA AZIONE POLITICO-RELIGIOSA [Juraj Križanić: a symposium/debate on his life, his works, and his political and religious activity]. *Balcanica [Italy] 1983 2(4): 51-75.* Introduces and summarizes the contributions of participants at a conference in Zagreb, 1-4 September 1983, to honor the tercentenary of the death of Juraj Križanić, a Croatian monk of the Catholic Church, who contributed to the study of Slavic languages and literatures and anticipated the formation of a unified Yugoslav national self-image and of ecumenical reconciliation between the Orthodox Eastern Church and the Roman Catholic Church. 17c

3708. Hamm, Josef. ENDSTATION KAHLENBERG 1683: SCHICKSAL EINES GELEHRTEN [Last stop, Kahlenberg 1683: a scholar's fate]. *Anzeiger der Österreichischen Akademie der Wissenschaften. Philosophisch-Historische Klasse [Austria] 1983 120(1-9): 299-314.* Relates the life and scholarly accomplishments of the Slavic philologist and historian Juraj Križanić (1618-83). 1618-83

3709. Kadić, Ante. MIROSLAV KRLEŽA ON KRIŽANIĆ—FROM HISTORY TO LEGEND. *Journal of Croatian Studies 1982 23: 33-39.* Miroslav Krleža (1893-1981) was a distinguished Croatian who wrote about Juraj Križanić (1618-83), a Croatian priest who dedicated his life to Pan-Slavism. Krleža romanticized to create a legend, but he also made the public aware of Križanić. With all their historical methodology, other writers did not accomplish this same end. 21 notes. 17c

3710. —. [JURAJ KRIŽANIĆ]. *Balcanica [Italy] 1983 2(3): 3-33.*

Jerkov, Antonio. GIORGIO KRIŽANIĆ, IL PENDOLO CROATO [Juraj Križanić, the dangling Croat], *pp. 3-30.* Analyzes the personality of Croatian Catholic priest Juraj Križanić (1617?-83), missionary to Russia, exile in Siberia, Dominican friar at Vilnius, chaplain to John III Sobieski's court in Warsaw, and casualty in an assault on the Turks besieging Vienna. Emphasizes his anticipatory pan-Slavism.

—. IL RITRATTO DI KRIŽANIĆ [Križanić's portrait], *pp. 30-32.* Discusses a portrait of Juraj Križanić as a character in the Polish artist Jan Matejko's (1838-93) 1888 painting of John III Sobieski's attack to lift the siege of Vienna. The painting hangs in the Vatican.

—. DUE COSE SU KRIŽANIĆ [Two things about Križanić], *pp. 32-33.* Errors in the margins of translations of "schismatic" books translated into Latin from Greek, English, and Russian in the Biblioteca Casanatense in Rome demonstrate that Juraj Križanić remained in Rome during the 1656 plague. 1642-83

Królikowski, Stefan

3711. Sajur, Tadeusz W. STEFAN KRÓLIKOWSKI (1881-1937): SYN CZERWONEJ WOLI [Stefan Królikowski (1881-1937): son of red freedom]. *Nowe Drogi [Poland] 1982 (9): 104-115.* Stefan Królikowski, active first in the Polish Socialist Party, then in the Polish Communist Party, represented the working class area of Warsaw in the Polish

Parliament until his emigration to the USSR in 1929, where he worked in the local government in Kazakhstan and as Party interpreter. 1920's-37

Kröll, Ignaz Gottlieb

3712. Hutz, Ferdinand. IGNAZ GOTTLIEB KRÖLL: NOTIZEN ZUM LEBEN EINES STEIRISCHEN BAROCKMALERS [Ignaz Gottlieb Kröll: notes on the life of a Styrian baroque artist]. *Blätter für Heimatkunde [Austria] 1983 57(4): 113-118.* Describes the life of the Styrian baroque artist Ignaz Gottlieb Kröll (d. 1737) whose frescoes appear in the Augustine monastery in Vorau, Austria. 18c

Kropotkin, Pëtr

3713. Markin, Viacheslav A. DEIATEL'NOST' P. A. KROPOTKINA V RUSSKOM GEOGRAFICHESKOM OBSHCHESTVE [P. A. Kropotkin's activities in the Russian Geographical Society]. *Voprosy Istorii Estestvoznaniia i Tekhniki [USSR] 1982 (2): 89-96.* Biography of Pëtr Kropotkin (1842-1921), noting his expeditions to Northeast Siberia and the Far East, 1864-67, sponsored by the Russian Geographical Society, the publication of his expeditionary results in the society's *Izvestiia,* and research in meteorology, climatology, orography, seismology, paleogeography, and quaternary glaciation. Arrested as an anarchist in 1873, he escaped and fled abroad in 1876, returning to Russia only after the March 1917 Revolution. Most of his studies were published in British and American journals and are little known in the USSR. A bibliography of his works was published in Moscow, 1980. 13 notes, 6 illus. 1862-73

Krüger, Friederike

3714. Bunners, Michael. UNTEROFFIZIER FRIEDERIKE KRÜGER UND IHR BIOGRAPH PASTOR HEINRICH RIEMANN [Sergeant Friederike Krüger and her biographer Pastor Heinrich Riemann]. *Militärgeschichte [East Germany] 1985 24(6): 506-514.* A biography of Friederike Krüger (1789-1848), a German woman from Friedland who fought heroically in the Napoleonic Wars, 1813-15, and Heinrich Riemann (1793-1872), another Friedlander who fought in the Napoleonic Wars, upon whose writings Friederike's biography is based. Riemann eulogized her during an 1863 commemoration and used her as an example of "people's war" in contrast to the careers of professional soldiers and "their" wars. 16 notes, illus., photo. 1813-72

Krupskaya, Nadezhda

3715. Bobrova, E. K. SOVMESTNYE DOKUMENTY V. I. LENINA I N. K. KRUPSKOI [Joint documents of V. I. Lenin and Nadezhda Krupskaya]. *Vestnik Leningradskogo U.: Seriia Istorii, Iazyka i Literatury [USSR] 1981 (3): 5-14.* V. I. Lenin and N. K. Krupskaya worked together on much material—preparatory notes for Lenin's works, translations of articles, original manuscripts by Krupskaya which Lenin revised. A woman of great erudition and devoted to Lenin and his revolutionary work, Krupskaya was able to act as an interpreter of Leninism. She took an active role in the preparation of his collected works and in the recording of his philosophical development. During his periods of exile she was in constant touch with him, and was thus able to further his revolutionary designs, and maintain his links with the outside world. Based on the works of Lenin and Krupskaya and on work of the Lenin Institute; 56 notes. 1900-24

3716. Kirillova, E. E. O ROLI BIBLIOTEK V KOMMUNISTICHESKOM VOSPITANII, V POD"EME KUL'TURNOGO UROVNIA SOVETSKIKH LIUDEI [On the role of libraries in Communist education, and the cultural elevation of the Soviet people: new documents of Nadezhda Krupskaya]. *Voprosy Istorii KPSS [USSR] 1983 (4): 42-51.* Krupskaya expressed her concern about libraries, citing them as chief institutions of Communist education and propaganda. She gave suggestions for their general improvement, system of registration, and selection of books, particularly in the rural libraries. She also recommended the ordinance on the libraries' preservation in 1926-32. Based on the documents of the Central Party Archives of the Institute of Marxism and Leninism; 12 notes. 1926-32

Krushanov, A. I.

3717. Kim, M. P.; Koval'chenko, I. D.; Iskenderov, A. A.; and Mandrik, A. T. V OTDELENII ISTORII AN SSSR: 60 LETIE A. I. KRUSHANOVA [In the history section of the USSR Academy of Sciences: the 60th birthday of A. I. Krushanov]. *Voprosy Istorii [USSR] 1981 (6): 123-124.* Andrei Ivanovich Krushanov (b. 1921), a prominent Soviet historian, was born and raised in the Krasnoiarsk district of the USSR, but spent his working life in the Soviet Far East. In 1958 he was appointed head of the Department of History, Archaeology, and Ethnography of the Far Eastern branch of the Siberian Academy of Sciences, and since 1965 he has been a professor at the Far Eastern University. His main research interests are in the history of the Soviet Far East, and he has published on such topics as the Civil War in the Far East. 1921-81

3718. Shilo, N. A.; Dikov, N. N.; Balitskii, V. G.; and Mandrik, A. T. K 60-LETIIU CHLENA-KORRESPONDENTA AN SSSR A. I. KRUSHANOVA [On the 60th birthday of A. I. Krushanov, Corresponding Member of the Academy of Sciences of the USSR]. *Istoriia SSSR [USSR] 1981 (3): 217-220.* Reviews the career of the Soviet historian A. I. Krushanov, a specialist on the Russian Far East. Krushanov has produced a series of studies on the political, social, and economic history of the Far Eastern region in the late 19th and 20th centuries. In addition to his scholarly work, Krushanov is an active communist and has performed numerous important political, cultural, and educational functions. 4 notes, ref. 19c-20c

Krylenko, N. V.

3719. Shabanov, V. M. REVOLIUTSIONNAIA DEIATEL'NOST' N. V. KRYLENKO V ARMII (K 100-LETII SO DNIA ROZHDENIIA) [N. V. Krylenko's revolutionary activity in the army on the centenary of his birth]. *Voenno-Istoricheskii Zhurnal [USSR] 1985 (6): 75-77.* Outlines the revolutionary activities before and after the 1917 revolution of N. V. Krylenko (1885-1938). He joined the Russian Social Democratic Party in 1904, carrying out clandestine propaganda work in the army. In October 1917 he became a member of *Revvoensovet* (Revolutionary Military Council). After the civil war, during which he fought on the western front, he took part in the reorganization of the Soviet army. Based on sources from the Central State Archive of Military History; photo, 6 notes. 1904-38

Krylov, Aleksei N.

3720. Frenkel, Viktor Ia. [CORRESPONDENCE BETWEEN A. N. KRYLOV AND S. F. OL'DENBURG] (Russian text). *Voprosy Istorii Estestvoznaniia i Tekhniki [USSR] 1982 (1): 97-104.*

—. PEREPISKA A. N. KRYLOVA S NEPREMENNYM SEKRETAREM AN SSSR AKADEMIKOM S. F. OL'DENBURGOM [Correspondence between Aleksei N. Krylov and academician Sergei F. Ol'denburg, permanent secretary of the Academy of Sciences of the USSR], *pp. 97-103.* An exchange of four letters, 23 June-10 August 1926, between A. N. Krylov (1863-1945), mathematician and founder of Soviet shipbuilding, and orientologist S. F. Ol'denburg (1863-1934) during their temporary stay abroad. The letters contain both scholarly and personal material and are now preserved in the archives of the Academy of Sciences of the USSR. 16 notes.

—. O PEREPISKE A. N. KRYLOVA I S. F. OL'DENBURGA [On the correspondence of A. N. Krylov and S. F. Ol'denburg], *pp. 103-104.* Comments on the Krylov-Ol'denburg correspondence, providing information on the correspondents, explaining the significance of the letters as archival material, and providing details of the present location of the originals. 1926

Krylov, N. I.

3721. Kazakov, K. MARSHAL SOVETSKOGO SOIUZA N. I. KRYLOV (K 80-LETIIU SO DNIA ROZHDENIIA) [Marshal of the Soviet Union N. I. Krylov: on the 80th anniversary of his birth]. *Voenno-Istoricheskii Zhurnal [USSR] 1983 (4): 54-58.* During World War II, the military talent of N. I. Krylov was exhibited to the full. At the outbreak of the war he was a colonel serving as commander of staff of the Dunai fortified district; subsequently he commanded the 21st and 5th Armies and took part in the fighting with Japan. In the postwar period he commanded military districts in the Urals in 1956, Leningrad in 1957, and Moscow in 1960 and in 1963 was appointed chief in command of strategic rocket troops. Secondary sources; 3 notes, 2 photos. 1903-83

Krymova, Nina

3722. Gardenina, I. NINA IL'INICHNA KRYMOVA 1902-1983 [Nina Il'inichna Krymova, 1902-83]. *Skandinavskii Sbornik [USSR] 1983 28: 217-219.* Obituary of Nina Krymova (1902-83), Soviet scholar and translator of Swedish and Danish literature. During the 1920's she worked as secretary to Alexandra Kollontai at the Soviet consulate in Norway. She was a member of the editorial committee of the Progress Publishing House and coauthor of the Russian-Danish dictionary. Photo. Swedish summary. 1902-83

Kubitschek, Juscelino

3723. Peregrino, Umberto. JUSCELINO KUBITSCHEK PERANTE A HISTÓRIA [Juscelino Kubitschek before history]. *Rev. do Inst. Hist. e Geog. Brasileiro [Brazil] 1979 (325): 61-89.* Juscelino Kubitschek's place among the Brazilian presidents of exceptional merit is assured by his creation of the new capital, Brasilia, which from the architectural and urbanistic point of view exemplifies the city of the future. 1955-69

Kucherov, Stepan G.

3724. Filimoshin, M. ADMIRAL S. G. KUCHEROV (K 80-LETIIU SO DNIA ROZHDENIIA) [Admiral S. G. Kucherov: the 80th anniversary of his birth]. *Voenno-Istoricheskii Zhurnal [USSR] 1982 (8): 94-96.* Stepan G. Kucherov (b. 1902) began his naval career in 1922 in the Balkan Fleet. Appointed in 1940 commander of the Northern Fleet, he brought it to the highest standard, insisting on vigilance to thwart Russia's enemies. He was an able commander in World War II. From April 1945 to February 1946 he was Naval Chief of Staff and oversaw the transition from war to peace. He participated in the Yalta and Potsdam conferences, commanded the Caspian Flotilla, 1946-48, and was at the General Staff naval training center, 1953-62. Based on Soviet military sources; 6 notes. 1922-62

Kuchin, Aleksandr S.

3725. Barr, William. ALEKSANDR STEPHANOVICH KUCHIN: THE RUSSIAN WHO WENT SOUTH WITH AMUNDSEN. *Polar Record [Great Britain] 1985 22(139): 401-412.* Reviews the career of the Russian mariner, oceanographer, and polar explorer Aleksandr S. Kuchin (1888-1912), who reached the South Pole with Roald Amundsen in 1911. 1888-1912

Kuczynski, Waldemar

3726. Kuczynski, Waldemar. REPORTAGE DERRIERE LES VERROUS [Report from behind bars]. *Esprit [France] 1983 (4): 101-114.* A member of the Solidarity Movement tells of his life in Poland and experiences during his confinement. Article translated from Polish. 1981

Kuga, Jānis

3727. Blūma, Dz. K. LATVIEŠU SKATUVES GLEZNOTĀJU DARBĪBA KRIEVIJĀ NO 1915. LIDZ 1919. GADAM [The activity of Latvian scene-painters in Russia from 1915 to 1919]. *Latvijas PSR Zinātņu Akad. Vēstis [USSR] 1982 (1): 72-79.* Describes the activities of the well-known Latvian scene painters and decorators Jānis Muncis, Niklāvs Strunke, Jānis Kuga and others during World War I, when they were evacuated from Latvia into Russia and worked at Latvian theaters in Moscow and Leningrad and at theaters organized by the Latvian Riflemen units close to the front lines. Based on archival documents, museum exhibits, and other primary sources; 32 notes. Russian summary. 1915-19

Kugelgen, Wilhelm von

3728. Fraser, Catherine Clarke. "The Autobiographies of Ludwig Richter, Ernst Rietschel and Wilhelm von Kugelgen: Fictionalization and Adoption of Goethe's Narrative Techniques." U. of Connecticut 1981. 214 pp. *DAI 1982 42(9): 4015-A.* DA8205163 19c

Kuhlmann, Frédéric

3729. Thépot, André. FREDERIC KUHLMANN: INDUSTRIEL ET NOTABLE DU NORD, 1803-1881 [Frédéric Kuhlmann: a factory owner and notable of northern France (1803-81)]. *Revue du Nord [France] 1985 67(265): 527-546.* Frédéric Kuhlmann appears as the rare example of a factory owner being a man of talent in three different fields: scientific research, technology and management. He knew how to set up in the north of France an industrial establishment perfectly adapted to the needs of the region. That strong foundation allowed him to stand against both national and international competition. Meanwhile, Kuhlmann came to be the advocate and supporter of the interests of his adoptive country. 1820's-81

Kuhn, Walter

3730. Rhode, Gotthold and Weczerka, Hugo. NACHRUF ZUM TODE VON WALTER KUHN (1903-1983) [Notice on the death of Walter Kuhn (1903-83)]. *Zeitschrift für Ostforschung [West Germany] 1983 32(2): 161-168.* Prints a biography as an obituary for Walter Kuhn (1903-83), one of the principal historians of Germans in Silesia in Poland. His work chronicled the local history of German-speaking ethnic groups over several centuries. 18 notes. 13c-20c

3731. —. PROF. DR. WALTER KUHN (1903-1983) [Dr. Walter Kuhn, (1903-83)]. *Europa Ethnica [Austria] 1983 40(4): 205.* A tribute to the Austrian professor Walter Kuhn (1903-83), who was well known for his work in many spheres of Austrian history. 1903-83

Kühnert, Wilhelm

3732. Barton, Peter F. IN MEMORIAM WILHELM KÜHNERT [In memory of Wilhelm Kühnert]. *Jahrbuch der Gesellschaft für die Gesch. des Protestantismus in Österreich [Austria] 1981 97(1-4): v-x.* A tribute to the Austrian academician, theologian, and leading Protestant church historian, Wilhelm Kühnert (1900-80). The author examines Kühnert's life and pays particular attention to his academic activities in the sphere of Protestant theology and history as well as to his work as a church minister. 1900-80

Kuk, Ivan

3733. Stres, Peter. PUBLICIST IVAN KUK (1823-1864) [The writer Ivan Kuk (1823-64)]. *Goriški Letnik [Yugoslavia] 1982 9: 53-58.* Ivan Kuk's eight stories and his articles in the Slovene newspapers *Vedez, Novice,* and *Prijatel* between 1840 and 1860 show his knowledge of Slovene culture and his sense of Slovene national awareness. English and Italian summaries. 1840-60

Kuklin, Georgi A.

3734. Drugovskaia, A. Iu. G. A. KUKLIN—ISTORIK RUSSKOGO REVOLIUTSIONNOGO DVIZHENIIA (NOVYE BIOGRAFICHESKIE MATERIALY) [G. A. Kuklin: historian of the Russian revolutionary movement. New biographical data]. *Vestnik Moskovskogo Universiteta, Seriia 8: Istoriia [USSR] 1984 (2): 26-35.* Outlines the political biography of Georgi A. Kuklin (1880-1907), founder of the first Bolshevik library and archive in Geneva in the 1900's. He contributed to the journal *Zhizn'* [Life] despite its anarcho-syndicalist bias with which the Bolsheviks were in disagreement. The Geneva library was transported to Soviet Russia in 1917. Although Kuklin's birth date is usually quoted as 1877, there is evidence to support the later date of 1880, such as the marriage certificate of his parents dated 1879. Based on material from the Central Party Archives of the Institute of Marxism-Leninism and Central State Archives of the October Revolution; 53 notes. 1880-1907

Kulab Saipradit

3735. Batson, Benjamin A. KULAB SAIPRADIT AND THE "WAR OF LIFE." *J. of the Siam Soc. [Thailand] 1981 69(1-2): 58-73.* Kulab Saipradit (1905-74) was a Thai writer who in his lifetime was active chiefly as a journalist but today is remembered for his novels and short stories. He was an outspoken critic of the establishment and spent time in jail. 17 notes. 1930's-74

Kulbak, Moshe

3736. Luria, Shalom. MSHORER BEIN MITOR L'MISGERET: AL MOSHE KULBAK V-YETSIRATO [A poet amid myth and mold: on Moshe Kulbak and his writings]. *Shvut [Israel] 1982 9: 69-93.* Describes the life and works of Moshe Kulbak, a Polish poet, playwright, and novelist. Although born in Vilnius, he began writing in Hebrew. The colors and expressions of Yiddish drew him to that language. In 1928, at age 32, he moved to Minsk where he hoped to further his talent. In 1937 he was sent to a labor camp and was never heard from again. He was posthumously rehabilitated in 1956. Based on Kulbak's works. 1896-1956

Kuliński, Tomasz

3737. Wojciechowski, Daniel. DZIAŁALNOŚĆ DUSZPASTERSKA BISKUPA KIELECKIEGO TOMASZA KULIŃSKIEGO (1870-1907) [The ministry of the Bishop of Kielce Tomasz Kuliński, 1870-1907]. *Nasza Przeszłość [Poland] 1982 (57): 9-44.* A pastoral biography of Tomasz Kuliński when he was the bishop of Kielce between 1870 and 1907. Based on documents at the Kielce Diocese Archives and contemporary press articles; 168 notes. 1870-1907

Kuliscioff, Anna

3738. Casalini, Maria. FEMINISMO E SOCIALISMO IN ANNA KULISCIOFF: 1890-1907 [Feminism and socialism in Anna Kuliscioff: 1890-1907]. *Italia Contemporanea [Italy] 1981 33(143): 11-43.* Russian socialist Anna Kuliscioff devoted her life to improving the condition of women workers in Italy. Kuliscioff's extensive correspondence with F. Turati, the texts of her reports at conferences, and her published works indicate the scope of her activity. While others in Italy, e.g. Catholic groups, wanted to secure protection for women workers with the aim of eventually getting them out of the work force, Kuliscioff's aim was to make women a more important component of the work force. As a medical doctor, she saw the problem not only in terms of needed legislation to safeguard the health of women workers, but also in terms of enforcement of existing legislation. Based on primary sources, including archival material from the International Institute for Social History, Amsterdam; 173 notes. 1890-1907

Kulomzin, A. N.

3739. Lieven, D. C. B. BUREAUCRATIC LIBERALISM IN LATE IMPERIAL RUSSIA: THE PERSONALITY, CAREER AND OPINIONS OF A. N. KULOMZIN. *Slavonic and East European Rev. [Great Britain] 1982 60(3): 413-432.* A. N. Kulomzin (1838-1921) exemplified the enlightened gentry liberalism that could be found in the Russian State Council in the 19th century. Highly cultivated and widely traveled, Kulomzin combined a social conscience with considerable expertise in agriculture, housing, and transport. For more than 20 years he was secretary to the Committee of Ministers, and for 11 years he also served on the Siberian Railway Committee, contributing to the Russian pioneering effort in Siberia. His mature political thought was colored by a British constitutionalism which by 1905 had lost much of its relevance to Russian conditions. Based on materials in the Central State Historical Archives and the Manuscript Division of the Lenin Library; 59 notes. 1882-1905

Kun, Béla

3740. Musatov, V. L. and Kolychev, V. G. PLAMENNYI REVOLIUTSIONER-INTERNATSIONALIST (K 100-LETIIU SO DNIA ROZHDENIIA BELA KUNA) [Ardent revolutionary and internationalist: tribute on the 100th anniversary of the birth of Béla Kun (1886-1939?)]. *Voprosy Istorii KPSS [USSR] 1986 (2): 119-123.* Biography of the founder of the Hungarian Communist Party and leader of the short-lived Hungarian Soviet Republic of 1919. He abandoned his early "leftist deviation" under Lenin's influence and remained his lifelong friend. As member of the Comintern, 1921-36, Kun zealously advanced the cause of European Communist parties, promoted international workers' movements, opposed the reactionary counterrevolutionary regime of Admiral Miklós Horthy in Hungary, and always regarded the Soviet Union as his second homeland, having fought in the Soviet Revolution, participated in the First All-Union

Congress of Soviets and been selected to the All-Russian Party Central Executive Committee. Based mainly on Lenin and Kun's works; 22 notes. 1917-30's

3741. —. KUN BÉLA SZÜLETÉSÉNEK CENTENÁRIUMA ELÉ [On the centenary of Béla Kun]. *Párttörténeti Közlemények [Hungary] 1985 31(3): 3-14.* Béla Kun was born on 20 February 1886. He became a member of the Hungarian Social Democratic Party in 1902 and in 1916 was a prisoner of war in Russia. In 1918 he initiated the formation of the Hungarian Section of the Russian Communist Party. In November 1918, he returned to Hungary and formed the Hungarian Party of Communists in Budapest. After the proclamation of the Hungarian Soviet Republic he became the leader in the Political Bureau of the Revolutionary Governing Council, later becoming the political initiator of the military expeditions of the Red Army. After the downfall of the Hungarian Soviet Republic he went abroad and fought for the revival of the Hungarian Communist movement. He died in 1937. 1910's-37

Kunfi, Zsigmond

3742. Jemnitz, János. KUNFI ZSIGMOND ÉS A NEMZETKÖZI MUNKÁSMOZGALOM [Zsigmond Kunfi and the international labor movement]. *Történelmi Szemle [Hungary] 1981 24(4): 675-685.* Zsigmond Kunfi was the theoretician of the Social Democratic Party, a man of literary and other interests. He sympathized with the French. He was editor of and frequent contributor to the journal *Szocializmus,* 1906-14. His writings are analyzed here. 1906-24

3743. Mucsi, Ferenc and Szabo, Ágnes. ZSIGMOND KUNFI (1879-1929) [Zsigmond Kunfi (1879-1929)]. *Acta Historica [Hungary] 1984 30(1-2): 181-207.* Traces the career of Hungarian journalist and organizer for the labor movement Zsigmond Kunfi. Focuses on his work with other intellectuals on periodicals, including *Népszava* and *Szocializmus* of the Social Democratic Party. Extract from the introduction to *Die Ausgewählten Schriften von Zsigmond Kunfi* (1984). 1902-29

Küng family

3744. Yoder, Don. THE KÜNG-GNÄGI CONNECTION. *Pennsylvania Mennonite Heritage 1983 6(1): 2-6.* 17c

*For abstract see **Gnägi family***

Kunzig, Johannes

3745. Kretzenbacher, Leopold. JOHANNES KÜNZIG (1897-1982) [Obituary of Johannes Künzig (1897-1982)]. *Südostdeutsches Arch. [West Germany] 1981-82 24-25: 190-193.* Presents an appreciation of Johannes Künzig, the eminent folklorist, who was an active professor in the Universities of Karlsruhe (1937-42) and Freiburg im Breisgau (1942-45). He made a substantial contribution to the development of folklore as an academic discipline, especially with regard to German and comparative folklore. 1897-1982

Kurchatov, Igor' V.

3746. Moskovchenko, N. Ia. and Frenkel, V. Ia. IGOR' VASIL'EVICH KURCHATOV O SEBE (K 80-LETIIU SO DNIA ROZHDENIIA) [Igor' Vasil'evich Kurchatov about himself: tribute on his 80th birthday]. *Voprosy Istorii Estestvoznaniia i Tekhniki [USSR] 1983 (1): 127-130.* Cites with explanatory commentary a curriculum vitae written in June 1934 by the Soviet physicist Igor' V. Kurchatov (1903-60) in which he describes his experiments on the conductivity of dielectric crystals and research on physical properties of semiconductors. 9 notes, biblio. 1925-34

Kuropatkin, Aleksei N.

3747. Pozefsky, Peter. GENERAL ALEKSEI NIKOLAEVICH KUROPATKIN AND THE IMPERIAL RUSSIAN ARMY. *UCLA Historical Journal 1985 6: 50-82.* A profile of General Aleksei N. Kuropatkin (1848-1925), focusing on his service as Russian Minister of War from 1898 to 1904. A combat veteran, Kuropatkin won the favor of Nicholas II, but the need for military reforms, the jealousy of rival officers, and the pitfalls of political life made his position frustrating and difficult. Initially committed to a Far East policy, Kuropatkin came to realize the importance of increasing Western defenses and instituting important military changes. By then the tsar was committed to expansion in the Far East. Kuropatkin was made commander, but defeats in the Russo-Japanese War proved his undoing. The necessity for modernizing Russia's army went unmet, with disastrous results then and later. Primary and secondary sources; 80 notes. 1898-1905

Kuropatwińska-Świdowa, Halina

3748. Rogala, Jan. HALINA KUROPATWIŃSKA-ŚWIDOWA (3 III 1903-22 VI 1982) [Halina Kuropatwińska-Świdowa (3 March 1903-22 June 1982)]. *Archeion [Poland] 1983 (76): 330-332.* An obituary of a historian at the State Archives of the City of Warsaw, 1960-68. Her main responsibility was assembling a library of publications concerning the history of Warsaw. She took an active role in the preparations of historical exhibitions in the Mazovia region in 1966, the millennium of the Christianization of Poland. Photo, note. 7c-20c

Kuševski, Vojslav

3749. Andonov-Poljanski, Hristo and Panov, Branko. PROFESOR DR VOJSLAV D. KUŠEVSKI [Vojslav D. Kuševski]. *Istorija [Yugoslavia] 1981 17(2): 7-12.* Reviews the life and work of Vojslav D. Kuševski, an eminent Macedonian historian and lecturer at Skopje University, on the occasion of his 60th birthday. 1940's-81

Kutakhov, Pavel S.

3750. Rudenko, S. GLAVNYI MARSHAL AVIATSII P. S. KUTAKHOV [Chief air marshal P. S. Kutakhov]. *Voenno-Istoricheskii Zhurnal [USSR] 1984 (8): 43-46.* Pavel S. Kutakhov (b. 1914) fought as a pilot in the defense of Murmansk in 1941-42. He flew 367 missions during the war. He completed officer and military training after the war, and in 1967, became the first deputy air commander. In 1969, he was named air commander and deputy defense minister. In 1972, he became air marshal. He still serves as a Supreme Soviet deputy and has been a member of the Central Committee of the Communist Party of the Soviet Union since 1971. 1941-84

Kuusinen, Otto

3751. Kol'cov, P. S. EIN WAHRER SOLDAT DER REVOLUTION: OTTO KUUSINEN [A true soldier of the revolution: Otto Kuusinen]. *Beiträge zur Gesch. der Arbeiterbewegung [East Germany] 1982 24(5): 737-745.* Traces the life, career, and political activities of the Finnish Communist leader Otto Kuusinen (1881-1964). The author pays particular attention to his activities in the Finnish Social Democratic Party, 1904-18, as a leader in the Finnish revolution of 1918, his flight to Russia in 1918, his work to establish the Communist Party in Finland in 1918, and his role within the international Communist movement, 1921-40. In addition the author discusses his activities within the Soviet Union, his writings on Marxism-Leninism, and his work as a member of the Academy of Sciences in the USSR. Secondary sources; 28 notes. 1881-1964

3752. Kol'tsov, P. S. VERNYI SOLDAT REVOLIUTSII [A true soldier of the revolution]. *Voprosy Istorii KPSS [USSR] 1981 (10): 89-92.* In honor of the 100th anniversary of the birth of Otto Kuusinen, an outline is given of his life, work, and contribution to the cause of socialism, from his birth in Laukaa in October 1881 to his death in May 1964, and subsequent burial next to Lenin's mausoleum in Red Square. Considers his childhood, the awakening of his interest in politics, his entry into the Social Democratic Party of Finland, his reactions to the Russian Revolution of 1917 and involvement in the Finnish revolution of 1918, V. I. Lenin's attitude toward him, his life in the USSR, and further political efforts and achievements there. Based on the works of Kuusinen and Lenin; 21 notes. 1900's-64

Küzmič, Mikloš

3753. Smej, Jože. PISMA MIKLOŠA KÜZMIČA ZEMLJIŠKEMU GOSPODU [Mikloš Küzmič's letters to the estate possessor]. *Časopis za Zgodovino in Narodopisje [Yugoslavia] 1981 17(2): 273-293.* During 1769-1801 Slovenian writer Mikloš Küzmič wrote letters describing economic conditions of his homeland as well as his own poverty, which prevented him from writing more books. Based on 11 letters by Mikloš Küzmič. 1769-1801

Kuzmin, Mikhail

3754. Cheron, George. "The Drama of Mixail Kuzmin." U. of California, Los Angeles 1982. 305 pp. *DAI 1983 43(7): 2363-A.* DA8229660 1910-36

Kuznetsov, Nikolai G.

3755. Kasatonov, V. VITSE-ADMIRAL N. G. KUZNETSOV (K 80-LETIIU SO DNIA ROZHDENIIA) [Vice-Admiral N. G. Kuznetsov: on the 80th anniversary of his birth]. *Voenno-Istoricheskii Zhurnal [USSR] 1982 (7): 93-95.* Nikolai G. Kuznetsov (1902-74) rose through the ranks to become an experienced naval leader. Shortly after his graduation from the Naval Academy in 1932 he was appointed naval attaché in Spain. On his return to the USSR in 1937 he commanded the Pacific Fleet and in 1939 became People's Commissar of the Soviet Navy and served his country brilliantly during the Great Patriotic War. From 1945 until his retirement in 1956 he held a number of posts including that of naval minister and first deputy defense minister. 2 notes, photo. 1902-74

3756. Smirnov, N. "IA SDELAL VYBOR..." ["I made a choice..."]. *Morskoi Sbornik [USSR] 1982 (7): 66-69.* Former Soviet Naval Commander in Chief (1950's) Admiral Nikolai G. Kuznetsov (b. 1902) participated in the Civil War in Russia in 1919 and later distinguished himself as a talented naval commander. As Soviet naval attaché, he commanded Soviet naval volunteers during the Civil War in Spain in 1937. 1919-82

Kuzyk, Mykola

3757. Kuzyk, Mykola. [IZ SPOHADIV ZV'IAZKOVOHO OUN] [From the memoirs of a member of the O. U. N.].

DOROHA DO SHVAITSARII: IZ SPOHADIV ZV'IAZKOVOHO OUN [The road to Switzerland: from the memoirs of a member of the O. U. N.]. *Sučasnist [West Germany] 1980 (11): 28-44.* The author describes his activities as a member of the underground Organization of Ukrainian Nationalists in the western Ukraine from 1940 until his arrest and imprisonment by the German forces in 1945.

PISLIA "VYZVOLENNIA": IZ SPOHADIV ZV'IAZKOVOHO OUN [After "liberation": from the memoirs of a member of the O. U. N.]. *Sučasnist [West Germany] 1981 (5): 65-80.* The author recalls his release from detention by the Germans in 1945 and describes his eventual emigration to Munich. 1940-45

Kwane

3758. Schoeman, Karel. "MY LIEVE VADER GOVERNOR": KWANE (JAN LETELE) EN SY BRIEF AAN SIR GEORGE GREY ["My beloved father Governor": Kwane (Jan Letele) and his letter to Sir George Grey]. *Quarterly Bulletin of the South African Library [South Africa] 1984 39(2): 67-72.* Gives the text of a letter in Dutch written to Sir George Grey in 1858 by Kwane ("Jan Letele"), chief of the Bamonaheng branch of the Bakwena living in the vicinity on the modern Zastron, Orange Free State, denying accusations of horse stealing made against him. Sketches Kwane's life up to 1869. English summary. 1820-68

Kyŏnghŏ

3759. Sorensen, Henrik Hjort. THE LIFE AND THOUGHT OF THE KOREAN SŎN MASTER KYŎNGHŎ. *Korean Studies 1983 7: 9-33.* The Korean Sŏn monk Kyŏnghŏ, although never an innovative thinker, helped to revitalize a moribund Buddhist tradition in Korea primarily through the depth of his learning and the force of his charismatic personality. Himself a personification of traditional Buddhist values, he sought particularly to instill them in the laity, thus helping to bridge the perennial gap between monk and common man. Based on writings of Kyŏnghŏ and secondary sources; 150 notes. 1850-1900

L

Laar, Johannes Jacobus van

3760. Snelders, H. A. M. THE DUTCH PHYSICAL CHEMIST J. J. VAN LAAR (1860-1938) VERSUS J. H. VAN'T HOFF'S "OSMOTIC SCHOOL." *Centaurus [Denmark] 1986 29(1): 53-71.* Throughout his life's work, Johannes Jacobus van Laar (1860-1938) championed the thermodynamic approach to chemical analysis while he opposed using the concept of osmotic pressure in developing a theory of solutions. Often polemic in tone, Van Laar's mathematically rigorous writings had little influence on the development of physical chemistry, even though many of his ideas eventually were universally accepted. He is perhaps best remembered for his constant confrontation of the Dutch chemical community led and influenced by the ideas of Jacobus Henricus 'Van't Hoff (1852-1911). Based on Van Laar's published writings; 60 notes. 1884-1938

Laatikainen, Taavetti

3761. Halila, Aimo. KOLME SUOMALAISTA SOTILASPEDAGOGIA [Three Finnish military pedagogues]. *Turun Hist. Arkisto [Finland] 1982 38: 390-408.* Presents biographical sketches of three leaders in Finnish military education: Samuel Möller (1743-1815), who taught at Haapaniemi military school 1780-99; General Frithiof Alfred Neovius (1830-95), director of the Finnish Cadet School at Hamina, 1871-85; and General Taavetti Laatikainen (1886-1954), director of the Cadet School during 1927-34. English summary. 1743-1954

LaBolina, Jack

See Vecchj, Augusto Vittorio

Labriola, Antonio

3762. Bazzani, Fabio. IL PROBLEMA LABRIOLA [The Labriola problem]. *Studi Storici [Italy] 1981 22(4): 917-933.* Antonio Labriola, Italian philosopher. Based on papers delivered at a conference organized by the Gramsci Institute in Florence, Italy, 15-17 October 1981. Primary sources; 2 notes. 1870-1904

3763. Femia, Joseph V. ANTONIO LABRIOLA: A FORGOTTEN MARXIST THINKER. *Hist. of Pol. Thought [Great Britain] 1981 2(3): 557-572.* Italian Marxist theoretician and true founder of Hegelian Marxism, Antonio Labriola (d. 1904) has enjoyed little scholarly attention. His *Essays on the Materialist Conception of History* (1896) and *Socialism and Philosophy* (1897) were a lively discussion of historical materialism and philosophical ideas. While providing an economic interpretation of history, Labriola did not dismiss the importance of ideology, accident, or chance. He denounced fatalism, Darwinism, and the Marxist notion of the inevitability of progress. Labriola sought a radicalization and historicization of knowledge with an aim toward practicality; finally, he called for a distinctly Marxian philosophy of life. Despite his admiration for Gramsci and Lenin, Labriola's relative obscurity stems from his vague, elliptic manner of presentation, occasional inconsistencies and equivocations, inability to collect his thought into a consistent whole, lack of a congenial audience, and his disregard for the Italian Socialist Party. 73 notes. 1890-1904

Lacan, Jacques

3764. Fisher, David James. LACAN'S AMBIGUOUS IMPACT ON FRENCH PSYCHOANALYSIS. *Contemporary French Civilization 1981-82 6(1-2): 89-114.* Compares French psychoanalyst Jacques Lacan with surrealist André Breton, discusses his unique approach to psychoanalytic technique and training, and assesses his impact on French psychoanalysis. 1925-80

LaCeppède, Jean de

3765. Plantié, Jacqueline and Rivière, Maguelone. JEAN DE LA CEPPÈDE "EN FAMILLE" D'APRÈS LES ARCHIVES NOTARIALES [Jean de La Ceppède, "family man," as seen in notary archives]. *Bibliothèque d'Humanisme et Renaissance [Switzerland] 1984 46(3): 549-571.* Departmental notary records shed much light on the life of poet Jean de La Ceppède (1550-1623), and particularly on his fiscal dealings with his mother, wives, and other family members. In 1596 he resolved two legal proceedings, one with his sister Jeanne concerning the settlement of their mother's estate, and one with his wife, Madeleine de Brancas, concerning the division of the couple's belongings. Other documents deal with La Ceppède's testamentary provisions for his children. Based extensively on governmental archives in Provence, and on other sources; 103 notes. 1577-1623

Lacordaire, Henri

3766. Carré, A.-M. LAMENNAIS ET LACORDAIRE [Lamennais and Lacordaire]. *Rev. des Deux Mondes [France] 1982 (8): 287-294.* Describes the links between the Dominican priest, Henri Lacordaire, and the revolutionary, Lamennais, and their involvement with the journal *L'Avenir,* which advocated the separation of Church and state. 1830-48

Lacoste, Constant

3767. Massie, Jean-François. NECROLOGIE: CONSTANT LACOSTE (1901-1981) [Obituary: Constant Lacoste (1901-81)]. *Rev. de Pau et du Béarn [France] 1981 (9): 69-74.* Recounts the career and describes the scientific and literary publications of Constant Lacoste, whose interests lay in the regional history of Pau and Béarn; gives a bibliography of works published since 1920. 1901-81

Laemmert, Eduardo

3768. Ferrez, Gilberto. A OBRA DE EDUARDO LAEMMERT [The work of Eduardo Laemmert]. *Rev. do Inst. Hist. e Geog. Brasileiro [Brazil] 1981 (331): 193-208.* Describes the life and work of Eduardo Laemmert, a German-born publisher who came to Brazil in 1827. He became one of the most notable Brazilian publishers, especially in the area of almanacs and scholarly books. The contents of Laemmert's major collection, the *Folhinas Laemmert,* noted for their historical "curiosities" are described and excerpted. Laemmert was one of the most important publishers in Brazil, and the publishing house he began still flourishes. Based on the works published by Laemmert, journals, and other secondary sources; 3 photos, tables, 10 notes, biblio. 1806-81

Laënnec, René

3769. Hanngren, Åke. RENÉ THÉOPHILE HYACINTHE LAENNEC (1781-1826) [René Théophile Hyacinthe Laënnec (1781-1826)]. *Nordisk Medicinhistorisk Årsbok [Sweden] 1981: 106-119.* On the occasion of René Laënnec's 200th birthday, recounts the achievements of this eminent French physician, inventor of the stethoscope and developer of the practice of auscultation. 1806-26

Lafarge, Marie Cappelle

3770. Douay, Serge. MARIE LAFARGE: EMPOISONNEUSE OU VICTIME? [Marie Lafarge: poisoner or victim?]. *Hist. Mag. [France] 1983 (38): 28-32.* Relates the famous controversial trial of Marie Lafarge, née Cappelle who, accused of giving poison to her husband, was sentenced to two years' imprisonment, in 1840, in spite of insufficient evidence of guilt. 1840-52

Lafargue, Paul

3771. Makarenko, E. M. MOLODOI LAFARG [The young Lafargue]. *Voprosy Istorii [USSR] 1981 (6): 115-122.* Outlines the first 27 years of the French Communist Paul Lafargue (1842-1911). Lafargue was born in the Cuban town of Santiago and moved with his family to Bordeaux in France when he was nine. He studied medicine at the Sorbonne and was active in the antimonarchist movement. In 1865 he started contributing to the radical newspaper *Rive Gauche.* He was eventually expelled from the Sorbonne for attending an international students' congress in Belgium. He then moved to London and studied to be an assistant surgeon at St. Bartholomew's hospital. One of his first patients was Karl Marx, whose daughter he later married. The couple settled in France and Lafargue became involved in the 1st International, promoting the ideas of his father-in-law. 48 notes. 1842-69

Lafayette, Marquis de

3772. Chambrun, Marquis de and Chambrun, Marquise de. THE LAFAYETTES. *Daughters of the American Revolution Magazine 1984 118(1): 14-17.* Provides a biographical sketch of the Marquis de Lafayette and his wife Adrienne. 1777-1834

3773. Kramer, Lloyd S. LAFAYETTE AND THE HISTORIANS: CHANGING SYMBOL, CHANGING NEEDS, 1834-1984. *Historical Reflections [Canada] 1984 11(3): 373-401.* Since his death, the Marquis de Lafayette (1757-1834) has been viewed diversely by historians. Until Bayard Tuckerman's biography (1889), historians saw him as a symbol of the American Revolution and its ideals, and found few faults. Interpretations by 20th-century historians have been more "critical" and "realistic." Louis Gottschalk's six-volume study (1935-73) remains the standard biography. Extremely thorough, although stopping in 1790, it discusses, as do other works, negative facets of Lafayette's life in France that led him to go to America. 106 notes. 18c-20c

Lafont, Henri

3774. Delarue, Jacques. LA BANDE BONNY-LAFONT [The Bonny and Lafont gang]. *Histoire [France] 1985 (80): 62-69.* 1940-44
*For abstract see **Bonny, Pierre***

Laforgue, Jules

3775. Murat, Jean. UN POETE FRANÇAIS A LA COUR DE BERLIN: JULES LAFORGUE [Jules Laforgue: a French poet at the court of Berlin]. *Rev. d'Allemagne [France] 1982 14(2): 267-276.* Jules Laforgue (1860-87) was employed by Empress Augusta (1811-90) as her reader and French instructor. In this capacity Laforgue had ample opportunity to observe the imperial court, Berlin, and Germany, but these bored him and his observations had only a limited effect on his literary output. 26 notes. 1881-86

LaGallienne, Eva

3776. Tumbleson, Treva Rose. "Three Female Hamlets: Charlotte Cushman, Sarah Bernhardt and Eva La Gallienne." U. of Oregon 1981. 343 pp. *DAI 1982 42(8): 3349-A.* 8201871 19c

Lagerlöf, Selma

3777. St. Andrews, B. A. INNOVATION AND TRADITION: SELMA LAGERLÖF AND THE SAGA. *North Dakota Quarterly 1985 53(3): 96-102.* Discusses the works of Selma Lagerlöf (1858-1940), Swedish novelist and winner of the 1909 Nobel Prize in literature, particularly through an analysis of Lagerlöf's innovative use in narrative of oral traditions. 1894-1940

Lai Zhide

3778. Schulz, Larry James. "Lai Chih-te (1525-1604) and the Phenomenology of the *Classic of Change (I Ching).*" Princeton U. 1982. 358 pp. *DAI 1982 43(4): 1257-A.* DA8221585 1599

Láing, Judit

3779. Láng, Judit. NEGYVENNÉGY [1944]. *Történelmi Szemle [Hungary] 1982 25(2): 276-319.* The diary of a young upper-class Jewish woman describes her daily life during the siege of the German-occupied city of Budapest. Her non-Jewish husband and her father's position as one of the leading lawmakers of Hungary made it possible for the family to stay alive during those years of persecution. 38 notes. 1944-45

Lair, Pierre Jacques Guillaume

3780. Nourisson, Roger. LE COLONEL LAIR ET LES OUVRIERS MILITAIRES DE LA MARINE [Colonel Lair and the naval military workers]. *Bull. Hist. de la Soc. de Sauvegarde du Château Impérial de Pont-de-Briques [France] 1981 (15-18): 303-309.* A biographical sketch of Colonel Pierre Jacques Guillaume Lair (1769-1830), highlighting his career and achievements in shipbuilding. He directed the building in Boulogne, Northern France, and in Antwerp, Belgium, of a fleet designed by Napoleon I to attempt a military landing in England. 1804-09

Lajpat Rai, Lala

3781. Bhatia, L. M. LALA LAJPAT RAI AND THE RAJ. *Indo-British Review [India] 1983 10(2): 63-64.* Recounts the adventures of fiery Lala Lajpat Rai (1865-1928) and his challenge to British rule in India, banishment to Burma in 1907, his return to India somewhat tempered, his travels to England and the United States, and his death in 1928 after being injured in a confrontation with the police. ca 1900-28

Lalayants, Isahak

3782. Gharibjanian, G. B. V. I. LENINI HAY ZINAKITSNĚRN U ASHAKĚRTNĚRĚ [V. I. Lenin's Armenian comrades-in-arms and disciples]. *Patma-Banasirakan Handes. Istoriko-Filologicheskii Zhurnal [USSR] 1980 (1): 13-20.* ca 1890-1917
*For abstract see **Avanesov***

Lalbhai, Kasturbhai

3783. Ray, Rajat Kanta. PEDHIS AND MILLS: THE HISTORICAL INTEGRATION OF THE FORMAL AND INFORMAL SECTORS IN THE ECONOMY OF AHMEDABAD. *Indian Econ. and Social Hist. Rev. [India] 1982 19(3-4): 387-396.* Reviews two studies of Gujarati entrepreneurship: Dwijendra Tripathi's business biography of Kasturbhai Lalbhai and Makrand Mehta's history of the cotton industry of Ahmedabad. Based on government reports and secondary sources; 19 notes. 1820-1980

Lalique, René

3784. McClinton, Katherine Morrison. RENE LALIQUE: ART NOUVEAU JEWELER AND GOLDSMITH. *Art & Antiques 1983 6(2): 90-95.* French jeweler, goldsmith, and glassmaker René Lalique created complex jewelry of high craftsmanship in the Art Nouveau tradition during the 1880's-1930's. 1880's-1930's

Lam Qua

3785. Gilman, Sander L. LAM QUA AND THE DEVELOPMENT OF A WESTERNIZED MEDICAL ICONOGRAPHY IN CHINA. *Medical History [Great Britain] 1986 30(1): 57-69.* In the 19th century, the Chinese felt that it was important to defend their traditional medicine against the Western tradition, due to growing European contempt for all oriental ideas. One such tradition was medical illustration, which in China tended to show structures subject to treatment rather than symptoms. Europeans have overemphasized the differences and ignored early Western influences. The artist Lam Qua, who was trained in Western artistic styles, did over one hundred portraits illustrating various pathological conditions. He is the best example of Western-style medical illustration in 19th century China, but his work clearly shows an amalgam of occidental and oriental concepts. Based on a study of Lam Qua's paintings and secondary works; 22 notes. 1820-51

LaMadelène, Henry and Jules de

3786. Scales, Derek P. THE LA MADELENE BROTHERS AND THEIR SCENES OF COUNTRY AND PROVINCIAL LIFE. *Australian J. of French Studies [Australia] 1980 17(3): 232-240.* Examines the professional careers and the narrative elements found in the works of Henry de LaMadelène (1825-87) and Jules de LaMadelène (1820-59). 1830-87

Lamartine, Alphonse de

3787. Letessier, Fernand. CINQ LETTRES INEDITES DE TOCQUEVILLE A LAMARTINE [Five unpublished letters by de Tocqueville to Lamartine]. *Rev. d'Hist. Littéraire de la France [France] 1983 83(3): 451-458.* Adduces new evidence on relations between Alexis de Tocqueville and Alphonse de Lamartine, 1842-56. 1842-56

3788. Winegarten, Renée. IN QUEST OF LAMARTINE: A POET IN POLITICS. *Encounter [Great Britain] 1982 59(2): 22-29.* Examines the religious ideas and liberal politics advocated by French poet Alphonse de Lamartine (1790-1869), especially from 1833 to the 1840's when Lamartine served in the *Chambre de Députés* and in other French political bodies. 1815-69

Lambarde, John

3789. Warnicke, Retha M. THE MERCHANT SOCIETY OF TUDOR LONDON: JOHN LAMBARDE—A CASE STUDY. *Indiana Social Studies Quarterly 1984 37(2): 57-69.* Outlines the career of one of 16th-century London's richest merchants, John Lambarde (1500-54), who acquired his wealth through the Drapers (a livery company with social and political functions), the purchase of property, and a prestigious marriage. 1517-54

Lambarde, William

3790. Terrill, Richard J. WILLIAM LAMBARDE: ELIZABETHAN HUMANIST AND LEGAL HISTORIAN. *Journal of Legal History [Great Britain] 1985 6(2): 157-178.* Having inherited the family manor before he was 20, William Lambarde (1536-1601) was able to pursue his scholarly interests and eventually became the senior member of a group of Elizabethan legal historians. He wrote both practical manuals and learned treatises, including an edition of Anglo-Saxon laws and a handbook for justices of the peace. Lambarde's most important work was *Archeion,* a historical survey of the English court system, which utilized humanist methodology, vigorously defended the prerogative courts, and emphasized the role of the monarch as the supreme authority in the state. Based largely on Lambarde's writings and secondary works; 56 notes. 1550's-1601

Lambert, Raymond-Raoul

3791. Cohen, Yerachmiel (Richard). A JEWISH LEADER IN VICHY FRANCE, 1940-1943: THE DIARY OF RAYMOND-RAOUL LAMBERT. *Jewish Social Studies 1981 43(3-4): 291-310.* The recently discovered diary of Raymond-Raoul Lambert (1894-1943), head of the *Judenrat* in Vichy France, offers important new information on the Jews of France under the Vichy Regime, the Union Générale des Israelites de France, and on Lambert himself, particularly his wartime activities. Based on the diary and other contemporary sources; 82 notes. 1940-43

Lambertz, Maximilian

3792. Bihiku, Koço. MAKSIMILIAN LAMBERTZ SI STUDIUES DHE POPULLARIZUES I LETËRSISË SHQIPETARE [Maximilian Lambertz: scholar and popularizer of the Albanian language]. *Studime Filologjike [Albania] 1982 36(4): 193-197. 9 notes.* 20c

3793. Haxhihasani, Qemal. KONTRIBUTI I MAKSIMILIAN LAMBERCIT NË FUSHËN E FOLKLORISTIKËS SHQIPTARE [Maximilian Lambertz's contribution to the study of Albanian folklore]. *Studime Filologjike [Albania] 1982 36(4): 187-192. 14 notes.* 20c

3794. Lafe, Emil. MAKSIMILIAN LAMBERCI: STUDIUËS I GJUHES SHQIPE [Maximilian Lambertz: scholar of the Albanian language]. *Studime Filologjike [Albania] 1982 36(4): 177-185.* The Austrian scholar Maximilian Lambertz was the first to study the history and evolution of the Albanian language and its dialects by living for years with Albanians in Albania and abroad. 20c

Lamennais, Félicité de

3795. Carré, A.-M. LAMENNAIS ET LACORDAIRE [Lamennais and Lacordaire]. *Rev. des Deux Mondes [France] 1982 (8): 287-294.* 1830-48
*For abstract see **Lacordaire, Henri***

Lamotte, Etienne

3796. Bareau, André. ETIENNE LAMOTTE 1903-1983 [Etienne Lamotte (1903-83)]. *T'oung Pao [Netherlands] 1983 69(1-3): i-ii.* Etienne Lamotte (1903-83), professor at the University of Louvain, specialized in the study of Buddhist works translated into Chinese or Tibetan and those preserved in the original Sanskrit or Pali. His major achievment was the translation of Chinese texts of Sanskrit works that were no longer extant. His numerous articles dealt mainly with the historical and doctrinal problems of Buddhism. 20c

Landauer, Gustav

3797. Böhr, Christoph. GEIST UND MACHT: ZUM SPANNUNGSVERHÄLTNIS VON PHILOSOPHIE UND POLITIK IM WERK UND LEBEN GUSTAV LANDAUERS [Intellect and power: the relationship between philosophy and politics in the writings and life of Gustav Landauer]. *Zeitschrift für Religions- und Geistesgeschichte [West Germany] 1984 36(3): 232-251.* Gustav Landauer (1870-1919) considered himself an anarchist and a socialist favoring a utopian society organized by confederate groups. His thinking centered on the question of the compatibility of intellect and power, especially in *Skepsis und Mystik* [Skepticism and mysticism] (1903), in which he developed a vision that was close to chiliasm. Landauer's theory for a synthesis of the intellect and power did not achieve wide acceptance. He himself failed to put his ideas into reality during the Munich Revolution in 1919. 1890-1919

Landseer, Edwin

3798. Rishel, Joseph. LANDSEER: QUEEN VICTORIA'S FAVORITE PAINTER COPIED IN AMERICA. *Nineteenth Cent. 1981 7(3): 42-46.* Biography of the popular English painter Sir Edwin Landseer. Documents his influence on American artists James Beard, William Holbrook Beard, Lilly Martin Spencer, Newbold Trotter, A. F. Tait, Thomas H. Hinkley, and Henry Bryan Hall. 19c

Lang, Matthäus

3799. Wurstbauer, L. "Matthäus Lang im Dienst der Maximilian I" [Matthäus Lang in the service of Maximilian I]. U. of Graz [Austria] 1979. *DAI-C 1982 43(4): 708-709; 7/4364c.* 1508-20

Lange, Helene

3800. Albisetti, James C. COULD SEPARATE BE EQUAL? HELENE LANGE AND WOMEN'S EDUCATION IN IMPERIAL GERMANY. *Hist. of Educ. Q. 1982 22(3): 301-317.* Helene Lange (1848-1930) struggled to make women's education equal to men's in imperial Germany. A study of this struggle throws light on both educational reform and on the German women's movement. Lange's "Yellow Brochure" of 1887 took issue with the assumption that women should be educated to serve their husbands. Contact with English education developed Lange's belief that education should prepare women for life. Basic to her program was the training of women both as teachers and as principals in women's schools. Although Lange was conservative, she contributed more to the position of women in German society than did many of the more radical feminists of her day. Based on primary documents and secondary sources; 66 notes. 1887-1914

Langenfeld, Friedrich Spee von

3801. Rupp, Walter. FRIEDRICH SPEE VON LANGENFELD [Friedrich Spee von Langenfeld]. *Stimmen der Zeit [West Germany] 1985 203(8): 547-554.* Gives a biographical account of Friedrich Spee von Langenfeld's (1591-1635) career as professor of moral theology, spiritual advisor, poet, theologian, and social critic of early 17th-century Germany. 1620-35

Langer, Felicia

3802. Bishara, Ghassan, interviewer. FELICIA LANGER. *Journal of Palestine Studies 1984 13(4): 69-87.* An interview with Felicia Langer, a Polish-born Israeli lawyer, noted for her defense of cases concerning the rights of the Palestinians in the occupied territories. 1965-82

Langsdorf, Grigori I.

3803. Lysenko, T. I. DOKUMENTY O ZHIZNI I DEIATEL'NOSTI AKADEMIKA G. I. LANGSDORF V SOVETSKIKH I ZARUBEZHNYKH ARKHIVAKH [Documents on the life and work of academician G. I. Langsdorf in Soviet and foreign archives]. *Sovetskie Arkhivy [USSR] 1981 (2): 33-36.* Examines the contents of documents kept in archives in the USSR, Brazil, the United States, and a number of European countries concerning the life and work of the Russian scholar, explorer, and diplomat Grigori I. Langsdorf (1774-1852). The bulk of the material is in the Soviet archives and covers his many voyages and expeditions, including the first Russian exploratory expedition to Brazil, 1821-29. The Brazilian material is mainly concerned with his activities as Russian consul general in Rio de Janeiro. Some 20 drawings pertaining to his world voyage of 1803-10 are kept in the Bancroft Library, United States, and other documents and drawings dealing with Langsdorf's life are in the Vienna Academy of Imaginative Art, the Deutches Zentralarchiv in Merzeburg, East Germany, and in the National Archive, Lisbon. 14 notes. 1774-1852

LaNoue, François de

3804. Huseman, William H.; Schalk, Ellery (commentary). THE *DISCOURS* OF FRANÇOIS DE LA NOUE: HUMANISTIC EDUCATION AND THE SURVIVAL OF THE FRENCH NOBILITY. *Pro. of the Ann. Meeting of the Western Soc. for French Hist. 1981 9: 50-60.* The French Huguenot military leader François de La Noue (1531-91) was also an important educational theorist, as shown by his *Discours Politiques et Militaires* (1587). In these essays La Noue attempted to strengthen the nobility of the sword against the rise in social and political power of businessmen and nobles of the robe. La Noue argued that nobles should be broadly educated in various humanistic studies. His ideas were not put into practice in his lifetime, but they did have significant influence in the 17th and 18th centuries. 9 notes. Comments on pp. 61-67. 1570-90

Lapeyre, Henri

3805. Ponsot, Pierre. HOMMAGE A HENRI LAPEYRE (1912-1984) [Homage to Henri Lapeyre (1912-84)]. *Cahiers d'Histoire [France] 1984 29(4): 323-325.* An obituary for historian of commerce Henri Lapeyre, who was a professor at the University of Grenoble until poor health forced his retirement. His work focused on 16th-century Spanish history. In particular, his research brought to light an entire collection of papers left by the Ruiz family, the great merchants of Medini del Campo. Lapeyre's *Famille de Marchands, les Ruiz* [The Ruiz family of merchants] was published in 1955, followed by *Géographie de l'Espagne Morisque* [Geography of Morisco Spain] in 1959 and *Les Monarchies Européennes au XVI*[e] *Siècle: Les Relations Internationales* [The European monarchies of the 16th century: international relations] in 1967. He was also the author of other works, journal publications, and contributions to academic congresses. 1930's-84

3806. Ruiz Martín, Felipe. HENRI LAPEYRE [Henri Lapeyre]. *Revista de Historia Económica [Spain] 1985 3(1): 127-132.* Henri Lapeyre (d. 1984) was one of the greatest French hispanists. His special subject was the reign of Philip II. During his many stays in Spain he was helpful to many local university students. Though his specialty was economic history, he loved to dwell upon political, institutional, and cultural aspects. He was a tireless worker and a kind and intelligent man. 16c

3807. Vazquez de Prada, Valentín. LA PERSONALIDAD Y LA OBRA DE UN GRAN HISPANISTA HENRI LAPEYRE (1910-1984) [The personality and works of a great Hispanist, Henri Lapeyre (1910-84)]. *Hispania [Spain] 1985 45(161): 633-640.* An appreciation of the life and works of Henri Lapeyre (1910-84), eminent French historian of the era of Philip II of Spain. 1910-84

LaPira, Giorgio

3808. Bocchini Camaiani, Bruna. ALCUNI PROBLEMI DI RICERCA STORIOGRAFICA SULLA CHIESA FIORENTINA CONTEMPORANEA [Some problems of historical research on the contemporary Florentine Church]. *Cristianesimo nella Storia [Italy] 1985 6(2): 381-394.* Reviews a number of recent works, concentrating on biographies and autobiographies of churchmen, and emphasizes the role of Giorgio La Pira. 1945-75

Lăpuşneanu, Alexander

3809. Pungă, Gh. NOI CONSIDERAŢII PRIVIND ÎNCEPUTUL DOMNIEI LUI ALEXANDRU LĂPUŞNEANU [The beginning of the reign of Alexander Lăpuşneanu]. *Anuarul Institutului de Istorie şi Arheologie "A. D. Xenopol" [Romania] 1981 18: 551-565.* The reign of Alexander Lăpuşneanu, voivode of Moldavia from 1552, was overshadowed from the start by the rivalry of Poland, Austria, and Turkey. Little attention has been paid to the difficult role inherited by the voivode from his immediate predecessors, including Petru Rareş, at a time when the Turkish sultan was exerting maximum pressure on central and southeast Europe. The complicated politics of 1550-52, based on documents already in print, are examined in detail. Primary sources; 125 notes. 1550-70

Lara y Sandoval, Pedro Manrique de

3810. Albeda Alonso, Jaime. EL DUQUE FORTE [The strong duke]. *Rev. de Hist. Militar [Spain] 1983 27(54): 11-18.* Details the rise of Pedro Manrique de Lara y Sandoval (1443-1515), first Duke of Nájera and confidant of Isabella I. He served the Castilian princes in campaigns and diplomatic missions, playing a key role in the marriage of Ferdinand and Isabella. As a reward, their Catholic majesties awarded him the first ducal title presented in their reign. 3 plates, 7 notes, biblio. 1443-1515

Lardner, Dionysius

3811. Hays, J. N. THE RISE AND FALL OF DIONYSIUS LARDNER. *Ann. of Sci. [Great Britain] 1981 38(5): 527-542.* Dionysius Lardner (1793-1859) rose to prominence in the 1830's as a scientific writer, lecturer, and British literary figure. He became popular by promoting the ideals of scientific self-education, technological progress, and the practical applicability of science. His rapid fall from public favor after 1840 resulted partly from his involvement in a marital scandal; prior to that scandal, however, his character had provoked satire, and his caution and even pessimism about some technological prospects had offended the confident hopes of the audiences of that time, confident hopes which Lardner had helped to create. 1830-59

Larivey, Pierre de

3812. Freeman, M. J. GILLES CORROZET ET LES DEBUTS LITTERAIRES DE PIERRE DE LARIVEY [Gilles Corrozet and the literary beginnings of Pierre de Larivey]. *Bibliothèque d'Humanisme et Renaissance [Switzerland] 1986 48(2): 431-437.* The Parisian poet and bookseller Gilles Corrozet (1510-68) was an important influence on Pierre de Larivey's (ca. 1540-1619) early career as a writer and translator. Larivey's earliest known work is a 1567 sonnet dedicated to Corrozet. The poem combines the common Renaissance imagery of the "industrious bee" with references to the Horatian concept of immortality through the written word, and serves as an homage to an early mentor. 16 notes. 1567-68

LaRoque, Antoine de

3813. Todd, Christopher. LA REDACTION DU "MERCURE DE FRANCE" (1721-1744): DUFRESNY, FUZELIER, LA ROQUE [The editors of the *Mercure de France* (1721-44): Dufresny, Fuzelier, La Roque]. *Rev. d'Hist. Littéraire de la France [France] 1983 83(3): 439-441.* Focuses on the years encompassing Antoine de La Roque's assumption of the post of editor and his collaboration with Charles-Rivière Dufresny and Louis Fuzelier. 1721-44

Larsen, Hemming

3814. Larsen, Hemming. PAA KINAKYSTEN MED S/S NORVIKEN AV BERGEN [On the China coast with S/S Norviken of Bergen]. *Sjøfartshistorisk Årbok [Norway] 1983: 161-174.* Provides the memoirs of the author, who was an engineer on board the S/S *Norviken* from June 1937 to December 1938, sailing the China coast. The ship was crewed by Chinese and guarded from pirates by former Soviet soldiers. On one occasion crew members smuggled silver coins, while on another the ship had to ride out a typhoon. 4 illus. 1937-38

Lartigue, Jacques-Henri

3815. Nilson, Lisbet. THE ANCIENT LITTLE BOY. *Horizon 1981 24(7-8): 40-49.* Chronicles the photographic career of Jacques-Henri Lartigue (b. 1894) and describes his early photographs 1901-20, which were not made public until 1963. 1901-81

LasCasas, Bartolomé de

3816. André-Vincent, Ph. I. FRAY BARTOLOME DE LAS CASAS Y LOS DERECHOS DEL HOMBRE [Brother Bartholomé de Las Casas and human rights]. *Rev. de Estudios Histórico-Jurídicos [Chile] 1981 6: 189-202.* Discusses the life of Bartholomé de Las Casas, and his influence on human rights in the Dominican Republic and Chile. 1514-66

3817. Donahue, Francis. PATRON SAINT OF LIBERATION THEOLOGY. *San José Studies 1986 12(2): 20-31.* Sketches the life of Friar Bartolemé de Las Casas of the 16th century, the first human rights activist in the New World, who is proposed for canonization by Latin America's liberation theologists, Christian Marxists at odds with Pope John Paul II. 16c-20c

3818. Pereña Vicente, Luciano. FRAY BARTOLOMÉ DE LAS CASAS, PROFETA DE LA LIBERACION [Father Bartolomé de las Casas, prophet of liberation]. *U. Humanistica [Colombia] 1981 (14): 93-108.* Bartolomé de las Casas advised Charles V that he could be emperor of the Indians of Latin America only with their consent, respecting their customs, government, and property. By 1565 he had enlisted the aid of Pope Pius V in defense of the Indians, and his *De Imperiatoria seu Regia Potestate* has been used ever since in defense of the oppressed the world over. 1540-66

Lasker-Schüler, Else

3819. Hessing, Jakob. ELSE LASKER-SCHÜLER: DICHTERIN OHNE GESCHICHTE. DIE JÜDISCHEN, CHRISTLICHEN UND DEUTSCHEN MYTHEN IN IHRER NACHKRIEGSREZEPTION [Else Lasker-Schüler: poetess without history. The Jewish, Christian, and German myths and her postwar reception]. *Bulletin des Leo Baeck Instituts [Israel] 1983 (65): 23-52.* Examines the life and literary career of Else Lasker-Schüler (1869-1945). She was born in Elberfeld, lived in Berlin between 1893 and 1933, and emigrated to Switzerland. She was in Jerusalem when World War II broke out and died there in 1945. Her poems and personal fate reflected the sufferings of the Jews in Germany. Particular attention is paid to an assessment of Else Lasker-Schüler's work and its reception since World War II, when an ahistorical image of both the poetess and her work has been presented. The author also traces the evolution of Lasker-Schüler's ideas and poetry as assessed by Werner Kraft, Ernst Ginsberg, and Gottfried Benn. Secondary sources; 70 notes. 1869-1945

Laski, Harold J.

3820. Ekirch, Arthur A., Jr. HAROLD J. LASKI: THE AMERICAN EXPERIENCE. *Am. Studies 1983 24(1): 53-68.* Examines the career and influence of Harold J. Laski, British political scientist. His circle of American friends became important to his career, and included Franklin D. Roosevelt, Felix Frankfurter, Roscoe Pound, and Oliver Wendell Holmes. Throughout his life Laski sought to advance his ideas of socialism and the predominance of local authority in various political circles in the United States, although by the late 1930's he embraced the idea of a stronger presidency. Based on Laski's writings and the Roosevelt, Frankfurter, Holmes and Pound Papers; 37 notes; illus. 1900-50

Lassenius, Helge Ragnar

3821. Lassenius, Tor-Erik. EN VASA STUDENT 1914-1918: UR HELGE LASSENIUS BREV OCH DAGBOK [A Vaasa student, 1914-18: from the letters and diary of Helge Lassenius]. *Hist. och Litteraturhistorisk Studier [Finland] 1982 57: 207-256.* A biography of a Swedish-speaking Finn, Helge Ragnar Lassenius (1895-1918), a native of Vaasa and a university student in Helsinki 1914-18, who was killed as a soldier in the White army during Finland's civil war in 1918. Based on family letters, Lassenius' diary, and secondary sources; 2 maps, photo, 8 notes. 1895-1918

Łaszewski, Michał Remigiusz

3822. Mazur, Zdzisław. MICHAŁ REMIGIUSZ ŁASZEWSKI (1682-1746) BISKUP POMOCNICZY WARMIŃSKI [Michał Remigiusz Łaszewski (1682-1746), auxiliary bishop of Warmia]. *Komunikaty Mazursko-Warmińskie [Poland] 1979 (2): 165-181.* A biography of Michał Remigiusz Łaszewski, canon and auxiliary bishop of Warmia from 1709 to 1746. Łaszewski came from a noble family from Pomerania and was educated in Poznan and Rome. As canon under bishops Andrzej Załuski and Teodor Potocki he played a role in attempts to lower taxes levied by Saxon, Russian, and Polish armies during the Northern War. He was the author of *Aristotles ad famam* (1702) and *Columna Excelsa Ecclesiae* (1730). Łaszewski was active in conversions of leading Lutherans to Catholicism and he accompanied his superior, Bishop Krzystof Andrzej Szembek, on diplomatic trips outside the diocese. 1682-1746

LaTour, Henri de

See Bouillon, Duc de

Latreille, André

3823. Dubosc, Guy. ANDRÉ LATREILLE, 1901-1984 [André Latreille (1901-1984)]. *Revue d'Histoire de l'Eglise de France [France] 1984 70(185): 273-275.* A memorial tribute to André Latreille, vice-president of the Ecclesiastical Historical Society of France, who died 25 July 1984. He had been a member of the society since 1936. In that year he had obtained his doctorate with a thesis on "Napoleon and the Holy See (1801-1808)." He taught at the University of Poitiers until the end of World War II when he moved to the University of Lyon, where he occupied the chair of contemporary history until his retirement in 1972. Besides having many articles published on French religious history, he wrote a number of books on the same subject and was the director of a multivolume history of Roman Catholicism in France. He was also the founder of the center for the study of religious history at the University of Lyon, which was later divided into two organizations, one dealing with European religion and the other with foreign missions. After the war he became an assistant to the ministry of the interior, and also a regular columnist in *Le Monde.* 8c-20c

3824. Pacaut, Marcel. ANDRE LATREILLE (1901-1984) [André Latreille (1901-84)]. *Cahiers d'Histoire [France] 1984 29(1): 3-9.* André Latreille founded the publication *Cahiers d'Histoire* in 1956. Professor of modern history at Lyon University from 1945 to 1971, he rejected the narrowing tendencies of particular historical schools and sought to integrate regional, national, and global history with an appropriate balance of attention. 1930's-84

Latzko, Andreas

3825. Szabó, János. AZ ELFELEDETT ANDREAS LATZKO [The forgotten Andreas Latzko]. *Helikon Világirodalmi Figyelő [Hungary] 1984 30(2-4): 302-309.* The Hungarian-born Andreas Latzko (1876-1943), who in 1917 emigrated to Switzerland, was one of the most successful writers in presenting the horrors of war and describing how normal human beings could be and were transformed into monsters. His first book, *Menschen im Krieg* [People in war], was published anonymously in Zurich and had been translated into 19 languages by 1920. It was banned by all the nations involved in World War I. His successive books were also banned by the same governments, even before their publication. His books, written in an honest, straightforward, and highly artistic style, richly deserve the interest of those who are involved in historical research of the Habsburg regime. 6 notes. 1917-30's

Lauder, John

3826. Furgol, Edward M. THE DIARY OF THE REV. JOHN LAUDER OF TYNNINGHAME. *Scottish Historical Review [Great Britain] 1985 64(1): 75-78.* The diary of John Lauder (ca. 1589-1662) is included in the kirk session record of Tynninghame parish, presbytery of Haddington. It is the only known instance of a kirk session record containing the minister's diary. Lauder was a member of the Covenanter clergy in the 1640's and in addition to his parish ministry served three stints as chaplain to the Covenanter armies. Brief mentions of the religious life of the Covenanter armies are made in the diary, which covers the period 1639-52. 20 notes. 1639-52

Lauerma, Matti

3827. Virrankoski, Pentti. MATTI LAUERMA KUUSIKYMMENVUOTIAS [Matti Lauerma 60 years old]. *Turun Hist. Arkisto [Finland] 1982 38: 7-10.* Surveys the scholarly work of Professor Matti Lauerma (b. 1922), a specialist in French and Finnish military history on the faculty of Turku University in Finland. 1922-82

Laurel, José P.

3828. Gripaldo, Rolando M. LAUREL: THE POLITICAL PHILOSOPHER AND THE MAN. *Philippine Studies [Philippines] 1982 30(4): 512-541.* Biography of political philosopher José P. Laurel (1891-1959), during World War II, president of the puppet Philippine Republic. During the war years Laurel "did not compromise his basic political ideas but merely tailored them to the exigencies of the period." 103 notes. 1942-45

Laurian, August Treboniu

3829. Achim, Silviu. AUGUST TREBONIU LAURIAN—A PATRIOT SCHOLAR. *Romania: Pages of History [Romania] 1985 10(2): 106-110.* Tells the story of August Treboniu Laurian—a great Romanian scholar, historian, and linguist; describes his contribution to Romanian independence and the impact of his writings. 1845-70

Laval, Pierre

3830. Chambrun, René de. PIERRE LAVAL [Pierre Laval]. *Revue des Deux Mondes [France] 1985 (2): 391-396.* Publishes an extract from an interview in which the author discussed the liberation of Paris and the actions of Pierre Laval, head of the Vichy Government, who was later condemned to death and executed. 1944

3831. Laborde, Jean. LAVAL: L'HOMME QUI EN SAVAIT TROP [Laval: the man who knew too much]. *Historama [France] 1985 (20): 20-25, 96.* Presents several opinions on the personality and work of Pierre Laval (1883-1945), French government leader and premier of Vichy France, said to have delivered France to Hitler during World War II. 1930-45

Lavallée, Francis

3832. Simon, Nicole. FRANCIS LAVALLEE (1800-1864), VICE-CONSUL DE FRANCIA EN TRINIDAD Y CORRESPONSAL DE LA SOCIEDAD DE GEOGRAFIA [Francis Lavallée (1800-64), vice-consul of France in Trinidad and correspondent of the Geographical Society]. *Revista de la Biblioteca Nacional José Martí [Cuba] 1983[i.e., 1984] 26(2): 81-99.* Francis Lavallée migrated from France to Cuba in 1819 and eventually became the French vice-consul in Trinidad, a Cuban interior city. Supporting himself as a surveyor, Lavallée played a very active role in the study of Cuban geography and helped produce some very important maps of the island. His work was particularly significant in attracting the attention of French geographers to Cuba. Based on archival sources at the French National Library; 38 notes. 1800-64

Laveran, Charles Louis Alphonse

3833. Jarcho, Saul. LAVERAN'S DISCOVERY IN THE RETROSPECT OF A CENTURY. *Bull. of the Hist. of Medicine 1984 58(2): 215-224.* In 1880, Charles Louis Alphonse Laveran (1845-1922) discovered the malarial plasmodium. In 1875, he had written a treatise on military epidemiology, and then on 6 November 1880 at a military hospital in Constantine, Algeria, he discovered the plasmodium of malaria. This was the first of many contributions by which he founded the science of parasitology, and a quarter of a century later, in 1907, he received the Nobel Prize. After having received no recognition from the army, in 1896 he left the military service and was welcomed into the Pasteur Institute, where he established a laboratory of tropical medicine. Based on Laveran's writings and secondary sources; 34 notes. 1875-1907

Lavrenev, Boris

3834. Arkhipenko, V. KOMANDIR "ZARI SVOBODY" [Commander of the *Zaria Svobody*]. *Voenno-Istoricheskii Zhurnal [USSR] 1982 (9): 46-53.* For several decades Boris Lavrenev's play *Razlom* [The break-up] was a popular item in the repertoire of the Soviet theater. The hero is Captain Bersenev, an officer in the Imperial Russian Navy. It is not generally known that Lavrenev based this character on Aleksandr A. Kondrat'ev, a naval officer whom he met in the 1920's. After studying law in St. Petersburg, Kondrat'ev took a naval commission in 1914 and served on the *Tsar Aleksandr II.* He later captained the vessel—which at the time of the Revolution became known as *Zaria Svobody* [dawn of freedom]—and subsequently advanced to commander of the Black Sea Fleet. 3 notes, photo. ca 1910-30

Lavrov, Petr

3835. Itenberg, B. S. LAVROV I "NARODNAIA VOLIA" [Lavrov and the People's Will]. *Istoricheskie Zapiski Akademii Nauk SSSR [USSR] 1984 (110): 196-231.* In 1870, Petr Lavrov was exiled to Paris and lived there for the rest of his life. Even away from his Russian homeland, Lavrov continued to fight for freedom of the people, playing a significant role in the People's Will movement. He became one of the kindest critics of his colleagues' work, publicizing their activities from abroad. 121 notes. 1870-1900

Lawless, Emily

3836. Brewer, Betty Webb. "Emily Lawless: An Irish Writer above All Else." U. of North Carolina, Chapel Hill 1982. 311 pp. *DAI 1983 43(11): 3600-A.* DA8308283 1880's-90's

Lawrence, D. H.

3837. Boulton, James T. D. H. LAWRENCE: LETTER-WRITER. *Renaissance and Modern Studies [Great Britain] 1985 29: 86-100.* A critical assessment of the letters written by D. H. Lawrence (1885-1930), ca. 1910-30, which included correspondence with Lady Cynthia Asquith, Edward Garnett, Bertrand Russell, and Aldous Huxley. ca 1910-30

3838. Kalnins, Mara. "TERRA INCOGNITA": LAWRENCE'S TRAVEL WRITINGS. *Renaissance and Modern Studies [Great Britain] 1985 29: 66-77.* D. H. Lawrence (1885-1930) in his travel writings, ca. 1912-27, not only chronicled his journeys to Europe, the Far East, Australia, and Mexico, but also revealed his fascination for human psychology and his profound and searching criticism of the contemporary technological age and its effect on the quality of human existence. ca 1912-27

3839. Owen, Frederick D. D. H. LAWRENCE'S ITALY: ALLUREMENTS AND CHANGES. *Contemporary Review [Great Britain] 1985 247(1438): 261-268.* During the period 1912-14 and for over five years during the 1920's the English novelist D. H. Lawrence resided in Italy, which "had the profoundest and most abiding effect on his life and writings." 1912-14

3840. Pugh, Bridget. LAWRENCE AND INDUSTRIAL SYMBOLISM. *Renaissance and Modern Studies [Great Britain] 1985 29: 33-49.* Describes the construction of the industrial landscape of late 19th- and early 20th-century Britain in the work of D. H. Lawrence (1885-1930). Particular attention is paid to Lawrence's historical perspective, his emphasis on the ills brought about by industrialization, his selectivity with regard to those aspects of industry he chose to represent, and the absence of any serious political matter. 1890's-1930

3841. Rota, Anthony. D. H. LAWRENCE. THE GEORGE LAZARUS COLLECTION OF BOOKS AND MANUSCRIPTS. *Renaissance and Modern Studies [Great Britain] 1985 29: 101-119.* Describes the George Lazarus collection of books and manuscripts by and about D. H. Lawrence and traces the origins of and background to this collection from the mid-1920's to 1980. The collection includes D. H. Lawrence's books, manuscripts, and letters as well as books and other material about Lawrence and foreign language editions of Lawrence's work. ca 1925-80

3842. Treacy, Carol Ferrara. "Art and the Artist in D. H. Lawrence." U. of South Carolina 1983. 269 pp. *DAI 1983 44(4): 1095-A.* DA8319304 1911-29

3843. Worthen, John. SHORT STORY AND AUTOBIOGRAPHY: KINDS OF DETACHMENT IN D. H. LAWRENCE'S EARLY FICTION. *Renaissance and Modern Studies [Great Britain] 1985 29: 1-15.* Discusses the autobiographical nature of many of the British writer D. H. Lawrence's (1885-1930) short stories written between 1907 and 1914, and suggests that the short stories which appeared in both the 1914 collection *The Prussian Officer* and the posthumous collection published in 1934 were chosen in a random fashion. 1907-34

Lawrence, T. E.

3844. Decaux, Alain. LAWRENCE, LE HEROS MASOCHISTE [Lawrence: the masochist hero]. *Historama [France] 1984 (1): 24-35.* English archaeologist, military officer, and writer T. E. Lawrence (1888-1935) identified himself with the Arab people, supporting their revolts, but, as a British agent, never betrayed his country's interests. He died in a motorcycle accident after self-imposed obscurity in his later life, part of which he spent as an enlisted man under the name of Shaw. 1911-35

3845. Reid, Brian Holden. LAWRENCE AND THE ARAB REVOLT. *History Today [Great Britain] 1985 35(May): 41-45.* Considers the legends surrounding the role of T. E. Lawrence (1888-1935) in influencing the Arab revolt against the Turks, 1916-18. Lawrence's efforts demonstrated that he was a shrewd diplomat and a clever military strategist. 1916-19

3846. Tames, Richard. LAWRENCE OF ARABIA. *British Heritage 1985 6(5): 24-33.* Sketches the career of T. E. Lawrence (1888-1935), archeologist, British secret agent, guerrilla leader, political adviser to Arab rulers, and author. 1911-35

Lawson, John

3847. Edwards, A. S. G. LAWSON'S *ORCHET*. *Transactions of the Cambridge Bibliographical Society [Great Britain] 1984 8(4): 477-488.* Two manuscripts of John Lawson's *Orchet*, one dated 1581, the other undated, shed light on Lawson's life and work. He was a feodary of the Court of Wards and indefatigable versifier, and the *Orchet* is an attempted versification of Fabyan's chronicle of English history from the earliest times to Henry VIII. Much about Lawson remains obscure, and "it is possible to feel that neither Elizabethan poetry nor Lawson himself are well served by disturbing the neglect of centuries." Based on manuscripts in the British Library, and the Pepys Library, Magdalene College, Cambridge; illus., 28 notes. 16c

Layard, Austen Henry

3848. Swails, John Washington, III. "Austen Henry Layard and the Near East, 1839-1880." U. of Georgia 1983. 268 pp. *DAI 1983 44(2): 550-A.* DA8314749 1839-80

Layman, C. H.

3849. Layman, C. H. DUTY IN BOMB ALLEY. *US Naval Inst. Pro. 1983 109(8): 35-40.* Recounts his experiences as commander of the frigate *Argonaut* during the Falklands campaign. 1982

Lazar' family

3850. Cherniavskaia, T. A. K ISTORII VOZNIKNOVENIIA KAPITALOV I GORNOZAVODSKOGO KHOZIAISTVA LAZAREVYKH [On the capital formation and the mining and metallurgical interests of the Lazar' family]. *Istoricheskie Zapiski Akad. Nauk SSSR [USSR] 1980 (105): 273-279.* 1450-1800

For abstract see ***Stroganov, Grigori***

Lazare, Bernard

3851. Garner, Reuben. BERNARD LAZARE. *Midstream 1986 32(6): 24-26.* Through his writings, Bernard Lazare (1865-1903) helped develop Jewish national consciousness in France by taking uncompromising positions against a rising tide of anti-Semitism and against the complacency of middle-class Jews themselves. 1890-1903

Le Duan

3852. Nikitin, A. S. STOIKII MARKSIST-LENINETS (K 75-LETIIU SO DNIA ROZHDENIIA GENERAL'NOGO SEKRETARIA TSK KPV LE ZUANA) [A steadfast Marxist-Leninist: on the 75th anniversary of the birthday of the General Secretary of the Communist Party of Vietnam, Le Duan]. *Voprosy Istorii KPSS [USSR] 1982 (4): 108-111.* Le Duan, born 7 April 1907, was the right-hand man of Ho Chi Minh. He learned the love of work from his carpenter father and of study from his mother. During his youth, Vietnam was swept by the antimonarchist movement. He joined the Communist Party in 1930, and in 1931 was imprisoned for a 20-year term by the colonial power. He was released in 1936 and continued revolutionary work. He was elected a member of the Party's permanent committee in 1939. The Democratic Republic of Vietnam was proclaimed 2 September 1945, and liberation wars were fought against France and the United States. China's betrayal is described. Le Duan was present at all the struggles and victories of Vietnam. He became a member of the Politburo in 1951 and General Secretary of the Party in 1976. He is an optimist, ardent Marxist-Leninist, patriot, internationalist, and friend of the USSR. Based on the collected works of Le Duan and Soviet sources; 19 notes. 1907-82

Lead, Jane Ward

3853. Sperle, Joanne Magnani. "God's Healing Angel: A Biography of Jane Ward Lead." Kent State U. 1985. 282 pp. *DAI 1985 46(5): 1289-A.* DA8514183 1640's-1704

Leander, Folke

3854. Ryn, Claes G. NON VIDERI SED ESSE: FOLKE LEANDER (1910-1981). *Modern Age 1983 27(1): 56-60.* An obituary of Swedish philosopher and educator Folke Leander (1910-81). Includes an account of his embracing American new humanism. 16 notes. 1930's-81

Leavis, F. R.

3855. Jacobson, Dan. F. R. LEAVIS. *American Scholar 1985 54(2): 221-226.* Explores the idiosyncratic personality of F. R. Leavis, expressing surprise that so little has been written of this man who was so influential among his 20th-century students who became well known poets, critics, reviewers, novelists, teachers, editors, and drama producers. 1930's-70's

Lebaudy, Jacques

3856. Croix, Robert de la. LE REVE INSENSE DE JACQUES IER LEBAUDY, "EMPEREUR DU SAHARA" [The mad dream of Jacques Lebaudy I, "Emperor of the Sahara"]. *Hist. Mag. [France] 1983 (40): 62-66.* Focuses on the quixotic attempt by wealthy Frenchman Jacques Lebaudy to establish an empire in the Sahara during the early 20th century. 1903-19

Lebed', D. Z.

3857. Levin, V. S. 90-RICHCHIA Z DNIA NARODZHENNIA D. Z. LEBEDIA [The 90th birthday anniversary of D. Z. Lebed']. *Ukrains'kyi Istorychnyi Zhurnal [USSR] 1983 (2): 130-133.* Brief biographical sketch on D. Z. Lebed' (1893-1937), one of the early Bolshevik leaders in the Dnieper region. He was influential in persuading the Dnieper railmen to support the Bolshevik cause. He contributed regularly to the Bolshevik paper *Pravda,* reporting mainly on the revolutionary fervor of Yekaterinoslav railroad workers. In his capacity as Second Secretary of the Ukraine Communist Party Central Committee, he opposed the development of Ukrainian culture in 1923, which he regarded as backward and rural. This was a great mistake on his part. Secondary sources, 7 notes. ca 1910-37

Lebedev, Aleksei

3858. Flerov, Nikolai. ALEKSEI LEBEDEV, MORIAK I POET [Aleksei Lebedev, sailor and poet]. *Morskoi Sbornik [USSR] 1982 (8): 93-95.* Describes the life and works of Aleksei Lebedev, a Marxist poet imbued with a love of the sea, the Motherland, the Communist Party, and the Leninist Communist Youth League. Based on memoirs and Lebedev's works. ca 1930-41

Leber, Julius

3859. Beck, Dorothea. THEODOR HAUBACH, JULIUS LEBER, CARLO MIERENDORFF, KURT SCHUMACHER: ZUM SELBSTVERSTÄNDNIS DER "MILITANTEN SOZIALISTEN" IN DER WEIMARER REPUBLIK [Theodor Haubach, Julius Leber, Carlo Mierendorff, Kurt Schumacher: toward an understanding of the "militant socialists" in the Weimar Republic]. *Archiv für Sozialgeschichte [West Germany] 1986 26: 87-123.* 1919-33
For abstract see ***Haubach, Theodor***

Lebret, Louis-Joseph

3860. Poulat, Émile and Bouteloupt, Colette. UN NOUVEAU FONDS D'ARCHIVES: LES PAPIERS DU PERE LEBRET [A new archival source: the papers of Father Lebret]. *Revue d'Histoire Ecclésiastique [Belgium] 1983 78(2): 468-472.* Provisional catalog of the papers of Louis-Joseph Lebret (1897-1966), naval officer and from 1922 Dominican religious, deposited in the Archives Nationales in 1982. As a social activist, his career and thought are essential to tracing the radicalization of the Christian social conscience in France. Notes the centers, institutions, and journal he founded, his career in the Centre National de la Recherche Scientifique, and his role in helping prepare the influential papal social encyclical *Populorum Progressio.* Archives Nationales, Paris. 20c

Lecha Vilasuso, Augusto

3861. Ackley, C. S. THE SPANISH SEVERSKY. *Am. Aviation Hist. Soc. J. 1981 26(1): 60-67.* 1920's-39
For abstract see ***Seversky, Alexander Procofieff de***

Leclerc, Jacques Philippe

3862. Repiton-Préneuf, Colonel. LECLERC EN INDOCHINE [Leclerc in Indochina]. *Rev. Hist. des Armées [France] 1982 (4): 30-46.* After the Japanese surrender in 1945, General Jacques Philippe Leclerc, Vicomte de Hauteclocque (1902-47) was appointed commander of French ground forces in Indochina with the mission of reestablishing French control. Since the Yalta agreements provided for the British to take over from the Japanese south of the 16th parallel and the Chinese to do likewise north of it, Leclerc worked with the former after he arrived in Saigon and received British assistance in his operations against the Vietminh forces. After returning the south to some degree of normality, Leclerc brought troops to Haiphong and negotiated with the Chinese for their withdrawal and with Ho Chi Minh (1890-1969) for the incorporation of Tonkin into the new French Union. Based on the rough draft of Leclerc's report; illus., 11 photos, 4 notes. 1945-46

3863. Vincent, Jean-Noël. KOUFRA 23 DECEMBRE 1940-1ER MAI 1941 [Al-Kufrah 23 December 1940-1 May 1941]. *Rev. Hist. des Armées [France] 1982 (4): 4-19.* At Fort Lamy, Chad, Colonel Jacques Philippe Leclerc (1902-47) prepared to attack the Italian post at Al-Kufrah in southeastern Libya. He organized a force consisting of one small battalion, a transportation company, and a detachment of the British Long Range Desert Group (LRDG). After leaving Ounianga, his initial operational base, his force began to come under attack by the Italians and the LRDG detachment had to be relieved. At Al-Kufrah, a night reconnaissance turned into a successful raid on the airfield, followed several days later by an attack that destroyed the Italian motorized company. Leclerc's final operation was the siege of the fort, which surrendered after nine days. The 29 Italians in the garrison became prisoners of war and 273 Libyans were sent home. Based on archives of the Army Historical Section; 5 photos, 2 maps, 52 notes, 2 appendixes. 1940-41

3864. —. DOCUMENTS. [Documents]. *Rev. Hist. des Armées [France] 1982 (4): 108-113.* The three previously unpublished documents are a letter from Colonel Jacques Philippe Leclerc (1902-47) to a friend in North Africa, a request from the Italian commander at Fort El-Tag requesting help for his wounded, and the rough draft of Leclerc's liberation proclamation to the people of Strasbourg, all three in photostatic copies and in print. 1941

Leclerc de Hauteclocque, Henri

3865. Massu, Jacques. LE LIEUTENANT HENRI LECLERC DE HAUTECLOCQUE [Lieutenant Henri Leclerc de Hauteclocque]. *Rev. Hist. des Armées [France] 1982 (4): 47-51.* Henri François Leclerc de Hauteclocque (1926-52) joined the resistance at the age of 17, then enlisted in the Colonial Infantry and fought with the 2d Armored Division in Alsace. Commissioned a second lieutenant in 1945, he was sent to Indochina and in 1947 was transferred to Chad. Later he spent a year in the Department of Defense in Paris, after which he requested assignment to Indochina; there he became a company commander and was killed in action at Trung-Khu a year later. Illus., map. 1942-52

LeCorbusier

3866. Khait, V. L. SOTSIAL'NO-UTOPICHESKIE TENDENTSII V ARKHITEKTURNOM SOZNANII ZAPADA XX VEKA [Utopian social tendencies in the 20th-century architectural consciousness of the West]. *Voprosy Filosofii [USSR] 1982 (6): 124-131.* 1920's-70's
For abstract see ***Gropius, Walter Adolph***

Lecuona, Ernesto

3867. Jacobson, Gloria Castiel. "The Life and Music of Ernesto Lecuona." U. of Florida 1982. 205 pp. *DAI 1983 43(9): 2920-A.* DA8302247 1930-65

Ledebour, Georg

3868. Keller, Elke. EIN ALTER SOZIALISTISCHER HAUDEGEN. GEORG LEDEBOUR [An old socialist fighter: Georg Ledebour]. *Beiträge zur Geschichte der Arbeiterbewegung [East Germany] 1984 26(4): 512-521.* Prints a biography of Georg Ledebour (1850-1947), editor and publisher of socialist periodicals and newspapers in Germany. Traces his involvement in Communist parties and movements and his devotion to the example of the Russian Revolution and the USSR. He spent World War II in exile in the USSR and the Balkans. He died in Switzerland. 51 notes. 1882-1947

Ledo, Joaquim Gonçalves

3869. Ipanema, Marcello de and Ipanema, Cybelle de. BICENTENARIO DE JOAQUIM GONÇALVES LEDO [Bicentenary of Joaquim Gonçalves Ledo]. *Rev. do Inst. Hist. e Geog. Brasileiro [Brazil] 1982 (334): 79-93.* Notes the bicentennial of the birth of Ledo, one of the most important figures in Brazil's independence movement, and notes some of the works being published that relate his life and achievements. The article briefly outlines Ledo's career, the offices he held, and his main accomplishments, especially his journalism in Rio de Janeiro, which helped pave the way for independence. The role of his newspaper, the *Echo*, is described in detail, including brief excerpts from his editorials. Brazilian archives materials and secondary sources; 35 notes. 1781-1846

Lee, Alan

3870. Mason, Tony. ALAN LEE. *Bull. of the Soc. for the Study of Labour Hist. [Great Britain] 1981 (43): 3.* An obituary for Alan Lee (d. 1981), a British historian, who was an authority on the history of British newspapers and whose general interest was 19th- and 20th-century British history. 1950's-81

Lee, Bruce

3871. Chiao, Hsiung-Ping. BRUCE LEE: HIS INFLUENCE ON THE EVOLUTION OF THE KUNG FU GENRE. *J. of Popular Film and Television 1981 9(1): 30-42.* Briefly traces the movie career of Chinese superstar and social phenomenon Bruce Lee (d. 1973), and focuses on his mastery of Kung Fu and his influence on US and other films of the Kung Fu genre during the 1970's. 1970-79

Lee, Richard

3872. Frow, Edmund and Frow, Ruth. CHARLES PIGOTT AND RICHARD LEE: RADICAL PROPAGANDISTS. *Bull. of the Soc. for the Study of Labour Hist. [Great Britain] 1981 (42): 32-35.* Examines the careers of these two lesser-known English radicals and pamphleteers of the 1790's and provides a bibliography of their works. 1790's

Leese, Arnold

3873. Morell, John. ARNOLD LEESE AND THE IMPERIAL FASCIST LEAGUE: THE IMPACT OF RACIAL FASCISM. Lunn, Kenneth and Thurlow, Richard C., ed. *British Fascism: Essays on the Radical Right in Inter-War Britain* (New York: St. Martin's Pr., 1980): 57-75. Discusses the ideology and career of Arnold Leese, prominent British anti-Semite, racial theorist, and founder of the Imperial Fascist League in the 1920's. 1924-47

LeFanu, Joseph Sheridan

3874. Hall, Wayne. LE FANU'S HOUSE BY THE MARKETPLACE. *Éire-Ireland 1986 21(1): 55-72.* Discusses Joseph Sheridan Le Fanu's years as editor of the *Dublin University Magazine*, 1861-69. Le Fanu's faltering financial circumstances were reflected both in the quality of his novels, serialized in the journal, which went from inspired to apathetic, and in the political opinions expressed in the journal, which began optimistically but by the end of Le Fanu's tenure had lapsed into a conservative despair over the Fenian movement. Based on correspondence and contemporary newspaper accounts; 16 notes. 1834-69

Lefebvre, Marcel

3875. Boisdeffre, Pierre de. L'HONORABLE RESISTANCE DE MONSEIGNEUR LEFEBVRE [The honorable resistance of Cardinal Lefebvre]. *Revue des Deux Mondes [France] 1985 (9): 643-652, (10): 70-79.* Part 1. Traces the life of French Cardinal Marcel Lefebvre, born in 1905 and ordained in 1929, and discusses his conservative interpretation of Catholicism, which led him to resist the liberal reforms introduced by Vatican II in 1962. Part 2. Describes Marcel Lefebvre's rebellion against the liberalism and modernism introduced into the Catholic Church by Popes John XXIII and Paul VI and his suspension from the Church in 1976 because of sharp criticism of the Vatican coming from his conservative Catholic seminary at Ecône. 1929-83

Lefebvre, Raymond

3876. Broue, Pierre. UN "BOLCHEVISTE" EN CURE À ALLEVARD [A "Bolshevist" in Allevard]. *Cahiers d'Hist. [France] 1980 25(3-4): 361-370.* Examines the career of radical cleric Raymond Lefebvre with particular attention to his activities in Allevard in 1919 and the reactions of the authorities to his presence there. Based on printed sources and departmental archives; prints the texts of 4 police reports on Lefebvre's activities, July-September, 1919; 7 notes. 1919

Leffler, Anne Charlotte

3877. Shogren, Melissa Lowe. "The Search for Self-Fulfillment: The Life and Writings of Anne Charlotte Leffler." U. of Washington 1984. *DAI 1986 46(8): 2307-A.* 1870's-92

Léger, Fernand

3878. Fabre, Gladys C. and Briot, Marie-Odile. AU MUSEE RATH APRES PARIS ET HOUSTON: LEGER ET L'ESPRIT MODERNE (1918-1931) [The Rath Museum after Paris and Houston: Léger and modern art, 1918-31]. *Mus. de Genève [Switzerland] 1982 (230): 13-16.* Discusses Fernand Léger's purist aesthetics and his pictorial representation of the technological innovations of the early 20th century. 1918-31

Lehl, Pauline Schlegel

3879. Lehl, Pauline et al. LETTERS TO PAULINE. *Journal of the American Historical Society of Germans from Russia 1985 8(4): 26-40.* Prints translations of an autobiographical statement by Pauline Schlegel Lehl (d. 1981). Lehl immigrated from German Russia to Oklahoma in 1913. Also prints letters written to her by relatives in Mikhaylovka, Sebryakovo, and Batumi, Russia between 1914 and 1931, describing the experiences of family and friends during the February 1917 revolution, the famine of the 1920's, and the first Five Year Plan. 1914-31

Lehmann, Rosamond

3880. Richardi, Janis Marie. "The Modern British *Bildungsroman* and the Woman Novelist: Dorothy Richardson, May Sinclair, Rosamond Lehmann, Elizabeth Bowen, and Doris Lessing." U. of North Carolina, Chapel Hill 1981. 245 pp. *DAI 1982 42(8): 3612-A.* 8200609 20c

3881. Siegel, Ruth. "Rosamond Lehmann: A Thirties Writer." Columbia U. 1985. 317 pp. *DAI 1986 46(8): 2303-A.* DA8523239 1930's

Leibniz, Gottfried von

3882. Wilson, Catherine. LEIBNIZ AND ATOMISM. *Studies in Hist. and Phil. of Sci. [Great Britain] 1982 13(3): 175-199.* A new account that examines the conceptual and religious difficulties of 17th-century atomic theory explains Leibniz's early acceptance of it in 1666 and his later rejection of it for a metaphysical explanation of the constituents of matter. 1666-95

Lejiņš, Paulis

3883. Valeskalns, P. P. IA. LEIN'SH—PERVYI PREZIDENT AKADEMII NAUK LATVIISKOI SSR: K STOLETIIU SO DNIA ROZHDENIIA [Paulis Lejiņš, the first president of the Latvian SSR Academy of Sciences: commemorating the 100th anniversary of his birth]. *Latvijas PSR Zinātņu Akad. Vēstis [USSR] 1983 (2): 115-116.* Commemorates the hundredth anniversary of the birth of the zoologist Paulis Lejiņš (1883-1959), professor of the University of Latvia and the Agricultural Academy of Latvia, who later became the first president of the Academy of Sciences of the Latvian SSR and the organizer of the Institute of Zootechnics and Zoohygiene of the Academy. Photo. 1940's-59

Leleux, Pierre Antoine

3884. Verna, Paul. PEDRO ANTONIO LELEUX: EL FRANCES EDECAN, SECRETARIO Y AMIGO DE CONFIANZA DE MIRANDA Y BOLIVAR [Pierre Antoine Leleux: French aide-de-camp, secretary, and confidential friend of Miranda and Bolívar]. *Bol. de la Acad. Nac. de la Hist. [Venezuela] 1982 65(257): 113-130.* Leleux (1781-1849) was born in Calais, France, and was working in a bookstore in London when he met the precursor of Spanish American independence, Francisco de Miranda. Subsequently he was aide-de-camp, secretary, and friend of both Miranda and Simón Bolívar. 1802-49

Lelewel, Joachim

3885. Sós, István. JOACHIM LELEWEL (1786-1861) [Joachim Lelewel (1786-1861)]. *Világtörténet [Hungary] 1979 (3): 88-105.* Polish historiographer Joachim Lelewel was deeply involved in questions of methodology. During the 1830's and 1840's, he lived in exile in France. In 1835, he published a monograph on medieval numismatics. Biblio., fig. 1820-61

Leliushenko, D. D.

3886. Rotmistrov, P. GENERAL ARMII D. D. LELIUSHENKO (K 80 LETIIU SO DNIA ROZHDENIIA) [General D. D. Leliushenko: on his 80th birthday]. *Voenno-Istoricheskii Zhurnal [USSR] 1981 23(10): 91-94.* Briefly outlines the military career of Soviet General D. D. Leliushenko (b. 1901). Leliushenko joined the Red Army in 1919 and fought in the Civil War. He saw action in Poland and Finland at the start of World War II. Leliushenko was an expert on armored forces, and in this capacity took part in a three-power conference in Moscow in September 1941. In October of that year he was put in charge of the 5th Army and later the 30th Army and played a major role in the defense of Moscow. After Stalingrad he took command of the 4th Tank Army and participated in the liberation of Silesia, Berlin, and Prague. He remained in uniform after the war, becoming a Ministry of Defense inspector in 1964. Among the many honors and medals he has received are four Orders of Lenin. Photo, 2 notes. 1901-80

Lenin, V. I.

3887. Antoniuk, D. I. ILIA NIKOLAEVICH ULIANOV [Ilia N. Ulianov]. *Voprosy Istorii KPSS [USSR] 1981 (7): 97-100.* 1831-86

*For abstract see **Ul'ianov, Il'ia N.***

3888. Bobrova, E. K. SOVMESTNYE DOKUMENTY V. I. LENINA I N. K. KRUPSKOI [Joint documents of V. I. Lenin and Nadezhda Krupskaya]. *Vestnik Leningradskogo U.: Seriia Istorii, Iazyka i Literatury [USSR] 1981 (3): 5-14.* 1900-24

*For abstract see **Krupskaya, Nadezhda***

3889. Bordukov, V. A. and Kobylianski, K. V. V. I. LENIN I REVOLIUTSIONNOE RABOCHEE DVIZHENIE V ITALII [V. I. Lenin and the revolutionary workers' movement of Italy]. *Voprosy Istorii [USSR] 1981 (7): 42-58.* Describes Lenin's role in the development of the Italian workers' movement, in strengthening the revolutionary forces within the Italian Socialist Party and, after the founding of the Italian Communist Party, in overcoming sectarianism, and making the Party the vanguard of the Italian working people. Also shows the impact of the October Revolution on the struggle of the Italian working people, the differentiation process, and the emergence of a revolutionary trend within the Italian Socialist Party. 1912-22

3890. Borodin, E. I. NOVYI FAKT BIOGRAFII V. I. LENINA [New detail for the biography of V. I. Lenin]. *Voprosy Istorii KPSS [USSR] 1984 (11): 120-124.* As indicated by the French newspaper *L'Humanité* of the time and memoirs of T. S. Krivov, published in *Ogonëk* 1956 (17): 7, the 1910 Paris celebration of the 70th birthday of the German Social Democrat August Bebel (1840-1911) was attended by V. I. Lenin, Russian, German, and Polish socialists gathered together, and Lenin delivered a speech praising Bebel's relentless pursuit of revolutionary goals and the ruthlessness of his struggle with opportunists in the German Social Democratic Party. Lenin's acquaintance with Bebel, originated by their correspondence of 1905, began at the 1907 Congress of the 2d International. Secondary sources; 25 notes. 1910

3891. Borodin, E. I. NOVYE SVEDENIIA O PREBYVANII V. I. LENINA V BRIUSSELE V 1909 G. [New evidence on V. I. Lenin's stay in Brussels in 1909]. *Voprosy Istorii KPSS [USSR] 1985 (8): 127-129.* Quotes a new source on Lenin's activities during his visit to Brussels, 23-26 October 1909, where he addressed a meeting of socialist journalists at the conference of the Second International. A letter from Vladimir E. Minakov to G. Chicherin reveals that Lenin also addressed two meetings of Russian, Polish, and Latvian political emigrés on 23 and 24 October. According to Minakov's letter, the only source on this subject, the address dealt with the ideology of counterrevolutionary liberalism. Based on sources from the Central Party Archive of the Institute of Marxism-Leninism; 23 notes. 1909

3892. Dalin, V. M. LENIN I OBRAZOVANIE FRANTSUZSKOI KOMPARTII [Lenin and the formation of the Communist Party of France]. *Frantsuzskii Ezhegodnik [USSR] 1980: 5-24.* V. I. Lenin took a particular interest in the formation of the French Communist Party and the development of revolutionary socialism in France. He was familiar with many of the political activists of France and he followed such political and social phenomena as the Dreyfus Affair with great interest, particularly from 1908 to 1912, when he lived in Paris. Lenin supported the faction of Jules Guesde in the Communist movement, although the two never met, in contrast to Karl Kautsky, the German Communist leader, who leaned toward Millerand. Rosa Luxemburg supported Lenin in this regard. Documentary evidence of Lenin's support of Guesde is presented, dating from the Congress of the Second International at Stuttgart in 1907 through the Fourth Congress of the Comintern in 1922. 85 notes. French summary. 1901-23

3893. Deich, G. M. EPISTOLIARNOE NASLEDIE V. I. LENINA I NEKOTORYE VOPROSY EVRISTIKI [The epistolary legacy of V. I. Lenin and some questions of heuristics]. *Voprosy Istorii KPSS [USSR] 1982 (4): 121-123.* G. D. Obichkin and M. Ia. Pankratova's *Letters of Vladimir Il'ich Lenin* are an important work examining Lenin's letters in the context of his writings. But in general not enough attention has been paid to his letters, which illuminate his ideas. Only seven letters to Nedezhda Krupskaya survive. Many were perhaps destroyed, such as those to N. Konstatinova, who burned Lenin's letters to her as a security measure. Of Krupskaya's letters to Lenin we know even less. Between Lenin and Maksim Gorky 54 letters survive, but the earliest is dated 1907, and we know that Lenin wrote to Gorky in 1905. We must also suppose that he wrote more letters to his family than we now possess. Much correspondence from Lenin's Pskov period has been lost. It is a rich field for research. Based on Lenin's collected works; 11 notes. 1905-24

3894. Fichtner, Emilija. NEUE ZEUGNISSE ÜBER LENINS LEITUNGSSTIL NACH DOKUMENTEN DES LENIN-SAMMELBANDES XXXIX [New evidence concerning Lenin's style of leadership from documents in Lenin's *Collected Works,* Vol. 39]. *Beiträge zur Gesch. der Arbeiterbewegung [East Germany] 1981 23(5): 696-701.* Examines new material which provides insights into V. I. Lenin's style of leadership as both Party leader and head of government, 1918-21. The author pays particular attention to the importance which Lenin attached to the idea of collective leadership. Based on Lenin's letters and secondary sources; 31 notes. 1918-21

3895. Gharibjanian, G. B. V. I. LENINI HAY ZINAKITSNĒRN U ASHAKĒRTNĒRĒ [V. I. Lenin's Armenian comrades-in-arms and disciples]. *Patma-Banasirakan Handes. Istoriko-Filologicheskii Zhurnal [USSR] 1980 (1): 13-20.* ca 1890-1917

For abstract see ***Avanesov***

3896. Haas, Leonard. NUEVOS CONOCIMIENTOS SOBRE LOS ANTEPASADOS DE LENIN [New knowledge about Lenin's ancestors]. *Folia Humanistica [Spain] 1982 20(232): 315-318.* Traces relatives of V. I. Lenin (Vladimir Il'ich Ul'ianov) through his father Il'ia Nikolaevich Ul'ianov (1831-86), and his mother Mariia Aleksandrovna Blank (1835-1916). 1605-1924

3897. Heller, Michel. KRASIN-SAVINKOV: UNE RENCONTRE SECRETE [Krasin-Savinkov: a secret encounter]. *Cahiers du Monde Russe et Soviétique [France] 1985 26(1): 63-67.* A letter of Boris Savinkov to Marshal Józef Piłsudski, which had remained unknown to historians until now, speaks of a secret encounter in London in December 1921 between Leonid B. Krasin, the representative of the Soviet Republic, and the very active enemy of Soviet power, Boris Savinkov. This letter throws new light on certain important aspects of V. I. Lenin's foreign policy, including the use he made of disinformation as an instrument of diplomacy. 1921

3898. Hertzfeldt, Renate. BRIEFE UND NOTIZEN W. I. LENINS FÜR G. W. TSCHITSCHERIN [V. I. Lenin's letters and notes to G. V. Chicherin]. *Beiträge zur Gesch. der Arbeiterbewegung [East Germany] 1981 23(4): 543-548.* Reproduces nine letters and notes written by Lenin between 1918 and 1921 to G. V. Chicherin, People's Commissioner for Foreign Affairs. They reflect the struggle of the new Soviet state for favorable external conditions for socialist reconstruction and provide new details concerning the search for a concrete outcome to the realization of the Soviet Republic's policies of peaceful coexistence and international solidarity. Based on Lenin's documents in the Institute for Marxism-Leninism, Moscow; 20 notes. 1918-21

3899. Iroshnikov, M. P. LENIN VEDET ZASEDANIE [Lenin conducts a session]. *Voprosy Istorii [USSR] 1981 (3): 91-101.* There has been little study of Lenin's method of conducting meetings; from 1917-21 he presided over more than 600, dealing with every aspect of Soviet affairs. His approach was characterized by precise and systematic attention to detail. Lenin's instructions led to the constant improvement in efficiency of the government apparatus; he demanded punctuality, brevity, and discipline. Thoroughly acquainted with all areas of government, Lenin participated actively in discussions and encouraged others to do so, insisting on collective decisions. 65 notes. 1917-22

3900. Jena, Detlef. ZUM BRIEFWECHSEL ZWISCHEN LENIN UND PLECHANOW (1900-1913) [The correspondence between V. I. Lenin and Georgi Plekhanov, 1900-13]. *Beiträge zur Gesch. der Arbeiterbewegung [East Germany] 1981 23(6): 892-904.* Examines the correspondence between Lenin and the Russian political philosopher Georgi Plekhanov (1857-1918), 1900-13. The letters provide insights into the evolution of Leninism, the struggle for the new style party, and differences with those displaying revisionist tendencies. In addition they help to trace the political biography of both Lenin and Plekhanov, as well as revealing Lenin's methodological approach to the evaluation of Plekhanov's total personality. Based on letters published in Lenin's complete works; 39 notes. 1900-13

3901. Kalashnikov, V. V. LENINSKAIA PROGRAMMA PROLETARSKOI REVOLIUTSII V ROSSII (O RABOTE V. I. LENINA "MATERIALY PO PERESMOTRU PARTIINOI PROGRAMMY") [Lenin's program of proletarian revolution in Russia: on V. I. Lenin's *Materials for the Review of the Party Program*]. *Vestnik Leningradskogo U.: Seriia Istorii, Iazyka i Literatury [USSR] 1982 (3): 5-12.* The Bolshevik Party's draft program, written by Lenin in Spring 1917, showed Lenin's approach to the Party's program, his concept of the proletarian revolution in Russia, and his conviction that socialism was the inevitable, objective result of capitalism's development. Bourgeois critics accuse Lenin of demogogic behavior for entering the revolution with certain generally democratic aims. This is nonsense, as the general aims were designed to gain the support of the masses prior to the installation of the dictatorship of the proletariat. Lenin, an excellent tactician and strategist, realized that the building of socialism in Russia would require intermediate stages. Based on Lenin's works and Party documents; 13 notes. 1917

3902. Ketola, Eino. V. I. LENININ PIILESKELY SUOMESSA 1917: AJOITUSKYSYMYKSIÄ [V. I. Lenin's time in hiding in Finland, 1917: questions of dates]. *Historiallinen Aikakauskirja [Finland] 1985 83(4): 259-267.* Establishes dates for the last illegal stay of V. I. Lenin in Finland during 1917. He arrived in Finnish Karelia on 12 August, moved to Helsinki on 21 August and to Viipuri on 6 October, returning to St. Petersburg on 20 October. Based on interviews and private papers in Finnish archives and publications in Russian and Finnish; 87 notes. 1917

3903. Khudaverdian, K. S. V. I. LĒNINĒ ĒV KULTURAKAN HĒGHAPOKHUTYUNĒ SSHM-UM [V. I. Lenin and the cultural revolution in the USSR]. *Patma-Banasirakan Handes. Istoriko-Filologicheskii Zhurnal [USSR] 1980 (1): 3-12.* Lenin greatly contributed to the development of Marxist cultural theory. He stressed particularly the interdependence of the socioeconomic and cultural problems. The democratization of culture and the resulting rise in the level of education alone could bring about the high productivity that was essential for victory over capitalism. But culture was a continuous process and the proletariat should build on, and not reject, the culture of past generations. Secondary sources; 17 notes. 1920's

3904. Kipp, Jacob W. LENIN AND CLAUSEWITZ: THE MILITARIZATION OF MARXISM, 1914-1921. *Military Affairs 1985 49(4): 184-191.* 1914-21
For abstract see ***Clausewitz, Karl von***

3905. Klevanskij, A. V. I. LENIN A BOJ ZA VYTVOŘENÍ KOMUNISTICKÉ STRANY ČESKOSLOVENSKA [Lenin and the struggle for the creation of the Communist Party in Czechoslovakia]. *Slovanský Přehled [Czechoslovakia] 1981 67(2): 97-116.* In the struggle for the creation of the Communist Party Bohumil Šmeral, one of the major founders, went to Russia to meet with Lenin. Lenin encouraged the Czech and German Communists in Czechoslovakia to unite. Czech Communist delegates came to the 2d Congress of the Communist International in 1920, before the formal establishment of the Communist Party in Czechoslovakia. A. Zápotocký was again encouraged by Lenin on Czechoslovakia's difficult nationality problems. Lenin also met the German Communist leaders, which led to the final cooperation and the formation of a multinational party in Czechoslovakia. 64 notes. 1916-21

3906. Komissarova, T. S. V. I. LENIN O ZADACHAKH KUL'TURNO-PROSVETITEL'NOI RABOTY V GODY GRAZHDANSKOI VOINY I INOSTRANNOI VOENNOI INTERVENTSII [V. I. Lenin on the tasks of cultural-educational work during the years of the civil war and foreign military intervention]. *Vestnik Leningradskogo U.: Seriia Istorii, Iazyka i Literatury [USSR] 1981 (2): 94-96.* Describes Lenin's close attention to out-of-school education and the teaching of illiterates in Soviet Russia during the first years of Bolshevik dictatorship, 1917-1921. He spoke at many conferences of teachers stressing that a socialist state could only be built on the correct cultural basis. Based on Lenin's writings; 13 notes. 1919-21

3907. Lavrov, V. M. MALOIZVESTNYE STRANITSY DEIATEL'NOSTI V. I. LENINA [Little-known pages from V. I. Lenin's life and activities]. *Novaia i Noveishaia Istoriia [USSR] 1986 (3): 21-29.* Describes Lenin's meetings with one of the leaders of the Communist Party of Austria, F. Koritchoner, and shows Lenin's ideological and theoretical influence on the Party's formation. Based on archival and secondary sources, published in the USSR and Austria. 1916-21

3908. Moskovski, P. V. and Semenov, V. G. LENIN V DANII [Lenin in Denmark]. *Voprosy Istorii [USSR] 1981 (4): 99-106.* Members of the Russian Social Democratic Workers' Party attempted to hold their conference in Copenhagen in 1907, and the 8th Congress of the 2d International was held there in 1910. Lenin followed the conference with work at the Royal Public Library in Copenhagen, subsequently making use of Danish material, especially agricultural statistics. He formed friendly contacts with Danish revolutionaries, in particular Trir, and was able to use Copenhagen as a channel for information about Russia during World War I. 45 notes. 1907-18

3909. Ovčarenko, N. E. LENINS KAMPF GEGEN DEN OPPORTUNISMUS IN DER INTERNATIONALEN ARENA IN DER PERIODE DER SCHAFFUNG DER PARTEI NEUEN TYPS [Lenin's struggle against opportunism in the international arena during the period in which the new style party was being created]. *Beiträge zur Gesch. der Arbeiterbewegung [East Germany] 1980 22(4): 500-512.* V. I. Lenin aimed to create a new type of proletarian party in Russia and to spread its ideas and principles together with the experiences of revolutionary strategy and tactics throughout the international socialist movement. The main opponents in Russia to the creation of this new party were the Mensheviks, the Russian opportunists. The author examines Lenin's struggle against international opportunism, 1904-10, which encompassed a wide range of theoretical, philosophical, tactical, and strategic questions concerning revolutionary struggle. Particular attention is paid to Lenin's writings during this period on the methodological and theoretical aspects of this struggle with regard to the sociopolitical character of opportunism, the ideological and political content of the struggle, and the international importance of the historical experiences of Leninism as a means of strengthening the unity of the Communist movement. Secondary sources; 40 notes. 1904-10

3910. Pavlov, V. K ISTORIOGRAFII LENINSKOGO VOENNOGO NASLEDIIA [Historiography of Lenin's military heritage]. *Voenno-Istoricheskii Zhurnal [USSR] 1982 (9): 71-74.* Reviews in broad terms historiography in the 1920's and early 1930's on V. I. Lenin's writings about military theory and his activity in the revolutions of 1905 and 1917. The first works fully to appreciate Lenin's contribution to the theory of armed uprising and the formation of popular revolutionary armies were by M. N. Pokrovski, E. M. Iaroslavski, V. A. Bystrianski and S. I. Gusev. These were also noteworthy in that they adopted a properly academic approach and listed Lenin's own sources. In his *Lenin: Theoretician and Exponent of Armed Uprising* and other works, Iaroslavski was the first to draw attention to Lenin's view that military science is a key aspect of the proletariat's class struggle. Later writers, such as M. V. Frunze, I. S. Unshlikh, A. S. Bubnov, K. E. Voroshilov, A. V. Luncharski, and N. I. Podvoiski analyzed in detail Lenin's role in the concrete preparation of cadres for the revolutionary army. 28 notes. 1914-35

3911. Protopopov, D. Z. V. I. LENIN I SOZDANIE SOIUZA SSR (VOSPOMINANIIA UCHASTNIKA I VSESOIUZNOGO S"EZDA SOVETOV) [V. I. Lenin and the founding of the USSR: reminiscences of a participant in the 1st All-Union Congress of Soviets]. *Istoriia SSSR [USSR] 1982 (6): 124-127.* In 1922 V. I. Lenin, though already seriously ill, took an active part in the discussion on the nationalities policy, criticizing Joseph Stalin's theses on "autonomization," which sought to deprive republics of their sovereignty. The author recalls how in December of that year he was elected a delegate to the 10th All-Russian Congress of Soviets at which the unification of the republics into a Union of Soviet Socialist Republics was ratified. Accordingly on 30 December the first session of the 1st All-Union Congress of Soviets was opened and a number of prominent Party members spoke. Biographical information on the author of the article is given. 9 notes. 1922

3912. Rachkovski, V. A. U ISTOKOV VYSSHEI SHKOLY (PO STRANITSAM BIOGRAFICHESKOI KHRONIKI V. I. LENINA) [At the origins of higher education: a survey of V. I. Lenin's biographical chronicle]. *Vestnik Leningradskogo Universiteta: Seriia Istorii, Iazyka i Literatury [USSR] 1985 (3): 20-25.* According to *Biograficheskaia Khronika V. I. Lenina* [The biographical chronicle of V. I. Lenin], reform of higher education in the spirit of the revolution was one of Lenin's major concerns in the 1918-19 period. In his frequent consultations with Anatoli Lunacharski, People's Commissar for Education, Lenin expressed special concern for drawing proletarian youth into the ranks of the new Soviet intelligentsia and for the ideological preparation of teachers in higher education. Secondary sources; 37 notes. English summary. 1918-19

3913. Savitskaia, R. M. NAUCHNAIA LENINIANA [Scientific Leniniana]. *Voprosy Istorii KPSS [USSR] 1981 (8): 126-134.* From 1970 to 1980 increased attention has been paid to the life and work of V. I. Lenin. The need for the publication of more books on the subject was stessed at the 24th, 25th, and 26th Communist Party Congresses and a series of plenary sessions of the Party's Central Committee. The last decade was also marked by several important anniversaries: the 100th and 110th anniversaries of Lenin's birth and the 60th anniversary of the Great October Socialist Revolution. A joint session of the Party Central Committee, the Supreme Soviet of the USSR, and of the Russian Federation in 1970 heard a keynote speech by the Party's General Secretary, Leonid Brezhnev, assessing Lenin's life and work. 43 notes. 1894-1981

3914. Shevel'ev, K. LIU ZERONG'S REMINISCENCES OF LENIN. *Far Eastern Affairs [USSR] 1980 (3): 172-176.* Liu Zerong (Liu Tse-jung), a former Chairman of the Central Executive Committee of the League of Chinese Workers in Russia, reminisces about V. I. Lenin and the early years of the Russian Revolution as well as about Lenin's charismatic political leadership. 1914-50's

3915. Shmorhun, P. M. V. I. LENIN I KYIVSKA PARTIINA ORHANIZATSIIA [V. I. Lenin and the Kiev party organization]. *Ukrains'kyi Istorychnyi Zhurnal [USSR] 1981 (11): 44-53.* Traces Lenin's interest in the Ukraine from childhood and his attention to revolutionary movements there. Following the October Revolution, in the most difficult conditions of the Civil War, Lenin maintained links with Kiev Bolsheviks, guiding their struggle against the Ukrainian Central Rada. 1880-1924

3916. Shumikhin, V. S. V. I. LENIN I BOL'SHEVISTSKAIA AGITATSIIA SREDI VOISK INTERVENTOV V GODY GRAZHDANSKOI VOINY [V. I. Lenin and Bolshevik agitation among interventionist troops during the Civil War]. *Voprosy Istorii KPSS [USSR] 1982 (2): 56-65.* Lenin showed himself to be a skillful military strategist during the Civil War by organizing ideological propaganda for foreign troops on Soviet soil and even beyond. Numerous letters, telegrams, Party archives, and memoirs shed light on Lenin's personal participation in instigating and organizing publications and leaflets in foreign languages to be distributed by airplane to interventionist troops or handed out among prisoners of war. Propaganda letters were even sent to US workers. The Bolshevik agitation proved effective not only among the enemy but also among internal counterrevolutionary forces. Primary sources; 64 notes. 1918-20

3917. Sitnikov, B. GORKI LENINSKIE [Gorki Leninskie]. *Voenno-Istoricheskii Zhurnal [USSR] 1982 (4): 80-83.* Gorki Leninskie, an estate near Moscow, is closely connected with the life and work of V. I. Lenin, who stayed at the house many times, 1918-24. During his visits he wrote many articles and met with important members of the Party and government. Lenin spent the last months of his life at Gorki and it was there that he died, 21 January 1924. A museum was opened at the estate in 1945. Based on secondary sources; 3 notes. 1918-81

3918. Stepanov, V. N. V. I. LENIN I SOZDANIE OBSHCHEROSSIISKOI ISKROVSKOI ORGANIZATSII [V. I. Lenin and the creation of the all-Russian *Iskra* organization]. *Voprosy Istorii KPSS [USSR] 1982 (2): 44-55.* Dedicated to 80th anniversary of *Iskra,* the first all-Russian Marxist paper, the author concentrates on organizational work by Lenin. The organization acted as a prototype of a revolutionary party, built on a centralist principle with a high level of revolutionary discipline among its members and supporters throughout Russia. Primary sources; 46 notes. 1900-05

3919. Stoljarowa, Ruth. DIE BIOGRAPHISCHE CHRONIK ÜBER LENINS LEBEN UND WIRKEN—EIN BEDEUTENDER BEITRAG ZUR LENINIANA. TEIL I: GESCHICHTE, CHARAKTER UND BEDEUTUNG DER AUSGABE [The biographical chronicle of Lenin's life and works—an important contribution to studies of Lenin. Part 1: history, characteristics, and importance of the publication]. *Beiträge zur Gesch. der Arbeiterbewegung [East Germany] 1983 25(5): 673-685.* The official biography of V. I. Lenin (12 volumes of which have been published since 1970) presents a chronological collection of facts about Lenin as a Marxist theoretician and revolutionary, as the founder of the Communist Party in the Soviet Union, as a leader of the world proletariat, and as a person. Examines the sources and types of archival and primary material that have been used in this work, and provides examples of new material concerning his life and work that has never before been published. This material reveals new evidence concerning the origins, publication, and distribution of Lenin's works and increases our knowledge of many dates in Lenin's life. Based on primary sources and archival material; 62 notes. Article to be continued. 1870-1924

3920. Stoljarowa, Ruth. BRIEFE UND TELEGRAMME DEUTSCHER GENOSSEN AN W. I. LENIN [Letters and telegrams to V. I. Lenin from German comrades]. *Beiträge zur Gesch. der Arbeiterbewegung [East Germany] 1980 22(2): 216-221, (3): 381-382.* Part 1. Reproduces previously unpublished telegrams and letters sent to Lenin, 1917-22, by German Communist Party members. These letters provide an insight into the high esteem in which Lenin was held. They include letters from Eduard Fuchs, Leo Jogiches-Tyszko, Jakob Eckert, Wilhelm Eich, and August Bebel. Part 2. Afterword. Based on letters and telegrams held in the Central Party Archives of the Institute for Marxism-Leninism, Moscow and secondary sources; 20 notes. 1917-22

3921. Taranev, N. M. OB UCHASTII V. I. LENINA V VYRABOTKE KONSTITUTSII RSFSR 1918 GODA [V. I. Lenin's contributions to drafting the RSFSR constitution of 1918]. *Voprosy Istorii [USSR] 1983 (4): 178-181.* Though not a member of the commission appointed in 1918 by the All-Russian Executive Committee (VTsIK) to write the Russian Federation's constitution, Lenin wrote or inspired the wording of numerous statutes, such as those dealing with fundamental rights (freedom of conscience, opinion, and assembly) as well as articles curtailing the rights of those who might harm the interests of the Socialist Revolution. He also edited and thoroughly revised the entire draft of this first Soviet constitution. 34 notes. 1918

3922. Titarenko, S. L. LENINSKOE TEORETICHESKOE NASLEDIE: NESOSTOIATEL'NOST' BURZHUAZNYKH INTERPRETATSII [Lenin's theoretical legacy: the bankruptcy of bourgeois interpretations]. *Voprosy Istorii KPSS [USSR] 1982 (4): 96-107.* Western imperialist circles, ever keen to slander V. I. Lenin, say that he was not a Marxist because he didn't know Marx's works. This is an absurd charge. Lenin knew all the major works of Marx. His writings and analysis of Russia's economic condition owed much to Marx. Lenin was a staunch supporter of Marx, and never compromised with anti-Marxists. Western circles say many of Lenin's works are "loosely based" on Marx's *The Growth of Capitalism in Russia.* The truth is that they are indeed based on Marx, but the word "loosely" implies not an inadequate knowledge of Marx, but the modifications of an original thinker. It is impossible to fault Lenin, whose works have captured the hearts and minds of people all over our planet. Based on Lenin's works and on Neil Harding's *Lenin's Political Thought;* 33 notes. 1880-1924

3923. Uhlmann, Maria. ZWEI NEUE LENINBRIEFE [Two new letters by Lenin]. *Beiträge zur Gesch. der Arbeiterbewegung [East Germany] 1981 23(3): 387-390.* Reproduces two hitherto unpublished letters by V. I. Lenin. The first document was written December 1917/January 1918 in reply to Hermann Fernau, a German liberal writer who in several books took issue with the standpoint of bourgeois pacifism concerning war and peace and particularly with the causes and outcome of World War I. The second letter was in reply to a letter from Emerson P. Jennings, an American industrial magnate. Jennings was the head of an engineering firm in Pennsylvania and in 1920 formed an association to foster trading links with the Soviet Union. In March 1921 he wrote to Lenin describing the aims of a trip to Moscow he had made in 1920, and in addition he reminded Lenin of the financial support he had procured for the political emigrants L. K. Martens and A. F. Nuorteva. Based on documents held in Moscow and secondary sources; 14 notes. 1917-21

3924. Vasser, M. M. LENINISM—REVOLIUTSIONNOE ZNAMIA NASHEI EPOKHI: STRANITSY ZHIZNI VOZHDIA [Leninism, the revolutionary banner of our era: pages from the life of the leader]. *Voprosy Istorii KPSS [USSR] 1981 (11): 33-44.* Reviews Volume 21 of *Vladimir Ilich Lenin: A Biographical Chronicle,* covering the period from 12 July to 30 November 1921. 7 notes. 1921

3925. Vinogradova, L. B. NOVYE STRANITSY LENINSKOGO NASLEDIIA [New pages in the Leninist heritage]. *Voprosy Istorii [USSR] 1981 (4): 110-116.* The 33d Lenin collection of documents and articles—texts, speeches, letters, notes, resolutions, and preparatory materials pertaining to V. I. Lenin—has just been published. It contains 264 documents relating to Lenin's life and work from 1894 to 1922. A number of documents reflect life and work from 1894 to 1922. Others display Lenin's concern with agrarian relations in Russia, with Western European countries, and with the United States. Others show him working for the unification of leftist, internationalist forces in the international workers movement on the eve of World War I and his efforts to improve the machinery of government, evolve a planned economy, and organize defense. 18 notes. 1894-1922

3926. Volkova, G. S. FORMIROVANIE REVOLIUTSIONNOGO MIROVOZZRENIIA V. I. LENINA I PEREDOVAIA RUSSKAIA LITERATURA [The formation of the revolutionary outlook of V. I. Lenin and progressive Russian literature]. *Voprosy Istorii KPSS [USSR] 1982 (4): 57-69.* Western reaction asserts that Lenin is outside the main Russian Marxist tradition. This is untrue, as, steeped in Russian literature, Lenin had been advocating scientific socialism from the late 1880's. Lenin was raised in a highly literate family and early studied Russian and foreign progressive literature. He greatly admired Chernyshevski, from whom he learned the importance of the peasantry in the revolutionary struggle, the significance of patriotism and internationalism, and the rejection of racism and nationalism. He learned to abhor liberalism. Lenin was not merely an imitator, but an original thinker who, having read and absorbed these works, accepted some ideas, rejected others, and synthesized a remarkable new whole—Leninism. Based on the works of Lenin and Brezhnev and Soviet studies and biographies; 78 notes. 1880-90

3927. —. BEZTSINNY VKLAD U LENINIANU (DO ZAVERSHENNIA VYKHODU U SVIT BIOKHRONIKY V. I. LENINA) [A priceless contribution to the study of Lenin: on the completed publication of the biochronology of V. I. Lenin]. *Ukrains'kyi Istorychnyi Zhurnal [USSR] 1982 (10):*

5-16. A review of the 12th and final volume of a chronological biography of V. I. Lenin, researched, compiled, and edited by a collective of academicians at the Institute of Marxism-Leninism of the Central Committee of the Communist Party of the Soviet Union. The collected volumes give details of Lenin's life from childhood to death, his revolutionary work, writings, Party and government documents, articles, speeches, letters, memoirs, monographs, and other examples of his activities. The biography annotates over 39,000 facts about Lenin, presents new information on him, and is intended to inspire the Soviet people to live as true Communists. 1870-1924

3928. —. 110 ANI DE LA NAŞTERE. LENIN ÎN AMINTIRILE TOVARĂŞILOR SĂI [110th anniversary of his birth: V. I. Lenin in his comrades' memories]. *Magazin Istoric [Romania] 1980 14(4): 40-42.* Excerpts from the two-volume anthology *Lenin—Oktiabr' Semnadtsatogo* [Lenin: October 1917] (1977), which presents reminiscences by many who had personal contact with V. I. Lenin during 1917. 1917

Lennander, K. G.

3929. Thorén, Lars. K. G. LENNANDER OCH KIRURGIEN I UPPSALA KRING SEKELSKIFTET [K. G. Lennander and surgery in Uppsala at the turn of the century]. *Nordisk Medicinhistorisk Årsbok [Sweden] 1984: 153-164.* K. G. Lennander was professor of surgery from 1891 to his death 1908 at the University of Uppsala. He devoted his life to the study and practice of surgery and worked hard in spite of a serious heart condition. His main research interest was the sensitivity of the peritoneal cavity and the treatment of appendicitis and peritonitis, in which he made important contributions to the science of surgery. In 1897 he was also the first to remove a foreign body (a bullet) from the brain after a preoperative localization by X-ray examination. One of Sweden's first internationally known surgeons, he maintained contact with surgery and colleagues abroad during all his active years. 1891-1908

Lennox, Charles

3930. Saggus, Charles D. OUR COUNTRY PATRONYMIC: THE THIRD DUKE OF RICHMOND (1735-1806). *Richmond County Hist. 1982 14(1): 4-9.* Biography of Charles Lennox, 3d Duke of Richmond (1735-1806) for whom Richmond County, Georgia was named, concluding that his character and pro-American stance during the American Revolution resulted in his being honored by having a county named after him. 1770's-80's

Lenoir, Alexandre

3931. Mellon, Stanley; Kennedy, Emmet (commentary). ALEXANDER LENOIR: THE MUSEUM VERSUS THE REVOLUTION. *Consortium on Revolutionary Europe 1750-1850: Pro. 1979: 75-91.* Examines the career of Alexandre Lenoir, who in 1791 was given the task of preserving various historic monuments (especially paintings and statues). Lenoir's Museum of French Monuments survived the Revolutionary and Napoleonic periods; it was abolished during the Restoration era. Lenoir's achievements in the 1790's were extraordinary. In the midst of much official destruction of remnants of the Old Regime he had the task of preserving many of the country's artistic treasures. In order not to be branded as an enemy of the Revolution, he had to make several compromises. The widespread vandalism of the period 1789-95 resulted from the fact that revolutionary leaders often criticized every aspect of the Old Regime. Comments, pp. 89-91. 11 notes. 1789-95

Lenoit, Anita

3932. Hispano, Cornelio. ANITA LENOIT, UNA EXQUISITA AVENTURA DEL LIBERTADOR [Anita Lenoit, an exquisite adventure of the Liberator]. *Rev. de la Soc. Bolivariana de Venezuela [Venezuela] 1980 37(125): 37-42.* 1812-68

*For abstract see **Bolívar, Simón***

Leonard, Józef

3933. Urbański, E. S. DR JÓZEF LEONARD W AMERYCE ŚRODKOWEJ (1880-1908) [Doctor Józef Leonard in Central America, 1880-1908]. *Zeszyty Hist. [France] 1982 (61): 129-140.* Sketches the biography of the Polish humanist and diplomat Józef Leonard, who spent most of his life in exile in Nicaragua, Honduras, and El Salvador, and surveys the impact of his ideas and personality on his pupils and friends. As director of a Nicaraguan school, Leonard became the mentor and lifelong friend of Nicaraguan poet Rubén Dario in whose memoirs he is fondly described. Leonard's diplomatic activities in Honduras in 1900-03 resulted in the great popularity of his political thought among a generation of politicians in Central America. Primary sources. 1900-08

Leonardo da Vinci

3934. Barolsky, Paul. WALTER PATER AND THE POETRY OF NOTHINGNESS. *Antioch Rev. 1982 40(4): 469-478.* 15c

*For abstract see **Botticelli***

3935. Carlsöö, Sven. LEONARDO DA VINCI SOM ANATOM [Leonardo da Vinci as anatomist]. *Nordisk Medicinhistorisk Årsbok [Sweden] 1985: 65-70.* Anatomy was only one of many fields in which the multitalented Leonardo da Vinci was involved. Like anatomists in ancient and medieval times, he studied the anatomy of animals in great detail. However, his systematic dissections and analyses of the human body earned him a place in the annals of anatomy. Among other things, he elucidated the ventricles of the brain and was the first to provide an accurate description of the maxillary sinus. But muscles and their function, human movements, and body balance predominated in his work on human anatomy. His masterly drawings represented an enormous step forward in the art of depicting anatomical details. And his captions for these drawings show, perhaps more than the drawings themselves, just what a great anatomist he really was. Even if his physiological hypotheses now seem unreasonable, his descriptions of muscular function were often both accurate and pioneering. 1470's-1519

Leonetti, Alfonso

3936. Broué, Pierre. FEROCI, SOUZO, MARTIN, LEONETTI, ALFONSO . . . [Feroci, Souzo, Martin, Leonetti, Alfonso . . .]. *Belfagor [Italy] 1985 40(6): 675-682.* A tribute to Italian Trotskyist historian Alfonso Leonetti, who also wrote under the pseudonyms mentioned in the title. Relates the events surrounding the Italian Communist Party's position on the Spanish Civil War, the formation of a Trotskyist group called Nuova Opposizione Italiana, and Leonetti's activities in the last years of his life. 1930's-84

3937. Santarelli, Enzo. ALFONSO LEONETTI [Alfonso Leonetti]. *Belfagor [Italy] 1983 38(3): 299-308.* Describes the career of one of the leading figures of Italian Marxism and his relations with the Communist Party, particularly after 1960. 1921-79

3938. Trotsky, Leon and Leonetti, Alfonso; Chitarin, Attilio, ed. PER UN NUOVO POLO RIVOLUZIONARIO [Toward a new revolutionary polarity]. *Belfagor [Italy] 1985 40(6): 683-699.* Presents correspondence, 1930-36, between Alfonso Leonetti and Leon Trotsky, focusing on Leonetti's split from the Italian Communist Party in 1935 over the amount of support to be given to the fight against fascism in Spain. 1930-36

Leonhard, Susanne

3939. Weber, Hermann. SUSANNE LEONHARD GESTORBEN [Susanne Leonhard dies]. *Internationale Wissenschaftliche Korrespondenz zur Geschichte der Deutschen Arbeiterbewegung [West Germany] 1984 20(2): 155-156.* Commemorates the German writer and radical socialist Susanne Leonhard (1895-1984), whose works included *Unterirdische Literatur im Revolutionären Deutschland während der Weltkriegs* [Underground literature in revolutionary Germany during the world war] (1919). 1919-84

Leonhardy, Leo

3940. Leonhardy, Wolfgang A. EIN FLIEGERLEBEN: DER "POUR LE MERITE"-TRÄGER LEO LEONHARDY [A flyer's life: "Pour le Merite" recipient Leo Leonhardy]. *Zeitschrift für Heereskunde [West Germany] 1984 48(313): 75-78.* Describes the career of German pilot Leo Leonhardy, who won the "Pour le Merite" award for flying 83 combat missions during World War I. ca 1900-28

Leonora Christina

3941. Skov, Sigvard. LEONORA CHRISTINA: HELGEN ELLER HØJFORRAEDER [Leonora Christina: heroine or traitor?]. *Historie [Denmark] 1982 14(2): 201-215.* Leonora Christina (1621-98), Countess of Schleswig-Holstein, was deeply involved in politics. Her husband, Corfits Ulfeldt (1606-64), was not a traitor but a cosmopolitan statesman like many others in his day. He and Leonora Christina were leading Danish proponents of aristocratic constitutional government in opposition to the absolutism established in 1660 by her half-brother, King Frederick III (1609-70). Probably their aim was to establish Leonora Christina as queen, with Ulfeldt as leader of an aristocratic regime in the style of Jan de Witt (1625-72) in the Netherlands. 36 notes. 1640-1700

Leonov, A. I.

3942. Popov, N. MARSHAL VOISK SVIAZI A. I. LEONOV (K 80-LETIIU SO DNIA ROZHDENIIA) [Marshal of signal troops, A. I. Leonov on his 80th birthday]. *Voenno-Istoricheskii Zhurnal [USSR] 1982 (5): 93-95.* Marshal A. I. Leonov was born 7 May 1902 into a working class family. In 1918 he joined the Red Army and in 1938 graduated from the Military Electro-Technical Academy. He participated in actions against the Japanese in 1939, for which he was awarded the Order of the Red Banner. In 1944-45, he commanded the signals troops of the 2d Ukrainian Front. In 1961, he became a marshal. He died in 1972. Based on secondary sources; 2 notes, 2 photos. 1902-82

Leont'ev, Aleksei K.

3943. —. PAMIATI ALEKSEIA KONSTANTINOVICHA LEONT'EVA (1920-1983) [In memory of Aleksei Konstantinovich Leont'ev (1920-83)]. *Vestnik Moskovskogo Universiteta, Seriia 8: Istoriia [USSR] 1984 (2): 93-96.* Obituary of Aleksei K. Leont'ev (1920-83), Soviet historian, co-author of the univeristy textbook of Russian history. Lists his publications. Secondary sources. 1920-83

Leopardi, Giacomo

3944. Bonadeo, Alfredo. LEOPARDI E LA RELIGIONE [Leopardi and religion]. *Italian Quarterly 1984 25(96): 37-47.* Giacomo Leopardi (1798-1837) distanced himself from Christianity, believing that it blocked the will to live, and turned constantly to classical writers who provided him with a model for an energetic religion. 1820's-37

Leopold III

3945. Maga, Timothy P. DIPLOMAT AMONG KINGS: JOHN CUDAHY AND LEOPOLD III. *Wisconsin Mag. of Hist. 1983-84 67(2): 82-98.* 1940
*For abstract see **Cudahy, John***

3946. Rémy, Colonel. LEOPOLD DE BELGIQUE, BOUC EMISSAIRE DE LA FRANCE? [Leopold of Belgium, France's scapegoat?]. *Hist. Mag. [France] 1984 (47): 32-37.* A former leader of the French resistance during the German occupation in World War II rehabilitates Leopold III of Belgium (1901-83), who capitulated on 28 May 1940 in the face of the German invasion of Belgium and comments on the false accusation of the king's treason levelled by Paul Reynaud (French premier at the time) and by the French press. 1940

Leopold William

3947. Haupt, Herbert. KULTUR- UND KUNSTGESCHICHTLICHE NACHRICHTEN VOM WIENER HOFE ERZHERZOG LEOPOLD WILHELMS IN DEN JAHREN 1646-1654 [Cultural and art historical reports on Archduke Leopold William's Vienna court during the years 1646-54]. *Mitteilungen des Österreichischen Staatsarchivs [Austria] 1980 33: 346-355.* Archduke Leopold William (1614-62) was one of the more prominent art patrons of the 17th century. He kept numerous artists and skilled craftsmen in his pay. The author has edited archival notes on the archduke's cultural endeavors in Vienna while he resided as governor in the Netherlands, 1646-54. The records consist of 64 entries, which mostly concern pay for services rendered. The entries have been provided with biographical footnotes on the artists and craftsmen mentioned. Based on documents in the Vienna Hofkammerarchiv. Entries not edited in this essay, can be found in Franz Mareš's *Kenntnis der Kunstbestrebung des Erzherzogs Leopold Wilhelm;* biblio. 1646-54

Lepe, Manuel

3948. Bender, Bea. THE CHARMED WORLD OF MANUEL LEPE: PRIMITIVE ART BY A MEXICAN MASTER. *Caribbean Review 1984 13(1): 41-43.* Describes the life and art of Manuel Lepe, a self-taught painter from Puerto Vallarta recognized as Mexico's national painter in 1975. 1936-83

LePen, Jean-Marie

3949. Shields, James G. JEAN-MARIE LE PEN AND THE NEW RADICAL RIGHT IN FRANCE. *Patterns of Prejudice [Great Britain] 1986 20(1): 3-10.* Discusses the rise in popularity of the French New Right politician Jean-Marie Le Pen and his Front National Party, especially since 1983.

His popularity has been linked to rising unemployment and crime as well as his attacks on Arabs, Jews, and blacks. 1980's

Lepse, Ivan I.

3950. Gel'berg, Ia. L. S MANDATOM SOVETSKIKH PROFSOIUZOV [With a mandate from the Soviet trade unions]. *Voprosy Istorii [USSR] 1981 (6): 181-184.* Examines the part played by Ivan I. Lepse (1888-1929), chairman of the USSR Central Committee of the Union of Metal Workers, in furthering the cause of trade unionism at various international trade union congresses during the 1920's. His first major overseas conference was as part of the Soviet delegation to the 56th British Trade Unions Congress at Hull in 1924. In 1925 he headed a delegation of Soviet trade unionists to China and in the same year he took part in the first Soviet trade union delegation to Japan. Based on documents in the Central State Archives of the October Revolution, USSR; 15 notes. 1924-25

3951. Zelov, N. S. IZ LICHNYKH FONDOV DELEGATOV I VSESOIUZNOGO S"EZDA SOVETOV [From the personal archives of the deputies of the 1st All-Union Congress of Soviets]. *Sovetskie Arkhivy [USSR] 1982 (6): 40-43.* 1920's
*For abstract see **Bogdanov, N. P.***

Lepsius, Johannes

3952. Goltz, Hermann. BOL'SHOI DRUG ARMIANSKOGO NARODA (V SVIAZI S NOVONAIDENNYMI DOKUMENTAMI I LEPSIUSA) [The great friend of the Armenian people: recently found documents of J. Lepsius]. *Patma-Banasirakan Handes. Istoriko-Filologicheskii Zhurnal [USSR] 1982 (4): 131-136.* In the archives of Johannes Lepsius (1858-1926), German orientalist, clergyman, community worker, who was a great friend of the Armenian nation, some material which reveals the wide extent of Lepsius's activities in defense of Armenians, particularly during the years of the Armenian genocide, 1914-18. Primary sources; photo, 6 notes. Armenian summary. 1896-1926

Lerminier, Eugène

3953. Smith, Bonnie G. THE RISE AND FALL OF EUGENE LERMINIER. *French Hist. Studies 1982 12(3): 377-400.* Eugène Lerminier (1803-57) soared to prominence in the early Orléanist monarchy as a legal scholar, lecturer, and journalist. Later branded as a shallow careerist because of his frequent doctrinal and political shifts, he lost his popular following by 1839. Yet he was important as an able newspaperman, academic, contributor to legal and German scholarship, and as a model for a number of Stendhalian fictional characters in 19th-century French literature. Based on Lerminier's published works and periodicals dating from the 1830's. 1823-57

Lermontov, Mikhail

3954. Goscilo, Helena. LERMONTOV'S DEBT TO LAVATER AND GALL. *Slavonic and East European Rev. [Great Britain] 1981 59(4): 500-515.* As "the first Russian writer to grapple with complex psychological issues in contemporary context," Mikhail Lermontov (1814-41) used the popular studies of Johann Kaspar Lavater (1741-1801) on physiognomy and the phrenological researches of Franz Josef Gall (1758-1826). The belief that external facial or cranial characteristics described a person's inner disposition and character influenced many 19th-century writers and pervades Lermontov's major fiction. 42 notes. 1772-1841

3955. Semczuk, Antoni. LEGENDY I DRAMATY RODZINNE (KARTKI Z DZIECIŃSTWA I LAT MŁODZIEŃCZYCH LERMONTOWA) [Legends and family dramas (notes from the childhood and youth of Lermontov)]. *Slavia Orientalis [Poland] 1980 29(3): 393-399.* Discusses the turbulent and quarrelsome family atmosphere of the writer Mikhail Lermontov (1814-41). His mother died broken-hearted after discovering the infidelities of her husband, who was rarely present during the writer's early years because of his addiction to wine, women, and gambling. Lermontov was witness to a long struggle over custody between his father and his despotic maternal grandmother. 1814-30's

Leroy, Pierre

3956. Lamy, E. AUTOBIOGRAPHIE AFRICAINE DE PIERRE LEROY, DERNIER GOUVERNEUR DE LA PROVINCE ORIENTALE DU CONGO BELGE [African autobiography of Pierre Leroy, last governor of Orientale province of the Belgian Congo]. *Bulletin des Séances de l'Académie Royale des Sciences d'Outre-Mer [Belgium] 1982 28(3): 269-285.* The five-volume autobiography of Pierre Leroy provides many insights into colonial life in Ruanda-Urundi and the Belgian Congo between 1938 and 1960. In particular the volume "Diary of Orientale province," covering the years 1958 to 1960, records the tumultuous, often tragic events of the preindependence period in the Congo. The activities of Patrice Lumumba, in his opposition to colonial rule, are highlighted. Reissue of these privately-printed memoirs would be welcome. 14 notes. 1938-60

LeSecq, Henri

3957. Masheck, Joseph. THINK-SHOTS. *Art in America 1984 72(3): 108-113.* Discusses the art of the 19th-century French photographer Henri Le Secq, who is best known for his landscape and architectural photographs, but who is now being recognized for his sophisticated still-life photographs. 19c

Leskov, Nikolay

3958. Muckle, James. NIKOLAY LESKOV: EDUCATIONAL JOURNALIST AND IMAGINATIVE WRITER. *New Zealand Slavonic Journal [New Zealand] 1984: 81-110.* Presents the life and career of Russian author Nikolay Leskov (1831-95). 1831-95

Leslie family

3959. Dukes, Paul. THE LESLIE FAMILY IN THE SWEDISH PERIOD (1630-5) OF THE THIRTY YEARS' WAR. *European Studies Rev. [Great Britain] 1982 12(4): 401-424.* Sir Thomas Urquhart of Cromarty (1605-60), in his *Eksuvalauron,* referred to several Scots mercenaries who had significant military careers on the Continent, including three generals from the Leslie family, founded by a knight from Hungary in 1067. Briefly traces the Leslie family history and details the exploits of the three generals, Alexander Leslie (1580-1661), later 1st Earl of Leven, Sir Alexander Leslie, who settled in Smolensk (d. 1660's), and Walter Leslie (1606-67), a Habsburg count, in their service in the Swedish, Polish, and Russian military campaigns in the 1620's and 1630's and specifically in the period 1630-35 in the Thirty Years War. 56 notes. 1630-35

Lesseps, Ferdinand de

3960. Dufresne, Claude. POUR LESSEPS, UN CANAL DE TROP [For Lesseps, it was one canal too many]. *Historama [France] 1984 (4): 40-45.* Relates the life of Ferdinand de Lesseps (1805-94), diplomat, engineer, and promoter of the Suez Canal, whose constant courage and audacity eventually led him to the unfortunate enterprise of the Panama Canal, which ended in scandal and bankruptcy. 1805-94

Lessing, Doris

3961. Lasch, Cristopher. DORIS LESSING AND THE TECHNOLOGY OF SURVIVAL. *Democracy 1983 3(2): 28-36.* Doris Lessing has alienated many of her former followers with her retreat from politics, turn to mysticism, science fiction, and study of nuclear survival since the 1960's. 1960's-80's

3962. Richardi, Janis Marie. "The Modern British *Bildungsroman* and the Woman Novelist: Dorothy Richardson, May Sinclair, Rosamond Lehmann, Elizabeth Bowen, and Doris Lessing." U. of North Carolina, Chapel Hill 1981. 245 pp. *DAI 1982 42(8): 3612-A.* 8200609 20c

Lessing, Gotthold Ephraim

3963. Schilson, Arno. ZWISCHEN GLAUBE UND VERNUNFT. ZUM 200. TODESTAG LESSINGS [Between belief and reason: on the 200th anniversary of Lessing's death]. *Stimmen der Zeit [West Germany] 1981 199(2): 103-116.* Describes Gotthold Ephraim Lessing's life and work, emphasizing the problems he dealt with and his philosophy toward them. 1740's-81

3964. Sturges, Beate. "Die Frau im Werk und Leben Lessings" [Women in Lessing's life and work]. Wayne State U. 1984. 188 pp. *DAI 1985 45(12): 3650-A.* DA8504925 1740's-70's

Lessing, Theodor

3965. Baron, Lawrence. DISCIPLESHIP AND DISSENT: THEODOR LESSING AND EDMUND HUSSERL. *Pro. of the Am. Phil. Soc. 1983 127(1): 32-49.* Theodor Lessing (1872-1933) studied under the philosophical phenomenalist Edmund Husserl (1859-1938) for just two semesters in 1906-07. This was a time when Husserl's own philosophical system was undergoing change. He was projecting his new positions in his lectures, and had not yet published them. In a couple of articles Lessing used a great deal of Husserl's terminology and new thought without giving the precise documentation which Husserl thought should have been given, and thus Lessing laid himself open to the charge of plagiarism. For his part, Lessing operated under the assumption that Husserl would be flattered by the employment of his phenomenological approach in his essay on value axiomatics, but such was not the case. The article traces Lessing's development in philosophy and points out the basic difference in the philosophical postures of the two men. Whereas Husserl was interested in philosophy per se, Lessing was not nearly so concerned about what he knew as what he did. Based on the writings of Husserl and Lessing, particularly the latter's article, "Studien zur Wertaxiomatik," *Archiv für Systematische Philosophie* (1908), and the Husserl Archief (Leuven, Belgium); 117 notes. 1890-1910

Lessner, Friedrich

3966. Friederici, Hans Jürgen. EINER VON DER ALTEN GARDE: FRIEDRICH LESSNER [One of the old guard: Friedrich Lessner]. *Beiträge zur Gesch. der Arbeiterbewegung [East Germany] 1981 23(6): 912-920.* Traces the life, career, and political activities of the German Socialist Friedrich Lessner (1825-1910). At the age of 14 Lessner was sent to Weimar to learn carpentry; the working conditions and pay were poor. In 1843 Lessner became a member of the Hamburg Workers Educational Association and here he became interested in politics. The author traces the development of Lessner's political activities, his work for the Communist League, his friendship with Marx and Engels, and his work for both the German and International working-class movement. Secondary sources; 28 notes. 1840's-1910

Leuthner, Karl

3967. Fletcher, Roger. SOCIALIST NATIONALISM IN CENTRAL EUROPE BEFORE 1914: THE CASE OF KARL LEUTHNER. *Can. J. of Hist. [Canada] 1982 17(1): 27-57.* Karl Leuthner (1869-1944) was a minor Social Democratic journalist and politician. He served as foreign affairs editor of the Viennese *Arbeiter-Zeitung* which was the official organ of the German Social Democratic Labor Party of Austria. He also contributed to other right-wing Social Democratic publications in Germany, and was instrumental in the dissemination of nationalist and imperialist ideas within the socialist movements of both Germany and Austria during the decade preceding the outbreak of World War I. Reviews Leuthner's socialism in the prewar context, his influence, his position in the Austrian Social Democratic Party, and his opinion of Germany's place in the global community from 1904 to 1914. Primary sources; 153 notes. 1904-14

3968. Fletcher, Roger. KARL LEUTHNER'S GREATER GERMANY: THE PRE-1914 PAN-GERMANISM OF AN AUSTRIAN SOCIALIST. *Can. Rev. of Studies in Nationalism [Canada] 1982 9(1): 57-79.* Karl Leuthner (1869-1944) was an Austrian journalist, parliamentarian, and public speaker. His anticlerical, anti-Habsburg, and anti-Russian pronouncements gave him a certain influence with the revisionist wing of the Socialist Party. He was best known for advocating German hegemony over the European continent and demanding global parity between this Greater Germany and the British Empire. Although Leuthner was not a proto-Nazi, such views as his helped deliver Germany to the right. 62 notes. 1869-1918

Levchenko, Zinaida

3969. Levchenko, Zinaida. PERSHI ROKY MOHO ZHYTTIA [The first years of my life]. *Sučasnist [West Germany] 1982 (1-2): 188-203.* Reminiscences of an impoverished childhood in wartime and postwar Ukraine. 1941-52

Levi, Primo

3970. Eberstadt, Fernanda. READING PRIMO LEVI. *Commentary 1985 80(4): 41-47.* Offers a brief portrait of noted author Primo Levi (b. 1919), an Italian Jew and survivor of Auschwitz. Also provides a critique of his literary work. 1930's-85

3971. Levi, Primo. PRIMO LEVI: QUESTIONS AND ANSWERS AT INDIANA UNIVERSITY. *Midstream 1986 32(4): 26-28.* Primo Levi, the distinguished Jewish-Italian writer, answered questions about his incarceration at Auschwitz death camp posed by Professor Alvin Rosenfeld and his Holocaust literature students. 1945

Levi, Raphael

3972. Schwartzchild, Steven and Schwartzchild, Henry. TWO LIVES IN THE JEWISH FRÜHAUFKLÄRUNG—RAPHAEL LEVI HANNOVER AND MOSES ABRAHAM WOLFF. *Leo Baeck Institute. Year Book [Great Britain] 1984 29: 229-276.* Profiles two German-Jewish savants and community leaders whose long lives spanned most of the 18th century. Raphael Levi (1683-1779) and Moses Abraham Wolff (1715-1802) had important connections in the intellectual and political circles of the Enlightenment period. Both of these "court Jews" are worthy of detailed studies because they are early representatives of what would become a significant movement within Central European Jewry to participate in the wider social and cultural world of the Gentiles. Photo, 326 notes. 18c

Levi-Civita, Tullio

3973. Roca, Antoni and Glick, Thomas F. ESTEVE TERRADAS (1883-1950) I TULLIO LEVI-CIVITA (1873-1941): UNA CORRESPONDENCIA [Esteve Terradas (1883-1950) and Tullio Levi-Civita (1873-1941): correspondence]. *Dynamis [Spain] 1982 2: 387-402.* The Italian mathematician Levi-Civita, whose calculations on the occasion of the solar eclipse in May 1919 helped give definitive shape to Einstein's general theory of relativity, gave a series of lectures in Madrid and Barcelona in 1921. Here published are five letters written to him by the Catalan mathematician Terradas in connection with the Catalan edition of those lectures. The letters are preceded by an introduction on Levi-Civita's work and the content of the lectures. 1920-22

Leviova, S. Z.

3974. —. S. Z. LEVIOVA [S. Z. Leviova]. *Novaia i Noveishaia Istoriia [USSR] 1981 (3): 223.* Sof'ia Zelikovna Leviova (1918-81) devoted her life to the editing and publication of the work of Marx and Engels and was responsible for the issue of their complete works in the original German, *Marx-Engels Gesamtausgabe,* and other projects. 1918-81

Lévis Mirepoix, Antoine de

3975. Castries, Duc de; Erlanger, Philippe; and Chaffanjon, Arnaud. LE DUC DE LEVIS-MIREPOIX [Antoine de Lévis Mirepoix]. *Nouvelle Rev. des Deux Mondes [France] 1981 (9): 520-530.* Eulogy and biography of the late duke, member of the Académie Française, who died at the age of 96 in 1981. 1909-81

Levski, Vasil

3976. Pavlovska, Tsvetana. ZA VZAIMNOTO VLIIANIE MEZHDU LEVSKI I BOTEV [On the reciprocal influences between Levski and Botev]. *Istoricheski Pregled [Bulgaria] 1982 38(4): 65-79.* 1865-73
For abstract see ***Botev, Khristo***

Lewes, George Henry

3977. Bell, Srilekha. GEORGE HENRY LEWES: A MAN OF HIS TIME. *J. of the Hist. of Biology [Netherlands] 1981 14(2): 277-298.* George Henry Lewes, the husband of George Eliot, was a minor scientist-philosopher who, in his writings, held fast to a teleogical, vitalist view of nature. Combining an urge to find a scientific law governing nature and society (positivism) with philosophical idealism, Lewes wanted to bend Darwinism to his own ideological prejudices. Along with many of his contemporaries, Lewes wanted a compromise between or a unity of idealism and materialism, constancy and change. 1817-78

Lewis, Arthur

3978. Kofi, Tetteh. ARTHUR LEWIS AND WEST AFRICAN DEVELOPMENT. *Social and Econ. Studies [Jamaica] 1980 29(4): 202-227.* Describes the role of Arthur Lewis in West African economic development. Finds these efforts fall into three areas: programming development strategies, articulating African development problems to the West, and advising African governments. Briefly critiques some of the criticism of Lewis's ideas. Secondary sources; 31 ref. 1940-80

Lewis, Bernard

3979. Nyang, Sulayman S. and Abed-Rabbo, Samir. BERNARD LEWIS AND ISLAMIC STUDIES: AN ASSESSMENT. *Search: Journal for Arab and Islamic Studies 1984 5(1-2): 1-24.* Prints a biography of Bernard Lewis, a student of Islamic history and culture in both Great Britain and the United States; his idiosyncratic interpretation of Arabic and Turkish sources was formed by his early devotion to the British Empire and serves to elicit unwarranted support for Israel against the Arab states. 1940-78

Lewis, C. S.

3980. Dorsett, Lyle. C. S. LEWIS: A PROFILE OF HIS LIFE. *Christian History 1985 4(3): 6-11.* Details events in the life of British writer and scholar C. S. Lewis (1898-1963), including his student years at Oxford during World War I, his friendship with British writer G. K. Chesterton, and his career as writer, Christian evangelist, and professor at Cambridge University from 1955 to 1963. 1898-1963

3981. Hart, Dabney. TEACHER, HISTORIAN, CRITIC, APOLOGIST. *Christian History 1985 4(3): 21-24.* Discusses the scholarly works of British writer C. S. Lewis, (1898-1963) including *The Allegory of Love* (on medieval literature), *A Preface to Paradise Lost* (introduction to the work of English poet John Milton), and *English Literature in the Sixteenth Century.* 15c-17c

3982. Kolbe, Martha Emily. "Three Oxford Dons as Creators of other Worlds for Children: Lewis Carroll, C. S. Lewis, and J. R. Tolkien." U. of Virginia 1981. 285 pp. *DAI 1982 43(5): 1532-A.* DA8219062 1865-1950's

3983. Matthews, Kenneth Ernest. "C. S. Lewis and the Modern World." U. of California, Los Angeles 1983. 188 pp. *DAI 1983 44(5): 1451-A.* DA8321951 1930's-63

Lewis, George Cornewall

3984. Palmer, Stanley H. SIR GEORGE CORNEWALL LEWIS, A DIFFERENT KIND OF ENGLISHMAN. *Éire-Ireland 1981 16(3): 118-133.* The English Whig government employed the young Lewis, 1833-36, to investigate "the conditions of the lower classes and the Roman Catholic church in Ireland." His report, published in book form in 1836, was a scholarly study of Irish agrarian violence that he hoped would enlighten the English government about needed reforms. The author describes Lewis's career and life and discusses his study of the "reactionary collective violence" of the Whiteboys, a protective "trades union" without explicit political aim that "employed violence against both persons and property" as a highly disciplined surrogate legal system countering the English-imposed system of absentee landlordism, high rents, compulsory tithes to the Church of Ireland, and low wages. Based on Lewis's study, *Parliamentary Papers,* and other sources; 46 notes. 1833-36

Leyds, Willem J.

3985. VanNiekerk, L. E. DR. W. J. LEYDS AS STAATSPROKUREUR VAN DIE ZUID-AFRIKAANSCHE REPUBLIEK (1884-1889) [Dr. W. J. Leyds as State Attorney of the South African Republic, 1884-89]. *South African Hist. J. 1981 13: 50-77.* Surveys Willem J. Leyds's career and his contributions to judicial administration, penology, and diplomacy in the Republic of South Africa. An incorruptible public servant, he was elected State Secretary at the age of 29. 1884-89

Lezama Lima, José

3986. Vitier, Cintio. DE LAS CARTAS QUE ME ESCRIBIO LEZAMA [From the letters Lezama wrote me]. *Casa de las Américas [Cuba] 1983 23(137): 106-113.* From his correspondence with the poet José Lezama Lima, Cintio Vitier culls some thoughts characteristic of Lezama's poetic universe. Lezama speaks of his poems, of literature, of the Cuban Revolution, of friendship, and of many other topics. Poetry was for him a coherent and unified universe, which not only transcended individual poems but embraced the experience of their creators. 22 notes. 1939-76

Lézardière, Pauline de

3987. Schweinzer, Silvia. UNE CONTRIBUTION A L'HISTORIOGRAPHIE DE L'ANCIEN REGIME: PAULINE DE LEZARDIERE ET SON OEUVRE [A contribution to the historiography of the old régime: Pauline de Lézardière and her work]. *Francia [West Germany] 1980 8: 573-594.* Traces the life and work of the French writer Pauline de Lézardière (1754-1835), who wrote *The Theory of the Political Laws of the French Monarchy* (1792). Examines her contribution to the historiography of the old régime. She was exiled to Holland in 1796, but returned to France in 1801 and continued her historical research and writing until her death in 1835. The author also discusses her personality and political ideology as revealed in her works and her personal letters, as well as describing her position within late 18th- and early 19th-century historiography and her methods of writing. A list of her works both published and unpublished is also included. Based on Pauline de Lézardière's writings and personal letters and secondary sources; 110 notes, appendix. 1754-1835

Lhuyd, Edward

3988. Roberts, Brynley F. EDWARD LHUYD Y CYMRO [Edward Lhuyd: Welshman]. *National Library of Wales Journal [Great Britain] 1985 24(1): 63-83.* The first of the National Museum of Wales Edward Lhuyd Lectures. Lhuyd, scholar and scientist, began his formal academic career in 1682 at Jesus College, Oxford. He made Oxford his home and from there wrote "Archaeologia Britannica" and developed his skills as a philologist and antiquarian. He had spent a great deal of time in Llanberis as a young naturalist and continued to visit regularly. He became an authority on the characteristic flora of the area as well as pursuing other interests such as the effects of weathering on the stony slopes of Nant Ffrancon and Nant Peris. Secondary sources; 40 notes. 17c

Li Ai Vee

3989. Kreis-Li, Edo. PEINTURE CHINOISE TRADITIONNELLE DE LI AI VEE, "OISEAUX, FLEURS ET INSECTES" [Li Ai Vee's traditional Chinese painting: "birds, flowers, and insects"]. *Mus. de Genève [Switzerland] 1984 (245): 19-21.* Describes the career and work of this renowned 20th-century artist, born in China, but who has lived in Switzerland since 1958. 1932-84

Li Desheng

3990. —. THE RISE OF LI TE-SHENG. *Issues & Studies [Taiwan] 1985 21(6): 136-145.* Li Desheng (Li Te-sheng, b. 1916), until 1985 commander of the Shengyang Military Region, has had a continuous career in the Chinese Communist army from 1930, when he joined the Party. Li's political experience and skill have enabled him to rise to high Party offices during the current regime even though he was formerly a supporter of the Cultural Revolution Group. He is a likely candidate for a high military post, but this promotion is not certain. Based on Chinese media reports; 8 notes. 1930-85

Li Huifen

3991. —. SOME NEW FACES ON THE 12TH CCP CENTRAL COMMITTEE. *Issues & Studies [Taiwan] 1983 19(2): 72-77, (3): 79-83.* 1976-82
*For abstract see **Hu Jintao***

Li Lian

3992. —. FOUR SECRETARIES OF THE CCP PROVINCIAL-LEVEL COMMITTEES. *Issues & Studies [Taiwan] 1983 19(6): 97-100.* 1960's-83
*For abstract see **Han Peixin***

Li Peng

3993. —. LI P'ENG—VICE PREMIER OF THE STATE COUNCIL. *Issues & Studies [Taiwan] 1985 21(9): 158-163.* Li Peng (Li P'eng, b. 1928) is a Moscow-trained technologist who joined the Chinese Communist Party in 1945 and has held responsible posts in the power industry and water conservation department. His recent rise has been rapid, as indicated by his official visits to the USSR and Soviet bloc nations and his appointments to the posts of vice premier of the State Council (1983) and minister in charge of the State Education Commission (1985). 1945-85

Li Yuqin

3994. Li, Yuqin. MY LIFE IN THE IMPERIAL PALACE. *Chinese Studies in History 1986 19(4): 82-101.* A translation of a memoir by Li Yuqin, who served as imperial consort to Pu Yi, last of the Qing emperors and puppet ruler of Manchukuo from 1943 to 1945. Her life at court was severely restricted. Based on the author's personal experience; 2 editor's notes. 1943-45

Liang Buting

3995. —. ONE MAYOR AND THREE GOVERNORS. *Issues & Studies [Taiwan] 1983 19(7): 72-75.* 1937-83
*For abstract see **Chen Xitong***

Liang Qichao

3996. Liu, Mei Ching. LIANG CH'I-CH'AO AND THE MEDIA: A HISTORIC RETROSPECTION. *Gazette: Int. J. for Mass Communication Studies [Netherlands] 1983 31(1): 35-45.* A narrative of the life and times of Liang Qichao (Liang Ch'i-ch'ao), one of China's first influential journalists. Having witnessed the humiliation of a backward China at the hands of foreign powers, he became a militant advocate of Chinese reform as a writer, editor, and publisher. His success led to influence with the young reform-minded Manchu emperor. Shortly thereafter, however, the emperor was deposed and Liang Qichao was forced into exile. His work, however, had prepared the way for the 1911 revolution. 1880's-1900

Liberman, Evsei G.

3997. Prociuk, Stephan G. LIBERMAN'S ECONOMIC REFORM PROPOSALS IN THE USSR. *Ukrainian Quarterly 1984 40(3): 241-254.* Traces the career of Ukrainian economist Evsei G. Liberman (1897-1983), emphasizing his call for relaxation of centralized planning and other economic reforms only partially and ineffectively implemented in the 1960's and 1970's. 1956-80

Liboi, Antonio

3998. Arian Levi, Giorgina. ANTONIO LIBOI, SOLDATO IN ALBANIA (1916-1919) [Antonio Liboi, soldier in Albania, 1916-19]. *Movimento Operaio e Socialista [Italy] 1982 5(3): 439-446.* Antonio Liboi was 21 years old when he was sent as a soldier to Albania in 1916. He was later a socialist and member of the Communist Party. From his reminiscences and other souvenirs preserved from his four years in that country it appears he had no idea why exactly he was there and what the meaning and import of the war was. 1915-18

Libri, Guglielmo

3999. Arrighi, Vanna. LE CARTE LIBRI DELLA BIBLIOTECA MORENIANA DI FIRENZE [The Libri papers in the Biblioteca Moreniana in Florence]. *Rassegna Storica Toscana [Italy] 1982 28(1): 115-131.* Describes some 15,000 documents and 2,000 letters belonging to the noted mathematician and bibliophile Guglielmo Libri (1802-69). 78 notes. 17c-1869

Liddell Hart, B. H.

4000. Morelock, Jerry D. THE LEGACY OF LIDDELL HART. *Military Review 1986 66(5): 65-75.* This biographical sketch of B. H. Liddell Hart, English military authority and writer, outlines the extent of his impact and influence on military affairs and thought from 1922 to the present as well as his worldwide influence on military and political leaders. Based on Liddell Hart's autobiography, memoirs, and other primary and secondary sources; illus., 2 photos, 42 notes. 1922-70

4001. Thorne, I. D. P. INTERPRETATIONS: LIDDELL HART AFTER FIFTEEN YEARS. *Journal of the Royal United Services Institute for Defence Studies [Great Britain] 1985 130(4): 48-51.* Basil H. Liddell Hart (1895-1970) was undoubtedly a superb historian, but there is room for criticism. His theory of the "indirect approach" while innovative gave no room for aggressiveness. His history of World War II did not consider Nazi political motives in evaluating their conduct of the war. In all his judgments, he failed to take into account the confusion of high command as a factor in war. Liddell Hart's position as a master historian will always be secure due to his history of World War I. Based on Liddell Hart's writings, interviews, and secondary sources; 31 notes. 1918-70

Liebermann, Max

4002. Grasshoff, Kurt. DER SPORT IM WERK DES IMPRESSIONISTISCHEN MALERS MAX LIEBERMANN (1847-1935) [Sport in the work of the Impressionist painter Max Liebermann (1847-1935)]. *Stadion [West Germany] 1982-83 8-9: 105-136.* Discusses motifs of sport in the work of Max Liebermann (1847-1935), a German Impressionist painter. Eight groups of pictures in respect to sport can be perceived: the bathing of boys in open water, horseback riding at the beach, tennis at Dutch seaside resorts, rowing and sailing on Alster and Wannsee, polo games, horseracing, wrestling, and children's games. As an Impressionist, Liebermann was especially interested in man in nature—his control over it, his movements, the reflection of the sun on the body, and nondepictable motifs of nature. Being part of bourgeois society and enjoying horseback riding and ice skating himself, his painting motifs were chosen from these circles. Based on the catalog of the Max Liebermann exhibition in the National Galerie (Staatliche Museen, Preussischer Kulturbesitz) in Berlin, 1979, and other secondary sources; 13 illus., 53 notes. 1860's-1935

Liebig, Justus

4003. Brock, W. H. LIEBIGIANA: OLD AND NEW PERSPECTIVES. *Hist. of Sci. [Great Britain] 1981 19(45): 201-218.* Little has been published on the German chemist Justus Liebig since his death in 1873 although his reputation in the 19th century was considerable, and many of his publications and manuscripts are available for study. He had diverse influences on many of the chemical disciplines and a role in the institutionalization of research. Much could be learned about Liebig's career and his relation to various chemical interest groups from investigation of vast archives of unread Liebigiana, documents which promise much new information on the development of chemical industries in Europe. Based on primary sources in the Gesellschaft Liebigs-Museum, Giessen, and the Bavarian state library, Munich; 58 notes. 1820-73

4004. Snelders, H. A. M. THE MULDER-LIEBIG CONTROVERSY ELUCIDATED BY THEIR CORRESPONDENCE. *Janus [Netherlands] 1982 69(3-4): 199-221.* The 21 available letters, dated 1838-46, of the Dutch chemist Gerrit Jan Mulder (1802-80) to his German colleague Justus Liebig (1803-73) give a detailed description of Mulder's research on albuminous substances. Liebig, although impressed with Mulder's results, doubted the essential part of sulfur and phosphorus in the albuminoid molecule and this led to a bitter polemic between the two. Based on the letters of Mulder to Liebig in the Bayerische Staatsbibliothek, Munich; 103 notes. 1838-46

Liebknecht, Karl

4005. John, Matthias. KARL LIEBKNECHT ALS STUDENT AN DER LEIPZIGER UNIVERSITÄT [Karl Liebknecht as a student at Leipzig University]. *Beiträge zur Gesch. der Arbeiterbewegung [East Germany] 1981 23(4): 556-561.* Discusses the influence of lectures and political activities at the University of Leipzig on German Communist Karl Liebknecht (1871-1919), who studied law, public finance, and administration there. Based on documents in the Leipzig University archives and secondary sources; 48 notes. 1890-93

Liebknecht, Wilhelm

4006. Kandel', E. P. VILGEL'M LIBKNEKHT—SOLDAT REVOLIUTSII [Wilhelm Liebknecht: soldier of the revolution]. *Novaia i Noveishaia Istoriia [USSR] 1982 (5): 88-108.* Wilhelm Liebknecht (1826-1900) participated in the German revolutionary democratic and republican movement from his student days. He played an active role in the French and German revolutions of 1848, was imprisoned, and subsequently exiled to Switzerland, and then to England, where he became a close collaborator of Marx and Engels and helped to found the periodical *Neue Zeit* (1859). He returned to Germany in 1861, and took a leading role in the struggle against Lassalist conceptions within the workers' movement. 2 photos. Article to be continued. 1848-1900

4007. Schröder, Wolfgang. IM RINGEN UM EINE POLITISCHE OPERATIONSBASIS: WILHELM LIEBKNECHTS VERHÄLTNIS ZU KARL MARX IN DEN "BERLINER JAHREN" 1862 BIS 1865 [The struggle for a political base of operations: Wilhelm Liebknecht's relationship with Karl Marx in the "Berlin years" 1862-65]. *Beiträge zur Gesch. der Arbeiterbewegung [East Germany] 1983 25(3): 368-383.* Wilhelm Liebknecht and Karl Marx became great friends, 1850-62, when Liebknecht also lived in England. In 1862 Liebknecht returned to Germany and went to live in Berlin, but had to limit his political activities because Bismarck had risen to power. He continued to correspond with Marx and discussed many aspects of his life in Berlin during the period 1862-65, including his work for the *Norddeutsche Allgemeine Zeitung,* 1862-63, which he decided to leave when it became apparent that the paper was an official organ for Bismarck, his plans for a political base of operations in Berlin, and his practical political activities within the German labor movement. Liebknecht founded the Berlin printers' union and was the most effective middleman between Marx and Engels and the German labor movement. In 1865 Liebknecht was expelled from Berlin. Based on correspondence between Marx and Liebknecht in the Central Party archives at the Institute for Marxism-Leninism in Moscow; 89 notes. 1862-65

Liévano Aguirre, Indalecio

4008. —. FALLECIMIENTO DEL ACADEMICO DE NUMERO DON INDALECIO LIEVANO AGUIRRE [Death of Academician Indalecio Liévano Aguirre]. *Bol. de Hist. y Antigüedades [Colombia] 1982 69(737): 353-382.*

—. NOTA BIBLIOGRAFICA [Bibliographic note], *pp. 355-357.* Brief bibliography of the work of the Colombian political leader, diplomat, and historian Indalecio Liévano Aguirre (1917-82).

Ocampo López, Javier. LIEVANO AGUIRRE Y EL REVISIONISMO HISTORICO [Liévano Aguirre and historical revisionism], *pp. 358-366.* Assesses Liévano's significance in Colombian historiography as a liberal critic of traditional liberal interpretations and pioneer in emphasis on socioeconomic factors. 7 notes.

Acosta Borrero, Pedro. INDALECIO LIEVANO AGUIRRE HISTORIADOR... HOMBRE DE SU TIEMPO [Indalecio Liévano Aguirre: historian and man of his time], *pp. 367-371.*

Tirado Mejía, Alvaro. DOS VIDAS PARALELAS. LIEVANO AGUIRRE Y ANTONIO GARCIA [Two parallel lives: Liévano Aguirre and Antonio García], *pp. 377-380.* Compares Liévano with the Colombian socialist economist and supporter of populist political movements Antonio García, whose death occurred within a month of Liévano's. Includes resolutions of tribute and newspaper articles on Liévano Aguirre. 1940's-82

Liffman, Herbert

4009. Liffman, Herbert. IN SEARCH OF MY IDENTITY. *Australian Journal of Politics and History [Australia] 1985 31(1): 10-28.* Personal memoirs of Herbert Liffman, born in 1908 at Aachen, Germany, graduate in economics and social sciences of Cologne University, who migrated to Australia in 1939 to get away from Nazism. Discusses his response to Australia and his search for identity. In Germany he had been German first, then Jewish. In Australia he chose cultural Judaism after meeting his wife. For 30 years he ran a small business providing magazines for waiting rooms, but did not prosper. Restitution compensation awarded by the German government in 1956 brought more material prosperity and permitted return trips to Europe. In his 60's he gave up business and became a teacher in a school of intelligent underachievers. He became tricultural—a Jew, emotionally attached to Australia, and still integrated with his German background. 1910's-80's

Ligeti, György

4010. Szigeti, István. A BUDAPEST INTERVIEW WITH GYÖRGY LIGETI. *New Hungarian Q. [Hungary] 1984 25(94): 205-210.* Prints a transcript of a radio interview with Hungarian composer György Ligeti (b. 1923). He was born in Dicsőszentmárton in Transylvania, moving to Kolozsvár at age six. Recounts his career in Hungary, Romania, Austria, and West Germany. Broadcast on Budapest Radio, 29 July 1983. 1940's-83

Ligne, Charles Joseph von

4011. Ricaumont, Jacques de. "LE PRINCE DE LIGNE" ["The Prince de Ligne"]. *Rev. des Deux Mondes [France] 1982 (7): 82-88.* Recounts the life and career of Charles Joseph von Ligne (1735-1814), soldier and diplomat, who epitomized the breeding and manners of the Old Regime. 1735-1814

Lilienblum, Moshe Lieb

4012. Kabakoff, Jacob. L'TOLDOT HAKHMEI YISRAEL B-RUSIA [Two autobiographies of Russian Jewish authors]. *Shvut [Israel] 1982 9: 99-101.* 1843-1912

*For abstract see **Deinard, Ephraim***

Lillienberg, Jean Georg

4013. Nilzén, Göran. JEAN GEORG LILLIENBERG: EN FRIHETSTIDA KARRIÄRIST [Jean Georg Lillienberg: a careerist in the age of liberty]. *Personhistorisk Tidskrift [Sweden] 1979 75(1-2): 62-71.* The 1776 autobiography by Lillienberg (1713-98), Swedish governor, chamberlain, member of the Riksdag, and count, relates the successful career of a Swedish civil servant in a dramatic historical period. To some extent Lillienberg avoids mentioning the part he played in politics on the side of the Hat Party, which greatly helped his career. 52 notes, 33 ref. 1713-76

Lima, Polita de

4014. Briceño Perozo, Mario. POLITA DE CORO [Polita of Coro]. *Bol. de la Acad. Nac. de la Hist. [Venezuela] 1983 66(262): 299-305.* Polita de Lima de Castillo (1869-1944) of Coro, state of Falcon, was a poet, playwright, novelist, and publicist. She was very active in the cultural life of her region. In 1913 she was awarded the title of "Princess of the Venezuelan Parnassus." 1880's-20c

4015. Sola Ricardo, Imra de. POLITA DE LIMA, PROMOTORA CULTURAL DE CORO [Polita de Lima, cultural promoter of Coro]. *Bol. de la Acad. Nac. de la Hist. [Venezuela] 1983 66(262): 401-408.* The writer Polita de Lima (1869-1944) was influential in the cultural life of Venezuela. Many of her works were translated into French and German. Some of her plays were staged in Spain. She was also a teacher, and later founded and administered a school for 45 years. 1890's-20c

Lima Sobrinho, Alexandre José Barbosa

4016. Barreto, Dalmo Freire. CINQUENTENARIO DA ELEIÇÃO DOS SOCIOS DR.S PEDRO CALMON E ALEXANDRE JOSE BARBOSA LIMA SOBRINHO [Fiftieth anniversary of the election of members Drs. Pedro Calmon and Alexandre José Barbosa Lima Sobrinho]. *Rev. do Inst. Hist. e Geog. Brasileiro [Brazil] 1981 (333): 71-92.* 1921-81
For abstract see ***Calmon, Pedro***

Limantour, Jose Yves

4017. Bazant, Jan. JOSEPH YVES LIMANTOUR (1812-1885) Y SU AVENTURA CALIFORNIANA. [Jose Yves Limantour (1812-85) and his California adventure. Part 2]. *Hist. Mexicana [Mexico] 1980 29(3): 352-374.* Continued from a previous article. In 1858, a US judge ruled that titles acquired by Jose Yves Limantour (1812-85) to prove ownership of half the land occupied by the city of San Francisco were fraudulent. Documents available at the University of Texas indicate that Limantour's titles were indeed genuine but obtained without approval of the Mexican government and consequently invalid. Although Limantour was the victim of injustice, it was an injustice that deprived him of property that he had acquired illegally. Based on documents located in the Nettie Lee Benson Latin American Collection of the University of Texas, Austin, and secondary works; 28 notes. 1848-53

Lin Boqu

4018. Iur'ev, M. LIN BOQU, AN OUTSTANDING CHINESE REVOLUTIONARY. *Far Eastern Affairs [USSR] 1983 (2): 130-138.* Reviews the life and political career of Lin Boqu (Lin Zuhan) (1886-1960), one of the founders of the Communist Party of China. 1886-1960

Lin Zheng

4019. —. ONE MAYOR AND THREE GOVERNORS. *Issues & Studies [Taiwan] 1983 19(7): 72-75.* 1937-83
For abstract see ***Chen Xitong***

Linchwe I

4020. Morton, R. F. LINCHWE I AND THE KGATLA CAMPAIGN IN THE SOUTH AFRICAN WAR, 1899-1902. *Journal of African History [Great Britain] 1985 26(2-3): 169-191.* During the Boer War, the Kgatla people and their leader, Linchwe I, became active participants—fighting on the British side against the Afrikaners. The author considers the Kgatla choice to support Briton over Boer, Linchwe's expectations when entering the war, the Kgatla role in the struggle, and the effects of their participation. The Kgatla community straddled two colonial worlds: part of Linchwe's people were resident in the Bechuanaland Protectorate under British administration, while the other part lived in the western Transvaal under Afrikaner rule. Linchwe fought alongside the British and led raids into the Transvaal in an effort to eliminate the Boer settlement and reestablish his control over the Kgatla under Afrikaner domination. Linchwe proved successful in his efforts to reunify his kingdom (following the British victory) and secure his political leadership against African rivals. Based on documents in the Botswana and South African National Archives and on published primary sources; 107 notes. 1899-1920

Linchwe II

4021. Grant, Sandy. A CHRONOLOGICAL CAREER SUMMARY: CHIEF LINCHWE II KGAFELA. *Botswana Notes and Records [Botswana] 1985 17: 47-52.* Since his installation as Chief of the Kgatla at the age of 27 in 1963, Linchwe II has figured prominently in the history of Botswana. Chief Linchwe has reformed social customs, while retaining the essence of his society and its political structure. As Kgatla ruler, he has resuscitated the age-regimental system and been heavily involved in church disputes. He has opposed the national government's policy of reducing the powers of local governments, befriended President Kaunda of Zambia, and served as Botswana's ambassador to the United States. Based on personal communications, documents from the Botswana National Archives, and the newspaper *Botswana Daily News;* 60 notes, biblio. 1935-84

Lindeman-Lindschöld, Erik

4022. Jägerskiöld, Stig. ERIK LINDEMAN-LINDSCHÖLD [Erik Lindeman-Lindschöld]. *Karolinska Förbundets Årsbok [Sweden] 1983: 119-179.* Describes the circumstances and experiences that brought Erik Lindeman, the son of a country smith, to a successful career at the Swedish court, culminating in his elevation as Count Erik Lindschöld, advisor to the king, in the 17th century. As preceptor to the king's son, Lindeman was responsible for the boy's upbringing and education, guiding him through nine years of studies and contacts abroad. There Lindeman made fruitful contacts with the heads of states and the prominent thinkers of his time, developing a culture and a drive surpassed by few in administration, politics, literature, science, and the arts. 97 notes. 17c

Lindman, Sven

4023. Anckar, Dag. SVEN LINDMAN IN MEMORIAM [In memory of Sven Lindman]. *Politiikka [Finland] 1983 25(1): 2-5.* Reviews the scholarly career of Sven O. G. Lindman (1910-83), professor of political science at the Swedish-language Turku University in Finland *(Åbo Akademi)* and a specialist in Finnish political history. 1910-83

4024. Anckar, Dag. SVEN LINDMAN [Sven Lindman]. *Statsvetenskaplig Tidskrift [Sweden] 1983 86(2): 153-156.* An obituary for the Finnish political scientist and political historian, Sven Olof Gustav Lindman (1910-83). 1910-83

4025. Lindman, Sven. MINA LÄROFÄDER: TILLBAKABLICK [My intellectual ancestors: looking backward]. *Statsvetenskaplig Tidskrift [Sweden] 1983 86(1): 1-5.* Autobiographical sketch of the intellectual development of Sven Lindman (b. 1910), emeritus professor of political science at Åbo Akademi in Turku, Finland. 1910-82

Lindo, José

4026. —. CORONEL JOSE LINDO, PROCER TOCUYANO [Colonel José Lindo, Tocuyan hero]. *Boletín de la Academia Nacional de la Historia [Venezuela] 1985 68(270): 526-537.* Reproduces several documents concerning Colonel José Lindo, from Tocuyo, Venezuela, who died in 1840 at the age of 34, while on active service. The documents include several applications for recognition of his services and other papers concerning his career. Text of documents in the National Archives of Colombia. 1806-40

Lindroth, Sten

4027. Eriksson, Gunnar. STEN LINDROTH 1914-1980 [Sten Lindroth 1914-80]. *Lychnos [Sweden] 1979-80: ix-xxiv.* This eulogy on Sten Lindroth, internationally known scholar and professor of the history of ideas and science at the University of Uppsala in Sweden, outlines his youth and early studies and focuses on his later research projects. A large part of his life's work is accounted for in a series of studies devoted to Swedish intellectual and technological history. In the 1950's, Lindroth began heading a huge project that was to cover the history of the Royal Swedish Academy of Sciences from its beginning in 1739 until 1818-20. His last, unfinished achievement was a general survey of sciences and learning in Sweden from the Middle Ages to the beginning of the 19th century. Lindroth was a member of the Swedish Academy and the editor of *Lychnos* since 1950. 1914-80

Lindsay, Anne

See Barnard, Anne

Lindsay, Lord

See Williams, Alexander

Lindsey, Robert L.

4028. Medoff, Rafael. MISSIONARIES IN ISRAEL. *Midstream 1985 31(7): 3-8.* Describes the activities and experiences of Baptist missionary Robert L. Lindsey, who served as pastor of the Baptist center in Jerusalem from 1945. 1945-85

Lindström, Erik Fritiof

4029. Hamberg, Lars. ERIK LINDSTRÖM, SCENARTISTEN [Erik Lindström, the stage artist]. *Historiska och Litteraturhistoriska Studier [Finland] 1986 61: 259-300.* A biographical sketch of the Finnish actor Erik Fritiof Lindström (1906-74), a member of the repertory company at the Swedish Theater in Helsinki, Finland, from 1926 to 1973. Based on interviews. 1906-74

Lingard, John

4030. Cattermole, P. H. "John Lingard: The Historian as Apologist." University of Kent at Canterbury [England] 1984. *DAI-C 1985 46(3): 614; 46/2944c.* 10c-19c

Lingen, Reinholdt Johan von

4031. Nilzén, Göran. REINHOLDT JOHAN VON LINGENS SJÄLVBIOGRAFISKA ANTECKNINGAR [Reinholdt Johan von Lingen's autobiographical records]. *Personhistorisk Tidskrift [Sweden] 1982 78(1-2): 3-124.* Reinholdt Johan von Lingen's (1708-85) autobiography concentrates on his years as a press-ganged member of the French navy, 1725-29; his military career in Saxony; his years in Russia, 1737-41, when he took part in the war against Turkey, and the years to 1744, when he was called back to Sweden to join the Hats in their war against Russia. In 1743 von Lingen brought the peace proposals from the peace conference in Åbo to Stockholm after a hazardous journey. Their timely arrival altered the political situation overnight and helped save Sweden from threatening civil war. His account is based on his diaries and notes and on official documents to which he had access and is in the main reliable. Based on the autobiography and supporting sources; introd., 3 maps, 92 notes, index of names. ca 1700-72

Liniers y Bremond, Santiago de

4032. Martinez Valverde, Carlos. SANTIAGO DE LINIERS EN EL RIO DE LA PLATA [Santiago de Liniers at Río de la Plata]. *Rev. de Hist. Militar [Spain] 1982 26(52): 7-46.* Admiral and General Santiago de Liniers y Bremond commanded the garrison forces of the Plata region standing before the British amphibious assault on Buenos Aires in 1806. Expelled from the city, Liniers retook the city with local forces two months later. He then organized regional forces on popular and national lines and repulsed a larger British invasion in 1807. Displaced as acting viceroy in 1809, he fell victim to the republican movement, which executed him the following year. Based on published sources; 16 illus., 2 maps, 3 appendixes, 74 notes, biblio. 1805-10

Linnaeus, Carolus

4033. Browne, Janet. BOTANY AND BOTANISTS. *Hist. of Sci. [Great Britain] 1984 22(2): 207-209.* Reviews Edward Lee Greene's *Landmarks of Botanical History* (1983) and Tore Frangsmyr's *Linnaeus: The Man and His Work* (1983). The first book is a reprint of Greene's original *Landmarks of Botany* along with a previously unpublished second volume and a valuable biographical and historical essay, all of which are concerned with pre-Linnean botany. The second book is a new selection of essays about Linnaeus that helps explain why he both antagonizes and excites historians of botany. 1400-1800

4034. Jonsell, Bengt. DANIEL SOLANDER—THE PERFECT LINNAEAN: HIS YEARS IN SWEDEN AND RELATIONS WITH LINNAEUS. *Archives of Natural History [Great Britain] 1984 11(3): 443-450.* Examines the personal relations between the Swedish-born naturalist Daniel Solander (1733-82) and the famous Swedish botanist Carolus Linnaeus (1707-82), one of the founders of modern systematic botany. Discusses how Solander came into contact with Linnaeus, his career as one of Linnaeus's pupils, and his experiences as a field botanist and plant collector. Solander turned down Linnaeus's offer of a chair in Natural History at St. Petersburg Academy in 1762, preferring to stay in England, where he had journeyed in 1760. Thereafter, relations between the two men were never restored. 3 fig., biblio. 1750-62

Linton, W. J.

4035. Gleckner, Robert F. W. J. LINTON, A LATTER-DAY BLAKE. *Bull. of Res. in the Humanities 1982 85(2): 208-227.* A political radical, artist, and dedicated practitioner-teacher of his work, W. J. Linton (1812-97), who shared William Blake's views, was an honored engraver in Great Britain and the United States. 1836-86

Lipertes, Demetres

4036. Michaēlidē, M. G. HO DĒMĒTRĒS LIPERTĒS KAI HĒ ALLĒLOGRAPHIA TOU ME TON HIERŌNYMO VARLAAM (1886-1893) [Demetres Lipertes and his correspondence with Jerome Varlaam, 1886-1893]. *Kypriakaí Spoudaí [Cyprus] 1980 44: 131-146.* Describes 16 letters exchanged between Demetres Lipertes, a Cypriot poet, with Jerome Varlaam, a Hellenist teaching in Larnaca. 1886-93

Lipgens, Walter

4037. Fehrenbach, Elisabeth. NEKROLOG: WALTER LIPGENS 12. 6. 1925-29. 4. 1984 [Obituary: Walter Lipgens, 12 June 1925-29 April 1984]. *Historische Zeitschrift [West Germany] 1984 239(3): 757-759.* Evaluates the career of

Walter Lipgens of Saarbrucken, especially his major work on European integration and earlier biographical studies on the Reformation and 18th-century subjects. 1925-84

Lipold, Marko Vincenc

4038. Ramovš, Anton and Kochansky-Devidé, Vanda. MARKO VINCENC LIPOLD (1816-1883), PRVI SLOVENSKI GEOLOG: ŽIVLJENJE IN DELO. OB STOLETNICI SMRTI [Marko Vincenc Lipold (1816-83), first Slovenian geologist: his life and work. On the centenary of his death]. *Zbornik za Zgodovino Naravoslovja in Tehnike [Yugoslavia] 1985 8: 9-63.* Reviews Lipold's family background, presents a family tree beginning in 1692 and describes his research and practical activity. After reading law and completing studies in mining engineering in 1842, he held several jobs in both fields, becoming second geologist at the new Vienna State Geological Institute in 1849. After 1867 he headed the mercury mine at Idrija in western Slovenia, where he continued his geological research while improving procedures and increasing output, always demonstrating great concern for the conditions of the miners. 1840's-83

4039. Ramovš, Anton. POČASTITEV MARKA VINCENCA LIPOLDA OB STOTI OBLETNICI NJEGOVE SMRTI [Commemorating Marko Vincenc Lipold on the centenary of his death]. *Zbornik za Zgodovino Naravoslovja in Tehnike [Yugoslavia] 1985 8: 147-152.* Address at the unveiling of a plaque in Mozirje, Slovenia commemorating the geologist Marko Vincenc Lipold (1816-83). 1816-83

Lipsius, Justus

4040. Mout, M. E. H. N. HEILIGE LIPSIUS, BID VOOR ONS [Holy Lipsius, pray for us]. *Tijdschrift voor Geschiedenis [Netherlands] 1984 97(2): 195-206.* Justus Lipsius (1547-1606) was a famous Dutch humanist, philologist, neostoic, and political thinker. Provides a brief review of two works, *Iusti Lipsi Epistolae* 2 vol. (1978-83) edited by A. Gerlo et al. and Gerhard Oestreich's *Neostoicism and the Early Modern State* (1982), which evaluate Lipsius's life and scholarship. 65 notes. ca 1570-1606

Lipsius, Richard Adlebert

4041. Suda, Max Josef. RICHARD A LIPSIUS' THEOLOGISCHE AUSEINANDERSETZUNG MIT HEGEL [Richard A. Lipsius's theological disagreement with Hegel]. *Jahrbuch der Gesellschaft für die Gesch. des Protestantismus in Österreich [Austria] 1980 96(1-3): 117-137.* Richard Adlebert Lipsius (1830-92) was professor of theology at the Protestant theological faculty in Vienna, 1861-65. The author describes Lipsius's academic career and theological writings, especially his most important work on Protestant dogma. He also discusses the influence of Kantian philosophy of Lipsius. He pays particular attention to Lipsius's disagreements with the philosophy of Hegel (1770-1831) and his debates with Alois Emanuel Biedermann, the Hegelian theologian. Secondary sources; 23 notes. 1830-92

Lipson, Alfred

4042. Lipson, Alfred. THE GAMBLE THAT SAVED SIXTY-FIVE. *Midstream 1985 31(4): 31-35.* The author recalls his escape from the ghetto of Radom when deportations commenced, together with 65 fellow workers. 1942

Lipszky, János

4043. Csendes, László. LIPSZKY JÁNOS HUSZÁRTISZT ÉLETÚTJA ÉS TÉRKÉPEI [Life and maps of János Lipszky, Hussar officer]. *Hadtörténelmi Közlemények [Hungary] 1982 29(3): 464-481.* Lipszky, who joined the Austro-Hungarian army at a very early age, gained all the necessary knowledge for producing high quality maps within the army. Attached to the mostly Hungarian Graeven Hussars, he served in Germany and Italy. In 1802 he was transferred to Pest as coordinator of all maps, which until then were all independently and sometimes inaccurately produced. In 1805 the standard 1:28,000 ratio was generally accepted in Hungary for the first time. Lipszky was considered the producer of the highest quality and most accurate maps of the period. 6 plates; 49 notes. 1766-1826

Lisboa, António Francisco

See Aleijadinho

Lisch, Friedrich

4044. Rakow, Peter-Joachim. FRIEDRICH LISCH (1801-1883)—EIN MECKLENBURGISCHER ARCHIVAR UND HISTORIKER [Friedrich Lisch (1801-83)—archivist and historian from Mecklenburg]. *Archivmitteilungen [East Germany] 1985 35(2): 59-62.* Describes Friedrich Lisch's successful transformation of the Mecklenburg-Schwerin official archive from a servant of the ruling elite, closed to the public, to an open institution available and catering to scholars and other interested parties during his lengthy tenure as its director, 1834-79. 1834-79

Lisle, Viscount

4045. Green, V. H. H. THE LISLES IN THEIR LETTERS. *Hist. Today [Great Britain] 1982 32(Mar): 43-47.* A collection known as the Lisle letters—numbering about 1,677 out of a total of some 3,000 surviving missives covering the years when Arthur Plantagenet, (Viscount Lisle) was lord deputy of Calais, 1533-40—have been collected into six volumes *(The Lisle Letters,* edited by Muriel St. Clare Byrne) that contain epistles written by Viscount Lisle, his wife Lady Elizabeth Lisle, and their agent, John Husee. 1533-40

Lisón de Tejada, Juan

4046. Hampe Martínez, Teodoro. EN TORNO AL LEVANTAMIENTO PIZARRISTA: LA INTERVENCION DEL OIDOR LISON DE TEJADA [On Pizarro's uprising: the intervention of Judge Lisón de Tejada]. *Revista de Indias [Spain] 1984 44(174): 385-414.* Analyzes the conduct of Lisón de Tejada, a member of the Audiencia of Lima, comparing him with other members, during the uprising against royal authority in Peru. Tejada was significant for supporting Francisco Pizarro and was the authority responsible for requesting royal confirmation of the rebel's governorship. Based on documents in the General Archive of the Indies (Seville), General Archive of Simancas, and Library of the Royal Palace (Madrid); 2 appendixes, 133 notes. 1543-49

List, Friedrich

4047. Schäffer, Volker. FRIEDRICH LISTS STUDIENJAHRE IM LICHT NEUER ARCHIVALIEN [Friedrich List's university years in the light of new documents]. *Zeits. für Württembergische Landesgeschichte [West Germany] 1981 40: 376-386.* Friedrich List studied law exclusively during his years at the University of Tübingen. Based on material from the University Archive, Tübingen; 53 notes. 1811-14

4048. Zalin, Giovanni. L'IMPRONTA DELLE TEMATICHE LISTIANE NELLE CONCEZIONI ECONOMICHE DEL SENATORE ROSSI: ANALOGIE E DISSONANZE [List's topics in Senator Rossi's economic thought: analogies and differences]. *Arch. Storico Italiano [Italy] 1982 140(1): 117-129.* Friedrich List (1789-1846) and Alessandro Rossi (1819-98) were two of the main supporters of protectionism in their countries. They thought protectionism was the only means for the second rank of countries to close the industrial gap with Great Britain. Secondary sources; 41 notes. 19c

List, Herbert

4049. Spender, Stephen. HERBERT LIST. *Horizon 1981 24(4): 54-63.* Memoirs of the anti-intellectual German photographer Herbert List and his circle of friends in Weimar Germany, 1929-33, called by Spender "the Children of the Sun." 1929-33

Lista y Aragón, Alberto

4050. Vásquez, George L. ALBERTO LISTA AND THE BIRTH OF SPANISH LIBERAL HISTORIOGRAPHY. *Iberian Studies [Great Britain] 1980 9(1): 32-39.* Discusses the life, career, and historiographical output of the Spanish liberal historian Alberto Lista y Aragón (1775-1848) and examines the weaknesses and shortcomings of liberal historiography in 19th-century Spain. 19c

Liszt, Daniel

4051. Walker, Alan. A BOY NAMED DANIEL. *New Hungarian Quarterly [Hungary] 1986 27(101): 204-220.* Chronicles the brief life of Daniel Liszt (1839-59), the son and third illegitimate child of Franz Liszt and the Countess Marie d'Agoult. Based on unpublished letters in the Bibliothèque Nationale (Paris), the Bayreuth Archives, and other primary and secondary sources; 49 notes, 4 illus., biblio. 1839-59

Liszt, Franz

4052. Porterfield, Christopher. LISZT'S ESCAPADES HAVE TENDED TO OBSCURE HIS GENIUS. *Smithsonian 1986 17(5): 112-124.* A biographical account of the unique genius of Franz Liszt. 1811-86

4053. Walker, Alan. LISZT AND VIENNA. *New Hungarian Quarterly [Hungary] 1985 26(100): 253-259.* The career of Franz Liszt was most intimately associated with the cities of Budapest, Rome, and Weimar. His association with Vienna, though less prominent, was equally important. This connection has been researched by Dezső Legány in *Franz Liszt: Unbekannte Presse und Briefe aus Wien, 1822-1886* (1984). 21 notes, biblio. 1822-86

Littré, Emile

4054. Petit, Annie. PHILOLOGIE ET PHILOSOPHIE DE L'HISTOIRE [Philology and philosophy of history]. *Revue de Synthèse [France] 1982 103(106-108): 215-243.* His philological training led lexicographer and historian Emile Littré (1801-81) to research methods and a conception of history which differed significantly from the positivist school with which he identified himself. 1820's-81

4055. Rey, Alain. LITTRE, DE L'HUMANISME AUX SCIENCES HUMAINES [Littré, from humanism to the human sciences]. *Revue de Synthèse [France] 1982 103(106-108): 163-176.* Discusses French lexicographer Emile Littré's (1801-81) democratic and pedagogical humanism and his implicit contribution to the search for a science of the human reality. 1820's-81

4056. Rullière, Roger. LES ETUDES MEDICALES D'EMILE LITTRE [The medical studies of Emile Littré]. *Revue de Synthèse [France] 1982 103(106-108): 255-262.* Emile Littré's (1801-81) medical studies influenced the direction of his later work. 1819-39

Litvinov, Maxim

4057. Laloy, Jean. L'U.R.S.S. ET L'EUROPE A L'ISSUE DE LA GUERRE: LE TEMOIGNAGE DE LITVINOV [The USSR and Europe at the end of the war: the testimony of Litvinov]. *Revue des Sciences Morales & Politiques [France] 1982 137(4): 640-651.* In 1944 the veteran Soviet diplomat Maxim Litvinov urged his government to follow a policy of cooperation with the Western allies in the postwar world. By 1946 he despaired of success because Communist ideology insisted upon an inevitable conflict with the capitalist powers. Discussion follows, pp. 651-654. 4 notes. 1944-46

Liu Huaqing

4058. —. LIU HUA-CH'ING—COMMANDER OF THE PLA NAVY. *Issues & Studies [Taiwan] 1985 21(5): 126-130.* Liu Huaqing (Liu Hua-ch'ing; b. 1917), a native of Hubei (Hupeh), engaged in Communist Party and guerrilla activities from his youth. He held increasingly responsible posts in the Red Army until his eclipse during the Cultural Revolution. Since 1975 Liu has had a number of high level assignments. In 1982 he was appointed commander of the Chinese navy. 1932-85

Liu Shaoqi

4059. Dittmer, Lowell. MUERTE Y TRANSFIGURACION: LA REHABILITACION DE LIU SHAOQI Y LA POLITICA CHINA CONTEMPORANEA [Death and transfiguration: Liu Shaoqi's rehabilitation and the contemporary Chinese politics]. *Estudios de Asia y Africa [Mexico] 1982 17(3): 369-417.* During the Cultural Revolution (1966-76), Liu Shaoqi (1898-1969) became the paramount symbol of every trend leading the country away from the right path. There is, however, new evidence about Liu's biography, in the light of his political rehabilitation in 1980. The author surveys the charges as originally presented against Liu and as "selected" and "edited" for his rehabilitation by the present Chinese leaders. This event is to be explained in terms of Chinese political culture as well as by the nature of Liu's contribution to the Party's organization and expansion, and by the political needs of the new rulers. Republished from the *Journal of Asian Studies.* Based on China and Hong Kong's media reports; 78 notes. 1930's-80

Liublinskaia, Aleksandra D.

4060. Bernadskaia, E. V.; Kiseleva, L. I.; Malinin, Iu. P.; and Somov, V. A. ALEKSANDRA DMITRIEVNA LIUBLINSKAIA (1902-1980) [Aleksandra Dmitrievna Liublinskaia (1902-80)]. *Srednie Veka [USSR] 1983 46: 291-323.* Describes the career of Soviet historian Aleksandra Liublinskaia and the historical research conducted together with her husband, Vladimir Sergeevich Liublinski, an authority on Voltaire. Her primary field of interest was the sociopolitical history of France, specifically the rise of absolutism in the early 17th century under Cardinal Richelieu (1585-1642). Her voluminous collection of documents, letters, card catalogs, lecture outlines, and unpublished studies have been transferred to the archives of the Leningrad branch of the Institute of USSR History, Academy of Sciences. 29 notes. 17c

Llano, Manuel

4061. Diezhandino Nieto, M. "Vida y Obra Periodistica de Manuel Llano" [Life and journalistic work of Manuel Llano]. U. of Navarre [Spain] 1984. 668 pp. *DAI-C 1986 47(2): 272; 47/1328c.* 1920's-39

Llimona, Josep

4062. Ainaud, Josep M. JOSEP LLIMONA, ESCULTOR MODERNISTA [Josep Llimona, a modern sculptor]. *Historia y Vida [Spain] 1984 17(196): 28-37.* A review of the life and work of Catalan sculptor Josep Llimona (1864-1934), one of the major figures of Modernism. Many of his statues can be seen in the streets of Barcelona. 1878-1934

Lloyd, Charles

4063. Kellogg, Joyce Louise. "The Life and Works of Charles Lloyd to 1800." Yale U. 1983 304 pp. *DAI 1983 44(2): 493-A.* DA83146189 1775-1839

Lloyd, Christopher

4064. Kemp, Peter; Watt, James; Knight, Roger; and Gueritz, Edward. PROFESSOR CHRISTOPHER LLOYD. *Mariner's Mirror [Great Britain] 1986 72(2): 113-115.* Four of Christopher Lloyd's (1897-1986) colleagues pay tribute to his devotion to naval and maritime history. 1930-86

Lloyd, Humphrey

4065. Spearman, T. D. HUMPHREY LLOYD, 1800-1881. *Hermathena [Ireland] 1981 (130-131): 37-52.* Discusses the career of Humphrey Lloyd, elected to the Erasmus Smith Chair of Natural and Experimental Philosophy at Trinity College, Dublin, in 1831, then becoming a senior fellow in 1843, and serving as vice-provost for five years prior to his election as provost in 1867. 1825-81

Lloyd, Jenkin

4066. Jones, Francis. THE FAMILIES OF BLAIDDBWLL. *Natl. Lib. of Wales J. [Great Britain] 1981 22(1): 27-37.* Stresses the need to assess the contribution of the lesser gentry to modern Welsh history and takes as an example the families descended from Jenkin Lloyd and Reynald Morris and their common stock, who inhabited the homestead of Blaiddbwll in Llanfyrnach, Pembrokeshire. Lineage is clarified and the process of land consolidation and sales examined. The estate remained with this line via heiresses until its sale in the late 19th century. Based on estate collections, wills, and genealogical sources. 1450-1887

Lloyd, Thomas Davies

4067. Morgan, Paul Bennett. BRONWYDD AND SIR THOMAS LLOYD. *National Library of Wales Journal [Great Britain] 1984 23(4): 377-405.* Traces the history of Bronwydd, a Victorian Gothic mansion in Ceredigion and the man who built it, Sir Thomas Davies Lloyd, Bart., Lord of Cemais (1820-77). Sir Thomas took over the Bronwydd estate from his father in 1845. He served as justice of the peace and as Deputy Lieutenant in Pembroke, Carmarthen, and Cardiganshire. He was High Sheriff of the country in 1851, was created a baronet in 1863, and sat as a Liberal Member of Parliament from 1865 until 1874. As a landlord he was renowned for his courtesy and generosity to tenants. Based on National Library of Wales documents; append., 85 notes, photo. 19c

Lloyd George, David

4068. Boyd, Newell D. THE EMERGENCE OF THE WELSH BOUNDER: DAVID LLOYD GEORGE'S ORATORICAL ATTACKS DURING THE ANGLO-BOER WAR. *Communication Monographs 1985 52(1): 78-91.* David Lloyd George's political career gained its first successes during the Boer War, when he managed to attack the war in his native Welsh oratory, gaining support in Wales and enough national attention to contribute to his rise within the political opposition. 1898-1902

4069. Gilbert, Bentley B. PACIFIST TO INTERVENTIONIST: DAVID LLOYD GEORGE IN 1911 AND 1914. WAS BELGIUM AN ISSUE? *Historical Journal [Great Britain] 1985 28(4): 863-885.* Recounts the internal political maneuvering that took place among England's leaders in the years leading up to World War I. Though British statesman David Lloyd George continued to make pacifist pronouncements in line with the views of his Liberal Party constituency up until the German invasion of Belgium in 1914, he had actually decided as early as 1911 that Britain must support France militarily to prevent Prussian domination of Europe. Based on diaries and correspondence; 89 notes. 1907-14

4070. McEwen, J. M. LLOYD GEORGE'S ACQUISITION OF THE *DAILY CHRONICLE* IN 1918. *J. of British Studies 1983 22(1): 127-144.* 1918
*For abstract see **Donald, Robert***

4071. McEwen, J. M. NORTHCLIFFE AND LLOYD GEORGE AT WAR, 1914-1918. *Hist. J. [Great Britain] 1981 24(3): 651-672.* Outlines the relationship between Alfred Harmsworth, Viscount Northcliffe, owner of the *Times, Daily Mail,* and *Evening News,* and other journals and newspapers and David Lloyd George, 1914-18. During World War I, Northcliffe was frequently called "The Most Powerful Man in the Country," while Lloyd George was "The Man Who Won the War." Not until 1918 did the Maurice debate and the Coupon election prove that Lloyd George's power was real while Northcliffe's was largely illusory. 67 notes. 1914-18

4072. Rintala, Marvin. RENAMED ROSES: LLOYD GEORGE, CHURCHILL, AND THE HOUSE OF LORDS. *Biography 1985 8(3): 248-264.* 1890's-1955
*For abstract see **Churchill, Winston***

Lobachevski, Nikolai

4073. Duffy, Charles Gavan. "Nicholas Ivanovich Lobachevsky, Philosopher of Science." Boston Coll. 1981. 263 pp. *DAI 1982 42(9): 4032-A.* DA8203977 1829-56

Lobanov, N. D.

4074. Lobanov, N. D. MY COLLECTION OF COSTUME AND STAGE DESIGNS BY RUSSIAN-BORN ARTISTS. *Russian Hist. 1981 8(1-2): 265-287.* Describes the author's entry into collecting costume and stage designs by Russian-born artists and some of his more interesting moments as a collector. Lists his exhibitions and the names of painters whose work is included. 19 illus., 7 notes. 1950's-70's

Lobato Velho Lopes, Rita

4075. Lobo, Francisco Bruno. DUAS PIONEIRAS—MADAME DUROCHER, RITA LOBATO [Two pioneering women: Madame Durocher and Rita Lobato]. *Rev. do Inst. Hist. e Geog. Brasileiro [Brazil] 1980 (328): 53-56.* 19c
For abstract see ***Durocher, Josephine Mathilde***

Lobengula

4076. Davidson, Apollon. IUG AFRIKI: ZHIZN' I SMERT' LOBENGULY [Southern Africa: the life and death of Lobengula]. *Aziia i Afrika Segodnia [USSR] 1984 (12): 52-55.* The study of African history is difficult because of the scarcity of information, but there are some descriptions of the Ndebele leader Lobengula and of his relations with the British colonizers of Matabeleland in the late 19th century. 1860's-94

Lobengula, Peter

4077. Shephard, Ben. LOBENGULA: A ROYAL GENTLEMAN OF COLOUR. *History Today [Great Britain] 1984 34(Apr): 36-41.* Describes the career of Peter Lobengula, an alleged son of the last Ndebele king, who lived in England by working as an actor and coal miner until his death in 1913. 1899-1913

Lobo, Antonio Leite Pereira da Gama

4078. Valladares, Francisco Canavarro de. PRIMEIRO COMANDANTE DA IMPERIAL GUARDA DE HONRA, ANTÔNIO LEITE PEREIRA DA GAMA LOBO [Antonio Leite Pereira da Gama Lobo, first commander of the imperial guard of honor]. *Revista do Instituto Histórico e Geográfico Brasileiro [Brazil] 1983 (340): 15-20.* Antonio Leite Pereira da Gama Lobo, of Cabeceiras de Basto, Portugal, embraced the military career and served in India and Brazil. He played a prominent role in Brazilian independence and was appointed first commander of the guard of honor of Emperor Pedro I. He was also an elected member of the provincial legislative assembly of São Paulo. 1814-50's

Lobov, S. M.

4079. Filimoshin, M. ADMIRAL FLOTA S. M. LOBOV (K 70-LETIIU SO DNIA ROZHDENIIA) [Admiral S. M. Lobov, on the 70th anniversary of his birth]. *Voenno-Istoricheskii Zhurnal [USSR] 1983 (2): 93-96.* S. M. Lobov (1913-77) graduated from the Frunze higher naval college in 1937 and served in the Pacific Fleet. He took part in the war with Japan in 1945 as a destroyer commander. In the postwar period he served in the Black and the North Seas and proved an able commander of the Northern fleet 1964-72. In 1972 he was appointed head of the Naval Section of the General Staff of the USSR Armed Forces. Secondary sources; 3 notes, 2 photos. 1937-77

Locke, Alain

4080. Helbling, Mark. AFRICAN ART: ALBERT C. BARNES AND ALAIN LOCKE. *Phylon 1982 43(1): 57-67.* 1920's
For abstract see ***Barnes, Albert C.***

Locke, John

4081. Mulligan, Lotte; Richards, Judith; and Graham, John K. A CONCERN FOR UNDERSTANDING: A CASE OF LOCKE'S PRECEPTS AND PRACTICE. *Hist. J. [Great Britain] 1982 25(4): 841-857.* John Locke's interest in the proper use of language for clear communication of meaning led him to the problem of establishing new meanings for old words. In his own use of "substance" and "essence" he wished to retain notions of things which were, according to his empirical philosophy, unknown and unknowable. He did this by redefining the words to exclude metaphysical speculations and rob them of scientific relevance. This device freed him from prevailing conventions without preventing him communicating distinct and innovative meanings. He shared with other innovatory 17th-century writers a preference for redefining old words rather than introducing new ones to clarify possible confusions. Based on Locke's writings and other 17th-century works; 92 notes. 1660's-1704

Locock, Charles

4082. Maulitz, Russell C. METROPOLITAN MEDICINE AND THE MAN-MIDWIFE: THE EARLY LIFE AND LETTERS OF CHARLES LOCOCK. *Medical Hist. [Great Britain] 1982 26(1): 25-46.* Reproduces 9 and summarizes 11 letters by Charles Locock (1799-1875), eminent physician and obstetrician, written during his life as a medical student. The letters provide an intriguing view of late Georgian English medicine, as practiced in London by a member of the small, cohesive community of medical students who were destined to move upward socially, and become leading physicians and consultants. 65 notes. 1818-55

Lodge, Oliver J.

4083. Hunt, Bruce. EXPERIMENTING ON THE ETHER: OLIVER J. LODGE AND THE GREAT WHIRLING MACHINE. *Historical Studies in the Physical and Biological Sciences 1986 16(1): 111-134.* Describes the experiments of British physicist Oliver J. Lodge (1851-1940) in the 1890's, in which he tried to determine if the ether, a hypothetical substance that physicists before Einstein posited as filling space and acting as a medium for the transmission of electromagnetic energy, could be set in motion. Lodge and many other scientists believed so strongly in the ether that when Lodge's experiments failed to detect it, they interpreted it as a sign of ether's perfect elusiveness rather than its nonexistence. Based on original papers and correspondence; 3 fig., 65 notes. 1887-1925

Loeffler, Friedrich

4084. Döhner, Leopold. FRIEDRICH LOEFFLER UND DIE ENTWICKLUNG DES INFEKTIONSSCHUTZES [Friedrich Loeffler and the development of anti-infection medicine]. *Wissenschaftliche Zeitschrift der Ernst-Moritz-Arndt-Universität Greifswald. Gesellschafts- und Sprachwissenschaftliche Reihe [East Germany] 1982 31(4): 45-50.* Discusses the contributions of the microbiologist and hygienist Friedrich Loeffler (1852-1915) toward protection against infection in human and veterinary medicine. 1852-1915

Loesche, Georg

4085. Barton, Peter F. GEORG LOESCHES AUTOBIOGRAPHIE [Georg Loesche's autobiography]. *Jahrbuch der Gesellschaft für die Geschichte des Protestantismus in Österreich [Austria] 1983 99(1): 3-29.* Reproduces a previously unpublished unfinished autobiography written by the German-born historian and academic Georg Loesche (1855-1932), who was noted for his work on the history of Protestantism in Austria. The autobiography covers Loesche's childhood and education, university studies, travels and studies in Italy, research and teaching, and his professional career. Based on Loesche's autobiography and secondary sources; 306 notes. 1860's-1932

Logan, Rayford Whittingham

4086. Franklin, John Hope. RAYFORD WHITTINGHAM LOGAN (1897-1982). *Hispanic Am. Hist. Rev. 1983 63(3): 596-597.* Rayford W. Logan was a historian, editor, columnist, and public servant, and spent the 28 years prior to his retirement in 1965 as chairman of the Department of History at Howard University. He was a productive scholar and prolific writer who produced works on US relations with Haiti, African history, Afro-American history, and international human rights. 1897-1982

Lohmann, George Alfred

4087. Langham-Carter, R. R. LOHMANN OF ENGLAND: A LONELY GRAVE ON THE KAROO. *Q. Bull. of the South African Lib. [South Africa] 1983 37(3): 255-262.* George Alfred Lohmann (1865-1901) is considered one of the greatest British cricketers. He played for Surrey, 1884-96, and was a supreme bowler and a pioneer in the use of the spin and turn and of the slower delivery. In 18 test matches against Australia and South Africa, Lohmann took 112 wickets at 10.75 runs each. He contracted tuberculosis in 1892 and moved to Matjiesfontein, South Africa, for his health, staying at the home of J. D. Logan, a cricket enthusiast. Although Lohmann remained actively involved in cricket, he died in 1901 of tuberculosis. Lohmann's grave at Matjiesfontein is described. 22 notes, photo. 1880's-1901

Loisy, Alfred

4088. Zambarbieri, Annibale. LOISY IN ITALIA: PROSPETTIVE GENERALI E IL "CASO" SEMERIA [Loisy in Italy: general considerations and the "case" of Semeria]. *Riv. de Storia della Chiesa in Italia [Italy] 1980 34(1): 123-162.* Discusses the influence that the French exegete and biblical scholar Alfred Loisy (1857-1940), who is generally regarded as the "father of Catholic Modernism" and who struggled against the thesis of the absolute infallibility of the Holy Bible, exercised in Italy around 1900. Also illuminates Loisy's friendship with the Barnabite friar Giovanni Semeria (1867-1931). Based on episcopal and private archives, libraries, and manuscript collections; 174 notes. 1850-1940

Lombardi, Riccardo

4089. Galeazzi, Marco. IL SOCIALISMO ITALIANO E LA POLITICA INTERNAZIONALE (1948-1949) [Italian socialism and international policy, 1948-49]. *Ponte [Italy] 1985 41(4): 77-93.* Italian socialist leader Riccardo Lombardi's position of nonalignment with Soviet socialism was criticized by Italian Communists and became a major obstacle to leftist unity in 1948, but his viewpoint was eventually adopted. 1948-49

Lomonosov, Mikhail

4090. Treshnikov, A. F. MIKHAIL LOMONOSOV AND THE NORTHERN SEA ROUTE. *Transactions of the Royal Society of Canada [Canada] 1982 20: 399-407.* Mikhail Lomonosov (1711-65) studied chemistry, physics, geology, engineering, philology, literature, geography, history, and economics at St. Petersburg. He became chief of the Geographical Department of the Russian Academy of Sciences in 1758 and was elected honorary member of the Swedish Academy of Science in 1761. His studies, many of which concentrated on a northern sea route and Russia's northern lands, were the basis for all subsequent Russian Arctic studies, from the first expedition in 1765 through current Soviet expeditions. 1740's-65

4091. Vernadski, V. I. PAMIATI M. V. LOMONOSOVA [In memory of M. V. Lomonosov]. *Voprosy Istorii Estestvoznaniia i Tekhniki [USSR] 1981 (4): 12-14.* A scientist, thinker, and poet, Mikhail Lomonosov was first appreciated only as a man of letters; his scholarly contributions were recognized later. 1720's-60's

4092. —. LOMONOSOV—UCHENYI I GRAZHDANIN [Lomonosov as a scholar and citizen]. *Voprosy Istorii Estestvoznaniia i Tekhniki [USSR] 1981 (4): 15-19.* A profile of Mikhail Lomonosov composed from observations and appreciations of his contemporaries and of Soviet and foreign scholars. 1720's-60's

Lon Nol

4093. Klinderová, Iva. LON NOLŮV VZESTUP A PÁD [Lon Nol's rise and fall]. *Nový Orient [Czechoslovakia] 1983 38(2): 42-44.* Examines the personal and political profile of Cambodian politician Lon Nol whose regime ended in April 1970 after five years of civil war. 1965-70

Londoño Londoño, Julio

4094. —. FALLECIMIENTO DEL ACADEMICO DE NUMERO GENERAL(R) DON JULIO LONDOÑO LONDOÑO [Death of the academician General Julio Londoño Londoño]. *Bol. de Hist. y Antigüedades [Colombia] 1980 67(729): 225-244.* Tribute to Colombian military officer and writer on history, geography, and geopolitics Julio Londoño Londoño (1901-80), which includes a biographical note, bibliography, and press notices. 1926-80

Londres, Albert

4095. Rabaut, Jean. ALBERT LONDRES, GRAND REPORTER [Albert Londres, a great reporter]. *Histoire [France] 1984 (70): 74-79.* An account of the life and career of Albert Londres (1884-1932), centering on the famous French newspaperman's descriptions and comments of places or events of great suffering, such as the prisons in French Guiana and North Africa, and misdeeds in the Russian Revolution, China, and Palestine. 1914-32

Long, John

4096. Palmer, Sarah. JOHN LONG A LONDON SHIPOWNER. *Mariner's Mirror [Great Britain] 1986 72(1): 43-61.* John Long, a Woolrich brick, stone, and coal dealer, owned all or part of 10 ships. Discusses the ships, the patterns of trade to Latin America and the Mediterranean, and the costs of doing business. Concludes that both risks and returns were high. Based on Long's business papers in the Public Record Office, London; 9 tables, 14 notes. 1814-26

Long Meg of Westminster

4097. Gartenberg, Patricia. AN ELIZABETHAN WONDER WOMAN: THE LIFE AND FORTUNES OF LONG MEG OF WESTMINSTER. *Journal of Popular Culture 1983 17(3): 49-58.* Long Meg of Westminster's proper name is unknown, but her supposed exploits during the reign of Henry VIII fueled popular plays, poems, and lore from the late 16th century well into the 17th century and beyond. 46 notes. 16c-17c

Longanesi, Leo

4098. Guarnieri, Silvio. LEO LONGANESI E IL DRAMMA DI UNA GENERAZIONE [Leo Longanesi and a generation's drama]. *Ponte [Italy] 1985 41(2): 83-109.* Considers the influence of Italian Fascist playwright Leo Longanesi on the generation of Italian dramatists who followed him. 1920's-70's

Longfield, Mountifort

4099. Tait, Alan A. MOUNTIFORT LONGFIELD 1802-1884: ECONOMIST AND LAWYER. *Hermathena [Ireland] 1982 (133): 15-28.* Mountifort Longfield, known for his legal scholarship, worked in economics, 1830-34, while at Trinity University in Dublin. 1830-72

Longo, Luigi

4100. Zangheri, Renato. LUIGI LONGO E LA NUOVA DEMOCRAZIA ITALIANA [Luigi Longo and the new Italian democracy]. *Studi Storici [Italy] 1981 22(4): 797-813.* The text of an address to the Italian parliament commemorating the death in 1981 of the Italian statesman and writer, Luigi Longo. Longo was an influential leader, particularly during the period of resistance to Fascism and following its fall. He advocated a new democracy to capture the centers of power that had been held in Italy by Fascism, based on a unity of the working class that would transcend party lines. It would gradually develop the social justice provided by the Italian constitution. Primary sources; 50 notes. 1936-76

Lönnrot, Elias

4101. Kaukonen, Väinö. KALEVALA OCH LÖNNROT [*Kalevala* and Lönnrot]. *Nordisk Tidskrift [Sweden] 1985 61(5): 365-371.* Discusses the Finnish folklorist, Elias Lönnrot (1802-84) as the creative author of the *Kalevala* epic, which he published in 1835. 19c

López, Alfonso

4102. Forero Benavides, Abelardo. LOS GRANDES HOMBRES QUE HE CONOCIDO [Great men I have known]. *Bol. de Hist. y Antigüedades [Colombia] 1981 68(734): 691-715.* On the basis of personal experiences, points out the distinctive traits of Alfonso López and Eduardo Santos, Liberal Party statesmen who became presidents of Colombia, Gabriel Turbay and Jorge Eliécer Gaitan, two Liberal Party leaders who failed to become president, and the outstanding Conservative Party figure, Laureano Gómez, who rose to the presidency also. 1920's-50's

López, Carlos Antonio

4103. Kaiser, Cathy. CARLOS ANTONIO LOPEZ AND THE BIRTH OF PARAGUAYAN DIPLOMACY. *Jahrbuch für Gesch. von Staat, Wirtschaft und Gesellschaft Lateinamerikas [West Germany] 1982 19: 238-253.* Consul Carlos Antonio López (nephew of President José de Francia) sought to open up Paraguay and to obtain access to the Río de la Plata river system by means of an alliance with the rebellious Argentine province of Corrientes and later through military campaigns. The alliance proved of little value and the campaigns ended in defeat. These events convinced Carlos Antonio López that military force might be unproductive in achieving desired results. Unfortunately, his teenage son, Francisco Solano López, whom he had groomed as chief military commander and as his future successor, remained attracted to military activity, sadly for Paraguay. Based on records in the Archivo Nacional de Asunción (Sección Histórica), Coleção Viconde do Rio Branco, Biblioteca Nacional (Rio de Janeiro), and printed primary sources; 45 notes. 1841-45

López, José Hilario

4104. Durán Pombo, Jaime. JOSE HILARIO LOPEZ Y LA RESTAURACION DEMOCRATICA DE LA NUEVA GRANADA [José Hilario López and the democratic resoration of New Granada]. *Bol. de Hist. y Antigüedades [Colombia] 1981 68(734): 578-644.* The close of the independence struggle ushered in a period of conflict between adherents of civil authority and the existing Colombian constitution, led by Vice-President Francisco de Paula Santander, and military and other malcontents who sought a revamping of institutions along the lines of the constitution drafted by Simón Bolívar for Bolivia. José Hilario López, who held a military command position in the Cauca region, belonged to the former group and supported Santander when a definitive break occurred between him and Bolívar. He rose in rebellion against Bolívar's subsequent dictatorship, and though he soon agreed to end the revolt, he again played a major role in the successful struggle of 1830-31 against the dictatorship of Rafael Urdaneta, which was an abortive revival of Bolívar's. 28 notes, biblio. 1825-31

4105. —. CARTAS DE JOSE HILARIO LOPEZ A PEDRO ALCANTARA HERRAN Y JOSE MARIA OBANDO [Letters of José Hilario López to Pedro Alcántara Herrán and José María Obando]. *Bol. de Hist. y Antigüedades [Colombia] 1982 69(736): 206-243.* Group of 37 letters from the future Liberal president José Hilario López (ca. 1800-69) to General Pedro Alcántra Herrán (1800-72) and one to General José María Obando (1795-1861), written at different places in Colombia and abroad and referring to personal questions, Colombian politics, observations of the United States and Europe, and López's diplomatic mission to the Holy See. 1837-41

Lopez Contreras, Eleazar

4106. Tablante Garrido, P. N. ELEAZAR LOPEZ CONTRERAS, PRESIDENTE-GENERAL EN JEFE-SENADOR VITALICIO [Eleazar Lopez Contreras: president, general-in-chief, senator for life]. *Bol. de la Acad. Nac. de la Hist. [Venezuela] 1983 66(264): 1059-1069.* Eleazar Lopez Contreras (1883-1973), president of Venezuela, 1936-41, and his military, political, and academic career, including personal and family data. 1900's-73

López de Gómara, Francisco

4107. Lewis, Robert E. EL TESTAMENTO DE FRANCISCO LOPEZ DE GOMARA Y OTROS DOCUMENTOS TOCANTES A SU VIDA Y OBRA [Francisco López de Gómara's last will and other documents]. *Revista de Indias [Spain] 1984 44(173): 61-79.* Publishes documents that correct errors repeated by several authors and adds new details throwing light on the last years of this chronicler from 1550 to 1559. The documents concern his family, daily life, economic conditions, travels, and his relationship with Martín Cortés. The most interesting document is his will dated in Soria, 1559. Based on documents in the General Archive of the Indies (Seville), General Archive of Simancas, National Historical Archive (Madrid), and Historical Archive of Protocols (Madrid); 2 appendixes, 53 notes. 1550-59

López de Mesa, Luis

4108. Gómez Martínez, Pablo. LUIS LOPEZ DE MESA [Luis López de Mesa]. *Boletín de la Academia Colombiana [Colombia] 1984 34(146): 284-289.* Luis López de Mesa (1884-1967), founder of the Colombian Academy, was impressive for his intellectual and moral personality and the rigor with which he pursued and cultivated the truth, especially in his historical writings. 1884-1967

4109. Guzmán Esponda, Eduardo. EL PROFESOR LOPEZ DE MESA [Professor López de Mesa]. *Boletín de la Academia Colombiana [Colombia] 1984 34(146): 275-278.* Pays tribute to Professor Luis López de Mesa (1884-1967), historian, diplomat, statesman, and man of letters and founder of the Colombian Academy. 1884-1967

4110. Lleras Restrepo, Carlos. UN COLOMBIANO EMINENTE: LUIS LOPEZ DE MESA [An eminent Colombian: Luis López de Mesa]. *Boletín de Historia y Antigüedades [Colombia] 1984 71(747): 792-818.* In addition to a distinguished career of public service, Luis López de Mesa enriched the literature of Colombian history with insightful biographical sketches of political and intellectual figures and probing examinations, in historical perspective, of the nation's problems and cultural idiosyncracies. 1910's-67

4111. Mejía Velilla, David. BREVES PALABRAS CONMEMORATIVAS DE DON LUIS LOPEZ DE MESA [A few words in memory of Don Luis López de Mesa]. *Boletín de la Academia Colombiana [Colombia] 1984 34(146): 279-283.* Describes the intellectual roots and outlook of Professor Luis López de Mesa (1884-1967), founder of the Colombian Academy, a historian and man of letters who cultivated the art of writing well as a central pursuit. 1884-1967

4112. Ocampo López, Javier. LUIS LOPEZ DE MESA: UN ESTUDIO SOBRE SU IDEARIO DE DARWINISMO SOCIAL PARA LA INTERPRETACION DE LA CULTURA COLOMBIANA [Luis López de Mesa: a study on his ideas of Social Darwinism for the interpretation of Colombian culture]. *Boletín de Historia y Antigüedades [Colombia] 1984 71(747): 841-869.* Classified in Colombian terms as a member of the modernizing "Centenary Generation," Luis López de Mesa also belonged to a larger movement in Latin America at the turn of the century that was heavily influenced by positivism and Social Darwinism. He was interested in the geographic and biological determinants of culture and in collective mentalities, as he sought to identify the roots of Colombian and Latin American historical frustrations. 20 notes. 1910's-67

4113. Santa, Eduardo. A PROPOSITO DE UN CENTENARIO: LOPEZ DE MESA Y LA CULTURA COLOMBIANA [Apropos a centenary: López de Mesa and Colombian culture]. *Boletín de Historia y Antigüedades [Colombia] 1984 71(747): 819-840.* Though trained as a medical doctor, Luis López de Mesa (1884-1967) specialized also in psychiatry and sociology and was the true founder of modern social studies in Colombia. As minister of education in the 1930's, he showed particular interest in rural areas. He also served as foreign minister in World War II. López de Mesa was a man of letters in the broadest humanistic sense. 5 notes. 1910's-67

López y López, Antonio

4114. González Echegaray, Rafael. LOS ASTILLEROS DE ANTONIO LOPEZ [The shipyards of Antonio López]. *Revista de Historia Naval [Spain] 1983 1(2): 91-106.* Antonio López y López, 1st Marquis of Comillas, who died in 1883, was a Spanish shipping entrepreneur who created the powerful Compañía Trasatlántica, which operated fast mail steamers between Spain and Cuba from the 1860s. López originally acquired British ships, but soon built two shipyards in Spain to build and repair vessels for his shipping line, one at Matagorda near Cádiz and one near Santander. 6 illus., 10 notes. 1866-83

Lorca, Federico García

4115. Martín, Sabas. LORCA: TEATRO PÓSTUMO [Lorca: posthumous theater]. *Cuadernos Hispanoamericanos [Spain] 1979 116(348): 647-656.* Shortly before his death the poet and dramatist Federico García Lorca (1899-1936) entrusted to his friend Rafael Martínez Nadal the draft of a play entitled *El Público,* which was published in 1978 with an unfinished play, *Comedia sin Título. El Publico* is a key work in the Lorca opus. *Comedia,* which probably antedates *El Público,* explores the theme of the arts and revolution. Based on the two plays and the writings of R. Martínez Nadal and M. Faffranque; 2 notes. 1930's

Lorentz, Stanisław

4116. Lorentz, Stanisław. AUTOBIOGRAFIA [Autobiography]. *Kwartalnik Hist. Nauki i Techniki [Poland] 1979 24(4): 731-756.* An autobiography of Stanisław Lorentz, since 1935 director of the Warsaw National Museum. He studied philosophy and the history of art under Zygmunt Batowski and Władysław Tatarkiewicz at Warsaw University, worked in the scientific branch of the Education Ministry, and was director of conservation of historical buildings in northeastern Poland. He is the author of *Natolin,* a book on 18th-century art and organized a number of important exhibitions in the 1950's and 1960's. 22 photos. 1930's-60's

Lorenz, Konrad

4117. Kalikow, Theodora J. KONRAD LORENZ'S ETHOLOGICAL THEORY: EXPLANATION AND IDEOLOGY, 1938-1943. *J. of the Hist. of Biol. [Netherlands] 1983 16(1): 39-73.* Influenced by Ernst Haeckel's ideas of cultural despair and biological decline, Konrad Lorenz's studies of animal behavior led him to join the Nazi Party. Although the Third Reich failed, Lorenz maintained the same values about science, society, and humanity's future that made him a Nazi. For Lorenz, the laws of biology and the laws of society were the same phenomena; hence, democracy, in its various forms, was merely a sickness of society. 104 notes. 1938-43

Lorenzo, Manuel

4118. Pérez Tenreiro, Tomás. NOTICIA SOBRE DON MANUEL LORENZO Y DON LORENZO MORILLO [Notice on Don Manuel Lorenzo and Don Lorenzo Morillo]. *Boletín de la Academia Nacional de la Historia [Venezuela] 1984 67(268): 691-698.* Manuel Lorenzo and Lorenzo Morillo were royalist soldiers who distinguished themselves in the campaigns following the battle of Carabobo. Although that battle sealed the fate of the Spanish resistance these men fought a guerrilla war against the patriotic forces in obedience to orders. The similarity of their names has caused confusion in their identity and careers, which is here cleared. Based on primary material in the Archive of Simancas. 1820's

Loriga, Mariella

4119. Loriga, Mariella. RICORDI DA IVREA: UNA CARRIERA FEMMINILE ALLA OLIVETTI [Memories of Ivrea: a woman's career at Olivetti]. *Memoria: Riv. di Storia delle Donne [Italy] 1982 (6): 14-23.* The author, a middle-class mother of two children separated from her husband, recounts her experiences as the director of a child care center at the Olivetti plant in the 1950's. Describes the social milieu of the plant and the town, and the reactions of the people to her efforts as director. 1956-61

Losik, Oleg

4120. Lashchenko, P. N. MARSHAL BRONETANKOVYKH VOISK O. A. LOSIK [Marshal of the Armored Forces O. A. Losik]. *Voenno-Istoricheskii Zhurnal [USSR] 1985 (12): 78-80.* A biography of Oleg Losik (b. 1915), marshal of the armored divisions of the Soviet army. He studied at the Saratov Tank School in 1935 and fought in the 1939 Russo-Finnish War. During World War II his 4th Tank Brigade served in many major operations. He was appointed head of the Military Academy of the Armored Forces in 1969. Secondary sources; 2 photos, note. 1935-85

Łosiński, Augustyn

4121. Fert, Stanisław. DZIAŁALNOŚĆ DUSZPASTERSKA BISKUPA KIELECKIEGO AUGUSTYNA ŁOSIŃSKIEGO (1910-1937) [The pastoral work of Augustyn Łosiński, bishop of Kielce, 1910-37]. *Nasza Przeszłość [Poland] 1979 (52): 227-255.* 1910-37

4122. Szafrański, Adam Ludwik. AUGUSTYN ŁOSIŃSKI, BISKUP KIELECKI (1910-1937) W ŚWIETLE LISTÓW PASTERSKICH, OPINII I FAKTÓW [Augustyn Łosiński, 1910-37, bishop of Kielce, in the light of pastoral letters, opinions, and facts]. *Nasza Przeszłość [Poland] 1983 (59): 215-240.* Sketches the biography of Bishop Augustyn Łosiński as it emerges from his private and public utterances. His controversial political stance made him unpopular with both the Polish Left and the Piłsudski government. 1910-37

Loucheur, Louis

4123. Carls, Stephen D.; Hall, Hines H. (commentary). LOUIS LOUCHEUR AND THE ECONOMIC MOBILIZATION OF FRANCE DURING WORLD WAR I. *Proceedings of the Annual Meeting of the Western Society for French History 1984 12: 208-217.* Louis Loucheur was a French industrialist who responded to the war crisis of 1914 by expanding significantly the production of heavy artillery shells. In 1916 the government appointed him undersecretary of state for munitions, and in 1917 he became armaments minister. He worked to maintain the country's supplies of coal and steel, and he supervised aircraft production. His boldness and his organizational skills marked the advent of a new class of manager-technicians in France. Comments, pp. 218-220. Based on documents in the Archives Nationales; 40 notes. 1914-18

4124. Carls, Stephen Douglas. "Louis Loucheur: A French Technocrat in Government, 1916-1920." U. of Minnesota 1982. 573 pp. *DAI 1982 43(4): 1259-A.* DA8221255 1916-20

Loudon, Baron von

See Ernst, Gideon

Loudon, John Claudius

4125. Simo, Melanie Louise. REVIEW ESSAY: JOHN CLAUDIUS LOUDON AND THE EARLY NINETEENTH CENTURY IN GREAT BRITAIN. *J. of Garden Hist. [Great Britain] 1983 3(1): 59-63.* Reviews Elisabeth B. MacDougall's *John Claudius Loudon and the Early Nineteenth Century in Great Britain* (1980), which discusses the life and works of John Claudius Loudon, a horticultural writer, in the context of his times. 1783-1843

Louis I Philippe

4126. Huart, Suzanne d'. LOUIS-PHILIPPE, DUC D'ORLEANS, SOUS L'EMPIRE: ECHECS ET REUSSITES [Louis Philippe, Duc d'Orléans, under the Empire: failures and successes]. *Rev. de l'Inst. Napoléon [France] 1980 (136): 3-18.* Recounts Louis Philippe's exile and his travels through North America and Europe, 1793-1815, and describes the political contacts the future monarch of France made during this period. 1793-1815

Louis II

4127. Burgess, Michele. A MAD KING'S LEGACY. *Westways 1985 77(5): 51-53.* Outlines the life of Louis II of Bavaria, highlighted by his support of Richard Wagner, which enabled Wagner to produce some of his greatest operatic works and by the translation of his fantasies into the building of the three magnificent castles that today stand as his memorial. 1845-85

4128. Decaux, Alain. LOUIS II, LE RÊVE ET LA FOLIE [Louis II: dream and madness]. *Hist. Mag. [France] 1984 (48): 36-48.* Recalls the adventurous private and political life of Louis II (1845-86), king of Bavaria, who was a dreamer and a homosexual, but probably not a bad king, contrary to his reputation, and who died tragically and mysteriously as a lunatic. 1845-86

Louis XI

4129. Decaux, Alain. ANNE DE BEAUJEU, "LA MOINS FOLLE FEMME DE FRANCE" [Anne of Beaujeu, "the least deluded woman of France"]. *Historama [France] 1985 (13): 36-42.* 1483-91
*For abstract see **Anne of France***

4130. Erlanger, Philippe. LOUIS XI AVANT LOUIS XI: LE RENARD DANS LE POULAILLER [Louis XI before he was Louis XI: the fox in the hen-house]. *Hist. Mag. [France] 1983 (42): 86-93.* Recounts the events of the reign of Louis XI of France (1423-83) and his attempts, while still the dauphin, to hasten the death of his father, Charles VII. 1423-83

Louis XII

4131. Love, Ronald S. CONTEMPORARY AND NEAR-CONTEMPORARY OPINION OF LOUIS XII, "PERE DU PEUPLE." *Renaissance and Reformation [Canada] 1984 8(4): 235-265.* Louis XII was called father of his people because he was a kindly man and ruled France internally with justice and order. In spite of the scandal of his divorce from a barren wife, Jeanne, and his lack of success in foreign policy, Louis XII was considered to be a good king while he was alive. He has been unduly obscured by his more dynamic and flamboyant predecessors, Louis XI and Charles VIII, and his successor, Francis I. Secondary sources; 133 notes. 1498-1515

Louis XIII

4132. Foisil, Madeleine. LOUIS XIII A TRAVERS LE STETHOSCOPE [Louis XIII through the stethoscope]. *Histoire [France] 1982 (42): 76-78.* Discussion of the *Journal d'Héroard,* a six-volume medical account of the health of Louis XIII during the first 26 years of his life, written by his doctor, Jean Héroard. 1601-27

4133. Micotti, Sara. UN'INFANZIA AMBIGUA: LUIGI XIII BAMBINO NEL "JOURNAL" DI HEROARD [An ambiguous infancy: Louis XIII in Heroard's journal]. *Quaderni Storici [Italy] 1984 19(3): 793-818.* This article, based on the *Journal* by Doctor Jean Heroard, relating Louis XIII's childhood and early youth, aims at a reconstruction of some material aspects of the life of a Dauphin of France. The starting point of its approach is the many-sided language of the *Journal.* It is an adult's writing concerning a child but nevertheless a well-grounded medical writing, conditioned yet by its attesting a royal experience. It allows one to follow closely an absolutely unique upbringing. The author's analysis considers the human environment surrounding the Dauphin and his educational relations, focusing on the ways in which socializing circumstances and encounters shaped his personality, his assumption of his royal engagements, his transformation from a royal baby into a baby-king. 1600-10

Louis XIV

4134. Berry, Joseph. LES DERNIERES HEURES DE LOUIS XIV [The last hours of Louis XIV]. *Histoire [France] 1984 (74): 96-97.* Gives a day-by-day account of the last month in the life of King Louis XIV, describing his sickness, decline, and death. 1715

Louis XVI

4135. Lever, Evelyne. L'ENFANCE CASTREE DE LOUIS XVI [The emasculated childhood of Louis XVI]. *Historama [France] 1985 (21): 60-66.* The education of Louis XVI as a child, when he was known as the Duc de Berry, was a series of lessons in how to defer to the authority of his older brother, the Duc de Bourgogne, who was being groomed to reign over France; Bourgogne died in 1760 at the age of 10, leaving Berry ill prepared for the task of government. 1754-65

4136. Roudil, Pierre, interviewer. LOUIS XVI ETAIT-IL COUPABLE? [Was Louis XVI guilty?]. *Hist. Mag. [France] 1983 (37): 22-27.* Adduces new evidence concerned with the arrest, trial, and execution of Louis XVI. 1792-93

Louis XVIII

4137. Chaussinand-Nogaret, Guy. LOUIS XVIII: UN LIBERAL PARMI LES ROIS [Louis XVIII: a liberal among kings]. *Histoire [France] 1983 (55): 87-89.* Describes, with illustrations, the personality of Louis XVIII (1755-1824): his accession to the throne, the influence of 19th-century nobles on his governments (1814-15; 1815-24), and the relative liberalism of his rule. ca 1795-1824

4138. Mansel, Philip. A KING AND HIS ENEMY: LOUIS XVIII AND TALLEYRAND. *Hist. Today [Great Britain] 1981 31(Oct): 43-48.* Details the decades-long struggle between Louis XVIII (1755-1824) and Charles Maurice de Talleyrand (1754-1838), beginning in 1789 when Talleyrand supported the French Revolution and the king (then Comte de Provence) supported the Counter-Revolution, until Louis XVIII died in 1824. 1789-1824

4139. Pogosian, V. A. PAVEL I I LIUDOVIK XVIII [Paul I and Louis XVIII]. *Frantsuzskii Ezhegodnik [USSR] 1980: 204-210.* Driven from one country to another after the French Revolution, the pretender to the throne of France, Louis XVIII, found himself in Blankenburg under the protection of the Duke of Brunswick in 1796. The Directory of France, however, insisted that Brunswick expel the "political vagabond," whereupon Paul I offered the pretender sanctuary in Russia. The tsar then invited the other monarchs of Europe to provide aid to Louis to support his retinue. Great Britain and Sicily promised to do what they could, but Spain, attempting to maintain good relations with France, refused to send aid to Louis openly. The French pretender left Blankenburg in February 1798 and traveled to Mitava in Courland, where he remained until 1801. 37 notes. French summary. 1796-1801

Louis-Philippe-Joseph

4140. Barker, Nancy Nichols; Censer, Jack (commentary). A BOURGEOIS OR A REACTIONARY PRINCE? THE CASE OF LOUIS-PHILIPPE-JOSEPH, DUKE OF ORLEANS. *Pro. of the Ann. Meeting of the Western Soc. for French Hist. 1981 9: 148-160.* Examines the wealth and the business enterprises of the Duc d'Orléans, later known as Philippe Egalité (1747-93). The great variety in the duke's interests makes it impossible to label him simply as a traditional feudal noble or as an early capitalist entrepreneur. He encouraged rational reforms in the administration of his properties, sponsored new industries, developed West Indies cotton plantations, and patronized scientists. Based on the private papers of the Orléans family deposited in the Archives Nationales; 35 notes. Comments, pp. 162-165. 1785-92

Love, Joseph Robert

4141. Lumsden, Joy. JOSEPH ROBERT LOVE, 1839-1914: WEST INDIAN EXTRAORDINARY. *Afro-Americans in New York Life and Hist. 1983 7(1): 25-39.* Discusses the travels and influences of Jamaican journalist, orator, clergyman, and patriot Joseph Robert Love in New York and other areas of the United States. 1839-1914

Low, David

4142. Smith, Adrian. LOW AND LORD BEAVERBROOK: CARTOONIST AND PROPRIETOR. *Encounter [Great Britain] 1985 65(5): 7-24.* Assesses the career of the cartoonist Sir David Low and his relationship with the newspaper proprietor Lord Beaverbrook, from his arrival in England in 1919 to his death in 1963. 1919-63

Loynes, Comtesse de

4143. Bornecque, Jacques-Henry. UN AMOUR DE MISTRAL [One of Mistral's loves]. *Rev. des Deux Mondes [France] 1982 (11): 294-309.* 1864-1913
*For abstract see **Mistral, Frédéric***

Lozer, Giuseppe

4144. Tramontin, Silvio. DON GIUSEPPE LOZER: UN PRETE PER L'UNITA SINDACALE [Don Giuseppe Lozer: a priest in favor of labor confederations]. *Civitas [Italy] 1985 36(2): 33-42.* Soon after he entered the priesthood in 1904, Don Giuseppe Lozer (1880-1974) founded a worker's credit union and a cooperative store and called for unity between Catholic and Socialist factions of the labor union movement for social reform; rejected by both Socialist and Fascist movements in the 1920's, he continued his activities independently and was imprisoned in 1944. After the war he founded a Secretariat of Poverty, but was forced to retire in 1957. 1904-57

Lu Jiaxi

4145. —. LU CHIA-HSI—NEW PRESIDENT OF THE CHINESE ACADEMY OF SCIENCES. *Issues & Studies [Taiwan] 1981 17(8): 71-76.* Lu Jiaxi (Lu Chia-hsi, b. 1915) of Fujian (Fukien) province, is a chemist and a graduate of Amoy University. From 1937 to 1945 he was in England and the United States studying and doing national defense research. After returning to China in 1945, he taught at Amoy University. In 1956 he joined an organization of the Chinese Communist Party. He has been active both academically and politically ever since. Zhou Enlai (Chou En-lai) protected him from serious persecution during the Cultural Revolution. Based on Mainland media reports; 20 notes. 1937-81

Lü Liuliang

4146. Fisher, Tom. LOYALIST ALTERNATIVES IN THE EARLY CH'ING. *Harvard Journal of Asiatic Studies 1984 44(1): 83-122.* 1635-70
*For abstract see **Huang, Zongxi***

Lu Xun

4147. Chan, Ping-leung. LU HSÜN AND COMMUNISM: MYTH AND REALITY. *Asian Thought & Soc. 1982 7(19): 53-78.* The diary and letters as well as literary production of Lu Xun (Lu Hsün, 1881-1936) shows that his connection with the Chinese Communist Party was one of sympathy rather than identification. 1909-42

4148. Chung, Tan. AH Q OR SUPERMAN? AN APPRAISAL OF THE APPRAISALS OF LU XUN. *China Report [India] 1982 18(2-3): 9-28.* Lu Xun (Lu Hsun, 1881-1936), one of China's great modern writers, was recognized by Mao for the political sophistication of his writing. After his death he was deified and seen as a kind of superman. He was more like the Ah Q character he created, who represented a combination of the best and the worst in the Chinese national character. Secondary sources; 52 notes. 1906-36

4149. Fedorenko, N. T. LU SIN (K 100-LETIIU SO DNIA ROZHDENIIA) [Lu Xun (Lu Hsün): on the 100th anniversary of his birth]. *Narody Azii i Afriki [USSR] 1982 (3): 70-77.* Lu Xun's (1881-1936) literary activity began in the years preceding China's 1911 revolution, and his later works bear witness to the fact that Lu Xun cared deeply about China's fate, the progress of the Chinese revolution, and a genuine abolition of class bondage. The October Revolution in Russia gave a new impetus to the Chinese proletariat, and this was reflected in Lu's works after 1918; he gradually approached the ideas of Marxism-Leninism. His activity in the 1930's was characterized by yet more active participation in China's social life, including various actions organized by the Chinese Communist Party. 1881-1981

4150. Goldman, Merle. THE POLITICAL USE OF LU XUN. *China Q. [Great Britain] 1982 (91): 446-461.* Lu Xun (Lu Hsün) was, and remains, so towering a figure in Chinese literature that each new group in power, or seeking power, has found it necessary to invoke his support. While opposing much of what Lu favored and, at times, actually purging his disciples, various contenders have presented a Lu Xun who fit their needs of the moment. While current treatment of Lu is more balanced than any heretofore, any bureaucracy is bound to be discomfited by the writer's refusal to accept injustice and his skillful use of satire. Based largely on Chinese materials from the era of the Cultural Revolution; 31 notes. 1936-82

4151. Jenner, W. J. F. LU XUN'S LAST DAYS AND AFTER. *China Q. [Great Britain] 1982 (91): 424-445.* Lu Xun (Lu Hsün) died early in the morning of 18 October 1936. His death, at a time when his health was thought to be improving, shocked his friends and colleagues across China and Japan and resulted in a burial committee which was appropriately international and politically mixed. Though too often used by current policymakers as a supportive symbol, Lu Xun continues to inspire the Chinese imagination. Based on Chinese and Japanese materials; 49 notes. 1936-82

4152. Lee, Mabel. SOLACE FOR THE CORPSE WITH ITS HEART GOUGED OUT: LU XUN'S USE OF THE POETIC FORM. *Papers on Far Eastern Hist. [Australia] 1982 (26): 145-174.* Examines the reasons why the Chinese writer Lu Xun (Lu Hsün) may have sought to deliberately conceal his love for the poems he wrote, 1900-35. First, he did not wish to increase his companion Xu Guangping's anxieties about him, for he was already in constant danger because of his association with Communists and his role in founding the League of Leftist Writers (1930) and the Alliance for the Protection of Human Rights (1933). Second, he may have sought to play down the importance he attached to his poetry because he did not wish to dampen the efforts of young poets who were striving to establish new poetic forms. Most of his poetic impulses were expressed in the classical style, and he only wrote about 40 poems altogether. The author provides a critical examination of Lu Xun's classical poetry and prose poems, 1900-35. Based on Lu Xun's letters and writings and secondary sources; 52 notes. 1900-35

4153. Murthy, Sheela. LU XUN: THE ARCH DISSENTER. *China Report [India] 1982 18(2-3): 29-39.* Chinese writer Lu Xun (1881-1936) attacked Chinese values on many levels. He criticized China's isolationism, blaming this for the country's cultural stagnation. He was hostile to Confucian ethics for their perpetuation of the feudal order under a polite veneer. He bemoaned the lack of love, sincerity, and virtue in the Chinese character. Society was not based on these but on propriety and obedience. He had a strong sympathy for the masses who were overtaxed and kept in place by Confucian ethics. In *The True Story of Ah Q* the writer portrayed the suffering of the Chinese masses at the hands of the landlord-gentry. In his later years he was increasingly attracted to Marxism-Leninism. Secondary sources; 37 notes. 1906-36

4154. Pankaj, N. M. LU XUN: A CULTURAL MOVEMENT. *China Report [India] 1982 18(2-3): 113-120.* The writings of Chinese author Lu Xun (Lu Hsun, 1881-1936) were an important force in China's transition from feudalism to modernity. His 1907 *Discourse on the Power of Mara Poetry*—in which he established a philosophy of rebelliousness, dissent, progressivism, and courage—criticizes Confucian moral authority and identifies kindred rebel spirits such as the poets Shelley and Byron. He had a wide following both in China and in India. The cultural movement he sparked in China was partly due to his endorsement by the Chinese Communist movement. Secondary sources; 14 notes. 1906-36

4155. Rawat, Mahua. LU XUN AND JAPAN. *China Report [India] 1982 18(2-3): 41-54.* Chinese writer Lu Xun (Lu Hsun, 1881-1936) lived in Japan from 1902 to 1909 where he studied medicine. He was influenced by the Japanese writers Natsume Soseki and Kuriyaga Hakuson, especially in the masterpieces he produced in the 1920's. He also influenced Japanese writers, notably Takeuchi Yoshimi (1910-77), one of the most prominent members of the Tokyo intellectual community. Lu Xun is widely read in modern Japan. Based on secondary sources; 54 notes. 1906-70's

4156. Thakur, Ravni. LU XUN'S FOREIGN INSPIRATIONS. *China Report [India] 1982 18(2-3): 55-67.* Chinese writer Lu Xun (Lu Hsun, 1881-1936) was influenced by many foreigners, including western Europeans like Schopenhauer, Nietzsche, Byron, Ibsen, and Shaw. He was also influenced by a number of Russian writers including Gogol, Pushkin, Andreev, Gorky, Tolstoy, Lunacharski, and Plekhanov. After 1925 he was increasingly influenced by Marxism and involved in the political development of China. Based on secondary sources; 32 notes. 1906-36

4157. Weiss, Ruth. LU XUN—HE SPEAKS TO US AND TO OUR DAY. *Eastern Horizon [Hong Kong] 1981 20(9): 29-33.* Discusses the life, literary and academic careers, and political views of Lu Xun (Lu Hsun, 1881-1936), whose real name was Zhou Shuren (Chou Shu-jen), a writer of short stories, and describes the numerous memorials and institutes created in his memory throughout China.
1920's-30's

Łubieńska, Róża

4158. Świąteczka, Maria. RÓŻA ŁUBIEŃSKA I JEJ DZIAŁALNOŚĆ SPOŁECZNA [Róża Łubieńska and her social work]. *Nasza Przeszłość [Poland] 1979 (51): 147-177.* Document-based outline of the life of Róża Łubieńska (1881-1954), Catholic social worker in Cracow. 1906-54

Lucaciu, Vasile

4159. Cotoțiu, Constantin and Horja, Gavril. VASILE LUCACIU, TRIBUN AL LUPTEI PENTRU DREPTURILE ŞI UNITATEA ROMÂNILOR [Vasile Lucaciu, a leader of the struggle for the rights and unity of the Romanian people]. *Revista de Istorie [Romania] 1982 35(7): 793-806.* Dr. Vasile Lucaciu (1852-1922) dedicated his life to the ideal of Romania's national unity. While serving as priest in the village of Şişeşti, he was politically active in Transylvania's struggle against Austro-Hungary and for its union with Romania. He served as general secretary of the Romanian National Party in Transylvania, Banat and Hungary. He was imprisoned several times by the Austro-Hungarian authorities because of being one of the authors of the Memorandum presented to the Court of Vienna in 1892. In 1917-19, V. Lucaciu was in charge of several diplomatic missions abroad, mainly in France, Italy, and the United States. 28 notes. French summary. 1852-1922

Lucas, N. B. C.

4160. Hannam, Charles. OUTSTANDING HISTORY TEACHERS: N. B. C. LUCAS. *Teaching History [Great Britain] 1984 (40): 18-19.* An outline of the life of the author's history teacher and headmaster of Midhurst Grammar School, N. B. C. Lucas, discussing his sensitivity and teaching skills. 20c

Luchitski, Ivan V.

4161. Obolenskaia, S. V. and Gurvich, S. N.. PIS'MA I. V. LUCHITSKOGO P. L. LAVROVU [Letters from I. V. Luchitski to P. L. Lavrov]. *Frantsuzskii Ezhegodnik [USSR] 1982: 225-235.* A biographical sketch of the Russian liberal populist historian Ivan V. Luchitski (1845-1918) precedes four (annotated) letters sent by him from Paris, November 1872-January 1873, to the populist sociologist and publicist Petr Lavrovich Lavrov (1823-1900), then in Zurich. Luchitski, who was doing research in France for his doctoral dissertation, became deeply interested in the political turmoil following the fall of the Paris Commune and the establishment of the Third Republic in September 1871. His letters deal primarily with the treatment of these events in politically diverse press organs. 49 notes. French summary.
1872-73

Luckner, Felix von

4162. DelaCroix, Robert. UN CORSAIRE DANS LA GRANDE GUERRE [A corsair in the great war]. *Historama [France] 1985 (20): 72-76.* Presents the adventures of Felix von Luckner, German naval officer and corsair who sailed in the South Atlantic and Pacific oceans during World War I raiding and capturing allied sailing ships while eluding the British fleet. ca 1916-19

Luden, Heinrich

4163. Friesen, Gerhard. NEMESIS UND DAS GALAKLEID DER JAKOBINER: EINE POLITISCH-LITERARISCHE KONTROVERSE ZWISCHEN HANS VON GAGERN UND HEINRICH LUDEN [Nemesis and the Jacobins' party dress: a political and literary conflict between Hans von Gagern and Heinrich Luden]. *Jahrbuch des Inst. für Deutsche Gesch. [Israel] 1982 11: 91-125.* Hans von Gagern (1766-1852) criticized the journalist Heinrich Luden (1780-1847) for his bad manners in criticizing the German League in his Weimar journal *Nemesis.* Luden's criticism of the league tested the policy of freedom of the press then being tried out in the principality of Saxe-Weimar, and complaints against Luden eventually led to his trial and imprisonment. Previously unpublished letters by Gagern and Luden show that Luden regarded Gagern's criticism as proof that the freedoms granted in Germany after the end of the Napoleonic Wars were specious and hollow. Gagern's letters show him to be caught in a no-man's-land between Metternich's conservatism and nationalist critics of Metternich, unable to join either. Based on original papers kept by the von Gagern family and by the German federal archives in Frankfurt; 66 notes, appendix containing the texts of 6 letters. Hebrew summary. 1816-18

Ludlolo, Nomapuleti Florah

4164. Becken, Hans-Jurgen. "GIVE ME WATER, WOMAN OF SAMARIA:" THE PILGRIMAGE OF SOUTHERN AFRICAN BLACKS IN THE 1980'S. *J. of Religion in Africa [Netherlands] 1983 14(2): 115-129.* Discusses faith healer Nomapuleti Florah Ludlolo of Cancele, Transkei. Commonly known as Ma-Radebe, she is also called the Black Madonna of Cancele, Mother of Cancele, and Mother Samaritan. Discusses pilgrimages to the holy place, objections to her healing, worship at Cancele, testimonies, intercessions, and devotional objects. A symbiotic, rather than a syncretic, relationship exists between African and Christian religion here. Based in part on five local interviews; 23 notes.
1980-83

Ludschuweit, J. F.

4165. Gerhardt, Wolf. DER RETTER VON SANSSOUCI: J. F. LUDSCHUWEIT [The savior of Sanssouci: J. F. Ludschuweit]. *Archivmitteilungen [East Germany] 1985 35(2): 49-50.* Describes the successful mission of Soviet army officer J. F. Ludschuweit to protect the cultural treasures and palaces of Sanssouci Park in Potsdam during the Soviet occupation of the city, 27 April 1945, treasures that had been ordered destroyed by the German commander in the city. 1945

Ludwig, Emil

4166. West, Franklin C. SUCCESS WITHOUT INFLUENCE: EMIL LUDWIG DURING THE WEIMAR YEARS. *Leo Baeck Institute. Year Book [Great Britain] 1985 30: 169-189.* Emil Ludwig (1881-1948), a highly assimilated German Jew, was one of the most popular and prolific writers living in Germany during the 1920's, although his historical works and biographies were scorned by most literary critics and professional historians. The disapproval of Ludwig's work paralleled his transformation from an enthusiastic German nationalist to an antimilitaristic internationalist after the first world war. Valid objections to Ludwig's superficial scholarship were often expressed along with aspersions to his Jewishness and liberal political beliefs. Based on the writings of Emil Ludwig and other primary sources; 4 photos, 139 notes. 1918-32

Ludwig II

4167. Handzic, Jeanne. THE DEATH OF KING LUDWIG II OF BAVARIA. *Historian [Great Britain] 1985 (7): 3-7.* Conventional historiography assumes that "mad" King Ludwig II of Bavaria, "mad" because of his extravagant living, killed his chief medical advisor Dr. Bernhard von Gudden, and then either committed suicide or died trying to escape, but modern research suggests that the king was not insane and was himself murdered, along with von Gudden, in 1886. 1886

Lueger, Karl

4168. Boyer, John W. KARL LUEGER AND THE VIENNESE JEWS. *Leo Baeck Inst. Year Book [Great Britain] 1981 26: 125-141.* Karl Lueger, mayor of Vienna from 1897 until 1910, was the head of the anti-Semitic Austrian Christian Socials (the petite bourgeoisie, property owners, teachers, merchants and shopkeepers, middle and lower government officers, and anti-Semitic members of the Catholic clergy). Despite his professed anti-Semitism and his skillful use of it in propaganda, Lueger never disliked Jews personally and maintained social and business contacts with wealthy Jews. He attacked Jews and their "offspring" capitalism at the same time that he admired wealth and intelligence, which he found widely among Viennese Jews. This contradiction arose from Lueger's cultural attitudes and from his view of the social system; he saw the Jew as an agent of cultural fragmentation and social disunity. The issue of economic competition remained the most compelling motive to employ anti-Semitism, and it became a convenient tool in his political maneuvers against Social Democrats and Catholic Labor. 42 notes. 1890-1910

4169. Brown, Karin Brinkmann. "Karl Lueger as Liberal: Democracy, Municipal Reform, and the Struggle for Power in the Vienna City Council 1875-1882." City U. of New York 1982. 315 pp. *DAI 1982 43(5): 1641-A.* DA8222934 1875-82

Luetgebrune, Walter

4170. Heydeloff, Rudolf. STARANWALT DER RECHTSEXTREMISTEN: WALTER LUETGEBRUNE IN DER WEIMARER REPUBLIK [Star attorney for extremists on the right: Walter Luetgebrune in the Weimar Republic]. *Vierteljahrshefte für Zeitgeschichte [West Germany] 1984 32(3): 373-421.* As successful defense lawyer for prominent rightist plotters and terrorists, Walter Luetgebrune (1879-1949) played a major role in the destruction of the Weimar Republic. In 1931 he became legal adviser to the SA and defended a number of SA and SS terrorists in court. After the Nazi seizure of power he became a top official in the Interior Ministry and was even considered for the position of justice minister. But his close ties to SA leader Ernst Röhm and his attempt to enrich himself by representing Jewish businessmen in the Aryanization of business brought his arrest during the 1934 Röhm Purge, followed by disbarment until 1937. Based on the Luetgebrune papers (AHA War Documents microfilms) and the author's dissertation (1977); 288 notes. 1918-49

Lugard, Frederick

4171. Crowder, Michael. LUGARD AND COLONIAL NIGERIA: TOWARDS AN IDENTITY? *History Today [Great Britain] 1986 36(Feb): 23-29.* Describes the role of Frederick Lugard in conquering Northern Nigeria and amalgamating the region with the south to form the British colony of Nigeria. Notes the ethnic and religious differences between the regions. 1900-14

4172. Mangan, J. A. "GENTLEMEN GALORE"—IMPERIAL EDUCATION FOR TROPICAL AFRICA: LUGARD THE IDEOLOGIST. *Immigrants & Minorities [Great Britain] 1982 1(2): 149-168.* Describes the views and career of Sir Frederick Lugard (1858-1945), former governor of Hong Kong and Nigeria. He was a great believer in the civilizing mission of Great Britain and the civilizing role of the English public school system, which he attempted to bestow on the empire's native races, whom he considered inferior but capable of improvement. 85 notes. 1900-28

Luis of Olot

4173. Delgado, Buenaventura. UN PEDAGOGO DESCONOCIDO: EL CAPUCHINO LUIS DE OLOT (1720-1794) [An unknown educator: the Capuchin Luis of Olot (1720-94)]. *Perspectivas Pedagógicas [Spain] 1983 13(51): 477-480.* The little-known works of Luis de Olot show him to have been a widely read, rigorous, and erudite scholar who should be recognized as an important figure in the history of education. 1720-94

Lukács, Georg

4174. Bessonov, B. N. and Narski, I. S. D'ERD' LUKACH KAK FILOSOF I SOTSIAL'NYI MYSLITEL' [Georg Lukács as philosopher and social thinker]. *Voprosy Filosofii [USSR] 1985 (3): 85-99.* Traces the philosophical, social, ideological, and political development of one of the most eminent Marxist theoreticians of the century. 1918-71

4175. Bolyki, János. LUKÁCS GYÖRGY ÉS FÜLEP LAJOS KAPCSOLATÁRÓL [The association between Georg Lukács and Lajos Fülep]. *Theologiai Szemle [Hungary] 1985 28(5): 309-311.* 1910-50
*For abstract see **Fülep, Lajos***

4176. Cases, Cesare. QUANDO LUKÁCS GUIDAVA. LE NOSTRE LETTERE 1958/64 [When Lukács led: our letters 1958-64]. *Belfagor [Italy] 1985 40(1): 55-74.* Edits, translates, introduces, and annotates selected correspondence between Georg Lukács and the author from the years 1958 to 1964. 1958-64

4177. Dürr, J. "Die Expressionismusdebatte: Untersuchungen zum Werk von Georg Lukács" [The debate on Expressionism: investigations on the work of Georg Lukács]. U. of Munich [West Germany] 1982. 410 pp. *DAI-C 1985 46(4): 844; 46/4046c.* 1910's-71

4178. Kiss, Endre. LUKÁCS, VIENNA, BELLE EPOQUE: ON THE SIGNIFICANCE OF VIENNA IN THE DEVELOPMENT OF YOUNG LUKÁCS. *East European Quarterly 1986 20(2): 141-155.* The art criticism of Viennese Impressionism by Georg Lukács revealed a philosophical mind that should be ranked with Wittgenstein's. The decisive concept in Lukács's early writing, especially in *Die Seele und die Formen* (1911), was grounded in the Austro-Hungarian culture of the period, which emphasized the requirement that the existential predicament should be simultaneously presented with the utmost methodological rigor and awareness. Based on Lukács's published works; 32 notes. 1900-15

4179. Novak, Zoltan. GYÖRGY LUKÁCS'S THEORETICAL AND POLITICAL ACTIVITY IN THE COURSE OF THE SOVIET REPUBLIC IN HUNGARY *Ann. U. Sci. Budapestinensis de Rolando Eötvös Nominatae: Sectio Phil. et Sociol. [Hungary] 1979 13: 127-163.* György (Georg) Lukács, a communist from 1918 and supporter of world revolution, misunderstood V. I. Lenin, proclaiming that revolutionary organs had to be created as state, not party, organs. 1915-25

4180. Urbán, Károly. LUKÁCS GYÖRGY A MAGYAR MUNKÁSMOZGALOMBAN (1918-1930) [The role of Georg Lukács in the Hungarian labor movement, 1918-30]. *Párttörténeti Közlemények [Hungary] 1985 31(1): 45-86.* Lukács joined the Communist Party in 1918, and between 1919 and 1921 was a member of the Central Committee of the Party, which by this time was forced to go underground. Although he had leading positions in Party politics throughout the 1920's, he was in many of his political undertakings extremely unsuccessful. Lukács always felt that he would be far happier and more appreciated as a scholar of the social sciences than a political figure. In 1930 he decided to leave the Party in order to accomplish his ambition. 84 notes. 1918-30

4181. Urbán, Károly. LUKÁCS GYÖRGY FELSZABADULÁS UTÁNI POLITIKAI PÁLYAKÉPÉHEZ [On the political career of Georg Lukács after the liberation]. *Párttörténeti Közlemények [Hungary] 1985 31(3): 56-108.* Provides a short survey of the development of Georg Lukács's political thinking between 1938 and 1945, paying particular attention to his new conception of democracy and people's democracy. Lukács imagined the process of democratic transformation as a slow but long-lasting transition to socialism and attached great hopes to gaining ground by the institutions of direct democracy. Lukács's idea of democracy was in contradistinction to the dogmatic interpretation of the dictatorship of the proletariat accepted by the Party leadership at the beginning of 1949, however, and his cultural-political conception based on the popular front policy was contrary to the new sectarian political objectives. His subsequent position is examined, especially his new era during the process of breaking with dogmatism. Based on secondary sources and various works by Lukács; 110 notes. 1930's-70's

4182. Vermes, Pamela. THE BUBER-LUKÁCS CORRESPONDENCE (1911-1921) *Leo Baeck Inst. Year Book [Great Britain] 1982 27: 369-378.* The 13 letters of this correspondence between Buber and the young Georg Lukács are of interest and somewhat surprising since Lukács is known as a Marxist. That he was attracted to religious ideas and beliefs for a time was known; that he actually communicated with a person of Buber's reputation suggests how seriously he treated them at that period of his life. The author translated the letters from the original German into English for this publication. Letters are found in the Lukács Archive of the Hungarian Academy of Sciences and in the Buber Archive of the Jewish National and University Library in Jerusalem. 1911-21

4183. Veszelák, Ferenc. MŰHELY ÉS ÖRÖKSÉG: BESZÉLGETÉS SZIKLAI LÁSZLÓVAL, A LUKÁCS ARCHÍVUM ÉS KÖNYVTÁR VEZETŐJÉVEL [Workshop and heritage: a conversation with László Sziklai, head of the Lukács archives and library]. *Társadalmi Szemle [Hungary] 1982 37(10): 68-72.* The intellectual legacy of George Lukács is used as a base to expand and establish essential research for the development of Marxist philosophy in Hungary. As the 100th anniversary of Lukács's birth is approaching, the occasion will be celebrated by offering his library of approximately 10,000 books, his manuscripts, and publications to interested individuals for study. 1918-71

4184. Zoltai, Dénes. LUKÁCS AND THE RENCONTRES INTERNATIONALES OF GENEVA. *New Hungarian Quarterly [Hungary] 1985 26(98): 68-76.* Discusses Hungarian Communist Georg Lukács's role in the peace movements among European intellectuals after World War II, focusing on his participation in the Rencontres Internationales in Geneva, cultural festivals first organized in 1946 to unite Europeans, often pointedly excluding citizens of the USSR. Bases treatment of the dilemma posed by his support of Soviet Communism and of European reconciliation in his autobiographical *My Road to Marx,* especially its postscript, and in his political theory. Primary sources; 23 notes. 1946-57

Lukacs, John

4185. Congdon, Lee. HISTORY AS PERSONAL KNOWLEDGE: JOHN LUKACS AND HIS WORK. *Continuity 1981 (3): 63-75.* By examining John Lukacs's life and writings, the historian can see how historical knowledge is achieved from disciplined inquiry carried on from a specific perspective. Lukacs was a Hungarian nationalist and believed that Europe was a series of nationalities that should be preserved. He opposed American and Russian domination in the European continent. These attitudes and ideas clearly emerged from his writings. 1945-80

Lukin, Nikolai M.

4186. Galkin, I. S. 100-LETIE SO DNIA ROZHDENIIA AKADEMIKA N. M. LUKINA [Centenary of the birth of Academician N. M. Lukin]. *Voprosy Istorii [USSR] 1985 (6): 95-102.* Surveys the academic career of Nikolai M. Lukin (1885-1940), Soviet historian and publicist. In the 1920's he wrote polemical articles for *Pravda* and a brochure on the relationship of church and state for mass distribution. His Paris research of 1927 yielded material for subsequent publications on the Paris Commune and the French Revolution. As President of the Soviet Academy of Sciences in the 1930's he initiated publication of a world history series. Secondary sources; 34 notes. 1917-40

4187. Galkin, I. S. AKADEMIK N. M. LUKIN [Academician N. M. Lukin]. *Novaia i Noveishaia Istoriia [USSR] 1982 (3): 197-207.* Nikolai M. Lukin, born 21 July 1885 into a family of village school teachers was a revolutionary professor at Moscow University and expert on Soviet Marxist history and on Western Europe and the United States. He entered the Historical Philology Department of Moscow University, and became a Bolshevik. He was arrested several times and exiled. He welcomed the Russian Revolution and in 1919 was entrusted with the education of the new cadres of historians. He faithfully interpreted Soviet history. He studied the works of Marx, Engels, and Lenin. He is honored as a great scholar and the teacher of the first generation of Soviet historians. 71 notes. 1885-1982

Lumsden, Louisa

4188. Vicinus, Martha. VIVERE INSIEME: *COLLEGE WOMEN* INGLESI TRA FINE '800 E INIZIO '900 [Living together: English college women at the turn of the century]. *Memoria: Riv. di Storia delle Donne [Italy] 1982 (4): 45-58.* 1870-1920

For abstract see ***Davies, Emily***

Lumumba, Patrice

4189. Lamy, E. AUTOBIOGRAPHIE AFRICAINE DE PIERRE LEROY, DERNIER GOUVERNEUR DE LA PROVINCE ORIENTALE DU CONGO BELGE [African autobiography of Pierre Leroy, last governor of Orientale province of the Belgian Congo]. *Bulletin des Séances de l'Académie Royale des Sciences d'Outre-Mer [Belgium] 1982 28(3): 269-285.* 1938-60

For abstract see ***Leroy, Pierre***

Luna Arbizú, José

4190. —. ENSAYO BIOGRAFICO SOBRE EL DOCTOR JOSE LUNA ARBIZU [A biographical essay about Dr. José Luna Arbizú]. *Anales de la Academia de Geografía e Historia de Guatemala [Guatemala] 1983 57: 225-242.*

Figueroa Marroquín, Horacio. *pp. 225-239.* A brief biography of José Luna Arbizú (1805-88) of the University of San Carlos medical faculty. A Salvadoran by birth, but educated in Guatemala City and Paris, he founded the first medical journal in Central America, 1845, was the first to use ether in Latin America, served as *protomédico* of Guatemala (1858-70), and was a noted teacher who introduced the latest drugs and techniques from France and Europe.

López Mayorical, Mariano. *pp. 240-242.* Provides a brief biography of Figueroa Marroquín. 1805-88

Lunacharski, Anatoli

4191. Nedava, Yosef. B'MA'AVAK AL IVRIT B'BRIT HA'MOATZOT—BEN ANATOLI LUNACHARSKY L'PROFESSOR S. Z. ZEITLIN [The struggle for Hebrew in the USSR: from Anatoli Lunacharski to Professor S. Z. Zeitlin]. *Shvut [Israel] 1980 7: 41-44.* Anatoli Lunacharski was a truly enlightened person in the intellectual world of prerevolutionary Russia. His position as Commissar of Education, 1917-29, placed him in a position to support Judaism, Jewish culture, Zionism, and the Hebrew language and their continuation in Russia. Lunacharski's support was not sufficient to ensure Hebrew's survival. The author describes one of the last attempts to rescue the Hebrew language in Russia, a 1928 effort by S. Z. Zeitlin, which met with failure. Lunacharski was under political pressure to avoid any activity that might encourage the Jews in creating a national identity. Based on archival material from Hebrew University and Hebrew Union College, interviews with Zeitlin; 2 portraits, 22 notes. 1918-28

Lundberg, Johan Wilhelm

4192. Jungmarker, Gunnar. SILHUETTÖREN OCH PORTRÄTTGRAVÖREN J. W. LUNDBERG ("LUNDEBERG"): ETT IDENTIFIKATIONSPROBLEM [The silhouettist and portrait engraver J. W. Lundberg (Lundeberg): a problem of identification]. *Personhistorisk Tidskrift [Sweden] 1979 75(3): 84-94.* The Swedish silhouettist, J. W. Lundberg, previously thought to have been a factory owner by that name, is now known to have been a clergyman, Johan Wilhelm Lundberg (1762-1814) from Göta, Sweden. A number of engravings from 1792-1806 and silhouette portraits from 1796-97 can be identified as his work. Court documents, in which his name appears as Lundeberg, show that he was sentenced to death for counterfeiting in 1812. The sentence was changed to forced labor, and Lundberg died two years later. One tinted drawing from 1796 is clearly by the clergyman Lundberg, and the remaining body of works carries the same signature. Based on works by J. W. Lundberg and Court Archives in Jönköping, Sweden; 5 illus., 10 notes, 10 ref. 1796-1806

Luria, Isaac

4193. Tamar, David. REISHITO SHEL HA'ARI BEMITSRAIM [The early activity of Rabbi Isaac Luria (Ha'ari) in Egypt]. *Zion [Israel] 1979 44: 229-240.* Discusses Rabbi Isaac Luria's residence in Egypt, 1542-70. Historic accounts of Luria's life are steeped in fables that began before his death in Safad in 1572 at the age of 38. Very few facts are known of his life in Egypt between the ages of eight and 36. The author throws light on this period by analyzing two commercial letters written in 1554 and, in particular, a letter of approbation written at some time between 1558 and 1560 by the rabbis of Egypt. It was soon after this letter that Luria retired to seclusion in a house near the Nile for six to seven years, where he devoted himself to the study of kabbalistic treatises. 51 notes. 1534-72

Lusardi, Cristoforo Matteo

4194. Pini, Ulisse Angelo. CRISTOFORO MATTEO LUSARDI OCULISTA GIRAMONDO [Cristoforo Matteo Lusardi, oculist and world traveler]. *Arch. Storico per le Province Parmensi [Italy] 1979 31: 271-274.* Lusardi da Cereseto da Compiano (1778-1853), eye doctor and surgeon, studied at the University of Pavia and spent a great part of his life journeying through Europe, especially France, Belgium, Switzerland, and Italy, performing hundreds of cataract and artificial pupil operations. 1803-53

Lütfi, Ahmed

4195. Aktepe, M. Münir. VAK'A-NÜVİS AHMED LÜTFÎ EFENDİ VE TÂİHİ HAKKINDA BÂZI BİLGİLER [The chronicler Ahmed Lütfi Efendi and some information regarding his *History*]. *Tarih Enstitüsü Dergisi [Turkey] 1979-80 10-11: 121-152.* Recounts the official career of Ahmed Lütfi Efendi (1816-1907), Ottoman court historian from 1865 until his death. Lütfi's official history covers the years 1825-76 and contains 15 volumes, of which seven were published during his lifetime and one after his death. Describes and gives the location of all 15 manuscript volumes and lists Lütfi's other works. 7 photos. 1816-1907

Luther, Martin

4196. Cabot, José Tomás. EL MARCO HISTORICO [The historical framework]. *Hist. y Vida [Spain] 1983 16(181): 6-12.* Summarizes Martin Luther's life and the historical events in Germany that helped to shape his ideas, and notes the influence of Luther's ideas in modern times. 1483-1555

4197. Congar, Yves Marie. "NOVO ET MIRO VOCABULO ET THEOLOGICO." LUTHER, REFORMATEUR DE LA THEOLOGIE ["Novo et miro vocabulo et theologico": Luther, a reformer of theology]. *Rev. d'Hist. et de Phil. Religieuses [France] 1983 63(1-2): 7-15.* Discusses Martin Luther's criticism of scholastic theology and his doctrinal reforms from 1509-40. 1509-40

4198. Kaufman, Peter Iver. LUTHER'S "SCHOLASTIC PHASE" REVISITED: GRACE, WORKS, AND MERIT IN THE EARLIEST EXTANT SERMONS. *Church Hist. 1982 51(3): 280-289.* Two early sermons of Martin Luther copied from a manuscript in Erfurt, Germany demonstrate the reformer's early endorsements of semi-Pelagian features of scholastic soteriology. These sermons delivered before 1512 discuss empowerment which, coupled with Luther's work on the Sentences and the Psalms, provide evidence that Luther's belief in divine generosity was present even in the soteriology of the early scholastic phase of his career. 51 notes. 1509-12

4199. Lehmann, Hartmut. MARTIN LUTHERS 500. GEBURTSTAG IM JAHRE 1983 [Martin Luther's 500th anniversary in 1983]. *Geschichte in Wissenschaft und Unterricht [West Germany] 1982 33(12): 748-751.* In 1980 the Martin Luther Committee formed in East Germany to prepare for the 1983 celebrations. Considers the various Luthers of past anniversary celebrations. In 1617 he was a Protestant hero. In 1717 he was the hero of the fundamentalist-pietist groups because of his profound knowledge of the Bible. In the late 18th century the rationalists celebrated him. In 1817 the national liberals eulogized him. In 1883 the conservatives praised him for his antisocialism, the liberals for his "culture." In 1933 German Christians looked to Luther for inspiration during their persecution by the Fascists. Since 1946 there has been an attempt to remove him from the tradition linking him with Frederick III, Bismarck, and Hitler. 1483-1983

4200. Lienhard, Marc. QUELQUES PUBLICATIONS RECENTES RELATIVES A MARTIN LUTHER [Current publications on Martin Luther]. *Revue d'Histoire et de Philosophie Religieuse [France] 1985 65(4): 461-480.* Reviews 30 publications honoring the 1983 Martin Luther jubilee, focusing on Luther's theology, ethics, social theory, place in the context of the Reformation in Germany, interpretations by later theologians, and importance to the ecumenical movement. 16c-20c

4201. Lotz, David. LUTHER: FROM ALPHA TO OMEGA. *Sixteenth Century Journal 1985 16(1): 135-138.* Reviews Marilyn H. Harran's *Luther on Conversion: The Early Years* (1983) and Mark U. Edwards, Jr.'s *Luther's Last Battles: Politics and Polemics* (1983). Harran studies the concept of conversion in young Luther in a praiseworthy way. Edwards probes the bitter conflicts of Luther's last years against the Catholics, Turks, Jews, and fellow Protestants, aiming neither to accuse or excuse. 1500-46

4202. McGrath, Alister E. *MIRA ET NOVA DIFFINITIO IUSTITIAE:* LUTHER AND SCHOLASTIC DOCTRINES OF JUSTIFICATION. *Archiv für Reformationsgeschichte [West Germany] 1983 74: 37-60.* An autobiographical fragment by Martin Luther dated 1545 and serving as a preface to the Wittenberg edition of his Latin works describes his concern with the phrase *iustitia dei* (the righteousness of God) in Romans 1.17. Originally he accepted the Aristotelian or Ciceronian meaning of righteousness as found in the theological literature of Gabriel Biel and emphasizing the punitive nature of God's justice against sinners. Later, however, Luther came to interpret "righteousness" as the mercy of God through which He justifies sinners. Based on an autobiographical fragment by Martin Luther dated 1545. 1545

4203. Meyer, Helmut. ZWINGLI UND LUTHER: EINHEIT UND GEGENSÄTZLICHKEIT ZWEIER REFORMATOREN [Zwingli and Luther: unity and contrariness of two reformers]. *Schweizer Monatshefte [Switzerland] 1984 64(10): 821-834.* Examines the personalities, common objectives and divergences of the two religious reformers Martin Luther and Ulrich Zwingli. 1505-29

4204. Neuhaus, Helmut. MARTIN LUTHER IN GESCHICHTE UND GEGENWART: NEUERSCHEINUNGEN ANLÄSSLICH DES 500. GEBURTSTAGES DES REFORMATORS [Martin Luther in history and the present: recent publications on the occasion of the 500th birthday of the reformer]. *Archiv für Kulturgeschichte [West Germany] 1984 66(2): 425-479.* Reviews 65 recent publications on Martin Luther and the Reformation, including biographical, artistic, general, and specific studies. 49 notes, biblio. 16c

4205. Sierra Valentí, Eduardo. PERSONALIDAD HUMANA [A human personality]. *Hist. y Vida [Spain] 1983 16(181): 13-19.* Examines the personal life of Martin Luther, including his family life and private happiness, and stresses that this aspect of Luther has been largely ignored in Spanish scholarship. 1483-1546

4206. Solov'ev, E. Iu. MARTIN LIUTER—VYDAIUSHCHIISIA DEIATEL' NEMETSKOI I EVROPEISKOI ISTORII [Martin Luther—an outstanding figure in German and European history]. *Voprosy Istorii [USSR] 1983 (10): 33-54.* Martin Luther was a religious ideologist of the German middle classes. His reformist ideas were in conformity with the epoch of the early bourgeois revolutions. Luther was one-sided in his agitation for an overthrow of church feudalism and the papacy; he opposed class struggle and peasant movements. At the same time his criticism of the Catholic Church, his recognition of the independence of the state, his religious and moral approval of labor and business initiative, and his support of universal primary education drew his teaching closer to the ideology and culture of the modern age. 1512-46

4207. Stayer, James M. THE ECLIPSE OF *YOUNG MAN LUTHER:* AN OUTSIDER'S PERSPECTIVE ON LUTHER STUDIES. *Canadian Journal of History [Canada] 1984 19(2): 167-182.* Reflects on the historiography of Martin Luther (1483-1546) after the publication of Erik H. Erikson's psychohistory *Young Man Luther: A Study in Psychoanalysis and History* (1958). Touches the methodology of historical biography as well as fashions in Luther studies. Although Luther scholars never liked Erikson's founding Luther's contributions to the Reformation on a tormented early life, Erikson actually interpreted the image of Luther accepted by most Luther scholars, rather than Luther's own source documents. When Luther scholars abandoned their image of a tormented youth as a projection onto the past of a tormented adult, they finally found grounds to reject Erikson's picture. 67 notes. 1505-19

4208. Thiel, Rudolf; Ignat, Petru; and Şerbănescu, Ana Maria. MARTIN LUTHER ŞI LUMEA GERMANĂ [Martin Luther and the German world]. *Magazin Istoric [Romania] 1983 17(11): 43-48; 60.* Based substantially on Rudolf Thiel's biography, discusses Luther's inner feelings and contradictions, reflecting the politics of 16th-century Germany in the light of their legacy for Germany. 1483-1555

4209. Wright, William J. PERSONALITY PROFILES OF FOUR LEADERS OF THE GERMAN LUTHERAN REFORMATION. *Psychohistory Review 1985 14(1): 12-22.* 16c
For abstract see ***John the Steadfast, Elector***

4210. —. TÉTELEK LUTHER MÁRTONRÓL, SZÜLETÉSÉNEK 500. ÉVFORDULÓJÁRA [Theses on Martin Luther, for the 500th anniversary of his birth]. *Theológiai Szemle [Hungary] 1982 25(2): 65-72.* 1482-1517

Luthuli, Albert

4211. Gorodnov, V. P. A LUTULI I N. MANDELA—IUZHNOAFRIKANSKIE PATRIOTY [A. Luthuli and N. Mandela, South African patriots]. *Narody Azii i Afriki [USSR] 1982 (4): 135-143.* Albert Luthuli (1898-1967) and Nelson Mandela (b. 1918) typify African patriotism and determination to prosecute the African national liberation struggle against racism. Their sociopolitical activity, their membership in the African National Congress brought them into close contact with their suffering compatriots. Both came from wealthy elites, but chose the path of struggle, eschewing the comfortable lives that their birth would have allowed them to achieve within racist society. They also rejected narrow tribalism, and insisted on a national struggle. Based on Luthuli's *Let My People Go,* (1962) and Mandela's *The Struggle is My Life,* (1978); 38 notes. 1918-82

Lutskaia, Natal'ia S.

4212. —. PAMIATI NATAL'I SERGEEVNY LUTSKOI [In memory of Natal'ia Sergeevna Lutskaia]. *Narody Azii i Afriki [USSR] 1985 (1): 215-217.* Profile of the professional life of N. S. Lutskaia (1916-84), faculty member of Moscow University and the Moscow Institute of Oriental Studies, senior fellow of the Academy of Sciences' Institute of Oriental Studies, and noted authority on North African history, politics, and national liberation movements. A list of over 50 of her major publications, compiled by S. D. Miliband, is appended. 1950's-82

Luxemburg, Rosa

4213. Adler, Georg. WISSENSCHAFTLICHE MITTEILUNGEN: NEUES ZUR BIOGRAPHIE ROSA LUXEMBURGS [Scholarly news: new information concerning the biography of Rosa Luxemburg]. *Beiträge zur Gesch. der Arbeiterbewegung [East Germany] 1981 23(1): 79-83.* Contains previously unpublished letters by and about Rosa Luxemburg pertaining to the judicial proceedings against her, Clara Zetkin, Franz Mehring, Peter Berten, and Heinrich Pfeiffer for publication of the periodical, *Die Internationale.* Based on material from Central Party Archives, Institute for Marxism-Leninism; 16 notes. 1916-18

4214. Bieńkowski, Władysław; with commentary by Iazhborovskaia, Inessa S. et al. BIOGRAFISTYKA POLSKIEGO RUCHU ROBOTNICZEGO [Biographical studies of the Polish labor movement]. *Z Pola Walki [Poland] 1984 27(1-2): 355-368.* 1880's-1970's
For abstract see ***Dzerzhinsky, Felix***

4215. Dziamski, Seweryn. RÓŻA LUKSEMBURG (W SZEŚĆDZIESIĘCIOLECIE ŚMIERCI) [Rosa Luxemburg: on the occasion of the 60th anniversary of her death]. *Studia Filozoficzne [Poland] 1979 (5): 53-65.* Describes the life of Rosa Luxemburg and her thought from the point of view of Marxist principles and discusses her views on social evolution, the rise and fall of capitalism, and nationalism. 1870-1919

4216. Keller, Elke. "ICH WAR, ICH BIN, ICH WERDE SEIN." ROSA LUXEMBURG ["I was, I am, I shall be." Rosa Luxemburg]. *Beiträge zur Gesch. der Arbeiterbewegung [East Germany] 1980 22(2): 253-263.* Traces the life, career, and political activities of Rosa Luxemburg (1871-1919), the Polish-born revolutionary and one of the founding members of the German Communist Party. Describes her early life in Warsaw and her flight to Switzerland in 1889 because of her membership in the revolutionary Proletarian Party. As a student in Zurich she became involved with the Polish Social Democratic Party and helped edit the party newspaper, 1893-96. In 1898 she moved to Berlin and became a member of the German Social Democratic Party. The author also examines her friendship with Clara Zetkin, Karl Kautsky, and August Bebel. She followed with interest the development of the Russian Revolution in 1905, and in 1907 became a teacher at a school in Berlin. She was held in custody during World War I but helped to form the Spartacus Party with Karl Liebknecht. In 1918 she was released from prison and helped to change the Spartacists into the German Communist Party. She and Liebknecht were arrested for their part in the Spartacist uprising in Berlin in 1919 and were killed by soldiers on their way to prison. Secondary sources; 39 notes. 1896-1919

4217. Lampe, Jürgen. BOJ ROSY LUXEMBURGOVÉ PROTI MILITARISMU A VÁLCE [Rosa Luxemburg's struggle against militarism and war]. *Hist. a Vojenství [Czechoslovakia] 1983 32(3): 56-63.* Examines the work and life of Rosa Luxemburg (1871-1919). After her escape to Switzerland in 1889, she struggled against Prussian and international militarism. At the 1907 Stuttgart Conference Luxemburg formulated the strategy and tactics of socialist parties in the antiwar movement. The foundation of the German Communist Party in 1918 and its program was basically her work. Her assassination did not stop the march of socialism in Germany. 17 notes. 1871-1919

4218. Laschitza, Annelies. DOKUMENTE UND MATERIALIEN: BRIEFE ROSA LUXEMBURGS AN KAMPFGEFÄHRTEN [Documents and materials: Rosa Luxemburg's letters to fellow-fighters]. *Beiträge zur Gesch. der Arbeiterbewegung [East Germany] 1981 23(1): 70-73.* Contains eight previously unpublished letters to Rosi Wolfstein and Friedrich Westmeyer, dated 1913 to 1918. 8 notes. 1913-18

4219. Mason, Tim. COMRADE AND LOVER: ROSA LUXEMBURG'S LETTERS TO LEO JOGICHES. *Hist. Workshop J. [Great Britain] 1982 (13): 94-109.* Rosa Luxemburg and Leo Jogiches met as revolutionary exiles in Switzerland in 1890, and sustained a political and emotional relationship until 1907. Considers their dual-faceted relationship in light of a selection of Rosa Luxemburg's letters to Jogiches, in *Rosa Luxemburg's Letters to Leo Jogiches* (1981), edited and translated by Elzbieta Ettinger. Based on *Rosa Luxemburg's Letters;* illus., 17 notes. 1890-1907

4220. Mullaney, Marie Marmo. GENDER AND THE SOCIALIST REVOLUTIONARY ROLE, 1871-1921: A GENERAL THEORY OF THE FEMALE REVOLUTIONARY PERSONALITY. *Historical Reflections [Canada] 1984 11(2): 99-151.* 1871-1921
For abstract see ***Balabanoff, Angelica***

4221. Rojahn, Jürgen. UM DIE ERNEUERUNG DER INTERNATIONALE: ROSA LUXEMBURG CONTRA PIETER JELLES TROELSTRA. ZUR HALTUNG DER RADIKALEN LINKEN IN DEUTSCHLAND NACH DEM 4. AUGUST 1914 [Toward the restoration of the International: Rosa Luxemburg versus Pieter Jelles Troelstra (on the attitude of the radical Left in Germany after 4 August 1914)]. *International Review of Social History [Netherlands] 1985 30(1): 2-150.* Reexamines the origins of the split in the European socialist parties after the fall of international socialism at the beginning of World War I, focusing not so much on the collapse of the Socialist International as the problem of its restoration. The positions of radical leftist Rosa Luxemburg (1870-1919) and the centrist-reformist Dutch socialist Pieter Jelles Troelstra (1860-1930) are used as a paradigm that contained the core of divergent tendencies of international socialism during the critical years of 1914 and 1915. Luxemburg attempted to keep international socialism alive by championing the struggle against imperialism. Troelstra, on the other hand, advocated the full democratization of individual national states before international socialism could be revived. Appendix contains three unpublished letters by Rosa Luxemburg and seven by Karl Liebknecht, written between August 1914 and January 1915, and addressed to socialists in neutral countries. Based on archival sources, largely from the International Institute for Social History, Amsterdam; 5 illus., 635 notes, appendix containing letters by Rosa Luxemburg and Karl Liebknecht. 1914-15

Luzac, Elie

4222. Velema, W. R. E. HOMO MERCATOR IN HOLLAND: ELIE LUZAC EN HET ACHTTIENDE-EEUWSE DEBAT OVER DE KOOPHANDEL [The merchant in Holland: Elie Luzac and the 18th-century debate over trade]. *Bijdragen en Mededelingen betreffende de Geschiedenis der Nederlanden [Netherlands] 1985 100(3): 427-444.* The Dutch writer Elie Luzac (1723-96) wrote extensively on trade and concluded that this economic activity was the most important for the well-being and happiness of a nation. Trade, he alleged, was the best road to happiness, tempered passions, and was an effective way of preventing war. The merchant was the hero of society. The Dutch Republic did not collapse because of a decline in commerce but because of high taxation and cultural factors. Primary materials; 75 notes. 18c

Luzzatto, Moses Hayyim

4223. Tishbi, Isaiah. DEMUTO SHEL RABBI MOSHE VALLE (RAMDU) UMA'AMADO BEHAVURAT RAMHAL [Rabbi Moses Valle and his status within the circle of Rabbi Moses Hayyim Luzzatto]. *Zion [Israel] 1979 44: 265-302.* 1696-1777
For abstract see ***Valle, Moses David***

Lyell, Charles

4224. Porter, Roy. CHARLES LYELL: THE PUBLIC AND PRIVATE FACES OF SCIENCE. *Janus [Netherlands] 1982 69(1-2): 29-50.* Deep tensions arose between the private and public dimensions of Charles Lyell's (1797-1875) career as geologist. He felt the public pulling him one way and his most respected colleagues another. To maintain his position in the scientific world of the 1860's, he advocated evolutionism. His scientific colleagues were distressed by the traditional orthodoxy expressed in his *Antiquity of Man* (1863) and in the 10th edition of his *Principles of Geology.* Based on Leonard Wilson's biography of Lyell, studies by Rudwick, Morrell, and Page, and other works; 109 notes. 1860's

Lyons, Francis Stewart Leland

4225. Foster, R. F. FRANCIS STEWART LELAND LYONS, 1923-1983. *Proceedings of the British Academy [Great Britain] 1984 70: 463-479.* The Irish historian Francis Stewart Leland Lyons (1923-83) was born in Londonderry, Northern Ireland, and educated at Trinity College, Dublin. From 1947 to 1951 he was a lecturer in history at Hull University, before returning to Trinity as Fellow and Lecturer. From 1964 to 1974 he was Professor of History at the University of Kent and from 1974 to 1980 Provost of Trinity. His books include *The Fall of Parnell* (1960), *John Dillon: a Biography* (1968), *Ireland since the Famine* (1971), and *Parnell* (1978). At the time of his death he was working on a biography of W. B. Yeats. Photo, 11 notes.
1840's-1970's

M

Ma Junwu

4226. Huang Chia-mu. MA CHÜN-WU TI TSAO CH'I SSU HSIANG YÜ YEN LUN [The early thoughts and writings of Ma Chün-wu]. *Bull. of the Inst. of Modern Hist. Acad. Sinica [Taiwan] 1981 10: 303-349.* Ma Junwu (Ma Chün-wu, 1881-1940) received a traditional education. Later exposure to Western learning and reformist thought and study in Japan changed his outlook. He joined Sun Yat-sen's followers and wrote extensively for revolutionary periodicals. After the 1911 revolution, he held important posts, through which he expressed his republicanism in national documents, such as the draft constitution. Based on Ma's writings; chart, 141 notes. 1881-1912

Macavei, Mihail

4227. Florian, T. MIHAIL MACAVEI 1882-1965 [Mihail Macavei (1882-1965)]. *Anale de Istorie [Romania] 1982 28(5): 96-99.* Macavei studied law in Paris and, returned to Romania, entered politics and became a member of Parliament (1914) as a National Liberal. Through the Socialist Party, he became ultimately a Communist. He was editor of *Socialismul* (1921), a supporter of the Workers and Peasants Bloc in 1924, fought fascism, and was imprisoned in 1939. He survived to welcome liberation in 1944, filled a number of party posts, and for a time was Romanian minister plenipotentiary in London. Portrait. 1900's-65

MacBride, Sean

4228. MacEvilly, Michael. SEAN MACBRIDE AND THE REPUBLICAN MOTOR LAUNCH *ST. GEORGE. Irish Sword [Ireland] 1984 16(62): 49-57.* Sean MacBride, an Irish revolutionary, politician, and statesman, was also involved in naval activities, largely smuggling of arms for the Irish Republican Army from 1921 to 1924. In December 1924, he undertook a difficult sea operation. He acquired a motor launch, the *St. George,* outfitted it, and gathered a crew to attempt the rescue of prisoners from an internment camp at Larne, County Antrim. The rescue attempt was unsuccessful because of storms. The boat was wrecked, but the crew was saved. Based on newspaper accounts and interviews and writings of the participants; 22 notes, illus. 1924

Macchi, Mauro

4229. Armani, Giuseppe. MAURO MACCHI NELL'EPISTOLARIO DI CARLO CATTANEO [Mauro Macchi in the letters of Carlo Cattaneo]. *Bol. della Domus Mazziniana [Italy] 1981 27(1): 175-188.* Macchi (1818-80) was a disciple of Cattaneo and in the latter's correspondence his figure and ideas stand out in relief. Their political relations were based on a deep human friendship which dated from the period when Macchi was the publicist's close collaborator and editorial assistant. Cattaneo had absolute trust in Macchi and he was often the source of parliamentary moves carried out by Macchi. Based on Cattaneo's published correspondence; 49 notes. 1850-69

4230. Tomasi, Tina. L'IMPEGNO DI MAURO MACCHI PER UN'EDUCAZIONE DEMOCRATICA [Mauro Macchi's commitment to democratic education]. *Bol. della Domus Mazziniana [Italy] 1981 27(1): 89-119.* Macchi (1818-80) entered the field of education early, but was soon expelled. He maintained a strong interest in it throughout his political, journalistic, and masonic activities. The article summarizes his ideas on the nonecclesiastical school, on popular education, on the education of women, and on the reform of the educational system. 50 notes. ca 1840-70

4231. —. MAURO MACCHI NEL CENTENARIO DELLA MORTE [Mauro Macchi on the centenary of his death]. *Bol. della Domus Mazziniana [Italy] 1981 27(2): 9-88, 189-195.*

DellaPeruta, Franco. MAURO MACCHI E LA DEMOCRAZIA ITALIANA (1850-1857) [Mauro Macchi and Italian democracy, 1850-57], *pp. 9-88.* Macchi is an important though little known figure in the history of the Risorgimento. He was a democrat in radical opposition to Mazzinianism and the Action Party. Appended are 48 letters to and from Macchi.

Montale, Bianca. INTERVENTO DI BIANCA MONTALE [Comments], *pp. 189-191.*

Parmentola, Vittorio. INTERVENTO DI VITTORIO PARMENTOLA [Comments], *p. 193.*

Lacaita, Carlo G. REPLICA DI CARLO LACAITA [Reply], *p. 195. Partly based on primary material in the Archivio Macchi of the Feltrinelli Library, Milan, National Library, Florence, and the Museo del Risorgimento, Genoa; 60 notes.* 1850-57

MacCulloch, John

4232. Flinn, Derek. JOHN MACCULLOCH, M.D., F.R.S. AND HIS GEOLOGICAL MAP OF SCOTLAND: HIS YEARS IN THE ORDNANCE, 1795-1826. *Notes and Records of the Royal Soc. of London [Great Britain] 1981 36(1): 83-102.* John MacCulloch, the first government-employed geologist in Great Britain, singlehandedly surveyed Scotland. He began his geological career in 1809 when assigned to locate limestone suitable for millstones. Additional miscellaneous duties led to geological and mineralogical surveys, and finally to the survey of Scotland in 1821. He believed his services were ill-used and undervalued; his survey of Scotland was not published until 1836, after his death. Based on documents from the Public Record Office at Kew and the Ordnance Survey Library at Southampton; 81 notes. 1795-1836

MacDiarmid, Hugh

4233. Harvie, Christopher. MACDIARMID THE SOCIALIST. *J. of the Scottish Labour Hist. Soc. [Great Britain] 1981 (16): 4-11.* Discusses the life, beliefs, and poetry of the 20th-century Scottish nationalist, socialist, and political activist Hugh MacDiarmid (pseudonym for Christopher Murray Grieve). 1910's-78

MacDonnell, Henry

4234. Ireland, John De Courcy. HENRY MACDONNELL, TENIENTE GENERAL IN THE SPANISH NAVY. *Irish Sword [Ireland] 1982 15(58): 23-29.* Henry MacDonnell started in 1760 as a cadet in Spain's Irish Regiment. He served until 1805 in North Africa, the West Indies, at Cadiz, and in the Battle of Trafalgar, except fo three years, 1788-91, when he was in the Swedish Navy. During his service with the Spanish he reached the rank of brigadier. MacDonnell was captured by the British at Trafalgar. Upon his return to Spain he served at various tasks for the navy but died in poverty in 1823. Based on dossier on MacDonnell's career from the Spanish naval archives; 2 notes. 1760-1823

Maceo y Grajales, Antonio

4235. Aguirre, Sergio. EN EL ANIVERSARIO DE LA MUERTE DE MACEO [On the anniversary of the death of Maceo]. *U. de La Habana [Cuba] 1979-80 (211): 67-81.* Outlines the life and career of Antonio Maceo y Grajales (1845-96), Cuban revolutionary hero of the war of 1895. 1845-96

Macfarlane, Walter Victor

4236. McIntyre, A. K. WALTER VICTOR MACFARLANE, 1913-82. *Historical Records of Australian Science [Australia] 1985 6(2): 247-265.* A zoologist, physiologist, ecologist, and physician, Macfarlane was a professor of physiology at the University of Queensland, the Australian National University, and, finally, the University of Adelaide. Based on personal recollections and interviews; biblio. 1940's-82

MacGill, Patrick

4237. Greacen, Robert. "TAKING THE DERRY BOAT": PATRICK MACGILL, NOVELIST. *Éire-Ireland 1981 16(1): 90-104.* Patrick MacGill (1890-1963), son of a potato farmer in the Glen of Glenties in County Donegal, Ireland, "took the Derry boat" to Scotland as a seasonal migrant laborer in the potato and turnip fields. In 1910 he became established as a successful poet. He later moved to London and took positions at the *Daily Express* and the Chapter Library at Windsor Castle. In his novels, 1914-34, MacGill voiced the protest of exploited rural workers of Ulster, but he was resented by some of them for the seeming anticlericalism and criticism of Ireland that contributed to his success. 26 notes. 1910-34

Mach, Ernst

4238. Sajner, Josef. ERNST MACHS BEZIEHUNGEN ZU SEINEM HEIMATORT CHIRLITZ (CHRLICE) UND ZU MÄHREN [Ernst Mach's relations to his native Chrlice and to Moravia]. *Bohemia [West Germany] 1983 24(2): 358-368.* The physicist and philosopher Ernst Mach (1838-1916) returned to his native Moravia as a youth to complete his secondary schooling (1852-55) at the Piarist *gymnasium* in Kroměříž (Kremsier). These formative years, which also familiarized him with the Czech language and people, are reflected in his surviving school record. Based on material in Moravian archives and published sources; 25 notes. 1838-1916

Machado de Assis, Joaquim Maria

4239. MacNicoll, Murray Graeme. SILVIO ROMERO AND MACHADO DE ASSIS: A ONE-SIDED RIVALRY (1870-1914). *Inter-American Rev. of Biblio. 1981 31(3): 366-377.* Sílvio Romero (1851-1914) was extremely critical of Brazilian author Joaquim Maria Machado de Assis (1839-1908), whom he considered to be overrated. Romero wrote articles which included criticism of Machado and in 1897 published *Machado de Assis.* He ignored Machado's aesthetic and technical skills and attacked him for romanticism, pessimism, and lack of nationalism. At times he resorted to personal criticism. Romero's son, Nelson Romero, revised *Machado de Assis,* and this shorter, less vindictive, version was published in 1936. One effect of Romero's animosity was that Machado and his works rose to the center of literary interest in Brazil. Based on a study of the works discussed; 30 notes. 1870-1914

Machado y Ruíz, Antonio and Manuel

4240. Ortíz, Fernando. UNA CIUDAD Y DOS POETAS [One city and two poets]. *Cuadernos Hispanoamericanos [Spain] 1984 (412): 126-133.* Biographies of Manuel (1874-1947) and Antonio Machado y Ruíz (1875-1939) run together until the mid-1890's. They were born into the liberal, anticlerical, and progressive strata of Seville and attended the Institución Libre de Enseñanza in Madrid, where the family moved in 1883. After 1895, Manuel became a leader of reactionary *fin-de-siècle* Seville, contributing to the Andalusian literary image, whereas Antonio increasingly concerned himself with Spanish problems involving Castile and the more real Andalusia of Baeza. Photo. 1880's-1947

Machalski, Tadeusz

4241. Smogorzewski, Kazimierz. NAJNOWSZA HISTORIA OD STRONY MAGLA [Contemporary history according to a mangler]. *Zeszyty Hist. [France] 1981 (57): 204-217.* Reviews the memoirs of General Tadeusz Machalski, a Polish army officer who was trained in the Austro-Hungarian army and took part in the 1914 war in Eastern Galicia and Italy and who later joined the Polish army. Machalski has a very personalized opinion of modern Polish history and its leading personalities. Machalski was a right-wing National Democrat, and as a professional soldier, he looked down on the legions formed by Piłsudski. As the ill-will was mutual, Machalski was denied promotion five times in the interwar era, which only increased his hostility toward the Piłsudski régime. 4 notes. 20c

Machiavelli, Niccolò

4242. Arrillaga Aldama, Luis. MAQUIAVELO: EL PODER QUE FUE Y NO PUDO SER [Machiavelli: the power that he was and could not be]. *Revista de Estudios Políticos [Spain] 1984 (38): 215-237.* The greatness of Niccolò Machiavelli consists in the fact that despite the particularistic conditioning of public life of his time and his own subordinate position in that arena, he was able to penetrate to the effective nature of political reality as independent from religious views, and to elaborate a political theory charged with a practical intent. 48 notes. 1469-1527

4243. Dietz, Mary G. TRAPPING THE PRINCE: MACHIAVELLI AND THE POLITICS OF DECEPTION. *American Political Science Review 1986 80(3): 777-799.* Machiavelli's most famous political work, *The Prince,* was a masterful act of political deception. Machiavelli's intention was a republican one: to undo Lorenzo de Medici by giving him advice that would jeopardize his power, hasten his overthrow, and allow for the resurgence of the Florentine republic. This interpretation returns *The Prince* to its specific historical context, considering Machiavelli's advice to Lorenzo on where to reside, how to behave, and whom to arm in light of the political reality of 16th-century Florence. Evidence external to *The Prince,* including Machiavelli's other writings and his own political biography, confirms his anti-Medicean sentiments, his republican convictions, and his proclivity for deception. Understanding *The Prince* as an act of political deception continues a tradition of reading Machiavelli as a radical republican. Moreover, it overcomes the difficulties of previous republican interpretations and provides new insight into the strategic perspective and Renaissance artistry Machiavelli employed as a theoretician. 1513

4244. Heers, Jacques. MACHIAVEL, POETE ET PAYSAN [Machiavelli, poet and peasant]. *Historama [France] 1985 (19): 82-87.* A biographical sketch of Niccolò Machiavelli (1469-1527) centering on the famous Italian philosopher, statesman, and author's disgrace, which was followed by his varied successful literary pursuits. 1512-27

4245. McIntosh, Donald. THE MODERNITY OF MACHIAVELLI. *Political Theory 1984 12(2): 184-203.* Argues that instrumentalism has remained the dominant ethical philosophy of the modern era and that Machiavelli was the first major thinker to adopt a completely instrumental stance. Machiavelli's ethic was irrational and the psychological roots of his instrumentalism were sexual. 16c

4246. McKenzie, Lionel A. ROUSSEAU'S DEBATE WITH MACHIAVELLI IN THE *SOCIAL CONTRACT. J. of the Hist. of Ideas 1982 43(2): 209-228.* Although Jean Jacques Rousseau tried to camouflage the relationship of his political thought to that of Niccolò Machiavelli, the effects of the latter's influence are detectable. They were united in their pessimism regarding the possibility of a libertarian society in which pursuit of the common good would not be extinguished. Machiavelli's reputation in the 18th century was still largely negative, although his problematic mode of republican theory had been somewhat revitalized by the positive valuation both Montesquieu and Diderot placed on the potential for a society based on the harmonizing conflict of self-interests. Rousseau could not adopt this socially hierarchical view of egotism in a republic and thus had to read and misread selectively Machiavelli's interpretation of the Roman Republic in order to highlight the ideal consensualized meaning of *virtù* for modern democracies governed by an interestless "general will." 46 notes. 1500-1760's

4247. Stephens, J. N. and Butters, H. C. NEW LIGHT ON MACHIAVELLI. *English Hist. Rev. [Great Britain] 1982 97(382): 54-69.* In order to better understand the origins of Machiavelli's ideas, "the sort of world from which they came, and their relationship to his public life . . .," six documents from the Florentine archives are reprinted in their original language and analyzed in a brief note. Two of the documents suggest that Machiavelli resided in Florence rather than abroad in the years before 1498 when he began his career in the Florentine chancery. Two other documents give a hint of Machiavelli's unpopularity prior to his dismissal from public office in 1512. An additional document suggests that Machiavelli had an "itch to tell the Medici how to rule (and not just in order to win their favor)...." The final document is used to characterize contemporary reaction to the *Prince* as similar to present day. Other documents in the archives provide details of his transitional periods in 1512-13 and 1524-26. Based upon documents in the Florentine State Archives; 56 notes. 1498-1527

4248. Cooper, Roslyn Pesman. MACHIAVELLI, FRANCESCO SODERINI AND DON MICHELOTTO. *Nuova Riv. Storica [Italy] 1982 66(3-4): 342-357.* In 1506 the Florentine Republic made the controversial appointment of Michele de Corella, Cesar Borgia's hangman and a most cruel and feared man, to the post of captain of the guard of the county and district. Current debate among historians seems to focus on Niccolò Machiavelli as the instigator of the establishment of a militia and the appointment of its captain. Rather than Macchiavelli it was the ambitious cardinal of Volterra, Francesco Soderini, who was responsible for the move. Based on primary material in the Florence State Archive; 115 notes. 1506-24

Macià, Francisco

4249. Jardí, Enric. MACIA EN EL 50 ANIVERSARIO DE SU MUERTE [Macià: the 50th anniversary of his death]. *Hist. y Vida [Spain] 1983 16(189): 104-117.* Reviews the life of Francisco Macià, the great Catalan military-man-turned-statesman, who served for a brief time as president of the Catalan Republic. 1859-1933

Maciu, Vasile

4250. —. VASILE MACIU 1904-1981 [Vasile Maciu (1904-81)]. *Revista de Istorie [Romania] 1981 34(3): 579-580.* Vasile Maciu was born in 1904 in Cavacal, studied history with Nicolae Iorga and was a secondary school teacher for 20 years. In 1949 he was appointed lecturer on modern Romanian history at the faculty of history in Bucarest and head of the modern history department of the Institute of History and Philosophy of the Academy. In 1954 he was granted the highest national award for his didactic and scientific activities. In 1963 he received a professorship at the same institution. His research papers covered the major aspects of Romanian modern history. In 1972-76, he was editor in chief of *Revista de Istorie.* His death in 1981 was a loss to historical research and his country. 1904-81

MacIver, H. R. H.

4251. Momčilović, Branko. PUKOVNIK H. R. H. MAKIVER, KOMANDANT SRPSKE KONJICE U SRPSKO-TURSKOM RATU 1876 [Colonel H. R. H. MacIver, commander of the Serbian cavalry in the Serbo-Turkish war of 1876]. *Zbornik za Istoriju [Yugoslavia] 1981 (23): 133-148.* The Scot H. R. H. MacIver was a professional soldier whose career on the field of battle spanned nearly every conflict of the mid-19th century. Born at sea in 1841, he was trained in military affairs in the British army in India, but left British service shortly after the Great Rebellion and became a staff officer to General Stonewall Jackson in the American Civil War. A decade later, he organized a cavalry force for Prince Milan of Serbia in the war against Turkey, and played a major role in the defeat of the Turks in the Morava valley. 1876

Mackau, Armand de

4252. Ireland, John de Courcy. MACKAU AND CASEY: TWO FRANCO-IRISH MINISTERS OF MARINE AND THE FRENCH NAVAL REVIVAL AFTER 1815. *Mariner's Mirror [Great Britain] 1982 68(2): 127-131.* 1815-65
For abstract see ***Casey, Joseph-Gregoire***

Mackay, John Henry

4253. Wucherpfennig, Wolf. JOHN HENRY MACKAY: DICHTER, ANARCHIST, HOMOSEXUELLER [John Henry Mackay: poet, anarchist, homosexual]. *Jahrbuch des Instituts für Deutsche Geschichte [Israel] 1983 12: 229-254.* John Henry Mackay (1864-1933) was born near Glasgow to a Scottish father and German mother. Because of his father's early death, John's mother returned to Germany where she remarried. The repressive atmosphere of his home and school left an indelible mark on John's personality and his philosophy of life. The antiauthoritarian author shunned patriotism, nationalism, legalism and revolutionary anarchy while advocating passive resistance, global love, equality, and individual freedom. Mackay's homosexual tendencies were first expressed in anonymous publications in 1908 and 1909. After the death of his mother, Mackay was outspoken about his ambivalence toward her. His political and philosophical convictions reflected those of his contemporaries Stirner and Tucker. Secondary sources; 47 notes. 1864-1933

Mackintosh, James

4254. Barazzone, Esther Lynn. "The Politic Philosopher: Sir James Mackintosh (1765-1832) and the Scottish Enlightenment." Columbia U. 1982. 354 pp. *DAI 1982 43(5): 1640-A.* DA8222341 1791-1832

Maclean, Donald

4255. —. PAMIATI DONAL'DA DONAL'DOVICHA MAKLEINA [Obituary: in memory of Donald Maclean]. *Mirovaia Ekonomika i Mezhdunarodnye Otnosheniia [USSR] 1983 (5): 157.* Donald Maclean, historian and expert on international politics, was born in England in 1913 and died in the USSR in 1983. He studied British politics and the international relations of the western nations. His Soviet work was written under the pseudonym S. Madzoevski. 1913-83

Macleay, Alexander

4256. King, Hazel. MAN IN A TRAP: ALEXANDER MACLEAY, COLONIAL SECRETARY OF NEW SOUTH WALES. *J. of the Royal Australian Hist. Soc. [Australia] 1982 68(1): 37-48.* In 1824, family needs and debts from speculative banking forced Alexander Macleay, a British civil service pensioner aged 56, to become colonial secretary in New South Wales. Macleay speculated in colonial pastoral ventures, accruing huge debts by 1845. A friend, Thomas Barker, returned the estate to solvency by 1859 and enabled Macleay by posthumous bequests, to attain his objective in coming to New South Wales to provide for his large family. Paper read before Royal Australian Historical Society, Sydney, 30 September 1980. Based on Macleay's papers in the Mitchell Library, Sydney and the Linnean Society, London, Colonial Office papers, London and Sydney, and other primary sources; 38 notes. 1767-1859

Macmillan, Harold

4257. Charmley, John. HAROLD MACMILLAN AND THE MAKING OF THE FRENCH COMMITTEE OF LIBERATION. *Int. Hist. Rev. [Canada] 1982 4(4): 553-567.* Most biographers of Harold Macmillan have given little space to his wartime career. Yet that experience was the effective starting point in his ministerial career. The author attempts to consider this least-known period of Macmillan's career in light of recently released archival material. His greatest accomplishment while he was serving as British resident minister in North Africa was bringing together generals Charles de Gaulle and Henri Giraud, disparate personalities and quite hostile to one another, to serve as co-chairmen of the Committee of National Liberation. Based on Macmillan's *Memoirs,* files from the Franklin D. Roosevelt Library, British Foreign Office, Prime Minister's Papers, Cabinet Records, and lesser used primary sources; 52 notes. 1940-44

Macran, Henry Stewart

4258. Furlong, E. J. ANOTHER STELLA. *Hermathena [Ireland] 1981 (130-131): 53-61.* Describes the author's conversations with Stella Macran, wife of Henry Stewart Macran (professor of moral philosophy at the University of Dublin, 1901-34), in which she reminisced about her husband. 20c

Madajczyk, Czesław

4259. Mańkowski, Zygmunt. O TWÓRCZOŚCI CZESŁAWA MADAJCZYKA [The writing of Czesław Madajczyk]. *Kwartalnik Hist. [Poland] 1981 88(3): 761-769.* Celebrates the 25th anniversary of Madajczyk's historical writing. A prolific author, Madajczyk's interest is in German policy in occupied Poland. His research concentrates on the period between the two world wars. In the field of general history his studies center on the Third Reich and fascism. 20c

Madero, Francisco I.

4260. LaFrance, David G. FRANCISCO I. MADERO AND THE 1911 INTERIM GOVERNORSHIP IN PUEBLA. *Americas (Academy of American Franciscan History) 1986 42(3): 311-331.* During the period between his victory in the revolution against Porfirio Díaz and his own inauguration as president of Mexico, Francisco I. Madero worked mainly with political moderates in the state of Puebla, many of whom had served the Díaz dictatorship. He sought to disarm his own revolutionary followers and entrusted civil and military authority to figures they distrusted, while failing to initiate expected socioeconomic reforms. His policies in Puebla reflected those in the nation as a whole and foreshadowed his eventual failure as a ruler. Based on contemporary newspapers, various Mexican archival collections, and published works; 101 notes. 1911

Madgearu, Virgil N.

4261. Preda, Eugen. DIN CULISELE UNUI ASASINAT POLITIC [Backstage of a political assassination]. *Magazin Istoric [Romania] 1982 16(11): 36-39, (12): 36-39, 52.* Recently released British documents show that Virgil N. Madgearu (1887-1940), assassinated 17 November 1940 by the Iron Guard, was a contact for the Romanian Resistance during World War II. 1940

Maestertius, Jacobus

4262. Feenstra, R. JACOBUS MAESTERTIUS (1610-1658): ZIJN JURIDISCH ONDERWIJS IN LEIDEN EN HET LEUVENSE DISPUTATIESYSTEEM VAN GERARDUS CORSELIUS [Jacobus Maestertius (1610-58): his teaching of law in Leiden and the Louvain disputation system of Gerardus Corselius]. *Tijdschrift voor Rechtsgeschiedenis [Netherlands] 1982 50(3): 297-335.* Covers the life and works of Jacobus Maestertius, baptized Sebastiaan Mesterton, who, after law studies at Louvain and Orléans universities, settled in Holland in 1631 to become professor of law at Leiden University, where he introduced a treatment of legal disputations used in Louvain by Gerardus Corselius (1568-1636). The analysis of Maestertius's treatises on the disputations he conducted, privately and publicly, between 1636 and 1657, is limited to their external aspects and followed, in the appendix, by a comparison of their contents with those reconstructed from Corselius's works. Primary sources; 175 notes, appendix. 1610-58

Mafai, Mario

4263. Lambarelli, Roberto. MARIO MAFAI, GENTILISSIMO ARTISTA ROMANO (1902-1965) [Mario Mafai, the most graceful of Roman artists (1902-65)]. *Studi Romani [Italy] 1985 33(3-4): 268-270.* Mario Mafai painted views of Rome in a tonalist, expressionist style from 1929 to 1947. 1929-47

Magera, Franz

4264. Hein, Martin. DAS SCHICKSAL DES FRANZ MAGERA: EIN BEITRAG ZUM VERHÄLTNIS VON REFORMATION UND TÜRKENKRIEGEN [Franz Magera's destiny: the relationship between the Reformation and Turkish wars]. *Arch. für Reformationsgeschichte [West Germany] 1982 73: 308-313.* The interest in the 16th-century advance of the Turks into southeastern Europe is amply reflected in the writings of the reformers as well as in their mutual correspondence. When, therefore, a Greek, Magera by name, turned up at the Diet of Ratisbon in 1541 and told the story of his expulsion by the Turks and reported about the fate of his family in captivity, the Protestants received him well and supported him. Until his death at the end of 1541 his name appears in several letters which intercede for him and recommend him. From these documents his past had to be inferred in a rather indirect way. More light is now shed on his person—shrouded in considerable darkness so far—by the letter published here. Magera himself wrote that letter to Wittenberg. It fills up his biography with important details. 16c

Magheru, Gheorghe

4265. Cernovodeanu, Paul and Ştefan, Marian. INTEGRUL ŞI MODESTUL CETĂŢEAN GHEORGHE MAGHERU [The upright and modest citizen Gheorghe Magheru]. *Magazin Istoric [Romania] 1980 14(3): 33-37, 61.* A brief biography of Wallachian General Gheorghe Magheru (1804-80), followed by excerpts from an unpublished letter of his concerning Romanian radicalism and revolutionary activities in 1848. 1804-80

Mahler, Gustav

4266. Schorske, Carl E. MAHLER AND KLIMT: SOCIAL EXPERIENCE AND ARTISTIC EVOLUTION. *Daedalus 1982 111(3): 29-50.* 1870-1907
*For abstract see **Klimt, Gustav***

Mahler-Werfel, Alma

4267. Liberman, Arnoldo. EL TECLADO DE LA PIEL [Skin as keyboard]. *Cuadernos Hispanoamericanos [Spain] 1985 (420): 185-193.* Alma Mahler-Werfel (1880-1964) was the wife or lover of several main figures in the European cultural circles of the interwar period: Mahler, Gropius, Werfel, and Kokoshka. Her home was regularly attended by Schönberg, Hauptmann, Alban Berg, and many others. She was highly regarded in Austrian society, which passionately longed for cultural supremacy, and where art was the ultimate measure of socioeconomic standing. Photo. ca 1910-64

Mahmud Hasan, Mawlana

4268. Hossain, A. H. M. Mujtaba. SHAIKHUL HIND MAWLANA MAHMUD HASAN: HIS CONTRIBUTIONS TO EDUCATION AND POLITICS. *Dhaka University Studies Part A [Bangladesh] 1984 (41): 41-53.* Shaikhul Hind was both an Islamic scholar and an armed revolutionist. He was a very well-known expositor of the Qur'an and of the Hadith who attracted students from many parts of the Islamic world. In 1917-20 he even gave a series of lectures on the Hadith in the Malta jail where he was confined for revolutionary activities. Politically, he regarded the British as enemies of Islam and supported Turkey in World War I because the sultan of that country was the caliph of Islam. 63 notes. 1880's-1947

Mahul, Emma

4269. Condorelli, Emma. EMMA MAHUL DES COMTES DEJEAN, UNE PETRARQUISTE OUBLIEE [Emma Mahul of the Comtes Dejean, a forgotten Petrarchist]. *Revue des Etudes Italiennes [France] 1985 31(1-4): 103-111.* Reconstructs the biography of a French student and translator of the poetry of Petrarch, Emma Dejean Mahul (ca. 1814-79), who received recognition for her work during her lifetime, but was virtually forgotten after her death. Includes a list of her correspondence, which has been preserved in the Biblioteca degli Zelanti d'Acireale (Sicily). 14c

Maintenon, Marquise de

4270. Chaussinand-Nogaret, Guy. LA MAINTENON OU CENDRILLON A LA COUR DU ROI SOLEIL [Madame de Maintenon, or Cinderella at the court of the Sun King]. *Histoire [France] 1982 (44): 91-93.* Marquise de Maintenon, formerly Françoise d'Aubigné, daughter of a criminal, and born in prison, after the death of her paralytic husband Paul Scarron, became governess to the children of Louis XIV and later his wife and queen of France, although the union remained secret. 1655-1719

Mair, John

4271. Burns, J. H. POLITIA REGALIS ET OPTIMA: THE POLITICAL IDEAS OF JOHN MAIR. *Hist. of Pol. Thought [Great Britain] 1981 2(1): 31-61.* The Scottish scholastic theologian and logician, John Mair (1467?-1550) formulated a model for civil government which reflected conciliarist and Parisian nominalism prevalent in the 14th and 15th centuries. In Mair's system, all power—whether inherited, confiscated, or exercized through a ruler—was sanctioned and legitimated through community acceptance and consent. While the ruler assumed extensive executive, legislative, and judicial power, sovereign rule was a public trust conferred on the ruler by the assembly representing the community. Mair's ecclesiastical thought influenced his model of civic polity and his acceptance of temporal, royal sovereignty stemmed from his acceptance of papal sovereignty over spiritual matters. Mair was inconclusive about the origins and nature of community; however, he assumed an idealistic, noncombative, Aristotelian order. 128 notes. 1500-20

Mais, Adolf

4272. Martischnig, Michael. ADOLF MAIS (1914-1982) [Adolf Mais, 1914-82]. *Burgenländische Heimatblätter [Austria] 1983 45(1): 1-8.* A tribute to the Austrian Museum director Adolf Mais (1914-82), whose work on the local history and customs of Burgenland and eastern and southeastern Europe was particularly important. He founded the Museum of Ethnography at the Kitsee Castle. 1914-82

Maister, Rudolf

4273. Ude, Lojze. RUDOLF MAISTER (OB 60-LETNICI BOJEV ZA SEVERNO SLOVENSKO MEJO) [Rudolf Maister: on the 60th anniversary of the military struggles for the northern Slovene frontier]. *Časopis za Zgodovino in Narodopisje [Yugoslavia] 1979 15(1-2): 370-383.* When on 29 October 1918 the independent State of Solvenes, Croats, and Serbs had been proclaimed in Zagreb and Ljubljana, Maister was the first to realize that the frontiers of the new state ought to be outlined by military occupation. On 1 November he seized the Austrian command at Maribor in the name of Yugoslavia. The November actions of Maister and of his soldiers, mobilization and disarmament of the Maribor Schutzwehr, introduced a spirit new to Slovene history. 1918-19

Maistre, Joseph de

4274. Guyon, Edouard-Félix. JOSEPH DE MAISTRE, DIPLOMATE SARDE, TEMOIN ET JUGE DE SON TEMPS (1792-1817) [Joseph de Maistre, Sardinian diplomat, witness and judge to his age, 1792-1817]. *Rev. d'Hist. Diplomatique [France] 1983 97(1-2): 75-107.* Maistre was for 15 years Sardinian minister at the court of St. Petersburg, where his rank was not high and where he lived for some time without the company of his family. This author describes his life at the court and the ideas contained in his official dispatches, which during the Risorgimento became a source book for the defenders of order, the throne, and the altar. 6 notes. 1792-1822

Maistrenko, Ivan

4275. Maistrenko, Ivan. HAMLET PROTY STALINA [Hamlet versus Stalin]. *Sučasnist [West Germany] 1980 (11): 17-27.* The author remembers his activities as lecturer in Western literature at the Kharkov Institute of Journalism in the Ukraine. 1931-36

Majerová, Marie

4276. Mourková, Jarmila. Z DOPISŮ IVANA OLBRACHTA [From the letters of Ivan Olbracht]. *Česká Literatura [Czechoslovakia] 1982 30(2): 176-179.* Five letters, reproduced verbatim, throw light on Olbracht's relations with Marie Majerová, a friend and fellow socialist, in the early days of socialist literature (1911), at the time when Olbracht fell foul of the Ruthenian gendarmerie (1933), and when Majerová retired from editing *Československo* (1950). The introduction quotes extensively from *Čin,* where Oldracht defends himself against the accusations of the gendarmerie in Ruthenia. 1911-50

4277. Olonová, Elvíra. Z ARCHÍVU MARIE MAJEROVÉ: K ČESKO-RUSKÝM LITERÁRNÍM VZTAHŮM [From the archive of Marie Majerová: Czech-

Russian literary relations]. *Česká Literatura [Czechoslovakia] 1982 30(2): 164-175.* Six letters from Majerová's corresondence with A. I. Tarasov-Rodionov (1885-1938), six items, articles and correspondence, from her contacts with Soviet publishing houses, and two drafts of memoirs on Mayakovsky and Babel', all reproduced verbatim, throw light on Majerová's Soviet contacts between the wars. 14 notes. 1930's

4278. Voráček, Jaroslav. MARIE MAJEROVÁ JAKO VYKLADAČKA LITERATURY PRO MLÁDEŽ [Marie Majerová as a critic of young people's literature]. *Česká Literatura [Czechoslovakia] 1982 30(1): 11-17.* Marie Majerová is one of few authors to have given systematic attention to children's literature, using criticism to influence authors and parents, formulating clearly the artistic aspects of literature for children, and stoutly defending the fairy tale as a useful genre. 15 footnotes from Majerová's journalistic writings on the subject. ca 1932-37

Majewski, Kazimierz

4279. Nowicka, Maria. KAZIMIERZ MAJEWSKI (1903-1981) [Kazimierz Majewski (1905-81)]. *Acta Poloniae Historica [Poland] 1982 (46): 287-288.* Kazimierz Majewski graduated at Lwów in 1925, where he became assistant professor of classical archaeology and an Aegean specialist. With the German occupation, he became a building worker. After the war he was professor of ancient history at Wrocław and in 1951 professor of medieval archaeology at Warsaw. He founded the Polish Archaeological Society and, through the Academy of Sciences, organized the Institute of the History of Material Culture. Although best known for his work on Greek antiquity, he covered Polish history from Roman times. Despite his research work, he gave priority to teaching. 1925-81

Majorkiewicz, Felicjan

4280. Siemaszko, Z. S. OKOLICZNOŚCI ROZPOCZĘCIA POWSTANIA WARSZAWSKIEGO [Circumstances surrounding the outbreak of the Warsaw Uprising]. *Zeszyty Historyczne [France] 1985 (72): 159-176.* A review article on Felicjan Majorkiewicz's *Lata Chmurne, Lata Dumne* [Stormy years, proud years] (1983), the memoirs of an officer in the Polish Home Army. The reviewer is most interested in Majorkiewicz's recollections of the circumstances surrounding the Warsaw Uprising in summer of 1944. 9 notes. 1940-44

Majumdar, Biman Behari

4281. Banerjee, Tarasankar. BIMAN BEHARI MAJUMDAR (1899-1969). *Journal of Indian History [India] 1982 60: 293-329.* Explores the life of B. B. Majumdar and interprets the importance of his writings on the developments of Indian historiography. Educated at Calcutta University, Majumdar was associated as a teacher and administrator with Jain and Patna Colleges. As a political historian, his works addressed the Pre-Gandhian period of Indian nationalism, institutional history, and the history of ideas. Deeply influenced by Pramathanath Banerjee and Marc Bloch, his works held a marked lucidity. 42 notes. 1899-1969

Makarios, Archbishop

4282. SantCassia, Paul. THE ARCHBISHOP IN THE BELEAGUERED CITY: AN ANALYSIS OF THE CONFLICTING ROLES AND POLITICAL ORATORY OF MAKARIOS. *Byzantine and Modern Greek Studies [Great Britain] 1982-83 8: 191-212.* The populism and political leadership of Archbishop Makarios in Cyprus between 1950 and 1977 depended primarily not upon any objectively rational ideal but upon the abstract ideal of Greek nationalism from which he could not be separated, even by failure. His political oratory thus remained constant, deriving from his ultimately contradictory roles as churchman and politician and his attempts to deal with the problems which that entailed. This usually involved a highly elaborate symbolism, which was achieved at the expense of clarity, and programs attempting to integrate Cypriots by reference to Greek cultural themes. Based on printed sources and secondary works; 32 notes. 1950-77

Makarov, A. G.

4283. Poletaev, O. GEROI GRAZHDANSKOI VOINY [Heroes of the Civil War]. *Voenno-Istoricheskii Zhurnal [USSR] 1982 (5): 68-71.* Gives short biographies of seven heroes of the Russian Civil War and quotes the texts of the directives awarding them Orders of the Red Banner. A. G. Makarov, for example, a regimental commander with the 1st Khar'kov Cadet Brigade against Makhno won his for action near the village of Andreevka on 14 December 1920. He won a second while commanding the 2d Trans-Volga Rifle Regiment in 1921. 8 photos, 5 notes. 1921-33

Makohon, Odarka

See Vil'de, Iryna

Maksymovych, Mykhailo

4284. Hrushevsky, Mikhail S. "MALOROSSIISKIIA PIESNI" MAKSYMOVYCHA I STOLITTIA UKRAINS'KOI NAUKOVOI PRATSI [*Little Russian Songs* of Maykosymovych and the centenary of Ukrainian scholarly work]. *Ukrains'kyi Istoryk 1984 21(1-4): 132-147.* Mykhailo Maksymovych's (1804-73) career as an ethnographer, historian, and philologist began with the publication of *Malorossiiskiia piesni* [Little Russian (Ukrainian) songs] (1827). This collection began a new epoch in Ukrainian scholarly endeavors, since it focused attention on the common people and provided an impetus for a deeper study of Ukrainian folklore. Reprinted from *Ukraina* 1927 6: 1-13. 1827-80's

Makushev, Vikenti V.

4285. Minkova, Liliana. PEREPISKA VIKENTIIA V. MAKUSHEVA S MARINOM DRINOVYM 1869-1878 GG. [Correspondence of Vikenti V. Makushev with Marin Drinov, 1869-78]. *Bulgarian Hist. Rev. [Bulgaria] 1981 9(1-2): 180-213.* 1869-78

*For abstract see **Drinov, Marin***

Malamaios family

4286. Mitakēs, D. OI MALAMAIOI EPI VAVAROKRATIAS [The Malamaios family during the Bavarian period]. *Ēpeirōtikē Hestia [Greece] 1982 (366-368): 673-685.* George Malamaios, the head of his family, and his three brothers—John, Kostas, and Panaiotis—distinguished themselves in the struggle in the Greek War of Independence. They served in the Greek government but eventually turned against King Otto (1833-62) and rebelled in 1836. It has been believed that all four perished in battle against Otto, but only John was killed and George did not take up arms. 13 letters, 35 notes. 1820-36

Malaparte, Curzio

4287. Barzini, Luigi. REMEMBERING CURZIO MALAPARTE. *Encounter [Great Britain] 1982 58(4): 85-87.* A brief memoir of the Italian writer Curzio Malaparte which discusses his relationship with the painter Orfeo Tamburi, his fascination with publicity, his political cynicism, and the Germanic origins of his world view. 1898-1957

4288. Evans, Arthur R., Jr. ASSIGNMENT TO ARMAGEDDON: ERNST JÜNGER AND CURZIO MALAPARTE ON THE RUSSIAN FRONT, 1941-43. *Central European Hist. 1981 14(4): 295-321.* 1920-45
*For abstract see **Jünger, Enrst***

Malaspina, Alessandro

4289. Manfredi, Dario. QUALI E QUANDO VERAMENTE FURONO LE IMPRESE NAUTICHE DI ALESSANDRO MALASPINA (CONTIBUTO ALLA BIOGRAFIA) [Where did Alessandro Malaspina's nautical expeditions take him and when did they take place? A contribution to a biography]. *Archivio Storico per le Province Parmensi [Italy] 1984 36: 89-109.* Following a review of biographical material available 1831-1940 on navigator Alessandro Malaspina, reconstructs his naval career in the service of the Royal Spanish Armada, 1774-89, which included expeditions in the Mediterranean Sea, the Atlantic and the Pacific Oceans, attempts to capture Gibraltar from the British in 1782, a voyage to the Philippines in 1783, and to the New World colonies in 1786 and 1789. 1774-89

Malatesta, Errico

4290. Levy, Carl. MALATESTA IN EXILE. *Ann. della Fondazione Luigi Einaudi [Italy] 1982 15: 245-280.* Errico Malatesta (1853-1932) was the leader of Italian anarchism for most of its important years. He lived most of his adult life in exile. His life abroad determined many aspects of the international history of anarchism and revolutionary syndicalism during the Second International. Based on primary material in the Central State Archive, Rome; 103 notes. 1881-1919

Maldonado, Fulgencio

4291. Pouncey, Lorene; Lentz, Rolf, transl. DR. DON FREY FULGENCIO MALDONADO (1586-1661), CHANTRE DE LA CATEDRAL DE AREQUIPA [Fulgencio Maldonado (1586-1661), precentor of the cathedral of Arequipa]. *Histórica [Peru] 1983 7(1): 123-133.* Fray Fulgencio Maldonado was an important figure in the social, cultural and religious life of Arequipa, Peru, in the 17th century. A member first of the Augustinian order and then of the Knights of Malta, he was appointed precentor of the cathedral in Arequipa in 1629. He founded the convent of La Recoleta in the city and left to it his important library. He was an eloquent preacher and learned as he was generous. Partly based on primary material in the Archivo General de Simancas; biblio. 17c

Maldonado, Juan

4292. García, Heliodoro. ESBOZO BIOGRAFICO Y LITERARIO DE JUAN MALDONADO [Biographical and literary sketch of Juan Maldonado]. *Hispania Sacra [Spain] 1982 34(70): 329-353.* Juan Maldonado (1483?-1554) was a Spanish humanist, friend of Italian scholars, correspondent of Erasmus, grammarian, and author of many edifying writings. 81 notes. 1500's-54

Malestroit, Yvonne-Aimée de

4293. Laurentin, René. LE RETOUR D'YVONNE-AIMEE DE MALESTROIT [The return of Yvonne-Aimée de Malestroit]. *Historama [France] 1985 (21): 68-72.* The study of Yvonne-Aimée de Malestroit (1902-52), born Yvonne Beauvais, mother-superior of a Normandy convent that was decorated by General Charles DeGaulle in 1949 for heroic service to the French Resistance, has been banned by the Catholic Church for the past 25 years because of the miraculous or visionary nature of the phenomena associated with her. 1923-49

Malet, Charles Ware

4294. Berlatsky, Joel. BRITISH IMPERIAL ATTITUDES IN THE EARLY MODERN ERA: THE CASE OF CHARLES WARE MALET IN INDIA. *Albion 1982 14(2): 139-152.* The career of Charles Ware Malet, a man ill equipped to deal with an alien culture, provides an apt illustration of British attitudes toward indigenous populations under colonial rule and of the purposes of British rule in the East. His early stereotypes of Indians as lazy and contemptible remained and hardened, accompanied by fears of native cunning and intrigue. Based on Malet's letters in the India Office Library, the Public Record Office, and the British Museum; 79 notes. 1690-1800

Malinovski, Rodion

4295. Petrov, M. NA SLUZHBE NARODU [Serving the nation]. *Voenno-Istoricheskii Zhurnal [USSR] 1982 (3): 35-44.* Describes the military career and personality of the Soviet World War II Commander Rodion Malinovski (1898-1967), minister of defense until his death. Despite many official duties and his unflagging devotion to the country's safety, he was also concerned with patriotic education of the soldiers and of Soviet youth. In many instances, he interceded personally in the cases of war invalids and widows. Primary sources; photo. 1941-67

Malinowski, Bronisław

4296. Średniawa, Bronisław. THE ANTHROPOLOGIST AS A YOUNG PHYSICIST: BRONISŁAW MALINOWSKI'S APPRENTICESHIP. *Isis 1981 72(264): 613-620.* Malinowski, pioneer anthropologist, attended the University of Cracow, 1902-06. He began as a student in physics, but gradually shifted his emphasis to psychology and philosophy. His doctoral dissertation, "On the Economy of Thinking," was directly related to all three of these fields. Several of his professors are described and the dissertation is summarized. 23 notes. 1902-06

Malkhasyants', Step'an

4297. Zak'aryan, A. H., ed. STEP'AN MALKHASYANTS'I NAMAKNERĔ KIWREGH SRAPYANIN [The letters of Step'an Malkhasyants' to Kiwregh Srapyan]. *Patma-Banasirakan Handes. Istoriko-Filologicheskii Zhurnal [USSR] 1986 (1): 190-200.* The text of 16 letters written by the philologist Step'an Malkhasyants' (1857-1947), mainly from St. Petersburg, to the linguist and mathematician Kiwregh Srapyan (1844-95). These letters provide information on their scholarly activities and personal and family circumstances. Based on documents in the Mashtots' Institute (Yerevan); 22 notes. Russian summary. 1883-89

Mallart, José

4298. Mallart, José. MEMORIAS DE UM ASPIRANTE A PSICOLOGO (AUTOBIOGRAFIA) [Memoirs of an aspiring psychologist (an autobiography)]. *Rev. de Hist. de la Psicología [Spain] 1981 2(2): 91-123.* Describes author's youth and training in Geneva and Berlin and the institutional setting of his work in Barcelona and Madrid in the early years of modern psychological studies in Spain. 1915-61

Malm, Hanna

4299. Lackman, Matti. MIKÄ KAATOI KULLERVO MANNERIN? [What brought down Kullervo Manner?]. *Historiallinen Aikakauskirja [Finland] 1981 79(3): 207-218.* 1929-35

*For abstract see **Manner, Kullervo***

Malozemov, Ivan Prokop'evich

4300. —. GEROI STALINGRADSKOI BITVY [Heroes of the battle of Stalingrad]. *Voenno-Istoricheskii Zhurnal [USSR] 1982 (9): 42-45.* 1942-43

*For abstract see **Bashkirov, Viacheslav Filippovich***

Malraux, André

4301. Bevan, David. ANDRÉ MALRAUX: FÉMINISTE [André Malraux: a feminist]. *Atlantis [Canada] 1982 7(2): 117-120.* Corrects the antifeminist reputation of André Malraux (1901-75). Malraux described some of the women characters of his novels as basically equal to men. This benevolent feeling became particularly noticeable after his reading, in 1928, D. H. Lawrence's *Lady Chatterley's Lover,* to which he prefaced the first edition in French translation, in 1932. 13 notes. 1963-76

Malthus, Thomas

4302. Flubacher, Joseph F. A NOTE ON AN ANNIVERSARY. *Forum for Social Economics 1985 (Spr): 61-63.* On the 150th anniversary of the death of Thomas Malthus, discusses his ideas on population growth and the poor, his neglect of the possibilities of technological development, especially agricultural, and his anticipation of the work of John Maynard Keynes. 1780's-1834

4303. Pullen, John M. CORRESPONDENCE BETWEEN MALTHUS AND HIS PARENTS. *History of Political Economy 1986 18(1): 133-154.* A review of 40 letters exchanged by Thomas Malthus and his parents, Daniel (1730-1800) and Henrietta (1733-1800). The letters were written in the period 1783-96 when Thomas was first at the Dissenting Academy at Warrington, then at the home of Gilbert Wakefield, a private tutor, and Jesus College, Cambridge. This correspondence provides insight into young Malthus's recreational activities, studies, and other intellectual pursuits. The letters also reflect the relationship between father and son. Daniel Malthus took an active interest in his son's education, and they frequently exchanged thoughts on appropriate studies. Based on the documents entitled *Life of Thomas Malthus,* a part of the collection of the University of Illinois Library at Urbana-Champaign, and other primary sources; 32 notes. 1783-96

Malý, J. J.

4304. Becka, Jiří. J. J. MALÝ (1890-1975) V RUSKÉM TURKESTANU A V BUCHARSKÉM EMIRÁTU [J. J. Malý (1890-1975) in Russian Turkestan and the Emirate of Bukhara]. *Slovanský Přehled [Czechoslovakia] 1982 68(2): 171-176.* J. J. Malý was a naturalist and chemist who in the 1920's and 1930's made several trips to Central Asia and published his observations, acquainting the Czech public, for the first time, with that part of the world. Besides providing topographical descriptions of Turkestan, especially Samarkand, where he spent six months, he made notes on the area's social customs, schooling, Moslem culture, and economic backwardness as well as changes being wrought under the Russians. 32 notes. 1920's-30's

Malynkovych, Volodymyr

4305. —. ROZMOVA Z VOLODYMYROM MALYNKOVYCHEM [Interview with Volodymyr Malynkovych]. *Sučasnist [West Germany] 1981 (11): 60-74.* Former dissident, Volodymyr Malynkovych, relates his experiences in the opposition movement and among dissidents in the Ukraine in the 1970's, giving details of their work to defend national rights. 1970-80

Mamba, Enoch

4306. Bundy, Colin. A VOICE IN THE BIG HOUSE: THE CAREER OF HEADMAN ENOCH MAMBA. *J. of African Hist. [Great Britain] 1981 22(4): 531-550.* Enoch Mamba (1861?-1916) was educated by the Methodists. His service as an interpreter in the Idutywa magistrate's office was highly praised and stood him in good stead in his next post as headman. His energy and his intrepid part in local controversies earned him general recognition as an outstanding headman. Mamba overreached himself and was dismissed in 1896. In spite of his being discredited, Mamba was active as a businessman and a politician during the next eight years and was reinstated as headman in Lota in 1904. His mature approach as administrator and politician together with his independent attitude made him one of the few Transkeian leaders to attain any status in South Africa. Based on archival and published sources; map, 60 notes. 1860-1916

Man, Hendrik de

4307. Glasneck, Johannes. HENDRIK DE MAN UND DIE KRISE REFORMISTISCHER THEORIE UND PRAXIS IN DEN DREISSIGER JAHREN [Hendrik de Man and the crisis of reformist theory and practice in the 1930's]. *Beiträge zur Gesch. der Arbeiterbewegung [East Germany] 1982 24(2): 199-210.* The Belgian socialist and writer Hendrik de Man (1885-1953) became President of the Belgian Workers' Party (POB) in 1939. However, in 1940 he told Belgian POB members not to offer any resistance to the Nazis who occupied Belgium. The author considers that de Man's actions were the result of the theories and politics that he had embraced in the 1920's and 1930's, which had found an echo in international social democracy and were the expression of the specific processes of evolution of reformism during this period. The author pays particular attention to the reformist theories outlined in de Man's *Psychology of Socialism* (1926). For de Man represented the prototype of the social democratic policy of capitulation in the face of fascism in the 1930's and was on the extreme right wing of the social democratic movement. Based on de Man's writings and secondary sources; 70 notes. 1926-40

Manakopoulos, Ioannis

4308. Spanos, Kōstas. ENNIA ANEKDOTA ENGRAFA TŌN OLYMPIŌN AGŌNISTŌN TOU 1821 I. D. MANAKOPOULOU KAI MIH. DĒMĒTRAKOPOULOU [Nine unpublished documents related to D. Manakopoulos and Mihail Demetrakopoulos, combatants of 1821, who were

from the area of Olympia]. *Makedonika [Greece] 1984 24: 197-208.* ca 1821
*For abstract see **Demetrakopoulos, Mihail***

Mañara, Miguel de

4309. Unceín Tamayo, Luis Alberto. "MIGUEL MAÑARA" TRICENTENARIO DE UN LIBRO EN LAS BIBLIOTECAS DE LOS PONTE, FAMILIARES DE BOLÍVAR ["Miguel Mañara" Tricentenary of a book in the library of the Pontes, Bolívar's relatives]. *Bol. de la Acad. Nac. de la Hist. [Venezuela] 1980 63(249): 143-149.* Commemorates Miguel de Mañara's (1626-79) centenary by noting other centenaries, including that of Robert Louis Stevenson's *Across the Plains: The Amateur Immigrant,* about his trip across the United States in 1879; Bishop Martí's book on his visit to Venezuela and the situation of the aborigines there in 1779; and Comtesse D'Aulnoy's account of her trip to Spain in 1679. 10 notes. 1679-1879

Manasseh of Ilya

4310. Barzilay, Isaac E. MANASSEH OF ILYA (1767-1831) AND THE EUROPEAN ENLIGHTENMENT. *Jewish Social Studies 1984 46(1): 1-8.* Discusses broader aspects of the thought of Manasseh of Ilya (1767-1831), particularly his ideas on unity, interdependence, and humanitarianism. Manasseh's views reflect a universalist approach shaped by both Jewish and European Enlightenment sources. 41 notes. 1767-1831

Mandela, Nelson

4311. Gorodnov, V. P. A LUTULI I N. MANDELA—IUZHNOAFRIKANSKIE PATRIOTY [A. Luthuli and N. Mandela, South African patriots]. *Narody Azii i Afriki [USSR] 1982 (4): 135-143.* 1918-82
*For abstract see **Luthuli, Albert***

Mandelstam, Nadezhda

4312. Rowse, A. L. THE MANDELSTAM EXPERIENCE. *Contemporary Review [Great Britain] 1986 249(1446): 21-26.* Discusses Nadezhda Mandelstam's memoirs of life in the USSR in the 1920's and 30's, entitled *Hope Against Hope* (1976), and her description not only to the reign of terror, of Stalin's purges, executions, and deportations, but also to the inner terror, the systematic attempt to kill the individual soul. 1920's-30's

Mandrou, Robert

4313. François, Etienne. NEKROLOG: ROBERT MANDROU 31.1.1921-25.3.1984 [Obituary: Robert Mandrou (31 January 1921-25 March 1984)]. *Historische Zeitschrift [West Germany] 1984 239(2): 496-499.* Summarizes the academic career of Robert Mandrou, former secretary of the journal *Annales,* co-founder of the Mission Historique Française en Allemagne (The French Historical Mission in Germany), and pioneer researcher on early modern witchcraft, popular culture, and the Fuggers' investment systems. 1921-84

4314. LeRoy Ladurie, Emmanuel. ROBERT MANDROU (1921-1984) [Robert Mandrou (1921-84)]. *Annales: Economies, Sociétés, Civilisations [France] 1985 40(2): 241-243.* Robert Mandrou was a historian with a very wide range of interests. Besides a history of French civilization, he wrote on German, Bohemian, and Russian historical subjects. He was interested both in structures and in sensibilities and mentalities. He was professor at the Ecole des Hautes Etudes and member of the editorial committee of *Annales.* He was an exceptional teacher and seminar animator. Note. 1921-84

Manet, Edouard

4315. Clesmeur, Jean-Paul de. MANET, LE PEINTRE PAR QUI LE SCANDALE ARRIVE [Manet, the painter who inaugurated the famous scandal]. *Hist. Mag. [France] 1983 (39): 38-44.* Focuses on the career of French painter Edouard Manet from 1858-65 and contemporary hostility to the works of the Impressionists. 1858-65

4316. Luján, Néstor. EDOUARD MANET [Edouard Manet]. *Hist. y Vida [Spain] 1983 16(184): 68-77.* Reviews Manet's life, discusses his views on art, and presents some of his works. 1832-83

4317. Robida, Michel. AUTOUR DE QUELQUES-UNS DES DERNIERS PORTRAITS DE MANET [Some of Manet's final portraits]. *Rev. des Deux Mondes [France] 1983 (5): 352-356.* Focuses on the painter Edouard Manet's (1832-83) final illness and his correspondence with, and several portraits of, Isabelle Lemonnier. 1870's-83

4318. Stuckey, Charles F. OLLER AND MANET. *Horizontes [Puerto Rico] 1985 28(56): 15-18.* 1858-77
*For abstract see **Oller, Francisco***

Manfredi, Giuseppe Salvatore

4319. Schippisi, Ranieri. GIUSEPPE SALVATORE MANFREDI (1895-1984) [Giuseppe Salvatore Manfredi (1895-1984)]. *Archivio Storico per le Province Parmensi [Italy] 1984 36: 36-39.* Regrets the passing of Giuseppe Salvatore Manfredi, historian of the Italian Risorgimento, founder of charitable Catholic social action organizations, and student of Manzoni. 1895-1984

Mangada, Julio

4320. Suero Roca, María Teresa. JULIO MANGADA Y EL ANTIFASCISMO [Julio Mangada and antifascism]. *Hist. y Vida [Spain] 1983 16(178): 44-57.* Discusses the role played by Mangada in the struggle to save the Spanish republic from the fascist movement. 1931-36

Mangan, John Clarence

4321. Shannon-Mangan, Ellen. A LETTER AND A POEM: NEW SOURCES FOR THE LIFE OF MANGAN. *Éire-Ireland 1986 21(1): 6-15.* Letters and poems of Irish poet John Clarence Mangan (1803-49), discovered during the 1970's and 1980's, shed light on his early development as a poet and on his political views. Mangan published several early poems in ladies' magazines under the pseudonymn James Tynan. A letter of 1844 contains the only known reference by Mangan to his mother. Based on manuscripts and microfilm in the National Library of Ireland, documents in the University College Dublin Archives, and other primary sources; 21 notes. 1821-90's

Manglard, Adrien

4322. Michel, Olivier. ADRIEN MANGLARD, PEINTRE ET COLLECTIONNEUR (1695-1760) [Adrien Manglard, painter and collector (1695-1760)]. *Mélanges de l'Ecole Française de Rome. Moyen Age-Temps Moderne [Italy] 1981 93(2): 823-926.* Traces the life and career of Adrien Manglard, a painter known for his seascapes and an art collector, from his birth in Lyon in 1695 to his death in Rome in 1760, focusing on his passion for collecting art. Provides a transcription of the inventory of his collection and several reproductions of his own paintings and discusses his relationship with his rival, Joseph Vernet. 1695-1760

Manley, Edna

4323. Boxer, David. EDNA MANLEY: SCULPTOR. *Jamaica Journal [Jamaica] 1985 18(1): 25-40.* A retrospective look at the 66-year career of Edna Manley, who is still actively producing art at the age of 85, and an attempt to assess the significance of major works. 23 illus. 1919-85

Manley, Roger

4324. Köster, Patricia. THE CORRESPONDENCE OF SIR ROGER MANLEY. *Bulletin of Bibliography 1985 42(4): 179-186.* Sir Roger Manley, linguist, translator and historian, was a soldier for England and, after his exile, for the Netherlands, who wrote numerous accounts and translations of histories and wars, in addition to 93 known letters, which are listed and in part annotated. 1644-86

Mann, Klaus

4325. Grunewald, Michel, ed. ANDRE GIDE—KLAUS MANN: EIN BRIEFWECHSEL [André Gide-Klaus Mann: letters]. *Rev. d'Allemagne [France] 1982 14(4): 581-682.* From 1926 to 1949, Klaus Mann, son of Thomas, and André Gide developed relations that were, at certain times, quite friendly. Seventy of the letters they wrote to each other have been kept, and they give a very precise idea of the mood of their relationship. 1926-49

Mann, Thomas

4326. Gelber, Mark H. THOMAS MANN AND ANTISEMITISM. *Patterns of Prejudice [Great Britain] 1983 17(4): 31-40.* Although German writer Thomas Mann never identified with Jews and wrote satirically about them, he was a vocal anti-Nazi and was active in pro-Jewish affairs in the Hitler years. 1920's-45

4327. Matamoro, Blas. THOMAS MANN, EN SUS DIARIOS [Thomas Mann in his diaries]. *Cuadernos Hispanoamericanos [Spain] 1981 124(371): 227-265.* The novelist Thomas Mann (1875-1955) kept a diary from early adolescence onwards. After he left Germany in 1933 some of his journals were passed to the Nazi authorities, but subsequently he regained them. Mann destroyed much of this material in 1945. The author quotes extracts from some of the surviving diaries, for the years 1918 to 1921 and 1933 to 1936. The diaries kept in the Thomas Mann archive in Zürich were opened in 1975. They add insight into Mann's ideological development, lifestyle, attitude toward Germany, views on society, World War I, Spengler, Nazism and Hitler, his relationship with his brother Heinrich, comments on his own writings, and his homosexual leanings. Based on Thomas Mann's diaries and correspondence. 1918-36

Manner, Kullervo

4328. Lackman, Matti. MIKÄ KAATOI KULLERVO MANNERIN? [What brought down Kullervo Manner?]. *Historiallinen Aikakauskirja [Finland] 1981 79(3): 207-218.* Traces the events from 1929 to 1935 through which the power of Kullervo Manner (b. 1880), chairman of the Finnish Communist Party in exile in the USSR, was eroded. In addition to tactical errors, Manner and his wife Hanna Malm expressed ideological views that contradicted those of Joseph Stalin and Stalin's Finnish supporter, Otto Ville Kuusinen (1881-1964). In 1935 Manner and Malm were expelled from the Party and sent to labor camps. Based on Finnish police archives, interviews, memoirs, and monographs; 68 notes. 1929-35

Mannerheim, Carl Gustav

4329. Manninen, Ohto. MANNERHEIM JA PUNAVANGIT [Mannerheim and the Red prisoners]. *Historiallinen Aikakauskirja [Finland] 1981 79(3): 195-206.* Some scholars claim that there was a dispute in the spring of 1918 between Finnish White Army General, Carl Gustav Mannerheim (1867-1951), and the Finnish White Senate concerning treatment of Finnish Red Army prisoners at the end of the civil war in Finland. Archival sources show that Mannerheim advocated rapid court martial and release of most prisoners, while the Senate advocated the slower legal procedures actually adopted. These differing views did not, however, lead to a direct confrontation between Mannerheim and the Senate. Based on public and private papers in the Finnish State Archives; 61 notes. 1918

Mannheim, Karl

4330. Wolff, Kurt H. KARL MANNHEIM: AN INTELLECTUAL ITINERARY. *Society 1984 21(3): 71-74.* Biographical profile of an Austrian-born German sociologist forced to flee to England in the 1930's. 1910's-47

Mannix, Daniel

4331. Kiernan, Colm. ARCHBISHOP DANIEL MANNIX OF MELBOURNE, 1864-1963. *Éire-Ireland 1984 19(3): 121-130.* Daniel Mannix, Roman Catholic Archbishop of Melbourne from 1913 to 1963, was posted to Australia from Ireland partly because his militant Irish nationalism embarrassed the Church. In Australia, Mannix was similarly involved controversially in politics throughout his long career, first as an outspoken opponent of World War I conscription, later as an advocate of Irish separation from Great Britain, finally as a successful crusader for state funding of Catholic schools. Mannix's policies split the Australian Labor Party in the 1950's and helped to keep the Liberals in power federally for over 20 years. Based on press reports and secondary sources; 17 notes. 1913-63

Manrique, Alonzo

4332. Wagner, Klaus. EL ARZOBISPO ALONZO MANRIQUE, PROTECTOR DEL ERASMISMO Y DE LOS REFORMISTAS EN SEVILLA [Archbishop Alonzo Manrique, protector of Erasmism and the Reformers in Seville]. *Bibliothèque d'Humanisme et Renaissance [Switzerland] 1983 45(2): 349-350.* The Grand Inquisitor Alonzo Manrique, Archbishop of Seville, was a friend of the circle of "Lutheran heretics" formed by Francisco Vargas, Juan Gil, and Constantino Ponce de la Fuente. He was responsible for their appointments to the pulpit and chapter of the Cathedral of Seville. Though the latter two enjoyed their benefices peacefully, the former's appointment was contested after the death of the archbishop. Partly based on primary material in the archives of the Cathedral of Seville; 8 notes. 1534-46

Manselli, Raoul

4333. Brezzi, Paolo. RAOUL MANSELLI [Raoul Manselli]. *Studi Romani [Italy] 1985 33(1-2): 89-90.* Provides an obituary of Raoul Manselli (1917-84), professor and researcher in medieval history. 1930's-84

Mansfield, Charlotte

4334. Baker, Colin. NYASALAND 1905-1909: THE JOURNEYS OF MARY HALL, OLIVIA COLVILLE AND CHARLOTTE MANSFIELD. *Soc. of Malawi J. [Malawi] 1982 35(1): 11-29.* 1905-09
For abstract see ***Colville, Olivia***

Mansfield, Katherine

4335. Else, Anne. FROM LITTLE MONKEY TO NEUROTIC INVALID: LIMITATION, SELECTION AND ASSUMPTION IN ANTONY ALPERS' *LIFE OF KATHERINE MANSFIELD. Women's Studies International Forum 1985 8(5): 497-505.* Describes the sexist interpretation of the life and work of British author Katherine Mansfield by Anthony Alpers in his 1980 biography. 1910's-23

Mantova Benavides, Marco

4336. Mayer, Thomas F. MARCO MANTOVA AND THE PADUAN RELIGIOUS CRISIS OF THE EARLY SIXTEENTH CENTURY. *Cristianesimo nella Storia [Italy] 1986 7(1): 41-61.* Marco Mantova Benavides's biography illustrates how humanism in the narrow sense of religion and politics could be combined into one personality. The Venetian defeat at Agnadello triggered a psychological crisis in Mantova that was compounded by reduced opportunities for the nobility in Venice's dependent territories. He struggled to attain a compromise between an active life and a more personal religion that expressed itself in Mantova's massive literary output. The institutional Church dissatisfied Mantova and he often expressed conciliarist leanings. His case also suggests a complex interplay between Venetian and Paduan religion, mediated through the university. Based on documents in the Robbins Law Library, University of California, Berkeley, Biblioteca Marciana, Venice, Biblioteca Apostolica Vaticana, and other primary and secondary sources; 62 notes. 1509-72

Manzoni, Alessandro

4337. Petrocchi, Giorgio. MANZONI E ROSMINI [Alessandro Manzoni and Antonio Rosmini-Serbati]. *Veltro [Italy] 1985 29(5-6): 595-604.* The history of the friendship and exchange of ideas between Alessandro Manzoni (1785-1873) and Antonio Rosmini-Serbati (1797-1855) as expressed in their exchange of numerous letters, which contained many discussions of philosophy (especially concerning the origin of the idea of being and the problem of language), between 1826 and 1855. 1826-55

Mao Dun

4338. Chen, Susan W. THE PERSONAL ELEMENT IN MAO TUN'S EARLY FICTION. *Harvard J. of Asiatic Studies 1983 43(1): 187-213.* Describes the early life of Chinese author Mao Dun (Mao Tun; pen name for Shen Yanbing, 1896-1981), based largely on Mao's own memoirs. Identifies personal elements in his literature, including his reaction to wrenching political changes and conflicts in China. Based on primary sources; 25 notes. 1916-28

Mao Zedong

4339. Chai, Trong R. MAO ZEDONG'S CONTROL OVER THE STATE COUNCIL OF CHINA. *Indian Pol. Sci. Rev. [India] 1981 15(2): 115-128.* By analyzing turnover patterns of ministers, vice-ministers, commission chairmen, and vice-chairmen in the State Council of China between 1949 and 1969, attempts to test the allegation that Mao Zedong lost control over government in the early 1960's and regained it later in the decade thanks to the Cultural Revolution. Research findings do not support the conventional view of Mao's authority to hire and fire bureaucrats and to maintain a high personnel mobility. Even during the Cultural Revolution turnover of personnel was not significantly higher than in other periods. 4 charts, 30 notes. 1949-69

4340. Das, Naranarayan. MAO: MAN AND MYTH. *China Report [India] 1982 18(1): 3-10.* A review of the philosophy and works of Mao Zedong. The writings of Karl Marx served Mao as a source of ideas, not as a blueprint to be slavishly followed. Most of his inconsistencies stem from Mao's consistent willingness to discard ideas if they proved to be unworkable. Mao's seeming inconsistencies on the questions of Sino-Soviet accord, Sino-American relations, and the Cultural Revolution were strictly tactical; there was no wavering in the matter of goals. 18 notes. 1930's-76

4341. Robinson, Jean C. INSTITUTIONALIZING CHARISMA: LEADERSHIP, FAITH & RATIONALITY IN THREE SOCIETIES. *Polity 1985 43(2): 181-203.* 1950's-76
For abstract see ***Castro, Fidel***

4342. Scalapino, Robert A. THE EVOLUTION OF A YOUNG REVOLUTIONARY—MAO ZEDONG IN 1919-1921. *J. of Asian Studies 1982 42(1): 29-62.* Traces Mao Zedong's intellectual development through two key years, when he edited two nationalist journals in Hunan, first *Xiang Liang Pinglun* then *Xin Hunan.* Traces the frustrations that led to his choice of Marxism-Leninism. His areas of substantive concern were the standard ones of liberalism, cast in a Chinese nationalist frame, underlaid with a perception of a decadent West. He moved in these years from Western liberalism to the beginning of his understanding of Marxism, and his perceived arena of activity went from China to Hunan to international and back. 17 notes, 41 ref. 1919-21

4343. Strong, Tracy B. and Keyssar, Helene. ANNA LOUISE STRONG: THREE INTERVIEWS WITH CHAIRMAN MAO ZEDONG. *China Quarterly [Great Britain] 1985 (103): 489-509.* A translation of interviews by Anna Louise Strong with Mao Zedong in March 1959, January 1964, and November 1965. Based on Strong's manuscripts of the interviews in the Beijing Library; 29 notes. 1959-65

Mao Zhiyang

4344. —. MAO CHIH-YUNG—THE FIRST SECRETARY OF THE CCP HUNAN PROVINCIAL COMMITTEE. *Issues & Studies [Taiwan] 1984 20(12): 76-82.* Mao Zhiyang (Mao Chih-yang, b. 1929), who became first secretary of the Hunan Provincial Committee in 1977, was active in denouncing Gang of Four crimes at the end of the Cultural Revolution. He has, however, also been identified with recent leftist tendencies in Hunan, and it appears that Hu Yaobang (Hu Yao-pang) may soon withdraw support from Mao in favor of other Hunanese Communists. Based on Chinese media reports; 11 notes. 1976-84

Marais, J. C. Nielen

4345. Schoeman, Karel. DIE VADER VAN DIE DIGTER: IETS OOR DIE LEWE VAN J. C. NIELEN MARAIS [The father of the poet: something about the life of J. C. Nielen Marais]. *Africana Notes and News [South Africa] 1983 25(6): 200-204.* Eugène Marais's fame as a poet has overshadowed that of his father, himself an interesting figure who caused quite a stir in his day. J. C. Nielen Marais became government secretary and treasurer-general of the Orange Free State in 1863, only to be found guilty in 1870 of embezzling government funds and sentenced to prison. His youngest son, the poet, was born a year later in Pretoria. 1863-70

Marañón, Gregorio

4346. Mesa, Carlos E. DON GREGORIO MARAÑÓN [Gregorio Marañón]. *Bol. de la Acad. Colombiana [Colombia] 1981 31(131): 44-49.* Gregorio Marañón (1887-1960) was a physician and man of letters. He worked many years at Madrid's General Hospital, became an outstanding historian, attained memberships in five Royal Academies, won uncountable decorations, and published 500 scholarly papers and 35 books in his elegant and simple style. 1887-1960

Marat, Jean Paul

4347. Goldschläger, Alain. MARAT, LECTEUR DE ROUSSEAU [Marat: a reader of Rousseau]. *U. of Ottawa Q. [Canada] 1981 51(1): 151-158.* Reviews the life of Jean Paul Marat (1743-93), highlighting the main traits of his character. Analyzes *Un Roman de Coeur ou les Aventures du Jeune Comte Potowski* (published posthumously in 1847), in which the famous leader of the French Revolution, greatly influenced by Jean Jacques Rousseau's thought, used the techniques and themes of the French philosopher's *Nouvelle Heloïse.* Emphasizes similarities in the creation of stereotyped human situations and characteristics, the typology of characters and facts, and the effort to communicate an ideology. Based on a paper delivered at the 25-27 October 1978 Conference on Jean Jacques Rousseau and 18th-century society at McGill University, Montreal, Canada; 18 notes. 1762-93

Marcel, Gabriel

4348. Titos Lomas, Francisco. GABRIEL MARCEL Y SU ENCUENTRO CON DIOS [Gabriel Marcel and his encounter with God]. *Estudios [Spain] 1982 38(138): 349-361.* Discusses the conversion of Gabriel Marcel to Catholicism and the nature of the existential Christianity that prevailed in his philosophy. 1889-1950

Marchesi, Concetto

4349. Zadro, Attilio. NEL CENTENARIO DI CONCETTO MARCHESI E MANARA VALGIMIGLI: I. L'ORIZZONTE POLITICO DI CONCETTO MARCHESI II. GLI ORIZZONTI FILOSOFICI DI MARCHESI E DI VALGIMIGLI [On the centenary of Concetto Marchesi and Manara Valgimigli: 1. The political horizon of Concetto Marchesi; 2. The philosophical horizons of Marchesi and Valgimigli]. *Quaderni per la Storia dell'U. di Padova [Italy] 1980 13: 115-138.* Both Marchesi (1878-1957), philologist and Communist, and Valgimigli (b. 1878), Greek scholar and Socialist, inscribed their scholarly and educational activity in the very midst of the historical events of their time; their philosophy was an active intellectual search and not a mere doctrine to be transmitted. 20c

Marchetti, Giuseppe

4350. Scarpa, Anton Maria. GIUSEPPE MARCHETTI IL GARIBALDINO UNDICENNE [Giuseppe Marchetti, the 11-year-old follower of Garibaldi]. *Rassegna Storica del Risorgimento [Italy] 1980 67(3): 297-307.* Giuseppe Marchetti at the age of 11, (1849-77) accompanied his father on a military campaign led by Giuseppe Garibaldi. He also fought alongside Garibaldi, 1866-67, when he distinguished himself. Based on material in the Turin State Archives. 1849-77

Marconi, Guglielmo

4351. Schueler, Donald G. THE INVENTOR MARCONI: BRILLIANT, DAPPER, TOUGH TO LIVE WITH. *Smithsonian 1982 12(12): 126-128, 130-132, 134, 136-138, 140, 142, 144-147.* Biography of Guglielmo Marconi, (1874-1937), examining his home life and character. 1890's-1937

Marcos, Ferdinand

4352. Neher, Clark D. POLITICAL CLIENTELISM AND INSTABILITY IN THE PHILIPPINES. *Asian Affairs: An American Review 1985 12(3): 1-23.* Defines clientelism as the structure of personal relationships in which the socioeconomic elite uses its resources and influence to benefit those of lower socioeconomic status, who reciprocate by offering their services and loyalty. Discusses President Ferdinand Marcos's presidency from 1965 to 1985, his relationship with the military and such opponents as Benigno Aquino, the assassination of the latter, the Philippine economy, and US political and economic influence. Presented at a conference on "Major Current Issues in East Asia," St. John's University, 1985. Based on published and unpublished Philippine government sources. 18 notes. 1950-85

Marcquis, Lazare

4353. Hamilton, Alastair. LAZARE MARCQUIS' LEIDEN YEARS. *Bibliothèque d'Humanisme et Renaissance [Switzerland] 1981 43(3): 567-571.* Lazare Marcquis (1574-1647), prominent Antwerp physician, spent eight hitherto undocumented years at the Protestant university at Leiden. He enrolled in May 1589 and was certainly still matriculated there in 1595. He probably stayed in Leiden until 1597, when he went to Padua to continue his medical studies. Because of Marcquis's Protestant activities in Leiden, these years were later played down by Catholic contemporaries and biographers. Based on university and municipal archives in Leiden and secondary sources; 34 notes. 1589-97

Marcuse, Herbert

4354. Katz, Barry Martin. "*Praxis* and *Poesis:* An Intellectual Biography of Herbert Marcuse." U. of California, Santa Cruz 1980. 313 pp. *DAI 1983 43(7): 2418-A.* DA8226320 1920-79

Maréchal, Pierre-Sylvain

4355. Kiiasov, S. E. SIL'VEN MARESHAL' POSLE PORAZHENIIA "ZAGOVORA RAVNYKH" (1796 G.) [Sylvain Maréchal after the defeat of the conspiracy of equals, 1796]. *Novaia i Noveishaia Istoriia [USSR] 1982 (9): 73-87.* The life of French writer, playwright, and journalist Pierre-Sylvain Maréchal was typical for a revolutionary of petit-bourgeois tendencies. 1796

Marek, Antonín

4356. Hnízdová, Květoslava. ANTONÍN MAREK A ČESKÉ NÁRODNÍ OBROZENÍ (K 200. VÝROČÍ JEHO NAROZENIN) [Antonín Marek and the Czech national revival: on the 200th anniversary of his death]. *Slovanský Přehled [Czechoslovakia] 1985 71(6): 484-491.* Antonín Marek belonged to the first generation of national awakeners and was particularly interested in the Czech language, as indicated by his poetry, but was also an activist who contributed to the development of cultural and theater societies in his region of Turnov. An early believer in the concept of a united Slavdom, he was especially interested in close ties with

Russia, though critical of serfdom and tsarist regime. He attended the Slavic Congress of 1848 and was active in the Slovanská Lípa society. 1780-1860

Maresca family

4357. Sinisi, Agnese. UNA FAMIGLIA MERCANTILE NAPOLETANA DEL XVIII SECOLO: I MARESCA DI SERRACAPRIOLA [An 18th-century Neapolitan merchant family: the Marescas of Serracapriola]. *Econ. e Storia [Italy] 1982 3(2): 139-203.* In the context of studies of social mobility in the old regime and the introduction of wealthy merchant families into the ranks of the traditional nobility, describes the rise of the Marescas, originally from Piana di Sorrento. The Maresca family belonged to the merchant class but were politically active in the early 18th century; later in the century they acquired titles of nobility and rich feudal lands. In the 19th century they occupied high government and political positions. Their history illustrates the typical stages of the political and social ascent of the merchant class in the 18th century. Based on primary material in the Naples State archive; 7 tables, 239 notes. 18c

Margaret of Anjou

4358. Lee, Patricia-Ann. REFLECTIONS OF POWER: MARGARET OF ANJOU AND THE DARK SIDE OF QUEENSHIP. *Renaissance Quarterly 1986 39(2): 183-217.* Reviews the life of Margaret of Anjou (1430-82), Henry VI's queen, to determine how she was used by Shakespeare to symbolize the archetypal figure of villainy. Studies contemporary sources to assess their evaluation of Margaret. Margaret was a major Lancastrian decisionmaker in the struggle with the Yorkists. 100 notes. ca 1429-82

Margaret of Austria

4359. Bonner, Shirley Harrold. "Margaret of Austria: Her Life and Learning in Europe's High Renaissance." U. of Pittsburgh 1981. 453 pp. *DAI 1982 43(5): 1449-A.* DA8213132 ca 1500-30

Margeret, Jacques

4360. Dunning, Chester S. L. QUAND UN FRANÇAIS REDECOUVRAIT LA RUSSIE [When a Frenchman rediscovered Russia]. *Revue Historique [France] 1984 272(2): 331-351.* Merchants trading through the White Sea in the 1580's were the first to reestablish contact between France and Russia. This opened the way for Captain Jacques Margeret (1560's-1620's?) and other French mercenary soldiers to enter Russian service. In 1607 Margeret published the first French description of Russia. His account was widely used by historians but contained some errors which become apparent from a detailed study of Margeret's career, presented here. Based on Margeret's writing and works of Russian historians; 93 notes. 1560-1620's

Margolin, Iuli

4361. Kutiiel', I. IULII MARGOLIN: DO DESIATYRICHCHIA Z CHASU SMERTY [Iuli Margolin: on the 10th anniversary of his death]. *Sučasnist [West Germany] 1981 (12): 60-71.* Biographical sketch devoted to the life and work of Iuli Margolin (1900-71), doctor of philosophy, Zionist, publicist, and litterateur, who made a valuable contribution to directing the struggle of Jews and Ukrainians alike against Russian Communist oppression. 1900-71

Maria Anna

4362. Rudan, Othmar. ERZHERZOGIN MARIA ANNA IN KLAGENFURT 1781-1789 [Archduchess Maria Anna in Klagenfurt, 1781-89]. *Carinthia I [Austria] 1980 170: 185-260.* Traces the life of the Archduchess Maria Anna (b. 1739), the second child of Emperor Francis I and Empress Maria Theresa, particularly the time she spent in the Elizabethan convent in Klagenfurt, 1781-89. 1781-89

María of Austria

4363. Castro, Manuel de. CONFESORES FRANCISCANOS DE LA EMPERATRIZ DOÑA MARIA DE AUSTRIA [Franciscan confessors of Empress María of Austria]. *Archivo Ibero-Americano [Spain] 1985 45(177-178): 113-152.* Provides biographical sketches of eight Franciscans who served as confessors for María of Austria (1528-1603), wife of Holy Roman Emperor Maximilian II. A profoundly religious woman, María demonstrated a great fondness for the Franciscan order. Widowed in 1576, she spent the last 20 years of her life in a Madrid convent. Her confessors included Fernando Cano, Pedro de Maldonado, Francisco de Córdoba, Juan de Espinosa, Francisco Guzmán, Antonio de Aguilar, Juan de Portocarrero, and Jerónimo de Gouvea. A documentary appendix provides five relevant letters from the Archivo General de Simancas. Based on archival and secondary sources; 165 notes, appendix. 1540's-1603

Maria Theresa

4364. Benda, Kálmán. MÁRIA TERÉZIA KIRÁLYNŐ A MAGYAR TÖRTÉNETÍRÁSBAN [Empress Maria Theresa in Hungarian historiography]. *Történelmi Szemle [Hungary] 1981 24(3): 485-492.* Traditionally, the romantic scene where the Hungarian nobility offered Maria Theresa their life and blood dominated historical representations. Despite some favors for Hungarians, the empress followed a policy of imperial centralization. Reforms were instituted. In the 1920's, Gyula Szekfü attributed the Enlightenment in Vienna, where many Hungarian aristocrats resided, to anti-Church French freethinkers, of whom the empress did not approve. Marxist historiography of the 1950's proposed a new interpretation of this period, accusing Vienna of crippling Hungary. Today views are different. Maria Theresa was a born ruler. She did exhibit some goodwill toward Hungary, but considered and treated it as but part of a large empire. A 1980 lecture in German in the Collegium Hungaricum, Vienna. Based on writings on Maria Theresa; biblio. note. 1741-80

4365. Kállay, István. EIN GEHEIMBERICHT ÜBER DEN TOD MARIA THERESIAS [A confidential report concerning the death of Empress Maria Theresa]. *Mitteilungen des Österreichischen Staatsarchivs [Austria] 1981 34: 342-344.* 1760's-1807
*For abstract see **Balassa, Franz***

Mariátegui, José Carlos

4366. Buşe, Constantin. VIAŢA ŞI OPERA LUI JOSÉ CARLOS MARIATEGUI (1895-1930) [The life and works of José Carlos Mariategui, 1895-1930]. *Revista de Istorie [Romania] 1980 33(12): 2315-2334.* Commemorates the 85th anniversary of the birth of José Carlos Mariategui, the great Marxist theoretician and propagandist from Latin America. Presents important aspects of his activity and works, emphasizing his contribution to the political and ideological education of the Peruvian proletariat and his role in the formation of the Communist Party and revolutionary unions. Mariategui's literary criticism occupied an important part in his writings, reflecting his belief in the formative role of literature in the life of the people. 149 notes. French summary. 1910's-30

4367. Cometta Manzoni, Aída. VIGENCIA DE JOSÉ CARLOS MARIÁTEGUI [The continued relevance of José Carlos Mariátegui]. *Rev. Nac. de Cultura [Venezuela] 1981 41(246): 79-89.* José Carlos Mariátegui (1895-1930), the outstanding Peruvian essayist, was a self-taught intellectual of extensive culture. In 1926, he founded the journal *Amauta,* which became popular in all of Latin America as the free voice of the new anticolonial thought sweeping the continent. Similarly successful was the journal *Labor,* which Mariátegui published 1928-30, effective in forming a proletarian class awareness among the Peruvian working masses. His two most important works were *La escena contemporánea* (1925), which describes the Europe of the years 1920-25, and *Siete ensayos de una realidad peruana* (1928), which presents a historical study of Peru's national problems from an economic perspective. Primary sources; 12 notes. 1914-30

Marie Antoinette

4368. Castelot, André. MARIE-ANTOINETTE TRAHISSAIT-ELLE? [Was Marie Antoinette guilty of treason?]. *Hist. Mag. [France] 1984 (48): 74-80.* Recalls the behavior of Marie Antoinette (1755-93), who died on the scaffold, stressing her frivolities, intrigues, and actions that favored the interests of Austria, her native country, often against those of France. 1775-93

4369. Davenport, Nancy. MAENAD, MARTYR, MOTHER: MARIE ANTOINETTE TRANSFORMED. *Consortium on Revolutionary Europe 1750-1850: Proceedings 1985 15: 66-84.* Over a span of nearly 100 years the image of Marie Antoinette was formed, reevaluated, and transformed by various individuals. While she was the dauphine and queen, contemporaries used Marie as a scapegoat for France's problems. She was portrayed as a promiscuous adulteress, a domineering wife, and a foreign-born traitor. After the Reign of Terror, however, Marie's reputation was reassessed. She soon became a martyr—almost Christlike in most cases—and the loving mother of France who protected the poor and innocent. Based on materials from the Bibliothèque Nationale and printed primary sources; 51 notes, 15 illus. 1774-1865

Marie Casimir

4370. Komaszyński, Michał. LEGENDA I PRAWDA O OSTATNICH LATACH JANA III [Legend and truth about the last years of John III]. *Śląski Kwartalnik Hist. Sobótka [Poland] 1980 35(2): 211-221.* Examines the truth of the popular belief that during the last years of John III Sobieski's rule, the effective control of state affairs lay in his wife Marie Casimir's hands. 1690-96

4371. Szkoda, Joanna. POSTAĆ MARII KAZIMIERY W HISTORIOGRAFII POLSKIEJ [Marie Casimir in Polish historiography]. *Śląski Kwartalnik Hist. Sobótka [Poland] 1980 35(2): 323-329.* Surveys the presentation of the private and public life of Marie Casimir, wife of John III Sobieski. 1670's-90's

Marighella, Carlos

4372. Antoine, Charles. LES DOMINICAINS DU BRESIL ET LA MORT DE MARIGHELLA [Brazilian Dominicans and the death of Marighella]. *Esprit [France] 1984 (3): 7-27.* An attempt to reconstruct the events surrounding the murder by the Brazilian police of the urban guerrilla leader Carlos Marighella in 1969. 1969

Marinello, Juan

4373. Corretjer, Juan Antonio. TRES INSTANTÁNEAS DE JUAN MARINELLO [Three snapshots of Juan Marinello]. *Casa de las Américas [Cuba] 1980 20(118): 97-100.* The author pays tribute to the memory of Cuban writer Marinello, by remembering his first meeting with him in Havana, a second meeting in prison, and a third encounter with his recorded voice reading his poetry and prose. 20c

Marinescu, Dimitrie

4374. Tudoran, Georgeta. DIMITRIE MARINESCU (1882-1916) [Dimitrie Marinescu (1882-1916)]. *Anale de Istorie [Romania] 1982 28(5): 92-95.* Marinescu was a prominent Romanian militant, an apprentice printer who took to politics, and as an editor and publicist stood unsuccessfully for Parliament in 1911 as a Social Democratic candidate. Subsequently he was arrested and imprisoned, before going to Germany to work with *Vorwärts.* In the face of World War I he stood for Romanian neutrality, and took an important part in various inter-Balkan socialist conferences in 1914-15 and at Zimmerwald. He was killed in battle in 1916. Portrait. ca 1900-16

Marinetti, Filippo Tommaso

4375. Roche-Pézard, Fanette. ANARCHIE VISUELLE A PARIS PENDANT LA BELLE EPOQUE: LA FORMATION ESTHETIQUE DE MARINETTI [Visual anarchy in Paris at the turn of the century: the aesthetic development of Marinetti]. *Pro. of the Ann. Meeting of the Western Soc. for French Hist. 1980 8: 395-401.* Studies the intellectual and literary formation of Italian anarchist writer Filippo Tommaso Marinetti during the period 1893-1909, when he lived mostly in France. Marinetti read the works of French syndicalists and symbolists. He was even more influenced, however, by the many small anarchist newspapers and pamphlets printed in Paris. From them he derived his emotional writing style and many of his ideas about futurism. 9 notes. 1893-1909

Mario, Alberto

4376. Bagatin, Pier Luigi. LA REPUBBLICA E L'IDEALE [The republic and the ideal]. *Veltro [Italy] 1985 29(5-6): 645-655.* Presents a brief biography of Italian journalist and patriot Alberto Mario (1825-83), collaborator of Mazzini in the struggle to unify and liberate Italy and found a republic on the basis of the libertarian humanist principles of John Stuart Mill. 1848-82

Mariotti, Giovanni

4377. Giuffrida, Ines. GIOVANNI MARIOTTI E I SUOI CORRISPONDENTI [Giovanni Mariotti and his correspondents]. *Archivio Storico per le Province Parmensi [Italy] 1983 35: 351-385.* Discusses the life and work of Giovanni Mariotti (1850-1935), a scholar of Parma history, numismatics, and archaeology, who became president of the Deputation of National History of Italy, and systematically lists the correspondents of his 2,402 surviving letters. 1870's-1935

Maritain, Jacques

4378. Campanini, Giorgio. MONTINI E MARITAIN [Montini and Maritain]. *Studium [Italy] 1984 80(3): 349-355.* Determines the degree to which French neo-Thomist philosopher Jacques Maritain influenced the thought of Giovanni Battista Montini, his Italian translator (later Pope Paul VI). 1919-39

4379. Riquet, Michel. L'HOMMAGE DE JEAN-PAUL II À JACQUES MARITAIN [John Paul II's tribute to Jacques Maritain]. *Rev. des Deux Mondes [France] 1983 (2): 277-284.* Relates and comments on the statements and messages of Pope John Paul II on French philosopher and theologian Jacques Maritain (1882-1973). ca 1916-73

4380. Schultz, Walter James. "Jacques Maritain's Social Critique and His Personalism." McMaster U. [Canada] 1982. *DAI 1983 43(10): 3345-A.* 20c

4381. Ward, Leo R. MEETING JACQUES MARITAIN. *Rev. of Pol. 1982 44(4): 483-488.* To those who knew him or saw him lecture Jacques Maritain possessed a touching humility and warmth. The correspondence he maintained with his pupil and disciple Yves Simon provides better insight into the man and a clearer perception of his Christian philosophy. 4 notes. 1930-60

Marjanović, Jovan

4382. Knežević, Djordje. DR JOVAN MARJANOVIĆ—IN MEMORIAM [Dr. Jovan Marjanović: an obituary]. *Jugoslovenski Istorijski Časopis [Yugoslavia] 1981 20(1-4): 1-5.* Jovan Marjanović (1922-80) was expelled from school in his native Belgrade because of membership in the illegal Communist Party. Despite ill health he enjoyed distinguished war service, editing underground partisan newspapers, and at one time ran the railway in the Bosnian town of Drvar. After World War II he graduated in economics from Belgrade University, edited the newspaper *Narodni Front* and worked in the Party archives in Belgrade. In 1958, he joined the history department at Belgrade University, where he remained until his death. Marjanović specialized in the modern history of Serbia, especially relations between the Serbian Chetnik leader Draža Mihailović and Britain and Germany. Photo. 1922-80

4383. Petranović, Branko. JOVAN MARJANOVIĆ [Jovan Marjanović]. *Jugoslovenski Istorijski Časopis [Yugoslavia] 1981 20(1-4): 5-14.* Assesses Jovan Marjanović's contribution to Yugoslav historiography on World War II. His impeccable attention to detail in examining sources has been an example to later generations of scholars, yet his meticulousness did not hamper a lively approach and writing style. Jovan Marjanović will be remembered for particularly useful work on unearthing archival material concerning the Yugoslav Communist Party in Moscow. Also of special interest are his works *Prilozi Istoriji Sukoba Narodnooslobodilačkog Pokreta i Četnika Draže Mihailovića u Srbiji 1941 Godine* [Contributions to the history of the conflict between the national liberation movement and Draža Mihailović's Chetniks in Serbia in 1941] and *Ustanak i Narodnooslobodilački Pokret u Srbiji 1941* [The uprising and the national liberation movement in Serbia in 1941]. He did much to promote the study of Yugoslav history abroad and took part in many international seminars. 1922-80

Marlborough, Duchess of

4384. Harris, Frances. ACCOUNTS OF THE CONDUCT OF SARAH, DUCHESS OF MARLBOROUGH, 1704-42. *British Lib. J. [Great Britain] 1982 8(1): 7-35.* Examines the various narratives written by Sarah, Duchess of Marlborough (1660-1744), relating to her life and conduct at the court of Queen Anne, 1704-11. In acounts drawn up after her dismissal from court in 1711, Sarah defends her management of the court offices which she held as mistress of the robes and keeper of the privy purse. Examines various versions vindicating her fall from favor written by Gilbert Burnett, Archibald Hutcheson, Whadcock Priest, and Benjamin Hoadly. Based on the Blenheim Papers of Sarah, Duchess of Marlborough Nos. 61414-80 at the British Library, London; 5 fig., 86 notes. 1704-42

Marlborough, 1st Duke of

4385. Barber, Peter. MARLBOROUGH AS IMPERIAL PRINCE, 1704-1717. *British Lib. J. [Great Britain] 1982 8(1): 46-79.* John, 1st Duke of Marlborough was made an imperial prince of the Holy Roman Empire by Leopold I in 1704 who hoped to retain Marlborough's support for the dynasty. The Duke accepted the title, mainly in order to enhance his authority with his continental military subordinates. He then exerted pressure for title and lands on the imperial ambassador at the English Court, Count Wratislaw, and, after many negotiations he acquired possession of the lordship of Mindelheim in 1706. Examines Marlborough's attachment to Mindelheim, his administration and treatment of his subjects there, 1706-17. Based on the Blenheim Papers held at the British Library, London; 4 fig., 182 notes. 1704-17

4386. Hudson, J. P. THE BLENHEIM PAPERS. *British Lib. J. [Great Britain] 1982 8(1): 1-6.* Describes the papers of John, 1st Duke of Marlborough (1650-1722), his wife Sarah (1660-1744), and his son-in-law Charles, 3d Earl of Sunderland (1674-1722), as well as those of other members of the Spencer, Churchill and related families, acquired by the British Library from the Marlborough family in 1978. They include correspondence between the 1st Duke of Marlborough and royalty, politicians, diplomats, naval and military commanders, and relate to the Duke's principality of Mindelheim, his personal finances, and the building works at Blenheim Palace. His wife's papers include correspondence with Queen Anne, and the papers of Charles Spencer, 3d Earl of Sunderland, comprise political, diplomatic, military and naval correspondence. Based on the Blenheim Papers Nos. 61101-61710 at the British Library, London; 2 notes. 1670-1740

Marley, Robert Nesta

4387. Reid, Hazel. BOB MARLEY: UP FROM BABYLON. *Freedomways 1981 21(3): 171-179.* Discusses the life and musical career of Jamaican Robert Nesta Marley (1945-81), commenting on the religious basis of his music and its political implications for the Third World. 1970's

Marlowe, Christopher

4388. Balet, Sebastià. MARLOWE: DRAMATURGO, INCREDULO Y ESPIA [Marlowe: playwright, nonbeliever, and spy]. *Historia y Vida [Spain] 1985 18(203): 104-113.* Discusses the life and work of English writer Christopher Marlowe (1564-93), including his religious views, his influence on the development of English theater in the Renaissance, and his tragic death. 1585-93

Marocchi, Arnaldo

4389. Dall'Olio, Enrico. ARNALDO MAROCCHI (1911-1983) [Arnoldo Marocchi (1911-83)]. *Archivio Storico per le Province Parmensi [Italy] 1983 35: 47-50.* Reviews the life and work of Monsignor Arnaldo Marocchi of the Church of Parma, who served as chancellor and archivist of the Curia and who was leader of the Catholic Action group. 1930's-83

Marpeck, Pilgram

4390. Klassen, William. THE LIMITS OF POLITICAL AUTHORITY AS SEEN BY PILGRAM MARPECK. *Mennonite Q. Rev. 1982 56(4): 342-369.* The view of Anabaptists as anarchists, expressed by G. R. Elton in *Reformation Europe, 1517-1559* (1964), is wrong, as shown by the life work and influence of Pilgram Marpeck, who held specific limits to political authority, but supported the state within these limits. 67 notes. 1527-44

Marr, Iuri Nikolaevich

4391. Mirzoyan, N. L. IURII NIKOLAEVICH MARR [Iuri Nikolaevich Marr]. *Patma-Banasirakan Handes. Istoriko-Filologicheskii Zhurnal [USSR] 1985 (3): 186-195.* Reviews the life of the orientalist Iuri Marr (1893-1935), some of whose archival material has not yet been published. Primary sources; photo, 24 notes. Armenian summary. 1893-1935

Marr, Nikolai

4392. Mnats'akanyan, S. Kh. HAYKAKAN CHARTARAPETUT'YAN HARTS'ERĚ NIKOGHAYOS MAṚI ASHKHATUT'IWNNERUM (TSNNDYAN 120-AMYAKI AṚT'IV) [Questions of Armenian architecture in the works of Nikolai Marr: on the 120th anniversary of his birth]. *Patma-Banasirakan Handes. Istoriko-Filologicheskii Zhurnal [USSR] 1985 (1): 21-31.* Nikolai Marr (1865-1934) was the first to distinguish the various periods of Armenian architecture and to demonstrate the continuity between the pagan and the Christian periods. He directed the excavation of Ani, the Bagratuni capital, for some 25 years. His work on the church of Ereruyk' is important for the study of basilica-type constructions. Some of his proposals, however, such as the characteristics of "Chalcedonian" structures, are not acceptable. Based on the N. Ia. Marr archive of the USSR Academy of Sciences, Leningrad; photo, 18 notes. Russian summary. 1892-1934

Marr, Wilhelm

4393. Levy, Richard S.; Jarausch, Konrad H. (commentary). 1848 AND THE DISCOVERY OF POLITICAL ANTI-SEMITISM IN GERMANY: THE CASE OF WILHELM MARR. *Consortium on Revolutionary Europe 1750-1850: Pro. 1981: 255-264.* A biographical sketch of activist-author-politician Wilhelm Marr, most widely known for his espousal of anti-Semitism. His early years were spent as a radical supporter of the German working class. When the performance of the *Volk* in the Revolution of 1848 convinced him that they were not worthy of his sacrifices, he sought another cause. He chose racism in general and anti-Semitism in particular. His major work was *The Victory of Jewry over Germandom* (1879). Comments, pp. 265-268. Based on Hamburg Staatsarchiv, microfilm, and secondary sources; 28 notes. 1839-79

4394. Zimmerman, Moshe. FROM RADICALISM TO ANTI-SEMITISM. *Jerusalem Quarterly [Israel] 1982 (23): 114-128.* Analyzes the interrelation between radicalism and anti-Semitism in the 19th century as illustrated by the career of the German radical Wilhelm Marr (b. 1819). 1840's-60's

Marsden, Samuel

4395. Griffiths, Tom. BOUNDARIES OF THE SACRED: THE WILLIAMS FAMILY IN NEW ZEALAND, 1823-30. *Journal of Religious History [Australia] 1984 13(1): 35-45.* The contrasting missionary styles of the Reverends Henry Williams and Samuel Marsden, both representing the Anglican Church Missionary Society among the Maori in New Zealand, dramatized the debate of how best to Christianize tribal peoples, whether to place greater emphasis on the material superiority of Christian civilization, as Marsden believed, or on the tenets of Christian faith and the gospel, as believed Williams. In the context of Protestant missionary activities there was a problem in separating European civilization from Christianity, as the definition of the sacred was difficult to communicate. Reverend Williams and his family were notable for their ability to set the example of the good Christian life without overemphasizing its material or economic dimensions. Based on archival and secondary sources; 55 notes. 1820-30

Marshall, Alexander

4396. Leith-Ross, Prudence. ALEXANDER MARSHALL: 17TH CENTURY BOTANICAL ARTIST. *British Heritage 1985 6(6): 44-49.* Reviews what little is known of the life and work of English artist Alexander Marshall (d. 1682), chiefly notable for his realistic paintings of flowers. 1649-82

Marshall, Alfred

4397. Coase, Ronald H. ALFRED MARSHALL'S MOTHER AND FATHER. *History of Political Economy 1984 16(4): 519-527.* John Maynard Keynes's memoir of English economist Alfred Marshall (1842-1924) had little to say about Marshall's parents. This was in part because the Marshall family had sought to conceal information about the lower-class origins of Alfred Marshall's mother, Rebecca Oliver, daughter of a Maidstone butcher, and about the economist's violent and tyrannical father, William Marshall. Based on correspondence of Alfred Marshall and family; 28 notes. 1830-1924

Marshall, David

4398. Yeo Kim Wak. DAVID MARSHALL: THE REWARDS AND SHORTCOMINGS OF A POLITICAL BIOGRAPHY. *Journal of Southeast Asian Studies [Singapore] 1985 16(2): 304-321.* David Marshall was a Singapore politician in the 1950's. At the height of his career he was chief minister of Singapore. Chan Heng Chee has written about him in *A Sensation of Independence: A Political Biography of David Marshall.* The reviewer calls it an accurate, convincing portrayal of Marshall's character, but is critical of her political analysis. 66 notes. 1945-78

Marshall, T. H.

4399. Halsey, A. H. T. H. MARSHALL: PAST AND PRESENT 1893-1981: PRESIDENT OF THE BRITISH SOCIOLOGICAL ASSOCIATION 1964-1969. *Sociology [Great Britain] 1984 18(1): 1-18.* A tribute to T. H. Marshall (1893-1981), assessing his work as a historian of the Industrial Revolution in Great Britain and as a sociologist. 1893-1981

Marshall, Tom

4400. MacRae, Donald G. TOM MARSHALL 1893-1981: A PERSONAL MEMOIR. *British J. of Sociol. [Great Britain] 1982 33(3): iii-vi.* Provides a personal tribute to the English economic historian, sociologist, and academic, Tom Marshall (1893-1981). 1893-1981

Marshman, John Clark

4401. Hussain, Md. Delwar. THE ROLE OF PROVIDENCE AND THE WRITING OF HISTORY: JOHN CLARK MARSHMAN (1794-1877): A CASE STUDY. *Dhaka University Studies Part A [Bangladesh] 1984 (41): 64-69.* Like any other literary activity, the writing of history is influenced by the intellectual environment in which it functions. Marshman was born in England but went to India at the age of five because his parents were Baptist missionaries there. He studied at the mission school and later became a teacher there and a prolific writer. One of his major themes was that the establishment of a British Empire in India was the unfolding of God's plan for that country. To Marshman, providence meant divine intervention in human affairs in order to realize God's own purposes in the world, and history was no more than the recording of this intervention. 17 notes. 19c

Marson, Una

4402. Smilowitz, Erika. UNA MARSON: WOMAN BEFORE HER TIME. *Jamaica J. [Jamaica] 1983 16(2): 62-68.* Una Marson (1905-65) was the first Jamaican woman to own, write, and edit a magazine. In England she was secretary of the League of Coloured People, wrote and directed a London play, was Emperor Haile Selassie's secretary, and was involved with feminist organizations. After returning to Jamaica, she became organizing secretary of the Pioneer Press in 1945, which influenced West Indian literature for several years. 1928-65

Martegani, Giacomo

4403. Dainelli, Luca. RICORDO DI UN GRANDE SACERDOTE ITALIANO: PADRE GIACOMO MARTEGANI S.J. [Remembering a great Italian priest: Giacomo Martegani, S.J.]. *Riv. di Studi Pol. Int. [Italy] 1981 48(3): 395-411.* Martegani was director of the Jesuit review *Civiltà Cattolica,* assistant to the General, and director of Vatican Radio. He was a man of God but deeply knowledgeable about and interested in Italian and international affairs. 1930's-81

Martel de Janville, Sibylle de

4404. Millstone, Amy B.; Chastain, James G. (commentary). GYP, ENFANT TERRIBLE OF THE FRENCH RIGHT, 1880-1905. *Pro. of the Ann. Meeting of the Western Soc. for French Hist. 1980 8: 382-389.* Most scholars of late 19th-century French history have assumed that right-wing groups and aristocratic women were generally unsympathetic to the women's movement. This assumption is contradicted by the example of Comtesse Sibylle de Martel de Janville (1849-1932), whose literary pseudonym was Gyp. Gyp was a best-selling novelist, a prominent journalist, and also a vehement anti-Dreyfusard, anti-Semite, Boulangiste, Bonapartist, and Catholic *ultra.* In addition, she was a committed advocate of equality for women in such matters as divorce and the woman's role in the family. Comments, pp. 390-394. 23 notes. 1880-1905

Martel Viniegra, Ignacio

4405. Martel Viniegra, Ignacio. UN BRILLANTISIMO EXITO DIPLOMATICO [A most brilliant diplomatic success]. *Rev. General de Marina [Spain] 1983 205(Nov): 653-657.* The author, as commander of the Spanish warship *Xauen* in 1941, secretly transported the Italian naval attaché from Las Palmas to Tenerife while at the same time he was ordered to give passage to the crew of a stranded British seaplane. He prevented the British aviators from learning the identity of the Italian passenger by entertaining them all by playing the accordion throughout the five-hour voyage. 1941

Martelanc, Vladimir

4406. Kacin-Wohinz, Milica. O VLADIMIRJU MARTELANCU [Vladimir Martelanc]. *Prispevki za Zgodovino Delavskega Gibanja [Yugoslavia] 1980 20(1-2): 130-137.* Gives a biography of Vladimir Martelanc (1905-44), a Slovene politician and publicist from Trieste. Discusses his works and stresses his activities as member of the Italian Communist Party. 1905-44

Martensen, Hans Lassen

4407. Lein, Bente Nilsen. BISKOP MARTENSEN OG DEN ETISK-KRISTLIGE SOSIALISME [Bishop Martensen and moral Christian socialism]. *Norsk Teologisk Tidsskrift [Norway] 1980 81(4): 233-248.* Hans Lassen Martensen was an important figure in his own lifetime though he has since been overshadowed by Kirkegaard. He believed that a moderate form of socialism could be reconciled with Christianity, although he felt much socialist criticism was justified. He rejected the socialist concept of a classless society and advocated what he termed "moral Christian socialism," which aimed to elevate the living standards of the working class to those of the middle class. 1849-84

Martí, José

4408. Fernández Retamar, Roberto. JOSE MARTI EN LOS ORIGENES DEL ANTIMPERIALISMO LATINOAMERICANO [José Martí and the origins of Latin American anti-imperialism]. *Casa de las Américas [Cuba] 1985 25(151): 3-11.* His consciously assumed Caribbean origins, wide Latin American experience, and years of exile in the United States enabled José Martí to be among the first to discover and voice his opposition to nascent American imperialism. Though a non-Marxist revolutionary, he was able to see the early development of what Lenin would later characterize as the last stage of capitalism. Ref. 1880-95

4409. Guillén, Nicolás. MARTI EN LA PLUMA DE GUILLEN [Martí in the writing of Guillén]. *Islas [Cuba] 1982 (71): 45-50.* Describes the personality of José Martí as presented in two articles written by Nicolás Guillén. 1853-95

4410. Hidalgo Paz, Ibrahím. NOTAS ACERCA DE LA HISTORIOGRAFIA MARTIANA EN EL PERIODO 1959-1983 [Notes concerning the Martiana historiography from 1959 to 1983]. *Revista de la Biblioteca Nacional José Martí [Cuba] 1985 27(1): 63-78.* The revolution of 1959 naturally inspired a new look at early radical roots in Cuba. Among these new interests had been a reexamination of José Martí (1853-95), the father of Cuban independence. Much of the new work on Martí has emphasized his radical ideology and the ties that his goals for Cuba have with the present government. Secondary sources. 1870's-95

4411. LeRiverend, Julio. BOLIVAR Y MARTI: DOS TIEMPOS, UNA HISTORIA [Bolívar and Martí: two moments, one history]. *Santiago [Cuba] 1984 (53): 27-58.* 19c

For abstract see ***Bolívar, Simón***

4412. Miranda, Olivia. PARALELO ENTRE VARELA Y MARTI: EL ANTICLERICALISMO [The parallel between Varela and Martí: anticlericalism]. *Rev. de la Biblioteca Nac. José Martí [Cuba] 1981 23(3): 167-204.* Félix Varela (1777-1853) and José Martí (1853-95) were two Cuban intellectuals whose ideas were very radical for their generation. Both expressed religious ideas that contained anticlerical sentiments. 23 notes, biblio. 19c

4413. Rosa, Leopoldo de la. LA FAMILIA MATERNA DE JOSE MARTI [The maternal family of José Martí]. *Rev. de Hist. Canaria [Spain] 1980 37(172): 245-247.* 1828-42

For abstract see ***Pérez Cabrera, Leonor***

Martí y Navarro, Mariano

4414. Iduate, Juan. DON MARIANO MARTI Y NAVARRO, CAPITAN JUEZ PEDANEO DE LA HANABANA [Don Mariano Martí y Navarro, captain and puisne judge of La Hanábana]. *Santiago [Cuba] 1982 (46): 137-182.* Mariano Martí, father of José Martí, was puisne judge and captain in the district which includes the Bay of Pigs when an illegal boatload of slaves was unloaded there in 1862. He ordered those responsible to be arrested but they were later released. Among the documents relating to the case two were written by his son, then a boy of nine. These are his earliest known manuscripts and they are evidence of a close lifelong relationship between father and son. Based on primary material in the National Archives; 54 notes, 27 documents in appendix, some in facsimile. 1862

Martineau, Harriet

4415. Chialant, Maria Teresa. STORIA DI UNA CARRIERA: HARRIET MARTINEAU [Story of a career: Harriet Martineau]. *Memoria: Riv. di Storia delle Donne [Italy] 1983 (8): 121-128.* Harriet Martineau's life and career were marked by a sense of duty and a call to sacrifice. Her choice of historical, political, and religious journalism over a career as a fiction writer exemplifies her will to discipline, and her decision to control and disguise her feelings rather than express them in her writing. Biblio. 19c

4416. Riedesel, Paul L. WHO *WAS* HARRIET MARTINEAU? *J. of the Hist. of Sociol. 1981 3(2): 63-80.* Reviews the life and writings of 19th-century English writer Harriet Martineau, especially the sociological aspects of her work. 1827-76

Martines, Marianna

4417. Fremar, Karen Lynn. "The Life and Selected Works of Marianna Martines (1744-1812)." U. of Kansas 1983. 267 pp. *DAI 1983 44(4): 905-A.* DA8317966 1750's-1812

Martínez de Tineo, Juan Victorino

4418. Acevedo, Edberto Oscar. EL GOBERNADOR MARTINEZ DE TINEO Y EL CHACO [Governor Martínez de Tineo and the Chaco]. *Revista de Historia Americana y Argentina [Argentina] 1983-84 12(23-24): 11-65.* A biography and discussion of Juan Victorino Martínez de Tineo, the governor of the province of Tucumán, and his activities during the mid-18th century, a period of dramatic change in the region and in the viceroyalty of the Río de la Plata. Narrates Martínez de Tineo's rise to the office, his administrative and military activities while governor, and the important events that occurred during his tenure, centering on his actions concerning the Chaco desert frontier. Based on archival documents and secondary sources. 1705-70

Martínez Moreno, Carlos

4419. Salisbury-Ginsburg, Liz. "Downfall of a Democracy: Carlos Martínez Moreno and the Uruguayan Experience." U. of California, Davis 1982. 192 pp. *DAI 1983 44(1): 182-A.* DA8311987 1929-73

Martínez Mutis, Aurelio

4420. Cacua Prada, Antonio. AURELIO MARTINEZ MUTIS. SU VIDA Y SU OBRA [Aurelio Martínez Mutis: his life and work]. *Boletín de Historia y Antigüedades [Colombia] 1984 71(747): 870-893.* The poet Aurelio Martínez Mutis, born in Bucaramanga in 1884, made his mark in Colombian letters with works exalting the values of the Roman Catholic religion, Colombian nationhood, and the Hispanic heritage. He lived for a time in southern South America and in his final years held a diplomatic assignment in France, where he died in 1954. 1884-1954

4421. Sánchez Camacho, Jorge. UN GRATO CENTENARIO: AURELIO MARTINEZ MUTIS [A kind centennial: Aurelio Martínez Mutis]. *Boletín de la Academia Colombiana [Colombia] 1985 35(147): 3-37.* Literary biography of the Colombian poet Aurelio Martínez Mutis (1884-1954) on the occasion of the first centennial of his birth. 1900's-54

Martínez Villena, Rubén

4422. Rodríguez, Pedro Pablo. RUBEN MARTINEZ VILLENA: EL MARXISMO ENTRA EN EL PENSAMIENTO ECONOMICO CUBANO [Rubén Martínez Villena: Marxism enters Cuban economic thought]. *Revista de la Biblioteca Nacional José Martí [Cuba] 1983[i.e., 1984] 26(2): 41-63.* Rubén Martínez Villena was the principal intellectual in Cuba's first Marxist party from 1927 to 1934. Although much of his work was not published during his life, he combined a strong anti-imperialist attitude in his writings with the economic theories of Marx and Lenin. To a great extent, he pioneered Marxist economic theories in Cuba. Secondary sources; 56 notes, biblio. 1900-34

4423. Yanes, Pedro Armando. "Rubén Martínez Villena: Conflictos entre Poesía y Política" [Rubén Martínez Villena: the conflicts between poetry and politics]. New York U. 1983. 238 pp. *DAI 1983 44(2): 497-A.* DA8313936 1899-1934

Martini, Giuseppe

4424. Boscolo, Alberto. CONTINUITÀ DI UNA CULTURA STORICA [Continuity of a historical culture]. *Nuova Riv. Storica [Italy] 1980 64(1-2): v-vii.* The new director of the journal and successor in the chair of Medieval History in the University of Milan pays tribute to the man who preceded him, Giuseppe Martini (d. 1979). The review, founded in 1917 to counteract the hypercritical philological scholarship of the time, will continue to play its role as a forum for discussion and debate. 1917-79

Martini, Martino

4425. Melis, Giorgio. CONVEGNO INTERNAZIONALE SU MARTINO MARTINI [International conference on Martino Martini]. *Mondo Cinese [Italy] 1981 9(4): 101-104.* The Jesuit Martini (1614-61) was a notable scholar, geographer, and historian of China. He defended Chinese practices in the famous controversy of the Chinese rites. His work and personality were recently discussed by scholars, two of whom came from the People's Republic of China, at a conference in his native Trento (9-11 October 1981). 1635-61

Márton, József

4426. Mikó, Pálné. A MAGYAR NYELV ÉS MÁRTON JÓZSEF A BÉTSI UNIVERSZITÁSBAN [The Hungarian language and József Márton at the University of Vienna]. *Magyar Tudomány [Hungary] 1983 28(7-8): 616-623.* József Márton was appointed professor of Hungarian literature at the University of Vienna in 1806 at the age of 35. He had been educated in Debrecen, Hungary and had spent 1795 in Jena, Prussia on a study tour where he perfected his knowledge of German. In Vienna he initially undertook the editing and compiling of a dictionary with Demeter Görög (1760-1833), the founder of the periodical *Magyar Hírmondó.* The Hungarian chair was established by imperial decree with the stipulations that it carry no pay or benefits and that students on scholarships be allowed to attend the lectures free. In the annual university catalog Márton's name was always listed last despite his considerable teaching and scholarly activities in Hungarian language and literature. Primary sources; 30 notes. 1806-40

Marton, L'udovít

4427. Rakovický, Viliam. Z HISTÓRIE JEDNEJ DIELNI [From the history of a workshop]. *Umění a Řemesla [Czechoslovakia] 1980 (4): 32-38.* Discusses the work and life of a little known locksmith L'udovít Marton around the 1850's. ca 1850

Martov, Julius

4428. Burbank, Jane. WAITING FOR THE PEOPLE'S REVOLUTION: MARTOV AND CHERNOV IN REVOLUTIONARY RUSSIA 1917-1923. *Cahiers du Monde Russe et Soviétique [France] 1985 26(3-4): 375-394.* 1917-23
*For abstract see **Chernov, Victor***

Martuszewski, Edward

4429. Wrzesiński, Wojciech. EDWARD MARTUSZEWSKI (1921-1982) [Edward Martuszewski (1921-82)]. *Komunikaty Mazursko-Warmińskie [Poland] 1983 (4): 589-592.* An obituary of Edward Martuszewski, historian of the Masuria region of Poland in the 19th century, whose work concerned issues in nationality policies in the region and has led to major revisions in the field. 19c

Marvell, Andrew

4430. Burdon, Pauline. THE SECOND MRS. MARVELL. *Notes and Queries [Great Britain] 1982 29(1): 33-44.* 1538-1647
*For abstract see **Alured, Lucy***

4431. Burdon, Pauline. MARVELL AND HIS KINDRED: THE FAMILY NETWORK IN THE LATER YEARS. *Notes and Queries [Great Britain] 1985 32(2): 172-180.* Tells the story of Andrew Marvell's relationships to the Thompson, Nelthorpe, and Popple families, examining their family ties, their friendships, and their impact on Marvell's later life. 17c

Marx, Eleanor

4432. Mullaney, Marie Marmo. GENDER AND THE SOCIALIST REVOLUTIONARY ROLE, 1871-1921: A GENERAL THEORY OF THE FEMALE REVOLUTIONARY PERSONALITY. *Historical Reflections [Canada] 1984 11(2): 99-151.* 1871-1921
*For abstract see **Balabanoff, Angelica***

Marx, Karl

4433. Abosch, Heinz. MARX, DER MENSCH [Marx, the person]. *Schweizer Monatshefte [Switzerland] 1982 62(2): 164-168.* New biographical research on Karl Marx and his family reveals Marx's ideas to be strongly influenced by 19th-century society, his family life being typically patriarchal and characterized by strong Victorian moral standards. 19c

4434. Himmelfarb, Gertrude. THE "REAL" MARX. *Commentary 1985 79(4): 37-43.* Attacks Bruce Mazlish's *The Meaning of Karl Marx* for glossing over such negative aspects of Marx's character as an obsession with scatology, anti-Semitism, and contempt for most of the human race. 1840's-83

4435. Huerta de Pacheco, Maria Antonieta. EL SIGLO XIX COMO CONTEXTO HISTORICO DEL PENSAMIENTO DE MARX [The 19th century as the historical context for Marx's thought]. *Universitas Humanistica [Colombia] 1983 12(20): 10-31.* The development of Karl Marx's theories are explained by reviewing the important events of the 19th century such as the consolidation of liberal politics, the consolidation of capitalism, social movements, and the position of the Church. Commentaries follow, pp. 31-34. 19c

4436. Jemnitz, János. MARX ÉS A FRANCIA MUNKÁSMOZGALOM MARX ÉLETÉNEK UTOLSÓ ÉVEIBEN [Marx and the French labor movement during the last years of his life]. *Párttörténeti Közlemények [Hungary] 1983 29(1): 73-96.* During the last years of his life, Karl Marx showed an interest in all new developments in French working-class movements. He read articles in all socialist journals and dailies and provided comments, which greatly influenced editorial policy as well as the basic concepts of the newly established workers' party. 83 notes. 1879-83

4437. Jemnitz, János. MARX ÉS AZ ANGOL, BELGA MUNKÁSMOZGALOM (1877-1883) [Marx and the labor movement in Belgium and England, 1877-83]. *Századok [Hungary] 1983 117(6): 1196-1224.* During the last years of his life Karl Marx was largely isolated from the working-class movement in England, which followed a path separate from that of European socialists. Nevertheless, Marx remained in contact with several leading English intellectuals who recognized his contribution to the workers' struggle. His role in Belgium was much more direct; even in his final years, Marx played an active part in the suppression of anarchist tendencies in the Belgian socialist movement. Secondary sources; 124 notes. 1877-83

4438. Kain, Philip J. THE YOUNG MARX AND KANTIAN ETHICS. *Studies in Soviet Thought [Netherlands] 1986 31(4): 277-301.* In both his search for a historical agent that would make possible the realization of morality in the world, and in his theory of communist society established by that historical agent, the young Karl Marx fell back on Immanuel Kant's concept of the categorical imperative. Based on the writings of Marx and Kant; 63 notes. 19c

4439. Kapp, Yvonne. KARL MARX'S CHILDREN. *New Left Rev. [Great Britain] 1983 (138): 69-84.* Only two of Marx's seven children survived him, due to the hardships of their early life. 1840's-83

4440. Machalek, Richard. KARL MARX: "A SWARTHY FELLOW FROM *TRIER.*" *Social Science Quarterly 1983 64(4): 778-785.* A biographical sketch introducing a symposium on Karl Marx. 1842-83

4441. Mah, Harold E. KARL MARX IN LOVE: THE ENLIGHTENMENT, ROMANTICISM AND HEGELIAN THEORY IN THE YOUNG MARX. *History of European Ideas [Great Britain] 1986 7(5): 489-507.* "Surviving documentary evidence does not support" the notion that the young Karl Marx (1818-83) was politically radicalized. Introduced early to Enlightenment thought, he rejected it for "the impassioned life of Romanticism," expressed in his love poems to his future wife. Then in 1837 he in turn rejected "the unworldly idealism of Romanticism" for "the realistic idealism of Hegelian philosophy." "For Marx, Hegelian philosophy had succeeded in reconciling the Enlightenment with Romanticism." By accepting Hegel, he "resolved the conflicts and tensions that characterized his early adulthood." Based on Marx's early writings; 72 notes. 1835-37

4442. McLellan, David. KARL MARX—HIS LIFE AND WORK. *Hist. Today [Great Britain] 1983 33(Mar): n.pp.* Chronology and bibliography of the life of Karl Marx, to be used in conjunction with one segment of a British television program titled *Today's History.* 1818-1983

4443. McLellan, David. MARX IN ENGLAND. *Hist. Today [Great Britain] 1983 33(Mar): 5-10.* Discusses the quality of Karl Marx's life while he lived in London; demonstrates how London and Marx were compatible and outlines the major influences upon Marx during his stay in England. 1849-83

4444. Mikhailov, M. I. KARL MARKS I FRIDRIKH ENGEL'S V KËL'NSKOM RABOCHEM SOIUZE [Marx and Engels in the Cologne workers' union]. *Novaia i Noveishaia Istoriia [USSR] 1985 (6): 19-33.* 1848-49
For abstract see ***Engels, Friedrich***

4445. Veszelák, Ferenc. FRANZ MEHRING: KARL MARX. ÉLETRAJZ [Franz Mehring: Karl Marx, a biography]. *Társadalmi Szemle [Hungary] 1983 38(3): 73-77.* Franz Mehring's biography of Marx, now in its third edition, was first published in Hungarian in 1925. The aim of this biography, directed mostly at the working class, was to introduce Marx's teachings in popular, easy to understand language, but at the same time in a scientific and accurate form. The book graphically describes Marx's everyday life, his struggle to publish his works, the deprivations and illnesses, and the difficulties of being a poverty-stricken immigrant. 2 notes, plate. 1843-1925

4446. Walentowicz, Halina. PERSPEKTYWY REWOLUCYJNE II POŁOWY XIX WIEKU W ŚWIETLE KORESPONDENCJI K. MARKSA I F. ENGELSA [Revolutionary prospects in the mid-19th century in the correspondence of Marx and Engels]. *Studia Filozoficzne [Poland] 1981 (2): 119-131.* 19c
For abstract see ***Engels, Friedrich***

4447. Watson, George. WAS MARX AN ANCIENT HISTORIAN? *Encounter [Great Britain] 1981 57(5): 57-61.* Marx was conversant with the classics and ancient history. 19c

4448. —. OSNOVOPOLOZHNIK NAUCHNOGO SOTSIALIZMA (MIROVAIA PECHAT' 1883 G. O KARLE MARKSE) [The great founder of scientific socialism (the world press on Marx in 1883)]. *Novaia i Noveishaia Istoriia [USSR] 1983 (2): 3-29.* This publication, prepared by the Institute of Marxism-Leninism under the Central Committee of the Communist Party of the Soviet Union, contains obituaries, articles, and biographical essays which appeared in the press of 19 countries, including Russia, in connection with the death of Karl Marx 14 March 1883. The Social Democratic, workers', democratic, and even liberal bourgeois press of that time highly praised Marx's life and activities, his great services to the working-class movement, and his contribution to the science of society. 1883

Masaryk, Jan

4449. Mayne, Richard. PRAGUE'S CRUEL SPRING: MASARYK, 1948. *Encounter [Great Britain] 1983 60(5): 76-85.* Discusses the heritage of Czechoslovak Jan Masaryk, the formation of his political ideologies, his participation in Czechoslovakian politics, and the mysteries surrounding his death in 1948. 1919-48

Masaryk, Tomáš

4450. Brodská, Zdenka. A PRAGUE HOMAGE TO THE MASARYK LEGACY. *Cross Currents 1986 5: 241-246.* Discusses the recent Czechoslovakian underground publication, *T. G. Masaryk and Our Times,* a cultural review of essays by Czech authors, including exiles, recalling the political legacy of Tomáš Masaryk (1850-1937), the first president of Czechoslovakia. 1870's-1937

4451. Leboucher, Marc. THOMAS MASARYK ET LA DEMOCRATIE [Tomáš Masaryk and democracy]. *Esprit [France] 1984 (7): 37-45.* Analyzes the career of the Czech leader Tomáš Masaryk (1850-1935), his intellectual debts, and his concept of the social democratic state. 1850-1935

4452. Noel, Leon. "LA TCHECOSLOVAQUIE D'AVANT MUNICH": THOMAS GARRIGUE MASARYK [Czechoslovakia before Munich: Tomáš Masaryk]. *Rev. des Deux Mondes [France] 1982 (6): 527-536.* Recounts the life and career of Masaryk (1850-1937), statesman and first president of Czechoslovakia. 1881-1935

4453. Pospisil, Raymond Harold. "Great Truths and Small Lies: Tomáš G. Masaryk and His Critics, 1886-1926." Indiana U. 1983. 185 pp. *DAI 1984 44(12): 3778-A.* DA8406838 1886-1926

4454. Schmidt-Hartmann, Eva. MASARYK UND UNSERE GEGENWART [Masaryk and our own times]. *Bohemia [West Germany] 1985 26(1): 104-110.* The essay volume *Tomáš G. Masaryk a Naše Současnost* [Tomáš Masaryk and our own times] (1980) was issued independently in Prague. Despite the condemnations of the present Communist regime, Masaryk (1850-1937) as a leader and thinker continues to engage many of the younger thinkers in Czechoslovakia. Frequently, the contributors tend to duplicate Masaryk's own formulations and his relative neglect of political and legal concepts. Yet their response to Masaryk's ethically grounded nationalism, which involves moral autonomy and fearless search for truth, remains impressive. 2 notes. 1882-1937

4455. Schmidt-Hartmann, Eva. T. G. MASARYK UND DIE VOLKSDEMOKRATIE [T. G. Masaryk and people's democracy]. *Bohemia [West Germany] 1982 23(2): 370-387.* Tomáš Masaryk (1850-1937), first president of Czechoslovakia, has commonly been identified with parliamentary democracy, but an analysis of his social thought since 1880 reveals patterns derived from the European utopian tradition. Masaryk distrusted human inertia more than governmental power. His scientific predilections led him to overestimate "science" as a key to correct political choices, while favoring protection of the common good at the expense of parliamentary pluralism and competition. After 1945, Czechoslovakia's adoption of people's democracy was a logical outgrowth of Masarykism, though Masaryk's successors could match neither his stature nor his moderating influence. Based on Masaryk's writings; 35 notes. 1880-1937

Maschke, Erich

4456. Schremmer, Eckart. NEKROLOG: ERICH MASCHKE (2. MÄRZ 1900-11. FEBRUAR 1982) [Obituary: Erich Maschke (2 March 1900-11 February 1982)]. *Hist. Zeits. [West Germany] 1982 235(1): 251-255.* Evaluates the career of Erich Maschke, the Heidelberg historian of medieval economy and social classes. A prisoner of war in Russia from 1945 to 1953, he completed his career in Heidelberg and after retirement directed the Wissenschaftliche Kommission für Deutsche Kriegsgefangenengeschichte [Scientific commission for the history of German prisoners of war], which produced 22 volumes of documentation on World War II and its aftermath. Based on personal acquaintance; 6 citations of Maschke's works. 1900-82

Masefield, John

4457. Hammer, Lee. "John Masefield in the Twentieth Century: A Reputation Study." Marquette U. 1985. 276 pp. *DAI 1985 46(6): 1634-A.* DA8516271 20c

Massaquoi, Momulu

4458. Smyke, Raymond J. MASSAQUOI OF LIBERIA (1870-1938). *Genève-Afrique [Switzerland] 1983 21(1): 73-105.* Details the life of Momulu Massaquoi (1870-1938) one of the rare Liberians of local (as opposed to American) origin to achieve prominence in government before 1980. The son of a prominent woman chief of the Vai people of the Sierra Leone border, Massaquoi served in various political and diplomatic offices and was a contender for the presidency in 1931. Based on oral sources in Liberia and archives in Europe and the United States; 16 notes, 2 photos. 1870-1938

Massari, Giuseppe

4459. Morelli, Emilia. LE FONTI DELLA BIOGRAFIA DI VITTORIO EMANUELE DI GIUSEPPE MASSARI [The sources of the biography of Victor Emmanuel by Giuseppe Massari]. *Rassegna Storica del Risorgimento [Italy] 1980 67(1): 14-57.* Examines the notes made by Giuseppe Massari when he was collecting material for a biography of Victor Emmanuel II. It is clear that Massari did not deliberately exclude discussion of left-wing politics, he simply did not know about them. Considers the information used in writing the personal section and attempts to understand Massari's methodology. Particularly important are the sections on the relations among the king and Giuseppe Mazzini and Garibaldi. 19c

Massé, Pierre

4460. Guitton, Henri. LA TRAVERSEE DU SIECLE [Across the century]. *Revue d'Economie Politique [France] 1984 94(3): 399-403.* Discusses the career of the French engineer and administrator, Pierre Massé (b. 1898) on the occasion of his autobiography, *Aléas et Progrès, entre Candide et Cassandre* (1984). 1920's-84

Massignon, Louis

4461. Basetti-Sani, Giulio. LOUIS MASSIGNON: CHRISTIAN ISLAMOLOGIST. *Hamdard Islamicus [Pakistan] 1985 8(1): 55-79.* Louis Massignon (1883-1963) was a French scholar and diplomat who developed great sympathy for Islam, interpreting it in terms of Abrahamic mysticism. He participated in pilgrimages to Muslim shrines in Morocco, Egypt, Syria, Palestine, Iraq, and Pakistan, became a priest of the Melkite (Byzantine Arabic) Rite of the Catholic Church, and was a constant supporter of the right of the Algerians and the Palestinians to self-determination. 1902-63

Massine, Leonide

4462. Fusillo , Lisa Ann. "Leonide Massine: Choreographic Genius with a Collaborative Spirit." Texas Woman's U. 1982. 237 pp. *DAI 1982 43(4): 957-A.* DA8219612 20c

Masson, André

4463. Beatty, Frances Fielding Lewis. "André Masson and the Imagery of Surrealism." Columbia U. 1981. 704 pp. *DAI 1983 44(1): 3-4-A.* DA8307547 1922-26

Mastrilli, Marcello

4464. Volpe, Angela. MARCELLO MASTRILLI: UNA VITA PER LE MISSIONI [Marcello Mastrilli: a life for the missions]. *Archivum Historicum Societatis Iesu [Italy] 1985 54(108): 333-345.* Excerpts chosen from unofficial letters of a 17th-century Jesuit missionary in East Asia, Marcello Mastrilli, reveal the apostolic fervor he and men of his time brought to their missionary tasks. 1630's

Mathiez, Albert

4465. Godechot, Jacques; Simakov, E. Iu., transl. AL'BER MAT'EZ [Albert Mathiez]. *Frantsuzskii Ezhegodnik [USSR] 1982: 165-173.* Warm personal tribute to French historian Mathiez (1874-1932) by a pupil, disciple, and admirer. Mathiez's *La Révolution Française* (1922) and lectures at the Sorbonne 1927-28 had a profound influence on Godechot's choice of profession and involvement in the history of the French Revolution. 13 notes. French summary. 1920's

Matinolli, Eero Antero

4466. Virrankoski, Pentti. MUISTOSANAT TURUN HISTORIALLISEN YHDISTYKSEN TUTKIJAJÄSENESTÄ DOSENTTI EERO ANTERO MATINOLLISTA (29.6.1924-9.6.1981) [Memorial for the research member of the Turku Historical Society, docent Eero Antero Matinolli (29 June 1924-9 June 1981)]. *Turun Hist. Arkisto [Finland] 1982 37: 280-282.* An obituary for Matinolli, specialist in Finnish clerical and cultural history of the 18th century. 1924-81

Matković, Anto

4467. Bojović, Jovan R. JEDAN RAZGOVOR SA ANTOM MATKOVIĆEM [A conversation with Anto Matković]. *Istorijski Zapisi [Yugoslavia] 1983 36(3-4): 161-182.* An interview with Anto Matković (1893-1980) on 26 June 1967. Matković, who was a founder of the Communist Party in Kotor, described his life as a Communist and freedom fighter between 1919 and 1944. He focused on his organization of the Communist Party in Kotor, his trials and periods of imprisonment, and the Yugoslav National Liberation struggle of 1941-44 in which he played a large part. 1919-44

Mátrai, László

4468. Hermann, István. MÁTRAI LÁSZLÓ 1909-1983 [László Mátrai (1909-83)]. *Magyar Tudomány [Hungary] 1984 29(3): 245-247.* Obituary for László Mátrai, Hungarian Marxist philosopher. Mátrai was a university professor and director of the University Library in Budapest. His most important area of work was the history of philosophy. He was a humanist philosopher whose interests also included classical psychology. 1930-83

Matsugi family

4469. Sasamoto, Shouji. KINSEI NO IMOJI TO MATSUGI KE *[Imoji* and the Matsugi family in the modern period]. *Rekishigaku Kenkyū [Japan] 1984 (534): 91-99.* In the early modern period, the influence of the Matsugi family on metalcasters *(imoji)* decreased. But in the late 17th century, when increased demand provoked severe competition among metalcasters they voluntarily rekindled a relationship with the family, which acted as their arbitrator. At the beginning of the 18th century, the Matsugi family strengthened its control over the casters by issuing licenses and utilizing the authority of the Imperial court. However, metalcasters remained an autonomous group. Using the Matsugi family as authority, they formed a price cartel in order to prevent competition and control the tinkers *(ikake).* Based on Matsugi family papers and other primary sources; 2 tables. 17c-1850

Matsuura Takeshirō

4470. Dettmer, Hans A. EIN JAPANISCHER FORSCHUNGSREISENDER DES 19. JAHRHUNDERTS: MATSUURA TAKESHIRŌ [A Japanese explorer of the 19th century: Matsuura Takeshirō]. *Oriens [Netherlands] 1981 27-28: 538-555.* Matsuura Takeshirō (1818-88), author of 240 titles, has been largely ignored by Japanese geographers and historians. He early developed a passion for mountain climbing and pilgrimages to shrines and temples. From 1844 to 1858 he dedicated himself to the exploration of Japan's northern border region, traveling extensively in Ezo (now Hokkaido—a name which he later proposed) and to Kita-Ezo (Sakhalin) and the southern Kurils. He prepared detailed illustrated journals for each of his journeys and later assisted also in the preparation of an atlas of Hokkaido. Based on *Teihon Matsuura Takeshirō,* 2 vol. (Tokyo: 1972-73) and other sources; 149 notes. 1818-88

Mattei, Enrico

4471. Charlier, Jean-Michel. LE SDECE A-T-IL ASSASSINE MATTEI? [Did the SDECE assassinate Mattei?]. *Historama [France] 1984 (3): 93-97.* Follows the career of Italian oil magnate Enrico Mattei from 1945 to his death in a plane crash in 1962, and subsequent investigation into the manner of his death, which might have been planned by the Mafia or by the French intelligence and counterespionage agency (SDECE). 1945-80

Matteotti, Giacomo

4472. Mack Smith, Denis. L'ASSASSINIO DI MATTEOTTI [The assassination of Giacomo Matteotti]. *Rassegna degli Archivi di Stato [Italy] 1983 43(2-3): 351-363.* Also published in English in the *Italian Quarterly* 1983 24(93). 1924-26

4473. Mack Smith, Denis. THE MURDER OF MATTEOTTI. *Italian Q. 1983 24(93): 11-20.* Describes the assassination of Giacomo Matteotti, Italian socialist, in 1924, and the consequent investigation. The author suggests that there is little doubt that Benito Mussolini was responsible for his political opponent's murder. 1924-26

4474. Mack Smith, Denis. L'AFFAIRE MATTEOTTI [The Matteotti affair]. *Histoire [France] 1983 (52): 10-18.* Describes the abduction and murder of opposition leader Giacomo Matteotti in 1924 by Mussolini henchmen as part of the violent terrorist activities conducted during the early years of Italian fascism. 1922-24

Matthews, John

4475. Thomas, Colin. LAND SURVEYORS IN WALES, 1750-1850: THE MATTHEWS FAMILY. *Bulletin of the Board of Celtic Studies [Great Britain] 1985 32: 216-232.* Discusses the activities of Edward Matthews (1727-1800) and more especially his son, John Matthews (1773-1848), whose business and domestic life is examined. The proprietors in North Wales for whom John Matthews worked are described, as are the difficulties of the surveying work and Matthews's activities in reassessing and valuing estates such as Lord Mostyn's at Bodidris and Corsygedol. Reference is also made to the importance of the work of John Matthews, Jr. (b. 1808). Based on a series of diaries, letters, and a ledger of surveying accounts, maps, and drawings at the University College of North Wales and documents at the Record Offices of Clwyd and Gwynedd, Wales, as well as secondary sources; 98 notes, fig. 1750-1850

Matthias

4476. Wacha, Georg. MATTHIAS ARCHIDUX AUSTRIAE [Matthias Archidux Austriae]. *Mitteilungen des Oberösterreichischen Landesarchivs [Austria] 1984 14: 231-240.* Discusses the personality of Austrian Archduke Matthias, King of Hungary from 1608 and Holy Roman Emperor, 1612-19. 3 plates. 1579-1619

Matthias, Erich

4477. —. [ERICH MATTHIAS]. *Int. Wiss. Korrespondenz zur Gesch. der Deutschen Arbeiterbewegung [West Germany] 1981 17(3): 409-418.*

Weber, Hermann. ERICH MATTHIAS 60 JAHRE [Erich Matthias at 60], *pp. 409-413.* Describes the life and research of Erich Matthias, a social and political scientist whose work on political parties is particularly valuable.

Kukuck, Horst-A. VERZEICHNIS DER SCHRIFTEN VON ERICH MATTHIAS [Listing of the publications of Erich Matthias], *pp. 413-418.* 1940's-81

Mattick, Paul

4478. Dingel, Frank. PAUL MATTICK (1904-1981) [Paul Mattick (1904-81)]. *Internationale Wissenschaftliche Korrespondenz zur Geschichte der Deutschen Arbeiterbewegung [West Germany] 1981 17(2): 190-197.* Discusses the life and theories of the German radical Communist Paul Mattick, who was active in German and American Communist parties and movements from the 1920's. 1918-81

Maurenbrecher, Max

4479. Fricke, Dieter. NATIONALSOZIALE VERSUCHE ZUR FÖRDERUNG DER KRISE DER DEUTSCHEN SOZIALDEMOKRATIE: ZUM BRIEFWECHSEL ZWISCHEN MAX MAURENBRECHER UND FRIEDRICH NAUMANN 1910-1913 [National socialist attempts at promoting a crisis in German social democracy: the correspondence between Max Maurenbrecher and Friedrich Naumann, 1910-13]. *Beiträge zur Gesch. der Arbeiterbewegung [East Germany] 1983 25(4): 537-548.* Traces the life, political activities, and writings of Max Maurenbrecher (1874-1930), assessing the part that he played in the transformation of the Social Democratic Party in Germany into a reformist labor party. The letters reproduced here were written by Maurenbrecher to Friedrich Naumann between 1910 and 1913, and illustrate Maurenbrecher's differences from other German socialists. In 1914 Maurenbrecher's politics went further to the right and he became a cofounder of the "Fatherland Society" in 1914. Based on Maurenbrecher's letters located in Potsdam and secondary sources; 50 notes. 1910-13

Mauriac, Claude

4480. Mauriac, Claude. LE RELIRE ET LE RETROUVER [To read him again and find him again]. *Revue des Deux Mondes [France] 1985 (8): 282-286.* A French novelist and critic brings back memories of his childhood, when, through his father, writer, member of the French Academy and Nobel Prize laureate François Mauriac, he knew André Maurois (1885-1967) and tells how he became a friend of the renowned biographer, novelist, and member of the French Academy, whom he admires greatly today. 1930's-67

Mauriac, François

4481. Chochon, Bernard. MAURIAC, SOURCIER TRAGIQUE DE L'ENFANCE DANS LE "BLOC-NOTES" [Mauriac, tragic diviner of childhood in the "Bloc-Notes"]. *Revue d'Histoire Littéraire de la France [France] 1985 85(6): 1011-1026.* Childhood was one of the themes of autobiographical reflection and metaphor in a series of newspaper columns by French novelist François Mauriac, published between 1952 and 1970 in *L'Express* and *Le Figaro Littéraire.* ca 1890's-1910

4482. Pereira, Paulette J. "The Impact of the German Occupation of France upon Four French Intellectuals: Charles Maurras, Pierre Drieu la Rochelle, Henry de Montherlant, and François Mauriac." Am. U. 1985. 221 pp. *DAI 1986 46(8): 2415-A.* DA8522268 1940-44

Maurice of Saxony

4483. Pérez Tenreiro, Tomás. MAURICIO DE SAJONIA [Maurice of Saxony]. *Bol. de la Acad. Nac. de la Hist. [Venezuela] 1983 66(264): 973-984.* Describes the career and ideas of this unusual 18th-century military leader and philanderer, whose ideas seem to have influenced Simón Bolívar's military conceptions, especially the notion that the science of war has no principles or rules and that none of the great captains who wrote on war had given any rules. Bolívar was accused of being irresponsible when he uttered a similar opinion. 4 notes. 1696-1750

Maurois, André

4484. Dordet, Danielle. MON AMI DU TRAIN [My train companion]. *Revue des Deux Mondes [France] 1985 (8): 358-364.* A French journalist recalls her intimate conversations with famous novelist and biographer André Maurois (1885-1967) during trips which, as a coincidence, they both happened to make regularly on the same trains. 1960's

4485. Droit, Michel. ETRE UNE VOLONTE [To have willpower]. *Revue des Deux Mondes [France] 1985 (8): 299-301.* Expresses his admiration for willpower and comments on this trait in André Maurois (1885-1967), who possessed it to a high degree, as evidenced by the famous French writer's courageous stand against adversity through his life. 1885-1967

4486. Dumoncel, Maurice. ANDRE MAUROIS ET L'ANGLETERRE [André Maurois and England]. *Revue des Deux Mondes [France] 1985 (8): 325-338.* A study of the efforts exercised by famous French novelist and biographer André Maurois (1885-1967), particularly through his literary works, to help the French understand the English and to promote friendly relations between France and England. 1918-40

4487. Gautier, Jean-Jacques. COURTES NOUVELLES, POEMES EN PROSE [Short stories, poems in prose]. *Revue des Deux Mondes [France] 1985 (8): 308-310.* Comments on the short stories and tales written by André Maurois (1885-1967), in which the famous French writer showed his particular style and attractive talents. ca 1930-60

4488. Guth, Paul. PREMIERE RENCONTRE [First meeting]. *Revue des Deux Mondes [France] 1985 (8): 287-292.* An account of a visit with André Maurois in his studio in 1951 and comments on the famous French biographer and novelist's philosophy, stressing his remarkable gifts of being a universal educator as well as a novelist. 1951

4489. Narkirier, Fedor. ANDRE MAUROIS ET L'U.R.S.S. [André Maurois and the USSR]. *Revue des Deux Mondes [France] 1985 (8): 339-357.* Twenty letters between André Maurois (1885-1967), French biographer, novelist, and critic, and Fedor Narkirier, Soviet author, from 1964 through 1967, on topics of French literature and intellectual life. 1964-67

4490. Rivoyre, Christine de. UNE AME ACCUEILLANTE [A friendly soul]. *Revue des Deux Mondes [France] 1985 (8): 293-298.* A writer who was literary director of the French magazine *Marie-Claire* during the 1950's and 1960's recalls her business relations with famous biographer and novelist André Maurois (1885-1967), who was a contributor to this magazine, and stresses his particularly affable and friendly personality. 1950's-60's

4491. Troyat, Henri. PERMANENCE D'ANDRE MAUROIS [A permanent remembrance about André Maurois]. *Revue des Deux Mondes [France] 1985 (8): 275-281.* A writer and member of the French Academy recalls events about his personal relations with famous French biographer and novelist, also a member of the French Academy, André Maurois, pen name of Emile Salomon Wilhelm Herzog (1885-1967). ca 1930-67

Maurras, Charles

4492. Pereira, Paulette J. "The Impact of the German Occupation of France upon Four French Intellectuals: Charles Maurras, Pierre Drieu la Rochelle, Henry de Montherlant, and François Mauriac." Am. U. 1985. 221 pp. *DAI 1986 46(8): 2415-A.* DA8522268 1940-44

Mavrocordat, Irina

4493. Spiridoneanu, Mircea. DIN VIENA MARELUI RĂZBOI [From Vienna during the Great War]. *Rev. Arhivelor [Romania] 1982 44(2): 169-179, (3): 264-271.* Part 1. From the diary of Irina Mavrocordat (1864-1955), wife of a Romanian diplomat in Vienna, covering part of November-December 1914. Includes political and personal gossip. Annotated and with a full introduction. Part 2. Further extracts from the Viennese diary of Irina Mavrocordat, wife of a Romanian diplomat, covering December 1914. 1914

Mavrokordatos, Alexander

4494. Cernovodeanu, Paul and Caratasu, Mihail. CORRESPONDANCE DIPLOMATIQUE D'ALEXANDRE MAVROCORDATO L'EXAPORITE, 1676-1703 (1) [The diplomatic correspondence of Alexander Mavrokordatos, the private counselor, 1676-1703. Part 1]. *Rev. des Etudes Sud-Est Européennes [Romania] 1982 20(1): 93-128.* After a biographical sketch of Alexander Mavrokordatos (1641-1709), analyzes in detail the correspondence, 1676-1703, of the Ottoman diplomat of Greek origin, which consists of 326 letters (210 in Greek and 116 in Italian or Latin). These are followed by the text of 19 of the letters, almost all addressed to Transylvania's chancellor, Mihaly Teleki. Based on Austrian, Hungarian, English, French, Romanian, and Turkish official and private archives and other primary sources; 4 photos, 123 notes. 1676-1703

Mavrokordatos, Constantine

4495. Vlad, Matei D. UN PRINCIPE LUMINAT PE TRONUL ŢĂRILOR ROMÂNE: CONSTANTIN MAVROCORDAT [An enlightened prince on the throne of the Romanian tsars: Constantin Mavrocordat]. *Magazin Istoric [Romania] 1981 15(11): 40-44.* For much of the period from 1730 until his death in 1769 Constantine Mavrocordat in various capacities ruled over Moldavia as the Phanariot nominee of the Ottoman sultan and was known for his reformist policies. 1730-69

Mawdudi, Abul 'Ala

4496. Barua, B. P. THE POLITICAL THEORY OF MAULANA MAUDUDI. *Indian Pol. Sci. Rev. [India] 1982 16(2): 225-233.* Mawlana Abul 'Ala Mawdudi (b. 1903) was a renowned Islamic thinker, writer, and publicist as well as an active politician. His movement, Jamaat-i-Islami, was one of the most significant forces in contemporary Islam and Pakistan. He played a central role in the controversy over the Islamic constitution of Pakistan and the debates over the definition of an Islamic state. Article traces the evolution of his thought. 44 notes. 1920-56

4497. Pochoy, Michel. LA VIE DE MAULANA SAIYYED ABUL A'LA MAUDOUDI [The life of Mawlana Sayyid Abul 'Ala Mawdudi]. *Afrique et l'Asie Modernes [France] 1985-86 (147): 17-31.* A deeper understanding of the Islamic integrist movement of the 1970's-80's can be gained from a consideration of Muslim nationalist leader Mawlana Sayyid Abul 'Ala Mawdudi (1903-79), who sought to create an Islamic state while India was still under British domination, and continued after the founding of Pakistan to campaign for the incorporation of Islamic law into its constitution. 1919-79

Maximilian I

4498. Scholz-Williams, Gerhild. THE LITERARY WORLD OF MAXIMILIAN I: AN ANNOTATED BIBLIOGRAPHY. *Sixteenth Cent. Biblio. 1982 (21): 1-67.* Entire issue devoted to Maximilian's literary activities and his influence on the literary production of his time with an introductory biography of the emperor (1459-1519) and a bibliography of secondary works. 1486-1519

4499. Vodosek, Peter. HERMANN WIESFLECKER: KAISER MAXIMILIAN I [Hermann Wiesflecker: Emperor Maximilian I]. *Österreich in Geschichte und Literatur [Austria] 1985 29(3-4): 159-162.* Critiques the work by the Austrian historian Hermann Wiesflecker, *Das Reich, Österreich und Europa an der Wende zur Neuzeit,* Bd. 1-5 [The empire, Austria, and Europe at the transition to modernity, vol. 1-5, 1971-81]. The first four volumes provide a biography of the Austrian Emperor Maximilian I and describe his youth and aspects of Austrian foreign and domestic policy during his rule from 1508-19. The fifth volume was proposed for publication in 1985 and was to place Maximilian I's life and rule in the context of the Austrian state, economy, and culture at the time he lived. 1508-19

4500. Wiesflecker, Hermann. MAXIMILIAN UND DIE PÄPSTE SEINER ZEIT [Maximilian and the popes of his time]. *Römische Hist. Mitteilungen [Austria] 1980 22: 147-165.* Considers the stormy relationships between the Holy Roman Emperor Maximilian I (1459-1519) and the popes who held office between 1493 and 1519. These disputes highlighted the struggles between Maximilian and the French to retain the support of the Holy See. Maximilian wanted to retain his authority over the papacy but the popes were concerned with securing the Holy See, retaining the freedom of the papacy, freeing Italy from foreign influences, and keeping peace among the Christian powers in order to unite against the Turks. Accordingly the popes tried to diminish Maximilian's influence on the Church and sought closer relationships with France. This was one of the factors which led to the separation between Rome and the Holy Roman Empire, which was also influenced by the Reformation in Germany. Secondary sources; note. 1493-1519

4501. Wiesflecker, Hermann. NEUE BEITRÄGE ZUM GESANDTSCHAFTSWESEN MAXIMILIANS I [New contributions to the diplomatic conduct of Maximilian I]. *Römische Hist. Mitteilungen [Austria] 1981 23: 303-317.* Maximilian I (1459-1519) sought more active diplomatic relationships with other European powers than his predecessors to pursue his aim of universal unity among the Christian powers. The author traces the origins of diplomacy in Italy, France, Burgundy, and especially Venice during the 15th century, and considers how Maximilian established and maintained his system of diplomatic links throughout Europe, 1493-1519. At first he had no regular ambassadors but relied on his court officials and noblemen. The most important matters were discussed by his close confidants, but he always made the final decisions. For less important business he made use of "neighbor" diplomacy. The countries in which he had particularly strong diplomatic ties were Switzerland and the Netherlands. The author also describes Maximilian's ambassadors, the communications network between the emperor's court and the ambassadors, and the cost of maintaining the embassies. Biblio. 1493-1519

Maximus

4502. Obolensky, Dimitri. ITALY, MOUNT ATHOS, AND MUSCOVY: THE THREE WORLDS OF MAXIMOS THE GREEK (C. 1470-1556). *Pro. of the British Acad. [Great Britain] 1981 67: 143-161.* The career of Maximus the Greek, born Michael Trivolis, spanned the three cultural worlds of Italy, Greece, and Muscovy. Studying theology in Florence, he was influenced by Platonism and Savonarola, but in 1505 or 1506 for unknown reasons joined the cosmopolitan monastery of Mount Athos, where he immersed himself in Byzantine religious and secular literature. Called to Russia in 1518 to translate Greek texts into Slavonic for use against heresy, he became embroiled in the controversy over monastic landholding and was imprisoned for 23 years. Released in about 1548, he continued to be a widely renowned writer and teacher at St. Sergius monastery in Zagorsk. Based on printed sources and secondary works; 64 notes. 1500's-56

May, Ernst

4503. Lane, Barbara Miller. ARCHITECTS IN POWER: POLITICS AND IDEOLOGY IN THE WORK OF ERNST MAY AND ALBERT SPEER. *Journal of Interdisciplinary History 1986 17(1): 283-310.* Both Ernst May, municipal architect for Frankfurt am Main, Germany, and Albert Speer, architect of the Third Reich, believed that the people's welfare was served by the guidance of the expert rather than by democratic process. Both achieved positions of power to achieve their goals, but they were builders first, politicians second. May's low-cost green-belt housing mixed local and international historical references with elements of the international style. He expected that the new architecture would affect behavior, and he sought to build a new society out of the best of the old. Speer's architecture was influenced by the modern movement but included details that harkened back to traditional styles. His architecture conveyed a sense of theater and preserved the appearance of the old in the service of new, monumental architecture. 11 photos, 25 notes. 1920's-45

May, Kenneth Ownsworth

4504. Jones, Charles V.; Enros, Philip C.; and Tropp, Henry S. KENNETH O. MAY, 1915-1977: HIS EARLY LIFE TO 1946. *Historia Mathematica 1984 11(4): 359-379.* Prints the first part of a biography of Kenneth Ownsworth May (1915-77), American historian of mathematics, who traveled to England, Europe, and the USSR in the late 1930's, returned to the United States, joined the Communist Party, served in the army in World War II, finished a PhD at the University of California, Berkeley, in 1946, and obtained an assistant professorship at Carleton College in Northfield, Minnesota. 1915-46

Maya, Rafael

4505. —. FALLECIMIENTO DEL ACADEMICO DE NUMERO DON RAFAEL MAYA [Death of the Academician Rafael Maya]. *Bol. de Hist. y Antigüedades [Colombia] 1980 67(730): 365-415.*

—. RAFAEL MAYA, NOTA BIOBIBLIOGRAFICA [Rafael Maya, biobibliographic note], *pp. 367-370.*

Santa, Eduardo. RECUERDOS DE RAFAEL MAYA [Recollections of Rafael Maya], *pp. 402-415.*

Obituary, biobibliography, and various tributes to Rafael Maya (1898-1980). He introduced new stylistic approaches to Colombian literature in the period between the wars and was a major poet and an exceptional prose writer and literary critic. 1920's-80

Mayakovski, Vladimir

4506. Marutian, M. L. K BIOGRAFII V. V. MAIAKOVSKOGO (PO MATERIALAM TSGALI SSR) [Toward a biography of Vladimir Mayakovski: based on materials of the Central State Archives of Literature and Art of the USSR]. *Sovetskie Arkhivy [USSR] 1983 (2): 44-47.* The archive of Vladimir Mayakovski has not yet been fully researched, as is shown by the analysis of little-known material presented in this article. Many of the letters to Mayakovski have yet to be published, and some of his correspondence, notes, and autographs have yet to be located. The work of the researcher is hampered by the fact that documents are scattered in a number of archives. This problem could be overcome by the compilation of a catalog of the author's works. Based on the Central State Archives of Literature and Art of the USSR and secondary sources; 44 notes. 1908-30

4507. Pallister, Janis L. APOLLINAIRE AND MAYAKOVSKY: SOME PARALLELS. *East European Quarterly 1985 19(1): 95-103.* ca 1900-30
*For abstract see **Apollinaire, Guillaume***

Mayer, Emile

4508. Lerner, Henri. LE COLONEL EMILE MAYER ET SON CERCLE D'AMIS [Colonel Emile Mayer and his circle of friends]. *Rev. Hist. [France] 1981 266(1): 75-94.* Colonel Emile Mayer (1851-1938) was one of the few military thinkers in France capable of influencing Charles de Gaulle. Mayer was one of the most flexible and independent minds in the French army between the 1890's and 1930's. He criticized official policies publicly, which alienated the high command. He influenced a wide circle of friends. He foresaw the preeminence of defense in World War I and of the airplane thereafter. Based on Mayer's writings; 57 notes. 1890's-1938

Mayer, Enrico

4509. Tramarollo, Giuseppe. ENRICO MAYER UN PEDAGOGISTA DEL RISORGIMENTO [Enrico Mayer, an educationalist of the Risorgimento]. *Risorgimento [Italy] 1983 35(1): 67-75.* The Risorgimento, a movement of national regeneration, produced many men involved with the problem of education. Enrico Mayer (1802-77) was especially interested in popular education. His philosophy is derived from a careful study of European systems of public and private education. Against the contemporary current of uncritical admiration of the English system, Mayer pointed out its implicit elitist character. 23 notes. 1820's-77

Mayer, Karol

4510. Meissner, Roman. ŚWIATOWY PRIORYTET KAROLA MAYERA W DZIEDZINIE RADIODIAGNOSTYKI—PRZYCZYNEK DO DZIEJÓW TOMOGRAFII [The world priority of Karol Mayer in diagnostic radiology: a contribution to the history of tomography]. *Kwartalnik Hist. Nauki i Techniki [Poland] 1982 27(1): 125-137.* Karol Mayer (1882-1946), a Hungarian-born Polish roentgenologist, professor, and head of the first radiology department in Poland (Poznań, 1921), has been unjustly bypassed by historians concerning his contributions to early tomography—today, as computed tomography, a valuable diagnostic method. By moving the X-ray tube to obtain a focused picture of the object, Mayer obtained the first ever heart tomogram. Based on archival, journal, and secondary sources; 10 illus., 24 notes. Russian and English summaries. 1920's-30's

Mayer, Otto

4511. Heyen, Erk Volkmar. OTTO MAYERS KIRCHENRECHT UND DIE VERFASSUNG DER EVANGELISCH-LUTHERISCHEN KIRCHE IN ELSASS-LOTHRINGEN UND POLEN [Otto Mayer's church law and the constitution of the Evangelical Lutheran Church in Alsace-Lorraine and Poland]. *Zeits. der Savigny-Stiftung für Rechtsgeschichte [West Germany] 1979 96(Kanonistische): 239-264.* Otto Mayer (1846-1924) is well known as a theorist of administrative law, but he has been forgotten as an authority on church law. As a minister and professor in Alsace-Lorraine until 1902, when he moved to Leipzig, he was deeply involved in the organization of the Protestant community in the newly reconquered territories. He expected that the church would be separated from the state in time, and he promoted the creation of a loose, tolerant synodical governance for ecclesiastical communities. In 1917 he prepared a draft of a constitution for the Evangelical and Augustana Church in Poland with theologian Franz Rendtorff. Based on original manuscript and printed sources; 49 notes, text of draft constitution. 1880-1917

Mayer, René

4512. Gerbet, Pierre. RENE MAYER, PRESIDENT DE LA HAUTE AUTORITE DE LA COMMUNAUTE EUROPEENNE DU CHARBON ET DE L'ACIER [René Mayer, President of the High Authority of the European Coal and Steel Community]. *Revue d'Histoire de la Deuxième Guerre Mondiale et des Conflits Contemporains [France] 1986 36(141): 95-110.* René Mayer was chosen president of the High Authority of the European Coal and Steel Community in 1955, after the retirement of its founder, Jean Monnet. Mayer was an excellent choice for a position which required diplomatic skill and political stature. Mayer had faith in the supranational principle and firm administrative skills which made the institutions of the community function. He was not always supported by the council and often sided with the Germans. He made two trips to the United States and promoted good relations with nonmembers of the community. He apparently lost interest or faith in supranationalism and resigned at the end of 1957, for which he received some criticism. Based on Mayer's journal; 18 notes. 1955-57

4513. Palewski, Gaston. PROPOS [Remarks]. *Rev. des Deux Mondes [France] 1983 (4): 128-136.* ca 1860-1983
For abstract see ***Chirac, Jacques***

4514. Pedroncini, Guy, ed. "JOURNAL" DE RENE MAYER (27 FEVRIER 1944-6 FEVRIER 1945) [René Mayer's journal, 27 February 1944 to 6 February 1945]. *Rev. d'Hist. de la Deuxième Guerre Mondiale et des Conflits Contemporaine [France] 1983 33(129): 69-97.* In 1944, while René Mayer was in exile in Algeria he began keeping notes for a more extensive journal which he never wrote. He continued to make notes on his daily work after his return to Paris after the liberation of France. The document was released for publication by his widow and reveals much about French public life in 1944-45. 1944-45

4515. Poidevin, Raymond. RENE MAYER ET LA POLITIQUE EXTERIEURE DE LA FRANCE (1943-1953) [René Mayer and French foreign policy (1943-53)]. *Revue d'Histoire de la Deuxième Guerre Mondiale et des Conflits Contemporains [France] 1984 34(134): 73-97.* Much of René Mayer's career between 1943 and 1953 concerned French foreign policy, especially the problems of Germany's role in the future of Europe. While serving as president of the council in 1953, he participated in a variety of important international discussions and agreements, including the policies of the European Coal and Steel Community, the European Defense Community, policies relating to the Indo-Chinese War, and the work of the United Nations. Based on Mayer's archives; 136 notes. 1943-53

Mayerhöfer, Heinz

4516. Ferenc, Tone. DNEVNIK NACISTIČNEGA FUNKCIONARJA NA ŠTAJERSKEM IZ POSLEDNJIH MESECEV VOJNE [Diary of the Nazi functionary in Styria from the last months of the war]. *Časopis za Zgodovino in Narodopisje [Yugoslavia] 1982 18(2): 43-97.* The personal diary of the Nazi functionary Heinz Mayerhöfer from Lower Styria has data from 1 November 1944 to 1 May 1945. At that time SA-Oberführer Mayerhöfer was the leader of the protective sections of the third (Brežice) and first (Ptuj) security territory of the police of Lower Styria and finally from February to the end of the war district leader of the Styrian patriotic league (Heimatbund) and councillor of the district of Celje. The diary was written in German, with a pencil into two exercise-books and has been kept in the archives of the Institute for the History of the Labor Movement at Ljubljana. 1944-45

Maynard, Constance

4517. Vicinus, Martha. VIVERE INSIEME: *COLLEGE WOMEN* INGLESI TRA FINE '800 E INIZIO '900 [Living together: English college women at the turn of the century]. *Memoria: Riv. di Storia delle Donne [Italy] 1982 (4): 45-58.* 1870-1920
For abstract see ***Davies, Emily***

Mayne, William

4518. Ward, S. G. P. MAJOR MONSOON. *J. of the Soc. for Army Hist. Res. [Great Britain] 1981 59(238): 65-70.* Chronicles the life of British soldier, William Mayne (1775-1843), especially his career as a military officer, which served as the basis for Charles Lever's acclaimed novels of war on the Iberian Peninsula. 1805-10

Mayo, George Elton

4519. Bourke, Helen. INDUSTRIAL UNREST AS SOCIAL PATHOLOGY: THE AUSTRALIAN WRITINGS OF ELTON MAYO. *Hist. Studies [Australia] 1982 20(79): 217-233.* An account of the early career and writings of George Elton Mayo, who left Australia in 1922 for the United States, where he was professor of industrial research at the Harvard Business School from 1926 to 1947 and became a pioneer in the human relations approach to labor studies. From 1911 to 1922 he taught philosophy at the University of Queensland, and there his basic approach to industrial problems evolved. In *Democracy and Freedom* (1919) he sought an alternative to the class conflict approach and focused on the need for understanding of a person's social role. He hoped "spontaneous co-operation" would succeed laissez-faire or that by devices like arbitration amelioration would be achieved. He turned to anthropology (and entertained Malinowski in Australia) and psychology. He concluded that revolutionaries were neurotics whose fantasy life dominated their concept of reality. He believed that the unconscious mind of the worker was more important than his rational intellect, and the solutions to labor problems were to be found in the social and psychological context of the workplace rather than in the processes of arbitration and collective bargaining. Based on Mayo's papers; 63 notes. 1880-1947

Mayreder, Rosa

4520. Reiss, Mary-Ann. ROSA MAYREDER: PIONEER OF AUSTRIAN FEMINISM. *International Journal of Women's Studies [Canada] 1984 7(3): 207-216.* Reviews the life and works of feminist Rosa Mayreder, author, painter, and musician. 1858-1938

Mazarin, Jules

4521. Bonney, Richard. THE PARADOX OF MAZARIN. *Hist. Today [Great Britain] 1982 32(Feb): 18-24.* Discusses the paradox of Cardinal Jules Mazarin, chief minister of Louis XIV from 1643 to 1661. Born Giulio Mazarini in Italy, he barely spoke or wrote French and was said by some to know little of France's domestic affairs; although he was a cardinal, he was never a priest, and he was also the target of intense criticism during "the great political upheaval of the Fronde between 1648 ad 1653." 1629-61

4522. Dessert, Daniel. MAZARIN: COMMENT LE POUVOUIR AMENE LA FORTUNE [Mazarin: how power brings fortune]. *Histoire [France] 1985 (81): 48-55.* An account of the wealth Cardinal Mazarin acquired thanks to his political position. 17c

4523. Grillon, Pierre. MAZARIN, UN HOMME DE PAIX A L'AGE BAROQUE [Mazarin, a man of peace in the baroque age]. *Rev. d'Hist. Diplomatique [France] 1982 96(1-2): 138-157.* Various reflections originating from an evaluation of the recent book by Georges Dethan, *Mazarin, un Homme de Paix à l'Âge Baroque* (1981). For many readers, this book about the private personality of Mazarin, a man who has been shamefully slandered, will be a revelation. 21 notes. 1630-61

Mazepa, Ivan

4524. Mackiw, Theodore. A BRIEF BIOGRAPHY OF MAZEPA: HETMAN OF UKRAINE AND PRINCE OF THE HOLY ROMAN EMPIRE, 1639-1709. *Ukrainian Review [Great Britain] 1984 32(1): 53-61, (2): 69-78; 1985 33(2): 67-72.* Continued from previous articles. Part 3. The Cossack Hetman Mazepa fought in the Great Northern War for Peter I of Russia, allied with Augustus II of Poland, against Charles XII of Sweden, freeing Livonia from Sweden and much of the Ukraine from a weakened Poland. Discusses negotiations behind Joseph I's granting Mazepa the title of Prince of the Holy Roman Empire. Part 4. Chronicles the obstructions of Sweden, Poland, and Russia to General Ivan Mazepa's independence movement aimed at a Ukrainian state under the protection of the Ottoman Empire. Part 5. Mazepa allied with Sweden so his rebellion against Russian oppression of Ukrainian Cossacks would be more effective. 1700-11

4525. [Mackiw, Theodore]. HETMAN MAZEPA V PRATSIIAKH M. HRUSHEVS'KOHO [Hetman Mazepa in the studies of Mikhail S. Hrushevsky]. *Ukrains'kyi Istoryk 1984 21(1-4): 111-122.* Discusses various works pertaining to Ivan Mazepa (1639-1709), portrays the Cossack hetman in the light of the views of his contemporaries, and analyzes the publications devoted to him by the renowned Ukrainian historian Mikhail Hrushevsky (1866-1934). While Hrushevsky's evaluation of Mazepa is critical and severe, it is at the same time quite objective. 57 notes. 1639-1709

4526. Mackiw, Theodore. A BRIEF BIOGRAPHY OF MAZEPA: HETMAN OF UKRAINE AND PRINCE OF THE HOLY ROMAN EMPIRE, 1639-1709. *Ukrainian Rev. [Great Britain] 1983 31(2): 60-71, (4): 63-72.* Part 1. The career of Ivan Mazepa, elected chief executive or *Hetman* of the Ukraine in 1687, and the international politics of the area. Part 2. Ivan Mazepa, as a well-educated youth of noble Ukrainian birth, was a page in the royal court of Poland in the 1650's and 1660's, and later became associated with leaders of the Ukraine, finally rising to the post of hetman and pledging fealty to Peter I of Russia, whom he served as a military leader and adviser while, as hetman, he labored to strengthen and unify the Ukraine. Based on many contemporary published US, European and Russian sources; 95 notes. Article to be continued. 1654-1708

Mazrui, Al-Amin bin Ali

4527. Pouwels, Randall L. SH. AL-AMIN B. ALI MUZRUI AND ISLAMIC MODERNISM IN EAST AFRICA, 1875-1947. *Int. J. of Middle East Studies [Great Britain] 1981 13(3): 329-345.* Discusses the contributions of Sheik Al-Amin bin Ali Mazrui (1890-1947), administrator, author, and educator, to the process of modernization and reform in East Africa. Sheik Al-Amin was convinced of the universality of Islam and its appeal to many varieties of people. Moreover he thought Moslems should become skilled in Western science and technology in order to progress. Based on interviews and other primary sources; 60 notes. 1875-1947

Mazzini, Giuseppe

4528. Caratti, Lorenzo. UN CURIOSO COLLEGAMENTO CHIAVARESE FRA LA FAMIGLIA DI GIUSEPPE GARIBALDI E QUELLA DI GIUSEPPE MAZZINI [A curious Chiavarese relationship between the family of Giuseppe Garibaldi and that of Giuseppe Mazzini]. *Rassegna Storica del Risorgimento [Italy] 1982 69(1): 8-14.* 1736-76

For abstract see ***Garibaldi, Giuseppe***

4529. Flora, Giuseppe. STUDI MAZZINIANI IN INDIA A PROPOSITO DI UN RECENTE VOLUME [Studies of Giuseppe Mazzini in India with regard to a recent volume]. *Rassegna Storica del Risorgimento [Italy] 1983 70(1): 40-45.* A review of Gita Srivastava's *Mazzini and His Impact on the Indian National Movement* (1982). 1857-1945

4530. Monsagrati, Giuseppe. LETTERE INEDITE DI GIUSEPPE MAZZINI (1834-1869) NELLA BIBLIOTECA VATICANA [Unpublished letters of Giuseppe Mazzini, 1834-69, in the Vatican Library]. *Bol. della Domus Mazziniana [Italy] 1981 27(1): 5-50.* Reproduces the texts of 30 letters of Mazzini written to various correspondents in Italian, French, and English. The longest is written to a Swiss correspondent, Jules Thrumann, explaining to him the philosophy of his movement and inviting him to express his reaction to it. 1834-69

Mazzolari, Primo

4531. Miccoli, Giovanni. DON PRIMO MAZZOLARI: UNA PRESENZA CRISTIANA NELLA CRONACA E NELLA STORIA [Don Primo Mazzolari: a Christian presence in journalism and history]. *Cristianesimo nella Storia [Italy] 1985 6(3): 561-598.* Primo Mazzolari's (1890-1959) career as a rural preacher and forceful writer depended on his experiences as an observer of the anti-Modernist struggle at Cremona before World War I and as a chaplain during and immediately after the war. 1909-26

Mbacké, Ahmadu Bamba

4532. Mbacké, Serigne Bachir; Mbacké, Khadim, transl. LES BIENFAITS DE L'ETERNEL OU LA BIOGRAPHIE DE CHEIKH AHMADOU BAMBA MBACKE [The kindness of the eternal or the biography of Sheikh Ahmadu Bamba Mbacké]. *Bull. de l'Inst. Fondamental d'Afrique Noire. Série B [Senegal] 1980 42(3): 554-631.* A biography of Ahmadu Bamba Mbacké that traces his life and its intellectual and moral qualities with the emphasis on his modesty, courage, scruples, and generosity as he progressed through the nine steps of developing his Muslim faith. Illus., 119 notes. 19c-20c

Mboya, Tom

4533. Goldsworthy, David. ETHNICITY AND LEADERSHIP IN AFRICA: THE "UNTYPICAL" CASE OF TOM MBOYA. *J. of Modern African Studies [Great Britain] 1982 20(1): 107-126.* An analysis of Tom Mboya's career that attacks both the liberal image of the Kenyan labor and political leader as nonethnic or antitribal and the radical view that depicts him as an instrument of Western capitalism. Mboya as General Secretary of the Kenya Federation of Labor and a leader in the Kenya African National Union before and after independence in 1963 skillfully managed the "tribal" factor in Kenyan economic and political life to succeed as a South Nyanza Luo in a predominantly Kikuyu movement and capital city. In his political and economic moves, Mboya served his own position and those of fellow Kenyans, rather than the interest of outside countries or parties. Based on the author's 1982 biography of Mboya and research in Kenya; 39 notes. 1951-69

McArthur, Norma

4534. Yen, D. E. NORMA MCARTHUR: A PERSONAL POSTSCRIPT. *Journal of Pacific History [Australia] 1984 19(1-2): 60-63.* Norma McArthur (1921-84) devoted a lifetime to significant contributions in the demography, prehistory, and history of the Pacific Islands. Rather than follow the implications of the current interpretations of the cultural history of Hawaiian settlement, she focused critically on the dynamics of population change. A list of her writings from 1946 to 1982 is appended. Biblio. 1946-84

McColvin, Lionel Roy

4535. Harrison, K. C.; deParis, P. M.; Collison, R. L.; and Maidment, W. R. MCCOLVIN: A REVISION STUDY. *Lib. Rev. [Great Britain] 1983 32(Sum): 113-144.* A tribute to Lionel Roy McColvin who headed Westminster's library system from 1938 until 1961. He was a defender of his profession and claimed in 1947 that "there must be libraries if civilization is to survive." 1938-61

McCulloch, William

4536. McCulloch, Samuel Clyde. PRINCE OF BIDDERS: WILLIAM MCCULLOCH SPENDS HIS FORTUNE. *J. of the Royal Australian Hist. Soc. [Australia] 1982 68(3): 205-221.* William McCulloch (1832-1909), a Scottish immigrant to the Victorian gold fields in 1852, soon deserted fossicking and developed transportation on the diggings. From this grew a transport empire that dominated shipping on the Murray River and omnibus and trams in Melbourne. McCulloch spent vast sums importing breeding stock (2,000 guineas for a cow) and considerably influenced the development of Shorthorn and Ayrshire cattle, Clydesdales, Lincoln sheep, and Greyhounds in colonial Victoria. He virtually founded coursing as a sport in Victoria. Based on McCulloch Company Papers in Victorian Public Library and Victorian colonial newspapers; 95 notes. 1881-90

McCulloh, Henry

4537. Bumsted, J. M. A FORGOTTEN PROPHET: HENRY MCCULLOH AND REFORM OF THE BRITISH EMPIRE. *Can. Rev. of Am. Studies [Canada] 1982 13(1): 1-14.* Henry McCulloh, a North Carolina land-grabber and 18th-century pamphleteer, argued foresightedly in the 1750's for reform of British imperial controls over Great Britain's North American colonials. He described tensions that could induce colonials to separate from the empire. However, British authorities ignored his reform proposals, partly because the exigencies of Britain's war with France obscured the alarming undercurrents of colonial tension to which McCulloh pointed. Equally a handicap was McCulloh's lack of influential patrons in Britain for his ideas, which clashed with the assumptions of the Whig oligarchs in the London government. Based on British Museum manuscript materials and secondary sources; 47 notes. 1750's

McGregor, Gregor

4538. Wilkinson, D. M. THE MCGREGORS OF NORTHERN WAIROA. *Auckland Waikato Hist. J. [New Zealand] 1983 (42): 8-10.* Typical of many New Zealand pioneers, Gregor McGregor bought his remote claim in 1840, sold off his kauri timber for ship's spars, then settled into the role of cattleman with his family. 1840-1930

McKay, Claude

4539. Cooper, Wayne Foley. "Stranger and Pilgrim: The Life of Claude McKay, 1890-1948." Rutgers U. 1982. 891 pp. *DAI 1983 43(10): 3392-A.* DA8305737 1890-1948

McKenzie, Robert Trelford

4540. MacRae, Donald G. ROBERT TRELFORD MCKENZIE 1917-1981. *British J. of Sociol. [Great Britain] 1982 33(1): v-viii.* A tribute to the Canadian political scientist, sociologist, historian, and broadcaster Robert Trelford McKenzie. After World War II McKenzie spent most of his time in England and some of his most important work concerned the British political system. 1937-81

McNally, Charles

4541. Kerr, Donal. CHARLES MCNALLY: O'CONNELLITE BISHOP-REFORMING PASTOR. *Arch. Hibernicum [Ireland] 1982 37: 11-20.* Summarizes the career of Charles McNally (1788-1864) who was the son of a farmer. For several decades at Maynooth he was a supporter of the Union government, but by the 1840's he had become a repealer. In internal Church affairs he was a determined reformer. Uses unpublished letters in Clogher and other diocesan archives. 1820's-40's

McNally, Leonard

4542. Pitcher, E. W. LEONARD MCNALLY: A FEW FACTS ON A MINOR IRISH AUTHOR OF THE EIGHTEENTH CENTURY. *Notes and Queries [Great Britain] 1981 28(4): 306-308.* Brief biography of Irish farcist and satirist Leonard McNally (1752-1820), focusing on a few of his works, particularly his contributions to literary magazines and some other writings besides his theatrical productions. 1770's-94

McNeill, John James

4543. Bolton, H. C. J. J. MCNEILL AND THE DEVELOPMENT OF OPTICAL RESEARCH IN AUSTRALIA. *Historical Records of Australian Science [Australia] 1983 5(4): 55-70.* John James McNeill (1916-80) played a significant role in the development of research in optics in Australia, particularly during the war years of 1939-45 when he contributed to the development of optical munitions such as rangefinders, telescope sights, and other instruments. Much of his time was spent at the Munitions Supply Laboratory (MSL) where he worked as a physicist in the fields of electricity, heat, thermometry, and optics. McNeill's work on microscopes helped expand the capabilities of the physics section of MSL, and after the war McNeill continued his research as leader of the Specialized Optics Section at the CSIRO Division of Chemical Physics in Clayton. Primary sources; 91 notes. 1916-80

M'Cormick, Robert

4544. Jones, A. G. E. ROBERT M'CORMICK: DEPUTY INSPECTOR-GENERAL ROYAL NAVY. *Great Circle [Australia] 1982 4(2): 84-91.* Describes Robert M'Cormick's career as ship surgeon on a number of expeditions made by the British navy during the 19th century, the most notable being the hydrographic survey of South America with Charles Darwin aboard the *Beagle* during 1831-32. 19c

Mecenseffy, Grete

4545. —. GRETE MECENSEFFY, 1898-1985. *Mennonite Quarterly Review 1986 60(1): 104.* Provides an obituary of Grete Mecenseffy, who served as a member of the theology faculty at the University of Vienna and was noted for her historical studies of Austrian Protestantism. 1898-1985

Mecham, Clifford Henry

4546. Fraser, John. CAPTAIN CLIFFORD HENRY MECHAM. *J. of the Soc. for Army Hist. Res. [Great Britain] 1982 60(243): 166-180.* Captain Clifford Henry Mecham served in the British Army in India and drew scenes which he had witnessed in the army. 1831-65

Médici, Catherine de

4547. Stephens, J. N. L'INFANZIA FIORENTINA DI CATERINA DE' MEDICI, REGINA DI FRANCIA [The Florentine childhood of Catherine de Médici, queen of France]. *Archivio Storico Italiano [Italy] 1984 142(3): 421-436.* Describes the early life of Catherine de Médici (1519-89), who was born and raised in Florence. Catherine was the daughter of Lorenzo de' Medici (1492-1519) and Madeleine de la Tour d'Auvergne, whose marriage was arranged to link the powerful Medici family into the French crown. Catherine was probably placed in the Convent of Santa Lucia in 1527, although some historians suggest that she was sent to the Convent of Santa Caterina in Siena. The documents indicate that the French court displayed a continuous interest in Catherine's well-being and education, as did Pope Clement VII, who sought to strengthen Franco-Vatican ties. In 1533, Catherine married Henry, son of Francis I of France. Based on documents in the Archivio di Stato di Firenze and other Italian and French archives; 83 notes. 1519-33

Medici, Lorenzo de

4548. Bourassin, Emmanuel. LORENZACCIO, LE PLUS RATE DES MEDICIS [Lorenzaccio, the most unsuccessful of the Medicis]. *Historama [France] 1985 (13): 86-91.* Recounts the history of Lorenzo (Lorenzaccio or Lorenzino) de Medici (1514-48). Born into a poor branch of the Medicis, his father died when Lorenzino was 11, and the family took to the streets for a living. He plotted against the life of his cousin Alessandro, Duke of Florence. Following Alessandro's assassination, the socially disagreeable Lorenzino lived in poverty in Venice and France, and was finally murdered at the instigation of Alessandro's successor, Cosimo de Medici. 1514-48

4549. Dietz, Mary G. TRAPPING THE PRINCE: MACHIAVELLI AND THE POLITICS OF DECEPTION. *American Political Science Review 1986 80(3): 777-799.* 1513

*For abstract see **Machiavelli, Niccolò***

Medici family

4550. Fubini, Riccardo. FICINO E I MEDICI ALL'AVVENTO DI LORENZO IL MAGNIFICO [Ficino and the Medici to the advent of Lorenzo the Magnificent]. *Rinascimento [Italy] 1984 24: 3-52.* 1450-93

*For abstract see **Ficino, Marsilio***

Medinger, Wilhelm von

4551. Krüger, Peter. WILHELM VON MEDINGER, DIE INTERNATIONALE ORDNUNG NACH 1918 UND DER SCHATTEN DES MANNES AUS DER MANCHA [Wilhelm von Medinger, the post-1918 international order, and the shadow of the man of La Mancha]. *Bohemia [West Germany] 1985 26(2): 257-276.* Having reached maturity under the Habsburg Empire, Wilhelm von Medinger (1878-1934) became a citizen of Czechoslovakia after World War I. An agricultural engineer and economic historian, he rejected the negativism of most Sudeten German politicians and, as deputy and senator, remained active in Czechoslovak statewide politics. As a participant in the Inter-Parliamentary Union and the International Federation of League of Nations Societies, he urged a leading role for the League of Nations in a movement of international dialogue and cooperation that would in time modify the untenable features of the 1919 peace settlement. Memorial lecture presented to the Collegium Carolinium in Munich, 11 January 1985. Based on Medinger's articles and other published sources; 55 notes. 1918-34

Medvedev, Roy

4552. Motyl, Alexander J. ROY MEDVEDEV: DISSIDENT OR CONFORMIST? *Survey [Great Britain] 1980 25(3): 74-85.* Roy Medvedev's status as a major dissident who has remained untouched by official Soviet persecution cannot be adequately explained by his standing as a revisionist Leninist. The more valid factor to observe is his Russianness and his identification with Russian nationalism, as evidenced in his writings on nationalities policy. As long as he continues to be a bulwark of the Soviet policy of internationalism and Russification, he will escape the fate that non-Russian dissidents have had to face. 28 notes. 1917-80

Meekings, C. A. F.

4553. Post, J. B. C. A. F. MEEKINGS, 1914-1977. *Journal of Legal History [Great Britain] 1985 6(1): 84-85.* Brief biographical sketch of C. A. F. Meekings, British legal archivist and historian. Note. 1914-77

Meester, Willem

4554. Roorda, D. J. DE LOOPBAAN VAN WILLEM MEESTER [The career of Willem Meester]. *Spiegel Hist. [Netherlands] 1981 16(11): 614-622.* An account of the life of Willem Meester (1643-1701), technician and inventor, and in particular his role in the sea war against Louis XIV. Meester achieved a degree of fame in the 1690's for his inventions aimed at neutralizing the Dunkirk privateers. His career ended suddenly in 1695, caught in the crosscurrents of European diplomacy, debt, and disappointed expectations. Primary sources; 11 illus. 1690's

Mehmed Sukri Paşa

4555. Kornrumpf, Hans-Jürgen. MEHMED SUKRI PASCHA, DER VERTEIDIGER VON EDIRNE 1912-13 [Mehmed Sukri Paşa, the defender of Edirne, 1912-13]. *Südost-Forschungen [West Germany] 1982 41 181-197.* Prints a German translation of the autobiography of Mehmed Sukri (1855-1916), who became a professional army officer and rose through the ranks to general and in 1908 to the highest level of the Ottoman army, Marshal. The rebellion of the Young Turks brought him temporarily into disfavor, but he was named area commander of the Edirne district at the outbreak of war in 1912. His courageous defense of that city against Bulgarian and Serbian armies was instrumental in his regaining a place of honor within the sultan's government and in retirement. 74 notes. 1855-1916

Mehring, Franz

4556. Katsch, Gunter and Schwendler, Gerhild. FRANZ MEHRINGS PROMOTION AN DER UNIVERSITÄT LEIPZIG [Franz Mehring's graduation at Leipzig University]. *Beiträge zur Gesch. der Arbeiterbewegung [East Germany] 1981 23(5): 706-713.* Provides a list of works, published 1956-76, on the life and political and academic accomplishments of German social historian Franz Mehring (1846-1919). The author pays particular attention to Mehring's intellectual and political development and his activities as a journalist, 1869-91. He describes Mehring's studies in Leipzig and his radical journalism, 1880-84. Based on documents held in the Karl Marx University in Leipzig and secondary sources; 25 notes. 1869-91

4557. Vlček, Radomir. FRANZ MEHRING (1846-1919) [Franz Mehring (1846-1919)]. *Slovanský Přehled [Czechoslovakia] 1983 69(6): 520-528.* Assesses the life and times of Franz Mehring, a student of Ferdinand Lasalle, and an early practitioner of the Marxist interpretation of history. A representative of the German Social Democratic left, he recognized the significance of the Bolshevik revolution, and, contrary to some interpretations of his contribution to socialism, such as that by George Lukacs, he had a positive impact on the Communist movement. His prolific writings are a worthwhile source of early Marxist origins and interpretations of historical trends. 30 notes. 1846-1919

Meijer, A.

4558. Veltheer, W. ERASMUS, IN DE GROND NIET SO SLECHT [Erasmus: a more favorable postmortem]. *Spiegel Hist. [Netherlands] 1982 17(4): 190-196.* 1480-1520

For abstract see ***Erasmus, Desiderius***

Meijers, Eduard Maurits

4559. Gilissen, John. L'APPORT DE MEIJERS A L'HISTOIRE DU DROIT [Meijer's contribution to the history of law]. *Tijdschrift voor Rechtsgeschiedenis [Netherlands] 1980 48(4): 355-371.* Surveys Eduard Maurits Meijers's career and publications relating to the history of law, in particular marriage and testaments, publication of sources, international private law, and studies and editions of medieval Roman law. French version of a paper given at a colloquium at the Faculty of Law at Leiden in January 1980, commemorating the centenary of the birth of Eduard Maurits Meijers (1880-1954); paper originally published in *Weekblad voor Privaatrecht* 1980 111(5504): 32-40. 49 notes. 1880-1954

Meili, Julius

4560. Penna, João Fernandes. JULIUS MEILI, O PAI DA NUMISMATICA BRASILEIRA [Julius Meili, father of Brazilian numismatics]. *Rev. do Inst. Hist. e Geog. Brasileiro [Brazil] 1981 (330): 23-27.* Julius Meili (1839-1907), a Swiss citizen, lived in Brazil as a merchant and consul for his country. He gathered an extraordinary collection of coins, medals, and banknotes. After returning to his country, he published between 1890 and 1905 various articles and catalogues which he distributed to museums, collectors and friends. 6 photos, biblio. 1870's-1907

Meindl, Erich

4561. Keimel, Reinhard. OB. ING. ERICH MEINDL: FLUGZEUGBAUER AUS ÖSTERREICH: EIN BEITRAG ZU 200 JAHRE LUFTFAHRT IN ÖSTERREICH [Senior Engineer Erich Meindl, Austrian aircraft builder: a contribution to 200 years of air flight in Austria]. *Blätter für Technikgeschichte [Austria] 1982-83 44-45: 7-169.* Describes the life of the Austrian aircraft engineer Erich Meindl (1906-80) and prints pictures, diagrams, and technical descriptions of the airplanes he designed on the occasion of the bicentennial celebration in Vienna of the first hot-air balloon flight in Austria. 1924-80

Meinecke, Friedrich

4562. Klueting, Harm. "VERNUNFTREPUBLIKANISMUS" UND "VERTRAUENSDIKTATUR": FRIEDRICH MEINECKE IN DER WEIMARER REPUBLIK ["Republicanism of the mind" and "dictatorship of confidence": Friedrich Meinecke in the Weimar Republic]. *Historische Zeitschrift [West Germany] 1986 242(1): 69-98.* During the era of the Weimar Republic, many persons involved in public life and academic careers accepted the republic intellectually but either remained monarchists at heart or emotionally uncommitted to republicanism for other reasons. After the passing of Ernst Troeltsch and Max Weber, Friedrich Meinecke was one of the most prominent republicans of the mind. He rationalized the authority of the republican president as a temporary plebiscitary grant by the populace. His use of the term "dictatorship" evolved over time, but was never intended to rationalize a permanent, totalitarian authority such as that applied by the Nazis. The content and motives of Meinecke's republicanism and his views of the republic in the later Weimar era are especially controversial. Based on works by Meinecke and those who evaluated them; 155 notes. 1919-33

4563. Nishimura, Teiji. MAINEKKE TO RITTĀ FUTATABI [A second study of Meinecke and Ritter]. *Shigaku Zasshi [Japan] 1985 94(8): 54-74.* Discusses the relationship of historians, Friedrich Meinecke (1862-1954) and Gerhard Ritter (1888-1967), referring to Klaus Schwabe, ed., *Gerhard Ritter: Ein Politischer in Seinen Briefen Herausgegeben* [Gerhard Ritter: A Political Historian's Letter-Collection] (1984), which includes nine letters from Ritter to Meinecke and 46 citations to Meinecke between 2 September 1927 and 10 September 1946. In his letters Ritter criticized Meinecke's idea of universalism in the world phenomenon. 1920's-40's

Meira, Olynto Jose

4564. Meira, Silvio. OLYNTO JOSE MEIRA, PRESIDENTE DE DUAS PROVINCIAS DO IMPERIO [Olynto Jose Meira, president of two provinces of the empire]. *Rev. do Inst. Hist. e Geog. Brasileiro [Brazil] 1981 (332): 235-264.* Describes the career of Olynto Jose Meira (1829-1917), president of the Brazilian provinces of Pará (1861) and Rio Grande do Norte (1863-66) and long-time participant in the politics of imperial Brazil. Meira's ancestry, education, and early writings are discussed, including the events leading up to his first appointment as provincial president. Documents are reproduced concerning his election and his governorships, especially in Rio Grande do Norte, where he had his greatest and longest-lasting success. After representing Rio Grande do Norte in the Brazilian Congress (1878-79), Meira retired from politics and devoted himself to agricultural and literary pursuits, becoming one of the most noted and respected Brazilians of his time. Photo. 1860's-1917

Meitner, Lisa

4565. Rife, Patricia Elizabeth. "Lisa Meitner: The Life and Times of a Jewish Woman Physicist." Union for Experimenting Coll. and U. 1983. 525 pp. *DAI 1984 45(3): 922-A.* DA8410853 1900-68

Mękarska-Bogdanowiczowa, Adela Paulina

4566. Wawrzykowska-Wierciochowa, Dionizja. ADELA PAULINA MĘKARSKA-BOGDANOWICZOWA [Adela Paulina Mękarska-Bogdanowiczowa]. *Z Pola Walki [Poland] 1982 25(3-4): 231-243.* Sketches the biography of a Polish socialist of French origins, Adela Paulina Mękarska-Bogdanowiczowa (1840-1901). Exiled from Poland and active in France during the Paris Commune, her involvement with the Polish emigre circles included help to newly arrived exiles and emigres, teaching French, and organizing worker socialist circles in Paris. 19c

Měkěrian, Měkěrtich

4567. Gabrielian, V. A. MĚKĚRTICH MĚKĚRIAN [Měkěrtich Měkěrian]. *Patma-Banasirakan Handes. Istoriko-Filologicheskii Zhurnal [USSR] 1983 (4): 239-240.* Obituary of Měkěrtich Měkěrian (1907-83), scholar, professor of Armenian literature at Erevan University, and ex-director of the Abeghian Literature Institute. His researches in Armenian literature cover the period from the 5th to the 20th centuries. Primary sources; photo. 1933-83

Melanchthon, Philipp

4568. Green, Lowell C. and Froehlich, Charles D., ed.; Hammer, William. MELANCHTHON IN ENGLISH: NEW TRANSLATIONS INTO ENGLISH WITH A REGISTRY OF PREVIOUS TRANSLATIONS, A MEMORIAL TO WILLIAM HAMMER (1909-1976). *Sixteenth Cent. Biblio. 1982 (22): 1-58.* Presents a translation of Philipp Melanchthon's letters dealing with Anglican and German churches, followed by translations of his inaugural address at the University of Wittenberg, *On Educational Reform,* 29 August 1518; his letter to Christoph Karlewitz, ca. 24 April 1538; his letter to the Elector Frederick, 1 November 1559; his opinion on the controversy over the Holy Supper at Heidelberg, 1 November 1559; includes a list of Melanchthon's works previously translated into English. 16c

4569. Wright, William J. PERSONALITY PROFILES OF FOUR LEADERS OF THE GERMAN LUTHERAN REFORMATION. *Psychohistory Review 1985 14(1): 12-22.* 16c

*For abstract see **John the Steadfast, Elector***

Melartin, Erik Gabriel

4570. Hietala, Marjatta. ERIK GABRIEL MELARTININ TOIMINTA JA MOTIIVIT VIIPURIN LÄÄNIN KOULULAITOKSEN PALVELUKSESSA VUOSINA 1805-1812 [The work and motives of Erik Gabriel Melartin in the service of the public education system in the province of Vyborg, 1805-12]. *Hist. Arkisto [Finland] 1983 (79): 131-182.* Examines the actions and motives of the Finnish school and church administrator, Erik Gabriel Melartin (1780-1847) during 1805-14, when he served as teacher and superintendent in the schools of Vyborg province in the Russian empire. Content analysis of Melartin's public papers and private correspondence shows that, contrary to previous assumptions, he was not at this time a Finnish nationalist or an educational ideologist. He was interested mainly in promoting his own bureaucratic career. Based on public and private papers in the Finnish State Archives, the University of Helsinki Library and Finnish Lutheran diocesan archives, and on secondary works; 3 tables, 2 graphs, 134 notes, 2 appendixes. English summary. 1805-14

Melik, Vasilij

4571. Grafenauer, Bogo. VASILIJ MELIK—ŠESTDESETLETNIK [Vasilij Melik—sexagenarian]. *Kronika [Yugoslavia] 1981 29(1): 59-61.* Biography of Vasilij Melik (b. 1921), professor of Slovene and Yugoslav history at the University of Ljubljana. He contributed significantly to the study of political elections in Slovene lands, 1861-1918. 1946-81

Melik'-Hakobyan, Hakob

See Raffi

Melikian, Spiridon

4572. Tadevossian, A. G. SPIRIDON MELIKIAN (TSĔNĔNDYAN 100-AMYAKI ARTIV) [Spiridon Melikian, on the centenary of his birth]. *Patma-Banasirakan Handes. Istoriki-Filologicheskii Zhurnal [USSR] 1981 (4): 22-31.* Spiridon Melikian (1880-1933) student of Komitas, composer, conductor and lecturer, devoted his life to Armenian music. While studying music in Berlin (1905-08) he had his copy of Komitas's collection of Armenian folk songs, which he published in 1931. His expeditions into Armenian villages yielded more than 1,000 folk songs which he set to music. In Tiflis (1909-21) and Erevan Conservatory (1923-33) he conducted choirs, taught theory, trained musicians, and prepared textbooks for music teachers. Apart from his compositions, he published *Analysis of Komitas's Work, Scales of Armenian Folk-songs,* and *Outline of Armenian Music.* Two volumes of his folk songs were published posthumously (1949, 1952). Primary sources; photo, 7 notes. Russian summary. 1880-1933

Melis, Federigo

4573. Barbieri, Gino. STORIA E CIVILTA RINASCIMENTALE NELL'OPERA DI FEDERIGO MELIS [History and Renaissance civilization in the work of Federigo Melis]. *Economia e Storia [Italy] 1984 5(2): 153-162.* Discusses the work of Federigo Melis on medieval and Renaissance economics and civilization and on the transformation of medieval mentality into Renaissance humanism. Melis was interested also in a scientific method for his historiography, and he had a passion for history as the pathway to the understanding of humanity. Based on a talk presented in 1984 at a congress in honor of the 10th anniversary of the death of Melis. 15c-16c

Mella, Julio Antonio

4574. Grobart, Fabio. EIN LEBEN FÜR DIE REVOLUTION. JULIO ANTONIO MELLA [A life for the revolution: Julio Antonio Mella]. *Beiträge zur Gesch. der Arbeiterbewegung [East Germany] 1980 22(5): 738-745.* Traces the life and political activities of the Cuban revolutionary hero Julio Antonio Mella (1903-29). The author describes Mella's early life and studies and considers in particular the influence of Salvador Díaz Miron, one of Mella's teachers at the Newton Academy, on the development of Mella's revolutionary ideas. In 1921 Mella became a student at Havana University and the leader of the Cuban students' movement. His activities coincided with a general awakening of democratic and anti-imperialist consciousness among both students and intellectuals and the members of the working-class movement. Mella became involved in the movement for university reform and the working-class movement and its organizations. He entered the Communist Party in 1924, where he met Carlos Baliño. In 1925 he was imprisoned, but after going on a hunger strike, he was released and left Cuba for Mexico. He soon became a leading member of the Mexican Communist Party, and in 1926 he published a book on José Marti, one of his revolutionary heroes since his schooldays. After various trips to Europe and the USSR, he returned to Mexico where he was killed by agents of Cuban dictator Gerardo Machado. Based on Mella's papers in Havana and secondary sources; 5 notes. 1903-29

Mellini, Giacomo

4575. Vanagolli, Gian Franco. UN MANOSCRITTO INEDITO DI GIACOMO MELLINI, UFFICIALE NAPOLEONICO [An unpublished manuscript of Giacomo Mellini, Napoleon's officer]. *Riv. Italiana di Studi Napoleonici [Italy] 1983 20(1): 55-70.* The document, preserved in the family archive, is a memoir in which Mellini, a veteran of Marengo and many other campaigns, applies for his retirement and a pension, and lists the reasons that entitle him to the same including praise by the Committee of Public Salvation, 18 months of captivity, and two wounds. Mellini adds that his health has been much weakened by 10 years of war and that his presence at home is required by pressing family affairs. Based on the text of Mellini's manuscript; 17 notes. 1793-1802

Memmo, Giovan Maria

4576. Scarpa, Emanuela. GIOVAN MARIA MEMMO PLAGIARIO DI MACHIAVELLI [Giovan Maria Memmo plagiarizer of Machiavelli]. *Pensiero Pol. [Italy] 1981 14(3): 421-439.* A reexamination of parallel passages in Memmo's *Dialogo* reconfirms it as a plagiary of Machiavelli's ideas in the *Discourses, The Prince,* and *The Art of War.* Primary sources; 21 notes. 1520-70

Mendel, Gregor

4577. Alay Henríquez, Faruk. GREGORIO MENDEL, EL GENIO INCOMPRENDIDO [Gregor Mendel, a misunderstood genius]. *Atenea [Chile] 1984 (450): 185-196.* Discusses the life and work of Gregor Mendel, focusing on the cultural context that surrounded him, his scientific background, and the reasons why his discovery of genetic laws was kept unknown for 34 years. 1840's-84

4578. Cabot, José Tomás. MENDEL Y EL "MENDELISMO" [Mendel and mendelianism]. *Historia y Vida [Spain] 1984 17(192): 4-14.* The life of Gregor Mendel, his work in genetics, and the failure of the scientific community to fully credit his discoveries until the 1930's. 1840-84

4579. George, Wilma. THE MENDEL ENIGMA, THE FARMER'S SON: THE KEY TO MENDEL'S MOTIVATION. *Arch. Int. d'Hist. des Sci. [Italy] 1982 32(109): 177-183.* Although Gregor Mendel was a monk and the son of a farm couple, he was not an unschooled and isolated genius. He had received scientific training and was a respected member of the European scientific community before initiating his pioneering genetic experiments. His farm background aroused his interests in the two most vital phenomena in a farmer's life, meteorology and plant genetics. He made important contributions to the understanding of both. 1841-84

4580. Kalmus, H. THE SCHOLASTIC ORIGINS OF MENDEL'S CONCEPTS. *Hist. of Sci. [Great Britain] 1983 21(1): 61-83.* Gregor Mendel's concepts and approach derive directly or indirectly from Aristotle's categories and metaphysics. His scholastic training contributed to his success where others had failed. Mendel started his work with the aim of explaining the possible role of hybrids in the creation of new species. Coincidence played a major role in his success. He brought together more than two disciplines; his achievement can be described as "multiple association." Based on primary sources; table, 91 notes. 1832-1909

Mendeleev, Dmitri I.

4581. Goriushkin, L. M. and Lozovski, I. T. MENDELEEV I SIBIR' [Mendeleev and Siberia]. *Izvestiia Sibirskogo Otdeleniia Akademii Nauk SSSR. Seriia Obshchestvennykh Nauk [USSR] 1982 (3): 48-59.* Dmitri I. Mendeleev was born in Tobolsk, Siberia, in 1834 and died in 1907. A graduate of Tobolsk University and a practical intellectual, he realized that Russia's, and especially Siberia's, agriculture, oil, iron, and other natural resources could both supply the world and sustain a vast Russian industry. Throughout his life he urged the Russian government to establish a radical educational system in Siberia so as to produce a highly qualified workforce for modern industrial needs. Mendeleev was active in the founding of the Tomsk Technological Institute. Based on accounts of Mendeleev's life, and especially on documents in the Central State Historical Archive of the USSR; 30 notes. 1850-1907

4582. Makarenia, A. A. and Kapustinskaia, K. A. O NAUCHNYKH SVIAZIAKH D. I. MENDELEYEVA I T. KARNELLI [The scientific contacts between D. I. Mendeleev and T. Carnelley]. *Voprosy Istorii Estestvoznaniia i Tekhniki [USSR] 1981 (2): 135-137.* The Periodic Table of chemical elements devised by the Russian scientist Dmitri I. Mendeleev was initially not universally accepted. One of Mendeleev's main supporters in Western Europe was the English chemist Thomas Carnelley (b. 1854), who had tried to formulate a periodic law of elements before Mendeleev's discovery. Mendeleev was impressed by Carnelley's research into elements' atomic weights, in particular the relation between atomic weights and magnetic properties. He was also helped by Carnelley's exhaustive work on physical chemical constants and his establishment of tables of melting and boiling points. The two scientists maintained correspondence, and Mendeleev gave Carnelley a glowing reference when he successfully applied for the chair of chemistry at the University of Dundee in 1882. Secondary sources. 1875-90

Méndez Núñez, Casto

4583. Marco, Miguel Angel de. MENDEZ NUÑEZ EN EL PLATA [Méndez Núñez on the River Plate]. *Revista de Historia Naval [Spain] 1984 2(5): 33-63.* Casto Méndez Núñez (1824-69) was a Spanish naval officer who successfully promoted his nation's interests in South America because he was an enterprising naval commander and because he was also sensitive to politics. He served at Montevideo as a young officer in 1847-48, and returned in 1864 in command of the *Numancia.* Uruguay was undergoing a civil war, and Méndez Núñez played a delicate political role between the rival factions. He then sailed in command of the Spanish fleet for the Pacific campaign that culminated in the battle of Callao in 1866, returning to the River Plate later that year. He safeguarded Spanish interests by taking command of the Plate Naval Station while Uruguay continued with civil strife that led to both rival leaders being killed in 1868. That same year Méndez Núñez returned to Spain in ill health and died the next year. Based on naval and diplomatic archives in Spain and Uruguay; 5 illus., 40 notes. 1847-68

Menegon, Giuseppe

4584. Corletto, Gianfranco. DON GIUSEPPE E IL DOKTOR KAISER [Don Giuseppe and Dr. Kaiser]. *Civitas [Italy] 1982 33(4): 95-99.* 1944
*For abstract see **Kaiser, Albrecht***

Mengele, Josef

4585. Varon, Benno Weiser. THE HUNT FOR MENGELE. *Present Tense 1983 10(4): 12-17.* It is an open secret that Josef Mengele, the notorious "Angel of Death" of Auschwitz, spent most of the post-World War II period in Paraguay, where he probably remains. 1945-82

4586. Zofka, Zdenek. DER KZ-ARZT JOSEF MENGELE: ZUR TYPOLOGIE EINES NS-VERBRECHERS [The concentration camp doctor Josef Mengele: typology of a Nazi criminal]. *Vierteljahrshefte für Zeitgeschichte [West Germany] 1986 34(2): 245-267.* Josef Mengele, the best known of the camp physicians at the Nazi extermination camp of Auschwitz because he performed a great number of medical experiments on living children, especially identical twins, was neither a fanatical Nazi or sadist. A doctor of both medicine and anthropology, he was rather a totally cold, cynical man who was driven by consuming ambition to make a name for himself as a medical researcher and racial anthropologist. Although he readily conformed to the brutal practices of Auschwitz and advocated the "Final Solution," he used Nazism mainly as a rationalization for his deadly experiments. Based on Berlin Document Center, Bundesarchiv and the Mengele papers from Brazil at Stern and Burda publishers; 60 notes. 1933-45

Menshikov, Aleksandr D.

4587. Borello, Rodolfo A. UNA NOVELA CORDOBESA MANUSCRITA DE 1822 [A manuscript novel of Córdoba of 1822]. *Boletín de la Academia Argentina de Letras [Argentina] 1983 48(187-188): 25-52.* 1822
*For abstract see **Rodríguez, Juan Justo***

Menshikov, M. A.

4588. Zagladin, V. V. SOVETSKII DIPLOMAT MEN'SHIKOV [The Soviet diplomat Menshikov]. *Voprosy Istorii [USSR] 1983 (1): 181-185.* Between 1930 and 1953 M. A. Menshikov (1902-76) held a number of important posts in foreign trade, including the post of minister. From 1953 to his retirement in 1968, he represented the USSR as its ambassador first in India then in the United States and was later RSFSR Minister of Foreign Affairs. M. A. Menshikov carried out his duties conscientiously and made a significant contribution to international detente. Secondary sources; 21 notes. 1930-68

Men'shikov, S. M.

4589. Men'shikov, M. A. IZ ZAPISOK DIPLOMATA: DVA SLOVA OB AVTORE [From a diplomat's diary: a few words about the author]. *Novaia i Noveishaia Istoriia [USSR] 1982 (3): 137-157.* S. M. Men'shikov held many positions in the Soviet state, being ambassador to the United States between 1958 and 1962. Franklin D. Roosevelt, though determined to maintain American power, was realistic regarding the USSR, and under his administration began the trend to peaceful coexistence. Men'shikov (1902-76) deals with Franklin Roosevelt and traditions of cooperation with the USSR; the commencement of diplomatic relations between the USSR and the United States; his own first journey to the United States in 1936; the war years; Washington; the president and the man; and conversations about Roosevelt and his traditions. He describes the immediate post-war years, consolidation of American power in Europe, formalities and subterfuges in US political life, Roosevelt's realism toward the USSR, the Kennedy years, and Lyndon B. Johnson's harder attitude. Based on the author's works, *Pravda,* and Soviet and American sources; 24 notes. 1936-62

Mensonides, Haye Mense

4590. Bordewijk, H. IN MEMORIAM DRS. H. M. MENSONIDES [In memory of Dr. Haye Mense Mensonides]. *Nederlands Archievenblad [Netherlands] 1983 87(4): 313-316.* A community archivist for The Hague, Mensonides was actively involved with the preservation of state and local records during and after World War II. He was also responsible for archival organization in Groningen and Leeuwarden, and was active in editing and writing many books. 1912-82

Menzinger, Moriz

4591. Rheinberger, Rudolf. MORIZ MENZINGER [Moriz Menzinger]. *Jahrbuch des Historischen Vereins für das Fürstentum Liechtenstein [Liechtenstein] 1982 82: 5-152.* The Liechtenstein landscape artist Moriz Menzinger (1832-1914) was born in Hungary and moved to Vaduz, Liechtenstein in 1833. He was educated in Feldkirch, Liechtenstein and Innsbruck, Austria, after which he commenced a military career. In 1870 he enrolled in the Academy of Fine Arts in Vienna while on leave from the military. After completing his studies at the academy he taught as a drawing instructor for military schools and resumed active military service in 1879 until he retired in 1889. He spent the last 25 years of his life in Überlingen, Germany. Menzinger produced a total of 175 watercolors and 490 pencil drawings, many of which used Liechtenstein as subject matter. Primary sources; 37 notes, 68 reproductions, appendix. 19c-1914

Mercier, Désiré Joseph

4592. Aubert, Roger. LE CARDINAL MERCIER ET L'ACADEMIE ROYALE DE BELGIQUE [Cardinal Mercier and the Royal Academy of Belgium]. *Académie Royale de Belgique. Bulletin de la Classe des Lettres et des Sciences Morales et Politiques [Belgium] 1983 69(6-9): 336-370.* Discusses the life and intellectual development of Désiré Joseph Mercier, Archbishop of Malines and member of the Belgian Royal Academy from 1899 to his death in 1926. As a philosopher faithful to the Christian Aristotelianism of Aquinas, he engaged in a polemic with materialism and experimental psychology. His writings deal with the major philosophical currents of his age, the pragmatism of William James and temporal notions of Henri Bergson. His last work treats Dante as poet and man of action and conviction, whose *Commedia* reveals in symbols "the Christian path to the purifying and fecund struggles of life, from time to eternity." Based on the works of Mercier, publications of the Belgian Royal Academy, and secondary sources; 112 notes. 1899-1926

Meredith, H. O.

4593. Putt, S. Gorley. A PACKET OF BLOOMSBURY LETTERS. *Encounter [Great Britain] 1982 59(5): 77-84.* Excerpts conversational letters from H. O. Meredith, who held the chair of economics at Queen's University in Belfast, 1911-40, and who has been identified as E. M. Forster's "first great love." 1911-40

Merekalov, Aleksei F.

4594. Bartel, Heinrich. ALEKSEJ FEDOROVIČ MEREKALOV: FRAGMENTE ZUR HISTORISCHEN BIOGRAPHIE EINES SOWJETDIPLOMATEN IN BERLIN 1938/39 [Aleksei Fedorovich Merekalov: fragments on the historical biography of a Soviet diplomat in Berlin 1938-39]. *Jahrbücher für Geschichte Osteuropas [West Germany] 1985 33(4): 518-545.* Although he was appointed Soviet ambassador in Berlin in May 1938, Aleksei F. Merekalov's name has been all but expunged from Soviet foreign office records. Assuming his position when German-Soviet relations were at an all-time low, he was unable to finalize credit arrangements with Germany or prevent the diplomatic isolation of the USSR at the Munich Conference. With the purges of the late 1930's and the liquidation of some 62% of the Soviet upper diplomatic corps, younger men with limited qualifications—among them Merekalov—found themselves in responsible diplomatic posts. Reasons for his recall from Berlin in April 1939 can only be surmised: Stalin did not feel he could rely on the inexperienced Merekalov and turned to a member of the Old Guard, Georgi Astakhov. Merekalov's loyalty to Stalin does not seem to have been an issue. In 1948 he held a position in the Ministry for Meat and Dairy Industries from which he retired at age 58 in 1958—the period of de-Stalinization of the state apparatus. Based on archival materials in the Politisches Archiv des Auswärtigen Amtes (Bonn), the Public Record Office (London), published documents in *Akten zur Deutschen Auswärtigen Politik* and *Dokumenty Vneshnej Politiki SSSR,* and other primary materials; 173 notes. 1938-39

Mérida, Carlos

4595. Luján Muñoz, Luis. CARLOS MERIDA, RAFAEL YELA GÜNTHER, CARLOS VALENTI, SABARTES Y LA PLASTICA CONTEMPORANEA DE GUATEMALA [Carlos Mérida, Rafael Yela Günther, Carlos Valenti, Sabartés and the contemporary plastic arts of Guatemala]. *Anales de la Academia de Geografía e Historia de Guatemala [Guatemala] 1982 56: 267-299.* Reviews the lives and works of four dynamic early 20th-century artists who were either born in or resided in Guatemala and had a great influence on Guatemalan artistic movements. Jaime Sabartés, a Spaniard who had been exposed to modernism in Europe, is credited with introducing the movement to Guatemala. Mérida, Yela Günther, and Valenti were, in turn, influenced by Sabartés. The new artistic movement in Guatemala included a nationalistic element in which Precolumbian and folkloric expressions were presented. Based on contemporary newspaper and journal articles, letters, and secondary sources; 5 illus., 5 fig., 66 notes. 1888-1981

Meriño, Fernando A. de

4596. Garcia, Lautico. MERIÑO, "MAS POLITICO QUE PRELADO?" [Meriño, "more a politician than a clergyman?"]. *Estudios Sociales [Dominican Republic] 1983 16(54): 9-29.* Examines the claim that Fernando A. de Meriño was more involved in politics than in religion by reviewing his life and works and concludes that although he was involved in Dominican politics, this stemmed from his religious convictions. 1858-1904

Merkel, Garlieb

4597. Heeg, Jürgen. DIE POLITISCHE PUBLIZISTIK GARLIEB MERKELS (1769-1850): EIN CHRONOLOGISCHER ÜBERBLICK [The political journalism of Garlieb Merkel (1769-1850): a chronological survey]. *Zeitschrift für Ostforschung [West Germany] 1984 33(1): 1-15.* In Merkel's journalistic activites there are two outstanding themes: the fight against serfdom in the Baltic provinces of Russia and the fight against Napoleon. In contrast to the older writers of the Enlightenment, Merkel was the first to espouse radical abolition of serfdom in Livonia and Estonia. His proposals for regulating the new rural conditions were essentially realized by the later rural reforms of 1804. As editor of the *Vossische Zeitung* in Berlin and as publisher of his own newspapers and magazines he became the creator of the modern newspaper feuilleton and changed the character of the newspaper scene in Germany and the Baltic provinces of Russia. In the literary field the militant Merkel criticized Goethe and Romanticism. Together with Kotzebue, Merkel printed his literary views in the *Freimüthige,* where, in 1805-06, he also voiced his opposition to Napoleon's policies. At this time in Germany there was no political press in the strict sense, so Merkel felt called upon to protect German interests, especially of Prussia. In many articles he tried to strengthen the patriotic attitude of the Prussian people against French conquest. After the Prussian defeats of Jena and Auerstedt, Merkel fled to Riga and continued to fight against Napoleon in the *Supplementblätter zum Freimüthigen* and the *Zuschauer.* Merkel was able to influence the Convention of Tauroggen of 1812 in a positive way. In the Baltic provinces Merkel set up the basis of a modern press system and advocated further reforms in his *Provinzblatt.* However, he exposed himself to the devastating judgment of his contemporaries and future generations by his harsh criticism of Goethe. 1796-1850

Merkel, Georg

4598. Zelenka, M. K. "Georg Merkel 1881-1976: Leben und Schaffen" [Georg Merkel (1881-1976): life and works]. U. of Vienna 1982. 319 pp. *DAI-C 1984 45(3) 580; 9/2347c.* 1910's-76

Merkle, Sebastian

4599. Ganzer, Klaus. DER BEITRAG SEBASTIAN MERKLES ZUR ENTWICKLUNG DES KATHOLISCHEN LUTHERBILDES [The contribution of Sebastian Merkle to the development of the Catholic image of Luther]. *Historisches Jahrbuch [West Germany] 1985 105(1): 171-188.* Sebastian Merkle (1862-1945) studied church history, was ordained a priest and later became professor of church history at the University of Würzburg. The center of his studies was the Catholic reform movement, especially the Council of Trent. His contributions decidedly influenced the Catholic views on Martin Luther. He defended Luther against unfair accusations by Catholic scholars and proved that many errors of the medieval Church mentioned by Luther were already noticed before the Reformation and that therefore Luther's criticism of the Catholic Church was too harsh. Many theses in Luther's teaching were basically catholic. Primary sources; 80 notes. 1880-1945

Merkulov, Aleksandr

4600. Kulizhnikov, G. and Zav'ialov, N. ARKTIKOI ODERZHIMYI [Captivated by the Arctic]. *Morskoi Sbornik [USSR] 1981 (10): 93-95.* Describes the work of Russian artist Aleksandr Merkulov (1904-73), who specialized in painting subjects relating to the Soviet Arctic. 1928-73

Merritt, Anna Lea

4601. Gorokhoff, Galina. ANNA LEA MERRITT, EXPATRIATE AMERICAN PAINTER. *Mag. Antiques 1983 123(6): 1221-1227.* Anna Lea Merritt was born in Philadelphia but made England her home and was known in the late 19th and early 20th centuries for her portraits, landscapes, floral scenes, and religious and allegorical works. 1870-1930

Mersenne, Marin

4602. Dear, Peter. MARIN MERSENNE AND THE PROBABILISTIC ROOTS OF "MITIGATED SCEPTICISM." *Journal of the History of Philosophy 1984 22(2): 173-205.* Discusses the life, education and the influences that may have bearing on the literary work of Marin Mersenne, a 17th-century Jesuit, seemingly bent upon softening the skepticism taught by Pyrrho. 1611-48

Mersfelder, Ade

4603. Paterson, Thomas. ARTIST IN STALAG III-B. *Am. Hist. Illus. 1983 18(4): 48-53.* Ade Mersfelder, a US infantryman captured in Tunisia in March 1943 by German and Italian forces, was incarcerated for two years in Stalag III-B at Furstenburg-Oder, Germany, during which time he made sketches of the prison and fellow prisoners. 1943-45

Mertz von Quirnheim, Hermann

4604. Wegner-Korfes, Sigrid. REALPOLITISCHE HALTUNG BEI OFFIZIEREN DER FAMILIEN MERTZ VON QUIRNHEIM, KORFES UND DIECKMANN [Realistic political attitudes of officers from the Mertz von Quirnheim, Korfes, and Dieckmann families]. *Militärgeschichte [East Germany] 1986 25(3): 226-233.* Hermann Mertz von Quirnheim, his son, Albrecht Mertz von Quirnheim (1905-44), and his sons-in-law Otto Korfes and Wilhelm Dieckmann (1893-1944) all eventually became opponents of the Nazi regime. Korfes was captured at Stalingrad and joined the National Committee "Free Germany." The younger Mertz von Quirnheim and Dieckmann were executed because of their complicity in the attempted assassination of Hitler on 20 July 1944. 45 notes. 1920's-44

Meshko, Oksana

4605. Meshko, Oksana. MEMOIRS OF OKSANA MESHKO. *Ukrainian Rev. [Great Britain] 1979 27(3): 36-50, (4): 22-50.* Part 2. Continues Oksana Meshko's memoirs covering her incarceration in a labor camp in the 1950's. Part 3. Completes Meshko's memoirs of persecution and imprisonment in the USSR, 1953-77. 1953-77

Messali Hadj

4606. Stora, Benjamin. LES *MEMOIRES* DE MESSALI HADJ: ASPECTS DU MANUSCRIT ORIGINAL [The *Memoirs* of Messali Hadj: aspects of the original manuscript]. *Revue de l'Occident Musulman et de la Méditerranée [France] 1983 (36): 75-101.* Discusses the differences between the manuscript of Messali Hadj's *Memoirs,* which covers 1898-1938, and the published version (1982). The vast manuscript is written in the discursive, circular style of an Arab folktale and also contains long quotations from newspaper articles, although Messali mainly relies on memory. Some of the major themes include Messali's religious outlook, his view of the colonial regime in Algeria, the relations between Arab nationalism and the French Left in the 1920's and 1930's, and the experience of Arab workers in France. Based on manuscript memoirs and secondary works; 93 notes. 1898-1938

Messerschmid, Felix

4607. Erdmann, Karl Dietrich. IN MEMORIAM FELIX MESSERSCHMID (1904-1981) [In memory of Felix Messerschmid (1904-81)]. *Gesch. in Wiss. und Unterricht [West Germany] 1981 32(6): 325-330.* This obituary of a prominent German historian by a longtime friend and collaborator reviews Messerschmid's contributions to the history of religion and to history teaching in Germany. In the latter area, Messerschmid served as chairman of the Union of History Teachers in Germany, 1955-67, and as one of the editors of *Geschichte in Wissenschaft und Unterricht* from its inception until his death. He also played a key role in the post-World War II debates over the function and content of political education in German schools. 1949-81

Mesterton, Sebastiaan

See Maestertius, Jacobus

Meston, Archibald

4608. Thorpe, William. ARCHIBALD MESTON AND ABORIGINAL LEGISLATION IN COLONIAL QUEENSLAND. *Hist. Studies [Australia] 1984 21(82): 52-67.* An analysis of the career and attitudes of Archibald Meston (1851-1924), chief architect of the Queensland Aborigines Protection and Restriction of the Sale of Opium Act, 1897 and Southern Protector of Aborigines in Queensland, 1898-1904. Born in Scotland, he was brought up in New South Wales farming country. He first went to Queensland in 1871 and went on to a career in business, journalism, and politics. In 1891 he joined the Brisbane Aborigines Protection Society and in 1895 and 1896 produced reports on Aborigines, which were embodied in the legislation. Many of his ideas reflected Victorian attitudes to race, manliness, superiority, and progress. He preferred the "real" rural Aborigine to urban, mixed-race peoples. Based on newspapers, archives, and monographs; 2 photos, 99 notes. 1890's-1904

Meštrović, Ivan

4609. Mulnix, Michael. MEŠTROVIĆ IN VIENNA. *Journal of Croatian Studies 1983 24: 36-50.* Describes the influence of Vienna on Ivan Meštrović during the formative years of his life. During this period he struggled with lack of acceptance, uncertainty over the direction his art should take, and conditions of extreme poverty. He emerged from this period as a nationalistic sculptor in the classical tradition. 23 notes. ca 1900-10's

4610. Porter, Dean A. NEW OBSERVATIONS ON IVAN MEŠTROVIĆ. *Journal of Croatian Studies 1983 24: 57-80.* Reviews Ivan Meštrović's life in Croatia, western Europe, and the United States as a sculptor, indicating his influences, projected works, completed works, the impact of his works, and his frustrations. Bemoans the lack of interest in Meštrović by art historians. 12 illus., 22 notes. 1904-82

Metternich, Klemens von

4611. Andics, Erzsébet. SZÉCHENYI ÉS METTERNICH [Széchenyi and Metternich]. *Történelmi Szemle [Hungary] 1982 25(3): 560-586.* István Széchenyi, the aristocratic statesman, fighting without compromise for what he believed was the best interests of Hungary, had an endless battle with Metternich. Both men misjudged each other and both tried to put their ideas into practice over the other's protest. Széchenyi's belief that an absolute dynasty or the Hungarian feudal aristocracy could be changed to accept his new ideas was hopelessly naive and caused his political demise. 136 notes. 1825-48

Mevorah, Nissim

4612. Mevorah, Barouh. DARKHO HA-YEHUDIT-BULGARIT SHEL PROFESOR NISIM MVORAKH [Nissim Mevorah's Jewish-Bulgarian life]. *Shvut [Israel] 1982 9: 102-103.* Outlines the life of Nissim Mevorah (1891-1968), a Bulgarian diplomat and a founder of the Bulgarian Communist Party. He was also a committed Zionist and active in resistance groups. He remained a fervent Zionist and died under house arrest because of his views. 21 notes. 1918-68

4613. Mevorah, Barouh. PROFESSOR NISSIM MEVORAH'S BULGARIAN-JEWISH WAY OF LIFE. *East European Quarterly 1985 19(1): 75-80.* A brief biographical sketch of a prominent Bulgarian Jew, Nissim Mevorah. He was the Bulgarian ambassador to the United States, 1944-48, and served in other important positions within Bulgaria. Based on secondary material and interviews; 21 notes. 1920's-70

Mexia de Fernangil, Diego

4614. Pociña, Andrés. EL SEVILLANO DIEGO MEXIA DE FERNANGIL Y EL HUMANISMO EN PERU A FINALES DEL SIGLO XVI [Seville's Diego Mexia de Fernangil and humanism in Peru at the end of the 16th century]. *Anuario de Estudios Americanos [Spain] 1983 40: 163-184.* Diego Mexia, one of Seville's most prominent 16th-century humanists, spent much of his life in Peru and New Spain, where he completed many of his important works. Based on published sources; 36 notes. 1560-1620

Meyer, Eduard

4615. Tenbruck, Friedrich H. MAX WEBER E EDUARD MEYER [Max Weber and Eduard Meyer]. *Comunità [Italy] 1985 39(187): 150-197.* Notes the influence of Eduard Meyer (1855-1930) on the political, historical, and sociological content of Max Weber's *Wirtschaft und Gesellschaft* (1922). 1884-1922

Meyer, Hannes

4616. Bassin, Arthur. WHAT IS SOCIALIST ARCHITECTURE? *Monthly Review 1985 37(2): 59-63.* Discusses the views of architect Hannes Meyer and notes that socialist architecture must be both creative and functional. 1930-84

Meyer, Kuno

4617. O'Luing, Sean. KUNO MEYER BY AUGUSTUS JOHN: A BRIEF HISTORY OF A FAMOUS PORTRAIT. *Studies [Ireland] 1982 71(284): 325-343.* An account of the portrait of Kuno Meyer, professor of German and Celtic studies in the University of Liverpool (1884-1911) and professor of Celtic philology at Berlin (1911-19), painted by Augustus John in Liverpool 1911. The portrait was sold to the National Gallery, Dublin in 1924. Based chiefly on the Meyer family letters and Richard Best's correspondence in the National Library of Ireland; photo, 61 notes. 1911-25

Meyerhold, Vsevolod

4618. Marowitz, Charles. MEYERHOLD ALONE. *Contemporary Rev. [Great Britain] 1982 240(1395): 208-212.* Refers to the harsh treatment of dramatist Vsevolod Meyerhold by the Soviet authorities in the 1930's, official policies on art and literature, and the removal of the imposed obscurity that marked the first 25 years after Meyerhold's death. 1930's-81

Meynell, Wilfrid

4619. Dudt, Charmazel. WILFRID MEYNELL: EDITOR, PUBLISHER, & FRIEND. *Victorian Periodicals Rev. [Canada] 1983 16(3-4): 104-108.* Describes the literary career of Wilfrid Meynell, best known as the founder of *Merry England,* a monthly publication designed to elevate the outlook of lower class readership. 1883-1948

Mezhlauk, Valeri I.

4620. Mezhlauk, F. K. DEIATEL'NOST' V. I. MEZHLAUKA V GODY GRAZHDANSKOI VOINY [The participation of V. I. Mezhlauk in the Civil War]. *Voenno-Istoricheskii Zhurnal [USSR] 1983 (2): 69-72.* The Soviet state and party functionary Valeri I. Mezhlauk (1893-1938) fought in the Civil War and showed great courage in the face of danger. He served as a member of the Revolutionary Military Council of the 5th, 10th, and 14th armies and also took part in the operations against Makhno and Grigor'ev. By the end of the war, when his military career came to an end, he was a member of the revolutionary council of the 2d Special Railway Labor Army. Secondary sources; 13 notes, 2 photos. 1917-20

4621. Voblov, I. V. 90-RICHCHIA Z DNIA NARODZHENNIA V. I. MEZHLAUKA [The 90th birthday anniversary of V. I. Mezhlauk]. *Ukrains'kyi Istorychnyi Zhurnal [USSR] 1983 (2): 127-130.* Valeri I. Mezhlauk (1893-1938) joined the progressive movement when still in his teens, and from 1917 was a member of the Communist Party. During the civil war he distinguished himself as an organizer, commissar, and commander. After the civil war he wholly devoted himself to the restoration of industry and, as a result, he rapidly advanced within the Party. He served as a deputy chairman of the USSR Gosplan, as a deputy prime minister, and, from 1937, as minister of heavy industry. At the 17th Party congress he was elected to the Politburo. 11 notes. 1893-1937

Mező, Imre

4622. Hegedüs Sándor. MEZŐ IMRE (1905-1956) [Imre Mező (1905-56)]. *Párttörténeti Közlemények [Hungary] 1981 27(3): 173-192.* Mezo, a tailor by profession, unable to find employment in Hungary, emigrated to Belgium in 1924. There he joined the Communist Party, which sent him to Spain in 1936 to fight against Franco in the International Brigade. After 1945 he returned to Hungary and was elected as a member of parliament and became a member of the Party committee in Budapest. He was shot in 1956 while protecting the entrance to his office against the counterrevolutionaries. 65 notes. 1905-56

Mgijima, Enoch

4623. Edgar, Robert. THE PROPHET MOTIVE: ENOCH MGIJIMA, THE ISRAELITES, AND THE BACKGROUND TO THE BULLHOEK MASSACRE. *Int. J. of African Hist. Studies 1982 15(3): 401-422.* A history of the South African prophet Enoch Mgijima and of his millennial church, which was destroyed when 200 of his followers were killed in a clash with police in 1921. Based on South African documents and interviews with survivors; 71 notes. 1868-1921

Miall, Louis Compton

4624. Baker, R. A. and Bayliss, R. A. LOUIS COMPTON MIALL: SCIENTIST AND EDUCATOR (1842-1921). *Notes and Records of the Royal Soc. of London [Great Britain] 1983 37(2): 201-234.* Biography of the scientist and educator especially known for his work in entomology and the history of science. 206 notes. 1842-1921

Miasnikian

4625. Gharibjanian, G. B. V. I. LENINI HAY ZINAKITSNĒRN U ASHAKĒRTNĒRĚ [V. I. Lenin's Armenian comrades-in-arms and disciples]. *Patma-Banasirakan Handes. Istoriko-Filologicheskii Zhurnal [USSR] 1980 (1): 13-20.* ca 1890-1917

For abstract see ***Avanesov***

Miasnikov, Gavril T.

4626. Avrich, Paul. BOLSHEVIK OPPOSITION TO LENIN: G. T. MIASNIKOV AND THE WORKERS' GROUP. *Russian Review 1984 43(1): 1-29.* Outlines the career and ideas of Gavril T. Miasnikov, a metalworker and Bolshevik since 1906, who was one of the most vocal but most obscure critics of the party. Loyal through the revolution and the civil war, Miasnikov was concerned with the drift toward authoritarianism and away from workers' democracy. In 1921 Miasnikov demanded unrestricted press freedom, which provoked a response from Lenin and eventually led to Miasnikov's banishment, surveillance, and expulsion from the party when his criticism continued. In 1923 he organized a "Workers' Group" that reiterated his principles of worker self-determination and self-management and gained support during the numerous strikes in mid-1923. The group was suppressed, however, and Miasnikov imprisoned. In 1928 he fled abroad, spending some time in Turkey where he continued to demand a return to workers' democracy. In 1930 he arrived in Paris where he remained until 1946, when he was lured back to Russia. There he was imprisoned and shot. 102 notes. 1917-46

Michael of Wallachia

4627. Boisnard, Georges. TEMOIGNAGES FRANÇAIS SUR MICHEL LE BRAVE (DANS LA CORRESPONDANCE DIPLOMATIQUE D'HENRI IV) [French testimony on Michael of Wallachia (Michael the Brave) in the diplomatic correspondence of Henry IV]. *Revue Roumaine d'Histoire [Romania] 1985 24(1-2): 137-146.* The character and victories of Romanian Prince Michael of Wallachia were often distorted in Western Europe due to inexact information and Habsburg propaganda. The correspondence of Henry IV with his diplomats in Constantinople, as collected in the nine volumes of the *Recueil de lettres missives de Henri IV,* published in Paris by J. Guadet, 1848-76, offer a more objective view of the marked impression of Michael as a decisive factor in the evolution of the complex political and military scene in Southeastern Europe. French pamphlets on Michael's triumphal entry into Alba Iulia in 1599, his death, and the victory at Gorăslău also appeared during 1601-02 in Lyons, attesting to the interconnection of Romanian events with the overall European situation. Based on the nine volumes by Jules Verger de Xivrey, the Romanian Hurmuzaki Documents, and secondary works; 60 notes. 1595-1602

4628. David, Gheorghe. IAŞI, 27 MAI 1600. MIHAI VITEAZUL, "DOMN AL ŢĂRII ROMÂNEŞTI, AL ARDEALULUI ŞI A TOATĂ ŢARA MOLDOVEI" [Iaşi, 27 May 1600: Michael the Brave "Lord of the Romanian lands, of Transylvania, and all the lands of Moldavia"]. *Magazin Istoric [Romania] 1983 17(11): 6-13.* The brief rule of Michael the Brave, Voivode of Moldavia May-September 1600, is highlighted in a review of the history of Iaşi and its court from 1400. 15c-19c

4629. Musat, Mircea. DOMN AL TUTUROR ROMÂNILOR [Prince of all the Romanians]. *Magazin Istoric [Romania] 1980 14(7): 29-32.* Michael the Brave was able to play off and defeat contending Hungarian and Ottoman forces, and briefly unite Moldavia, Wallachia, and Transylvania, thus becoming the ruler of a united Romania. 1590-1600

4630. Nägler, Thomas. MIHAI VITEAZUL ÎN CONŞTIINTA CRONICARILOR ŞI ILUMINIŞTILOR SAŞI [Michael the Brave through the eyes of Saxon chroniclers]. *Magazin Istoric [Romania] 1981 15(11): 8-11.* Michael of Wallachia briefly united Wallachia and Transylvania. 1590-1600

Michałek, Władysław

4631. Pawlak, Karol. WŁADYSŁAW MICHAŁEK (25 VI 1916-10 IX 1980) [Władysław Michałek, 25 June 1916—10 September 1980]. *Archeion [Poland] 1982 (74): 247-248.* Obituary of Władysław Michałek (1916-80), Polish archivist employed at the Kalisz Regional State Archives since its foundation in 1955. Secondary sources. 1916-80

Michałowski, Kazimierz

4632. Gawlikowski, Michał. KAZIMIERZ MICHALOWSKI (1901-1981) [Kazimierz Michałowski (1901-81)]. *Acta Poloniae Historica [Poland] 1982 (45): 297-298.* Kazimierz Michałowski was professor of classical archaeology at Warsaw, a chair created for him after his publication in 1932 of the report on excavations at Delos. He had trained in Germany and later in Athens, after long years as a prisoner of war. He was determined to secure for Poland a place in the history of classical archaeology, and this, despite World War II, he did through the excavations he organized in Egypt, Syria, Cyprus, and Nubia, not to mention his seminars at home and his work for the Warsaw Museum. 1932-81

Michałowski, Władysław

4633. Bednarski, Zenobiusz. DR MED. WŁADYSŁAW MICHAŁOWSKI 23 V 1919-12 I 1980 [Władysław Michałowski, M.D., 23 May 1919-12 January 1980]. *Archiwum Historii i Filozofii Medycyny [Poland] 1985 48(3): 373-378.* Biography of Władysław Michałowski (1919-80), Polish physician active in the Gdańsk and Olsztyn health services, listing his publications. 1945-80

Michalski, Konstanty

4634. Michalski, Konstanty; Świerzawski, Wacław, intro. KRONIKA KAPLICY W SICHOWIE ORAZ KAZANIA SICHOWSKIE *[A Chronicle of the Sichów Chapel* and *Sichów Homilies]. Nasza Przeszłość [Poland] 1981 (56): 13-74.* Contains a chronicle of the Sichów Chapel written by Konstanty Michalski (1879-1947) between 8 September 1940 and 3 September 1944 and transcripts of homilies he delivered there in 1941 and 1942 when he was serving as chaplain to the Radziwiłł family on their Sichów estate near Staszów. 1940-44

4635. Popiel, Jadwiga. WSPOMNIENIE O KSIĘDZU REKTORZE KONSTANTYM MICHALSKIM JAKO TŁO DO "KRONIKI KAPLICY SICHOWSKIEJ" [Memoir about Father Rector Konstanty Michalski: the background of *A Chronicle of the Sichów Chapel]. Nasza Przeszłość [Poland] 1981 (56): 75-82.* Portrays Konstanty Michalski (1879-1947) between 1939 and 1944, when the priest was keeping his chronicle of the chapel on the Radziwiłł family's estate of Sichów near Staszów. 1939-44

4636. Wojtkowski, Julian. NAJPIĘKNIEJSZE LATA ŻYCIA: KS. KONSTANTY MICHALSKI CM (1940-1944) [The most beautiful years of his life: Father Konstanty Michalski, 1940-44]. *Nasza Przeszłość [Poland] 1981 (56): 83-91.* Describes the activities of Konstanty Michalski (1879-1947) as a patriotic Pole, priest, and philosopher during the years of Germany's occupation of Poland in World War II. 1940-44

Micheelsen, Hans Friedrich

4637. Braun, William Henry. "The Life and Sacred Choral Music of Hans Friedrich Micheelsen (1902-1973)." Ball State University 1984. 283 pp. *DAI 1985 45(8): 2432-2433-A.* DA8417071 1930-73

Michel, Louise

4638. Efremova, N. P. GEROINIA PARIZHSKOI KOMMUNY [The heroine of the Paris Commune]. *Voprosy Istorii [USSR] 1981 (7): 183-188.* Biographical sketch of the French anarchist Louise Michel (1833-1905). Born of peasant stock, she eventually became a teacher and opened a school for poor children in Montmartre, Paris. She took part in the first International in 1864. As a result of her part in the Paris Commune she was deported by the authorities to the island of Noumea. She was amnestied in 1880 and returned to Europe to live in London and Paris, where she carried on her political activities. 38 notes. 1850's-1905

4639. Mullaney, Marie Marmo. GENDER AND THE SOCIALIST REVOLUTIONARY ROLE, 1871-1921: A GENERAL THEORY OF THE FEMALE REVOLUTIONARY PERSONALITY. *Historical Reflections [Canada] 1984 11(2): 99-151.* 1871-1921
*For abstract see **Balabanoff, Angelica***

Michelangelo

4640. Barolsky, Paul. WALTER PATER AND THE POETRY OF NOTHINGNESS. *Antioch Rev. 1982 40(4): 469-478.* 15c
*For abstract see **Botticelli***

Middleton, Alice

4641. Geritz, Albert J. MORE'S REMARRIAGE: OR, DAME ALICE VINDICATED. *Indiana Social Studies Quarterly 1984 37(2): 47-56.* Describes the second marriage of Thomas More (1478-1535), English statesman and philosopher, to Alice Middleton (ca. 1470-?) in 1511. The second Mrs. More is often depicted as a "simple-minded, bourgeois social climber who was unlearned in the classics and inclined to be shrewish." In truth, she was a woman with the strength of character to raise a large family, supervise a busy household, and challenge her humanist husband on moral and practical issues. 1511-30's

Middleton, James Smith

4642. Barker, Bernard. A NEW LABOUR ARCHIVE: THE MIDDLETON COLLECTION. *History Workshop Journal [Great Britain] 1985 (20): 164-174.* Describes the documents preserved on the life and activities of Labour Party leader James Smith Middleton. Middleton was a key figure in Labour politics from 1903 to 1944. These research sources, which include letters, photographs, and personal papers, have recently been cataloged for the Ruskin College archives. They provide a vivid description of the development of the British labor movement and its most important personalities, including Keir Hardie, Harold Laski, Ramsay MacDonald, and Hugh Gaitskell. Based on the Middleton Papers at Ruskin College, Oxford; 17 notes, 3 photos. 20c

Mieli, Aldo

4643. Pogliano, Claudio. ALDO MIELI, STORICO DELLA SCIENZA (1879-1950) [Aldo Mieli, historian of science (1879-1950)]. *Belfagor [Italy] 1983 38(5): 537-557.* Discusses the work and publishes a bibliography of Aldo Mieli, who wrote about the history of science and directed *Archeion,* a UNESCO-funded journal on the historiography of science. 5c BC-19c

Mier, Servando

4644. Mendirichaga Cueva, Tomás. LA INICIACIÓN MASÓNICA DEL PADRE MIER [Father Mier's Masonic initiation]. *Humánitas [Mexico] 1908 21: 495-520.* Dominican father Servando Teresa de Mier returned to Mexico in 1817 as part of the efforts of Mexico toward independence from Spain, but shortly afterward was imprisoned by the Inquisition for heresy and for being a Mason; while he had been initiated in a secret lodge in Cadiz in 1811, it was not certain that it was a Masonic lodge, until recently discovered documents proved it and Mier's involvement. 1812-17

Mierendorff, Carlo

4645. Beck, Dorothea. THEODOR HAUBACH, JULIUS LEBER, CARLO MIERENDORFF, KURT SCHUMACHER: ZUM SELBSTVERSTÄNDNIS DER "MILITANTEN SOZIALISTEN" IN DER WEIMARER REPUBLIK [Theodor Haubach, Julius Leber, Carlo Mierendorff, Kurt Schumacher: toward an understanding of the "militant socialists" in the Weimar Republic]. *Archiv für Sozialgeschichte [West Germany] 1986 26: 87-123.* 1919-33
For abstract see ***Haubach, Theodor***

Mierzecki, Henryk

4646. Mierzecki, Henryk. CZASY I KLIMATY [The times and their climate]. *Kwartalnik Hist. Nauki i Techniki [Poland] 1981 26(3-4): 503-532.* Fragment from the memoirs of Henryk Mierzecki (1891-1977). Covers the period of 1919-39 and describes the process by which labor medicine became an autonomous discipline. Mierzecki, who wrote more than 130 books and articles, was a founder of the discipline of dermatology. 5 notes, 8 photos. Russian and German summaries. 1919-39

Miglinieks, Pēteris

4647. Zalāne, Paulīne. PĒTERIS MIGLINIEKS—LĀPA TUMSĀ: VELTĪTS PĒTERA MIGLINIEKA NĀVES 100 GADU ATCERI, 1883-1983 [Pēteris Miglinieks—a torch in darkness: the 100th anniversary of his death, 1883-1983]. *Akad. Dzīve 1983 25: 30-36.* In his capacity as village secretary, Pēteris Miglinieks inspired his countrymen in Latgale to resist exploitation by landowners and the Russian bureaucracy. 1850's-83

Mihăescu, Haralambie

4648. Domi, Mahir and Demiraj, Shaban. NEKROLOGJI HARALLAMB MIHĔJESKU (HARALAMBIE MIHĂESCU) 1907-1985 [Obituary of Haralambie Mihăescu 1907-85]. *Studime Filologjike [Albania] 1985 39(4): 177-181.* The Romanian Academician Professor Haralambie Mihăescu, who died on 25 February 1985, was a philologist studying Balkan languages but he wrote also about Albanian history. 1907-85

Mika, Johann Marian

4649. Haubelt, Josef. BOLZANŮV UČITEL JAN MARIAN MIKA [Bolzano's teacher, Johann Marian Mika]. *Sborník Hist. [Czechoslovakia] 1982 28: 159-203.* Johann Marian Mika (1754-1816), canon at Strahov monastery, was professor of pastoral theology at the University of Prague, 1786-1804. Despite his social conservatism, he was influenced by the Enlightenment and tended to justify points of Catholic doctrine by their moral effects. In Church-state relations he favored the Josephine reforms. These views influenced his student, Bernhard Bolzano (1781-1848), who in 1805 became professor of religion. Bolzano's success in combining rationalism with Catholic faith, and his appeal to Czech intellectual youth in the earlier 19th century owe something to Mika's teaching and example. Based on manuscript records at the Strahov Library in Prague and on published sources; 127 notes. Russian and German summaries. 1754-1816

Mikak

4650. Taylor, J. Garth. THE TWO WORLDS OF MIKAK, PART I. *Beaver [Canada] 1983 314(3): 4-13.* In 1767, Mikak, a beautiful, highly intelligent, young Inuit woman, was kidnapped with her son, and taken to England. After being introduced to "the power, splendor and generosity of the English nation," she was returned to her people. Subsequently she exercised significant control over her people—in part because of her wealth, in part because of her knowledge of "other nations," and lastly because of her intelligence. Her influence was a significant factor in the success of the Moravian missionaries in southern Labrador in particular. 6 photos, map. 1767-70

Mikhailov, A. D.

4651. Pelevin, Iu. A. KONSPIRATIVNAIA DEIATEL'NOST' A. D. MIKHAILOVA V "ZEMLE I VOLE" I "NARODNOI VOLE" [Conspiratorial activity of A. D. Mikhailov in Land and Freedom and People's Will]. *Vestnik Moskovskogo Universiteta, Seriia 8: Istoriia [USSR] 1986 (2): 53-64.* Describes the conspiratorial methods used by A. D. Mikhailov, Russian radical during the 1870's, in the Land and Freedom and People's Will revolutionary organizations. Based on Central State Historical Archive, Central State Archive of October Revolution, and Central State Archive of Literature and Art; 91 notes. 1870's

Miklukho-Maklai, Nikolai N.

4652. Komissarov, B. N. RANNIE GODY N. N. MIKLUKHO-MAKLAIA [N. N. Miklukho-Maklai's early years]. *Sovetskaia Etnografiia [USSR] 1983 (1): 128-138.* Describes the schooldays of the travel writer and ethnologist Nikolai N. Miklukho-Maklai in St. Petersburg, recalling his participation in demonstrations organized by progressive students. 1850's-70

Mikoyan, Anastas I.

4653. Mosolov, V. G. VERNYI SYN PARTII, POSLEDOVATEL'NYI INTERNATSIONALIST [Faithful son of the Party, undeviating internationalist]. *Voprosy Istorii KPSS [USSR] 1986 (2): 150-153.* On 22 November 1985, the Institute of Marxism-Leninism held a testimonial for Anastas I. Mikoyan (1895-1978). K. V. Gusev delivered a tribute to Mikoyan's outstanding Party and political service. M. P. Mchedlov retraced Mikoyan's biography from 1915 and his political career, including the US and Cuba missions in 1962 and election to the post of president of the Presidium of the Supreme Soviet of the USSR in 1964. D. G. Sturua conveyed his personal recollections of Mikoyan. 1915-64

Mikszáth, Kálmán

4654. Rejtő, István. MIKSZÁTH KÁLMÁN ÉS A *MAGYAR HÍRLAP* [Kálmán Mikszáth and the *Magyar Hírlap]. Magyar Könyvszemle [Hungary] 1983 99(4): 332-344.* Kálmán Mikszáth (1847-1910), renowned author and journalist, left the *Pesti Hírlap,* a newspaper which supported the ruling party, in 1891. The reason for the split was Mikszáth's friendship with and support of Prime Minister Kálmán Tisza (18-30-1902), who had resigned 13 March 1890. With chief editor Gyula Horváth he founded the *Magyar Hírlap* on 21 March 1891, which aligned itself with the opposition party in Parliament. Because of political differences with Gyula Horváth, he returned to the *Pesti Hírlap* on 1 September 1891. Based primarily on Mikszáth's *Collected Works, Magyar Hírlap* and *Pesti Hírlap;* 55 notes. German summary. 1890-91

Mikucki, Sylwiusz

4655. Perzanowski, Zbigniew. SYLWIUSZ MIKUCKI (24 I 1898 - 23 VII 1983) [Sylwiusz Mikucki, 24 January 1898*-23 July 1983]. *Studia Historyczne [Poland] 1984 27(3): 555-557.* Presents accomplishments of Sylwiusz Mikucki, a historian of the University of Cracow, especially in heraldry and the methods of analysis of medieval documents. Pays attention to his other professional activities in the University of Cracow and the Polish Academy of Sciences. 1920's-83

Mikuž, Metod

4656. Stiplovšek, Miroslav. IN MEMORIAM PROFESORJU DR. METODU MIKUŽU [In memoriam: Professor Metod Mikuž]. *Zgodovinski Časopis [Yugoslavia] 1983 37(1-2): 117-120.* Obituary for Dr. Metod Mikuž (1909-82), Slovene historian and resistance fighter. 1946-82

Milaković, Dimitrije

4657. Vukmanović, Savo. DIMITRIJE MILAKOVIĆ [Dimitrije Milaković]. *Istorijski Zapisi [Yugoslavia] 1980 33(3): 99-110.* Dimitrije Milaković (1805-58), as Njegoš's private secretary, played a major role in both the cultural and political life of Montenegro. Administering Njegoš's presses, Milaković published Njegoš's first works in Cetinje in 1834. For the next 20 years, he wrote, published, or edited the most important works of Montenegrin literature. Milaković's grammar texts were the first attempt to bring literacy to the small principality. His most important work, however, was his *History of Montenegro* (1856). Politically, Milaković aided in exposing plots aimed at removing Njegoš from his throne in 1836. Based on the archives of the State Museum, Cetinje and secondary sources; 34 notes. 1805-58

Milanés, Adolfo

4658. Pabón Núñez, Lucio. VALORES INTELECTUALES DE OCAÑA: EL ROMANTICO ADOLFO MILANES Y EL CRITICO LUIS EDUARDO PAEZ COURVEL [Intellectual assets of Ocaña: the romantic Adolfo Milanés and the critic Luis Eduardo Páez Courvel]. *Bol. de Hist. y Antigüedades [Colombia] 1982 69(739): 848-880.* During the first half of the 20th century Adolfo Milanés (1882-1930) and Luis Eduardo Páez Courvel (1906-50) upheld the cultural and intellectual traditions of the city of Ocaña, as poets and prose writers. One of Páez Courvel's most notable works of criticism is his analysis of the work of his friend Milanés. He also wrote history and was a regional Conservative Party leader. ca 1900-50

Miletić, Svetozar

4659. Panković, Dušan. UDEO SVETOZARA MILETIĆA U POKRETANJU LISTA *MATICA* [Svetozar Miletić's part in starting the journal *Matica*]. *Zbornik za Istoriju [Yugoslavia] 1982 (25): 109-112.* The Novi Sad lawyer-journalist Svetozar Miletić played the leading role in the founding of the most important Serbian cultural institution of the 19th century, the journal *Matica Srpska.* In December 1864 he presented a program for *Matica* to the members of the literary committee of the *Matica Srpska,* which outlined his vision of the proper role of an intellectual journal, its financial basis, and its trusteeship by the cultural leaders of the nation. The program of Miletić is appended. 11 notes. 1864

Miliutin, Dmitri A.

4660. Czövek, István. ARCKÉPEK A 19. SZÁZADI OROSZ POLITIKA MŰHELYÉBŐL. (A. M. GORCSAKOV (1798-1883) ÉS D. A. MILJUTYIN (1816-1912)) [Portraits from the workshop of 19th-century Russian policy: A. M. Gorchakov (1798-1883) and D. A. Miliutin (1816-1912)]. *Századok [Hungary] 1984 118(4): 709-729.* 1820-81
For abstract see ***Gorchakov, Aleksandr***

Mill, John Stuart

4661. Kinzer, Bruce L. J. S. MILL AND IRISH LAND: A REASSESSMENT. *Historical Journal [Great Britain] 1984 27(1): 111-127.* Evaluates and amplifies an earlier article by Lynn Zastoupil describing how John Stuart Mill's position on the political status of Ireland was influenced by his moral philosophy. From 1825 to the 1860's, Mill reflected an ambivalence in his attitude to the Irish and their problems. Initially, he demonstrated a sympathy for the Irish peasants, characterizing the system of land tenure as responsible for their misery. Late in his career, however, agitation and revolt in Ireland led Mill to reassess his position and emphasize Britain's responsibility for reform. In his political speeches and his *England and Ireland* (1868), Mill advanced the view that the union of the two countries be maintained. Separation would indicate English moral failure and would not do justice to Ireland. Irish problems would have to be solved in a British context. Based on Mill's writings and secondary sources; 71 notes. 1825-60's

4662. Pugh, Evelyn L. FLORENCE NIGHTINGALE AND J. S. MILL DEBATE WOMEN'S RIGHTS. *J. of British Studies 1982 21(2): 118-138.* 1860-67
For abstract see ***Nightingale, Florence***

Miller, Hugh

4663. Rosie, George. *Hugh Miller: Outrage and Order—A Biography and Selected Writings.* Edinburgh: Mainstream, 1981. 236 pp. 1830's-56

Miller, John

4664. Craig, Robin. CAPTAIN JOHN MILLER OF THE *BLACK JOKE. Great Circle [Australia] 1984 6(1): 43-46.* Summarizes the account of the life of John Miller, a Scottish sailor born in 1802 and retired in 1865, from his autobiography, focusing on his travels in East Asia and Australia aboard the *Black Joke* and other ships. 1819-48

Miller, William

4665. Cayo Córdova, Percy. BOLIVAR Y MILLER [Bolívar and Miller]. *Boletín de Historia y Antigüedades [Colombia] 1985 72(748): 177-221.* The British officer William Miller after the Napoleonic wars went to serve in the Spanish American independence struggle, in Argentina, Chile, and eventually Peru, where he played an important part as collaborator first of José de San Martín and then of Simón Bolívar. For reasons of health and because he felt his services not wholly appreciated, he returned to England in 1826. He later returned to Peru and participated in its postindependence political struggles. 76 notes. 1817-61

Milosz, Czeslaw

4666. Hoffmann, M. Norberta. CZESLAW MILOSZ—EIN "APOKALYPTISCHER VISIONAR" [Czeslaw Milosz—an "apocalyptical visionary"]. *Stimmen der Zeit [West Germany] 1984 202(8): 557-568.* Chronicles the reception, life, and work of the Polish writer Czeslaw Milosz with an analysis of the thematic and philosophical portrayal of his apocalyptic vision in his poetry and his employment of language. 1933-83

Mindszenty, József

4667. Gergely, Jenő. MINDSZENTY JÓZSEF [József Mindszenty]. *Társadalmi Szemle [Hungary] 1983 38(4): 80-88.* Mindszenty, jailed by Nazis and liberated in 1945 by the Russian army, turned out to be one of the greatest enemies of democratic Hungary and the USSR. His opinion that religion and politics cannot be separated caused him to denounce publicly several official regulations to the point where the government had to place him in jail. It was only after his release in 1970, when he left the country, that the Catholic Church and the government were able to work together. Till his death in Vienna in 1975 Mindszenty agitated for a counterrevolution and the liberation of Hungary. 1918-75

Minimus, Lord

4668. García Font, J. PEQUEÑA HISTORIA DE GRANDES ENANOS [A small story of big dwarfs]. *Historia y Vida [Spain] 1984 17(199): 68-79.* 1c-19c
For abstract see ***Cornelius of Lithuania***

Mints, I. I.

4669. Poliakov, Iu. A. AKADEMIK ISAAK IZRAILEVICH MINTS (K 85-LETIIU SO DNIA ROZHDENIIA) [Academician Isaak Izrailevich Mints: tribute on his 85th birthday]. *Istoriia SSSR [USSR] 1981 (1): 212-215.* Biography of this Soviet historian, commissar of the Air Force Academy in the early 1920's, member of the Academy of Sciences since 1946, head of its Commission on the History of World War II, and founder in 1957 of the Scientific Council on the History of the Great October Revolution. His major work, a three-volume history of the Revolution, was published in 1967-73. 2 notes. 1920's-70's

4670. Samsonov, A. M.; Poliakov, Iu. A.; and Khesin, S. S. AKADEMIKU ISAAKU IZRAILEVICHU MINTSU—90 LET [To Academician Isaak Izrailevich Mints on his 90th birthday]. *Istoriia SSSR [USSR] 1986 (2): 108-112.* Celebrates the 90th birthday of the distinguished Soviet historian I. I. Mints. Born in the Ukraine in 1896, Mints joined the Bolshevik Party in April 1917 and participated in both the Russian Revolution and Civil War. In 1923 Mints enrolled in the historical department of the Institute of Red Professors in Moscow, from which he graduated in 1926. A specialist on the revolution and Civil War, Academician Mints has garnered numerous honors and awards as a leading Soviet scholar, scientific organizer, propagandist, and teacher. 1910's-86

4671. —. AKADEMIKU I. I. MINTSU 85 LET [Academician I. I. Mints's 85th birthday]. *Novaia i Noveishaia Istoriia [USSR] 1981 (2): 199-202.* Biographical sketch of Soviet historian I. I. Mints. His major research interests include the October Revolution, the Russian Civil War, and Soviet foreign policy. He has contributed to major works on the history of diplomacy and the Russian Civil War and won the Lenin Prize in 1974 for his book *Istoriia Velikogo Oktiabria* [A History of the Great October Revolution]. He became a member of the Academy of Sciences in 1946. Photo. 1821-1981

Miramón, Alberto

4672. Lee López, Alberto. ALBERTO MIRAMON. NOTA BIOBIBLIOGRAFICA [Alberto Miramón: Biobibliographic note]. *Bol. de Hist. y Antigüedades [Colombia] 1981 68(733): 267-277.* Brief summary of career of Alberto Miramón (1910-81) as historian and diplomatic representative, followed by listing of his books, unpublished monographs, and articles. 1910-81

Miranda, Francisco de

4673. Armas Chitty, J. A. de. FRANCISCO DE MIRANDA, UN HOMBRE SOLO [Francisco de Miranda, a solitary man]. *Bol. de la Acad. Nac. de la Hist. [Venezuela] 1983 66(261): 27-31.* Francisco de Miranda (1750-1816) the precursor of Spanish American independence who sought help for his designs all over Europe, was a lonely man and apparently a failure but his figure dominates later history. The obstacles to his success were many: the avarice of the slaveholders, the fanaticism of the clergy, the indiscipline of his troops. Finally his indecision and capitulation made him a captive of members of his own republican party. 1750-1816

4674. Burelli Rivas, Régulo. MIRANDA EN PEKIN [Miranda in Peking]. *Rev. de la Soc. Bolivariana de Venezuela [Venezuela] 1982 39(134): 41-44.* Presents a biographical sketch of General Francisco de Miranda for the dedication ceremony in which a portrait of Miranda was presented in China. 1750-1810

4675. Rivero, Manuel Rafael. HOMENAJE AL PRECURSOR, EL GENERALISIMO FRANCISCO DE MIRANDA [Tribute to the precursor, Generalissimo Francisco de Miranda]. *Bol. de la Acad. Nac. de la Hist. [Venezuela] 1982 65(257): 1-11.* This speech, delivered on the occasion of the inauguration of Miranda's statue in Paris, 29 March 1982, recalls his connection with France and the French Revolution. Miranda was one of the most universal Americans of his time; he fought in the cause of liberty, first in Europe and then in his native land. His name is inscribed on the Arc de Triomphe, Place de l'Etoile, Paris. 1750-1816

4676. Salcedo-Bastardo, J. L. MIRANDA: DOSCIENTOS AÑOS DE TRABAJO POR LA LIBERTAD Y POR AMÉRICA [Miranda: 200 years of work for freedom and for America]. *Bol. de la Acad. Nac. de la Hist. [Venezuela] 1981 64(254): 264-278.* Francisco de Miranda was the first Latin American. During the 1781 campaign of Pensacola in the American Revolution, in which he took part, he conceived the ideas of a fatherland and America as a unit. He worked and fought for these ideas in Paris and in London as well as in America. Lecture read at a special session of the National Academy of History, Caracas, 7 May 1981. 1781

Mīrghanī, Shaykh

4677. Grandin, Nicole. LE SHAYKH MUHAMMAD 'UTHMÂN AL-MÎRGHANÎ (1793-1853): UN DOUBLE LECTURE DE SES HAGIOGRAPHIES [Shaykh Muḥammad 'Uthmān al-Mīrghanī (1793-1853): a double reading of his hagiographies]. *Archives de Sciences Sociales des Religions [France] 1984 58(1): 139-155.* Studies the life and work of Shaykh Muḥammad 'Uthmān al-Mīrghāni (1793-1853) on the basis of three hagiographic texts dating from the latter half of the nineteenth century. In 1840, the Shaykh founded the Mirghaniyya brotherhood, one of the most important in Sudan. Faithful to traditional themes and codes, these texts were written and used by the Shaykh's descendants to legitimize and extend the organisation as established by its founder, i.e. to justify the domination of a family of religious notables, the Mīrghāni, over all the brotherhood's members. 19c

Mishima, Yukio

4678. Bachs, Agustí. EL "INCIDENTE" MISHIMA [The Mishima "incident"]. *Historia y Vida [Spain] 1984 17(200): 97-103.* Reviews the suicide of Japanese writer Yukio Mishima, who committed *seppuku* after having held hostage an important member of the Japanese Army, General Mashita, with the help of four other members of his Tate-no-kai organization. Also examines his work and life. 1945-70

4679. Chan, Stephen. MISHIMA—AGAINST A POLITICAL INTERPRETATION. *Contemporary Review [Great Britain] 1985 247(1436): 133-135.* Examines the life and work of the Japanese writer Yukio Mishima who died after an abortive coup d'etat in 1970. Particular reference is made to Paul Schrader's film about Mishima's life and it is asserted that "insofar as Mishima was a political animal, he believed there could be no politics without culture." 1970

4680. McAdams, Dan P. FANTASY AND REALITY IN THE DEATH OF YUKIO MISHIMA. *Biography 1985 8(4): 292-317.* Themes of blood, passion, night, anality, and homosexuality are explored in the writings of the Japanese novelist Yukio Mishima, who committed ritual suicide in 1970. The writings of Sigmund Freud, W. R. D. Fairbairn, Harry Stack Sullivan, and David Bakan inform the psychological interpretation. 1925-70

Mistral, Frédéric

4681. Bornecque, Jacques-Henry. UN AMOUR DE MISTRAL [One of Mistral's loves]. *Rev. des Deux Mondes [France] 1982 (11): 294-309.* Describes the career of 19th-century French literary figure Frédéric Mistral, concentrating on his relationship with the Comtesse de Loynes, 1864-74. 1864-1913

Mistral, Gabriela

4682. Vargas Saavedra, Luis. GABRIELA MISTRAL: ORACIONES DE LA MUERTE [Gabriela Mistral: death's prayers]. *Revista Universitaria [Chile] 1985 (15): 63-68.* Describes the relation between the life and work of Chilean poet Gabriela Mistral, focusing on one tragic event, the death by suicide of the poet's nephew and adopted son, whom she called Yin-Yin. 1925-54

Mitchell, William E.

4683. Christienne, Charles. DEUX PENSEURS AERONAUTIQUES: ADER ET MITCHELL [Two aviation theorists: Ader and Mitchell]. *Rev. Hist. des Armées [France] 1982 (1): 24-41.* 1896-1926
*For abstract see **Ader, Clement***

Mitelman, Šelomoh

4684. Mitelman, Šelomoh; Ša'ul, Eliševʻa, transl. ʻAD LE-WARŠAH ʻIM HA-ṢAVAʼ HA-POLANY MIKTAVIYM ŠEL ḤAYIYAL YEHUDY ŠE-NAFAL BE-ḤAZYT WARŠAH [To Warsaw with the Polish army: letters of a Jewish soldier who died on the Warsaw front]. *Yalkut Moreshet Periodical [Israel] 1985 (40): 161-183.* Presents the letters written by Šelomoh Mitelman of Lublin, who served in the Polish army, during his unit's travels from the USSR to Warsaw, 13 March-10 October 1944, dealing with the topics of life, war, and the slaughter of Jews. 1944

Mitgau, Hermann

4685. Kuss, Horst. GENEALOGIE ALS GESELLSCHAFTSWISSENSCHAFT: HERMANN MITGAU (1895-1980) [Genealogy as a social science: Hermann Mitgau (1895-1980)]. *Blätter für Deutsche Landesgeschichte [West Germany] 1982 118: 261-263.* Hermann Mitgau (1895-1980), late professor of history teaching and Lower Saxon provincial history at the Teachers' College in Göttingen, pioneered in three major areas: 1) historical sociology and genealogy as a social science; 2) Lower Saxon provincial history; and 3) the social history of German students. The common denominator for all of his research was "the fate of the generations in the development of society." 1895-1980

Mitre, Bartolomé

4686. Burns, E. Bradford. BARTOLOMÉ MITRE: THE HISTORIAN AS NOVELIST, THE NOVEL AS HISTORY. *Inter-American Rev. of Biblio. 1982 32(2): 155-167.* Bartolomé Mitre (1821-1906), Argentine historian, novelist, and statesman, was part of the Generation of 1837. His novel *Soledad,* published in 1847, is treated as a historical allegory of South American independence and progress. It illustrates his romantic tenets, European biases, and concept of the hero as central in history. These concepts are also evident in his historical works *Historia de Belgrano y de la Independencia Argentina* [History of Belgrano and Argentine independence] and *Historia de San Martin y de la Emancipación Sudamericana* [History of San Martin and South American independence], which were written much later. The interrelationships between literature and history in the writings of Vicente Fidel López and Jorge Isaacs is also briefly discussed. Based on the works discussed; 33 notes. 1821-1906

Mitscherlich, Eilhardt

4687. Melhado, Evan M. MITSCHERLICH'S DISCOVERY OF ISOMORPHISM. *Hist. Studies in the Physical Sci. 1980 11(1): 87-123.* Provides an analysis of the discovery of isomorphism in 1819 by Eilhardt Mitscherlich (1794-1863), in light of the impact of earlier scientific traditions. Initially versed in stoichiometry, Mitscherlich began to acquire a knowledge of crystallography only after he observed his first isomorph. Mitscherlich bridged the two fields, creatively overcoming the obstacles each field presented. 116 notes. 1801-19

Mitterrand, François

4688. Antonian, Armen and Wall, Irwin. THE FRENCH COMMUNISTS UNDER FRANÇOIS MITTERRAND. *Political Studies [Great Britain] 1985 23(2): 254-273.* Describes the course of French President François Mitterrand's alliance with the Parti Communiste Français (PCF) from 1981 to 1984. The PCF, weakened by electoral losses, formed a coalition with Mitterrand's Socialist Party in hopes of promoting leftist reforms. Mitterrand's implementation of an austerity policy in 1982 alienated the Left, and continued austerity policies led to departure of the PCF from the coalition in July 1984. Based on French newspaper accounts; 66 notes. 1981-84

4689. Singer, Daniel. MITTERRAND'S ACHIEVEMENTS. *Monthly Review 1986 38(2): 20-25.* François Mitterrand, who came to power promising a break with capitalism, ultimately secured the applause of the capitalist social sector due to his praise of private enterprise. 1981-86

Mjøen, J. A.

4690. Roll-Hansen, Nils. DEN NORSKE DEBATTEN OM RASEHYGIENE [The Norwegian debate on eugenics]. *Hist. Tidsskrift [Norway] 1980 59(3): 259-283.* In 1915 J. A. Mjøen put forward his proposals for achieving racial and social purity and became the leader of the popular eugenics movement. He was strongly opposed by the scientific establishment, but more for his inadequate scientific knowledge than for the nature of the theories. During the debates, which continued into the 1930's, many radical proposals, such as the enforced sterilization of the criminal and the socially weak, found strong support among scientists, but criticism of the popular eugenics movement was stronger in Norway than in the rest of Scandinavia and in the United States. Based on contemporary sources; 91 notes. English summary. 1908-40

Modena, Leon

4691. Adelman, Howard Ernest. "Success and Failure in the Seventeenth Century Ghetto of Venice: The Life and Thought of Leon Modena, 1571-1648." Brandeis U. 1985. 1221 pp. *DAI 1985 46(6): 1656-A.* DA8517022 1571-1648

Modigliani, Amadeo

4692. Areán, Carlos. EN EL CENTENARIO DE MODIGLIANI [On the centenary of Modigliani]. *Cuadernos Hispanoamericanos [Spain] 1985 (415): 111-121.* Despite the psychopathic features of his personality, Amadeo Modigliani (1884-1920) was able to acquire a vast artistic culture, consolidating a strictly personal style which recognizes the past and reelaborates it freely. He abandoned the landscape to center on the human figure, achieving that classicist expressionism for which he is so widely acclaimed. 3 photos. 1884-1920

Modliński, Eugeniusz

4693. Zieliński, Tadeusz. EUGENIUSZ MODLIŃSKI 1903-1984 [Eugeniusz Modliński (1903-84)]. *Państwo i Prawo [Poland] 1984 39(6): 93-95.* An obituary of a professor in labor law at the Maria Curie-Skłodowska University, Lublin, a leading Polish expert on social security and insurance laws. 1930's-84

Moerloose, Isabella de

4694. Roodenburg, Herman W. THE AUTOBIOGRAPHY OF ISABELLA DE MOERLOOSE: SEX, CHILDREARING AND POPULAR BELIEF IN SEVENTEENTH CENTURY HOLLAND. *Journal of Social History 1985 18(4): 517-540.* Discusses the autobiography of Isabella de Moerloose, *Vrede Tractaet Gegeven van de Hemel door Vouwenzaet* [Peace tract, given by heaven through woman's seed], published in 1695. Her extensive descriptions of personal life afford a rare glimpse of daily life and social customs of members of the lower classes in early modern Europe. Analyzes Moerloose's descriptions of childhood superstitions and punishment, her adult family life, and sexual relations with her husband in the context of other contemporary testimony to illuminate social conditions of the period. Based on Moerloose's book and secondary sources; 131 notes. 1660's-95

Moffett, Samuel Austin

4695. Lee, Jong Hyeong. "Samuel Austin Moffett: His Life and Work in the Development of the Presbyterian Church of Korea 1890-1936." Union Theological Seminary, Virginia 1983. 322 pp. *DAI 1983 44(6): 1825-A.* DA8324445 1890-1936

Mohammed VI

4696. Bacqué-Grammont, Jean-Louis and Mammeri, Hasseine. SUR LE PELERINAGE ET QUELQUES PROCLAMATIONS DE MEHMED VI EN EXIL [Concerning the wanderings and several proclamations from exile of Mohammed VI]. *Turcica [France] 1982 14: 226-247.* Mohammed VI (1861-1926) succeeded his brother as Turkish sultan in 1918, but four years later was forced out of Turkey by the revolution. During the remaining four years of his life, Mohammed wandered from Malta to Arabia to Italy. From these places he addressed open letters to his former subjects and to various Western European governments claiming his legitimate right to rule in Turkey. Contains texts of several of these letters. Based on documents in Archives of Ministry of Foreign Affairs in Paris; 60 notes. 1922-26

Möhlmann, Günther

4697. Goetting, Hans. GÜNTHER MÖHLMANN [Günther Möhlmann]. *Archivar [West Germany] 1985 38(2): 267-270.* Provides an obituary of Günther Möhlmann (1910-84), archivist and former director of the Aurich State Archives of East Frisia. 1910-84

Mohr, Wolfgang

4698. Franke, Herbert. WOLFGANG MOHR. [Wolfgang Mohr]. *Oriens Extremus [West Germany] 1980 27(2): 151-153.* Wolfgang Mohr (1903-79), professor of Chinese newspaper history and newspaper and colloquial Chinese at Ludwig-Maximilian University, Munich, became interested in the Far East while still a student of mechanical engineering in Berlin. He worked in Shanghai from 1932 to 1956. After finally obtaining an exit visa in 1956, he joined the University of Munich. Concurrently, he coauthored *Verträge der Volksrepublik China mit Anderen Staaten* [Treaties of the People's Republic of China with other countries], Institut für Asienkunde, Hamburg, completed a history of the Chinese daily press, and began a history of the overseas Chinese press. Lists his published works. 1903-79

Moi, Daniel Arap

4699. Katz, Stephen. THE SUCCESSION TO POWER AND THE POWER OF SUCCESSION: NYAYOISM IN KENYA. *Journal of African Studies 1985 12(3): 155-161.* Daniel Arap Moi's rise to power in Kenya began in 1966, when the ruling Kenya African National Union (KANU) in its Limuru party conference brought his Kalenjin group into the national power structure. Moi became vice-president in 1969 and succeeded President Jomo Kenyatta following the latter's death in office in August 1978. He consolidated his power by defeating an effort to change the constitution and thereby eliminate his favorable status as acting president, winning the national post-Kenyatta election, and dismantling the paramilitary *ngorokos* unit of his opponents. Subsequently, Moi and his supporters have developed and disseminated nyayoism as a national ideology—that Kenya should follow in the "footsteps" of Kenyatta. Nyayoism as a doctrine incorporates positive notions of stability, prosperity, and honesty. However, linking the regime's political opponents to anti-nyayoist activities has also been used to repress them. Based on newspapers and secondary sources; 33 notes. 1966-82

4700. Stamp, Patricia. KENYA'S YEAR OF DISCONTENT. *Current Hist. 1983 82(482): 102-105, 126-127.* Presents a political and economic profile of Kenya under President Daniel Arap Moi, demonstrating how the leader's thoughts and actions are in harmony with those of his people. 1982-83

Moiseenko, Pëtr A.

4701. Volkovinskii, V. N. MALOIZVESTNYE DOKUMENTY TSGAOR USSR O P. A. MOISEENKO [Little-known sources on P. A. Moiseenko in the Central State Archives of the October Revolution of the Ukrainian Soviet Socialist Republic]. *Sovetskie Arkhivy [USSR] 1983 (6): 40-42.* Views material on the last years of the Soviet revolutionary Pëtr A. Moiseenko found in the Ukrainian Archives of the October Revolution. Moiseenko (1852-1923) spent the 1921-23 period in Kharkov, then capital of the Soviet Ukraine, working for the All-Ukrainian Central Executive Committee in the propaganda section. Sources for this period show him busy with his memoirs and conducting correspondence with workers and trade unionists of the region. Based on material from the Central State Archives of the October Revolution of the Ukrainian Soviet Socialist Republic; 14 notes. 1912-23

Molière

4702. Herzel, Roger. LE JEU "NATUREL" DE MOLIÈRE ET DE SA TROUPE [The natural acting of Molière and his company]. *Dix-Septième Siècle [France] 1981 33(3): 279-283.* Molière was not successful as a tragic actor but very successful as comedian. Although he played the buffoon, he appeared natural in comparison with some others in his company. Molière took into consideration which of his colleagues was going to play each role as he wrote his plays. 11 notes. 1660-70

Molina, Tirso de

4703. Vázquez, Luis. TIRSO NO RESIDIO EN SEGOVIA LOS AÑOS 1615-1616 [Tirso did not reside in Segovia during the years 1615-16]. *Estudios [Spain] 1982 38(138): 433-437.* Provides proof that Tirso de Molina did not live in the Convent of Mercy at Segovia. 1614-20

Molina Campos, Florencio

4704. Kenny, Matt. THE WORLD OF THE GAUCHO. *Américas (Organization of American States) 1985 37(5): 2-7, 51.* Summarizes the career of Argentine painter Florencio Molina Campos, whose sympathetic and humorous depictions of the people, animals, and way of life of the Argentine pampas earned him great popularity in the 1930's-50's. 1926-57

Molina family

4705. Wells, Allen. FAMILY ELITES IN A BOOM-AND-BUST ECONOMY: THE MOLINAS AND PEÓNS OF PORFIRIAN YUCATAN. *Hispanic Am. Hist. Rev. 1982 62(2): 224-253.* Between 1850 and 1910 a henequen economy developed in Yucatan due to the increased demand in the United States for binder twine and the invention of the decorticator, which made henequen profitable. Two of the powerful henequen families are discussed. The Molina family had no landed wealth but rose to power through Olegario Molina, who, in 1887, founded the export house Olegario Molina y Compañía. In 1902 he contracted with International Harvester to be their sole agent for henequen and was elected governor of Yucatan. The large Peón family's wealth was based on landed estates. The Peón y Peón wing of the family's conversion from cattle to henequen stabilized their position when Augusto Luis Peón y Peón in the 1880's and 1890's gained control of some rail transportation and built warehouses to hold henequen for better prices. While different in background, both types of families were easily assimilated into the henequen oligarchy of about 30 families. Based partly on documents in Archivo Notarial del Estado de Yucatán and Archivo General del Estado de Yucatán, both in Mérida, Yucatan, and International Harvester Company Archives, Chicago, Illinois; table, 6 fig., 50 notes. 1850-1911

Molina Orantes, Adolfo

4706. —. NOTA NECROLOGICA: DOCTOR ADOLFO MOLINA ORANTES, 1915-1980 [Dr. Adolfo Molina Orantes: an obituary]. *Anales de la Soc. de Geog. e Hist. de Guatemala [Guatemala] 1980 53: 5-9.* Dr. Molina Orantes (d. 1980), president of the Geographical and Historical Society at the time of his death, was a jurist and professor of law, former director of the School of Diplomacy, a contributor to the *Anales,* and author of numerous studies on international law and its historical aspects. 1915-80

Molinari, Gustave de

4707. Hart, David M. GUSTAVE DE MOLINARI AND THE ANTI-STATIST LIBERAL TRADITION: PART I. *J. of Libertarian Studies 1981 5(3): 263-290.* Describes the 18th-century antistatist liberal thinkers, notably Adam Smith and Jean-Baptiste Say, who influenced the thought of Gustave de Molinari (1819-1912), and recounts Molinari's career against the turbulent background of 19th-century Paris. Article to be continued. 1840-1912

Molland, Einar

4708. Schørring, Jens Holger. EINAR MOLLAND OG DEN TYSKE KIRKEKAMP: TEKST OG KOMMENTAR TIL EINAR MOLLANDS BREV FRA TYSKLAND TIL JENS NØRREGAARD I 1934 [Einar Molland and the German ecclesiastical controversy: text of and commentary on Einar Molland's letters from Germany to Jens Nørregaard in 1934]. *Norsk Teologisk Tidsskrift [Norway] 1981 82(4): 189-225.* The Norwegian theologian Einar Molland (1908-76) spent 1933-34 in Germany and took part in the controversy regarding the position of the church and the nature of Christian doctrine in Nazi Germany. His letters to his Danish colleague demonstrate his wide-ranging concerns and learning. Molland's first-hand account of the issues and participants in the dispute demonstrates that there was no clear division into two camps, but that, contrary to current opinion, the picture was far more complex. The letters also show that Molland had a real understanding of the social dangers, which he, no doubt, transmitted to his colleagues after his return to Norway. Based on contemporary and secondary sources; 71 notes. ca 1930-45

Möllendorff, Paul Georg von

4709. Leifer, Walter. PAUL-GEORG VON MOELLENDORFF AND THE OPENING OF KOREA. *Asian & Pacific Q. of Cultural and Social Affairs [South Korea] 1982 14(2): 1-23.* Moellendorff was the first European to serve as a high ranking advisor to the Korean government. His initial task was to organize a Korean customs service along the lines of the English-run Chinese customs service. Within a short time, his duties expanded. He had the opportunity to become both a reformer and a diplomat. Between 1882 and 1885, he initiated an English-language school, arranged for a partial geological survey of the Korean peninsula, and brought agriculture, sericulture, coinage, and glass production experts to the Hermit Kingdom. The rebellion of Kim Okkyun in 1884 and the machinations of Russia and England led Moellendorff into a brief diplomatic career. In December 1885, he left the Korean government's employ. The activities of his detractors and a Russian Korean crisis that some claimed he created occasioned his departure from Seoul. Based on German sources, including Moellendorff's diary; 31 notes. 1880's

Möller, Samuel

4710. Halila, Aimo. KOLME SUOMALAISTA SOTILASPEDAGOGIA [Three Finnish military pedagogues]. *Turun Hist. Arkisto [Finland] 1982 38: 390-408.* 1743-1954
For abstract see ***Laatikainen, Taavetti***

Molnár, Albert Szenci

4711. Vásárhelyi, Judit. SZENCI MOLNÁR ALBERT PÁLYÁJA [The life and work of Albert Szenci Molnár]. *Theologiai Szemle [Hungary] 1984 27(3): 153-159.* Charts the life of Calvinist humanist Albert Szenci Molnár who was the first to translate the bible into Hungarian and also produced translations of hymns and psalm books, some of which are still in use today. Based on secondary sources appraising Albert Szenci Molnár's career on the 350th anniversary of his death. 1574-1634

Molnár, Erik

4712. Pach, Zsigmond Pál. A TÖRTÉNETÍRÓ MOLNÁR ERIK [Erik Molnár the historiographer]. *Történelmi Szemle [Hungary] 1981 24(4): 513-520.* A survey of the historical activities of Erik Molnár, (d. 1966), who began publishing historical articles in the mid-1930's. As a Marxist and internationalist, he was interested in the international situation of the working class. He wrote on social classes in the Revolution of 1848 and on the history of Hungarian society from antiquity to the defeat of Mohács (1526). In the last 17 years of his life, he was director of the Institute of Historical Science of the Hungarian Academy of Sciences, 1949-66. Lecture at the memorial session for Erik Molnár, 27 November 1981, in Kecskemét; 32 notes. 1930-66

Molnár, Ferenc

4713. Voit, Krisztina. MOLNÁR FERENC ÉS A FRANKLIN TÁRSULAT [Ferenc Molnár and the Franklin Society]. *Magyar Könyvszemle [Hungary] 1982 98(3): 220-229.* Describes the relationship between Ferenc Molnár (1878-1952) and the Franklin Society from 1905 to 1932. Molnár signed a contract on 3 February 1905 with the Franklin Society, and in 1907 one of his most successful works *A Pál Utcai Fiúk* [The boys of Pál street] appeared. In 1937 Molnár left the Franklin Society for Atheneum, although the Franklin Society continued to publish editions of his works to which it held exclusive rights. Based primarily on manuscripts in the National Archives; 21 notes. French summary. 1905-43

Moloney, Alfred

4714. Ashdown, Peter. THE COLONIAL ADMINISTRATORS OF BELIZE: SIR ALFRED MOLONEY (1891-1897). *Belizean Studies [Belize] 1986 14(2): 1-10.* Discusses Sir Alfred Moloney's reign as governor of Belize from 1891 to 1896, emphasizing his unsuccessful attempts to institute economic and agricultural reform and to diversify the economy. 1891-96

Mommsen, Theodor

4715. Christ, Karl. THEODOR MOMMSEN UND SEIN BIOGRAPH [Theodor Mommsen and his biographer]. *Hist. Zeits. [West Germany] 1981 233(2): 363-370.* 1817-1903
For abstract see ***Wickert, Lothar***

Monash, John

4716. Pedersen, P. A. SOME THOUGHTS ON THE PRE-WAR MILITARY CAREER OF JOHN MONASH. *J. of the Royal Australian Hist. Soc. [Australia] 1981 67(3): 212-226.* Sir John Monash's reputation as a military commander dates from World War I, and his pre-1914 career is often ignored, although during this period he developed his key qualities—an interest in the link between technology and weaponry and an appreciation of the commander-soldier relationship. Based on the Monash papers at Monash University and secondary sources; 80 notes. 1880-1914

4717. Pederson, Peter Andreas. "The Development of Sir John Monash as a Military Commander." U. of New South Wales [Australia] 1982. *DAI 1983 44(2): 553-A.* 1918

Monchanin, Jules

4718. Petit, Jacques. UN NON-CONFORMISTE DES ANNEES 20: JULES MONCHANIN [A nonconformist in the 1920's: Jules Monchanin]. *Cahiers d'Hist. [France] 1981 26(3): 271-287.* Analyzes the life, religious dedication, and philosophy of theologian Jules Monchanin (1895-1937) of Lyons. Focuses on his pacifist philosophy, critical intelligence, and interest in communism. Based on the archives of the Rhone Department and those of the municipality of Lyons; biblio., 72 notes. 1920's

Monckton Milnes, Richard

4719. Campbell, Ian. CONVERSATIONS WITH CARLYLE: THE MONCKTON MILNES DIARIES. *Prose Studies [Great Britain] 1985 8(1): 48-57.* Discusses the diaries of 1st Baron Houghton (Richard Monckton Milnes), in which are recorded conversations with his friend English author Thomas Carlyle during the period 1838-45. 1838-45

Mond, Georges

4720. Mond, Georges. TÉMOIGNAGE: 1944: VARSOVIE FACE AUX ALLEMANDS ET AUX RUSSES [Testimony: 1944: Warsaw face to face with the Germans and the Russians]. *Histoire [France] 1982 (42): 86-89.* Memoirs of the secretary general of the Polish Historical and Literary Society in France, a survivor of the Warsaw Uprising of 1944. The insurrection's failure was due as much to the Russians' lack of support as to the Germans' efforts to suppress it. 1944-45

Mondolfo, Ugo Guido

4721. Ambrosoli, Luigi. UGO GUIDO MONDOLFO [Ugo Guido Mondolfo]. *Risorgimento [Italy] 1983 35(3): 217-235.* A member of the famous Florentine group of intellectuals, Ugo Guido Mondolfo fought for educational and political reform and against political favoritism. A long-time leading member of the Socialist Party, he wrote for *Critica Sociale* on various problems such as socialist history and the need for gradualism in reforms in order to integrate capitalism into socialism, and the danger of a fusion of the Socialist Party with the Communist Party. Text presented at a conference on the Mondolfo brothers in 1983 at Milan; 40 notes. 1870-1950

Monfort, Benito

4722. Whitehead, H. G. BENITO MONFORT, 1716-1785: A TENTATIVE LIST OF HOLDINGS IN THE REFERENCE DIVISION OF THE BRITISH LIBRARY. *British Library Journal [Great Britain] 1984 10(1): 51-62.* Studies the career of Benito Monfort y Besades (1716-85) one of Spain's most well-known printers. A review of his major accomplishments is presented. Several modern day criticisms of his work are discussed and refuted. A chronological list of his works which are held at the British Library is included. Based on a review of Montfort's major printings and critiques by D. B. Updike; 5 notes, 5 fig. 18c

Moniz, Egas

4723. Calmon, Pedro. EGAS MONIZ E SEUS DESCENDENTES DO BRASIL [Egas Moniz and his Brazilian descendants]. *Rev. do Inst. Hist. e Geog. Brasileiro [Brazil] 1980 (327): 317-323.* Recalls the almost legendary figure of the tutor of the first king of Portugal, Afonso Henriques. Includes data on his descendants, especially some who emigrated to the new world. Gives the names of some descendants still living in Brazil. Secondary sources. 12c-20c

Monnet, Denis

4724. Edmonds, Bill. A STUDY IN POPULAR ANTI-JACOBINISM: THE CAREER OF DENIS MONNET. *French Hist. Studies 1983 13(2): 215-251.* The career of the weaver Denis Monnet (1750-93) sheds light on the widespread popular support for the anti-Jacobin cause in Lyon during 1793. Monnet was "politicized" by the moderate Girondins early in the Revolution and had adopted their horror of revolutionary violence and extremism. He was also influenced by his desire to maintain the position of political power he had acquired as part of the Girondist political system. Based on documents in the Departmental Archives of the Rhône, Communal Archives of Lyon, and the Archives Nationales; 2 tables, 113 notes. 1750-93

Monroy, Antonio de

4725. Ríos Miramontes, M. Teresa. EL ARZOBISPO MONROY: NOTAS PARA SU BIOGRAFIA [Archbishop Monroy: notes for his biography]. *Archivo Ibero-Americano [Spain] 1984 44(175): 327-350.* Examines the career of Antonio de Monroy (1634-1715). Born in Santiago de Querétaro, Mexico, Monroy entered the Dominican order at age 19. After holding a variety of academic posts in Mexico City, he was named general of the Dominican order in 1676. Nine years later he was appointed archbishop of Santiago de Compostela in Spain, a post he held until his death. Monroy maintained amicable relations with Charles II and sided with Philip V during the succession struggle. Using his power and resources to aid victims of famine and epidemic in 1695 and 1710, Monroy also made many donations to religious bodies throughout Santiago and Galicia. The cathedral in Santiago received several physical improvements during Monroy's tenure as archbishop. Based on archival materials and secondary sources; 2 photos, 124 notes. 1650's-1715

Montagu, Elizabeth

4726. Hanson, Marjorie. "Elizabeth Montagu: A Biographical Sketch and a Critical Edition of Her Writings." U. of Southern California 1982. *DAI 1982 42(12): 5128-5129-A.* 18c

Montagu, Lily H.

4727. Umansky, Ellen M. THE ORIGINS OF LIBERAL JUDAISM IN ENGLAND: THE CONTRIBUTION OF LILY H. MONTAGU. *Hebrew Union College Annual 1984 55: 309-322.* Describes the role of Lily H. Montagu, principal founder of the Jewish Religious Union, which was organized in 1902 in order to revitalize Jewish religious life in England. Without minimizing the contributions of Claude Montefiore and others in the ideological development of liberal Judaism, attempts to show how Montagu was indispensable in the everyday leadership role she assumed during the formative stage of the Anglo-Jewish reform movement. 55 notes. 1895-1915

Montagu, 1st Duke of

4728. Metzger, Edward Charles. "Ralph, First Duke of Montagu—The Artful Contriver, 1638-1709." State U. of New York, Buffalo 1983. 448 pp. *DAI 1983 44(1): 261-A.* DA8312430 1638-1709

Montague, Mary Wortley

4729. Perry, Ruth. TWO FORGOTTEN WITS. *Antioch Rev. 1981 39(4): 431-438.* ca 1690-1762
*For abstract see **Astell, Mary***

Montaigne, Michel de

4730. Henry, Patrick. MONTAIGNE: CENSORSHIP AND DEFENSIVE WRITING. *Pro. of the Ann. Meeting of the Western Soc. for French Hist. 1980 8: 90-102.* Despite the fact that in 1581 the Roman Censor ordered him to delete or alter references to six different subjects that appeared in his *Essays* (1580), Michel de Montaigne continued to write on these topics in subsequent editions of the work. These subjects included the role of fortune in human affairs and the works of various heretical poets. Nevertheless, Montaigne did fear the dangerous eye of the Church. He gave misleading titles to several sections of the book and used a variety of rhetorical tricks to disguise his true beliefs. Because of these ruses and also because Montaigne's brand of skepticism was popular at the time, the *Essays* did not appear on the Index of Prohibited Books until 1676. 29 notes. 1580-81

Montalvo, Juan

4731. Bueno, Salvador. A PROPOSITO DEL SESQUICENTENARIO DE JUAN MONTALVO [On the 150th anniversary of Juan Montalvo]. *Casa de las Américas [Cuba] 1982 23(135): 140-146.* Juan Montalvo (1832-89) was born in Ambato, Ecuador and died in exile in Paris. Ecuador, having received its independence in 1830, was building its basic institutions. As a polemicist and public orator, Montalvo fought against all forms of military and Church tyranny. He was one of the creators not only of Ecuadorian but of Latin American consciousness. 1850's-89

Montalvo, Lorenzo

4732. Cruz Hermosilla, Emilio de la. LORENZO MONTALVO, FIGURA SEÑERA DE LA ARMADA [Lorenzo Montalvo, unique figure of the navy]. *Rev. General de Marina [Spain] 1982 202(Jan): 17-23.* Lorenzo Montalvo, Count of Macuriges, a career administrative officer in the Spanish navy, lived from 1710 to 1778, mostly in Cuba. He organized the defenses and supply of Havana under British attack in 1762, owned and cultivated an estate near Guantánamo, and was the personal representative of the crown to oversee the functioning of government in Cuba. His descendents have been a significant force in the subsequent history of Cuba. 3 illus. 1730's-78

Montansier, La

See Brunet, Marguerite

Montefiore, Moses

4733. Raphael, Chaim. THE PHENOMENAL LIFE OF SIR MOSES MONTEFIORE. *Commentary 1984 77(4): 51-54.* Discusses the piety and ironically limited religious and ethnic comprehension of English Jewish philanthropist Sir Moses Montefiore (1784-1885), who as a symbol of Jewish power helped to inspire the Zionist movement without ever understanding its significance for the future of the world's Jews. ca 1800-85

Montes Matoso, Luis

4734. Arruda, Virgílio. LUIS MONTES MATOSO, HISTORIADOR E JORNALISTA (UMA VIDA POR CONHECER E UMA OBRA POR PUBLICAR) [Louis Montes Matoso, historian and journalist: a life for knowledge and a work to be published]. *Anais da Acad. Portuguesa da Hist. [Portugal] 1980 26(2): 73-127.* Surveys the life and career of Luis Montes Matoso, an 18th-century Portuguese journalist, churchman, editor, and literary figure. Notes his career at the University of Coimbra, in several religious orders (especially the Franciscans), and his work in and devotion to his home city of Santarém, which included the writing of several histories and diaries about the city. Briefly mentions most of his major works and activities, and notes the need for publication and emendation of his works. Based mostly on original documents and secondary works dealing with Portuguese literature; 53 notes. 1701-60

Montespan, Marquise de

4735. Decker, Michel de. MME DE MONTESPAN NOIRCIE PAR LES JALOUX? [Mademoiselle de Montespan tarnished by jealous ones?]. *Historama [France] 1985 (14): 72-77.* Examines the life of Marquise de Montespan (Françoise Athénaïs de Rochechouart de Mortemart) as Louis XIV's favorite mistress, noting her role in court life and rumors about her poisoning several notables. 1667-1771

Montesquieu, Charles de

4736. Beyer, Charles. L'OPTIMISME DE MONTESQUIEU FACE A LA CRISE DU DROIT DES GENS AU XVIIIe SIECLE [Montesquieu's optimism in the face of the 18th-century crisis in the law of peoples]. *Revue des Sciences Morales et Politiques [France] 1985 140(4): 537-548.* Charles de Montesquieu continued to believe in a universal law of peoples that would ultimately prevail despite the Machiavellian behavior of rulers in his time. He was confident that some future generation would embrace his enlightened concept of human rights, in practice as well as in theory. Discussion and response follow, pp. 548-550. Based on Montesquieu's published works. 1725-55

4737. Pomeau, René. MONTESQUIEU MONDAIN ET PHILOSOPHE, D'APRES UNE CORRESPONDENCE INEDITE [The worldly and philosophical Montesquieu, according to a group of unpublished letters]. *Rev. des Travaux de l'Acad. des Sci. Morales & Pol. et Comptes Rendus de ses Séances [France] 1981 134(2): 239-259.* Sixty-eight letters of Montesquieu recently discovered in private archives cast new light on his life and work, 1734-39, revealing a great deal about his social connections, activities in Paris, and personality, but less about his philosophical thought. Includes comments by Pierre Antoine Perrod, Roland Mousnier, Pierre Clarac, René Poirier, Ferdinand Alquié, Pierre-Georges Castex, and Henri Guitton; 12 notes. 1734-39

Montesquieu, Pierre de

4738. Bordes, Maurice. D'ARTAGNAN ET LES D'ARTAGNAN DANS L'HISTOIRE ET LE ROMAN [D'Artagnan and the "D'Artagnans" in history and novel]. *Information Historique [France] 1984 46(3): 105-112.* 1611-1725

*For abstract see **Batz, Charles de***

Montesquiou, Robert de

4739. Dumas, François Ribadeau. LE MIROBOLANT COMTE ROBERT, BARON DE CHARLUS [The stupendous Comte Robert, the Baron de Charlus]. *Historama [France] 1984 (5): 57-61.* Describes the eccentric and flamboyant lifestyle of Robert de Montesquiou, which is reflected in the novels of Marcel Proust and Joris- Karl Huysmans, and the French *demi-monde* of the late 19th and early 20th centuries. 1895-1919

Montgomery, Bernard

4740. Bidwell, Shelford. MONTY: MASTER OF THE BATTLEFIELD OR THE MOST OVERRATED GENERAL? *Journal of the Royal United Services Institute for Defence Studies [Great Britain] 1984 129(2): 62-63.* Reviews Nigel Hamilton's *Monty: Master of the Battlefield, 1942-1944* (1983). This book is largely based on oral accounts and General Bernard Montgomery's papers and, thus, provides insight into the character and abilities of Great Britain's most controversial World War II military leader. 1942-44

Montgomery, Gabriel de

4741. Jestaz, Philippe. LE PROCES DE MONTGOMERY [The Montgomery trial]. *Rev. Hist. de Droit Français et Étranger [France] 1981 59(3): 361-382.* Count Gabriel de Montgomery (1530?-74), a warrior and captain of the Scottish guards, accidentally killed his king, Henry II of France, during a tournament and was captured and executed 15 years later for this offense and others he had been accused of in the meantime during a turbulent part of his life. In particular, he had allegedly participated in a conspiracy against Huguenot leader Admiral Gaspard de Coligny (1519-72). Based mainly on French memorialists and witnesses; biblio., 107 notes. 1559-74

Montherlant, Henry de

4742. Billecocq, André. HENRY DE MONTHERLANT ET LE PATRONAGE DU BON CONSEIL [Henry de Montherlant and the Patronage du Bon Conseil]. *Nouvelle Rev. des Deux Mondes [France] 1981 (10): 79-86.* An account of the period in the life of Henry de Montherlant (1895-1972) when he attended the Patronage du Bon Conseil, a Catholic club for young people, mentioned briefly in his *Relève du Matin* (1920). 1911-20

4743. Pereira, Paulette J. "The Impact of the German Occupation of France upon Four French Intellectuals: Charles Maurras, Pierre Drieu la Rochelle, Henry de Montherlant, and François Mauriac." Am. U. 1985. 221 pp. *DAI 1986 46(8): 2415-A.* DA8522268 1940-44

Montini brothers

4744. Montini, Lodovico. IGINO RIGHETTI E IL FRATELLI MONTINI [Igino Righetti and the Montini brothers]. *Studium [Italy] 1985 81(1): 67-72.* 1925-60's
For abstract see ***Righetti, Igino***

Montt, Manuel

4745. Matte Varas, Joaquín. MANUEL MONTT [Manuel Montt]. *Rev. Chilena de Hist. y Geog. [Chile] 1980 (148): 314-320.* A short biography of Manuel Montt, a prominent politician and president of Chile. 1809-80

Moody, Theodore William

4746. Martin, F. X. THEODORE WILLIAM MOODY. *Hermathena [Ireland] 1984 (136): 5-7.* Provides an obituary of Theodore William Moody (1906-84), historian of Ireland, noted for his prolific scholarship and his teaching at Trinity College. 1906-84

4747. Mulvey, Helen F. THEODORE WILLIAM MOODY (1907-84): AN APPRECIATION. *Irish Historical Studies [Ireland] 1984 24(94): 121-130.* Obituary of Moody, a Fellow of Trinity College, Dublin, founder of *Irish Historical Studies,* and originator of *A New History of Ireland* (1976-). 1940's-84

Mook, Hubertus Johanes van

4748. Maas, P. F. DR. H. J. VAN MOOK, ONZE LAATSTE LANDVOOGD, TOT ONTSLAG GEDWONGEN (AUGUSTUS/OKTOBER 1948) [Dr. H. J. van Mook, our last governor, forced to resign, August-October 1948]. *Acta Pol. [Netherlands] 1982 17(3): 367-384.* Records the circumstances that caused Hubertus Johanes van Mook (b. 1894) to lose his post as lieutenant governor general of Indonesia (1945-48). Van Mook, born in Dutch East India and conversant with its affairs, wanted temporary restoration of order by the Dutch before Indonesia's independence and the problems of decolonization solved from the Indonesian standpoint, which brought him into conflict with Dutch government policies. Criticized for his autocratic actions and domineering ways, and without party support in the Netherlands, Van Mook was ousted by the newly formed cabinet. Based on Van Mook-Drees correspondence in Drees Archives; 68 notes. 1945-48

Moore, George

4749. Becker, R. S. GEORGE MOORE: AN EXILE FROM THE NOUVELLE ATHENES. *Éire-Ireland 1986 21(2): 146-151.* The Nouvelle Athènes, a cafe-restaurant in the Place de Pigalle of Paris, was a meeting place for French writers and painters in the 1870's. George Moore spent time there in his youth. He admired Honoré de Balzac because, like the writers of the Nouvelle Athènes, he embraced no school. In his own iconoclasm and individuality Moore transcended even that of the writers of this Paris cafe. Based on letters and other writings of George Moore and secondary sources; 31 notes. 1870's-80's

Moore, Henry

4750. Kingsley, April. THE IMAGES OF TIME. *Horizon 1983 26(2): 42-47.* Biography of the English sculptor Henry Moore, born in 1898, and discussion of his solid, sensuous sculptures. 1898-1982

Moore, Richard

4751. Mardis, Allen, Jr. RICHARD MOORE, CARPENTER. *Virginia Magazine of History and Biography 1984 92(4): 416-422.* Richard Moore was the first governor of Bermuda. Little is known about the man, but there is evidence that the officeholder was the same Richard Moore who was an English carpenter, member of the Company of Carpenters trade guild, and author of a book entitled *The Carpenters Rule.* Based on 17th-century naval histories, shipwrights' company records, trade guild manuscripts, and carpenters' company records; 28 notes. 1596-1617

Moore, Richard Benjamin

4752. Tudor, J. Cameron. RICHARD BENJAMIN MOORE: AN APPRECIATION. *Caribbean Studies [Puerto Rico] 1979 19(1-2): 169-174.* Tribute to Richard Benjamin Moore, president of the Afro-American Institute, scholar, author, orator, and bibliophile. Moore was a major figure in the development of Afro-American studies in the United States and the Caribbean. Reviews his principal publications and organizational work. 1930's-78

Moosberg, Hilda

4753. —. HILDA MOOSBERG [Hilda Moosberg]. *Eesti NSV Teaduste Akadeemia Toimetised. Ühiskonnateadused [USSR] 1985 34(4): 403.* Hilda Moosberg (1903-85) was a professor of history at Tartu University and a corresponding member of the History Institute of the Estonian Academy of Sciences. Her research and writing included the history of the revolutionary movement in Estonia in the 19th and early 20th centuries. Toward the end of her career Moosberg was engaged as the chief editor of the *Scandinavian Anthology.* Additionally, Moosberg was active in community affairs and promoted the welfare of the town of Tartu as well as that of Tartu University. 19c-20c

Móra, Ferenc

4754. Sáráné Lukátsy, Sarolta. MÓRA FERENC KÖNYVTÁRIGAZGATÓI TEVÉKENYSÉGE 1920 UTÁN [The library administrative activities of Ferenc Móra after 1920]. *Magyar Könyvszemle [Hungary] 1981 97(1-2): 108-120.* Hungary after the Treaty of Trianon was beset by inflation, poverty, and a general decline of cultural life. Against this background with almost no government support Ferenc Móra (1879-1934) managed to increase both the collections and the clientele of the Somogyi Library at Szeged. He founded the Müzeumbarátok Egyesület [Friends of the Museum], whose sole aim was promoting cultural life and whose dues were used for the acquisition of rare books of both national and local interest. The growth of the collection was encouraged by gifts, one of the most important of which was the 42-volume 1789 edition of Frigyes Nagy's collected works donated by József Szalay. Móra also collected archival materials related to Szeged. His strong commitment the service increased to patronage of the library to 30 million a year by the end of the 1920's. Based primarily on Ferenc Móra's works; 16 notes. French summary. 1920-34

Moraczewski, Jędrzej

4755. Gołota, Janusz. DZIAŁALNOŚĆ JĘDRZEJA MORACZEWSKIEGO W LATACH 1905-1914 [The activities of Jędrzej Moraczewski in the years 1905-14]. *Kwartalnik Hist. [Poland] 1982 89(2-3): 315-330.* The little interest of researchers in the activities of Jędrzej Moraczewski in the Polish socialist movement in Austria contrasts with the large amount of archival material on this topic. Moraczewski began his political activity in 1905, when the issue of the day was electoral reform. He helped to organize demonstrations and meetings, at which he often spoke. The introduction of electoral reform for the Austrian parliament in 1907 marked a turning point in his life. He was one of six Polish socialists to win election to parliament in 1907, and he won reelection in 1911. Henceforth, his activities centered on the parliamentary forum in Vienna and local affairs in his electoral district. Based on the Moraczewski papers and other archival sources; 67 notes, Russian summary. 1905-14

Morant, Robert Laurie

4756. Taylor, Tony. "AN EARLY ARRIVAL OF THE FASCIST MENTALITY": ROBERT MORANT'S RISE TO POWER. *Journal of Educational Administration and History [Great Britain] 1985 17(2): 48-62.* Robert Laurie Morant (1863-1920), the ambitious British educational administrator, became Permanent Secretary of the Board of Education in April 1903. The author considers Morant's character and analyzes his rapid rise to power, 1895-1903. 1895-1903

Morazán, Francisco

4757. Kuzmishchev, A. V. F. MORASAN I BOR'BA ZA EDINOE TSENTRAL'NOAMERIKANSKOE GOSUDARSTVO [Francisco Morazán and the struggle for a united Central American state, 1821-30]. *Voprosy Istorii [USSR] 1984 (10): 77-93.* The article deals with Morazán's biography and his role in the establishment and leadership of a united Central American state in the 1820's. The author sees close similarity between the struggle against reaction and obscurantism waged by this major military and political figure in the first half of the 19th century and the antioligarchic and anti-imperialist struggle waged today by the peoples of the region. 1820's

4758. Lewis, William. THE STRUGGLE FOR CENTRAL AMERICA. *Mankind 1981 6(11): 8-11, 38-39, (12): 8-13, 38-39.* Part 1. MORAZAN. Recounts the story of Francisco Morazan (1792-1842) who, from Central America's separation from Spain in 1821 until his execution, led the unsuccessful struggle to unite Guatemala, Honduras, El Salvador, Nicaragua, and Costa Rica into the "Federation of Central America." Morazan, a Honduran, faced numerous obstacles: an 1836 cholera epidemic; opposition from wealthy Spaniards and Conservative Catholics; uprisings in Costa Rica and Nicaragua; and, finally, the rise of Rafael Carrera, a Guatemalan Indian who began a successful campaign to oust Morazan in 1838. Part 2. WALKER'S WAR IN NICARAGUA. In 1854 William Walker led an unsuccessful expedition to establish a free state in Mexico. Later that year he mounted a small invasion force and went to the aid of Nicaraguan liberals in their struggle against the conservatives. By June he had proclaimed himself dictator, but other Central American nations soon united against him. He was forced to flee to the United States. He raised another invasion force in July 1860, but he was quickly defeated, captured, and executed on 12 September 1860. Secondary sources; 3 photos, map, 20 ref., 7 illus., 9 notes. Article to be continued. 1821-60

Mordaunt, Charles

4759. Bakshian, Aram, Jr. "A HANGDOG WHOM I DEARLY LOVE": THE THIRD EARL OF PETERBOROUGH. *Hist. Today [Great Britain] 1981 31(Oct): 14-19.* Biography of Charles Mordaunt, 3d Earl of Peterborough (1658-1735), a mischievous "soldier, sailor, courtier, conspirator, diplomat, wit and rake," with a focus on his exploits as General and Commander-in-Charge of the Forces of the Fleet and as General and Commander-in-Chief of Allied forces in Spain, particularly his capture of Barcelona, and his hatred of the Duke of Marlborough. 1680's-1735

More, Thomas

4760. Bradshaw, Brendan. THE CONTROVERSIAL SIR THOMAS MORE. *Journal of Ecclesiastical History [Great Britain] 1985 36(4): 535-569.* Assesses recent revisionist scholarship on More's controversial career from 1516 to 1534, including close literary analysis of More's writings leading to conclusions of internal coherence consistent with the situations addressed. Rejects the revisionist charge of More's rigid conservatism, finding instead that in religion he was a cautious reformer and that as chancellor he was an enemy of corruption and inefficiency. Discusses More's opposition to the Reformation, which was based on his commitment to Erasmian humanism. 94 notes. 16c

4761. March'adour, Germain. SAINT THOMAS MORE (1477-1535) AND SAINT FRANCIS OF ASSISI (1182-1226). *Cithara 1985 25(1): 5-18.* Discusses the life of Saint Thomas More and his book *Utopia;* his vision resembled that of Saint Francis of Assisi, although instead of being a monk, More was a cosmopolitan, affluent, family man. ca 1200-26

4762. Ramsay, G. D. A SAINT IN THE CITY: THOMAS MORE AT MERCERS' HALL, LONDON. *English Hist. Rev. [Great Britain] 1982 97(383): 269-288.* Describes the "City career" of Thomas More, which lasted from 1509, when he was admitted to the Mercers' Company, to 1518, when he resigned from the municipal office of undersheriff. However, he was available thereafter for an occasional service. Recognized as a bright young talented lawyer, More was probably recruited by the Mercers' to take part in internal and external negotiations. He participated in negotiations involving the Staplers, the Merchant Adventurers, and other mercantile interests with each other and with representatives from Antwerp, the Netherlands, and the Hanseatic League. Based primarily on a published edition of *Acts of Court of the Mercers' Company.* 1509-18

Morel, Eugène

4763. Benoit, Gaetan. EUGÈNE MOREL AND CHILDREN'S LIBRARIES IN FRANCE. *Journal of Library History 1985 20(3): 267-286.* Eugène Morel (1869-1934), although known primarily for his scholarly and academic work, was an early advocate for establishing free public libraries especially geared to the needs of the children of France. He expressed his concept of the children's library as an institution used for recreation, education, and research in his 1910 book *La Librairie Publique.* Based on an American model, Morel's ideas were not put into practice until L'Heure Joyeuse, the first French children's library, was opened in Paris in 1934. Based on Morel's published works and other primary sources; 79 notes. 1908-24

Morelly, Etienne-Gabriel

4764. Antonetti, Guy. ETIENNE-GABRIEL MORELLY: L'ECRIVAIN ET SES PROTECTEURS [Etienne-Gabriel Morelly: the writer and his patrons]. *Rev. d'Hist. Littéraire de la France [France] 1984 84(1): 19-52.* Follows the career of this 18th-century man of letters, describing his relations with his powerful patrons and discussing references to contemporary events in French history in Morelly's political works. 18c

4765. Antonetti, Guy. ETIENNE-GABRIEL MORELLY: L'HOMME ET SA FAMILLE [Etienne-Gabriel Morelly: the man and his family]. *Rev. d'Hist. Littéraire de la France [France] 1983 83(3): 390-402.* Recounts the discovery of the 1716 marriage contract of Etienne-Gabriel Morelly, author of *Code de la Nature,* and adduces other baptismal, marriage, and notarial documents concerning Morelly's family which describe various aspects of 18th-century French domestic life. 1716

Moreno, Juan Nepomuceno

4766. Rausch, Jane M. THE TAMING OF A COLOMBIAN CAUDILLO: JUAN NEPOMUCENO MORENO OF CASANARE. *Americas (Academy of American Franciscan History) 1986 42(3): 275-288.* Juan Nepomuceno Moreno, who has received scant attention from historians, rose to leadership among the patriot forces on the eastern plains of what is now Colombia and served as military commandant of Casanare province during the period of Gran Colombian union. He eventually backed the annexation of Casanare to Venezuela, in the belief that Venezuela would pay more attention to the region's needs than the government in Bogotá. Venezuela rejected the proposal, and Moreno then played a key role in support of liberal forces in the struggle for control of New Granada at the breakup of Gran Colombia. He never sought to extend his personal influence at national level. Based on published primary and secondary sources; fig., 46 notes. 1814-39

Morgan, Augustus de

4767. Pycior, Helena M. THE THREE STAGES OF AUGUSTUS DE MORGAN'S ALGEBRAIC WORK. *Isis 1983 74(272): 211-226.* Historians have offered conflicting interpretations of Augustus de Morgan's (1806-71) contributions to and attitudes toward abstract algebra. The reason is that over a period of roughly 20 years his attitude toward algebra and symbolical algebra in particular changed considerably. His work seems to have passed through three distinctive stages, from support of traditional mathematics and algebra through espousal of an extremely modern and abstract approach to disillusionment with symbolical algebra as a useless art. 41 notes. 1828-49

Morgan, Sydney

See Owenson, Sydney

Morgenrood, Philip Dominicus

4768. Morgenrood, Pierre. PHILIP DOMINICUS MORGENROOD: THE SQUIRE OF "WIJNBERG'S HOOGTE". *Q. Bull. of the South African Lib. [South Africa] 1983 37(4): 287-297, 38(1): 19-30.* Parts 1-2. A short biography of Philip Dominicus Morgenrood, a Cape Town shop assistant for a general dealership, who inherited his employer's holdings. While prospering in business, he became active in the affairs of the local Lutheran Church, which was disrupted by a doctrinal dispute. Based on records in the Cape archives and secondary sources. 1810-82

Morgenthau, Hans J.

4769. Eckstein, George. HANS MORGENTHAU: A PERSONAL MEMOIR. *Social Res. 1981 48(4): 641-652.* Traces the relationship of the author with Hans J. Morgenthau from 1931 to the 1960's, focusing on Morgenthau's life in Germany during the rise of Nazism, his academic career in the United States, and his views on US society and foreign policy, especially during the Vietnam War; and includes excerpts from his autobiography. 1930's-60's

Morillo, Lorenzo

4770. Pérez Tenreiro, Tomás. NOTICIA SOBRE DON MANUEL LORENZO Y DON LORENZO MORILLO [Notice on Don Manuel Lorenzo and Don Lorenzo Morillo]. *Boletín de la Academia Nacional de la Historia [Venezuela] 1984 67(268): 691-698.* 1820's
*For abstract see **Lorenzo, Manuel***

Morlan, Frederick H.

4771. Sloan, James J. THE FIRST AIR DEPOT: COLOMBEY-LES-BELLES, FRANCE, 1918. *Am. Aviation Hist. Soc. J. 1981 26(3): 221-230.* Discusses the aeronautic career of Captain Frederick H. Morlan, aircraft acceptance and replacement officer for the 1st Air Depot at Colombey-les-Belles, France, during World War I; provides photographs of depot personnel and aircraft taken by Morlan during 1918-19. 1918-19

Moro, Aldo

4772. Komolova, N. P. GIBEL' AL'DO MORO [Death of Aldo Moro]. *Novaia i Noveishaia Istoriia [USSR] 1981 (3): 140-160.* A detailed appraisal of the last two decades of the political career of Aldo Moro, sometime prime minister and leader of the Italian Christian Democrats, abducted and murdered by ultra-left-wing terrorists in 1978. He had appeared to be on the edge of reconstituting a political understanding with the Communist Party, such as had existed briefly at the end of the war. 112 notes. 1947-78

4773. Moss, David. THE KIDNAPPING AND MURDER OF ALDO MORO. *European J. of Sociol. [Great Britain] 1981 22(2): 265-295.* Political terrorism became a feature of Italian politics in the 1970's, culminating in the 1978 murder of Aldo Moro, the leader of the Christian Democrats, by the Red Brigades. The kidnapping is interpreted as a tactic appropriate to the pursuit of political identity. It was a ritual with a solidaristic function for the Red Brigades. It established the continuity of the group and created a frame for subsequent symbolic actions (communiqués and show-trials). Biblio. 1970-78

4774. Ruffilli, Roberto. RELIGIONE, DIRITTO E POLITICA NEGLI ANNI QUARANTA: ALDO MORO [Religion, law, and politics in the 1940's: Aldo Moro]. *Politico [Italy] 1981 46(1-2): 5-40.* Examines recent historiography on the role of Aldo Moro in the postwar emergence of the Christian Democratic Party in Italy. Reconstructs the party's origins in the intellectual currents of the Catholic Action movement, 1943-47. 1940's

Morozov, Savva T.

4775. Pak, B. I. SAVVA TIMOFEEVICH MOROZOV. *Soviet Studies in Hist. 1981-82 20(3): 74-95.* Discusses the life and activity of Savva Morozov, leading capitalist in Russia, Bolshevik sympathizer, and friend of Maxim Gorky and actress M. F. Andreeva. He made generous contributions to the Bolshevik cause. There was a strike in his factory in 1905 that caused his family to remove him as head of the company. He committed suicide. Originally published in *Istoriia SSSR* 1980 (6) (see entry 34A:3068). Secondary sources; 104 notes. 1900-05

Morrell, W. P.

4776. McIntyre, W. David. IMPERIAL JUBILEE: W. P. MORRELL'S CONTRIBUTIONS TO IMPERIAL HISTORY. *New Zealand J. of Hist. [New Zealand] 1982 16(1): 56-67.* After a brief summary of Morrell's career, analyzes his contributions to imperial history and describes his influence on the author's own teaching and research. Based on publications by or about Morrell and other secondary works; 32 notes. 1899-1982

Morris, E. Wynne

4777. Roberts, David H., ed. PART 3—CONCLUSION: LIVERPOOL TO MELBOURNE: A PASSENGER'S LOG. S.S. GLENOGIL 1897. *Nautical Research Journal 1984 30(3): 125-128.* The end of a description of a voyage from England to Australia contained in a diary kept by passenger E. Wynne Morris, who was on his way to work at a sheep station. 1897

Morris, Reynald

4778. Jones, Francis. THE FAMILIES OF BLAIDDBWLL. *Natl. Lib. of Wales J. [Great Britain] 1981 22(1): 27-37.* 1450-1887
*For abstract see **Lloyd, Jenkin***

Morris, William

4779. Evans, Timothy. WILLIAM MORRIS AND THE STUDY OF MATERIAL CULTURE. *Folklore Forum 1982 15(1): 69-86.* Provides a description of the accomplishments of William Morris (1834-96), the many-faceted English genius, and an annotated bibliography of 25 of his works that are relevant to the study of material culture. 1877-94

4780. Frye, Northrop. THE MEETING OF PAST AND FUTURE IN WILLIAM MORRIS. *Studies in Romanticism 1982 21(3): 303-318.* Discusses the poetry and fiction of William Morris (1834-96), in relationship to his agitation for socialism. Examines Morris's motives for writing and identifies distinct periods in his literary career. 1859-96

4781. Hussain, Shawkat. WILLIAM MORRIS: MEDIEVALISM AND SOCIALISM. *Dacca U. Studies Part A [Bangladesh] 1981 (34): 1-14.* William Morris was an upper middle-class English capitalist who espoused the cause of the working class. He admired Karl Marx and preached revolutionary socialism, but he was also a medievalist. Morris argued for a social order that provided a decent life for all. He defined this decent life as having four elements: a healthy body; an active mind in sympathy with the past, the present, and the future; an occupation fit for a healthy body and an active mind; and a beautiful world to live in. Morris recognized that captialist society rooted in the search for profits was unable to provide such a life, but he thought that the revolutionary proletariat could. Inherent in Morris's vision is the rejection of the machine so that workers can rediscover the joy of creative labor. Based on Morris's writings and secondary sources; 46 notes. 1850-1914

4782. Zaitsev, V. P. MORRIS—ODIN IZ PIONEROV SOTSIALISTICHESKOGO DVIZHENIIA V ANGLII [William Morris, one of the pioneers of the British socialist movement]. *Voprosy Istorii [USSR] 1985 (6): 177-181.* Outlines the biography of William Morris (1834-96), British writer, artist, and utopian socialist. Under the influence of John Ruskin's aesthetics, he initiated mass aesthetic education during the 1860's. In the 1880's he became associated with Karl Marx and Friedrich Engels and participated in the foundation of British socialism. His *News from Nowhere* (1891), an account of a socialist Britain set in the future, shows the anarchist bent of Morris's socialism in his later years. Secondary sources; 40 notes. 1850's-96

Mosberg, Hilda Ivanovna

4783. Svanidze, A. A. and Chernysheva, O. V. KHIL'DA IVANOVNA MOSBERG I SOVETSKAIA SKANDINAVISTIKA [Hilda Ivanovna Mosberg and Soviet Scandinavian studies]. *Skandinavskii Sbornik [USSR] 1983 28: 208-212.* Tribute to Hilda Ivanovna Mosberg (b. 1883), Soviet Scandinavian historian and renowned scholar of Southern Estonian. She represented Tartu University at several international conferences and was the editor of *Skandinavskii Sbornik,* 1962-77. Photo. Swedish summary. 1883-1983

Mosca, Gaetano

4784. Gottarelli, Alberto. STUDI RECENTI SU GAETANO MOSCA E LA DOTTRINA DELLA CLASSE POLITICA [Recent studies on Gaetano Mosca and the doctrine of the political class]. *Politico [Italy] 1986 51(1): 115-120.* Reviews recent studies on Gaetano Mosca (1858-1941), Italian political scientist, and on his theory of the ruling class. Notes Mosca's influence on later intellectuals, emphasizing his concept that there are two classes: the rulers and the ruled. According to Mosca's theory, all societies are governed by minorities, who constitute the "political class." Mosca's writings remain an important source for political theory and for evaluating contemporary political systems. Based on Mosca's writings and secondary sources; 9 notes. 1880's-1984

Moscati, Ruggero

4785. Curato, Federico. RUGGERO MOSCATI STORICO DEL MEZZOGIORNO E DELL'ITALIA UNITA [Ruggero Moscati historian of the Mezzogiorno and of united Italy]. *Risorgimento [Italy] 1982 34(2): 85-97.* Ruggero Moscati (1908-81) was a member of the governing council of the Istituto Nazionale per la Storia del Risorgimento Italiano. This is a tribute to his memory and an account of his scholarly work and teaching career. 28 notes. 1908-81

4786. Galasso, Giuseppe. RUGGERO MOSCATI (1908-1981) [Ruggero Moscati (1908-81)]. *Rassegna Storica del Risorgimento [Italy] 1982 69(1): 3-7.* Surveys the work of the Italian historian, Ruggero Moscati, whose interests included the history of Italian international relations, the institutional and social history of southern Italy, the history of Italian liberalism, and the history of archival development. 1932-80

Mosconi, Enrique

4787. Sollberg, Carl E. ENTREPRENEURSHIP IN PUBLIC ENTERPRISE: GENERAL ENRIQUE MOSCONI AND THE ARGENTINE PETROLEUM INDUSTRY. *Business Hist. Rev. 1982 56(3): 380-399.* Enrique Mosconi was the first director general of Yacimientos Petroliferos Fiscales (YPF), the Argentine state oil company that became the first vertically integrated government-owned petroleum enterprise outside the Soviet Union and the largest firm in Argentina. Assuming control of the infant company in 1922, Mosconi promoted the concept of petroleum nationalism, but he failed in an effort to have government authorities establish YPF as a monopoly. He was fired in 1930 when a military coup placed in power a regime more receptive to the interest of privately owned oil companies. Based on public and periodical Argentine sources; 3 illus., table, 32 notes. 1922-30

Mosellanus

4788. Kremer, Ulrich Michael. MOSELLANUS: HUMANIST ZWISCHEN KIRCHE UND REFORMATION [Mosellanus: humanist between Church and Reformation]. *Arch. für Reformationsgeschichte [West Germany] 1982 73: 20-34.* As a youthful biblical humanist, Mosellanus discovered between 1518 and 1520 his own point of departure for the solution to the problem of the reform of education. Like Melanchthon, who until that time had not stepped forward as a theologian, Mosellanus saw the reform of spirituality as a function of a successful reform of education. His approach to the solution of this dual problem consisted in the stress on the original languages of the Bible and departure from the monopoly of Latin as the language of theology. At the same time, however, he found time to write a successful little book on the enhancement of Latinity, a fact with which his opponents did not properly credit him. They saw in him the grammarian who, as the proponent of the faculty of the arts, led the controversy of the masters against the doctors. Unlike Melanchthon who shared his background and goals, he did not succeed in establishing himself as a recognized theologian. The reason must be sought in his appointment at Leipzig which placed more restrictions on him than had to be faced by Melanchthon. Consequently, he soon found himself in the role of Erasmus, without, however, having Erasmus' virtual immunity derived from his high international prestige. His tendency to peaceful mediation and his irenicism which grew from his humanist convictions and his weak physical constitution, were denounced by the reformers as Erasmian, while his enemies on the theological faculty did not forgive his stress on the Greek language. It is questionable whether he might have developed into a significant voice on behalf of moderation in the religious controversy as our own ecumenical age prefers. One suspects that his early death in 1524 spared him further disappointment. 1518-24

Moser, Mentona

4789. Schiel, Ilse. VORWÄRTS, IMMER VORWÄRTS! MENTONA MOSER [Forward, ever forward! Mentona Moser]. *Beiträge zur Geschichte der Arbeiterbewegung [East Germany] 1985 27(3): 377-384.* Provides a biography of the Swiss revolutionary Mentona Moser (1874-1971). Born into a wealthy upper middle class family she turned to social work while in England and then to activism in the Swiss Social Democratic Party. After the beginning of World War I Moser joined the Swiss Communist Party and became increasingly internationalist in her views; from the mid-1920's she was very active in the German radical labor movement. During World War II and afterwards she worked in Switzerland and East Germany. 24 notes. ca 1900-71

Moses, Julius

4790. Nadav, Daniel S. JULIUS MOSES' KAMPF GEGEN DAS ABTREIBUNGSGESETZ WÄHREND DER WEIMAR REPUBLIK [Julius Moses's fight against the abortion law during the Weimar Republic]. *Jahrbuch des Instituts für Deutsche Geschichte [Israel] 1985 14: 261-276.* Julius Moses was a physician and a member of the Social Democratic Party in the Reichstag of the Weimar Republic. From 1920-32 Moses fought for the repeal of the abortion law paragraph 218 by all available means: from the speaker's podium, in political and legislative committees, and in political journals. Although some leading Social Democrats were opposed to legalization of abortion, Moses managed to have the law amended in 1926. A total repeal of the abortion law was blocked by the Nazi seizure of power. Based on Reichstag documents, periodicals, and secondary sources; 49 notes, illus. 1920-32

Moskalenko, Kirill S.

4791. Leliushenko, D. MARSHAL SOVETSKOGO SOIUZA K. S. MOSKALENKO (K 80-LETIIU SO DNIA ROZHDENIIA) [Marshal of the Soviet Union K. S. Moskalenko: on the 80th anniversary of his birth]. *Voenno-Istoricheskii Zhurnal [USSR] 1982 (5): 63-67.* Kirill S. Moskalenko was born in May 1902 in the village of Grishino. At 18 he joined the 6th Division of the 1st Cavalry Army as a private and by 1941 had risen to become a major general. His military talents were particularly in evidence during World War II, during which he held several army commands. Moskalenko is now deputy minister of defense. Based on TsAMO and secondary sources; 2 photos. 1902-82

Mosley, Oswald

4792. Thurlow, Richard C. THE RETURN OF JEREMIAH: THE REJECTED KNOWLEDGE OF SIR OSWALD MOSLEY IN THE 1930'S. Lunn, Kenneth and Thurlow, Richard C., ed. *British Fascism: Essays on the Radical Right in Inter-War Britain* (New York: St. Martin's Pr., 1980): 100-111. Examines the career of Sir Oswald Mosley, leader of the British Union of Fascists during the 1930's, focusing on the practical nature of his economic ideas, many of which were eventually adopted by the British government. 1923-40

Mosquera, Tomás Cipriano de

4793. Mosquera, Jaime. PRESENTACION DEL LIBRO "MEMORIA SOBRE EL LIBERTADOR SIMON BOLIVAR" [Presentation of the book *Memoir on the Liberator Simón Bolívar*]. *Bol. de la Acad. Nac. de la Hist. [Venezuela] 1981 64(256): 996-1000.* 1783-1830
*For abstract see **Bolívar, Simón***

Mosse, Albert

4794. Mosse, Werner E. ALBERT MOSSE: A JEWISH JUDGE IN IMPERIAL GERMANY. *Leo Baeck Inst. Year Book [Great Britain] 1983 28: 169-184.* Albert Mosse (1846-1925) was the first of two unbaptized Jews to be appointed to high judicial office in Germany. His career illustrates at the same time opportunities for Jews and the reality of discrimination against them in the Prussian judicial service. Based on the Albert Mosse collection in the archives of the Leo Baeck Institute, New York; 43 notes, 2 photos. 19c

Mota, Francisco

4795. Abascal López, Jesús. ELOGIO A FRANCISCO MOTA [Tribute to Francisco Mota]. *Santiago [Cuba] 1983 (50): 91-99.* Spanish-born Francisco Mota (b. 1914) emigrated to Spanish America after the civil war and in 1952 settled in Havana. He edited and contributed to many periodicals and is the author of many volumes of history and bibliographical research. This tribute was read at a special session honoring him on the 50th anniversary of his literary career. 1932-82

Moule, Horace

4796. Buckler, William E. THE HARDY-MOULE AFFAIR WITH A READING OF FOUR HARDY POEMS. *Biography 1982 5(2): 136-142.* 1866-73
*For abstract see **Hardy, Thomas***

Moulin, Jean

4797. —. L'"ENIGME" JEAN MOULIN [The Jean Moulin "enigma"]. *Histoire [France] 1983 (55): 98-102.* Interview with Jean-Pierre Azéma, who discusses the mysterious causes and circumstances of the death of founder of the National Council of the Resistance Jean Moulin (1899-1943), buried in the Paris Pantheon (1964) as a national hero. 1943

Moult, George and Francis

4798. Sakula, Alex. DOCTOR NEHEMIAH GREW (1641-1712) AND THE EPSOM SALTS. *Clio Medica [Netherlands] 1984 19(1-2): 1-22.* 1660's-1712
*For abstract see **Grew, Nehemiah***

Moulton, William

4799. Moulton, Harold K. A METHODIST FAMILY: MINISTERIAL SUCCESSION AND INTERMARRIAGE. *Pro. of the Wesley Hist. Soc. [Great Britain] 1981 43(3): 49-58.* Traces the continuous succession of father and son in the Methodist ministry in the Moulton family since William Moulton (1769-1835) was ordained in 1794 and explores the family's connections with other families exhibiting similar successions. 17c-20c

Mounier, Emmanuel

4800. Arnal, Oscar L. EMMANUEL MOUNIER AS PARADIGM OF THE CATHOLIC AVANT-GARDE (1930-1950). *Hist. Reflections [Canada] 1983 10(3): 377-386.* Reviews John Hellman's *Emmanuel Mounier and the New Catholic Left, 1930-1950* (1981), the best study of the French personalist yet to appear in English. Although somewhat overstating Mounier's ties to fascism, and of necessity treating the context of liberal Catholicism too briefly (due to his focus on Mounier), Hellman's work is a "monumental achievement," integrating, with rich literary skill, biography and intellectual history. Biographic parallels between Hellman and Mounier are also drawn. 10 notes. 1930-50

4801. Comte, Bernard. EMMANUEL MOUNIER DEVANT VICHY ET LA REVOLUTION NATIONALE EN 1940-41: L'HISTOIRE REINTERPRETEE [Emmanuel Mounier, Vichy, and the national revolution in 1940-41: a reinterpretation]. *Revue d'Histoire de l'Eglise de France [France] 1985 71(187): 253-279.* Editor of the magazine *Esprit* in Lyons during 1940-41, Emmanuel Mounier has been accused recently by revisionist scholars of having embraced Vichy ideology and served its propaganda machine. These allegations are based on faulty methodology, and they distort reality. Mounier's diverse activities must be assessed globally with due regard for their evolution over time. His overriding concern was spiritual, not political. The profound coherence that emerges is the struggle against Nazism. Based on published notebooks and correspondence of Mounier and secondary sources; 82 notes. 1940-41

Mounsey, James

4802. Appleby, John H. "RHUBARB" MOUNSEY AND THE SURINAM TOAD—A SCOTTISH PHYSICIAN-NATURALIST IN RUSSIA. *Archives of Natural History [Great Britain] 1982 11(1): 137-152.* Biographical sketch of the life and scientific work of the Scottish physician James Mounsey (1710-73), employed at the court of Russia's Empress Elisabeth and her successor Peter III. As director of the Medical Chancery in Russia, he reorganized the medical services. While in Russia, he was involved in the establishment of the development cycles of the Surinam toad, which he believed to progress from frog to fish, a belief which he later discarded. Dismissed by Catherine the Great, he returned to Scotland and became known as 'Rhubarb' Mounsey, for his introduction to Britain of seeds of medicinal rhubarb from Russia. Based on documents in the Royal Society Archives, the Manchester University Library, and other primary sources; 3 fig., 44 notes, biblio. 1710-73

Mountbatten, Louis

4803. Brown, David. MOUNTBATTEN AS FIRST SEA LORD. *Journal of the Royal United Services Institute for Defence Studies [Great Britain] 1986 131(2): 63-68.* The tenure of Lord Louis Mountbatten (1900-79) as First Sea Lord of the British Navy from 1954 to 1959 was during a period of economic retrenchment in the government. Instead of fighting against naval reductions, Mountbatten took the lead in cutting the navy through his Way Ahead Committee made up of naval personnel. The committee eliminated obsolete vessels, reserves, and civilian personnel but preserved the building program so that in the end it produced a smaller and less costly but more modern and capable navy. Mountbatten's fights for funding, however, created friction between the services and his efficient cost-cutting methods made the navy a target for cuts in the future. Based on information from Mountbatten's secretary Vice Admiral Ronald Brockman, Admiralty documents, and secondary sources; photo, 23 notes. 1954-59

4804. Campbell-Johnson, Alan. SUPREME COMMAND: EARL MOUNTBATTEN OF BURMA. *Encounter [Great Britain] 1985 65(1): 51-57.* Discusses the career of Earl Mountbatten of Burma in the period 1944-47 in the light of Philip Ziegler's biography, *Mountbatten* (1985). 1944-47

4805. Dickins, Douglas. MOUNTBATTEN. *British Heritage 1984 5(2): 22-33.* Chronicles the life of Earl Louis Mountbatten, great grandson of Queen Victoria, who attained the highest command in the British Navy and achieved fame throughout the empire. 1920's-79

4806. Kedourie, Elie. SCUTTLING AN EMPIRE. *Commentary 1985 80(6): 45-50.* Louis Mountbatten's biography indicates that he was ignorant of the character of politics in the Third World, and that like other Englishmen of his time his ideas of the Commonwealth were based on illusion combined with a sense of defeatism. 1939-79

4807. Tarling, Nicholas. LORD MOUNTBATTEN AND THE RETURN OF CIVIL GOVERNMENT TO BURMA. *J. of Imperial and Commonwealth Hist. [Great Britain] 1983 11(2): 197-226.* "Lord Mountbatten regarded Burma as his 'first failure.'" This study deals with the early return to Burma of a civil governor after the surrender of Japan and the fruitless attempts to bring Burma back to being "a willing partner of the Empire." Perhaps Mountbatten's mistake was not calling for the return of civil government but rather in trying to follow a policy that had only a remote chance of being accepted back in Britain. Based on materials in the India Office records, the Foreign Office and War Office papers at the Public Record Office, London, and various printed secondary materials; 108 notes. 1940's

Moura, Maria Lacerda de

4808. Leite, Miriam Lifchitz Moreta. A BRAZILIAN FEMINIST AND HER CONTRIBUTION TO THE PACIFIST CAUSE. *Women's Studies Int. Forum 1983 6(4): 371-373.* Between the wars, Maria Lacerda de Moura was a pioneering Brazilian voice in feminism and pacifism, who was driven into seclusion for her activism. 1919-45

Mourouzes family

4809. Koudounarēs, A. L. OIKOGENEIA MOUROUZĒ [The Mourouzes family]. *Kypriakaí Spoudaí [Cyprus] 1981 45: 161-170.* Traces the genealogy of the distinguished Karageorgiades family back to the Byzantine Mourouzes family. The earliest known members settled in Trebizond after the fall of Constantinople to the 4th Crusade in 1204, and members of the family still lived in Trebizond in the 17th century. During the 18th and early 19th centuries a branch of the Mourouzes family lived in Istanbul and served the sultan as dragomans or hospodars of the Romanian principalities. The founder of the Cypriot branch of the family was George Mourouzes, a former Grand Dragoman who was exiled to Cyprus in 1796 and murdered the next year. The author hypothesizes that his granddaughter married a Karageorgiades. Based primarily on obituaries in local Cypriot newspapers and other primary sources; 3 photos. 1204-1980

Mous, Antoon Theodorus

4810. Jacobs, J. Y. H. A. TER NAGEDACHTENIS VAN PROF. DR. A. TH. MOUS [In memory of A. Th. Mous]. *Archief voor de Geschiedenis van de Katholieke Kerk in Nederland [Netherlands] 1980 22(2): 118-121.* A tribute to the scholarship, teaching ability, and personality of Antoon Theodorus Mous (1927-1980), late professor of medieval and modern Church history at the Catholic Theological University, Amsterdam. Born in Amsterdam, Mous was ordained in Haarlem in 1952, received his doctorate from the Gregorian University in Rome, taught at Warmond High Seminary, 1961-67, and then at the Catholic Theological University. He was editorial secretary to the Archief, 1961-80, which published his doctoral thesis and other writings. 1952-80

Mozart, Wolfgang Amadeus

4811. Kramnick, Isaac. AN APOLITICAL *AMADEUS. Dissent 1985 32(3): 339-341.* That Mozart was politically involved is seen by his membership in the progressive Freemasons; this and the subject matter of *The Magic Flute* and *The Marriage of Figaro* and radical politics explain his vulgarity as a rejection of the social system—a side to Mozart which Peter Shaffer's movie *Amadeus* ignores. 18c

4812. Mila, Massimo. LA FORTUNA DI MOZART [The destiny of Mozart]. *Belfagor [Italy] 1985 40(6): 647-658.* Reviewing Gernot Gruber's 1985 work *Mozart in der Nachwelt,* discusses how Mozart has fared with the changing times. The two centuries since his death have seen a great variety of interpretation given to his life and work, which usually reflected the preoccupations of their age. 1760's-91

Mueller, George J.

4813. Mueller, George J. THE LORD IN BRAZIL. *Concordia Hist. Inst. Q. 1983 56(2): 71-83.* A narrative of a Lutheran pastor's 24 years of ministry, mostly in rural Brazil, where, from 1936 to 1960, 18th-century living conditions prevailed. 1936-60

Mugnier, Abbé

4814. Diesbach, Ghislain de. *JOURNAL* DE L'ABBE MUGNIER [The *Journal* of Abbé Mugnier]. *Revue des Deux Mondes [France] 1985 (4): 86-96.* Reviews the recent publication of the *Journal* of Abbé Mugnier (1853-1944) and describes his beginnings as a country priest, his correspondence, and his immense knowledge of history, art, and literature. 1870's-1944

Muhammad, Aziz

4815. Mikhailov, M. P. SAMOOTVERZHENNYI BORETS ZA INTERESY NARODA [A selfless fighter for the interests of the people]. *Voprosy Istorii KPSS [USSR] 1984 (7): 114-116.* Tribute to Aziz Muhammad, First Secretary of the Communist Party of Iraq, on his 60th birthday. He was born in northern Iraq at a time when his country was fighting against colonialism and monarchical reaction. He joined the Party in 1945 and was imprisoned in the years 1948-58. He joined the Central Committee after the revolution of 1958 and the Politburo in 1959. He was elected First Secretary in 1964 and helped rebuild the Party following the Ba'athist repression of 1963, but when the Baath Party came to power a second time in 1968, the Communists cooperated with them, going underground again after 1979. 1924-84

Muhammad Sultan Pasha.

4816. Hunter, F. Robert. THE MAKING OF A NOTABLE POLITICIAN: MUHAMMAD SULTĀN PASHA (1825-1884). *Int. J. of Middle East Studies [Great Britain] 1983 15(4): 537-544.* Traces the rise to power of the Egyptian politician Muhammad Sultan Pasha, a prominent member of Egypt's provincial elite of village mayors or headmen. 2 tables, 19 notes. 1825-84

Mukhamedzhanov, Khasan Mukhamedzhanovich

4817. —. GEROI GRAZHDANSKOI VOINY [Heroes of the Civil War]. *Voenno-Istoricheskii Zhurnal [USSR] 1982 (8): 57-60.* 1917-69
For abstract see ***Appar, Petr Andreevich***

Mukhtar al-Kunti, Sidi al-

4818. Batran, Aziz. AL-SHAIKH AL-MUKHTĀR AL-KUNTĪ AL-KABĪR WA-DAWRUHU FĪ NASHR AL-ISLĀM WA-AL-TARĪQAH AL-QĀDIRIYAH FĪ AL-SAHRĀ' WA-GHARB IFRIQIYĀ [The Grand Sheikh al-Mukhtar al-Kunti and his role in disseminating Islam and the Qadiriyya order in the Sahara and West Africa]. *Majallat Al-Buhūth Al-Tārīkhiya [Libya] 1981 3(2): 313-328.* Sidi al- Mukhtar al-Kunti was born in 1729 at Azwad in southern Algeria to an important religious family. By the age of 20 he was an outstanding religious scholar and became an itinerant teacher as well as following the family tradition in the caravan trade. He used his wealth to found religious schools and help the needy and was instrumental in spreading the Qadiriyya brotherhood. In 1753 he founded his famous religious school in Azwad. He was responsible for codifying and spreading the teachings of the Qadiriyya Sufis. At his death in 1811 his fame stretched to all the Sahara kingdoms, Mauritania, and West Africa. Based on his own works and some classical sources; 54 notes. 1729-1811

Mulder, Gerrit Jan

4819. Snelders, H. A. M. THE MULDER-LIEBIG CONTROVERSY ELUCIDATED BY THEIR CORRESPONDENCE. *Janus [Netherlands] 1982 69(3-4): 199-221.* 1838-46

For abstract see ***Liebig, Justus***

Muller, Christof F. J.

4820. Liebenberg, B. J. PROFESSOR C. F. J. MULLER AS HISTORIKUS [Professor C. F. J. Muller as a historian]. *Kleio [South Africa] 1980 12(1-2): 5-13.* Professor C. F. J. Muller, head of the department of history at the University of South Africa, 1946-79, made his reputation as a historian for his work on the Great Trek. He published four works, of which his first, *Die Britse Owerheid en die Groot Trek,* (1949) remains probably the best known. With careful, painstaking research he put the historical study of the Great Trek on a respectable academic footing, he searched assiduously for new documentation and consequently shed new light on many aspects of the Great Trek and corrected many previous mistakes. Uses primary sources and Prof. Muller's own publications; 10 notes. 1946-79

4821. Zyl, M. C. van. PROFESSOR C. F. J. MULLER: DIE EINDE VAN 'N ERA [Professor C. F. J. Muller: the end of an era]. *Kleio [South Africa] 1980 12(1-2): 1-4.* In 1979 Professor Christof F. J. Muller retired from the history department of the University of South Africa after 33 years. Born in Stellenbosch in 1916, he spent much of his early life there, graduating from the university with first-class honors in 1936. He completed his doctorate on the Great Trek, on which he became an expert, and began his teaching career in 1945. He joined the department of history at the University of South Africa in 1946 and under him the department grew; by 1979 it numbered 29 academic staff. Primary sources; photo. 1916-79

Müller, Heinrich

4822. Blank, A. S. TRI MAGISTRA "CHERNOGO ORDENA" [Three heads of the Black Order]. *Voprosy Istorii [USSR] 1982 (9): 105-117.* Traces the history of the SS (Schutzstaffel) in Germany and its connections with owners of large capital, who traded political support for orders for military production. Three leaders looked at are: Heinrich Müller (1896-?1945), head of the Gestapo, 1936-45, who may still be alive; Karl Wolf (b. 1900), head of the Führer's staff from 1936, a man of impeccable manners and speech who was important in making contact with the capitalists and in negotiating for a possible separate peace; Walter Schellenberg (b. 1911), a brilliant intellectual who was head of intelligence and involved in many operations, including a plot to kill Stalin. Based on memoirs and secondary sources; 69 notes. 1936-45

Munch, Edvard

4823. Areán, Carlos. DOS EXPOSICIONES MODELICAS: CEZANNE Y MUNCH [Two exemplary exhibitions: Cézanne and Munch]. *Cuadernos Hispanoamericanos [Spain] 1984 (409): 151-158.* 1860's-1944

For abstract see ***Cézanne, Paul***

Munch, Peter

4824. Staur, Carsten. P. MUNCH OG FORSVARSSPØRGSMÅLET CA. 1900-1910 [Peter Munch and Danish defense policy 1900-10]. *Historisk Tidsskrift [Denmark] 1981 81(1): 101-121.* Although he started his career as a Radical Liberal leader by opposing the Danish Defense Law of 1909, Peter Munch became the Danish Minister of Defense 1913-20 and Foreign Minister, 1929-40. This apparent contradiction is analyzed here in conjunction with his general opinion on Danish defense and foreign policy. Munch pointed out that the greatest danger to the country was a future (primarily naval) war between England and Germany, in which the Danish straits might constitute an important factor. He claimed that the strategic importance of these areas was diminishing, and thus that the key to Danish neutrality lay in German confidence in the credibility of the declared Danish neutrality. This credibility could only be obtained if Denmark renounced all military arrangements over and above a minor frontier guard. Munch regarded a Danish military defense against a German attack as a total futility, and maintained that the only possible defense was a cultural one based on a strong and true national feeling. Later, during World War I, Munch revised some of these ideas; together with the foreign minister, Erik Scavenius, he devised a new concept of neutrality which made it possible for the Danish government to conduct a pro-German foreign policy within the framework of classical neutrality. 1900-10

Muncis, Jānis

4825. Blūma, Dz. K. LATVIEŠU SKATUVES GLEZNOTĀJU DARBĪBA KRIEVIJĀ NO 1915. LIDZ 1919. GADAM [The activity of Latvian scene-painters in Russia from 1915 to 1919]. *Latvijas PSR Zinātņu Akad. Vēstis [USSR] 1982 (1): 72-79.* 1915-19

For abstract see ***Kuga, Jānis***

Munck, Claes Johan

4826. Degerman, Henrik. C. J. MUNCK: GUSTAVIAN I PJÄXOR: ETT STYCKE SJUTTONHUNDRATALS MILJÖ [C. J. Munck: a Gustavian in boots: a slice of life in the 1700's]. *Historiska och Litteraturhistoriska Studier [Finland] 1984 59: 137-156.* A biographical sketch of the Finnish nobleman and army officer, Claes Johan Munck (1764-1839), including his activities in management of his estate and in local community affairs. Based on private and local archives and on memoirs; illus., biblio. 1764-1839

Münichreiter, Karl

4827. Winkler, Elisabeth. KARL MÜNICHREITER—EIN BEISPIEL ZUR PRAXIS POLITISCHER JUSTIZ IM AUSTROFASCHISMUS [Karl Münichreiter—an example of the practice of political justice under Austrian fascism]. *Zeitgeschichte [Austria] 1985 12(11-12): 411-424.* Describes the political climate and events leading to the uprising on 12 February 1934 in Hietzing, a suburb of Vienna, in which Karl Münichreiter, member of the Defense League and of the Social Democratic Party, was arrested. Gives a detailed account of the uprising itself and of Münichreiter's trial. The purported purpose of Münichreiter's death sentence, handed down in 1934, was to act as a scare tactic. However, the sentence illustrates the dictatorial desire of Dollfuss's fascist regime to undermine workers' organizations and to persecute political protest brutally. Münichreiter's trial was grossly unfair: inconsistencies in testimony abounded and proof of guilt was never established. 77 notes. 1933-34

Münster, Sebastian

4828. Lebeau, Jean. *NOVUS ORBIS.* LES COSMOGRAPHES ALLEMANDS DU XVIe SIÈCLE ET LES GRANDES DECOUVERTES *[Novus Orbis:* German cosmographers of the 16th century and the great discoveries]. *Rev. d'Allemagne [France] 1981 13(2): 197-215.* 1520-50
*For abstract see **Boemus, Johannes***

Münter, Frederik

4829. Wojtowicz, Jerzy. FRYDERYK MÜNTER—DUŃSKI PODRÓŻNIK, WOLNOMULARZ I DZIAŁACZ OŚWIECENIA. SZKIC Z DZIEJÓW KOMUNIKACJI SPOŁECZNEJ [Frederik Münter—Danish traveller, Freemason, and agent of the Enlightenment: essay on the history of social communication]. *Kwartalnik Hist. Nauki i Techniki [Poland] 1983 28(2): 329-344.* Intellectual biography of Frederik Münter. Born in Denmark, but connected more with the culture of the German Enlightenment, his personal and intellectual contacts with Freemasonry in Vienna, Copenhagen, Rome, and Florence are examined. 45 notes. 1780's-1830

Münzer, Thomas

4830. Bainton, Roland H. THOMAS MÜNTZER, REVOLUTIONARY FIREBRAND OF THE REFORMATION. *Sixteenth Cent. J. 1982 13(2): 3-15.* Thomas Münzer's sermons against superstitions, the cult of saints, papists, and Franciscans incited his listeners to violence and prompted Luther to respond with the tract *Against Rebellious Spirits.* Central to Münzer's thought was the belief that under the leadership of the elect, whom he believed could be clearly identified, the godless could be eliminated and a Christian society created. Münzer's *Werke,* secondary sources; appendix on terminology in Luther and Münzer, illus., 26 notes. ca 1525

Murchison, Roderick

4831. Secord, James A. KING OF SILURIA: RODERICK MURCHISON AND THE IMPERIAL THEME IN NINETEENTH-CENTURY BRITISH GEOLOGY. *Victorian Studies 1982 25(4): 413-442.* The career of British geologist Roderick Murchison (1792-1871) represents a vital link between science, militarism, and imperialism. Murchison turned to geology after a frustrating military career. The publication of his key works, *The Silurian System* and *The Geology of Russia,* made him a leading scientific figure. During his later years, while president of the Royal Geographic Society, he eagerly promoted British overseas expansion and involvement. Based on Murchison's writings and addresses; 2 illus., chart, 56 notes. 1825-71

Murdoch, William

4832. Durkan, John. WILLIAM MURDOCH AND THE EARLY JESUIT MISSION IN SCOTLAND. *Innes Review [Great Britain] 1984 35(1): 3-11.* Born in 1539, William Murdoch was formed in Catholic Scotland and believed that his Jesuit mission could reverse the Protestant Reformation effected by the Lords of Congregation, provided they maintained the support of the Catholic earls. 1562-1607

Murga y Mugartegui, Gonzalo de

4833. Fernández Gaytán, José. DON GONZALO DE MURGA Y MUGARTEGUI: MARINO, ESCRITOR Y VIAJERO [Don Gonzalo de Murga y Mugartegui: sailor, writer, and traveller]. *Rev. General de Marina [Spain] 1981 201(Aug): 69-79.* Gonzalo de Murga y Mugartegui (1830-82) was a young Spanish naval officer when he was named to the Hydrographic Office, which he soon came to head. He was widely read, a world traveller, and a writer on many subjects, but he never held a rank above lieutenant. 2 illus.; 7 notes. 1830-82

Murgescu, Ioan

4834. Mocioiu, Nicolae. DOCUMENTE INEDITE PRIVIND ACTIVITATEA LUI IOAN MURGESCU [Unpublished documents concerning the activities of Ioan Murgescu]. *Rev. Arhivelor [Romania] 1980 42(1): 98-104.* Publishes 10 official documents relating to the experience at the Ecole Navale de Brest of the future Romanian admiral, Ioan Murgescu and his brief service in the French navy. Documents preserved at the Service Historique de la Marine, Paris. 1864-68

Murillo Toro, Manuel

4835. —. CONMEMORACION DEL PRIMER CENTENARIO DE LA MUERTE DEL DOCTOR MANUEL MURILLO TORO [Commemoration of the first centennial of the death of Dr. Manuel Murillo Toro]. *Bol. de Hist. y Antigüedades [Colombia] 1980 67(731): 613-671.*

Murillo Toro, Manuel. [LETTERS] (Spanish text), *pp. 613-646.* Reprints a group of letters of Manuel Murillo Toro (1816-80), Liberal leader and publicist who twice served as president of Colombia. Based on materials from the Archivo de la Academia Colombiana de Historia.

Riaño, Camilo. EN EL CENTENARIO DE LA MUERTE DE MANUEL MURILLO TORO [On the centennial of the death of Manuel Murillo Toro], *pp. 647-655.* A brief biographical sketch. Biblio.

Cruz Santos, Abel. MANUEL MURILLO TORO, HACENDISTA [Manuel Murillo Toro, public financier], *pp. 656-661.* Biography. Reproduced from Vol. 15, Part 1, *Economía y Hacienda Pública* of the collaborative *Historia Extensa de Colombia.*

Cacua Prada, Antonio. EL DR. MANUEL MURILLO TORO, FUNDADOR DEL DIARIO OFICIAL [Dr. Manuel Murillo Toro, founder of the *Diario Oficial], pp. 662-671.* Evokes Manuel Murillo Toro's career as a journalist. 1816-80

Murillo, Gerardo

See Atl, Dr.

Murra, John V.

4836. Murra, John V.; Rowe, John Howland, introd. AN INTERVIEW WITH JOHN V. MURRA: INTRODUCTION BY JOHN HOWLAND ROWE. *Hispanic American Historical Review 1984 64(4): 633-653.* Reviews the career of an anthropologist whose major works concern the historical ethnology of the Inca Empire, from his youth in pre-World War II Romania and Croatia to teaching posts in the United States, France, and Mexico. An early acceptance of Marxism led Murra to describe the Inca mode of production as "feudal," but later influences, such as British social anthropology, intervened in *Formaciones Económicas y Políticas del Mundo Andino* (1975). Biblio., 8 notes. 15c-18c

Murray, Daniel

4837. Purcell, Mary and Sheehy, David. DUBLIN DIOCESAN ARCHIVES: MURRAY PAPERS (6). *Archivium Hibernicum [Ireland] 1986 41: 3-63.* Part 6. Completes the calendar of the papers of Daniel Murray, the Roman Catholic Archbishop of Dublin (1768-1852) in the Dublin Diocesan

Archives. Correspondence for the years 1850-52 is listed along with various undated letters from laypersons, priests, and nuns and various charitable organizations. Further papers relating to the great Irish potato famine (1847-50) are included. An index to the calendar will be published in the next issue. 1823-52

Murray, Gilbert

4838. Lloyd-Jones, Hugh. GILBERT MURRAY. *Am. Scholar 1981-82 51(1): 55-72.* Gilbert Murray (1866-1957) was active in international affairs and scholarship, but was not completely at home in either milieu. Although the world changed and turned against the liberal values that he fought for all of his life, he never became embittered and never wavered in his loyalty to what he believed. 1890's-1950's

Murray, Hubert Leonard

4839. Jinks, Brian. BLAMING THE VICTIM: LEONARD MURRAY AND THE SUSPENSION OF CIVIL ADMINISTRATION IN PAPUA. *Australian J. of Pol. and Hist. [Australia] 1982 28(1): 44-55.* On 6 February 1942, after the first bombing of Port Moresby, the Australian government suspended the civil administration in Papua. Authority was assumed by Major General Basil Morris, commanding officer of the garrison at the start of the war. The author seeks to restore the reputation of Hubert Leonard Murray, the civil administrator, claiming that the army was poorly disciplined, that Murray was bound by orders from Canberra, and that the military authorities tended to blame the civil administration for a breakdown of government. An inquiry conducted in 1944 by John Vincent Barry was, it argued, biased against Murray. Based on Australian archives and private papers; 14 notes. 1942-44

Murray, John

4840. Miller, Stuart T. JOHN MURRAY: "A BOLD AND SKILFUL ENGINEER." *Industrial Archaeol. Rev. [Great Britain] 1982 6(2): 102-111.* Traces the development of Sunderland harbor, 1832-59, and describes the influence which the engineer John Murray (1804-82) had on engineering at Sunderland during this period. 1832-59

4841. Ogden, Mark. LORD DUNMORE EMERGES FROM THE SHADOWS. *Daughters of the Am. Revolution Mag. 1982 116(5): 366-369.* Discusses the life of John Murray, 4th Earl of Dunmore, one of King George III's outstanding colonial governors, especially his activities as governor of Virginia on the eve of the American Revolution. 18c

Musatti, Cesare

4842. Musatti, Cesare. IL MIO MONDO GIOVANILE NELL'ANTICA PADOVA [My young world in old Padua]. *Belfagor [Italy] 1986 41(1): 81-94.* A personal recollection of intellectual life, especially studies under Vittorio Benussi, at the University of Padua before the rise of Fascism. 1915-40

Muscettola Family

4843. Visceglia, Maria Antonietta. FORMAZIONE E DISSOLUZIONE DI UN PATRIMONIO ARISTOCRATICO: LA FAMIGLIA MUSCETTOLA TRA XVI E XIX SECOLO [Formation and dissolution of an aristocratic patrimony: the Muscettola Family from the 16th to the 19th centuries]. *Mélanges de l'Ecole Française de Rome. Moyen Age-Temps Moderne [Italy] 1980 92(2): 555-624.* Chronicles the births, deaths, marriages, finances, property, and social conditions of the Neapolitan Muscettola Family. 16c-19c

Musicescu, Maria-Ana

4844. Pippidi, Andrei. MARIA-ANA MUSICESCU (1910-1980) [Maria-Ana Musicescu, 1910-80]. *Rev. des Études Sud-Est Européennes [Romania] 1980 18(3): 519-520.* Obituary of archaeologist and art historian, Maria-Ana Musicescu, an instrumental figure in the creation of the Institut d'Études Sud-Européennes in Bucharest, researcher and critic in Romanian art from the Middle Ages through the 18th century, author of monographs on art history and translator of Rilke's *Letters to a Young Poet* into Romanian. 1910-80

Mussolini, Benito

4845. Decaux, Alain. LA MARCHE SUR ROME? JUSTE UN EPOUVANTAIL [The march on Rome? Just a bugbear]. *Hist. Mag. [France] 1983 (42): 14-27.* Recounts the life of Benito Mussolini (1883-1945) until the march on Rome in 1922. 1883-1922

4846. DeGrazia, Victoria. IL FASCINO DEL PRIAPO: MARGHERITA SARFATTI BIOGRAFA DEL DUCE [Priapic fascination: Margherita Sarfatti as Il Duce's biographer]. *Memoria: Riv. di Storia delle Donne [Italy] 1982 (4): 149-154.* 1922-37
*For abstract see **Sarfatti, Margherita***

4847. Meier, Viktor. 100. GEBURTSTAG MUSSOLINIS, 40. JAHRESTAG SEINES STURZES [Centennial of Benito Mussolini's birthday, 40th anniversary of his defeat]. *Schweizer Monatshefte [Switzerland] 1983 63(7-8): 568-574.* Review article on Mussolini's life, ideas, and actions in their political context. 1883-1943

Musy, Jean Marie

4848. Lewin, Isaac. ATTEMPTS AT RESCUING EUROPEAN JEWS WITH THE HELP OF POLISH DIPLOMATIC MISSIONS DURING WORLD WAR II: PART IV. *Polish Review 1984 29(4): 71-86.* A detailed account of Jean Marie Musy's (1876-1952) mission as former president of Switzerland to save the remaining European Jews in the closing months of World War II. Musy, in October 1944, met with Heinrich Himmler (1900-45) who agreed to free all Jews held in concentration camps on territory occupied by Germany in return for five million Swiss francs, which were to be used for buying medical and food supplies for Germany. As a result of this agreement, 1,200 Jews entered Switzerland in February 1945. Further exchanges did not occur because of Adolf Hitler's direct opposition and intervention. Musy's efforts, with Himmler's cooperation, next centered on attempts at keeping the remaining Jews held in camps alive until liberation. Primary sources. 1944-45

Mutis, José C.

4849. Bateman, Alfredo. LOS PERSONAJES DE LA EXPEDICION BOTANICA [Personages of the Botanical Expedition]. *Boletín de Historia y Antigüedades [Colombia] 1984 71(747): 907-964.* 18c-19c
*For abstract see **Caballero y Góngora, Antonio***

4850. Esteva de Sagrera, Juan. LA EXPEDICION INTERMINABLE: J. C. MUTIS [The interminable expedition: J. C. Mutis]. *Hist. y Vida [Spain] 1983 16(186): 36-44.* José

C. Mutis (1732-1802) spent many years gathering valuable information about plants of the New World (especially New Granada) and was instrumental in the discovery of quinine, yet much of his work remains unpublished. 1750's-1802

Mwasi

4851. Vansina, Jan. MWASI'S TRIALS. *Daedalus 1982 111(2): 49-70.* Discusses the plight of Mwasi, the wife of a student, Mobali, at Lovanium University in Zaire after his abduction into the army on 3 June 1971, in a government crackdown on the intelligentsia. 1971

Mynsinger von Frundeck, Joachim

4852. Schumann, Sabine. JOACHIM MYNSINGER VON FRUNDECK: HUMANIST—RECHTSGELEHRTER—POLITIKER (1514-1588) [Joachim Mynsinger von Frundeck: humanist, legal scholar, politician (1514-88)]. *Archiv für Kulturgeschichte [West Germany] 1980-81 62-63: 159-193.* Arguing that the stable period between the Peace of Augsburg and the outbreak of the Thirty Years War allowed the development of consolidated territorial states run for princes by bureaucrats drawn largely from a mostly bourgeois educated elite, summarizes the life and career of Mynsinger, chancellor for the archduke of Brunswick-Lüneburg, as an example of the central role played by individuals of humanistic training in the furtherance of absolutism. The essay is composed of three chronological sections focusing on Mynsinger as a law student and legal scholar, chancellor, and private scholar and political advisor. 68 notes. 1530's-88